Heat packs, neck
Standard terry cover
Neck terry cover
Fluorimethane
Cold spray
Ice bags
Ice bags, Cramer
Kwik-heat pack
Cramer Atomic Rub Down
Flexi-wrap (small, large)
Flexi-wrap handles
Lotion, 1 gal

First Aid
Cotton rolls (nose plugs)
Tongue depressors
Pocket masks
Cotton tip applicators
Cotton tip applicators (sterile)
Sani Cloths
Latex gloves (med., large)
Cotton balls
Skin-preps
Save-A-Tooth
Penlights
Biohazard bags
Safety goggles

Taping Accessories
Heel and lace pads
Tape Adherent Spray
Tape remover

Sharps
Stainless steel prep blades
Scalpel blades, #10, #11 (sterile)
Scissors bandage
Scissors, small
Tweezers

Tweezers (sterile)
Suture sets
Nail clippers (large, small)
Tape cutters
Stethoscopes
Shark refill blades

Inhalants
Afrin

Antiseptics
Triadine
Peroxide
Rubbing alcohol
Betasept, small bottles
Betasept, 1 gal jug
Antimicrobial skin cleaner
Super Quin 9
Zorbidide Spray

Skin Treatments
Polysporin
Bacitracin
1% Tolnaftate Powder
Lamisil
1% Hydrocortisone
Second skin
Collodion
2% Miconazole
10% hydrocortisone
Baby powder
Tincture of benzoin

Eye Treatment
Dacriose Irrigation
Saline
Eye wash
ReNu contact cleaning agent
Penlights

Teeth Treatment
Blue mouth guards, 25/box
Clear mouth guards, 25/box

Oral Medications
Acetaminophen bottle
Acetaminophen, 2 pk
Cepastat
Chlorpheniramine, 4 mg
Diphenhydramine, 25 mg
Ibuprofen bottle
Ibuprofen, 2 pk
Immodium AD
Pepto-Bismol tabs
Q-fed pkg
Sudodrin, 2 pk
Titralac
Robitussin DM

Crutches
Large
Medium
Small
Large aluminum

Water
Bottle carriers
Water bottles
Coolers (3, 7, 10 gal)
Chest

Other
Stools
Spray bottles
Bucket
Cloth towels

principles of
Athletic Training

tenth edition

ANCIENT TRAINING ROOM

The palaestra, a sand-covered open courtyard, was surrounded by small rooms where athletes bathed, oiled, and dressed. Right figure, a youth leaves his outer garment with an attendant; center figure, a competitor oils his body before entering the palaestra; left figure, an attendant removes a thorn from an injured athlete.

principles of
Athletic Training

tenth edition

Daniel D. Arnheim, D.P.E., A.T.C.
Fellow, American College of Sports Medicine
Professor Emeritus of Physical Education
California State University
Long Beach, California

William E. Prentice, Ph.D., A.T.C., P.T.
Professor, Coordinator of the Sports Medicine Specialization,
Department of Exercise and Sport Science
Clinical Professor, Division of Physical Therapy,
Department of Medical Allied Health Professions
Associate Professor, Department of Orthopaedics
School of Medicine
The University of North Carolina
Chapel Hill, North Carolina

Boston   Burr Ridge, IL   Dubuque, IA   Madison, WI   New York   San Francisco   St. Louis
Bangkok   Bogotá   Caracas   Lisbon   London   Madrid
Mexico City   Milan   New Delhi   Seoul   Singapore   Sydney   Taipei   Toronto

McGraw-Hill Higher Education

A Division of The **McGraw-Hill** *Companies*

PRINCIPLES OF ATHLETIC TRAINING, TENTH EDITION

Copyright © 2000, 1997, 1993, 1989, 1985, 1981, 1977, 1973, 1969, 1963 by The McGraw-Hill Companies, Inc. All rights reserved. Printed in the United States of America. Except as permitted under the United States Copyright Act of 1976, no part of this publication may be reproduced or distributed in any form or by any means, or stored in a data base or retrieval system, without the prior written permission of the publisher.

 This book is printed on recycled, acid-free paper containing 10% postconsumer waste.

3 4 5 6 7 8 9 0 VNH/VNH 0 9 8 7 6 5 4 3 2 1

ISBN 0–07–109255–2

Vice president and editorial director: *Kevin T. Kane*
Publisher: *Edward E. Bartell*
Executive editor: *Vicki Malinee*
Senior developmental editor: *Michelle Turenne*
Senior marketing manager: *Pamela S. Cooper*
Senior project manager: *Gloria G. Schiesl*
Senior production supervisor: *Mary E. Haas*
Coordinator of freelance design: *Michelle D. Whitaker*
Photo research coordinator: *John C. Leland*
Senior supplement coordinator: *David A. Welsh*
Compositor: *ElectraGraphics, Inc.*
Typeface: *10/12 Meridien*
Printer: *Von Hoffmann Press, Inc.*

Freelance cover designer: *Paul Uhl; Design Associates*
Cover image: © *Al Bello/Tony Stone Images*

The credits section for this book begins on page C-1 and is considered
an extension of the copyright page.

This text was revised based on the most up-to-date research and suggestions made by individuals knowledgeable in the field of athletic training. The author and publisher disclaim any responsibility for any adverse effects or consequences from the misapplication or injudicious use of information contained within this text. It is also accepted as judicious that the athletic trainer performing his or her duties is, at all times, working under the guidance of a licensed physician.

Library of Congress Cataloging-in-Publication Data

Arnheim, Daniel D.
    Principles of athletic training / Daniel D. Arnheim, William E.
  Prentice. — 10th ed.
     p.   cm.
   ISBN 0–07–109255–2
    1. Physical education and training.   I. Prentice, William E.
  II. Title.
  RC1210.A75   2000
  617.1'027—dc21   99–20214
                                 CIP

www.mhhe.com

BRIEF

Contents

DETAILED

Contents

Applications at a Glance

Since the first edition of this text was published in 1963, the profession of athletic training has experienced amazing growth, not only in numbers but also in the associated body of knowledge. During those years the authors of this text have taken it as a personal responsibility to provide the reader with the most current research-based and clinically based information available in athletic training and sports medicine. Thus *Principles of Athletic Training* has always been considered the leading text in this field. The changes and additions in this tenth edition are a reflection of our commitment and our passion toward continuing this tradition.

A great deal of thought and planning always goes into the revision of *Principles of Athletic Training*. As in development of previous editions, the tenth edition development included serious consideration and incorporation of suggestions made by students as well as detailed feedback from reviewers and other respected authorities in the field. Consequently, this tenth edition reflects the major dynamic trends in the field of athletic training and sports medicine. Furthermore, it is our hope that this newest edition will help to prepare the student to become a competent professional who will continue to enhance the ongoing advancement of the athletic training profession.

The essential philosophy of this edition of *Principles of Athletic Training* remains the same as that of past editions. The text is designed to lead the student from general foundations to specific concepts relative to injury prevention, evaluation, management, and rehabilitation. As the student progresses from beginning to end, he or she will gradually begin to understand the complexities of the profession of athletic training and sports medicine. A major premise in this edition, as in past editions, is that the student should be able to apply the appropriate techniques and concepts in the day-to-day performance of his or her job.

WHO IS IT WRITTEN FOR?

Principles of Athletic Training should be used by athletic trainers in courses concerned with the scientific and clinical foundations of athletic training and sports medicine. Practicing athletic trainers, physical therapists, and other health care professionals involved with physically active individuals will also find this text valuable.

WHAT'S NEW IN THIS EDITION?

Addressing the Education Council Competencies

In 1998, the National Athletic Trainers Association created the Education Council and charged it with the responsibility for identifying knowledge and skills that must be included in educational programs that prepare the student to enter the athletic training profession. To meet this charge, the Education Council has developed a list of competencies categorized according to twelve domains that constitute the role of the athletic trainer. The authors feel very strongly that for *Principles of Athletic Training* to continue to be the most widely used and comprehensive textbook available for the entry-level athletic trainer, these competencies needed to be included. Thus, one goal in this tenth edition was to make certain that every single competency identified by the Education Council is specifically addressed in this text. To the best of our abilities this has been accomplished.

Additional Features

In addition to the inclusion of material that addresses specific competencies, *Principles of Athletic Training* has undergone significant changes in content with this newest edition. The changes and additions reflect the ever-increasing body of knowledge that is expanding the scope of practice for the athletic trainer.

- The order of presentation of the chapters has been reorganized into five sections: Professional Development and Responsibilities; Risk Management; Pathology of Injury; Management Skills; and Specific Sports Conditions.

- Expanded information on the roles of various professionals included in the sports medicine team and updated information on the reorganization of the NATABOC performance domains along with a discussion of the Education Council's expansion of the clinical competencies into twelve domains are included in Chapter 1, *The Athletic Trainer and the Sports Medicine Team*.

- Chapter 2, *Health Care Administration in Athletic Training*, has expanded its discussion on the role of the athletic trainer as an administrator and personnel manager.

- Chapter 3, *Legal Concerns and Insurance Issues*, is now a new, separate chapter that deals with two topics that are becoming more critical to the athletic trainer in today's society. Recommendations are made for athletic trainers to avoid liability.

- Chapter 4, *Training and Conditioning Techniques*, has been revised to reflect the current philosophies regarding periodization as well as discuss the relationship between the athletic trainer and a strength and conditioning coach.

- Nutrition is a topic that is always of particular interest to the athlete. Chapter 5, *Nutritional Considerations*, has been revised to explain the newly released Dietary Recommended Intakes and the changes to the Recommended Dietary Allowances. In addition, new discussions include considerations for the athlete who is consuming fast foods and for the use of herbs to enhance performance.

- Chapter 6, *Environmental Considerations*, contains the latest information on the dangers of lightning. Also included are position statements from various organizations about conducting practices and competitions under potentially threatening environmental conditions.

- Chapter 7, *Protective Sports Equipment*, and Chapter 8, *Bandaging and Taping*, have been updated to show the latest types of protective equipment available and to include the current recommended taping techniques.

- Chapter 9, *Mechanisms and Characteristics of Sports Trauma*, and Chapter 10, *Tissue Response to Injury*, cover the pathology of the injury process and have been updated to include the most current information on the healing process.

- Chapter 11, *Psychosocial Intervention for Sports Injuries and Illnesses*, now focuses on both the psychological and social impact of athletic injuries, including rehabilitation and intervention strategies used by the athletic trainer to facilitate the athlete's return to activity.

- Chapter 12, *On-the-Field Acute Care and Emergency Procedures*, has been reorganized to concentrate on those situations that require the athletic trainer to make decisions for appropriate emergency care while focusing on specific procedures to follow.

- Chapter 13, *Off-the-Field Injury Evaluation*, has been expanded to include discussions of various special tests that can be used in the assessment process.

- The latest available statistics on HIV and AIDS have been added to Chapter 14, *Bloodborne Pathogens*. In addition, the recent NATA position statement on bloodborne pathogens can be found in Appendix B.

- New information on ultrasound and electrical stimulating currents has been included in Chapter 15, *Using Therapeutic Modalities*.

- Chapter 16, *Using Therapeutic Exercise in Rehabilitation*, now provides detailed discussion of the important components of a rehabilitation program, including minimizing swelling, controlling pain, maintaining or improving flexibility, restoring or increasing strength, reestablishing neuromuscular control, regaining balance, maintaining levels of cardiorespiratory fitness, and incorporating functional progressions. This chapter is also the basis for potential rehabilitation techniques that may be used in the three phases of the healing process addressed in Part V, Specific Sports Conditions.

- A discussion of pharmacokinetics has been added to Chapter 17, *Pharmacology, Drugs, and Sports*. Also included are updates and expansions of previous tables and protocols as well as a new table on medications for treating asthma.

- Chapters 18 through 28 cover specific sports injuries to regional areas of the body. The chapters, expanded to include new information, are fully comprehensive within the scope of practice in athletic training. The chapter for each body region includes sections on anatomy, prevention, assessment, management of specific injuries, and rehabilitation (when appropriate). These sections consistently discuss the associated etiology, symptoms and signs, and management of each injury identified. Coverage of rehabilitation techniques includes mobilization, flexibility exercises, muscular strength, neuromuscular control, functional progressions (when appropriate), and guidelines for return to activity.
- A new Chapter 23 now offers separate coverage of the elbow.
- Chapter 29, *Additional Health Conditions*, includes new and expanded content on the immune system, muscular system disorders, nervous system disorders, and types of anemia.
- Web sites are included at the end of appropriate chapters as an additional resource; students can obtain further information as well as link to other Web sites.

PEDAGOGICAL AIDS

Numerous pedagogical devices are included in this edition:

- *Chapter objectives*   Goals begin each chapter to reinforce important key concepts to be learned.
- *Margin information*   Key concepts, selected definitions, helpful training tips, and illustrations are placed in the margins throughout the text for added emphasis and ease of reading and studying.
- *Anatomy*   Where applicable, extensive discussion of anatomy is presented and illustrated throughout the text.
- *Focus boxes*   Important information has been highlighted and boxed to make key information easier to find and to enhance the text's flexibility and appearance.
- *Critical thinking exercises*   Case studies are included in every chapter that encourage the student to apply the content presented to the clinical setting.
- *Color throughout text*   Color is used throughout the text to accentuate and clarify illustrations and textual material.
- *New photographs and line drawings*   Many new photographs and color line drawings have been added.
- *Color illustrations*   Fourteen full-color photographs are included in Chapter 28 to depict common skin disorders.
- *Management plans*   In selected chapters, sample management plans are presented as examples of treatment procedures.
- *Chapter summaries*   Each chapter's salient points are summarized to reinforce key content.
- *Review questions and class activities*   Located at the end of each chapter, review questions and class activities are provided to enhance the learning process.
- *References*   References have been extensively updated to provide the most complete and current information available.
- *Annotated bibliography*   For students and instructors who want to expand on the information presented in each chapter, an annotated bibliography has been provided.
- *A detailed glossary*   An extensive list of key terms and their definitions is presented in one convenient location to reinforce information.
- *Appendixes*   The appendixes contain the NATA's Code of Ethics, Bloodborne Pathogens Guidelines, and Helmet Removal Guidelines. Also included is Canada's *Food Guide for Healthy Living* and the Recommended Nutrient Intake (RNI).

- *End pages* Front and back end pages inside the covers of the text provide helpful lists of suggested supplies for the athletic trainer along with charts for metric and Celsius conversions.

ANCILLARIES

- **Instructor's Manual and Test Bank**
  Developed specifically for the tenth edition, *The Instructor's Manual* was prepared by Meredith Busby, M.A., A.T.C. It includes:
  - Brief chapter overviews
  - Learning objectives
  - Key terminology
  - Discussion questions
  - Class activities
  - Worksheets
  - Worksheet answer keys
  - Test bank
  - Appendixes of additional resources
  - Transparency masters
  - Perforated format, ready for immediate use

In total, approximately 2,000 examination questions are included. Reviewed by instructors of the course for accuracy and currency, the questions for each chapter consist of true-false, multiple choice, and completion test questions. The worksheets in each chapter also include a separate *Test Bank* of matching, short answer, listing, essay, and personal or injury assessment questions that can be used as self-testing tools for students or as additional sources for examination questions.

- **Computerized Test Bank**
  A computerized version of the *Test Bank* from the *Instructor's Manual* is available for both IBM and Macintosh to qualified adopters. This software provides a unique combination of user-friendly aids and enables the instructor to select, edit, delete, or add questions and construct and print tests and answer keys.

- **Transparencies**
  Fifty-four acetate transparencies of important illustrations, tables, and charts are available to maximize the instructor's teaching and the student's learning process and are available to qualified adopters.

- **Photo CD**
  Photographs used in the text are available on CD-ROM, most in full color, to qualified adopters.

WEB RESOURCES

- **McGraw-Hill's Athletic Training Supersite**
  The athletic training supersite provides a wide variety of information for instructors and students, from text information to the latest technology. It includes competency locations found in *Principles of Athletic Training* as well as professional organization, convention, and career information. Visit the Web site at www.mhhe.com/hper/physed/athletictraining.

  Additional features of the supersite include:
  - *Up Close and Personal*

This link identifies the people who work on the athletic training list at McGraw-Hill, which conventions are attended, how to become a reviewer, and how to submit a book proposal.

- *By the Book*

  To log on to the Arnheim/Prentice *Principles of Athletic Training* home page, see the description and Web site address below. Link to the on-line catalog to find the perfect text or ancillary for your course.

- *Personalize Your Course*

  This section includes sample simulations, journal articles, and additional features to assist in preparation for certification examination and for the profession of athletic training.

- *Especially McGraw-Hill*

  This feature links to the many resources that McGraw-Hill has to offer, including the Web-based course management tool, the McGraw-Hill Learning Architecture, as well as regular updates to the Cox AIDS booklet.

- **Principles of Athletic Training** **Home Page**

  Developed specifically for the tenth edition, a Power Point Presentation has been prepared by Jeffrey A. Bonacci, D.A., A.T.C., and William O. Kauth, Ph.D., A.T.C., both of Illinois State University; it can be downloaded from this home page. Also included here are links to PageOut and PageOut Lite, McGraw-Hill's Web-based programs that can be used to help create your own Web site. Visit the *Principles of Athletic Training* home page at www.mhhe.com/hper/physed/arnheim_prin.

ACKNOWLEDGMENTS

Since the revision of the ninth edition of *Principles of Athletic Training,* McGraw-Hill has become the new publisher of this text. Fortunately, several of the many Mosby editors and production personnel who have contributed to the metamorphosis of this text over the years now work for McGraw-Hill. Once again, we want to express our deepest gratitude to our developmental editor, Michelle Turenne, who has truly been the glue holding this whole project together. Her input and dedication to this project has been indispensable, and her loyalty to us as authors has never been questioned. Our editor, Vicki Malinee, has been a "rock" in keeping us focused, and we cannot thank her enough for her efforts on our behalf.

During the revision process for the tenth edition, we relied heavily on input solicited from our reviewers. Many personal thanks are extended to:

Thomas W. Kaminski
University of Florida

Dan Foster
University of Iowa

Shari D. Bartz
University of Alabama at Birmingham

Sally D. Mays
University of North Carolina

Kim A. Bissonnette
University of Rhode Island

Patrick J. Sexton
Mankato State University

Ben G. Vance
Graceland College (Iowa)

Richard G. Dievert
University of Ohio

Mark H. Gibson
University of Wisconsin–La Crosse

Peter Koehneke
Canisius College (New York)

Sara D. Brown
Boston University

David Middlemas
William Paterson University
(New Jersey)

Many thanks must also be extended to our Focus Group participants, who were invaluable in developing the technology accompaniments for the tenth edition. They include:

Daniel Sedory
University of New Hampshire

Gerald Bell
University of Illinois

Ed Ferreira
Fresno State University

Bobby Patton
Southwest Texas State University

Donald Fuller
East Tennessee State University

Kent Scriber
Ithaca College

Jim Gallaspy
University of Southern Mississippi

R.T. Floyd
University of West Alabama

Rob Doyle
Eastern Illinois University

Katie Grove
Indiana University

Carl R. Cramer
Barry University

Katie Walsh
East Carolina University

Charles Redmond
Springfield College (Massachusetts)

Roger D. Clark
Western Illinois University

Michelle Sandrey
Indiana State University

Ken Wright
University of Alabama–Tuscaloosa

Scott Barker
California State University at Chico

Takanori Yoshinaga
Seagulls Football Team (Tokyo, Japan)

We also wish to extend our sincere appreciation to our technical reviewers for their critique of selected chapters. Their input was most valuable to the completion of this edition.

John Anderson, Ph.D.
Department of Nutrition
The University of North Carolina
at Chapel Hill

Patsy Huff, Pharm.D.
Pharmacy, Student Health Service
The University of North Carolina
at Chapel Hill

Thomas Brickner, M.D.
Sports Medicine, Student Health Service
The University of North Carolina
at Chapel Hill

Jill Rosenblum, J.D.
Legal Department, UNC Hospitals
The University of North Carolina
at Chapel Hill

Finally, Dan would like to extend a special thank you to Gloria Schiesl and the production staff at McGraw-Hill Higher Education, who helped make this edition possible. Bill would like to thank his wife, Tena, and their sons, Brian and Zachary, for putting up with the old man during the revision of this edition.

Daniel D. Arnheim
William E. Prentice

Professional Development and Responsibilities

The Athletic Trainer and the Sports Medicine Team

When you finish this chapter you should be able to

- Describe the historical foundations of athletic training.
- Identify the differences between professional organizations dedicated to athletic training and sports medicine.
- Differentiate among the roles and responsibilities of the athletic trainer, the team physician, and the coach.
- Explain the function of support personnel in sports medicine.
- Identify various employment settings for the athletic trainer.
- Discuss the certification and licensure of the athletic trainer.
- Discuss the role of the physical therapist in sports medicine.

An athletic trainer is concerned with the well-being of the athlete and generally assumes the responsibility for overseeing the total health care for the athlete. Participation in sports places the athlete in a situation in which injury is likely to occur. Fortunately, most of the injuries are not serious and lend themselves to rapid rehabilitation, but the athletic trainer must be capable of dealing with any type of trauma or catastrophic injury.

Although millions of individuals participate in organized and recreational sports, there is a relatively low incidence of fatalities and catastrophic injuries among them. A major problem, however, lies with the millions of sports participants who incur injuries or illnesses that could have been prevented and who later, as a consequence, develop more serious chronic conditions. Athletes in organized sports have every right to expect that their health and safety be kept as the highest of priorities. The field of athletic training, as a specialization, provides a major link between the sports program and the medical community for the implementation of injury prevention, emergency care, and rehabilitative procedures (Figure 1-1).[44]

HISTORICAL PERSPECTIVES

Early History

The history of athletic training draws on the histories of exercise, medicine, physical therapy, physical education, and sports.

The drive to compete was important in many early societies. Sports developed over a period of time as a means of competing in a relatively peaceful and nonharmful way. Early civilizations show little evidence of highly organized sports. Some evidence indicates that in Greek and Roman civilizations there were coaches, trainers (people who helped the athlete reach top physical condition), and physicians to assist the athlete in reaching optimum performance.[41] Many of the roles that emerged during this early period are the same in modern sports.

For many centuries after the fall of the Roman Empire there was a complete lack of interest in sports activities. Not until the beginning of the Renaissance did these activities slowly gain popularity. Athletic training as we know it came into existence during the late nineteenth century with the firm establishment of intercollegiate and interscholastic athletes in the United States. The first athletic trainers of this era were hangers-on who "rubbed down" the athlete. Because they possessed no technical knowledge, their athletic training techniques usually consisted of a rub, the application of some type of counterirritant, and occasionally the prescription of various home remedies and poultices. Many of those earlier athletic trainers were persons of questionable background and experience. As a result, it has taken many years for

Figure 1-1

The field of athletic training is a major link between the sports program and the medical community.

the athletic trainer to attain the status of a well-qualified allied health care professional.[41]

Evolution of the Contemporary Athletic Trainer

The terms *training* and *athletic training, trainer* and *athletic trainer* are confused more often outside than inside the United States. Historically, training implies the act of coaching or teaching. In comparison, athletic training has traditionally been known as the field that is concerned with the athlete's health and safety. A trainer refers to someone who trains dogs or horses or functions in coaching or teaching areas. The athletic trainer is one who is a specialist in athletic training. Athletic training has evolved over the years to play a major role in the health care of the physically active in general and the athlete in specific. This evolution occurred rapidly after World War I and the appearance of the athletic trainer in intercollegiate athletics. During this period, the major influence in developing the athletic trainer as a specialist in preventing and managing athletic injuries resulted from the work of Dr. S. E. Bilik, a physician who wrote the first major text on athletic training and care of athletic injuries, called *The Trainer's Bible*, in 1917.[6]

In the early 1920s the Cramer family in Gardner, Kansas, started a chemical company and began producing a liniment to treat ankle sprains. Over the years, the Cramers realized that there was a market for products to treat injured athletes. In an effort to enhance communication and facilitate an exchange of ideas among coaches, trainers, and athletes, Cramer began publication of the *First Aider* in 1932. The members of this family were instrumental in early development of the athletic training profession and have always played a prominent role in the education of student athletic trainers.[41]

During the late 1930s an effort was made, primarily by several college and university trainers, to establish a national organization named the National Athletic Trainers' Association (NATA). After struggling for existence from 1938 to 1944, the association essentially disappeared during the difficult years of World War II.

Between 1947 and 1950 university athletic trainers once again began to organize themselves into separate regional conferences, which would later become district organizations within NATA. In 1950 some 101 athletic trainers from the various conferences met in Kansas City, Missouri, and officially formed the National Athletic Trainers' Association. The primary purpose for its formation was to establish professional standards for the athletic trainer.[41] Since 1950 many individuals have made contributions to the development of the profession.

The growth of the profession of athletic training has been remarkable. Today NATA has more than 23,000 members, and the certified athletic trainer is widely recognized as a well-qualified allied health care provider.

SPORTS MEDICINE AND ATHLETIC TRAINING

The Field of Sports Medicine

Sports medicine encompasses many different fields of study related to sport.

Sports medicine has become a term that has many connotations depending on which group is using it. It is a generic term that encompasses many different areas of sports related to both performance and injury. Among the areas of specialization within sports medicine are athletic training, biomechanics, exercise physiology, the practice of medicine relative to the athlete, physical therapy, sports nutrition, and sports psychology. The American College of Sports Medicine (ACSM) has defined sports medicine as multidisciplinary, including the physiological, biomechanical, psychological, and pathological phenomena associated with exercise and sports.[1] The clinical application of the work of these disciplines is performed to improve and maintain an individual's functional capacities for physical labor, exercise, and sports. The term also includes the prevention and treatment of diseases and injuries related to exercise and sports.

Growth of Professional Sports Medicine Organizations

Many professional organizations that are dedicated to achieving health and safety in sports have developed in the twentieth century.

The twentieth century brought with it the development of a number of professional organizations dedicated to athletic training and sports medicine. Professional organizations have many goals: (1) to upgrade the field by devising and maintaining a set of professional standards, including a code of ethics; (2) to bring together professionally competent individuals to exchange ideas, stimulate research, and promote critical thinking; and (3) to give individuals an opportunity to work as a group with a singleness of purpose, thereby making it possible for them to achieve objectives that, separately, they could not accomplish. The organizations listed below are presented in chronological order according to their year of establishment.

 *Focus*

Addresses of professional organizations

American Academy of Pediatrics, Sports Committee, 141 NW Point Boulevard, Elk Grove Village, IL 60007-1098. http://www.aap.org/

American Academy of Family Physicians, 8880 Ward Parkway, Kansas City, MO 64114. http://home.aafp.org/

American Board of Physical Therapy Specialists, American Physical Therapy Association, 1111 N. Fairfax St., Alexandria, VA 22314. http://apta.edoc.com/

American College of Sports Medicine, 401 W. Michigan St., Indianapolis, IN 46202-3233. http://www.acsm.org/

American Orthopaedic Society for Sports Medicine, 6300 N. River Road, Suite 200, Rosemont, IL 60018. http://www.sportsmed.org/

National Athletic Trainers' Association, 2952 Stemmons Freeway, Dallas, TX 75247. http://www.nata.org/

National Collegiate Athletic Association, Competitive Safeguards and Medical Aspects of Sports Committee, 6201 College Boulevard, Overland Park, KS 66211-2422. http://www.ncaa.org/

The National Federation of State High School Athletic Associations, 11724 Plaza Circle, P.O. Box 20626, Kansas City, MO 64195. http://nfshsa.org/

National Strength and Conditioning Association, P.O. Box 38909, Colorado Springs, CO 80937-8909. http://www.nsca-lift.org/

Addresses for these organizations are in *Focus Box:* "Addresses of professional organizations."

Several of these professional organizations also disseminate information to the general public relative to safe participation in sport activities in the form of guidelines or position statements. *Focus Box:* "Guidelines and position statements" lists the guidelines and position statements that are published by several different organizations.

International Federation of Sports Medicine

Among the first major organizations was the Federation Internationale de Medecine Sportive (FIMS). It was created in 1928 at the Olympic Winter Games in St. Moritz, Switzerland, by Olympic medical doctors with the principal purpose of promoting the study and development of sports medicine throughout the world. FIMS is made up of the national sports medicine associations of more than 100 countries. This organization is multidisciplinary and includes many disciplines that are concerned with the physically active individual. To some degree the ACSM has patterned itself after this organization.

American Academy of Family Physicians

The American Academy of Family Physicians (AAFP) was founded in 1947 to promote and maintain high quality standards for family doctors who are providing continuing comprehensive health care to the public. AAFP is a medical association of more than 85,000 members. Many team physicians are members of this organization. It publishes the *American Family Physician.*

National Athletic Trainers' Association

Before the formation of the National Athletic Trainers' Association in 1950, athletic trainers occupied a somewhat insecure place in the athletic program. Since that time, as a result of the raising of professional standards and the establishment of a code of ethics, there has been considerable professional advancement. The stated mission of NATA is

> To enhance the quality of health care for the physically active through education and research in prevention, evaluation, management, and rehabilitation of injuries.

The association accepts as members only those trainers who are properly qualified and who are prepared to subscribe to a code of ethics and to uphold the standards of the association. NATA currently has more than 23,000 members. It publishes a quarterly journal, *The Journal of Athletic Training,* and holds an annual convention at which members have an opportunity to keep abreast of new developments and to exchange ideas through clinical programs. The organization is constantly working to improve both the quality and the status of athletic training.

American College of Sports Medicine

As discussed previously, the ACSM is interested in the study of all aspects of sports. Established in 1954, ACSM's membership is composed of medical doctors, doctors of philosophy, physical educators, athletic trainers, coaches, exercise physiologists, biomechanists, and others interested in sports. The organization holds national and regional conferences and meetings devoted to exploring the many aspects of sports medicine, and it publishes a quarterly magazine, *Medicine and Science in Sports and Exercise*. This journal includes articles in French, Italian, German, and English and provides complete translations in English of all articles. It reports recent developments in the field of sports medicine on a worldwide basis.

American Orthopaedic Society for Sports Medicine

The American Orthopaedic Society for Sports Medicine (AOSSM) was created in 1972 to encourage and support scientific research in orthopedic sports medicine; the organization works to develop methods for safer, more productive, and more

1-1

Critical Thinking E x e r c i s e

A student athletic trainer has been given a class assignment to put together a list of various sports medicine organizations and to define the missions of those organizations.

? Where can the student find the most information about these organizations?

Focus

Guidelines and position statements

National Collegiate Athletic Association (NCAA) guidelines

Sports Medicine Administration

Medical Evaluations, Immunizations, and Records

Dispensing Prescription Medication

Lightning Safety

Medical Disqualification of the Student-Athlete

Skin Infections in Wrestling

Prevention of Heat Illness

Weight Loss-Hypohydration

Assessment of Body Composition

Eating Disorders—Anorexia and Bulimia

Menstrual Cycle Dysfunction

Bloodborne Pathogens and Intercollegiate Athletics

Nontherapeutic Drugs

Nutritional Ergogenic Aids

The Use of Local Anesthetics in College Athletics

The Use of Injectable Corticosteroids in Sports Injuries

Cold Stress

"Burners" (Brachial Plexus Injuries)

Concussion and Second-Impact Syndrome

Participation by the Impaired Student-Athlete

Participation by the Pregnant Student-Athlete

The Student-Athlete with Sickle Cell Trait

Protective Equipment

Eye Safety in Sports

Use of Trampoline and Minitramp

Mouth Guards

Use of the Head as a Weapon in Football and Other Contact Sports

Guidelines for Helmet Fitting and Removal in Athletics

National Athletic Trainers' Association (NATA)

Helmet Removal

Bloodborne Pathogens Guidelines

Clinical/Industrial/Corporate

Secondary School Athletic Trainers

Governmental Affairs

American Academy of Pediatrics (AAP)

Recommendations for Participation in Competitive Sports

Climatic Heat Stress and the Exercising Child

Anabolic Steroids and the Adolescent Athlete

Strength Training, Weight and Power Lifting, and Bodybuilding by Children and Adolescents

Risks in Distance Running for Children

Knee Brace Use by Athletes

Organized Athletics for Preadolescent Children

Amenorrhea in Adolescent Athletes

Infant Exercise Programs

Exercise for Children Who are Mentally Retarded

Physical Fitness and the Schools

American College of Sports Medicine (ACSM)

Female Athlete Triad

Heat and Cold Illnesses during Distance Running

Weight Loss in Wrestlers

The Use of Blood Doping as an Erogenic Aid

Exercise and Fluid Replacement

Osteoporosis and Exercise

Exercise for Patients with Coronary Artery Disease

Physical Activity, Physical Fitness, and Hypertension

The Recommended Quality and Quantity of Exercise for Developing and Maintaining Cardiorespiratory and Muscular Fitness in Healthy Adults

The Prevention of Thermal Injuries during Distance Running

The Use of Anabolic-Androgenic Steroids in Sports

Proper and Improper Weight Loss Programs

The Use of Alcohol in Sports

Physical Fitness in Children and Youth

enjoyable fitness programs and sports participation. Through programs developed by the AOSSM, members receive specialized training in sports medicine, surgical procedures, injury prevention, and rehabilitation. AOSSM's 1,200 members are orthopedic surgeons and allied health professionals committed to excellence in sports medicine. Its official bimonthly publication is the *American Journal of Sports Medicine.*

National Strength and Conditioning Association

The National Strength and Conditioning Association (NSCA) was formed in 1978 to facilitate a professional exchange of ideas in strength development as it relates to the improvement of athletic performance and fitness and to enhance, enlighten, and advance the field of strength and conditioning.

NSCA has a membership of more than 14,500 professionals, including strength and conditioning coaches, personal trainers, exercise physiologists, athletic trainers, researchers, educators, sport coaches, physical therapists, business owners, exercise instructors, fitness directors, and students training to enter the field. In addition, the NSCA Certification Commission offers two of the finest and the only nationally accredited certification programs: the Certified Strength and Conditioning Specialist (CSCS) and the NSCA Certified Personal Trainer (NSCA-CPT). NSCA publishes both the *Journal of Strength and Conditioning Research* and *Strength and Conditioning.*

American Academy of Pediatrics, Sports Committee

The American Academy of Pediatrics, Sports Committee, was organized in 1979. Its primary goal is to educate all physicians, especially pediatricians, about the special needs of children who participate in sports. Between 1979 and 1983, this committee developed guidelines that were incorporated in a report, *Sports Medicine: Health Care for Young Athletes,* edited by Nathan J. Smith, M.D.

American Physical Therapy Association, Sports Physical Therapy Section

In 1981, the Sports Physical Therapy Section of the American Physical Therapy Association (APTA) was officially established. The mission of the Sports Physical Therapy Section is "to provide a forum to establish collegial relations between physical therapists, physical therapist assistants, and physical therapy students interested in sports physical therapy." The Section promotes prevention, recognition, treatment, and rehabilitation of injuries in an athletic and physically active population; provides educational opportunities through sponsorship of continuing education programs and publications; promotes the role of the sports physical therapist to other health professionals; and supports research to further establish the scientific basis for sports physical therapy. The Section's official journal is the *Journal of Orthopaedic and Sports Physical Therapy.*[21]

NCAA Committee on Competitive Safeguards and Medical Aspects of Sports

The National Collegiate Athletic Association (NCAA) Committee on Competitive Safeguards and Medical Aspects of Sports collects and develops pertinent information about desirable training methods, prevention and treatment of sports injuries, utilization of sound safety measures at the college level, drug education, and drug testing; disseminates information and adopts recommended policies and guidelines designed to further the objectives just listed; and supervises drug-education and drug-testing programs.

Other Health-Related Organizations

Many other health-related professions such as dentists, podiatrists, and chiropractors have, over the years, become interested in the health and safety aspects of sports. Besides national organizations that are interested in athletic health and safety, there are state and local associations that are extensions of the larger bodies. National, state, and local sports organizations have all provided extensive support to the reduction of illness and injury risk to the athlete.

Other Sports Medicine Journals

Other journals that provide an excellent service to the field of athletic training and sports medicine are *The International Journal of Sports Medicine*, which is published in English by Thieme-Stratton, Inc., New York; *The Journal of Sports Medicine and Physical Fitness*, published by Edizioni Minerva Medica SPA, ADIS Press Ltd., Auckland 10, New Zealand; the *Journal of Sport Rehabilitation* and *Athletic Therapy Today*, both published by Human Kinetics Publishers, Inc., Champaign, Illinois; the *Physician and Sportsmedicine*, published by McGraw-Hill, Inc., New York; *Physical Therapy* and *Clinical Management*, both published by the American Physical Therapy Association, Fairfax, Virginia; *Physical Medicine and Rehabilitation Clinics* and *Clinics in Sports Medicine*, both published by W. B. Saunders, Philadelphia; *Sports Medicine Update*, published by the Healthsouth Corporation, Birmingham, Alabama; and *Training and Conditioning*, published by MAG, Inc., Ithaca, New York.

THE SPORTS MEDICINE TEAM

The provision of health care to the athlete requires a group effort to be most effective.[44] The sports medicine team involves a number of individuals, each of whom must perform specific functions relative to caring for the injured athlete. Those people having the closest relationship with the injured athlete are the athletic trainer, the team physician, and the coach.

THE ATHLETIC TRAINER

Of all the professionals charged with injury prevention and health care provision for the athlete, perhaps none is more intimately involved than the athletic trainer.[44] The athletic trainer is the one individual who deals with the athlete throughout the period of rehabilitation, from the time of the initial injury until the athlete's complete, unrestricted return to practice or competition.[44] The athletic trainer is most directly responsible for all phases of health care in an athletic environment, including preventing injuries from occurring, providing initial first aid and injury management, evaluating injuries, and designing and supervising a timely and effective program of rehabilitation that can facilitate the safe and expeditious return of the athlete to activity.

The athletic trainer must be knowledgeable and competent in a variety of specialties encompassed under the umbrella of "sports medicine" if he or she is to be effective in preventing and treating injuries to the athlete.[13] The specific roles and responsibilities of the athletic trainer differ and to a certain extent are defined by the situation in which he or she works.[37]

Roles and Responsibilities of the Athletic Trainer

NATABOC performance domains   In 1999 the NATA Board of Certification (NATABOC) completed the latest role delineation study, which redefined the profession of athletic training.[38] This study was designed to examine the primary tasks performed by the entry-level athletic trainer and the knowledge and skills required to perform each task. The panel determined that the roles of the practicing athletic trainer could be divided into six major areas, or performance domains: (1) prevention of athletic injuries; (2) recognition, evaluation, and assessment of injuries; (3) immediate care of injuries; (4) treatment, rehabilitation, and reconditioning of athletic injuries; (5) health care administration; and (6) professional development and responsibility.

Education Council competencies   In 1998, the leadership of NATA established the Education Council to dictate the course of educational preparation for the student athletic trainer.[47] The focus of this Education Council has shifted to competency-based education at the entry level, and thus the Council has signifi-

Athletic training must be considered as a specialization under the broad field of sports medicine.

The primary sports medicine team consists of the coach, the athletic trainer, and the team physician.

Six performance domains of the athletic trainer:
- Prevention of athletic injuries
- Recognition, evaluation, assessment
- Immediate care
- Treatment, rehabilitation, and reconditioning
- Organization and administration
- Professional development and responsibility

cantly expanded and reorganized the clinical competencies identified in the NATA's previous document, the 1993 *Competencies in Athletic Training*. Whereas NATABOC defined the minimum knowledge base that an entry-level athletic trainer should possess to be able to work in the profession, the Education Council was charged with determining the competencies that should be taught in accredited educational programs.

The twelve domains established by the Education Council include (1) acute care of injury and illness, (2) assessment and evaluation, (3) general medical conditions and disabilities, (4) health care administration, (5) nutritional aspects of injury and illnesses, (6) pathology of illness and injuries, (7) pharmacological aspects of injury and illnesses, (8) professional development and responsibility, (9) psychosocial intervention and referral, (10) risk management and injury prevention, (11) therapeutic exercise, and (12) therapeutic modalities. These competencies are required for both curriculum development and education of students enrolled in entry-level athletic training education programs. As can be seen in *Focus Box:* "Domains and competencies," it is obvious that a great deal of overlap exists between the six performance domains identified by the NATABOC and the twelve competency domains established by the Education Council.[36]

Injury Prevention and Risk Management

Participation in competitive sports places the athlete into situations in which injuries are possible at any given time. One major responsibility of the athletic trainer is to make the competitive environment as safe as possible to minimize the risk of injury. If injury can be prevented initially, there will be no need for first aid and subsequent rehabilitation.

The athletic trainer can minimize the risk of injury by (1) ensuring appropriate training and conditioning of the athlete; (2) monitoring environmental conditions to ensure safe participation; (3) selecting, properly fitting, and maintaining protective

1-2

Critical Thinking E x e r c i s e

A student of athletic training must develop a sound knowledge base in and demonstrate competent performance skills in six major domains: prevention of athletic injuries; recognition, evaluation, and assessment of injuries; immediate care of injuries; treatment, rehabilitation, and reconditioning of athletic injuries; health care administration; and professional development and responsibility.

? How can student athletic trainers best prepare themselves to be competent professional athletic trainers?

Focus

Domains and competencies

Six performance domains established by the NATABOC*

Prevention of athletic injuries
Recognition, evaluation, and assessment of injuries
Immediate care of injuries
Treatment, rehabilitation, and reconditioning of athletic injuries
Health care administration
Professional development and responsibility
*Based on the 1999 Role Delineation Study

Education competencies established by the Education Council

Acute care of injury and illness
Assessment and evaluation
General medical conditions and disabilities
Health care administration
Nutritional aspects of injury and illnesses
Pathology of illness and injuries
Pharmacological aspects of injury and illnesses
Professional development and responsibility
Psychosocial intervention and referral
Risk management and injury prevention
Therapeutic exercise
Therapeutic modalities

equipment; (4) making certain that the athlete is eating properly; and (5) making sure the athlete is using medications appropriately while discouraging substance abuse.

Developing training and conditioning programs　Perhaps the most important aspect of injury prevention is making certain that the athlete is fit and thus able to handle the physiological and psychological demands of athletic competition. The athletic trainer works with the coaches to develop and implement an effective training and conditioning program for the athlete (see Chapter 4). It is essential that the athlete maintain a consistently high level of fitness during the preseason, the competitive season, and the off-season. This consistent level of fitness is critical not only for enhancing performance parameters but also for preventing injury and reinjury. An athletic trainer must be knowledgeable in the area of applied physiology of exercise, particularly with regard to strength training, flexibility, improvement of cardiorespiratory fitness, maintenance of body composition, weight control, and nutrition. Many colleges and most professional teams employ full-time strength coaches to oversee this aspect of the total program. The athletic trainer, however, must be acutely aware of any aspect of the program that may have a negative impact on an athlete or group of athletes and must offer constructive suggestions for alternatives when appropriate. At the high-school level, the athletic trainer may be totally responsible for designing, implementing, and overseeing the fitness and conditioning program for the athletes.

Ensuring a safe playing environment　To the best of his or her ability, the athletic trainer must ensure a safe environment for competition. This task may include duties not typically thought to belong to the athletic trainer, such as collecting trash, picking up rocks, or removing objects (e.g., hurdles, gymnastics equipment) from the perimeter of the practice area, all of which might pose potential danger to the athlete. The athletic trainer should call these potential safety hazards to the attention of an administrator. The interaction between the athletic trainer and a concerned and cooperative administrator can greatly enhance the effectiveness of the sports medicine team.

The athletic trainer should also be familiar with potential dangers associated with practicing or competing under inclement weather conditions, such as high heat and humidity, extreme cold, or electrical storms. Practice should be restricted, altered, or canceled if weather conditions threaten the health and safety of the athlete. If the team physician is not present, the athletic trainer must have the authority to curtail practice if the environmental conditions become severe (see Chapter 6).

Selecting, fitting, and maintaining protective equipment　The athletic trainer works with coaches and equipment personnel to select protective equipment and is responsible for maintaining its condition and safety (see Chapter 7). Because liability lawsuits have become the rule rather than the exception, the athletic trainer must make certain that high-quality equipment is purchased and that it is constantly being worn, maintained, and reconditioned according to specific guidelines recommended by the manufacturers.

Protective equipment and devices can consume a significant portion of the athletic budget. The individual who is responsible for purchasing protective equipment is usually inundated with marketing literature on a variety of braces, supports, pads, and other types of protective equipment. Decisions on purchasing specific pieces or brands should be based on research data that clearly document effectiveness in reducing or preventing injury (Figure 1-2).

Equipment is expensive, and schools are certainly subject to budgeting restrictions. However, purchasing decisions made about protective equipment should always be made in the best interest of the athlete. Most colleges and professional teams hire full-time equipment managers to oversee this area of responsibility, but the athletic trainer must be knowledgeable about and aware of the equipment being worn by each athlete.

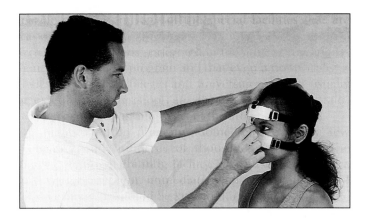

Figure 1-2

The athletic trainer should be responsible for taping and also for fitting of protective devices.

The design, building, and fitting of specific protective orthopedic devices are also responsibilities of the athletic trainer. Once the physician has indicated the problem and how it may be corrected, the athletic trainer should be able to construct an orthopedic device to correct it.

Explaining the importance of nutrition   Good nutrition can have a substantial impact on health and well-being. Poor nutritional habits can certainly have a negative effect on an athlete's ability to perform at the highest level possible. Yet for all the attention that athletes, coaches, and athletic trainers direct at practicing sound nutritional habits, good nutritional decisions are still subjected to a tremendous amount of misunderstanding, misinformation, and occasionally, quackery. An athletic trainer is often asked for advice about matters related to diet, weight loss, and weight gain, and is occasionally asked about disordered eating. The athletic trainer does not need to be an expert on nutrition but must possess some understanding of the basic principles of nutrition.

Using medications appropriately   The athlete, like any other individual in the population, may benefit greatly from using medications prescribed for various medical conditions by qualified physicians. Under normal circumstances an athlete would be expected to respond to medication just like anyone else would. However, because of the nature of physical activity, the athlete's situation is not normal; intense physical activity requires that special consideration be given to the effects of certain types of medication.

For the athletic trainer who is overseeing the health care of the athlete, some knowledge of the potential effects of certain types of drugs on performance is essential. Occasionally, the athletic trainer must make decisions regarding the appropriate use of medications based on knowledge of the indications for use and of the possible side effects in athletes who are involved in training and conditioning as well as in injury rehabilitation programs. The athletic trainer must be cognizant of the potential effects and side effects of over-the-counter and prescription medications on the athlete during rehabilitation as well as during competition.

In addition, the athletic trainer should also be aware of the problems of substance abuse, both in ergogenic aids that may be used in an effort to enhance performance and in the abuse of so-called recreational or street drugs. The athletic trainer may be involved in drug testing of the athlete and should thus be responsible for educating the athlete in drug use and substance abuse.

Recognition, Evaluation, and Assessment of Athletic Injuries

Frequently, the athletic trainer is the first person to see an athlete who has sustained an injury. The athletic trainer must be skilled in recognizing the nature and extent of an injury through competency in injury evaluation. Once the injury has been evaluated, the athletic trainer must be able to provide the appropriate first aid and then refer the athlete to appropriate medical personnel.

Conducting physical examinations The athletic trainer, in cooperation with the team physician, should obtain a medical history and conduct physical examinations of the athletes before participation as a means of screening for existing or potential problems (see Chapter 2). The medical history should be reviewed closely and clarification given to any point of concern.

The preparticipation examination should include measurement of height, weight, blood pressure, and body composition. The physician examination should concentrate on cardiovascular, respiratory, abdominal, genital, dermatological, and ear, nose, and throat systems and may include blood work and urinalysis. A brief orthopedic evaluation would include range of motion, muscle strength, and functional tests to assess joint stability. When the athletic trainer knows at the beginning of a season that an athlete has a physical problem that may predispose that athlete to an injury during the course of the season, he or she may immediately implement corrective measures that may significantly reduce the possibility of additional injury.

The athletic trainer must be able to efficiently and accurately evaluate an injury. Information obtained in this initial evaluation may be critical later on when swelling, pain, and guarding mask some of the functional signs of the injury.

It is essential that the athletic trainer be alert and observe, as much as possible, everything that goes on in practice. Invaluable information regarding the nature of an injury can be obtained by seeing the mechanism of the injury.

The subsequent off-the-field examination should include (1) obtaining a brief medical history of exactly what happened, according to the athlete, (2) observation, (3) palpation, (4) special tests that might include range of motion, muscle strength, joint stability, or a brief neurological examination. Information obtained in this initial examination should be documented by the athletic trainer and given to the physician once the athlete is referred. The team physician is ultimately responsible for providing an accurate diagnosis of an injury. The initial evaluation often provides the basis for this diagnosis (see Chapter 13).

Understanding the pathology of injury and illness The athletic trainer must be able to recognize the various types of musculoskeletal and nervous system injuries that can occur in the physically active population. Based on this knowledge of different injuries, the athletic trainer must possess some understanding of both the sequence and time frames for the various phases of healing, realizing that certain physiological events must occur during each of the phases (see Chapter 10). Anything done during training and conditioning or during a rehabilitation program that interferes with this healing process will likely delay a return to full activity. The healing process must have an opportunity to accomplish what it is supposed to. At best the athletic trainer can only try to create an environment that is conducive to the healing process. Little can be done to speed up the process physiologically, but many things may be done both during training and conditioning and during rehabilitation to impede healing.

Referring to medical care After the initial management of an injury, the athletic trainer should routinely refer the athlete to the team physician for further evaluation and accurate diagnosis. If an athlete requires treatment from medical personnel other than the team physician, such as a dentist or opthalmologist, the athletic trainer should arrange appointments as necessary. Referrals should be made after consultation with the team physician.

Referring to support services If needed, the athletic trainer must be familiar with and should have access to a variety of personal, school, and community health service agencies including community-based psychological and social support services available to the athlete. With assistance and direction from these agencies, the athletic trainer together with the athlete should be able to formulate a plan for appropriate intervention following injury.

Immediate Care of Injury and Illness

The athletic trainer is often responsible for the initial on-the-field injury assessment following acute injury. Once this initial assessment is done, the athletic trainer then must assume responsibility for administering appropriate first aid to the injured athlete and for making correct decisions in the management of acute injury (see Chapter 12). Although the team physician is frequently present at games or competitions, in most cases he or she cannot be at every practice session, where injuries are more likely to occur. Thus the athletic trainer must possess sound skills not only in the initial recognition and evaluation of potentially serious or life-threatening injuries but also in emergency care.

The athletic trainer should be certified in cardiopulmonary resuscitation by the American Red Cross, the American Heart Association, or the National Safety Council. Athletic trainers should also be certified in first aid by the American Red Cross or the National Safety Council. Many athletic trainers have gone beyond these essential basic certifications and have completed emergency medical technician (EMT) requirements.

Emergency care procedures should be established by the athletic trainer in cooperation with local rescue squads and the community hospitals that can provide emergency treatment. Emergency care is expedited and the injured athlete's frustration and concern is lessened if arrangements regarding transportation, logistics, billing procedures, and appropriate contacts are made before an injury occurs.

Treatment, Rehabilitation, and Reconditioning

An athletic trainer must work closely with and under the supervision of the team physician with respect to designing rehabilitation and reconditioning protocols that make use of appropriate therapeutic exercise, rehabilitative equipment, manual therapy techniques, or therapeutic modalities. The athletic trainer should then assume the responsibility of overseeing the rehabilitative process, ultimately returning the athlete to full activity (see Chapter 15).

Designing rehabilitation programs   Once the team physician has evaluated and diagnosed an injury, the rehabilitation process begins immediately. In most cases, the athletic trainer will design and supervise an injury rehabilitation program, modifying that program based on the healing process. It is critical for an athletic trainer to have a sound background in anatomy. Without this background, an athletic trainer cannot evaluate an injury. And if the athletic trainer cannot evaluate an injury, there is no point in the athletic trainer knowing anything about rehabilitation because he or she will not know at what phase the injury is in the healing process. The athletic trainer must also understand how to incorporate therapeutic modalities and appropriate therapeutic exercise techniques if the rehabilitation program is to be successful.

Supervising rehabilitation programs   Too often in the past the athletic trainer has routinely referred the injured athlete to a physical therapist who supervises the rehabilitation program. Although physical therapists are well qualified for this task, there is no reason for the well-trained athletic trainer to avoid this responsibility. In fact, the athletic trainer should have a better understanding of how to design a series of activities related to the sport that allow the athlete to gradually progress to complete functional return.

Incorporating therapeutic modalities   Athletic trainers use a wide variety of therapeutic modalities in the treatment and rehabilitation of sport-related injuries. Modality use may involve a relatively simple technique such as using an ice pack as a first-aid treatment for an acute injury or may involve more complex techniques such as the stimulation of nerve and muscle tissue by electrical currents. Certainly, therapeutic modalities are useful tools in injury rehabilitation, and when used appropriately, these modalities can greatly enhance the athlete's chances for a safe and

1-3

Critical Thinking E x e r c i s e

A basketball player suffers a grade 2 ankle sprain during midseason of the competitive schedule. After a three-week course of rehabilitation, most of the pain and swelling has been eliminated. The athlete is anxious to get back into practice and competitive games as soon as possible, and subsequent injuries to other players have put pressure on the coach to force the athlete's return. Unfortunately the athlete is still unable to perform functional tasks (cutting and jumping) essential in basketball.

? Who is responsible for making the decision regarding when the athlete can fully return to practice and game situations?

rapid return to athletic competition. It is essential for the athletic trainer to possess knowledge regarding the scientific basis and the physiologic effects of the various modalities on a specific injury. Modalities, though important, are by no means the single most critical factor in injury treatment. Therapeutic exercise that forces the injured anatomic structure to perform its normal function is the key to successful rehabilitation. However, therapeutic modalities play an important role in reducing pain and are extremely useful as an adjunct to therapeutic exercise.

Offering psychosocial intervention   The psychological aspect of how the individual athlete deals with an injury is a critical yet often neglected aspect of the rehabilitation process. Injury and illness produce a wide range of emotional reactions. Therefore the athletic trainer needs to develop an understanding of the psyche of each athlete. Athletes vary in terms of pain threshold, cooperation and compliance, competitiveness, denial of disability, depression, intrinsic and extrinsic motivation, anger, fear, guilt, and the ability to adjust to injury. Principles of sport psychology may be used to improve total athletic performance through visualization, self-hypnosis, and relaxation techniques. The athletic trainer plays a critical role in social support for the injured athlete.[5]

Organization and Administration

The athletic trainer is responsible for the organization and administration of the training room facility, including the maintenance of health and injury records for each athlete, requisition and inventory of necessary supplies and equipment, the supervision of assistant or student trainers, and the establishment of policies and procedures for day-to-day operation of the athletic training program (see Chapter 2).[50]

Record keeping   Accurate and detailed record keeping—including medical histories, preparticipation examinations, injury reports, treatment records, and rehabilitation programs—are critical for the athletic trainer, particularly in light of the number of lawsuits directed toward malpractice in health care. Although record keeping may be difficult and time consuming for the athletic trainer who treats and deals with a large number of patients each day, it is an area that simply cannot be neglected.

Ordering equipment and supplies   Although tremendous variations in operating budgets exist, depending on the level and the institution, decisions regarding how available money may best be spent are always critical. The athletic trainer must keep on hand a wide range of supplies to enable him or her to handle whatever situation may arise. At institutions in which severe budgetary restrictions exist, prioritization based on experience and past needs must become the mode of operation. A creative athletic trainer can make do with very little equipment, which should include at least a taping and treatment table, an ice machine, and a few free weights. Like in other professions, the more tools available for use, the more effective the practitioner can be, as long as there is an understanding of how those tools are used most effectively.

Supervising personnel   In an athletic training environment, the quality and efficiency of the assistant and student trainers in carrying out their specific responsibilities is absolutely essential.[15] The person who supervises these assistants has a responsibility to design a reasonable work schedule that is consistent with other commitments and responsibilities they have outside the training room. It is the responsibility of the head athletic trainer to provide an environment in which assistant and student trainers can continually learn and develop professionally.[2]

Establishing policies for operation of an athletic training program   Although the athletic trainer must be able to easily adjust and adapt to a given situation, it is essential that specific policies, procedures, rules, and regulations be established to ensure smooth and consistent day-to-day operation of the athletic training program. A plan should be established for emergency management of injury. Appropriate channels for referral after injury and emergency treatment should be used consistently.

Policies and procedures must be established and implemented that reduce the likelihood of exposure to infectious agents by following universal precautions, which can prevent the transmission of infectious diseases.

Professional Development and Responsibilities

The athletic trainer should assume personal responsibility for continuously expanding his or her own knowledge base and expertise within the chosen field. This professional development may be accomplished by attending continuing education programs offered at state, district, and national meetings. Athletic trainers must also routinely review professional journals and consult current textbooks to stay abreast of the most up-to-date techniques. The athletic trainer should also make an effort to be involved professionally with national, regional, or state organizations that are committed to enhancing continued growth and development of the profession.

The athletic trainer as an educator   The athletic trainer must take time to help educate student athletic trainers. The continued success of any profession lies in its ability to educate its students. Education should not simply be a responsibility, it should be a priority.

To be an effective educator, the athletic trainer needs an understanding of the basic principles of learning and methods of classroom instruction. The athletic trainer should seek and develop competence in presenting information to students through the use of a variety of instructional techniques. The athletic training educator should also make an effort to stay informed about the availability of relevant audiovisual aids, multimedia, newletters, journals, workshops, and seminars that can enhance the breadth of the students' educational experience. The athletic trainer must also be able to evaluate student knowledge and competencies through development and construction of appropriate tests.[2]

Students of athletic training must be given a sound academic background in a curriculum that stresses the competencies that are outlined in this chapter. They must be able to translate the theoretical base presented in the classroom into practical application in a clinical setting if they are to be effective in treating patients. The athletic training educator accomplishes this application by organizing appropriate laboratory and/or clinical experiences in order to evaluate the students' clinical competencies.[16]

The athletic trainer must also educate the general public, in addition to a large segment of the various allied medical health care professions, as to exactly what athletic trainers are and the scope of their roles and responsibilities. This educating is perhaps best accomplished by organizing workshops and clinics in athletic training, holding professional seminars, meeting with local and community organizations, publishing research in scholarly journals, and most important, doing a good and professional job of providing health care to the injured athlete.

The athletic trainer as a counselor   The athletic trainer should take responsibility for informing parents and coaches about the nature of a specific injury and how it may affect the ability of the athlete to compete. The athletic trainer should be concerned primarily with counseling and advising the athlete not only with regard to prevention, rehabilitation, and treatment of specific injuries but on any matter that might be of help to the athlete.[31,32] Perhaps one of the most rewarding aspects of working as an athletic trainer can be found in the relationships that the trainer develops with individual athletes.

During the period of time that athletes are competing, the athletic trainer has the opportunity to get to know them very well on a personal basis because he or she spends a considerable amount of time with them. Athletes often develop a degree of respect and trust in the athletic trainer's judgment that carries over from their athletic life into their personal life. It is not uncommon for an athletic trainer to be

1-4

Critical Thinking E x e r c i s e

A young athletic trainer has taken his first job at All-American High School. The school administrators are extremely concerned about the number of athletes who get hurt playing various sports. They have charged the athletic trainer with the task of developing an athletic training program that can effectively help prevent the occurrence of injury to athletes in all sports at that school.

? What actions can the athletic trainer take to reduce the number of injuries and to minimize the risk of injury in the competitive athletes at that high school?

asked questions about a number of personal matters, at which point he or she crosses a bridge from athletic trainer to friend and confidant. This considerable responsibility is perhaps best handled by first listening to the problems, presenting several options, and then letting the athlete make his or her own decision. Certainly, the role of counselor and advisor cannot be taken lightly.[17]

Personal Qualities of the Athletic Trainer

An athletic trainer's personal qualities:
- Stamina and ability to adapt
- Empathy
- Sense of humor
- Ability to communicate
- Intellectual curiosity
- Ethics

There is probably no field of endeavor that can provide more work excitement, variety of tasks, and personal satisfaction than athletic training. A person contemplating going into this field must love sports and must enjoy the world of competition, in which there is a level of intensity seldom matched in any other area.

An athletic trainer's personal qualities, not the facilities and equipment, determine his or her success. Personal qualities are the many characteristics that identify individuals in regard to their actions and reactions as members of society. Personality is a complex of the many characteristics that together give an image of the individual to those with whom he or she associates. The personal qualities of athletic trainers are important because they in turn work with many complicated and diverse personalities. Although no attempt has been made to establish a rank order, the qualities discussed in the following paragraphs are essential for a good athletic trainer.

Stamina and Ability to Adapt

Athletic training is not the field for a person who likes an 8-to-5 job. Long, arduous hours of often strenuous work will sap the reserve strength of anyone not in the best of physical and emotional health. Athletic training requires abundant energy, vitality, and physical and emotional stability.[48] Every day brings new challenges and problems that must be solved. The athletic trainer must be able to adapt to new situations with ease. A problem that can happen in any helping profession and does on occasion occur among athletic trainers is burnout. This problem can be avoided if addressed early.

As a member of a helping profession, the athletic trainer is subject to burnout.

A problem with burnout   The term *burnout* is commonly used to describe feelings of exhaustion and disinterest toward work.[18] Clinically, burnout is most often associated with the helping professions; however, it is seen in athletes and other types of individuals engaged in physically or emotionally demanding endeavors.[9] Most persons who have been associated with sports have known athletes, coaches, or athletic trainers who just drop out.[10] Such workers have become dissatisfied with and disinterested in the profession to which they have dedicated a major part of their lives. Signs of burnout include excessive anger, blaming others, guilt, being tired and exhausted all day, sleep problems, high absenteeism, family problems, and self-preoccupation.[18] Persons experiencing burnout may cope by consuming drugs or alcohol.

The very nature of athletic training is one of caring about and serving the athlete. When the emotional demands of work overcome the professional's resources to cope, burnout may occur. Too many athletes to care for, the expectations of coaches to return an injured athlete to action, difficulties in caring for chronic conditions, and personality conflicts involving athletes, coaches, physicians, or administrators can leave the athletic trainer physically and emotionally drained at the end of the day. Sources of emotional drain include little reward for one's efforts, role conflicts, lack of autonomy, and a feeling of powerlessness to deal with the problems at hand. Commonly, the professional athletic trainer is in a constant state of high emotional arousal and anxiety during the working day.

Individuals entering the field of athletic training must realize that it is extremely demanding. Even though the field is often difficult, they must learn that they cannot be "all things to all people." They must learn to say no when their health is at stake, and they must make leisure time for themselves beyond their work.[11] Perhaps most important, athletic trainers must make time to spend with their family, friends, and loved ones.

Empathy

Empathy refers to the capacity to enter into the feeling or spirit of another person. Athletic training is a field that requires both the ability to sense when an athlete is in distress and the desire to alleviate that stress.

Sense of Humor

Many athletes rate having a sense of humor as the most important attribute that an athletic trainer can have. Humor and wit help release tension and provide a relaxed atmosphere. The athletic trainer who is too serious or too clinical will have problems adapting to the often lighthearted setting of the sports world.

Communication

Athletic training requires a constant flow of both oral and written communication. As an educator, psychologist, counselor, therapist, and administrator, the athletic trainer must be a good communicator.

Intellectual Curiosity

The athletic trainer must always be a student. The field of athletic training is so diverse and ever changing that it requires constant study. The athletic trainer must have an active intellectual curiosity. Through reading professional journals and books, communicating with the team physician, and attending professional meetings, the athletic trainer stays abreast of the field.

Ethical Practice

The athletic trainer must act at all times with the highest standards of conduct and integrity.[28] To ensure this behavior, NATA has developed a code of ethics, which was approved at the NATA annual symposium in 1993,[34] and has subsequently been expanded. The complete code of ethics appears in Appendix A. The five basic ethics principles are as follows:

1. Members shall respect the rights, welfare, and dignity of all individuals.
2. Members shall comply with the laws and regulations governing the practice of athletic training.
3. Members shall accept the responsibility for the exercise of sound judgment.
4. Members shall maintain and promote high standards in the provision of services.
5. Members shall not engage in conduct that constitutes a conflict of interest or that adversely reflects on the profession.

Members who act in a manner that is unethical or unbecoming to the profession can ultimately lose their certification.

Professional Memberships

It is essential that an athletic trainer become a member of and be active in professional organizations. Such organizations are continuously upgrading and refining the profession. They provide an ongoing source of information about changes occurring in the profession and include NATA, district associations within NATA, various state athletic training organizations, and ASCM. Some athletic trainers are also physical therapists. Over the years a closer relationship has developed between NATA and the American Physical Therapy Association. Increasingly, physical therapists are becoming interested in working with physically active individuals.

As a professional, the athletic trainer must be a member of and be active in professional organizations.

The Athletic Trainer and the Athlete

The major concern of the athletic trainer should always be the athlete. If it were not for athletes, the physician, the coach, and the athletic trainer would have nothing to do in sports. It is essential to realize that decisions made by the physician, coach, and athletic trainer ultimately affect the athlete. Athletes are frequently caught in the middle between coaches telling them to do one thing and medical staff telling them to do something else. Thus the injured athlete must always be informed and made aware of the why, how, and when that collectively dictate the course of an injury rehabilitation program.

The athletic trainer should educate the student athlete about injury prevention and management. Athletes should learn about techniques of training and conditioning that may reduce the likelihood of injury. They should be well informed about their injuries and taught how to listen to what their bodies are telling them to prevent reinjury.

In a high-school setting, the athletic trainer must also take the time to explain to and inform the parents about injury management and prevention. With an athlete of high school age, the parents' decisions regarding health care must be taken into consideration.

Each role and responsibility is critical if the athletic trainer is to be as effective as possible in treating people with injuries related to participation in sports.[40] Though a number of authorities can significantly affect the health care of the athlete, the athletic trainer is certainly an integral part of the sports medicine team.

RESPONSIBILITIES OF THE TEAM PHYSICIAN

The athletic trainer works primarily under the supervision of the team physician, who is ultimately responsible for directing the total health care of the athlete (Figure 1-3). In cooperation with the team physician, the athletic trainer must make decisions that ultimately have a direct effect on the athlete who has sustained an injury.

From the viewpoint of the athletic trainer, there are a number of roles and responsibilities that the team physician should assume with regard to injury prevention and the health care of the athlete.[30,45] (See *Focus Box:* "Duties of the team physician.")

First, the physician should be a supervisor and an advisor to the athletic trainer. However, the athletic trainer must be given flexibility to function independently in the decision-making process and must often act without the advice or direction of the physician. Therefore it is critical that the team physician and the athletic trainer share philosophical opinions regarding injury management and rehabilitation programs; this cohesion will help minimize any discrepancies or inconsistencies that

Figure 1-3

In treating the athlete, the athletic trainer carries out the directions of the physician.

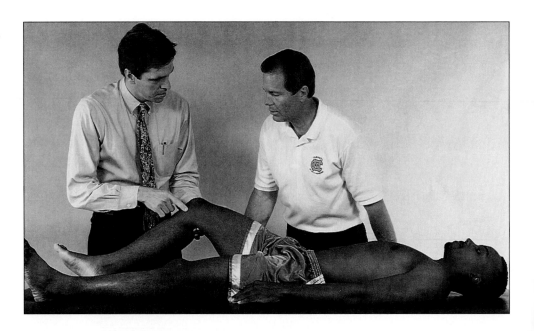

Focus

Duties of the team physician

- Seeing that a complete medical history of each athlete is compiled and is readily available
- Determining through a physical examination the athlete's health status
- Diagnosing and treating injuries and other illnesses
- Directing and advising the athletic trainer about health matters
- Acting, when necessary, as an instructor to the athletic trainer, assistant athletic trainer, and student athletic trainers about special therapeutic methods, therapeutic problems, and related procedures
- If possible, attending all games, athletic contests, scrimmages, and practices
- Deciding when, on medical grounds, athletes should be disqualified from participation and when they may be permitted to reenter competition
- Serving as an advisor to the athletic trainer and the coach and, when necessary, as a counselor to the athlete
- Working closely with the school administrator, school dentist, athletic trainer, coach, and health services personnel to promote and maintain consistently high standards for the care of the athlete

may exist. Most athletic trainers would prefer to work with rather than for a team physician.

Compiling Medical Histories

The team physician should be responsible for compiling medical histories and conducting physical examinations for each athlete, both of which can provide critical information that may reduce the possibility of injury. Preparticipation screening done by both the athletic trainer and physician are important in establishing baseline information to be used for comparison should injury occur during the season.

Diagnosing Injury

The team physician should assume responsibility for diagnosing an injury and should be keenly aware of the program of rehabilitation as designed by the athletic trainer after the diagnosis. Athletic trainers should be capable of doing an accurate initial evaluation after acute injury. Input from that evaluation may be essential to the physician, who may not see the patient for several hours or perhaps days after the injury. However, the physician has been trained specifically to diagnose injuries and to make recommendations to the athletic trainer for treatment based on that diagnosis. The athletic trainer, with a sound background in injury rehabilitation, designs and supervises an effective rehabilitation scheme. These two closely related yet distinct roles require both cooperation and close communication if they are to be optimized.

Team physicians must have absolute authority in determining the health status of an athlete who wishes to participate in the sports program.

Deciding on Disqualification and Return to Play

The physician determines when a recommendation should be made that an athlete be disqualified from competition on medical grounds and must have the final say as to when an injured athlete may return to activity. Any decision to allow an athlete to resume activity should be based on recommendations from the athletic trainer. An athletic trainer often has an advantage in that he or she knows the injured athlete well, including how the athlete responds to injury, how the athlete moves, and how hard to push to return the athlete safely to activity. The physician's judgment must be based not only on medical knowledge but also on knowledge of the psychophysiological demands of a particular sport.[26]

Attending Practices and Games

A team physician should make an effort to attend as many practices, scrimmages, and competitions as possible. This attendance obviously becomes difficult at an institution that has twenty or more athletic teams. Thus the physician must be readily available should the athletic trainer (who generally is at most practices and games) require consultation or advice.

If the team physician cannot attend all practice sessions and competitive events or games, it is sometimes possible to establish a plan of rotation involving a number of physicians. In this plan, any one physician need be present at only one or two activities a year. The rotation plan has proved practical in situations in which the school district is unable to afford a full-time physician or has so limited a budget that it must ask for volunteer medical coverage. In some instances, the attending physician is paid a per-game stipend.

Committing to Sports and the Athlete

Most important, the team physician must have a strong love of sports and must be generally interested in and concerned for the young people who compete. Colleges and universities typically employ someone to act as a full-time team physician. High schools most often rely on a local physician from within the community who volunteers his or her time. To serve as a team physician for the purpose of enhancing social standing in the community can be a frustrating and potentially dangerous situation for everyone involved in the athletic program.

When a physician is asked to serve as a team physician, arrangements must be made with the employing educational institution about specific required responsibilities. Policies must be established regarding emergency care, legal liability, facilities, personnel relationships, and duties.[46] It is essential that the team physician at all times promotes and maintains consistently high quality care for the athlete in all phases of the sports medicine program.

THE COACH

The coach is directly responsible for preventing injuries by seeing that the athlete has undergone a preventive injury conditioning program. The coach must ensure that sports equipment, especially protective equipment, is of the highest quality and is properly fitted. The coach must also make sure that protective equipment is properly maintained. A coach must be keenly aware of what produces injuries in his or her particular sport and what measures must be taken to avoid them (Figure 1-4). A coach should be able to apply proper first aid when called on to do so, especially for serious head and spinal injuries.

It is essential that a coach have a thorough understanding of the skill techniques and environmental factors that may adversely affect the athlete. Poor biomechanics in skill areas such as throwing and running can lead to overuse injuries of the arms and legs, and overexposure to heat and humidity may cause death. Just because a coach is experienced in coaching does not mean that he or she knows proper skill techniques. It is essential that coaches engage in a continual process of education to further their knowledge in their particular sport. When a sports program or specific sport is without an athletic trainer, the coach often takes over this role.

Coaches work closely with athletic trainers; therefore both must develop an awareness and an insight into each other's problems so that they can function as effectively as possible. The athletic trainer must develop patience and must earn the respect of the coaches so that his or her judgment in all athletic training matters is fully accepted. In turn, the athletic trainer must avoid questioning the abilities of the coaches in their particular fields and must restrict opinions to athletic training matters. To avoid frustration and hard feelings, the coach must coach, and the athletic trainer must conduct athletic training matters. In terms of the health and well-being

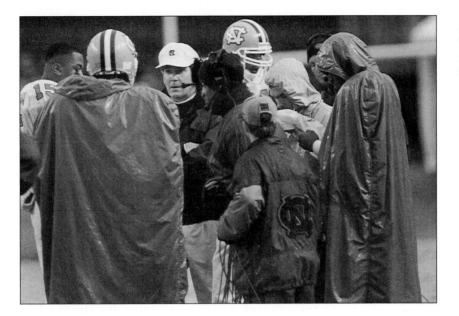

Figure 1-4

The coach is directly responsible for preventing injuries in his or her sport.

of the athlete, the physician and the athletic trainer have the last word. This position must be backed at all times by the athletic director.

REFERRING THE ATHLETE TO OTHER MEDICAL AND NONMEDICAL SUPPORT SERVICES AND PERSONNEL

In certain situations, an athlete may require treatment from or consultation with a variety of both medical and nonmedical services or personnel other than the athletic trainer or team physician. After the athletic trainer consults with the team physician about a particular matter, either the athletic trainer or the team physician can arrange for appointments as necessary. When referring an athlete for evaluation or consultation, the athletic trainer must be aware of the community-based services available and the insurance or managed care plan coverage available for that athlete.

A number of support health services and personnel may be used by a sports program. These services and personnel may include school health services; nurses; physicians including orthopedists, neurologists, internists, family medicine specialists, ophthalmologists, pediatricians, and psychiatrists; dentists; podiatrists; physician's assistants; physical therapists; strength and conditioning specialists; biomechanists; exercise physiologists; nutritionists; sports psychologists; or social workers.

School Health Services

Colleges and universities maintain school health services that range from a department operating with one or two nurses and a physician available on a part-time basis to an elaborate setup comprised of a full complement of nursing services with a staff of full-time medical specialists and complete laboratory and hospital facilities. At the high-school level, health services are usually organized so that one or two nurses conduct the program under the direction of the school physician, who may serve a number of schools in a given area or district. This organization poses a problem because it is often difficult to have qualified medical help at hand when it is needed. Local policy determines the procedure for referral for medical care. If such policies are lacking, the athletic trainer should see to it that an effective method is established for handling all athletes requiring medical care or opinion. The ultimate source of health care is the physician. The effectiveness of athletic health care service can be evaluated only to the extent to which it meets the following criteria:

Support personnel concerned with the athlete's health and safety:
- Nurse
- School health services
- Physician
- Dentist
- Podiatrist
- Physician's assistant
- Biomechanist
- Strength and conditioning coach
- Sport psychologist
- Physical therapist
- Exercise physiologist
- Nutritionist
- Social worker

1. Availability at every scheduled practice or contest of a person qualified and delegated to render emergency care to an injured or ill participant
2. Planned access to a physician by phone or nearby presence for prompt medical evaluation of the health care problems that warrant this attention
3. Planned access to a medical facility, including plans for communication and transportation

The Nurse

As a rule, the nurse is not usually responsible for the recognition and management of sports injuries. However, in certain institutions that lack an athletic trainer, the nurse may assume the majority of the responsibility in providing health care for the athlete. The nurse works under the direction of the physician and in liaison with the athletic trainer and the school health services.

Physicians

A number of physicians with a variety of specializations can aid the sports medicine team in treating the athlete.

Orthopedist   The orthopedist is responsible for treating injuries and disorders of the musculoskeletal system. Many colleges and universities have a team orthopedist on their staff.

Neurologist   A neurologist specializes in treating disorders of and injuries to the nervous system. There are common situations in athletics in which consultation with a neurologist would be warranted, such as for head injury or peripheral nerve injury.

Internist   An internist is a physician who specializes in the practice of internal medicine. An internist treats diseases of the internal organs by using measures other than surgery.

Family Medicine Physician   A physician who specializes in family medicine supervises or provides medical care to all members of a family. Many team physicians in colleges and universities and particularly at the high-school level are engaged in family practice.

Ophthalmologist   Physicians who manage and treat injuries to the eye are ophthalmologists. An optometrist evaluates and fits patients with glasses or contacts.

Pediatrician   A pediatrician cares for or treats injuries and illnesses that occur in young physically active children and adolescents.

Psychiatrist   Psychiatry is a medical practice that deals with the diagnosis, treatment, and prevention of mental illness.

Dentist

The role of team dentist is somewhat analogous to that of team physician. He or she serves as a dental consultant for the team and should be available for first aid and emergency care. Good communication between the dentist and the athletic trainer should ensure a good dental program. There are three areas of responsibility for the team dentist:
1. Organizing and performing the preseason dental examination
2. Being available to provide emergency care when needed
3. Conducting the fitting of mouth protectors

Podiatrist

Podiatry, the specialized field dealing with the study and care of the foot, has become an integral part of sports health care. Many podiatrists are trained in surgical procedures, foot biomechanics, and the fitting and construction of orthotic devices for the shoe. Like the team dentist, a podiatrist should be available on a consulting basis.

Physician's Assistant

Physician's assistants (PAs) are trained to assume some of the responsibilities for patient care traditionally done by a physician. They assist the physician by conducting preliminary patient evaluations, arranging for various hospital-based diagnostic tests, and dispensing appropriate medications. A number of athletic trainers have also become PAs in recent years.

Physical Therapist

Some athletic trainers use physical therapists to supervise the rehabilitation programs for injured athletes while the athletic trainer concentrates primarily on getting a player ready to practice or compete. In many sports medicine clinics, athletic trainers and physical therapists work in teams, jointly contributing to the supervision of a rehabilitation program. A number of athletic trainers are also physical therapists. Physical therapists can be certified as a Sports Certified Specialist (SCS).

Strength and Conditioning Specialist

Many colleges and universities and some high schools employ full-time strength coaches to advise athletes on training and conditioning programs. Athletic trainers should routinely consult with these individuals and advise them about injuries to a particular athlete and exercises that should be avoided or modified relative to a specific injury. Strength coaches can be certified by the National Strength and Conditioning Association as CSCSs.

Biomechanist

An individual who possesses some expertise in the analysis of human motion can also be a great aid to the athletic trainer. The biomechanist uses sophisticated video and computer-enhanced digital analysis equipment to study movement. By advising the athlete, coach, and athletic trainer on matters such as faulty gait patterns or improper throwing mechanics, the biomechanist can reduce the likelihood of injury to the athlete.

Exercise Physiologist

The exercise physiologist can significantly influence the athletic training program by giving input to the trainer regarding training and conditioning techniques, body composition analysis, and nutritional considerations.

Nutritionist

Increasingly, individuals in the field of nutrition are becoming interested in athletics. Some large athletic training programs engage a nutritionist as a consultant who plans eating programs that are geared to the needs of a particular sport. He or she also assists individual athletes who need special nutritional counseling.

Sports Psychologist

The sports psychologist can advise the athletic trainer on matters related to the psychological aspects of the rehabilitation process. The way the athlete feels about the injury and how it affects his or her social, emotional, intellectual, and physical dimensions can have a substantial effect on the course of a treatment program and how quickly the athlete may return to competition. The sports psychologist uses different intervention strategies to help the athlete cope with injury. Sport psychologists can seek certification through the Association for the Advancement of Sport Psychology.

Social Worker

Occasionally athletes or their families may need a referral for social support services within the community. Social workers can offer counseling and support for a variety of personal or family difficulties, such as substance abuse, family planning, and other social concerns.

EMPLOYMENT SETTINGS FOR THE ATHLETIC TRAINER

Athletic trainers work in a number of different settings:
- Secondary schools
- School districts
- Colleges and universities
- Professional sports
- Sports medicine clinics
- Industrial settings

Opportunities for employment as an athletic trainer have changed dramatically during recent years.[3] Since the 1950s the traditional employment setting for the athletic trainer has been in an athletic training room at the college, university, or professional levels. During the 1980s—primarily because of intensive public relations efforts by NATA—the majority of jobs available were at the high-school level.[7] Today the largest percentage of certified athletic trainers are employed in sports medicine clinics or in industry, areas that until recently had been considered nontraditional settings.

Secondary Schools

It would be ideal to have certified athletic trainers serve every secondary school in the United States.[22] Many of the physical problems that occur later from improperly managed sports injuries could be avoided initially if proper care from an athletic trainer had been provided. Many times a coach does all his or her own athletic training, although in some cases, a coach is assigned additional athletic training responsibilities and is assisted by a student athletic trainer. If a secondary school hires an athletic trainer, it is very often in a faculty-trainer capacity. This individual is usually employed as a teacher in one of the school's classroom disciplines and performs athletic training duties on a part-time or extracurricular basis.[43] Thus, student athletic trainers who hope to find a position in a secondary-school setting should be encouraged to seek teacher certification.[14] In this instance compensation usually is on the basis of released time from teaching, a stipend as a coach, or both.[25] Salaries for the secondary-school athletic trainer are continuing to improve.[4]

Another means of obtaining high-school or community-college athletic training coverage is using a certified graduate student from a nearby college or university. The graduate student receives a graduate assistantship with a stipend paid by the secondary school or community college. In this situation both the graduate student and the school benefit.[21] However, this practice may prevent a school from employing a certified athletic trainer on a full-time basis.

Based on a proposal from the American Academy of Pediatrics, in 1998 the American Medical Association adopted a policy calling for certified athletic trainers to be employed in all high-school athletic programs. Although this policy was simply a recommendation and not a requirement, it was a very positive statement supporting the efficacy of athletic trainers in the secondary schools.

School Districts

Some school districts have found it effective to employ a centrally placed certified athletic trainer. In this case the athletic trainer, who may be full- or part-time, is a nonteacher who serves a number of schools. The advantage is savings; the disadvantage is that one individual cannot provide the level of service usually required by a typical school.

Colleges or Universities

At the college or university level, the athletic training positions vary considerably from institution to institution. In smaller institutions, the athletic trainer may be a half-time teacher in physical education and half-time athletic trainer. In some cases, if the athletic trainer is a physical therapist rather than a teacher, he or she may spend part of the time in the school health center and part of the time in athletic training. Increasingly at the college level, athletic training services are being offered to members of the general student body who participate in intramural and club sports. In most colleges and universities, the athletic trainer is full-time, does not teach, works in the department of athletics, and is paid by the institution.

Professional Teams

The athletic trainer for professional sports teams usually performs specific team athletic training duties for six months out of the year; the other six months are spent in off-season conditioning and individual rehabilitation. The athletic trainer working with a professional team is involved with only one sport and is paid according to contract, much like a player. Playoff and championship money may add substantially to the yearly income.

Sports Medicine Clinics

For years, sports medicine clinics have been considered a nontraditional setting for employment as an athletic trainer. Today, more athletic trainers are employed in sports medicine clinics than in any other employment setting. The role of the athletic trainer varies from one clinic to the next. Most clinical athletic trainers see patients with sports-related injuries during the morning hours in the clinic. In the afternoons, athletic trainers' services are contracted out to local high schools or small colleges for game or practice coverage. For the most part, private clinics have well-equipped facilities in which to work, and salaries for their trainers are generally somewhat higher than in the more traditional settings. In many sports medicine clinics, the athletic trainer may be responsible for formulating a plan to market or promote athletic training services offered by that clinic throughout the local community.[19]

Industrial Settings

It is becoming relatively common for corporations or industries to employ athletic trainers to oversee fitness and injury rehabilitation programs for their employees. The athletic trainer working in an industrial setting must have a sound understanding of the principles and concepts of workplace ergonomics, including inspecting, measuring, and observing dimensions of the work space as well as specific tasks that are performed at the workstation. Once a problem has been identified, the athletic trainer must be able to implement proper adjustments to workplace ergonomics to reduce or minimize possible risks for injury. In addition to these responsibilities, athletic trainers may be assigned to conduct wellness programs and provide education and individual counseling. It is likely that many job opportunities will exist for the athletic trainer in industry in the next few years.

Treating the Physically Active

In these various employment settings, athletic trainers no longer treat only athletes but instead a physically active population. Physically active individuals may include not only what we have traditionally referred to as athletes in their late teens or twenties, but also both adolescents and older adults who engage in physical activities either recreationally or competitively.

The Adolescent Athlete

Children have always been physically active. But in today's society, playtime or physical activity for many adolescents is focused on organized competition. Certainly many relevant sociological issues arise in answer to questions such as, how old should children be when they begin to compete, or when should a child begin training and conditioning? Skeletally immature adolescent athletes present a particular challenge to the athletic trainer involved in some aspect of their health care. Young athletes cannot be dealt with either physically or emotionally in the same manner as adult athletes. Thus the athletic trainer must be aware of patterns of growth and development and all the special considerations that this process brings with it.

The Aging Athlete

Aging involves a lifelong series of changes in physiological and performance capabilities. These capabilities increase as a function of the growth process throughout adolescence, peak sometime between the ages of eighteen and forty years, then steadily decline with increasing age. However, this decline may be due as much to the sociological constraints of aging as to biological effects. In most cases, after age thirty-five, qualities such as muscular endurance, coordination, and strength tend to decrease. Recovery from vigorous exercise requires a longer amount of time. Regular physical activity, however, tends to delay and in some cases prevent the appearance of certain degenerative processes.

It is possible for individuals to maintain a relatively high level of physiological function if they maintain an active lifestyle. Consistent participation in vigorous physical activity can result in improvement of many physiological parameters regardless of age. The effects of exercise on the aging process and the long-term health benefits of exercise have been convincingly documented.

Generally, exercise is considered a safe activity for most individuals. ACSM has recommended that individuals under age forty who are apparently healthy with no significant risks can generally begin an exercise program without further medical evaluation, as long as the exercise program progresses gradually and moderately and no unusual signs or symptoms develop.[1] Individuals who are over age forty or who are at high risk should have a complete medical examination and undergo an exercise test before beginning an exercise program.

RECOGNITION AND ACCREDITATION OF THE ATHLETIC TRAINER AS AN ALLIED HEALTH PROFESSIONAL

1-6

Critical Thinking Exercise

A second-semester college sophomore has decided that she is interested in becoming a certified athletic trainer. She happens to be in an institution that offers an advanced master's degree in athletic training yet does not offer an entry-level CAAHEP-approved curriculum. However, the institution does sponsor an internship program that currently has about fifteen students.

? How can this student most effectively achieve her goal of becoming a certified athletic trainer?

In June 1991 the American Medical Association (AMA) officially recognized athletic training as an allied health profession. The primary purpose of this recognition was for accrediting educational programs. The AMA's Committee on Allied Health Education and Accreditation (CAHEA) was charged with the responsibility of developing essentials and guidelines for academic programs to use in preparation of individuals for entry into the profession through the Joint Review Committee on Athletic Training (JRC-AT). As of 1993, all entry-level athletic training education programs became subject to the CAHEA accreditation process.[12]

In June 1994 CAHEA was dissolved and was replaced immediately by the Commission on Accreditation of Allied Health Education Programs (CAAHEP). Currently eighteen professional review committees are sponsored by the forty-nine separate organizations—including NATA—that make up CAAHEP. The CAAHEP is recognized as an accreditation agency for allied health education programs by the U.S. Department of Education. Entry-level college and university athletic training education programs at both the undergraduate and graduate levels that were at one time approved by NATA and subsequently by CAHEA are now accredited by CAAHEP. The JRC-AT is currently made up of representatives from NATA, the American Academy of Pediatrics, the American Orthopaedic Society for Sports Medicine, and the American Academy of Family Physicians.

The effects of CAAHEP accreditation are not limited to the educational aspects. In the future, this recognition may potentially affect regulatory legislation, the practice of athletic training in nontraditional settings, and insurance considerations. This recognition will continue to be a positive step in the development of the athletic training profession.

Accredited Athletic Training Education Programs

As of 1999, seventy-nine institutions across the United States offer entry-level athletic training education programs that have been accredited by CAAHEP, while twenty-two others are still in the process of changing from accreditation by NATA to CAAHEP accreditation.[29] In addition, thirteen graduate programs in athletic training that in the past were approved by the Professional Education Committee of NATA will now be approved by the Advanced Graduate Education Committee of the Education Council. The approved advanced graduate athletic training education programs are designed to enhance the academic and clinical preparation of individuals who are already certified athletic trainers or those who have completed the requirements for certification.

Other Health Care Organization Accrediting Agencies

Although CAAHEP is the accrediting organization for athletic training, there are other organizations that accredit various health care agencies and organizations.

Joint Commission on Accreditation of Healthcare Organizations

The Joint Commission on Accreditation of Healthcare Organizations (JCAHO) is the nation's largest standards-setting and accrediting body in health care. JCAHO accredits more than 18,000 health care organizations and programs in the United States. Its mission is to improve the quality of care provided to the public through the provision of health care accreditation and related services that support performance improvement in health care organizations.

Rehabilitation Accreditation Commission (CARF)

The Rehabilitation Accreditation Commission (CARF) is an accrediting organization that promotes quality rehabilitation services by establishing standards of quality for organizations to use as guidelines in developing and offering their programs or services to consumers. CARF uses the standards to determine how well an organization is serving its consumers and how it can improve. CARF standards are developed with input from consumers, rehabilitation professionals, state and national organizations, and funders. Every year the standards are reviewed and new ones are developed to keep pace with changing conditions and current consumer needs.

REQUIREMENTS FOR CERTIFICATION AS AN ATHLETIC TRAINER

An athletic trainer who is certified by NATA is a highly qualified paramedical professional educated and experienced in dealing with the injuries that occur with participation in sports. Candidates for certification are required to have an extensive background of both formal academic preparation and supervised practical experience in a clinical setting, according to CAAHEP guidelines. The guidelines listed in *Focus Box: "NATA certification"* have been established by the National Athletic Trainers Association Board of Certification (NATABOC).[39]

The Certification Examination

Once the requirements have been fulfilled, applicants are eligible to sit for the certification examination.[20] The certification examination has been developed by NATABOC in conjunction with Columbia Assessment Services, Inc., and is administered five times each year at various locations throughout the United States.[39] The examination consists of three sections: a written portion, an oral-practical portion, and a written-simulation portion. The examination tests for knowledge and skill in six major domains: (1) prevention of athletic injuries; (2) recognition, evaluation, and assessment of injuries; (3) immediate care of injuries; (4) treatment, rehabilitation, and reconditioning of athletic injuries; (5) health care administration; and (6) professional development and responsibility. Successful performance on the certification examination leads to NATABOC certification as an athletic trainer with the credential of **ATC.** (For the latest information on certification requirements, contact the NATABOC website at www.nataboc.org.)

Continuing Education Requirements

To ensure ongoing professional growth and involvement by the certified athletic trainer, NATABOC has established requirements for continuing education.[35] To maintain certification, all certified trainers must document a minimum of eight continuing education units (CEUs) attained during each three-year recertification term.

Focus

NATA certification

Purpose of certification

The National Athletic Trainers' Association Board of Certification (NATABOC) was established in 1970 to implement a program of certification for entry-level athletic trainers. The purpose of the certification program is to establish standards for entry into the profession of athletic training.

To attain certification as an athletic trainer, an applicant must fulfill the following core requirements and must either complete a CAAHEP-accredited entry-level program or an internship program.

Core requirements

Note: If one or more of the core requirements are not fulfilled at the time of application, the application will be returned.

1. The athletic training student must have a high school diploma to begin accumulating directly supervised clinical hours that are to be used to meet requirements for NATABOC certification.
2. Proof of graduation (an official transcript) at the baccalaureate level from an accredited college or university located in the United States of America. Foreign-degreed applicants who wish to credit this degree toward a bachelor's degree requirement will be evaluated, at the candidate's expense, by an independent consultant selected by the NATABOC. Students who have begun their last semester or quarter of college are eligible to take the certification examination before graduation, provided the other core and section requirements have been fulfilled at the time of application. Verification of intent to graduate must be provided to the Board of Certification by the dean or department chairperson of the college or university the applicant is attending. Certification will not be issued until an official transcript indicating date of degree is received by the Board of Certification.
3. Proof of current American National Red Cross Standard First Aid Certification and current Basic CPR (American Red Cross or American Heart Association); EMT equivalent instead of First Aid and CPR will be accepted. Both cards must be current at the time of application.
4. At the time of application, all candidates for certification (curriculum and internship) must verify that at least 25 percent of their athletic training experience hours credited in fulfilling the certification requirements were attained in actual (on location) practice or game coverage with one or more of the following sports: football, soccer, hockey, wrestling, basketball, gymnastics, lacrosse, volleyball, and rugby.
5. Endorsement of certification application by a NATA-certified athletic trainer.
6. Subsequent passing of the certification examination (written, oral-practical, and written-simulation sections).

Section requirements

CAAHEP-accredited program

The candidate must graduate from an undergraduate or graduate program accredited by the Commission on Accreditation of Allied Health Education Programs (CAAHEP). Students applying to take the certification exam must complete formal instruction in the following core curriculum subject areas:

Human anatomy
Human physiology
Psychology
Kinesiology/biomechanics
Exercise physiology
Prevention of athletic injuries/illness
Evaluation of athletic injuries/illness
First aid and emergency care
Therapeutic modalities
Therapeutic exercise
Personal community health
Nutrition
Administration of athletic training programs

It is recommended that students complete coursework in physics, chemistry, pharmacology, research design, and statistics. In addition, students are required to complete a minimum of 800 clinical hours under the direct supervision of a NATA-certified athletic trainer at that college or an affiliated site. Applicants who are applying for NATA certification from a CAAHEP-accredited undergraduate or graduate program must receive their degree from that college or university.

Continued

Focus

NATA certification—cont'd

*Internship programs**

If a student does not attend a CAAHEP-accredited program, he or she may still be eligible for certification by completing an internship. At the time of application, each internship candidate must present documentation of attaining at least 1,500 hours of athletic training experience under direct supervision of a NATA-certified athletic trainer. These hours must have been attained over a minimum of two calendar years and not more than five years. Of these 1,500 hours, at least 1,000 hours must be attained in a traditional athletic setting at the interscholastic, intercollegiate, or professional sports level. The additional 500 hours may be attained from an allied clinical setting or sport camp setting under the direct supervision of a NATA-certified athletic trainer. Each candidate must present, via official transcript, proof of completion of formal course work, no more than seven years before the date of application, with at least one course in each of the following areas:

Health (e.g., nutrition, drugs/substance abuse, health education)

Human anatomy

Kinesiology/biomechanics

Human physiology

Physiology of exercise

Basic athletic training

Advanced athletic training (a course in therapeutic modalities or rehabilitation may satisfy the advanced course requirement)

   Basic and advanced athletic training courses must be successfully completed in a college or university in the United States or taught by a NATA-certified athletic trainer in a foreign college or university for credit. The remaining core courses may be accepted from foreign universities as deemed acceptable by NATABOC.

*As of the year 2004, the NATABOC will no longer recognize internship programs as a means of obtaining certification. Thus, all applicants for certification must have completed a CAAHEP accredited program.

CEUs may be awarded for attending symposiums, seminars, workshops, or conferences; serving as a speaker, panelist, or certification exam model; participating in the United States Olympic Committee (USOC) program; authoring a research article in a professional journal; completing a NATA journal quiz; completing postgraduate course work; and obtaining CPR, first aid, or EMT certification. All certified athletic trainers must also demonstrate proof of CPR certification at least once during the three-year term.

STATE REGULATION OF THE ATHLETIC TRAINER

During the early 1970s, the leadership of NATA realized the necessity of obtaining some type of official recognition by other medical allied health organizations of the athletic trainer as a health care professional. Laws and statutes specifically governing the practice of athletic training were nonexistent in most states.

   Based on this perceived need, the athletic trainers in many individual states organized their efforts to secure recognition by seeking some type of regulation of the athletic trainer by state licensing agencies. To date, this ongoing effort has resulted in thirty-seven of the fifty states enacting some type of regulatory statutes governing the practice of athletic training.[33]

   Rules and regulations governing the practice of athletic training vary tremendously from state to state. Regulation may be in the form of certification, registration, licensure, or exemption (see *Focus Box:* "State regulation of the athletic trainer").

   For the most part, legislation regulating the practice of athletic training has been positive and to some extent protects the athletic trainer from litigation. However, in some instances, regulation has restricted the limits of practice for the athletic trainer. The leadership of NATA has strongly encouraged athletic trainers in all states to seek some form of state regulation.

Forms of state regulation:
- Certification
- Registration
- Licensing
- Exemption

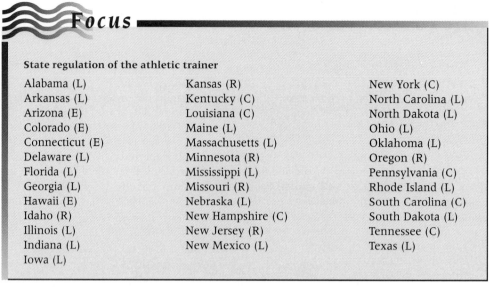

State regulation of the athletic trainer

Alabama (L)	Kansas (R)	New York (C)
Arkansas (L)	Kentucky (C)	North Carolina (L)
Arizona (E)	Louisiana (C)	North Dakota (L)
Colorado (E)	Maine (L)	Ohio (L)
Connecticut (E)	Massachusetts (L)	Oklahoma (L)
Delaware (L)	Minnesota (R)	Oregon (R)
Florida (L)	Mississippi (L)	Pennsylvania (C)
Georgia (L)	Missouri (R)	Rhode Island (L)
Hawaii (E)	Nebraska (L)	South Carolina (C)
Idaho (R)	New Hampshire (C)	South Dakota (L)
Illinois (L)	New Jersey (R)	Tennessee (C)
Indiana (L)	New Mexico (L)	Texas (L)
Iowa (L)		

E, Exempt from existing licensure standards; C, certification; R, registration; L, licensure. For additional information about individual state regulating boards, contact http://www.nata.org/ on the Web.

Licensure

Licensing limits the practice of athletic training to those who have met minimal requirements established by a state licensing board. Through this licensing board the state limits the number of individuals who can perform functions related to athletic training as dictated by the practice act. Requirements for licensure vary from state to state but most require a specific educational and training background, evidence of good moral character, letters of recommendation from current practitioners, and minimal acceptable performance on a licensing examination. Licensure is the most restrictive of all the forms of regulation. Individuals who are providing health care services to an athlete cannot call themselves athletic trainers in that particular state unless they have met the requirements for licensure.[8]

Certification

State certification as an athletic trainer differs from certification as an athletic trainer by NATABOC. An individual who has passed the NATABOC exam does not automatically obtain a state certification. Although certification does not restrict the use of the title of athletic trainer to those certified by the state, it can restrict performance of athletic training functions to only those individuals who are state certified. State certification indicates that a person possesses the basic knowledge and skills required in the profession and has passed a certification examination. Many states that offer certification use the NATABOC exam as a criterion for granting state certification.[8]

Registration

Registration means that before an individual can practice athletic training, he or she must register in that state. Registration means that the individual has paid a fee for being placed on an existing list of practitioners. The state may or may not have a mechanism for assessing competency. However, registration does prevent individuals who are not registered with the state from calling themselves athletic trainers.[8]

Exemption

Exemption means that a state recognizes that athletic trainers perform functions similar to those of other licensed professions (e.g., physical therapy) yet still allows them to practice athletic training despite the fact that they do not comply with the practice acts of other regulated professions. Exemption is most often used in those states in which there are not enough practitioners to warrant the formation of a state regulatory board.[8]

THE PHYSICAL THERAPIST AND THE ATHLETIC TRAINER

As the certified athletic trainer continues to gain recognition among health care professionals, interest on the part of many individuals with backgrounds in other health-related professions likewise continues to increase. In particular, it is not unusual to find a physical therapist interested in sports and athletics who is working toward certification as an athletic trainer.[24] Conversely, the certified trainer who is interested in working with patients outside the athletic population is often looking toward licensure as a physical therapist.

Historically, the relationship between athletic trainers and physical therapists has been less than cooperative. Many reasons underlie this lack of cooperation, but the main reason over the years has been failure to clarify the roles of each group in injury rehabilitation.

Athletic trainers have been trained to deal specifically with those injuries that occur in sports, whereas physical therapists have a much broader expertise in injury rehabilitation across many different patient populations. The physical therapist who has not been exposed to the athletic training environment is as inefficient in that setting as is the athletic trainer working with stroke patients in a rehabilitation setting.

The academic curricula required for the athletic trainer and for the physical therapist are similar, particularly in the basic sciences and in the clinical methods courses. The physical therapy curriculum provides a significantly broader background in treating patients of all ages who have a wide variety of physical problems. However, the physical therapist functioning in an athletic training environment must receive additional clinical instruction beyond that which is typically offered in a physical therapy curriculum. Otherwise the period of adjustment and orientation to a nontraditional physical therapy setting is often difficult.

The individual who achieves both certification as an athletic trainer and licensure as a physical therapist is extremely well qualified to function in various sports medicine settings, including both the private clinic and the colleges and universities. Today, the person who holds a dual credential is in high demand in the job market.

Certification as a Sports Physical Therapist

In the late 1970s the sports physical therapy section of the American Physical Therapy Association (APTA) began identifying competencies specific to the practice of physical therapy in a sports medicine setting. In 1985 the Professional Examination Service was contracted by APTA to develop a specialty examination based on specifically identified competencies.[27]

Candidates for the examination must fulfill the minimal criteria as outlined in the document *Minimal Criteria for Therapist to Sit for the Initial Certification Examination.* These criteria include the completion of a required number of hours of clinical practice in patient care, education, and administration. In addition, written evidence of competency in these areas and research must be submitted.

FUTURE DIRECTIONS FOR THE ATHLETIC TRAINER

The athletic training profession has made remarkable gains during the past two decades. Today, certified athletic trainers possess a strong, highly structured academic background in addition to a substantial amount of closely supervised clinical experience in their chosen area of expertise. The athletic trainer continues to gain credibility and recognition as a health care professional trained to deal with injuries that occur in sports.

Future directions for athletic training will be determined by the efforts of NATA and its membership. Athletic trainers must continue to enhance their visibility through research efforts and scholarly publication.[23,42] Certified athletic trainers must strive to develop some comprehension of basic research design and statistical analysis and thus be able to interpret new research.[49]

Athletic trainers should make themselves available for local and community meetings to discuss the health care of the athlete. They must continue to provide and refine quality educational programs for student athletic trainers. Most important, athletic trainers must continue efforts in injury prevention and provide appropriate, high-quality health care to athletes who are injured while participating in a sport.

SUMMARY

- Athletic training is a specialization within sports medicine, with its major concern being the health and safety of athletes. The primary athletic training team consists of the coach, the athletic trainer, and the team physician. The coach must ensure that both the equipment that is worn and the environment are the safest possible, that all injuries and illnesses are properly cared for, that skills are properly taught, and that conditioning is at the highest level.

- The athletic trainer must be a highly educated, well-trained professional. The athletic trainer must be certified and, if possible, have a state license to practice. The successful athletic trainer loves sports and the competitive environment. He or she must have an abundance of vitality and emotional stability, empathy for people who are in physical or emotional pain, a sense of humor, the ability to communicate, and a desire to learn. All the athletic trainer's actions must follow the highest standards of conduct.

- The team physician can be in varied specializations. Team physicians, depending on their time commitment to a specific sports program, can perform a variety of responsibilities. Some key responsibilities are conducting the preparticipation health examination; diagnosing and treating illnesses and injuries; advising and teaching the athletic training staff; attending games, scrimmages, and practices; and counseling the athlete about health matters.

Web Sites

National Athletic Trainers' Association: http://www.nata.org/

This site describes the athletic training profession, how to become involved in athletic training, and the role of an athletic trainer.

American Sports Medicine Institute: http://www.asmi.org/

The American Sports Medicine Institute's mission is to improve through research and education the understanding, prevention, and treatment of sports-related injuries. In addition to stating this mission, the site provides access to current research and journal articles.

American Academy of Orthopaedic Surgeons: http://www.aaos.org/

This site provides some general public information as well as information to its members. The public information as well as information to its members. The public information is in the form of patient education brochures; the site also includes a description of the organization and a definition of orthopedics.

The American Orthopaedic Society for Sports Medicine: http://www.sportmed.org/

This site is dedicated to educating health care professionals and the general public about sports medicine. The site provides access to the American Journal of Sports Medicine *and a wide variety of links to related sites.*

Athletic Trainer.com: http://athletictrainer.com/

This Web site is specifically designed to give information to athletic trainers, including students, and those interested in athletic training. It provides access to interesting journal articles and links to several informative Web sites.

NCAA: http://www.ncaa.org/

This site gives general information about the NCAA and the publications that the NCAA circulates. This site may be useful for those working in the collegiate setting.

Solutions to Critical Thinking EXERCISES

1-1 The student should be able to find all necessary information by simply going to the Internet and contacting these organizations via the World Wide Web.

1-2 Students of athletic training must be like sponges, willing to soak up whatever knowledge they can attain to make themselves more efficient in performing their chosen profession. That knowledge may come from attending classes, reading books or journals, attending lectures and conferences, and actively learning the tricks of the trade during the hours spent in the training room and on the field. Students must be able to apply theoretical knowledge to a practical setting if they are to be competent clinicians.

1-3 Ultimately the team physician is responsible for making that decision. However, that decision must be made based on collective input from the athletic trainer, the coach, and the athlete. Remember that everyone on the sports medicine team has the same ultimate goal, that being to return the athlete to full competitive levels as quickly and safely as possible.

1-4 To help prevent injury, the athletic trainer should (1) arrange for physical examinations and preparticipation screenings to identify conditions that predispose an athlete to injury, (2) ensure appropriate training and conditioning of the athlete, (3) monitor environmental conditions to ensure safe participation, (4) select and maintain properly fitting protective equipment, and (5) educate parents, coaches, and athletes about the risks inherent to sport participation.

1-5 To some extent, the role of the clinical athletic trainer is dictated by that state's regulation of the practice of athletic training. Certainly the clinical and academic preparation of athletic trainers should enable them to effectively evaluate an injured patient and guide that patient through a rehabilitative program. The athletic trainer should treat only those individuals who have sustained injury related to physical activity and not patients with neurological or orthopedic conditions. The athletic trainer may work part-time in the clinic and then cover one or several high schools around the area. The athletic trainer and physical therapist should work as a team to maximize the effectiveness of patient care.

1-6 To be eligible for certification through the internship route, the student must complete 1,500 hours of directly supervised clinical experience and course work in each of seven areas. It is possible to complete this work in two years, although realistically it will be difficult. At this point, she may find it necessary to spend an additional year completing the requirements. An alternative would be for her to transfer to an institution that offers an entry-level CAAHEP-approved program in which she must complete course work covering fourteen subject matter areas and 800 hours of directly supervised clinical experience.

REVIEW QUESTIONS AND CLASS ACTIVITIES

1. How do modern athletic training and sports medicine compare with early Greek and Roman approaches for the care of the athlete?
2. What professional organizations are important to the field of athletic training?
3. Why is athletic training considered a team endeavor? Contrast the coach's, athletic trainer's, and team physician's roles in athletic training.
4. What qualifications should the athletic trainer have in terms of education, certification, and personality?
5. What are the various employment opportunities available to the athletic trainer?
6. Explain the criteria for becoming certified as an athletic trainer.

REFERENCES

1. American College of Sports Medicine: 1987 annual meeting, Las Vegas, Nev, May 27–30, 1987.
2. Anderson M, Larson G, Luebe J: Student and supervisor perceptions of the quality of supervision in athletic training education, *J Ath Train* 32(4):328, 1997.
3. Arnold B, Gansneder B, VanLunen B: Importance of selected athletic trainer employment characteristics in collegiate, sports medicine clinic, and high school settings, *J Ath Train* 33(3):254, 1998.
4. Arnold B, VanLunen B, Gansneder B: 1994 athletic trainer employment and salary characteristics, *J Ath Train* 31(3):215, 1996.
5. Barefield S, McCallister S: Social supports in the athletic training room: athletes' expectations of staff and student athletic trainers, *J Ath Train* 32(4):333, 1997.
6. Bilik SE: *The trainer's bible*, New York, 1956, Reed (originally published 1917).
7. Buxton B, Okasaki E, Ho K: Legislative funding of athletic training positions in public secondary schools, *J Ath Train* 30(2):115, 1995.
8. Campbell D, Konin J: Regulation of athletic training. In Konin J: *Clinical athletic training*, Thorofare, NJ, 1997, Slack.
9. Campbell D, Miller M, Robinson W: The prevalence of burnout among athletic trainers, *Ath Train* 20(2):110, 1985.
10. Capel S: Attrition of athletic trainers, *Ath Train* 25(1):34, 1990.
11. Capel S: Psychological and organizational factors related to burnout in athletic trainers, *Ath Train* 21(4):322, 1986.
12. Committee on Allied Health Education and Accreditation: *Essentials and guidelines for an accredited educational program for athletic trainers*, Chicago, 1992, American Medical Association.
13. Cramer C: A preferred sequence of competencies for athletic training education programs, *Ath Train* 25(2):123, 1990.
14. Curtis N: Teacher certification among athletic training students, *J Ath Train* 30(4):349, 1995.
15. Curtis N, Helion J, Domsohn M: Student athletic trainer perceptions of clinical supervisor behaviors: a critical incident study, *J Ath Train* 33(3): 249, 1998.
16. Fuller D: Critical thinking in undergraduate athletic training education, *J Ath Train* 32(3):242, 1997.
17. Furney SR, Patton B: An examination of health counseling practices of athletic trainers, *Ath Train* 21(4):294, 1985.
18. Geick J: Athletic training burnout: a case study, *Ath Train* 21(1):43, 1986.
19. Gray R: The role of the clinical athletic trainer. In Konin J: *Clinical athletic training*, Thorofare, NJ, 1997, Slack.
20. Harrelson G, Gallaspy J, Knight H: Predictors of success on the NATABOC certification examination, *J Ath Train* 32(4):323, 1997.
21. Hossler P: How to acquire athletic trainers on the high school level, *Ath Train* 20(3):199, 1985.
22. Knight K: Athletic trainers for secondary schools, *Ath Train* 23(4):313, 1988.
23. Knight K: Research in athletic training: a frill or a necessity, *Ath Train* 23(3):212, 1988.
24. Knight K: Roles and relationships between sports PTs and ATCs, *Ath Train* 23(2):153, 1988.
25. Lephart S, Metz K: Financial and appointment trends of the athletic trainer clinician/educator, *Ath Train* 25(2):118, 1990.
26. Loeffler RD: On being a team physician, *Sports Med Digest* 9(2):1, 1987.

27. Malone T: Sports physical therapy specialization, *J Orthop Sports Phys Ther* 7(5):273, 1986.

28. Mangus BC, Ingersoll CD: Approaches to ethical decision making in athletic training, *Ath Train* 25(4):340, 1990.

29. Mathies A, Denegar C, Arnhold R: Changes in athletic training education as a result of changing from NATA-PEC to CAAHEP, *J Ath Train* 30(2):129, 1995.

30. Mellion MB, Walsh WM: The team physician. In Mellion MB, editor: *Sports medicine secrets*, St. Louis, 1994, Mosby.

31. Misasi S, Davis C, Morin G: Academic preparation of athletic trainers as counselors, *J Ath Train* 31(1):39, 1996.

32. Moulton M, Molstad S, Turner A: The role of counseling collegiate athletes, *J Ath Train* 32(2):148, 1997.

33. National Athletic Trainers' Association Governmental Affairs Committee: Personal communication, July 1998.

34. National Athletic Trainers' Association: New NATA code of ethics approved, *NATA News* 4(7):15, 1992.

35. National Athletic Trainers' Association Board of Certification, Continuing Education Office: *Continuing education file 1997–99*, Dallas, 1997, NATABOC.

36. National Athletic Trainers' Association Board of Certification: Role delineation matrix, *Certification Update* Fall (3):6, 1994.

37. National Athletic Trainers' Association Board of Certification: *Role delineation study of the entry level athletic trainer certification examination*, Philadelphia, 1994, Davis.

38. National Athletic Trainers' Association Board of Certification: *Role delineation study*, Raleigh, NC, 1995, Columbia Assessment Services.

39. National Athletic Trainers' Association Board of Certification: *Study guide for the NATABOC entry level athletic trainer certification examination*, Philadelphia, 1993, Davis.

40. National Athletic Trainers' Association Professional Education Committee: *Competencies in athletic training*, Dallas, 1992, National Athletic Trainers' Association.

41. O'Shea M: *A history of the National Athletic Trainers' Association*, Greenville, NC, 1980, National Athletic Trainers' Association.

42. Osternig L: Research in athletic training: the missing ingredient, *Ath Train* 23(3):323, 1988.

43. Prentice W, Mischler B: A national survey of employment opportunities for athletic trainers in the public schools, *Ath Train* 21(3):215, 1986.

44. Prentice W: The athletic trainer. In Mueller F, Ryan A, editors: *Prevention of athletic injuries: the role of the sports medicine team*, Philadelphia, 1991, Davis.

45. Rich BS: All physicians are not created equal: understanding the educational background of the sports medicine physician, *J Ath Train* 28(2):177, 1993.

46. Schneiderer L: A survey of appointing and utilizing intercollegiate athletic team physicians, *Ath Train* 22(3):211, 1987.

47. Starkey C: Reforming athletic training education, *J Ath Train* 32(2):113, 1997.

48. Staurowsky E, Scriber K: An analysis of selected factors that affect the work lives of athletic trainers employed in accredited educational programs, *J Ath Train* 33(3):244, 1998.

49. Whitehill W, Norton P, Wright K: Navigating the library maze: introductory research and the athletic trainer, *J Ath Train* 31(1):50, 1996.

50. Winterstein A: Organizational commitment among intercollegiate head athletic trainers: examing our work environment, *J Ath Train* 33(1):54, 1998.

ANNOTATED BIBLIOGRAPHY

Bilik SE: *The trainer's bible*, ed 9, New York, 1956, Reed.

A classic book, first published in 1917, by a major pioneer in athletic training and sports medicine.

National Athletic Trainers' Association Board of Certification: *Role delineation study of the entry level athletic trainer certification examination*, Philadelphia, 1994, Davis.

Contains a complete discussion of the 1993 role delineation study that redefined the responsibilities of the athletic trainer.

National Athletic Trainers' Association: *Code of ethics 1993*, National Athletic Trainers' Association, Dallas, 1993, National Athletic Trainers' Association.

Contains a revision of the previous code of ethics; includes ethical principles, membership standards, and certification standards.

O'Shea ME: *A history of the National Athletic Trainers' Association*, Greenville, NC, 1980, National Athletic Trainers' Association.

An interesting text about the history of NATA that should be read by any student interested in athletic training as a career.

Health Care Administration
in Athletic Training

When you finish this chapter you should be able to

- Describe a functional, well-designed athletic training facility.
- Identify policies and procedures that should be enforced in the athletic training room.
- Explain budgetary concerns for ordering supplies and equipment.
- Explain the importance of the preparticipation physical examination.
- Identify the necessary records that must be maintained by the athletic trainer.
- Describe current systems for gathering data on injuries.

Operating an effective athletic training program requires careful organization and administration regardless of whether the setting is in a high school, college, or university, at the professional level, or in a clinical or industrial setting. Besides being a clinical practitioner, the athletic trainer must be an administrator who performs both managerial and supervisory duties. This chapter looks at the administrative tasks required of the athletic trainer for successful operation of the program, including facility design, policies and procedures, budget considerations, personnel management, administration of physical examinations, record keeping, and collecting injury data.

ESTABLISHING A SYSTEM FOR ATHLETIC TRAINING HEALTH CARE

Developing a Strategic Plan

Perhaps the first step in establishing an athletic training program is to determine why there is a need for such a program and what the function of this program should be within the total scope of the athletic program.[25] These two basic questions in the strategic planning process must be answered by administrators, athletic directors, or school boards who in most cases will ultimately be responsible for funding and supporting the athletic training program. The depth of the commitment from these decision makers toward providing quality health care will to a large extent determine the size of the staff, the size of the facility, and the scope of operation of the athletic training program. A clearly written mission statement will help focus the direction of the program and should be an outcome of the strategic planning process.[15]

Strategic planning for an athletic training program should involve many individuals including administrators, student-athletes, coaches, physicians, staff athletic trainers, parents, and community-based health leaders. Including many individuals in the planning process will help to secure allies who are committed to seeing the program be successful.[25]

Strategic planning should be an ongoing process that takes a critical look at the strengths and weaknesses of the program and then takes immediate action to correct deficiencies. The *WOTS UP* analysis—which looks at *W*eaknesses, *O*pportunities, *T*hreats, and *S*trengths underlying planning[27]—is a useful and effective technique in strategic planning for existing athletic training programs.

Developing a Policies and Procedures Manual

Once the strategic planning process is complete and some consensus has been reached by those involved in the process, the next step is to create a detailed policies and procedures manual for use by everyone who is involved with providing some aspect of health care for the athlete, including the athletic training staff and student trainers, team physicians, other allied health personnel, coaches, and administrators. The manual should include much of the information presented later in this chapter in the section titled "Athletic Training Program Operations." In addition, if the institution's budget permits, an abbreviated version of this manual, outlining the rules for using the athletic training room, should be prepared and distributed to the athletes and their parents.

DESIGNING AN ATHLETIC TRAINING FACILITY

Maximizing use of facilities and effectively using equipment and supplies are essential to the function of any athletic program. The athletic training facility must be specially designed to meet the many requirements of the athletic training program (Figure 2-1).[18] The size and the layout of the athletic training facility will vary significantly depending on the scope of the athletic training program, including the size and number of teams and athletes and what sports are offered. The clinical setting has a much broader patient population, and thus the requirements for equipment and supplies will be somewhat different.[18] To accommodate the various functions of an athletic training program, the athletic training room must serve as a health care center for athletes.[11]

Size

The size of the athletic training room can range anywhere from a large storage closet in some high schools or middle schools to 15,000-square-foot sports medicine complexes in some universities. Certainly the size of the facility can have a major impact on how the athletic training program is managed. But the most important consideration is to organize the athletic training program in a manner that most efficiently takes advantage of the space that happens to be available. When designing a new athletic training facility, the athletic trainer should interact closely with design architects relative to specific needs of the institution and the number of athletes who will be served.

Location

The athletic training facility should have an outside entrance from the athletic field or court. This arrangement makes it unnecessary to bring injured athletes in through the building and possibly through several doors; it also permits access when the rest of the building is not in use. A double door at each entrance is preferable to allow easy passage of a wheelchair or a stretcher. A ramp at the outside entrance is safer and far more functional than are stairs.

The athletic training room should be near the locker rooms if possible so that showers are readily available to athletes coming in for treatment following practice. Toilet facilities should be located adjacent to the athletic training room and should be readily accessible through a door in the training room.

Because the athletic training facility is where emergency treatment is given, its light, heat, and water sources should be independent from those for the rest of the building.

Illumination

The athletic training facility should be well lighted throughout. Lighting should be planned with the advice of a technical lighting engineer. Ceilings and walls acting as reflective surfaces aid in achieving an equable distribution and balance of light. Natural lighting through windows or skylights can certainly be helpful.

Special Service Sections

Apart from the storage and office space, a portion of the athletic training room should be divided into special sections, preferably by half walls or partial glass walls. Space, however, may not permit a separate area for each service section, and an overlapping of functions may be required.

The training facility is a multipurpose area used for first aid, therapy and rehabilitation, injury prevention, medical procedures such as the physical examination, and athletic training administration.

2-1

Critical Thinking Exercise

The members of the school board at All-American High School voted to allocate $25,000 to renovate a 25′ × 40′ storage space and to purchase new equipment for an athletic training room. The athletic trainer has been asked to provide the school principal with a wish list of what should be included in this facility. The physical renovation will cost approximately $17,000.

? How may this space be best used, and what type of equipment should be purchased to maximize the effectiveness of this new facility?

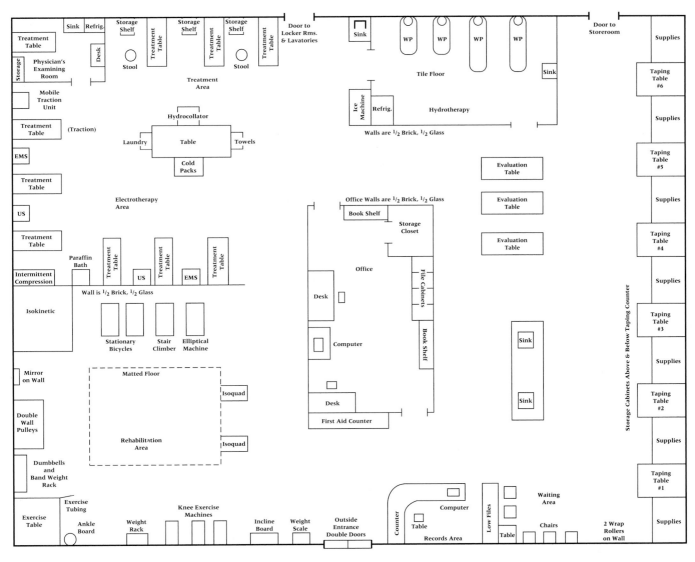

Figure 2-1

The ideal training room facility should be well designed to maximize its use.

Treatment Area

The treatment area should include four to six treatment tables, preferably of adjustable height, that can be used during the application of ice packs or hydrocollator packs or for manual therapy techniques such as massage, mobilization, or proprioceptive neuromuscular facilitation (PNF). Three or four adjustable stools on rollers should also be readily available. The hydrocollator unit and ice bags should be easily accessible to this area.

Electrotherapy Area

The electrotherapy area is used for treatment by ultrasound, diathermy, or electrical stimulating units. Equipment should include at least two treatment tables, several wooden chairs, one or two dispensing tables for holding supplies, shelves, and a storage cabinet for supplies and equipment. The area should contain a sufficient number of grounded outlets, preferably in the walls and several feet above the floor. It is advisable to place rubber mats or runners on each side of the treatment tables as a precautionary measure. This area must be under supervision at all times, and the storage cabinet should be kept locked when not in use.

Hydrotherapy Area

In the hydrotherapy area, the floor should slope toward a centrally located drain to prevent standing water. Equipment should include two or three whirlpool baths (one permitting complete immersion of the body), several lavatories, and storage shelves. Because some of this equipment is electrically operated, considerable precaution must be observed. All electrical outlets should be placed four to five feet above the floor and should have spring-locked covers and water spray deflectors. All cords and wires must be kept clear of the floor to eliminate any possibility of electrical shock. To prevent water from entering the other areas, a slightly raised, rounded curb should be built at the entrance to the area. When an athletic training room is planned, ample outlets must be provided—under no circumstances should two or more devices be operated from the same outlet. All outlets must be properly grounded using ground fault interrupters (GFI).

Exercise Rehabilitation Area

Ideally, an athletic training facility should accommodate injury reconditioning under the strict supervision of the athletic trainer. Selected pieces of resistance equipment should be made available. Depending on the existing space, dumbbells and free weights; exercise machines for knee, ankle, shoulder, hip, and so forth; isokinetic equipment; devices for balance and proprioception; and space for using surgical tubing may all be available for use.

Taping, Bandaging, and Orthotics Area

Each athletic training room should provide a place in which taping, bandaging, and applying orthotic devices can be executed. This area should have three or four taping tables adjacent to a sink and a storage cabinet.

Physician's Examination Room

In colleges and universities, the team physician has a special room in which examinations and treatments may be given. This room contains an examining table, sink, locking storage cabinets, refrigerator, and small desk with a telephone. At all times, this facility must be kept locked to outsiders.

Records Area

Some space, either in the office or at the entrance to the training room, should be devoted to record keeping. Record-keeping facilities may range from a filing system to a more sophisticated computer-based system. Records should be accessible to sports medicine personnel only.

Storage Facilities

It is essential to have adequate storage space available for supplies and equipment.

Many athletic training facilities lack ample storage space. Often, storage facilities are located a considerable distance away, which is extremely inconvenient. In addition to the storage cabinets and shelves provided in each of the three special service areas, a small storage closet should be placed in the athletic trainer's office. All these cabinets should be used for the storage of general supplies as well as for the small, specialized equipment used in the respective areas. A large walk-in closet, 80 to 100 square feet in area, is a necessity for the storage of bulky equipment, medical supplies, adhesive tape, bandages, and protective devices (Figure 2-2). A refrigerator for the storage of frozen water in styrofoam cups for ice massage and other necessities is also an important piece of equipment. Many athletic trainers prefer to place the refrigerator in their office, where it is readily accessible but still under close supervision. In small sports programs, a large refrigerator will probably be sufficient for all ice needs. If at all possible, an ice-making machine should be installed in an auxiliary area to provide an ample and continuous supply of ice for treatment purposes.

Athletic Trainer's Office

A space at least ten feet by twelve feet is ample for the athletic trainer's office. The office should be located so that all areas of the training room can be well supervised without the athletic trainer's having to leave the office. Glass partitions on two sides permit the

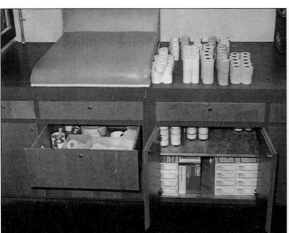

Figure 2-2

An effective athletic training program must have appropriate storage facilities that are highly organized.

athletic trainer, even while seated at the desk, to observe all activities. A desk, chair, tackboard for clippings and other information, telephones, and record file are the basic equipment. In some cases a computer is also housed in this office. The office should have an independent lock-and-key system so that it is accessible only to authorized personnel.

Additional Areas

If space is available, several other areas could potentially be included as part of a training room facility.

Pharmacy Area

A separate room that can be secured for storing and administering medications is helpful. All medications, including over-the-counter drugs, should be kept under lock and key. If prescription medications are kept in the training room, only the team physician or pharmacist from a campus health center should have access to the storage cabinet. Records for administering medications to athletes should be kept in this area. It is essential to adhere to individual state regulations regarding the storage and administration of medications (see Chapter 17).

Rehabilitation Pool

It is rare that a pool is located in the training room; however, if the facility has the space and can afford one, a pool can be an extremely useful rehabilitation tool. The pool should be accessible to individuals with various types of injuries. It should have a graduated depth to at least seven feet, the deck should have a nonslip surface, and the filter system should be in a separate room.[24]

X-Ray Room

A separate room for x-ray equipment must have lead shielding in the walls. The x-ray room must be large enough to house all the necessary equipment (x-ray unit, processing unit, etc.).

ATHLETIC TRAINING PROGRAM OPERATIONS

It is imperative that every athletic training program develop policies and procedures that carefully delineate the daily routine of the program.

The Scope of the Athletic Training Program

A major consideration in any athletic training program is to determine who is to be served by the athletic training staff. The individual athlete, the institution, and the community are considered.

Every athletic training program must develop policies and procedures that carefully delineate the daily routine of the program.

The Athlete

The athletic trainer must decide the extent to which the athlete will be served. For example, will prevention and care activities be extended to athletes for the entire year, including summer and other vacations, or only during the competitive season? Also, the athletic trainer must decide what care will be rendered. Will it extend to all systemic illnesses or to just musculoskeletal problems?

The Institution

A policy must be established as to who, other than the athletes, will be served by the athletic training program. Often, legal concerns and the school liability insurance dictate who beyond the athlete is to be served. A policy should make it clear whether students other than athletes, athletes from other schools, faculty, and staff are to receive care. If so, how are they to be referred and medically directed? Also, it must be decided whether the athletic training program will act as a clinical setting for student athletic trainers.

The Community

A decision must be made as to which, if any, outside group or person in the community will be served by the athletic training staff. Again, legality and the institution's insurance program must be taken into consideration. If a policy is not delineated in this matter, outside persons may abuse the services of the athletic training facilities and staff.

Clinical and Industrial Setting Considerations

The athletic trainer working in the clinical or industrial setting will likely be working with patients other than high school or college athletes. The scope of practice within an individual clinic may include pediatric, work hardening, orthopedic, or even occasionally, neurological patients. Athletic trainers in the clinical setting should be assigned to work only with patient populations that may generally be classified as physically active. Clinical administrators should not require athletic trainers to treat other patient populations because athletic trainers have no formal education or training geared toward those patient problems.

Athletic trainers in the industrial setting, in addition to overseeing preventive and rehabilitation programs, are frequently asked to take on responsibility for employee fitness programs. Therefore a more advanced understanding of the principles of training and conditioning will be necessary (see Chapter 4).

Providing Coverage

Facility Personnel Coverage

A major concern of any athletic department is whether proper personnel coverage is provided for the athletic training facility and specific sports. If a school has a full-time athletic training staff, an athletic training facility could, for example, operate from 7 A.M. to 10 P.M. Mornings are commonly reserved for treatments and exercise rehabilitation; early afternoons are for treatment, exercise rehabilitation, and preparation for practice or a contest; and late afternoons and early evenings are spent in injury management. High schools with limited available supervision may be able to provide athletic training facility coverage only in the afternoons and during vacation periods.

Sports Coverage

Ideally, all sports should have a certified, or at least a student, athletic trainer in attendance at all practices and contests, both at home and away. Many colleges and universities have sufficient personnel to provide coverage to a variety of sports simultaneously. At the high school level, however, only one or occasionally two athletic trainers may be available to cover every sport that the high school offers. Thus it is impossible for the athletic trainer to be in several places at one time. The athletic trainer in this difficult situation must make some decisions about where the greatest need for coverage is, based on the potential risk of a particular sport and the number of athletes involved.

Hygiene and Sanitation

The practice of good hygiene and sanitation is of the utmost importance in an athletic training program. The prevention of infectious diseases is a direct responsibility of the athletic trainer, whose duty it is to see that all athletes are surrounded by the most hygienic environment possible and that each individual is practicing sound health habits. Chapter 14 discusses the management of bloodborne pathogens. The athletic trainer must be aware of and adhere to guidelines for the operation of an athletic care facility as dictated by the Occupational Safety and Health Administration (OSHA).

Good hygiene and sanitation are essential for an athletic training program.

The Athletic Training Facility

The athletic training room should be used only for the prevention and care of sports injuries. Too often the athletic training facility becomes a meeting or club room for the coaches and athletes. Unless definite rules are established and practiced, room cleanliness and sanitation become an impossible chore. Unsanitary practices or conditions must not be tolerated. The following are some important athletic training room policies:

1. No cleated shoes are allowed. Dirt and debris tend to cling to cleated shoes; therefore cleated shoes should be removed before athletes enter the athletic training facility.
2. Game equipment is kept outside. Because game equipment such as balls and bats adds to the sanitation problem, it should be kept out of the athletic training room. Coaches and athletes must be continually reminded that the athletic training room is not a storage room for sports equipment.
3. Shoes must be kept off treatment tables. Because of the tendency of shoes to contaminate treatment tables, they must be removed before any care is given to the athlete.
4. Athletes should shower before receiving treatment. The athlete should make it a habit to shower before being treated if the treatment is not an emergency. This procedure helps keep tables and therapeutic modalities sanitary.
5. Roughhousing and profanity should not be allowed. Athletes must be continually reminded that the athletic training facility is for injury care and prevention. Horseplay and foul language lower the basic purpose of the athletic training room.
6. No food or smokeless tobacco should be allowed.

General cleanliness of the athletic training room cannot be stressed enough. Through the athletic trainer's example, the athlete may develop an appreciation for cleanliness and in turn develop wholesome personal health habits. Cleaning responsibilities in most schools are divided between the athletic training staff and the maintenance crew. Care of permanent building structures and trash disposal are usually the responsibilities of maintenance, whereas upkeep of specialized equipment falls within the province of the training staff.

Division of routine cleaning responsibilities may be organized as follows:

1. Maintenance crew
    a. Sweep floors daily.
    b. Clean and disinfect sinks and built-in tubs daily.
    c. Mop and disinfect hydrotherapy area twice a week.
    d. Refill paper towel and drinking cup dispensers as needed.
    e. Empty wastebaskets and dispose of trash daily.

2. Athletic training staff
    a. Clean and disinfect treatment tables daily.
    b. Clean and disinfect hydrotherapy modalities daily.
    c. Clean and polish other therapeutic modalities weekly.

The Gymnasium

Maintaining a clean environment in sports is a continual battle in the athletic training setting. Practices such as passing a common towel to wipe off perspiration, using common water dispensers, or failing to change dirty clothing for clean are prevalent violations of sanitation in sports. The following is a suggested cleanliness checklist that may be used by the athletic trainer:
1. Facilities cleanliness
    a. Are the gymnasium floors swept daily?
    b. Are drinking fountains, showers, sinks, urinals, and toilets cleaned and disinfected daily?
    c. Are lockers aired and sanitized frequently?
    d. Are mats cleaned routinely (wrestling mats and wall mats cleaned daily)?
2. Equipment and clothing issuance
    a. Are equipment and clothing fitted to the athlete to avoid skin irritations?
    b. Is swapping of equipment and clothes prevented?
    c. Is clothing laundered and changed frequently?
    d. Is wet clothing allowed to dry thoroughly before the athlete wears it again?
    e. Is individual attention given to proper shoe fit and upkeep?
    f. Is protective clothing provided during inclement weather or when the athlete is waiting on the sidelines?
    g. Are clean, dry towels provided each day for each individual athlete?

The Athlete

To promote good health among the athletes, the athletic trainer should encourage sound health habits. The following checklist may be a useful guide for coaches, athletic trainers, and athletes:
1. Are the athletes medically cleared to participate?
2. Is each athlete insured?
3. Does the athlete promptly report injuries, illnesses, and skin disorders to the coach or the athletic trainer?
4. Are good daily living habits of resting, sleeping, and proper nutrition practiced?
5. Do the athletes shower after practice?
6. Do they dry thoroughly and cool off before departing from the gymnasium?
7. Do they avoid drinking from a common water dispenser?
8. Do they avoid using a common towel?
9. Do they avoid exchanging gym clothes with teammates?
10. Do they practice good foot hygiene?
11. Do they avoid contact with teammates who have a contagious disease or infection?

Emergency Telephone

The accessibility of an emergency telephone adjacent to all major activity areas is also essential. It should be possible to use this telephone to call outside for emergency aid and to contact the athletic training facilities when additional assistance is required. Two-way radios or, preferably, cellular or digital telephones provide the greatest flexibility in the communication system and should be bought if the budget permits.

Budgetary Concerns

A major problem often facing athletic trainers is a budget of sufficient size.

One of the major problems faced by athletic trainers is to obtain a budget of sufficient size to permit them to perform a creditable job of athletic training. Most high schools provide only limited budgetary provisions for athletic training except for the purchase of tape, ankle wraps, and a training bag that contains a minimum amount of supplies. Many fail to provide a room and any of the special facilities that are needed to establish an effective athletic training program. Some school boards and administrators fail to recognize that the functions performed in the athletic training facility are an essential component of the athletic program and that even if no specialist is used, the facilities are nonetheless necessary. Colleges and universities are not usually faced with this problem to the extent that high schools are. By and large, athletic training at the college level is recognized as an important aspect of the athletic program.

Budgetary needs vary considerably within programs; some require only a few thousand dollars, whereas others spend hundreds of thousands of dollars. The amount spent on building and equipping a training facility, of course, is entirely a matter of local option. In purchasing equipment, immediate needs and availability of personnel to operate specialized equipment should be kept in mind.

The budget process should be a continuous process involving prioritizing, planning, documenting and evaluating the goals of the athletic training program and formulating a plan for how available resources can be utilized and expended during the next budget period.[24]

Budget records should be kept on file so that they are available for use in projecting the following year's budgetary needs. The records present a picture of the distribution of current funds and serve to substantiate future budgetary requests.

Supplies

The supplies that the athletic trainer uses to carry out daily tasks may be classified as either expendable or nonexpendable. Some athletic trainers spend much of their budget on expendable supplies that cannot be reused. Supplies that are expendable are used for injury prevention, first aid, and management. Examples of expendable supplies are adhesive tape, adhesive bandages, and hydrogen peroxide. Nonexpendable supplies are those that can be reused. Examples are compression wraps, scissors, and neoprene sleeves. An annual inventory must be conducted at the end of the year or before the ordering of supplies. Accurate records must be kept to justify future requests.

Equipment

The term *equipment* refers to items that may be used by the athletic training room for a number of years. Equipment may be further divided into fixed and nonfixed. Fixed equipment does not necessarily mean that it cannot be moved but that it is not usually removed from the athletic training facility. Examples of fixed equipment are ice machines, treatment tables, isokinetic machines, and electrical therapeutic modalities. Nonfixed equipment includes things like crutches, coolers, and training kits.

Equipment may be fixed or nonfixed.

Purchasing Systems

Purchasing of supplies and equipment must be done through either direct buy or competitive bid. For expensive purchases, an institutional purchasing agent is sent out to competing vendors who quote a price on specified supplies or equipment. Orders are generally placed with the lowest bidder. Smaller purchases or emergency purchases may be made directly from one single vendor.[23]

Purchasing may be done through direct buy or competitive bid.

An alternative to purchasing expensive equipment is to arrange for a lease. Many manufacturers and distributors are now willing to lease equipment on a monthly or yearly basis. Over the long run, purchasing equipment will be less costly. In the short term, however, if a large capital expenditure is not possible, a leasing agreement should be considered.[24]

Additional Budget Considerations

In addition to supplies and equipment, the athletic trainer must also consider other costs that may be included in the operation of an athletic training program; these include telephone and postage, contracts with physicians or clinics for services, professional liability insurance, memberships in professional organizations, the purchase of professional journals or textbooks, travel and expenses for attending professional meetings, and clothing to be worn in the training room.[24,25]

Developing a Risk Management Plan

The athletic trainer, working in conjunction with the appropriate administrative personnel, must be responsible for developing a risk management plan that covers security issues, fire safety, electrical and equipment safety, and emergency injury management.

Security Issues

The athletic trainer must decide who will have access to the athletic training room facility. In addition to the staff athletic trainers, the team physician must have keys to access the athletic training room. Student athletic trainers may also be given keys as necessary at the collegiate level; at the high school level, however, student athletic trainers should only be in the athletic training room when directly supervised. At the collegiate level, coaches do not need to have access to the athletic training room; but at the high school level, coaches might need to have a key to get into the facility at times when the athletic trainer may not be available. Access to areas of the building other than the athletic training room should be strictly limited.

Fire Safety

The athletic trainer should establish and have clearly posted a plan for evacuating the athletic training facility should a fire occur. Smoke detectors and fire alarm systems must be periodically tested and inspected to make certain that they are functioning normally.

Electrical and Equipment Safety

Electrical safety in the athletic training setting should be of maximal concern to the athletic trainer. Unnecessary accidents can be avoided by taking some basic precautions and acquiring some understanding of the power distribution system and electrical grounds. *Focus Box:* "Safety when using electrical equipment" lists considerations for electrical safety.

Emergency Injury Management

In cooperation with existing community-based emergency health care delivery systems, the athletic trainer should develop a systematic plan for accessing the emergency medical system and subsequent transportation of the injured athlete to an emergency care facility. Meetings should be scheduled periodically with EMTs or paramedics who work in the community to make certain that they understand the role of the athletic trainer as a provider of emergency health care. It is important to communicate the special considerations for dealing with athletic equipment issues before an emergency arises. Chapter 12 discusses the emergency management plan in detail.

Accessing Community-Based Health Services

In addition to the community-based emergency medical services personnel, the athletic trainer should become familiar with existing local and regional community health services and agencies that may be accessed should a need arise to refer an athlete to psychological or sociological services. Referrals should be made with input and assistance from the team physician. The family of an athlete requiring referral for psychological or sociological counseling must be informed of the existing problems, particularly when minors are involved.

Human Resource and Personnel Issues

The importance of putting together the sports medicine team was discussed in Chapter 1. Any team is only as good as the group of individuals who make up that team. Recruiting, hiring, and retaining the most qualified personnel is essential if the athletic training program is to be effective.

2-2

Critical Thinking Exercise

The principal at All-American High School has received a mandate from the school board to develop a risk management plan for the athletic program. The principal asks the athletic trainer to chair a committee to develop this plan.

? What considerations are important for inclusion in this risk management plan?

2-3

Critical Thinking Exercise

State University has an opening for an assistant athletic trainer in its Department of Athletics. The athletic director has asked the head athletic trainer to be in charge of the recruitment and hiring process for the new position.

? What factors must be considered in hiring a new employee?

Focus

Safety when using electrical equipment

- The entire electrical system of the building or athletic training room should be designed or evaluated by a qualified electrician.
- Problems with the electrical system may exist in older buildings or in situations in which rooms have been modified to accommodate therapeutic devices (e.g., putting a whirlpool in a locker room in which the concrete floor is always wet or damp).
- It should not be assumed that all three-pronged wall outlets are automatically grounded to the earth. The ground must be checked. Ground fault interrupters (GFI) should be installed, particularly in those areas in which water may be present (i.e., whirlpools).
- The athletic trainer should become very familiar with the equipment being used and with any potential problems that may exist or develop. Any defective equipment should be immediately removed from the clinic. The plug should not be jerked out of the wall by pulling on the cable.
- Extension cords or multiple adapters should never be used.
- Equipment should be reevaluated on a yearly basis and should conform to National Electrical Code guidelines. A clinic or training room that is not in compliance with this code has no legal protection in a lawsuit.
- Common sense should always be exercised when using electrotherapeutic devices. A situation that appears to be potentially dangerous may in fact result in injury or death.

Specific policies dealing with recruitment, hiring and firing, performance evaluations, and promotions are mandated by federal law.[10] The policies relative to recruitment and hiring clearly mandate that all qualified applicants should receive equal consideration regardless of their race, gender, religion, or nationality. Athletic trainers who are in positions to hire new staff must strictly adhere to these mandates.

Once an individual has been hired, it is important for everyone on the sports medicine team to clearly understand what individual roles and responsibilities are within that team. Individual job descriptions and job specifications that describe qualifications, accountability, a code of conduct, and the scope of that position should be written. A well-defined organizational chart should be created to show the chain of command.[25]

The head athletic trainer must serve as a supervisor for the staff assistants, graduate students, and undergraduate student athletic trainers.[16] The supervisor should strive to improve job performance and enhance professional development of those being supervised. *Focus Box:* "Models of supervision for head athletic trainer" defines supervisory models.[25]

Performance evaluations should be routinely done at regularly scheduled intervals to analyze the quality of the work being performed. Evaluations should focus first on the positive aspects of job performance and then on any weaknesses.[16]

Each of these policies relative to personnel issues should be included in the policies and procedures manual.

RECORD KEEPING

Record keeping is a major responsibility of the athletic training program. Some athletic trainers object to keeping records and filling out forms, stating that they have neither the time nor the inclination to be bookkeepers. Nevertheless, because lawsuits are currently the rule rather than the exception, accurate and up-to-date records are an absolute necessity. Medical records, injury reports, treatment logs,

Keeping adequate records is of major importance in the athletic training program.

Focus

Models of supervision for the head athletic trainer

Clinical supervision—Involves direct observation of the assistant trainers in the performance of their written job responsibilities, followed by an analysis of strengths and weaknesses and a collaborative effort to correct weaknesses.

Developmental supervision—A mentoring approach in which the head athletic trainer works in a collaborative manner with the assistants, helping them to develop professionally while meeting the needs of the day-to-day athletic training program.

Inspection production supervision—An authoritative management style in which the head athletic trainer demands that lines of authority be strictly maintained to accomplish the stated goals of the athletic training program.

Preparticipation health examination:
- Medical history
- Physical examination
- Maturity assessment
- Orthopedic screening

2-4

Critical Thinking Exercise

All-American High School offers eighteen sports, six in the fall, six in the winter, and six in the spring. There are a total of approximately 500 athletes, and approximately 200 of them are involved in the fall sports. The athletic trainer is charged with the responsibility of arranging and administering preparticipation examinations so that each athlete can be cleared for competition.

? How can the athletic trainer most efficiently set up the preparticipation exams to clear 200 athletes for competition in the fall sports?

personal information cards, injury evaluations and progress notes, supply and equipment inventories, and annual reports are essential records that should be maintained by the athletic trainer.

Administering Preparticipation Examinations

The first piece of information that the athletic trainer should collect on each athlete is obtained from an initial preparticipation examination done prior to the start of practice. The primary purpose of the preparticipation exam is to identify an athlete who may be at risk before he or she participates in a specific sport.[12] The preparticipation examination should consist of a medical history, a physical examination, a brief orthopedic screening, and in some situations, wellness screening. Information obtained during this examination will establish a baseline to which comparisons may be made after injury. It may also reveal conditions that could warrant disqualification from certain sports. The examination will also satisfy insurance and liability issues. The preparticipation exam may be administered on an individual basis by a personal physician, or it may be done using a station examination system with a team of examiners.[4]

Examination by a Personal Physician

Examination by a personal physician has the advantage of yielding an in-depth history and an ideal physician-patient relationship. A disadvantage of this type of examination is that it may not be directed to detection of factors that predispose the athlete to a sports injury.[28]

Station Examination

The most thorough and sport-specific type of preparticipation examination is the station examination.[20] This method can provide the athlete with a detailed examination in a short period of time. A team of nine people is needed to examine thirty or more athletes. The team should include two physicians, two medically trained nonphysicians (nurse, athletic trainer, physical therapist, or physician's assistant), and five managers, student athletic trainers, or assistant coaches (Table 2-1).[28]

Medical History

A medical history form should be completed before the physical examination and orthopedic screening; its purpose is to identify any past or existing medical problems.[1] This form should be updated for each athlete every year. Medical histories should be closely reviewed by both the physician and the athletic trainer so that

TABLE 2-1 Suggested Station Preparticipation Examination

Station	Points Noted	Personnel
1. Individual history; height, weight, body composition	"Yes" answers are probed in depth; height and weight relationships	Physician, nurse, or athletic trainer
2. Blood pressure, pulse	Upper limits: age 6 to 11—130/80; 12 and older—140/90; right arm is measured while athlete is seated	Student athletic trainer or manager
3. Snellen test, vision	Upper limits of visual acuity— 20/40	Student athletic trainer or manager
4. Skin, mouth, ears, nose, throat	Suspicious-looking skin infections or rashes, dental prosthesis or caries, abnormalities of the ears, nose, throat	Physician, nurse, or athletic trainer
5. Chest, heart, lungs, breasts	Heart abnormalities (e.g., murmurs, latent bronchospasm), clarity of lungs	Physician
6. Lymphatics, abdomen, male genitalia	Adenopathy (cervical and axillary), abnormalities of genitalia, hernia	Physician or physician's assistant
7. Orthopedics	Postural asymmetry, decreased range of motion or strength, abnormal joint laxity	Physician, athletic trainer, physical therapist, or nurse practitioner
8. Urinalysis	After its collection in a plastic cup, urine is tested in a lab for sugar and protein	Student athletic trainer or manager
9. Blood work	Lab test to determine hematocrit	Nurse or physician
10. Review	History and physical examination reports are evaluated and the following decisions are made: (a) No sports participation (b) Limited participation (no participation in specific sports such as football or ice hockey) (c) Clearance withheld until certain conditions are met (e.g., additional tests are taken, rehabilitation is completed) (d) Full, unlimited participation is allowed	Physician and athletic trainer

MEDICAL HISTORY FORM

HEAD
1. Do you experience headaches? _____
   If yes, how frequently do they appear? _____
   Where are they located? _____
   Do you take any medicine to relieve them? _____
   If yes, what do you use? _____
2. Do you have any episodes of dizziness, seizures, or
   convulsions? _____
3. Have you ever fainted? _____
4. Have you ever had a head or neck injury? _____
   If yes, did you lose consciousness? _____
   If yes, how long? _____
   Were you under the care of a doctor? _____
   Were you hospitalized? _____
   Paralysis? _____ Numbness, tingling, or weakness of any extrem-
   ity? _____
   How long before you resumed normal activity? _____

EYES
1. Have you ever had a problem with your eyes? Trauma? _____
   Loss of vision? _____ Pink eye? _____ Pain? _____

EARS
1. Have you ever had a problem with your ears? _____
   Infection? _____ Swimmer's ear? _____ Pain? _____
   Drainage? _____ Loss of hearing? _____

NOSE
1. Have you ever had a problem with your nose? _____
   Broken? _____ Sneezing? _____ Nosebleeds? _____

THROAT
1. How often do you have colds or sore throats? _____

SKIN
1. Do you ever have a skin rash? _____
   If yes, explain. _____

CHEST
1. Do you ever have chest pain? _____
   If yes, explain. _____
2. Do you have chronic cough? _____ Asthma? _____
   Hay fever? _____ Have you ever coughed up blood? _____

HEART
1. Have you ever been told you had a heart murmur? _____
   If yes, explain. _____
2. Have you ever been told you had elevated blood pressure? _____
   If yes, explain. _____
3. Is heart disease present in your family? _____
   If yes, explain. _____
4. Have you ever been told that a member of your family died suddenly or had a heart attack at a young age? _____

GI
1. Do you have trouble with heartburn? _____ Indigestion? _____
   Nausea? _____ Vomiting? _____ Constipation? _____
   Diarrhea? _____ Have you ever vomited blood? _____
   If yes, explain. _____
2. Have you ever passed blood in your stools? _____
   If yes, explain. _____

GU
1. Have you ever noted burning on urination? _____
   Urgency? _____ Frequency? _____ Wake up at night to
   pass urine? _____ Penile discharge? _____ Passed blood
   on urination? _____ Kidney stone? _____

SKELETAL
1. Have you ever had arthritis? _____
   Sprained ankle? _____ If yes, explain. _____
   Knee injury? _____ If yes, explain. _____
   Shoulder injury? _____ If yes, explain. _____
   Broken bone? _____ If yes, explain. _____
   Neck injury? _____ If yes, explain. _____
   Back trouble? _____ If yes, explain. _____
   Have you ever had surgery? _____ If yes, explain. _____
   Have you ever had a dislocation? If yes, explain. _____
2. Does any joint feel as if it is slipping? _____
3. Do you have a pin, plate, screw, or anything metal in your
   body? _____ If yes, explain. _____

GENERAL
1. Do you have any drug allergies? _____
2. Are you allergic to insect bites? _____
3. Are you allergic to anything? _____
4. Have you ever had hepatitis? _____ Mononucleosis? _____
   Diabetes? _____ Does any family member have diabetes? _____
5. Have you ever had any serious disease? _____ If yes, explain. _____
6. Have you ever had heat exhaustion or heat stroke? _____
   If yes, explain. _____
7. Has any member of your family ever had head exhaustion or heat
   stroke? _____
8. Has any member of your family been told they were allergic to
   medication used as anesthesia? _____
9. Have you ever been allergic to local anesthetics used by doctors
   or dentists? _____
10. Has your weight changed in the last three months? _____
    If yes, explain. _____

Figure 2-3

Sample medical history examination form

personnel may be prepared should some medical emergency arise. Necessary participation release forms and insurance information should be collected along with the
medical history (Figure 2-3).[13]

Physical Examination

The physical examination should include assessment of height, weight, body composition, blood pressure, pulse, vision, skin, dental, ear, nose, throat, heart and lung
function, abdomen, lymphatics, genitalia, maturation index, urinalysis, and blood
work (Figure 2-4).[14]

Maturity Assessment

Maturity assessment should be part of the physical examination as a means of protecting the young, physically developing athlete.[5] The most commonly used methods
are the circumpubertal (sexual maturity), skeletal, and dental assessments. Of the
three, Tanner's five stages of assessment, indicating maturity of secondary sexual
characteristics, is the most expedient for use in the station method of examination.[29]
The Tanner approach evaluates pubic hair and genitalia development in boys and
pubic hair and breast development in girls (Figure 2-5). Other indicators that may be
noted are facial and axillary hair. Stage one indicates that puberty is not evident, and
stage five indicates full development. The crucial stage in terms of collision and high-
intensity noncontact sports is stage three, in which there is the fastest bone growth.
In this stage, the growth plates are two to five times weaker than the joint capsule
and tendon attachments.[5] Young athletes in grades seven to twelve must be matched
by maturity, not age.[17]

Name _____ SS# _____ Date _____

Height _____ Weight _____ Percent body fat _____

Check if negative

  1. Blood pressure _____ / _____
  2. Pulse _____
  3. Vision
       Without glasses R 20/_____ L 20/_____
       With glasses R 20/_____ L 20/_____
  4. Skin _____
  5. Dental/mouth _____
  6. Ears _____
  7. Nose _____
  8. Throat _____
  9. Chest
       Heart rhythm _____
       Lungs _____
       Breasts _____
 10. Abdomen
       Liver _____
       Spleen _____
       Kidneys _____
       Stomach _____
       Bowel _____
 11. Lymphatics
       Cervical _____
       Axillary _____
       Femoral _____
 12. Genitalia _____
 13. Maturation Index _____
 14. Urinalysis
       Protein _____
       Sugar _____
 15. Blood
       Hematocrit _____
 16. Other _____
Disposition
       No participation
       Limited participation
       Clearance withheld
       Cleared for participation
Comments _____
_____
_____

_____

Physician's signature

_____

Date

Figure 2-4

Sample physical examination form

Orthopedic Screening

Orthopedic screening may be done as part of the physical examination or separately by the athletic trainer. An example of a quick orthopedic screening examination appears in Figure 2-6 and usually will take about ninety seconds.[2] A more detailed orthopedic examination may be conducted to assess strength, range of motion, and stability at various joints (Figure 2-7).

Figure 2-5

Tanner Stages of Maturity[29]

Males
Stage 1. **No evidence of pubic hair**
Stage 2. **Slightly pigmented hair laterally at the base of the penis. Usually straight.**
Stage 3. **Hair becomes darker and coarser, begins to curl, and spreads over the pubic region.**
Stage 4. **Hair is adult in type but does not extend onto thighs.**
Stage 5. **Hair extends onto the thighs and frequently up the linea alba.**

Females
Stage 1. **No evidence of pubic hair.**
Stage 2. **Long, slightly pigmented, downy hair along the edges of the labia.**
Stage 3. **Darker, coarser, slightly curled hair spread sparsely over the mons pubis.**
Stage 4. **Adult type of hair but it does not extend onto thighs.**
Stage 5. **Adult distribution including spread along the medial aspects of the thighs.**

Wellness Screening

Some preparticipation exams include a screening for wellness. The purpose is to determine whether the athlete is engaging in healthy lifestyle behaviors. A number of wellness screening tools are available. Figure 2-8 provides an example of a wellness screening questionnaire.

Sport Disqualification

As discussed previously, sports participation involves risks. Certain injuries or conditions warrant concern on the part of both the athlete and sports medicine personnel relative to continued participation in sport activities.[9] Table 2-2 lists those conditions.[3] Sports medicine physicians can only recommend that an athlete voluntarily retire from participation. The Americans with Disabilities Act of 1990 dictates that the individual athlete is the only person who can make the final decision. Most conditions that potentially warrant disqualification should be identified by a preparticipation examination and noted in the medical history.[20]

Figure 2-6

The orthopedic screening examination. Equipment that may be needed includes reflex hammer, tape measure, pin, and examining table.

Orthopedic Screening Examination	
Activity and Instruction	**To Determine**
Stand facing examiner	Acromioclavicular joints; general habitus
Look at ceiling, floor, over both shoulders; touch ears to shoulders	Cervical spine motion
Shrug shoulders (examiner resists)	Trapezius strength
Abduct shoulders 90° (examiner resists at 90°)	Deltoid strength
Full external rotation of arms	Shoulder motion
Flex and extend elbows	Elbow motion
Arms at sides, elbows 90° flexed; pronate and supinate wrists	Elbow and wrist motion
Spread fingers; make fist	Hand or finger motion and deformities
Tighten (contract) quadriceps; relax quadriceps	Symmetry and knee effusion; ankle effusion
"Duck walk" four steps (away from examiner with buttocks on heels)	Hip, knee, and ankle motion
Stand with back to examiner	Shoulder symmetry; scoliosis
Knees straight, touch toes	Scoliosis, hip motion, hamstring tightness
Raise up on toes, raise heels	Calf symmetry, leg strength

Orthopedic Screening Form

Name: _____   SS#: _____

FLEXIBILITY	Check if Normal
Shoulder:	Abduction
	Adduction
	Flexion
	Extension
	Internal rot.
	External rot.
Hip:	Ext. (flex knee)
	Flex. (flex knee)
	Ext. (str. leg)
	Flex. (str. leg)
	Abduction
	Adduction
Knee:	Flexion
	Extension
Ankle:	Dorsiflexion
	Plantar flexion
Trunk:	Flexion
	Extension
	Rotation
	Lat. Flexion
Joint Stability	
Knee:	Lachman
	Pivot shift
	Anterior drawer
	Posterior drawer
	Valgus
	Varus
	McMurray
	Apley's grind
Ankle:	Anterior drawer
	Talor tilt
Leg Length	
Posture:	Pelvis height
	Shoulder height
	Spine
Previous Injury:	

Comments:

Figure 2-7

Sample of a detailed orthopedic screening examination form

1. Circle the appropriate response for each question.
2. Add the total number of points for each section.

Behavior	Almost Always	Sometimes	Almost Never
Tobacco Use			
If you never smoke or use tobacco products, enter a score of 10 for this section and go to the next section on Alcohol and Drugs.			
1. I avoid smoking cigarettes and chewing tobacco.	2	1	0
2. I smoke only low-tar and low-nicotine cigarettes, or I smoke a pipe or cigars.	2	1	0
		Tobacco Use Score:	_____
Alcohol and Drugs			
1. I avoid drinking alcoholic beverages or I drink no more than one or two a day.	4	1	0
2. I avoid using alcohol or other drugs (especially illegal drugs) as a way of handling stressful situations or problems in my life.	2	1	0
3. I am careful not to drink alcohol when taking certain medicines (e.g., medicine for sleeping, pain, colds, and allergies) or when pregnant.	2	1	0
4. I read and follow the label directions when using prescribed and over-the-counter drugs.	2	1	0
		Alcohol and Drug Score:	_____
Eating Habits			
1. I eat a variety of foods each day, such as fruits and vegetables, whole grain breads and cereals, lean meats, dairy products, dry peas and beans, and nuts and seeds.	4	1	0
2. I limit my intake of fat, saturated fat, and cholesterol (including fat in meats, eggs, butter, and other dairy products, shortenings, and organ meats such as liver).	2	1	0
3. I limit the amount of salt I eat by cooking with only small amounts, not adding salt at the table, and avoiding salty snacks.	2	1	0
4. I avoid eating too much sugar (especially frequent snacks of sticky candy or soft drinks).	2	1	0
		Eating Habits Score:	_____
Exercise/Fitness Habits			
1. I maintain a desired weight, avoiding overweight and underweight.	3	1	0
2. I do vigorous exercises for 15–30 minutes at least three times a week (examples include running, swimming, and brisk walking).	3	1	0
3. I do exercises that enhance my muscle tone for 15–30 minutes at least three times a week (examples include yoga and calisthenics).	2	1	0
4. I use part of my leisure time participating in individual, family, or team activities that increase my level of fitness (such as gardening, bowling, golf, and baseball).	2	1	0
		Exercise/Fitness Score:	_____

Behavior	Almost Always	Sometimes	Almost Never
Stress Control			
1. I have a job or do other work that I enjoy.	2	1	0
2. I find it easy to relax and to express my feelings freely.	2	1	0
3. I anticipate and prepare for events or situations likely to be stressful for me.	2	1	0
4. I have close friends, relatives, or others with whom I can discuss personal matters and call on for help when needed.	2	1	0
5. I participate in group activities (such as church and community organizations) or hobbies that I enjoy.	2	1	0
		Stress Control Score:	_____
Safety			
1. I wear a seat belt when riding in a car.	2	1	0
2. I avoid driving while under the influence of alcohol and other drugs.	2	1	0
3. I obey traffic rules and the speed limit when driving.	2	1	0
4. I am careful when using potentially harmful products or substances (such as household cleaners, poisons, and electrical devices).	2	1	0
5. I avoid smoking in bed.	2	1	0
6. I am not sexually active or I have sex with only one mutually faithful, uninfected partner, or I always engage in safer sex (using condoms) and I do not share needles to inject drugs.	2	1	0
		Safety Score:	_____

What your Scores Mean

Scores of 9 and 10: Excellent. Your answers show that you are aware of the importance of this area to your health.

Scores of 6 to 8: Good. Your health practices in this area are good, but there is room for improvement.

Scores of 3 to 5: Fair. Your health risks are showing.

Scores of 0 to 2: Poor. Your answers show that you may be taking serious and unnecessary risks with your health. Perhaps you are not aware of the risks and what to do about them. You can easily get the information and help you need to improve, if you wish.

If you have questions or concerns you should consult your athletic trainers for advice.

Figure 2-8

Wellness screening questionnaire

Injury Reports and Injury Disposition

An injury report serves as a record for future reference (Figure 2-9). If the emergency procedures followed are questioned at a later date, an athletic trainer's memory of the details may be somewhat hazy, but a report completed on the spot provides specific information. In a litigation situation, an athletic trainer may be asked questions about an injury that occurred three years in the past. All injury reports should be filed in the athletic trainer's office. It is well advised to make the reports out in triplicate so that one copy may be sent to the school health office, one to the physician, and one retained.

TABLE 2-2 Recommendations for Participation in Competitive Sports

	Contact		Noncontact		
	Contact/ Collision	Limited Contact/ Impact	Moderately Strenuous	Strenuous	Nonstrenuous
Atlantoaxial instability	No	No	Yes*	Yes	Yes

*Swimming: no butterfly, breast stroke, or diving starts

Acute illnesses	*	*	*	*	*

*Needs individual assessment, e.g., contagiousness to others, risk of worsening illness

Cardiovascular					
Carditis	No	No	No	No	No
Hypertension					
Mild	Yes	Yes	Yes	Yes	Yes
Moderate	*	*	*	*	*
Severe	*	*	*	*	*
Congenital heart disease	†	†	†	†	†

*Needs individual assessment
†Patients with mild forms can be allowed a full range of physical activities; patients with moderate or severe forms or who are postoperative should be evaluated by a cardiologist before athletic participation.

Eyes					
Absence or loss of function of eye	*	*	*	*	*
Detached retina	†	†	†	†	†

*Availability of American Society for Testing and Materials (ASTM)-approved eye guards may allow competitor to participate in most sports, but this must be judged on an individual basis.
†Consult ophthalmologist

Inguinal hernia	Yes	Yes	Yes	Yes	Yes
Kidney: Absence of one	No	Yes	Yes	Yes	Yes
Liver: Enlarged	No	No	Yes	Yes	Yes
Musculoskeletal disorders	*	*	*	*	*

*Needs individual assessment

Neurologic status					
History of serious head or spine trauma, repeated concussions, or craniotomy	*	*	Yes	Yes	Yes
Convulsive disorder					
Well controlled	Yes	Yes	Yes	Yes	Yes
Poorly controlled	No	No	Yes†	Yes	Yes††

*Needs individual assessment
†No swimming or weight lifting
††No archery or riflery

Ovary: Absence of one	Yes	Yes	Yes	Yes	Yes
Respiratory status					
Pulmonary insufficiency	*	*	*	*	Yes
Asthma	Yes	Yes	Yes	Yes	Yes

*May be allowed to compete if oxygenation remains satisfactory during a graded stress test

Sickle cell trait	Yes	Yes	Yes	Yes	Yes
Skin: Boils, herpes, impetigo, scabies	*	*	Yes	Yes	Yes

*No gymnastics with mats, martial arts, wrestling, or contact sports until not contagious

Spleen: Enlarged	No	No	No	Yes	Yes
Testicle: Absent or undescended	Yes*	Yes*	Yes	Yes	Yes

*Certain sports may require protective cup

Figure 2-9

Athletic injury record form

Name _____ Sport _____ Date: ___ / ___ / ___ Time: _____ Injury number: _____

Player I.D. _____ Age: _____ Location: _____ Intercollegiate-nonintercollegiate

Initial injury   Recheck   Reinjury   Preseason—Practice—Game   Incurred while participating in sport: yes ___ no ___

Description: How did it happen? _____

Initial impression: _____

Site of injury	Body part	Structure	Treatment _____
1 Right	1 Head	25 MP joint	1 Skin	_____
2 Left	2 Face	26 PIP joint	2 Muscle
3 Proximal	3 Eye	27 Abdomen	3 Fascia
4 Distal	4 Nose	28 Hip	4 Bone
5 Anterior	5 Ear	29 Thigh	5 Nerve
6 Posterior	6 Mouth	30 Knee	6 Fat pad
7 Medial	7 Neck	31 Patella	7 Tendon
8 Lateral	8 Thorax	32 Lower leg	8 Ligament
9 Other	9 Ribs	33 Ankle	9 Cartilage
	10 Sternum	34 Achilles tendon	10 Capsule
	11 Upper back	35 Foot	11 Compartment
Site of evaluation	12 Lower back	36 Toes	12 Dental
1 SHS	13 Shoulder	37 Other	13 _____
2 Athletic Trn Rm.	14 Rotator cuff		
3 Site-Competition	15 AC joint		Medication _____
4 _____	16 Glenohumeral		
	17 Sternoclavicular	Nontraumatic	Nature of injury
Procedures	18 Upper arm	1 Dermatological	1 Contusion
1 Physical exam	19 Elbow	2 Allergy	2 Strain
2 X-ray	20 Forearm	3 Influenza	3 Sprain
3 Splint	21 Wrist	4 URI	4 Fracture
4 Wrap	22 Hand	5 GU	5 Rupture
5 Cast	23 Thumb	6 Systemic infect.	6 Tendonitis
6 Aspiration	24 Finger	7 Local infect.	7 Bursitis
7 Other		8 Other	8 Myositis
			9 Laceration	Prescription dispensed
			10 Concussion	1 Antibiotics 5 Muscle relaxant
			11 Avulsion	2 Antiinflammatory 6 Enzyme
			12 Abrasion	3 Decongestant 7 _____
Disposition	Referral	Disposition of injury	13 _____	4 Analgesic
1 SHS	1 Arthrogram	1 No part.		Injections
2 Trainer	2 Neurological	2 Part part.		
3 Hospital	3 Int. Med.	3 Full part.	Degree	1 Steroids
4 H.D.	4 Orthropedic		1° 2° 3°	2 Antibiotics
5 Other	5 EENT			3 Steriods-xylo
	6 Dentist			4 _____
	7 Other			

Previous injury _____

The Treatment Log

Each athletic facility should have a sign-in log available for the athlete who receives any service. Emphasis is placed on recording the treatments for the athlete who is receiving daily therapy for an injury. Like accident records and injury dispositions, these records often have the status of legal documents and are used to establish certain facts in a civil litigation, an insurance action, or a criminal action after injury.

Personal Information Card

Always on file in athletic trainer's office is the athlete's personal information card. This card is completed by the athlete at the time of the health examination and serves as a means of contacting the family, personal physician, and insurance company in case of emergency.

Injury Evaluation and Progress Notes

Injuries should be evaluated by the athletic trainer, who must record information obtained in some consistent format. The SOAP format (Subjective, Objective, Assessment, Plan for treatment) is a concise method of recording the initial evaluation and progress notes for the injured athlete and is discussed in detail in Chapter 13. The subjective portion of the SOAP note refers to what the athlete tells the athletic trainer about the injury relative to the history or what he or she felt. The objective portion documents information that the athletic trainer gathers during the evaluation, such as range of motion, strength levels, patterns of pain, and so forth. The assessment records the athletic trainer's professional opinion about the injury based on information obtained during the subjective and objective portions. The plan for treatment indicates how the injury will be managed and includes short- and long-term goals for rehabilitation.

Supply and Equipment Inventory

A major responsibility of the athletic trainer is to manage a budget, most of which is spent on equipment and supplies. Every year an inventory must be conducted and recorded on such items as new equipment needed, equipment that needs to be replaced or repaired, and the expendable supplies that need replenishing.

Annual Reports

Most athletic departments require an annual report on the functions of the athletic training program. This report serves as a means for making program changes and improvements. It commonly includes the number of athletes served, a survey of the number and types of injuries, an analysis of the program, and recommendations for future improvements.

Release of Medical Records

The athletic trainer may not release an athlete's medical records to anyone without written consent. If the athlete wishes to have medical records released to professional sports organizations, insurance companies, the news media, or any other group or individual, the athlete must sign a waiver that specifies which information is to be released.

THE COMPUTER AS A TOOL FOR THE ATHLETIC TRAINER

Like in all other facets of our society, computers in athletic training have become indispensable tools (Figure 2-10). Athletic trainers who have access to a computer find that a great deal of information can be efficiently stored for immediate and future use because of large storage and retrieval capacities. Software packages are available to help store and retrieve any type of relevant records or information.[22]

2-5

Critical Thinking Exercise

The athletic trainer has requested that the school purchase a new computer to be housed in the athletic training room. The administrator indicates that funds are tight; however, the athletic trainer is asked to develop a written proposal to justify the purchase.

? What information can the athletic trainer include in the request that could justify purchasing a new computer for the athletic training room?

Companies facilitate the record-keeping process.

Figure 2-10

Computers are becoming an essential tool in athletic training.

2-6

Critical Thinking Exercise

A basketball coach at All-American High School is concerned about what seems to be an abnormally high frequency of ankle sprains on her varsity team. Her philosophy is to require all her players to wear high-top shoes, yet the budget will not permit all players' ankles to be taped by the athletic trainer for practices and games. Together the coach and athletic trainer decide to purchase a number of lace-up ankle braces in an attempt to reduce the number of ankle sprains.

? How can the athletic trainer determine if the braces are helping decrease the frequency of ankle sprains in these basketball players?

Record keeping is a time-consuming but essential chore for all athletic trainers regardless of whether they work at a college or university, at a high school, in the clinical setting, or in industry. Several software packages are available specifically for managing injury records in the athletic training setting. Among these are the Integrated Injury Tracking System (Micro Integration Services); Athletic Injury Management (Cramer, Inc.); Sports Injury Monitoring System (Med Sport Systems, Inc.); and SportsWare Injury Tracking System (Computer Sports Medicine Inc.).[24,25]

A problem that must be addressed by the athletic trainer is ensuring security and protecting the confidentiality of medical records stored on a computer. Databases that contain such information should be accessible only to the athletic trainer or team physician and should be protected by some type of password required for entry into the database.

Besides record keeping, computer software can be used for word processing, budget planning, management of a personal schedule or calender, or the creation of a database from which injury data can be organized, retrieved, or related to specific injury situations or to other injury records for analysis. Other software can provide analysis and information relative to nutrition, body composition, injury risk profiles based on other anthropometric measures, and the recording of isokinetic evaluation and exercise.[26]

The use of educational software to assist in teaching and in the academic preparation of student athletic trainers has become an integral component of the educational program. New software continues to become available, and the use of CD-ROM, with its interactive capabilities, has made the multimedia presentation of instructional material, and thus learning, more interesting and memorable for the student.

The Internet and the World Wide Web have brought about great impacts and changes. The current world is one in which any kind of information desired is immediately accessible to anyone who knows how to use the system. The sports medicine community in general and the athletic trainer specifically can access Web sites and home pages that have direct application to clinical practice, to the education of student athletic trainers, and to the general base of knowledge that is relevant to the athletic training field. The use of E-mail to share information and to communicate immediately with colleagues has opened up a new world of possibilities for education.[22] Because computers will continue to become more integral to the athletic training program, student athletic trainers must receive some formal instruction in the use of computers both for purposes of record keeping and for information retrieval.

COLLECTING INJURY DATA

Because of the vast number of physically active individuals involved with organized and recreational sports, some knowledge relative to the number and types of injuries sustained during participation in these activities is essential. Although methods are much improved over the past, many weaknesses exist in systematic data collection and analysis of sports injuries.[19]

The Incidence of Injuries

An **accident** is defined as an unplanned event capable of resulting in loss of time, property damage, injury, disablement, or even death.[21] An **injury** may be defined as damage to the body that restricts activity or causes disability to such an extent that the athlete is not able to practice or compete the next day.[21] In general, the incidence of sports injuries can be studied epidemiologically from many points of view—in terms of age at occurrence, gender, body regions that sustain injuries, or the occurrence in different sports. Sports are usually classified according to the risk, or chances, of injuries occurring under similar circumstances and are broadly divided into contact and noncontact sports.[3] Contact sports can be subdivided into contact/collision, limited contact/impact, and strenuous. Contact/collision sports have a higher risk potential for fatalities, catastrophic neck injuries, and severe musculoskeletal injuries when compared with other sports. Noncontact sports are subdivided into those that are either moderately strenuous or nonstrenuous; noncontact sports have a low incidence of injury (Table 2-3).

Athletes in all sports, recreational and organized, who participate in sports in the span of one year face a 50 percent chance of sustaining some injury. Of the 50 million estimated sports injuries per year, 50 percent require only minor care and no restriction of activity.[7] Approximately 90 percent of injuries are muscle contusions, ligament sprains, and muscle strains; however, 10 percent of these injuries lead to microtrauma complications and eventually to a severe, chronic condition in later life.

Of the sports injuries that must be medically treated, sprains or strains, fractures, dislocations, and contusions are the most common.[8] In terms of the body regions most often injured, the knee has the highest incidence, with the ankle second and the upper limb third. For both males and females the most commonly injured body

accident
An act that occurs by chance or without intention.

injury
An act that damages or hurts.

Risk of injury is determined by the type of sport—collision, contact, or noncontact.

The epidemiological approach toward injury data collection provides the most information.

TABLE 2-3 **Classification of Sports**

Contact		Noncontact		
Contact/ Collision	**Limited Contact/ Impact**	**Strenuous**	**Moderately Strenuous**	**Non-strenuous**
Boxing	Baseball	Aerobic dance	Badminton	Archery
Field hockey	Basketball	Crew	Curling	Golf
Football	Bicycling	Fencing	Table tennis	Riflery
Ice hockey	Diving	Field (discus,		
Lacrosse	Field (high jump,	javelin, shot put)		
Martial arts	pole vault)	Running/track		
Rodeo	Gymnastics	Swimming		
Soccer	Horseback riding	Tennis		
Wrestling	Skating (ice, roller)	Weight lifting		
	Skiing (cross country,			
	downhill, water)			
	Softball			
	Squash/handball			
	Volleyball			

part is the knee, followed by the ankle; however, males have a much higher incidence of shoulder and upper-arm injuries than do females.[8]

Catastrophic Injuries

Although millions of individuals participate in organized and recreational sports, there is a relatively low incidence of fatalities or catastrophic injuries. Ninety-eight percent of individuals with injuries requiring hospital emergency room medical attention are treated and released.[19] Deaths have been attributed to chest or trunk impact with thrown objects, other players, or nonyielding objects (e.g., goalposts). Deaths have occurred when players were struck in the head by sports implements (bats, golf clubs, hockey sticks) or by missiles (baseballs, soccer balls, golf balls, hockey pucks). Death has also resulted when an individual received a direct blow to the head from another player or the ground. On record are a number of sports deaths in which a playing structure, such as a goalpost or backstop, fell on a participant.

The highest incidence of indirect sports death stems from heatstroke. Less common indirect causes include cardiovascular and respiratory problems or congenital conditions not previously known. Catastrophic injuries leading to cervical injury and quadriplegia are seen mainly in American football. Although the incidence is low for the number of players involved, it could be lowered even further if more precautions were taken.

In most popular organized and recreational sports activities, the legs and arms have the highest risk factor for injury, with the head and face next. Muscle strains, joint sprains, contusions, and abrasions are the most frequent injuries sustained by the active sports participant.[8] The major goal of this text is to provide the reader with the fundamental principles necessary for preventing and managing illnesses and injuries common to the athlete.

Current National Injury Data-Gathering Systems

The state of the art of sports injury surveillance is at this time unsatisfactory.[6] Currently, most local, state, and federal systems are concerned with the accident or injury only after it has happened, and they focus on injuries requiring medical assistance or those that cause time loss or restricted activity.

The ideal system takes an epidemiological approach that studies the relationship of various factors that influence the frequency and distribution of sports injuries.[21] When considering the risks inherent in a particular sport, both extrinsic and intrinsic factors must be studied.[24] Thus information is gleaned from both epidemiological data and the individual measurements of the athlete. The term *extrinsic factor* refers to the type of activity that is performed, the amount of exposure to injury, factors in the environment, and the equipment. The term *intrinsic factor* refers directly to the athlete and includes age, gender, neuromuscular aspects, structural aspects, performance aspects, and mental and psychological aspects.

Over the years, a number of athletic injury surveillance systems have been implemented; most have collected data for a few years and then ceased to exist. The currently active systems that are most often mentioned are the National Safety Council, the Annual Survey of Football Injury Research, the National Electronic Injury Surveillance System (NEISS), the NCAA Injury Surveillance System, the National Center for Catastrophic Sports Injury Research, and the National High School Sports Injuries Registry.

National Safety Council

The National Safety Council* is a nongovernmental, nonprofit public service organization. It draws sports injuries data from a variety of sources, including educational institutions.

---

*National Safety Council, 444 N. Michigan Avenue, Chicago, IL 60611.

Annual Survey of Football Injury Research

In 1931 the American Football Coaches Association (AFCA) conducted its first Annual Survey of Football Fatalities. Since 1965 this research has been conducted at the University of North Carolina. In 1980 the survey's title was changed to Annual Survey of Football Injury Research. Every year, with the exception of 1942, data have been collected about public school, college, professional, and sandlot football. Information is gathered through personal contact interviews and questionnaires.[19] The sponsoring organizations of this survey are the AFCA, the NCAA, and the National Federation of State High School Athletic Associations (NFSHSA).

This survey classifies football fatalities as direct or indirect. Direct fatalities are those resulting directly from participation in football. Indirect fatalities are produced by systemic failure caused by the exertion of playing football or by a complication that arose from a nonfatal football injury.

National Center for Catastrophic Sports Injury Research

In 1977 the NCAA initiated the National Survey of Catastrophic Football Injuries. As a result of the injury data collected from this organization, several significant rule changes have been incorporated into collegiate football. Because of the success of this football project, the research was expanded to all sports for both men and women, and a National Center for Catastrophic Sports Injury Research was established at the University of North Carolina under the direction of Dr. Fred Mueller. With support from the NCAA, the NFSHSA, the AFCA, and the Section on Sports Medicine of the American Association of Neurological Sciences, this center compiles data on catastrophic injuries at all levels of sport.[19]

NCAA Injury Surveillance System

The NCAA Injury Surveillance System was established in 1982 primarily for the purpose of studying the incidence of football injuries so that rule change recommendations could be made to reduce injury rate. Since that time this system has been greatly expanded and now collects data on most major sports. For the most part, athletic trainers are primarily involved in the collection and transmission of injury data.

National Electronic Injury Surveillance System

In 1972 the federal government established the Consumer Product Safety Act (CPSA), which created and granted broad authority to the Consumer Product Safety Commission to enforce the safety standards of more than 10,000 products that may be risky to the consumer.[6] To perform this mission, the National Electronic Injury Surveillance System (NEISS)** was established. Data on injuries related to consumer products are monitored twenty-four hours a day from a selected sample of 5,000 hospital emergency rooms nationwide. Sports injuries represent 25 percent of all injuries reported by NEISS. It should be noted that a product may be related to an injury but not be the direct cause of that injury.

Once a product is considered hazardous, the commission can seize the product or create standards to decrease the risk.[6] Also, manufacturers and distributors of sports recreational equipment must report to the commission any product that is potentially hazardous or defective.[6] The commission can also research the reasons that a sports or recreational product is hazardous.

National High School Sports Injuries Registry

In fall 1995 the National High School Sports Injuries Registry began tracking injuries in ten different sports at 150 to 200 high schools in each sport. The registry is under

---

**National Electronic Injury Surveillance System, U.S. Consumer Products Safety Commission, Directorate for Epidemiology, National Injury Information Clearinghouse, Washington, DC.

the direction of Dr. John Powell and is being administered by Med Sport Systems and funded by NATA. Data collection continued through spring 1998.

Using Injury Data

Valid, reliable sports injury data can materially help decrease injuries. If properly interpreted, the data can be used to modify rules, assist coaches and players in understanding risks, and help manufacturers evaluate their product against the overall market.[21] The public, especially parents, should understand the risks inherent in a particular sport, and insurance companies that insure athletes must know risks in order to set reasonable costs.

SUMMARY

- The administration of a program of health care for the athlete demands a significant portion of the athletic trainer's time and effort. The efficiency and success of the athletic training program depend in large part on the administrative abilities of the athletic trainer in addition to the clinical skills required to treat the injured athlete.
- The athletic training program can certainly be enhanced by designing or renovating a facility to maximize the potential use of the space available. Space designed for injury treatment, rehabilitation, modality use, office space, physician examination, record keeping, and storage of supplies should be designated within each facility.
- The athletic training program may best serve the athlete, the institution, and the community by establishing specific policies and regulations governing the use of available services.
- Budgets should allow for the purchase of equipment and supplies essential for providing appropriate preventive and rehabilitative care for the athlete.
- Preparticipation exams must be given to athletes and should include a medical history, a general physical examination, and orthopedic screenings.
- The athletic trainer must maintain accurate and up-to-date medical records in addition to the other paperwork that is necessary for the operation of the athletic training program.
- Computers are extremely useful tools that enable athletic trainers to retrieve and store a variety of records.
- A number of data collection systems tabulate the incidence of sports injuries. The systems mentioned most often are the National Safety Council, the Annual Survey of Football Injury Research, the National Electronic Injury Surveillance System, the NCAA Injury Surveillance System, the National Center for Catastrophic Sports Injury Research, and the National High School Sports Injuries Registry.

Solutions to Critical Thinking EXERCISES

2-1 The training room should have specific areas designated for taping and preparation, treatment and rehabilitation, and hydrotherapy. It should have an office for the athletic trainer and adequate storage facilities positioned within the space to allow for an efficient traffic flow. Equipment purchases might include four or five treatment tables and two or three taping tables (these could be made in-house, if possible), a large-capacity ice machine, a combination ultrasound/electrical stimulating unit, a whirlpool, and various free weights and exercise tubing.

2-2 The athletic trainer should work in conjunction with the appropriate administrative personnel to develop a risk management plan that includes the areas of security issues, fire safety, electrical and equipment safety, and emergency injury management.

2-3 Federal law mandates specific policies for recruitment, hiring, and firing. All qualified applicants should receive equal consideration regardless of their race, gender, religion, or nationality. The head athletic trainer must strictly adhere to these mandates.

2-4 The preparticipation examination should consist of a medical history, a physical examination, and a brief orthopedic screening. The preparticipation physical may be effectively adminis-tered using a station examination system with a team of ex-aminers. A station examination can provide the athlete with a detailed examination in a short period of time. A team of peo-ple is needed to examine this many athletes. The team should include several physicians, medically trained nonphysicians (nurses, athletic trainers, physical therapists, or physician's as-sistants), and managers, student athletic trainers, or assistant coaches.

2-5 The athletic trainer should explain that the computer can be used for maintaining medical records, doing word processing, planning a budget, managing a personal schedule or calender, and creating a database containing injury data that can be or-ganized, retrieved, or related to specific injury situations or to other injury records for analysis. Additional software can pro-vide the athletic trainer with analysis and information about nutrition, body composition, and injury risk profiles. The com-puter could also be used for E-mail and for accessing informa-tion from the Internet.

2-6 The athletic trainer should do a simple study in which one-half of the players are randomly placed in the ankle braces while the other half continues to play in their high-top shoes. By comparing the number of ankle injuries in the group wearing the braces with those in the group without the braces, the ath-letic trainer can make some decision as to the effectiveness of the braces in preventing ankle injuries. Collecting and analyz-ing injury data is helpful in determining the efficacy of many of the techniques used by the athletic trainer.

REVIEW QUESTIONS AND CLASS ACTIVITIES

1. What are the major administrative functions that an ath-letic trainer must perform?
2. Design two athletic training facilities—one for a high school and one for a large university.
3. Observe the activities in the athletic training facility. Pick both a slow time and a busy time to observe.
4. Why do hygiene and sanitation play an important role in athletic training? How should the athletic training facility be maintained?
5. Fully equip a new medium-size high school, college ath-letic training facility, or clinical facility. Pick equipment from current catalogs.
6. Establish a reasonable budget for a small high school, a large high school, and a large college or university.
7. Identify the groups of individuals to be served in the ath-letic training facility.
8. Organize a preparticipation health examination for ninety football players.
9. Record keeping is a major function in athletic training. What records are necessary to keep? How can a computer help?
10. Debate what conditions constitute good grounds for medi-cal disqualification from a sport.
11. Discuss the epidemiological approach to recording sports injury data.

REFERENCES

1. Abdenour TE, Weir NJ: Medical assessment of the prospective stu-dent athlete, *Ath Train* 21:122, 1986.
2. American Academy of Pediatrics Policy Statement: Recommenda-tions for participation in competitive sports, *Physician Sportsmed* 16(5):51, 1988.
3. American Academy of Pediatrics: *Sports medicine: health care for young athletes,* Elk Grove Village, Ill, 1991, American Academy of Pediatrics.
4. Bonci CM, Ryan R: Pre-participation screening in intercollegiate athletics, *Postgrad Adv Sports Med* 3:3, 1988.
5. Caine DJ, Broekhoff J: Maturity assessment: a viable preventive measure against physical and psychological insult to the young athlete? *Physician Sportsmed* 15(3):67, 1987.
6. Damron CF: Injury surveillance systems for sports. In Vinger PF, Hoerner EF, editors: *Sports injuries,* Boston, 1986, Year Book Medi-cal Publishers.
7. Dean CH, Hoerner EF: Injury rates in team sports and individual recreation. In Vinger PF, Hoerner EF, editors: *Sports injuries,* Boston, 1986, Year Book Medical Publishers.
8. DeHaven JE, Lintner DM: Athletic injuries: comparison by age, sport, and gender, *Am J Sports Med* 14(3):218, 1986.
9. Dorsen PJ: Should athletes with one eye, kidney, or testicle play contact sports? *Physician Sportsmed* 14(7):130, 1986.
10. Equal Opportunity Commission: *Uniform guidelines on employee selection procedures,* Washington, DC, 1979, Bureau of National Affairs.
11. Forseth EA: Consideration in planning small college athletic train-ing facilities, *Ath Train* 21(1):22, 1986.
12. Herbert D: Professional considerations related to conduct of preparticipation exams, *Sports Med Stand Malpract Report* 6(4):49, 1994.
13. Jones R: The preparticipation, sport-specific athletic profile exami-nation, *Semin Adolesc Med* 3:169, 1987.
14. Kibler W: *The sports participation fitness examination,* Champaign, Ill, 1990, Human Kinetics.
15. Knells S: Leadership and management techniques and principles for athletic training, *J Ath Train* 29(4): 328, 1994.
16. Konin J, Donley P: The athletic trainer as a personnel manager. In Konin J: *The clinical athletic trainer,* Gaithersburg, Md, 1997, Slack.
17. McKeag DB: Preseason physical examination for the prevention of sports injuries, *Sports Med* 2:413, 1985.
18. Moyer-Knowles J: Planning a new athletic facility. In Konin J: *The clinical athletic trainer,* Gaithersburg, Md, 1997, Slack.
19. Mueller F: Catastrophic sports injuries. In Mueller F, Ryan A: *Pre-vention of athletic injuries: the role of the sports medicine team,* Philadel-phia, 1991, Davis.
20. Myers GC, Garrick JG: The preseason examination of school and college athletes. In Strauss RH, editor: *Sports medicine,* Philadelphia, 1984, Saunders.
21. Powell J: Epidemiologic research for injury prevention programs in sports. In Mueller F, Ryan A: *Prevention of athletic injuries: the role of the sports medicine team,* Philadelphia, 1991, Davis.
22. Rankin J: Technology and sports health care administration, *Ath-letic Therapy Today* 2(5):14, 1997.
23. Rankin J: Financial resources for conducting athletic training programs in the collegiate and high school settings, *J Ath Train* 27(4):344, 1992.
24. Rankin J, Ingersoll C: *Athletic training management: concepts and ap-plications,* St Louis, 1995, Mosby.
25. Ray R: *Management strategies in athletic training,* Champaign, Ill, 1994, Human Kinetics.
26. Ray R, Shire TL: An athletic training program in the computer age, *Ath Train* 21:212, 1986.
27. Steiner G: *Strategic planning,* New York, 1979, Free Press.
28. Swander H: *Preparticipation physical examination,* Kansas City, 1992, American Academy of Family Physicians, American Academy of Pediatrics, American Orthopedic Society for Sports Medicine, American Osteopathic Academy for Sports Medicine.
29. Tanner M: *Growth of adolescence,* ed 2, Oxford, England, 1962, Black-well Scientific Publications.

ANNOTATED BIBLIOGRAPHY

Konin J: *The clinical athletic trainer,* Gaithersburg, Md, 1997, Slack.

A unique, practical book that specifically addresses the administration of a health care program for athletic trainers working in a clinical setting.

Rankin J, Ingersoll C: *Athletic training management: concepts and applications,* St Louis, 1995, Mosby.

Designed for upper-division undergraduate or graduate students interested in all aspects of organization and administration of an athletic training program.

Ray R: *Management strategies in athletic training,* Champaign, Ill, 1994, Human Kinetics.

The first text that covered the principles of organization and administration as they apply to many different employment settings in athletic training; contains many examples and case studies based on principles of administration presented in the text.

Legal Concerns and Insurance Issues

When you finish this chapter you should be able to

- Explain the legal considerations for the athletic trainer acting as a health care provider.
- Define the legal concepts of torts, negligence, and assumption of risk.
- Discuss measures that can be taken by both the coach and athletic trainer to minimize chances of litigation.
- Discuss product liability.
- Identify the essential insurance requirements for protection of the athlete.
- Discuss the types of insurance necessary to protect the athletic trainer acting as a health care provider.

LEGAL CONCERNS OF THE COACH AND ATHLETIC TRAINER

In recent years negligence suits against teachers, coaches, athletic trainers, school officials, and physicians arising out of sports injuries have increased both in frequency and in the amount of damages awarded.[8,20] An increasing awareness of the many risk factors present in physical activities has had a major effect on the athletic trainer in particular. **Liability** means being legally responsible for the harm one causes another person.[13] A great deal of care must be taken in following athletic training procedures to reduce the risk of being sued by an athlete and being found liable for negligence.[15]

The Standard of Reasonable Care

Negligence is the failure to use ordinary or reasonable care—care that persons would normally exercise to avoid injury to themselves or to others under similar circumstances. The *standard of reasonable care* assumes that an individual is neither exceptionally skillful nor extraordinarily cautious, but is a person of reasonable and ordinary prudence. Put another way, it is expected that an individual will bring a commonsense approach to the situation at hand and will exercise due care in its handling. In most cases in which someone has been sued for negligence, the actions of a hypothetical, reasonably prudent person are compared with the actions of the defendant to ascertain whether the course of action followed by the defendant was in conformity with the judgment exercised by such a reasonably prudent person.[14]

The standard of reasonable care requires that an athletic trainer will act according to the standard of care of an individual with similar educational background or training.[10] An athletic trainer who has many years of experience, who is well educated in his or her field, and who is certified or licensed must act in accordance with those qualifications.

Torts

Torts are legal wrongs committed against the person or property of another.[13] Such wrongs may emanate from an *act of omission*, wherein the individual fails to perform a legal duty, or from an *act of commission*, wherein he or she commits an act that is not legally his or hers to perform. In either instance, if injury results, the person can be held liable. In the case of omission an athletic trainer may fail to refer a seriously injured athlete for the proper medical attention. In the case of commission, the athletic trainer may perform a medical treatment not within his or her experience, training, or education from which serious medical complications develop.

liability
The state of being legally responsible for the harm one causes another person.

negligence
The failure to use ordinary or reasonable care.

torts
Legal wrongs committed against a person.

A baseball batter was struck with a pitched ball directly in the orbit of the right eye and fell immediately to the ground. The athletic trainer ran to the player to examine the eye. There was some immediate swelling and discoloration around the orbit, but the eye appeared to be normal. The player insisted that he was fine and told the trainer he could continue to bat. After the game the athletic trainer told the athlete to go back to his room, put ice on his eye, and check in tomorrow. That night the baseball player began to hemorrhage into the anterior chamber of the eye and suffered irreparable damage to his eye. An ophthalmologist stated that if the athlete's eye had been examined immediately after the injury, the bleeding could have been controlled and there would not have been any damage to his vision.

? If the athlete brings a lawsuit against the athletic trainer, what must the athlete prove if he is to win a judgment?

3-2

Critical Thinking Exercise

? How should the first-aid care provided by a certified athletic trainer differ from the care that may be provided by a lay person?

Negligence

When an athletic trainer is sued by an athlete, the complaint typically is for the tort of negligence. Negligence is alleged when an individual (1) does something that a reasonably prudent person would not do or (2) fails to do something that a reasonably prudent person would do under circumstances similar to those shown by the evidence.[1] To be successful in a suit for negligence, an athlete must prove that the athletic trainer had a duty to exercise reasonable care, that the athletic trainer breached that duty by failing to use reasonable care, and that there is a reasonable connection between the failure to use reasonable care and the injury suffered by the athlete or that the athletic trainer's action made the injury worse. If the athletic trainer breaches a duty to exercise reasonable care, but there is no reasonable connection between the failure to use reasonable care and the injury suffered by the athlete, the athlete's suit for negligence will not succeed.

An example of negligence is when an athletic trainer, through improper or careless handling of a therapeutic agent, seriously burns an athlete. Another illustration, occurring all too often in sports, is one in which a coach or an athletic trainer moves a possibly seriously injured athlete from the field of play to permit competition or practice to continue and does so either in an improper manner or before consulting those qualified to know the proper course of action. Should a serious or disabling injury result, the coach or the athletic trainer may be found liable. Liability is the state of being legally responsible for the harm one causes another person.[13]

Athletic trainers employed by an institution have a duty to provide athletic training care to athletes at that institution. Clinical athletic trainers have a greater choice of whom they may choose to treat as a patient. Once the athletic trainer assumes the duty of caring for an athlete, the athletic trainer has made an obligation to make sure that appropriate care is given.

A person possessing more training in a given field or area is expected to possess a correspondingly higher level of competence than, for example, a student is. An individual will therefore be judged in terms of his or her performance in any situation in which legal liability may be assessed. It must be recognized that liability per se in all its various aspects is not assessed at the same level nationally but varies in interpretation from state to state and from area to area. Athletic trainers therefore should know and acquire the level of competence expected in their particular area. In essence, negligence is conduct that results in the creation of an unreasonable risk of harm to others.[19]

Statutes of Limitation

A *statute of limitation* sets a specific length of time that individuals may sue for damages from negligence. The length of time to bring suit varies from state to state, but in general plaintiffs have between one and three years to file suit for negligence. The statute of limitations begins to run on a plaintiff's time to file a lawsuit for negligence either from the time of the negligent act or omission that gives rise to the suit or from the time of the discovery of an injury caused by the negligent act or omission. Some states permit an injured minor to file suit up to three years after the minor reaches the age of eighteen. Therefore, an injured minor athlete's cause of action for negligence against an athletic trainer remains valid for many years after the negligent act or omission occurred or after the discovery of an injury caused by the negligent act or omission.

Assumption of Risk

An athlete assumes the risk of participating in an activity when he or she knows of and understands the dangers of that activity and voluntarily chooses to be exposed to those dangers. An assumption of risk can be expressed in the form of a waiver signed by an athlete or his or her parents or guardian or can be implied from the conduct of an athlete under the circumstances of his or her participation in an activity.

Assumption of risk may be asserted as a defense to a negligence suit brought by an injured athlete. The athletic trainer bears the burden of proving that an athlete assumed the risk by producing the document signed by the athlete or his or her parents or guardian or by proving that the athlete knew the risk of the activity and understood and voluntarily accepted that risk.

Assumption of risk, however, is subject to many and varied interpretations by courts, especially when a minor is involved, because he or she is not considered able to render a mature judgment about the risks inherent in the situation. Although athletes participating in a sports program are considered to assume a normal risk, this assumption in no way excuses those in charge from exercising reasonable care and prudence in the conduct of such activities or from foreseeing and taking precautionary measures against accident-provoking circumstances. In general, courts have been fairly consistent in upholding waivers and releases of liability for adults unless there is evidence of fraud, misrepresentation, or duress.[13]

Reducing the Risk of Litigation

The coach or athletic trainer can significantly decrease risk of litigation by paying attention to several key points.[11] The coach should follow these guidelines:

1. Warn athletes of the potential dangers inherent in their sports.[4]
2. Supervise regularly and attentively.
3. Properly prepare and condition athletes.
4. Properly instruct athletes in the skills of their sports.
5. Ensure that proper and safe equipment and facilities are used by athletes at all times.[5]

The athletic trainer should do as follows:

1. Work to establish good personal relationships with athletes, parents, and coworkers.
2. Establish specific policies and guidelines for operation of an athletic training facility, and maintain qualified and adequate supervision of the training room, its environs, facilities, and equipment at all times.
3. Develop and carefully follow an emergency plan.
4. Become familiar with the health status and medical history of the athletes under his or her care so as to be aware of particular problems that could present a need for additional care or caution.
5. Keep factually accurate and timely records that document all injuries and rehabilitation steps, and set up a record retention policy that allows records to be kept and used in defense of litigation that may be brought by athletes. A record retention system needs to keep records for long enough to defend against suits brought by athletes after they attain the age of eighteen.
6. Document efforts to create a safe playing environment.
7. Have a detailed job description in writing.
8. Obtain, from athletes and from parents or guardians when minors are involved, written consent for providing health care.
9. Maintain confidentiality of medical records.
10. Exercise extreme caution in the administration, if allowed by law, of nonprescription medications; athletic trainers may not dispense prescription drugs.
11. Use only those therapeutic methods that he or she is qualified to use and that the law states may be used.
12. Not use or permit the presence of faulty or hazardous equipment.
13. Work cooperatively with the coach and the team physician in the selection and use of sports protective equipment, and insist that the best be obtained, properly fitted, and properly maintained.
14. Not permit injured players to participate unless cleared by the team physician. Players suffering a head injury should not be permitted to reenter the game. In

assumption of risk
The individual, through express or implied agreement, assumes that some risk or danger will be involved in the particular undertaking. In other words, a person takes his or her own chances.

3-3
Critical Thinking Exercise

A college athletic trainer is cleaning out a filing cabinet and decides to throw some older medical files away. Concern is expressed, however, about how long these files should be maintained for legal purposes.

? What is the statute of limitations for a college-age athlete to file suit?

some states a player who has suffered a concussion may not continue in the sport for the balance of the season.

15. Develop an understanding with the coaches that an injured athlete will not be allowed to reenter competition until, in the opinion of the team physician or the athletic trainer, he or she is psychologically and physically able. Athletic trainers should not allow themselves to be pressured to clear an athlete until he or she is fully cleared by the physician.

16. Follow the express orders of the team physician at all times.

17. Purchase professional liability insurance that provides adequate financial coverage and be aware of the limitations of the policy.

18. Know the limitations of his or her expertise as well as the applicable state regulations and restrictions that limit the athletic trainer's scope of practice.

19. Use common sense in making decisions about an athlete's health and safety.

In the case of an injury the athletic trainer must use reasonable care to prevent additional injury until further medical care is obtained.[14] (See Chapter 12 for additional comments.)

Product Liability

Manufacturers of athletic equipment have a duty to design and produce equipment that will not cause injury as long as it is used as intended. An express warranty is the manufacturer's written statement that a product is safe. Warning labels on football helmets inform the player of possible dangers inherent in using the product. Athletes must read and sign a form indicating that they have read and understand the warning. The National Operating Committee on Standards for Athletic Equipment (NOCSAE) establishes minimum standards for equipment that must be met to ensure its safety.

INSURANCE REQUIREMENTS

During the past forty years the insurance industry has undergone a significant evolutionary process. Health care reform initiated in the 1990s has focused on the concept of *managed care* in which costs of a health care provider's medical care are closely monitored and scrutinized by insurance carriers. Often preapproval is required prior to health care delivery.

Since 1971 there has been a significant increase in the number of lawsuits filed, caused in part by the steady increase in individuals who have become active in sports. The costs of insurance have also significantly increased during this period. More lawsuits and much higher medical costs are causing a crisis in the insurance industry.[7] Medical insurance is a contract between an insurance company and a policyholder in which the insurance company agrees to reimburse a portion of the total medical bill after some deductible has been paid by the policyholder. The major types of insurance about which individuals concerned with athletic training and sports medicine should have some understanding are general health insurance, catastrophic insurance, accident insurance, and liability insurance as well as insurance for errors and omissions. There is a need to protect adequately all who are concerned with sports health and safety. *Focus Box:* "Common insurance terminology" lists some of the more common insurance terms.

General Health Insurance

Every athlete should have a *general health insurance* policy that covers illness, hospitalization, and emergency care. Some institutions offer primary insurance coverage in which all medical expenses are paid for by the athletic department. The institutions pay an extremely high premium for this type of coverage. Most institutions offer *secondary insurance* coverage, which pays the athlete's remaining medical bills once the athlete's personal insurance company has made its payment. Secondary insurance always includes a deductible that will not be covered by the plan.

Focus

Common insurance terminology

Allowable Charge: The maximum amount, according to the individual policy, that insurance will pay for each procedure or service performed.

Beneficiary: A person eligible to receive the benefits of a specific policy or program.

Benefits: Services that an insurer, government agency, or health care plan offers to pay for an insured individual.

Case Management Services: The process in which the attending physician or agent coordinates the care given to a patient by other health care providers and/or community organizations.

Claim: A form sent to an insurance company requesting payment for covered medical expenses. Information includes the insured's name and address, procedure codes, diagnostic codes, charges, and date of service.

Clean Claim: A filed claim with all the necessary information that may be immediately processed.

Contract: A legally binding agreement between an insurance company and a physician describing the duties of both parties.

Copayment: A provision in an insurance policy requiring the policyholder to pay a specified percentage of each medical claim.

Customary Fees: The average fee charged for a specified service or procedure in a defined geographic area.

Deductible: The amount owed by the insured on a yearly basis before the insurance company will begin to pay for services rendered.

Dependent: A person legally eligible for benefits based on his or her relationship with the policyholder.

Exclusions: Specified medical services, disorders, treatments, diseases, and durable medical equipment that is listed as uncovered or not reimbursable in an insurance policy.

Explanation of Benefits (EOB): An insurance report accompanying all claim payments that explains how the insurance company processed a claim.

Fee Schedule: A comprehensive listing of the maximum payment amount that an insurance company will allow for specified medical procedures performed on a beneficiary of the plan.

Gatekeeper: The primary care physician assigned by the insurer that oversees the medical care rendered to a patient and initiates all specialty and ancillary services.

Participating Provider: A health care provider who has entered into a contract with an insurance company to provide medical services to the beneficiaries of a plan. The provider agrees to accept the insurance company's approved fee and will only bill the patient for the deductible, copayment, and uncovered services.

Policyholder: The person who takes out the medical insurance policy.

Premium: A periodic payment made to an insurance company by an individual policy.

Third Party Administrator: An independent organization that collects premiums, pays claims, and provides administrative services within a health care plan.

UCR Allowable Charge: Usual, customary, and reasonable charge that represents the maximum amount an insurance company will pay for a given service based on geographical averages.

Many athletes are covered under some type of *family health insurance* policy. However, the school or university must make certain that personal health insurance is arranged for or purchased by athletes not covered under family policies.[17] A form letter directed to the parents of all athletes should be completed and returned to the institution to make certain that appropriate coverage is provided (Figure 3-1). Some so-called comprehensive plans do not cover every health need. For example, they may cover physicians' care but not hospital charges. Many of these plans require

Every athlete should have a general health insurance policy that covers illness, hospitalization, and emergency care.

Figure 3-1

Sample insurance information form

Insurance Information on Student Athletes

Student's Name _____ Date of Birth _____ Sport _____

Home Address _____

Home Phone _____

Social Security or Student ID Number _____ Sex: M ___ F ___

Family Doctor _____ Phone _____

Address _____

Policy Holder _____ Relation to Student _____

Employer _____

Address _____

Home Phone _____ Work Phone _____

Names of Insurance Companies _____

Address of Insurance Company _____

Certificate Number _____ Group _____ Type _____

Should my son/daughter require services beyond those covered by the Sports Medicine Program, I give permission to the Division of Sports Medicine to file a claim for such services with the above health insurer.

I understand that any insurance payments I receive must be returned to be placed on my child's account.

Parent's Signature _____ Date _____

large prepayments before the insurance takes effect. Supplemental policies such as accident insurance and catastrophic insurance are designed to take over where general health insurance stops.

Accident Insurance

Besides general health insurance, low-cost *accident insurance* is available to the student. It often covers accidents on school grounds while the student is in attendance. The purpose of this insurance is to protect against financial loss from medical and hospital bills, encourage an injured student to receive prompt medical care, encourage prompt reporting of injuries, and relieve a school of financial responsibility.

The school's general insurance may be limited; thus accident insurance for a specific activity such as sports may be needed to provide additional protection.[7] This type of coverage is limited and does not require knowledge of fault, and the amount it pays is limited. For serious sport injuries requiring surgery and lengthy rehabilitation, accident insurance is usually not adequate. This inadequacy can put families with limited budgets into a real financial bind. Of particular concern is insurance that does not adequately cover catastrophic injuries.

Professional Liability Insurance

Most individual schools and school districts have general liability insurance to protect against damages that may arise from injuries occurring on school property. Liability insurance covers claims of negligence on the part of individuals. Its major concern is whether supervision was reasonable and if unreasonable risk of harm was perceived by the sports participant.[17]

Because of the amount of litigation based on alleged negligence, premiums have become almost prohibitive for some schools. Typically, a victim's lawsuit has taken a shotgun approach, suing the coach, athletic trainer, physician, school administrator, and school district. If a protective piece of equipment is involved, the product manufacturer is also sued.

All athletic trainers should carry *professional liability insurance* and must clearly understand the limits of coverage. Liability insurance typically covers negligence in a civil case. If a criminal complaint is filed, however, liability insurance will not cover the athletic trainer.

Catastrophic Insurance

Although catastrophic injuries in sports participation are relatively uncommon, when they do occur the consequences to the athlete, family, and institution, as well as society, can be staggering.[16] In the past when available funds have been completely diminished, the family was forced to seek funding elsewhere, usually through a lawsuit. Organizations such as the National Collegiate Athletic Association (NCAA) and National Association of Intercollegiate Athletics (NAIA) provide plans that deal with the problem of a lifetime that requires extensive medical and rehabilitative care because of a permanent disability.[3]

Benefits begin when expenses have reached $25,000 and are then extended for a lifetime. A program at the secondary school level is offered to districts by the National Federation of State High School Associations (NFSHSA). This plan provides medical, rehabilitation, and transportation costs in excess of $10,000 not covered by other insurance benefits.[17] Costs for catastrophic insurance are based on the number of sports and the number of hazardous sports offered by the institution.

To offset the shotgun approach of lawsuits and to cover what is not covered by a general liability policy, *errors and omissions liability insurance* has evolved. It is designed to cover school employees, officers, and the district against suits claiming malpractice, wrongful actions, errors and omissions, and acts of negligence.[17] Even when working in a program that has good liability coverage, each person within that program who works directly with students must have his or her own personal liability insurance.

Insurance that covers the athlete's health and safety can be complex. The coach and the athletic trainer must ensure that every athlete is adequately covered by a reliable insurance company. In some athletic programs the filing of claims becomes the responsibility of the athletic trainer. This task can be highly time consuming, taking the athletic trainer away from his or her major role of working directly with the athlete. Because of the intricacies and time involved with claim filing and follow-up communications with parents, doctors, and vendors, a staff person other than the athletic trainer should be assigned this responsibility.

Third-Party Reimbursement

Third-party reimbursement is the primary mechanism of payment for medical services in the United States.[18] The policyholder's insurance company reimburses health care professionals for services performed. Medical insurance companies may provide group and individual coverage for employees and dependents. Managed care involves a prearranged system for delivering health care that is designed to control costs while continuing to provide quality care. To cut payout costs, many insurance companies pay for preventive care (to reduce the need for hospitalization) and limit where the individual can go for care. A number of different health care systems have been developed to contain costs.

Health Maintenance Organizations

Health maintenance organizations (HMOs) provide preventive measures and limit where the individual can receive care. Except in emergencies, permission must be obtained before the individual can go to another provider. HMOs generally pay

---

Because of the amount of litigation for alleged negligence, all professionals involved with the sports program must be fully protected by professional liability insurance.

3-4

Critical Thinking Exercise

During a high school gymnastics meet, a gymnast fell off the uneven parallel bars and landed on her forearm. The athletic trainer suspected a fracture and decided an x ray was needed. The gymnast's parents had general health insurance through a PPO, but because the gymnast was in severe pain, she was sent to the nearest emergency room to be treated. Unfortunately, the emergency facility was not on the list of preferred providers, and the insurance company denied the claim. The athletic trainer assured the parents that the school would take care of whatever medical costs were not covered by their insurance policy.

? Because the PPO denied the claim, what type of insurance policy should the school carry to cover the medical costs?

Third-party reimbursement involves reimbursement by the policyholder's insurance company for services performed by health care professionals.

Third party payers:
- Private insurance carriers
- HMOs
- PPOs

100 percent of the medical costs as long as care is rendered at an HMO facility. Many supplemental policies do not cover the medical costs that would normally be paid by the general policy. Therefore an athlete treated outside the HMO may be ineligible for any insurance benefits. Many HMOs determine fees using a capitation system, which limits the amount that will be reimbursed for a specific service. It is essential for the athletic trainer to understand the limits of and restrictions on coverage at his or her institution.

Preferred Provider Organizations

Preferred provider organizations (PPOs) provide discount health care but also limit where a person can go for treatment of an illness. The athletic trainer must be apprised in advance as to where the ill athlete should be sent. Athletes sent to a facility that is not on the approved list may be required to pay for care, whereas if they are sent to a preferred facility, all costs are paid.[7] PPOs may provide added services, such as physical therapy, more easily and at no cost or at a much lower cost than would another insurance policy. PPOs pay on a fee-for-service basis.

Point of Service Plan

The point of service plan is a combination of the HMO and PPO plans. It is based on an HMO structure, yet it allows members to go outside the HMO to obtain services. This flexibility is allowed only with certain conditions and under special circumstances.

Indemnity Plan

An indemnity plan is the most traditional form of billing for health care. It is a fee-for-service plan that allows the insured party to seek medical care without restrictions on utilization or cost. The provider charges the patient or a third-party payer for services provided. Charges are based on a set fee schedule.

Capitation

Capitation is a form of reimbursement used by managed care providers in which members make a standard payment each month regardless of how much service is rendered to the member by the provider.

Third-Party Reimbursement for Athletic Trainers

Currently, athletic trainers who are not also licensed physical therapists have difficulty obtaining third-party reimbursement for health care services provided. Because most athletic trainers are now employed in clinical or industrial settings, this lack of reimbursement has become a major concern for the future of athletic trainers working in for-profit private clinics. State licensing or credentialing of the athletic trainer has, to date, helped very little with obtaining reimbursement. In general, insurance companies have not been willing to cover services provided by the athletic trainer. Athletic trainers working in the clinical setting perform many of the same functions as physical therapists in the clinic and are also responsible for obtaining referrals to the clinic through contacts in local high schools. Certainly, securing third-party reimbursement for athletic training services must be a priority, especially for the clinical athletic trainer.[18]

In 1995 NATA established the Reimbursement Advisory Group to monitor managed care changes and to help the athletic trainer secure a place as a health care provider. Specifically this group was charged with the responsibility of developing a model for approaching third-party payers for the reimbursement of athletic training services, of educating athletic trainers on issues related to reimbursement, and perhaps most important, of designing and implementing a data-based clinical outcomes study.[6] In 1996 NATA initiated the Athletic Training Outcomes Assessment project designed to present supporting data that measures the results of interventions involving

3-5

Critical Thinking Exercise

An athletic trainer working in a clinic is seeking third-party reimbursement for athletic training services performed. The trainer is experiencing difficulty in obtaining reimbursement from certain payers due to an uncertainty of the effectiveness of the treatment program.

? What can the athletic trainer do to address the concerns of the third-party payers?

athletic training procedures. This three-year study was designed to provide data that focused on functional outcomes including assessing the patients' perceptions of their functional capabilities and their overall satisfaction with their treatment program; assessing the physical, emotional, and social well-being of patients; assessing health care cost effectiveness relative to time lost from activity due to injury; and assessing the number of treatments.[9] The results of this study (summarized in Figure 3-2) are critical in securing reimbursement for athletic training services because the majority of third-party payers currently require outcomes research when evaluating a contract.[2,12]

Insurance Billing

The athletic trainer must file insurance claims immediately and correctly.[18] Athletic trainers working in educational settings can facilitate this process by collecting insurance information on every athlete at the beginning of the year. Letters should be drafted to the parents of all athletes explaining the limits of the school insurance policy and what the parents must do to process a claim if injury does occur. Schools with secondary policies should stress that the parents must submit all bills to their insurance company before they submit the remainder to the school. In educational institutions, most claims will be filed with a single insurance company, which will pay for medical services provided by individual health care providers.

When filing an insurance claim to submit for reimbursement, athletic trainers will find that a standard form labeled HCFA-1500 is accepted by most carriers (Blue Cross/Blue Shield uses Form UB-92). These forms must be completed in detail with as much information as possible. Experience dictates that the more accurately and thoroughly these forms are completed, the quicker and higher the rate of reimbursement.

Athletic trainers working in the clinical setting should understand that the clinic must be able to collect reimbursement from third-party payers for services provided. The athletic trainer should request approval from insurance companies before treating patients. The athletic trainer must bill the patient's insurance company according to the Current Procedural Terminology (CPT) codes published by the American Medical Association, which lists appropriate number codes for specific procedures or services delivered to the patient. In 1994 the American Physical Therapy Association proposed a new coding scheme that specifically addressed the inequities of the physical therapy and sports medicine reimbursement system.[18]

SUMMARY

- A great deal of care must be taken in following coaching and athletic training procedures that conform to the legal guidelines governing liability for negligence.
- Liability is the state of being legally responsible for the harm one causes another person. It assumes that an athletic trainer would act according to the standard of care of any individual with similar educational background and training.
- An athletic trainer who fails to use reasonable care—care that persons would normally exercise to avoid injury to themselves or to others under similar circumstances—may be found liable for negligence.
- Although athletes participating in a sports program are considered to assume a normal risk, this assumption in no way exempts those in charge from exercising reasonable care.
- Athletic trainers can significantly decrease risk of litigation by making certain that they have done everything possible to provide a reasonable degree of care to the injured athlete.
- The major types of insurance about which athletic trainers should have some understanding are general health insurance, catastrophic insurance, accident insurance, liability insurance, and insurance for errors and omissions.
- Third-party reimbursement is the primary mechanism of payment for medical services in the United States. A number of different health care systems—including

---

- Overall satisfaction with certified athletic trainers: 3.89
- Pre-treatment ability to participate in sports or recreational activities: 1.75
- Post-treatment ability to participate in sports or recreational activities: 3.31
- Athletic training methods produce excellent overall outcomes with the best results in functional outcomes (particularly in sport, recreation, wellness, and work activities), and in physical outcomes (i.e. range of motion, pain relief).
- The most effective modalities appear to be cold packs, ice massage, heat packs, therapeutic exercise, functional activity exercise, electrotherapy, and taping/bracing.

Figure 3-2

Athletic Training Outcomes Assessment project summary findings (0 = lowest rating, 4 = highest rating)

3-6

Critical Thinking Exercise

? When filing an insurance claim for an athlete following injury, what can an athletic trainer do to improve the reimbursement rate as well as to speed up the process?

health maintenance organizations, preferred provider organizations, point of service plans, indemnity plans, and capitation plans—have been developed to contain costs.

- It is essential that the athletic trainer file insurance claims immediately and correctly.

Web Sites

Legal Information Institute at Cornell: http://www.law.cornell.edu/topics/sports.html

This Web site is part of a series of legal information and specifically addresses law in sport; the information is rather technical in nature. The relevant area to sports medicine is addressed in the area titled "Torts."

Cramer First Aider: http://www.ccsd.k12.wy.us/cchs_web/cramerfirstaider/fstaider.htm

The Cramer First Aider is a newsletter published by Cramer that provides information about current topics in sports medicine. For information relevant to this chapter, go to the section titled "Legal Issues."

Solutions to Critical Thinking EXERCISES

3-1 An athletic trainer who assumes the duty of caring for an athlete has an obligation to make sure that appropriate care is given. If the athletic trainer fails to provide an acceptable standard of care, there is a breach of duty on the part of the athletic trainer, and the athlete must then prove that this breach caused the injury or made the injury worse.

3-2 A person possessing more training in a given field or area is expected to possess a correspondingly higher level of competence than a lay person is. A certified athletic trainer will therefore be judged in terms of his or her performance in any situation in which legal liability may be assessed.

3-3 The athlete would typically have between one and three years to file suit for negligence. The statute of limitations begins to run on a plaintiff's time to file a lawsuit for negligence either from the time of the negligent act or omission that gives rise to the suit or from the time of the discovery of an injury caused by the negligent act or omission.

3-4 Besides general health insurance, low-cost accident insurance often covers accidents on school grounds while the athlete is competing. The purpose of this insurance is to protect against financial loss from medical and hospital bills, encourage an injured athlete to receive prompt medical care, encourage prompt reporting of injuries, and relieve a school of financial responsibility.

3-5 The athletic trainer could initiate an outcomes research project designed to present supporting data that measures the results of interventions involving athletic training procedures. This research project would assess the athletes' perceptions of their functional capabilities and overall satisfaction with their treatment program, the cost-effectiveness of the health care relative to time lost from activity due to injury, and the number of

treatments. The majority of third-party payers currently require outcomes research when evaluating a contract.

3-6 The athletic trainer should file an insurance claim for reimbursement using the standard form labeled HCFA-1500. The form should be completed in detail with as much information as possible. The athletic trainer who completes these forms accurately and thoroughly probably experience a quicker and higher rate of reimbursement.

REVIEW QUESTIONS AND CLASS ACTIVITIES

1. What are the athletic trainer's major legal concerns for negligence and for assumption of risk?
2. What measures can an athletic trainer take to minimize the chances of litigation should an athlete be injured?
3. Invite an attorney who is familiar with sports litigation to class to discuss how athletic trainers can protect themselves from lawsuits.
4. Discuss what the athletic trainer must do to provide reasonable and prudent care in dealing with an injured athlete.
5. Why is it necessary for an athlete to have both general health insurance and accident insurance?
6. Briefly discuss the various methods of third-party reimbursement.
7. Why should an athletic trainer carry individual liability insurance?
8. What are the critical considerations for filing insurance claims?

REFERENCES

1. Appenzeller H: *Sports and the law: contemporary issues,* Charlottesville, Va, 1985, Michie.
2. Benjamin K: Outcomes research and the allied health professional, *J Allied Health* 24:3, 1995.
3. Berg R: Catastrophic injury insurance, an end to costly litigation, *Ath J* 8:10, 1987.
4. Borkowski RP: Coaches and the courts, *First Aider* 54:1, 1985.
5. Borkowski RP: Lawsuit less likely if safety comes first, *First Aider* 55:11, 1985.
6. Campbell D: Workshop on third party reimbursement, *NATA News* 3:34, 1996.
7. Chambers RL: Insurance types and coverage: knowledge to plan for the future (with a focus on motor skill activities and athletics), *Phys Educ* 44:233, 1986.
8. Clement A: Patterns of litigation in physical education instruction. Paper presented at the American Association of Health, Physical Education, and Dance, National Convention and Exposition, Cincinnati, April 1986.
9. De Carlo M: Reimbursement for health care services. In Konin J: *Clinical athletic training,* Thorofare, NJ, 1997, Slack.

10. Drowatzky JN: Legal duties and liability in athletic training, *Ath Train* 20:11, 1985.

11. Graham L: Ten ways to dodge the malpractice bullet, *Ath Train* 20(2):117, 1985.

12. Harada N, Sofaer S, Kominski G: Functional status outcomes in rehabilitation: implications for prospective payment, *Medical Care* 31:345, 1993.

13. Hawkins J, Appenzeller H: Legal aspects of sports medicine. In Mueller F, Ryan A: *Prevention of athletic injuries: the role of the sports medicine team,* Philadelphia, 1991, FA Davis.

14. Herbert D: *Legal aspects of sports medicine,* Canton, Ohio, 1990, Professional Reports Corporation.

15. Leverenz L, Helms L: Suing athletic trainers, parts I and II, *Ath Train* 25(3):212, 1990.

16. Mueller F: Catastrophic sports injuries. In Mueller F, Ryan A: *Prevention of athletic injuries: the role of the sports medicine team,* Philadelphia, 1991, FA Davis.

17. Rankin J, Ingersoll C: *Athletic training management: concepts and applications,* St. Louis, 1995, Mosby.

18. Ray R: *Management strategies in athletic training,* Champaign, Ill, 1994, Human Kinetics.

19. Yasser R: Calculating risk, *Sports Med Digest* 9(2):5, 1987.

20. Wong G: *Essentials of amateur sports law,* Westport, Conn, 1994, Praeger.

ANNOTATED BIBLIOGRAPHY

Appenzeller H: *Sports and law: contemporary issues,* Charlottesville, Va, 1985, Michie.

Exposes sports litigation from the perspectives of the athletic director, athlete, athletic trainer, coach, officials, and products liability expert. A chapter on the athletic trainer emphasizes the use of modalities and how this use relates to the practice of physical therapy in different states.

Champion W: *Sports law in a nutshell,* St. Paul, 1993, West.

Translates difficult legal concepts into terminology that a lay person can understand.

Herbert D: *Legal aspects of sports medicine,* Canton, Ohio, 1990, Professional Reports Corporation.

A discussion of sports medicine, policies, procedures, responsibilities of the sports medicine team, informed consent, negligence, insurance and risk management, medications, drug testing, and other topics.

Rowell JC: *Understanding medical insurance: a step-by-step guide,* Albany, NY, 1994, Delmar.

Provides a comprehensive resource for dealing with issues related to insurance.

PART

II

Risk Management

Training and Conditioning Techniques

When you finish this chapter you should be able to

- Discuss the role of the athletic trainer and the strength and conditioning coach in getting an athlete fit.
- Describe the concept of periodization and identify the various training periods within a macrocycle.
- Identify the principles of conditioning.
- Discuss the importance of the warm-up and cooldown periods.
- Describe the importance of flexibility, strength, and cardiorespiratory endurance for both athletic performance and injury prevention.
- Identify specific techniques and principles for improving flexibility, muscular strength, and cardiorespiratory endurance.
- Discuss fitness testing and identify specific tests to assess various fitness parameters.

Preventing injury to the athlete is one of the primary functions of the athletic trainer. To compete successfully at a high level, the athlete must be fit. An athlete who is not fit is more likely to sustain an injury. Both coaches and athletic trainers recognize that improper conditioning is one of the major causes of sports injuries (Figure 4-1). Thus coaches and athletic trainers should work cooperatively to supervise training and conditioning programs that minimize the possibility of injury and maximize performance.[34]

It takes time and careful preparation to bring an athlete into competition at a level of fitness that will preclude early-season injury. The athletic trainer must possess sound understanding of the principles of training and conditioning relative to flexibility, strength, and cardiorespiratory endurance.

Lack of physical fitness is one of the primary causes of sports injury.

THE RELATIONSHIP BETWEEN ATHLETIC TRAINERS AND STRENGTH AND CONDITIONING COACHES

The responsibility for making certain that an athlete is fit for competition depends on the personnel who are available to oversee this aspect of the athletic program. At the professional level and at most colleges and universities, a full-time strength and conditioning coach is employed to conduct both team and individual training sessions. Many but not all strength coaches are certified by the National Strength and Conditioning Association. In these situations, it is essential that both the athletic trainers and the team coaches communicate freely, working in close cooperation with the strength coaches to ensure that the athletes achieve an optimal level of fitness.

The specific role of the athletic trainer is to critically review the training and conditioning program as designed by the strength and conditioning coach and to be extremely familiar with what is expected of the athletes on a daily basis. The athletic trainer should feel free to offer suggestions and make recommendations that are in the best interest of the athletes' health and well-being. If it becomes apparent that a particular exercise or a specific training session seems to be causing an inordinate number of injuries, the athletic trainer should inform the strength and conditioning coach of the problem so that some alternative exercise can be substituted.

If an athlete is injured and is undergoing a rehabilitation program, it should be the responsibility of the athletic trainer to communicate to the strength and

Figure 4-1

Modern sports programs often require elaborate conditioning facilities and equipment to apply sound injury prevention methods.

conditioning coach how the conditioning program should be limited and/or modified. The athletic trainer must respect the role of the strength and conditioning coach in getting the athlete fit. However, the responsibility for rehabilitating an injured athlete clearly belongs to the athletic trainer.

In the majority of high school settings, a strength and conditioning coach is not available; the responsibility for ensuring that the athlete gets fit lies with the athletic trainer and the team coaches. In this situation the athletic trainer very often assumes the role of a strength and conditioning coach in addition to his or her athletic training responsibilities. The athletic trainer frequently finds it necessary not only to design training and conditioning programs but also to oversee the weight room and to educate young, inexperienced athletes about getting themselves fit to compete. The athletic trainer must demand the cooperation of the team coaches in supervising the training and conditioning program.

PERIODIZATION IN TRAINING AND CONDITIONING

No longer do serious athletes engage only in preseason conditioning and in-season competition. Sports conditioning is a year-round endeavor. *Periodization* is an approach to conditioning that brings about peak performance while reducing injuries and overtraining in the athlete through a training and conditioning program that is followed throughout the various seasons. Periodization takes into account that athletes have different needs relative to training and conditioning during different seasons and modifies the program according to individual needs (Table 4-1).

Sports conditioning often falls into three seasons: off-season, preseason, and in-season.

Macrocycle

Periodization organizes a training and conditioning program into cycles. The complete training period, which could be a year in the case of seasonal sports or perhaps four years for an Olympic athlete, is referred to as a *macrocycle*. With seasonal sports the macrocycle can be divided into a preseason, an in-season, and an off-season. Throughout the course of the macrocycle, intensity, volume, and specificity of training are altered so that an athlete can achieve peak levels of fitness for competition. As competition approaches, training sessions change gradually and progressively from high-volume, low-intensity, non-sport-specific activity to low-volume, high-intensity, sport-specific training.[50]

Mesocycle

Within the macrocycle are a series of *mesocycles,* each of which may last for several weeks or even months. A mesocycle is further divided into *transition, preparatory,* and *competition* periods.[50]

TABLE 4-1 Periodization Training

Season	Period/Phase	Type of Training Activity
Off-season sports	Transition period	Unstructured Recreational
	Preparatory period	Cross-training
	Hypertrophy/endurance phase	Low intensity High volume Non-sport-specific
	Strength phase	Moderate intensity Moderate volume More sport-specific
Preseason	Power phase	High intensity Decreased volume Sport-specific
In-season	Competition period	High intensity Low volume Skill-training Strategic

Transition period   The transition period begins after the last competition and comprises the early part of the off-season. The transition period is generally unstructured, and the athlete is encouraged to participate in sport activities on a recreational basis. The idea is to allow the athlete to escape both physically and psychologically from the rigor of a highly organized training regimen.

Preparatory period   The preparatory period occurs primarily during the off-season when there are no upcoming competitions. The preparatory period has three phases: the hypertrophy/endurance phase, the strength phase, and the power phase.

During the hypertrophy/endurance phase, which occurs in the early part of the off-season, training is at a low intensity with a high volume of repetitions, using activities that may or may not be directly related to a specific sport. The goal is to develop a base of endurance on which more intense training can occur. This phase may last from several weeks to two months.

During the strength phase, which also occurs during the off-season, the intensity and volume progress to moderate levels. Weight-training activities should become more specific to the sport or event.

The third phase, or power phase, occurs in the preseason. The athlete trains at a high intensity at or near the level of competition. The volume of training is decreased so that full recovery is allowed between sessions.

Competition period   In certain cases the competition period may last for only a week or less. With seasonal sports, however, the competition period may last for several months. In general this period involves high-intensity training at a low volume. As training volume decreases, an increased amount of time is spent on skill training or strategy sessions. During the competition period, it may be necessary to establish *microcycles,* which are periods lasting from one to seven days. During a weekly microcycle, training should be intense early in the week and should progress to moderate and finally light the day before a competition. The goal is to make sure that the athlete will be at peak levels of fitness and performance on days of competition.[50]

Cross Training

The concept of cross training is an approach to training and conditioning for a specific sport that involves substitution of alternative activities that have some carryover value to that sport. For example, a swimmer could engage in jogging, running, or aerobic exercise to maintain levels of cardiorespiratory conditioning. Cross training is

4-1

Critical Thinking Exercise

Following the end of the competitive season, a college football player took the months of December and January off from intense training. He played only basketball and occasionally rode an exercise bike, thus completing the transitional period of the macrocycle. It is now time for him to begin the preparatory phase of training.

? What activities should he begin with, and how should these activities progress over the next several months?

particularly useful in both the transition and early preparatory periods. It adds variety to the training regimen, thus keeping training during the off-season more interesting and exciting. It must be stressed, however, that while cross training can be effective in maintaining levels of cardiorespiratory endurance, it is not sport-specific and thus should not be used during the preseason.

PRINCIPLES OF CONDITIONING

The following principles should be applied in all programs of training and conditioning to minimize the likelihood of injury:

1. *Warm-up/cooldown.* Take time to do an appropriate warm-up before engaging in any activity. Do not neglect the cooldown period after a training bout.
2. *Motivation.* Athletes are generally highly motivated to work hard because they want to be successful in their sport. By varying the training program and incorporating techniques of periodization, the program can remain enjoyable rather than becoming routine and boring.
3. *Overload.* To see improvement in any physiological component, the system must work harder than it is accustomed to working. Logan and Wallis identified the SAID principle, which directly relates to the principle of overload.[33] SAID is an acronym for specific adaptation to imposed demands. The SAID principle states that when the body is subjected to stresses and overloads of varying intensities, it will gradually adapt over time to overcome whatever demands are placed on it. Although overload is a critical factor in training and conditioning, the stress must not be great enough to produce damage or injury before the body has had a chance to adjust specifically to the increased demands.
4. *Consistency.* The athlete must engage in a training and conditioning program on a consistent, regularly scheduled basis if it is to be effective.
5. *Progression.* Increase the intensity of the conditioning program gradually and within the individual athlete's ability to adapt to increasing workloads.
6. *Intensity.* Stress the intensity of the work rather than the quantity. Coaches and athletic trainers too often confuse working hard with working for long periods of time. They make the mistake of prolonging the workout rather than increasing tempo or workload. The tired athlete is prone to injury.
7. *Specificity.* Specific goals for the training program must be identified. The program must be designed to address specific components of fitness (i.e., strength, flexibility, cardiorespiratory endurance) relative to the sport in which the athlete is competing.
8. *Individuality.* The needs of individual athletes vary considerably. The successful coach is one who recognizes these individual differences and adjusts or alters the training and conditioning program accordingly to best accommodate the athlete.
9. *Minimize stress.* Expect that athletes will train as close to their physiological limits as they can. Push the athletes as far as possible but consider other stressful aspects of their lives and allow them time to be away from the conditioning demands of their sport.
10. *Safety.* Make the training environment safe. Take time to educate athletes regarding proper techniques, how they should feel during the workout, and when they should push harder or back off.

WARM-UP AND COOLDOWN

Warm-Up

It is generally accepted that a period of warm-up exercises should take place before a training session begins, although a review of the literature reveals little data-based research to support the efficacy of a warm-up. Nevertheless, most athletic trainers would agree empirically that a warm-up period is a precaution against unnecessary musculoskeletal injuries and possible muscle soreness.[49,52] A good warm-up may also improve certain aspects of performance.[2,44]

The function of the warm-up is to prepare the body physiologically for some upcoming physical work. The purpose is to gradually stimulate the cardiorespiratory system to a moderate degree, thus producing an increased blood flow to working skeletal muscles and resulting in an increase in muscle temperature.

Moderate activity speeds up the metabolic processes that produce an increase in core body temperature. An increase in the temperature of skeletal muscle alters the mechanical properties of muscle. The elasticity of the muscle (the length to which the muscle can be stretched) is increased, whereas the viscosity (the rate at which the muscle can change shape) is decreased.

The warm-up should begin with two to three minutes of whole body activities using large muscle groups (e.g., light jogging, riding an exercise bike) to elevate the metabolic rate and raise core temperature.[44] Once the athlete breaks into a light sweat indicating that core temperature has been increased, a period of stretching exercises should follow. Stretching exercises should be sport-specific and related to the activity to be performed. For example, a soccer player uses the upper extremity considerably less than the lower extremity, so his or her stretching exercises should be directed more toward the lower extremity.

After stretching, the intensity of the warm-up should be increased gradually by performing sport-specific skills related to the activity in which the athlete is going to participate. For example, a basketball player should warm up by shooting layups and jump shots and by dribbling; a tennis player should hit forehand and backhand shots and serves.

The warm-up should last approximately ten to fifteen minutes. The athlete should not wait longer than fifteen minutes to begin the activity after the warm-up, although the effects will generally last up to about forty-five minutes. Thus the third-string football player who warms up before the game and then does nothing more than stand around until he gets into the game during the fourth quarter is running a much higher risk of injury. This player should be encouraged to stay warmed up and ready to play throughout the course of a game. In general, continued sweating is a good indication that the body has been sufficiently warmed up and is ready for more strenuous activity.

Cooldown

Following a workout or training session, a cooldown period is essential. The cooldown period enables the body to cool and return to a resting state. Such a period should last about five to ten minutes.

Although the value of warm-up and workout periods is well accepted, the importance of a cooldown period afterward is often ignored. Again, experience and observation indicate that persons who stretch during the cooldown period tend to have fewer problems with muscle soreness after strenuous activity.[49]

IMPROVING AND MAINTAINING FLEXIBILITY

Flexibility is the ability to move a joint or series of joints smoothly and easily throughout a full range of motion.[3] Flexibility can be discussed in relation to movement involving only one joint, such as the knees, or movement involving a whole series of joints, such as the spinal vertebral joints, which must all move together to allow smooth bending or rotation of the trunk.

An athlete who has a restricted range of motion will realize a decrease in performance capabilities. For example, a sprinter with tight, inelastic hamstring muscles loses some speed because the hamstring muscles restrict the ability to flex the hip joint, thus shortening stride length.

Lack of flexibility results in uncoordinated or awkward movements and predisposes the athlete to muscle strain.[8] Low back pain is frequently associated with tightness

4-3

Critical Thinking Exercise

A track athlete constantly complains of feelings of tightness in her lower extremity during workouts. She states that she has a difficult time during her warm-up and cannot seem to "get loose" until her workout is almost complete. She feels that she is always on the verge of "pulling a muscle."

? What should the athletic trainer recommend as a specific warm-up routine that should consistently be done before this athlete begins her workout?

Warming up involves general body warming and warming specific body areas for the demands of the sport.

Proper cooling down decreases blood and muscle lactic acid levels more rapidly.

Conditioning should be performed gradually, with work added in small increments.

The "tight," or inflexible, athlete performs with a considerable handicap in terms of movement.

Figure 4-2

Flexibility can be an important factor in decreasing sports injuries.

of the musculature in the lower spine and also of the hamstring muscles. Most activities require relatively normal amounts of flexibility.[46] However, some activities, such as gymnastics, ballet, diving, karate, and yoga, require increased flexibility for superior performance (Figure 4-2).

Good flexibility is essential to successful physical performance.[53] Most athletic trainers feel that maintaining good flexibility is important in prevention of injury to the musculotendinous unit, and they will generally insist that stretching exercises be included as part of the warm-up before the athlete engages in strenuous activity.

Factors That Limit Flexibility

A number of factors may limit the ability of a joint to move through a full, unrestricted range of motion. The *bony structure* may restrict the endpoint in the range. An elbow that has been fractured through the joint may deposit excess calcium in the joint space, causing the joint to lose its ability to fully extend. However, in many instances bony prominences stop movements at normal endpoints in the range.

Excessive *fat* may also limit the ability to move through a full range of motion. An athlete who has a large amount of fat on the abdomen may have severely restricted trunk flexion when asked to bend forward and touch the toes. The fat may act as a wedge between two lever arms, restricting movement wherever it is found. *Skin* might also be responsible for limiting movement. For example, an athlete who has had some type of injury or surgery involving a tearing incision or laceration of the skin, particularly over a joint, will have inelastic scar tissue formed at that site. This scar tissue is incapable of stretching with joint movement. *Muscles and their tendons,* along with their surrounding fascial sheaths, are most often responsible for limiting range of motion. An athlete who performs stretching exercises for the purpose of improving flexibility about a particular joint is attempting to take advantage of the highly elastic properties of a muscle. Over time it is possible to increase the elasticity, or the length that a given muscle can be stretched. Athletes who have a good deal of movement at a particular joint tend to have highly elastic and flexible muscles. *Connective tissue* surrounding the joint, such as ligaments on the joint capsule, may be subject to contractures. Ligaments and joint capsules do have some elasticity; however, if a joint is immobilized for a period of time, these structures tend to lose some elasticity and shorten. This condition is most commonly seen after surgical repair of an unstable joint, but it can also result from long periods of inactivity.

It is also possible for an athlete to have relatively slack ligaments and joint capsules. These individuals are generally referred to as being loose-jointed. Examples of loose-jointedness would be an elbow or knee that hyperextends beyond 180 degrees (Figure 4-3). Frequently the instability associated with loose-jointedness may present as great a problem in movement as ligamentous or capsular contractures.

Skin contractures caused by scarring, ligaments, joint capsules, and musculotendinous units are each capable of improving elasticity to varying degrees through

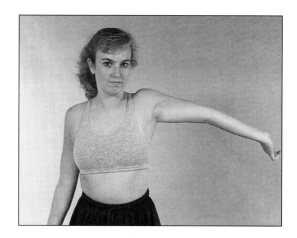

Figure 4-3

Excessive joint motion can predispose to injury.

stretching over time. With the exception of bony structure, age, and gender, all the other factors that limit flexibility may be altered to increase range of joint motion.

Active and Passive Range of Motion

Active range of motion, also called *dynamic flexibility,* refers to the degree to which a joint can be moved by a muscle contraction, usually through the midrange of movement. Dynamic flexibility is not necessarily a good indicator of the stiffness or looseness of a joint because it applies to the ability to move a joint efficiently, with little resistance to motion.[39]

Passive range of motion, sometimes called *static flexibility,* refers to the degree to which a joint may be passively moved to the endpoints in the range of motion. No muscle contraction is involved to move a joint through a passive range.

When a muscle actively contracts, it produces a joint movement through a specific range of motion. However, if passive pressure is applied to an extremity, it is capable of moving farther in the range of motion. It is essential in sport activities that an extremity be capable of moving through a nonrestricted range of motion. For example, a hurdler who cannot fully extend the knee joint in a normal stride is at considerable disadvantage because stride length and thus speed will be reduced significantly (Figure 4-4).

Passive range of motion is important for injury prevention. In many sports situations, a muscle is forced to stretch beyond its normal active limits. If the muscle does not have enough elasticity to compensate for this additional stretch, the musculotendinous unit will likely be injured.

Figure 4-4

Good flexibility is essential to successful performance in many sport activities.

Stretching Techniques

The maintenance of a full, nonrestricted range of motion has long been recognized as critical to injury prevention and as an essential component of a conditioning program.[24] See *Focus Box:* "Guidelines and precautions for stretching." The goal of any effective flexibility program should be to improve the range of motion at a given articulation by altering the extensibility of the musculotendinous units that produce movement at that joint. Exercises that stretch these musculotendinous units over a period of time increase the range of movement possible about a given joint.[18]

Stretching techniques for improving flexibility have evolved over the years. The oldest technique for stretching is called ballistic stretching, which makes use of repetitive bouncing motions. A second technique, known as static stretching, involves stretching a muscle to the point of discomfort and then holding it at the point for an extended time. This technique has been used for many years. A third technique involves a group of stretching techniques known collectively as proprioceptive neuromuscular facilitation (PNF) that uses alternating contractions and stretches.[40]

Focus

Guidelines and precautions for stretching

The following guidelines and precautions should be incorporated into a sound stretching program:

Warm up using a slow jog or fast walk before stretching vigorously.

To increase flexibility, the muscle must be overloaded or stretched beyond its normal range but not to the point of pain.

Stretch only to the point where you feel tightness or resistance to stretch or perhaps some discomfort. Stretching should not be painful.

Increases in range of motion will be specific to whatever joint is being stretched.

Exercise caution when stretching muscles that surround painful joints. Pain is an indication that something is wrong and should not be ignored.

Avoid overstretching the ligaments and capsules that surround joints.

Exercise caution when stretching the low back and neck. Exercises that compress the vertebrae and their disks may cause damage.

Stretching from a seated position rather than a standing position takes stress off the low back and decreases the chances of back injury.

Stretch those muscles that are tight and inflexible.

Strengthen those muscles that are weak and loose.

Always stretch slowly and with control.

Be sure to continue normal breathing during a stretch. Do not hold your breath.

Static and PNF techniques are most often recommended for individuals who want to improve their range of motion.

Ballistic stretching should be done only by those who are already flexible or are accustomed to stretching and done only after static stretching.

Stretching should be done at least three times per week to see minimal improvement. It is recommended that you stretch five or six times per week to see maximum results.

Researchers have had considerable discussion about which of these techniques is most effective for improving range of motion.

Agonist versus Antagonist Muscles

Prior to a discussion of the three different stretching techniques, it is essential to define the terms *agonist* and *antagonist*. Most joints in the body are capable of more than one movement. The knee joint, for example, is capable of flexion and extension. Contraction of the quadriceps group of muscles on the front of the thigh causes knee extension, whereas contraction of the hamstring muscles on the back of the thigh produces knee flexion.

To achieve knee extension, the quadriceps group contracts while the hamstring muscles relax and stretch. The muscle that contracts to produce a movement, in this case the quadriceps, is referred to as the agonist muscle. The muscle being stretched in response to contraction of the agonist muscle is called the antagonist muscle. In knee extension, the antagonist muscle would be the hamstring group. Some degree of balance in strength between agonist and antagonist muscle groups is necessary for normal smooth, coordinated movement and for reducing the likelihood of muscle strain caused by muscular imbalance.

Ballistic Stretching

Ballistic stretching involves a bouncing movement in which repetitive contractions of the agonist muscle are used to produce quick stretches of the antagonist muscle. The ballistic stretching technique, although apparently effective in improving range

ballistic stretching
Older stretching technique that uses repetitive bouncing motions.

of motion, has been criticized because increased range of motion is achieved through a series of jerks or pulls on the resistant muscle tissue. If the forces generated by the jerks are greater than the tissues' extensibility, muscle injury may result.

Successive forceful contractions of the agonist that results in stretching of the antagonist may cause muscle soreness. For example, forcefully kicking a soccer ball fifty times may result in muscular soreness of the hamstrings (antagonist muscle) as a result of eccentric contraction of the hamstrings to control the dynamic movement of the quadriceps (agonist muscle). Ballistic stretching that is controlled usually does not cause muscle soreness.[43]

Static Stretching

The **static stretching** technique is a widely used and effective technique of stretching. This technique involves passively stretching a given antagonist muscle by placing it in a maximal position of stretch and holding it there for an extended time. Recommendations for the optimal time for holding this stretched position vary, ranging from as short as three seconds to as long as sixty seconds.[27] Recent data indicate that thirty seconds may be an optimal time to hold the stretch. The static stretch of each muscle should be repeated three or four times.[6]

Much research has been done comparing ballistic and static stretching techniques for the improvement of flexibility. It has been shown that both static and ballistic stretching are effective in increasing flexibility and that there is no significant difference between the two. However, static stretching offers less danger of exceeding the extensibility limits of the involved joints because the stretch is more controlled. Ballistic stretching is apt to cause muscular soreness, whereas static stretching generally does not and is commonly used in injury rehabilitation of sore or strained muscles.[39]

Static stretching is certainly a much safer stretching technique, especially for sedentary or untrained individuals. However, many physical activities involve dynamic movement. Thus stretching as a warm-up for these types of activity should begin with static stretching followed by ballistic stretching, which more closely resembles the dynamic activity.

PNF Stretching Techniques

The **PNF** techniques were first used by physical therapists for treating patients who had various types of neuromuscular paralysis.[20] Only recently have PNF stretching exercises been used as a stretching technique for increasing flexibility.

A number of different PNF techniques are currently being used for stretching, including slow-reversal-hold-relax, contract-relax, and hold-relax techniques.[27] All involve some combination of alternating contraction and relaxation of both agonist and antagonist muscles. All three techniques use a ten-second push phase followed by a ten-second relax phase.

Using a hamstring stretching technique as an example (Figure 4-5), the slow-reversal-hold-relax technique would be done as follows:[40]

- With the athlete lying supine with the knee extended and the ankle flexed to 90 degrees, the athletic trainer passively flexes the hip joint to the point at which there is slight discomfort in the muscle.
- At this point the athlete begins pushing against the athletic trainer's resistance by contracting the hamstring muscle.
- After pushing for ten seconds, the hamstring muscles are relaxed and the agonist quadriceps muscle is contracted while the athletic trainer applies passive pressure to further stretch the antagonist hamstrings. This action should move the leg so that there is increased hip joint flexion.
- The relaxing phase lasts for ten seconds, after which the athlete pushes against the athletic trainer's resistance, beginning at this new joint angle.
- The push-relax sequence is repeated at least three times.

static stretching
Passively stretching an antagonist muscle by placing it in a maximal stretch and holding it there.

proprioceptive neuromuscular facilitation (PNF)
Stretching techniques that involve combinations of alternating contractions and stretches.

Figure 4-5

The slow-reversal-hold-relax technique for stretching the hamstring muscles.

The contract-relax and hold-relax techniques are variations on the slow-reversal-hold-relax method. In the contract-relax method, the hamstrings are isotonically contracted so that the leg actually moves toward the floor during the push phase. The hold-relax method involves an isometric hamstring contraction against immovable resistance during the push phase. During the relax phase, both techniques involve relaxation of hamstrings and quadriceps while the hamstrings are passively stretched. This same basic PNF technique can be used to stretch any muscle in the body. The PNF stretching techniques are perhaps best performed with a partner, although they may also be done using a wall as resistance (see Chapter 16).[40]

Neurophysiologic Basis of Stretching

All three stretching techniques are based on a neurophysiologic phenomenon involving the *stretch reflex* (Figure 4-6).[40] Every muscle in the body contains mechanoreceptors that when stimulated inform the central nervous system of what is happening with that muscle. Two of these receptors are important in the stretch reflex: the *muscle spindles* and the *Golgi tendon organs*. Both types of receptors are sensitive to changes in muscle length. The Golgi tendon organs are also affected by changes in muscle tension.

When a muscle is stretched, the muscle spindles are also stretched, sending a volley of sensory impulses to the spinal cord that informs the central nervous system that the muscle is being stretched. Impulses return to the muscle from the spinal cord, which causes the muscle to reflexively contract, thus resisting the stretch.[40] If the stretch of the muscle continues for an extended period of time (at least six seconds), the Golgi tendon organs respond to the change in length and the increase in tension by firing off sensory impulses of their own to the spinal cord. The impulses from the Golgi tendon organs, unlike the signals from the muscle spindle, cause a reflex relaxation of the antagonist muscle. This reflex relaxation serves as a protective mechanism that will allow the muscle to stretch through relaxation before the extensibility limits are exceeded, causing damage to the muscle fibers.[40]

With the jerking, bouncing motion of ballistic stretching, the muscle spindles are being repetitively stretched; thus there is continuous resistance by the muscle to further stretch. The ballistic stretch is not continued long enough to allow the Golgi tendon organs to have any relaxing effect.

The static stretch involves a continuous sustained stretch lasting anywhere from six to sixty seconds, which is sufficient time for the Golgi tendon organs to begin responding to the increase in tension. The impulses from the Golgi tendon organs have the ability to override the impulses coming from the muscle spindles, allowing the

CROSS SECTION OF SPINAL CORD

Figure 4-6

Stretch reflex. The muscle spindle produces a reflex resistance to stretch, and the Golgi tendon organ causes a reflex relaxation of the muscle in response to stretch.

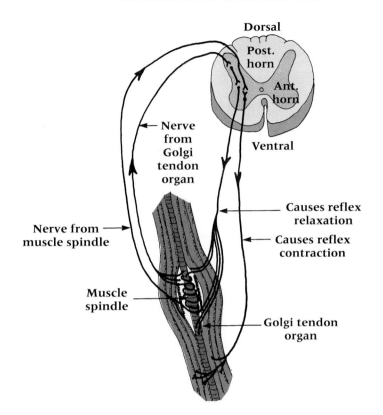

muscle to reflexively relax after the initial reflex resistance to the change in length. Thus lengthening the muscle and allowing it to remain in a stretched position for an extended period of time is unlikely to produce any injury to the muscle.

The effectiveness of the PNF techniques may be attributed in part to these same neurophysiologic principles. The slow-reversal-hold technique discussed previously takes advantage of two additional neurophysiologic phenomena.[40] The maximal isometric contraction of the muscle that will be stretched during the ten-second push phase again causes an increase in tension, which stimulates the Golgi tendon organs to effect a reflex relaxation of the antagonist even before the muscle is placed in a position of stretch. This relaxation of the antagonist muscle during contractions is referred to as **autogenic inhibition.**

During the relaxing phase the antagonist is relaxed and passively stretched while a maximal isotonic contraction of the agonist muscle pulls the extremity further into the agonist pattern. In any synergistic muscle group, a contraction of the agonist causes a reflex relaxation in the antagonist muscle, allowing it to stretch and protecting it from injury. This phenomenon is referred to as *reciprocal inhibition* (Figure 4-7). Thus with the PNF techniques the additive effects of autogenic inhibition and reciprocal inhibition should theoretically allow the muscle to be stretched to a greater degree than is possible with static stretching or the ballistic technique.[40]

autogenic inhibition
The relaxation of the antagonist muscle during contractions.

Practical Application

Although all three stretching techniques have been demonstrated to effectively improve flexibility, there is still considerable debate as to which technique produces the greatest increases in range of movement. The ballistic technique is seldom recommended because of the potential for causing muscle soreness. However, it must be added that most sport activities are ballistic in nature (e.g., kicking, running), and those activities use the stretch reflex to enhance performance. In highly trained

Figure 4-7

A contraction of the agonist will produce relaxation in the antagonist.

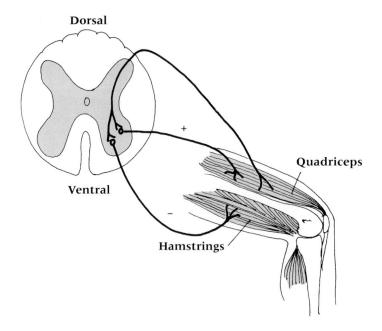

individuals, it is unlikely that ballistic stretching will result in muscle soreness. Static stretching is perhaps the most widely used technique. It is a simple technique and does not require a partner. A fully nonrestricted range of motion can be attained through static stretching over time.[48]

The PNF stretching techniques are capable of producing dramatic increases in range of motion during one stretching session. Studies comparing static and PNF stretching suggest that PNF stretching is capable of producing greater improvement in flexibility over an extended training period.[40] The major disadvantage of PNF stretching is that a partner is required for stretching, although stretching with a partner may have some motivational advantages. An increasing number of athletic teams are adopting the PNF technique as the method of choice for improving flexibility.

The Relationship between Strength and Flexibility

It is often said that strength training has a negative effect on flexibility.[18] For example, someone who develops large bulk through strength training is often referred to as muscle-bound. The term *muscle-bound* has negative connotations in terms of the ability of that athlete to move. We tend to think of athletes who have highly developed muscles as having lost much of their ability to move freely through a full range of motion. Occasionally an athlete develops so much bulk that the physical size of the muscle prevents a normal range of motion. It is certainly true that strength training that is not properly done can impair movement; however, weight training, if done properly through a full range of motion, will not impair flexibility. Proper strength training probably improves dynamic flexibility and, if combined with a rigorous stretching program, can greatly enhance powerful and coordinated movements that are essential for success in many athletic activities. In all cases a heavy weight-training program should be accompanied by a strong flexibility program.

Measuring Range of Motion

Accurate measurement of the range of joint motion is difficult. Various devices have been designed to accommodate variations in the size of the joints and the complexity of movements in articulations that involve more than one joint. Of these devices, the simplest and most widely used is the goniometer (Figure 4-8). A goniometer is a large protractor with measurements in degrees. By aligning the two arms parallel to the longitudinal axis of the two segments involved in motion about a specific joint, it is

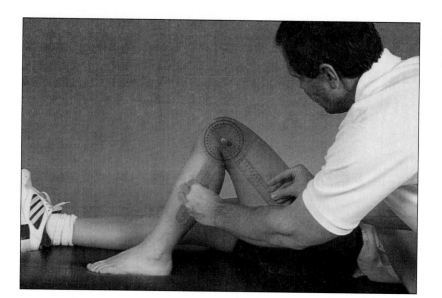

Figure 4-8

A goniometer can be used to measure joint angles.

possible to obtain relatively accurate measures of range of movement. The goniometer has its place in a rehabilitation setting, where it is essential to assess improvement in joint flexibility for the purpose of modifying injury rehabilitation programs.[20,37]

THE IMPORTANCE OF MUSCULAR STRENGTH, ENDURANCE, AND POWER

The development of **muscular strength** is an essential component of a training program for every athlete. By definition, strength is the ability of a muscle to generate force against some resistance. Most movements in sports are explosive and must include elements of both strength and speed if they are to be effective. If a large amount of force is generated quickly, the movement can be referred to as a **power** movement. Without the ability to generate power, an athlete will be limited in his or her performance capabilities.[39,45]

Muscular strength is closely associated with muscular endurance. **Muscular endurance** is the ability to perform repetitive muscular contractions against some resistance for an extended period of time. As muscular strength increases, there tends to be a corresponding increase in endurance.[14] For example, an athlete can lift a weight twenty-five times. If muscular strength is increased by 10 percent through weight training, it is likely that the maximum number of repetitions would be increased because it is easier for the athlete to lift the weight.

muscular strength
The maximum force that can be applied by a muscle during a single maximum contraction.

muscular endurance
The ability to perform repetitive muscular contractions against some resistance.

Skeletal Muscle Contractions

Skeletal muscle is capable of three different types of contraction: *isometric contraction, concentric contraction,* and *eccentric contraction.*[42] An isometric contraction occurs when the muscle contracts to increase tension but there is no change in length of the muscle. Considerable force can be generated against some immovable resistance even though no movement occurs. In concentric contraction the muscle shortens in length as a contraction is developed to overcome or move some resistance. In eccentric contraction the resistance is greater than the muscular force being produced and the muscle lengthens while continuing to contract. Concentric and eccentric contractions are both considered to be dynamic movements.[42]

Skeletal muscle is capable of three types of contractions:
- Isometric
- Concentric
- Eccentric

Fast-Twitch versus Slow-Twitch Fibers

All fibers in a particular motor unit are either *slow-twitch* or *fast-twitch* fibers, each of which has distinctive metabolic and contractile capabilities. Slow-twitch fibers are also referred to as type I fibers. They are more resistant to fatigue than are

There are three basic types of muscle fibers:
- Slow-twitch type I
- Fast-twitch type IIa
- Fast-twitch type IIb

fast-twitch fibers; however, the time required to generate force is much greater in slow-twitch fibers.[35] Because they are relatively fatigue resistant, slow-twitch fibers are associated primarily with long-duration, aerobic-type activities.

Fast-twitch fibers (also referred to as type II fibers) are capable of producing quick, forceful contractions but have a tendency to fatigue more rapidly than do slow-twitch fibers. Fast-twitch fibers are useful in short-term, high-intensity activities, which mainly involve the anaerobic system. Fast-twitch fibers are capable of producing powerful contractions, whereas slow-twitch fibers produce a long-endurance type of force. There are two subdivisions of fast-twitch fibers. Although both types of fast-twitch fibers are capable of rapid contraction, type IIa fibers are moderately resistant to fatigue whereas type IIb fibers fatigue rapidly and are considered the "true" fast-twitch fibers.[25]

Any given muscle contains both types of fibers, and the ratio in an individual muscle varies with each person.[35] Those muscles whose primary function is to maintain posture against gravity require more endurance and have a higher percentage of slow-twitch fibers. Muscles that produce powerful, rapid, explosive strength movements tend to have a much greater percentage of fast-twitch fibers. Because this ratio is genetically determined, it may play a large role in determining ability for a given sport activity. Sprinters and weight lifters, for example, have a large percentage of fast-twitch fibers in relation to slow-twitch fibers.[10] Conversely, marathon runners generally have a higher percentage of slow-twitch fibers.

The metabolic capabilities of both fast-twitch and slow-twitch fibers may be improved through specific strength and endurance training. It now appears that there can be an almost complete change from slow-twitch to fast-twitch and from fast-twitch to slow-twitch fiber types in response to training.[35]

Factors That Determine Levels of Muscular Strength

Muscular strength is proportional to the cross-sectional diameter of the muscle fibers. The greater the cross-sectional diameter or the bigger a particular muscle, the stronger it is, and thus the more force it is capable of generating. The size of a muscle tends to increase in cross-sectional diameter with weight training. This increase in muscle size is referred to as **hypertrophy.**[28] Conversely, a decrease in the size of a muscle is referred to as **atrophy.**

Size of the Muscle

Strength is a function of the number and diameter of muscle fibers composing a given muscle. The number of fibers is an inherited characteristic; thus an athlete with a large number of muscle fibers to begin with has the potential to hypertrophy to a much greater degree than does someone with relatively fewer fibers.[15]

Neuromuscular Efficiency

Strength is also directly related to the efficiency of the neuromuscular system and the function of the motor unit in producing muscular force. Initial increases in strength during a weight-training program can be attributed primarily to increased neuromuscular efficiency.[36]

Biomechanical Factors

Strength in a given muscle is determined not only by the physical properties of the muscle itself but also by biomechanical factors that dictate how much force can be generated through a system of levers to an external object. If we think of the elbow joint as one of these lever systems, we would have the biceps muscle producing flexion of this joint (Figure 4-9). The position of attachment of the biceps muscle on the lever arm, in this case the forearm, will largely determine how much force this muscle is capable of generating.[21] If there are two persons, **A** and **B,** and **B** has a biceps attachment that is farther from the center of the joint than is **A**'s, then **B** should be

hypertrophy
Enlargement of a muscle caused by an increase in the size of its cells in response to training.

atrophy
Decrease of a muscle caused by the decrease in the size of its cells because of inactivity.

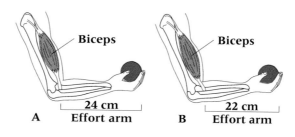

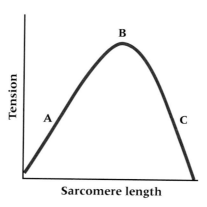

Figure 4-9

The position of attachment of the muscle tendon on the arm can affect the ability of that muscle to generate force. **B** should be able to generate greater force than **A** because the tendon attachment is closer to the resistance.

Figure 4-10

Because of the length-tension relation in muscle, the greatest tension is developed at point **B** with less tension developed at points **A** and **C**.

able to lift heavier weights because the muscle force acts through a longer lever (moment) arm and thus can produce greater torque around the joint.

The length of a muscle determines the tension that can be generated.[21] By varying the length of a muscle, different tensions may be produced. This length-tension relationship is illustrated in Figure 4-10. At position **B** in the curve, the interaction of the crossbridges between the actin and myosin myofilaments within the sarcomere is at a maximum. Setting a muscle at this particular length will produce the greatest amount of tension. At position **A** the muscle is shortened, and at position **C** the muscle is lengthened. In either case the interaction between the actin and myosin myofilaments through the crossbridges is greatly reduced and the muscle is not capable of generating significant tension.

Overtraining

Overtraining can have a negative effect on the development of muscular strength. The statement "if you abuse it you will lose it" is applicable. Overtraining can result in psychological breakdown (staleness) or physiological breakdown, which may involve musculoskeletal injury, fatigue, or sickness. Engaging in proper and efficient resistance training, eating a proper diet, and getting appropriate rest can minimize the potential negative effects of overtraining.

Reversibility

If strength training is discontinued or interrupted, the muscle will atrophy, decreasing in both strength and mass. Adaptations in skeletal muscle that occur in response to resistance training may begin to reverse in as little as forty-eight hours. It does appear that consistent exercise of a muscle is essential to prevent reversal of the hypertrophy that occurs due to strength training.

Physiology of Strength Development

A number of theories have been proposed to explain why a muscle hypertrophies in response to strength training.[28] Some evidence exists that the number of muscle fibers increase because fibers split in response to training.[30] However, this research has been conducted in animals and should not be generalized to humans. It is generally accepted that the number of fibers is genetically determined and does not seem to increase with training.

Another hypothesis is that because the muscle is working harder in weight training, more blood is required to supply that muscle with oxygen and other nutrients. Thus the number of capillaries is increased. This hypothesis is only partially correct; few new capillaries are formed during strength training, but a number of dormant capillaries may become filled with blood to meet this increased demand for blood supply.

A third theory to explain this increase in muscle size seems the most credible. Muscle fibers are composed primarily of small protein filaments, called myofilaments, which are the contractile elements in muscle. These myofilaments increase in both size and number as a result of strength training, causing the individual muscle fibers themselves to increase in cross-sectional diameter.[35] This increase is particularly true in men, although women also see some increase in muscle size.[47] More research is needed to further clarify and determine the specific causes of muscle hypertrophy.

Other Physiological Adaptations to Resistance Exercise

In addition to muscle hypertrophy there are a number of other physiological adaptations to resistance training.[9] The strength of noncontractile structures, including tendons and ligaments, is increased. The mineral content of bone is increased, making the bone stronger and more resistant to fracture. Maximal oxygen uptake is improved when resistance training is of sufficient intensity to elicit heart rates at or above training levels. There is also an increase in several enzymes important in aerobic and anaerobic metabolism.[10,35]

Techniques of Resistance Training

There are a number of different techniques of resistance training for strength improvement, including isometric exercise, progressive resistance exercise, isokinetic training, circuit training, and plyometric exercise. Regardless of which of these techniques is used, one basic principle of training is extremely important. For a muscle to improve in strength, it must be forced to work at a higher level than it is accustomed to. In other words, the muscle must be *overloaded*. Without overload the muscle will be able to maintain strength as long as training is continued against a resistance the muscle is accustomed to. To most effectively build muscular strength, weight training requires a consistent, increasing effort against progressively increasing resistance.[16] Progressive resistance exercise is based primarily on the principles of overload and progression. If this principle of overload is applied, all five training techniques will produce improvement of muscular strength over a period of time.

Isometric Exercise

isometric exercise
Contracts the muscle statically without changing its length.

An i**sometric exercise** involves a muscle contraction in which the length of the muscle remains constant while tension develops toward a maximal force against an immovable resistance.[5] The muscle should generate a maximal force for ten seconds at a time, and this contraction should be repeated five to ten times per day. Isometric exercises are capable of increasing muscular strength; unfortunately, strength gains are specific to the joint angle at which training is performed. At other angles, the strength curve drops off dramatically because of a lack of motor activity at that angle.

Another major disadvantage of isometric exercises is that they tend to produce a spike in systolic blood pressure that can result in potentially life-threatening cardiovascular accidents.[41] This sharp increase in blood pressure results from holding one's breath and increasing intrathoracic pressure. Consequently, the blood pressure experienced by the heart is increased significantly. This phenomenon has been referred to as the Valsalva effect. To avoid or minimize this increase in pressure, it is recommended that breathing be continued during the maximal contraction.

Isometric exercises are useful in the rehabilitation of certain injuries; this use is discussed in later chapters.

Progressive Resistance Exercise

A second technique of resistance training is perhaps the most commonly used and most popular technique for improving muscular strength. *Progressive resistance exercise* training uses exercises that strengthen muscles through a contraction that overcomes some fixed resistance produced by equipment such as dumbbells, barbells, or various weight machines (Figure 4-11). Progressive resistance exercise uses isotonic contractions in which force is generated while the muscle is changing in length.[12]

Isotonic contractions   Isotonic contractions may be either concentric or eccentric. An athlete who is performing a biceps curl offers a good example of an isotonic contraction. To lift the weight from the starting position, the biceps muscle must contract and shorten in length. This shortening contraction is referred to as a **concentric,** or **positive, contraction.** If the biceps muscle does not remain contracted when the weight is being lowered, gravity will cause the weight to simply fall back to the starting position. Thus, to control the weight as it is being lowered, the biceps muscle must continue to contract while at the same time gradually lengthening. A contraction in which the muscle is lengthening while still applying force is called an **eccentric,** or **negative, contraction.**[22]

concentric (positive) contraction
The muscle shortens while contracting against resistance.

eccentric (negative) contraction
The muscle lengthens while contracting against resistance.

It is possible to generate greater amounts of force against resistance with an eccentric contraction than with a concentric contraction. This greater force is because eccentric contractions require a much lower level of motor unit activity to achieve a certain force than do concentric contractions. Because fewer motor units are firing to produce a specific force, additional motor units may be recruited to generate increased force. In addition, oxygen utilization is much lower during eccentric exercise than during comparable concentric exercise. Thus eccentric contractions are less resistant to fatigue than are concentric contractions. The mechanical efficiency of eccentric exercise may be several times higher than that of concentric exercise.[42]

Concentric contractions function to accelerate movement, whereas eccentric contractions act to decelerate motion. For example, the hamstrings must contract eccentrically to decelerate the angular velocity of the lower leg during running. Likewise, the external rotators in the rotator cuff muscles surrounding the shoulder contract eccentrically to decelerate the internally rotating humerus during throwing. Because of the excessive forces involved with these eccentric contractions, injury to the

A

B

Figure 4-11

A, Barbells and dumbbells are free weights that assist the athlete in developing isotonic strength. **B,** Many machine exercise systems provide a variety of exercise possibilities for the athlete.

muscles are quite common. Thus, eccentric exercise must be routinely incorporated in the strength training program in order to prevent injury to those muscles that act to decelerate movement.

Free weights versus machine weights   Various types of exercise equipment can be used with progressive resistance exercise, including free weights (barbells and dumbbells) or exercise machines such as those made by Universal, Nautilus, Cybex, Eagle, and Body Master. Dumbbells and barbells require the use of iron plates of varying weights that can be easily changed by adding or subtracting equal amounts of weight to both sides of the bar. The exercise machines have a stack of weights that are lifted through a series of levers or pulleys. The stack of weights slides up and down on a pair of bars that restrict the movement to only one plane. Weight can be increased or decreased simply by changing the position of a weight key.

There are advantages and disadvantages to both free weights and machines. The exercise machines are relatively safe to use in comparison with free weights. It is also a simple process to increase or decrease the weight on exercise machines by moving a single weight key, although changes can generally be made only in increments of ten or fifteen pounds. The iron plates used with free weights must be added or removed from each side of the barbell or dumbbell.

Figure 4-12 shows examples of different isotonic strengthening exercises.

Spotting for free weight exercises   When training with free weights, it is essential to have a partner who can assist the lifter in performing a particular exercise. This assistance is particularly critical when the weights to be lifted are extremely heavy. A *spotter* has three functions: to protect the lifter from injury, to make recommendations on proper lifting technique, and to help motivate the lifter. *Focus Box:* "Proper spotting techniques" provides some guidelines for correct spotting techniques.

Isotonic training   Regardless of which type of equipment is used, the same principles of **isotonic** training may be applied. In progressive resistance exercise, it is essential to incorporate both concentric and eccentric contractions. Research has clearly demonstrated that the muscle should be overloaded and fatigued both concentrically and eccentrically for the greatest strength improvement to occur.[29,35]

When training specifically for the development of muscular strength, the concentric, or positive, portion of the exercise should require one to two seconds and the

isotonic exercise
Shortens and lengthens the muscle through a complete range of motion.

Focus

Proper spotting techniques
- Make sure the lifter uses the proper grip.
- Check to see that the lifter is in a safe, stable position.
- Make sure the lifter moves through a complete range of motion at the appropriate speed.
- Make sure the lifter inhales and exhales during the lift.
- When spotting dumbbell exercises, spot as close to the dumbbells as possible above the elbow joint.
- Make sure the lifter understands how to get out of the way of missed attempts, particularly with overhead techniques.
- Stand behind the lifter.
- If heavy weights exceed the limits of your ability to control the weight, use a second spotter.
- Communicate with the lifter to know how many reps are to be done, whether a liftoff is needed, and how much help the lifter wants in completing a rep.
- Always be in a position to protect both the lifter and yourself from injury.

eccentric, or negative, portion of the lift should require two to four seconds. The ratio of negative to positive should be approximately one to two. Physiologically, the muscle will fatigue much more rapidly concentrically than eccentrically.

Athletes who have trained with both free weights and machines realize the difference in the amount of weight that can be lifted. Unlike the machines, free weights have no restricted motion and can thus move in many different directions, depending on the forces applied. With free weights, an element of muscular control on the part of the lifter to prevent the weight from moving in any direction other than vertical will usually decrease the amount of weight that can be lifted.[51]

One problem often mentioned in relation to isotonic training is that the amount of force necessary to move a weight through a range of motion changes according to the angle of pull of the contracting muscle. The amount of force is greatest when the angle of pull is approximately 90 degrees. In addition, once the inertia of the weight has been overcome and momentum has been established, the force required to move the resistance varies according to the force that the muscle can produce through the range of motion. Thus, it has been argued that a disadvantage of any type of isotonic exercise is that the force required to move the resistance is constantly changing throughout the range of movement.

Certain exercise machines are designed to minimize this change in resistance by using a cam system (Figure 4-13). The cam has been individually designed for each piece of equipment so that the resistance is variable throughout the movement. The cam system attempts to alter resistance so that the muscle can handle a greater load: at the points at which the joint angle or muscle length is at a mechanical disadvantage, the cam reduces the resistance to muscle movement. Whether this design does what it claims is debatable. This change in resistance at different points in the range is called accommodating resistance, or variable resistance.

Progressive Resistance Exercise Techniques

Perhaps the single most confusing aspect of progressive resistance exercise is the terminology used to describe specific programs. The following list of terms and their operational definitions may help clarify the confusion:

- Repetitions—number of times a specific movement is repeated.
- Repetitions maximum (RM)—maximum number of repetitions at a given weight.
- One repetition maximum (1RM)—The maximum amount of weight that can be lifted one time.
- Set—a particular number of repetitions.
- Intensity—the amount of weight or resistance lifted.
- Recovery period—the rest interval between sets.
- Frequency—the number of times an exercise is done in one week.

A considerable amount of research has been done in the area of resistance training to determine optimal techniques in terms of the intensity or the amount of weight to be used, the number of repetitions, the number of sets, the recovery period, and the frequency of training. It is important to realize that there are many different effective techniques and training regimens. Regardless of specific techniques used, it is certain that to improve strength the muscle must be overloaded in a progressive manner.[37] This overload is the basis of progressive resistance exercise. The amount of weight used and the number of repetitions must be enough to make the muscle work at a higher intensity than it is used to. This overload is the single most critical factor in any strength-training program. The strength-training program must also be designed to meet the specific needs of the athlete.

There is no such thing as an optimal strength-training program. Achieving total agreement on a program of resistance training that includes specific recommendations relative to repetitions, sets, intensity, recovery time, and frequency among researchers or other experts in resistance training is impossible. However, the

Figure 4-12

Examples of isotonic strength training exercises shown with appropriate spotting techniques where needed. **A,** Parallel squat. **B,** Power clean. **C,** Bench press. **D,** Military press. **E,** Dead lift. **F,** Snatch. **G,** Leg press. **H,** Leg curl. **I,** Toe raise. **J,** Arm curl. **K,** Tricep extension.

A

B

C   **D**

E   **F**

G

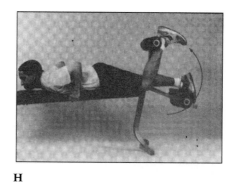

H

I

J

K

following general recommendations will provide an effective resistance-training program.

For any given exercise, the amount of weight selected should be sufficient to allow six to eight repetitions maximum (RM) in each of three sets with a recovery period of sixty to ninety seconds between sets. Initial selection of a starting weight may require some trial and error to achieve this 6 to 8 RM range. If at least three sets of six repetitions cannot be completed, the weight is too heavy and should be reduced. If it is possible to do more than three sets of eight repetitions, the weight is too light and should be increased.[7] Progression to heavier weights is determined by the ability to perform at least 8 RM in each of three sets. An increase of about 10 percent of the current weight being lifted should still allow at least 6 RM in each of three sets.

Occasionally, athletes may be tested at 1RM to determine the greatest amount of weight that can be lifted one time. Extreme caution should be exercised when trying to determine 1RM. Attention should be directed toward making sure the athlete has had ample opportunity to warm up and that the lifting technique is correct before attempting a maximum lift. Determining 1RM should be done very gradually to minimize the chances of injuring the muscle.

A particular muscle or muscle group should be exercised consistently every other day. Thus the frequency of weight training should be at least three times per week but no more than four times per week. It is common for serious weight trainers to lift every day; however, they exercise different muscle groups on successive days. For example, Monday, Wednesday, and Friday may be used for upper body muscles, whereas Tuesday, Thursday, and Saturday are used for lower body muscles.

Training for muscular strength versus endurance   Muscular endurance is the ability to perform repeated muscle contractions against resistance for an extended period of time. Most weight-training experts believe that muscular strength and muscular endurance are closely related.[39] As one improves, the other tends to improve also.

When weight training for strength, heavier weights with a lower number of repetitions should be used. Conversely, endurance training uses relatively lighter weights with a greater number of repetitions.

Endurance training should consist of three sets of ten to fifteen repetitions using the same criteria for weight selection, progression, and frequency as recommended for progressive resistance exercise.[5] Thus, suggested training regimens for muscular strength and endurance are similar in terms of sets and numbers of repetitions. Persons who possess great levels of strength tend to also exhibit greater muscular endurance when asked to perform repeated contractions against resistance.

Isokinetic Exercise

isokinetic exercise
Resistance is given at a fixed velocity of movement with accommodating resistance.

An **isokinetic exercise** involves a muscle contraction in which the length of the muscle is changing while the contraction is performed at a constant velocity.[38] In theory, maximal resistance is provided throughout the range of motion by the machine. The

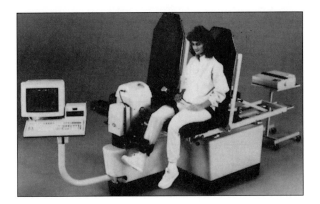

Figure 4-14

During isokinetic exercising the amount of resistance depends on the extent of force applied by the athlete.

resistance provided by the machine will move only at some preset speed regardless of the force applied to it by the individual. Thus the key to isokinetic exercise is not the resistance but the speed at which the resistance can be moved.

Several isokinetic devices are available commercially; Cybex, Biodex, and Kin-Com are among the more common isokinetic machines (Figure 4-14). In general, isokinetic devices rely on hydraulic, pneumatic, and mechanical pressure systems to produce constant velocity of motion. The majority of isokinetic devices are capable of resisting both concentric and eccentric contractions at a fixed speed to exercise a muscle.

A major disadvantage of these units is their cost. Many come with a computer and printing device and are used primarily as diagnostic and rehabilitative tools in the treatment of various injuries.

Isokinetic devices are designed so that regardless of the amount of force applied, the resistance can be moved only at a certain speed. That speed will be the same whether maximal force or only half the maximal force is applied. Consequently, when training isokinetically, it is absolutely necessary to exert as much force against the resistance as possible (maximal effort) for maximal strength gains to occur. This need for maximal effort is one of the major problems with an isokinetic strength-training program.

Anyone who has been involved in a weight-training program knows that on some days it is difficult to find the motivation to work out. Because isokinetic training does not require a maximal effort, it is easy to "cheat" and not go through the workout at a high level of intensity. In a progressive resistance exercise program, one knows how much weight has to be lifted with how many repetitions. Thus, isokinetic training is often more effective if a partner system is used as a means of motivation toward a maximal effort.

When isokinetic training is done properly with a maximal effort, it is theoretically possible that maximal strength gains are best achieved through the isokinetic training method in which the velocity and force of the resistance are equal throughout the range of motion. However, there is no conclusive research to support this theory. Whether changing force capability is in fact a deterrent to improving the ability to generate force against some resistance is debatable.

In the athletic training setting, isokinetics are perhaps best used as a rehabilitative and diagnostic tool rather than as a training device.[19]

Circuit Training

Circuit training employs a series of exercise stations that consist of various combinations of weight training, flexibility, calisthenics, and brief aerobic exercises. Circuits may be designed to accomplish many different training goals. With circuit training one moves rapidly from one station to the next and performs whatever exercise is to be done at that station within a specified time period. A typical circuit would consist of eight to twelve stations, and the entire circuit would be repeated three times.

circuit training
Exercise stations that consist of various combinations of weight training, flexibility, calisthenics, and aerobic exercises.

Circuit training is most definitely an effective technique for improving strength and flexibility. Certainly, if the pace or the time interval between stations is rapid and if workload is maintained at a high level of intensity with heart rate at or above target training levels, the cardiorespiratory system may benefit from this circuit. However, little research evidence shows that circuit training is effective in improving cardiorespiratory endurance. It should be and is most often used as a technique for developing and improving muscular strength and endurance.

Calisthenic Strengthening Exercises

Calisthenics, or free exercise, is one of the more easily available means of developing strength. Isotonic movement exercises can be graded according to intensity by using gravity as an aid, by ruling gravity out, by moving against gravity, or by using the body or body part as a resistance against gravity. Most calisthenics require the athlete to support the body or move the total body against the force of gravity. Push-ups are a good example of a vigorous antigravity free exercise. To be considered maximally effective, the isotonic calisthenic exercise, as in all types of exercise, must be performed in an exacting manner and in full range of motion. In most cases, ten or more repetitions are performed for each exercise and are repeated in sets of two or three.

Some free exercises use an isometric, or holding, phase instead of a full range of motion. Examples of these exercises are back extensions and sit-ups. When the exercise produces maximum muscle tension, it is held between six and ten seconds and then repeated one to three times.

Plyometric Exercise

Plyometric exercise is a technique that includes specific exercises that encompass a rapid stretch of a muscle eccentrically, followed immediately by a rapid concentric contraction of that muscle for the purpose of facilitating and developing a forceful explosive movement over a short period of time.[1,13] The greater the stretch put on the muscle from its resting length immediately before the concentric contraction, the greater the resistance the muscle can overcome. Plyometric exercises emphasize the speed of the eccentric phase. The rate of stretch is more critical than the magnitude of the stretch. An advantage to plyometric exercises is that they can help develop eccentric control in dynamic movements.[11]

Plyometric exercises involve hops, bounds, and depth jumping for the lower extremity and the use of medicine balls and other types of weighted equipment for the upper extremity. Depth jumping is an example of a plyometric exercise in which an individual jumps to the ground from a specified height and then quickly jumps again as soon as ground contact is made.[13]

Plyometrics place a great deal of stress on the musculoskeletal system. The learning and perfection of specific jumping skills and other plyometric exercises must be technically correct and specific to the athlete's age, activity, physical development, and skill development.

Strength Training for the Female Athlete

Strength training is critical for the female athlete.[31] Significant muscle hypertrophy in the female athlete is dependent on the presence of the hormone testosterone. Testosterone is considered a male hormone, although all women possess some testosterone in their systems. Women with higher testosterone levels tend to have more masculine characteristics such as increased facial and body hair, a deeper voice, and the potential to develop a little more muscle bulk.[35]

With weight training, the female sees some remarkable gains in strength initially, even though muscle bulk does not increase. For a muscle to contract, an impulse must be transmitted from the nervous system to the muscle. Each muscle fiber is innervated by a specific motor unit. An athlete who overloads a particular muscle by engaging in weight training forces that muscle to work efficiently. Efficiency is

---

plyometric exercise
This type of exercise maximizes the myotatic, or stretch, reflex.

4-5

Critical Thinking Exercise

A high school shot-putter has been working intensely on weight training to improve his muscular power. In particular he has been concentrating on lifting extremely heavy free weights using a low number of repetitions (three sets of six to eight repetitions). Although his strength has improved significantly over the last several months, he is not seeing the same degree of improvement in his throws even though his coach says that his technique is very good.

? The athlete is frustrated with his performance and wants to know if there is anything else he can do in his training program that might enhance his performance.

achieved by getting more motor units to fire, causing a stronger contraction of the muscle. Consequently, it is not uncommon for a female to see extremely rapid gains in strength when a weight-training program is first begun. These tremendous initial strength gains, which can be attributed to improved neuromuscular system efficiency, tend to plateau, and minimal improvement in muscular strength will be realized during a continuing strength-training program. These initial neuromuscular strength gains are also seen in men, although their strength will continue to increase with appropriate training.

Perhaps the most critical difference between males and females regarding physical performance is the ratio of strength to body weight. The reduced *strength-to-body-weight ratio* in women is the result of their higher percentage of body fat. The strength-to-body-weight ratio may be significantly improved through weight training by decreasing the percentage of body fat while increasing lean weight.

CARDIORESPIRATORY ENDURANCE

By definition, **cardiorespiratory endurance** is the ability to perform whole-body large muscle activities for extended periods of time. The cardiorespiratory system provides a means by which oxygen is supplied to the various tissues of the body.[23] Athletes find cardiorespiratory endurance critical both for performance and for preventing undue fatigue that may predispose to injury.

Transport and Utilization of Oxygen

Basically, transport of oxygen throughout the body involves the coordinated function of four components: the heart, the lungs, the blood vessels, and the blood. The improvement of cardiorespiratory endurance through training occurs because of the increased capability of each of these four elements to provide necessary oxygen to the working tissues. The greatest rate at which oxygen can be taken in and used during exercise is referred to as *maximum aerobic capacity* ($\dot{V}O_2max$).[19] The performance of any activity requires a certain rate of oxygen consumption that is about the same for all persons, depending on the level of fitness. Generally, the greater the rate, or intensity of the performance, of an activity, the greater the oxygen consumption. Each person has his or her own maximal rate of oxygen consumption. That person's ability to perform an activity (or to fatigue) is closely related to the amount of oxygen required by that activity and is limited by the maximal rate of oxygen consumption of which the person is capable. Apparently, the greater the percentage of maximum oxygen consumption required during an activity, the less time the activity may be performed (Figure 4-15).

The maximal rate at which oxygen can be used is a genetically determined characteristic; a person inherits a certain range of maximum aerobic capacity, and the

cardiorespiratory endurance
Ability to perform activities for extended periods of time.

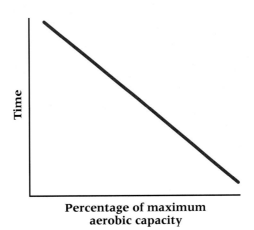

Figure 4-15

The greater the percentage of maximum aerobic capacity required during an activity, the less time the activity may be performed.

more active that person is, the higher the existing maximum aerobic capacity will be in that range.[23] A training program allows an athlete to increase maximum aerobic capacity to its highest limit within that athlete's range. Maximum aerobic capacity is most often presented in terms of the volume of oxygen used relative to body weight per unit of time (ml/kg/min). A normal maximum aerobic capacity for most college-age athletes would fall somewhere in the range of 45 to 60 ml/kg/min.[10] A world-class male marathon runner may have a maximum aerobic capacity in the 70 to 80 ml/kg/min range.

Three factors determine the maximal rate at which oxygen can be used: external respiration, involving the ventilatory process, or pulmonary function; gas transport, which is accomplished by the cardiovascular system (i.e., the heart, blood vessels, and blood); and internal respiration, which involves the use of oxygen by the cells to produce energy. Of these three factors the most limiting is generally the ability to transport oxygen through the system; thus the cardiovascular system limits the overall rate of oxygen consumption. A high maximum aerobic capacity within an athlete's inherited range indicates that all three systems are working well.

Effects on the Heart

The heart is the main pumping mechanism, circulating oxygenated blood throughout the body to the working tissues. As the body begins to exercise, the muscles use oxygen at a much higher rate, and the heart must pump more oxygenated blood to meet this increased demand. The heart is capable of adapting to this increased demand through several mechanisms. Heart rate shows a gradual adaptation to an increased workload by increasing proportionally to the intensity of the exercise and will plateau at a given level after about two to three minutes (Figure 4-16).

Monitoring heart rate is an indirect method of estimating oxygen consumption. In general, heart rate and oxygen consumption have a linear relationship, although at very low intensities and at high intensities this linear relationship breaks down (Figure 4-17).[32] During higher intensity activities, maximal heart rate may be achieved before maximal oxygen consumption, which will continue to rise.[35] The greater the intensity of the exercise, the higher the heart rate. Because of these existing relationships it should become apparent that the rate of oxygen consumption can be estimated by taking heart rate.[10]

A second mechanism by which the heart is able to adapt to increased demands during exercise is to increase the stroke volume, the volume of blood being pumped out with each beat.[10] The heart pumps out approximately 70 ml of blood per beat. Stroke volume can continue to increase only to the point at which there is simply not enough time between beats for the heart to fill up. This point occurs at about 40 percent of maximal heart rate, and above this level increases in the volume of blood being pumped out per unit of time must be caused entirely by increases in heart rate (Figure 4-18).[35]

Figure 4-16

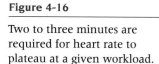

Two to three minutes are required for heart rate to plateau at a given workload.

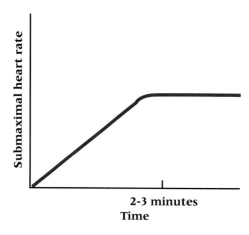

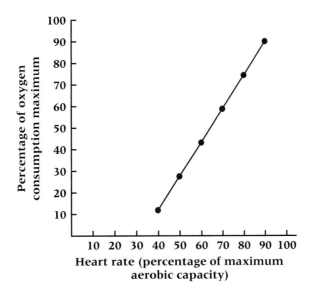

Figure 4-17

Maximal heart rate is achieved at about the same time as maximum aerobic capacity.

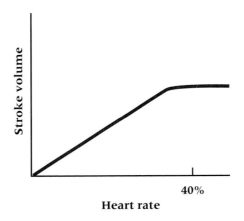

Figure 4-18

Stroke volume plateaus at 40 percent of maximal heart rate.

Stroke volume and heart rate together determine the volume of blood being pumped through the heart in a given unit of time. Approximately 5 L of blood are pumped through the heart during each minute at rest. This figure is referred to as the cardiac output, which indicates how much blood the heart is capable of pumping in exactly one minute. Thus, cardiac output is the primary determinant of the maximal rate of oxygen consumption possible (Figure 4-19). During exercise, cardiac output increases to approximately four times that experienced during rest in the normal individual and may increase as much as six times in the elite endurance athlete.

A **training effect** that occurs with regard to cardiac output of the heart is that the stroke volume increases while exercise heart rate is reduced at a given standard exercise load. The heart becomes more efficient because it is capable of pumping more blood with each stroke. Because the heart is a muscle, it will hypertrophy to some extent, but this hypertrophy is in no way a negative effect of training.

training effect
Stroke volume increases while heart rate is reduced at a given exercise load.

Training Effect

$$\frac{\text{Cardiac}}{\text{output}} = \frac{\text{Increased}}{\text{stroke volume}} \times \frac{\text{Decreased}}{\text{heart rate}}$$

Effects on Work Ability

Cardiorespiratory endurance plays a critical role in the athlete's ability to resist fatigue. Fatigue is closely related to the percentage of maximum aerobic capacity that a particular workload demands.[39] For example, Figure 4-20 presents two athletes, **A** and **B**. Athlete **A** has a maximum aerobic capacity of 50 ml/kg/min, whereas

Figure 4-19

Cardiac output limits maximum aerobic capacity.

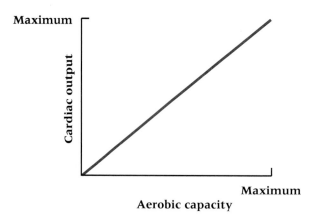

Figure 4-20

Athlete **A** should be able to work longer than Athlete **B** as a result of lower utilization of maximum aerobic capacity.

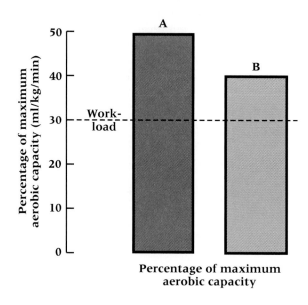

athlete **B** has a maximum aerobic capacity of only 40 ml/kg/min. If both **A** and **B** are exercising at the same intensity, **A** will be working at a much lower percentage of maximum aerobic capacity than **B** is. Consequently, **A** should be able to sustain his or her activity over a much longer period of time. Athletic performance may be impaired if the ability to use oxygen efficiently is impaired. Thus, improvement of cardiorespiratory endurance should be an essential component of any training program.

The Energy Systems

Various sports activities involve specific demands for energy. For example, sprinting and jumping are high-energy activities, requiring a relatively large production of energy for a short time. Long-distance running and swimming, on the other hand, are mostly low-energy activities per unit of time, requiring energy production for a prolonged time. Other physical activities demand a blend of both high- and low-energy output. These various energy demands can be met by the different processes in which energy can be supplied to the skeletal muscles.

ATP: The Immediate Energy Source

Energy is produced from the breakdown of nutrient foodstuffs.[35] This energy is used to produce adenosine triphosphate (ATP), which is the ultimate usable form of energy for muscular activity. ATP is produced in the muscle tissue from blood glucose or glycogen. Glucose is derived from the breakdown of dietary carbohydrates. Glucose not needed

TABLE 4-2 Comparison of Aerobic versus Anaerobic Activities

	Mode	Relative Intensity	Performance	Frequency	Duration	Miscellaneous
Aerobic activities	Continuous, long-duration, sustained activities	Less intense	60% to 80% of maximum range	At least three but not more than six times per week	20 to 60 min	Less risk to sedentary or older individuals
Anaerobic activities	Explosive, short-duration, burst-type activities	More intense	85% to 100% range	Three to four days per week	10 sec to 2 min	Used in sport and team activities

immediately is stored as glycogen in the resting muscle and liver. Stored glycogen in the liver can later be converted back to glucose and transferred to the blood to meet the body's energy needs. Fats and proteins can also be metabolized to generate ATP.

Once much of the muscle and liver glycogen is depleted, the body relies more heavily on fats stored in adipose tissue to meet its energy needs. The longer the duration of an activity, the greater the amount of fat that is used, especially during the later stages of endurance events. During rest and submaximal exertion, both fat and carbohydrates are used as energy substrate in approximately a 60 percent to 40 percent ratio.[35]

Regardless of the nutrient source that produces ATP, it is always available in the cell as an immediate energy source. When all available sources of ATP are depleted, more must be regenerated for muscular contraction to continue.

Aerobic versus Anaerobic Metabolism

Two major energy systems function in muscle tissue: anaerobic and aerobic metabolism. Each of these systems generates ATP. During sudden outbursts of activity in intensive, short-term exercise, ATP can be rapidly metabolized to meet energy needs. After a few seconds of intensive exercise, however, the small stores of ATP are used up. The body then turns to glycogen as an energy source. Glycogen can be metabolized within the muscle cells to generate ATP for muscle contractions.

Both ATP and muscle glycogen can be metabolized without the need for oxygen. Thus this energy system involves anaerobic metabolism (occurring in the absence of oxygen). As exercise continues, the body has to rely on the metabolism of carbohydrates (more specifically, glucose) and fats to generate ATP. This second energy system requires oxygen and is therefore referred to as aerobic metabolism (occurring in the presence of oxygen).

In most activities both aerobic and anaerobic systems function simultaneously. The degree to which the two major energy systems are involved is determined by the intensity and duration of the activity. If the intensity of the activity is such that sufficient oxygen can be supplied to meet the demands of working tissues, the activity is considered to be aerobic. Conversely, if the activity is of high enough intensity or the duration is such that there is insufficient oxygen available to meet energy demands, the activity becomes anaerobic. Consequently, an oxygen debt is incurred that must be paid back during the recovery period. For example, short bursts of muscle contraction, as in running or swimming sprints, use predominantly the anaerobic system. However, endurance events depend a great deal on the aerobic system. Most sports use a combination of both anaerobic and aerobic metabolism (Table 4-2).

Training Techniques for Improving Cardiorespiratory Endurance

Cardiorespiratory endurance may be improved through a number of different methods. Largely, the amount of improvement possible will be determined by initial levels of cardiorespiratory endurance.

4-6

Critical Thinking Exercise

A female soccer player has a grade 1 ankle sprain that is likely to keep her out of practice for about a week. She has worked extremely hard on her fitness levels and is concerned that not being able to run for an entire week will hurt her cardiorespiratory fitness.

? What types of activity should the athletic trainer recommend during her rehabilitation period that can help her maintain her existing level of cardiorespiratory endurance?

Continuous Training

Continuous training involves four considerations:

- *Mode* or type of activity
- *Frequency* of the activity
- *Duration* of the activity
- *Intensity* of the activity

Mode   The type of activity used in continuous training must be aerobic. Aerobic activities are those that elevate the heart rate and maintain it at that level for an extended time. Aerobic activities generally involve repetitive, whole-body, large-muscle movements performed over an extended time. Examples of aerobic activities are running, jogging, walking, cycling, swimming, rope skipping, stair climbing, and cross-country skiing. The advantage of these aerobic activities as opposed to more intermittent activities such as racquetball, squash, basketball, or tennis is that aerobic activities are easy to regulate by either speeding up or slowing down the pace. Because the given intensity of the workload elicits a given heart rate, these aerobic activities allow athletes to maintain heart rate at a specified or target level. Intermittent activities involve variable speeds and intensities that cause the heart rate to fluctuate considerably. Although these intermittent activities improve cardiorespiratory endurance, they are much more difficult to monitor in terms of intensity.

Frequency   To see at least minimal improvement in cardiorespiratory endurance, it is necessary for the average person to engage in no less than three sessions per week. If possible, one should aim for four or five sessions per week. A competitive athlete should be prepared to train as often as six times per week. Everyone should take off at least one day per week to allow for both psychological and physiological rest.

Duration   For minimal improvement to occur, an individual must participate in at least twenty minutes of continuous activity with the heart rate elevated to its working level. Recent evidence suggests that even shorter exercise bouts of as little as twelve minutes may be sufficient to show improvement. Generally, the greater the duration of the workout, the greater the improvement in cardiorespiratory endurance. The competitive athlete should train for at least forty-five minutes with the heart rate elevated to training levels.

Intensity   Of the four factors being considered, the most critical factor is the intensity of training, even though recommendations regarding training intensities vary. Intensity is particularly critical in the early stages of training, when the body is forced to make a lot of adjustments to increase workload demands.

Because heart rate is linearly related to the intensity of the exercise and to the rate of oxygen consumption, it becomes a relatively simple process to identify a specific workload (pace) that will make the heart rate plateau at the desired level. By monitoring heart rate, we know whether the pace is too fast or too slow to get heart rate into a target range.[4]

Several formulas identify a target training heart rate.[4] Exact determination of maximal heart rate involves exercising an individual at a maximal level and monitoring the heart rate using an electrocardiogram. This process is difficult outside a laboratory. However, an approximate estimate of maximal heart rate for both males and females is 220 beats per minute. Maximal heart rate is related to age. As age increases, maximal heart rate decreases. Thus, a relatively simple estimation of maximal heart rate (HR) would be Maximal HR = 220 − Age. If an athlete is working at 70 percent of maximal rate, the target heart rate can be calculated by multiplying $0.7 \times (220 - \text{Age})$.

Another commonly used formula that takes into account current level of fitness is the Karvonen equation.[26]

$$\text{Target training HR} = \text{Resting HR} + (0.6\,[\text{Maximal HR} - \text{Resting HR}])$$

Regardless of the formula used, to see minimal improvement in cardiorespiratory endurance, the heart rate should be elevated to at least 70 percent of its maximal rate.[10] A trained individual ought to be able to sustain a heart rate at the 85 percent level.

Interval Training

Unlike continuous training, interval training involves more intermittent activities. **Interval training** consists of alternating periods of relatively intense work and active recovery. It allows for performance of much more work at a more intense workload over a longer period of time than does working continuously.[34]

It is most desirable in continuous training to work at an intensity of about 60 percent to 80 percent of maximal heart rate. Obviously, sustaining activity at a relatively high intensity over a twenty-minute period would be extremely difficult. The advantage of interval training is that it allows work at this 80 percent or higher level for a short period of time followed by an active period of recovery during which an individual may be working at only 30 percent to 45 percent of maximum heart rate.[17] Thus, the intensity of the workout and its duration can be greater than with continuous training.

Most sports are anaerobic, involving short bursts of intense activity followed by a sort of active recovery period (for example, football, basketball, soccer, or tennis). Training with the interval technique allows the athlete to be more sport-specific during the workout. With interval training the overload principle is applied by making the training period much more intense.

There are several important considerations in interval training. The training period is the amount of time that continuous activity is actually being performed, and the recovery period is the time between training periods. A set is a group of combined training and recovery periods, and repetitions are the number of training and recovery periods per set. Training time or distance refers to the rate or distance of the training period. The training-recovery ratio indicates a time ratio for training versus recovery.

An example of interval training would be a soccer player running sprints. An interval workout would involve running ten,120-yard sprints with a 45-second walking recovery period between each sprint. During this training session the soccer player's heart rate would probably increase to 85 percent to 90 percent of maximal level during the dash and should probably fall to the 30 percent to 45 percent level during the recovery period.

Fartlek Training

Fartlek, a training technique that is a type of cross-country running, originated in Sweden. Fartlek literally means "speed play." It is similar to interval training in that the athlete must run for a specified period of time; however, specific pace and speed are not identified. The course for a fartlek workout should be some type of varied terrain with some level running, some uphill and downhill running, and some running through obstacles such as trees or rocks. The object is to put surges into a running workout, varying the length of the surges according to individual purposes. One advantage of fartlek training is that because the terrain is always changing, the course may prevent boredom and may actually be relaxing.

To improve cardiorespiratory endurance, fartlek training must elevate the heart rate to at least minimal training levels. Fartlek may best be utilized as an off-season conditioning activity or as a change-of-pace activity to counteract the boredom of training using the same activity day after day.

Equipment for Improving Cardiorespiratory Endurance

The extent and variety of fitness and exercise equipment available to the consumer is at times mind boggling. Prices of equipment can range from $2 for a jump rope to $60,000 for certain computer-driven isokinetic devices. It is certainly not necessary to purchase expensive exercise equipment to see good results. Many of the same physiological benefits can be achieved from using a $2 jump rope as from running

interval training
Alternating periods of work with active recovery.

Guidelines for choosing exercise equipment

Exercise bicycle

Most models work only the lower body, but some have pumping handlebars for arms and shoulders. Some can be programmed for various workouts, such as climbing hills. Some models let you pedal backward, which enhances the work on your hamstring muscles. Look for

- smooth pedaling motion
- a comfortable seat
- handlebars that adjust to your height
- pedal straps to keep your feet from slipping and to make your legs work on the up-stroke too
- easy-to-adjust workload
- solid construction

Treadmill

Some machines have adjustable inclines to simulate hills and make workouts more strenuous. Some can be programmed for various preset workouts. Look for

- easily adjustable speed and incline
- a running surface that is wide and long enough for your stride and that absorbs shock well
- a strong motor that can handle high speeds and a heavy load

Stair climber

Some larger models simulate real stair climbing. But most home models have pedals that work against your weight as you pump your legs; this feature puts less strain on your knees since you don't take real steps. Some people prefer pedals that remain parallel to the floor; others like pivoting pedals. Models with independent pedals provide a more natural stepping motion. Look for

- smooth stepping action
- large comfortable pedals with no wobble
- easily adjustable resistance
- comfortable handlebars or rails for balance

Rowing machine

A rowing machine provides a fuller workout than does running or cycling because it tones muscles in the upper body. Most machines have hydraulic pistons to provide variable resistance; many larger models use a flywheel. Piston models have hydraulic arms and are cheaper and more compact than are flywheel models, which have a smoother action that is usually more like real rowing. One new model actually has a flywheel in a water tank to mimic real rowing. Look for

- seats and oars that move smoothly
- footrests that pivot

Cross-country ski machine

These machines work most muscle groups. They simulate the outdoor sport: your feet slide in the tracks, and your hands pull on cords or poles, either independently or in synchronized movements. Machines with cords rather than poles may provide an especially strenuous upper-body workout. Look for

- a base that is long enough to accommodate your stride
- adjustable leg and arm resistance
- smooth action

Focus

Fitness testing

Muscle strength, power, endurance

One repetition maximum tests
Timed push-ups
Timed sit-ups
Chin-ups
Bar dips
Flexed arm hang
Vertical jump

Flexibility

Sit and reach test
Trunk extension test
Shoulder lift test

Cardiorespiratory endurance

Cooper's 12-minute walk/run
1.5 mile run
Harvard step test

Speed

6-second dash
10 to 60 yard dash

Agility

T-test
Edgren side step
SEMO agility test

Balance

Stork test

Fitness testing references

Baumgartner T, Jackson A: *Measurement for evaluation in physical education and exercise science,* Dubuque, Iowa, 1999, WCB/McGraw-Hill.

Prentice W: *Fitness and wellness for life,* ed 6, Dubuque, Iowa, 1999, WCB/McGraw-Hill.

Semenick D: Testing procedures and protocols. In Baechle T, editor: *Essentials of strength training and conditioning,* Champaign, Ill, 1994, Human Kinetics.

on a $10,000 treadmill. *Focus Box:* "Guidelines for choosing exercise equipment" identifies and discusses some of the more widely used pieces of exercise equipment.

FITNESS ASSESSMENT

Fitness testing provides the coach, athletic trainer, or strength and conditioning coach with information relative to the effectiveness of the conditioning program for an individual athlete. Testing may be done in a pretest/posttest format to determine significant improvement from some baseline measure. Tests may be used to assess flexibility, muscular strength, endurance, power, cardiorespiratory endurance, speed, balance, or agility, depending on the stated goals of the training and conditioning program. A variety of established tests can be used to assess these parameters. *Focus Box:* "Fitness testing" lists various tests that can be administered along with recommended references to consult for specific testing procedures and for in-depth testing directions.

SUMMARY

- Proper physical conditioning for sports participation should prepare the athlete for a high-level performance while helping to prevent injuries inherent to that sport.

- Year-round conditioning is essential in most sports to assist in preventing injuries. Periodization is an approach to conditioning that attempts to bring about peak performance while reducing injuries and overtraining in the athlete by developing a training and conditioning program to be followed throughout the various seasons.

- Physical conditioning must follow the SAID principle, which is an acronym for specific adaptation to imposed demands. Conditioning must work toward making the body as lean as possible, commensurate with the athlete's sport.

- A proper warm-up should precede conditioning, and a proper cooldown should follow. It takes at least fifteen to thirty minutes of gradual warm-up to bring the body to a state of readiness for vigorous sports training and participation. Warming up consists of a general, unrelated activity followed by a specific, related activity.

- Optimum flexibility is necessary for success in most sports. Too much flexibility can allow joint trauma to occur, and too little flexibility can result in muscle tears or strains. Ballistic stretching exercises should be avoided. The safest means of increasing flexibility are static stretching and the proprioceptive neuromuscular facilitation (PNF) technique, consisting of slow-reversal-hold-relax, contract-relax, and hold-relax methods.

- Strength is the capacity to exert a force or the ability to perform work against a resistance. There are numerous means to develop strength, including isometric, isotonic, and isokinetic muscle contraction. Isometric exercise generates heat energy by forcefully contracting the muscle in a stable position that produces no change in the length of the muscle. Isotonic exercise involves shortening and lengthening a muscle through a complete range of motion. Isokinetic exercise allows resisted movement through a full range at a specific velocity. Circuit training uses a series of exercise stations to improve strength and flexibility. Plyometric training uses a quick eccentric contraction to facilitate a more explosive concentric contraction.

- Cardiorespiratory endurance is the ability to perform whole-body, large-muscle activities repeatedly for long periods of time. Maximal oxygen consumption is the greatest determinant of the level of cardiorespiratory endurance. Most sport activities involve some combination of both aerobic and anaerobic metabolism. Improvement of cardiorespiratory endurance may be accomplished through continuous, interval, or fartlek training.

Web Sites

Health and Fitness Worldguide Forum:
http://www.worldguide. com/Fitness/hf.html

The information provided includes anatomy, strength, cardiovascular exercise, nutrition, and sports medicine.

Stretching and Flexibility: Everything you never wanted to know:
http://www.cs.huji.ac.il/papers/rma/stretching_toc. html

This paper by Brad Appleton gives detailed information on stretching and stretching techniques. It includes normal ranges of motion, flexibility, how to stretch, the physiology of stretching, and the types of stretching including PNF.

Mesomorphosis Interactive: Cardiovascular Exercise Principles and Guidelines: http://mesomorphosis.com/tackett/cardio1.htm

The topics that are discussed include warm-up, stretching, cooldown, frequency of exercise, and duration of exercise. There are also links to related pages that may be informative.

Fitness World: http://www.fitnessworld.com

The information at this site is about fitness in general and includes access to Fitness Management magazine.

Solutions to Critical Thinking EXERCISES

4-1 During the early part of the preparatory period, training should be at a low intensity with a high volume of repetitions, using activities that may or may not be directly related to football. This phase may last from several weeks to two months. The intensity and volume of these activities progress to moderate levels. Weight-training activities should eventually become more specific to football. Just before the preseason, the athlete trains at a high intensity. The volume of training is decreased so that full recovery is allowed between sessions.

4-2 Although athletes should make every effort to maintain existing levels of fitness during the rehabilitation period, it is imperative that to improve their fitness to competitive levels, athletes in any sport must practice or engage in that specific activity. The football player must begin a heavy strength-training program for the upper body immediately in the postseason and continue to progressively return to heavy lifting with the lower extremity as soon as the healing process will allow. It is essential for this player to progressively increase the intensity and variety of conditioning drills that specifically relate to performance at his particular position.

4-3 The warm-up should begin with a five- to seven-minute slow jog during which the athlete should break into a light sweat. At that point, she should engage in stretching (using either static or PNF techniques), concentrating on quadriceps, hamstrings, groin, and hip abductor muscles. Each specific stretch should be repeated four times, and the stretch should be held for fifteen to twenty seconds. Once the workout begins, the athlete should gradually and moderately increase the intensity of her activity. She may also find it effective to stretch during the cooldown period after the workout.

4-4 Weight training will not have a negative effect on flexibility as long as the lifting technique is done properly. Lifting the weight through a full range of motion will serve to improve strength and simultaneously maintain range of motion. A female swimmer is not likely to bulk up to the point at which range of motion will be affected by muscle size. It is also important to recommend that this athlete continue to incorporate active stretching into her training regimen.

4-5 The shot put, like many other dynamic movements in sport, requires not only great strength but also the ability to generate that strength rapidly. To develop muscular power, this athlete must engage in dynamic, explosive training techniques, which will help him develop his ability. Power lifting techniques should be helpful. Plyometric exercises using weights for added resistance will help him improve his speed of muscular contraction against some resistive force.

4-6 Because this athlete suffers from a lower extremity injury in which weight bearing is limited, alternative activities such as swimming or riding a stationary exercise bike should be incorporated into her rehabilitation program immediately. If the pressure on her ankle when riding an exercise bike is too painful, she may find it helpful initially to use a bike that incorporates upper extremity exercise. The athletic trainer should recommend that this soccer player engage in a minimum of thirty minutes of continuous training as well as some higher intensity interval training to maintain both aerobic and anaerobic fitness.

REVIEW QUESTIONS AND CLASS ACTIVITIES

1. Why is year-round conditioning so important for injury prevention?

2. In terms of injury prevention, list as many advantages as you can for conditioning.

3. How does the SAID principle relate to sports conditioning and injury prevention?

4. What is the value of proper warm-up and cooldown to sports injury prevention?

5. Critically observe how a variety of sports use warm-up and cooldown procedures.

6. Compare ways to increase flexibility and how they may decrease or increase the athlete's susceptibility to injury.

7. How may increasing strength decrease susceptibility to injury?

8. Compare different techniques of increasing strength. How may each technique be an advantage or a disadvantage to the athlete in terms of injury prevention?

9. Discuss the relationships among maximal oxygen consumption, heart rate, stroke volume, and cardiac output.

10. Differentiate between aerobic and anaerobic training methods.

11. How is continuous training different from interval training?

REFERENCES

1. Allerheiligen W: Speed development and plyometric training. In Baechle T, editor: *Essentials of strength training and conditioning*, Champaign, Ill, 1994, Human Kinetics.

2. Allerheiligen W: Stretching and warm-up. In Baechle T, editor: *Essentials of strength training and conditioning*, Champaign, Ill, 1994, Human Kinetics.

3. Alter M: *The science of stretching*, Champaign, Ill, 1996, Human Kinetics.

4. American College of Sports Medicine: *Guidelines for exercise testing and prescription*, Philadelphia, 1995, Lea & Febiger.

5. Baker D, Wilson G, Carlyon B: Generality vs. specificity: a comparison of dynamic and isometric measures of strength and speed-strength, *Eur J Appl Physiol* 68:350, 1994.

6. Bandy W, Irion J: The effect of time on static stretch in the flexibility of the hamstring muscles, *J Orthop Sports Phys Ther* 74:845, 1994.

7. Berger R: *Conditioning for men*, Boston, 1973, Allyn & Bacon.

8. Blanke D: Flexibility. In Mellion M, editor: *Sports medicine secrets*, Philadelphia, 1994, Hanley & Belfus.

9. Booth F, Thomason D: Molecular and cellular adaptation of muscle in response to exercise: perspectives of various models, *Physiol Rev* 71:541, 1991.

10. Brooks G, Fahey T, White T: *Exercise physiology: human bioenergetics and its applications*, Mountain View, Calif, 1996, Mayfield.

11. Chu D: *Jumping into plyometrics*, Champaign, Ill, 1992, Human Kinetics.

12. DeLorme TL, Watkins AL: *Progressive resistance exercise*, New York, 1951, Appleton-Century-Crofts.

13. Duda M: Plyometrics: a legitimate form of power training, *Physician Sportsmed* 16:213, 1988.

14. Dudley GA, Fleck SJ: Strength and endurance training: are they mutually exclusive? *Sports Med* 4(2):79, 1987 (review).

15. Faulkner J, Green H, White T. Response and adaptation of skeletal muscle to changes in physical activity. In Bouchard C, Shepard R, Stephens J, editors: *Physical activity, fitness, and health*, Champaign, Ill, 1994, Human Kinetics.

16. Fleck S, Kraemer W: *Designing resistance training programs*, Champaign, Ill, 1997, Human Kinetics.

17. Gaesser GA, Wilson LA: Effects of continuous and interval training on the parameters of the power-endurance time relationship for high-intensity exercise, *Int J Sports Med* 9(6):417, 1988.

18. Girouard C, Hurley B: Does strength training inhibit gains in range of motion from flexibility training in older adults? *Med Sci Sports Exerc* 2:1444, 1995.

19. Green J, Patla A: Maximal aerobic power: neuromuscular and metabolic considerations, *Med Sci Sports Exerc* 24:3846, 1992.

20. Green W: *The clinical measurement of joint motion*, Rosemont, Ill, 1994, American Academy of Orthopedic Surgeons.

21. Harman E: The biomechanics of resistance exercise. In Baechle T, editor: *Essentials of strength training and conditioning*, Champaign, Ill, 1994, Human Kinetics.

22. Hather B, Tesch P, Buchanan P: Influence of concentric actions on skeletal muscle adaptations to resistance training, *Acta Physiol Scanda* 99:105, 1991.

23. Hawley J, Myburgh K, Noakes T: Maximal oxygen consumption: a contemporary perspective. In Fahey T, editor: *Encyclopedia of sports medicine and exercise physiology*, New York, 1995, Mayfield.

24. Hendrick A: Flexibility and the conditioning program, *Natl Strength Cond Assoc J* 15(4):62, 1993.

25. Hickson R, Hidaka C, Foster C: Skeletal muscle fiber type, resistance training, and strength-related performance, *Med Sci Sports Exerc* 26:593, 1994.

26. Karvonen MJ, Kentala E, Mustala O: The effects of training on heart rate: a longitudinal study, *Ann Med Exp Biol* 35:305, 1957.

27. Knott M, Voss P: *Proprioceptive neuromuscular facilitation*, ed 3, New York, 1985, Harper & Row.

28. Kraemer W: General adaptation to resistance and endurance training programs. In Baechle T, editor: *Essentials of strength training and conditioning*, Champaign, Ill, 1994, Human Kinetics.

29. Kraemer W, Fleck S: *Strength training for young athletes*, Champaign, Ill, 1993, Human Kinetics.

30. Kraemer W, Patton J, Gordon S: Compatibility of high-intensity strength and endurance training on hormonal and skeletal muscle adaptations, *J App Physiol* 78:976, 1995.

31. Kuramoto A, Payne V: Predicting muscular strength in women, *Research Quarterly* 66:168, 1995.

32. Latin R, Elias B: Predictions of maximum oxygen uptake from treadmill walking and running, *J Sports Med Phys Fitness* 33:3439,1993.

33. Logan GA, Wallis EL: Recent findings in learning and performance. Paper presented at the Southern Section Meeting, California Association for Health, Physical Education, and Recreation, Pasadena, Calif, 1960.

34. MacDougall D, Sale D: Continuous vs. interval training: a review for the athlete and coach, *Can J Appl Sport Sci* 6:93, 1981.

35. McArdle W, Katch F, Katch V: *Exercise physiology, energy, nutrition, and human performance*, Philadelphia, 1996, Lea & Febiger.

36. McComas A: Human neuromuscular adaptations that accompany changes in activity, *Med Sci Sports Exerc* 26(12):1498, 1994.

37. Norkin C, White D: *Measurement of joint motion: a guide to goniometry*, Philadelphia, 1995, F. A. Davis.

38. Perrin DH: *Isokinetic exercise and assessment*, Champaign, Ill, 1993, Human Kinetics.

39. Prentice W: *Fitness and wellness for life*, ed 6, Dubuque, Iowa, 1999, WCB/McGraw-Hill.

40. Prentice W: Proprioceptive neuromuscular facilitation techniques. In Prentice W: *Rehabilitation techniques in sports medicine*, Dubuque, Iowa, 1999, WCB/McGraw-Hill.

41. Rehfeldt H et al: Force, endurance time, and cardiovascular responses in voluntary isometric contractions of different muscle groups, *Biomed Biochim Acta* 48(5-6):S509, 1989.

42. Sanders M: Weight training and conditioning. In Sanders B: *Sports physical therapy*, Norwalk, Conn, 1997, Appleton & Lange.

43. Sharkey J: Is ballistic stretching back? *Ultra Fit Australia* 22:22,1995.

44. Shellock F, Prentice WE: Warm-up and stretching for improved physical performance and prevention of sport related injury, *Sports Med* 2:267, 1985.

45. Soest A, Bobbert M: The role of muscle properties in control of explosive movements, *Biol Cybern* 69:195, 1993.

46. Stamford B: A stretching primer, *Physician Sportsmed* 22(9):85, 1994.

47. Staron R, Karapondo D, Kramer W: Skeletal muscle adaptations during the early phase of heavy resistance training in men and women, *J App Physiol* 76:1247, 1994.

48. Surburg P: Flexibility: training program design. In Miller P, editor: *Fitness programming and physical disability*, Champaign, Ill, 1995, Human Kinetics.

49. van Mechelen P: Prevention of running injuries by warm-up, cooldown, and stretching, *Am J Sports Med* 21(5):711, 1993.

50. Wathen D: Periodization: concepts and applications. In Baechle T, editor: *Essentials of strength training and conditioning*, Champaign, Ill, 1994, Human Kinetics.

51. Weltman A, Stamford B: Strength training: free weights vs. machines, *Physician Sportsmed* 10:197, 1982.

52. Wessel J, Wan A: Effect of stretching on intensity of delayed-onset muscle soreness, *I Sports Med* 112:83, 1994.

53. Worrell T, Smith T, Winegardner J: Effect of hamstring stretching on hamstring muscle performance, *J Orthop Sports Phys Ther* 20(3):154, 1994.

ANNOTATED BIBLIOGRAPHY

Alter M: *The science of stretching*, Boston, 1996, Houghton Mifflin.

This text explains the principles and techniques of stretching and details the anatomy and physiology of muscle and connective tissue. It includes guidelines for developing a flexibility program, illustrated stretching exercises, and warm-up drills.

Anderson B: *Stretching*, Bolinas, Calif, 1966, Shelter.

An extremely comprehensive best-selling text on stretching exercises for the entire body.

Baechle T, editor: *Essentials of strength training and conditioning*, Champaign, Ill, 1994, Human Kinetics.

A book from the National Strength Coaches Association that explains the science, theory, and practical application of various aspects of conditioning in a very concise, easily understood text.

Brooks G, Fahey T, White T: *Exercise physiology: human bioenergetics and its applications*, Mountain View, Calif, 1996, Mayfield.

An up-to-date, advanced text in exercise physiology that contains a comprehensive listing of the most current journal articles relative to exercise physiology.

Chu D: *Jumping into plyometrics*, Champaign, Ill, 1992, Human Kinetics.

This text helps the athlete develop a safe plyometric training program with exercises designed to improve quickness, speed, upper body strength, jumping ability, balance, and coordination. It is well illustrated.

Foss M, Keteyian S: *Fox's physiological basis for exercise and sport*, Dubuque, Iowa, 1998, McGraw-Hill.

A complete text that discusses the rationale and physiological principles underlying various aspects of an exercise program. Cardiorespiratory endurance is among several facets of fitness emphasized in this text.

Prentice W: *Fitness and wellness for life*, ed 6, Dubuque, Iowa, 1999, WCB/McGraw-Hill.

A comprehensive fitness text that covers all aspects of a training and conditioning program.

Nutritional Considerations

When you finish this chapter you should be able to

- Identify the six classes of nutrients and describe their major functions.
- Explain the importance of good nutrition in enhancing performance and preventing injuries.
- Describe the advantages or disadvantages of supplementing nutrients in the athlete's diet.
- Explain the advantages and disadvantages of a preevent meal.
- Explain the distinction between body weight and body composition.
- Explain the principle of caloric balance and how to assess it.
- Assess body composition using skinfold calipers.
- Describe methods for losing and gaining weight.
- List the signs of bulimia and anorexia nervosa.

The relation of nutrition, diet, and weight control to overall health and fitness is an issue of critical importance to an athlete. Athletes who practice sound nutritional habits reduce the likelihood of injury by maintaining a higher standard of healthful living. We know that eating a well-balanced diet can positively contribute to the development of strength, flexibility, and cardio-respiratory endurance.[57] Unfortunately, misconceptions, fads, and in many cases superstitions regarding nutrition affect dietary habits, particularly in the athletic population.[49]

Many athletes associate successful performance with the consumption of special foods or supplements. An athlete who is performing well may be reluctant to change dietary habits regardless of whether the diet is physiologically beneficial to overall health.[31] There is no question that the psychological aspect of allowing the athlete to eat whatever he or she is most comfortable with can greatly affect performance. The problem is that these eating habits tend to become accepted as beneficial and may become traditional when in fact they may be physiologically detrimental to athletic performance. Thus, many nutrition "experts" tend to disseminate nutritional information based on traditional rather than experimental information.[12] The athletic trainer must possess a strong knowledge base in nutrition so that he or she may serve as an informational resource for the athlete.

NUTRITION BASICS

Nutrition is the science of the substances that are found in food that are essential to life. A substance is essential if it must be supplied by the diet.[58] There are six classes of nutrients: carbohydrates (CHO), fats, proteins, vitamins, minerals, and water. Nutrients are necessary for three major roles: growth, repair, and maintenance of all tissues; regulation of body processes; and production of energy.[55]

Nutrient density describes foods that supply adequate amounts of vitamins and minerals in relation to their caloric value. The so-called junk foods provide excessive amounts of calories from fat and sugar in relation to vitamins and minerals and therefore are not nutrient dense. However, many people live on junk foods that displace more nutrient-dense foods from their diet. This behavior is not healthful in the long run.[55]

The six classes of nutrients are carbohydrates, fats, proteins, vitamins, minerals, and water.

Nutrient-dense foods supply adequate amounts of vitamins and minerals in relation to caloric value.

ENERGY SOURCES

Carbohydrates

Athletes have increased energy needs. Carbohydrates are the body's most efficient source of energy and should be relied on to fill that need.[18] For the athlete, carbohydrate intake should account for 55 percent to 70 percent of total caloric intake. The following sections describe different forms of carbohydrates and their role in the production of energy and the maintenance of health.[55]

Sugars

Carbohydrates are sugar, starches, or fiber.

Carbohydrates are classified as simple (sugars) or complex (starch and most forms of fiber). Sugars are further divided into monosaccharides and disaccharides. Monosaccharides, single sugars, are found mostly in fruits, syrups, and honey. Glucose (blood sugar) is a monosaccharide. Milk sugar (lactose) and table sugar (sucrose) are combinations of two monosaccharides and are called disaccharides. Because sugar contributes little in the way of other nutrients, the amount of sugar eaten should account for less than 15 percent of the total caloric intake.

Starches

Starches are complex carbohydrates. A starch is made up of long chains of glucose units. During the digestion process, the starch chain is broken down and the glucose units are free to be absorbed. Food sources of starch, such as rice, potatoes, and breads, often provide vitamins and minerals in addition to serving as the body's principal source of glucose. Many people believe that starchy foods contribute to obesity. However, most of these foods are eaten with fats from butter, margarine, sauces, and gravies that make the food more enjoyable but contribute an excess of calories.

Glycolysis is the process that breaks down glucose to produce energy.

The body cannot use starches and many sugars directly from food for energy. It must obtain the simple sugar glucose (blood sugar). During digestion and metabolism, starches and disaccharide sugars are broken down and converted to glucose. The glucose that is not needed for immediate energy is stored as glycogen in the liver and muscle cells. Glucose can be released from glycogen later if needed. The body, however, can store only a limited amount of glucose as glycogen. Any extra amount of glucose is converted to body fat. When the body experiences an inadequate intake of dietary carbohydrate, it uses protein to make glucose, but the protein is then diverted from its own important functions. Therefore, a supply of glucose must be kept available to prevent the use of protein for energy. This is called the protein-sparing action of glucose.

Fiber

In recent years, researchers have given considerable attention to the importance of fiber in the diet. Fiber forms the structural parts of plants and is not digested by humans. Fiber is not found in animal sources of food. There are two kinds of dietary fiber: soluble and insoluble. Soluble fiber includes gums and pectins; cellulose is the primary insoluble form. Sources of soluble fiber are oatmeal, legumes, and some fruits. Food sources of insoluble fiber include whole grain breads and bran cereals.

Because it is not digested, fiber passes through the intestinal tract and adds bulk. Fiber aids normal elimination by reducing the amount of time required for wastes to move through the digestive tract, which is believed to reduce the risk of colon cancer. Also, increased fiber intake is thought to reduce the risk of coronary artery disease. Soluble forms of fiber bind to cholesterol passing through the digestive tract and prevent its absorption, which can reduce blood cholesterol levels. Foods rich in saturated fats (meats, in particular) often take the place of fiber-rich foods in the diet, thus increasing cholesterol absorption and formation. Consumption of adequate amounts of fiber has been associated with lowered incidences of obesity, constipation, colitis, appendicitis, and diabetes.

The recommended amount of fiber in the diet is approximately twenty-five grams per day.[53] Unfortunately, the average person consumes only ten to fifteen grams per day. Fiber intake should be increased by increasing the amount of whole grain cereal products and fruits and vegetables in the diet rather than by using fiber supplements. Excessive consumption of fiber may cause intestinal discomfort as well as increased losses of calcium and iron.

Fats

Fats are another essential component of the diet. They are the most concentrated source of energy, providing more than twice the calories per gram when compared with carbohydrates or proteins. Fat is used as a primary source of energy. Some dietary fat is needed to make food more flavorful and for sources of the fat-soluble vitamins. Also, a minimal amount of fat is essential for normal growth and development.

Dietary fat represents approximately 40 percent to 50 percent of the total caloric intake. A substantial amount of the fat is from saturated fatty acids. This intake is believed to be too high and may contribute to the prevalence of obesity, certain cancers, and coronary artery disease. The recommended intake should be limited to less than 30 percent of total calories, with saturated fat reduced to less than 10 percent of total calories.[53]

Saturated versus Unsaturated Fat

Both plant and animal foods provide sources of dietary fat. About 95 percent of the fat consumed is in the form of triglycerides. Depending on their chemical nature, fatty acids may be saturated or unsaturated. The unsaturated fatty acids can be subdivided into monounsaturates or polyunsaturates. Therefore the terms *saturated, monounsaturated,* and *polyunsaturated* are used to describe the chemical nature of the fat in foods. The triglycerides that make up food fats are usually mixtures of saturated and unsaturated fatty acids but are classified according to the type that predominates. In general, fats containing more unsaturated fatty acids are from plants and are liquid at room temperature. Saturated fatty acids are derived mainly from animal sources.

Other Fats

Phospholipids and sterols represent the remaining 5 percent of fats. Phospholipids include lecithin; cholesterol is the best known sterol. Cholesterol is consumed in the diet from animal foods; it is not supplied by plant sources of food. Generally, it is wise to avoid eating foods high in cholesterol. Although cholesterol is essential to many body functions, the body can manufacture cholesterol from CHO, proteins, and especially saturated fat. Thus there is little if any need to consume additional amounts of cholesterol in the diet. The American Heart Association recommends consuming less than 300 mg per day.

One type of unsaturated fatty acid seems to serve as a protective mechanism against certain disease processes. The omega-3 fatty acids apparently have the capability of reducing the likelihood of diseases such as heart disease, stroke, and hypertension. These fatty acids are found in cold-water fish. However, experts do not recommend the use of fish oil supplements as a source of omega-3 fatty acids.

Fat Substitutes

Fat-free products containing artificial fat substitutes, such as Simplese and Olean, are now available to the consumer. These products contain no cholesterol and 80 percent fewer calories than similar products made with fat. Despite FDA approval of these fat substitutes, some individuals have reported abdominal cramping and diarrhea when using them.[8]

5-1

Critical Thinking Exercise

A female softball player has been told by her coach that she is slightly overweight and needs to lose a few pounds. The athlete has been watching television and reading about how important it is to limit the dietary intake of fat for losing weight. She has decided to go on a diet that is essentially fat free and is totally convinced that this will help her lose weight.

? What should the athletic trainer tell her about avoiding the excessive intake of fat as a means of losing weight?

Fats may be saturated or unsaturated.

Dietary recommendations: CHO, 60 percent; fats, 25 percent; proteins, 15 percent.

Proteins

Proteins make up the major structural components of the body. They are needed for growth, maintenance, and repair of all body tissues. In addition, proteins are needed to make enzymes, many hormones, and antibodies that help fight infection. In general, the body prefers not to use much protein for energy; instead it relies on fats and carbohydrates. Protein intake should be around 12 percent to 15 percent of total calories.

Amino Acids

Proteins are made up of amino acids.

The basic units that make up proteins are smaller compounds called amino acids. Most of the body's proteins are made up of about twenty amino acids. Amino acids can be linked together in a wide variety of combinations, which is why there are so many different forms and uses of proteins. Most of the amino acids can be produced as needed in the body. The others cannot be made to any significant degree and therefore must be supplied by the diet. The amino acids obtained through food are referred to as the essential amino acids. The amount of protein as well as the levels of the individual essential amino acids is important for determining the quality of diet. A diet that contains large amounts of protein will not support growth, repair, and maintenance of tissues if the essential amino acids are not available in the proper proportions.[37]

Most of the proteins from animal foods contain all the essential amino acids that humans require and are called complete, or high-quality, proteins. Incomplete proteins, that is, those sources of protein that do not contain all the essential amino acids, usually are from plant sources of food.

Protein Sources and Need

5-2

Critical Thinking Exercise

A volleyball player complains that she constantly feels tired and lethargic even though she thinks that she is eating well and getting a sufficient amount of sleep. A teammate has suggested that the player begin taking vitamin supplements, which the teammate claims gives her more energy and makes her more resistant to fatigue. The athlete comes to the athletic trainer to ask advice about what kind of vitamins she needs to take.

? What facts should the athletic trainer explain to the athlete about vitamin supplementation, and what recommendations should be made?

Most athletes do not have difficulty meeting protein needs because the typical diet is rich in protein, and many athletes consume more than twice the recommended levels of protein. There is no advantage to consuming more protein, particularly in the form of protein supplements. If more protein is supplied than needed, the body must convert the excess to fat for storage. This conversion can create a situation in which excess water is removed from cells, leading to dehydration and possible damage to the kidneys or liver. Protein supplements may also create imbalances of the chemicals that make up proteins, the amino acids, which is not desirable. A condition of the bones, osteoporosis, has been linked to a diet that contains too much protein.[5]

Increased physical activity increases a person's need for energy, not necessarily for protein.[39] The increases in muscle mass that result from conditioning and training are associated with only a small increase in protein requirements that can easily be met with the usual diet. Therefore no supplements are needed by an athlete.

REGULATOR NUTRIENTS

Vitamins

Although vitamins are required in extremely small amounts when compared with water, proteins, carbohydrates, and fats, they perform essential roles, primarily as regulators of body processes.[5] Thirteen vitamins have specific roles in the body, many of which are still being explored. In the past, letters were assigned as names for vitamins. Today, most are known by their scientific names. Vitamins are classified into two groups: fat-soluble vitamins, which are dissolved in fats and stored in the body, and water-soluble vitamins, which are dissolved in watery solutions and are not stored. Table 5-1 lists the vitamins and indicates their primary functions.

Fat-Soluble Vitamins

Fat-soluble vitamins: A, D, E, and K.

Vitamins A, D, E, and K are fat soluble. They are found in the fatty portions of foods and in oils. Because they are stored in the body's fat, it is possible to consume excess amounts and show the effects of vitamin poisoning.

TABLE 5-1 Vitamins

Vitamin	Major Function	Most Reliable Sources	Deficiency	Excess (Toxicity)
A	Maintains skin and other cells that line the inside of the body; bone and tooth development; growth; vision in dim light	Liver, milk, egg yolk, deep green and yellow fruits and vegetables	Night blindness; dry skin; growth failure	Headaches, nausea, loss of hair, dry skin, diarrhea
D	Normal bone growth and development	Exposure to sunlight; fortified dairy products; eggs and fish liver oils	Rickets in children—defective bone formation leading to deformed bones	Appetite loss, weight loss, failure to grow
E	Prevents destruction of polyunsaturated fats caused by exposure to oxidizing agents; protects cell membranes from destruction	Vegetable oils, some in fruits and vegetables, whole grains	Breakage of red blood cells leading to anemia	Nausea and diarrhea; interferes with vitamin K if vitamin D is also deficient; not as toxic as other fat-soluble vitamins
K	Production of blood-clotting substances	Green leafy vegetables; normal bacteria that live in intestines produce K that is absorbed	Increased bleeding time	
Thiamin	Needed for release of energy from carbohydrates, fats, and proteins	Cereal products, pork, peas, and dried beans	Lack of energy, nerve problems	
Riboflavin	Energy from carbohydrates, fats, and proteins	Milk, liver, fruits and vegetables, enriched breads and cereals	Dry skin, cracked lips	
Niacin	Energy from carbohydrates, fats, and proteins	Liver, meat, poultry, peanut butter, legumes, enriched breads and cereals	Skin problems, diarrhea, mental depression, and eventually death (rarely occurs in U.S.)	Skin flushing, intestinal upset, nervousness, intestinal ulcers
B$_6$	Metabolism of protein; production of hemoglobin	White meats, whole grains, liver, egg yolk, bananas	Poor growth, anemia	Severe loss of coordination from nerve damage
B$_{12}$	Production of genetic material; maintains central nervous system	Foods of animal origin	Neurological problems, anemia	
Folate (Folic acid)	Production of genetic material	Wheat germ, liver, yeast, mushrooms, green leafy vegetables, fruits	Anemia	
C (Ascorbic acid)	Formation and maintenance of connective tissue; tooth and bone formation; immune function	Fruits and vegetables	Scurvy (rare); swollen joints, bleeding gums, fatigue, bruising	Kidney stones, diarrhea
Pantothenic acid	Energy from carbohydrates, fats, proteins	Widely found in foods	Not observed in humans under normal conditions	
Biotin	Use of fats	Widely found in foods	Rare under normal conditions	

Water-Soluble Vitamins

Water-soluble vitamins: C, thiamin, riboflavin, niacin, B_6, B_{12}, folate, biotin, and panothenic acid.

The water-soluble vitamins consist of vitamin C, known as ascorbic acid, and the B-complex vitamins, most now referred to by their scientific names. B-complex vitamins include thiamin, riboflavin, niacin, B_6, folate, B_{12}, biotin, and pantothenic acid. Although vitamins are not metabolized for energy, thiamin, riboflavin, niacin, biotin, and pantothenic acid are used to regulate the metabolism of CHO, proteins, and fats to obtain energy. Vitamin B_6 regulates the body's use of amino acids. Folate and vitamin B_{12} are important in normal blood formation. Vitamin C is used for building bones and teeth, maintaining connective tissues, and strengthening the immune system. Unlike fat-soluble vitamins, water-soluble vitamins cannot be stored to any significant extent in the body and should be supplied in the diet each day.[5]

Antioxidants

Antioxidants: vitamin C, vitamin E, and beta-carotene.

Certain nutrients, called antioxidants, may prevent premature aging, certain cancers, heart disease, and other health problems.[30] An antioxidant protects vital cell components from the destructive effects of certain agents, including oxygen. Vitamin C, vitamin E, and beta-carotene are antioxidants. Beta-carotene is a plant pigment that is found in dark green, deep yellow, or orange fruits and vegetables. The body can convert beta-carotene to vitamin A. In the early 1980s, researchers reported that smokers who ate large quantities of fruits and vegetables rich in beta-carotene were less likely to develop lung cancer than were other smokers.[28] Since that time, more evidence is accumulating about the benefits of a diet rich in the antioxidant nutrients.[19]

Some experts believe that athletes should increase their intake of antioxidants, even if it means taking supplements. Others are more cautious.[27,28] Excess beta-carotene pigments circulate throughout the body and may turn the skin yellow. However, the pigment is not believed to be toxic like its nutrient cousin, vitamin A is. On the other hand, increasing intake of vitamins C and E is not without some risk. Excess vitamin C is not well absorbed; the excess is irritating to the intestines and creates diarrhea. Although less toxic than vitamins A or D, too much vitamin E causes health problems.

Vitamin Deficiencies

The illness that results from a lack of any nutrient, especially those nutrients, such as vitamins, needed in small amounts, is referred to as a deficiency disease.[44] Vitamin deficiency diseases are rare. Adequate amounts of the different vitamins, as with other nutrients, can be obtained if a wide variety of foods is eaten. For most people, vitamin supplements are a waste of money and can cause toxic effects if too many are taken. Many individuals think that vitamins are "foods" and are safe. However, in large doses, vitamins have druglike effects on the body. Table 5-1 describes some of vitamins' toxicity problems.

Minerals

More than twenty mineral elements have an essential role in the body and therefore must be supplied in the diet. These essential minerals are listed in Table 5-2. Most minerals are stored in the body, especially in the liver and bones. Magnesium is needed in energy-supplying reactions; sodium and potassium are important for the transmission of nerve impulses. Iron plays a role in energy metabolism but is also combined with a protein to form hemoglobin, the compound that transports oxygen in red blood cells. Calcium has many important functions: it is necessary for proper bone and teeth formation, blood clotting, and muscle contraction. In general, minerals have roles that are too numerous to detail within the scope of this book. Eating a wide variety of foods is the best way to obtain the minerals needed in the proper concentrations.[5]

TABLE 5-2 Minerals

Mineral	Major Role	Most Reliable Sources	Deficiency	Excess
Calcium	Bone and tooth formation; blood clotting; muscle contraction; nerve function	Dairy products	May lead to osteoporosis	Calcium deposits in soft tissues
Phosphorus	Skeletal development; tooth formation	Meats, dairy products, and other protein-rich foods	Rarely seen	
Sodium	Maintenance of fluid balance	Salt (sodium chloride) added to foods and sodium-containing preservatives		May contribute to the development of hypertension
Iron	Formation of hemoglobin; energy from carbohydrates, fats, and proteins	Liver and red meats, enriched breads and cereals	Iron-deficiency anemia	Can cause death in children from supplement overdose
Copper	Formation of hemoglobin	Liver, nuts, shellfish, cherries, mushrooms, whole grain breads and cereals	Anemia	Nausea and vomiting
Zinc	Normal growth and development	Seafood and meats	Skin problems, delayed development, growth problems	Interferes with copper use; may decrease high-density lipoprotein levels
Iodine	Production of the hormone thyroxin	Iodized salt, seafood	Mental and growth retardation; lack of energy	
Fluorine	Strengthens bones and teeth	Fluoridated water	Teeth are less resistant to decay	Damage to tooth enamel

Water

Water is the most essential of all the nutrients and should be the nutrient of greatest concern to the athlete.[55] It is the most abundant nutrient of the body, accounting for approximately 60 percent of the body weight. Water is essential for all the chemical processes that occur in the body, and an adequate supply of water is necessary for energy production and normal digestion of other nutrients. Water is also necessary for temperature control and for elimination of waste products of nutrient and body metabolism. Too little water leads to dehydration, and severe dehydration frequently leads to death. The average adult requires a minimum of 2.5 liters of water per day. (See *Focus Box*: "Directions for fluid ingestion.")

The body has a number of mechanisms designed specifically to maintain body water at near-normal level. Too little water leads to accumulation of solutes in the blood. These solutes signal the brain that the body is thirsty while signaling the kidney to conserve water. Excessive water dilutes these solutes, which signals the brain to stop drinking and the kidneys to get rid of the excess water.

Water is the only nutrient that is of greater importance to the athlete than to those people who are more sedentary, especially when the athlete is engaging in prolonged exercise carried out in a hot, humid environment. Such a situation may cause excessive sweating and subsequent losses of large amounts of water. Restriction of water during this time will result in dehydration. Symptoms of dehydration include fatigue, vomiting, nausea, exhaustion, fainting, and possibly death.

Replacing fluid after heavy sweating is far more important than replacing electrolytes.

Focus

Directions for fluid ingestion

When conditioning, training, or competing, the athlete should:

- Drink a pint (500 to 600 ml) of cold (40° to 50° F) water fifteen to thirty minutes before exercise.
- Avoid highly sugared drinks ingested within an hour of exercise (this drink elevates blood glucose and insulin and may lead to hyperglycemia).
- Ingest fluid that contains less than or equal to 2.5 g glucose per 100 ml water.
- Ingest fluid that contains a low concentration of ions (e.g., less than 0.2 g of sodium chloride and less than 0.2 g of potassium per quart [1000 ml] of fluid).

Electrolyte Requirements

Electrolytes: sodium, chloride, potassium, magnesium, and calcium.

Electrolytes, including sodium, chloride, potassium, magnesium, and calcium, are electrically charged ions. They maintain the balance of water outside the cell. Electrolyte replenishment may be needed when a person is not fit, suffers from extreme water loss, participates in a marathon, or has just completed an exercise period and is expected to perform at near-maximum effort within the next few hours. In most cases, electrolytes can be sufficiently replaced with a balanced diet, which can, if necessary, be salted slightly more than usual. Free access to water (ad libitum) before, during, and after activity should be the rule. Electrolyte losses are primarily responsible for muscle cramping and intolerance to heat. Sweating results not only in body water loss but in some electrolyte loss as well.[13]

In most cases, plain water is an effective and inexpensive means of fluid replacement for most types of exercise. Commercial drinks, rather than adequately hydrating the athlete, may in fact hinder water absorption because of their high sugar content. Drinks containing too much glucose, fructose, or sucrose are hypertonic and may draw water from blood plasma into the intestinal tract, dehydrating the athlete even more.[13] Electrolytes provided by commercial sports drinks are not needed unless the athlete is engaging in events such as ultramarathons.[40]

polymers
Natural or synthetic substances formed by the combination of two or more molecules of the same substance.

A new group of sports drinks that uses glucose **polymers** has been introduced. These drinks have the advantage of not causing the hypertonic problems of other commercial solutions. These drinks are most appropriate for highly intense and prolonged events that severely deplete glycogen stores.[43]

During cold weather, water is not as critical as in hot weather. Therefore a stronger electrolyte solution that allows a slower, more steady release of fluid from the stomach should be used. In hot weather or in cold weather, thirst is not an indicator of hydration.

NUTRIENT REQUIREMENTS AND RECOMMENDATIONS

A nutrient requirement is that amount of the nutrient that is needed to prevent the nutrient's deficiency disease. Nutrient needs vary among individuals within a population. A recommendation for a nutrient is different from the requirement for a nutrient. Scientists establish recommendations for nutrients and calories based on extensive scientific research and assessment of present dietary intakes.[22]

The US RDA helps consumers compare nutritional values of foods.

The U.S. Recommended Daily Allowances (US RDA) were designed to help consumers compare the nutritional value of many food products (Table 5-3A). Currently the RDAs are being changed to Dietary Reference Intakes (DRI). The term *RDA* is still being used as the actual amount recommended, and for some nutrients, these recommendations have not changed since 1989. However, several old RDAs have been downgraded and are now called Adequate Intakes (AI) because of insufficient knowledge to establish new DRIs (Table 5-3B).[22]

TABLE 5-3A Recommended Dietary Allowances,ᵃ Revised 1989 (Abridged) from the Food and Nutrition Board, National Academy of Sciences—National Research Council
Designed for the maintenance of good nutrition of practically all healthy people in the United States

Category	Age (year) or Condition	Weight (kg)	(lb)	Height (cm)	(in)	Protein (g)	Vitamin A (μg RE)ᶜ	Vitamin E (mg α-TE)ᵈ	Vitamin K (μg)	Vitamin C (μg)	Iron (mg)	Zinc (mg)	Iodine (μg)	Selenium (μg)
Males	15–18	66	145	176	69	59	1,000	10	65	60	12	15	150	50
	19–24	72	160	177	70	58	1,000	10	70	60	10	15	150	70
	25–50	79	174	176	70	63	1,000	10	80	60	10	15	150	70
	51+	77	170	173	68	63	1,000	10	80	60	10	15	150	70
Females	15–18	55	120	163	64	44	800	8	55	60	15	12	150	50
	19–24	58	128	164	65	46	800	8	60	60	15	12	150	55
	25–50	63	138	163	64	50	800	8	65	60	15	12	150	55
	51+	65	143	160	63	50	800	8	65	60	10	12	150	55
Pregnant						60	800	10	65	70	30	15	175	65
Lactating	1st 6 months					65	1,300	12	65	95	15	19	200	75
	2nd 6 months					62	1,200	11	65	90	15	16	200	75

ᵃThe allowances, expressed as average daily intakes over time, are intended to provide for individual variations among most normal persons as they live in the United States under usual environmental stresses. Diets should be based on a variety of common foods in order to provide other nutrients for which human requirements have been less well defined.

ᵇWeights and heights of Reference Adults are actual medians for the U.S. population of the designated age. The use of these figures does not imply that the height-to-weight ratios are ideal.

ᶜRetinol equivalents. 1 retinol equivalent = 1 μg retinol or 6 μg β-carotene.

ᵈα-tocopherol equivalents. 1 mg d-α tocopherol = 1 α-TE.

TABLE 5-3B Dietary Reference Intakes: Recommended Levels for Individual Intake from the Food and Nutrition Board, Institute of Medicine—National Academy of Sciences

Life-Stage Group	Calcium (mg/d)	Phosphorus (mg/d)	Magnesium (mg/d)	(μg/d)[a,b]	Fluoride (mg/d)	Thiamin (mg/d)	Riboflavin (mg/d)	Niacin (mg/d)[c]	B_6 (mg/d)	Folate (μg/d)[d]	B_{12} (μg/d)	Pantothenic Acid (mg/d)	Biotin (μg/d)	Choline[e] (mg/d)
Males														
14–18 yr	1,300*	1,250	410	5*	3*	1.2	1.3	16	1.3	400	2.4	5*	25*	550*
19–30 yr	1,000*	700	400	5*	4*	1.2	1.3	16	1.3	400	2.4	5*	30*	550*
31–50 yr	1,000*	700	420	5*	4*	1.2	1.3	16	1.3	400	2.4	5*	30*	550*
51–70 yr	1,200*	700	420	10*	4*	1.2	1.3	16	1.7	400	2.4[f]	5*	30*	550*
>70 yr	1,200*	700	420	15*	4*	1.2	1.3	16	1.7	400	2.4[f]	5*	30*	550*
Females														
14–18 yr	1,300*	1,250	360	5*	3*	1.0	1.0	14	1.2	400[g]	2.4	5*	25*	400*
19–30 yr	1,000*	700	310	5*	3*	1.1	1.1	14	1.3	400[g]	2.4	5*	30*	425*
31–50 yr	1,000*	700	320	5*	3*	1.1	1.1	14	1.3	400[g]	2.4	5*	30*	425*
51–70 yr	1,200*	700	320	10*	3*	1.1	1.1	14	1.5	400[g]	2.4[f]	5*	30*	425*
>70 yr	1,200*	700	320	15*	3*	1.1	1.1	14	1.5	400	2.4[f]	5*	30*	425*
Pregnancy														
≤18 yr	1,300*	1,250	400	5*	3*	1.4	1.4	18	1.9	600[h]	2.6	6*	30*	450*
19–30 yr	1,000*	700	350	5*	3*	1.4	1.4	18	1.9	600[h]	2.6	6*	30*	450*
31–50 yr	1,000*	700	360	5*	3*	1.4	1.4	18	1.9	600[h]	2.6	6*	30*	450*
Lactation														
≤18 yr	1,300*	1,250	360	5*	3*	1.5	1.6	17	2.0	500	2.8	7*	35*	550*
19–30 yr	1,000*	700	310	5*	3*	1.5	1.6	17	2.0	500	2.8	7*	35*	550*
31–50 yr	1,000*	700	320	5*	3*	1.5	1.6	17	2.0	500	2.8	7*	35*	550*

NOTE: This table presents Recommended Dietary Allowances (RDAs) in bold type and Adequate Intakes (AIs) in ordinary type followed by an asterisk (*). RDAs and AIs may both be used as goals for individual intake. RDAs are set to meet the needs of almost all (97 to 98 percent) individuals in a group. For healthy breastfed infants, the AI is the mean intake. The AI for other life-stage groups is believed to cover their needs, but lack of data or uncertainty in the data prevent clear specification of this coverage.

[a] As cholecalciferol. 1 μg cholecalciferol = 40 IU vitamin D.

[b] In the absence of adequate exposure to sunlight.

[c] As niacin equivalents. 1 mg of niacin = 60 mg of tryptohan.

[d] As dietary folate equivalents (DFE). 1 DFE = 1 μg food folate = 0.6 μg of folic acid (from fortified food or supplement) consumed with food = 0.5 μg of synthetic (supplemental) folic acid taken on an empty stomach.

[e] Although AIs have been set for choline, there are few data to assess whether a dietary supply of choline is needed at all stages of the life cycle, and it may be that the choline requirement can be met by endogenous synthesis at some of these stages.

[f] Since 10 to 30 percent of older people may malabsorb food-bound B_{12}, it is advisable for those older than 50 years to meet their RDA mainly by consuming foods fortified with B_{12} or a B_{12}-containing supplement.

[g] In view of evidence linking folate intake with neural tube defects in the fetus, it is recommended that all women capable of becoming pregnant consume 400 μg of synthetic folic acid from fortified foods and/or supplements in addition to intake of food folate from a varied diet.

[h] It is assumed that women will continue consuming 400 μg of folic acid until their pregnancy is confirmed and they enter prenatal care, which ordinarily occurs after the end of the periconceptional period—the critical time for formation of the neural tube.

Figure 5-1

A food label provides
nutritional information.

Nutrition Facts	
Serving Size 1/2 cup (114g)	
Servings Per Container 4	
Amount Per Serving	
Calories 260	Calories from Fat 120
	% Daily Value*
Total Fat 13g	20%
Saturated Fat 5g	25%
Cholesterol 30mg	10%
Sodium 660mg	28%
Total Carbohydrate 31g	11%
Dietary Fiber 0g	0%
Sugars 5g	
Protein 5g	
Vitamin A 4%	Vitamin C 2%
Calcium 15%	Iron 4%

*Percent Daily Values are based on a 2000
Calorie diet. Your daily values may be
higher or lower depending on your calorie
needs.

	Calories: 2000	2500
Total Fat	Less than 65g	80g
Sat. Fat	Less than 20g	25g
Cholesterol	Less than 300mg	300mg
Sodium	Less than 2,400mg	2,400mg
Total Carbohydrate	300g	375g
Dietary Fiber	25g	30g

Calories per gram
Fat 9 • Carbohydrate 4 • Protein 4

Food Labels

Food labels on packages help consumers make more informed food selections (Figure 5-1). Concern over the amount of fat, cholesterol, sodium, and fiber in the typical American diet led the drive for a more health-conscious label. For more than a decade, the US RDA appeared on nutrient labels. In the early 1990s, the old food labels were replaced by a new format that presents the information in the form of percentages of daily values based on a standard 2,000 calories.[21]

THE FOOD PYRAMID

Most people are familiar with the basic four food groups plan, which was introduced in the mid-1950s. More recently, the basic four has been redesigned into a food pyramid concept that is believed to do a better job in educating Americans about the relationship of food choices to health.[26] Figure 5-2 shows the food pyramid. For most of the food groupings, the pyramid specifies the minimum number of servings that should be eaten daily and shows examples of foods. Carbohydrate-rich foods (the breads and cereals group) form the foundation of the diet. The other food groups are shown according to their relative importance in a healthy diet. One major change from the basic four plan is that the fruits and vegetables are separated into two distinct groups, each with a specified number of servings. Note that fats and

Figure 5-2

The food pyramid offers examples of appropriate food selections important to an athlete's diet.

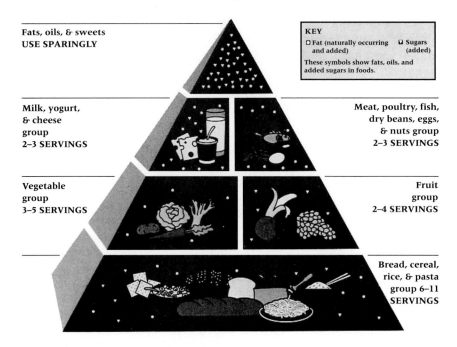

Food Guide Pyramid
A Guide to Daily Food Choices

sugars form the small apex of the pyramid, which indicates that foods rich in fat and sugar should provide the smallest proportion of total calories. No minimum number of servings is suggested because many people consume far too much fat and sugars.

NUTRITION AND PHYSICAL ACTIVITY

Vitamin requirements do not increase during exercise.

Athletes often believe that exercise increases requirements for nutrients such as proteins, vitamins, and minerals and that it is possible and desirable to saturate the body with these nutrients.[7] There is no scientific basis for ingesting levels of these nutrients above RDA or DRI levels.[58] Exercise increases the need for energy, not for proteins, vitamins, and minerals.[48] Additionally, many athletes use nutritional practices as an ergogenic aid to improve various aspects of performance (see Chapter 17).[23] Thus it is necessary to explore some of the more common myths that surround the subject of nutrition's role in physical performance.

Vitamin Supplementation

Many athletes believe that taking large amounts of vitamin supplements can lead to superior health and performance.[24] A megadose of a nutrient supplement is essentially an overdose; the amount ingested far exceeds the RDA levels.[50] The rationale used for such excessive intakes is that if taking a pill that contains the RDA for each vitamin and mineral makes an athlete healthy, taking a pill that has ten times the RDA should make the athlete ten times healthier.

An example of a popular practice among athletes is to take megadoses of vitamin C. Such doses do not prevent the common cold or slow aging. They do cause diarrhea and possibly the development of painful kidney stones. An athlete has no increased need for vitamin C. Fruits, juices, and vegetables are reliable sources of vitamin C that also supply other vitamins and minerals.[5]

Taking megadoses of vitamin E has become popular among people of all ages. The vitamin functions to protect certain fatty acids in cell membranes from being damaged.[5] There is not much evidence to support the notion that this vitamin can extend life expectancy or enhance physical performance. Vitamin E does not enhance sexual ability, prevent graying hair, or cure muscular dystrophy. A person can obtain adequate amounts of vitamin E by consuming whole-grain products, vegetable oils, and nuts.

The B-complex vitamins that are involved in obtaining energy from CHO, fats, and proteins are often abused by athletes who believe that vitamins provide energy. Any increased need for these nutrients is easily fulfilled when the athlete eats more nutritious foods while training. If athletes do not increase their food consumption, they will lose weight because of their high level of caloric expenditure.

Mineral Supplementation

Obtaining adequate levels of certain minerals can be a problem for some athletes.[10] Calcium and iron intakes may be low for those athletes who do not include dairy products, red meats, or enriched breads and cereals in their diet. To prevent wasting their money and overdosing, however, athletes must be careful to first determine whether they need extra minerals. The following sections explore some minerals that can be low in the diet and some suggestions for improving the quality of the diet so that supplements may not be necessary.

Calcium Deficiency

Calcium is the most abundant mineral in the body. It is essential for bones and teeth as well as for muscle contraction and conduction of nerve impulses. However, the importance of obtaining adequate calcium supplies throughout life has become more recognized. If calcium intake is too low to meet needs, the body can remove calcium from the bones. Over time, the bones become weakened and appear porous on X-ray films. These bones are brittle and often break spontaneously. This condition is called **osteoporosis** and is estimated to be eight times more common among women than men. It becomes a serious problem for women after menopause.[5]

osteoporosis
A decrease in bone density.

The AI for young adults is 1,000 mg (an eight-ounce glass of milk contains about 300 mg of calcium). Unfortunately about 25 percent of all females in the United States consume less than 300 mg of calcium per day, well below the RDA. High-protein diets and alcohol consumption also increase calcium excretion from the body. Exercise causes calcium to be retained in bones, so physical activity is beneficial. However, younger females who exercise to extremes so that their normal hormonal balance is upset are prone to develop premature osteoporosis.[34] Calcium supplementation, preferably as calcium carbonate or citrate rather than phosphate, may be advisable for females who have a family history of osteoporosis.

Milk products are the most reliable sources of calcium. Many athletes complain that milk and other dairy products upset their stomach. They may lack an enzyme, called lactase, that is needed to digest milk sugar, lactose. This condition is referred to as lactose intolerance, or **lactase deficiency.**[55] The undigested lactose enters the large intestine, where the bacteria that normally reside there use it for energy. The bacteria produce large quantities of intestinal gas, which causes discomfort and cramps. Many lactose-intolerant people also suffer from diarrhea. Fortunately, scientists have produced the missing enzyme, lactase. Lactase is available without prescription in forms that can be added to foods before eating or taken along with meals.

lactase deficiency
Difficulty digesting dairy products.

Iron Deficiency

Iron deficiency is also a common problem, especially for young females. Lack of iron can result in iron-deficiency **anemia** (see Chapter 29). Iron is needed to properly form hemoglobin. With anemia, the oxygen-carrying ability of the red blood cells is reduced so that muscles cannot obtain enough oxygen to generate energy. Anemia leaves a person feeling tired and weak. Obviously, an athlete cannot compete at peak level while suffering from an iron deficiency.

anemia
Lack of iron.

5-3

Critical Thinking Exercise

A high-school football player has become interested in body building. He is most interested in seeing an increase in muscle mass. He is religious about his weight training but has heard that increasing protein intake will cause the muscles to hypertrophy more quickly.

? What advice can the athletic trainer give him about taking commercially produced protein supplements?

Protein Supplementation

Athletes often believe that more protein is needed to build bigger muscles.[35] It is true that a relatively small amount of protein is needed by athletes who are developing muscles in a training program. Many athletes, particularly those who are training with heavy weights or who are bodybuilders, routinely take protein supplements that are commercially produced and marketed.[17,25] To build muscle, athletes should consume 1 to 1.5 grams of extra protein per kilogram (0.5 to 0.7 grams per pound) of body weight every day. This range goes from slightly above to about double the protein RDA (0.8 grams per kilogram of desirable body weight). Anyone eating a variety of foods, but especially protein-rich foods, can easily meet the higher amounts. Thus, athletes do not need protein supplements because their diets typically exceed even the most generous protein recommendations.[4] An active adult will most likely require 0.6 grams per pound, or 66 percent more than the RDA.

Creatine Supplementation

Creatine is a naturally occurring organic compound synthesized by the kidneys, liver, and pancreas. Creatine can also be obtained from the ingestion of meat and fish that contain approximately five grams per kilogram. Creatine has an integral role in energy metabolism.[6]

There are two main types of creatine: free creatine and phosphocreatine. Phosphocreatine is stored in skeletal muscle and is used during anaerobic activity to produce ATP with the assistance of the enzyme creatine kinase. With creatine supplementation, phosphocreatine depletion is delayed and performance is enhanced through the maintenance of the normal metabolic pathways.[38]

The positive physiological effects of creatine include increasing the resynthesis of ATP, thus allowing for increased intensity in a workout; functioning as a lactic acid buffer, thus prolonging maximal effort and improving exercise recovery time during maximal intensity activities; stimulating protein synthesis; decreasing total cholesterol while improving the HDL-to-LDL ratio; decreasing total triglycerides; and increasing fat-free mass.[42] Side effects of creatine supplementation include weight gain and occasional muscle cramping; however, there are apparently no other known long-term side effects.

It has been suggested that an initial loading phase should consist of twenty grams of creatine and 120 ounces of water each day for six days. The recommended amount for improving performance after the loading phase is five to ten grams per day for four weeks.[6] Oral supplementation with creatine may enhance muscular performance during high-intensity resistance exercise.[38,54]

Sugar and Performance

Ingesting large quantities of glucose in the form of honey, candy bars, or pure sugar immediately before physical activity may have a significant impact on performance.[14] As carbohydrates are digested, large quantities of glucose enter the blood. This increase in blood sugar (glucose) levels stimulates the release of the hormone insulin. Insulin allows the cells to use the circulating glucose so that blood glucose levels soon return to normal.[47] It was hypothesized that a decline in blood sugar levels was detrimental to performance and endurance. However, recent evidence indicates that the effect of eating large quantities of carbohydrates is beneficial rather than negative.[16,48]

Nevertheless, some athletes are sensitive to high-carbohydrate feedings and experience problems with increased levels of insulin. Also, some athletes cannot tolerate large amounts of the simple sugar fructose. For these individuals, too much fructose leads to intestinal upset and diarrhea. Athletes should test themselves with various high-carbohydrate foods to see if they are affected (but not before a competitive event).[48]

Caffeine

Caffeine is a central nervous system stimulant. Most people who consume caffeine in coffee, tea, or carbonated beverages are aware of its effect of increasing alertness and decreasing fatigue. Chocolate contains compounds that are related to caffeine and have the same stimulating effects. However, large amounts of caffeine cause nervousness, irritability, increased heart rate, and headaches. Also, headaches are a withdrawal symptom experienced when a person tries to stop consuming caffeinated products.[44]

Although small amounts of caffeine do not appear to harm physical performance, cases of nausea and light-headedness have been reported. Caffeine enhances the use of fat during endurance exercise, thus delaying the depletion of glycogen stores.[20] This delay would help endurance performance. Caffeine also helps make calcium more available to the muscle during contraction, allowing the muscle to work more efficiently. However, Olympic officials rightfully consider caffeine to be a drug. It should not be present in an Olympic competitor's blood in levels greater than that resulting from drinking five or six cups of coffee.

Alcohol

Alcohol provides energy for the body; each gram of pure alcohol (ethanol) supplies seven calories. However, sources of alcohol provide little other nutritional value with regard to vitamins, minerals, and proteins. The depressant effects of alcohol on the central nervous system include decreased physical coordination, slowed reaction times, and decreased mental alertness. Also, this drug increases the production of urine, resulting in body water losses (diuretic effect). Therefore, use of alcoholic beverages by the athlete cannot be recommended before, during, or after physical activity.[33]

Organic, Natural, or Health Foods

Many athletes are concerned about the quality of the foods they eat—not just the nutritional value of the food but also its safety. Organic foods are grown without the use of synthetic fertilizers and pesticides. Those who advocate the use of organic farming methods claim that these foods are nutritionally superior and safer than the same products grown using chemicals such as pesticides and synthetic fertilizers.[26]

Technically, the description of organic food is meaningless. All foods (except water) are organic, that is, contain the element carbon. Organically produced foods are often more expensive than the same foods that have been produced by conventional means. There is no advantage to consuming organic food products. They are not more nutritious than foods produced by conventional methods. Nevertheless, for some athletes, the psychological benefit of believing that they are doing something good for their bodies justifies the extra cost.

Natural foods have been subjected to little processing and contain no additives such as preservatives or artificial flavors.[55] Processing can protect nutritional value. Preservatives save food that would otherwise spoil and have to be destroyed. Furthermore, many foods in their natural form are poisonous. The green layer often found under the skin of potatoes is poisonous if eaten in large amounts. Poisonous mushrooms and molds in peanuts cause liver cancer.

Both organic and natural foods could be described as health foods. However, there is no benefit derived from eating a diet consisting of health foods, even for the athlete.

Herbs

The use of herbs as natural alternatives to drugs and medicines has clearly become a trend among American consumers. Most herbs, as edible plants, are safe to ingest as foods; as natural medicines, they are claimed to have few side effects, although occasionally a mild, allergy-type reaction may occur.[44]

Most widely used herbs and purposes for use

dong quai—to treat menstrual symptoms

echinacea—to promote wound healing and strengthen immune system

garlic—as an antibiotic, antibacterial, antifungal agent to prevent and relieve coronary-artery disease by reducing total blood cholesterol and triglyceride levels and raising HDL levels

ginkgo biloba—to improve blood circulation, especially in the brain

ginseng—to reduce impotence, weakness, lethargy, and fatigue

kava—to reduce anxiety, relax muscle tension, produce analgesic effects, act as a local anesthetic, provide antibacterial benefit

saw palmetto—to treat inflamed prostate; also used as a diuretic and as a sexual enhancement agent

St. John's wort—used as an antidepressant; also used to treat nervous disorders, depression, neuralgia, kidney problems, wounds, and burns

valerian—to treat insomnia, anxiety, stress

yohimbe—to increase libido and blood flow to sexual organs in the male

Herbs can offer the body nutrients that are reported to nourish the brain, glands, and hormones. Unlike vitamins, which work best when taken with food, herbs do not need to be taken with other foods since herbs provide their own digestive enzymes.[51]

Herbs in their whole form are not drugs. As medicine, herbs are essentially body balancers that work with the body's functions so that it can heal and regulate itself. Herbal formulas can be general for overall strength and nutrient support or specific to a particular ailment or condition.

Hundreds of herbs are widely available today at all quality levels. They are readily available at health food stores. However, unlike both food and medicine, no federal or governmental controls regulate the sale of herbs and ensure the quality of the products being sold.[29] Extreme caution must be exercised by the consumer of herbal products.

Focus Box: "Most widely used herbs and purposes for use" lists the most popular and widely used herbal products sold in health food stores. Some additional potent and complex herbs, such as capsicum, lobelia, sassafras, mandrake tansy, canada snake root, wormwood, woodruff, poke root, and rue may be useful in small amounts and as catalysts, but should not be used alone.

Vegetarianism

Vegetarians: total vegetarians, lactovegetarians, ovolacto-vegetarians, and semi-vegetarians.

Vegetarianism has emerged as an alternative to the usual American diet. All vegetarians use plant foods to form the foundation of their diet; animal foods are either totally excluded or included in a variety of eating patterns.[15] Athletes who choose to become vegetarians do so for economic, philosophical, religious, cultural, or health reasons. Vegetarianism is no longer considered to be a fad if it is practiced intelligently. However, the vegetarian diet may create deficiencies if nutrient needs are not carefully considered. Athletes who follow this eating pattern must plan their diet carefully so that their calorie needs are met.[15] Types of vegetarian dietary patterns are categorized as follows:

- *Total vegetarians, or vegans:* People who consume plant but no animal foods; meat, fish, poultry, eggs, and dairy products are excluded from their diet. This diet is adequate for most adults if they give careful consideration to obtaining enough calories, vitamin B_{12}, and the minerals calcium, zinc, and iron.
- *Lactovegetarians:* Individuals who consume milk products along with plant foods; meat, fish, poultry, and eggs are excluded from their diet. Iron and zinc levels can be low in this form of vegetarianism.

- *Ovolactovegetarians:* People who consume dairy products and eggs in their diet along with plant foods; meat, fish, and poultry are excluded. Again, obtaining sufficient iron could be a problem.
- *Semivegetarians:* People who consume animal products but exclude red meats. Plant products still form an important part of the diet. This diet is usually adequate.

Preevent Nutrition

The importance and content of the preevent meal has been heatedly debated among coaches, athletic trainers, and athletes.[12] The trend has been to ignore logical thinking about what should be eaten before competition in favor of upholding the tradition of "rewarding" the athlete for hard work by serving foods that may hamper performance. For example, the traditional steak-and-eggs meal before football games is great for coaches and trainers; however, the athlete gains nothing from this meal. The important point is that too often people are concerned primarily with the preevent meal and fail to realize that those nutrients consumed over several days before competition are much more important than what is eaten three hours before an event. The purpose of the preevent meal should be to provide the competitor with sufficient nutrient energy and fluids for competition while taking into consideration the digestibility of the food and, most important, the eating preferences of the individual athlete. (See *Focus Box:* "The pregame meal".) Figure 5-3 gives examples of preevent meals.

Athletes should be encouraged to become conscious of their diet. However, no experimental evidence indicates that performance may be enhanced by altering a diet that is basically sound. There are a number of ways that a nutritious diet may be achieved, and the diet that is optimal for one athlete may not be the best for another. In many instances, the individual will be the best judge of what he or she should or should not eat in the preevent meal or before exercising. It seems that a person's best guide is to eat whatever he or she is most comfortable with.

Liquid Food Supplements

Recently, liquid meals have been recommended as extremely effective preevent meals and are being used by high school, college, university, and professional teams with some indications of success.[46] These supplements supply from 225 to 400 calories per average serving. Athletes who have used these supplements report

5-4

Critical Thinking Exercise

A recreational runner has been training to run his first marathon. He feels good about his level of conditioning but wants to make certain that he does everything that he can do to maximize his performance. He is concerned about eating the right type of foods both before and during the marathon to help ensure that he does not become excessively fatigued.

? What recommendations should the athletic trainer make regarding glycogen supercompensation, the preevent meal, and food consumption during the event?

MEAL 1	
³/₄ c Orange juice	³/₄ c Orange juice
¹/₂ c Cereal with 1 tsp sugar	1–2 Pancakes with:
1 Slice whole wheat toast with:	1 tsp Margarine
1 tsp Margarine	2 tbsp Syrup
1 tsp Honey or jelly	8 oz Skim or lowfat milk
8 oz Skim or lowfat milk	Water
Water	(Approximately 450–500 kcal)
(Approximately 450–500 kcal)	

MEAL 2	
1 c Vegetable soup	1 c Spaghetti with tomato sauce and cheese
1 Turkey sandwich with:	¹/₂ c Sliced pears (canned) on 1/4 c cottage cheese
2 Slices bread	1–2 Slices (Italian) bread with 1–2 tsp margarine
2 oz Turkey (white or dark)	(avoid garlic)
1 oz Cheese slice	¹/₂ c Sherbet
2 tsp Mayonnaise	1–2 Sugar cookies
8 oz Skim or lowfat milk	4 oz Skim or lowfat milk
Water	Water
(Approximately 550–600 kcal)	(Approximately 700 kcal)

Figure 5-3

Sample preevent meals.

Focus

The pregame meal

- Try to achieve the largest possible storage of carbohydrates (glycogen) in both resting muscle and the liver. This storage is particularly important for endurance activities but may also be beneficial for intense, short-duration exercise.

- A stomach that is full of food during contact sports is subject to injury. Therefore, the type of food eaten should allow the stomach to empty quickly. Carbohydrates are easier to digest than are fats or proteins. A meal that contains plenty of carbohydrates will leave the stomach and be digested faster than a fatty meal. It would be wise to replace the traditional steak-and-eggs preevent meal with a low-fat one containing a small amount of pasta, tomato sauce, and bread.

- Foods should not cause irritation or upset to the gastrointestinal tract. Foods high in cellulose and other forms of fiber, such as whole grain products, fruits, and vegetables, increase the need for defecation. Highly spiced foods or gas-forming foods (such as onions, baked beans, or peppers) must also be avoided because any type of disturbance in the gastrointestinal tract may be detrimental to performance. Carbonated beverages and chewing gum also contribute to the formation of gas.

- Liquids consumed should be easily absorbed and low in fat content and should not act as a laxative. Whole milk, coffee, and tea should be avoided. Water intake should be increased, particularly if the temperature is high.

- A meal should be eaten approximately three to four hours before the event or before exercising. This timing allows for adequate stomach emptying, but the individual will not feel hungry during activity.

- Any food that is disliked should not be eaten. Most important, the individual must feel psychologically satisfied by any preevent meal. If not, performance may be impaired more by psychological factors than by physiological factors.

- Prolonged fasting and diet programs that severely restrict caloric intake are scientifically undesirable and can be medically dangerous.

- Fasting and diet programs that severely restrict caloric intake result in the loss of large amounts of water, electrolytes, minerals, glycogen stores, and other fat-free tissue (including proteins within fat-free tissues), with minimal amounts of fat loss.

- Mild calorie restriction (500 to 1,000 calories less than the usual daily intake) results in a smaller loss of water, electrolytes, minerals, and other fat-free tissue and is less likely to cause malnutrition.

- Dynamic exercise of large muscles helps maintain fat-free tissue, including muscle mass and bone density, and results in losses of body weight. Weight loss resulting from an increase in energy expenditure is primarily in the form of fat weight.

- A nutritionally sound diet resulting in mild calorie restriction coupled with an endurance exercise program, along with behavioral modification of existing eating habits, is recommended for weight reduction. The rate of sustained weight loss should not exceed 1 kg (2 lb) per week.

- To maintain proper weight control and optimal body fat levels, a lifetime commitment to proper eating habits and regular physical activity is required.

elimination of the usual pregame symptoms of dry mouth, abdominal cramps, leg cramps, nervous defecation, and nausea.

Under ordinary conditions, it usually takes approximately four hours for a full meal to pass through the stomach and the small intestine. Pregame emotional tension often delays the emptying of the stomach; therefore the undigested food mass remains in the stomach and upper bowel for a prolonged time, even up to or through the actual period of competition, and frequently results in nausea, vomiting, and cramps. This unabsorbed food mass is of no value to the athlete. Team physicians who have experimented with the liquid food supplements say that a major advantage to the supplements is that they clear both the stomach and the upper bowel before game time, thus making available the caloric energy that would otherwise still be in an unassimilated state. There is merit in the use of such food supplements for pregame meals.[46]

Eating Fast Foods

Eating fast food is a way of life in American society.[36] Athletes, especially young athletes, have for the most part grown up as fast-food junkies. Furthermore, travel budgets and tight schedules dictate that fast food is a frequent choice for coaches on road trips. Aside from occasional problems with food flavor, the biggest concern in consuming fast foods, as can be seen in Table 5-4, is that 40 percent to 50 percent of the calories consumed are from fats. To compound this problem, these already sizable meals are now being "supersized" at a more affordable price for those who want maximum fat, salt, and calories in a single sitting.[44]

On the positive side, fast-food restaurants have broadened their menus to include whole wheat breads and rolls, salad bars, and low-fat milk products. Many of the larger fast-food restaurants provide nutritional information for consumers upon request or from well-stocked racks.[44] *Focus Box:* "Tips for selecting fast foods" provides suggestions for eating more healthfully at fast-food restaurants.

Glycogen Supercompensation

For endurance events, maximizing the amount of glycogen that can be stored, especially in muscles, may make the difference between finishing first or at the end of the pack. Athletes can increase glycogen supplies in muscle and liver by reducing the training program a few days before competing and by significantly increasing

Focus

Tips for selecting fast foods

- Limit deep-fried foods such as fish and chicken sandwiches and chicken nuggets, which are often higher in fat than plain burgers are. If you are having fried chicken, remove some of the breading before eating.
- Order roast beef, turkey, or grilled chicken, where available, for a lower fat alternative to most burgers.
- Choose a small order of fries with your meal rather than a large one, and request no salt. Add a small amount of salt yourself if desired. If you are ordering a deep-fat-fried sandwich or one that is made with cheese and sauce, skip the fries altogether and try a plain baked potato (add butter and salt sparingly) or a dinner roll instead of a biscuit; or, try a side salad to accompany your meal instead.
- Choose regular sandwiches instead of "double," "jumbo," "deluxe," or "ultimate." And order plain types rather than those with the works, such as cheese, bacon, mayonnaise, and special sauce. Pickles, mustard, ketchup, and other condiments are high in sodium. Choose lettuce, tomatoes, and onions.
- At the salad bar, load up on fresh greens, fruits, and vegetables. Be careful of salad dressings, added toppings, and creamy salads (potato salad, macaroni salad, coleslaw). These can quickly push calories and fat to the level of other menu items or higher.
- Many fast-food items contain large amounts of sodium from salt and other ingredients. Try to balance the rest of your day's sodium choices after a fast-food meal.
- Alternate water, low-fat milk, or skim milk with a soda or a shake.
- For dessert, or a sweet-on-the-run, choose low-fat frozen yogurt where available.
- Remember to balance your fast-food choices with your food selections for the whole day.

TABLE 5-4 Fast-Food Choices and Nutritional Value

Food	Calories	Protein (g)	CHO (g)	Fat (g)	Calories from Fat (%)	Cholesterol (mg)	Sodium (mg)
Hamburgers							
McDonald's hamburger	263	12.4	28.3	11	38.6	29.1	506
Dairy Queen single hamburger w/cheese	410	24	33	20	43.9	50	790
Hardee's 1/4 pound cheeseburger	506	28	41	26	46.2	61	1,950
Wendy's double hamburger, white bun	560	4.1	24	34	54.6	125	575
McDonald's Big Mac	570	24.6	39.2	35	55.2	83	45
Burger King Whopper sandwich	640	27	42	41	57.6	94	842
Jack in the Box Jumbo Jack	485	26	38	26	48.2	64	905
Chicken							
Arby's chicken breast sandwich	592	28	56	27	41.0	57	1,340
Burger King chicken sandwich	688	26	56	40	52.3	82	1,423
Dairy Queen chicken sandwich	670	29	46	41	55.0	75	870
Church's Crispy Nuggets (one; regular)	55	3	4	3	49.0	—	125
Kentucky Fried Chicken Nuggets (one)	46	2.82	2.2	2.9	56.7	11.9	140
Fish							
Church's Southern fried catfish	67	4	4	4	53.7	—	151
Long John Silver's Fish & More	978	34	82	58	53.3	88	2,124
McDonald's Filet-O-Fish	435	14.7	35.9	25.7	53.1	45.2	799
Others							
Hardee's hot dog	346	11	26	22	57.2	42	744
Jack in the Box taco	191	8	1.6	11	51.8	21	406
Arby's roast beef sandwich (regular)	350	22	32	15	38.5	39	590
Hardee's roast beef sandwich	377	21	36	17	40.5	57	1,030
French fries							
Arby's french fries	211	2	33	8	34.1	6	30
McDonald's french fries (regular)	220	3	26.1	11.5	47.0	8.6	109
Wendy's french fries (regular)	280	40	35	14	45.0	15	95
Shakes							
Dairy Queen	710	14	120	19	24.0	50	260
McDonald's							
Vanilla	352	9.3	59.6	8.4	21.4	30.6	201
Chocolate	383	9.9	65.5	9	21.1	29.7	300
Strawberry	362	9	62.1	8.7	22.3	32.2	207
Soft drinks							
Coca-Cola	154	—	40	—	—	—	6
Diet Coke	0.9	—	0.3	—	—	—	16
Sprite	142	—	36	—	—	—	45
Tab	1	—	1	—	—	—	30
Diet Sprite	3	—	0	—	—	—	9

carbohydrate intake during the week before the event.[45] By reducing training for at least forty-eight hours before the competition, the body is able to eliminate any metabolic waste products that may hinder performance. The high-carbohydrate diet restores glycogen levels in muscle and the liver. This practice is called **glycogen supercompensation.** The basis for the practice is that the quantity of glycogen stored in muscle directly affects the endurance of that muscle.[42]

Glycogen supercompensation is accomplished over a six-day period divided into three phases. In phase 1 (days 1 and 2), training should be hard and dietary intake of carbohydrates restricted. During phase 2 (days 3 through 5), training is cut back and the individual eats plenty of carbohydrates. Studies have indicated that glycogen stores may be increased from 50 percent to 100 percent, theoretically enhancing endurance during a long-term event. Phase 3 (day 6) is the day of the event, during which a normal diet must be consumed.

The effect of glycogen supercompensation in improving performance during endurance activities has not as yet been clearly demonstrated. It has been recommended that glycogen supercompensation not be done more than two to three times during the course of a year. Glycogen supercompensation is only of value in long-duration events that produce glycogen depletion, such as a marathon.[44]

Fat Loading

Some endurance athletes tried fat loading in place of carbohydrate loading.[40] Their intent was to have a better source of energy at their disposal. The deleterious effects of this procedure outweigh any benefits that may be derived. Associated with fat loading is cardiac protein and potassium depletion, causing arrhythmias and increased levels of serum cholesterol as a result of the ingestion of butter, cheese, cream, and marbled beef.

WEIGHT CONTROL AND BODY COMPOSITION

Gain or loss of weight in an athlete often poses a problem because the individual's ingrained eating habits are difficult to change. The athletic trainer's inability to adequately supervise the athlete's meal program in terms of balance and quantity further complicates the problem. An intelligent and conscientious approach to weight control requires, on the part of both athletic trainer and athlete, some knowledge of what is involved. Such understanding allows athletes to better discipline themselves as to the quantity and kinds of foods they should eat.

Body Composition

Ideal body weight is most often determined by consulting age-related height and weight charts such as those published by life insurance companies. Unfortunately, these charts are inaccurate because they involve broad ranges and often fail to take individual body types into account. Because these charts are based solely on gross body weight, their accuracy is questionable. Health and performance, rather than body weight, may best be related to body composition.[41]

Body composition refers to both the fat and nonfat components of the body. That portion of total body weight that is composed of fat tissue is referred to as the percentage of body fat. The total body weight that is composed of nonfat or lean tissue, which includes muscles, tendons, bones, and connective tissue, is referred to as lean body weight. Body composition measurements provide an accurate determination of precisely how much weight an athlete may gain or lose.[11]

The average college-age female has between 20 percent and 25 percent of her total body weight made up of fat. The average college-age male has between 12 percent and 15 percent body fat. Male endurance athletes may get their fat percentage as low as 8 percent to 12 percent, and female endurance athletes may reach 10 percent to 18 percent. Body fat percentage should not go below 3 percent in males and 12 percent in females, because below these percentages the internal organs tend

glycogen supercompensation
High-carbohydrate diet.

to lose their protective padding of essential fat, potentially subjecting them to injury.[9]

Being overweight and being obese are different conditions. Being overweight implies having excess body weight relative to physical size and stature. Being overweight may not be a problem unless a person is also overfat, which means that the percentage of total body weight that is made up of fat is excessive. **Obesity** implies an extreme amount of excessive fat, much greater than what would be considered normal. Females with body fat above 30 percent and males with body fat above 20 percent are considered to be obese.[9]

Two factors determine the amount of fat in the body: the number of fat, or adipose, cells and the size of the adipose cell. Proliferation, or hyperplagia, of adipose cells begins at birth and continues to puberty. It is thought that after early adulthood the number of fat cells remains fixed, although some evidence suggests that the number of cells is not necessarily fixed.[42] Adipose cell size also increases gradually, or hypertrophies, to early adulthood and can increase or decrease as a function of caloric balance. In adults, weight loss or gain is primarily a function of the change in cell size, not cell number. Obese adults tend to exhibit a great deal of adipose cell hypertrophy.

The **adipose cell** stores triglyceride (a form of liquid fat). This liquid fat moves in and out of the cell according to the energy needs of the body, which are determined to some extent by activity type. The greatest amount of fat is used in activities of moderate intensity and long duration. The greater the amount of triglyceride contained in the adipose cell, the greater the amount of total body weight composed of fat. One pound of body fat is made up of approximately 3,500 calories stored as triglyceride within the adipose cell.

Assessing Body Composition

Among the several methods of assessing **body composition** are hydrostatic, or underwater, weighing; measurement of electrical impedance; and measurement of skinfold thickness.[2]

The method of measuring the thickness of skinfolds is based on the fact that about 50 percent of the fat in the body is contained in the subcutaneous fat layers and is closely related to total fat. The remainder of the fat in the body is found around organs and vessels and serves a shock-absorptive function. The skinfold technique measures the thickness of the subcutaneous fat layer with a skinfold caliper (Figure 5-4). Its accuracy is relatively low; however, expertise in measurement is easily developed and the time required for this technique is considerably less than for the others. It has been estimated that error in skinfold measurement is plus or minus 3 percent to 5 percent.[42]

obesity
Excesive amount of body fat.

adipose cell
Stores triglyceride.

body composition
Percent body fat plus lean body weight.

Figure 5-4

Measuring body composition. **A,** Triceps skinfold. **B,** Subscapular skinfold.

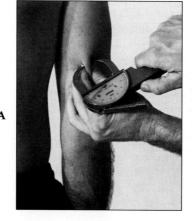

A

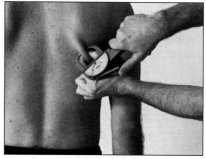

B

Researchers have offered several different techniques for measuring body composition via skinfolds. A technique proposed by McArdle and coworkers, which measures the triceps skinfold and the subscapular skinfold, is widely used.[42]

Assessing Caloric Balance

Changes in body weight are almost entirely the result of changes in caloric balance.

Caloric balance = Number of calories consumed − Number of calories expended

Calories may be expended by three different processes: basal metabolism; work (work may be defined as any activity that requires more energy than sleeping); and excretion. If more calories are consumed than expended, this positive caloric balance results in weight gain. Conversely, weight loss results from a negative caloric balance in which more calories are expended than are consumed.

Caloric balance is determined by the number of calories consumed regardless of whether the calories are contained in fat, carbohydrate, or protein. There are differences in the caloric content of these foodstuffs:

Carbohydrate = 4 calories per gram

Protein = 4 calories per gram

Fat = 9 calories per gram

Alcohol = 7 calories per gram

Recently, there has been an emphasis on limiting fat intake as a means of controlling weight.[32] Certain foods that contain little or no fat may still contain a significant number of calories if the foods are high in carbohydrate or protein; thus an individual who is limiting fat intake can still be in positive caloric balance.[1]

Estimations of caloric intake for college athletes range between 2,000 and 5,000 calories per day. Estimations of caloric expenditure range between 2,200 and 4,400 calories on the average. Energy demands will be considerably higher in endurance-type athletes, who may require as many as 7,000 calories per day.[41] Caloric balance may be calculated by maintaining accurate records of both the number of calories consumed in the diet and the number of calories expended for metabolic needs and in activities performed during the course of a day.

METHODS OF WEIGHT LOSS

An individual has several ways to go about losing weight: dieting, increasing the amount of physical exercise, or a combination of diet and exercise.

Weight loss through dieting alone is difficult, and in most cases dieting alone is an ineffective means of weight control. Long-term weight control through dieting alone is successful only 2 percent of the time.[55] About 35 percent to 45 percent of weight decrease due to dieting results from a loss of lean tissue. The minimum caloric intake should not go below 1,000 to 1,200 calories per day for a female and not below 1,200 to 1,400 calories per day for a male.[56]

Weight loss through exercise involves an 80 percent to 90 percent loss of fat tissue with almost no loss of lean tissue. Weight loss through exercise alone is almost as difficult as losing weight through dieting. However, exercise will not only result in weight reduction but may also enhance cardiorespiratory endurance, improve strength, and increase flexibility.[9] For these reasons, exercise has some distinct advantages over dieting in any weight-loss program.

The most efficient method of decreasing the percentage of body weight that is fat is through some combination of diet and exercise. A moderate caloric restriction combined with a moderate increase in caloric expenditure will result in a negative caloric balance. This method is relatively fast and easy compared with either of the other methods because habits are being moderately changed.

In any weight-loss program, the goal should be to lose 1.5 to 2 pounds per week. Weight loss of more than 4 to 5 pounds per week may be attributed to dehydration

Positive caloric balance leads to weight gain; negative caloric balance leads to weight loss.

as opposed to a loss of body fat.[9] A weight-loss program must emphasize the long-haul approach. It generally takes a long time to put on extra weight, and there is no reason to expect that true loss of excess body fat can be accomplished in a relatively short time. The American College of Sports Medicine has made specific recommendations for weight loss.[3]

METHODS OF WEIGHT GAIN

The aim of a weight-gaining program should be to increase lean body mass, that is, muscle as opposed to body fat. Muscle mass should be increased only by muscle work combined with an appropriate increase in dietary intake. Muscle mass cannot be increased by the intake of any special food or vitamin.

The recommended rate of weight gain is approximately one to two pounds per week. Each pound of lean body mass gained represents a positive caloric balance. This positive balance is an intake in excess of an expenditure of approximately 2,500 calories. One pound of fat represents the equivalent of 3,500 calories; lean body tissue contains less fat, more protein, and more water and represents approximately 2,500 calories. To gain one pound of muscle, an excess of approximately 2,500 calories is needed; to lose one pound of fat, approximately 3,500 calories in excess of intake must be expended in activities. Adding 500 to 1,000 calories daily to the usual diet will provide the energy needs of gaining one to two pounds per week and fuel the increased energy expenditure of the weight-training program. Weight training must be part of the weight-gaining program. Otherwise, the excess intake of energy will be converted to fat.

EATING DISORDERS

There is an epidemic in our society, especially in sports. This problem is the inordinate concern with being overweight. Out of this obsession has emerged the eating disorders bulimia and anorexia nervosa. Both these disorders are increasingly seen in athletes.[52]

Bulimia

The bulimic person is commonly female, ranging in age from adolescence to middle age. It is estimated that 1 out of every 200 American girls, ages twelve to eighteen years (1 percent to 2 percent of the population), will develop patterns of bulimia, anorexia nervosa, or both.[56] The bulimic individual typically gorges herself with thousands of calories after a period of starvation and then purges herself through induced vomiting and further fasting or through the use of laxatives or diuretics. This secretive binge-eating–purging cycle may go on for years.

Typically the bulimic athlete is white and belongs to a middle-class or upper-middle-class family. She is perfectionistic, obedient, overcompliant, highly motivated, successful academically, well liked by her peers, and a good athlete.[52] She most commonly participates in gymnastics, track, and dance. Male wrestlers and gymnasts may also develop bulimia. (See *Focus Box:* "Identifying the athlete with an eating disorder.")

Binge-purge patterns of eating can cause stomach rupture, disruption of heart rhythm, and liver damage. Stomach acids brought up by vomiting cause tooth decay and chronically inflame the mucous lining of the mouth and throat.

Anorexia Nervosa

It has been estimated that 30 percent to 50 percent of all individuals diagnosed as having anorexia nervosa also develop some symptoms of bulimia. Anorexia nervosa is characterized by a distorted body image and a major concern about weight gain. As with bulimia, anorexia nervosa affects mostly females. It usually begins in adolescence and can be mild without major consequences or can become life threatening. As many as 15 percent to 21 percent of individuals diagnosed as anorexic ultimately die from this disorder. Despite being extremely thin, the athlete sees herself as too

5-5

Critical Thinking Exercise

An ice hockey attackman has an excellent level of fitness and has superb skating ability and stick work. He is convinced that the only thing keeping him from moving to the next level is his body weight. In recent years he has engaged more in weight-training activities to improve his muscular endurance and, to a lesser extent, to increase his strength.

? What recommendations should the athletic trainer make for him to be successful in his weight-gaining efforts?

5-6

Critical Thinking Exercise

A tennis coach observes that one of her players has lost a significant amount of weight. Along with this loss of weight, this athlete's level of play has begun to decrease. The coach becomes seriously concerned when another player tells the coach that she thinks her roommate was purposely throwing up after a team meal on a recent road trip. After briefly questioning the athlete about her eating habits, the coach asks the athletic trainer to become involved in dealing with this situation.

? How should the athletic trainer respond to this request?

Focus

Identifying the athlete with an eating disorder

The athlete with an eating disorder may display the following signs:

- Social isolation and withdrawal from friends and family
- A lack of confidence in athletic abilities
- Ritualistic eating behavior (e.g., organizing food on plate)
- An obsession with counting calories
- An obsession with constantly exercising, especially just before a meal
- An obsession with weighing self
- A constant overestimation of body size
- Patterns of leaving the table directly after eating to go into the restroom
- Problems related to eating disorders (e.g., malnutrition, menstrual irregularities, or chronic fatigue)
- Family history of eating disorders

fat. These individuals deny hunger and are hyperactive, engaging in abnormal amounts of exercise such as aerobics or distance running.[52] In general, the anorexic individual is highly secretive, and the coach and athletic trainer must be sensitive to eating problems. Early intervention is essential. Any athlete with signs of bulimia or anorexia nervosa must be confronted in a kind, empathetic manner by the coach or athletic trainer. When detected, individuals with eating disorders must be referred for psychological or psychiatric treatment. Unfortunately, simply referring an anorexic person to a health education clinic is not usually effective. The key to treatment of anorexia seems to be getting the patient to realize that a problem exists and that he or she could benefit from professional help. The individual must voluntarily accept such help if treatment is to be successful.[44]

Female Athlete Triad Syndrome

Female athlete triad syndrome is a potentially fatal problem that involves a combination of an eating disorder (either bulimia or anorexia), amenorrhea, and osteoporosis (diminished bone density). The incidence of this syndrome is uncertain; however, some studies have suggested that eating disorders in female athletes may be as high as 62 percent in certain sports, with amenorrhea being common in at least 60 percent of female athletes. However, the major risk of this syndrome is that the bone lost in osteoporosis may not be regained.[5]

SUMMARY

- The classes of nutrients are carbohydrates, fats, proteins, vitamins, minerals, and water. Carbohydrates, fats, and proteins provide the energy required for muscular work during activity and also play a role in the function and maintenance of body tissues. Vitamins are substances found in food that have no caloric value but are necessary to regulate body processes. Vitamins may be either fat soluble (vitamins A, D, E, and K) or water soluble (B-complex vitamins and vitamin C). Minerals are necessary in most physiological functions of the body. Water is the most essential of all the nutrients and should be of great concern to anyone involved in physical activity.
- A nutritious diet consists of eating a variety of foods in amounts recommended in the food pyramid. A diet that meets those recommended amounts does not need nutrient supplementation.
- Protein supplementation during weight training is not necessary if a nutritious diet is maintained. Many males and especially females may require calcium

supplementation to prevent osteoporosis. It may be necessary to supplement the diet with extra iron to prevent iron-deficiency anemia.

- Organic or natural foods have no beneficial effect on performance. Vegetarian diets can provide all the essential nutrients if care is taken and the diet is well thought out and properly prepared.
- The preevent meal should be higher in carbohydrates, easily digested, eaten three to four hours before an event, and psychologically pleasing.
- Glycogen supercompensation involves maximizing resting stores of glucose in the muscle, blood, and liver before a competitive event.
- Body composition indicates the percentage of total body weight composed of fat tissue versus the percentage composed of lean tissue. The size and number of adipose cells determine percentage of body fat. Percentage of body fat can be assessed by measuring the thickness of the subcutaneous fat at specific areas of the body with a skinfold caliper.
- Changes in body weight are caused almost entirely by a change in caloric balance, which is a function of the number of calories taken in and the number of calories expended. Weight can be lost either by increasing caloric expenditure through exercise or by decreasing caloric intake through dieting. Diets generally do not work. The recommended technique for losing weight involves a combination of moderate calorie restriction and a moderate increase in physical exercise during the course of each day. Weight gain should be accomplished by increasing caloric intake and engaging in a weight-training program. It is possible to gain weight and lose fat, thus changing body composition. Equal volumes of muscle weigh more than fat.
- Anorexia is a disease in which a person suffers a pathological weight loss because of a psychological aversion to food and eating. Bulimia is an eating disorder that involves binging and subsequent purging.

Web Sites

Food and Nutrition Information Center: http://www.nalusda.gov/fnic

This site is part of the information centers at the National Agricultural Library and offers access to information on healthy eating habits, food composition, and many additional resources.

Yahoo Health and Nutrition Information: http://www.yahoo.com/Health/Nutrition

This site includes diet analysis information, nutritional facts, and links to many other informative sites.

Eating Disorders: http://www.mirror_mirror.org/eatdis.htm

Eating disorder information can be found here, including information about anorexia, bulimia, and overeating as well as information about how to access support groups.

Athletes and Eating Disorders: http://www.uq.net.au/~zzedainc/n3frames.html

This site is part of the Eating Disorders Resources Web site; it gives some statistics from a recent NCAA study and has a section on the coaches' responsibility. The site also includes information about warning signs and the female athlete triad.

The American Dietetic Association: http://www.eatright.org

This site includes access to the journal published by the American Dietetic Association and provides informative nutritional tips as well as gateways to nutrition and to related sites.

Solutions to Critical Thinking EXERCISES

5-1 The important consideration for weight control is the total number of calories that are consumed relative to the total number of calories expended. It makes no difference whether the calories consumed are CHO, fat, or protein. Fat contains more than twice the number of calories that either CHO or protein contains, so an athlete can eat significantly more food and still have about the same caloric intake if the diet is high in CHO. This athlete should be told that it is also essential to consume at least some fat, which is necessary for the production of several enzymes and hormones.

5-2 For an athlete who is truly consuming anything close to a well-balanced diet, vitamin supplementation is generally not necessary. However, if taking a one-a-day type of vitamin supplement makes the athlete feel better, there will be no harm. Her tiredness could be related to a number of medical conditions (e.g., mononucleosis). An iron-deficiency anemia may be detected through a laboratory blood test. The athletic trainer should refer the athlete to a physician for blood work.

5-3 A small amount of protein (slightly above to about double the protein RDA) is needed for developing muscles in a training program. However, an athlete can easily meet these necessary higher amounts by eating a variety of foods, especially protein-rich foods. Thus, athletes do not need protein supplements because their diets typically exceed protein recommendations.

5-4 The amount of glycogen that can be stored in muscle and liver can be increased by reducing the training program a few days before competing and by significantly increasing carbohydrate intake during the week before the event. Nutrients consumed over several days before competition are much more important than what is eaten three hours before an event. The purpose of the preevent meal should be to provide the competitor with sufficient nutrient energy and fluids for competition while taking into consideration the digestibility of the food. Glucose-rich drinks taken at regular intervals are beneficial for highly intense and prolonged events that severely deplete glycogen stores.

5-5 This athlete must understand the importance of adding lean tissue muscle mass rather than increasing his percentage of body fat. His caloric intake must be increased so that he is in a positive caloric balance of about 500 calories per day. Additional calorie intake should consist primarily of CHO. Additional supplementation with protein is not necessary. It is absolutely essential that this athlete incorporate a weight-training program using heavy weights that will overload the muscle, forcing it to hypertrophy over a period of time.

5-6 Treating eating disorders is difficult even for health care professionals specifically trained to counsel these individuals. The athletic trainer should approach the athlete, not with accusation, but with support, showing concern about her weight loss and expressing a desire to help her secure appropriate counseling. Remember that the athlete must first be willing to admit that she has an eating disorder before treatment and counseling will be effective. Eliciting the support of close friends and family can help with treatment.

REVIEW QUESTIONS AND CLASS ACTIVITIES

1. What is the value of good nutrition in terms of an athlete's performance and injury prevention?
2. Ask coaches of different sports about the type of diet they recommend for their athletes and their rationale for doing so.
3. Have a nutritionist talk to the class about food myths and fallacies.
4. Have each member of the class prepare a week's food diary; then compare it with other class members' diaries.
5. What are the daily dietary requirements according to the food pyramid? Should the requirements of the typical athlete's diet differ from them? If so, in what ways?
6. Have the class debate the value of vitamin and mineral supplements.
7. Describe the advantages and disadvantages of supplementing iron and calcium.
8. Is there some advantage to preevent nutrition?
9. Are there advantages or disadvantages in the vegetarian diet for the athlete?
10. What is the current thinking on the value of creatine as a nutritional supplement?
11. What is the primary concern of using herbs?
12. Discuss the importance of athletes monitoring their body composition.
13. Explain the most effective technique for losing weight.
14. Contrast the signs and symptoms of bulimia and anorexia nervosa. If an athletic trainer is aware of an athlete who may have an eating disorder, what should he or she do?

REFERENCES

1. Allred J: Too much of a good thing? An overemphasis on eating low-fat foods may be contributing to the alarming increase in overweight among US adults, *J Am Diet Assoc* 95:417, 1995.
2. Amato H, Wenos D: Bioelectrical impedance of hydration effects on muscular strength and endurance in college wrestlers, *J Ath Train* 28(2):170, 1993.
3. American College of Sports Medicine: Proper and improper weight loss programs, *Med Sci Sports Exerc* 15:ix, 1983.
4. American Dietetic Association and Canadian Dietetic Association: Position of the American Dietetic Association and Canadian Dietetic Association: nutrition for physical fitness and athletic performance of adults, *J Am Diet Assoc* 93:691, 1993.
5. Anderson J, Stender M, Rodando P: Nutrition and bone in physical activity and sport. In Wolinsky I, Hickson J: In *Nutrition in exercise and sport*, Boca Raton, 1998, CRC Press.
6. Balsom P, Soderlund K, Ekblom B: Creatine in humans with special reference to creatine supplementation, *Sports Med* 18:268, 1994.
7. Beltz S, Doering P: Efficacy of nutritional supplements used by athletes, *Clin Pharm* 12:900, 1993.
8. Blackburn H: Olestra and the FDA, *N Engl J Med* 334(15):984, 1996.
9. Brownell KD, Steen SN, Wilmore JH: Weight regulation practices in athletes: analysis of metabolic and health effects, *Med Sci Sports Exerc* 19(6):546, 1987 (review).
10. Burke L, Read R: Dietary supplements in sport, *Sports Med* 15(1):4365, 1993.
11. Champaign BN: Body fat distribution: metabolic consequences and implications for weight loss, *Med Sci Sport Exerc* 22:291, 1990.
12. Clark K: Working with college athletes, coaches, and trainers at a major university, *Int J Sports Med* 4:135, 1994.
13. Cole K, Grandjean R, Sobszak R: Effect of carbohydrate composition on fluid balance, gastric emptying, and exercise performance, *Int J Sports Nutr* 3:408, 1993.
14. Coleman E: Eating before exercise, *Sports Med Digest* 16(4):6, 1995.
15. Coleman E: Nutritional concerns of vegetarian athletes, *Sports Med Digest* 17(2):1–3, 1995.
16. Costill D, Hargreaves M: Carbohydrate nutrition and fatigue, *Sports Med* 13(2):86, 1992.
17. Cowart V: Dietary supplements: alternatives to anabolic steroids? *Physician Sportsmed* 20(3):24, 1993.
18. Coyle EF, Coyle E: CHOs that speed recovery from training, *Physician Sportsmed* 21:111, 1993.
19. Diplock A: Antioxidant nutrients and disease prevention: an overview, *Am J Clin Nutr* 53:189S, 1991.
20. Dodd S, Herb R, Powers S: Caffeine and exercise performance: an update, *Sports Med* 15:14, 1993.
21. Food and Drug Administration: Food labeling: reference daily intakes, *Federal Register* 59(2):427, 1994.
22. Food and Nutrition Board, National Academy of Sciences—National Research Council: Recommended dietary allowances, ed 12, Washington, DC, 1998, US Government Printing Office.
23. Grandjean A: Practices and recommendations of sports nutritionists, *Int J Sports Nutr* 3:232, 1993.
24. Greenwalt D, Krabbe J, Derrickson B: Current trends in sports supplementation, Dixon, Ill, 1997, ISP Nutrition.
25. Grunewald K, Bailey R: Commercially marketed supplements for body-building athletes, *Sports Med* 15(2):90, 1993.
26. Gutherie H, Picciano M: *Human nutrition*, St Louis, 1994, Mosby.
27. Hennekens C, Buring L, Peto R, editors: Antioxidant vitamins—benefits not yet proved, *N Engl J Med* 330:1080, 1994.
28. Herbert V: The antioxidant supplement myth, *Am J Clin Nutr* 60:157, 1994.
29. Herbert V: Health claims in food labeling and advertising: literal truths but false messages; deceptions by omission of adverse facts, *Nutr Today* 19:25, 1987.
30. Hoffman R, Garewal H: Antioxidants and the prevention of coronary heart disease, *Arch Int Med* 155:241, 1995.
31. Holt W: Nutrition and athletes, *Am Fam Physician* 47:1757, 1993.
32. Horton T et al: Fat and carbohydrate overfeeding in humans: different effects on energy storage, *Am J Clin Nutr* 62:19, 1995.
33. Jackson C: *Nutrition for recreational athletes*, Boca Raton, 1995, CRC Press.

34. Kirshner E, Lewis R, O'Connor P: Bone mineral density and dietary intake of college gymnasts, *Med Sci Sports Exerc* 24(4):543, 1995.

35. Kleiner S: The beef on food myths, *Physician Sportsmed* 20(10):23, 1992.

36. Kleiner S: Nutrition on the run, *Physician Sportsmed* 23(2):15, 1995.

37. Kreider R: Amino acid supplementation and exercise performance: analysis of the proposed ergogenic value, *Sports Med* 16(3):190, 1993.

38. Krieder R, Ferreira M, Wilson M: Effects of creatine supplementation on body composition, strength, and sprint performance, *Med Sci Sports Exerc* 30(1):73, 1998.

39. Lemon P, Proctor D: Protein intake and athletic performance, *Sports Med* 12(5):313, 1991.

40. Lindamen A: Eating for endurance and ultraendurance, *Physician Sportsmed* 20(3):87, 1992.

41. Lohman T: *Advances in body composition assessment*, Champaign, Ill, 1992, Human Kinetics.

42. McArdle W, Katch F, Katch V: *Exercise physiology: energy, nutrition, and human performance*, Philadelphia, 1994, Lea & Febiger.

43. Millard-Stafford M: Fluid replacement during exercise in the heat: review and recommendations, *Sports Med* 13(4):223, 1992.

44. Payne W, Hahn D: *Focus on health*, ed 2, Dubuque, 1998, McGraw-Hill.

45. Rauch L, Rodger I, Wilson J: The effects of carbohydrate loading on muscle glycogen content and cycling performance, *Int J Sports Med* 5(l):25, 1995.

46. Reimers K: The role of liquid supplements in weight gain, *Strength Cond* 17(l):64, 1995.

47. Schlabach G: Carbohydrate strategies for injury prevention, *J Ath Train* 29(3):244, 1994.

48. Sherman WM, Peden MC, Wright DA: Carbohydrate feedings 1 hour before exercise improves exercise performance, *Am J Clin Nutr* 54:866, 1991.

49. Short S: Health quackery: our role as professionals, *J Am Diet Assoc* 94:607, 1994.

50. Sobal J, Marquat L: Vitamin/mineral supplementation use among athletes: a review of the literature, *Int J Sports Med* 4:320, 1994.

51. Springer K, Hager M: Beyond vitamins, *Newsweek*, April 25, 1994.

52. Thornton JS: Feast or famine: eating disorders in athletes, *Physician Sportsmed* 18:116, 1990.

53. US Department of Agriculture and US Department of Health and Human Services: *Nutrition and your health: dietary guidelines for Americans*, ed 4, Washington, DC, 1995.

54. Volek J, et al: Creatine supplementation enhances muscular performance during high-intensity resistance exercise, *J Am Diet Assoc* 97:765, 1997.

55. Wardlaw GM, Insel PM: *Perspectives in nutrition*, ed 3, St Louis, 1996, Mosby.

56. Wiita B, Stombaugh I, Bush J: Nutrition knowledge and eating patterns of young female athletes, IOHPERD 66(3):33, 1995.

57. Williams C, Devlin J: Foods, nutrition, and sport performance, London, 1992, E & FN Spon.

58. Williams M: *Nutrition for fitness and sports*, Dubuque, Iowa, 1992, William C Brown.

59. Williams M: The use of nutritional ergogenic aids in sports: is it an ethical issue? *Int J Sport Nutr* 4:120, 1994.

ANNOTATED BIBLIOGRAPHY

American Dietetic Association, Dyrugff R: *Complete food and nutrition guide*, Minnetonka, Minn, 1996, Chronimed Publishing.

This extensive text is packed with information concerning every aspect of eating and food safety. This book is highly recommended for individuals who aspire to the highest understanding of healthful eating.

Barrett S, Herbert V: *The vitamin pushers: how the "health food" industry is selling America a bill of goods*, Buffalo, 1994, Prometheus Books.

This book outlines how the health-food companies have created a multi-billion-dollar industry, mostly by preying on the fears of uninformed consumers.

Clark N: *Sport nutrition guidebook: eating to fuel your active lifestyle*, Champaign, 1990, Leisure Press.

Real-life case studies of nutritional advice are given to athletes; the book also provides recommendations for pregame meals.

Cooper K: *Antioxidant revolution*, Nashville, 1994, Thomas Nelson.

This text discusses the latest research on antioxidants and tells how they can decrease the risk of cancer and heart disease, delay premature aging, and power the immune system to fight disease.

Crayhom R: *Nutrition made simple: a comprehensive guide to the latest findings in optimal nutrition*, New York, 1994, M Evans.

Topics in this book include what constitutes a healthy diet, how energy can be increased, which healthy fats are essential for weight loss and disease prevention, and the role of antioxidants.

Wardlaw GM, Insel PM: *Perspectives in nutrition*, ed 3, St Louis, 1996, Mosby.

This comprehensive text deals with all aspects of nutrition.

Williams M: *Nutrition for fitness and sport*, Dubuque, 1992, William C Brown.

This excellent and comprehensive guide provides the concepts of sound nutrition for individuals engaging in sport or fitness activities.

Environmental Considerations

When you finish this chapter you should be able to

- Describe the physiology of hyperthermia and the clinical signs of heat stress and how they can be prevented.
- Identify the causes of hypothermia and the major cold disorders and how they can be prevented.
- Describe the problems that high altitude might present to the athlete and how they can be managed.
- Explain how an athlete should be protected from exposure to the sun.
- Describe precautions that should be taken in an electrical storm.
- List the problems that are presented to the athlete by air pollution and how they can be avoided.
- Discuss what effect circadian dysrhythmia can have on athletes and the best procedures for handling any problems that arise.
- Discuss the effect of artificial versus natural turf on the incidence of injury.

Environmental stress can adversely affect an athlete's performance and in some instances can pose a serious health threat. The environmental categories that are of major concern to athletic trainers and coaches, particularly those involved in outdoor sports, include hyperthermia, hypothermia, altitude, exposure to the sun, electrical storms, air pollution, and circadian dysrhythmia (jet lag).

HYPERTHERMIA

A major concern in sports is the problem of **hyperthermia.** Over the years, hyperthermia has caused a number of deaths among football players and distance runners in high school and college.[1]

It is vitally important that the athletic trainer and the coaching staff have knowledge about temperature and humidity factors to assist them in planning practice. The athletic trainer must clearly understand when environmental heat and humidity are at a dangerous level and make recommendations to the coaches accordingly. In addition, the clinical symptoms and signs of heat stress must be recognized and managed properly.

Heat Stress

Regardless of the level of physical conditioning, athletes must take extreme caution when exercising in hot, humid weather. Prolonged exposure to extreme heat can result in heat illness.[28] Heat stress is preventable, but each year many athletes suffer illness and even death from some heat-related cause.[5] Athletes who exercise in hot, humid environments are particularly vulnerable to heat stress.[42]

The physiological processes in the body will continue to function only as long as body temperature is maintained within a normal range.[23] Maintenance of normal temperature in a hot environment depends on the ability of the body to dissipate heat. Body temperature can be affected by five factors, described in the following sections.

Metabolic Heat Production

Normal metabolic function in the body results in the production and radiation of heat. Consequently, metabolism will always cause an increase in body heat that depends on the intensity of the physical activity. The higher the metabolic rate, the more heat produced.

hyperthermia
Elevated body temperature.

Heat can be gained or lost through:
- Metabolic heat production
- Conductive heat exchange
- Convective heat exchange
- Radiant heat exchange
- Evaporative heat loss

Conductive Heat Exchange

Physical contact with other objects can result in either a heat loss or heat gain. A football player competing on artificial turf on a sunny August afternoon will experience an increase in body temperature simply by standing on the turf.

Convective Heat Exchange

Body heat can be either lost or gained depending on the temperature of the circulating medium. A cool breeze will always tend to cool the body by removing heat from the body surface. Conversely, if the temperature of the circulating air is higher than the temperature of the skin, body heat increases.

Radiant Heat Exchange

Radiant heat from sunshine causes an increase in body temperature. Obviously, the effects of this radiation are much greater in the sunshine than in the shade.[18] On a cloudy day, the body also emits radiant heat energy; thus, radiation may result in either heat loss or heat gain. During exercise the body attempts to dissipate heat produced by metabolism by dilating superficial arterial and venous vessels, thus channeling blood to the superficial capillaries in the skin.

Evaporative Heat Loss

Sweat glands in the skin allow water to be transported to the surface, where it evaporates, taking large quantities of heat with it. When the temperature and radiant heat of the environment become higher than body temperature, loss of body heat becomes highly dependent on the process of sweat evaporation.

A normal person can sweat off about one quart of water per hour for about two hours.[31] Sweating does not cause heat loss. The sweat must evaporate for heat to be dissipated. But the air must be relatively free of water for evaporation to occur. Heat loss through evaporation is severely impaired when the relative humidity reaches 65 percent and virtually stops when the humidity reaches 75 percent.

It should be obvious that heat-related problems have the greatest chance of occurring on days when the sun is bright and the temperature and relative humidity are high. However, cramps, heat exhaustion, and heatstroke can occur whenever the body's ability to dissipate heat is impaired.

Monitoring the Heat Index

The athletic trainer must exercise common sense when overseeing the health care of athletes training or competing in the heat. Obviously, when the combination of heat, humidity, and bright sunshine is present, extra caution is warranted. The universal wet bulb globe temperature (WBGT) index provides the athletic trainer with an objective means for determining necessary precautions for practice and competition in hot weather.[27] The index incorporates readings from several different thermometers. The dry bulb temperature (DBT) is recorded from a standard mercury thermometer. The wet bulb temperature (WBT) uses a wet wick or piece of gauze wrapped around the end of a thermometer that is swung around in the air. Globe temperature (GT) measures the sun's radiation and has a black metal casing around the end of the thermometer. Once the three readings have been taken, the following formula is used to calculate the WBGT index:

> The WBGT index measures heat and humidity.

$$WBGT = 0.1 \times DBT + 0.7 \times WBT + GT \times 0.2$$

Using this formula yields an index on which recommendations relative to outdoor activity are based (Table 6-1).

The DBT and WBT can be easily measured using either of two instruments: a physiodyne (Figure 6-1A) or a sling psychrometer (Figure 6-1B). Both instruments

TABLE 6-1 Universal WBGT Index

WBGT Index for Outdoor Activities (Wet Bulb Global Temperature)		
Range	Signal Flag	Activity
82–84.9	Green	Alert for possible increase in index
85–87.9	Yellow	Active practice curtailed (unacclimated athletes)
88–89.9	Red	Active practice curtailed (all athletes except most acclimated)
90+		All training stopped; team meetings or demonstrations

calculate the difference between DBT and WBT, which is the relative humidity. Either instrument is inexpensive and easy to use.

Heat Illnesses

Exercising in a hot, humid environment can cause various forms of heat illness, including heat rash, heat syncope, heat cramps, heat exhaustion, and heatstroke (heat hyperexia).

Heat Rash

Heat rash, also called prickly heat, is a benign condition associated with a red, raised rash accompanied by sensations of prickling and tingling during sweating. It usually occurs when the skin is continuously wet with unevaporated sweat. The rash is generally localized to areas of the body covered with clothing. Continually toweling the body can help prevent the rash from developing.[38]

Heat Syncope

Heat syncope, or heat collapse, is associated with rapid physical fatigue during overexposure to heat. It is usually caused by standing in heat for long periods or by not being accustomed to exercising in the heat. It is caused by peripheral vasodilation of superficial vessels, hypotension, or a pooling of blood in the extremities, which

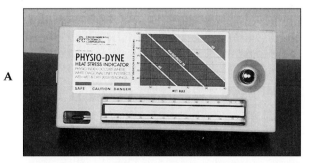

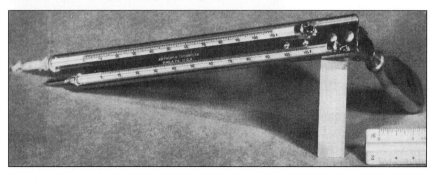

Figure 6-1

A, A physiodyne, or **B,** a sling psychrometer may be used to determine the WBGT heat index.

results in dizziness, fainting, and nausea. Heat syncope is quickly relieved by laying the athlete down in a cool environment and replacing fluids.[38]

Heat Cramps

Heat cramps occur because of some imbalance between water and electrolytes.

Heat cramps are extremely painful muscle spasms that occur most commonly in the calf and abdomen, although any muscle can be involved (Table 6-2). The occurrence of heat cramps is related to excessive loss of water and several electrolytes or ions (sodium, chloride, potassium, magnesium, and calcium), which are each essential elements in muscle contraction.

Profuse sweating involves losses of large amounts of water and small quantities of sodium, potassium, magnesium, and calcium, thus destroying the balance in concentration of these elements within the body. This imbalance will ultimately result in painful muscle contractions and cramps. The person most likely to get heat cramps is one who is in fairly good condition but who simply overexerts in the heat.

Heat cramps may be prevented by adequate replacement of sodium, chloride, potassium, magnesium, calcium, and most important, water. Ingestion of salt tablets is not recommended. Simply salting food a bit more heavily can replace sodium; bananas are particularly high in potassium; and calcium is present in milk, cheese, and dairy products. The immediate treatment for heat cramps is ingestion of large quantities of water and mild stretching with ice massage of the muscle in spasm. An athlete who experiences heat cramps will generally not be able to return to practice or competition for the remainder of the day because cramping is likely to reoccur.

Heat Exhaustion

Heat exhaustion results from dehydration.

Heat exhaustion results from inadequate replacement of fluids lost through sweating (Table 6-2). Clinically, the victim of heat exhaustion will collapse and manifest profuse sweating, pale skin, mildly elevated temperature (102° F), dizziness, hyperventilation, and rapid pulse.

It is sometimes possible to spot athletes who are having problems with heat exhaustion. They may begin to develop heat cramps. They may become disoriented and light-headed, and their physical performance will not be up to their usual standards when fluid replacement has not been adequate. In general, persons in poor physical condition who attempt to exercise in the heat are most likely to get heat exhaustion.

Immediate treatment of heat exhaustion requires ingestion and eventually intravenous replacement of large quantities of water.[32] It is essential for the athletic trainer to obtain a rectal temperature to differentiate heat exhaustion from heatstroke. In heat exhaustion, the rectal temperature will be around 102° F. If possible, the athlete should be placed in a cool environment, although it is more critical to replace fluids.

Heatstroke

Unlike heat cramps and heat exhaustion, heatstroke is a serious, life-threatening emergency (Table 6-2). The specific cause of heatstroke is unknown. It is clinically characterized by sudden collapse with loss of consciousness; flushed, hot skin with less sweating than would be seen with heat exhaustion; shallow breathing; a rapid, strong pulse; and most important, a core temperature of 106° F or higher. The heatstroke victim experiences a breakdown of the thermoregulatory mechanism caused by excessively high body temperature; the body loses the ability to dissipate heat through sweating.

Heatstroke can occur suddenly and without warning. The athlete will not usually experience signs of heat cramps or heat exhaustion. The possibility of death from heatstroke can be significantly reduced if body temperature is lowered to normal within forty-five minutes. The longer that the body temperature is elevated to 106° F or higher, the higher the mortality rate.

6-1

Critical Thinking Exercise

A wrestler collapses during a match and exhibits signs of profuse sweating, pale skin, mildly elevated temperature (102° F), dizziness, hyperventilation, and rapid pulse. When questioned by the athletic trainer, the wrestler indicates that earlier in the day he took diuretic medication to facilitate water loss in an effort to help him make weight.

? What type of heat illness is the athlete experiencing, and what does the athletic trainer need to do to manage this situation appropriately?

TABLE 6-2 Heat Disorders: Treatment and Prevention

Disorders	Cause	Clinical Features and Diagnosis	Treatment	Prevention
Heat cramps	Hard work in heat; sweating heavily; imbalance between water and electrolytes	Muscle twitching and cramps, usually after midday; spasms in arms, legs, abdomen	Ingesting large amounts of water, mild stretching, and ice massage of affected muscle	Acclimatize athlete properly; provide large quantities of water; increase intake of calcium, sodium, and potassium slightly
Heat exhaustion	Prolonged sweating; inadequate replacement of body fluid losses; diarrhea; intestinal infection	Excessive thirst, dry tongue and mouth; weight loss; fatigue; weakness; incoordination; mental dullness; small urine volume; slightly elevated body temperature; high serum protein and sodium; reduced swelling	Bed rest in cool room, IV fluids if drinking is impaired; increase fluid intake to 6 to 8 L/day; sponge with cool water; keep record of body weight; keep fluid balance record; provide semiliquid food until salination is normal	Supply adequate water and other liquids Provide adequate rest and opportunity for cooling
Heatstroke	Thermoregulatory failure of sudden onset	Abrupt onset, preceded by headache, vertigo, and fatigue; flushed skin; relatively less sweating than seen with heat exhaustion; pulse rate increases rapidly and may reach 160 to 180; respiration increases; blood pressure seldom rises; temperature rises rapidly to 105° or 106° F (40° to 41° C); athlete feels as if he or she is burning up; diarrhea, vomiting; circulatory collapse may produce death; could lead to permanent brain damage	Heroic measures to reduce temperature must be taken immediately (e.g., sponge cool water and air fan over body, massage limbs); remove to hospital as soon as possible	Ensure proper acclimatization, proper hydration Educate those supervising activities conducted in the heat Adapt activities to environment Screen participants with past history of heat illness for malignant hyperthermia

Heatstroke is a life-threatening emergency.

Every first-aid effort should be directed to lowering body temperature.[43] Get the athlete into a cool environment. Strip all clothing off the athlete, sponge him or her down with cool water, and fan with a towel. Do not immerse the athlete in cold water. It is imperative that the victim be transported to a hospital as quickly as possible. Do not wait for an ambulance; transport the victim in whatever vehicle happens to be available. The replacement of fluid is not critical in initial first aid.

Malignant hyperthermia Malignant hyperthermia is a rare muscle disorder that causes hypersensitivity to anesthesia and hot environments. This disorder causes muscle temperatures to increase faster than core temperatures, and its symptoms are similar to those of heatstroke. The athlete complains of muscle pain after exercise, and rectal temperature remains elevated for ten to fifteen minutes after exercise. Muscle biopsy is necessary for diagnosis. Athletes with malignant hyperthermia should be disqualified from competing in hot, humid environments.[21]

Preventing Heat Illness

The prevention of hyperthermia involves:
- Gradual acclimatization
- Identification of susceptible individuals
- Lightweight uniforms
- Routine weight record keeping
- Unrestricted fluid replacement
- Well-balanced diet
- Routine temperature and humidity readings

The athletic trainer should understand that heat illness is preventable if he or she exercises some common sense and caution. An athlete can only perform at an optimal level when dehydration and hyperthermia are minimized by the ingestion of ample volumes of fluid during exercise and by common-sense precautions in keeping cool.[32] *Focus Box:* "NCAA guidelines for preventing heat illness" summarizes NCAA-recommended guidelines for preventing heat illness.[35] The following factors should be considered when planning a training or competitive program that is likely to take place during hot weather.

Fluid and Electrolyte Replacement

During hot weather it is essential that athletes continually replace fluids lost through evaporation by drinking large quantities of water.[8] Even low levels of dehydration (e.g., less than 2 percent loss of body weight) impair cardiovascular and thermoregulatory response and reduce the capacity for exercise.[32]

Sweating occurs whether or not the athlete drinks water, and if the sweat losses are not replaced by fluid intake over a period of several hours, dehydration results. An average runner may lose from 1.5 to 2.5 liters of water per hour through active sweating; much greater amounts can be lost by football players in warm-weather activity.[1] Consuming fluid in volumes approximating sweat loss maintains important physiological functions and significantly improves exercise performance, even during exercise lasting only one hour.[32]

ad libitum
To the amount desired.

Even if athletes take replacement fluids **ad libitum,** seldom is more than 50 percent of their fluid loss replaced.[33] Athletes usually find it uncomfortable to exercise

Focus

NCAA guidelines for preventing heat illness
- Obtain athletes' medical histories of previous heat illnesses
- Allow a period of seven to ten days for acclimatization
- Instruct athletes to wear appropriate clothing during the acclimatization period
- Take regular measurements of the WBGT index
- Encourage athletes to adequately replace fluids
- Record body weight of athletes before and after practice
- Identify susceptible athletes
- Constantly monitor athletes for signs of heat illness

Figure 6-2

Athletes must have unlimited access to water, especially in hot weather.

vigorously on a full stomach. The problem in fluid replacement is how rapidly the fluid can be eliminated from the stomach into the intestine, from which it can enter the bloodstream. Cold drinks (45° to 55° F [7.2° to 12.8° C]) tend to empty more rapidly from the stomach than do warmer drinks; they are not more likely to induce cramps, nor do they offer any particular threat to a normal heart.

Athletes must have unlimited access to water. There is no acceptable reason for allowing or causing an athlete to become hypohydrated.[35] Failure to permit ad libitum access will not only undermine an athlete's performance, but may also predispose the athlete to unnecessary heat-related illnesses (Figure 6-2).

A number of adverse physiological and potentially pathological effects can be caused by hypohydration, including reduced muscular strength and endurance, decreased blood and plasma volume, altered cardiac function, impaired thermoregulation, decreased kidney function, reduced glycogen stores, and loss of electrolytes.[35]

Commercially prepared drinks   Commercially prepared drinks may be used in fluid replacement. Ingestion of hypertonic solutions containing simple sugars and electrolyes tends to slow gastric emptying, thus depriving the working cell of much-needed fluid.[26] A cell needs water to function normally and may be damaged if sufficient amounts of water are not available. A solution that contains only 5 percent glucose will significantly retard the replacement of lost fluids.[8] Thus, ingestion of drinks containing simple sugars and electrolytes during activity is not recommended, although the drinks may be useful for replenishing fluids and electrolytes before and after activity in the heat. Athletes may find it necessary to replace glucose during activities that last longer than forty-five minutes, and in this case the drinks may be beneficial.[29]

The new generation of commercially manufactured drinks has reduced the negative effects of simple sugar solutions on gastric emptying by using a polymerized form of glucose. This process maximizes carbohydrate content while making the solution less hypertonic. Thus, a 5 percent solution of polymerized glucose provides the athlete with more water and carbohydrates than does a drink containing simple sugars.[26]

Gradual Acclimatization

Gradual acclimatization is probably the single most effective method of avoiding heat stress. Acclimatization should involve not only becoming accustomed to heat but also becoming acclimatized to exercising in hot temperatures.[28] A good preseason conditioning program, started well before the advent of the competitive season and carefully graded as to intensity, is recommended.[35] Progressive exposure should occur over a seven- to ten-day period.[35] During the first five or six days, an 80 percent acclimatization can be achieved on the basis of a two-hour practice period in the morning and a two-hour practice period in the afternoon. Each practice period should be broken down into twenty minutes of work alternated with twenty minutes of rest in the shade.

Identifying Susceptible Individuals

Athletes with a large muscle mass are particularly prone to heat illness.[30] Body build must be considered when determining individual susceptibility to heat stress. Overweight individuals may have as much as 18 percent greater heat production than underweight individuals because metabolic heat is produced proportionately to surface area. It has been found that heat illness victims tend to be overweight. Death from heatstroke increases at a ratio of approximately four to one as body weight increases.[30]

Women are apparently more physiologically efficient in body temperature regulation than men are; although women possess as many heat-activated sweat glands as men do, they sweat less and manifest a higher heart rate when working in heat.[26] Although slight differences exist, the same precautionary measures apply to both genders.

Other individuals who are susceptible to heat stress include those with relatively poor fitness levels, those with a history of heat illness, and anyone with a febrile condition.[35]

Uniforms

Uniforms should be selected on the basis of temperature and humidity. Initial practices should be conducted in short-sleeved T-shirts, shorts, and socks, and athletes should be moved gradually into short-sleeved net jerseys, lightweight pants, and socks as acclimatization proceeds. All early-season practices and games should be conducted in lightweight uniforms with short-sleeved net jerseys and socks. Rubberized suits should never be used.[35]

Weight Records

Careful weight records of all players must be kept. Weights should be measured both before and after practice for at least the first two weeks of practice. If a sudden increase in temperature or humidity occurs during the season, weight should be recorded again for a period of time. A loss of 3 percent to 5 percent of body weight will reduce blood volume and could lead to a health threat.[46]

Temperature and Humidity Readings

Dry bulb and wet bulb temperature readings should be taken on the field before practice to monitor the heat index.[27] Modifications to the practice schedule should be made according to the severity of existing environmental conditions. The purchase of a physiodyne or sling psychrometer for this purpose is recommended (see Figure 6-1).

Clinical Indications and Treatment

Focus Box: "Environmental conduct of sports, particularly football" and Table 6-2 list the clinical symptoms of the various hyperthermia conditions and the indications for treatment. Although the Focus Box calls particular attention to some of the procedures for football, the precautions in general apply to all sports. Because of the specialized equipment worn by the players, football requires special consideration. Many football uniforms are heat traps and serve to compound the environmental heat problem, which is not true of lighter uniforms.

6-2

Critical Thinking Exercise

A high school football coach in southern Louisiana is concerned about the likelihood that several of his players will suffer heat-related illness during preseason football practice in the first two weeks of August. The school has recently hired an athletic trainer, and the coach has come to the athletic trainer to ask what can be done to minimize the risk of heat-related illnesses.

? What recommendations or intervention strategies can the athletic trainer implement to help the athletes avoid heat-related illnesses?

Environmental conduct of sports, particularly football

I. General warning
   A. Most adverse reactions to environmental heat and humidity occur during the first few days of training.
   B. It is necessary to become thoroughly acclimatized to heat to successfully compete in hot or humid environments.
   C. Occurrence of a heat injury indicates poor supervision of the sports program.
II. Athletes who are most susceptible to heat injury
   A. Individuals unaccustomed to working in the heat.
   B. Overweight individuals, particularly large linemen.
   C. Eager athletes who constantly compete at capacity.
   D. Ill athletes who have an infection, fever, or gastrointestinal disturbance.
   E. Athletes who receive immunization injections and subsequently develop temperature elevations.
III. Prevention of heat injury
   A. Take complete medical history and provide physical examination.
      1. Include history of previous heat illnesses or fainting in the heat.
      2. Include inquiry about sweating and peripheral vascular defects.
   B. Evaluate general physical condition and type and duration of training activities for previous month.
      1. Extent of work in the heat.
      2. General training activities.
   C. Measure temperature and humidity on the practice or playing fields.
      1. Make measurements before and during training or competitive sessions.
      2. Adjust activity level to environmental conditions.
         a. Decrease activity if hot or humid.
         b. Eliminate unnecessary clothing when hot or humid.
   D. Acclimatize athletes to heat gradually.
      1. Acclimatization to heat requires work in the heat.
         a. Use recommended type and variety of warm weather workouts for preseason training.
         b. Provide graduated training program for first seven to ten days and other abnormally hot or humid days.
      2. Adequate rest intervals and water replacement should be provided during the acclimatization period.
   E. Monitor body weight loss during activity in the heat.
      1. Body water should be replaced as it is lost.
         a. Allow additional water as desired by players.
         b. Provide salt on training tables (no salt tablets should be taken).
         c. Weigh athletes each day before and after training or competition.
            (1) Treat athlete who loses excessive weight each day.
            (2) Treat well-conditioned athlete who continues to lose weight for several days.
   F. Monitor clothing and uniforms.
      1. Provide lightweight clothing that is loose fitting at the neck, waist, and sleeves; use shorts and T-shirt at beginning of training.
      2. Avoid excessive padding and taping.
      3. Avoid use of long stockings, long sleeves, double jerseys, and other excess clothing.
      4. Avoid use of rubberized clothing or sweatsuits.
      5. Provide clean clothing daily—all items.
   G. Provide rest periods to dissipate accumulated body heat.
      1. Rest athletes in cool, shaded area with some air movement.
      2. Avoid hot brick walls or hot benches.
      3. Instruct athletes to loosen or remove jerseys or other garments.
      4. Provide water during the rest period.
IV. Trouble signs: stop activity!

Headache	
Nausea	Diarrhea
Mental slowness	Cramps
Incoherence	Seizures
Visual disturbance	Rigidity
Fatigue	Weak, rapid pulse
Weakness	Pallor
Unsteadiness	Flush
Collapse	Faintness
Unconsciousness	Chill
Vomiting	Cyanotic appearance

Guidelines for Athletes Who Intentionally Lose Weight

Wrestlers or other athletes who purposely dehydrate themselves as a means of making weight are predisposing themselves to heat-related illness and may in fact be creating a potentially life-threatening situation. Weight loss to make some predetermined weight limit should absolutely not be accomplished through dehydration. The process must be gradual over a period of several weeks, even months, and should result from a reduction in the percentage of body fat relative to lean body mass. The NCAA and many state high school federations have recently established guidelines for weight loss and set policies for how and when a wrestler can officially weigh in.

HYPOTHERMIA

Many sports played in cold weather do not require heavy protective clothing; thus, weather becomes a factor in injury susceptibility.

Cold weather is a frequent adjunct to many outdoor sports in which the sport itself does not require heavy protective clothing; consequently, the weather becomes a pertinent factor in injury susceptibility.[48] In most instances, the activity itself enables the athlete to increase the metabolic rate sufficiently to function physically in a normal manner and dissipate the resulting heat and perspiration through the usual physiological mechanisms. An athlete may fail to warm up sufficiently or may become chilled because of relative inactivity for varying periods of time demanded by the particular sport either during competition or training; consequently, the athlete is exceedingly prone to injury. Low temperatures alone can pose some problems, but when such temperatures are further accentuated by wind, the chill factor becomes critical (Figure 6-3).[39] For example, a runner proceeding at a pace of 10 mph directly into a wind of 5 mph creates a chill factor equivalent to a 15-mph headwind.

A third factor, dampness or wetness, further increases the risk of hypothermia. Air at a temperature of 50° F is relatively comfortable, but water at the same tem-

Figure 6-3

Low temperatures can pose serious problems for the athlete, but wind chill could be a critical factor.

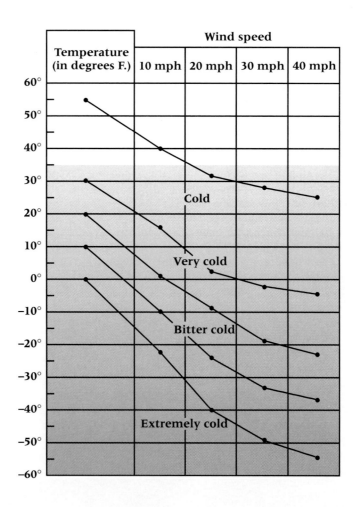

perature is intolerable. The combination of cold, wind, and dampness creates an environment that easily predisposes the athlete to hypothermia.

Sixty-five percent of the heat produced by the body is lost through radiation. This loss occurs most often from the warm, vascular areas of the head and neck, which may account for as much as 50 percent of total heat loss.[35] Twenty percent of heat loss is through evaporation, of which two thirds is through the skin and one third is through the respiratory tract.[47]

As an athlete's muscular fatigue builds up during strenuous physical activity in cold weather, the rate of exercise begins to drop and may reach a level wherein the body heat loss to the environment exceeds the metabolic heat protection, resulting in definite impairment of neuromuscular responses and exhaustion. A relatively small drop in body core temperature can induce shivering sufficient to materially affect an athlete's neuromuscular coordination. Shivering ceases below a body temperature of 85° to 90° F (29.4° to 32.2° C). Death is imminent if the core temperature rises to 107° F (41.6° C) or drops to between 77° and 85° F (25° and 29° C).

Low temperatures accentuated by wind and dampness can pose major problems for athletes.

Prevention

Apparel for competitors must be geared to the weather.[15] The function of such apparel is to provide a semitropical microclimate for the body and to prevent chilling. Several fabrics available on the market are waterproof and windproof but permit the passage of heat and allow sweat to evaporate. The clothing should not restrict movement, should be as lightweight as possible, and should consist of material that will permit the free passage of sweat and body heat that would otherwise accumulate on the skin or the clothing and provide a chilling factor when activity ceases. The athlete should routinely dress in thin layers of clothing that can easily be added or removed as the temperature decreases or increases. Continuous adjustment of these layers will reduce sweating and the likelihood that clothing will become damp or wet. Again, wetness or dampness plays a critical role in the development of hypothermia. To prevent chilling, athletes should wear warm-up suits before exercising, during activity breaks or rest periods, and at the termination of exercise. Activity in cold, wet, and windy weather poses some problems because such weather reduces the insulating value of clothing; consequently, the individual may be unable to achieve energy levels equal to the subsequent body heat losses. Runners who wish to continue outdoor work in cold weather should use lightweight insulating clothing and, if breathing cold air seems distressful, should use ski goggles and a ski face mask or should cover the mouth and nose with a free-hanging cloth.[2]

Inadequate clothing, improper warm-up, and a high chill factor form a triad that can lead to musculoskeletal injury, chilblains, frostbite, or the minor respiratory disorders associated with lower tissue temperatures. For work or sports in temperatures below 32° F (0° C), it is advisable to add a layer of protective clothing for every 5 mph of wind.

As is true in a hot environment, athletes exercising in a cold environment need to replace fluids. Dehydration causes reduced blood volume, which means less fluid is available for warming the tissues.[34,35] Athletes performing in a cold environment should be weighed before and after practice, especially in the first two weeks of the season.[34] Severe overexposure to a cold climate occurs less often than hyperthermia does in a warm climate; however, it is still a major risk of winter sports, long-distance running in cold weather, and swimming in cold water.[15]

Common Cold Injuries

Local cooling of the body can result in tissue damage ranging from superficial to deep. Exposure to a damp, freezing cold can cause frost nip. In contrast, exposure to dry temperatures well below freezing more commonly produces a deep, freezing type of frostbite.

Below-freezing temperatures may cause ice crystals to form between or within the cells and may eventually destroy the cell. Local capillaries can be injured, blood clots may form, and blood may be shunted away from the injury site to ensure the survival of the nonaffected tissue.

Cold injuries in sports include:
- Frost nip
- Frostbite

Frost Nip

Frost nip involves ears, nose, cheeks, chin, fingers, and toes. It commonly occurs when there is a high wind, severe cold, or both. The skin initially appears very firm, with cold, painless areas that may peel or blister in twenty-four to seventy-two hours. Affected areas can be treated early by firm, sustained pressure of the hand (without rubbing), by blowing hot breath on the spot, or if the injury is to the fingertips, by placing them in the armpits.

Frostbite

Chilblains result from prolonged and constant exposure to cold for many hours. In time, there is skin redness, swelling, tingling, and pain in the toes and fingers. This adverse response is caused by problems of peripheral circulation and can be avoided by preventing further cold exposure.

Superficial frostbite involves only the skin and subcutaneous tissue. The skin appears pale, hard, cold, and waxy. Palpating the injured area will reveal a sense of hardness but with yielding of the underlying deeper tissue structures. When rewarming, the superficial frostbite will at first feel numb, then will sting and burn. Later the area may produce blisters and be painful for a number of weeks.[36]

Deep frostbite is a serious injury indicating tissues that are frozen. This medical emergency requires immediate hospitalization. As with frost nip and superficial frostbite, the tissue is initially cold, hard, pale or white, and numb. Rapid rewarming is required, including hot drinks, heating pads, or hot water bottles that are 100° to 110° F (38° to 43° C). During rewarming, the tissue will become blotchy red, swollen, and extremely painful. Later the injury may become gangrenous, causing a loss of tissue.

ALTITUDE

Most athletic events are not conducted at extreme altitudes. For example, Mexico City's elevation, which is 7,600 feet high, is considered moderate, yet at this height there is a 7 percent to 8 percent decrease in maximum oxygen uptake.[45] This loss in maximum oxygen uptake represents a 4 percent to 8 percent deterioration in an athlete's performance in endurance events, depending on the duration of effort and lack of wind resistance. Often, the athlete's body compensates for this decrease in maximum oxygen uptake with corresponding tachycardia.[45] When the body is suddenly without its usual oxygen supply, hyperventilation can occur. Many of these responses result from the athlete having fewer red blood cells than necessary to adequately capture the available oxygen in the air.[7]

Most athletic events are not conducted at high altitudes.

Adaptation to Altitude

A major factor in altitude adaptation is the problem of oxygen deficiency. With a reduction in barometric pressure, the partial pressure of oxygen in inspired air is also low. Under these circumstances, the existing circulating red blood cells become less saturated, depriving tissue of needed oxygen.[25]

An individual's adaptation to high altitude depends on whether he or she is a native, resident, or visitor to the area. Natives of areas with high altitudes (e.g., the Andes and Nepal) have a larger chest capacity, more alveoli, more capillaries that transport blood to tissue, and a higher red blood cell level.[7] In contrast, the resident or the individual who stays at a high altitude for months or years makes a partial adaptation. His or her later adaptation includes the conservation of glucose, an increased number of mitochondria (the sources of energy in a cell), and increased formation of hemoglobin. In the visitor or the person who is in an early stage of adaptation to high altitude, a number of responses represent a physiological struggle. The responses include increased breathing, increased heart action, increased hemoglobin in circulating blood, increased blood alkalinity, and increased myoglobin as well as changes in the distribution of blood flow and cell enzyme activity.

There are many uncertainties about when to have an athlete go to an area of high altitude to train and compete.[6] Experts believe that having the athlete arrive two to three weeks before competition provides the best adjustment period, whereas others believe that, for psychological as well as physiological reasons, bringing in the athlete three days before competition is enough time.[45] This shorter adjustment period allows for the recovery of the acid-base balance in the blood but does not provide enough time for the athlete to achieve a significant adjustment in blood volume and maximum cardiac output.[45]

Altitude Illnesses

Coaches and athletic trainers must understand that some of their athletes may become ill when suddenly subjected to high altitudes.[51] These illnesses include acute mountain sickness, pulmonary edema, and when present in some athletes, an adverse reaction to the sickle cell trait.

Acute Mountain Sickness

One out of three individuals who go from a low to a moderate altitude of 7,000 to 8,000 feet will experience mild to moderate symptoms of acute mountain sickness. Symptoms include headache, nausea, vomiting, sleep disturbance, and dyspnea, which may last up to three days.[45] These symptoms have been attributed to a tissue disruption in the brain that affects the sodium and potassium balance. This imbalance can cause excess fluid retention within the cells and the subsequent occurrence of abnormal pressure.[45]

Pulmonary Edema

At an altitude of 9,000 to 10,000 feet, high-altitude pulmonary edema may occur. Characteristically, lungs at this altitude will accumulate a small amount of fluid within the alveolar walls.[45] In most individuals this fluid is absorbed in a few days, but in some it continues to collect and forms pulmonary edema. Symptoms of high-altitude pulmonary edema are dyspnea, cough, headache, weakness, and in some cases, unconsciousness.[45] The treatment of choice is to move the athlete to a lower altitude as soon as possible and give oxygen. The condition rapidly resolves once the athlete is at a lower altitude.[44]

Sickle Cell Trait Reaction

Approximately 8 percent to 10 percent of African Americans (approximately 2 million persons) have the sickle cell trait. In most, the trait is benign. The sickle cell trait relates to an abnormality of the structure of the red blood cell and its hemoglobin content.[12] When the abnormal hemoglobin molecules become deoxygenated as a result of exercise at a high altitude, the cells tend to clump together. This process causes an abnormal sickle shape to the red blood cell, which can be easily destroyed. This condition can cause an enlarged spleen, which in some cases has been known to rupture at high altitudes (see Chapter 29).[45]

OVEREXPOSURE TO SUN

Athletes, along with coaches, athletic trainers, and other support staff, frequently spend a great deal of time outdoors in direct sunlight. Precautions to protect these individuals from overexposure to ultraviolet light by applying sunscreens are often totally ignored.

Long-Term Effects on Skin

The most serious effects of long-term exposure to ultraviolet light are premature aging of the skin and skin cancer.[10] Lightly pigmented individuals are more susceptible to these maladies. Premature aging of the skin is characterized by dryness, cracking, and a decrease in the elasticity of the skin. Skin cancer is the most common malignant tumor found in humans and has been epidemiologically and clinically

6-3

Critical Thinking E x e r c i s e

A track athlete from Florida is traveling to Colorado to compete in a week-long track meet. She is concerned because she will be competing at a much higher altitude than she has been training at in Florida. She wants to make certain that she has a chance to adapt to the higher altitude.

? What should the athletic trainer recommend to maximize her ability to compete at the higher altitude?

associated with exposure to ultraviolet radiation. Damage to DNA is suspected as the cause of skin cancer, but the exact cause is unknown. The major types of skin cancer are basal cell carcinoma, squamous cell carcinoma, and malignant melanoma. Fortunately, the rate of cure exceeds 95 percent with early detection and treatment.[10]

Using Sunscreens

SPF
Sun protection factor.

Sunscreens applied to the skin can help prevent many of the damaging effects of ultraviolet radiation. A sunscreen's effectiveness in absorbing the sunburn-inducing radiation is expressed as the sun protection factor (**SPF**). An SPF of 6 indicates that an athlete can be exposed to ultraviolet light six times longer than without a sunscreen before the skin will begin to turn red. Higher numbers provide greater protection. However, athletes who have a family or personal history of skin cancer may experience significant damage to the skin even when wearing an SPF-15 sunscreen. Therefore, these individuals should wear an SPF-30 sunscreen.

Sunscreen should be worn regularly by athletes, coaches, and athletic trainers who spend time outside, particularly if the individual has a fair complexion, light hair, blue eyes, or skin that burns easily. People with dark complexions should also wear sunscreens to prevent sun damage.

Sun exposure causes a premature aging of skin (wrinkling, freckling, prominent blood vessels, coarsening of skin texture), induces the formation of precancerous growths, and increases the risk of developing basal and squamous cell skin cancers. Because 60 percent to 80 percent of our lifetime sun exposure is often obtained by age twenty, everyone over six months of age should use sunscreens.

Sunscreens are needed most between the months of March and November but should be used year-round. They are needed most between the hours of 10 A.M. and 4 P.M. and should be applied fifteen to thirty minutes before sun exposure. Although clothing and hats provide some protection from the sun, they are not a substitute for sunscreens (a typical white cotton T-shirt provides an SPF of only 5). Reflected sunlight from water, sand, and snow may effectively increase sun exposure and risk of burning.

ELECTRICAL STORMS

Research indicates that lightning is the number two cause of death by weather phenomena, accounting for 110 deaths per year.[50] Each institution should designate a chain of command to establish who should monitor both the weather forecast and changing weather of a threatening nature and to determine who makes the decision to remove a team from the practice field.[49] A person who hears thunder or sees lightning is in immediate danger and should seek a protective safe shelter in an indoor facility at once. An indoor facility is recommended as the safest protective shelter. However, if an indoor facility is not available, an automobile is a relatively safe alternative. If neither of these options is available, the following guidelines are recommended. Avoid standing under large trees and telephone poles. If the only alternative is a tree, choose a small grove of trees in a wooded area that is not on a hill. As a last alternative, find a ditch, ravine, or valley. In all instances outdoors, assume a crouched position. Avoid standing water and metal objects at all times (metal bleachers, metal cleats, umbrellas, etc.).[4]

The most dangerous storms give little or no warning.

The most dangerous storms give little or no warning; thunder and lightning are not heard or seen. Lightning is always accompanied by thunder, although 20 percent to 40 percent of thunder cannot be heard because of atmospheric disturbances. The **flash-to-bang** method provides an estimation of how far away lightning is occurring.[4] To calculate the number of miles away the lightning is, count the number of seconds from the time the lightning is sighted until the bang occurs and divide by five.[35] When the count is at 30 seconds, there is inherent danger and conditions should be closely monitored. When the count is 15 seconds, everyone should leave the field immediately and seek safe shelter.[35]

flash-to-bang
Number of seconds from lightning flash until the sound of thunder divided by five.

At times, the only natural forewarning that might precede a strike is when a person feels the hair stand on end and the skin tingle. At this point, the person is in imminent danger of being struck by lightning and should drop to the ground and assuming a crouched position immediately. A person should not lie flat. Should a ground strike occur nearby, lying flat increases the body's surface area that is exposed to the current traveling through the ground.[50]

The National Severe Storms Service recommends that thirty minutes should pass after the last sound of thunder is heard or lightning strike is seen before play is resumed.[35] This time is sufficient to allow the storm to pass and move out of lightning strike range. The perilous misconception that it is possible to see lightning coming and have time to act before it strikes could prove to be fatal. In reality, the lightning that is seen flashing is actually the return stroke flashing upward from the ground to the cloud, not downward. Seeing lightning strike means it has already hit.[50]

AIR POLLUTION

Air pollution is a major problem common in urban areas with large industries and heavy automobile traffic. Because athletes are outside for long periods of time during training or competition, they may be more susceptible to the effects of air pollution than is a sedentary individual who remains indoors.[3] There are two types of pollution: photochemical haze and smog. Photochemical haze consists of nitrogen dioxide and stagnant air that are acted on by sunlight to produce ozone.[3] Smog is produced by the combination of carbon monoxide and sulphur dioxide, which emanates from the combustion of a fossil fuel such as coal.

Ozone

Ozone is a form of oxygen in which three atoms of the element combine to form the molecule O_3. It is produced by a reaction of oxygen (O_2), nitrogen oxides, and hydrocarbon plus sunlight.[16]

When individuals are engaged in physical tasks requiring minimum effort, an increase in ozone in the air does not usually reduce functional capacity in normal work output. However, when individuals increase their work output (e.g., during exercise), their work capacity is decreased. The athlete may experience shortness of breath, coughing, chest tightness, pain during deep breathing, nausea, eye irritation, fatigue, lung irritation, and a lowered resistance to lung infections. Over a period of time, individuals may to some degree become desensitized to ozone. Asthmatics are at greater risk when ozone levels increase.

Sulfur Dioxide

Sulfur dioxide (SO_2) is a colorless gas that is a component of burning coal or petroleum. As an air contaminant it causes an increased resistance to air movement in and out of the lungs, a decreased ability of the lungs to rid themselves of foreign matter, shortness of breath, coughing, fatigue, and increased susceptibility to lung diseases. Sulfur dioxide causes an adverse effect mostly on asthmatics and other sensitive individuals. Nose breathing lessens the effects of sulfur dioxide because the nasal mucosa acts as a sulfur dioxide scrubber.[13]

Carbon Monoxide

Carbon monoxide (CO) is a colorless, odorless gas. In general, it reduces hemoglobin's ability to transport oxygen and restricts the release of oxygen to the tissue. Besides interfering in performance during exercise, carbon monoxide exposure interferes with various psychomotor, behavioral, and attention-related activities.[13]

Prevention

To avoid problems created by air pollution, the athlete must stop or significantly decrease physical activity during periods of high pollution. If activity is conducted, it should be performed when commuter traffic has lessened and when ambient

6-5
Critical Thinking Exercise

A lacrosse team is practicing on a remote field with no indoor facility in close proximity. The weather is rapidly worsening with the sky becoming dark and the wind blowing harder. Twenty minutes are left in the practice session, and the coach is hoping to finish practice before it begins to rain. Suddenly, there is a bolt of lightning and an immediate burst of thunder.

? How should the athletic trainer manage this extremely dangerous situation?

Air pollution is a major problem common in urban areas with large industries and heavy automobile traffic.

Carbon monoxide (CO) reduces hemoglobin's ability to transport and release oxygen in the body.

temperature has lowered. Ozone levels rise during dawn, peak at midday, and are much reduced after the late-afternoon rush hour. Running should be avoided on roads containing a concentration of auto emission and carbon monoxide.[16]

CIRCADIAN DYSRHYTHMIA (JET LAG)

Jet power has made it possible to travel thousands of miles in just a few hours. Athletes and athletic teams are now quickly transported from one end of the country to the other and to foreign lands. For some athletes, such travel induces a particular physiological stress, resulting in a syndrome that is identified as circadian dysrhythmia and that reflects a desynchronization of the athlete's biological and biophysical time clock.[14]

The term *circadian* (from the Latin *circa dies,* "about a day") implies a period of time of approximately twenty-four hours. The body maintains many cyclical mechanisms (circadian rhythms) that follow a pattern (e.g., the daily rise and fall of body temperature or the tidal ebb and flow of the cortical steroid secretion, which produces other effects on the metabolic system that are in themselves cyclical in nature). Body mechanisms adapt at varying rates to time changes. Some adjust immediately (e.g., protein metabolism), whereas others take time (e.g., the rise and fall of body temperature, which takes approximately eight days to adjust). Other body mechanisms, such as the adrenal hormones, which regulate metabolism and other body functions, may take as long as three weeks. Even intellectual proficiency, or the ability to think, clearly is cyclical.

The term *jet lag* refers to the physical and mental effects caused by traveling rapidly across several time zones.[41] It results from disruption of both circadian rhythms and the sleep-wake cycle. As the length of travel increases over several time zones, the effects of jet lag become more profound.

Disruption of circadian rhythms has been shown to cause fatigue, headache, problems with the digestive system, and changes in blood pressure, heart rate, hormonal release, endocrine secretions, and bowel habits. Any of these changes may have a negative effect on athletic performance and may predispose the athlete to injury.[9]

Younger individuals adjust more rapidly to time zone changes than do older people, although the differences are not great. The stress induced in jet travel occurs only when flying either east or west at high speed. There is 30 percent to 50 percent faster adaptation in individuals flying westward than in individuals flying eastward.[20] Travel north or south has no effect on the body unless several time zones are crossed in an east or west progression. The changes in time zones, illumination, and environment prove somewhat disruptive to the human physiological mechanisms, particularly when a person flies through five or more time zones, as occurs in some international travel.[20] Some people are more susceptible to the syndrome than are others, but the symptoms can be sufficiently disruptive to interfere with an athlete's ability to perform maximally in a competitive event.[22] In some cases, an athlete will become ill for a short period of time with anorexia, severe headache, blurred vision, dizziness, insomnia, or extreme fatigue. The negative effects of jet lag can be reduced by paying attention to the guidelines in *Focus Box:* "Minimizing the effects of jet lag."

ARTIFICIAL TURF

Artificial turf was first used in the Houston Astrodome in 1966 and was first marketed under the trade name AstroTurf. The artificial surface was said to be more durable, offer greater consistency, require less maintenance, be more "playable" during inclement weather, and offer greater performance characteristics such as increased speed and resiliency. Since the late 1960s, a number of companies have manufactured synthetic surfaces that are variations of AstroTurf. Today, artificial turfs being manufactured include Southwest Resources (AstroTurf, Polypro, Polyknit, Omniturf), Eidelgras, Desso, Kony Green, and Ssupergrass.

6-6

Critical Thinking E x e r c i s e

A college tennis team from the West Coast must travel to the East Coast to play a scheduled match. The coach has done a lot of traveling and knows that traveling from west to east seems to be more difficult than traveling east to west. This match is important, and the tennis coach asks the athletic trainer for advice to help the athletes minimize the effects of jet lag.

? What can the athletic trainer recommend to help the athletes adjust to the new time zone in as short a time as possible?

Focus

There has been an ongoing debate over the advantages and disadvantages of artificial surfaces versus natural surfaces.[24] The literature does not contain enough conclusive evidence to indicate that an artificial surface is more likely to cause injury than a natural surface is.[11,24,37,40] Empirically, it seems that most athletes, coaches, and athletic trainers agree that injuries are more likely to occur on artificial surfaces than on natural grass, and most of these individuals would rather practice and play on natural grass. In recent years, the trend in many colleges, universities, and professional arenas has been to move away from artificial surfaces and replace them with natural grass. New hybrid grasses are now available that are more durable.

It has been argued that synthetic surfaces lose their inherent shock absorption capability as they age.[24] Training injuries are more likely to occur if training always takes place on artificial turf.[17] Higher speeds are said to be possible on artificial surfaces; thus, injuries involving collision can potentially be more severe because of increased force on impact.[11] A shoe that does not stick to the artificial surface but still provides solid footing will significantly reduce the likelihood of injury.[19]

Two injuries that seem to occur more frequently in athletes competing on an artificial surface are abrasions and turf toe (a hyperextension of the great toe). The incidence of abrasions can be greatly reduced by wearing pads on the elbows and knees. Turf toe is less likely to occur if the shoe has a stiff, firm sole.

SUMMARY

- Environmental stress can adversely affect an athlete's performance as well as pose a serious health problem.
- Hyperthermia is one of sport's major concerns. In times of high temperatures and humidity, caution should always be exercised. The key to preventing heat-related illness is rehydration, acclimatization, and common sense. Losing 5 percent or more of body weight because of fluid loss could pose a potential health problem.
- Cold weather requires athletes to wear the correct apparel and to warm up properly before engaging in sports activities. The wind chill factor must always be considered when performing. As is true in a hot environment, athletes in cold conditions must ingest adequate fluids. Alcohol must be avoided at all times. Extreme cold exposure can cause conditions such as frost nip, chilblains, and frostbite.

- An athlete going from a low to a high altitude in a short time may encounter problems with performance and may perhaps experience some health problems. Researchers are unsure about how much time it takes for adaptation to occur and about when to bring the athlete to the higher altitude, especially for an endurance event. Many athletic trainers believe that three days at the higher altitude will provide enough time for adaptation to occur. Others believe that a much longer time period is needed. An athlete who experiences a serious illness because of his or her presence at a particular altitude must be returned to a lower altitude as soon as possible.

- Air pollution can produce a major decrement to performance and, in some cases, can cause illness. Increased ozone levels can cause respiratory distress, nausea, eye irritation, and fatigue. Sulfur dioxide, a colorless gas, can also cause physical reactions in some athletes and can be a serious problem for asthmatics. Carbon monoxide, a colorless and odorless gas, reduces hemoglobin's ability to use oxygen and, as a result, adversely affects performance.

- Travel through different time zones can place a serious physiological stress on the athlete. This stress is called circadian dysrhythmia, or jet lag. This disruption of biological rhythm can adversely affect performance and may even produce health problems. The athletic trainer must pay careful attention to helping the athlete acclimatize to time-zone shifting.

- There is inconclusive evidence that the incidence of injury on artificial surfaces is higher than on natural surfaces, although most coaches, athletes, and athletic trainers seem to prefer practicing and playing on natural grass. Two frequently seen injuries that occur on artificial turf are turf toe and abrasions.

Web Sites

Sports Medicine: Dressing for the cold: http://www.olympic-usa.org/inside/in_1_3_5_4.html

This site gives a brief description of how to dress for cold weather.

Cramer First Aider: http://www.ccsd.k12.wy.us/cchs_web/cramerfirstaider/fstaider.htm

Heat stroke and Heat Exhaustion: http://www.city.swift-current.sk.ca/info/heat.htm

This site gives a description of the signs, symptoms, and treatment of heat illness.

Hypothermia and Cold Weather Injuries: http://www.princeton.edu/~oa/hypocold.html

This site describes the body's mechanism for temperature regulation and includes the signs, symptoms, and treatment of common cold illnesses.

Kool tie: http://www.kooltie.com/illness.htm

This site discusses heat exhaustion, cramps, and stroke including the causes, common signs and symptoms, and care.

Solutions to Critical Thinking EXERCISES

6-1 The wrestler is experiencing heat exhaustion, which results from inadequate fluid replacement or dehydration. If conscious, the athlete should be forced to drink large quantities of water. By far the most rapid method of fluid replacement is for a physician to use an IV (fluids administered intravenously). It is desirable but not necessary to move the athlete to a cooler environment. The athlete should be counseled about the dangers of using diuretic medication.

6-2 The athletic trainer should explain to the coach that heat-related illnesses are for the most part preventable. The athletes should come into preseason practice at least partially acclimatized to working in a hot, humid environment and during the first week of practice should become fully acclimatized. Temperature and humidity readings should be monitored, and practice modified according to conditions. Practice uniforms should maximize evaporation and minimize heat absorption to the greatest extent possible. Weight records should be maintained to identify individuals who are becoming dehydrated. Most important, the athletes must keep themselves hydrated by constantly drinking large quantities of water both during and between practice sessions.

6-3 The safest recommendation would be for the athlete to travel to Colorado two to three weeks before the event. If this arrival time is not practical, she should be in Colorado for at least three days before her first event.

6-4 The sun protection factor (SPF) indicates the sunscreen's effectiveness in absorbing the sunburn-inducing radiation. An SPF of 15 indicates that an athlete can be exposed to ultraviolet light 15 times longer than without a sunscreen before the skin will begin to turn red. Therefore the athlete needs to understand that a higher SPF does not indicate a greater degree of protection. She must simply apply the sunscreen with an SPF of 15 twice as often as would be necessary with a sunscreen with an SPF of 30.

6-5 As soon as lightning is observed, the athletic trainer should immediately end practice and get the athletes under cover. If an indoor facility is not available, automobiles are a relatively safe alternative. The athletes should avoid standing under large trees or telephone poles. As a last alternative, athletes should assume a crouched position in a ditch or ravine. If possible, athletes should avoid any standing water or metal objects around the fields.

6-6 Most important, the athletes should leave for the trip well rested. The day before leaving, the athletes should go to bed and get up three hours earlier than normal. Athletes should reset their watches according to the new time zone once they board the plane. During the trip they should drink plenty of fluids to prevent dehydration, but they should avoid caffeine. Their largest meal should be eaten earlier in the day. On arrival, athletes should immediately adopt the local time schedule for training, eating, and sleeping, and they should get as much sunlight as possible. Training sessions should be done earlier in the day.

REVIEW QUESTIONS AND CLASS ACTIVITIES

1. How do temperature and humidity cause heat disorders?
2. What steps should be taken to avoid heat disorders?
3. Describe the symptoms and signs of the most common heat disorders.
4. How is heat lost from the body to produce hypothermia?
5. What should an athlete do to prevent heat loss?
6. Identify the physiological basis for the body's susceptibility to a cold disorder.
7. Describe the symptoms and signs of the major cold disorders affecting athletes.
8. How should athletes protect themselves from the effects of ultraviolet radiation from the sun?
9. What precautions can be taken to minimize the possibility of injury during an electrical storm?
10. What concerns should an athletic trainer have when athletes are to perform an endurance sport at high altitudes?
11. What altitude illnesses might be expected among some athletes, and how should those illnesses be managed?
12. What adverse effects could high air concentrations of ozone, sulfur dioxide, and carbon monoxide have on the athlete? How should they be dealt with?
13. How can the adverse effects of circadian dysrhythmia be avoided or lessened?
14. What are two common injuries in athletes who compete on artificial turf?

REFERENCES

1. ACSM position statement on prevention of thermal injuries during distance running, *Med Sci Sports Exerc* 19(5):529, 1987.
2. Armstrong LE, Epstein Y, Greenleaf JE: Heat and cold illnesses during distance running, *Med Sci Sports Exerc* 28(12), 1996.
3. Atkinson G: Air pollution and exercise, *Sports Exercise and Injury* 3(1):2, 1997.
4. Bennett B: A model lightning safety policy for athletics, *J Ath Train* 32(3):251, 1997.
5. Bernard TE: Risk management for preventing heat illness in athletes, *Athletic Therapy Today* 1(4):19, 1996.
6. Bovard R, Schoene RB, Wappes JR: Don't let altitude sickness bring you down, *Physician Sportsmed* 23(2):87, 1995.
7. Coote JH: Medicine and mechanisms in altitude sickness: recommendations, *Sports Med* 20(3):148, 1995.
8. Coyle E: Fluid and carbohydrate replacement during exercise: how much and why? *Sports Science Exchange* 7(50):1, 1994.
9. Davis JO et al: *Jet lag and athletic performance*, Colorado Springs, 1986, United States Olympic Committee Sports Medicine Council.
10. Davis M: Ultraviolet therapy. In Prentice W, editor: *Therapeutic modalities in sports medicine*, Dubuque, Iowa, 1999, WCB/McGraw-Hill.
11. Duda M: More grid injuries on grass, *Physician Sportsmed* 16(4):41, 1988.
12. Eichner ER: Sickle cell trait, exercise, and altitude, *Physician Sportsmed* 14(11):144, 1986.
13. Folinsbee LJ: Air pollution and exercise. In Welsh RP, Shephard RJ, editors: *Current therapy in sports medicine 1985–1986*, Philadelphia, 1985, Decker.
14. French J: Circadian rhythms, jet lag, and the athlete. In Torg J, Shephard R, editors: *Current therapy in sports medicine*, St Louis, 1995, Mosby.
15. Fritz R, Perrin D: Cold exposure injuries: prevention and treatment. In Ray R, editor: *Clinics in sports medicine*, Philadelphia, 1989, Saunders.
16. Gong H: How pollution and airborne allergens affect exercise, *Physician sportsmed* 23(7):35, 1995.
17. Grose K, Mickey C, Bierhals A: Conditioning injuries associated with artificial turf in two preseason football training programs, *J Ath Train* 32(4):304, 1997.
18. Gutierrez G: Solar injury and heat illness, *Physician sportsmed* 23(7):43, 1995.
19. Heidt RS, Dormer SG, Crawley PW: Differences in friction and torsional resistance in athletic shoe–turf surface interfaces, *Am J Sports Med* 24(6):834, 1996.
20. Herbert DL: Does "jet lag" for teams traveling west-to-east adversely affect performance? *Sports Med Stand Malpract Report* 8(3):43, 1996.
21. Hunter SL et al: Malignant hyperthermia in a college football player, *Physician Sportsmed* 15(12):77, 1987.
22. Johnson R, Tulin B: *Travel fitness*, Champaign, Ill, 1995, Human Kinetics.
23. Knochel JP: Management of heat conditions, *Athletic Therapy Today* 1(4):30, 1996.
24. Kraeger DR: Playing surfaces in sports. In Baker CL et al, editors: *The Hughston Clinic sports medicine book*, Baltimore, 1995, Williams & Wilkins.
25. Levine B, Stray-Gundersen J: Exercise at high altitudes. In Torg J, Shephard R, editors: *Current therapy in sports medicine*, St Louis, 1995, Mosby.
26. McArdle WD, Katch FI, Katch VL: *Exercise physiology*, Philadelphia, 1996, Lea & Febiger.
27. McCann DJ, Adams WC: Wet bulb globe temperature index and performance in competitive distance runners, *Med Sci Sports Exerc* 29(7):955, 1997.
28. Mellion MB, Shelton GL: Thermoregulation, heat illness, and safe exercise in the heat. In Mellion MB, editor: *Office sports medicine*, ed 2, Philadelphia, 1996, Hanley & Belfus.
29. Montain SJ, Maughan RJ, Sawka MN: Fluid replacement strategies for exercise in hot weather, *Athletic Therapy Today* 1(4):24, 1996.
30. Murphy RJ: Heat illness in the athlete, *Ath Train* 19:1, 1984.
31. Murray B: Fluid replacement: the American College of Sports Medicine position stand. *Sports Science Exchange* 9(4):1, 1996.
32. Murray R: Dehydration, hyperthermia, and athletes: science and practice, *J Ath Train* 31(3):248, 1996.
33. Murray R: Guidelines for fluid replacement during exercise. *Australian Journal of Nutrition and Dietetics* 53(4 suppl):S17, 1996.
34. Murray R: Practical advice for exercising in cold weather. In Murray R: *Endurance training for performance*, Barrington, Ill, 1995, Gatorade Sports Science Institute.

35. *NCAA sports medicine handbook, 1998–1999*, Overland Park, Kan, 1998, National Collegiate Athletic Association.

36. Nelson WE, Gieck J II, Kolb P: Treatment and prevention of hypothermia and frostbite, *Ath Train* 18:330, 1983.

37. Noncontact knee injuries in the NFL: the role of field surface and footwear. *Sports Med Digest* 19(4):37, 1997.

38. Pandolf K: Avoiding heat illness during exercise. In Torg J, Shephard R, editors: *Current therapy in sports medicine*, St Louis, 1995, Mosby.

39. Pate RR: *Sports science exchange—special considerations for exercise in cold weather*, Chicago, 1988, Gatorade Sports Science Institute.

40. Powell JW: Incidence of injury associated with playing surfaces in the National Football League 1980–1985, *Ath Train* 22:202, 1987.

41. Reilly T, Atkinson G, Waterhouse J: Travel fatigue and jet lag, *Journal of Sports Sciences* 15(3):365, 1997.

42. Ryan A: Heat stress. In Mueller F, Ryan A, editors: *Prevention of athletic injuries: the role of the sports medicine team*, Philadelphia, 1991, Davis.

43. Sandor RP: Heat illness: on-site diagnosis and cooling. *Physician Sportsmed* 25(6):35, 1997.

44. Schoene RB, Bracker MD: High-altitude pulmonary edema: the disguised killer, *Physician Sportsmed* 16(8):103, 1988.

45. Shephard RJ: Adjustment to high altitude. In Welsh RP, Shephard RJ, editors: *Current therapy in sports medicine 1985–1986*, Philadelphia, 1985, Decker.

46. Thein L: Environmental conditions affecting the athlete, *J Orthop Sports Phys Ther* 21(3):158, 1995.

47. Thompson RL, Hayward JS: Wet-cold exposure and hypothermia: thermal and metabolic responses to prolonged exercise in rain, *J App Physiol* 81(3):1128, 1996.

48. Vellerand A: Exercise in the cold. In Torg J, Shephard R, editors: *Current therapy in sports medicine*, St Louis, 1995, Mosby.

49. Walsh K, Hanley M, Graner S: A survey of lightning policy in selected division I colleges, *J Ath Train* 32(3):206, 1997.

50. Walters F: Position stand on lightning and thunder: the Athletic Health Care Services of the District of Columbia Public Schools, *J Ath Train* 28(3):201, 1993.

51. White-Clergerie AM: Mountaineering without oxygen: courting death? *Physician Sportsmed* 15(3):38, 1987.

ANNOTATED BIBLIOGRAPHY

Haymes EM, Wells CL: *Environment and human performance*, Champaign, Ill, 1986, Human Kinetics.

This text examines sports performance during a variety of environmental conditions. Two hundred and fifty references are reported.

Strauss RH, editor: *Sports medicine*, Philadelphia, 1996, Saunders.

This book provides four pertinent chapters on the subject of environmental disorders that could affect the athlete.

Johnson R, Tulin B: *Travel fitness*. Champaign, Il, 1995, Human Kinetics.

Chapters include health and fitness in transit; coping with jet lag; getting to sleep; taking your workout on the road; avoiding excess baggage; how to eat right on your next trip; managing your travel stress; and coming home strong.

NCAA sports medicine handbook, 1999–2000, Overland Park, Kan, 1999, National Collegiate Athletic Association.

This handbook contains guidelines and recommendations for preventing heat illness and hypohydration, for cold, for stress, and for lightning safety.

Protective Sports Equipment

When you finish this chapter you should be able to

- Fit selected protective equipment properly (e.g., football helmets, shoulder pads, and running shoes).
- Differentiate between good and bad features of selected protective devices.
- Compare the advantages and disadvantages of customized versus commercial foot and ankle protective devices.
- Describe the controversies surrounding the use of certain protective devices—are they in fact weapons against opposing players, or do they really work?
- Rate the protective value of various materials used in sports to make pads and orthotic devices.
- List the steps in making a customized foam pad with a thermomoldable shell.

Modifications and improvements in sports equipment are continually being made, especially for sports in which injury is common. In this chapter, both commercial and preventive, or **prophylactic,** techniques are discussed. Protective sports equipment should be used for preventing initial injury and reinjury.

prophylactic
Refers to prevention, preservation, or protection.

COMMERCIAL EQUIPMENT

Proper selection and proper fit of sports equipment are essential in the prevention of many sports injuries, particularly in direct contact and collision sports such as football, hockey, and lacrosse, but also in indirect contact sports such as basketball and soccer. Whenever protective sports equipment is selected and purchased, a major decision in the safeguarding of the athletes' health and welfare is being made.

Currently there is serious concern about the standards for protective sports equipment, particularly material durability standards. Who should set these standards is one uncertainty; other concerns include the mass production of equipment, equipment testing methods, and the requirements for wearing protective equipment. Some people are concerned that a piece of equipment that is protective to one athlete might in turn be used as a weapon against another athlete.

Standards are also needed for protective equipment maintenance, both to keep it in good repair and to determine when to throw it away. Too often old, worn-out, and ill-fitting equipment is passed down from the varsity players to the younger and often less-experienced players, compounding their risk of injury. Coaches must learn to be less concerned with the color, look, and style of a piece of equipment and more concerned with its ability to prevent injury. Many national organizations are addressing these issues (see *Focus Box:* "Protective sports equipment regulatory organizations"). Engineering, chemistry, biomechanics, anatomy, physiology, physics, computer science, and other related disciplines are applied to solve problems inherent in safety standardization of sports equipment and facilities.

Commercial stock and custom protective devices differ considerably. Stock devices are premade and prepackaged and are for immediate use. Customized devices are constructed according to the individual characteristics of an athlete. Stock items may cause sizing problems. In contrast, a custom device can be specifically sized and made to fit the protection and support needs of the individual. Both commercial and customizing devices are discussed in this chapter.

Old, worn-out, ill-fitting equipment should never be passed down to younger, less-experienced players; it compounds their chances for injury.

Focus

Protective sports equipment regulatory organizations

Athletic Equipment Manager Association (AEMA)
723 Keil Court
Bowling Green, OH 43402
(419) 352-1207

National Association of Intercollegiate Athletics (NAIA)
1221 Baltimore
Kansas City, MO 64105
(816) 842-5050

National Collegiate Athletic Association (NCAA)
P.O. Box 1906
Nall at 63rd Street
Mission, KS 66201
(913) 384-3220

National Federation of State High School Associations (NFSHSA)
P.O. Box 20626
11724 Plaza Circle
Kansas City, MO 64195
(816) 464-5400

American National Standards Institute (ANSI)
1430 Broadway
New York, NY 10018
(212) 354-3300

United States Olympic Committee (USOC)
1750 E. Boulder Street
Colorado Springs, CO 80909
(719) 632-5551

HEAD PROTECTION

Direct collision sports such as football and hockey require special protective equipment, especially for the head. Football provides more frequent opportunities for body contact than does hockey, but hockey players generally move faster and therefore create greater impact forces. Besides direct head contact, hockey has the added injury elements of swinging sticks and fast-moving pucks. Other sports using fast-moving projectiles are baseball, with its pitched ball and swinging bat, and track and field, with the javelin, discus, and shot, which can also produce serious head injuries. In recent years most helmet research has been conducted for football and ice hockey; however, some research has been performed on baseball headgear.

Football Helmets

Football helmets must withstand repeated blows that are of high mass and low velocity.

The National Operating Committee on Standards for Athletic Equipment (NOCSAE) has developed standards for football helmet certification. An approved helmet must protect against concussive forces that may injure the brain. Collision that causes concussion is usually with another player or the turf.[13,21]

Schools must provide the athlete with quality equipment, especially football helmets. All helmets must have NOCSAE certification. A helmet that is certified is not necessarily completely fail-safe. Athletes as well as their parents must be apprised of the dangers that are inherent in any sport, particularly football.[13]

To make this danger especially clear, NOCSAE has adopted the following recommended warning to be placed on all football helmets:

WARNING: Do not strike an opponent with any part of this helmet or face mask. This is a violation of football rules and may cause you to suffer severe brain or neck injury, including paralysis or death. Severe brain or neck injury may also occur accidentally while playing football. NO HELMET CAN PREVENT ALL SUCH INJURIES. USE THIS HELMET AT YOUR OWN RISK.

Each player's helmet must have this visible, exterior warning label or a similar one ensuring that players have been made aware of the risks involved in the game of American football. The warning label must be attached to each helmet by both the manufacturer and the reconditioner.[7] It is important to have each player read this warning, after which it is read aloud by the equipment manager. The athlete then signs a statement, agreeing that he understands this warning.

A popular type of helmet is the air and fluid helmet (Figure 7-1). When fitting helmets, always wet the player's hair to simulate playing conditions; this makes the initial fitting easier. Closely follow the manufacturer's directions for a proper fit. (See *Focus Box:* "Properly fitting the helmet.") The football helmet must be routinely checked for proper fit, especially in the first few days that it is worn. A check for snugness should be made by inserting a tongue depressor between the head and the liner. Fit is proper when the tongue depressor is resisted firmly when moved back and forth. If air bladder helmets are used by a team that travels to a different altitude and air pressure, the helmet fit must be routinely rechecked.

Chin straps are also important in maintaining the proper head and helmet relationship. Two basic types of chin straps are in use today: a two-snap and a four-snap strap. Many coaches prefer the four-snap chin strap because it keeps the helmet from tilting forward and backward. The chin strap should always be locked so that it cannot be released by a hard external force to the helmet (Figure 7-2).

Jaw pads are also essential to keep the helmet from rocking laterally. They should fit snugly against the player's cheekbones. Certification of a helmet's ability to withstand the forces of the game is of no avail if the helmet is not properly fitted or maintained.

Ice Hockey Helmets

Like football helmets, ice hockey helmets have undergone a concerted effort of upgrading and standardizing.[13] Blows to the head in ice hockey, in contrast to in football, are usually singular rather than multiple. An ice hockey helmet must withstand

7-2
Critical Thinking E x e r c i s e

C- and B-level high school football players are issued their equipment. These athletes and their parents know very little about the equipment's potential for preventing injury. The athletic trainer is given the responsibility to reduce legal liability by educating the players and their parents about the equipment safety limits.

? What steps does the athletic trainer take?

7-3
Critical Thinking E x e r c i s e

The athletic trainer explains the helmet's limitations to a football team.

? Why does the football helmet have a warning label?

Focus

Properly fitting the helmet

In general, the helmet should adhere to the following fit standards:
- The helmet should fit snugly around all parts of the player's head (front, sides, and crown), and there should be no gaps between the pads and the head or face.
- It should cover the base of the skull. The pads placed at the back of the neck should be snug but not to the extent of discomfort.
- It should not come down over the eyes. It should set (front edge) $^3/_4$ inch (1.91 cm) above the player's eyebrows (approximately two finger widths).
- The ear holes should match.
- It should not shift when manual pressure is applied.
- It should not recoil on impact.
- The chin strap should be an equal distance from the center of the helmet. Straps must keep the helmet from moving up and down or side to side.
- The cheek pads should fit snugly against the sides of the face.
- The face mask should be attached securely to the helmet, allowing a complete field of vision, and positioned three finger widths from the nose.

Figure 7-1

The air- and fluid-filled padded football helmet.

Figure 7-2

Fitting a football helmet.
A, Pull down on face mask; helmet must not move.
B, Turn helmet to position on the athlete's head. **C,** Push down on helmet; there must be no movement. **D,** Try to rock helmet back and forth; there must be no movement.
E, Check for a snug jaw pad fit.
F, Proper adjustment of the chin strap is necessary to ensure proper helmet fit.

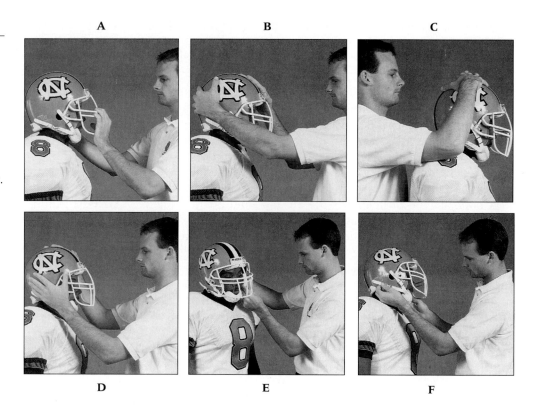

A   B   C

D   E   F

Even high-quality helmets are of no use if not properly fitted or maintained.

Ice hockey helmets must withstand the high-velocity impact of a stick or puck and the low-velocity forces from falling or hitting a sideboard.

Figure 7-3

There is some question about how well baseball batting helmets protect against high-velocity impacts.

not only high-velocity impacts (e.g., being hit with a stick or a puck, which produces low mass and high velocity) but also the high-mass–low-velocity forces produced by running into the sideboard or falling on the ice. In each instance, the hockey helmet, like the football helmet, must be able to spread the impact over a large surface area through a firm exterior shell and, at the same time, be able to decelerate forces that act on the head through a proper energy-absorbing liner. It is essential for all hockey players to wear protective helmets that carry the stamp of approval from the Canadian Standards Association (CSA).

Baseball Batting Helmets

Like ice hockey helmets, the baseball batting helmet must withstand high-velocity impacts.[13] Unlike football and ice hockey, baseball has not produced a great deal of data on batting helmets. It has been suggested, however, that baseball helmets do little to adequately dissipate the energy of the ball during impact (Figure 7-3). A possible answer is to add external padding or to improve the helmet's suspension. The use of a helmet with an ear flap can afford some additional protection to the batter. Each runner and on-deck batter is required to wear a baseball or softball helmet that carries the NOCSAE stamp, which is similar to the warning on football helmets.

FACE PROTECTION

Devices that provide face protection fall into four categories: full face guards, mouth guards, ear guards, and eye protection devices.

Face Guards

Face guards are used in a variety of sports to protect against flying or carried objects during a collision with another player (Figure 7-4). Since the adoption of face guards and mouth guards for use in football, mouth injuries have been reduced more than 50 percent (Figure 7-5), but the incidence of neck injuries has increased

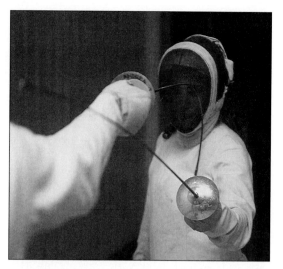

Figure 7-4

Sports such as fencing require complete face protection.

Figure 7-5

Face guards used for football.

significantly. The catcher in baseball, the goalie in hockey, and the lacrosse player should all be adequately protected against facial injuries, particularly lacerations and fractures (Figure 7-6).

A great variety of face masks and bars is available to the player, depending on the position played and the protection needed. In football, no face protection should have less than two bars. Proper mounting of the face mask and bars is imperative for maximum safety. All mountings should be made in such a way that the bar attachments are flush with the helmet. A 3-inch (7.62 cm) space should exist between the top of the face guard and the lower edge of the helmet. No helmet should be drilled more than one time on each side, and this drilling must be done by a factory-authorized reconditioner. Attachment of a bar or face mask not specifically designed for the helmet can invalidate the manufacturer's warranty.

Ice hockey face masks have been shown to reduce the incidence of facial injuries. In high school, face masks are required not just for the goalie but for all players. The rule stipulates that helmets be equipped with commercial plastic-coated wire mask guards, which must meet standards set by the Hockey Equipment Certification Council (HECC) and the American Society for Testing Materials (ASTM).[7] The openings in the guard must be small enough to prevent a hockey stick from entering. Plastic guards such as polycarbonate face shields have been approved by the HECC, ASTM, and the CSA Committee on Hockey Protective Equipment. The rule also requires that goalkeepers wear commercial throat protectors in addition to face protectors. The National Federation of High School Associations (NFHSA) rule is similar to the NCAA rule that requires players to wear face guards. There should be a space of 1 to 1.5 inches (3.81 cm) between the player's nose and the face guard. As with the helmet shell, pads, and chin strap, the face guard must be checked daily for defects.

In sports, the face may be protected by:
- Face guards
- Mouth guards
- Ear guards
- Eye protection devices

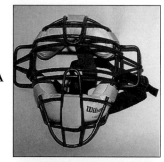

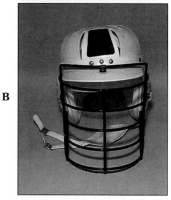

Figure 7-6

A, Baseball catcher's mask. **B,** Lacrosse helmet and faceguard.

A properly fitted mouth guard protects the teeth, absorbs blows to the chin, and can prevent concussion.

Laryngotracheal Protection

A laryngotracheal injury, though relatively uncommon, can be fatal.[13] Baseball catchers, lacrosse goalies, and ice hockey goalies are most at risk. Throat protection should be mandatory for these sports.

Mouth Protection

The majority of dental traumas can be prevented if the athlete wears a correctly fitted, customized, intraoral mouth guard (Figure 7-7) In addition to protecting the teeth, the intraoral mouth guard absorbs the shock of chin blows and helps prevent a possible cerebral concussion. Mouth guards serve also to prevent lacerations to lips and cheeks and fractures to the mandible. The mouth protector should give the athlete proper and tight fit, comfort, unrestricted breathing, and unimpeded speech during competition. A loose mouthpiece will soon be ejected onto the ground or left unused in the locker room. The athlete's air passages should not be obstructed in any way by the mouthpiece. It is best when the mouthpiece is retained on the upper jaw and projects backward only as far as the last molar, thus permitting speech. Maximum protection is afforded when the mouth guard is composed of a flexible, resilient material and is formed to fit to the teeth and upper jaw.

Cutting down mouth guards to cover only the front four teeth should never be permitted. It invalidates the manufacturer's warranty against dental injuries, and a cut-down mouth guard can easily become dislodged and lead to an obstructed airway, which poses a serious, life-threatening situation for the athlete.

The three types of mouth guards generally used in sports are the stock variety, the commercial mouth guard formed after submersion in boiling water, and the custom fabricated type, which is formed over a model made from an impression of the athlete's maxillary arch.[13]

Many high schools and colleges now require that mouth guards be worn at all times during participation. For example, the NCAA football rules mandate that all players wear a properly manufactured mouth guard. A time-out is charged to a team if a player fails to wear the mouth guard. To assist enforcement, official mouth guards are increasingly made in the most visible color possible—yellow.[13] It is important that coaches and athletic trainers measure the arch length of the mouth guards to ensure adequate protection for the athlete and to be in compliance with the NCAA rule.[13]

Ear Guards

With the exception of wrestling, water polo, and boxing, most contact sports do not make a special practice of protecting the ears. All these sports can cause irritation of the ears to the point that permanent deformity can ensue. To avoid this problem, special ear guards should be routinely worn (Figure 7-8).

Eye Protection Devices

The National Society to Prevent Blindness estimates that the highest percentage of eye injuries are sports or play related. Most injuries are from blunt trauma. Protective devices must be sport-specific.

Figure 7-7

Moldable and customized mouth protectors.

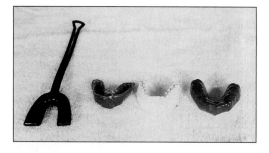

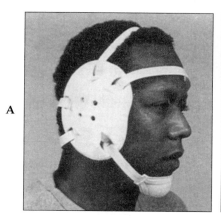

A

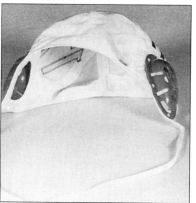

B

Figure 7-8

Ear protection. **A,** Wrestler's ear guard. **B,** Water polo player's ear protection.

Glasses

For the athlete who must wear corrective lenses, glasses can be both a blessing and a nuisance. They may slip on sweat, get bent when hit, fog from perspiration, detract from peripheral vision, or be difficult to wear with protective headgear. Even with all these disadvantages, properly fitted and designed glasses can provide adequate protection and withstand the rigors of the sport. If the athlete has glass lenses, they must be case-hardened to prevent them from splintering on impact. When a case-hardened lens breaks, it crumbles, eliminating the sharp edges that may penetrate the eye. The cost of this process is relatively low. The only disadvantages involved are that the weight of the glasses is heavier than average and they may be scratched more easily than regular glasses.

Another possible sports advantage of glass lenses is a process through which the lenses can become color tinted when exposed to ultraviolet rays from the sun and then return to a clear state when removed from the sun's rays. These lenses are known as photochromic lenses.

Plastic lenses for glasses are becoming increasingly popular with athletes. They are much lighter in weight than glass lenses; however, they are much more prone to scratching.

Contact Lenses

In many ways the athlete who is able to wear contact lenses without discomfort can avoid many of the inconveniences of glasses. The greatest advantage to contact lenses is probably the fact that they "become a part of the eye" and move with it.

Contact lenses come mainly in two types: the corneal type, which covers just the iris of the eye, and the scleral type, which covers the entire front of the eye, including the white. Peripheral vision as well as astigmatism and corneal waviness is improved through the use of contact lenses. Unlike regular glasses, contact lenses do not normally cloud during temperature changes. They also can be tinted to reduce glare. For example, yellow lenses can be used against ice glare and blue ones against glare from snow. One of the main difficulties with contact lenses is their high cost compared with regular glasses. Some other serious disadvantages of wearing contact lenses are the possibility of corneal irritation caused by dust getting under the lens and the possibility of a lens becoming dislodged during body contact. In addition, only certain individuals are able to wear contacts with comfort, and some individuals are unable to ever wear them because of certain eye idiosyncrasies. Athletes currently prefer the soft, hydrophilic lenses to the hard type. Adjustment time for the soft lenses is shorter than for the hard, they can be more easily replaced, and they are more adaptable to the sports environment. There are also disposable lenses and lenses that can be worn for an extended period. In the last few years, the cost of contact lenses has dropped significantly.

Figure 7-9

Athletes playing sports that involve small, fast projectiles should wear the closed type of eye guards.

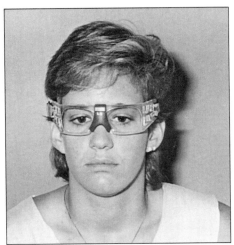

Eye protection must be worn by all athletes who play sports that use fast-moving projectiles.

Eye and Glass Guards

It is essential that athletes take special precautions to protect their eyes, especially in sports that use fast-moving projectiles and implements, such as handball or racquetball (Figure 7-9). Besides the more obvious sports of ice hockey, lacrosse, and baseball, the racquet sports also cause serious eye injury. Athletes not wearing glasses should wear closed eye guards to protect the orbital cavity. Athletes who normally wear glasses with plastic or case-hardened lenses are to some degree already protected against eye injury from an implement or projectile; however, greater safety is afforded by the metal-rimmed frame that surrounds and fits over the athlete's glasses. The protection that the guard affords is excellent, but it hinders vision in some planes. Polycarbonate eye shields that have recently been developed can be attached to football face masks, hockey helmets, and baseball and softball helmets.

Neck Protection

Experts in cervical injuries consider the major value of commercial and customized cervical collars to be mostly a reminder to the athlete to be cautious rather than to provide a definitive restriction.

TRUNK AND THORAX PROTECTION

Trunk and thorax protection is essential in many contact and collision sports. Sports such as football, ice hockey, and lacrosse use extensive body protection. Areas that are most exposed to impact forces must be properly covered with some material that offers protection against soft-tissue compression. Of particular concern are the external genitalia and the exposed bony protuberances of the body that have insufficient soft tissue for protection, such as shoulders, ribs, and spine (Figures 7-10 and 7-11).

As discussed earlier, the problem that arises in the wearing of protective equipment is that, although it is armor against injury to the athlete wearing it, it can also serve as a weapon against all opponents. Standards must become more stringent in determining what equipment is absolutely necessary for body protection and at the same time is not itself a source of trauma. Proper fit and proper maintenance of equipment are essential.

Football Shoulder Pads

Manufacturers of shoulder pads have made great strides toward protecting the football player against direct force to the shoulder muscle complex (Figure 7-12). There are two general types of pads: flat and cantilevered. The player who uses the shoulder a great deal in blocking and tackling requires the bulkier cantilevered type,

Figure 7-10

Full-body protection. Baseball chest protector for catchers.

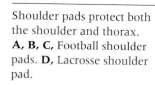

Figure 7-11

Shoulder pads protect both the shoulder and thorax. **A, B, C,** Football shoulder pads. **D,** Lacrosse shoulder pad.

whereas the quarterback or the ball receiver uses the flat type. Over the years, the shoulder pad's front and rear panels have been extended along with the cantilever. The following are rules for fitting the football shoulder pad:

- The width of the shoulder is measured to determine the proper size of pad.
- The inside shoulder pad should cover the tip of the shoulder in a direct line with the lateral aspect of the shoulder.
- The epaulets and cups should cover the deltoid muscle and allow movements required by the athlete's specific position.
- The neck opening must allow the athlete to raise the arm overhead but not allow the pad to slide back and forth.
- If a split-clavicle shoulder pad is used, the channel for the top of the shoulder must be in the proper position.

Straps underneath the arm must hold the pads firmly in place, but not so they constrict soft tissue. A collar and drop-down pads may be added to provide more protection.

Some athletic trainers use a combination of football and ice hockey shoulder pads to prevent injuries high on the upper arm and shoulder. A pair of supplemental shoulder pads are placed under the football pads (Figure 7-13). The deltoid cap of the hockey pad is connected to the main body of the hockey pad by an adjustable lace. The distal end of the deltoid cap is held in place by a Velcro strap. The chest pad is adjustable to ensure proper fit for any size athlete. The football shoulder pads are placed over the hockey pads. The athletic trainer should observe for a proper fit. Larger football pads may be needed.

Breast Support

Until recently the primary concern for female breast protection had been against external forces that could cause bruising. With the vast increase in the number of physically active women, concern has been redirected to protecting the breasts against movement that stems from running and jumping. This movement is a particular problem for women with large breasts. Many girls and women in the past may have avoided vigorous physical activity because of the discomfort felt from the uncontrolled movement of their breasts. Manufacturers are making a concerted effort to develop specialized bras for women who participate in all types of physical activity. The athletic clothing industry has produced an array of stylish, comfortable, and

Figure 7-12

Football shoulder pads should be made to protect the player against direct force to the entire shoulder complex.

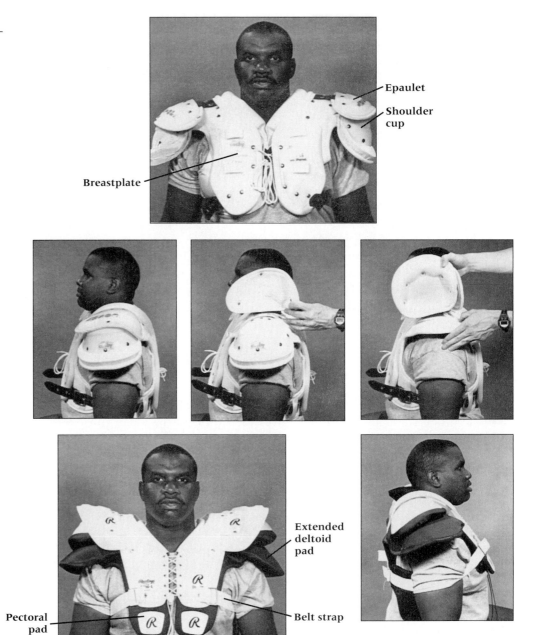

Epaulet

Shoulder cup

Breastplate

Extended deltoid pad

Pectoral pad

Belt strap

To be effective, a bra should hold the breasts tightly to the chest.

supportive sports bras. A bra should hold the breasts to the chest and prevent stretching of the Cooper's ligament, which causes premature sagging (Figure 7-14).

Most regular bras do not provide sufficient support to prevent excessive breast motion, and many are poorly designed. Sports bras fall into two categories:

1. Bras with good upward support; they have wide bands of elastic material under the breasts and wide shoulder straps that are attached close to the hooks in the back (Figure 7-15A).
2. Compressive bras, which function like wide elastic bandages, binding the breasts to the chest wall (Figure 7-15B).

To be effective, a bra should hold the breasts to the chest and prevent stretching of the Cooper's ligament, which causes premature sagging (see Figure 7-14). Metal parts (snaps, fasteners, underwire support) rub and abrade the skin. Nonsupport bras lack sufficient padding, and seams over nipples compound the rubbing of the bra on the nipple, which can lead to irritation.

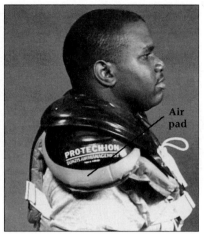

A   B

Figure 7-13

Customized foam is placed on the underside of the shoulder pad to provide additional protection.

For women with small breasts, no special type of bra is required except to protect the nipple area. Women with medium-sized breasts generally prefer the compressive bras, but women with a size C cup or larger should wear a firm, supportive bra. Fabric, fabric weight, and firmness of construction depend on the intensity of activity, support needed, sensitivity to the fabric, and climate. In contact sports, additional padding may be placed inside the cup if needed. Women competing in ice hockey, for example, wear protective plastic chest pieces that attach to their shoulder pads to protect the breast tissue from contusions. Women should look for a bra with these features:

- No irritating seams or fasteners next to the skin
- Nonslip straps
- Good support or compression that holds the breasts close to the body
- Firm, durable construction

Thorax

Manufacturers such as Bike Company and Casco provide equipment for thorax protection. Many of the thorax protectors and rib belts can be modified by replacing stock pads with customized thermomoldable plastic protective devices.[13] Recently, many lightweight pads have been developed to protect the athlete against external

Figure 7-14

Stretching of Cooper's ligament causes premature sagging.

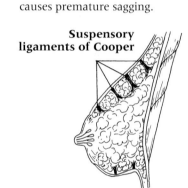

Suspensory ligaments of Cooper

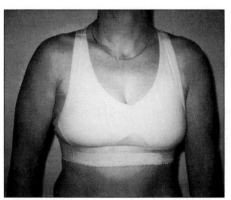

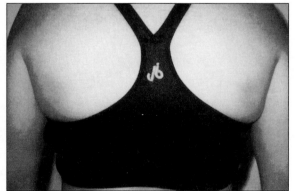

A   B

Figure 7-15

Female athletes should wear sports bras made of elastic material. **A,** Support bra. **B,** Compressive bra.

Figure 7-16

Protective rib belt.

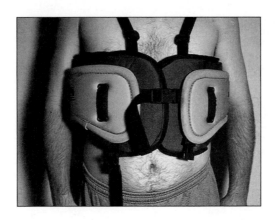

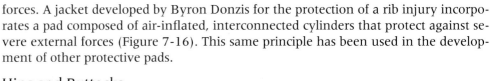

forces. A jacket developed by Byron Donzis for the protection of a rib injury incorporates a pad composed of air-inflated, interconnected cylinders that protect against severe external forces (Figure 7-16). This same principle has been used in the development of other protective pads.

Hips and Buttocks

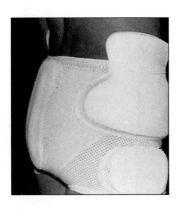

Figure 7-17

Girdle-style hip and coccygeal pad.

Pads in the region of the hips and buttocks are often needed in collision and high-velocity sports such as hockey and football. Other athletes needing protection in this region are amateur boxers, snow skiers, equestrians, jockeys, and water skiers. Two popular commercial pads are the girdle and belt types (Figure 7-17).

Groin and Genitalia

Sports involving high-velocity projectiles (e.g., hockey, lacrosse, and baseball) require cup protection for male participants. It comes as a stock item that fits into place in a jockstrap, or athletic supporter (Figure 7-18).

LIMB PROTECTION

Limbs, like other areas of the body, can be exposed a great deal to sports injuries and can require protection or, where there is weakness, support. Compression and mild soft-tissue support can be provided by neoprene sleeves, and hard bony areas of the body can be protected by commercial pads (Figure 7-19). In contrast, the athlete with a history of injury that needs special protection and support may require a commercial brace.

Footwear

Footwear can mean the difference between success, failure, or injury in competition. It is essential that the coach, athletic trainer, and equipment personnel make every effort to fit their athletes with proper shoes and socks.

Socks

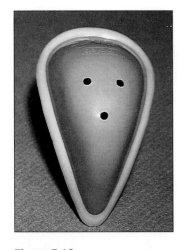

Figure 7-18

A cup, held in place by an athletic supporter, used for protecting the genitals against high-velocity projectiles.

Poorly fitted socks can cause abnormal stresses on the foot. For example, socks that are too short crowd the toes, especially the fourth and fifth ones. Socks that are too long can wrinkle and cause skin irritation. All athletic socks should be clean, dry, and without holes to avoid irritations. Manufacturers are now providing different types of socks for various sports. The composition of the sock's material also should be noted. Cotton socks can be too bulky, whereas a combination of materials such as cotton and polyester is less bulky and dries faster.

Shoes

Even more damaging than improperly fitted socks are improperly fitted shoes. Chronic abnormal pressures to the foot can often cause permanent structural deformities as well as potentially dangerous calluses and blisters. Besides these local problems, improperly fitted shoes result in mechanical disturbances that affect the body's total postural balance and may eventually lead to pathological conditions of the muscles and joints. Worn or broken-down shoes predispose the athlete to injuries of the foot and leg. Badly worn shoes have also been known to create hip and low back problems.

Shoe composition   The bare human foot is designed to function on uneven surfaces. Shoes were created to protect against harmful surfaces, but they should never interfere with natural functioning. Sports shoes, like all shoes, are constructed of different parts, each of which is designed to provide function, protection, and durability. Each sport places unique stresses and performance demands on the foot. In general, all sport shoes, like street shoes, are made of similar parts—soles, uppers, heel counters, and toe boxes.[19]

Sole   The sole, or bottom, of a shoe is divided into a center, middle, and inner section, each of which must be sturdy and flexible and provide a degree of cushioning.[19] Most shoes have three layers on the sole: a thick spongy layer, which absorbs the force of the foot strike under the heel; a midsole, which cushions the midfoot and toes; and a hard rubber layer, which comes in contact with the ground. The average runner's feet strike the ground between 1,500 and 1,700 times per mile. Thus, it is essential that the force of the heel strike be absorbed by the spongy layer to prevent overuse injuries from occurring in the ankles and knees. Heel wedges are sometimes inserted either on the inside or outside surface of the sole underneath the heel counter to accommodate and correct for various structural deformities of the foot that may alter normal biomechanics of the running gait.

Shoe upper   The upper part of the shoe is made of some combination of nylon and leather. The uppers should be lightweight, capable of quick drying, and well ventilated. The uppers should have some type of extra support in the saddle area, and there should also be some extra padding in the area of the Achilles tendon just above the heel counter.

Heel counter   The heel counter is the portion of the shoe that prevents the foot from rolling from side to side at heel strike. The heel counter should be firm but well fitted to minimize movement of the heel up and down or side to side. A good heel counter may prevent ankle sprains and painful blisters.[19]

Toe box   There should be plenty of room for the toes in the fitness shoe. Most experts recommend a $^{1}/_{2}$- to $^{3}/_{4}$-inch distance between toes and the front of the shoe. Most shoe salespersons can recommend a specific shoe for the athlete's foot. The best way to make sure there is adequate room in the toe box is to have the foot measured before the shoe is tried on (Figure 7-20).[19]

Shoe fitting   Fitting sports footgear is always difficult, mainly because the individual's left foot varies in size and shape from the right foot. Therefore measuring both feet is imperative. To fit the sports shoe properly, the athlete should approximate the conditions under which he or she will perform, such as wearing athletic socks, jumping up and down, or running. It is also desirable to fit the athlete's shoes

All athletic socks should be clean and dry and without holes. Socks of the wrong size can irritate the skin.

Figure 7-19

Neoprene elbow sleeve.

7-4

C*ritical Thinking* Exercise

A high school basketball player asks the athletic trainer for advice on purchasing a pair of basketball shoes.

? What fitting factors must be taken into consideration when purchasing basketball shoes?

Figure 7-20

Parts of a well-designed sport shoe.

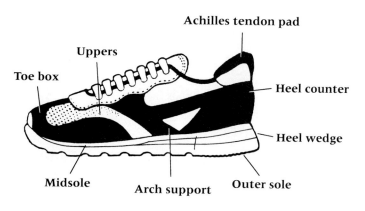

Achilles tendon pad
Uppers
Toe box
Heel counter
Heel wedge
Midsole   Arch support   Outer sole

Focus

Proper running shoe design and construction

To avoid injury to the athlete, the running shoe should meet the following requirements:[13]

- Have a strong heel counter that fits well around the foot and locks the shoe around the foot.
- Always have good flexibility in the forefoot where toes bend.
- Preferably have a fairly high heel for the athlete with a tight Achilles tendon.
- Have a midsole that is moderately soft but does not flatten easily.
- Have a heel counter that is high enough to surround the foot but still allows room for an orthotic insert, if needed.
- Have a counter that is attached to the sole to avoid the possibility of its coming loose from attachment.
- Always be of quality construction.

at the end of the day to accommodate the gradual increase in size that occurs from the time of awakening. The athlete must carefully consider this shoe choice because he or she will be spending countless hours in those shoes (see *Focus Box:* "Proper running shoe design and construction" for suggestions about shoe fitting).[5]

During performance conditions the new shoe should feel snug but not too tight. The sports shoe should be long enough that all toes can be fully extended without being cramped. Its width should permit full movement of the toes, including flexion, extension, and some spreading. A good point to remember is that the wide part of the shoe should match the wide part of the foot to allow the shoe to crease evenly when the athlete is on the balls of the feet. The shoe should bend (or "break") at its widest part; when the break of the shoe and the ball joint coincide, the fit is correct. However, if the break of the shoe is in back or in front of the normal bend of the foot (metatarsophalangeal joint), the shoe and the foot will oppose one another, causing abnormal skin and structural stresses to occur. Two measurements must be considered when fitting shoes: the distance from the heel to the metatarsophalangeal joint and the distance from the heel to the end of the longest toe. An individual's feet may be equal in length from the heels to the balls of the feet but different between heels and toes. It should be noted that one type of shoe is not appropriate for all athletes in a particular sport. Shoes therefore should be selected for the longer of the two measurements. Other factors to consider when buying the sports shoe are the stiffness of the sole and the width of the shank, or narrowest part of the sole. A shoe with a too rigid, nonyielding sole places a great deal of extra strain on the foot tendons. A shoe with too narrow a shank also causes extra strain because it fails to adequately support the athlete's inner, longitudinal arches.[19]

A properly fitted shoe will bend where the foot bends.

Figure 7-21

Variations in cleated shoes: the longer the cleat, the higher the incidence of injury.

TABLE 7-1 Shoe Comparisons

	Tennis	Aerobic	Running
Flexibility	Firm sole, more rigid than running shoe	Sole between running and tennis shoe	Flexible ball of foot
Uppers	Leather or leather with nylon	Leather or leather with nylon	Nylon or nylon mesh
Heel flare	None	Very little	Flared for stability
Cushioning	Less than a running shoe	Between running and tennis shoe	Heel and sole well padded
Soles	Polyurethane	Rubber or polyurethane	Carbon-based material for greater durability
Tread	Flattened	Flat or pivot dot	Deep grooves for grip

The specially soled shoe   The cleated, or specially soled, sports shoe presents some additional problems in fitting. For example, American football uses the multi–short-cleated, soccer-type polyurethane sole with cleats no longer than 0.5 inches (1.27 cm) (Figure 7-21). Specially soled shoes are also worn when playing on a synthetic surface. Whenever cleated shoes are used, the cleats must be properly positioned under the two major weight-bearing joints and must not be felt through the soles of the shoes (see Table 7-1 for shoe comparisons).[19]

Commercial Foot Pads

Commercial foot pads are intended for use by the general public and are not usually designed to withstand the rigors of sports activities. Commercial pads that are suited for sports are generally not durable enough for hard, extended use. If money is no object, the ready-made commercial pad, which is replaced more often, has the advantage of saving time. Commercial pads are manufactured for almost every type of common structural foot condition, ranging from corns and bunions to fallen arches and pronated feet. Excessive foot pronation often leads to overuse injuries. Available to the athlete commercially are preorthotic and arch supports (Figure 7-22). Products such as Scholl 610.2, Spenco arch supports, Shea devices, and Foothotics Ready

Figure 7-22

Commercially manufactured orthotic devices.

Figure 7-23

Heel cups and pads and lifts of orthopedic felt.

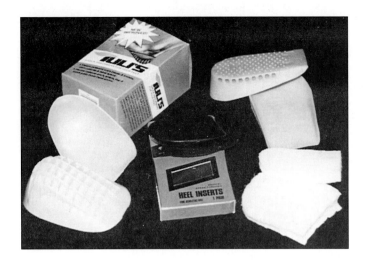

Indiscriminate use of commercial foot orthotics may give the athlete a false sense of security.

7-5

Critical Thinking E x e r c i s e

A basketball player with a history of ankle sprains needs support during practice.

? Which type of ankle support is cost-efficient and most reliable: tape or commercial supports?

Figure 7-24

Commercial ankle supports for an injured ankle.

to Dispense orthotics are commonly used before more formal customized orthotic devices are made. These products offer a compromise to the custom-made foot orthotics by providing some biomechanical control.[5] Indiscriminate use of these aids, however, may intensify the pathological condition or cause the athlete to delay seeing the team physician or team podiatrist for evaluation.[6]

For the most part, foot devices are fabricated and customized from a variety of materials such as foam, felt, plaster, aluminum, and spring steel (see the section titled "Construction of Protective and Supportive Devices," later in this chapter). The heel cup, designed to reduce tissue shearing and shock (Figure 7-23), is one item that began as a prefabricated device but now is commercial.

Commercial Ankle Supports

Commercial ankle stabilizers, either alone or in combination with ankle taping, are becoming increasingly popular in sports (Figure 7-24).[4] There has been significant debate regarding the efficacy of ankle supports in the prevention of ankle sprains. The majority of studies has indicated that bracing is effective in reducing ankle injury,[11,17,20] while other studies have shown no effects or even negative effects.[12,15] Bracing probably has little or no effect on performance; any change in performance is due to the athlete's perception of support and comfort.[2] When compared with an-

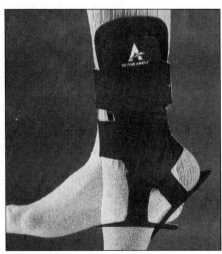

kle taping, these devices do not loosen significantly during exercise.[4] Recent studies have focused on the proprioceptive effects and how ankle braces influence balance, postural sway, and joint position sense.[9]

Shin and Lower Leg

The shin is an area of the body that is commonly neglected in contact and collision sports. Commercially marketed hard-shelled, molded shin guards are used in field hockey and soccer (Figure 7-25).

Thigh and Upper Leg

Thigh and upper leg protection is necessary in collision sports such as hockey and football. Generally, pads slip into ready-made pockets in the sports suit or uniform (Figure 7-26). To prevent abnormal slipping within the pocket and to protect from injury, customized pads are constructed.

Knee Supports and Protective Devices

In terms of the number of sports injuries, knees come just after ankles and feet. As a result of the variety and high frequency of knee afflictions, many protective and supportive devices have been devised. The devices most frequently used in sports today are sleeves, pads, and braces.

Elastic knee pads or guards are extremely valuable in sports in which the athlete falls or receives a direct blow to the anterior aspect of the knee. An elastic sleeve containing a resilient pad may help dissipate an anterior striking force but fails to protect the knee against lateral, medial, or twisting forces.

Knee Braces

There are a number of different knee braces on the market. Some consist of vertical rigid strips held in an elastic sleeve; others are elastic sleeves that contain rigid hinges to be placed on either side of the knee joint. Whether these braces protect against initial or recurrent injury is extremely questionable. Braces of the wraparound type with rigid strips contained in less elastic material hold the knee more firmly in place (Figure 7-27).

Prophylactic knee brace The American Academy of Orthopaedic Surgeons (AAOS) and the American Orthopaedic Society for Sports Medicine have both voiced reservations about knee braces.[16] Knee braces are classified into three types: prophylactic, functional, and rehabilitative. Chapter 20 discusses the latter two types of braces; the prophylactic knee brace is addressed here.

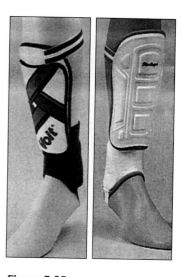

Figure 7-25

Soccer shin guards.

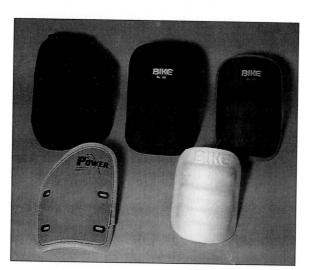

Figure 7-26

Protective thigh pads.

Figure 7-27

A prophylactic knee brace designed to protect against a lateral force and to distribute load away from joint.

Figure 7-28

Neoprene knee sleeve.

Figure 7-29

The hand is an often-neglected area of the body in sports.

The AAOS Committee on Sports Medicine indicates that the ideal prophylactic knee brace should have all the following criteria:[16]

- It should adapt to various anatomic shapes and sizes.
- It should supplement the stiffness of the knee, reducing loads from contact and noncontact stresses.
- It should be cost-effective and durable.
- It should not interfere with normal knee function.
- It should not harm other players.
- It should not increase injuries to the lower extremity.
- It should have documented efficacy in preventing injuries.

Currently no brace on the market fulfills all these criteria. Therefore, use of the prophylactic knee brace is controversial and should be employed on an individual basis.[16]

Recent research has indicated that these prophylactic braces positively influence proprioception and joint position sense,[8] but have little or no effect on performance.[10] Other popular knee devices are sleeves composed of elastic or neoprene material. Sleeves of this type provide mild soft-tissue support and to some extent retain body heat and help reduce edema caused by tissue compression (Figure 7-28).

Hand, Wrist, and Elbow Protection

Like the lower limbs, the upper limbs require initial protection from injury as well as prevention of further injury after a trauma. One of the finest physical instruments, the human hand, is perhaps one of the most neglected in terms of injury, especially in sports.[1] Special attention must be paid to protecting the integrity of all aspects of the hand when it encounters high-speed projectiles or receives external forces that contuse or shear (Figure 7-29).[3] Constant stress to the hand, as characterized by the force received by the hand of the baseball catcher, can lead to irreversible pathological damage in later life. The wrist and the elbow are also vulnerable to sports trauma and often need compression or support for protection (Figure 7-30).[18]

CONSTRUCTION OF PROTECTIVE AND SUPPORTIVE DEVICES

The athletic trainer who can construct protective and supportive devices is extremely valued in sports. The primary materials used are sponge rubber, felt, adhesive sponge rubber, adhesive felt, gauze pads, cotton, lamb's wool, and plastic.

Custom Pad and Orthotic Materials

Many different materials are available to the athletic trainer desiring to protect or support an injured area. In general, these materials can be divided into soft and hard materials (Figure 7-31).

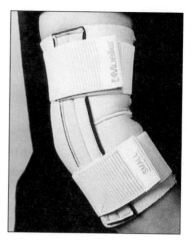

Figure 7-30

Commercial wrist and elbow pads and braces.

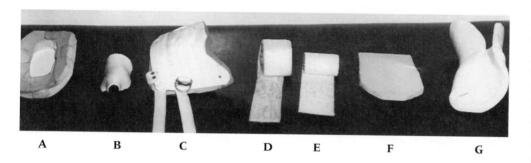

A   B   C   D   E   F   G

Figure 7-31

Types of sports orthoses. **A,** Orthoplast with a foam rubber doughnut. **B,** Ortho-plast splint. **C,** Orthoplast rib protector with a foam rubber pad. **D,** Fiberglass material for splint construction. **E,** Plaster of paris material for cast construction. **F,** Foam rubber pad. **G,** Aloplast foam moldable material for protective pad construction.

Soft Materials

The major soft-material mediums found in training rooms are lamb's wool, cotton, gauze pads, adhesive felt or adhesive foam rubber felt, and an assortment of foam rubber in bulk.

Lamb's wool is a material commonly used on and around the athlete's toes when circular protection is required. In contrast to cotton, lamb's wool does not pack but keeps its resiliency over a long period of time.

Gauze padding is less versatile than other pad materials. It is assembled in varying thicknesses and can be used as an absorbent or protective pad.

Cotton is probably the cheapest and most widely used material in sports. It has the ability to absorb, to hold emollients, and to offer a mild padding effect.

Adhesive felt (moleskin) or *sponge rubber* material contains an adhesive mass on one side, thus combining a cushioning effect with the ability to be held in a specific spot by the adhesive mass. It is a versatile material that is useful on all body parts.

Felt is a material composed of matted wool fibers pressed into varying thick-nesses that range from 1/4 to 1 inch (0.6 to 2.5 cm). Its benefit lies in its comfort-able, semiresilient surface, which gives a firmer pressure than most sponge rubbers. Because felt absorbs perspiration, it clings to the skin, and it has less tendency to move than sponge rubber does (Figure 7-32). Because of its absorbent qualities, felt must be replaced daily. Currently, it is used as support and protection for some foot conditions.

Foams are currently the major materials used for providing injury protection in sports. They come in many different thicknesses and densities (Figure 7-33). They are usually resilient, nonabsorbent, and able to protect the body against compressive forces. Some foams are open celled, whereas others are closed. The closed-cell type

Figure 7-32

Orthopedic felt, both $^1/_2$- and $^1/_4$-inch wide, with broad-blade knife and large scissors for contouring.

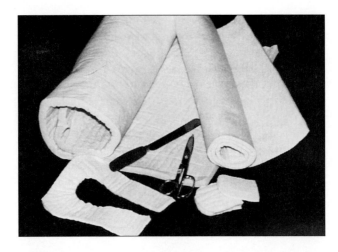

Figure 7-33

Foam assortment: *left,* thermo-moldable; *center,* closed celled; *right,* open celled.

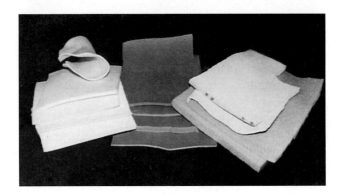

is preferable in sports because it rebounds and returns to its original shape quickly. Foams can be easily worked through cutting, shaping, and faceting. Some foams are thermomoldable and, when heated, become highly pliant and easy to shape. When cooled, they retain the shape in which they were formed. A new class of foams are composed of viscoelastic polymers; Sorbothane is one example. This foam has a high energy-absorbing quality, but it also has a high density, making it heavy (Figure 7-34). Used in inner soles in sports shoes, foam helps prevent blisters and also effectively absorbs vertical, front-to-back, and rotary shock caused by the foot. Foams generally range from $^1/_8$ to $^1/_2$ inch (0.3 to 1.25 cm) in thickness.

Nonyielding Materials

A number of hard, nonyielding materials are used in athletic training for making protective shells and splints.

Thermomoldable plastics   Plastic materials are becoming widely used in sports medicine for customized orthotics. They can brace, splint, and shield a body area. They can provide casting for a fracture, support for a foot defect, or a firm, nonyielding surface to protect a severe contusion.

Plastics used for these purposes differ in their chemical composition and reaction to heat. The three major categories are heat-forming plastics, heat-setting plastics, and heat-plastic foams.

Heat-forming plastics are of the low-temperature variety and are the most popular in athletic training. When heated to 140° to 180° F (60° to 82.2° C), depending on the material, the plastic can be accurately molded to a body part. Aquaplast (polyester sheets) and Orthoplast (synthetic rubber thermoplast) are popular types.

Heat-setting plastics require relatively higher temperatures for shaping. They are

Heat-forming plastics of the low-temperature variety are the most popular in athletic training.

Figure 7-34

Sorbothane products: *left,* sheet stock and insoles; *right,* knee pads.

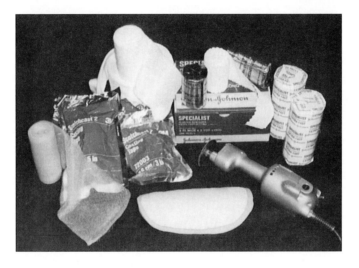

Figure 7-35

Casting material: *left,* fiberglass; *right,* plaster, including cast saw used to trim pictured shin guard.

rigid and difficult to form, usually requiring a mold rather than being formed directly to the body part. High-impact vinyl (polyvinyl chloride), Kydex (polyvinyl chloride acrylic), and Nyloplex (heat-plastic acrylic) are examples of the more commonly used thermoforming plastics.

Heat-plastic foams are plastics that have differences in density as a result of the addition of liquids, gas, or crystals. They are commonly used as shoe inserts and other body padding. Aloplast and Plastazote (polyethylene foams) are two commonly used products.

Usually the plastic is heated until soft and malleable. It is then molded into the desired shape and allowed to cool, thereby retaining its shape. Various pads and other materials can also be fastened in place. The rules and regulations of various sport activities may place limitations in the use of rigid thermomoldable plastics.

Casting materials   Applying casts to injured body areas has long been a practice in sports medicine. The material of choice is fiberglass, which uses resin and a catalytic converter, plus water, to produce hardening. Besides casts, this material makes effective shells for splints and protective pads. Once hardened, the fiberglass is trimmed to shape with a cast saw (Figure 7-35).

Tools Used for Customizing

Many different tools are needed to work with the various materials used to customize protective equipment. These tools include adhesives, adhesive tapes, heat sources, and shaping tools.

Figure 7-36

Glues and adhesive tapes.

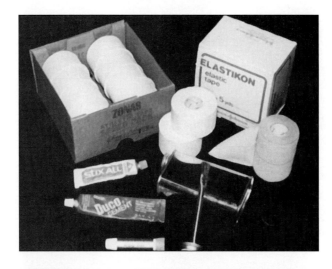

Figure 7-37

Fastening materials, including Velcro, Wet Wrap, leather, laces, rubber wraps, and hardware.

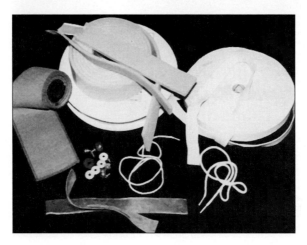

Adhesives   A number of adhesives are used in constructing custom protective equipment. Many cements and glues join plastic to plastic or join other combinations of materials (Figure 7-36).

Adhesive tape   Adhesive tape is a major tool in holding various materials in place. Linen and elastic tape can hold pads to a rigid backing or to adhesive felt (moleskin) and can be used to protect against sharp edges.

Heat sources   To form thermomoldable plastics, a heat source must be available. Three sources are commonly found in training rooms: the commercial moist heat unit, a hot air gun or hair dryer, and an electric skillet or portable oven with a temperature control. The usual desired temperature is 160° F (71° C) or higher.

Shaping tools   Commonly, the tools required to shape custom devices are heavy-duty scissors, sharp-blade knives, and cast saws.

Fastening material   Once formed, customized protective equipment often must be secured in place. Fastening this equipment requires the availability of a great variety of different materials. For example, if something is to be held securely, cotton herringbone–weave straps that are cut and riveted to the device may be desired. On the other hand, a Velcro fastener can be used when a device must be continually put on and removed. Leather can be cut and riveted in place to form hinge straps with buckles attached. Various types of laces can be laced through eyelets to hold something in place (Figure 7-37). Tools that allow for this type of construction include a portable drill, a hole punch, and an ice pick.

Focus

How to construct a hard-shell pad

1. Select proper material and tools, which might include
   a. Thermomoldable plastic sheet
   b. Scissors
   c. Felt material
2. Palpate and mark the margins of the tender area that needs protection.
3. Cut a felt piece to fit in the area of tenderness.
4. Heat plastic until malleable.
5. Place heated plastic over felt and wrap in place with an elastic wrap.
6. When cooled, remove elastic wrap and felt pad.
7. Trim shell to desired shape; a protective shell has now been made to provide a "bubble" relief.
8. If needed, add a softer inner layer of foam to distribute and lessen force further.
   a. Cut a doughnut-type hole in softer foam material the same size as the injury site.
   b. Cut foam the same shape as the hard shell.
   c. Use tape or an adhesive to affix the foam to the shell.

Customized Hard-Shell Pads

A hard-shell pad is often required for an athlete who has acquired an injury, such as a painful contusion (bruise), that must be completely protected from further injury. *Focus Box:* "How to construct a hard-shell pad" provides the procedures needed to customize such a pad.

Custom Foot Orthotics

The athlete with serious biomechanical foot problems often requires a customized foot orthotic device.[14] Measurement for this device is usually performed by an orthopedic surgeon or podiatrist. Foot orthotic devices prescribed by a professional are semisoft, semirigid, and rigid.

Semisoft orthotic device This orthotic device is similar in its construction to the preorthotic device. The major advantages of this device are that it is easily made in the doctor's office, is inexpensive, and is almost immediately comfortable because it has a short break-in period. The device can easily be modified with cork shims.

Proper construction of a semisoft orthotic device requires the use of the correct size blank that has the appropriate thickness and density. The foot is measured on the blank, which is then shaped and smoothed by a drum grinding wheel.[14]

Semirigid orthotic device The semirigid orthotic device is constructed from malleable plastics such as polyethylene, polypropylene, and polyvinyl chloride. As the name implies, semirigid orthotic devices will give under great force.

To make this device, the foot is cast in a neutral position; the cast is then sent to an outside laboratory for construction. The break-in period for this orthotic device is much longer than for the semisoft device.

Rigid orthotic device The rigid orthotic device is the most expensive and most difficult one to construct, although it provides the most rigid control. It is made from a cast of the foot in a neutral position. Rigid acrylic plastic is heated and pressed over the mold. Of all three orthotic devices, the rigid one is the most difficult to fit, and its use has the highest degree of complications.[14]

7-6

Critical Thinking Exercise

A soccer player has incurred a number of contusions to the right quadriceps muscle.

? How does the athletic trainer customize a hard-shell protective thigh pad for the soccer player?

Figure 7-38

A dynamic splint for the hand and fingers.

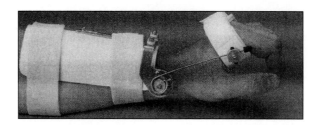

Dynamic Splints

Occasionally it is necessary to fabricate and apply a dynamic splint in treating injuries to the hand and fingers (Figure 7-38). Most often, an occupational therapist would make a dynamic splint; however, the athletic trainer is certainly capable of designing such a splint. A dynamic splint is used to provide long-duration tension on a healing structure (usually a tendon) so that it can return to normal function. Dynamic splints use a combination of thermoplastic material, Velcro, and pieces of rubber band or elastic to provide dynamic assistance.

SUMMARY

- The proper selection and proper fitting of sports equipment are essential in the prevention of many sports injuries. Because of the number of current litigations, sports equipment standards regarding the durability of the material and the fit and wear requirements of the equipment are of serious concern. Manufacturers must foresee all possible uses and misuses of their equipment and warn the user of any potential risks.

- Sports professionals must be concerned about head protection in many collision and contact sports. The football helmet must be used only for its intended purpose and not as a weapon. To avoid unwarranted litigation, a warning label must be placed on the outside of the helmet indicating that the helmet is not fail-safe and must be used as intended. Proper fit is also a major requirement.

- Face protection is of major importance in sports that have fast-moving projectiles, use implements that are in close proximity to other athletes, and facilitate body collisions. Protecting teeth and eyes is of particular significance. The customized mouth guard, fitted to individual requirements, provides the best protection for the teeth and also protects against concussions. Eyes must be protected against projectiles and sports implements. The safest eye guard for the athlete wearing contact lenses or glasses is the closed type that completely protects the orbital cavity.

- Many sports require protection of various parts of the athlete's body. American football players, ice hockey players, and baseball catchers are examples of players who require body protection. Commonly, the protection is for the shoulders, chest, thighs, ribs, hips, buttocks, groin, genitalia (male athletes), and breasts (female athletes).

- Quality sportswear, properly fitted, is essential to prevent injuries. Socks must be clean, without holes, and made of appropriate materials. Shoes must be suited to the sport and must be fitted to the largest foot. The wide part of the foot must match the wide part of the shoe. If the shoe has cleats, they must be positioned at the metatarsophalangeal joints.

- Currently, there are many stock pieces of specialized, protective equipment on the market. They may be designed to support ankles, knees, or other body parts. In addition to stock equipment, athletic trainers often construct customized equipment out of a variety of materials to pad injuries or support feet. Professionals such as orthopedists and podiatrists may devise orthopedic footwear and orthotic devices to improve the biomechanics of the athlete's foot.

Web Sites

Riddell: http://riddell1.com/index.htm

Riddell is an equipment manufacturing company, and this site gives information about the safety of the products they sell and the necessary standards for safety equipment.

Red Cross Tips: http://www.redcross.org/tips/april/aprtip98. html

The April 1998 tip for the American Red Cross is sports eye safety. This site gives tips on eye safety and safety equipment for the eyes.

Healthyway Sporting Protective Eyewear: http://www1. sympatico.ca/healthyway/HEALTHYWAY/feature_vis3c.html

This site emphasizes the importance of protective eyewear for young athletes and provides links to related informative sites.

National Operating Committee on Standards for Athletic Equipment: http://www.nocsae.com

Solutions to Critical Thinking EXERCISES

7-1 The student athletic trainer must acquire the following protective equipment competencies:
- Identify good-quality and poor-quality commercial protective equipment
- Properly fit commercial protective equipment
- Construct protective and supportive devices

7-2 The athletic trainer initiates the following steps:
1. A team meeting is called in which the athletic trainer fully explains the risks entailed in the use and fitting of the equipment.
2. Any defective pieces of equipment are immediately reported and repaired.
3. A letter is sent out to each parent or guardian explaining equipment limitations. This letter is signed and returned to the athletic trainer.
4. A meeting of parents, team members, and coaches is called in which the athletic trainer further explains equipment limitations.

7-3 The athletic trainer explains that the helmet cannot prevent serious neck injuries. Striking an opponent with any part of the helmet or face mask can place abnormal stress on cervical structures. Most severe neck injuries occur from striking an opponent with the top of the helmet; this action is known as axial loading.

7-4 The athletic trainer provides the following advice:
- Shoes are purchased to fit the larger foot.
- Athlete wears athletic socks when fitting shoes.
- Shoes are purchased at the end of the day.
- Shoes feel snug but comfortable when the athlete jumps up and down and performs cutting motions.
- Shoe length and width allow full toe function.
- Wide part of foot matches wide part of shoe.
- Shoe bends at its widest part.
- Each foot is measured from the heel to the end of the largest toe.

7-5 A verified commercial ankle support provides more consistent support for a longer period of time and is more cost-efficient.

7-6 To construct a hard-shell protective thigh pad, the athletic trainer follows these steps:
1. Mark the area on the athlete to be protected.
2. Cut a foam piece to temporarily cover the injury.
3. Heat thermomoldable plastic and place over the foam piece to form a bubble.
4. Cut a plastic sheet to form to the athlete's thigh.
5. Create a doughnut-shaped foam lining to surround the injury.
6. Secure the foam doughnut to the plastic piece.
7. Secure the pad in place with elastic wrap.

REVIEW QUESTIONS AND CLASS ACTIVITIES

1. What are the legal responsibilities of the equipment manager, coach, and athletic trainer in terms of protective equipment?
2. Have the equipment manager of your sports program talk to your class about the purchase and fitting of equipment (e.g., football helmets and shoulder pads).
3. What are the differences between the helmet that protects against a fast-moving projectile and the one that protects against hard blows from an opponent?
4. What are the advantages of a custom-made mouth guard over the stock type?
5. What sports require ear guards?
6. Why are proper eye protection devices necessary in different sports? Identify the different types and their corresponding sports.
7. Which sports require trunk protection? Why? Which types of equipment are necessary?
8. Why is proper breast support so important to the woman with large breasts?
9. On what basis should different sports shoes be evaluated?
10. How should sports shoes be fitted?
11. When would you suggest that a commercial foot pad be used by an athlete?
12. Have the class debate one of the following topics: the benefits of prophylactic taping versus the uselessness of prophylactic taping; commercial ankle supports versus no supports; and the current trend of using prophylactic knee braces versus not using braces.
13. What are the advantages and disadvantages of the fitted knee brace?
14. What is the relative value of commercial braces for the hand, wrist, and elbow?
15. You are given the responsibility to purchase materials that can be used for general padding or that can be customized into special pads or other protective devices. What materials would you buy and why?
16. What steps would you take in making a hard-shell plastic pad?

REFERENCES

1. Alexy C, De Carlo M: Rehabilitation and use of protective devices in hand and wrist injuries. In Rettig AC, editor: *Hand and wrist injuries. Clinic in sports medicine,* vol 17, no 3, July 1998.
2. Beriau M, Cox W, Manning J: Effects of ankle braces upon agility course performance in high school athletes, *J Ath Train* 29(3):224, 1994.
3. Bouvette C et al: A new protective soft splint for contact sports, *J Sport Rehabil* 3(4):282, 1994.

4. Davis PF, Trevino SG: Ankle injuries. In Baxter DE, editor: *The foot and ankle in sport,* St Louis, 1995, Mosby.

5. Frey C: The shoe in sports. In Baxter DE, editor: *The foot and ankle in sport,* St Louis, 1995, Mosby.

6. Hermann TJ: Taping and padding of the foot and ankle. In Sammarco GI, editor: *Rehabilitation of the foot and ankle,* St Louis, 1995, Mosby.

7. Hodgson VR, Thomas LM: *Biomechanical study of football head impacts using a head model—condensed version.* Final report prepared for National Operating Committee on Standards for Athletic Equipment (NOCSAE), 1975.

8. Kaminski TW, Perrin D: Effect of prophylactic knee bracing on balance and joint position sense, *J Ath Train* 31(2):131, 1996.

9. Kinzey SJ, Ingersoll CD, Knight KL: The effects of selected ankle appliances on postural control, *J Ath Train* 32(4):300, 1997.

10. Liggett C, Tandy R, Young J: The effects of prophylactic knee bracing on running gait, *J Ath Train* 30(2):159, 1995.

11. Lindley T: Taping and semirigid bracing may not affect ankle functional range of motion, *J Ath Train* 30(2):109, 1995.

12. Locke A et al: Long-term use of a soft-shell prophylactic ankle stabilizer on speed, agility, and vertical jump performance, *J Sport Rehabil* 6(3):235, 1997.

13. Lord JL: Protective equipment in high-risk sports. In Berrer RB, editor: *Sports medicine for the primary care physician,* ed 2, Boca Raton, Fla, 1994, CRC Press.

14. Massie D: Use and fabrication of temporary orthotics, *J Ath Train* 29(4):309, 1994.

15. Metcalfe RC, Schlabach GA, Looney MA et al: A comparison of moleskin tape, linen tape, and lace-up brace on joint restriction and movement performance, *J Ath Train* 32(2):136, 1997.

16. Montgomery DL: Prophylactic knee braces. In Torg JS, Shephard RJ, editors: *Current therapy in sports medicine,* St Louis, 1995, Mosby.

17. Paris D, Vardaxis V, Kokkaliaris J: Ankle ranges of motion during extended activity periods while taped and braced, *J Ath Train* 30(3):223, 1995.

18. Pincivero D, Rijke A, Heinrichs K et al: The effects of a functional elbow brace on medial joint stability: a case study, *J Ath Train* 29(3):232, 1994.

19. Prentice W: *Fitness and wellness for life,* ed 6, Dubuque, 1999, WCB/McGraw-Hill.

20. Sharpe SR, Knapik J, Jones B: Ankle braces effectively reduce recurrence of ankle sprains in female soccer players, *J Ath Train* 32(1):21, 1997.

21. Zemper E: Analysis of cerebral concussion frequency with the most commonly used models of football helmets, *J Ath Train* 29(1):44, 1994.

ANNOTATED BIBLIOGRAPHY

Baxter DE, editor: *The foot and ankle in sport,* St Louis, 1995, Mosby.

This in-depth medical text covers all aspects of foot and ankle conditions in sport.

Hunter S, Dolan M, Davis M: *Foot orthotics in therapy and sport,* Champaign, Ill, 1995, Human Kinetics.

This text takes a detailed look at the fabrication of orthotic devices.

Nicholas JA, Hirshman EB, editors: *The upper extremity in sports medicine,* St Louis, 1990, Mosby.

This book includes a special chapter on protective equipment for the shoulder, elbow, wrist, and hand.

Bandaging and Taping

When you finish this chapter you should be able to

- Explain the need for and demonstrate the application of roller bandages.
- Explain the need for and demonstrate the application of triangular and cravat bandages.
- Demonstrate site preparation for taping.
- Demonstrate basic skill in the use of taping in sports.
- Demonstrate the skillful application of tape for a variety of musculoskeletal problems.

Bandaging and taping are major skills used in the protection and management of the injured athlete. Each of these skill areas requires a great deal of practice before a high level of proficiency can be attained.

BANDAGING

A **bandage,** when properly applied, may contribute to recovery from sports injuries. Bandages carelessly or improperly applied may cause discomfort, allow wound contamination, and/or hamper repair and healing. In all cases bandages must be firmly applied—neither so tight that circulation is impaired nor so loose that the **dressing** is allowed to slip.

Bandage Materials

Bandages used on sports injuries consist of gauze, cotton cloth, and elastic wrapping.

Gauze materials are used in three forms: as sterile pads for wounds, as padding in the prevention of blisters on a taped ankle, and as a roller bandage for holding dressings and compresses in place.

Cotton cloth is used primarily for cloth ankle wraps and for triangular and cravat bandages. It is soft, is easily obtained, and can be washed many times without deterioration.

The *elastic roller bandage* is extremely popular in sports because of its extensibility, which allows it to conform to most parts of the body. Elastic wraps are active bandages; they let the athlete move without restriction. They act as controlled compression bandages where hemorrhage or swelling must be prevented and can also help support soft tissue.

A *cohesive elastic bandage* exerts constant, even pressure. It is lightweight and contours easily to the body part. The bandage is composed of two layers of nonwoven rayon, which are separated by strands of spandex material. The cohesive elastic bandage is coated with a substance that makes the material adhere to itself, eliminating the need for metal clips or adhesive tape to hold it in place.

Roller Bandages

Roller bandages are made of many materials; gauze, cotton cloth, and elastic wrapping are predominantly used in the training room. The width and length vary according to the body part to be bandaged. The sizes most frequently used are the 2-inch (5 cm) width by 6-yard (5.5 m) length for hand, finger, toe, and head bandages; the 3-inch (7.5 cm) width by 10-yard (9 m) length for the extremities; and the 4-inch (10 cm) or 6-inch (15 cm) width by 10-yard (9 m) length for thigh, groin, and trunk. For ease and convenience in the application of the roller bandage, the

bandage
Strip of cloth or other material used to cover a wound.

dressing
Covering, protective or supportive, that is applied to an injury or wound.

Wrinkles or seams in roller bandages may irritate skin.

strips of material are first rolled into a cylinder. When a bandage is selected, it should be a single piece that is free from wrinkles, seams, and any other imperfections that may cause skin irritation.[9]

Application

To apply a roller bandage, hold it in the preferred hand with the loose end extending from the bottom of the roll.

Application of the roller bandage must be executed in a specific manner to achieve the purpose of the wrap. When a roller bandage is about to be placed on a body part, the roll should be held in the preferred hand with the loose end extending from the bottom of the roll. The back surface of the loose end is placed on the part and held in position by the other hand. The bandage cylinder is then unrolled and passed around the injured area. As the hand pulls the material from the roll, it also standardizes the bandage pressure and guides the bandage in the proper direction. To anchor and stabilize the bandage, a number of turns, one on top of the other, are made. Circling a body part requires the operator to alternate the bandage roll from one hand to the other and back again.

To provide maximum benefit, a roller bandage should be applied uniformly and firmly but not too tightly. Excessive or unequal pressure can hinder the normal blood flow within the part. The following points should be considered when using the roller bandage:

1. A body part should be wrapped in the position of maximum muscle contraction to ensure unhampered movement or circulation.
2. It is better to use a large number of turns with moderate tension than a limited number of turns applied too tightly.
3. Each turn of the bandage should be overlapped by at least one half of the overlying wrap to prevent the separation of the material while engaged in activity. Separation of the bandage turns tends to pinch and irritate the skin.
4. When limbs are wrapped, fingers and toes should be scrutinized often for signs of circulation impairment. Abnormally cold or cyanotic phalanges are signs of excessive bandage pressure.

Begin anchoring bandages at the smallest part of the limb.

The usual anchoring of roller bandages consists of several circular wraps directly overlying each other. Whenever possible, anchoring is commenced at the smallest circumference of a limb and is then moved upward. Wrists and ankles are the usual sites for anchoring bandages of the limbs. Bandages are applied to these areas in the following manner:

1. The loose end of the roller bandage is laid obliquely on the anterior aspects of the wrist or ankle and held in this position. The roll is then carried posteriorly under and completely around the limb and back to the starting point.
2. The triangular portion of the uncovered oblique end is folded over the second turn.
3. The folded triangle is covered by a third turn, which finishes a secure anchor.

After a roller bandage has been applied, it is held in place by a locking technique. The method most often used to finish a wrap is to firmly tie or pin the bandage or place adhesive tape over several overlying turns.

Once a bandage has been put on and has served its purpose, removal can be performed either by unwrapping or by carefully cutting with bandage scissors. Whatever method of bandage removal is used, extreme caution must be taken to avoid additional injury.

Cloth ankle wrap   Because tape is so expensive, the ankle wrap is an inexpensive and expedient means of mildly protecting ankles (Figure 8-1).

Materials needed   Each muslin wrap should be $1^1/_2$ to 2 inches (3.8 to 5 cm) wide and 72 to 96 inches (180 to 240 cm) long to ensure complete coverage and protection. The purpose of this wrap is to give mild support against lateral and medial motion of the ankle. It is applied over a sock.

Position of the athlete   The athlete sits on a table, extending the leg and positioning the foot at a 90-degree angle. To avoid any distortion, it is important that the ankle be neither overflexed nor overextended.

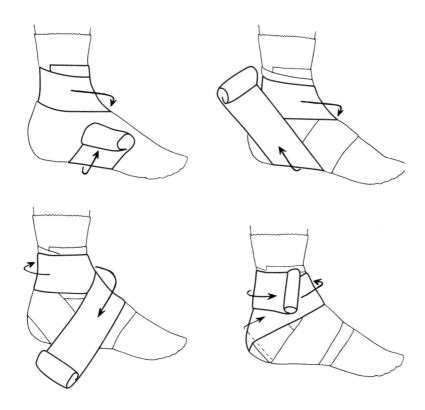

Figure 8-1

Ankle wrap.

Procedure

1. Start the wrap above the instep around the ankle, circle the ankle, and move it at an acute angle to the inside of the foot.
2. From the inside of the foot, move the wrap under the arch, coming up on the outside and crossing at the beginning point, where it continues around the ankle, hooking the heel.
3. Move the wrap up, inside, over the instep, and around the ankle, hooking the opposite side of the heel. This completes one series of the ankle wrap.
4. Complete a second series with the remaining material.
5. For additional support, two heel locks with adhesive tape may be applied over the ankle wrap.

Elastic Wrap Techniques

Any time an elastic wrap is applied to the athlete, always check for and avoid decreased circulation and blueness of the extremity, and check for a blood capillary refill.

Ankle and foot spica   The ankle and foot **spica** bandage (Figure 8-2) is primarily used in sports for the compression of new injuries and for holding wound dressings in place.

Materials needed   Depending on the size of the ankle and foot, a 2-inch (5 cm) or 3-inch (7.5 cm) wrap is used.

Position of the athlete   The athlete sits with ankle and foot extended over a table.

Procedure

1. Place an anchor around the foot near the metatarsal arch.
2. Bring the elastic bandage across the instep and around the heel, and return to the starting point.
3. Repeat the procedure several times, with each succeeding revolution progressing upward on the foot and the ankle.
4. Overlap each spica over the preceding layer by approximately three fourths.

Spiral bandage   The spiral bandage (Figure 8-3) is widely used in sports for covering a large area of a cylindrical part.

Check circulation after applying an elastic wrap.

spica
A figure-eight bandage with one of the two loops larger than the other.

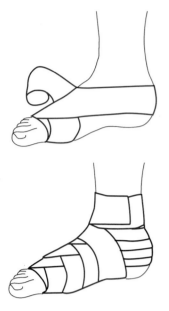

Figure 8-2

Ankle and foot spica.

8-1

Critical Thinking E x e r c i s e

A baseball player strains his right groin while running the bases.

? Which elastic wrap should be applied when the athlete returns to his sport and why?

Materials needed   Depending on the size of the area, a 3-inch (7.5 cm) or 4-inch (10 cm) wrap is required.

Position of the athlete   If the wrap is for the lower limb, the athlete bears weight on the opposite leg.

Procedure

1. Anchor the elastic spiral bandage at the smallest circumference of the limb and wrap upward in a spiral against gravity.
2. To prevent the bandage from slipping down on a moving extremity, fold two pieces of tape lengthwise and place on the bandage at either side of the limb, or spray tape adherent on the part.
3. After the bandage is anchored, carry it upward in consecutive spiral turns, each overlapping the other by at least 1/2 inch.
4. Terminate the bandage by locking it with circular turns, which are then firmly secured by tape.

Groin support   The following procedure is used to support a groin strain and hip adductor strains (Figure 8-4).

Materials needed   One roll of extra-long 6-inch (15 cm) elastic bandage, a roll of 1 1/2-inch (3.8 cm) adhesive tape, and nonsterile cotton.

Position of the athlete   The athlete stands on a table with weight placed on the uninjured leg. The affected limb is relaxed and internally rotated. This procedure is different from that described in Figure 8-5, in which the wrap was used for pressure only.

Procedure

1. Place a piece of nonsterile cotton or a felt pad, if needed, over the injured site to provide additional compression and support.
2. Start the end of the elastic bandage at the upper part of the inner aspect of the thigh and carry it posteriorly around the thigh. Then bring it across the lower abdomen and over the crest of the ilium on the opposite side of the body.
3. Continue the wrap around the back, repeating the same pattern and securing the wrap end with a 1 1/2-inch (3.8 cm) adhesive tape.

Variations of this method can be seen in Figure 8-5 (to support injured hip flexors) and Figure 8-6 (to limit the movement of the buttocks).

Shoulder spica   The shoulder spica (Figure 8-7) is used mainly for the retention of wound dressings and for moderate muscular support.

Materials needed   One roll of extra-long 4-inch (10 cm) to 6-inch (15 cm) elastic wrap, 1 1/2-inch (3.8 cm) adhesive tape, and padding for axilla.

Figure 8-3

Spiral bandage.

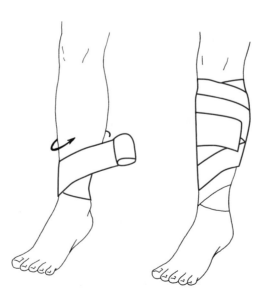

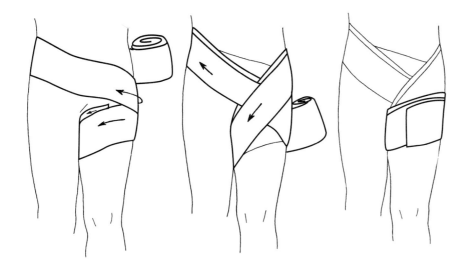

Figure 8-4

Elastic groin support.

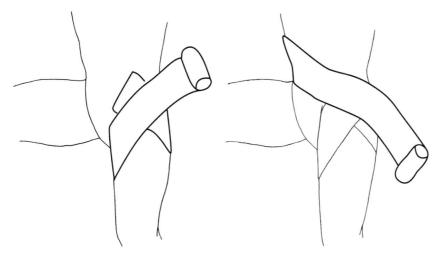

Figure 8-5

Hip spica for hip flexors.

Position of the athlete   The athlete stands with his or her side toward the operator.
Procedure
1. Pad the axilla well to prevent skin irritation and constriction of blood vessels.
2. Anchor the bandage by one turn around the affected upper arm.
3. After anchoring the bandage around the arm on the injured side, carry the wrap around the back under the unaffected arm and across the chest to the injured shoulder.
4. Encircle the affected arm again by the bandage, which continues around the back. Every figure-eight pattern moves progressively upward with an overlap of at least half of the previous underlying wrap.

Elbow figure-eight bandage   The elbow figure-eight bandage (Figure 8-8) can be used to secure a dressing in the antecubital fossa or to restrain full extension in hyperextension injuries. When it is reversed, it can be used on the posterior aspect of the elbow.

Materials needed   One 3-inch (7.5 cm) elastic roll and 1¹/₂-inch (3.8 cm) adhesive tape.

Position of the athlete   The athlete flexes his or her elbow between 45 degrees and 90 degrees, depending on the restriction of movement required.
Procedure
1. Anchor the bandage by encircling the lower arm.
2. Bring the roll obliquely upward over the posterior aspect of the elbow.

8-2

Critical Thinking E x e r c i s e

A wrestler sustains a left shoulder point injury. The athletic trainer cuts a sponge rubber doughnut to protect the shoulder point from further injury.

? How is the doughnut held in place?

Figure 8-6

Method used to limit
movement of buttocks.

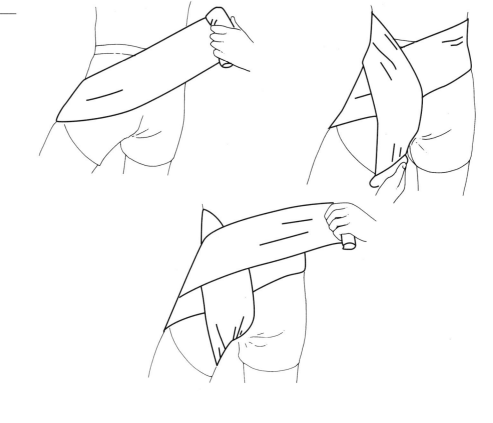

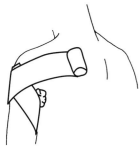

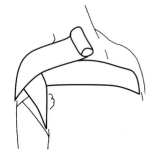

Figure 8-7

Elastic shoulder spica.

Triangular and cravat bandages
allow ease and speed of
application.

3. Carry the roll obliquely upward, crossing the antecubital fossa; then pass once again completely around the upper arm and return to the beginning position by again crossing the antecubital fossa.
4. Continue the procedure as described, but for every new sequence move upward toward the elbow one half the width of the underlying wrap.

Gauze hand and wrist figure eight   A figure-eight bandage (Figure 8-9) can be used for mild wrist and hand support and for holding dressings in place.

Materials needed   One roll of $^{1}/_{2}$-inch (1.25 cm) gauze, $^{1}/_{2}$-inch (1.25 cm) tape, and scissors.

Position of the athlete   The athlete positions his or her elbow at a 45-degree angle.
Procedure
1. The anchor is executed with one or two turns around the palm of the hand.
2. The roll is then carried obliquely across the anterior or posterior portion of the hand, depending on the position of the wound, to the wrist, which it circles once; then it is returned to the primary anchor.
3. As many figure eights as needed are applied.

Triangular and Cravat Bandages

Triangular and cravat bandages, usually made of cotton cloth, may be used if roller types are not applicable or available. The triangular and cravat bandages are primarily used as first aid devices.[5] They are valuable in emergency bandaging because of their ease and speed of application. In sports the more diversified roller bandages are usually available and lend themselves more to the needs of the athlete. The principal use of the triangular bandage in athletic training is for arm slings. There are two basic kinds of slings, the cervical arm sling and the shoulder arm sling, and each has a specific purpose.

Cervical arm sling   The cervical arm sling (Figure 8-10) is designed to support the forearm, wrist, and hand. A triangular bandage is placed around the neck and under the bent arm that is to be supported.

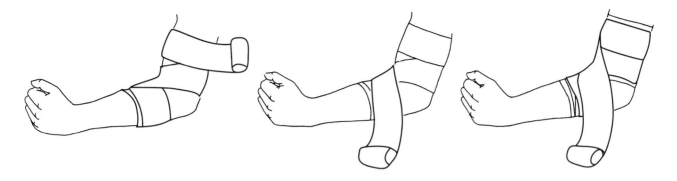

Figure 8-8

Elastic elbow figure-eight bandage.

Figure 8-9

Hand and wrist figure-eight bandage.

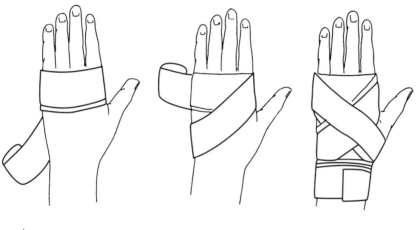

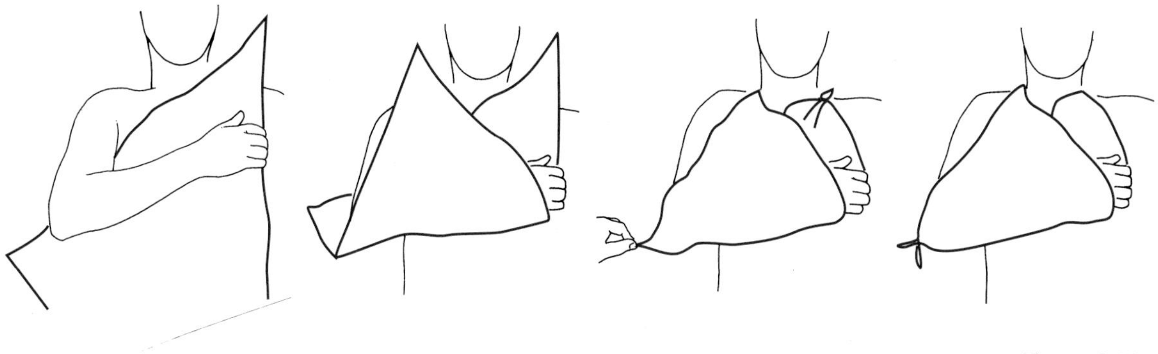

Figure 8-10

Cervical arm sling.

Materials needed   One triangular bandage.

Position of the athlete   The athlete stands with the affected arm bent at approximately a 70-degree angle.

Procedure

1. Position the triangular bandage under the injured arm with the apex facing the elbow.
2. Carry the end of the triangle nearest the body over the shoulder of the uninjured arm. The other end is allowed to hang down loosely.
3. Pull the loose end over the shoulder of the injured side.
4. Tie the two ends of the bandage in a square knot behind the neck. For the sake of comfort, the knot should be on either side of the neck, not directly in the middle.

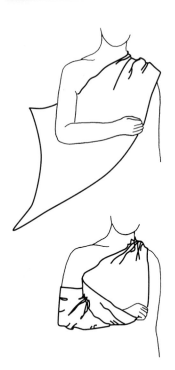

Figure 8-11

Shoulder arm sling.

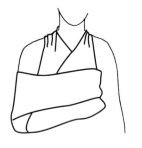

Figure 8-12

Sling and swathe.

5. Bring the apex of the triangle around to the front of the elbow and fasten by twisting the end, then tying in a knot.

If greater arm stabilization is required than that afforded by a sling, an additional bandage can be swathed about the upper arm and body.

Shoulder arm sling   The shoulder arm sling (Figure 8-11) is suggested for forearm support when there is an injury to the shoulder girdle or when the cervical arm sling is irritating to the athlete.

Materials needed   One triangular bandage and one safety pin.

Position of the athlete   The athlete stands with his or her injured arm bent at approximately a 70-degree angle.

Procedure

1. Place the upper end of the shoulder sling over the uninjured shoulder side.
2. Bring the lower end of the triangle over the forearm and draw it between the upper arm and the body, swinging it around the athlete's back and then upward to meet the other end, where a square knot is tied.
3. Bring the apex end of the triangle around to the front of the elbow and fasten with a safety pin.

Sling and swathe   The sling and swathe combination is designed to stabilize the arm securely in cases of shoulder dislocation or fracture (Figure 8-12).

TAPING

Historically, taping has been an important part of athletic training. In recent years athletic taping has become decreasingly important as an adjunct to sports medicine because current research questions long-thought ideas about the effectiveness of taping.[7,12,15] The psychological effect of taping on the athlete is currently unknown.

Tape Usage

Injury Care

When used for sports injuries, adhesive tape offers a number of possibilities:
- Retention of wound dressings.
- Stabilization of compression bandages that control external and internal hemorrhaging.
- Support of recent injuries to prevent additional insult that might result from the activities of the athlete.
- Stabilization of an injury while the athlete is undergoing an exercise rehabilitation procedure.

Injury Protection

Protecting against acute injuries is another major use of tape support. This protection can be achieved by limiting the motion of a body part or by securing some special device.

Linen Adhesive Tape

Modern adhesive tape has great adaptability for use in sports because of its uniform adhesive mass, adhering qualities, and lightness and because of the relative strength of the backing materials.[8] All these qualities are of value in holding wound dressings in place and in supporting and protecting injured areas. This tape comes in a variety of sizes; widths of 1, 1½, and 2 inches (2.5, 3.75, and 5 cm) are commonly used in sports medicine. When linen tape is purchased, factors such as cost, grade of backing, quality of adhesive mass, and properties of unwinding should be considered.

Tape Grade

Linen-backed tape is most often graded according to the number of longitudinal and vertical fibers per inch of backing material. The heavier and more costly backing contains 85 or more longitudinal fibers and 65 vertical fibers per square inch. The lighter, less expensive grade has 65 or fewer longitudinal fibers and 45 vertical fibers.

Adhesive Mass

As a result of improvements in adhesive mass, certain essentials should be expected from tape. It should adhere readily when applied and should maintain this adherence in the presence of profuse perspiration and activity. Besides sticking well, the mass must contain as few skin irritants as possible and must be able to be removed easily without leaving a mass residue or pulling away the superficial skin.

Winding Tension

The winding tension of a tape roll is important to the operator. Sports place a unique demand on the unwinding quality of tape; if tape is to be applied for protection and support, there must be even and constant unwinding tension. In most cases, a proper wind needs little additional tension to provide sufficient tightness.

Stretch Tape

Increasingly, tape with varying elasticity is being used in sports medicine, often in combination with linen tape. Because of its conforming qualities, stretch tape is used for small, angular body parts, such as the feet, wrist, hands, and fingers. As with linen tape, stretch tape comes in a variety of widths.

> Increasingly, tape with varying elasticity is being used in sports medicine.

Tape Storage

When storing tape, take the following steps:
1. Store in a cool place such as in a low cupboard.
2. Stack so that the tape rests on its flat top or bottom to avoid distortion.

> Store tape in a cool place, and stack it flat.

Using Adhesive Tape in Sports

Preparation for Taping

Special attention must be given when applying tape directly to the skin. Perspiration and dirt collected during sport activities will prevent tape from properly sticking to the skin. Whenever tape is used, the skin surface should be cleansed with soap and water to remove all dirt and oil. Also, hair should be shaved to prevent additional irritation when the tape is removed. If additional adherence or protection from irritation is needed, a preparation containing rosin and a skin toughener offers astringent action and dries readily, leaving a tacky residue to which tape will adhere firmly.[10]

> Skin should be cleansed and hair should be shaved before tape is applied.

Taping directly on skin provides maximum support. However, applying tape day after day can lead to skin irritation. To overcome this problem, many athletic trainers sacrifice some support by using a protective covering on the skin. The most popular covering is a moderately elastic commercial underwrap material that is extremely thin and fits snugly to the contours of the part to be taped. One commonly used underwrap material is polyester and urethane foam, which is fine, porous, extremely lightweight, and resilient. Proper use of an underwrap requires the part to be shaved and sprayed with a tape adherent. Underwrap material should be applied only one layer thick.

Proper Taping Technique

The correct tape width depends on the area to be covered. The more acute the angles, the narrower the tape must be to fit the many contours. For example, the fingers and toes usually require $1/2$- or 1-inch (1.25 or 2.5 cm) tape; the ankles require $1^1/2$-inch (3.75 cm) tape; and the larger skin areas such as thighs and back can accommodate 2- to 3-inch (5 to 7.5 cm) tape with ease.

NOTE: Supportive tape improperly applied can aggravate an existing injury or can disrupt the mechanics of a body part, causing an initial injury to occur.

Tearing Tape

Athletic trainers use various techniques in tearing tape (Figure 8-13). The tearing method should permit the operator to keep the tape roll in hand most of the time.[10] The following is a suggested procedure:

Figure 8-13

Methods of tearing linen-backed tape.

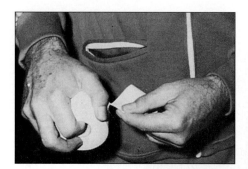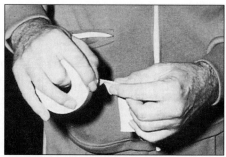
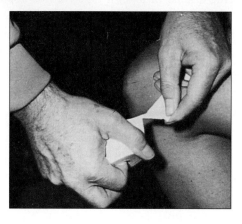

1. Hold the tape roll in the preferred hand with the index finger hooked through the center of the tape roll and the thumb pressing its outer edge.
2. With the other hand, grasp the loose end between the thumb and index finger.
3. With both hands in place, pull both ends of the tape so that it is tight. Next, make a quick, scissorslike move to tear the tape. In tearing tape, the movement of one hand is away from the body and the other hand toward the body. Remember, do not try to bend or twist the tape to tear it.

To tear tape, move hands quickly in opposite directions.

When tearing is properly executed, the torn edges of the linen-backed tape are relatively straight, without curves, twists, or loose threads sticking out. Once the first thread is torn, the rest of the tape tears easily. Learning to tear tape effectively from many different positions is essential for speed and efficiency. Many tapes other than the linen-backed type cannot be torn manually but require a knife, scissors, or razor blade.

Rules for Tape Application

The following are a few of the important rules to be observed in the use of adhesive tape. In practice the athletic trainer will identify others.

1. *If the part to be taped is a joint, place it in the position in which it is to be stabilized.* If the part is musculature, make the necessary allowance for contraction and expansion.
2. *Overlap the tape at least half the width of the tape below.* Unless tape is overlapped sufficiently, the active athlete will separate it, exposing the underlying skin to irritation.
3. *Avoid continuous taping.* Tape continuously wrapped around a part may cause constriction. It is suggested that one turn be made at a time and that each encirclement be torn to overlap the starting end by approximately 1 inch. This rule is particularly true of the nonyielding linen-backed tape.
4. *Keep the tape roll in the hand whenever possible.* By learning to keep the tape roll in the hand, seldom putting it down, and by learning to tear the tape, an operator can develop taping speed and accuracy.

5. *Smooth and mold the tape as it is laid on the skin.* To save additional time, tape strips should be smoothed and molded to the body part as they are put in place; this is done by stroking the top with the fingers, palms, and heels of both hands.

6. *Allow tape to fit the natural contour of the skin.* Each strip of tape must be placed with a particular purpose in mind. Linen-backed tape is not sufficiently elastic to bend around acute angles but must be allowed to fall as it may, fitting naturally to the body contours. Failing to allow this fit creates wrinkles and gaps that can result in skin irritations.

7. *Start taping with an anchor piece and finish by applying a lock strip.* Commence taping, if possible, by sticking the tape to an anchor piece that encircles the part. This placement affords a good medium for the stabilization of succeeding tape strips so that they will not be affected by the movement of the part.

8. *Where maximum support is desired, tape directly over skin.* In cases of sensitive skin, prewrap may be used as tape bases. With prewrap, some movement can be expected between the skin and the base.[2]

9. *Do not apply tape if skin is hot or cold from a therapeutic treatment.*

Removing Adhesive Tape

Tape usually can be removed from the skin by hand, by tape scissors or tape cutters, or by chemical solvents.[10]

Manual removal   When pulling tape from the body, be careful not to tear or irritate the skin. Tape must not be wrenched in an outward direction from the skin but should be pulled in a direct line with the body (Figure 8-14). Remember to remove the skin carefully from the tape and not to peel the tape from the skin. One hand gently pulls the tape in one direction, and the opposite hand gently presses the skin away from the tape.

> Peel the skin from the tape, not the tape from the skin.

Use of tape scissors or cutters   The characteristic tape scissors have a blunt nose that slips underneath the tape smoothly without gouging the skin. Take care to avoid cutting the tape too near the site of the injury, lest the scissors aggravate the condition. Cut on the uninjured side.

Taping Supplies

Effective taping requires the availability of numerous supplies:

1. Razor—hair removal
2. Soap—cleaning skin
3. Alcohol—oil removal from skin

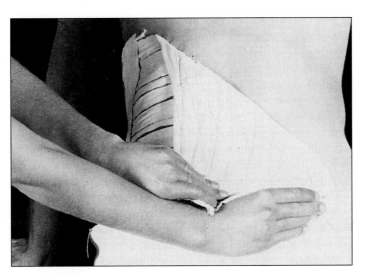

Figure 8-14

Remove tape by pulling in a direct line with the body.

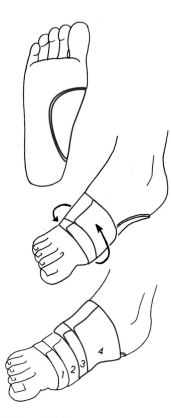

Figure 8-15

Arch taping technique no. 1, including an arch pad and circular tape strips.

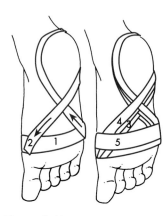

Figure 8-16

Arch taping technique no. 2 (X taping).

4. Adhesive spray—tape adherent
5. Prewrap material—skin protection
6. Heel and lace pads
7. White zinc oxide tape (linen-backed tape) ($^1/_2$ inch, 1 inch, $1^1/_2$-inch, and 2 inch [1.25 cm, 2.5 cm, 3.8 cm, and 5 cm])
8. Adhesive and stretch tape (1 inch, 2 inch, and 3 inch [2.5 cm, 5 cm, and 7.5 cm])
9. Felt and foam padding material
10. Tape scissors
11. Tape cutters
12. Elastic bandages (2 inch, 3 inch, 4 inch, and 6 inch [5 cm, 7.5 cm, 10 cm, and 15 cm])

Common Taping Procedures

The Arch

Arch technique no. 1: with pad support   Arch taping with pad support strengthens weakened arches (Figure 8-15). NOTE: The longitudinal arch should be lifted.

Materials needed   One roll of $1^1/_2$-inch (3.8 cm) tape, tape adherent, and a $^1/_8$- or $^1/_4$-inch (0.3 or 0.6 cm) adhesive foam rubber pad or wool felt pad, cut to fit the longitudinal arch.

Site preparation   Clean foot of dirt and oil; if hairy, shave dorsum of foot. Spray area with tape adherent.

Position of the athlete   The athlete lies face down on the table with the foot that is to be taped extending approximately 6 inches (15 cm) over the edge of the table. To ensure proper position, allow the foot to hang in a relaxed position.

Procedure
1. Place a series of strips of tape directly around the arch or, if added support is required, around an arch pad and the arch. The first strip should go just above the metatarsal arch (1).
2. Each successive strip overlaps the preceding piece about half the width of the tape (2 through 4).

CAUTION: Avoid putting on so many strips of tape that the action of the ankle is hampered.

Arch technique no. 2: the X for the longitudinal arch   Use the figure-eight method for taping the longitudinal arch (Figure 8-16).

Materials needed   One roll of 1-inch (2.5 cm) tape and tape adherent.

Site preparation   Same as for arch technique no. 1.

Position of the athlete   The athlete lies face down on the table with the affected foot extending approximately 6 inches (15 cm) over the edge of the table. To ensure proper position, allow the foot to hang in a relaxed position.

Procedure
1. Lightly place an anchor strip around the ball of the foot, making certain not to constrict the action of the toes (1).
2. Start tape strip 2 from the lateral edge of the anchor. Move it upward at an acute angle, cross the center of the longitudinal arch, encircle the heel, and descend. Then cross the arch again and end at the medial aspect of the anchor (2). Repeat three or four times (3 and 4).
3. Lock the taped Xs with a single piece of tape placed around the ball of foot (5).

After all the X strips are applied, cover the entire arch with $1^1/_2$-inch (3.8 cm) circular tape strips.

Arch technique no. 3: the X teardrop arch and forefoot support   As its name implies, this taping both supports the longitudinal arch and stabilizes the forefoot into good alignment (Figure 8-17).

Materials needed   One roll of 1-inch (2.5 cm) tape and tape adherent.

Position of the athlete   The athlete lies face down on the table with the foot to be taped extending approximately 6 inches (15 cm) over the edge of the table.

Procedure

1. Place an anchor strip around the ball of the foot (1).
2. Start tape strip 2 on the side of the foot, beginning at the base of the great toe. Take the tape around the heel, crossing the arch and returning to the starting point (2).
3. The pattern of the third strip of tape is the same as the second strip except that it is started on the little toe side of the foot (3). Repeat two or three times (4 and 5).
4. Lock each series of strips by placing tape around the ball joint (6). A completed procedure usually consists of a series of three strips.

Arch technique no. 4: fan arch support   The fan arch technique supports the entire plantar aspect of the foot (Figure 8-18).

Materials needed   One roll of 1-inch (2.5 cm) tape, one roll of 1¹/₂-inch (3.8 cm) tape, and tape adherent.

Position of athlete   The athlete lies face down on the table with the foot to be taped extending approximately 6 inches (15 cm) over the edge of the table.

Procedure

1. Using the 1-inch (2.5 cm) tape, place an anchor strip around the ball of the foot (1).
2. Starting at the third metatarsal head, take the tape around the heel from the lateral side and meet the strip where it began (2 and 3).
3. Start the next strip near the second metatarsal head and finish it on the fourth metatarsal head (4).
4. Begin the last strip on the fourth metatarsal head and finish it on the fifth metatarsal head (5). The technique, when completed, forms a fan-shaped pattern covering the metatarsal region (6).
5. Lock strips using 1¹/₂-inch (3.8 cm) tape and encircling the complete arch (7 through 11).

LowDye technique   The LowDye technique is an excellent method for managing the fallen medial longitudinal arch, foot pronation, arch strains, and plantar fasciitis.[14] Moleskin is cut in 3-inch (7.5 cm) strips to the shape of the sole of the foot. It should cover the head of the metatarsal bones and the clacaneus bone (Figure 8-19).

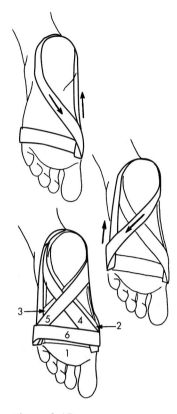

Figure 8-17

Teardrop arch taping technique no. 3 with double X and forefoot support.

Figure 8-18

Fan arch taping technique.

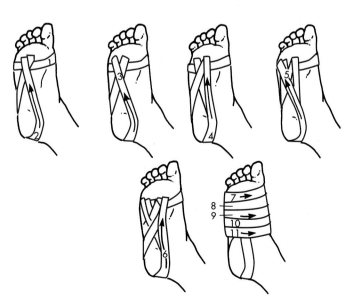

Figure 8-19

LowDye taping technique.

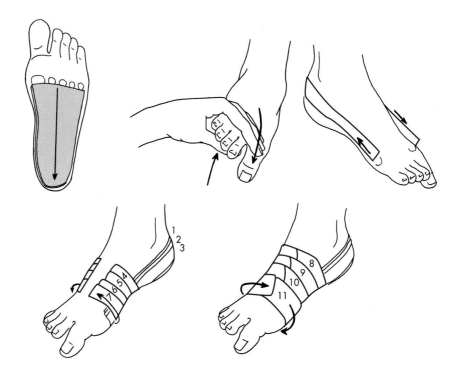

8-4

Critical Thinking E x e r c i s e

A football lineman has a severe right foot pronation with a fallen medial longitudinal arch. He is subject to arch strains.

? What taping technique is designed for this situation?

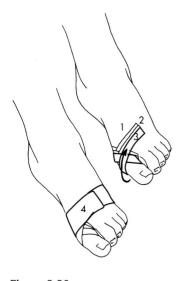

Figure 8-20

Taping for a sprained great toe.

Materials needed   One roll of 1-inch (2.5 cm) tape, one roll of 2-inch (5 cm) tape, and moleskin.

Position of the athlete   The athlete sits with the foot in a neutral position with the great toe and medial aspect of the foot in plantar flexion.

Procedure

1. Apply the moleskin to the sole of the foot, pulling it slightly downward before attaching it to the clacaneus.
2. Grasp the forefoot with the thumb under the distal 2 to 5 metatarsal heads, pushing slightly upward, with the tips of the second and third fingers pushing downward on the first metatarsal head. Apply two or three 1-inch (2.5 cm) tape strips laterally, starting from the distal head of the first metatarsal bone (1 through 3). Keep these lateral strips below the outer malleolus.
3. Secure the moleskin and lateral tape strip by circling the forefoot with four 2-inch (5 cm) strips (4 through 7). Start at the lateral dorsum of the foot, circle under the plantar aspect, and finish at the medial dorsum of the foot. Apply four strips of 2-inch stretch tape that encircle the arch (8 through 11).

A variation of this method is to use two 2-inch (5 cm) moleskin strips, one at the ball of the foot and the other at the base of the fifth metatarsal. Cross the strips and extend them along the plantar surface of the foot. For anchors, apply 2-inch (5 cm) elastic tape around the forefoot, lateral to medial, giving additional support.[14]

The Toes

The sprained great toe   This procedure is used for taping a sprained great toe (Figure 8-20).

Materials needed   One roll of 1-inch (2.5 cm) tape and tape adherent and one roll of 1½-inch tape.

Site preparation   Clean foot of dirt and oil, shave hair from toes, and spray area with tape adherent.

Position of the athlete   The athlete assumes a sitting position.

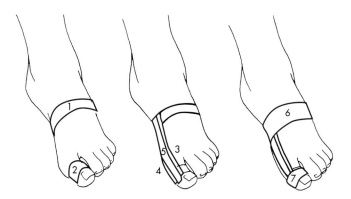

Figure 8-21

Bunion taping.

Procedure

1. The greatest support is given to the joint by a half-figure-eight taping (1 through 3). Start the series at an acute angle on the top of the foot and swing down between the great and first toes, first encircling the great toe and then coming up, over, and across the starting point. Repeat this process, starting each series separately.
2. After the required number of half-figure-eight strips are in position, place one and one-half inch lock piece around the ball of the foot (4).

Bunions

Materials needed   One roll of 1-inch (2.5 cm) tape, tape adherent, and ¼-inch (0.6 cm) sponge rubber or felt (Figure 8-21).

Position of the athlete   The athlete assumes a sitting position.

Procedure

1. Cut the ¼-inch sponge rubber to form a wedge between the great and second toes.
2. Place anchor strips to encircle the midfoot and distal aspect of the great toe (1 and 2).
3. Place two or three strips on the medial aspect of the great toe to hold the toe in proper alignment (3 through 5).
4. Lock the ends of the strips with tape (6 and 7).

Turf toe   Turf toe taping is designed to prevent excessive hyperextension of the metatarsophalangeal joint (Figure 8-22).

Materials needed   One roll of 1½-inch (3.8 cm) adhesive tape, one roll of 1-inch (2.5 cm) adhesive tape, and tape adherent.

Site preparation   Hair is shaved off the top of the forefoot and great toe. Spray the area with tape adherent.

Position of the athlete   The great toe is placed into a neutral position.

Procedure

1. Apply a one 1-inch (2.5 cm) tape strip around the great toe. Using 1½-inch (3.8 cm) tape, apply two arch anchors to the midarch area.
2. On the middle of the great toe, attach three 1-inch (2.5 cm) tape strips to create a checkrein.
3. Attach the checkrein to the arch anchor tapes, strip-crossing the metatarsophalangeal joint line.
4. Lock both ends of the checkrein in place.

Hammer, or clawed, toes   This technique is designed to reduce the pressure of the bent toes against the shoe (Figure 8-23).[13]

Materials needed   One roll of ½- or 1-inch (1.25 or 2.5 cm) adhesive tape and tape adherent.

Position of the athlete   The athlete sits on the table with the affected leg extended over the edge.

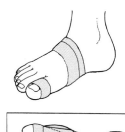

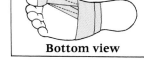

Bottom view

Figure 8-22

Turf toe taping.

Figure 8-23

Hammer, or clawed, toe taping.

Figure 8-24

Fractured toe taping.

Procedure

1. Tape one affected toe; then lace under the adjacent toe and over the next toe.
2. Tape can be attached to the next toe or can be continued and attached to the fifth toe.

Fractured toes   This technique splints the fractured toe with a nonfractured one (Figure 8-24).

Materials needed   One roll of $\frac{1}{2}$- or 1-inch (1.25 or 2.5 cm) tape, $\frac{1}{8}$-inch (0.3 cm) sponge rubber, and tape adherent.

Position of the athlete   The athlete assumes a sitting position.

Procedure

1. Cut a $\frac{1}{8}$-inch (0.3 cm) sponge rubber wedge and place it between the affected toe and a healthy one.
2. Wrap two or three strips of tape around both toes.

The Ankle Joint

The combination of foam prewrap plus tape provides significantly better ankle support during exercise than does taping directly on the skin. Both procedures diminish over time, but prewrap appears to decline more slowly. It is most effective immediately after initial application because it provides some minor resistance to ankle inversion movements.

Ankle joint taping is most appropriate for sports with short bursts of at-risk activity, such as high jumping, and for endurance sports, such as soccer or basketball. Ankle braces may be as effective as ankle taping.[7]

Routine noninjury taping

Materials needed   One roll of $1\frac{1}{2}$-inch (3.8 cm) tape, tape adherent, and underwrap (Figure 8-25).

Figure 8-25

Routine noninjury ankle taping.

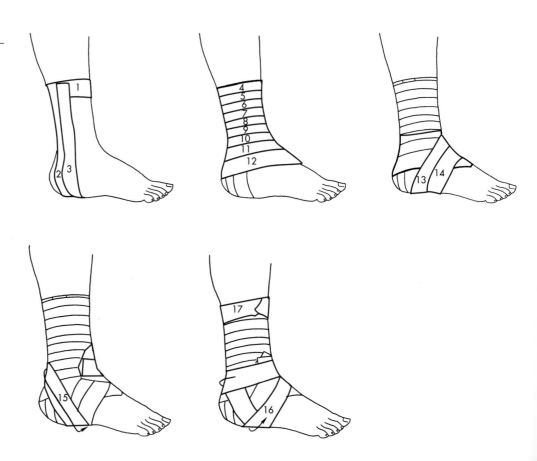

Site preparation   Ankle taping applied directly to the athlete's skin affords the greatest support; however, when applied and removed daily, skin irritation will occur. To avoid this problem, apply an underwrap material. Before taping, follow these procedures:

1. Clean foot and ankle thoroughly.
2. Shave all the hair off the foot and ankle.
3. Apply a coating of tape adherent to protect the skin and offer an adhering base.
4. Apply a gauze pad coated with friction-reducing material such as grease over the instep and to the back of the heel.
5. If underwrap is used, apply a single layer. The tape anchors extend beyond the underwrap and adhere directly to the skin.
6. Do not apply tape if skin is cold or hot from a therapeutic treatment.

Position of the athlete   The athlete sits on the table with the leg extended and the foot held at a 90-degree angle.

Procedure

1. Place an anchor around the ankle approximately 5 or 6 inches (12.5 or 15 cm) above the malleolus.
2. Apply two strips in consecutive order, starting behind the outer malleolus, taking care that the second strip overlaps the first by half the width of the tape (2 and 3).
3. After applying the strips, wrap seven or eight circular strips around the ankle, from the point of the anchor downward, until the malleolus is completely covered (4 through 12).
4. Apply two or three arch strips from lateral to medial, giving additional support to the arch (13 and 14).
5. Additional support is given by a heel lock. Starting high on the instep, bring the tape along the ankle at a slight angle, hooking the heel, leading under the arch, then coming up on the opposite side, and finishing at the starting point. Tear the tape to complete half of the heel lock (15). Repeat on the opposite side of the ankle (16). Finish with a band of tape around the ankle (17).

Closed basket weave (Gibney) technique   The closed basket weave, or Gibney, technique offers strong tape support and is primarily used in athletic training for newly sprained or chronically weak ankles (Figure 8-26).

Materials needed   One roll of 1½-inch (3.8 cm) tape, underwrap, and tape adherent.

Position of the athlete   The athlete sits on the table with the leg extended and the foot at a 90-degree angle.

Procedure

1. Place one anchor piece around the ankle approximately 5 or 6 inches (12.5 or 15 cm) above the malleolus just below the belly of the gastrocnemius muscle. Place a second anchor around the instep directly over the styloid process of the fifth metatarsal (1 and 2).
2. Apply the first strip posteriorly to the malleolus and attach it to the ankle anchor (3). NOTE: When applying strips, pull the foot into eversion for an inversion strain and into a neutral position for an eversion strain.
3. Start the first Gibney directly under the malleolus and attach it to the foot anchor (4).
4. In an alternating series, place three strips and three Gibneys on the ankle with each piece of tape overlapping at least half of the preceding strip (5 through 8).
5. After applying the basket weave series, continue the Gibney strips up the ankle, thus giving circular support (9 through 15).
6. For arch support, apply two or three circular strips laterally to medially (16 and 17).
7. After completing the conventional basket weave, apply two or three heel locks to ensure maximum stability (18 and 19).

Figure 8-26

Closed basket weave ankle taping.

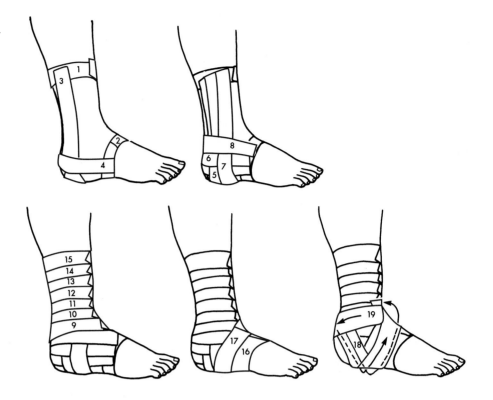

Open basket weave This modification of the closed basket weave, or Gibney, technique is designed to give freedom of movement in dorsiflexion and plantar flexion while providing lateral and medial support and giving swelling room. Taping in this pattern may be used immediately after an acute sprain in conjunction with a pressure bandage and cold applications because it allows for swelling (Figure 8-27).

Materials needed One roll of 1½-inch (3.8 cm) tape and tape adherent.

Position of the athlete The athlete sits on the table with the leg extended and the foot held at a 90-degree angle.

Procedure

1. The procedures are the same as for the closed basket weave (see Figure 8-26) with the exception of incomplete closures of the Gibney strips (11 through 17).

2. Lock the gap between the Gibney ends with two pieces of tape running on either side of the instep (18 through 21). NOTE: Application of a 1½-inch (3.8 cm) elastic bandage over the open basket weave affords added control of swelling; however, the athlete should remove it before going to bed. Apply the elastic bandage distal to proximal to prevent swelling from moving into the toes.

Of the many ankle taping techniques in use today, those using combinations of strips, basket weaves, and heel locks offer the best support.

Continuous-stretch tape technique This technique provides a fast alternative to other taping methods for the ankle (Figure 8-28).[6]

Materials needed One roll of 1½-inch (3.8 cm) linen tape, one roll of 2-inch (5 cm) stretch tape, tape adherent, and underwrap.

Position of the athlete The athlete sits on the table with the leg extended and the foot at a 90-degree angle.

Procedure

1. Place one anchor strip around the ankle approximately 5 to 6 inches (12.5 cm to 15 cm) above the malleolus (1).

2. Apply three strips, covering the malleolli (2 through 4).

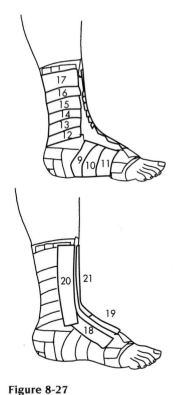

Figure 8-27

Open basket weave ankle taping.

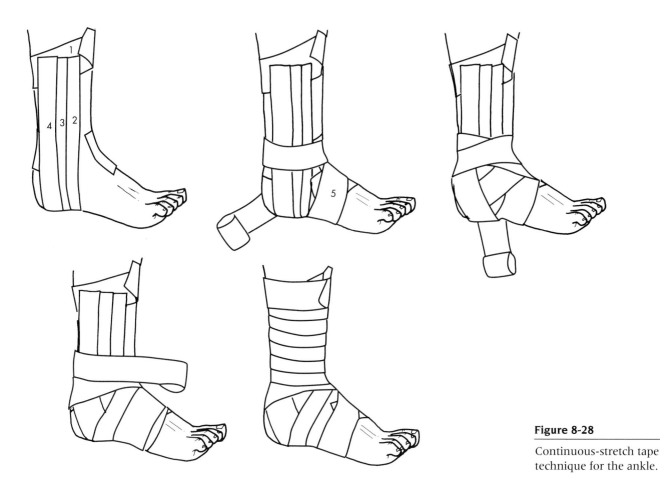

Figure 8-28

Continuous-stretch tape
technique for the ankle.

3. Start the stretch tape in a medial-to-lateral direction around the midfoot and continue it in a figure-eight pattern to above the lateral malleolus (5).
4. Continue to stretch tape across the midfoot, then across the heel.
5. Apply two heel locks, one in each direction.
6. Next, repeat a figure-eight pattern followed by a spiral pattern, filling the space up to the anchor.
7. Use the lock technique at the top with a linen tape strip.

The Lower Leg

Achilles tendon   Achilles tendon taping is designed to prevent the Achilles tendon from overstretching (Figure 8-29).

Materials needed   One roll of 3-inch (7.5 cm) elastic tape, one roll of 1^{1}/2-inch (3.8 cm) linen tape, and tape adherent.

Site preparation   Clean and shave the area, spray with tape adherent, and apply underwrap to the lower one third of the calf.

Position of the athlete   The athlete kneels or lies face down with the affected foot hanging relaxed over the edge of the table.

Procedure
1. Apply two anchors with 1^{1}/2-inch (3.8 cm) tape, one circling the leg loosely approximately 7 to 9 inches (17.5 to 22.5 cm) above the malleoli, and the other encircling the ball of the foot (1 and 2).
2. Cut two strips of 3-inch (7.5 cm) elastic tape approximately 8 to 10 inches (20 to 25 cm) long. Moderately stretch the first strip from the ball of the athlete's foot along its plantar aspect up to the leg anchor (3). The second elastic strip (4) follows the course of the first, but cut it and split it down the middle

8-5

Critical Thinking E x e r c i s e

A cross-country runner steps in a hole and suffers a lateral sprain to the right ankle.

? What taping technique should be selected to provide ankle joint support while still allowing for swelling?

Figure 8-29

Achilles tendon taping.

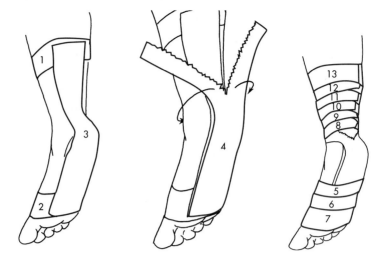

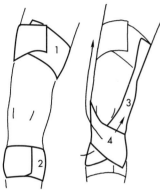

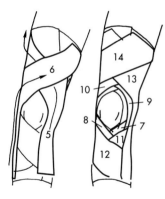

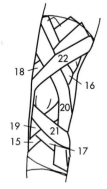

Figure 8-30

Collateral ligament knee taping.

lengthwise. Wrap the cut ends around the lower leg to form a lock. CAUTION: Keep the wrapped ends above the level of the strain.

3. Complete the series by placing two or three lock strips of elastic tape (5 through 7) loosely around the arch and five or six strips (8 through 13) around the athlete's lower leg.

Note that locking too tightly around the lower leg and foot will tend to restrict the normal action of the Achilles tendon and create more tissue irritation.

A variation on this method is to use three 2-inch (5 cm) elastic strips in place of strips 3 and 4. Apply the first strip at the plantar surface of the first metatarsal head and end it on the lateral side of the leg anchor. Apply the second strip at the plantar surface of the fifth metatarsal head and end it on the medial side of the leg anchor. Center the third strip between the other two strips and end it at the posterior aspect of the calf. Lock the strips with anchors of 3-inch (7.5 cm) elastic tape around the forefoot and lower calf.[1]

The Knee

Medial collateral ligament   Like athletes with ankle instabilities, athletes with unstable knees should never use tape and bracing as a replacement for proper exercise rehabilitation.[3] If properly applied, taping can help protect the knee and aid in the rehabilitation process (Figure 8-30).[6]

Materials needed   One roll of 2-inch (5 cm) linen tape, one roll of 3-inch (7.5 cm) elastic tape, a 1-inch (2.5 cm) heel lift, lubricant, gauze pad, tape adherent, and underwrap.

Site preparation   Clean, shave, and dry skin to be taped. Cover skin wounds. Lubricate the hamstring and popliteal areas and apply tape adherent.

Position of the athlete   The athlete stands on a 3-foot (90 cm) table with the injured knee held in a moderately relaxed position by a 1-inch (2.5 cm) heel lift. The hair is completely removed from an area 6 inches (15 cm) above to 6 inches (15 cm) below the patella.

Procedure
1. Lightly encircle the thigh and leg at the hairline with a 3-inch (7.5 cm) elastic anchor strip (1 and 2).
2. Precut twelve elastic tape strips, each approximately 9 inches (22.5 cm) long. Stretching them to their utmost, apply them to the knee as indicated in Figure 8-30 (3 through 14).
3. Apply a series of three strips of 2-inch (5 cm) linen tape (15 through 22). Some individuals find it advantageous to complete a knee taping by wrapping

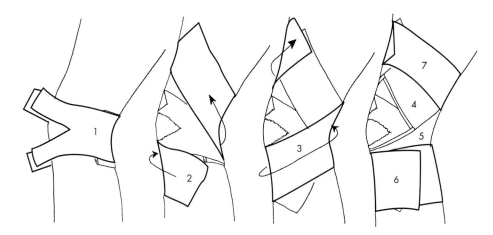

Figure 8-31

Rotary taping.

with an elastic wrap, thus providing an added precaution against the tape's coming loose from perspiration.

NOTE: Tape must not constrict the patella.

Rotary taping for instability of an injured knee   The rotary taping method is designed to provide the knee with support when it is unstable from injury to the medial collateral and anterior cruciate ligaments (Figure 8-31).

Materials needed   One roll of 3-inch (7.5 cm) elastic tape, tape adherent, 4-inch (10 cm) gauze pad, lubricant, scissors, and underwrap.

Position of the athlete   The athlete sits on the table with the affected knee flexed 15 degrees.

Procedure

1. Cut a 10-inch (25 cm) piece of elastic tape with both the ends snipped. Place the gauze pad in the center of the 10-inch (25 cm) piece of elastic tape to limit skin irritation and protect the popliteal nerves and blood vessels.

2. Put the gauze with the elastic tape backing on the popliteal fossa of the athlete's knee. Stretch both ends of the tape to the fullest extent and tear them. Place the divided ends firmly around the patella and interlock them (1).

3. Starting at a midpoint on the gastrocnemius muscle, spiral a 3-inch (7.5 cm) elastic tape strip to the front of the leg, then behind, crossing the popliteal fossa, and around the thigh, finishing anteriorly (2).

4. Repeat procedure 3 on the opposite side (3).

5. Apply three or four spiral strips for added strength (4 and 5).

6. Once they are in place, lock the spiral strips with two strips around the thigh and two around the calf (6 and 7).

NOTE: Tracing the spiral pattern with linen tape yields more rigidity.

Hyperextension   Hyperextension taping is designed to prevent the knee from hyperextending and also may be used for a strained hamstring muscle or for slackened cruciate ligaments (Figure 8-32).

Materials needed   One roll of 2½-inch (6.25 cm) tape or 2-inch (5 cm) elastic tape, cotton or a 4-inch (10 cm) gauze pad, tape adherent, underwrap, and a 2-inch (5 cm) heel lift.

Position of the athlete   The athlete's leg should be completely shaved, including the area above midthigh and below midcalf. The athlete stands on a 3-foot (90 cm) table with the injured knee flexed by a 2-inch (5 cm) heel lift.

Procedure

1. Place four anchor strips at the hairlines, two around the thigh and two around the leg (1 through 4). The strips should be loose enough to allow for muscle expansion during exercise.

2. Place a gauze pad at the popliteal space to protect the popliteal nerves and blood vessels from constriction by the tape.

Figure 8-32

Hyperextension taping.

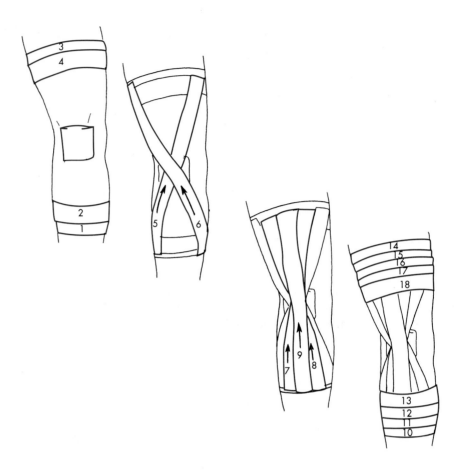

3. Start the supporting tape strips by forming an X over the popliteal space (5 and 6).

4. Cross the tape with two more strips, and place one up the middle of the leg (7 through 9).

5. Complete the technique by applying four or five locking strips around the thigh and calf (10 through 18).

6. Apply an additional series of cross strips if the athlete is heavily muscled. Lock the additional supporting strips in place with two or three strips around the thigh and leg.

Patellofemoral taping (McConnell technique)   Patellofemoral orientation may be corrected to some degree by using tape. The McConnell technique evaluates four components of patellar orientation: glide, tilt, rotation, and anteroposterior (AP) orientation.[11]

The glide component looks at side-to-side movement of the patella in the groove. The tilt component assesses the height of the lateral patellar border relative to the medial border. Patellar rotation is determined by looking for deviation of the long axis of the patella from the long axis of the femur. Anteroposterior alignment evaluates whether the inferior pole of the patella is tilted either anteriorly or posteriorly relative to the superior pole. Correction of patellar position and tracking is accomplished by passive taping of the patella in a more biomechanically correct position.[16] In addition to correcting the orientation of the patella, the tape provides a prolonged gentle stretch to soft-tissue structure that affects patellar movement.[11]

Materials needed   Two special types of extremely sticky tape are required. Fixomull and Leuko Sportape are manufactured by Biersdorf Australia, Ltd.

Site preparation   Clean and shape, and apply tape adherent.

Position of the athlete   The athlete should be seated with the knee in full extension.

Procedure

1. Two strips of Fixomull are extended from the lateral femoral condyle just posterior to the medial femoral condyle around the front of the knee. This tape is used as a base to which the other tape may be adhered. Leuko Sportape is used from this point on to correct patellar alignment (Figure 8-33).
2. To correct a lateral glide, attach a short strip of tape one thumb's width from the lateral patellar border, pushing the patella medially in the frontal plane. Crease the skin between the lateral patellar border and the medial femoral condyle and secure the tape on the medial side of the joint (Figure 8-34).
3. To correct a lateral tilt, flex the knee to 30 degrees, adhere a short strip of tape beginning at the middle of the patella, and pull medially to lift the lateral border. Again, crease the skin underneath and adhere it to the medial side of the knee (Figure 8-35).
4. To correct an external rotation of the inferior pole relative to the superior pole, adhere a strip of tape to the middle of the inferior pole, pulling upward and medially while internally rotating the patella with the free hand. The tape is attached to the medial side of the knee (Figure 8-36).
5. For correcting AP alignment in which there is an inferior tilt, take a 6-inch piece of tape, place the middle of the strip over the upper one half of the patella, and attach it equally on both sides to lift the inferior pole (Figure 8-37).
6. Once patellar taping is completed, the athlete should be instructed to wear the tape all day during all activities. The athlete should periodically tighten the strips as they loosen.

NOTE: The McConnell technique for treating patellofemoral pain also stresses the importance of more symmetrical loading of the patella through reeducation and strengthening of the vastus medialis.[11]

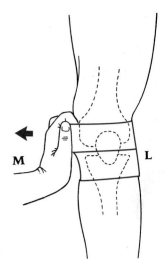

Figure 8-33

The McConnell patellar technique uses a base to which additional tape is adhered.

The Elbow

Elbow restriction   Taping the elbow prevents hyperextension (Figure 8-38).

Materials needed   One roll of $1\frac{1}{2}$-inch (3.8 cm) tape, tape adherent, and 2-inch (5 cm) elastic bandage.

Site preparation   Clean and shave area and apply adherent.

Position of the athlete   The athlete stands with the affected elbow flexed at 90 degrees.

Procedure

1. Apply two anchor strips loosely around the arm using a 2-inch (5 cm) elastic bandage (1 and 2).
2. Construct a checkrein by cutting a 10-inch (25 cm) and a 4-inch (10 cm) strip of tape and placing the 4-inch (10 cm) strip against the center of the 10-inch (25 cm) strip, blanking out that portion. Place the checkrein so that it spans the two anchor strips with the blanked-out side facing downward. Leave the checkrein extended 1 to 2 inches past the anchor strips on both ends. This allows anchoring of the checkreins with circular strips to secure against slippage (3 and 4).
3. Place five additional 10-inch (25 cm) strips of tape over the basic checkrein.
4. Finish the procedure by securing the checkrein with three lock strips on each end (5 through 10). A figure-eight elastic wrap applied over the taping will prevent the tape from slipping because of perspiration.

NOTE: A variation of this method is to fan the checkreins, dispersing the force over a wider area (Figure 8-39).

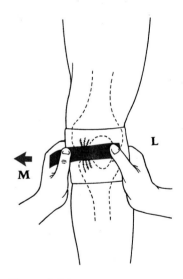

Figure 8-34

McConnell patellar technique to correct a lateral glide.

The Wrist and Hand

Wrist technique no. 1   This wrist taping technique is designed for mild wrist strains and sprains (Figure 8-40).

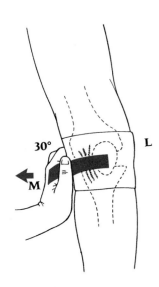

Figure 8-35

McConnell patellar technique to correct a lateral tilt.

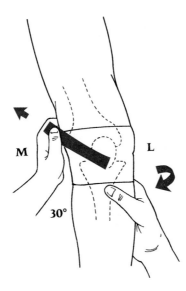

Figure 8-36

McConnell patellar technique to correct external rotation of the inferior pole.

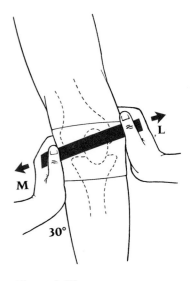

Figure 8-37

McConnell patellar technique to correct AP alignment with an inferior tilt.

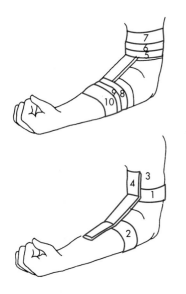

Figure 8-38

Elbow restriction taping.

Materials needed   One roll of 1-inch (2.5 cm) tape and tape adherent.

Site preparation   Clean, shave, and apply adherent.

Position of the athlete   The athlete stands with the affected hand flexed toward the injured side and the fingers moderately spread to increase the breadth of the wrist for the protection of nerves and blood vessels.

Procedure

1. Starting at the base of the wrist, bring a strip of 1-inch (2.5 cm) tape from the palmar side upward and around both sides of the wrist (1).
2. In the same pattern, with each strip overlapping the preceding one by at least half its width, lay two additional strips in place (2 and 3).

Wrist technique no. 2   This wrist taping technique stabilizes and protects badly injured wrists (Figure 8-41).

Materials needed   One roll of 1-inch (2.5 cm) tape and tape adherent.

Position of the athlete   The athlete stands with the affected hand flexed toward the injured side and the fingers moderately spread to increase the breadth of the wrist for the protection of nerves and blood vessels.

Procedure

1. Apply one anchor strip around the wrist approximately 3 inches (7.5 cm) from the hand (1); wrap another anchor strip around the spread hand (2).
2. With the wrist bent toward the side of the injury, run a strip of tape from the anchor strip near the little finger obliquely across the wrist joint to the wrist anchor strip. Run another strip from the anchor strip and the index finger side across the wrist joint to the wrist anchor. This forms a crisscross over the wrist joint (3 and 4). Apply a series of four or five crisscrosses, depending on the extent of splinting needed (5 through 8).
3. Apply two or three series of figure-eight tapings over the crisscross taping (9 through 11). Starting by encircling the wrist once, carry a strip over the back of the hand obliquely upward across the back of the hand to where the figure-eight started. Repeat this procedure to ensure a strong, stabilizing taping.

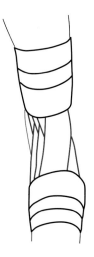

Figure 8-39

Fanned checkrein technique.

Bruised hand   The following method is used to tape a bruised hand (Figure 8-42).

Materials needed   One roll of 1-inch (2.5 cm) adhesive tape, one roll of $^1/_2$-inch (1.25 cm) tape, $^1/_4$-inch (0.6 cm) thick sponge rubber pad, and tape adherent.

Position of the athlete   The fingers are spread moderately.

Procedure

1. Lay the protective pad over the bruise and hold it in place with three strips of $^1/_2$-inch (1.25 cm) tape laced through the webbing of the fingers.
2. Apply a basic figure-eight bandage made of 1-inch (2.5 cm) tape.

Sprained thumb   Sprained thumb taping is designed to give protection to the muscle and joint as well as support to the thumb (Figure 8-43).[4]

Materials needed   One roll of 1-inch (2.5 cm) tape and tape adherent.

Position of the athlete   The athlete should hold the injured thumb in a relaxed, neutral position.

Procedure

1. Place an anchor strip loosely around the wrist and another around the distal end of the thumb (1 and 2).
2. From the anchor at the tip of the thumb to the anchor around the wrist, apply four splint strips in a series on the side of greater injury (dorsal or palmar side) (3 through 5) and hold them in place with one lock strip around the wrist and one encircling the tip of the thumb (6 and 7).

Figure 8-40

Wrist taping technique no. 1.

Figure 8-41

Wrist taping technique no. 2.

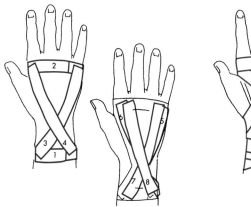
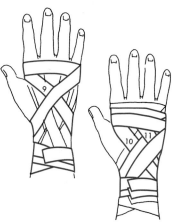

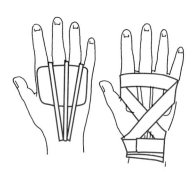

Figure 8-42

Bruised hand taping.

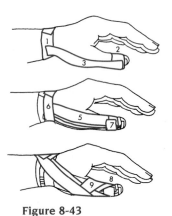

Figure 8-43

Sprained thumb taping.

Figure 8-44

Thumb spica.

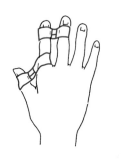

Figure 8-45

Finger and thumb checkreins.

3. Add three thumb spicas. Start the first spica on the radial side at the base of the thumb; carry it under the thumb, completely encircling it; cross the strip and continue around the wrist; finish at the starting point. Each of the subsequent spica strips should overlap the preceding strip by at least $2/3$ inch (1.7 cm) and move downward on the thumb (8 and 9).

The thumb spica with tape provides an excellent means of protection during recovery from an injury (Figure 8-44).

Finger and thumb checkreins   The sprained finger or thumb may require the additional protection afforded by a restraining checkrein (Figure 8-45).[4]

Materials needed   One roll of 1-inch (2.5 cm) tape.

Position of the athlete   The athlete spreads the injured fingers widely but within a range that is free of pain.

Procedure

1. Bring a strip of 1-inch (2.5 cm) tape around the middle phalanx of the injured finger over to the adjacent finger and around it also. The tape left between the two fingers, which are spread apart, is called the checkrein.

2. Add strength with a lock strip around the center of the checkrein.

SUMMARY

- Common types of bandages used in sports are arm slings, of which the cervical and shoulder types are the most common, and roller, triangular, and cravat bandages for wrist aid.
- Common roller bandages are gauze, used for wounds; cotton cloth ankle wraps; and elastic wraps.
- Like tape, roller bandages must be applied uniformly, firmly but not so tightly as to impede circulation.
- Historically, taping has been an important aspect of athletic training. Sports tape is used in a variety of ways—as a means of holding a wound dressing in place, as support, and as protection against musculoskeletal injuries.
- For supporting and protecting musculoskeletal injuries, two types of tape are currently used: linen and stretch.
- Sports tape must be stored in a cool place and must be stacked on the flat side of each roll.
- The skin of the athlete must be carefully prepared before tape is applied. The skin should first be carefully cleaned; then all hair should be removed. An adherent may be applied, followed by an underwrap material, if necessary, to help prevent skin irritation.
- Tape must be applied in a manner that provides the least amount of irritation and the maximum support. All tape applications require great care that the proper materials are used, that the proper position is ensured, and that procedures are carefully followed.

Web Sites

Solutions to Critical Thinking EXERCISES

8-1 The athletic trainer applies a 6-inch (15 cm) elastic wrap as a hip adductor restraint. This technique is designed to prevent the groin from being overstretched and the hip adductors re-injured.

8-2 The athletic trainer applies tape and a 4-inch (10 cm) elastic shoulder spica to hold the doughnut in place.

8-3 The athletic trainer applies a sling and swathe combination. This combination stabilizes the shoulder joint and upper arm.

8-4 The LowDye technique is designed to assist in the management of foot pronation and fallen medial longitudinal arch, which predisposes the athlete to arch strain.

8-5 Initially, for a sprained ankle, the athletic trainer selects the open basket weave taping technique. This technique in conjunction with a pressure bandage and cold application can also control swelling.

8-6 The McConnell taping technique can be employed to correct a lateral patellar glide.

REVIEW QUESTIONS AND CLASS ACTIVITIES

1. What are some common types of bandages used in sports medicine today?
2. Observe the athletic trainer when he or she is dressing wounds in the training room.
3. Demonstrate proper use of the roller, triangular, and cravat bandages.
4. What types of tape are available? What is the purpose of each type? What qualities should you look for in selecting tape?
5. How should you prepare an area to be taped?
6. How should you tear tape?
7. How should you remove tape from an area? Demonstrate the various methods and cutters that can be used to remove tape.
8. Bring the different types of tape to class. Discuss their uses and the qualities to look for in purchasing tape. Have the class practice tearing tape and preparing an area for taping.
9. Take each joint or body part and demonstrate the common taping procedures used to give support to that area. Have the students pair up and practice these tapings on each other. Discuss the advantages and disadvantages of using tape as a supportive device.

REFERENCES

1. Austin K et al: *Taping techniques*, Chicago, 1994, Mosby-Wolfe.
2. Benefit of ankle taping is short-lived with or without prewrap, *Sports Med Digest* 19(1):130, 1997.
3. Brownstein B: Migration and design characteristics of functional knee braces, *J Sport Rehabil* 7(1):33, 1998.
4. Deivert R: Functional thumb taping procedure, *J Ath Train* 29(4):357, 1994.
5. Hafen BQ: *First aid for health emergencies*, ed 5, St Paul, Minn, 1998, West Publishing.
6. Handling KA: Taping procedure for an unstable knee, *Ath Train* 16:371, 1984.
7. Lindley T: Taping and semirigid bracing may not affect ankle functional range of motion, *J Ath Train* 30(2):109, 1995.
8. Metcalfe RC, Schlabach GA, Looney MA et al: A comparison of moleskin tape, linen tape, and lace-up brace on joint restriction and movement performance, *J Ath Train* 32(2):136, 1997.
9. Parcel GS: *Basic emergency care of the sick and injured*, ed 5, St Louis, 1994, Mosby.
10. *Manual of athletic taping*, Phildelphia, 1995, FA Davis/Sports Medicine Council of British Columbia.
11. McConnell J: The management of chondro-malacia patella: a long-term solution, *Aust J Physiother* 32:215, 1986.
12. Paris D, Vardaxis V, Kokkaliaris J: Ankle ranges of motion during extended activity periods while taped and braced, *J Ath Train* 30(3):223, 1995.
13. Reuter B: Taping the hammer toe, *J Ath Train* 30(2):178, 1995.
14. Schulthies S, Draper D: A modified low-dye taping technique to support the medial longitudinal arch and reduce excessive pronation, *J Ath Train* 30(3):266, 1995.
15. Simoneau GG, Degner RM, Kramper CA et al: Changes in ankle joint proprioception resulting from strips of athletic tape applied over the skin, *J Ath Train* 32(2):141, 1997.
16. Somes S et al: Effects of patellar taping on patellar position in the open and closed kinetic chain: a preliminary study, *J Sport Rehabil* 6(4):299, 1997.

ANNOTATED BIBLIOGRAPHY

Austin K et al: *Taping techniques*, Chicago, 1994, Mosby-Wolfe.
  This book is an illustrated atlas of taping.

First aider, Cramer Products, Gardner, Kan.
  This periodical, published seven times throughout the school year, contains useful taping and bandaging techniques that have been submitted by readers.

Kenney R, Berry R: *Sports therapy guide*, Ontario, 1991, Sports Medix.
  This text is a well-illustrated guide to taping for the athletic trainer.

Manual of athletic taping, Philadelphia, 1995, FA Davis/Sports Medicine Council of British Columbia.
  This manual provides a good overview of athletic taping with clear and concise directions.

Perrin D: *Athletic taping*, Champaign, Ill, 1995, Human Kinetics.
  This text is a complete book of athletic taping for the practitioner.

Sports Medicine Guide, Mueller Sports Medicine, 1 Quench Dr, Prairie du Sac, Wisc 53578.
  Published four times a year, this quarterly often presents, along with discussions on specific injuries, many innovative taping and bandaging techniques.

Pathology of Injury

Mechanisms and Characteristics of Sports Trauma

When you finish this chapter you should be able to

- Explain the biomechanical factors in sports injuries.
- Describe the major biomechanical forces occurring in sports injuries.
- Identify the most common exposed skin injuries.
- Explain the normal structures of soft tissue and the specific mechanical forces that cause skin, internal soft-tissue, synovial joint, and bone injuries.
- Define the terms that describe the major injuries incurred during sports participation.
- Describe how epiphyseal injuries occur.
- Explain how microtraumas and overuse injuries occur.

M any factors produce mechanical injuries or trauma in sports. *Trauma* is defined as a physical injury or wound sustained in sport and produced by an external or internal force (Figure 9-1). This chapter provides a foundation for the identification, understanding, and management of sports injuries. It examines mechanical forces and tissue characteristics of sports injuries and the classification of these injuries.

A physical injury or wound sustained in sport and produced by an external or internal force is called trauma.

MECHANICAL INJURY

"Force or mechanical energy is that which changes the state of rest or uniform motion of matter. When a force applied to any part of the body results in a harmful disturbance in function and or structure, a mechanical injury is said to have been sustained."[12] Injuries related to sports participation can be caused by external forces directed on the body or can occur internally within the body. Understanding sports injuries requires a knowledge of tissue susceptibility to trauma and the mechanical forces involved.

Tissue Properties

Tissues have relative abilities to resist a particular load. The stronger the tissue, the greater magnitude of load it can withstand. Strength pressure, or power, is often used to imply a force. A force can be defined as a push or pull.[13] Tissue properties

9-1

Critical Thinking Exercise

To effectively present and manage sports injuries, the athletic trainer must understand tissue susceptibility to sports trauma.

? What should the athletic trainer know about tissue properties?

Figure 9-1

A sport injury can be sustained from an external or internal force.

load

Outside force or forces acting on tissue.

stress

The internal reaction or resistance to an external load.

strain

Extent of deformation of tissue under loading.

viscoelastic

Any material whose mechanical properties vary depending on rate of load.

Human tissue is viscoelastic—it has both viscous and elastic properties.

yield point

Elastic limit of tissue.

mechanical failure

Elastic limit of tissue is exceeded, causing tissue to break.

The five tissue mechanical stresses that can lead to sports injuries are tension, stretching, compression, shearing, and bending.

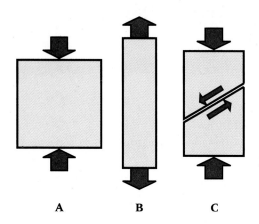

Figure 9-2

Mechanical forces that can cause injury. **A,** Compression. **B,** Tension. **C,** Shear.

are described according to engineering terminology. A **load** can be a singular or group of outside or internal forces acting on the body. The resistance to a load is called a mechanical **stress,** and the internal response is a deformation, or change in dimensions. Deformation is also defined as a mechanical **strain.** All human tissue is **viscoelastic;** it has both viscous and elastic properties, allowing for deformation. Tissue such as bone is brittle and has fewer viscoelastic properties when compared to soft tissue. Tissue also is anisotropic, responding with greater or lesser strength depending on the direction of the load that is being applied. When tissue is deformed to the extent that its elasticity is almost fully exceeded, a **yield point** has been reached. When the yield point has been exceeded, **mechanical failure** occurs, resulting in tissue damage.[2]

There are five primary tissue stresses leading to sports injuries: tension, stretching, compression, shearing, and bending.

Tension is that force that pulls or stretches tissue.

Stretching beyond the yield point leads to rupturing of soft tissue or fracturing of a bone. Examples of stretching injuries are sprains, strains, and avulsion fractures.

Compression is a force that, with enough energy, crushes tissue. When the force can no longer be absorbed, injury occurs. Constant submaximum compression over a period of time can cause the contacted tissue to develop abnormal wear. Compression occurs when a muscle or bone is stretched directly or when cartilage bone is directly loaded. Arthritic changes, fractures, and contusions are commonly caused by compression force.

Shearing is a force that moves across the parallel organization of the tissue. Injury occurs once shearing has exceeded the inherent strength of a tissue. Shearing stress can result in skin injuries such as blisters, rips of the hands, abrasions, or vertebral disk injuries (Figure 9-2).

Bending is a force on a horizontal beam or bone that places stresses within the structure, causing it to bend or strain.[13] This force is known as three-point bending (Figure 9-3). Compression occurs parallel to the beam's length if the force is on the concave side, and tension occurs if the force is on the convex side. Shear stress is also caused in two directions within the bending beam.[13] Bending strain can also occur perpendicular to or along the length of a beam, with compression, tension, and shearing occurring. Injuries to the hip and femur are examples of this type of bending strain. A torsion, or twisting, load causes compression and tension in a spiral pattern, with shearing stresses occurring parallel to the long axes. An example of a torsion injury is the spiral fracture that occurs in skiing (Figure 9-4).[10]

SOFT-TISSUE TRAUMA

Soft tissue, or nonbony tissue, is categorized as noncontractile and contractile. Noncontractile tissues are skin, joint capsules, ligaments, fascia, cartilage, dura mater, and nerve roots. Contractile tissues are those structures that are a part of the muscle, its tendon, or its bony insertion.[3]

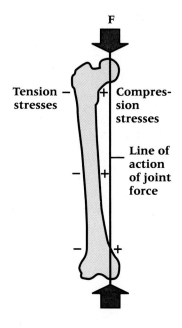

Figure 9-3

Bending strain. Compression and tension stress caused by a bending of the femur.

SKIN INJURIES

Generally, trauma that happens to the skin is visually exposed and is categorized as a skin wound. It is defined as a break in the continuity of the soft parts of body structures caused by a trauma to these tissues.

Anatomical Characteristics

The skin, or integument, is the external covering of the body. It represents the body's largest organ system and consists of two layers—the epidermis and the dermis (corium). Because of the soft, pliable nature of skin, it can be easily traumatized. (See Chapter 28 for an in-depth discussion of skin anatomy.)

Injurious Mechanical Forces

Numerous mechanical forces can adversely affect the skin's integrity. These forces are friction or rubbing, scraping, compression or pressure, tearing, cutting, and penetrating.

Wound Classification

Wounds are classified according to the mechanical force that causes them (Table 9-1).

Friction Blister

Continuous rubbing over the surface of the skin causes a collection of fluid below or within the epidermal layer called a blister.

Abrasion

Abrasions are common conditions in which the skin is scraped against a rough surface. The epidermis and dermis are worn away, exposing numerous blood capillaries.

Skin Bruise

When a blow compresses or crushes the skin surface and produces bleeding under the skin, the condition is identified as a bruise, or contusion.

Laceration

A laceration is a wound in which the flesh has been irregularly torn.

Skin Avulsion

Skin that is torn by the same mechanism as a laceration to the extent that tissue is completely ripped from its source is an avulsion injury.

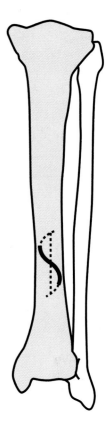

Figure 9-4

A torsion force could lead to a spiral fracture.

9-2

Critical Thinking Exercise

A baseball player slides into home base, severely scraping the skin on the left side.

? What is the force and type of injury produced?

TABLE 9-1 Soft-Tissue Trauma

Primary Tissue	Type	Mechanical Forces	Condition
Skin	Acute	Rubbing/friction	Blister
		Compression/contusion	Bruise
		Tearing	Laceration
		Tearing/ripping	Avulsion
		Penetrating	Puncture
Muscle/tendon	Acute	Compression	Contusion
		Tension	Strain
	Chronic	Tension/shearing	Myositis/fasciitis
		Tension	Tendinitis/tenosynovitis
		Compression/tension	Bursitis
		Compression/tension	Ectopic calcification—myositis ossificans, calcific tendinitis

Incision

An incision wound is one in which the skin has been sharply cut.

Puncture Wound

Puncture wounds, as the name implies, are penetrations of the skin by a sharp object.

NOTE: The care of skin wounds is discussed in Chapter 28.

SKELETAL MUSCLE INJURIES

Skeletal muscles have an extremely high percentage of sports injuries.

Anatomical Characteristics

Muscles are composed of contractile cells, or fibers, that produce movement. Muscle fibers possess the ability to contract as well as the properties of irritability, conductivity, and elasticity. Three types of muscles are within the body—smooth, cardiac, and striated. Of major concern in sports medicine are conditions that affect striated, or skeletal, muscles. Within the fiber cell is a semifluid substance called sarcoplasm (cytoplasm). Myofibrils are surrounded by the endomysium, fiber bundles are surrounded by the perimysium, and the entire muscle is covered by the epimysium (Figure 9-5). The epimysium, perimysium, and endomysium may be combined with the fibrous tendon. The fibrous wrapping of a muscle may become a flat sheet of connective tissue (aponeurosis) that attaches to other muscles. Tendons and aponeuroses are extremely resilient to injuries. They will pull away from a bone, a bone will break, or a muscle will tear before tendons and aponeuroses are injured.[18] Skeletal muscles are generally well supplied with blood vessels that permeate throughout their structure. Arteries, veins, lymph vessels, and bundles of nerve fibers spread into the perimysium. A complex capillary network goes throughout the endomysium, coming into direct contact with the muscle fibers.

Muscle Injury Classification

Acute Muscle Injuries

The two categories of acute muscle injuries are contusions and strains.

Contusions   A bruise, or contusion, is received because of a sudden traumatic blow to the body. The intensity of a contusion can range from superficial to deep tissue compression and hemorrhage (Figure 9-6).

Interrupting the continuity of the circulatory system results in a flow of blood and lymph into the surrounding tissues. A hematoma (blood tumor) is formed by the localization of the extravasated blood into a clot, which becomes encapsulated by a connective tissue membrane. The speed of healing of a contusion, as with all soft-tissue injuries, depends on the extent of tissue damage and internal bleeding.

9-3

Critical Thinking E x e r c i s e

A shortstop is hit in the shin by a batted ball that took a bad hop.

? What is the force and type of injury sustained by this athlete?

Figure 9-5

Connective tissue related to a skeletal muscle.

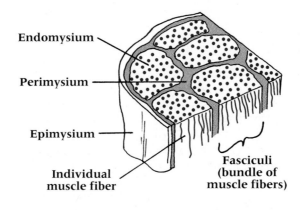

Endomysium

Perimysium

Epimysium

Individual
muscle fiber

Fasciculi
(bundle of
muscle fibers)

A contusion can penetrate to the skeletal structures, causing a bone bruise. The extent to which an athlete may be hampered by this condition depends on the location of the bruise and the force of the blow. Typical in cases of severe contusion are the following:

1. The athlete reports being struck a hard blow.
2. The blow causes pain and a transitory paralysis caused by pressure on and shock to the motor and sensory nerves.
3. Palpation often reveals a hard area, indurated because of internal hemorrhage.
4. Ecchymosis, or tissue discoloration, may take place.

Muscle contusions are usually rated by the extent to which the muscle is able to produce range of motion in a part (see Chapter 10). A blow to a muscle can be so great that the related fascia is ruptured, allowing muscle tissue to protrude through it.

Strains   A strain is a stretch, tear, or rip in the muscle or adjacent tissue such as the fascia or muscle tendons (Figure 9-7). The cause of muscle strain is often obscure. Most often a strain is produced by an abnormal muscular contraction. The cause of this abnormality has been attributed to many factors. One popular theory suggests that a fault in the reciprocal coordination of the agonist and antagonist muscles takes place. The cause of this fault or incoordination is a mystery. However, possible explanations are that it may be related to a mineral imbalance caused by profuse sweating, to fatigue metabolites collected in the muscle itself, or to a strength imbalance between agonist and antagonist muscles.

A strain may range from a minute separation of connective tissue and muscle fibers to a complete tendinous avulsion or muscle rupture (grade 1, 2, or 3). The resulting pathology is similar to that of the contusion or sprain, with capillary or blood vessel hemorrhage. A grade 1 strain is accompanied by local pain, which is increased by tension of the muscle, and a minor loss of strength. There is mild swelling, ecchymosis, and local tenderness.[18] A grade 2 strain is similar to the mild strain but has moderate signs and symptoms and impaired muscle function.[16]

A grade 3 strain has signs and symptoms that are severe, with a loss of muscle function and, commonly, a palpable defect in the muscle.[16] The muscles that have the highest incidence of strains in sports are the hamstring group, gastrocnemius, quadriceps group, hip flexors, hip adductor group, spinalis group of the back, deltoid, and rotator cuff group of the shoulder.

Tendon Injuries

The tendon contains wavy parallel collagenous fibers that are organized in bundles surrounded by a gelatinous material that decreases friction. A tendon attaches a muscle to a bone and concentrates a pulling force in a limited area. Tendons can produce and maintain a pull from 8,700 to 18,000 pounds per square inch. When a tendon is loaded by tension, the wavy collagenous fibers straighten in the direction of the load; when the tension is released, the collagen returns to its original shape. In tendons, collagen fibers will break if their physiological limits have been reached. A breaking point occurs after a 6 percent to 8 percent increase in length. Because a tendon is usually double the strength of the muscle it serves, tears commonly occur at the muscle belly, musculotendinous junction, or bony attachment. Clinically, however, a constant abnormal tension on tendons increases elongation by the infiltration of fibroblasts, which will cause more collagenous tissue to be produced. Repeated microtraumas can evolve into chronic muscle strain that resorbs collagen fibers and eventually weakens the tendon. Collagen resorption occurs in the early period of sports conditioning and during the immobilization of a part. During resorption, collagenous tissues are weakened and susceptible to injury; therefore a gradually paced conditioning program and early mobilization in the rehabilitation process are necessary.

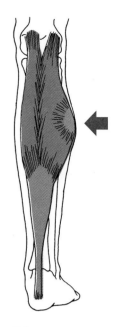

Figure 9-6

A contusion is caused by a severe compression force.

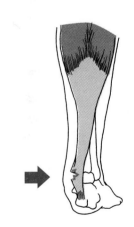

Figure 9-7

A strain is produced by severe tension force.

9-4

Critical Thinking Exercise

While performing an arm tackle, a football player severely injures his upper arm.

? What injury mechanism has occurred, and what is the subsequent injury produced?

Muscle Cramps and Spasms

Muscle cramps and spasms lead to muscle and tendon injuries. A cramp is a painful involuntary contraction of a skeletal muscle or muscle group. Cramps have been attributed to a lack of water or other electrolytes in relation to muscle fatigue. A spasm is a reflex reaction caused by trauma of the musculoskeletal system. The two types of cramps or spasms are the **clonic** type, with alternating involuntary muscular contraction and relaxation in quick succession, and the **tonic** type, with rigid muscle contraction that lasts a period of time. Muscle cramps or spasms may lead to a muscle strain.

Overexertion Muscle Problems

One constant problem in physical conditioning and training is overexertion. Even though the gradual pattern of overloading the body is the best way for ultimate success, many athletes and even coaches believe that if there is no pain, there is no gain.

Exercise overdosage is reflected in muscle soreness, decreased joint flexibility, and general fatigue twenty-four hours after activity. Four specific indicators of possible overexertion are acute muscle soreness, delayed muscle soreness, muscle stiffness, and muscle cramping.

Muscle soreness   Overexertion in strenuous muscular exercise often results in muscular pain. Most people, at one time or another, have experienced muscle soreness, usually resulting from some physical activity to which they are unaccustomed. The older a person gets, the more easily muscle soreness seems to develop.[6]

There are two types of muscle soreness. The first type is *acute-onset muscle soreness,* which accompanies fatigue. This muscle pain is transient and occurs during and immediately after exercise. The second type of soreness involves delayed muscle pain that appears approximately twelve hours after injury. This *delayed-onset muscle soreness* becomes most intense after twenty-four to forty-eight hours and then gradually subsides so that the muscle becomes symptom-free after three or four days. This second type of pain is described as a syndrome of delayed muscle pain leading to increased muscle tension, swelling, stiffness, and resistance to stretching.[5]

Delayed-onset muscle soreness is thought to result from several possible causes. It may occur from very small tears in the muscle tissue, which seems to be more likely with eccentric or isometric contractions. It may also occur because of disruption of the connective tissue that holds muscle tendon fibers together.

Muscle soreness may be prevented by beginning an exercise at a moderate level and gradually increasing the intensity of the exercise over time. Treatment of muscle soreness usually involves static or PNF stretching activities. Like other conditions discussed in this chapter, muscle soreness can be treated with ice applied within the first forty-eight to seventy-two hours.[5]

Muscle stiffness   Muscle stiffness does not produce pain. It occurs when a group of muscles have been worked hard for a long period of time. The fluids that collect in the muscles during and after exercise are absorbed into the bloodstream at a slow rate. As a result, the muscle becomes swollen, shorter, and thicker and therefore resists stretching. Light exercise, massage, and passive mobilization assist in reducing stiffness.

Muscle cramps   Like muscle soreness and stiffness, muscle cramps can be a problem related to hard conditioning. The most common cramp is tonic, in which there is continuous muscle contraction. It is caused by the body's depletion of essential electrolytes or an interruption of synergism between opposing muscles. Clonic, or intermittent, contraction, stemming from nerve irritation, may rarely occur.

Muscle guarding   Following injury, the muscles that surround the injured area contract to, in effect, splint that area, thus minimizing pain by limiting movement. Quite often this splinting is incorrectly referred to as a muscle spasm. The terms

---

The two major types of muscle soreness associated with severe exercise are acute and delayed.

tonic
Muscle contraction characterized by constant contraction that lasts for a period of time.

clonic
Involuntary muscle contraction characterized by alternate contraction and relaxation in rapid succession.

spasm and *spasticity* are more correctly associated with increased tone or contractions of muscle that occur because of some upper motor neuron lesion in the brain. Thus, *muscle guarding* is a more appropriate term for the involuntary muscle contractions that occur in response to pain following musculoskeletal injury.[6]

Chronic Musculotendinous Injuries

Chronic injuries usually progress slowly over a long period of time. Often, repeated acute injuries can lead to a chronic condition. A constant irritation caused by poor performance techniques or a constant stress beyond physiological limits can eventually result in a chronic condition. These injuries are often attributed to overuse microtraumas.[15]

Chronic muscle injuries are representative of a low-grade inflammatory process with a proliferation of fibroblasts and scarring. The acute injury that is improperly managed or that allows an athlete to return to activity before healing has completely occurred can cause chronic injury. The student should be especially knowledgeable about five chronic muscle conditions: myositis, tendinitis, tenosynovitis, ectopic calcification, and muscle atrophy and contracture.

Myositis/fasciitis   In general, the term *myositis* means inflammation of muscle tissue. More specifically, it can be considered a fibrositis, or connective tissue inflammation. Fascia that supports and separates muscle can also become chronically inflamed after injury. A typical example of this condition is plantar fasciitis.

Tendinitis   Tendinitis has a gradual onset, diffuse tenderness because of repeated microtraumas, and degenerative changes. Obvious signs of tendinitis are swelling and pain.

Tenosynovitis   Tenosynovitis is inflammation of the synovial sheath surrounding a tendon. In its acute state there is rapid onset, articular crepitus, and diffuse swelling. In chronic tenosynovitis the tendons become locally thickened, with pain and articular crepitus present during movement (Figure 9-8).

Ectopic calcification   Voluntary muscles can become chronically inflamed, resulting in myositis. An **ectopic** calcification known as myositis ossificans can occur in a muscle that directly overlies a bone. Two common sites for this condition are the quadriceps region of the thigh and the brachial muscle of the arm. In myositis ossificans, osteoid material that resembles bone rapidly accumulates. If there is no repeated injury, the growth may subside completely in nine to twelve months, or it may mature into a calcified area, at which time surgical removal can be accomplished with little fear of recurrence. Occasionally, tendinitis leads to deposits of minerals, primarily lime, and is known as *calcific tendinitis*.

Atrophy and contracture   Two complications of muscle and tendon conditions are atrophy and contracture. Muscle atrophy is the wasting away of muscle tissue. Its main cause in athletes is immobilization of a body part, inactivity, or loss of nerve stimulation. A second complication in sport injuries is muscle contracture, an abnormal shortening of muscle tissue in which there is a great deal of resistance to passive stretch. A contracture is associated with a joint that, because of muscle injury, has developed unyielding and resisting scar tissue.

SYNOVIAL JOINTS

A joint in the human body is defined as the point at which two bones join together. A joint must also transmit forces between participating bones.[12]

Anatomical Characteristics

The joint consists of cartilage and fibrous connective tissue. Joints are classified as immovable (synarthrotic), slightly movable (amphiarthrotic), and freely movable (diarthrotic). Diarthrotic joints are also called synovial articulations. Because of their ability to move freely and thus become more susceptible to trauma, joints are of major concern to the coach, the athletic trainer, and the physician. Anatomical

9-5

C*ritical Thinking* Exercise

A tennis player with a pronounced topspin style of hitting a backhand stroke sustains a painful elbow.

? What are the forces and type of elbow injury sustained by the tennis player, and what are ways to prevent this problem?

tendinitis
Inflammation of tendon-muscle attachments, tendons, or both.

ectopic
Located in a place different from normal.

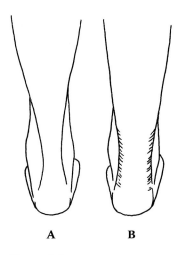

A   **B**

Figure 9-8

Tenosynovitis is an inflammation of the sheath covering a tendon. **A,** Normal. **B,** Strained.

Figure 9-9

General anatomy of a
diarthrodial joint.

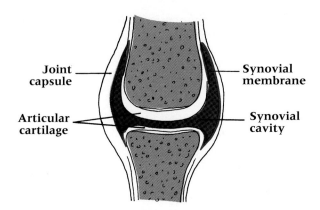

Figure 9-9

General anatomy of a
diarthrodial joint.

Joint capsule

Articular cartilage

Synovial membrane

Synovial cavity

characteristics of the synovial articulations consist of four features: they have a capsule or ligaments; the capsule is lined with a synovial membrane; the opposing bone surfaces contain hyaline cartilage; and there is a joint space (joint cavity) containing a small amount of fluid (synovial fluid) (Figure 9-9). In addition, there are nerves and blood supplied to the synovial articulation, and there are muscles that cross the joint or are intrinsic to it.[18]

Joint Capsule

Bones of the diarthrotic joint are held together by a cuff of fibrous tissue known as the capsule, or capsular ligament. It consists of bundles of collagen and functions primarily to maintain a relative joint position. It is extremely strong and can withstand cross-sectional forces of 500 kg/cm2. Parts of the capsule become slack or taut depending on the joint movements.

Ligaments

Ligaments are sheets or bundles of collagen fibers that form a connection between two bones. Ligaments fall into two categories: ones that are considered intrinsic and ones that are extrinsic to the joint. Intrinsic ligaments occur where the articular capsule has become thickened in some places. Extrinsic ligaments are separate from the capsular thickening.

Ligaments and capsules, found in synovial joints, are similar in composition to tendons; however, ligaments and capsules contain elastic fibers and collagen fibers that have a wavy, irregular, spiral configuration. Ligaments are strongest in their middle and weakest at their ends. When an intact ligament is traumatically stretched, the injury often produces an avulsion-type fracture or tear at the ends rather than in the middle. Avulsion fractures are more common when bone tissue is comparatively weaker than ligamentous tissue, for instance, in older individuals or postmenopausal women in whom significant osteoporosis has occurred or in children in whom the epiphyseal plates are relatively wide and soft.

A major factor in ligamentous injury is the viscoelastic tissue properties of ligaments and capsules. Viscoelasticity refers to extensibility when loaded that is time dependent. Constant compression or tension causes ligaments to deteriorate, whereas intermittent compression and tension increases strength, especially at the bony attachment. Chronic inflammation of ligamentous, capsular, and fascial tissue causes a shrinkage of collagen fibers; therefore, repeated microtraumas over time make capsules and ligaments highly susceptible to major acute injuries.

Ligaments act as protective backups for the joint. Primary protection occurs from the dynamic aspect of muscles and their tendons.[1] In a fast-loading situation, ligament failure ultimately will occur; however, the capsule and ligament provide maximum protection during rapid movements. Nevertheless, capsular and ligamentous tissues are highly sensitive to movement deprivation stress through joint immobilization.[1] Capsular and ligamentous tissue respond to Roux's law of functional adaptation: an organ will adapt itself structurally to an alteration, quantitative or qualitative, of function.[16]

Synovial Membrane and Synovial Fluid

Lining the synovial articular capsule is a synovial membrane made of connective tissue with flattened cells and villi (small projections) on its inner aspect. Fluid is secreted and absorbed by the synovial membrane. Synovial fluid has the consistency of egg white and acts as a joint lubricant. It has the ability to vary its viscosity. During slow movement, the fluid thickens; during fast movement it thins. This variation in viscosity is produced by the presence of hyaluronic acid.

Articular Cartilage

Cartilage, a connective tissue, provides firm and flexible support. It occurs throughout the body and consists of three types: hyaline, fibrous, and elastic. Cartilage is a semifirm connective tissue with a predominance of ground substance in the extracellular matrix. Within the ground substance are varying amounts of collagenous and elastic fibers. Cartilage has a bluish white or gray color and is semiopaque. It has no direct blood or nerve supply. Hyaline cartilage composes part of the nasal septum, the larynx, the trachea, the bronchi, and the articular ends of bones of the synovial joints. Fibrocartilage makes up the vertebral disks, symphysis pubis, and menisci of the knee joint. Elastic cartilage is found in the external ear and the eustachian tube.

As mentioned previously, the ends of the bones in a diarthrotic joint are covered by hyaline cartilage, which cushions the bone ends. Its general appearance is smooth and pearly. Hyaline cartilage acts like a sponge in relation to synovial fluid. As movement occurs, the articular cartilage helps provide both static and dynamic stability; it also absorbs and squeezes out the fluid as pressures vary between the joint surfaces. Because of its great strength, cartilage can be deformed without damage and can still return to its original shape. However, cartilaginous degeneration, producing microtrauma, may occur during the abnormal compressional forces that take place over time. Hyaline cartilage has no direct blood supply; it receives its nourishment from the synovial fluid, or more specifically, from the synovial membrane located at its edges. Deeper aspects of the cartilage are fed by spaces (lacunae) in the adjacent bone. The articular cartilage provides three major functions: motion control, stability, and load transmission.

Motion Control

The shape of the articular cartilage determines what motion will occur. An enarthrodial joint, or a ball-and-socket joint such as the hip, is considered a universal joint, allowing movement in all planes. In contrast, a hinge joint such as the interphalangeal joint allows movement in only one plane.

Stability

Bones that form a joint normally closely match with one another and produce varying degrees of stability depending on their particular shape.

Load Transmission

The articular cartilage assists in transmitting a joint load smoothly and uniformly. The atmospheric pressure within the joint space must be kept constant at all times.

Additional Synovial Joint Structures

Fat

In some joints, such as the knee and elbow, pads of fat lie between the synovial membrane and the capsule. These pads of fat tend to fill in the spaces between the bones that form joints. As movement occurs, they move in and out of these spaces.

Articular Disks

Some diarthrotic joints have an additional fibrocartilaginous disk. These disks vary in shape and are connected to the capsule. They are found in joints in which two planes of movement exist, and they may act as spreaders of the synovial fluid between the joint surfaces. In some joints, a fibrocartilagenous disk is referred to as a meniscus.

Nerve Supply

The articular capsule, ligaments, outer aspects of the synovial membrane, and fat pads of the synovial joint are well supplied with nerves. The inner aspect of the synovial membrane, cartilage, and articular disks, if present, have nerves as well. Mechanoreceptors (encapsulated nerve endings) provide information about the relative position of the joint and are found in the fibrous capsule and ligaments. Mechanoreceptors are myelinated, whereas nonmyelinated fibers are pain receptors or blood vessel suppliers.

Types of Synovial Joints

Synovial joints are subdivided into six types: ball-and-socket, hinge, pivot, ellipsoidal, saddle, and gliding. Ball-and-socket joints allow all possible movement (e.g., shoulder and hip joints). Hinge joints allow only flexion and extension (e.g., elbow joint). Pivot joints permit rotation around an axis (e.g., cervical atlas and axis, proximal ends of radius and ulna). Ellipsoidal joints have an elliptical convex head in an elliptical concave socket (e.g., wrist joint). Saddle-shaped joints are reciprocally concavo-convex (e.g., carpometacarpal joint of the thumb). Gliding joints allow a small amount of gliding back and forth or sideways (e.g., joints between the carpal and tarsal bones and all the joints between the articular processes of the vertebrae).

Functional Synovial Joint Characteristics

Synovial joints differ in their ability to withstand trauma, depending on their skeletal, ligamentous, and muscular organization. Table 9-2 provides a general guide to the relative strength of selected articulations in terms of sports participation.

Synovial Joint Stabilization

Muscle tension is important in limiting synovial joint movement. Limitation may be the result of contacting another body. When the joint capsule is overstretched, a reflex contraction of muscles in the area occurs to prevent overstretching. This reac-

TABLE 9-2 General Relative Strength Grades in Selected Articulations

Articulation	Skeleton	Ligaments	Muscles
Ankle	Strong	Moderate	Weak
Knee	Weak	Moderate	Strong
Hip	Strong	Strong	Strong
Lumbosacral	Weak	Strong	Moderate
Lumbar vertebrae	Strong	Strong	Moderate
Thoracic vertebrae	Strong	Strong	Moderate
Cervical vertebrae	Weak	Moderate	Strong
Sternoclavicular	Weak	Weak	Weak
Acromioclavicular	Weak	Moderate	Weak
Glenohumeral	Weak	Moderate	Moderate
Elbow	Moderate	Strong	Strong
Wrist	Weak	Moderate	Moderate
Phalanges (toes and fingers)	Weak	Moderate	Moderate

tion demonstrates Hilton's law, which states that the joint capsule, the muscles moving that joint, and the skin overlying the insertion of the muscles have the same nerve supply. Ligaments, for the most part, are not extensible but can be extended as a result of the collagen fibers being arranged in bundles at right angles to one another. As the angles of the bundles are changed, ligaments can be extended without lengthening the collagen fiber.

Ligaments and capsular structures are highly important to joint stability. Characteristically, joints that are shallow and relatively poor fitting must depend on their capsular structures or muscles for major support. The knee is an example of an articulation that lacks bony congruence and depends mainly on muscles and ligaments for its support.

Besides moving limbs, muscles also provide joint stabilization to a greater or lesser extent and absorb the forces of load transmission. Muscles help stabilize joints in the following ways: muscles that cross joints assist in maintaining proper articular alignment; and some muscles attach directly to the articular capsule (shunt muscles) and, when stretched, also tighten the capsule. By becoming taut, the shunt muscles prevent the articulations from separating and also assist in maintaining proper alignment.

Articular Capsule and Ligaments

Capsular and ligamentous tissue helps maintain anatomical integrity and structural alignment of synovial joints. Unlike tendons, however, these tissues contain elastic fibers, and their collagenous fibers, although having many configurations, are irregular and have a spiral arrangement. Ligaments, which attach bone to bone, are generally strongest in the middle and weakest at the ends. Compared to ligaments and capsular tissues, with their fast, protective response, muscles respond much more slowly. For example, a muscle begins to develop protective tension within just a few hundredths of a second when overly stretched, but will not fully respond until approximately one tenth of a second has elapsed.

Synovial Joint Trauma

A major factor in joint injuries is the viscoelastic tissue properties of ligaments and capsules (Table 9-3). Constant compression or tension can cause ligaments or capsular tissue to deteriorate. In contrast, intermittent compression and tension will, over time, increase overall strength, including that of the bony attachments of the connective tissue. Like tension forces, torsional or twisting forces that exceed the relative strength of collagen fibers can produce injury. Although occurring less often, a shearing action that cuts across the collagen fiber can traumatize capsular and ligamentous tissue. Tissue damage may occur when articular cartilage fails to properly transmit the applied loads. In other words, the bones and hyaline cartilage that form a joint become out of accordance with each other's compressional forces over a period of time and predispose the joint to degenerative changes.

TABLE 9-3 Synovial Joint Trauma

Primary Tissue	Type	Mechanical Forces	Condition
Capsule	Acute	Tension/compression	Sprains Dislocation/subluxation Synovial swelling
	Chronic	Tension/compression/ shearing	Capsulitis Synovitis Bursitis
Articular cartilage (hyaline)	Chronic	Compression/shearing	Osteochondrosis Traumatic arthritis

9-7

Critical Thinking Exercise

A basketball player steps on another player's foot and sustains a lateral ankle injury.

? What forces are applied, and what type of injury has been incurred?

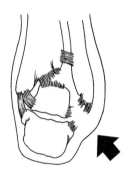

Figure 9-10

A sprain mainly involves injury to ligamentous and capsular tissue; however, muscle tendons can be secondarily strained.

Synovial Joint Injury Classification

Acute Joint Injuries

The major injuries that happen to synovial joints are sprains, subluxations, and dislocations.

Sprains   The sprain, one of the most common and disabling injuries seen in sports, is a traumatic joint twist that results in stretching or total tearing of the stabilizing connective tissues (Figure 9-10). When a joint is forced beyond its normal anatomical limits, microscopic and gross pathologies occur. Specifically, there is injury to ligaments and to the articular capsule and synovial membrane. According to the extent of injury, sprains are graded in three degrees. A grade 1 sprain is characterized by some pain, minimum loss of function, mild point tenderness, little or no swelling, and no abnormal motion when tested. With a grade 2 sprain there is pain, moderate loss of function, swelling, and in some cases slight to moderate instability.[16] A grade 3 (or severe) sprain is extremely painful, with major loss of function, severe instability, tenderness, and swelling. A grade 3 sprain may also represent a subluxation that has been reduced spontaneously.

Effusion of blood and synovial fluid into the joint cavity during a sprain produces joint swelling, local temperature increase, pain or point tenderness, and skin discoloration (ecchymosis). Ligaments and capsules, like tendons, can experience forces that completely rupture or produce an avulsion fracture. Ligaments and capsules heal slowly because of a relatively poor blood supply; however, their nerves are plentiful, often producing a great deal of pain when injured.

The joints that are most vulnerable to sprains in sports are the ankles, knees, and shoulders. Sprains occur least often to the wrists and elbows. Because it is often difficult to distinguish between joint sprains and tendon strains, the examiner should expect the worst possible condition and manage it accordingly. Repeated joint twisting can eventually result in chronic inflammation, degeneration, and arthritis.

Acute synovitis   The synovial membrane of a joint can be acutely injured by a contusion or a sprain. Irritation of the membrane causes an increase in fluid production, and swelling occurs. The result is joint pain during motion, along with skin sensitivity from pressure at certain points. In a few days, with proper care, effusion and extravasated blood are absorbed, and swelling and pain diminish.

Subluxations, dislocations, and diastasis   Dislocations are second to fractures in terms of disabling the athlete. The highest incidence of dislocations involves the fingers and, next, the shoulder joint (Figure 9-11). Dislocations, which result primarily from forces causing the joint to go beyond its normal anatomical limits, are divided into two classes: subluxations and luxations. Subluxations are partial dislocations in which an incomplete separation between two articulating bones occurs. Luxations are complete dislocations, presenting a total disunion of bone apposition between the articulating surfaces. A diastasis is of two types: a disjointing of two bones parallel to one another, such as the radius and ulna; and the rupture of a "solid" joint, such as the symphysis pubis.[1] A diastasis commonly occurs with a fracture.

Figure 9-11

A point that is forced beyond its anatomical limits can become **A,** partially dislocated (subluxated); or **B,** completely dislocated (luxated).

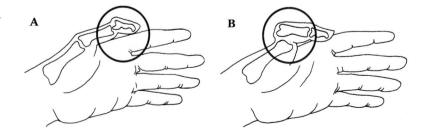

Several factors are important in recognizing and evaluating dislocations:

1. There is a loss of limb function. The athlete usually complains of having fallen or of having received a severe blow to a particular joint and then suddenly being unable to move that part.

2. Deformity is almost always apparent. Because the deformity can often be obscured by heavy musculature, it is important for the examiner to palpate the injured site to determine the loss of normal body contour. Comparison of the injured side with its normal counterpart often reveals distortions.

3. Swelling and point tenderness are immediately present.

At times, X-ray examination of the dislocation, as with a fracture, is the only absolute diagnostic measure. First-time dislocations or joint separations may result in a rupture of the stabilizing ligamentous and tendinous tissues surrounding the joint and in avulsion, or pulling away from the bone. Trauma is often so violent that small chips of bone are torn away with the supporting structures, or the force may separate growth epiphyses or cause a complete fracture of the neck in long bones. These possibilities indicate the importance of administering complete and thorough medical attention to first-time dislocations. It has often been said, "Once a dislocation, always a dislocation." In most cases this statement is true because once a joint has been either subluxated or completely luxated, the connective tissues that bind and hold it in its correct alignment are stretched to such an extent that the joint will be extremely vulnerable to subsequent dislocations. Chronic, recurring dislocations may take place without severe pain because of the somewhat slack condition of the stabilizing tissues.

A first-time dislocation should always be considered and treated as a possible fracture. Once the examiner has ascertained that the injury is a dislocation, a physician should be consulted for further evaluation. However, before the patient is taken to the physician, the injury should be properly splinted and supported to prevent any further damage.

A first-time dislocation should always be considered a possible fracture.

Chronic Joint Injuries

Like other chronic physical injuries or problems occurring from sports participation, chronic synovial joint injuries stem from microtraumas and overuse. The two major categories in which they fall are osteochondrosis and traumatic arthritis (osteoarthritis or inflammation of surrounding soft tissues such as the bursal capsule and the synovium).[8] Another general expression for the chronic synovial conditions of the child or adolescent is articular epiphyseal injury. A major cause of chronic joint injury such as osteoarthritis is failure of the muscle to control or limit deceleration. Athletes can avoid such injuries by avoiding chronic fatigue and training when tired and by wearing protective gear to enhance active absorption of impact forces.[14]

Osteochondrosis   Osteochondrosis is a category of conditions of which the causes are not well understood. In general, the term refers to degenerative changes in the ossification centers of the epiphyses of bones, especially during periods of rapid growth in children. Synonyms for this condition are, if it is located in a point such as the knee, *osteochondritis dissecans* and, if located at a tubercle or tuberosity, *apophysitis*. Apophyseal conditions are discussed in the section on skeletal trauma in this chapter.

One suggested cause of osteochondrosis is aseptic necrosis, in which circulation to the epiphysis has been disrupted. Another suggestion is that trauma causes particles of the articular cartilage to fracture, eventually resulting in fissures that penetrate to the subchondral bone. If trauma to a joint occurs, pieces of cartilage may be dislodged, which can cause joint locking, swelling, and pain. If the condition occurs in an apophysis, there may be an avulsion fracture and fragmentation of the epiphysis along with pain, swelling, and disability.

Traumatic arthritis   Traumatic arthritis is usually the result of microtraumas. With repeated trauma to the articular joint surfaces, the bone and synovium

9-8

Critical Thinking Exercise

A young female gymnast has a pronounced knee malalignment. She complains of a left knee locking, pain, and swelling.

? What is the gymnast's possible condition?

thicken, and pain, muscle spasm, and articular crepitus, or grating on movement, occur. Joint insult leading to arthritis can come from repeated sprains that leave a joint with weakened ligaments. There can be malalignment of the skeleton, which stresses joints, or it can arise from an irregular joint surface that stems from repeated articular chondral injuries. Loose bodies that have been dislodged from the articular surface can also irritate and produce arthritis. Athletes with joint injuries that are improperly immobilized or who are allowed to return to activity before proper healing has occurred may eventually be afflicted with arthritis.

Bursitis, capsulitis, and synovitis   The soft tissues that are an integral part of the synovial joint can develop chronic problems.

Bursitis   The bursa is the fluid-filled sac found in places at which friction might occur within body tissues. Bursae provide protection between tendons and bones, between tendons and ligaments, and between other structures where there is friction. Sudden irritation can cause acute **bursitis,** and overuse of muscles or tendons as well as constant external compression or trauma can result in chronic bursitis. The signs and symptoms of bursitis include swelling, pain, and some loss of function. Repeated trauma may lead to calcific deposits and degeneration of the internal lining of the bursa. Bursitis in the knee, elbow, and shoulder is common among athletes.

Capsulitis and synovitis   After repeated joint sprains or microtraumas, a chronic inflammatory condition called capsulitis may occur. Usually associated with capsulitis is synovitis. Synovitis also occurs acutely, but a chronic condition can arise with repeated joint injury or with joint injury that is improperly managed. Chronic synovitis involves active joint congestion with edema. As with the synovial lining of the bursa, the synovium of a joint can undergo degenerative tissue changes. The synovium becomes irregularly thickened, exudation occurs, and a fibrous underlying tissue is present. Several movements may be restricted, and there may be joint noises such as grinding or creaking.

SKELETAL TRAUMA

Bone provides shape and support for the body. Like soft tissue, bone can be traumatized during sports participation.

Anatomical Characteristics

Bone is a specialized type of dense connective tissue consisting of bone cells (osteocytes) that are fixed in a matrix, which consists of an intercellular material. The outer surface of a bone is composed of compact tissue, and the inner aspect is composed of a more porous tissue known as cancellous bone (Figure 9-12). Compact tissue is tunneled by a marrow cavity. Throughout the bone run countless branching canals, which contain blood vessels and lymphatic vessels. These canals form the haversian system. On the outside of a bone is a tissue covering, the periosteum, which contains the blood supply to the bone.

Bone Functions

Bones perform five basic functions: body support, organ protection, movement (through joints and levers), calcium reservation, and formation of blood cells (hematopoiesis).

Types of Bone

Bones are classified according to their shapes. Classifications include bones that are flat, irregular, short, and long. Flat bones are in the skull, the ribs, and the scapulae; irregular bones are in the vertebral column and the skull. Short bones are primarily in the wrist and the ankle. Long bones, the most commonly injured bones in sports, consist of the humerus, ulna, femur, tibia, fibula, and phalanges.

Flat, irregular, and short bones have the same inner cancellous bone over which there is a layer of compact bone. A few irregular and flat bones (e.g., the vertebrae

---

Athletes with improperly immobilized joint injuries or who are allowed to return to activity before proper healing has occurred may eventually be afflicted with arthritis.

bursitis
Inflammation of bursa at sites of bony prominences between muscle and tendon.

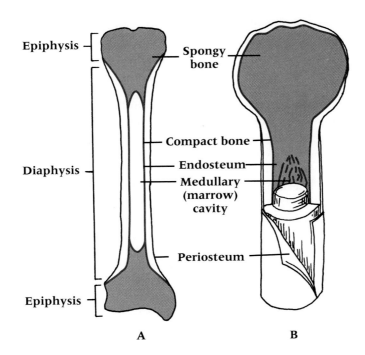

Figure 9-12

Anatomical characteristics of bone. **A,** Longitudinal section. **B,** Cutaway section.

and the sternum) have some space in the cancellous bone that is filled with red marrow and sesamoid bones.

Gross Structures

The gross structures of bone that are visible to the naked eye include the diaphysis, epiphysis, articular cartilage, periosteum, medullary (marrow) cavity, and endosteum. The diaphysis is the main shaft of the long bone. It is hollow, cylindrical, and covered by compact bone. The epiphysis is located at the ends of long bones. It is bulbous in shape, providing space for the muscle attachments. The epiphysis is composed primarily of cancellous bone, giving it a spongelike appearance. As discussed previously, the ends of long bones have a layer of hyaline cartilage that covers the joint surfaces of the epiphysis. This cartilage provides protection during movement and cushions jars and blows to the joint. A dense, white, fibrous membrane, the periosteum, covers long bones except at joint surfaces. Many fibers, called Sharpey's fibers, emanate from the periosteum and penetrate the underlying bone. Interlacing with the periosteum are fibers from the muscle tendons. Throughout the periosteum on its inner layer exist countless blood vessels and osteoblasts (bone-forming cells). The blood vessels provide nutrition to the bone, and the osteoblasts provide bone growth and repair. The medullar cavity, a hollow tube in the long bone diaphysis, contains a yellow, fatty marrow in adults. Lining the medullar cavity is the endosteum.

Microscopic Structures

Calcium salts impregnate the intercellular substance of bone, making it hard. Osteocytes are found in small, hollow spaces called lacunae. Running throughout the bone is the haversian system, consisting of a central tube (haversian canal) with alternate layers of intercellular matrix surrounding it in concentric cylinders. Haversian systems are the structural units of compact bone. Compact and cancellous bones differ in their structures. In compact bone, interspersed lamellae fill the spaces between adjacent haversian systems. In cancellous bone, numerous open spaces are located between thin processes called trabeculae. Trabeculae act like a scaffold, joining cancellous bone. They arrange themselves along the line of greatest stress, providing additional structural strength to the bone. The blood circulation connects the periosteum with the haversian canal through the Volkmann's canal. The medullary cavity and the bone marrow are supplied directly by one or more arteries.

Bone Growth

Bone ossification occurs from the synthesis of bone's organic matrix by osteoblasts, followed immediately by the calcification of this matrix.

The epiphyseal growth plate is a cartilaginous disk located near the end of each long bone. Growth of the long bones depends on these plates. Ossification in long bones begins in the diaphysis and in both epiphyses. It proceeds from the diaphysis toward each epiphysis and from each epiphysis toward the diaphysis. The growth plate has layers of cartilage cells in different stages of maturity, with immature cells at one end and mature ones at the other end. As the cartilage cells mature, immature osteoblasts replace them later to produce solid bone.

Epiphyseal growth plates are often less resistant to deforming forces than are ligaments of nearby joints or the outer shaft of the long bones; therefore, severe twisting or a blow to an arm or leg can result in growth disruption. Injury can prematurely close the growth plate, causing a loss of length in the bone. Growth plate dislocation can also cause deformity of the long bone.[11]

Bone diameter increases as a result of the combined action of osteoblasts and osteoclasts. Osteoblasts build new bone on the outside of the bone; at the same time, osteoclasts increase the medullary cavity by breaking down bony tissue. Once a bone has reached its full size, there occurs a balance of bone formation and bone destruction, or osteogenesis and resorption, respectively. This process of balance may be disrupted by factors in sports conditioning or participation. These factors may cause greater osteogenesis than resorption. Conversely, resorption may exceed osteogenesis in situations in which the athlete is out of shape but overtrains. On the other hand, women whose estrogen is decreased as a result of training may experience bone loss (see Chapter 29).[3] In general, bone loss begins to exceed bone gain by ages thirty-five to forty. Gradually, bone is lost in the endosteal surfaces and then is gained on the outer surfaces. As the thickness of long bones decreases, they are less able to resist the forces of compression. This process also leads to increased bone porosity, known as osteoporosis.

Like other structures in the human body, bones are morphologically, biochemically, and biomechanically sensitive to both stress and stress deprivation. Therefore, bone's functional adaptation follows Wolff's law;[19] that is, every change in the form and function of a bone, or in its function alone, is followed by certain definite changes in its internal architecture and equally definite secondary alterations in its mathematical laws.

Bone Injuries

Because of its viscoelastic properties, bone will bend slightly. However, bone is generally brittle and is a poor shock absorber because of its mineral content. This brittleness increases under tension forces more than under compression forces.

Many factors of bone structure affect its strength. Anatomical strength or weakness can be affected by a bone's shape and its changes in shape or direction. A hollow cylinder is one of the strongest structures for resisting both bending and twisting, stronger than a solid rod, which has much less resistance to such forces.[9] This may be why bones such as the tibia are primarily cylinders. Most spiral fractures of the tibia occur at its middle and distal third, where the bone is most solid (Figure 9-13).

Anatomical Weak Points

Stress forces become concentrated at points at which a long bone suddenly changes shape and direction. Long bones that change shape gradually are less prone to injury than those that change suddenly. The clavicle, for example, is prone to fracture because it changes from round to flat at the same point at which it changes direction.

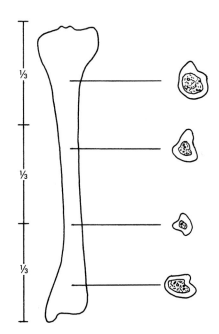

Figure 9-13

Anatomical strengths or weaknesses of a long bone can be affected by its shape, changes of direction, and hollowness.

Load Characteristics

Long bones can be stressed or loaded to fail by tension, compression, bending, twisting (torsion), and shearing. These forces, either singularly or in combination, can cause a variety of fractures. For example, spiral fractures are caused by twisting, whereas oblique fractures are caused by the combined forces of axial compression, bending, and torsion. Transverse fractures occur by bending (Figure 9-14).

Another stress factor is the amount of the load. An increase in energy causes a more complex fracture. Energy is used in deforming the bone and breaking the bony tissue, and some energy becomes dissipated in adjacent soft tissue.[10] The rate of

Long bones can be stressed by tension, compression, bending, torsion, and shearing.

MECHANISM	PATTERN	APPEARANCE
Bending	Transverse	
Torsion	Spiral	
Compression plus bending	Oblique-transverse or butterfly	
Compression plus bending plus torsion	Oblique	
Variable	Comminuted	
Compression	Metaphyseal compression	

Figure 9-14

Mechanisms, patterns, and appearances of acute bone fractures.

energy at which a force is applied to a long bone can cause tissue failure. Depending on the type of bony tissue, more energy is required to cause an abrupt fracture than to cause a fracture to develop over a period of time.[5]

A bone's magnitude of stress and strain is most prevalent at its outer surface and gradually decreases to zero at its center.[14]

Bone Trauma Classification

Bone trauma can generally be classified as periostitis, acute fractures, stress fractures, and epiphyseal conditions.

Periostitis   An inflammation of the periosteum can result from various sports traumas, mainly contusions. Periostitis often appears as skin rigidity of the overlying muscles. It can occur as an acute episode or can become chronic.

Acute bone fractures   A bone fracture can be a partial or complete interruption in a bone's continuity; it can occur without external exposure or can extend through the skin, creating an external wound (open fracture). Fractures can result from direct trauma; in other words, the bone breaks directly at the site where a force is applied. A fracture that occurs some distance from where force is applied is called an indirect fracture. A sudden, violent muscle contraction or repetitive abnormal stress to a bone can also cause a fracture. Fractures must be considered one of the most serious hazards of sports and should be routinely suspected in musculoskeletal injuries. The next sections present more detailed descriptions of acute fractures.

Depressed fracture   Depressed fractures occur most often in flat bones such as those found in the skull. They are caused by falling and striking the head on a hard, immovable surface or by being hit with a hard object. Such injuries also result in gross pathology of soft areas.

Greenstick fracture   Greenstick fractures are incomplete breaks in bones that have not completely ossified, such as the bones of adolescents. This injury occurs most frequently in the convex bone surface while the concave surface remains intact. The name is derived from the similarity of the fracture to the break in a green twig taken from a tree.

Impacted fracture   Impacted fractures can result from a fall from a height, which causes a long bone to receive, directly on its long axis, a force of such magnitude that the osseous tissue is compressed. This stress telescopes one part of the bone on the other. Impacted fractures require immediate splinting by the athletic trainer and traction by the physician to ensure a normal length of the injured limb.

Longitudinal fracture   Longitudinal fractures are those in which the bone splits along its length. They are often the result of an athlete jumping from a height and landing in such a way as to impact force or stress to the long axis.

Oblique fracture   Oblique fractures are similar to spiral fractures. Oblique fractures occur when one end of the bone receives sudden torsion or twisting while the other end is fixed or stabilized.

Serrated fracture   Serrated fractures, in which the two bony fragments have a sawtooth, sharp-edged fracture line, are usually caused by a direct blow. Because of the sharp and jagged bone edges, extensive internal damage, such as the severance of vital blood vessels and nerves, often occurs.

Spiral fracture   Spiral fractures have an S-shaped separation. They are common in football and skiing, sports in which the foot is firmly planted when the body is suddenly rotated in an opposing direction.

Transverse fracture   Transverse fractures occur in a straight line, more or less at right angles to the bone shaft. A direct outside blow usually causes this injury.

Comminuted fracture   Comminuted fractures consist of three or more fragments at the fracture site. This injury could be caused by a hard blow or a fall in an awkward position. These fractures impose a difficult healing situation because of the displacement of the bone fragments. Soft tissues are often interposed between the fragments, causing incomplete healing. Such cases may need surgical intervention.

9-9

Critical Thinking Exercise

An alpine skier catches his right ski tip and severely twists the lower leg.

? What type of serious injury could be created by this mechanism?

Contrecoup fracture   Contrecoup fractures occur on the side opposite to the point at which trauma was initiated. Fracture of the skull is, at times, a contrecoup fracture. An athlete may be hit on one side of the head with such force that the brain and internal structures compress against the opposite side of the skull, causing a fracture.

Blowout fracture   Blowout fractures occur to the wall of the eye orbit as the result of a blow to the eye.

Avulsion fracture   An avulsion fracture is the separation of a bone fragment from its cortex at an attachment of a ligament or tendon. This fracture usually occurs as a result of a sudden, powerful twist or stretch of a body part. A ligamentous avulsion can occur, for example, when a sudden eversion of the foot causes the deltoid ligament to avulse bone away from the medial malleolus. A tendinous avulsion can occur when an athlete falls forward while suddenly bending a knee, which causes a patellar fracture. The stretch of the patellar tendon pulls a portion of the inferior patellar pole apart. Figure 9-15 illustrates a tendinous avulsion of the sartorius muscle.

Stress fractures   Stress fractures have been variously called march, fatigue, and spontaneous fractures, although stress fracture is the most commonly used term. The exact cause of this fracture is not known, but there are a number of likely possibilities: an overload caused by muscle contraction, an altered stress distribution in the bone accompanying muscle fatigue, a change in the ground reaction force such as movement from a wood surface to a grass surface, or the performance of a rhythmically repetitive stress that leads up to a vibratory summation point. The last possibility is favored by many authorities.[17] Rhythmic muscle action performed over a period of time at a subthreshold level causes the stress-bearing capacity of the bone to be exceeded, hence, a stress fracture. A bone may become vulnerable to fracture during the first few weeks of intense physical activity or training. Weight-bearing bones undergo bone resorption and become weaker before they become stronger. The sequence of events, suggested by Stanitski, McMaster, and Scranton,[17] results from increased muscular forces plus an increased rate of remodeling that leads to bone resorption and rarefaction, which progresses to produce increasingly more severe fractures. The four progressively severe fractures are focal microfractures, periosteal or endosteal response (stress fractures), linear fractures (stress fractures), and displaced fractures.

Typical causes of stress fractures in sports are as follows:
1. Coming back into competition too soon after an injury or illness.
2. Going from one event to another without proper training in the second event.
3. Starting initial training too quickly.
4. Changing habits or the environment (e.g., running surfaces, the bank of a track, or shoes).

Susceptibility to fracture can also be increased by a variety of postural and foot conditions. Flatfeet, a short first metatarsal bone, or a hypermobile metatarsal region can predispose an athlete to stress fractures (see Chapter 18).

Early detection of the stress fracture may be difficult. Because of their frequency in a wide range of sports, stress fractures always must be suspected in susceptible body areas that fail to respond to usual management. Until there is an obvious reaction in the bone, which may take several weeks, X-ray examination may fail to reveal any change. Although nonspecific, a bone scan can provide early indications in a given area.

The major signs of a stress fracture are swelling, focal tenderness, and pain. In the early stages of the fracture, the athlete complains of pain when active but not at rest. Later, the pain is constant and becomes more intense at night. Percussion, by light tapping on the bone at a site other than the suspected fracture, will produce pain at the fracture site.

The most common sites of stress fracture are the tibia, fibula, metatarsal shaft, calcaneus, femur, pars interarticularis of the lumbar vertebrae, ribs, and humerus (Figure 9-16).

9-10

Critical Thinking E x e r c i s e

A long jumper experiences a sudden sharp pain in the region of the left ischial tuberosity during a jump.

? What injuries are possible through this mechanism?

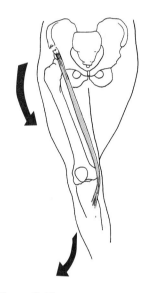

Figure 9-15

Tendinous avulsion fracture of the sartorius muscle.

Figure 9-16

The most common stress fracture sites.

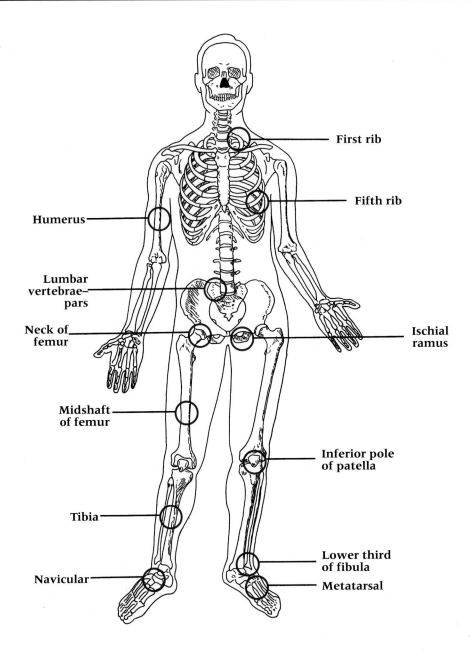

First rib

Fifth rib

Humerus

Lumbar vertebrae–pars

Neck of femur

Ischial ramus

Midshaft of femur

Inferior pole of patella

Tibia

Lower third of fibula

Navicular

Metatarsal

The management of stress fractures varies with the individual athlete, injury site, and extent of injury. Stress fractures that occur on the compression side of bone heal more rapidly and are managed more easily compared with those on the tension side. Stress fractures on the tension side can rapidly produce a complete fracture.

Epiphyseal conditions   Three types of epiphyseal growth site injuries can be sustained by children and adolescents performing sports activities. They are injury to the epiphyseal growth plate, articular epiphyseal injuries, and apophyseal injuries. The most prevalent age range for these injuries is from ten to sixteen years.

Epiphyseal growth plate injuries (Figure 9-17) have been classified by Salter-Harris into five types as follows:[4]

- Type I—complete separation of the epiphysis in relation to the metaphysis without fracture to the bone.
- Type II—separation of the growth plate and a small portion of the metaphysis.
- Type III—fracture of the epiphysis.
- Type IV—fracture of a portion of the epiphysis and metaphysis.

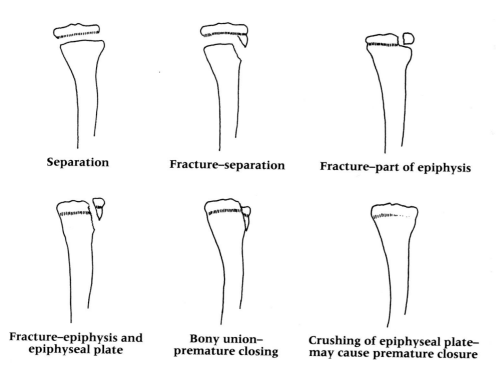

Separation　　　**Fracture–separation**　　　**Fracture–part of epiphysis**

Fracture–epiphysis and epiphyseal plate　　　**Bony union–premature closing**　　　**Crushing of epiphyseal plate–may cause premature closure**

Figure 9-17

Salter-Harris classification of long bone epiphyseal injuries in children.

- Type V—no displacement of the epiphysis, but the crushing force can cause a growth deformity.

Apophyseal injuries   The young, physically immature athlete is particularly prone to apophyseal injuries. The apophyses are traction epiphyses in contrast to the pressure epiphyses of the long bones. These apophyses serve as origins or insertions for muscles on growing bone that provide bone shape but not length. Common apophyseal avulsion conditions found in sports are Sever's disease and Osgood-Schlatter's disease (see Chapter 20).

A musculoskeletal injury to a child or adolescent should always be considered a possible epiphyseal condition.

NERVE TRAUMA

A number of abnormal nerve responses can be attributed to athletic participation or injury. The most frequent type of nerve injury is neuropraxia produced by a direct flow. A laceration can cut nerves, causing complications in healing of the injury. Fractures and dislocation can avulse or abnormally compress nerves.

Anatomical Characteristics

Nerve tissue provides sensitivity and communication from the central nervous system (brain and spinal cord) to the muscles, sensory organs, various systems, and the periphery. The basic nerve cell is the neuron. The neuron cell body contains a large nucleus and branched extensions called dendrites, which respond to neurotransmitter substances released from other nerve cells. From each nerve cell arises a single axon, which conducts the nerve impulses. Large axons found in peripheral nerves are enclosed in neurilemmal sheaths composed of Schwann cells and satellite cells, which are tightly wound around the axon. In the central nervous system, various types of neuroglial cells including astrocytes, oligodendrocytes, ependymal cells, and microglia function collectively to bind neurons together and provide a supportive framework for the nervous tissue.

Nerve Injuries

The two main forces that cause major nerve injury responses are compression and tension. As with injuries to other tissues in the body, the injurious forces to nerves may be acute or chronic.

Physical trauma to nerves in general produces pain as part of the inflammatory process (see Chapter 10). Any number of traumas directly affecting nerves can also produce a variety of sensory responses, including pain. For example, a sudden nerve stretch or pinch can produce muscle weakness as well as a sharp burning pain that radiates down a limb. Neuritis, a chronic nerve problem, can be caused by a variety of forces that usually have been repeated or continued for a long period of time. Symptoms of neuritis can range from minor nerve problems to paralysis.

Pain that is felt at a point of the body other than its actual origin is known as referred pain.[7] Another potential cause of referred pain is a trigger point, which occurs in the muscular system but refers pain to some other distant body part.

BODY MECHANICS AND INJURY SUSCEPTIBILITY

A careful study of the mechanical structure of the human body yields amazement that humans can move so effectively in the upright posture. Not only must constant gravitational force be overcome, but the body also must be manipulated through space by a complex system of somewhat inefficient levers, fueled by a machinery that operates at an efficiency level of approximately 30 percent. The bony levers that move the body must overcome considerable resistance in the form of inertia and muscle viscosity and must work in most instances at an extremely unfavorable angle of pull. All these factors mitigate the effectiveness of lever action to the extent that most movement is achieved at an efficiency level of less than 25 percent.

When determining the mechanical reasons for sports injuries to the musculoskeletal system, many factors stand out. Hereditary, congenital, or acquired defects may predispose an athlete to a specific type of injury. Anomalies in anatomical structure or in body build (somatotype) may make an athlete prone to injuries. The habitually incorrect application of skill is a common cause of overuse injuries.

Microtrauma and Overuse Syndrome

Injuries as a result of abnormal and repetitive stress and microtraumas fall into a class with certain identifiable syndromes. Such stress injuries frequently result in either limitation or curtailment of sports performance. Most of these injuries in athletes are directly related to the dynamics of running, throwing, or jumping. The injuries may result from constant and repetitive stresses placed on bones, joints, or soft tissues; from forcing a joint into an extreme range of motion; or from prolonged strenuous activity. Some of the injuries falling into this category may be relatively minor; still, they can be disabling.[19] Among injuries classified as repetitive stress and microtrauma are Achilles tendinitis; splints; stress fractures, particularly of the fibula and second and fifth metatarsal bones; Osgood-Schlatter's disease; runner's and jumper's knee; patellar chondromalacia; apophyseal avulsion, especially in the lower extremities of growing athletes; and intertarsal neuroma.

Postural Deviations

Postural deviations are often a major underlying cause of sports injuries. Postural malalignment may be the result of unilateral muscle and soft-tissue asymmetries or bony asymmetries. As a result, the athlete engages in poor mechanics of movement (pathomechanics). Many sports activities are unilateral, thus leading to asymmetries in body development. The resulting imbalance is manifested by a postural deviation as the body seeks to reestablish itself in relation to its center of gravity. Often, such deviations are a primary cause of injury. For example, a consistent pattern of knee injury may be related to asymmetries within the pelvis and the legs (short-leg syndrome). Unfortunately, not much in the form of remedial work is usually performed. As a result, an injury often becomes chronic—sometimes to the point that participation in a sport must be halted. When possible, the athletic trainer should seek to ameliorate or eliminate faulty postural conditions through therapy, working under the direction of an orthopedist or other qualified medical personnel. A number of postural conditions offer genuine hazards to athletes by making them exceedingly prone to specific injuries. Some of the more important are discussed in the chapters on foot and leg anomalies, spinal anomalies, and various stress syndromes.

SUMMARY

- "When a force applied to any part of the body results in a harmful disturbance in function or structure, a mechanical injury is said to have been sustained."[12] Engineering terminology is used to describe tissue properties and sport injuries. Examples of this terminology are *load, stress, deformation, viscoelastic, anisotropic, yield point,* and *tissue failure.*

- The five primary stresses leading to tissue trauma are tension, stretching, compression, shearing, and bending. Bending strain can produce a torque on a bone followed by injury. A torsion, or twisting, load can produce a spiral fracture along the long axis of a bone.

- Soft tissue (nonbony tissue) is categorized as noncontractile and contractile (muscle) tissues.

- Skin trauma can occur from a variety of forces (e.g., friction, scraping, compression, tearing, cutting, and puncturing) that produce blisters, skin bruises, lacerations, skin avulsions, incisions, and puncture wounds.

- Skeletal muscle trauma from sports participation can involve any aspect of the muscle-tension unit. Forces that injure muscles are compression, tension, and shearing. Acute muscle injuries include contusions and strains. Avulsion fractures and muscle ruptures can occur from an acute episode. Chronic muscle conditions are myositis, fasciitis, tendinitis, and tenosynovitis. Chronic muscle irritation can cause ectopic calcification; muscle disuse can cause atrophy; and immobilization can cause joint contracture.

- Sports injuries to the synovial joints are common. Anatomically, synovial joints have relative strengths or weaknesses based on their ligamentous or capsular type and their muscle arrangements. Forces that can injure synovial joints are tension, compression, torsion, and shear. Sprains involve acute injury to ligaments or the joint capsule. A grade 3 sprain may cause ligament rupture or an avulsion fracture. Acute synovial joint injuries that go beyond the third degree may result in a dislocation. Two major chronic synovial joint conditions are osteochondrosis and traumatic arthritis. Other chronic conditions are bursitis, capsulitis, and synovitis.

- Because of their shape, long bones are anatomically susceptible to fractures caused by changes in direction of the force applied to them. Mechanical forces that cause injury are compression, tension, bending, torsion, and shear. Bending and torsional forces are forms of tension. Acute fractures include avulsion, blowout, comminuted, depressed, greenstick, impacted, longitudinal, oblique, serrated, spiral, transverse, and contrecoup types. Stress fractures are commonly the result of overload to a given bone area. Stress fractures are apparently caused by an altered stress distribution or by the performance of a rhythmically repetitive action that leads to a vibratory summation and thus a fracture. Three major epiphyseal injuries in sports occur to the growth plate, the articular cartilage, and the apophysis.

- Nerve trauma can be produced by overstretching or compression. Like other injuries, nerve injuries can be acute or chronic. The sudden stretch of a nerve can cause a burning sensation. A variety of traumas to nerves can produce acute pain or a chronic pain such as neuritis.

- An athlete with faulty body mechanics has an increased potential for injury.

Web Sites

Biomechanics World Wide: http://www.per.ualberta.ca/biomechanics

This site enables the reader to search the biomechanics journals for recent information regarding mechanism of injury.

Solutions to Critical Thinking EXERCISES

9-1 All human tissue has viscous and elastic properties. The resistance of tissue is dependent on its viscoelastic characteristic and the types of forces that are applied.

9-2 The friction force produced by sliding into home base causes a serious abrasion skin injury.

9-3 The ball created a compressive force that crushed tissue, causing a secondary contusion.

9-4 The football player has sustained a tension force to the long head of the biceps tendon that caused a rupture or severe strain.

9-5 The mechanism of this elbow injury is repeated tension to the extensor tendons attached to the lateral epicondyle, causing microtraumas. Stress to this area can be reduced by increasing the grip circumference and flattening the backhand stroke.

9-6 Repeated contusions to the quadriceps could produce an ectopic calcification known as myositis ossificans.

9-7 In stepping on another player's foot, the basketball player produces an abnormal ankle torsion and lateral ankle tension, stretching and tearing ligaments.

9-8 Knee malalignment produces abnormal compression and shearing forces on the lateral menisci, which can lead to osteochondritis dissecans and osteochondritis.

9-9 Catching the ski tip produces a torsional force that could cause a boot-top spiral fracture.

9-10 During the jump, a powerful stretch of the biceps femoris could cause a serious strain or an avulsion fracture in the region of the ischial tuberosity.

REVIEW QUESTIONS AND CLASS ACTIVITIES

1. Describe the mechanics that produce noncontractile and contractile sports injuries.
2. Describe the mechanical forces that injure skin.
3. What forces injure muscle tissue?
4. Describe all types of acute muscle injuries.
5. Describe all types of chronic muscle injuries.
6. Describe the major acute injuries occurring to joints.
7. What mechanical forces traumatize the musculotendinous unit and the synovial joint? How are the forces similar to one another, and how are they different?
8. What forces gradually weaken tendons and ligaments?
9. Contrast two chronic synovial joint injuries.
10. List the structural characteristics that make a long bone susceptible to fracture.
11. What mechanical forces cause acute fracture of a bone?
12. How do stress fractures probably occur?
13. Describe the most common epiphyseal conditions that result from sports participation.
14. What are the relationships of postural deviations to sports injuries?
15. Discuss the concept of pathomechanics as it relates to microtraumas and overuse syndromes.

REFERENCES

1. Akeson WH et al: The biology of ligaments. In Hunter LY, Funk FJ Jr, editors: *Rehabilitation of the injured knee*, St Louis, 1984, Mosby.
2. American Academy of Orthopaedic Surgeons: *Athletic training and sports medicine*, Park Ridge, Ill, 1991, American Academy of Orthopaedic Surgeons.
3. Barak T et al: Basic concepts of orthopaedic manual therapy. In Gould JA III, Davies GJ, editors: *Orthopaedic and Sports Physical Therapy*, ed 2, St Louis, 1990, Mosby.
4. Blavelt CT, Nelson FRT: *A manual of orthopaedic terminology*, ed 4, St Louis, 1990, Mosby.
5. Byrnes WB, Clarkson PM: Delayed onset muscle soreness and training. In Katch FL, Freedson PS, editors: *Clinics in sports medicine*, vol 5, Philadelphia, 1986, Saunders.
6. Evans WJ: Exercise-induced skeletal muscle damage, *Physician Sportsmed* 15(1):89, 1987.
7. Fine PG: The biology of pain. In Heil J, editor: *Psychology of sport injury*, Champaign, Ill, 1993, Human Kinetics.
8. Geesink RGT et al: Stress response of articular cartilage, *Int J Sports Med* 5:100, 1984.
9. Gonza ER: Biomechanics of long bone injuries. In Gonza ER, Harrington IJ, editors: *Biomechanics of musculoskeletal injury*, Baltimore, 1982, Williams & Wilkins.
10. Gould JA III, Davies GJ, editors: *Orthopaedic and sports physical therapy*, ed 2, St Louis, 1990, Mosby.
11. Hirsch CS, Lumwalt RE: Injuries caused by physical agents. In Kissane JM, editor: *Anderson's pathology*, ed 9, vol 1, St Louis, 1990, Mosby.
12. Huson A: Mechanics of joints, *Int J Sports Med* 5:83, 1984.
13. Leaveau BF: Basic biomechanics in sports and orthopaedic therapy. In Gould JA III, Davies GJ, editors: *Orthopaedic and sports physical therapy*, ed 2, St Louis, 1990, Mosby.
14. Markey KL: Stress fractures. In Hunter-Griffin LY, editor: *Overuse injuries. Clinics in sports medicine*, vol 6, Philadelphia, 1987, Saunders.
15. Porth CM: *Pathophysiology*, ed 4, Philadelphia, 1994, Lippincott.
16. Roux W: *Die entwichlungsmechanic*, Leipzig, Germany, 1905, Englemann.
17. Stanitski CL, McMaster JH, Scranton PE: On the nature of stress fractures, *Am J Sports Med* 6:391, 1978.
18. Thibodeau GA, Patton KT: *Anatomy and physiology*, ed 3, St Louis, 1996, Mosby.
19. Wolff J: *Das geset der transformation der knockan*, Berlin, 1892, Hirschwald.

ANNOTATED BIBLIOGRAPHY

Blavelt CT, Nelson RRT: *A manual of orthopaedic terminology*, ed 4, St Louis, 1990, Mosby.

This resource book is for all individuals who need to identify medical words or their acronyms.

Booher JM, Thibodeau GA: *Athletic injury assessment*, St Louis, forthcoming, Times Mirror/Mosby College.

This text is an excellent guide to the recognition, assessment, classification, and evaluation of athletic injuries.

Brown LO, Yavorsky P: Locomotor biomechanics and pathomechanics: a review, *J Orthop Sports Phys Ther* 9:3, 1987.

This journal article offers a review of current knowledge regarding clinical anatomy and arthrokinematics of the foot and ankle.

Gunta KE: Alterations in skeletal functions: trauma and infection. In Porth CM, editor: *Pathophysiology,* Philadelphia, 1994, Lippincott.

Chapter 56 is dedicated to major soft and bony tissue trauma and infection.

Peacinn M, Bojanic I: *Overuse injuries of musculoskeletal system,* Boca Raton, Fla, 1993, CRC Press.

This comprehensive text describes overuse injuries of tendons, tendon sheaths, bursae, muscles, muscle-tendon functions, cartilage, and nerves.

Williams JGP: *Color atlas of injury in sport,* Chicago, 1990, Mosby.

This excellent visual guide to the area of sports injuries covers the nature and incidence of sport injury, types of tissue damage, and regional injuries caused by a variety of sports activities.

Tissue Response to Injury

When you finish this chapter you should be able to

- Describe the major events of acute and chronic inflammation.
- Identify the process of repair and regeneration.
- List the differences between soft-tissue and bone healing.
- Identify the management concepts designed for healing and pain modulation.
- List the major characteristics of a stress fracture.
- Explain pain perception.
- Describe pain transmission and management.

This chapter presents the reaction of vascularized living tissue to sports trauma, including the inflammatory response and the healing process. It provides a foundation for therapeutically managing the sports injury (Figure 10-1).[16]

THE INFLAMMATORY RESPONSE

Inflammatory response can be acute or chronic (Figure 10-2). Acute inflammation has a short onset and a short duration. It consists of hemodynamic changes, production of an exudate, and the presence of granular leukocytes.[22] Chronic inflammation has a long onset and a long duration. It displays a presence of nongranular leukocytes and a more extensive formation of scar tissue.

The Roman physician Celsus in the first century A.D. described the local reactions to an injury, which are now known as the cardinal signs of inflammation. They are *rubor* (redness), *tumor* (swelling), *color* (heat), and *dolor* (pain). Galen, a Greek physician in the second century A.D., added a fifth cardinal sign, *functio laesa* (loss of function).

Acute Inflammation

Acute musculoskeletal injuries sustained in sports generally fall into three phases: the acute, reactive, or substrate inflammatory phase; the repair and regeneration phase; and the remodeling phase.[6]

Phase I: Acute Phase

The acute phase of inflammation is the initial reaction of body tissue to an irritant or injury and is characteristic of the first three or four days after injury. Acute inflammation is the fundamental reaction designed to protect, localize, and rid the body of some injurious agent in preparation for healing and repair. The main causes of inflammation are trauma, chemical agents, thermal extremes, and pathogenic organisms.[24] The tissue irritants leading to the inflammatory process impose a number of vascular, cellular, and chemical responses.

An external or internal injury is associated with tissue death. In an acute phase, cellular death occurs from the actual trauma. After trauma, cellular death may continue as a result of a lack of oxygen in the area. Continued death also occurs when the digestive enzymes of engulfing phagocytes spill over and kill normal cells. This fact points to the major importance of proper immediate care using rest, ice, compression, and elevation (RICE).[10,23]

Vascular response

First hour At the time of trauma, before the usual signs of inflammation appear, a transitory **vasoconstriction** occurs, causing decreased blood flow. At the moment of vasoconstriction, coagulation begins to seal broken blood vessels and is followed

---

Acute phase:
- Redness
- Heat
- Swelling
- Pain
- Loss of function

Cellular death continues after initial injury because of the following:
- Lack of oxygen caused by disruption of circulation
- Digestive enzymes of the engulfing phagocytes that spill over to kill normal cells

vasoconstriction
Decrease in the diameter of a blood vessel.

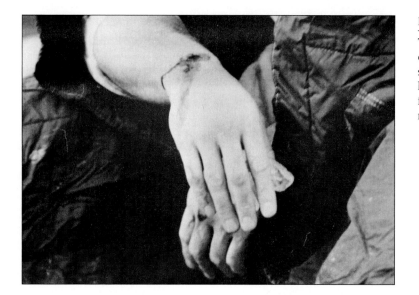

Figure 10-1

Tissue healing and the cause of pain are not clearly understood. However, what is not known must be studied as a foundation for proper injury management.

by the activation of chemical influences. Vasoconstriction is replaced by the dilation of venules, arterioles, and capillaries in the immediate area of the injury.

Second hour   **Vasodilation** brings with it a slowing of blood flow, increased blood viscosity, and stasis, which leads to swelling (edema). With dilation also comes exudation of plasma and concentration of red blood cells (hemoconcentration). Much of the plasma **exudate** results from fluid seepage through the intact vessel lining, which becomes more **permeable,** and from higher pressure within the vessel. Permeability is relatively transient in mild injuries, lasting only a few minutes. Slightly more severe situations may have a delayed response with a late onset of permeability. In such cases, permeability may not appear for many hours and then appears with some additional irritation and a display of rapid swelling lasting for an extended period. Permeability changes occur mainly in capillary and small venules.

A redistribution of leukocytes occurs within the intact vessels, caused in part by a slowing of circulation. These leukocytes move from the center of the blood flow to become concentrated and then line up and adhere to the endothelial walls. This process is known as margination, or pavementing, and occurs mainly in venules. The leukocytes pass through the wall of the blood vessel by ameboid action, known as diapedesis, and are directed to the injury site by chemotaxis (a chemical attraction to

vasodilation
Increase in the diameter of a blood vessel.

exudate
Fluid with a high protein content and containing cellular debris that comes from blood vessels and accumulates in the area of the injury.

permeable
Permitting the passage of a substance through a vessel wall.

Figure 10-2

Severe pain can be the outcome of serious sports injuries.

mast cells
Connective tissue cells that contain heparin and histamine.

leukocytes
Consist of two types—granulocytes (e.g., basophils and neutrophils) and agranulocytes (e.g., monocytes and lymphocytes).

phagocytosis
Process of ingesting microorganisms, other cells, or foreign particles, commonly performed by monocytes (white blood cells).

Chemical mediators:
- Histamine
- Serotonin
- Bradykinin
- Prostaglandins
- Leukotrienes

10-1

Critical Thinking E x e r c i s e

A wrestler receives a sudden twist to his right shoulder, causing a grade 2 strain to the teres minor muscle.

? What hemodynamic changes occur in the first hour of this acute injury?

Complement system:
- Leukocyte chemotaxis
- Phagocytosis

Blood coagulation: Thromboplastin + Calcium = Prothrombin = Thrombin = Fibrinogen = Insoluble fibrin clot

the injury). Ameboid motion is a slow process; it takes about six hours.[26] An injury also leads to an increase in lymph flow because of a high interstitial tissue pressure.

Cellular response In phase I of acute inflammation, **mast cells** and **leukocytes** are in abundance. Mast cells are connective tissue cells that contain heparin (a blood anticoagulant) and histamine; mast cells are the first line of defense. Basophils, monocytes, and neutrophils are the major leukocytes. Basophil leukocytes, believed to bring anticoagulant substances to tissues that are inflamed, are present during both acute and chronic inflammatory healing phases. The neutrophils, representing about 60 percent to 70 percent of the leukocytes, arrive at the injury site before the larger monocytes. Neutrophils emigrate from the bloodstream through diapedesis and **phagocytosis** to ingest smaller debris than do monocytes. Phagocytosis is the process of ingesting material such as bacteria, dead cells, and other debris associated with disease, infection, or injury. Opsonin is a protein substance in the blood serum that coats microorganisms and other cells, making them more amenable to phagocytosis. The phagocyte commonly accomplishes this process by projecting cytoplasmic pseudopods, which engulf the object and ingest the particle through enzymes. When the neutrophil disintegrates, it gives off enzymes called lysozomes, which digest engulfed material. These enzymes act as irritants and continue the inflammatory process. Neutrophils also have chemotactic properties, attracting other leukocytes to the injured area (Figure 10-3). The monocyte, which is a nongranular leukocyte, arrives on the scene after the neutrophils, about five hours after injury. Monocytes transform themselves into large macrophages that have the ability to ingest large particles of bacteria or cellular debris.

Chemical mediators Chemical mediators for the inflammatory process are stored and given off by various cells. Histamine, the first chemical to appear in inflammation, is given off by blood platelets, basophil leukocytes, and mast cells. It is a major producer of arterial dilation and capillary permeability. Serotonin is a powerful vasoconstrictor found in platelets and mast cells. With an increase in blood, there is an increase in local metabolism. Permeability occurs because the contraction of the endothelial cells of the capillary wall produces a gap between cells. Gaps allow plasma to leak plasma proteins, platelets, and leukocytes. Plasma proteases, with their ability to produce polypeptides, act as chemical mediators. A major plasma protease in inflammation is bradykinin, which increases permeability and causes pain.[28]

Heparin is also given off by mast cells and basophils and temporarily prevents blood coagulation. In addition, in the early stages of acute injury, prostaglandins and leukotrienes are produced. Both these substances stem from arachidonic acid; however, prostaglandins are produced in almost all body tissues. They are stored in the cell membranes' phospholipids. Leukotrienes alter capillary permeability and, it is believed, play a significant role, along with prostaglandins, in all aspects of the inflammatory process. Prostaglandins apparently encourage as well as inhibit inflammation, depending on the conditions that are prevalent at the time.[20] Table 10-1 summarizes the chemical responses to the various kinds of inflammation.

Complement system The complement system is a series of enzymatic proteins in normal serum that, in the presence of a specific sensitizer, destroys bacteria and other cells. Fourteen components combine with the antigen-antibody complex to effect cell lysis. Once activated, the components are involved in a great number of immune defense mechanisms, including anaphylaxis, leukocyte chemotaxis, and phagocytosis.

Bleeding and exudate The extent of fluid in the injured area is highly dependent on the extent of damaged vessels and the permeability of the intact vessel. Blood coagulates in three stages. In the initial stage, thromboplastin is formed. In the second stage, prothrombin is converted into thrombin under the influence of thromboplastin with calcium. In the third stage, thrombin changes from soluble fibrinogen into insoluble fibrin. The plasma exudate then coagulates into a network of fibrin and localizes the injured area.

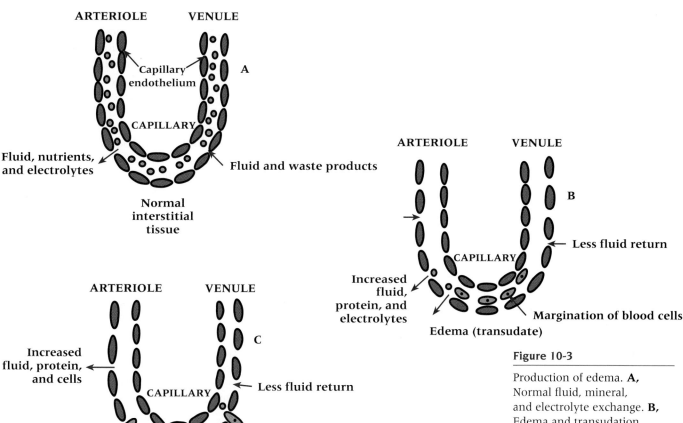

Figure 10-3

Production of edema. **A,** Normal fluid, mineral, and electrolyte exchange. **B,** Edema and transudation. In response to an injury, pressure balance is disrupted, and there is oozing of fluids, proteins, and electrolytes through the blood vessel walls. **C,** Edema and exudate. As inflammation continues, neutrophils and other blood cells emigrate into the surrounding tissue to form an exudate.

Phase II: Repair Phase

The term *repair* is synonymous with healing, whereas *regeneration* refers to the restoration of destroyed or lost tissue. Healing, which extends from the inflammatory phase (forty-eight to seventy-two hours to approximately six weeks), occurs when the area has become clean through the removal of cellular debris, erythrocytes, and the fibrin clot. Tissue repair is accomplished through three processes: by resolution, in which there is little tissue damage and normal restoration; by the formation of granulation tissue, occurring if resolution is delayed; and by regeneration,

TABLE 10-1 Inflammation and Chemical Response

Inflammation Response	Mediators
Vasoconstriction	Serotonin from platelets and most cells
Vasodilation	Histamine from platelets, basophils, and most cells
	Prostaglandin from arachidonic acid
	Leukotrienes from arachidonic acid
	Bradykinin from body fluids
Margination and pavementing	Loss of microcirculation and increase in blood viscosity
Emigration of leukocytes	Leukocytes pass through capillary walls (diapedesis)
Chemotaxis	Leukocytes attract other leukocytes
Phagocytosis	Leukocytes, debris, complement, opsonization

Tissue repairs:
- By resolution
- By granulation tissue
- By regeneration

10-2

Critical Thinking E x e r c i s e

An athlete sustained a grade 2 lateral ankle sprain three weeks ago. It was given proper immediate and follow-up care.

? What repair has taken place during this time?

Tissue repair depends on:
- Elimination of debris
- Regeneration of endothelial cells
- Production of fibroblasts

Remodeling depends on the amount and type of scar tissue present.

synthesis
Process of forming or building up.

lysis
Process of breaking down.

the replacement of tissue by the same tissue. The formation of scar tissue after trauma is a common occurrence; however, because scar tissue is less viable than normal tissue, the less scarring the better. When mature, scar tissue represents tissue that is firm, fibrous, inelastic, and devoid of capillary circulation. The type of scar tissue known as adhesion can complicate the recovery of joint or organ disabilities. Healing by scar tissue begins with an exudate, a fluid with a large content of protein and cellular debris that collects in the area of the injury site. From the exudate, a highly vascular mass develops known as granulation tissue. Infiltrating this mass is a proliferation of immature connective tissue (fibroblasts) and endothelial cells. Gradually the collagen protein substance that stems from fibroblasts forms a dense, fibrous scar. Collagenous fibers have the capacity to contract approximately three to fourteen weeks after an injury and even as long as six months afterward in more severe cases.

During this stage, two types of healing occur. Primary healing, healing by first intention, takes place in an injury that has even and closely opposed edges, such as a cut or incision. With this type of injury, if the edges are held in very close approximation, a minimum of granulation tissue is produced. Secondary healing, healing by secondary intention, results when there is a gaping lesion and large tissue loss leading to replacement by scar tissue. External wounds such as lacerations and internal musculoskeletal injuries commonly heal by secondary intention.

Regeneration   The ability to regenerate is associated with nutrition, general health of the individual, and most important, the type of tissue that has been injured. Repair and regeneration depend on three major factors: elimination of debris, the regeneration of endothelial cells, and the production of fibroblasts, which compose connective tissue throughout the body and form the basis of scar tissue.

In a traumatic event, injured blood vessels become deprived of oxygen and die. Before repair and regeneration can occur, debris must be removed by phagocytosis. Stimulated by hypoxia and the action of macrophages, capillary buds begin to form in the walls of the intact vessels (Figure 10-4). From these buds grow immature vessels that form connections with other vessels. As these vessels become mature, more oxygenated blood is brought to the injured area. From the perivascular cells come the fibroblasts (immature fibrocytes) that migrate to the injury and form collagen substances, often within a few days of the injury. The development of collagen is stimulated by lactic acid and vitamin C as well as the proper amount of oxygen.[30]

Phase III Remodeling Phase

Remodeling of the traumatized area overlaps that of repair and regeneration. Normally, in acute injuries, the first three to six weeks are characterized by increased production of scar tissue and increased strength of its fibers. Strength of scar tissue continues to increase from three months to two years after injury. Ligamentous tissue takes as long as one year to become completely remodeled. To avoid a rigid, nonyielding scar, a physiological balance must be maintained between **synthesis** and **lysis.** There is simultaneous synthesis of collagen by fibroblasts and lysis by collagenase enzymes.[30] The tensile strength of collagen apparently is specific to the mechanical forces imposed during the remodeling phase. Forces applied to the ligament during rehabilitative exercise will develop strength specifically in the direction that force is applied. If too early or excessive strain is placed on the injury, the healing process is extended. Proper healing of muscles and tendons requires careful consideration of when to mobilize the site. Early mobilization can assist in producing a more viable injury site; on the other hand, too long a period of immobilization can delay healing. The ideal of collagen remodeling is to have the healed area contain a preponderance of mature collagenous fibers that have a number of cross-linkages. As stated, collagen content and quality may be deficient for months after injury.[27]

Macrophage   Polymorphonuclear leukocytes   Mast cell   Fibrocyte (fibroblast)

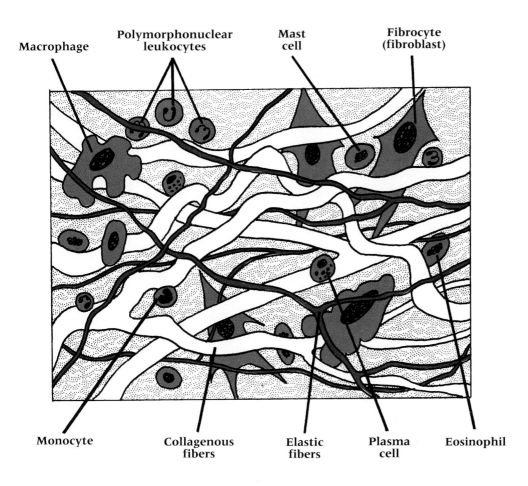

Monocyte   Collagenous fibers   Elastic fibers   Plasma cell   Eosinophil

Figure 10-4

Stimulated by hypoxia and the action of macrophages, capillary buds begin to form in the walls of the intact vessels.

Chronic Inflammation

The chronic muscle and joint problem is an ever-present, self-perpetuating concern in sports. If an acute inflammation reaction fails to be resolved in one month, it is termed a *subacute inflammation.* If it lasts for months or even years, the condition is termed *chronic.* Chronic inflammation results from repeated acute microtraumas and overuse. Prominent features that are distinct from acute inflammation are proliferation of connective tissue and tissue degeneration. The primary cells evident during chronic inflammation are lymphocytes, plasma cells, and macrophages (monocytes) in contrast to the neutrophil leukocytes found in acute inflammation. It has been suggested that lymphocytes, although not normally phagocytic, may be used to stimulate fibroblasts to heal and to form scar tissue. The role of plasma cells is not clearly understood, however.

Macrophages, present in both acute and chronic inflammation, are definitely phagocytic and actively engaged in repair and healing.[6]

Major chemicals found during chronic inflammation are the kinins (especially bradykinin), which also cause vasodilation, increased permeability, and pain. Prostaglandin, also seen in chronic conditions, causes vasodilation. Prostaglandin can be inhibited by aspirin and nonsteroidal antiinflammatory drugs (NSAIDs).

SOFT-TISSUE HEALING

Cell Structure and Function

All organisms, from the most simple to the most complex, are composed of cells. The properties of a specific soft tissue of the body are derived from the structure and function of the cells. Individual cells contain a nucleus surrounded by cytoplasm

Chronic inflammation can stem from repeated acute microtraumas and overuse.

10-3

Critical Thinking Exercise

A lacrosse player complains of a swollen ankle that never became completely resolved since a sprain was sustained nine months ago.

? What is the reason for this chronic swelling?

and are enclosed by a cell membrane that selectively allows substances to enter and leave the cell. The nucleus contains chromosomes, which consist of DNA and protein. The functional and structural elements within the cell are called organelles and include mitochondria, ribosomes, endoplasmic reticulum, centrioles, and Golgi apparatus.

All tissues of the body can be defined as soft tissue except for bone. The human body has four types of soft tissue: epithelial tissue, which consists of the skin and the lining of vessels and many organs; connective tissue, which consists of tendons, ligaments, cartilage, fat, blood vessels, and bone; muscle, which can be skeletal, cardia, or visceral; and nervous tissue, which consists of the brain, spinal cord, and nerves.[27]

Soft tissue can undergo changes and adaptations as a result of healing and of the rehabilitative process following injury. Soft-tissue adaptations include:

- metaplasia—coversion of one kind of tissue into a form that is not normal for that tissue
- dysplasia—abnormal development of tissue
- hyperplasia—excessive proliferation of normal cells in the normal tissue arrangement
- atrophy—a decrease in the size of tissue due to cell death and resorption or decreased cell proliferation
- hypertrophy—an increase in the size of a tissue without necessarily increasing the number of cells

Cartilage Healing

Articular cartilage has limited capacity to heal. Cartilage has little or no direct blood supply.[29] When chondrocytes are destroyed and the matrix is disrupted, healing is variable. Articular cartilage that fails to clot and has no perichondrium heals and repairs slowly. On the other hand, if the affected area includes the subchondral bone, which has a greater blood supply, granulation tissue is formed and the healing process proceeds normally.[19]

Ligament Healing

Ligament healing follows the same course of healing as other vascular tissue. If proper immediate and follow-up management is done, a sprained ligament will undergo the acute, repair, and remodeling phases in approximately the same time period as other vascular tissues.[4]

During the repair phase, collagen or connective tissue fibers are arranged in a random woven pattern with little organization. Gradually a scar is formed. In the next months, the scar matures, and collagen fibers realign in reaction to joint stress and strains. Full ligament healing with scar maturation may take as long as twelve months.[2]

Skeletal Muscle Healing

Skeletal muscles cannot undergo the mitotic activity required to replace cells that have been injured. In other words, regeneration of new myofibers is minimal. Skeletal muscle healing and repair follow the same process as other soft tissue developing tensile strength according to Wolff's law.[25,27]

Nerve Healing

Because of the special nature of nerve cells, they cannot regenerate after they have died. Regeneration can take place within a nerve fiber. The closer the injury is to the nerve cell, the more difficult regeneration becomes.

For nerve regeneration to occur, an optimal environment must be present. If peripheral nerve regeneration occurs, it is at a rate of only 3 to 4 mm per day. Injured nerves within the central nervous system do not regenerate as well as peripheral nerves do.[7]

Modifying Soft-Tissue Healing

The healing process is unique in each athlete. In addition, different tissues vary in their ability to regenerate. For example, cartilage regenerates to some degree from the perichondrium, striated muscle is limited in its regeneration, and peripheral nerve fibers can regenerate only if their damaged ends are opposed. Usually connective tissue will readily regenerate, but as is true of all tissue, this possibility is dependent on the availability of nutrients.

Age and general nutrition can play a role in healing. The older athlete may be more delayed in healing than younger athletes are. The injuries of an athlete with a poor nutritional status may heal more slowly than normal. Athletes with certain organic disorders may heal slowly. For example, blood conditions such as anemia and diabetes often inhibit the healing process.

Management Concepts

Many of the current treatment approaches are designed to enhance the healing process. Current treatments use drugs to combat inflammation, thermal agents, therapeutic modalities, mobilization, and exercise rehabilitation.

Drugs to treat inflammation   There is a current trend toward the use of antiprostaglandin medications, or nonsteroidal antiinflammatory drugs (NSAIDs). The intent of this practice is to decrease vasodilation and capillary permeability.

Therapeutic modalities   Both cold and heat are used for different conditions. In general, heat stimulates acute inflammation and cold acts as an inhibitor. Conversely, in chronic conditions, heat may serve as a depressant.

A number of electrical modalities are used for the treatment of inflammation stemming from sports injuries. These procedures include penetrating heat devices such as microwave and ultrasound therapy and electrical stimulation, including transcutaneous electrical nerve stimulation (TENS) and electrical muscle stimulation (EMS).

Therapeutic exercise   A major aim of soft-tissue rehabilitation through exercise is pain-free movement, full-strength power, and full extensibility of associated muscles. The ligamentous tissue, if related to the injury, should become pain free and have full tensile strength and full range of motion. The dynamic joint stabilizers should regain full strength and power.[14]

Immobilization of a part after injury or surgery is not always good for all injuries. When a part is immobilized over an extended period of time, adverse biochemical changes occur in collagenous tissue. Early mobilization used in exercise rehabilitation that is highly controlled may enhance the healing process (see Chapter 16).[23]

Methods to modify soft-tissue healing include:
- Drugs to treat inflammation
- Superficial thermal agents
- Therapeutic modalities
- Exercise and rehabilitation

FRACTURE HEALING

Those concerned with sports must fully realize the potential seriousness of a bone fracture. Coaches often become impatient for the athlete with a fracture to return to competition and sometimes become unjust in their criticism of the physician for being conservative. Time is required for proper bone union to take place.

The osteoblast is the cellular component of bone and forms its matrix; the osteocyte both forms and destroys bone, and osteoclasts destroy and resorb bone. The constant ongoing remodeling of bone is caused by osteocytes; osteoclasts are related mainly to pathological responses (Figure 10-5). Osteoclasts come from the cambium layer of the periosteum, which is the fibrous covering of the bone, and are involved in bone healing. The inner cambium layer, in contrast to the highly vascular and dense external layer, is more cellular and less vascular. It serves as a foundation for blood vessels and provides a place for attaching muscles, tendons, and ligaments.[23] Skeletal fractures are discussed under the general headings of acute fractures and stress fractures of the bone.

Figure 10-5

Bone is a complex organ in both growth and healing.

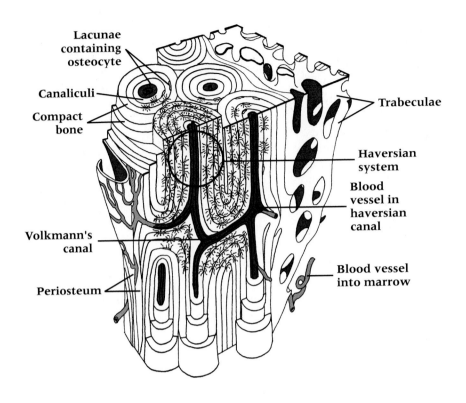

Lacunae containing osteocyte

Canaliculi

Compact bone

Volkmann's canal

Periosteum

Trabeculae

Haversian system

Blood vessel in haversian canal

Blood vessel into marrow

Acute Fractures of the Bone

acute fracture healing

Phase I: acute phase
- Trauma
- Hemorrhage
- Bone death

Phase II: repair and regeneration phase
- Granulation
- Woven bone
- Soft callus
- Hard callus

Phase III: remodeling phase
- Resorption of callus
- Trabecular bone
- Bone

Acute fracture healing follows the same three phases that soft tissue does but is more complex. In general acute fracture healing has five stages: hematoma formation, cellular proliferation, callus formation, ossification, and remodeling.[18]

Hematoma Formation

Acute inflammation usually lasts approximately four days. When a bone fractures, there is trauma to the periosteum and surrounding soft tissue. With hemorrhaging, a hematoma accumulates in the medullary canal and surrounding soft tissue in the first forty-eight to seventy-two hours. The exposed ends of vascular channels become occluded with clotted blood accompanied by dying of the osteocytes, disrupting the intact blood supply. The dead bone and related soft tissue begin to elicit a typical inflammatory reaction, including vasodilation, plasma exudate, and inflammatory cells.

Cellular Formation

The hematoma in a bone fracture, like in a soft-tissue injury, begins its organization in granulation tissue and gradually builds a fibrous junction between the fractured ends. At this time the environment is acid, but it will slowly change to neutral or slightly alkaline. A major influx of capillary buds that carry endosteal cells from the bone's cambium layer occurs. These cells first produce a fibrous callus, then cartilage, and finally a woven bone. When there is an environment of high oxygen tension, fibrous tissue predominates, whereas when oxygen tension is low, cartilage develops. Bone will develop at the fracture site when oxygen tension and compression are in the proper amounts.

Callus Formation

The soft callus, in general, is an unorganized network of woven bone formed at the ends of the broken bone that is later absorbed and replaced by bone. At the soft-callus stage, both internal and external calluses are produced that bring an influx of

10-4

Critical Thinking Exercise

A field hockey player falls and sustains an acute fracture of the left humerus.

? What are the healing events typical of this acute bone fracture?

osteoblasts that begin to immobilize the fracture site. The internal and external calluses are formed by bone fragments that grow to bridge the fracture gap. The internal callus grows rapidly to create a rigid immobilization. Beginning in three to four weeks, and lasting three or four months, the hard callus forms. Hard callus is depicted by a gradual connecting of bone filament to the woven bone at the fractured ends. Less than satisfactory immobilization produces a cartilagenous rather than bony union.

Ossification

With adequate immobilization and compression, the bone ends become crossed with a new haversian system that will eventually lead to the laying down of primary bone. The ossification stage is the completion of the laying down of bone. The fracture has been bridged and firmly united. Excess callus has been resorbed by osteoclasts.

Remodeling

Remodeling occurs after the callus has been resorbed and trabecular bone is laid down along the lines of stress. Complete remodeling may take many years. The influence of bioelectrical stimulation (piezoelectric effect) is the basis for development of new trabecular bone to be laid down at the point of greatest stress. This influence is predicated on the fact that bone is electropositive on its convex side and electronegative on its concave side. The convex is considered the tension side, whereas the concave is the compression side. Significantly, osteoclasts are drawn to a positive electrical charge and osteoblasts to a negative electrical charge. Remodeling is considered complete when a fractured bone has been restored to its former shape or has developed a shape that can withstand imposed stresses.

Management of Acute Fractures

In the treatment of acute fractures, the bones commonly must be immobilized completely until X-ray studies reveal that the hard callus has been formed. It is up to the physician to know the various types of fractures and the best form of immobilization for each specific fracture. Fractures can keep an athlete out of participation in his or her particular sport for several weeks or months, depending on the nature, extent, and site of the fracture. During this period, certain conditions can seriously interfere with the healing process:

- If there is a *poor blood supply to the fractured area* and one of the parts of the broken bone is not properly supplied by the blood, that part will die and union or healing of the fracture will not take place. This condition is known as avascular necrosis and often occurs in the head of the femur, the navicular bone in the wrist, the talus in the ankle, and isolated bone fragments. The condition is relatively rare among vital, healthy, young athletes except in the navicular bone of the wrist.

- *Poor immobilization of the fracture site,* resulting from poor casting by the physician and permitting motion between the bone parts, may not only prevent proper union but may also, in the event that union does transpire, cause deformity to develop.

- *Infection* can materially interfere with the normal healing process, particularly in the case of a compound fracture, which offers an ideal situation for development of a severe streptococcal or staphylococcal infection. The increased use of modern antibiotics has considerably reduced the prevalence of these infections coincidental with or immediately after a fracture. The closed fracture is not immune to contamination because infections within the body or poor blood supply can render it susceptible. If the fracture site should become and remain infected, the infection could interfere with the proper union of the bone.

Conditions that interfere with fracture healing:
- Poor blood supply
- Poor immobilization

- Soft parts that become positioned between the severed ends of the bone—such as muscle, connective tissue, or other soft tissue immediately adjacent to the fracture—can prevent proper bone union, often necessitating surgical cleansing.

Healing of Stress Fractures

As discussed in Chapter 9, stress fractures may be created by cyclic forces that adversely load a bone at a susceptible site. Fractures may be the result of axial compression or tension created by the pull of muscles. Stress on ligamentous and bony tissue can be positive and increase relative strength or can be negative and lead to tissue weakness. Bone produces an electrical potential in response to the stress of tension and compression. As a bone bends, tension is created on its convex side along with a positive electrical charge; conversely, on the concave or compressional side, a negative electrical charge is created. Torsional forces produce tension circumferentially. Constant tension caused by axial compression or stress by muscular activity can result in an increase in bone resorption and, subsequently, a microfracture. In other words, if the osteoclastic activity is greater than the osteoblastic activity, the bone becomes increasingly susceptible to stress fractures.[8]

Like the healing of acute fractures, healing of stress fractures involves restoring a balance of osteoclastic and osteoblastic activity. Achieving this balance requires recognition of the situation as early as possible. Stress fractures that go unhealed will eventually develop into complete cortical fractures that may, over a period of time, become displaced. A decrease in activity and elimination of other factors in training that cause stress will allow the bone to remodel and to develop the ability to withstand stress.

PAIN

Pain is one of the major indicators of the presence of injury. Many complex factors are inherent in pain, including anatomical structures; physiological reactions; and psychological, social, cultural, and cognitive factors.[11] The experience of pain is an individual experience and is subjective.[15]

Nociception

Pain receptors, known as nociceptors or free nerve endings, are sensitive to extreme mechanical, thermal, and chemical energy.[13] They are commonly found in meninges, periosteum, skin, teeth, and some organs.

A nociceptive neuron transmits pain information to the spinal cord via the unmyelinated C fibers and the myelinated A-delta fibers. The smaller C fibers carry impulses at a rate of 0.5 to 2.0 m per second, and the larger A-delta fibers carry impulses at a rate of 5 to 30 m per second. When a nociceptor is stimulated, a neuropeptide (substance P) is released that initiates an electrical impulse along the afferent fiber toward the spinal cord.[13] The faster A-delta afferent fiber impulse moves up the spinal cord at a moderately rapid speed to the thalamus, which gives a precise location of the acute pain, perceived as being bright, sharp, or stabbing.[2] In contrast, the slower conducting, smaller, unmyelinated C fibers are concerned with pain that is diffused, dull, aching, and unpleasant.[11,15] The C fiber impulse also terminates in the thalamus, with projections to the limbic cortex that provide an emotional aspect to this pain. Nociceptive stimuli are at or close to an intensity that produces tissue damage.[11]

Endogenous Analgesics

The nervous system is powered electrochemically. Chemicals known as neurotransmitters are released by a presynaptic cell. This is called a neurotransmitter. Two types of chemical neurotransmitters that mediate pain are the endorphins and serotonin. Both are generated by noxious stimuli, which activate inhibition of pain transmission.[15]

10-5

Critical Thinking Exercise

A female cross-country runner sustains a stress fracture of her left tibia. Her left leg is 3/4 inch shorter than the right leg.

? What is a possible cause of this injury?

10-6

Critical Thinking Exercise

A butterfly swimmer has been experiencing low back pain for more than six months. The pain is described as aching and throbbing.

? What type of pain is this athlete experiencing?

Stimulation of the periaqueductal gray area (PGA) of the midbrain and the raphe nucleus in the pons and medulla causes analgesia. Analgesia is produced by the stimulation of opioids, which are morphine-like substances manufactured in the PGA and in many other areas of the central nervous system. These endogenous opioid peptides are known as endorphins and enkephalins.

Noradrenergic neurons stimulating norepinephrine can also inhibit pain transmission. Serotonin has also been identified as a neuromodulator.[11]

Pain Categories

Pain can be described according to a number of different categories, such as pain sources, fast versus slow pain, acute versus chronic, and projected (referred) pain.[11,30]

Pain Sources

Pain sources are cutaneous, deep somatic, visceral, and psychogenic. Cutaneous pain is usually sharp, bright, and burning and can have a fast or slow onset. Deep somatic pain stems from structures such as tendons, muscles, joints, periosteum, and blood vessels. Visceral pain originates from internal organs. Visceral pain is diffused at first and later may be localized, as in appendicitis. In psychogenic pain, the individual feels pain but the cause is emotional rather than physical.[5]

Fast versus Slow Pain

As discussed earlier, fast pain is localized and carried through A-delta axons located in the skin. Slow pain, in contrast, is perceived as aching, throbbing, or burning. It is conducted through the C fibers.

Acute versus Chronic Pain

Acute pain is pain that is less than six months in duration. Tissue damage occurs and serves as a warning to the athlete. Chronic pain, on the other hand, has a duration longer than six months. The International Association for the Study of Pain describes chronic pain as that which continues beyond the usual normal healing time.[11,17]

Projected (Referred) Pain

One major category of pain that professionals in the field of sports medicine and athletic training commonly encounter is projected, or referred, pain. Such pain occurs away from the actual site of irritation. This pain has been called an error in perception. Each projected pain site must also be considered unique to each individual. Symptoms and signs vary according to the nerve fibers affected. Response may be motor, sensory, or both. The larger myelinated fibers (A-alpha) are the most sensitive to pressure (e.g., in a nerve root) and can produce paresthesia. Three types of referred pain common to athletes are myofascial, sclerotomic, and dermatomic pain.

Myofascial pain   **Trigger points** are small hyperirritable areas within a muscle in which nerve impulses bombard the central nervous system and are expressed as a referred pain. Acute and chronic musculoskeletal pain can be caused by myofascial trigger points. Such pain sites have variously been described as fibrositis, myositis, myalgia, myofasciitis, and muscular strain.

There are two types of trigger points: active and latent. The active trigger point is hyperirritable and causes an obvious complaint. The latent trigger point, on the other hand, is dormant, producing no complaint except perhaps a loss of range of motion. The trigger point does not follow a usual area of distribution such as sclerotomes, dermatomes, or peripheral nerves. The trigger point pain area is called the reference zone, which could be close to the point of irritation or a considerable distance from it.

Sclerotomic and dermatomic pain   Deep pain, which can be either slow or fast, may originate from sclerotomic, myotomic, or dermatomic nerve irritation or injury.

trigger points
Small hyperirritable areas within a muscle.

A sclerotome is an area of bone or fascia that is supplied by a single nerve root. Myotomes are muscles supplied by a single nerve root. Dermatomes also are in an area of skin supplied by a single nerve root.

Sclerotomic pain is often transmitted by the unmyelinated C fibers. Irritation of these fibers can cause deep, aching, and poorly localized pain. Sclerotomic pain impulses can be projected to regions in the brain such as the hypothalamus, limbic system, and reticular formation and can cause depression, anxiety, fear, or anger. Autonomic changes, such as changes in vasomotor tone, blood pressure, and sweating, may also occur.

Irritation of the A-delta fiber can produce dermatomic pain. This pain, in contrast to sclerotomic pain, is sharp and well localized. Unlike sclerotomic pain, dermatomic pain projects mainly to the thalamus and is relayed directly to the cortex, skipping autonomic and affective responses.

Variations in Pain Sensitivity

There are numerous variations in sensitivity to the pain stimuli. Hyperexcitability of sensory nerve fibers can cause hyperesthesia. Unpleasant sensations from severe nerve irritation produces paresthesia. Analgesia is the absence of pain.

Pain modulation   Because pain is a mixture of both physiological and psychological factors, management can be a major challenge for the athletic trainer. In most cases, pain in the athletic training setting is acute.

Pain assessment   Assessing pain can be a difficult task for the athletic trainer. The Agency for Health Care Policy and Research (AHCPR) indicates that the patient's self-report is the best reflection of pain and discomfort.[1]

Methods for pain assessment include the numerical value scale, the visual analog scale, and verbal descriptor scales. The numeric value scale is most commonly used in sports medicine. The athlete is asked to rate his or her pain on a scale of 1 to 10, with 1 representing the least pain and 10 representing the worst possible pain. The visual analog scale uses a line 10 cm in length. One end is labeled "no pain" and the other end is labeled "severe pain." The athlete then marks along the line to indicate the pain's severity.[13] This same approach can be used to determine the effectiveness of treatment. In other words, one end of the line indicates no pain relief and the other, complete pain relief. Verbal descriptor scales use words such as *none, slight, mild, moderate,* and *severe*.

Pain treatment   The athletic trainer is primarily concerned with acute pain. A number of approaches are used separately or in combination. Common to musculoskeletal injuries is the cyclic condition of pain-spasm-hypoxia-pain. Disruption of this cycle can occur through a variety of means: heat or cold, electrical stimulation–induced analgesia, or selected pharmacological approaches.

Heat and cold   Heat and cold are commonly used to address pain in sports medicine. Heat increases blood circulation through blood vessel dilation, reduces nociception and ischemia caused by muscle spasm, and may release endogenous opioids.[11]

In acute injury, cold is applied to cause vasoconstriction and prevent extravasation of blood into the tissues. Pain is relieved by reducing swelling and muscle spasm.

Induced analgesia   Sports therapy offers several electrical devices designed to reduce pain. They are discussed in some detail in Chapter 15. Two that are discussed here are TENS using the gate theory and acupuncture.

The gate theory   The gate theory sets forth the idea that the spinal cord is organized in such a way that pain or other sensations may be experienced.[29] An area located in the dorsal horn causes inhibition of the pain impulses ascending to the cortex for perception. The area, or gate, within the dorsal horn is composed of T cells and the substantia gelatinosa. T cells are neurons that organize stimulus input and transmit the stimulus to the brain. The substantia gelatinosa functions as a gate con-

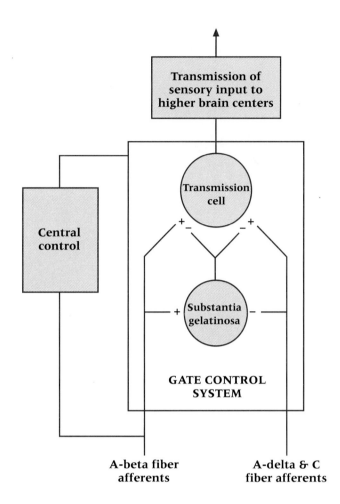

Figure 10-6

Scheme of the pain-modulating system in the dorsal horn of the spinal cord.

trol system. It determines the stimulus input sent to the T cells from peripheral nerves. If the stimulus from a noxious material exceeds a certain threshold, pain is experienced (Figure 10-6). Apparently the smaller and slower nerve fibers carry pain impulses, and larger and faster nerve fibers carry other sensations. Impulses from the faster fibers arriving at the gate first inhibit pain impulses. In other words, stimulation of large, rapidly conducting fibers can selectively close the gate against the smaller pain fiber input. This concept explains why acupuncture, acupressure, cold, heat, and chemical skin irritation can provide some relief against pain. It also provides a rationale for the current success of TENS.

Acupuncture   Acupuncture dates back thousands of years to ancient China. Acupuncture has been found to cause analgesia when needles are applied to specific points on the body.

Acupuncture points lie along a series of meridians that run throughout the body. These points are named according to the meridian on which they lie. Whenever there is pain or illness, certain points on the surface of the body become tender. When pain is eliminated or the disease is cured, these tender points apparently disappear. According to acupuncture theory, stimulation of specific points through needling can dramatically reduce pain in areas of the body known to be associated with a particular point. Thousands of acupuncture points have been identified by the Chinese.

Pharmacological agents   The athlete may be prescribed oral or injectable medications for pain. The most common of these medications are analgesics and antiinflammatory agents.[9]

Critical Thinking Exercise

A gymnast is receiving TENS for chronic low back pain.

? What is the purpose of administering TENS for the chronic pain?

Figure 10-7

Coping with pain in sports is as much psychological as it is physical.

Psychological Aspect of Pain

Pain, especially chronic pain, is a subjective, psychological phenomenon. When painful injuries are treated, the total athlete must be considered, not just the pain or condition. Even in the most well-adjusted person, pain will create emotional changes. Constant pain will often cause self-centeredness and an increased sense of dependency.

Athletes, like nonathletes, vary in their pain thresholds (Figure 10-7). Some can tolerate enormous pain, whereas others find mild pain almost unbearable. Pain is perceived as being worse at night because persons are alone, more aware of themselves, and devoid of external diversions. Personality differences can also cause differences in pain toleration. For example, athletes who are anxious, dependent, and immature have less tolerance for pain than those who are relaxed and emotionally in control.

A number of theories about how pain is produced and perceived by the brain have been advanced. Only in the last few decades has science demonstrated that pain is both a psychological and physiological phenomenon and is therefore unique to each individual. Sports activities demonstrate this fact clearly. Through conditioning, an athlete learns to endure the pain of rigorous activity and to block the sensations of a minor injury.

SUMMARY

- Inflammation can be acute or chronic based on vascular and cellular events and biochemical mediators.
- Acute soft-tissue healing consists of the acute phase, the repair and regeneration phase, and the remodeling phase. The acute phase lasts three to four days. During initial trauma, transitory vasoconstriction occurs, followed by vasodilation and increased permeability. Through the process of chemotaxis, leukocytes, by means of diapedesis, are attracted to the injured area. Throughout the acute phase, major

cellular and chemical events are occurring. A complement system that consists of enzymatic proteins is also involved. An integral part of the acute phase is blood coagulation, which occurs in three stages.

- The second phase of soft-tissue healing, repair and regeneration, extends from the inflammatory phase of forty-eight to seventy-two hours to approximately six weeks. It consists of resolution, development of granulation tissue, and finally, regeneration of lost tissue, depending on the extent of the injury. The two types of healing are primary, or first intention, and secondary, or second intention. Secondary healing develops more granulation tissue and subsequently has a greater possibility of producing more scar tissue. Remodeling is the final phase of the healing process of soft tissue. Remodeling refers to a balance of tissue synthesis and lysis. To maximize this phase, concern must be given to determining the extent of immobilization and mobilization of the injured part.

- Inflammation that lasts for a long period of time is chronic, lasting for months or even years. It may occur as a result of acute microtrauma and overuse. The cells that are typically involved are lymphocytes, plasma cells, and monocytes. Scar tissue and degeneration are associated with chronic inflammation. A number of factors such as nutrition and blood supply can modify the healing process. Anti-inflammatory drugs, thermal agents, therapeutic modalities, and proper exercise procedures can positively alter the healing process.

- Fractures can be acute or stress related. Healing of an acute fracture follows the phases of acute soft-tissue healing, with the exception of replacing osteocytes. Proper management, including immobilization when called for, is essential for bone healing and remodeling.

- Pain is both a psychological and physiological phenomenon. Pain perception is subjective and may be described as fast or slow. Acute pain is designed to protect the body, whereas chronic pain serves no useful purpose. Chronic pain is believed to be caused by a noxious stimulus that affects the high-threshold nociceptors in various tissue. Pain is managed by interrupting some aspect of the pain-spasm-ischemia-hypoxia-pain cycle. Interruption can be accomplished by certain drugs and by therapeutic approaches such as TENS.

Web Sites

Cramer First Aider: http://www.ccsd.k12.wy.us/cchs_web/cramerfirstaider/fstaider.htm

Solutions to Critical Thinking EXERCISES

10-1 Initially, a transitory vasoconstriction with the start of blood coagulation of the broken blood vessels occurs. Dilation of the vessels in the region of injury follow, along with activation of chemical mediators via key cells.

10-2 A grade 2 lateral ankle sprain implies that the joint capsule and ligaments are partially torn. At three weeks the injury has been cleaned of debris and is undergoing the process of secondary healing. Granulation tissue fills the torn areas, and fibroblasts are beginning to form scar tissue.

10-3 The athlete's injury in its acute phase was not allowed to heal properly. As a result, the injury became chronic, with a proliferation of scar tissue, lymphocytes, plasma cells, and macrophages.

10-4 Uncomplicated acute bone healing goes through five stages: hematoma formation, cellular proliferation, callus formation, ossification, and remodeling.

10-5 Because it is shorter, the left leg has the greater stress during running. This stress creates an increase of tension on the tibia's concave side, causing an increase in osteoclastic activity.

10-6 The pain is considered to be chronic, deep somatic pain stemming from the low back muscles. It is conducted primarily by the C-type nerve fibers.

10-7 The concept of TENS is to stimulate the large, rapidly conducting nerve fibers in order to inhibit the smaller and slower nerves that carry pain impulses.

REVIEW QUESTIONS AND CLASS ACTIVITIES

1. Identify the outward signs of inflammation.
2. Describe the vascular, cellular, chemical, and complement system events that occur during acute soft-tissue healing.
3. How does soft tissue repair and regenerate itself after an acute injury?
4. What are the major implications of soft-tissue remodeling after injury?

5. Differentiate between acute and chronic inflammatory processes.
6. What are the reasons for using drugs, thermal agents, therapeutic modalities, and exercise rehabilitation during the healing process?
7. Differentiate between acute soft-tissue healing and acute bone-fracture healing.
8. How does a stress fracture heal?
9. How does pain occur? Why is it generally described as pain perception?
10. What is projected, or referred, pain?
11. What are the major management concepts used in treating pain?

REFERENCES

1. Acute Pain Management Guideline Panel: *Acute pain management: operative or medical procedures and trauma,* AHCPR Pub. No. 92-0032, Rockville, Md, 1992, Agency for Health Care Policy and Research, Public Health Service, US Department of Health and Human Services.
2. Arnozky SP: Physiological principles of ligament injuries and healing. In Scott WN, editor: *Ligament and extensor tensor mechanism injuries of the knee,* St Louis, 1991, Mosby.
3. Bandy W, Dunleavy K: Adaptability of skeletal muscle: response to increased and decreased use. In Zachazewski J, Magee D, Quillen W, editors: *Athletic injuries and rehabilitation,* Philadelphia, 1996, WB Saunders.
4. Booher JM, Thibodeau GA: *Athletic injury assessment,* ed 2, St Louis, 1995, Mosby.
5. Bromm B, Desmedt JE: *Pain and the brain from nociception to cognition,* New York, 1995, Raven.
6. Bryant, MW: Wound healing, *CIBA Clinical Symposia* 29(30):2, 1997.
7. Butler D: Nerve structure, function, and physiology. In Zachazewski J, Magee D, Quillen W, editors: *Athletic injuries and rehabilitation,* Philadelphia, 1996, WB Saunders.
8. Clancy W: Tendon trauma and overuse injuries. In Leadbetter W, Buckwalter J, Gordon S, editors: *Sports-induced inflammation,* Park Ridge, Ill, 1990, American Academy of Orthopaedic Surgeons.
9. Clark WG: *Goth's medical pharmacology,* ed 13, St Louis, 1992, Mosby.
10. Cox D: Growth factors in wound healing, *J Wound Care* 2 (6):339, 1993.
11. Curtis SM, Curtis RL: Somatosensory function and pain. In Porth CM, editor: *Pathophysiology,* ed 4, Philadelphia, 1994, Lippincott.
12. Daly TJ: The repair phase of wound healing—reepithelialization and contraction. In Kloth LC, McCulloch JM, Feedar JH, editors: *Wound healing: alternatives in management,* Philadelphia, 1990, Davis.
13. Denegar CR, Donley PB: Managing pain with therapeutic modalities. In Prentice WE, editor: *Therapeutic modalities in sports medicine,* ed 4, Dubuque, Iowa, 1999, WCB/McGraw-Hill.
14. de Vries HA: Quantitative EMG investigation and treatment. In Zachazewski J, Magee D, Quillen W, editors: *Athletic injuries and rehabilitation,* Philadelphia, 1996, WB Saunders.
15. Fine PG: The biology of pain. In Heil J, editor: *Psychology of sport injury,* Champaign, Ill, 1993, Human Kinetics.
16. Goldenberg M: Wound care management: proper protocol differs from athletic trainer's perception, *J Ath Train* 31(6):12, 1996.
17. Grichnick K, Ferrante FM: The difference between acute and chronic pain, *Mt Sinai J Med* 58:217, 1991.
18. Gunta KE: Alterations in skeletal function: trauma and infection. In Porth CM, editor: *Pathophysiology,* ed 4, Philadelphia, 1994, Lippincott.
19. Houghlum P: Soft tissue healing and its impact on rehabilitation, *J Sport Rehabil* 1 (1):19, 1992.
20. Kloth CL, Miller KH: The inflammatory response. In Kloth LE, McCulloch JM, Feedar JA, editors: *Wound healing: alternatives in management,* Philadelphia, 1990, Davis.
21. Knight KL: *Cryotherapy in sport injury management,* Champaign, Ill, 1995, Human Kinetics.
22. Larocco M: Inflammation and immunity. In Porth CM, editor: *Pathophysiology,* ed 4, Philadelphia, 1994, Lippincott.
23. Loitz-Ramage B, Zernicke R: Bone biology and mechanics. In Zachazewski J, Magee D, Quillen W, editors: *Athletic injuries and rehabilitation,* Philadelphia, 1996, WB Saunders.
24. Madri JA: Inflammation and healing. In Kissane JM, editor: *Anderson's pathology,* ed 9, vol 1, St Louis, 1990, Mosby.
25. Malone T,. Garrett W, and Zachazewski J: Muscle: deformation, injury, and repair. In Zachazewski J, Magee D, Quillen W, editors: *Athletic injuries and rehabilitation,* Philadelphia, 1996, WB Saunders.
26. Porth CM: Cellular adaptation/injury and wound healing/repair. In Porth CM, editor: *Pathophysiology,* ed 4, Philadelphia, 1994, Lippincott.
27. Prentice WE: Understanding and managing the healing process through rehabilitation. In Prentice WE, editor: *Rehabilitation techniques in sports medicine,* ed 3, Dubuque, Iowa, 1999, WCB/McGraw-Hill.
28. Thibodeau GA, Patton KT: *Anatomy and physiology,* ed 2, St Louis, 1993, Mosby.
29. Wahl S, Renstrom P: Fibrosis in soft-tissue injuries. In Leadbetter W, Buckwalter J, Gordon S, editors: *Sports-induced inflammation,* Park Ridge. Ill, 1990, American Academy of Orthopaedic Surgeons.
30. Walker J: Cartilage of human joints. In Zachazewski J, Magee D, Quillen W, editors: *Athletic injuries and rehabilitation,* Philadelphia, 1996, WB Saunders.

ANNOTATED BIBLIOGRAPHY

Kissane JM, editor: *Anderson's pathology,* ed 9, vol 1, St Louis, 1990, Mosby.

This major text in pathology discusses inflammation and healing in depth.

Kloth LE, McCulloch JM, Feedar JA: *Wound healing: alternatives in management,* Philadelphia, 1990, Davis.

This book offers an excellent discussion of factors influencing wound healing, evaluation, and methods of treatment.

Porth CM: *Pathophysiology,* ed 4, Philadelphia, 1994, Lippincott.

This in-depth text on the physiology of altered health contains an excellent discussion on inflammation, healing, and pain.

Management Skills

Psychosocial Intervention for Sports Injuries and Illnesses

When you finish this chapter you should be able to

- Describe why and under what circumstances sports participation is a psychological stressor.
- Explain all the aspects of overtraining and staleness that stem from sports.
- Define the conflict adjustments that may occur as a result of becoming overstressed in sports.
- Identify physiological responses to stress.
- Describe how an athlete may respond psychologically to injuries or illnesses.
- Describe the roles of coaches, athletic trainers, and physicians who work with an overly stressed athlete.

Certainly, the injured or ill athlete experiences physical disability. But for many athletes, the psychological and sociological consequences of injury can be as debilitating as the physical injuries. These psychological and sociological reactions combined with the physical injury itself can have an adverse impact on the athlete's successful return to competition. The sports medicine team and the coach must understand how the psyche, especially feelings and emotions, enter into an athlete's reactions to serious injury or illness and ultimately to the rehabilitation process (Figure 11-1).[22]

Athletes, no matter what sport they participate in, react to serious injury and illness in a very personal way. Each athlete makes unique adaptations to these challenges. Some athletes view an injury or illness as devastating; others take such a setback in stride.[7] Some athletes have problems with emotional control after sustaining a serious injury or illness. The athletic trainer must be apprised that returning an athlete to full, all-out competition requires the athlete to be completely ready psychologically as well as physically. Success in sports performance requires fundamental skills such as speed, attention, concentration, stress management and the ability to perform cognitive strategies.

Some athletes have a tendency toward sustaining injuries, whereas other athletes under similar circumstances stay injury free.[1] Countless physical and psychosocial factors can interact to predispose an athlete to injury as well as influence the effectiveness of the rehabilitation process.[1] No one personality type can be associated with accident-proneness. However, athletes who are risk takers seem to be more prone to injury. These athletes have a higher competition anxiety, demonstrate sensation-seeking behaviors, and have a high motivation for success but do not have the appropriate coping skills to address these stressors.[1]

SPORT AS A STRESSOR

Stress is not something that an athlete can do to his or her body, but it is something that the brain tells the athlete is happening.[19] When change occurs, the brain interprets that change and tells the body how to react to it. Stress does not always imply a morbid change, but could also be associated with intense pleasure.

A number of studies on adverse stress have shown a relationship between life events or personal losses and physical injury among athletes who engage in high-intensity sports.[1] Negative stress tends to decrease the athlete's attentional focus and

stress
The positive and negative forces than can disrupt the body's equilibrium.

Figure 11-1

Sports participation can cause the athlete to experience either negative or positive stress.

create muscle tension, which may lead to a reduction in flexibility, problems in coordination, and an overall decrease in movement efficiency. A loss of attentional focus can cause the athlete to miss important cues.

All living organisms are endowed with the ability to cope effectively with stressful situations. Without stress, there would be very little constructive activity or positive change.[19] Negative stress can contribute to poor health, whereas positive stress can enhance growth and development. A healthy life must have a balance of stress; too little stress causes a rusting out, and too much can cause burnout.[19]

Every day athletes place their bodies in countless stress situations. Their bodies undergo numerous "flight-or-fight" reactions to avoid injury or other physically and emotionally threatening situations.

Sports participation is both a physical and an emotional stressor.

Physical Response to Stress

Wortman and Silver indicate that many stress responses are apparent when athletes adjust to a physical injury and/or undergo a program of rehabilitation.[30]

Stress is a psychosomatic phenomenon. A serious sports injury is a major stressor. Physiologic responses to a stressor are autonomic, immunologic, and neuroregulatory. Hormonal responses are reflected by an increase in the secretion of cortisol. Negative stress can produce fear and anxiety. Initially, in an acute reaction to a negative stress situation, secretions from the adrenal gland sharply increase, creating the well-known flight-or-fight response. With adrenaline in the bloodstream, pupils dilate, hearing becomes more acute, muscles become more responsive, and blood pressure increases to facilitate the absorption of oxygen. In addition to these responses, respiration and heart rate increase to further prepare the body for action.

In general, there are two kinds of stress: acute and chronic. During acute stress, the threat is immediate and response is instantaneous. Physiologically the primary reaction in the acute stage is produced by the epinephrine and norepinephrine of the adrenal medulla. Chronic stress leads to an increase of blood corticoids from the adrenal cortex.

An athlete who is taken out of a sport because of an injury or illness reacts in a personal way. The athlete who has trained diligently, has looked forward to a successful season, and is suddenly thwarted in that goal by an injury or illness can be emotionally devastated.

At the time of serious injury or illness, the athlete may normally fear the experience of pain or possible disability. The athlete may feel a sense of anxiety about suddenly becoming disabled and unable to continue sport participation.[14] An injury or illness is a stressor that results from an external or internal sensory stimulus. Coping with the stressor depends on the athlete's cognitive appraisal.

PSYCHOLOGICAL REACTIONS TO INJURY

The psychological reaction of an athlete who has suddenly sustained an injury will depend upon the length of recovery. The athlete's reactions are typical for anyone who has experienced a sudden serious loss. The injured athlete initially may be in shock and unable to grasp the full consequences of the injury.[16] The athlete may not believe that he or she is vulnerable and not impervious to injury. The athlete may feel a loss of self-esteem or a sense of worthlessness and self-reproach (Figure 11-2). Besides a sense of loss, the injured athlete experiences a number of physical, emotional, and social reactions (see Figure 11-3).[24]

Although some athletes experience minimal mood disturbances after a serious sports injury, others experience depression.[24] Deep depression may become a risk for suicide.[25] The profile of an at-risk athlete is as follows:

- The athlete belongs to the high-risk age group, between fifteen and twenty-four years of age.
- The athlete sustains a serious injury requiring surgery.
- The athlete is faced with a long rehabilitation period.
- The athlete is faced with being replaced by a teammate.

Athletes facing a severe injury that requires surgery with a long period of rehabilitation and an uncertainty of returning to competition may also experience behavioral signs such as exaggerated pain complaints, sleep disturbances, feelings of fatigue, and moodiness.[13] The injured athlete often becomes anxious and loses his or her dedication to the rehabilitation process.[11]

Personality Factors Leading to Injury

Ruling out high-risk situations, some athletes seem to receive an inordinate number of injuries. Athletes who are anxious, tense, restless, and nervous may be more prone to some injuries.[8] A sense of insecurity reflected in low self-confidence and low self-esteem may predispose an athlete to injury.[8] Athletes who are undisciplined in developing skills in their sport and who lack structure in their personal and social life may be accident-prone.[8]

11-1

Critical Thinking Exercise

A world-class sprinter tears her left hamstring muscle, which eliminates her from the Olympic trials.

? What could be the psychological ramifications to this athlete?

11-2

Critical Thinking Exercise

A seventeen-year-old world-class gymnast sustains a major knee injury after a horizontal bar dismount. The injury may end his career. As a result of this injury, the athlete becomes very depressed.

? What should the athletic trainer be concerned with in terms of this athlete's emotional stability?

Figure 11-2

A sports injury can cause the athlete psychological reactions characteristic of a sudden loss.

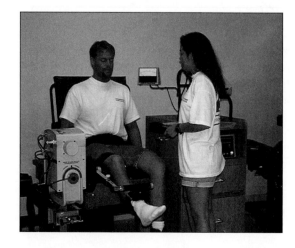

Length of rehabilitation	Reaction to injury	Reaction to rehabilitation	Reaction to return
Short (<4 weeks)	Shock Relief	Impatience Optimism	Eagerness Anticipation
Long (>4 weeks)	Fear Anger	Loss of vigor Irrational thoughts Alienation	Acknowledgment
Chronic (recurring)	Anger Frustration	Dependence or independence Apprehension	Confident or skeptical
Termination (career-ending)	Isolation Grief process	Loss of athletic identity	Closure and renewal

Figure 11-3

Progressive reactions of athletes based on severity of injury and length of rehabilitation.

SOCIOLOGICAL RESPONSE TO INJURY

Following injury, particularly one that requires long-term rehabilitation, athletes may have problems adjusting socially and may feel alienated from the rest of the team. Athletes with an injury that requires weeks or months of rehabilitation before they can return to competition often feel that the coaches have ceased to care, that teammates have no time to spend with them, that friends are no longer around, and that their social life consists of time put into rehabilitation. Such athletes feel that they have received little support from coaches and teammates.[7]

Injured athletes may understand that the coach cares but has no expertise in injury management and must be concerned with getting the team ready without them. The athletic trainer has no expertise in coaching but is primarily interested in rehabilitating injuries. Injured athletes may feel unable to maintain or regain normal relationships with teammates. The injured athlete is a reminder that injury can happen, and teammates may pull away from that constant reminder. Friendships based on athletic identification are now compromised because the athletic identification is gone; friends and team members relate to injured athletes only in terms of what they did yesterday or as injured teammates, not as individuals. Injured athletes no longer feel the team camaraderie that provides a sense of belonging or importance. Athletes who can remain involved with the team, however, feel less isolated and less guilty about not being able to help the team.[7]

Providing Social Support

The loss of social support can be lessened by the organization of support groups or similar injury groups or by mentoring by athletes who have completed rehabilitation successfully. After injury, athletes need the support of teammates to prevent feelings of negative self-worth and loss of identity. Support groups need to stress the importance of the athlete as a person as well as a team member.[7]

A supporting relationship between the athlete and the athletic trainer is critical to successful rehabilitation. Establishing this relationship may be difficult. Injured athletes often question many aspects of the rehabilitation procedure. They question the doctor's diagnosis; they question the athletic trainer for working them too much, and the coach for not paying attention to them. They wonder whether they are thought of as malingerers. They doubt that the athletic trainer, coach, or teammates know how important competition is to them.

Toward the end of rehabilitation, the athlete should begin sport-specific drills during practice time with his or her athletic team. The athlete then begins to reenter the team culture and is not isolated from the team environment. Thus, the athlete puts more effort into functional, sport-specific situations that are generally less boring. In so doing, the athlete gains a more realistic appreciation of the skills needed to attain preinjury performance levels. The rehabilitation routine is more easily tolerated by athletes if they can see some carryover to their particular sport.[7]

OVERTRAINING

Overtraining occurs because of an imbalance between a physical load placed on an athlete and his or her coping capacity.[1,6] Both physiological and psychological factors underlie overtraining. Overtraining can lead to staleness and eventually burnout.

Staleness

anxiety
A feeling of uncertainty or apprehension.

There are countless reasons why some athletes become stale. The athlete could be training too hard and long without proper rest. Staleness is often attributed to emotional problems stemming from daily worries, fears, and anxieties. **Anxiety** is one of the most common mental and emotional stress producers. It is reflected by a nondescript fear, a sense of apprehension, and restlessness. Typically, the anxious athlete is unable to describe the problem. The athlete feels inadequate in a certain situation but is unable to say why. Heart palpitations, shortness of breath, sweaty palms, constriction in the throat, and headaches may accompany anxiety. Children who are pushed too hard by parents may acquire a number of psychological problems. They may even fail purposely in their sport just to rid themselves of the painful stress of achieving. A coach who acts like a drill sergeant—one who continually gives negative reinforcements—will likely cause athletes to develop symptoms of overstress. Athletes are more prone to staleness if the rewards of their efforts are minimal. A losing season commonly causes many athletes to become stale.

Symptoms of Staleness

catecholamine
Active amines, epinephrine and norepinephrine, that affect the nervous and cardiovascular systems.

Staleness is evidenced by a wide variety of symptoms: a deterioration in the usual standard of performance, chronic fatigue, apathy, loss of appetite, indigestion, weight loss, and inability to sleep or rest properly.[8] Often, athletes will exhibit higher blood pressure or an increased pulse rate, both at rest and during activity, as well as increased **catecholamine** excretions. All these signs indicate adrenal exhaustion. Stale athletes become irritable and restless, have to force themselves to practice, and exhibit signs of boredom and lassitude about everything connected with the activity (see *Focus Box:* "Recognizing signs of staleness in athletes").[4]

Athletes who show signs of staleness also increase their potential for both acute and overuse injuries and infections.[8] Stress fractures and tendinitis are typical injuries that can occur during a time of staleness.

Emotional Stress

Sports are stressors to the athlete. An athlete often walks a fine line between reaching and maintaining peak performance and overtraining. Besides performance concerns, many peripheral stressors can be imposed on the athlete, such as unreasonable expectations by the athlete, the coaches, or the parents. Worries that stem from school, work, and family can also be major causes of emotional stress.

The Coach

The coach is often the first person to notice that an athlete is overstressed. The athlete whose performance is declining and whose personality is changing may need a training program that is less demanding. A good talk with the athlete by the coach might reveal emotional and physical problems that need to be dealt with by a counselor, psychologist, or physician.

Focus

Recognizing signs of staleness in athletes

An athlete who is becoming stale will often display some or most of the following signs:

- Show a decrease in performance level.
- Have difficulty falling asleep.
- Be awakened from sleep for no apparent reason.
- Experience a loss of appetite and a loss of weight; conversely, the athlete may overeat because of chronic worry.
- Have indigestion.
- Have difficulty concentrating.
- Have difficulty enjoying sex.
- Experience nausea for no apparent reason.
- Be prone to head colds or allergic reactions.
- Show behavioral signs of restlessness, irritability, anxiety, or depression.
- Have an elevated resting heart rate and elevated blood pressure.
- Display psychosomatic episodes of perceiving bodily pains such as sore muscles, especially before competing.

The Athletic Trainer

Injury prevention is both psychological and physiological. The athlete who enters a contest while angry, frustrated, or discouraged or while undergoing some other disturbing emotional state is more prone to injury than is the individual who is better adjusted emotionally. The angry player, for example, wants to vent ire in some way and therefore often loses perspective of desirable and approved conduct. In the grip of emotion, skill and coordination are sacrificed, resulting in an injury that otherwise would have been avoided.

Although athletic trainers are typically not educated as professional counselors or psychologists, they must nevertheless be concerned with the feelings of the athletes they work with. No one can work closely with human beings without becoming involved with their emotions and, at times, their personal problems. The athletic trainer is usually a caring person and, as such, is placed in numerous daily situations in which close interpersonal relationships are important. The athletic trainer must have appropriate counseling skills to confront an athlete's fears, frustrations, and daily crises and to refer individuals with serious emotional problems to the proper professionals. To help reduce the athlete's muscle tension caused by stress, the athletic trainer provides education in relaxation techniques.

> The athletic trainer must have some counseling skills.

Overtraining must be recognized early and dealt with immediately. A short interruption of training should be carried out over a three- to five-day period.[6] The athlete should perform a lower amount of work but with the same intensity.[6] When the athlete shows signs of a full recovery, a gradual return to the same workload can be initiated. Competition must be stopped. An abrupt cessation of training, however, can produce a serious physiological and psychological condition known as sudden exercise abstinence syndrome (see *Focus Box:* "Sudden exercise abstinence syndrome").

The Physician

The team physician, like the coach and the athletic trainer, plays an integral part with the athlete who is overly stressed. Many psychophysiological responses thought to be emotional are in fact caused by some undetected physical dysfunction. Therefore, referral to the physician must be routine.

11-3

Critical Thinking Exercise

A football player is forced to stop playing at midseason because of a shoulder injury.

? What psychological and physiological problems might this athlete experience by suddenly stopping his participation?

Focus

> **Sudden exercise abstinence syndrome[6]**
>
> Symptoms include the following:
> - Heart palpitations
> - Irregular heartbeat
> - Chest pain
> - Disturbed appetite and digestion
>
> - Sleep disorders
> - Increased sweating
> - Depression
> - Emotional instability

Burnout

Burnout is a syndrome related to physical and emotional exhaustion that leads to a negative self-concept, negative job or sport attitudes, and loss of concern for the feeling of others. Burnout stems from overwork and can affect both the athlete and the athletic trainer.

Burnout can be detrimental to an athlete's general health; it is reflected in frequent headaches, gastrointestinal disturbances, sleeplessness, and chronic fatigue. Athletes suffering from burnout may experience feelings of depersonalization, increased emotional exhaustion, a reduced sense of accomplishment, a cynicism, and a depressed mood.[27]

REACTING TO ATHLETES WITH INJURIES

Even though athletic trainers are proficient in counseling in the areas of injury prevention, injury rehabilitation, and nutrition, they are not usually academically trained for other areas. To meet other counseling needs of the student-athlete, the athletic trainer needs additional academic preparation or should refer the athlete to a sports psychologist.[23]

No matter what reaction the injured athlete displays, the athletic trainer should respond to the athlete as a person, not an injury. Sometimes an athlete can be difficult to be around, especially in the early stages of a serious injury. The injury may suddenly force the athlete to be dependent and helpless.[16] The athlete may regress to a childlike behavior, crying or displacing anger toward the person administering first aid. Table 11-1 provides some suggestions on rendering emotional first aid. During this time, comfort, care, and communication should be given freely.[18]

The sports medicine team must be honest, supporting, and respectful of the injured athlete during the time of disability. They need to understand the athlete at a deeper level and how he or she is coping with this major stress event.[13] A number of questions should be answered. Does the doctor-patient relationship contain confidence, trust, and optimism?[18] Does the athlete fear a pending surgery in terms of more pain or inability to continue in the sport?[18] How long is the recovery? What is the possibility of reinjury?[18] Is forced retirement possible? If so, how well will the athlete adjust? What are the athlete's attitudes toward rehabilitation?

The Catastrophic Injury

A permanent functional disability is a catastrophic injury. Intervention must be directed toward the psychological impact of the trauma and the ability of the athlete to cope during medical treatment.[12] A catastrophic injury profoundly affects all aspects of the athlete's functioning.

PSYCHOLOGICAL FACTORS IN THE REHABILITATION PROCESS

A successful program of rehabilitation takes the athlete's psyche into consideration. Success in treatment that involves therapeutic modalities and exercise rehabilitation depends on rapport, cooperation, and learning (Figure 11-4).[4]

11-4

Critical Thinking Exercise

A seriously injured athlete displays outward signs of being depressed. She talks little and displays mental confusion. She refuses to respond to the athletic trainer's questions.

? How should the athletic trainer respond to this athlete? What should the athletic trainer avoid?

TABLE 11-1 Emotional First Aid

Type of Emotional Reaction	Outward Signs	Trainer's Reactions	
		Yes	**No**
Normal	Weakness, trembling Nausea, vomiting Perspiration Diarrhea Fear, anxiety Heart pounding	Be calm and reassuring	Avoid pity
Overreaction	Excessive talking Argumentativeness Inappropriate joke telling Hyperactivity	Allow athlete to vent emotions	Avoid telling athlete he or she is acting abnormally
Underreaction	Depression; sitting or standing numbly Little or no talking Devoid of emotion Confusion Failure to respond to questions	Be empathetic; encourage talking to express feelings	Avoid being abrupt; avoid pity

Rapport

The term *rapport* means a relationship of mutual trust and understanding. Athletes must thoroughly trust their athletic trainer or therapist to achieve maximum rehabilitation, and they must believe that at all times their best interests are being considered.[13]

Cooperation

A highly motivated athlete begrudges every moment spent out of action and can become somewhat difficult to handle if the rehabilitative process moves slowly. Often, the athlete blames the physician or the athletic trainer for not doing all that he or she can. To avoid this situation, the athlete must be taught early in the rehabilitative

The psychology of sports rehabilitation must include establishing:

- Rapport
- A sense of cooperation
- Exercise rehabilitation as an educational process
- Competitive confidence

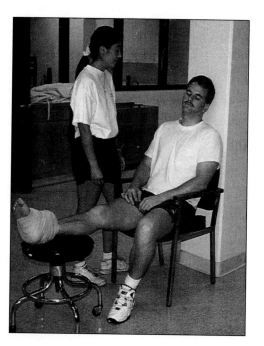

Figure 11-4

Treatment success requires rapport, cooperation, and learning.

process that healing is a cooperative undertaking. It must be established that the athlete, physician, and athletic trainer are a team, all working toward the same end—the return of the athlete to full function as soon as physiologically possible. To ensure this atmosphere, the athlete must feel free to vent frustrations, to ask questions, and to expect clear answers about any aspect of the rehabilitative process. The athlete must feel a major responsibility to come into the training room on time and not skip appointments. He or she must be motivated to perform all exercises correctly and to perform all home assignments on a regular basis.

Many injured athletes lack patience. Nevertheless, patience and desire are necessary adjuncts in securing a reasonable rate of recovery.

Sports Rehabilitation as an Educational Process

To ensure maximum positive responses from the athlete in all aspects of rehabilitation, continual education must occur. All education is provided in layman's language or is commensurate with the athlete's background and education. The following is a list of educational matters that athletic trainers or therapists must address carefully:

1. Describe the injury clearly, using anatomy charts or other visual aids. The athlete must fully understand the nature of his or her injury and its prognosis based on similar cases. A false hope for a fast comeback should not be engendered if a full recovery is doubtful.
2. Explain how the healing process occurs, and estimate the time needed for such healing.
3. Describe in detail the consequences of not following proper procedures.
4. Describe an overall rehabilitative plan, including progressive steps or phases within the plan.
5. Explain each physical modality or exercise, how it works, and its specific purpose.
6. Make the athlete aware that recovery depends as much on his or her attitude toward the rehabilitative process as on what therapy is being given. A positive attitude leads to a conscientious and persistent effort to speed recovery.
7. Realize that the athlete needs to see immediate results.[5]
8. Plan rehabilitation around the athlete's schedule.[5]
9. Ensure that the rehabilitation facility is convenient to the athlete.
10. Monitor the athlete regularly.

Psychological Approaches in the Phases of Rehabilitation

The rehabilitation process incorporates both therapeutic modalities and exercise rehabilitation. During each phase of rehabilitation, the athletic trainer or therapist must address specific psychological issues of the athlete.

Immediate Postinjury Period

The immediate postinjury period is a time of fear and denial for the athlete, who often has severe pain and disability. Emotional first aid must be administered. An accurate diagnosis must be given by the physician, with a full explanation given to the athlete and family members. As much as possible, the athlete needs to know the course of treatment, the prognosis, and the plan to attain goals. The athlete must know from the beginning that he or she is an integral part of rehabilitation.

Early Postoperative Period

When surgery is performed, the athlete becomes a disabled patient. Each phase of the healing process and the purpose of each treatment procedure should be explained to the athlete. The athlete is encouraged to maintain aerobic conditioning by exercising the noninjured body parts.

11-5

Critical Thinking Exercise

A football athlete is undergoing physical rehabilitation after major knee surgery. The process of rehabilitation will take twelve to eighteen months.

? What psychological aspects of the rehabilitation process must be considered by the athletic trainer?

Focus

Factors indicating overcompliance
- Mild degree of denial
- Obsessive-compulsive and impulsive tendencies
- Excessive risk taking
- Behavior masking an underlying fear
- Strong need to prove worthiness

Advanced Postoperative or Rehabilitation Period

While the athlete rehabilitates the injured body part, he or she continues to condition unaffected body regions both aerobically and anaerobically. The athlete must feel that he or she is in control and can make choices. An increase in the athlete's confidence is built on small successes. Milestones must be kept realistic, and positive verbal reinforcement must be given by the coach, peers, and sports medicine team.[26]

This period places greater emphasis on movement patterns that mimic a specific sport. Athletes need reassurance that they will be able to return to their sport and once again achieve success. Their fear of failure and anxiety is dealt with by positive reinforcement.[26]

Overrehabilitation Compliance

Athletic trainers or therapists are often faced with an athlete who overcomplies with the rehabilitation process. Such overcompliance produces treatment setbacks and possible reinjury (see *Focus Box:* "Factors indicating overcompliance").[10]

Poor Rehabilitation Compliance

The opposite extreme of overrehabilitation is found among athletes who comply poorly with the rehabilitation process.[11] Poor adherence could be indicative of a number of factors (see *Focus Box:* "Factors that cause poor compliance").

INITIAL SPORTS REENTRY PERIOD

Often, an athlete returns to participation physically ready but psychologically ill prepared. Although few athletes will admit it, they return to participation feeling anxious about getting hurt again. This feeling may, in some ways, be a self-fulfilling prophecy. In other words, anxiety can lead to muscle tension, which in turn can lead to disruption of normal coordination, thus producing conditions that are favorable

Focus

Factors that cause poor compliance[12]
- Scheduling problems
- School, financial, or family concerns
- Misunderstanding of treatment rationale
- Mistrust of treatment choices
- Mistrust of rehabilitation specialists
- Fear of pain or reinjury

for reinjury or for injury to another body part.[20] The following are suggestions for helping an athlete regain competitive confidence:

1. The athletic trainer allows the athlete to regain full performance by progressing in small increments. Return might include, first, performing all the necessary skills away from the team. This action may be followed by engaging in a highly controlled, small-group practice and then attempting participation in full-team noncontact practice. The athlete should be encouraged to express freely any anxiety that may be felt and to engage in full contact only when anxiety is at a minimum.

2. The athletic trainer can teach the athlete the technique of systematic desensitization. The athlete first learns to consciously relax as much as possible through the Jacobson progressive relaxation method (described later in this chapter).[14] When relaxation can be achieved at will, the athlete, with the help of the athletic trainer, develops a fear hierarchy related to returning to the sport and going all out. Each fear-related step is imagined while the athlete is fully relaxed. If the athlete experiences fear or anxiety at a specific step, the thought processes are halted while the athlete restores total relaxation and holds it until the anxiety has passed. The athlete then continues to the next, more anxiety-producing step and repeats the relaxation process until no anxiety is felt. The athlete who completes the entire list of steps without anxiety and who has completed the proper physical rehabilitation is ready for competition.

Mental Training Techniques

Mental training techniques have long been used to enhance sports skills. Many of these techniques are appropriate for athletes in the process of healing and rehabilitating a serious injury or illness.

Athletic trainers and therapists can assist athletes to positively respond to their injuries via specific mental training techniques. It should be noted that serious emotional instabilities must be referred to a professional psychologist. Some techniques that are available are quieting the anxious mind, mental and emotional assessment, pain control, and healing approaches.

Quieting the Anxious Mind

Fear and anxiety are always present to some degree in a serious sports injury or illness. Fear of pain, loss of control, and unknown consequences of disability can create physical and emotional tensions in an athlete. Two techniques to deal with anxiety and tension that can be taught to the athlete are meditation and progressive relaxation.

Meditation

Meditators focus on a constant mental stimulus such as a phrase, a sound, or a single word repeated silently or audibly, or they gaze steadily at some object. In the passive attitude of meditation, a "don't work at it" approach is taken. As thoughts come into the consciousness, they are quietly turned away, and the individual returns to the focus of attention. The meditator takes a comfortable position with the various major body areas relaxed. To effectively conduct a meditation session, a quiet environment is essential. Normally, the eyes are closed unless the meditator is focusing on some external object (see *Focus Box:* "The meditation technique").

Progressive Relaxation

Progressive muscle relaxation is probably the most extensively used technique for relaxation today.[13] It can be considered intense training in the awareness of tension and tension's release. Progressive relaxation may be practiced in a reclining position or while seated in a chair. Each muscle group is tensed from five to seven seconds, then relaxed for twenty to thirty seconds. In most cases, one repetition of the procedure is sufficient; however, if tension remains in the area, repeated contraction and

11-6

Critical Thinking E x e r c i s e

An athlete sustains a chronic back injury.

? How can the athletic trainer help the athlete deal with the chronic pain?

 **Focus**

The meditation technique

Quieting the body

The athlete sits comfortably in a position that maintains a straight back; the head is erect and the hands are placed loosely on each leg or on the arm of a chair with both feet firmly planted on the floor. To ensure a relaxed state, the meditator should mentally relax each body part, starting at the feet. If a great deal of tension is present, Jacobson's relaxation exercise might be appropriate, or several deep breaths are taken in and exhaled slowly and completely, allowing the body to settle more and more into a relaxed state after each emptying of the lungs.

The meditative technique

Once the athlete is in a quiet environment and fully physically relaxed, the meditative process can begin. With each exhalation the athlete emits a repetitive self-talk of a short word such as "one" or "peace." The word is repeated for ten to twenty minutes. Such words as "peace" or "relaxed" are excellent relaxers; however, Benson[2] has suggested that the word "one" produces the same physiological responses as any other word. If extraneous thoughts occur, the athlete just returns to the meditation process.

After meditating

After repeating the special word, the athlete comes back to physical reality slowly and gently. As awareness increases, physical activity should also increase. Moving too quickly or standing up suddenly might produce light-headedness or dizziness.

relaxation is permitted. The sequence of tensing and releasing is systematically applied to the following body areas: the dominant hand and forearm; dominant upper arm; nondominant hand and forearm; nondominant upper arm; forehead; eyes and nose; cheeks and mouth; neck and throat; chest; back; respiratory muscles; abdomen; dominant upper leg, calf, and foot; and nondominant upper leg, calf, and foot. Throughout the session, a number of expressions for relaxing may be used: "Let the tension dissolve. Let go of the tension. I am bringing my muscles to zero. Let the tension flow out of my body."

After the athlete has become highly aware of the tension in the body, the contraction is gradually decreased until little remains. At this point, the athlete focuses on one area and mentally wills the tension to decrease to zero, or complete relaxation. Jacobson's progressive relaxation normally takes longer than the time allowed in a typical session or than the individual would want to spend. A short form can be developed that, although not as satisfactory, helps the individual become better aware of the body (see *Focus Box:* "Jacobson's progressive relaxation"). The essence of Jacobson's method to recognize muscular tension and the conscious release of that tension.

Cognitive Restructuring

Some injured athletes practice irrational thinking and negative self-talk. This habit can hinder the treatment progress. An important approach to negative thoughts is cognitive restructuring. Two successful methods to thought restructuring are refuting irrational thoughts and thought stopping.[3]

Refuting Irrational Thoughts

This method is designed to deal with a person's internal dialogue. Psychologist Albert Ellis developed a system to change irrational ideas and beliefs.[3] His system is called rational emotive therapy. The basic premise is that actual events do not create

Focus

Jacobson's progressive relaxation

Beginning instructions
1. Get into a position that is relaxed and comfortable.
2. Breathe in and out easily and allow yourself to relax as much as possible.
3. Make yourself aware of your total body and the tensions that your muscles might have within them.

Arm relaxation

1. Clench your right fist. Increase the grip more and more until you feel the tension created in your hand and forearm.
2. Slowly open your fist and allow the tension to flow out slowly until there is no tension left in your hand and forearm.
3. Feel how soft and relaxed the hand and forearm are, and contrast this feeling with the left hand.
4. Repeat this procedure with the left hand, gripping hard and bringing the tension into the fist and forearm.
5. Bend your right elbow and bring tension into the right biceps, tensing it as hard as you possibly can and observing the tightness of the muscle.
6. Relax and straighten the arm, allowing the tension to flow out.
7. Repeat the tension and relaxation technique with the left biceps.

The head

1. Wrinkle your forehead as hard as you can and hold that tension for five seconds or longer.
2. Relax and allow the forehead and face to completely smooth out.
3. Frown and feel the tension that comes in between the eyes and eyebrows.
4. Let go to a completely blank expression. Feel the tension flow out of your face.
5. Squint your eyes tighter and tighter, feeling the tension creep into the eyes.
6. Relax and gently allow your eyes to be closed without tension.
7. Clench your jaw, bite down hard, harder. Notice the tension in your jaw.
8. Relax. When you are relaxed, allow your lips to be slightly parted and your face to be completely without expression, without wrinkles or tension.
9. Stick your tongue up against the roof of your mouth as hard as possible, feeling the tension in the tongue and the mouth. Hold that tension.
10. Relax, allowing the face and the mouth to be completely relaxed. Allow the tongue to be suspended lightly in the mouth. Relax.
11. Form an O with your lips. Purse the lips hard together so that you feel the tension around the lips only.
12. Relax, allowing the tension to leave around the lips. Allow your lips to be slightly parted, and allow tension to be completely gone from the face.

The neck and shoulders

1. Press your head back against the mat or chair and feel the tension come into the neck region. Hold that tension. Be aware of it, sense it.
2. Slowly allow the tension to leave, decreasing the amount of pressure applied until the tension has completely gone and there is as much relaxation as possible.
3. Bring your head forward so that your chin is pressing against your chest and tension is brought into the throat and back of the neck. Hold that tension.
4. Slowly return to the beginning position and feel the tension leave the neck. Relax completely.
5. Shrug your shoulders upward, raising your shoulders as far as you can toward your ears, hunching your head between your shoulders. Feel the tension creep into your shoulders. Hold that tension.
6. Slowly let the tension leave by returning the shoulders to their original position. Allow the tension to completely leave the neck and shoulder region. Have a sense of bringing the muscles to zero, where they are completely at ease and without strain.

Respiration and the trunk

1. When the body is completely relaxed and you have a sense of heaviness, allow tension to move to your respiration. Fill the lungs completely and hold your breath for five seconds, feeling the tension come into the chest and upper back muscles.
2. Exhale slowly, allowing the air to go out slowly as you feel the tension being released slowly.
3. While your breath is coming slowly and easily, sense the contrast of the breath holding to the breath that is coming freely and gently.

Continued

 *Focus*

Jacobson's progressive relaxation—cont'd

4. Tighten the abdominal muscles by pressing downward on the stomach. Note the tension that comes into the abdominal region, the respiratory center, and the back region.
5. Relax the abdominal area and feel the tension leave the trunk region.
6. Slightly arch the back against the mat or back of the chair. This should be done without hyperextending or straining. Feel the tension that creeps into and along the spine. Hold that tension.
7. Gradually allow the body to sink back into its original position. Feel the tension leave the long muscles of the back.
8. Flatten the lower back by rolling the hips forward. Feel the tension come into the lower back by rolling the hips forward. Hold that tension. Try to isolate that tension from all the other parts of your body.
9. Gradually return to the original position, and feel the tension leave the body. Be aware of any tension that might have crept into body regions that you have already relaxed. Allow your mind to scan your body; go back over the areas that you have released from tension and become aware of whether any tension has returned.

The buttocks and thighs

1. Tense your buttocks for five seconds. Try to isolate just the contraction of the buttocks region.
2. Slowly allow the buttocks to return to their normal state, relaxing completely.
3. Contract your thighs by straightening your knees. Hold that contraction, feeling the tension, isolating the tension just to that region, focusing just on the thigh region.
4. Slowly allow the tension to leave the region, bringing the entire body to a relaxed state, especially the thighs.
5. To bring the tension to the back of the thighs, press your heels as hard as you can against the floor or mat, slightly bending the knees; bring the tension to the hamstring region and the back of the thighs. Hold this tension, study it, concentrate on it. Try to isolate the tension from other tensions that might have crept into the body.
6. Relax. Allow the tension to flow out. Return your legs to the original position, and let go of all the tensions of the body.

The lower legs and feet

1. With the legs fully extended, point your feet downward as hard as possible, bringing tension into both calves. Hold that tension. Hold it as hard as you can without cramping.
2. Slowly allow the foot to return to a neutral position, and allow relaxation to occur within the calf muscle. Bring it to zero, if possible—no tension.
3. Curl the toes of the feet downward as hard as you can without pointing the foot downward, isolating the tension just in the bottoms of the feet and toes. Hold that tension. Isolate the tension, if possible, from the calves. Hold it, feel the tension on the bottoms of your feet.
4. Slowly relax and allow the tension to release from the foot as the toes straighten out.
5. Curl the toes backward toward the kneecaps and bring the foot back into dorsiflexion so that you feel the tension in the tops of the toes, the tops of the feet, and the shin. Hold that tension. Be aware of it, study the tension.
6. After five seconds or longer, return to a neutral state where the foot is completely relaxed and the toes have returned to their normal position. Feel the tension leave your body.

emotions; rather, it is the self-talk after the event that does. In other words, irrational self-talk causes anxiety, anger, and depression.

Athletes who are under severe stress should explore their self-talk. Following are two examples:

1. *Facts and events:* A tennis player, after surgical repair of her shoulder, is impatient about the speed of recovery. Emotions of anger and depression are present.

   Negative self-talk:
      "I was stupid to get hurt."
      "Why me? Why did I have to get hurt?"
      "I have never been laid up before. It's not fair!"
   Positive self-talk:
      "I was hurt and now I am doing my best to get well."
      "Every day I am getting better."
      "The athletic trainers are doing their best for me."

2. *Facts and events:* A football player blows a knee out and requires surgery. Emotions of anger and denial are present.
   Negative self-talk:
   "I was blindsided and no penalty was called."
   "I could have avoided such a serious injury if the coaches coached better."
   Positive self-talk:
   "I am hurt, but because of my good fitness level I will recover quickly."
   "I plan to do everything I am told to recover quickly."

Thought Stopping

Thought stopping is an excellent cognitive technique for helping the athlete overcome worries and doubts. The anxious athlete, especially one that is hurt, will often repeat negative, unproductive, and unrealistic statements during self-talk, such as "I am no good to anyone now that I am hurt" or "Everyone on the team is going to pass me by while I am recovering." Thought stopping consists of focusing on the undesired thoughts and stopping them with the command "stop" or a loud noise. After the thought interruption, a positive statement is inserted, such as "My shoulder is healing and I'll play as well as or maybe better than before."[17]

Therapeutic Imagery

Imagery, or visualization, can be a beneficial tool in the rehabilitation process. Imagery is seeing with the mind's eye; it encourages the athlete to focus on a goal, such as rehearsal of rehabilitation, pain control, and stimulating the healing process.[10,21]

Rehearsing the Rehabilitation Process

The athlete starts by becoming as relaxed as possible and then proceeds to imagine with eyes closed important events in the rehabilitation process. All senses of the imagination are used: sight, sound, touch, and kinesthesia.[21] The athlete can visualize being successful at the following important rehabilitative steps:
- Leaving the hospital
- Starting and carrying out active rehabilitation
- Enduring the healing process
- Returning to practice
- Participating in full practice without fear
- Competing without fear

Focus

Healing images

Treatment modalities
- Ultrasound increases circulation, bringing healthy new tissue to the area.
- Cold application inhibits pain.

Exercise rehabilitation
- Muscle fibers increase in number and become stronger.
- Joint range of motion—joints become fully functional.

Medications
- Antiinflammatories decrease inflammation and swelling.
- Pain medication inhibits pain.

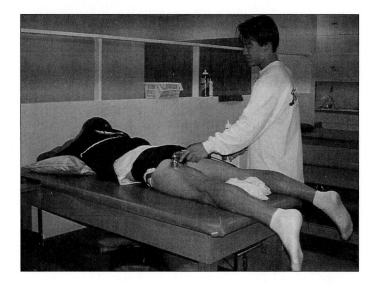

Figure 11-5

Educating the athlete about pain is a major goal in the healing process.

Imagery can be used specifically to enhance each treatment approach. A foundation to imagery is the education that the athletic trainer or therapist provides the athlete while treatment is given.[9] The athlete imagines that the treatment is positively affecting the body (see *Focus Box:* "Healing images").[10]

HEALING PROCESS AND PAIN CONTROL

Improving the Healing Process

It is important that the athlete be educated about the physiological process of healing (Figure 11-5). Once the healing process is understood, the athlete is instructed to imagine it taking place during therapy and throughout the day. An athlete fighting infection can imagine the body's phagocytes as "Pac Men" gobbling up infectious material. An athlete with torn tissue can visualize clot formation and organization followed by tissue regeneration and healing.

Techniques for Coping with Pain

The injured athlete can be taught relatively simple techniques to inhibit pain and discomfort. At no time should pain be completely inhibited because pain is a protective mechanism. The athlete can reduce pain in three ways: reducing muscle tension, diverting attention away from the pain, or changing the pain sensation to another sensation.

Tension Reduction

The pain response can be associated with general muscular tension stemming from anxiety or from the pain-spasm-pain cycle of the specific injury. In both these situations, muscle tension increases the sensation of pain. Conversely, relaxation methods that reduce muscle tension can also decrease the awareness of pain. Both the Benson[2] and Jacobson[14] techniques of stress reduction can be advantageous in pain reduction.

Attention Diversion

A positive method for decreasing pain perception is to divert attention from the injury. This method can be performed in a painful injury and can be beneficial. The athletic trainer or therapist should engage the athlete in mental problem solving, such as adding or subtracting a column of numbers or counting spots on the floor. The athlete can also divert pain by fantasizing about pleasant events, such as sunbathing at the beach, sailing, or skiing.

11-7

Critical Thinking E x e r c i s e

An athlete sustains a major knee injury.

? What mental activities can the athlete perform to enhance the healing process?

Altering the Pain Sensation

Imagination is one of the most powerful forces available to human beings. Negative imagination can be a major cause of illness, stress, and muscular tension, whereas positive imagination can produce wellness and counteract stress.

Through imagination, the athlete can alter pain sensation to another sensation. For example, immersing a body part in ice-cold water can change the pain to a sensation of cold dampness. The athlete can visualize that the injured part is relaxed and comfortable instead of painful. Imagining a peaceful scene at a pleasant spot such as the beach or mountains can both relax the athlete and divert attention from the pain.

SUMMARY

- The injured or ill athlete not only experiences physical disability but also major psychological reactions. Sport can be a major psychophysiological stressor.
- The athlete who sustains a serious injury may experience psychological characteristics of sudden loss, including denial, anger, bargaining, depression, and acceptance. Injury can cause physical, emotional, social, and self-concept reactions by the athlete.
- Some athletes, because of personality factors, experience an inordinate number of injuries and illnesses. Anxiety, low self-esteem, and poor discipline may lead an athlete to be accident-prone.
- Overtraining and staleness result in a physical load being placed on the athlete's ability to cope. Athletes who are pushed or who push themselves too hard may experience burnout. These conditions generate a higher incidence of overuse injuries.
- At all times, the injured or ill athlete must be treated as a person, not a condition. Comfort, care, and good communication should be the approach of the health care providers.
- The rehabilitation process requires mutual trust, understanding, and cooperation. Rehabilitation must be an educational process. Education is carried out through each phase of rehabilitation. Health care personnel may encounter athletes who overcomply or poorly comply.
- Many mental training aids can help the injured athlete through the rehabilitation process and reentry to competition. Some of these aids are systematic desensitization, mental and emotional assessment, refuting irrational thoughts, and thought stopping.

Web Sites

Health and Sports Psychology: http://www.cmhc.com/guide/pro07.htm

This site explores sport psychology and provides links to many health-related sites.

Sports Psychology General Information Page: http://www.mc.maricopa.edu/users/estabrook/html/sport_psychology.html

Go to the bottom of this page to access specific topics in sports psychology.

Exercise and Sport Psychology: http://www.psyc.unt.edu/apadiv47

This site belongs to the sports and exercise division of the American Psychological Association.

Solutions to *Critical Thinking* E X E R C I S E S

11-1 This athlete may experience the psychological reaction to a sudden loss: disbelief, anger, bargaining, depression, and finally, resignation.

11-2 This athlete fits the profile of a suicide risk. He is in a high-risk age group. He has been a successful athlete who now faces surgery and a period of long rehabilitation. He is also facing the possible end of his career, or if he is able to return, he faces being replaced by another athlete.

11-3 The athletic trainer should be aware of the possibility of sudden exercise abstinence syndrome. In this syndrome, the athlete may experience heart palpitations, irregular heartbeat, chest pain, problems with appetite and digestion, sleep disorders, increased sweating, depression, and in some cases, emotional instability.

11-4 The athletic trainer should be empathetic and encourage the athlete to talk and express her feelings. The athletic trainer should avoid being abrupt and avoid showing pity.

11-5 The athletic trainer must develop mutual trust and understanding with the athlete. The athlete must realize that rehabilitation is a cooperative undertaking. Continual education must occur throughout the rehabilitation process.

11-6 The athletic trainer can help the athlete better cope with pain by instructing her in the techniques of tension (stress) reduction, attention diversion, and imaging, such as being in a peaceful place, or by immersing the injury into cold water.

11-7 The athletic trainer teaches the athlete to visualize that healing is maximized through all its stages. All treatment procedures are visualized as being fully effective.

REVIEW QUESTIONS AND CLASS ACTIVITIES

1. What is the importance of psychology to sports injuries?
2. How does stress relate to athlete injuries and illnesses?
3. Discuss the psychology of loss in sports injuries.
4. Describe the physical, emotional, social, and self-concept factors in sports injuries.
5. As an athletic trainer, how would you psychologically assist the athlete about to undergo major knee surgery?
6. Discuss overtraining, staleness, and overuse injuries.
7. What actions would you take with an athlete who is stale?
8. Psychologically, how should an athletic trainer react to serious injury immediately after injury and during the disability?
9. Psychologically, what makes for a successful rehabilitation climate?
10. Discuss psychological problems common to the rehabilitation process and possible ways of intervening.
11. What mental training techniques might be employed to assist the athlete who is fearful and anxious?
12. Practice teaching mental training techniques.

REFERENCES

1. Ahern DK, Lohr BA: Psychological factors in sports injury rehabilitation. In Fadald PD, Hulstyn MS, editors: *Primary care of the injured athlete*, part III, vol 16, no 4, Philadelphia, 1997, WB Saunders.
2. Benson HH: *Beyond the relaxation response*, New York, 1984, Times.
3. Ellis A: *A new guide to rational living*, North Hollywood, Calif, 1975, Wilshire.
4. Faris GJ: Psychological aspects of athletic rehabilitation. In Harvey JS, editor: *Symposium on rehabilitation of the injured athlete. Clinics in sports medicine*, vol 4, no 3, Philadelphia, 1988, Saunders.
5. Fisher AC: Athletic trainer's attitudes and judgments of injured athletes' rehabilitation adherence, *J Ath Train* 28(1):43, 1993.
6. Froehlich J: Overtraining. In Heil J, editor: *Psychology of sport injury*, Champaign, Ill, 1993, Human Kinetics.
7. Gieck JJ, Hedgpeth EB: Considerations for rehabilitation of the injured athlete. In Prentice WE, editor: *Rehabilitation techniques in sports medicine*, ed 3, Dubuque, Iowa, 1999, WCB/McGraw-Hill.
8. Graham DJ: Personality traits relevant to the cause and treatment of athletic injuries, *Sports Med Digest* 15(2):1, 1993.
9. Heil J: Mental training in injury management. In Heil J, editor: *Psychology of sport injury*, Champaign, Ill, 1993, Human Kinetics.
10. Heil J: A psychologist's view of the personal challenge of injury. In Heil J, editor: *Psychology of sport injury*, Champaign, Ill, 1993, Human Kinetics.
11. Heil J: Specialized treatment approaches: problems in rehabilitation. In Heil J, editor: *Psychology of sport injury*, Champaign, Ill, 1993, Human Kinetics.
12. Heil J: Specialized treatment approaches: severe injury. In Heil J, editor: *Psychology of sport injury*, Champaign, Ill, 1993, Human Kinetics.
13. Heil J: Sport psychology, the athlete at risk, and the sports medicine team. In Heil J, editor: *Psychology of sport injury*, Champaign, Ill, 1993, Human Kinetics.
14. Jacobson E: *Progressive relaxation*, ed 2, Chicago, 1938, University of Chicago Press.
15. Koutedakis Y, Sharp NC: Seasonal variations of injury and overtraining in elite athletes, *Cl J Sports Med* 8(1):18, 1998.
16. Mary JR: Psychological sequelae and rehabilitation of the injured athlete, *Sports Med Digest* 12(11):1, 1990.
17. McGuire R: Emotional healing, training, and conditioning, *J Ath Train* 4(4):4, 1994.
18. McKay M et al: *Thoughts and feelings*, Richmond, Calif, 1981, New Harbinger Publications.
19. Pelletier KR: *Mind as healer, mind as slayer*, New York, 1977, Dell.
20. Petrie G: Injury from the athlete's point of view. In Heil J, editor: *Psychology of sport injury*, Champaign, Ill, 1993, Human Kinetics.
21. Richardson PA, Latuda LM: Therapeutic imagery and athletic injuries, *J Ath Train* 30(1):10, 1995.
22. Rotella RJ: Psychological care of the injured athlete. In Kulund DN, editor: *The injured athlete*, Philadelphia, 1988, Lippincott.
23. Selye H: *Stress without distress*, New York, 1974, Lippincott.
24. Sharon P et al: Academic preparation of athletic trainers as counselors, *J Ath Train* 31(1), 1996.
25. Shell D, Ferrante AP: Recognition of adjustment disorders in college athletes: a case study, *Cl J Sports Med* 6(1), 1996.
26. Smith AM, Milliner EK: Injured athletes and the risk of suicide, *J Ath Train* 29(4):337, 1994.
27. Smith AM et al: Emotional responses of athletes to injury, *Mayo Clin Proc* 65:38, 1990.
28. Steadman J: A physician's approach to the psychology of injury. In Heil J, editor: *Psychology of sport injury*, Champaign, Ill, 1993, Human Kinetics.
29. Wandling BJ, Smith BS: Burnout in orthopedic physical therapists, *J Orthop Sports Phys Ther* 26(1), 1997.
30. Wortman CB, Silver RC: The myth of coping with loss, *J Consulting and Clinical Psychology* 57:349, 1989.

ANNOTATED BIBLIOGRAPHY

Heil J, editor: *Psychology of sport injury*, Champaign, Ill, 1993, Human Kinetics.

This text provides an in-depth look at the psychology of sport injury for sports psychologists.

Kreider RB et al: *Overtraining in sport*, Champaign, Ill, 1998, Human Kinetics.

This excellent secondary reference covers the psychological, immunologic, nutritional, and psychological considerations of overtraining in sport.

Selye H: *Stress without distress*, New York, 1974, Lippincott.

This book is a practical guide to understanding the role of stress in life.

Taylor J, Taylor S: *Psychological approaches to sports injury rehabilitation*, Gaithersburg, Md, 1997, Aspen.

This text provides practical techniques and strategies for sports rehabilitation.

On-the-Field Acute Care and Emergency Procedures

When you finish this chapter you should be able to

- Establish a plan for handling an emergency situation at your institution.
- Explain the importance of knowing cardiopulmonary resuscitation and how to manage an obstructed airway.
- Describe the types of hemorrhage and their management.
- Assess the types of shock and their management.
- Describe the emergency management of musculoskeletal injuries.
- Describe techniques for moving and transporting the injured athlete.

Time becomes critical in an emergency situation.

Most sports injuries do not result in life-or-death emergency situations, but when such situations do arise, prompt care is essential. An emergency is defined as an unexpected serious occurrence that may cause injuries that require immediate medical attention.[30] Time becomes the critical factor, and assistance to the injured individual must be based on knowledge of what to do and how to do it, on how to perform effective firstaid immediately. There is no room for uncertainty, indecision, or error. A mistake in the initial management of injury can prolong the length of time required for rehabilitation and can potentially create a life-threatening situation for the athlete.

THE EMERGENCY PLAN

The prime concern of emergency aid is to maintain cardiovascular function and, indirectly, central nervous system function.[2] Failure of either of these systems may lead to death. The key to emergency aid in the sports setting is the initial evaluation of the injured athlete. Time is of the essence, so this evaluation must be done rapidly and accurately so that proper aid can be rendered without delay. In some instances, these first steps not only will be lifesaving but also may determine the degree and extent of permanent disability.

As discussed in Chapters 1 and 3, the sports medicine team—the athletic trainer, the team physician, and the coach—must at all times act reasonably and prudently. This behavior is especially important during emergencies.

All sports programs must have an emergency plan.

All sports programs must have a prearranged emergency plan that can be implemented immediately when necessary.[9,10] The following issues must be addressed when developing the emergency system:

1. Phones should be readily accessible. Cellular or digital phones are best because the athletic trainer can carry one at all times. If cellular phones are not available, the location of the telephone should be well known by student athletic trainers, coaches, and athletes and should be clearly marked. Use 911 if available.
2. The athletic trainer should be familiar with the community-based emergency health care delivery plan, including existing communication and transportation policies. It is also critical for the athletic trainer to be familiar with emergency care facility admission and treatment policies, particularly when rendering emergency care to a minor. The athletic trainer should specifically designate someone to make an emergency phone call. Most emergency medical systems can be accessed by dialing 911, which connects the caller to a dispatcher who has access to rescue squad, police, and fire personnel.

The person making the emergency phone call must provide the following information:

a. Type of emergency situation
b. Type of suspected injury
c. Present condition of the athlete
d. Current assistance being given (e.g., cardiopulmonary resuscitation)
e. Location of telephone being used
f. Exact location of emergency (give names of streets and cross streets) and how to enter facility

3. Keys to gates or padlocks must be easily accessible. Both the athletic trainer and the coach should have the appropriate key.
4. Separate emergency plans should be developed for each sport's fields, courts, or gymnasiums.
5. The athletic trainer should inform all coaches, athletic directors, school nurses, and maintenance personnel of the emergency plan at a meeting held annually before the beginning of the school year. Each individual must know his or her responsibilities should an emergency occur.
6. Someone should be assigned to accompany the injured athlete to the hospital.

Cooperation between Emergency Care Providers

Individuals providing emergency care to the injured athlete must cooperate and act professionally. Occasionally, disagreement arises between rescue squad personnel, the physician, and the athletic trainer over exactly how the injured athlete should be handled and transported. The athletic trainer is usually the first individual to deal with the emergency situation. The athletic trainer has generally had more training and experience in moving and transporting an injured athlete than the physician has. If the rescue squad is called and responds, the emergency medical technicians (EMTs) should have the final say on how that athlete is to be transported while the athletic trainer assumes an assistive role.

To alleviate potential conflicts, the athletic trainer should establish procedures and guidelines and should arrange practice sessions at least once a year that include everyone responsible for handling an injured athlete.[2] Rescue squad personnel may not be experienced in dealing with someone who is wearing a helmet or other protective equipment. The athletic trainer should make sure before an incident occurs that the EMTs understand the correct management of athletes wearing various types of athletic equipment.

Parent Notification

If the injured athlete is a minor, the athletic trainer should try to obtain consent from the parent to treat the athlete during an emergency.[14] Consent may be given in writing either before or during an emergency. This consent is notification that the parent has been informed about what the athletic trainer thinks is wrong and what the athletic trainer intends to do, and parental permission is granted to give treatment for a specific incident. If the athlete's parents cannot be contacted, the predetermined wishes of the parent given at the beginning of a season or school year can be enacted. If no informed consent exists, implied consent on the part of the athlete to save the athlete's life takes precedence.

PRINCIPLES OF ON-THE-FIELD INJURY ASSESSMENT

The athletic trainer cannot deliver appropriate acute medical care to the injured athlete until some systematic assessment of the situation has been made on the playing field or court where the injury occurs. This *on-the-field* assessment helps determine the nature of the injury and provides direction in the decision-making process concerning the emergency care that must be rendered (Figure 12-1). The

Figure 12-1

Flowchart showing the appropriate emergency procedures for the injured athlete.

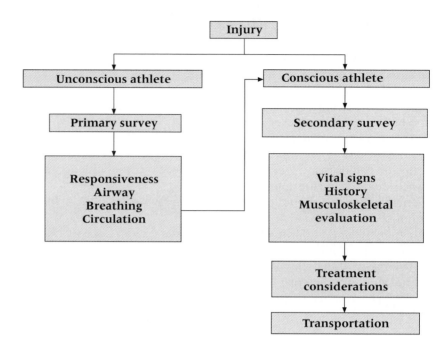

on-the-field assessment may be subdivided into a primary survey and a secondary survey.

The primary survey, which is done initially, determines the existence of potentially life-threatening situations, including problems with airway, breathing, and circulation and with severe bleeding and shock. The primary survey takes precedence over all other aspects of victim assessment and should be used to correct life-threatening situations.[18] Any athlete who has a life-threatening situation should be transported to an emergency care facility as soon as possible.

Once the primary survey has ruled out the existence of a life-threatening injury or illness, the secondary survey takes a closer look at the injury sustained by the athlete. The secondary survey gathers specific information about the injury from the athlete, systematically assesses vital signs and symptoms, and allows for a more detailed evaluation of the injury. The secondary survey is done to uncover problems that do not pose an immediate threat to life but that may do so if they remain uncorrected.[18]

An injured athlete who is conscious and stable will not require a primary survey. However, the unconscious athlete must be monitored for life-threatening problems throughout the assessment process.

Dealing with the Unconscious Athlete

The state of unconsciousness provides one of the greatest dilemmas for the athletic trainer. Whether to move the athlete and allow the game to resume or to await the arrival of a physician is a decision that too often is resolved hastily and without much forethought. Unconsciousness may be defined as a state of insensibility in which the athlete exhibits a lack of conscious awareness. This condition can be brought about by a blow to either the head or the solar plexus, or it may result from general shock. It is often difficult to determine the exact cause of unconsciousness (Table 12-1).

The unconscious athlete must always be considered to have a life-threatening injury, which requires an immediate primary survey. The following guidelines should be used when working with the unconscious athlete:

1. The athletic trainer should immediately note the body position and determine the level of consciousness and unresponsiveness.

TABLE 12-1 Evaluating the Unconscious Athlete

Functional Signs		Selected Conditions					
	Fainting	Concussion	Grand Mal Epilepsy	Brain Compression and Injury	Heatstroke	Diabetic Coma	Shock
Onset	Usually sudden	Usually sudden	Sudden	Usually gradual	Gradual or sudden	Gradual	Gradual
Mentality	Complete unconsciousness	Confusion or unconsciousness	Unconsciousness	Unconsciousness, gradually deepening	Delirium or unconsciousness	Drowsiness, later unconsciousness	Listlessness, later unconsciousness
Pulse	Feeble and fast	Feeble and irregular	Fast	Gradually slower	Fast and feeble	Fast and feeble	Fast and feeble
Respiration	Quick and shallow	Shallow and irregular	Noisy, later deep and slow	Slow and noisy	Difficult	Deep and sighing	Rapid and shallow, with occasional deep sigh
Skin	Pale, cold, and clammy	Pale and cold	Livid, later pale	Hot and flushed	Hot and relatively dry	Livid, later pale	Pale, cold, and clammy
Pupils	Equal and dilated	Equal	Equal and dilated	Unequal	Equal	Equal	Equal and dilated
Paralysis	None	None	None	May be present in leg, arm, or both	None	None	None
Convulsions	None	None	None	Present in some cases	Present in some cases	None	None
Breath	N/A	N/A	N/A	N/A	N/A	Acetone smell	N/A
Special features	Giddiness and sway before collapse	Signs of head injury, vomiting during recovery	Bites tongue, voids urine and feces, may injure self while falling	Signs of head injury, delayed onset of symptoms	Vomiting in some cases	In early stages, headache, restlessness, and nausea	May vomit; early stages shivering, thirst, defective vision, and ear noises

2. Airway, breathing, and circulation should be established immediately.

3. Injury to the neck and spine should always be considered a possibility in the unconscious athlete.[5]

4. If the athlete is wearing a helmet, it should never be removed until neck and spine injury have been unequivocally ruled out. However, the face mask must be cut away and removed to allow for cardiopulmonary resuscitation (CPR).

5. If the athlete is supine and not breathing, airway, breathing, and circulation (ABC) should be established immediately.

6. If the athlete is supine and breathing, nothing should be done until consciousness returns.

7. If the athlete is prone and not breathing, he or she should be logrolled carefully to the supine position and ABC should be established immediately.

8. If the athlete is prone and breathing, nothing should be done until consciousness returns, then the athlete should be carefully logrolled onto a spine board because CPR could be necessary at any time.

9. Life support for the unconscious athlete should be monitored and maintained until emergency medical personnel arrive.

10. Once the athlete is stabilized, the athletic trainer should begin a secondary survey.

THE PRIMARY SURVEY

Treatment of Life-Threatening Injuries

Life-threatening injuries take precedence over all other injuries sustained by the athlete. Situations that are considered life-threatening include those that require cardiopulmonary resuscitation (i.e., obstruction of the airway, no breathing, no circulation), profuse bleeding, and shock.

Overview of Emergency Cardiopulmonary Resuscitation

A careful evaluation of the injured person must be made to determine whether CPR should be conducted. This overview of adult CPR is not intended to be used by persons who are not certified in CPR. Because of the serious nature of CPR, recertification should routinely be sought through the American Red Cross, the American Heart Association, or the National Safety Council.

First, establish unresponsiveness of the athlete by tapping or gently shaking his or her shoulder and shouting, "Are you okay?" Note that shaking should be avoided if there is a possible neck injury. If the athlete is unresponsive, the emergency medical system (EMS) should be activated immediately by sending someone to dial 911. Carefully position the athlete in the supine position. If the athlete is in a position other than supine, he or she must be carefully rolled over as a unit, avoiding any twisting of the body, because CPR can be administered only with the athlete lying flat on the back with knees straight or slightly flexed (see Figure 12-6). In cases of suspected cervical spine injury, care must be taken to minimize cervical movement during logrolling. Then proceed with CPR.[18]

Equipment Considerations

Protective equipment worn by an athlete may complicate lifesaving CPR procedures. The presence of a football, ice hockey, or lacrosse helmet as well as a face mask and various types of shoulder pads will obviously make CPR more difficult if not impossible. Over the years, significant debate has raged in the sports medicine community regarding removal of the helmet in an athlete with suspected cervical spine injury, and a number of differing opinions have been expressed. [6,11,13,16,17,19,20,22,24,25,26,27,29]

It has been proposed that removing the face mask should be the first step.[25] The face mask does not hinder the evaluation of the airway, but it may hinder

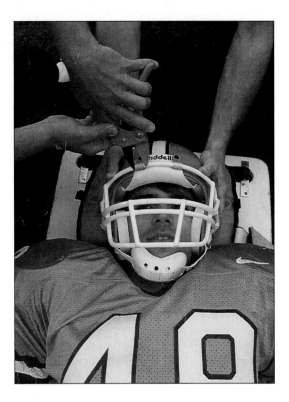

Figure 12-2

Various clipping devices such as the Anvil Pruner, the Trainer's Angel, and the FM extractor have been recommended for their effectiveness in quickly cutting plastic clips.

treatment.[3] Various instruments have been recommended to remove the face mask, including electric screwdrivers, which work well as long as the screws are not rusted, wire cutters, bolt cutters, trainer's scissors, and scalpels, none of which work very well. Two devices, the Anvil Pruner and the Trainer's Angel, have been recommended for their effectiveness in quickly cutting the plastic clips (Figure 12-2).[19] It has also been suggested that the athletic trainer must be proficient in removing the face mask within thirty seconds.[19] Studies comparing the efficacy of using these various devices suggest that the Anvil Pruner seems to be easier to use than the Trainer's Angel.[13] Furthermore, using a Trainer's Angel seems to cause more motion in the cervical spine than either a manual or powered screwdriver.[27] Recently the FM Extractor has been introduced as another tool for removing the face mask.

In 1992 the Occupational Safety and Health Administration (OSHA) mandated the use of a barrier device or pocket mask to protect the athletic trainer from transmission of bloodborne pathogens during CPR (see Figure 13-4B). It is possible to slip the pocket mask under the face mask, attach the one-way mouthpiece or valve through the bars of the face mask, and begin CPR within five to ten seconds without removing the face mask.[26] Also, use of a pocket mask appears to cause less extraneous motion in the cervical spine than does the use of either screwdrivers or the Trainer's Angel to remove the face mask.[27]

As mentioned earlier, controversy exists as to whether the helmet and shoulder pads should be left in place or removed.[20] The decision to remove the helmet and shoulder pads before initiating CPR should be based on the potential of injury to the cervical spine. If it is reasonably certain that no injury has occurred to the cervical spine, both the helmet and shoulder pads can be quickly removed before initiating CPR. If injury to the cervical spine is a possibility, care must be taken to minimize movement of the head and neck while CPR is being performed. The current recommendation, if cervical spine injury is a possiblity, is to leave the helmet and shoulder pads in place.[16,17] (See Appendix C for the NATA position statement.)

The athletic trainer must either remove both the helmet and shoulder pads or leave them both in place. Removing one or the other independently will force the cervical spine into either flexion or extension. If they are left in place, the face mask should be dealt with as recommended previously, and the jersey and shoulder pad strings or straps should be cut, spreading the shoulder pads apart so that the chest may be compressed according to CPR guidelines. Although removal of the helmet and shoulder pads has been recommended,[4] it seems that no matter how much care is taken, removal would create unnecessary movement of the cervical spine and would delay initiation of CPR, neither of which is best for the injured athlete. If cervical neck injury is suspected, yet the athlete is conscious and breathing and does not require CPR, the athlete should be transported with the helmet, chin strap, and shoulder pads in place. The face mask should be removed in case CPR becomes necessary.

The ABCs of CPR

The ABCs of CPR are easily remembered and indicate the sequential steps used for basic life support:[1,18]

1. A—airway opened
2. B—breathing restored
3. C—circulation restored

Frequently, when A is restored, B and C will resume spontaneously, and it is then unnecessary to perform them. In some instances, the restoration of A and B obviates the necessity for step C. When performing CPR on an adult victim, the following sequence should be followed.

Opening the airway   Open the airway by using the head tilt–chin lift method.[32] Lift under the chin with one hand while pushing down on the victim's forehead with the other, avoiding the use of excessive force. The tongue is the most common cause of airway obstruction; the forward lift of the jaw raises the tongue away from the back of the throat, thus clearing the airway.

NOTE: On victims with suspected head or neck injuries, perform a modified jaw thrust maneuver by grasping each side of the lower jaw at the angles, thus displacing the lower mandible forward as the head is tilted backward.[32] In executing this maneuver, both elbows should rest on the same surface as that on which the victim is lying. Should the lips close, they can be opened by retracting the lower lip with a thumb. If the victim is not breathing, additional forward displacement of the jaw may help.

Establishing breathing

1. To determine if the victim is breathing, maintain the open airway, place your ear over the victim's mouth, observe the chest, and look, listen, and feel for breath sounds.
2. With the hand that is on the athlete's forehead, pinch the nose shut, keeping the heel of the hand in place to hold the head back (if there is no neck injury) (Figure 12-3). Taking a deep breath, place your mouth over the athlete's mouth to provide an airtight seal and give two slow, full breaths at a rate of $1^1/_2$ to 2 seconds per inflation. Observe the chest rise and fall. Remove your mouth, and listen for the air to escape through passive exhalation. If the airway is obstructed, reposition the victim's head and try again to ventilate. If still obstructed, give up to five abdominal thrusts followed by a finger sweep with the index finger to clear objects from the mouth. Be careful not to push the object further into the throat. Continue to repeat this sequence until ventilation occurs.

If available, a bag/valve mask may be used for artificial respiration. Although the bag/valve mask is easy to use, some instruction and practice in its use is recommended (Figure 12-4A). NOTE: OSHA has mandated the use of barrier shields by athletic trainers to minimize the risk of transmitting bloodborne pathogens (Figure 12-4B). These shields have a plastic or silicone sheet that spreads over the face and separates the athletic trainer from the athlete. Some models have a tubelike mouthpiece, which may help in situations in which the athlete is wearing a face mask.

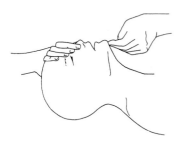

Figure 12-3

Head tilt–chin lift technique for establishing an airway.

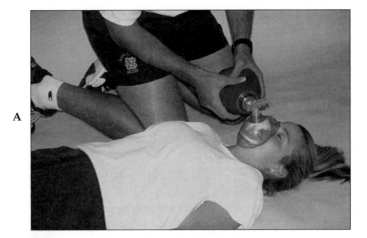

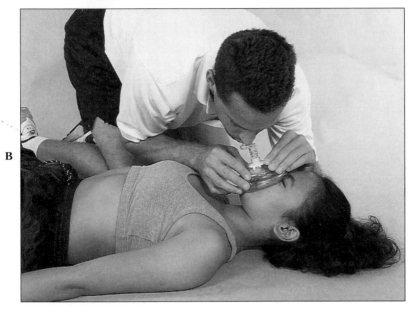

Figure 12-4

A, A bag/valve mask can be used for respiration. **B,** A barrier mask protects the athletic trainer from potential exposure to bloodborne pathogens.

Establishing circulation

1. To determine pulselessness, locate the Adam's apple with the index and middle fingers of the hand closest to the head. Then slide the fingers down into the groove on the side of the body on which you are kneeling to locate the carotid artery. Palpate the carotid pulse with one hand (allow five to ten seconds) while maintaining head tilt with the other.

2. Maintain open airway. Position yourself close to the side of the athlete's chest. With the middle and index fingers of the hand closest to the waist, locate the lower margin of the athlete's rib cage on the side next to you (Figure 12-5).

3. Run the fingers up along the rib cage to the xiphoid notch, where the ribs meet the sternum.

4. Place the middle finger on the notch and the index finger next to it on the lower end of the sternum.

5. Next, the hand closest to the athlete's head is positioned on the lower half of the sternum next to the index finger of the first hand that located the notch; the heel of that hand is placed on the long axis of the sternum.

6. The first hand is then removed from the notch and placed on top of the hand on the sternum so that the heels of both hands are parallel and the fingers are directed straight away from the athletic trainer (Figure 12-6).

7. Fingers can be extended or interlaced, but they must be kept off the chest wall.

Figure 12-5

With the middle and index fingers of the hand closest to the waist, the lower margin of the victim's rib cage is located. The fingers are then run along the rib cage to the notch where the ribs meet the sternum. The middle finger is placed on the notch with the index finger next to it on the lower end of the sternum.

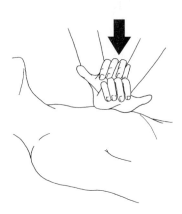

Figure 12-6

The heel of the headward hand is placed on the long axis of the lower half of the sternum next to the index finger of the first hand. The first hand is removed from the notch and placed on top of the hand on the sternum.

All coaches and athletic trainers must have current CPR certification.

8. Elbows are kept in a locked position with arms straight and shoulders positioned over the hands, enabling the thrust to be straight down.

9. In a normal-sized adult, enough force must be applied to depress the sternum $1\frac{1}{2}$ to 2 inches (4 to 5 cm). After depression, there must be complete release of the sternum to allow the heart to refill. The time of release should equal the time of compression. For one rescuer, compression must be given at the rate of 80 to 100 times per minute, maintaining a rate of fifteen chest compressions to two full breaths.

10. After four cycles of fifteen compressions and two breaths (15:2), or about one minute, recheck the pulse at the carotid artery (allow five seconds) while maintaining head tilt. If no pulse is found, continue the 15:2 cycle beginning with chest compressions.

Every coach and athletic trainer should be certified in CPR and should take a refresher examination at least once a year. All assistants should be certified as well.

Obstructed Airway Management

Choking is a possibility in many sports activities; for example, an athlete may choke on a mouth guard, a broken bit of dental work, chewing gum, or even a chaw of tobacco. When such emergencies arise, early recognition and prompt, knowledgeable action are necessary to avert a tragedy. An unconscious athlete can have an obstructed airway when the tongue falls back in the throat, thus blocking the upper airway. Blood clots resulting from head, facial, or dental injuries may impede normal breathing, as may vomiting. When complete airway obstruction occurs, the individual is unable to speak, cough, or breathe. If the athlete is conscious, there is a tremendous effort made to breathe, the head is forced back, and the face initially is flushed and then becomes cyanotic as oxygen deprivation occurs. If partial airway obstruction is causing the choking, some air passage can be detected, but during a complete obstruction no air movement is discernible.

To relieve airway obstruction caused by foreign bodies, two maneuvers are recommended: the Heimlich maneuver and finger sweeps of the mouth and throat.

Heimlich maneuver   As with CPR, the Heimlich maneuver (subdiaphragmatic abdominal thrusts) requires practice before proficiency is acquired. The Heimlich maneuver offers two methods of obstructed airway management, depending on whether the victim is in an erect position or has collapsed and is either unconscious or too heavy to lift. For the conscious victim, the standing Heimlich maneuver (Method A) is performed until he or she is relieved. In cases of unconsciousness, five abdominal thrusts are applied, followed by a finger sweep with an attempt at ventilation (Method B).

Method A   Stand behind and to one side of the athlete. Place both arms around the waist just above the belt line, and permit the athlete's head, arms, and upper trunk to hang forward (Figure 12-7A). Grasp one of your fists with the other, placing the thumb side of the grasped fist immediately below the xiphoid process of the sternum, clear of the rib cage. Now sharply and forcefully thrust the fists into the abdomen, inward and upward, several times. This "hug" pushes up on the diaphragm, compressing the air in the lungs, creating forceful pressure against the blockage, and thus usually causing the obstruction to be promptly expelled. Repeat the maneuver until the athlete is relieved or becomes unconscious. If the athlete loses consciousness, activate the EMS system, perform a finger sweep, open the airway, and try to ventilate. If the airway is still obstructed, reposition the head and try again. Then give up to five abdominal thrusts. Repeat this sequence as long as necessary.

Method B   If the athlete is on the ground or on the floor, place him or her on the back and straddle the victim's thighs, keeping your weight centered over your knees. Place the heel of one hand against the back of your other hand and push sharply into the abdomen just above the umbilicus (note the position, Figure 12-7B). Repeat this maneuver up to five times, and then repeat the finger sweep.

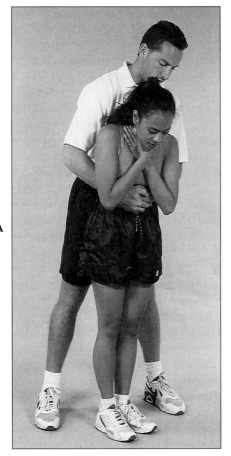

Figure 12-7

The Heimlich maneuver for an obstructed airway. **A,** Manual thrust maneuver for the conscious athlete. **B,** Manual thrust maneuver for the unconscious athlete.

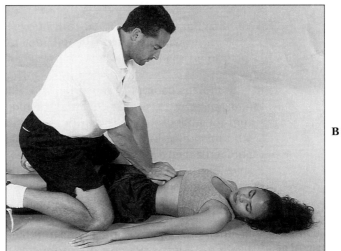

A

B

Care must be taken in either of these methods to avoid extreme force or applying force over the rib cage because fractures of the ribs and damage to the organs can result.

Finger sweeping   If a foreign object such as a mouth guard is lodged in the mouth or the throat and is visible, it may be possible to remove or release it with the fingers. Care must be taken that the probing does not drive the object deeper into the throat. It is usually impossible to open the mouth of a conscious victim who is in distress, so the Heimlich maneuver should be used immediately. In the unconscious athlete, turn the head either to the side or face up, open the mouth by grasping the tongue and the lower jaw, hold them firmly between the thumb and fingers, and lift—an action that pulls the tongue away from the back of the throat and from the impediment. If this action is difficult to do, the crossed finger method can usually be used effectively. The index finger of the free hand (or if both hands are used, an assistant can probe) should be inserted into one side of the mouth along the cheek deeply into the throat; using a hooking maneuver, attempt to free the impediment, moving it into a position from which it can be removed (Figure 12-8). Attempt to ventilate after each sweep until the airway is open. Once the object is removed, if the athlete is not already breathing, attempt to ventilate.

Using a Defibrillator

In most states, athletic trainers can be certified to use an automated external defibrillator (AED) in situations in which the victim has no pulse. These portable defibrillators are simple to operate. The athletic trainer must simply follow a series of voice

Figure 12-8

A finger sweep of the mouth is essential in attempting to remove a foreign object from a choking victim.

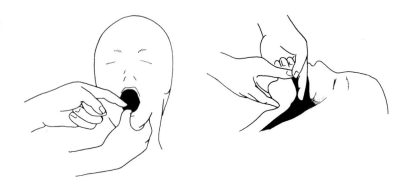

Critical Thinking Exercise

A soccer player jumps to win a head ball and an opponent's head smashes his right eyebrow, creating a significant laceration. The athlete is conscious but is bleeding profusely from the wound.

? What techniques may be most effectively used to control the bleeding, and what should be done to close the wound?

External bleeding can usually be managed through direct pressure, elevation, or pressure points.

Figure 12-9

Direct pressure for the control of bleeding is applied with the hand over a sterile gauze pad.

and auditory prompts without requiring the users discretion or judgment to perform the procedure. The AMA estimates that 2,000 lives could be saved annually by using an AED.

Control of Hemorrhage

An abnormal discharge of blood is called a hemorrhage. The hemorrhage may be venous, capillary, or arterial and may be external or internal. Venous blood is characteristically dark red with a continuous flow; capillary bleeding exudes from tissue and is a reddish color; and arterial bleeding flows in spurts and is bright red. NOTE: The athletic trainer must be concerned with exposure to bloodborne pathogens and other diseases when coming into contact with blood or other body fluids. It is essential to take universal precautions to minimize this risk. Disposable latex gloves should be used routinely whenever the athletic trainer comes into contact with blood or other body fluids. This topic is discussed in detail in Chapter 14.

External Bleeding

External bleeding stems from open skin wounds such as abrasions, incisions, lacerations, punctures, or avulsions (see Chapter 28 for further discussion). The control of external bleeding includes the use of direct pressure, elevation, and pressure points.[31]

Direct pressure   Pressure is directly applied with the hand over a sterile gauze pad. The pressure is applied firmly against the resistance of a bone (Figure 12-9).

Elevation   Elevation, in combination with direct pressure, provides an additional means for the reduction of external hemorrhage. Elevating a hemorrhaging part against gravity reduces hydrostatic blood pressure and facilitates venous and lymphatic drainage, which slows bleeding.

Pressure points   When direct pressure combined with elevation fails to slow hemorrhage, the use of pressure points may be the method of choice. Eleven points on each side of the body have been identified for controlling external bleeding; the two most commonly used are the brachial artery in the upper limb and the femoral artery in the lower limb. The brachial artery is compressed against the medial aspect of the humerus, and the femoral artery is compressed as it is detected within the femoral triangle (Figure 12-10).

Internal Hemorrhage

Internal hemorrhage is invisible to the eye unless manifested through some body opening or identified through X-ray studies or other diagnostic techniques. Its danger lies in the difficulty of diagnosis. When internal hemorrhaging occurs, either subcutaneously such as in a bruise or contusion, intramuscularly, or in joints, the athlete may be moved without danger in most instances. However, the detection of bleeding within a body cavity such as the skull, thorax, or abdomen is of the utmost importance because it could mean the difference between life and death. Because the symptoms are obscure, internal hemorrhage is difficult to diagnose properly. As a result, athletes with internal injuries require hospitalization under complete and constant observation by a medical staff to determine the nature and extent of the injuries. All severe hemorrhaging will eventually result in shock and should therefore be treated on this premise. Even if the athlete shows no outward indication of shock, he or she should be kept quiet and body heat should be maintained at a constant and suitable temperature. (See the following section on shock for the preferred body position.)

Shock

With any injury, shock is a possibility.[31] But when severe bleeding, fractures, or internal injuries are present, the development of shock is more likely. Shock occurs when a diminished amount of blood is available to the circulatory system, that is, when the vascular system loses its capacity to hold the fluid portion of the blood within its system because of dilation of the blood vessels within the body and disruption of the osmotic fluid balance. When shock occurs, a quantity of only plasma moves from the blood vessels into the tissue spaces of the body, leaving the blood cells within the vessels, causing stagnation, and slowing the blood flow. As a result, not enough oxygen-carrying blood cells are available to the tissues, particularly those of the nervous system. With this general collapse of the vascular system comes widespread tissue death, which will eventually cause the death of the individual unless treatment is given.

Certain conditions, such as extreme fatigue, extreme exposure to heat or cold, extreme dehydration of fluids and mineral loss, or illness, predispose an athlete to shock. In a situation in which there is a potential shock condition, there are other signs by which the athletic trainer should assess the possibility of the athlete's lapsing into a state of shock as an aftermath of the injury. The most important clue to potential shock is the recognition of a severe injury. It may happen that none of the usual signs of shock is present.[31]

The main types of shock are hypovolemic, respiratory, neurogenic, psychogenic, cardiogenic, septic, anaphylactic, and metabolic.[1]

Hypovolemic shock stems from trauma in which there is blood loss. Decreased blood volume causes a decrease in blood pressure. Without enough blood in the circulatory system, organs are not properly supplied with oxygen.

Respiratory shock occurs when the lungs are unable to supply enough oxygen to the circulating blood. Trauma that produces a pneumothorax or an injury to the breathing control mechanism can produce respiratory shock.

Neurogenic shock is caused by the general dilation of blood vessels within the cardiovascular system. When it occurs, the typical six liters of blood can no longer fill the system. As a result, the cardiovascular system can no longer supply oxygen to the body.

Psychogenic shock refers to what is commonly known as fainting (syncope). It is caused by a temporary dilation of blood vessels that reduces the normal amount of blood in the brain.

Cardiogenic shock refers to the inability of the heart to pump enough blood to the body.

Septic shock occurs from a severe, usually bacterial, infection. Toxins liberated from the bacteria cause small blood vessels in the body to dilate.

Anaphylactic shock is the result of a severe allergic reaction caused by foods, insect stings, or drugs or by inhaling dusts, pollens, or other substances.

Metabolic shock happens when a severe illness such as diabetes goes untreated. Another cause is an extreme loss of bodily fluid (e.g., through urination, vomiting, or diarrhea).

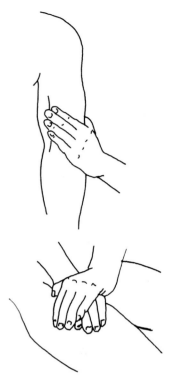

Figure 12-10

The two most common sites for direct pressure are the brachial artery and the femoral artery.

12-3

Critical Thinking Exercise

A wrestler is thrown to the mat and suffers an open fracture of both the radius and ulna in the forearm. There is significant bleeding from the wound. The athlete begins to complain of light-headedness, his skin is pale and feels cool and clammy, and his pulse becomes rapid and weak.

? What potential problem may be developing, and how should the athletic trainer manage this situation?

Symptoms and Signs

The major signs of shock are moist, pale, cool, clammy skin; weak and rapid pulse; a respiratory rate that becomes increased and shallow; decreased blood pressure; and in severe situations, urinary retention and fecal incontinence.[7,18] If conscious, the athlete may display a disinterest in his or her surroundings or may display irritability, restlessness, or excitement. There may also be extreme thirst.

Management

Depending on the causative factor for the shock, the following emergency care should be given:
1. Maintain body temperature as close to normal as possible.
2. Elevate the feet and legs eight to twelve inches for most situations. However, shock positioning varies according to the type of injury.[7] For a neck injury, for example, the athlete should be immobilized as found; for a head injury, his or her head and shoulders should be elevated; and for a leg fracture, his or her legs should be kept level and should be raised after splinting.

Shock can also be compounded or even initially produced by the psychological reaction of the athlete to an injury situation. Fear or the sudden realization that a serious situation has occurred can result in shock. In the case of a psychological reaction to an injury, the athlete should be instructed to lie down and avoid viewing the injury. The athlete should be handled with patience and gentleness, but firmness as well. Spectators should be kept away from the injured athlete. Reassurance is of vital concern to the injured individual. The person should be given immediate comfort through the loosening of clothing. Nothing should be given by mouth until a physician has determined that no surgical procedures are indicated.

THE SECONDARY SURVEY

After the primary survey has determined that no life-threatening injuries or illnesses presently exist, and the athlete appears to be in stable condition, the athletic trainer should conduct an on-the-field secondary survey to assess the existing injury more precisely.

Recognizing Vital Signs

The ability to recognize physiological signs of injury is essential to the proper handling of potentially critical injuries. When evaluating the seriously ill or injured athlete, the coach, athletic trainer, or physician must be aware of nine response areas: heart rate, breathing rate, blood pressure, temperature, skin color, pupils of the eye, movement, the presence of pain, and unconsciousness.

Pulse

The pulse is the direct extension of the functioning heart. In emergency situations, pulse is usually determined at the carotid artery at the neck or the radial artery in the wrist (Figure 12-11). A normal pulse rate per minute for adults ranges between

---

Signs of shock:
- Blood pressure is low
- Systolic pressure is usually below 90 mm Hg
- Pulse is rapid and weak
- Athlete may be drowsy and appear sluggish
- Respiration is shallow and extremely rapid
- Skin is pale, cool, and clammy

Vital signs to observe:
- Pulse
- Respiration
- Blood pressure
- Temperature
- Skin color
- Pupils
- State of consciousness
- Movement
- Abnormal nerve response

Figure 12-11

Pulse rate taken at **A,** the carotid artery, and **B,** the radial artery.

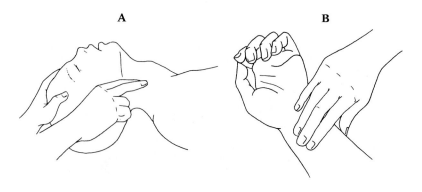

A   B

60 and 80 beats, and in children, between 80 to 100 beats; however, trained athletes usually have slower pulses than the typical population.

An alteration of a pulse from normal may indicate the presence of a pathological condition. For example, a rapid but weak pulse could mean shock, bleeding, diabetic coma, or heat exhaustion. A rapid and strong pulse may mean heatstroke or severe fright; a strong but slow pulse could indicate a skull fracture or stroke; and no pulse means cardiac arrest or death.[7]

Respiration

The normal breathing rate per minute is approximately 12 breaths in adults and 20 to 25 breaths in children. Breathing may be shallow (indicating shock), irregular, or gasping (indicating cardiac involvement). Frothy blood being coughed up indicates a chest injury, such as a fractured rib, that has affected a lung. The athletic trainer should look, listen, and feel: look to ascertain whether the chest is rising or falling; listen for air passing in and out of the mouth, nose, or both; and feel where the chest is moving.

Blood Pressure

Blood pressure, as measured by the sphygmomanometer, indicates the amount of pressure exerted against the arterial walls. It is indicated at two pressure levels: systolic and diastolic. **Systolic blood pressure** occurs when the left ventricle contracts, thereby pumping blood, and **diastolic blood pressure** is the residual pressure present in the arteries when the heart is between beats. The normal systolic pressure for fifteen- to twenty-year-old males ranges from 115 to 120 mm Hg (millimeters of mercury). The diastolic pressure usually ranges from 75 to 80 mm Hg. The normal blood pressure for females is usually 8 to 10 mm Hg lower than in males for both systolic and diastolic pressures. Between the ages of fifteen and twenty, a systolic pressure of 135 mm Hg and above may be excessive; 110 mm Hg and below may be considered too low. The outer ranges for diastolic pressure should not exceed 60 and 85 mm Hg, respectively. A lowered blood pressure could indicate hemorrhage, shock, heart attack, or internal organ injury.

Blood pressure is measured by applying the cuff circumferentially around the upper arm just proximal to the elbow (Figure 12-12). The cuff should be inflated to 200 mm Hg, which occludes blood flow in the brachial artery distal to the cuff in the cubital fossa. The cuff should be slowly deflated with the stethoscope in place; the first beating sound is recorded as systolic pressure. The cuff continues to be deflated until the beating sound disappears; diastolic pressure is then recorded.

systolic blood pressure
The pressure caused by the heart's pumping.

diastolic blood pressure
The residual pressure when the heart is between beats.

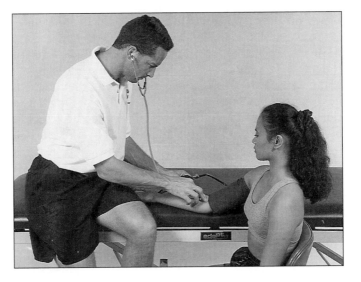

Figure 12-12

Blood pressure is measured using a sphygmomanometer and a stethoscope.

Figure 12-13

Thermometer for measuring tympanic membrane temperature.

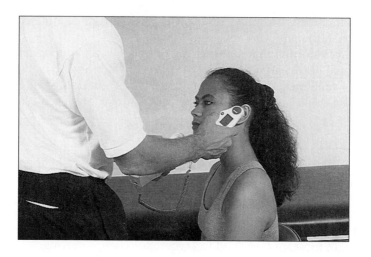

Temperature

To convert Fahrenheit to centigrade (Celsius): °C = (°F − 32) ÷ 1.8

To convert centigrade to Fahrenheit: °F = (1.8 × °C) + 32

Body temperature is maintained by water evaporation and heat radiation. It is normally 98.6° F (37° C). Temperature is measured with a thermometer, which is placed under the tongue, in the armpit, against the tympanic membrane in the ear, or, in case of unconsciousness, in the rectum. Core temperature is most accurately measured in the rectum or at the tympanic membrane in the ear (Figure 12-13). Changes in body temperature can be reflected in the skin. For example, hot, dry skin might indicate disease, infection, or overexposure to environmental heat. Cool, clammy skin could reflect trauma, shock, or heat exhaustion; cool, dry skin is possibly the result of overexposure to cold.

A rise or fall of internal temperature may be caused by a variety of circumstances such as the onset of a communicable disease, cold exposure, pain, fear, or nervousness. Characteristically, a lowered body temperature is accompanied by chills with chattering teeth, blue lips, goose bumps, and pale skin.

Skin Color

For individuals who are lightly pigmented, the skin can be a good indicator of the state of health. In this instance, three colors are commonly identified in medical emergencies: red, white, and blue. A red skin color may indicate heatstroke, high blood pressure, or elevated temperature. A pale, ashen, or white skin can mean insufficient circulation, shock, fright, hemorrhage, heat exhaustion, or insulin shock. Skin that is bluish in color (cyanotic), primarily noted in lips and fingernails, usually means an airway obstruction or respiratory insufficiency.

Assessing skin color in a dark-skinned athlete is more difficult. These individuals normally have pink coloration of the nail beds and inside the lips, mouth, and tongue. When a dark-skinned person goes into shock, the skin around the mouth and nose will often have a grayish cast, and the tongue, the inside of the mouth, the lips, and the nail beds will have a bluish cast. Shock resulting from hemorrhage will cause the tongue and inside of the mouth to become a pale, grayish color instead of blue. Fever in these athletes can be noted by a red flush at the tips of the ears.[7]

Pupils

Some athletes normally have irregular and unequal pupils.

The pupils of the eyes are extremely sensitive to situations affecting the nervous system. Although most persons have pupils of regular outline and equal size, some individuals normally have pupils that may be irregular and unequal. This disparity requires the athletic trainer to know which athletes deviate from the norm.

A constricted pupil may indicate that the athlete is using a central nervous system depressant drug. If one or both pupils are dilated, the athlete may have sustained a head injury; may be experiencing shock, heatstroke, or hemorrhage; or may have ingested a stimulant drug (Figure 12-14). The pupils' response to light should also be noted. If one or both pupils fail to accommodate to light, there may be brain injury or alcohol or drug poisoning. When examining an athlete's pupils, the examiner should note the presence of contact lenses. Pupil response is more critical in evaluation than pupil size.

State of Consciousness

When recognizing vital signs, the examiner must always note the athlete's state of consciousness. Normally the athlete is alert, is aware of the environment, and responds quickly to vocal stimulation. Head injury, heatstroke, and diabetic coma can alter the athlete's level of conscious awareness.

Movement

The inability to move a body part can indicate a serious central nervous system injury that has involved the motor system. An inability to move one side of the body (hemiplegia) could be caused by a head injury or cerebrovascular accident (stroke). Bilateral tingling and numbness or sensory or motor deficits of the upper extremity may indicate a cervical spine injury. Weakness or inability to move the lower extremities could mean an injury below the neck, and pressure on the spinal cord could lead to limited use of the limbs.[7,18]

Abnormal Nerve Response

The injured athlete's pain or other reactions to adverse stimuli can provide valuable clues to the coach or athletic trainer. Numbness or tingling in a limb with or without movement can indicate nerve or cold damage. Blocking of a main artery can produce severe pain, loss of sensation, or lack of a pulse in a limb. A complete lack of pain or of awareness of serious but obvious injury may be caused by shock, hysteria, drug usage, or a spinal cord injury. Generalized or localized pain in the injured region probably means there is no injury to the spinal cord.

Musculoskeletal Assessment

A logical process must be used to evaluate accurately the extent of a musculoskeletal injury. The athletic trainer must be aware of the major signs that reveal the site, nature, and above all, severity of the injury. Detection of these signs can be facilitated by understanding the mechanism or traumatic sequence and by methodically inspecting the injury. Knowledge of the mechanism of an injury is extremely important in determining which area of the body is most affected. When the injury mechanism has been determined, the examiner proceeds to the next phase: physical inspection of the affected region. At this point, information is gathered by what is seen, heard, and felt.

In an attempt to understand the mechanism of injury, a brief history of the complaint must be taken. The athlete is asked, if possible, about the events leading up to the injury and how it occurred. The athlete is further asked what was heard or felt when the injury took place. Sounds occurring at the time of injury or during manual inspection yield pertinent information about the type and extent of pathology present. Such uncommon sounds as grating or harsh rubbing may indicate fracture. Joint sounds may be detected when either arthritis or internal derangement is present. Areas of the body that have abnormal amounts of fluid may produce crepitus when palpated or moved. Such sounds as a snap, crack, or pop at the moment of injury often indicate bone fracture or injury to ligaments or tendon.

The athletic trainer makes a visual observation of the injured site, comparing it to the uninjured body part. The initial visual examination can disclose obvious deformity, swelling, and skin discoloration.

Finally, the region of the injury is gently palpated. Feeling, or palpating, a part with trained fingers can, in conjunction with visual and audible signs, indicate the

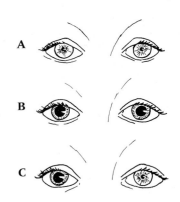

Figure 12-14

The pupils of the eyes are extremely sensitive to situations affecting the nervous system. **A,** Normal pupils. **B,** Dilated pupils. **C,** Irregular pupils.

nature of the injury. Palpation is started away from the injury and gradually moves toward it. As the examiner gently feels the injury and surrounding structures with the fingertips, several factors can be revealed: the extent of point tenderness, the extent of irritation (whether it is confined to soft tissue alone or extends to the bony tissue), and deformities that may not be detected by visual examination alone.

Assessment Decisions

After a quick on-site injury inspection and evaluation, the athletic trainer makes the following decisions:

1. The seriousness of the injury.
2. The type of first aid and immobilization necessary.
3. Whether the injury warrants immediate referral to a physician for further assessment.
4. The manner of transportation from the injury site to the sidelines, training room, or hospital.

All information about the initial history, signs, and symptoms of the injury must be documented, if possible, so that they may be described in detail to the physician.

Immediate Treatment

Musculoskeletal injuries are extremely common in sports. The athletic trainer must be prepared to provide appropriate first aid immediately to control hemorrhage and associated swelling. Every first aid effort should be directed toward one primary goal—reducing the amount of swelling resulting from the injury.[23] If swelling can be controlled initially, the amount of time required for injury rehabilitation will be significantly reduced. Initial management of musculoskeletal injuries should include rest, ice, compression, and elevation (RICE).

Rest   Rest after any type of injury is an extremely important component of any treatment program. Once a body part is injured, it immediately begins the healing process.[23] If the injured part is not rested and is subjected to external stresses and strains, the healing process never takes place. Consequently, the injured part does not heal, and the time required for rehabilitation is greatly increased. The number of days necessary for resting varies with the severity of the injury. Parts of the body that have experienced minor injury should rest for approximately seventy-two hours before a rehabilitation program is begun.

Ice (cold application)   The initial treatment of acute injuries should use cold.[12] Therefore ice is used for most conditions involving strains, sprains, and contusions. Cold is most commonly used immediately after injury to decrease pain and promote local constriction of the vessels (vasoconstriction), thus controlling hemorrhage and edema.[23] Cold applied to an acute injury will lower metabolism and tissue demands for oxygen and will reduce hypoxia.[12] This benefit extends to uninjured tissue, preventing injury-related tissue death from spreading to adjacent normal cellular structures. Cold is also used in the acute phase of inflammatory conditions such as bursitis, tenosynovitis, and tendinitis conditions in which heat may cause additional pain and swelling. Cold is also used to reduce the muscle guarding that accompanies pain. Its pain-reducing (analgesic) effect is probably one of its greatest benefits. One explanation of the analgesic effect is that cold slows the speed of nerve transmission, so the pain sensation is reduced. It is also possible that cold bombards pain receptors with so many cold impulses that pain impulses are lost. With ice treatments, the athlete usually reports an uncomfortable sensation of cold, followed by burning, then an aching sensation, and finally complete numbness.

Because the subcutaneous (under the skin) fat slowly conducts the cold temperature, applications of cold for short periods of time will be ineffective in cooling deeper tissues. For this reason, longer treatments of at least twenty minutes are recommended. It should be noted, however, that prolonged application of cold can cause tissue damage.[12]

Decisions that can be made from the secondary survey:
- Seriousness of injury
- Type of first aid required
- Whether injury warrants physical referral
- Type of transportation needed

Rest, ice, compression, and elevation (RICE) are essential in the emergency care of musculoskeletal injuries.

Cold treatments seem to be more effective in reaching deep tissues than most forms of heat are. Cold applied to the skin is capable of significantly lowering the temperature of tissues at a considerable depth. The temperature to which the deeper tissues can be lowered depends on the type of cold that is applied to the skin, the duration of its application, the thickness of the subcutaneous fat, and the region of the body to which it is applied.[12] Ice packs should be applied to the area for at least seventy-two hours after an acute injury. With many injuries, regular ice treatments may be continued for several weeks.

For best results, ice packs (crushed ice and towel) should be applied over a compression wrap. Frozen gel packs should not be used directly against the skin because they reach much lower temperatures than do ice packs. A good rule of thumb is to apply a cold pack to a recent injury for a twenty-minute period and repeat every 1 to 1½ hours throughout the waking day. Depending on the severity and site of the injury, cold may be applied intermittently for one to seventy-two hours. For example, a mild strain will probably require one day of twenty-minute periods of cold application, whereas a severe knee or ankle sprain might need three to seven days of intermittent cold. If the severity of an injury is in doubt, the best approach is to extend the time that ice is applied.

Compression   In most cases immediate compression of an acute injury is considered an important adjunct to cold and elevation and in some cases may be superior to them. Placing external pressure on an injury assists in decreasing hemorrhage and hematoma formation by mechanically reducing the space available for swelling to accumulate.[17] Fluid seepage into interstitial spaces is retarded by compression, and absorption is facilitated. However, application of compression to an anterior compartment syndrome or to certain injuries involving the head and neck is contraindicated.

Many types of compression are available. An elastic wrap that has been soaked in water and frozen in a refrigerator can provide both compression and cold when applied to a recent injury. Pads can be cut from felt or foam rubber to fit difficult-to-compress body areas. For example, a horseshoe-shaped pad placed around the malleolus in combination with an elastic wrap and tape provides focal compression to reduce ankle edema (Figure 12-15).[33] Although cold is applied intermittently, compression should be maintained throughout the day and if possible throughout the night. Because of the pressure buildup in the tissues, the athlete may find it painful to leave a compression wrap in place for a long time. However, it is essential to leave the wrap in place in spite of significant pain because compression is so important in the control of swelling. The compression wrap should be left in place for at least seventy-two hours after an acute injury. In many chronic overuse problems, such as tendinitis, tenosynovitis, and particularly bursitis, the compression wrap should be worn until all swelling is almost entirely gone.

Elevation   Along with cold and compression, elevation reduces internal bleeding. The injured part, particularly an extremity, should be elevated to eliminate the effects of gravity on blood pooling in the extremities.[23] Elevation assists the veins, which drain blood and other fluids from the injured area, returning them to the central circulatory system. The greater the degree of elevation, the more effective the reduction in swelling. In an ankle sprain, for example, the leg should be placed so that the ankle is virtually straight up in the air. The injured part should be elevated as much as possible during the first seventy-two hours.

Focus Box: "Technique for initial management of the acute musculoskeletal injury" indicates an appropriate technique for initial management of the acute musculoskeletal injury regardless of what body part is involved.

Emergency Splinting

Any suspected fracture should always be splinted before the athlete is moved.[8] Transporting a person with a fracture without proper immobilization can result in increased tissue damage, hemorrhage, and shock.[15] Conceivably, a mishandled

---

12-4

Critical Thinking Exercise

A field hockey player trips over an opponent's stick, planter flexing and inverting her ankle, and she falls to the turf with a grade 2 ankle sprain. She has immediate effusion and significant pain. On examination, there appears to be some laxity in the ankle joint. The athletic trainer transports the athlete to the training room so that the ankle sprain can be managed properly.

? What specifically should the athletic trainer do to most effectively control the initial swelling associated with this injury?

A suspected fracture must be splinted before the athlete is moved.

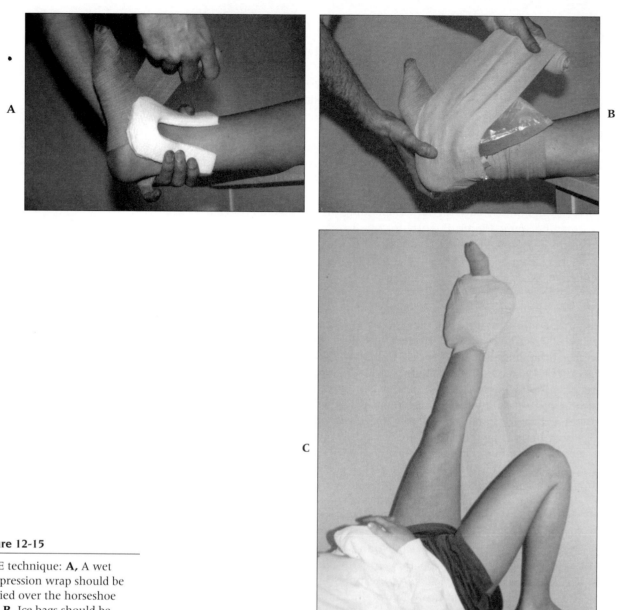

Figure 12-15

RICE technique: **A,** A wet compression wrap should be applied over the horseshoe pad. **B,** Ice bags should be secured in place by a dry compression wrap. **C,** The leg should be elevated during the initial treatment period.

fracture could cause death. Therefore a thorough knowledge of splinting techniques is important. The application of splints should be a simple process through the use of commercial emergency splints.[8,15] The athletic trainer usually does not have to improvise a splint because such devices are readily available in most sports settings.

Rapid form vacuum immobilizer   The rapid form vacuum immobilizer is a relatively new type of splint that is widely used by both EMTs and athletic trainers. It consists of styrofoam chips contained inside an airtight cloth sleeve that is pliable. This splint can be molded to the shape of any joint or angulated fracture through the use of Velcro straps. A handheld pump sucks the air out of the sleeve, giving it a cardboardlike rigidity. This splint is most useful for injuries that are angulated and must be splinted in the position in which they are found (Figure 12-16A).

Focus

Technique for initial management of the acute musculoskeletal injury

1. Apply a compression wrap directly over the injury, using a pad for focal compression if appropriate. Wrapping should start distally and continue proximally. Tension should be firm and consistent. It may be helpful to wet the elastic wrap to facilitate the passage of cold from ice packs. A dry compression wrap should be left in place for at least seventy-two hours or until there is little chance of continued swelling.
2. Surround the injured area entirely with ice packs or bags, and secure them in place. The ice should be left on for twenty minutes initially and then one hour off and thirty minutes on as much as possible over the next twenty-four hours. During the following forty-eight-hour period, ice should again be applied as often as possible.
3. The injured part should be elevated for most of the initial seventy-two-hour period after injury. It is particularly important to keep the injury elevated while sleeping. This elevation also allows the damaged part to rest after the injury. The initial management of an injury is extremely important to reduce the length of time required for rehabilitation.

Air splint   An air splint is a clear plastic splint that is inflated with air around the affected part and can be used for extremity splinting, but its use requires some special training. This splint provides support and moderate pressure to the body part and affords a clear view of the site for X-ray examination. The inflatable splint should not be used if it will alter a fracture deformity (Figure 12-16B).

Half-ring splint   For fractures of the femur, the half-ring traction splint offers the best support and immobilization but takes considerable practice to master. An open fracture must be carefully dressed to avoid additional contamination (Figure 12-16C).

Whatever the material used, the principles of good splinting remain the same. Two major concepts of splinting are to splint from one joint above the fracture to one joint below the fracture and to splint where the athlete lies. If at all possible, do not move the athlete until he or she has been splinted.

Splinting of lower-limb fractures   Fractures of the ankle or leg require immobilization of the foot and knee. Any fracture involving the knee, thigh, or hip needs splinting of all the lower-limb joints and one side of the trunk.

Splinting of upper-limb fractures   Fractures around the shoulder complex are immobilized by a sling and swathe bandage, with the upper limb securely bound to the body. Upper-arm and elbow fractures must be splinted, with immobilization effected in a straight-arm position to lessen bone override. Lower-arm and wrist fractures should be splinted in a position of forearm flexion and should be supported by a sling. Hand and finger dislocations and fractures should be splinted with tongue depressors, roller gauze, or aluminum splints.[28]

Splinting of the spine and pelvis   Injuries involving a possible spine or pelvic fracture are best splinted and moved using a spine board. Recently, a total body rapid form vacuum immobilizer has been developed for dealing with spinal injuries (Figure 12-17). The effectiveness of this piece of equipment as an immobilization device has yet to be determined.

MOVING AND TRANSPORTING THE INJURED ATHLETE

Moving, lifting, and transporting the injured athlete must be executed with the use of techniques that will prevent further injury. Moving or transporting the athlete improperly causes more additional injuries than does any other emergency procedure.[18,21] There is no excuse for poor handling of the injured athlete. Planning should

Great caution must be taken when transporting the injured athlete.

Figure 12-16

Examples of splints. **A,** Rapid form vacuum immobilizer. **B,** Air splint. **C,** Half-ring splint.

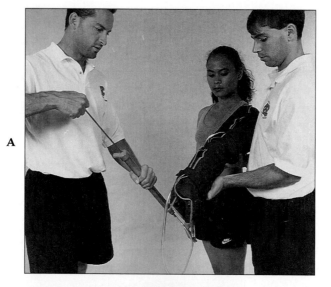

A

B

C

Figure 12-17

Athletic mattress total body immobilizer.

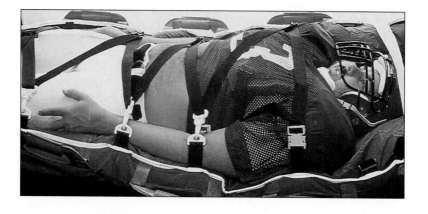

take into consideration all the possible transportation methods and the necessary equipment to execute them. Capable and well-trained personnel, spine boards, stretchers, and a rescue vehicle may be needed to transport the injured athlete. Special consideration must be given to extracting the injured athlete from a pool.

Placing the Athlete on a Spine Board

In cases of suspected cervical spine injury, the athletic trainer should generally access the EMS and wait until the rescue squad arrives before attempting to move the athlete. The only exception would be if the athlete is not breathing, and logrolling the athlete onto the back is required for CPR.

A suspected spinal injury requires extremely careful handling and is best left to properly trained paramedics or EMTs or to athletic trainers who are well trained and have access to the proper equipment for transport. (See the back inside cover of this text for a list of emergency equipment that should be available on the sidelines.) If such personnel are not available, moving should be done under the express direction of a physician, and a spine board should be used (Figure 12-18). The most important principle in transporting an individual on a spine board is to maintain the head and neck in alignment with the long axis of the body. In such cases, it is best to have one individual whose sole responsibility is to ensure and maintain proper positioning of the head and neck until the head is secured to a spine board.

Primary emergency care involves helping the athlete maintain normal breathing, treating for shock, and keeping the athlete quiet and in the position found until medical assistance arrives. Ideally, transportation should not be attempted until a physician has examined the athlete and has given permission to move him or her. Neck stabilization must be maintained throughout transportation, first to the emergency vehicle, then to the hospital, and throughout the hospital procedure.

These steps should be followed when moving an athlete with suspected neck injury:

1. The examiner must determine whether the athlete is breathing and has a pulse.
2. A spine board is retrieved for moving the athlete.
3. If the athlete is lying prone, he or she must be logrolled onto the back for CPR or to be secured to the spine board. An athlete with a possible cervical fracture is transported face up. An athlete with a spinal fracture in the lower trunk area may be transported face down.
   a. All extremities are placed in an axial alignment (see Figure 12-18A).
   b. To roll the athlete over requires four or five persons, with the captain of the team protecting the athlete's head and neck. The neck must be stabilized and must not be moved from its original position, no matter how distorted it may appear.
   c. The spine board is placed close to the side of the athlete (see Figure 12-18B).
   d. Each assistant is responsible for one of the athlete's body segments. One assistant is responsible for turning the trunk, another the hips, another the thighs, and the last the lower legs.
4. With the spine board close to the athlete's side, the captain gives the command to logroll him or her onto the board as one unit (see Figure 12-18C).
5. On the board, the athlete's head and neck continue to be stabilized by the captain (see Figure 12-18D).
6. If the athlete is a football player, the helmet is not removed; however, the face guard is removed or lifted away from the face for possible CPR. NOTE: To remove the face guard, the plastic fasteners holding it to the helmet should be removed.
7. Next, the head and neck are stabilized on the spine board by a chin strap secured to metal loops. Finally, the trunk and lower limbs are secured to the spine board by straps (see Figure 12-18E and F).

Figure 12-18

A, When moving an unconscious athlete, first establish whether the athlete is breathing and has a pulse. An unconscious athlete must always be treated as having a serious neck injury. If lying prone, the athlete must be turned over for CPR or be secured to a spine board for possible cervical fracture. One coach or athletic trainer (the captain) stabilizes the athlete's neck and head. **B,** The spine board is placed as close to the athlete as possible. **C,** Each assistant is responsible for one of the athlete's segments. When the coach or athletic trainer (captain) gives the command "roll," the athlete is moved as a unit onto the spine board. *(continued)*

If the athlete is face up, the straddle-slide method can be used to move the athlete onto a spine board. Four or five persons are needed: a captain stationed at the athlete's head and three or four assistants. One assistant is in charge of lifting the athlete's trunk, one the hips, and one the legs. At the captain's lift command, the athlete is lifted while the fourth assistant slides a spine board under the athlete between the feet of the captain and the assistants (Figure 12-19).

Ambulatory Aid

Ambulatory aid is that support or assistance given to an injured athlete who is able to walk (Figure 12-20). Before the athlete is allowed to walk, he or she should be carefully scrutinized to make sure that the injuries are minor. Whenever serious in-

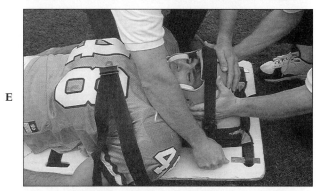

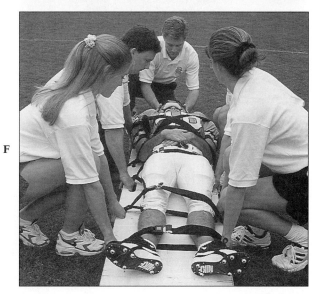

Figure 12-18—cont'd

D, The face mask is cut away while the captain continues to stabilize the athlete's neck. **E,** The head and neck are stabilized onto the spine board by means of a chin strap secured to metal loops. **F,** The trunk and lower limbs are secured to the spine board by straps. *(continued)*

juries are suspected, walking should be prohibited. Complete support should be given on both sides of the athlete by two individuals who are approximately the same height. The athlete's arms are draped over the assistants' shoulders, and their arms encircle his or her back.

Manual Conveyance

Manual conveyance may be used to move a mildly injured individual a greater distance than could be walked with ease (Figure 12-21). Any decision to carry the athlete, like a decision to use ambulatory aid, must be made only after a complete examination to determine the existence of potentially serious conditions. The most convenient carry is performed by two assistants.

Figure 12-18—cont'd

G, All carriers assume a position to stand. **H,** Once the carriers are standing, the athlete may be transported.

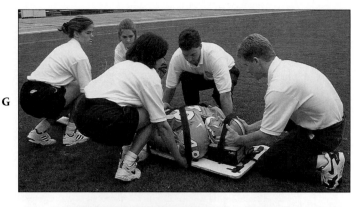

Figure 12-19

An alternative method of placing the athlete on a spine board is the straddle-slide method.

Stretcher Carrying

Whenever a serious injury is suspected, the best and safest mode of transportation for a short distance is by stretcher. With each segment of the body supported, the athlete is gently lifted and placed on the stretcher, which is carried adequately by a minimum of four assistants, two supporting either side (Figure 12-22). Any person with an injury serious enough to require the use of a stretcher must be carefully examined before being moved.

A limb injury must be splinted properly before the athlete is transported. Athletes with shoulder injuries are more comfortably moved in a semisitting position, unless

Figure 12-20

The ambulatory aid method of transporting a mildly injured athlete.

Figure 12-21

Manual conveyance method for transporting a mildly injured athlete.

Figure 12-22

Whenever a serious injury is suspected, a stretcher is the safest method for transporting the athlete.

other injuries preclude such positioning. If injury to the upper extremity is such that flexion of the elbow is not possible, the individual should be transported on a stretcher with the limb properly splinted and carried at the side, with adequate padding placed between the arm and the body.

Pool Extraction

Removing an injured athlete from a swimming pool requires some special consideration on the part of the athletic trainer.

1. The injured athlete who has not sustained a head or neck injury should be told to roll onto his or her back in the water and then towed to the edge of the pool using a cross-chest technique (Figure 12-23).
2. If the athlete is not breathing, a single rescuer should get the athlete out of the water and onto the deck as quickly as possible to perform CPR. If two rescuers

Figure 12-23

Cross-chest technique for towing an injured athlete.

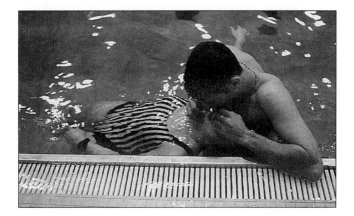

Figure 12-24

Rescue breathing should begin in the water.

are present, resuscitation should begin immediately while the athlete is still in the water. With the athlete supine in the water, one rescuer supports the shoulders and head while the other performs a jaw thrust to open the airway and begins rescue breathing if necessary. The athlete should be moved onto the deck where CPR is continued as rapidly as possible (Figure 12-24).

3. Athletes with a suspected head or cervical neck injury and who are unconscious require special precaution. The athletic trainer should approach the athlete in the water carefully to minimize wave action, which causes unnecessary movement of the head and neck. The athletic trainer, using a head-chin support technique, which uses the forearms to splint the chest and upper back and the hands to stabilize the head and neck, rolls the athlete onto his or her back and maintains the athlete in a horizontal position until help arrives (Figure 12-25A). NOTE: If

A

B

C

Figure 12-25

In suspected head or cervical neck injury, **A,** use a head-chin support technique; **B,** place the spine board under the athlete; **C,** secure the athlete to the board.

(continued)

D

Figure 12-25—cont'd

D and **E,** lift the spine board out of the water.

E

Critical Thinking E x e r c i s e

A diver, attempting a 2¹/₂ inward dive on a 3-meter board, hits her head on the end of the board. She lands on her face in the water, is briefly submerged, but floats quickly to the surface. She is conscious but disoriented; she has a bump on her forehead but is not bleeding. A teammate nearby jumps immediately in the water and, using a cross-chest technique, tows her about 10 feet to the side of the pool.

? The athletic trainer is concerned about both a head and neck injury. What precautions should be taken when removing the injured athlete from the pool?

Properly fitting a crutch or cane is essential to avoid placing abnormal stresses on the body.

necessary, a second rescuer can provide CPR in this position. The athlete should be secured to the spine board while still in the water. The spine board should be placed diagonally under the victim from the side with the foot end of the board going down into the water first. The board is slid under the victim and allowed to rise directly under the victim (Figure 12-25B). Once on the spine board, the athlete's head should be stabilized by one rescuer while the other rescuers strap the athlete onto the board, securing the victim's head (Figure 12-25C). When lifting the spine board out of the water, the rescuer at the head should be in charge and the spine board should be removed head first (Figure 12-25D).

PROPER FIT AND USE OF THE CRUTCH OR CANE

Weight bearing may be contraindicated for an athlete with a lower-limb injury, in which case a crutch or cane should be used for ambulation. The athletic trainer must be responsible for properly fitting the crutch or cane to the injured athlete and then for providing instruction in use. If the crutch or cane is not properly fitted, the athlete may experience discomfort in the axilla from excessive pressure as well as pain in the low back. Faulty mechanics in the use of the crutch or cane when ambulating and particularly when ascending or descending stairs can cause the athlete to fall.

Fitting the Athlete

The adjustable wooden crutch is well suited to the athlete. For a correct fit, the athlete should wear low-heeled shoes and stand with good posture and the feet close together. The crutch length is determined first by placing the tip 6 inches (15 cm) from the outer margin of the shoe and 2 inches (5 cm) in front of the shoe. The underarm crutch brace is positioned 1 inch (2.5 cm) below the anterior fold of the axilla. Next, the hand brace is adjusted so that it is even with the athlete's hand when the elbow is flexed at approximately a 30-degree angle (Figure 12-26).

Fitting a cane to the athlete is relatively easy. Measurement is taken from the superior aspect of the greater trochanter of the femur to the floor while the athlete is wearing street shoes.

Walking with the Crutch or Cane

Many elements of crutch walking correspond with walking. The technique commonly used in sports injuries is the tripod method. In this method, the athlete swings through the crutches without making any surface contact with the injured limb or by partially bearing weight with the injured limb. The following sequence is performed:

1. The athlete stands on one foot, with the affected foot completely elevated or partially bearing weight.
2. Placing the crutch tips 12 to 15 inches (30 to 37.5 cm) ahead of the feet, the athlete leans forward, straightens the elbows, pulls the upper crosspiece firmly against the side of the chest, and swings or steps between the stationary crutches (Figure 12-27). The athlete should avoid placing the major support in the axilla.
3. After moving through, the athlete recovers the crutches and again places the tips forward.

An alternative method is the four-point crutch gait. In this method, the athlete stands on both feet. One crutch is moved forward, and the opposite foot is stepped forward. The crutch on the same side as the foot that moved forward is moved to just ahead of the foot. The opposite foot steps forward, followed by the crutch on the same side, and so on.

The tripod gait that is used for crutch walking on a level surface is also used on stairs. In going up stairs, the unaffected support leg moves up one step while the body weight is supported by the hands on the crutches. The full weight of the body is transferred to the support leg, and the crutch tips and affected leg are moved to that step. In going down stairs, the crutch tips and the affected leg move down one step, followed by the support leg. If a handrail is available, the athlete uses the tripod gait with both crutches held by the outside hand.

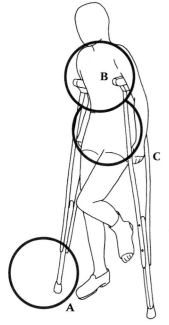
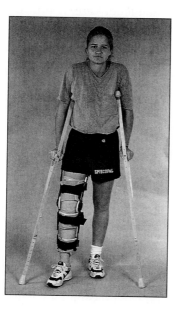

Figure 12-26

The crutch must be properly fitted to the athlete. **A,** The crutch tips are placed 6 inches (15 cm) from the outer margin of the shoe and 2 inches (5 cm) in front of the shoe. **B,** The underarm crutch brace is positioned 1 inch (2.5 cm) below the anterior fold of the axilla. **C,** The hand brace is placed even with the athlete's hand, with the elbow flexed approximately 30 degrees.

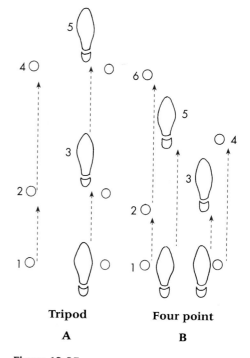

Tripod

A

Four point

B

Figure 12-27

Crutch gait. **A,** Tripod method. **B,** Four-point gait.

12-6

Critical Thinking E x e r c i s e

A fencer has a grade 2 ankle sprain. After spending an hour in the training room applying ice, compression, and elevation, the athletic trainer decides that the athlete should be sent home on crutches. The athlete indicates some reluctance to the crutches because he has never used them before.

? What instructions should the athletic trainer give the athlete so that he can correctly and safely ambulate on crutches?

Crutch walking will generally follow a progression from non–weight bearing (NWB) to touch down weight bearing (TDWB) to partial weight bearing (PWB) to full weight bearing (FWB). The rate of progression will be dictated by limitations of the injury as well as capabilities of the individual athlete.

In walking with a cane or a single crutch, the athlete should hold the cane in the hand on the injured side and move the cane forward simultaneously with the uninjured leg.

EMERGENCY EMOTIONAL CARE

Besides responding to the emergency physical requirements of an injury, the athletic trainer must respond appropriately to the emotions engendered by the situation. The American Psychiatric Association has set forth major principles for the emergency care of emotional reactions to trauma.[7] Those principles are as follows:

1. Accept everyone's right to personal feelings, because everyone comes from a unique background and has had different emotional experiences. Do not tell the injured person how he or she should feel. Show empathy, not pity.
2. Accept the injured person's limitations as real.
3. Accept your own limitations as a provider of first aid.

In general, the athletic trainer dealing with an injured athlete's emotions should be empathetic and calm and should make it obvious that the athlete's feelings are understood and accepted.

SUMMARY

- An emergency is defined as "an unforeseen combination of circumstances and the resulting state that calls for immediate action."[7] The primary concern of emergency aid is to maintain cardiovascular function and, indirectly, central nervous system function. All sports programs should have an emergency system that is activated whenever an athlete is seriously injured.
- The athletic trainer must make a systematic assessment of the injured athlete to determine appropriate emergency care. A primary survey assesses and deals with life-threatening situations. Once stabilized, the secondary survey makes a more detailed assessment of the injury.
- The mnemonic for cardiopulmonary resuscitation is ABC: A, airway opened; B, breathing restored; C, circulation restored. In adult CPR, the ratio of compression to breaths is 15 to 2, with 80 to 100 compressions per minute. An obstructed airway is relieved by use of the Heimlich maneuver, the finger sweep of the throat, or both.
- Hemorrhage can occur externally and internally. External bleeding can be controlled by direct pressure, by applying pressure at pressure points, and by elevation. Internal hemorrhage can occur subcutaneously, intramuscularly, or within a body cavity.
- Shock can occur from a variety of situations. Shock can be hypovolemic, respiratory, neurogenic, psychogenic, cardiogenic, septic, anaphylactic, and metabolic. Symptoms include pale skin, dilated eyes, weak and rapid pulse, and rapid, shallow breathing. Management includes maintaining normal body temperature and slightly elevating the feet.
- Rest, ice, compression, and elevation (RICE) should be used for the immediate care of a musculoskeletal injury. Ice should be applied for at least twenty minutes every 1 to 1½ hours, and compression and elevation should be continuous for at least seventy-two hours after injury.
- Any suspected fracture should be splinted before the athlete is moved. Commercial rapid form vacuum immobilizers and air splints are most often used in an athletic training setting.
- Great care must be taken in moving the seriously injured athlete. The unconscious athlete must be handled as though he or she has a cervical fracture. Moving an athlete with a suspected serious neck injury must be performed only by persons

specifically trained to do so. A spine board should be used for transport to avoid any movement of the cervical region.

- When removing an injured athlete from a swimming pool, the athletic trainer should make every effort to minimize movement of the head and cervical spine while placing the athlete on a spine board in the water.
- The athletic trainer should be responsible for the proper fitting and instruction in the use of crutches or a cane by an athlete with an injury to the lower extremity.
- Athletes who are injured will respond emotionally to the situation. Their feelings must be understood and fully accepted by the coach and the athletic trainer.

Web Sites

American Red Cross: http://www.redcross.org/what.html

The American Red Cross offers many emergency services and training. This site describes those services, introduces the information provided in various training opportunities, and explains how to obtain that training,

American Heart Association: http://www.amhrt.org

World Wide Wounds: The Electronic Journal of Wound Management Practice: http://www.smtl.co.uk/World-Wide-Wounds

This site lists interesting and informative information for health care professionals on the current management of wounds.

Cervical Spine Stabilization: http://www.trauma.org/spine/cspine-stab.html

This brief article describes the considerations with cervical spine stabilization.

First Aid with Parasol EMT: http://www.parasolemt.com.au

This site provides a comprehensive on-line first aid reference.

Solutions to Critical Thinking EXERCISES

12-1 Because of the mechanism of injury, the athletic trainer should suspect that the athlete has a cervical neck injury. The head should be stabilized throughout. Because the athlete is prone and breathing, the athletic trainer should do nothing until consciousness returns. An on-field exam should determine the athlete's neurological status. Then the player should be carefully logrolled onto a spine board because CPR could be necessary at any time. The face mask should be removed in case CPR is required. The helmet and shoulder pads should be left in place. The athlete should then be transported to the emergency facility. Remember, in this situation the worst mistake the athletic trainer can make is not exercising enough caution.

12-2 The athletic trainer must first take precautions to protect against the transmission of bloodborne pathogens. The wound should be cleaned with soap and water. The athletic trainer applies direct pressure using a gauze pad and applies cold. If the athlete is not dizzy, he should remain in a sitting position. The athlete should be referred to a physician for suturing. Sterile strips or a butterfly bandage may also be applied, although sutures will generally leave a smaller scar. All blood-contaminated supplies should be disposed of in a clearly marked biohazard bag.

12-3 The athlete may be going into hypovolemic shock secondary to hemorrhage and trauma, which can be a life-threatening situation. The athletic trainer should first direct someone to dial 911 to access the emergency medical system. Next, the athletic trainer must control the bleeding by using direct pressure, elevation, and pressure points. If bleeding is controlled and the rescue squad has not arrived, the forearm should be immobilized in a rapid form vacuum immobilizer. The athlete should be supine, and his feet elevated in the shock position. His body temperature should be maintained.

12-4 The ankle should be wrapped with a wet elastic compression wrap. Ice should be applied to both sides of the joint over the compression wrap and secured. The ankle should be elevated such that the leg is above 45 degrees at a minimum. The compression wrap, ice, and elevation should be maintained initially for at least thirty minutes but not longer than an hour. The athletic trainer should also make some determination as to whether a fracture is suspected and make the appropriate referral.

12-5 The athletic trainer should most likely place the athlete on a spine board and secure her before extracting her from the pool. Several people may be required to get the athlete appropriately positioned on the spine board while still in the water. The athlete should be given a brief neurological exam to determine the extent of the injury. The athlete should then be transported to an emergency facility in a rescue vehicle.

12-6 The athlete trainer should instruct the athlete in the tripod gait, in which the athlete swings through the crutches without making any surface contact with the injured limb. The tripod gait is also used on stairs. In negotiating stairs, the rule of thumb is go up with the good leg first, followed by crutches, and to go down with the crutches first, followed by the good leg. If the stairs have a handrail, the athlete can hold both crutches with his outside hand. Crutch walking will generally follow a progression: NWB to TDWB to PWB to FWB.

REVIEW QUESTIONS AND CLASS ACTIVITIES

1. What considerations are important in a well-planned system for handling emergency situations?
2. Discuss the rules for managing and moving an unconscious athlete.
3. What are the life-threatening conditions that should be evaluated in the primary survey?
4. What are the ABCs of life support?

5. Identify the major steps in giving CPR and managing an obstructed airway. When might these procedures be used in a sports setting?

6. List the basic steps in assessing a musculoskeletal injury.

7. What techniques should be used to stop external hemorrhage?

8. Numerous types of shock can occur from a sports injury or illness; list them and their management.

9. What first aid procedures are used to decrease hemorrhage, inflammation, muscle spasm, and pain from a musculoskeletal injury?

10. Describe the basic concepts of emergency splinting.

11. How should an athlete with a suspected spinal injury be transported?

12. What techniques can be used to transport an athlete with a suspected musculoskeletal injury?

13. Discuss the methods for extracting an injured athlete from a swimming pool.

14. Explain how to properly fit crutches.

15. Describe methods that should be used when dealing with an injured athlete's emotional response to the injury.

REFERENCES

1. American Red Cross: *First aid: responding to emergencies,* St Louis, 1996, Mosby.

2. Dick BH, Anderson JM: Emergency care of the injured athlete. In Zachazewski JE et al, editors: *Athletic injuries and rehabilitation,* Philadelphia, 1996, WB Saunders.

3. Feld F: Management of the critically injured football player, *J Ath Train* 28(3):206, 1993.

4. Feld F: Technology and emergency care, *Athletic Therapy Today* 2(5):28, 1997.

5. Fessey J: First aid for head and spinal injuries in sport, *Physiotherapy in Sport* 20(3):4, 1997.

6. Fuchs E: Face mask removal time of four face mask extrication devices. Master's thesis, San Jose State University, 1994.

7. Hafen BQ, Karren KJ, Frandsen KJ: *First aid for colleges and universities,* Boston, 1996, Allyn and Bacon.

8. Hay JM: Taping, splinting, and fitting of athletic equipment. In Baker CL et al, editors: *The Hughston Clinic sports medicine book,* Baltimore, Md, 1995, Williams & Wilkins.

9. Herbert D: Plan to save lives: create and rehearse an emergency response plan, *ACSM's Health & Fitness Journal* 1(5):34, 1997.

10. Herbert DL: Developing a comprehensive sports medicine emergency care plan, *Sports Med Stand Malprac Report* 7(4):49, 1995.

11. Kleiner DM: Football helmet face mask removal, *Athletic Therapy Today* 1(1):11, 1996.

12. Knight K: *Cryotherapy in sport injury management,* Champaign, Ill, 1995, Human Kinetics.

13. Knox KE, Kleiner DM: The efficiency of tools used to retract a football helmet face mask, *J Ath Train* 32(3):211, 1997.

14. Martin DE: Emergency medicine and the underage athlete, *J Ath Train* 29(3):200, 1994.

15. Meredith RM, Butcher JD: Field splinting of suspected fractures: preparation, assessment, and application. *Physician Sportsmed* 25(10):29, 1997.

16. National Athletic Trainers' Association: *Position stand: helmet removal guidelines,* Dallas, 1998, National Athletic Trainers' Association.

17. National Collegiate Athletic Association: Guidelines for helmet fitting and removal. In Benson M, editor: *1997-1998 NCAA sports medicine handbook,* Overland Park, Kan, 1997, National Collegiate Athletic Association.

18. National Safety Council: *First aid and CPR,* Boston, 1997, Jones & Bartlett.

19. Ortolani A: Helmets and face masks, *J Ath Train* 27(4):294, 1992 (letter).

20. Palumbo MA, Hulstyn MJ, Fadale PD: The effect of protective football equipment on alignment of the injured cervical spine: radiographic analysis in a cadaveric model, *Am J Sports Med* 24(4):446, 1996.

21. Parcel GS: *Basic emergency care of the sick and injured,* ed 4, St Louis, 1990, Mosby.

22. Patel M, Rund D: Emergency removal of football helmets, *Physician Sportsmed* 22(9):57, 1994.

23. Prentice WE: Considerations in designing a rehabilitation program, In Prentice WE: *Rehabilitation techniques in sports medicine,* Dubuque, 1999, WCB/McGraw-Hill.

24. Prinsen R, Syrotuik D, Reid D: Position of the cervical vertebrae during helmet removal and cervical collar application in football and hockey, *Cl J Sports Med* 5(3):155, 1995.

25. Putman L: Alternative methods for football helmet fask mask removal, *J Ath Train* 27(2):107, 1992.

26. Ray R: Helmets and face masks, *J Ath Train* 27(4):294, 1992 (letter).

27. Ray R, Luchies C, Bazuin D: Airway preparation techniques for the cervical spine–injured football player, *J Ath Train* 30(3):217, 1995.

28. Sailer SM, Lewis SB: Rehabilitation and splinting of common upper-extremity injuries in athletes, *Clin Sports Med* 14(2):411, 1995.

29. Segan RD, Cassidy C, Bentkowski J: A discussion of the issue of football helmet removal in suspected cervical spine injuries, *J Ath Train* 28(4):294, 1993.

30. *Taber's Cyclopedic Medical Dictionary,* Philadelphia, 1997, FA Davis.

31. United States Olympic Committee/American Red Cross: *Sport safety training: injury prevention and care handbook,* St Louis, 1997, Mosby Lifeline.

32. Veenema KR, Swenson EJ: Laryngeal trauma: securing the airway on the field, *Physician Sportsmed* 23(1):71, 1995.

33. Wilkerson GB: External compression for controlling traumatic edema, *Physician Sportsmed* 13:96, 1985.

ANNOTATED BIBLIOGRAPHY

American Red Cross: *First aid: responding to emergencies,* St Louis, 1996, Mosby.

Hafen BQ, Karren KJ, Frandsen KJ: *First aid for colleges and universities,* Boston, 1996, Allyn & Bacon.

National Safety Council: *First aid and CPR,* Boston, 1997, Jones & Bartlett.

All three of these texts are standard, well-written, and extremely well-illustrated texts that deal with first aid and emergency procedures. Although most of the information is directed at the general population, the principles and techniques can certainly be applied to the injured athlete. Any one of the three will provide an excellent resource for the athletic trainer.

Off-the-Field Injury Evaluation

When you finish this chapter you should be able to

- Differentiate between evaluation and diagnosis.
- Define terminology used in injury evaluation.
- Discuss the HOPS off-the-field evaluation scheme.
- Describe the process for documenting the findings of an off-the-field or progress evaluation.
- Discuss additional diagnostic techniques available to the athletic trainer through the team physician.

EVALUATION OF SPORTS INJURIES

Injury evaluation is an essential skill for the athletic trainer. In athletic training, four distinct evaluations are routinely conducted: the *preparticipation examination,* done prior to the start of preseason practice, was discussed in Chapter 2; the initial *on-the-field injury assessment,* which was discussed in great detail in Chapter 12, is done immediately after acute injury to determine the immediate course of acute care, necessary first aid, and handling of emergency situations; a more detailed *off-the-field injury evaluation* is done in the training room, clinic, emergency room, or physician's office after appropriate first aid has been rendered; and a *progress evaluation* is done periodically throughout the rehabilitative process for determining the progress and effectiveness of a specific treatment regimen. This chapter concentrates on the off-the-field evaluation and the progress evaluation.

INJURY EVALUATION VERSUS DIAGNOSIS

Although athletic trainers recognize and evaluate sports injuries, by law they cannot make a diagnosis. A diagnosis denotes what disease, injury, or syndrome a person has or is believed to have. Making a diagnosis is usually reserved for individuals specifically licensed by a state to do so. Health professionals such as physicians are generally permitted to diagnose. Health professionals restricted to diagnosing one body area are dentists, who are limited to diagnosing mouth disorders; podiatrists, who are limited to diagnosing foot disorders; and optometrists, who are limited to determining refractory problems of the eyes and prescribing lenses to increase the efficiency of vision. Chiropractors usually base their diagnoses on the relationship of the body's structure to its overall function. In some states, nurse practitioners may make limited diagnoses.

There is a fine line between the evaluation of an injury and its diagnosis. Debating this difference serves no useful purpose other than to confound the distinction further. In situations in which time is of the essence, as is often the case in sports injuries, the ability to evaluate quickly, accurately, and decisively is vitally important. In such situations, the athletic trainer must remain within the limits of his or her ability and training and must act in full accord with professional ethics.

BASIC KNOWLEDGE REQUIREMENTS

The athletic trainer who is examining an athlete with a sports injury must have a general knowledge of normal human anatomy and biomechanics and an understanding of the major hazards inherent in a particular sport. Without this information, accurate assessment becomes impossible.

Athletic trainers recognize and evaluate sports injuries, but by law they cannot make diagnoses.

The examiner of sports injuries must have a thorough knowledge of human anatomy and its function and of the hazards inherent in sports.

Normal Human Anatomy

Surface Anatomy

Understanding typical surface or topographical anatomy is essential when evaluating a possible injury. Key surface landmarks provide the examiner with indications of the normal or injured anatomical structures lying underneath the skin.[8]

Body planes and anatomical directions   Associated with surface anatomy is the understanding of body planes and anatomical directions. Body planes are used as points of reference from which positions of body parts are indicated. The three most commonly mentioned planes are the midsagittal, transverse, and frontal (or coronal) planes (Figure 13-1). Anatomical directions refer to the relative position of one part to another (Figure 13-2).

Abdominopelvic quadrants   The abdominopelvic quadrants are the four corresponding regions of the abdomen that are divided for evaluative and diagnostic purposes (Figure 13-3).

Musculoskeletal System Anatomy

Anyone examining the musculoskeletal system for sports injuries must have an in-depth knowledge of both structural and functional anatomy.[11] This knowledge encompasses the major joints and bony structures as well as skeletal musculature. A knowledge of neural anatomy is also of major importance, particularly that which is involved in movement control and sensation, along with the neural factors that influence superficial and deep pain.

Standard musculoskeletal terminology for bodily positions and deviations When assessing the musculoskeletal system, a standard terminology must be used to convey precise information to others who may become professionally involved with the athlete. These terms are found in Table 13-1.

Figure 13-1

Knowledge of body planes helps provide points of reference.

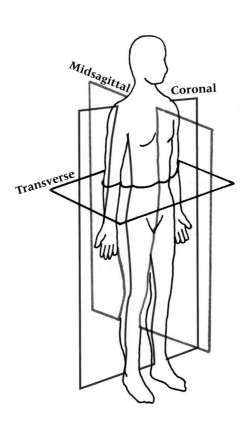

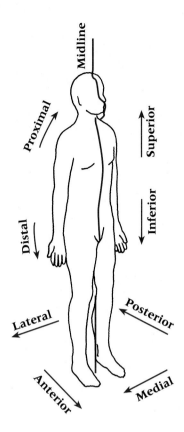

Figure 13-2

Anatomical directions refer to the relative position of one body part to another.

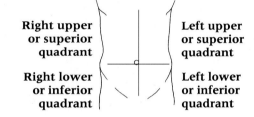

| Right upper or superior quadrant | Left upper or superior quadrant |
| Right lower or inferior quadrant | Left lower or inferior quadrant |

Figure 13-3

Knowledge about the four abdominopelvic quadrants helps in injury assessment.

Biomechanics

The understanding of biomechanics is the foundation for the assessment of musculoskeletal sports injuries. **Biomechanics** is the application of mechanical forces, which may stem from within or outside the body, to living organisms. Of major concern is pathomechanics, which may precede an injury. **Pathomechanics** refers to mechanical forces that are applied to the body because of a structural body deviation, leading to faulty alignment. Pathomechanics often cause overuse syndromes.

Understanding the Sport

The more that the examiner of sports injuries knows about how a sport is performed and its potential for trauma, the better his or her injury assessment can be.[23] To fully understand injuries that occur in a sport, the examiner needs a detailed knowledge of the correct kinesiological and biomechanical principles that should be applied. Violation of these principles can lead to repetitive and overuse syndromes. Understanding how an acute or chronic injury might occur helps the examiner focus more directly on tissues that have been affected.

Descriptive Assessment Terms

When evaluating sports injuries, examiners use selected terms to describe and characterize what is being learned about the condition. Students should become familiar with these terms.

Etiology refers to the cause of an injury or disease. In sports medicine, the term *mechanism* is often exchanged for etiology. **Pathology** refers to the structural and functional changes that result from the injury process.

After developing an understanding of an injury's etiology, the examiner ascertains symptoms and signs. **Symptom** refers to a perceptible change in an athlete's body or its functions that indicates an injury or disease. Symptoms are subjective and are

biomechanics
Application of mechanical forces to living organisms.

pathomechanics
Mechanical forces that are applied to a living organism and adversely change the body's structure and function.

etiology
Cause of disease.

pathology
Structural and functional changes that result from injury.

symptom
Change that indicates injury or disease.

TABLE 13-1 Standard Orthopedic Definitions for Positions and Deviations

Term	Definition
Abduction	To draw away or deviate from the midline of the body
Adduction	To deviate toward or draw toward the midline of the body
Eversion	Turning outward
Extension	To straighten; when the part distal to a joint extends, it straightens; joint angle decreases toward 0 degrees
External rotation	Rotary motion in the transverse plane away from the midline
Flexion	To bend; when a joint is flexed, the part distal to the joint bends; joint angle increases toward 180 degrees
Internal rotation	Rotary motion in the transverse plane toward the midline
Inversion	Turning inward
Pronation	Applied to the foot and assuming the foot is in a prone position, it refers to a combination of eversion and abduction movements, resulting in a lowering of the medial margin of the foot; applied to the hand, it means the palm is turned downward
Supination	To assume a supine position; applied to the foot, it refers to raising the medial margin of the foot; applied to the hand, it refers to turning the palm upward
Valgus	Deviation of a part or portion of the extremity distal to a joint toward the midline of the body
Varus	Deviation of a part or portion of an extremity distal to a joint away from the midline of the body

sign
Indicator of a disease.

diagnosis
Name of a specific condition.

prognosis
Predicted outcome of an injury.

sequela
Condition resulting from disease or injury.

syndrome
Group of symptoms that indicate a condition or disease.

described by the athlete to the coach, athletic trainer, or physician. In comparison, a **sign** is objective, a definitive and obvious indicator for a specific condition. Signs are often determined when the athlete is examined.

After it is inspected, an injury may be assigned a *grade*. Grade 1, 2, or 3 corresponds to an injury that is mild, moderate, or severe, respectively. Sometimes the term *degree* is used in place of grade, depending on the examiner's preference.

Diagnosis denotes the name of a specific condition. To establish the diagnosis of an athlete's injury or illness, all aspects of the condition must be studied. Once all the possible information has been gathered about the athlete's condition, a **prognosis** is made. A prognosis is a prediction of the course of the condition. In other words, the athlete is told what is to be expected as the injury heals. The amount of pain, swelling, or loss of function is discussed. Prognosis also refers to the projected outcome of an illness or injury and to the length of time predicted for complete recovery. For the athlete, prognosis translates into "the length of time before I can compete."

Sequela refers to a condition following and resulting from a disease or injury. Sequela is the development of an additional condition as a complication of an existing disease or injury. For example, pneumonia might result from a bout with the flu, or osteoarthritis might follow a severe joint sprain.

The term **syndrome** is used throughout the text and refers to a group of symptoms and signs that, together, indicate a particular injury or disease.

THE OFF-THE-FIELD INJURY EVALUATION PROCESS

The on-the-field injury assessment is done on the field immediately after injury to rule out those injuries that may potentially become life threatening, to assess musculoskeletal injuries, and to determine how the athlete should be transported from the field. Once the athlete has been transported from the site of initial injury, away from the excitement and confusion inherent in an athletic arena, a more detailed off-the-field injury evaluation is performed. This detailed evaluation may be per-

 *Focus*

Off-the-field evaluation sequence

History
   Past
   Present
      Injury location
      Pain characteristics
      Joint responses
      Determining whether the injury is acute or chronic
Observation
Palpation
   Bony palpation
   Soft-tissue palpation
Special Tests
   Movement assessment
      Active range of motion
      Passive range of motion
         Normal endpoints
         Abnormal endpoints
      Resisted motions
      Goniometric measurement of joint range
   Manual muscle testing
   Neurologic examination
      Cerebral function
      Cerebellar function
      Cranial nerve function
      Sensory testing
      Reflex testing
      Determining projected referred pain
      Testing joint stability
      Testing accessory motions
      Testing functional performance
      Postural examination
      Anthropometric measurements
      Volumetric measurements

formed on the sidelines, in the training room, in an emergency room, or in a sports medicine clinic. An injury may be evaluated immediately after the athlete has left the playing field when it is still in an acute phase, or evaluation make take place several hours or perhaps even days following acute injury.

The evaluation scheme is divided into four broad categories: history, observation, palpation, and a number of special tests that provide additional information about the extent of injuries. This evaluation scheme is sometimes referred to as the **HOPS** format (see *Focus Box:* "Off-the-field evaluation sequence"). The following discussion provides an overview of some of the steps and techniques that can be used in the evaluation process. (Chapters 18 through 27 provide the reader with specific injury assessment procedures.)

HOPS
- History
- Observation
- Palpation
- Special tests

History

Obtaining as much information as possible about the injury is of major importance to the examiner.[9] Understanding how the injury may have occurred and listening to the complaints of the athlete and to the athlete's answers to key questions can

History of musculoskeletal injuries

Information to obtain:

- Chief complaints and present problems
- If pain is present, its location, character, duration, variation, aggravation, distribution or radiation, intensity, and course
- Is the pain increased or decreased by specific activities or stresses?
- What situation or trauma caused the problem?
- Has the problem occurred before? If so, when, and how was it treated? Was treatment successful?

13-2

Critical Thinking Exercise

A fencer comes into the training room complaining of pain in his shoulder that he has had for about a week. He indicates that he first hurt the shoulder when lifting weights but did not think it was a bad injury. During the past week he has not been able to lift because of pain. He has continued to fence during practice, but his shoulder seems to be getting worse instead of better.

? What is the standard evaluation scheme that the athletic trainer should use?

provide important clues to the exact nature of the injury. The examiner becomes a detective in pursuit of as much accurate information as possible, which will lead to a determination of the true nature of the injury (see *Focus Box:* "History of musculoskeletal injuries"). From the history, the examiner develops strategies for further examination and possible immediate and follow-up management.[3]

When obtaining a history, the examiner should do the following:

- Be calm and reassuring.
- Express questions that are simple, not leading.
- Listen carefully to the athlete's complaints.
- Maintain eye contact to try and see what the athlete is feeling.
- Record exactly what the athlete said without interpretation.

Questions might be stated under specific headings in an attempt to get as complete a historical picture as possible. In many cases, a history becomes clear-cut because the mechanism, trauma, and pathology are obvious; in other situations, symptoms and signs may be obscured.

Past History of Injury

It is important to first obtain information about previous or preexisting injuries that the athlete may have had. The athletic trainer who is working with an athlete or group of athletes on a daily basis often has the advantage of being familiar with their medical history. Nevertheless, the first piece of information that should be obtained in an off-the-field injury evaluation would be

- Has this ever happened before? If so, when?

Present Injury

If conscious and coherent, the athlete is encouraged to describe the injury in detail. If the athletic trainer did not see the injury happen, he or she should try to get the athlete to describe in detail the mechanism of the injury.

- What is the problem?
- How did it occur?
- When did it occur?
- Did you fall? How did you land?
- Which direction did your joint move?
- Did you hear or feel something when it occurred?

If the athlete is unable to describe accurately how the injury occurred, perhaps a teammate or someone who observed the event can do so.

Injury location   The athlete should be asked to locate the area of complaint by pointing to it with one finger only. If the athlete can point to a specific pain site, the injury is probably localized. If the exact pain site cannot be indicated, the injury may be generalized and nonspecific.

Pain characteristics   The athlete should describe as accurately as possible exactly what the pain feels like.

- What type of pain is it? Nerve pain is sharp, bright, or burning. Bone pain tends to be localized and piercing. Pain in the vascular system tends to be poorly localized, aching, and referred from another area. Muscle pain is often dull, aching, and referred to another area.[18]
- Where is the pain? Determining pain origin makes the evaluation of musculoskeletal injuries difficult. The deeper the injury site, the more difficult it is to match the pain with the site of trauma. This factor often causes treatment to be performed at the wrong site. Conversely, the closer the injury is to the body surface, the better the elicited pain corresponds with the site of pain stimulation.[17]
- Does the pain change at different times? Pain that subsides during activity usually indicates a chronic inflammation. Pain that increases in a joint throughout the day indicates a progressive increase in edema.
- Does the athlete feel sensations other than pain? Pressure on nerve roots can produce pain or a sensation of "pins and needles" (paresthesia). What movement, if any, causes pain or other sensations?

Joint responses

- If the injury is related to a joint, is there instability?
- Does the joint feel as though it will give way?
- Does the joint lock and unlock?

Positive responses may indicate that the joint has a loose body that is catching or that is inhibiting the normal muscular support in the area.

Determining whether the injury is acute or chronic   The examiner should ask the athlete how long he or she has had the symptoms and how frequently they appear.

Observation

The examiner gains knowledge and understanding of the athlete's major complaint not only from a history but also through general observation, often done at the same time the history is taken. What is observed is commonly modified by the athlete's major complaints. The following are suggested as specific points to observe:

- How does the athlete move?
- Is there a limp?
- Are movements abnormally slow, jerky, and asynchronous?
- Is movement not possible in a body part?
- Is the body held stiffly to protect against pain?
- Does the athlete's facial expression indicate pain or lack of sleep?
- Are there any obvious body asymmetries?
- Is there an obvious deformity?
- Does soft tissue appear swollen or wasted as a result of atrophy?
- Are there unnatural protrusions or lumps such as occur with a dislocation or fracture?
- Is there a postural malalignment?
- Are there abnormal sounds such as crepitus when the athlete moves?
- Does a body area appear inflamed?
- Is there swelling, heat, or redness?

Palpation

Some examiners use palpation in the beginning of the examination procedure, whereas others use it only when they believe they have identified the specific injury site by other assessment means.[6,18] In some cases, palpation would be beneficial at both the beginning and the end of the examination. The two areas of palpation are bony and soft tissue. Like all examination procedures, palpation must be performed systematically. The examiner starts with very light pressure, followed by gradually deeper pressure, and usually begins away from the site of complaint and gradually moves toward it.

Bony Palpation

Both the injured and noninjured sites should be palpated and compared. The sense of touch might reveal an abnormal gap at a joint, swelling on a bone, joints that are misaligned, or abnormal protuberances associated with a joint or a bone.

Soft-Tissue Palpation

Through palpation, with the athlete as relaxed as possible, the examiner can assess normal soft-tissue relationships. Tissue deviations such as swelling, lumps, gaps, abnormal muscle tension, and temperature variations can be detected. The palpation of soft tissue can detect where ligaments or tendons have torn. The examiner can determine variations in the shape of structures, differences in tissue tightness and textures, differentiation of tissue that is pliable and soft from tissue that is more resilient. Involuntary muscle twitching or tremors may also be felt. Excessive skin dryness and moisture can also be noted. The examiner can become aware of abnormal skin sensations such as diminished sensation (dysesthesia), numbness (anesthesia), or increased sensation (hyperesthesia). Like bony palpation, soft-tissue palpation must be performed on both sides of the body for comparison.

Special Tests

Special tests have been designed for almost every body region as means for detecting specific pathologies. They are often used to substantiate what has been learned from the history, observation, and palpation portions of the evaluation process.

Movement Assessment

If a joint or soft-tissue lesion exists, the athlete is likely to complain of pain on movement. Cyriax has developed a method for locating and identifying a lesion by applying tension selectively to each of the structures that might produce this pain.[6] Tissues are classified as contractile or inert. Contractile tissues include muscles and their tendons; inert tissues include bones, ligaments, joint capsules, fascia, bursae, nerve roots, and dura mater.

If a lesion is present in contractile tissue, pain will occur on active motion in one direction and on passive motion in the opposite direction. Thus, a muscle strain would cause pain on both active contraction and passive stretch. Contractile tissues are tested through the midrange by an isometric contraction against maximum resistance. The specific location of the lesion within the musculotendinous unit cannot be identified by the isometric contraction.[5]

A lesion of inert tissue will elicit pain on active and passive movement in the same direction. A sprain of a ligament will result in pain whenever that ligament is stretched either through active contraction or passive stretching. It is not possible to identify a specific lesion of inert tissue by looking at movement patterns alone; other special tests must be done to identify injured structures.[3]

Active range of motion   Movement assessment should begin with **active range of motion** (AROM). The athletic trainer should evaluate quality of movement, range of movement, motion in other planes, movement at varying speeds, and strength throughout the range but in particular at the endpoint. A complaint of pain on active motion will not distinguish contractile pain from inert pain, so the athletic trainer must proceed with an evaluation of both passive and resistive motion. An athlete who seems to be pain free in each of these tests throughout a full range should be tested by applying passive pressure at the endpoint.

Passive range of motion   When **passive range of motion** (PROM) is being assessed, the athlete must relax completely and allow the athletic trainer to move the extremity to reduce the influence of the contractile elements. Particular attention

---

13-3

Critical Thinking Exercise

An athletic trainer is evaluating a volleyball player who complains of pain in her elbow. During the evaluation, manual muscle testing and active and passive range of motion tests reveal pain when the elbow is moved into extension both actively and passively. However, there is no pain when the elbow is moved actively into flexion.

? Does the injury more likely involve the ligament or the musculotendinous unit?

Movement examination includes:
- Active movement
- Passive movement
- Resisted isometric movement

active range of motion
Joint motion that occurs because of muscle contraction.

passive range of motion
Movement that is performed completely by the examiner.

should be directed toward the sensation of the athlete at the end of the passive range. The athletic trainer should categorize the "feel" of the endpoints as described in the following sections.[6]

Normal endpoints   Normal endpoints include the following:

- Soft-tissue approximation—soft and spongy, a gradual painless stop (e.g., knee flexion)
- Capsular feel—an abrupt, hard, firm endpoint with only a little give (e.g., endpoint of hip rotation)
- Bone to bone—a distinct and abrupt endpoint when two hard surfaces come in contact with one another (e.g., elbow in full extension)
- Muscular—a springy feel with some associated discomfort (e.g., end of shoulder abduction)

Abnormal endpoints   Abnormal endpoints include the following:

- Empty feel—movement is definitely beyond the anatomical limit, and pain occurs before the end of the range (e.g., a complete ligament rupture)
- Spasm—involuntary muscle contraction that prevents motion because of pain; also called guarding (e.g., back spasms)
- Loose—occurs in extreme hypermobility (e.g., previously sprained ankle)
- Springy block—a rebound at the endpoint (e.g., meniscus tear)

Throughout the passive range of movement, the athletic trainer is looking for limitation in movement and the presence of pain. An athlete's report of pain before the end of the available range probably indicates acute inflammation in which stretching and manipulation are both contraindicated as treatments. Pain occurring synchronous with the end of the range indicates that the condition is subacute and has progressed to some inert tissue fibrosis. If no pain occurs at the end of the range, the condition is chronic and contractures have replaced inflammation.[24]

Resisted motions   The purpose of resisted movement is to evaluate the status of the contractile tissues. The athlete is asked to perform an isometric contraction near the midrange of movement to avoid pinching other inert structures around the joint. Assessing resisted motion is different from manual muscle testing, in which muscle strength is evaluated throughout a full range of motion. Muscular contraction is under neural control; thus lesions of the nervous system may affect the strength of muscular contraction. Cyriax has designed the following system for differentiating lesions through assessment of muscular contraction.[6]

Resisted movement requires an isometric contraction at the midpoint in the range.

1. Strong and painless—normal muscle
2. Strong and painful—minor lesion in some part of the muscle or tendon
3. Weak and painless—complete rupture of muscle or tendon or some nervous system disorder
4. Weak and painful—a gross lesion of contractile tissue
5. Pain on repetition—a single contraction is strong and painless, but repetition produces pain as would exist in some vascular disorder
6. All muscles painful—may indicate a serious emotional or psychological problem

Goniometric measurement of joint range   Goniometry, which measures joint range of motion, is an essential procedure during the early, intermediate, and late stages of injury. Full range of motion of an affected body part is a major criterion for the return of the athlete to participation. Active and passive joint range of motion can be measured using goniometry (Figure 13-4).

Although a number of different types of goniometers are on the market, the most commonly used are ones that measure 0 to 180 degrees in each direction. The arms of the instrument are usually 12 to 16 inches (30 to 40 cm) long, with one arm stationary and the other fully movable.[5,10]

When measuring joint range of motion, the goniometer should generally be placed along the lateral surface of the extremity being measured. The 0, or starting, position for any movement is identical to the standard anatomical position. The

Figure 13-4

Goniometric measurement of hip joint flexion.

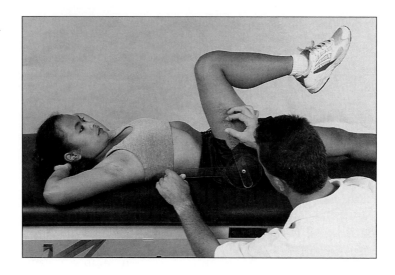

athlete should move the joint either actively or passively through the available range to the endpoint. The stationary arm of the goniometer should be placed parallel with the longitudinal axis of the fixed reference part. The movable arm should be placed along the longitudinal axis of the movable segment. (NOTE: The axis of rotation will change throughout the range as movement occurs. Thus the axis of rotation is located at the intersection of the stationary and movable arms.) A reading in degrees of motion should be taken and recorded as either active or passive range of motion for that specific movement. Accuracy and consistency in goniometric measurement require practice and repetition.

The normal available range of motion for specific movements at individual joints is indicated in Table 13-2. Specific goniometric measurement techniques for each joint are described in Chapters 18 through 25.

Manual Muscle Testing

Manual muscle testing is an integral part of the physical examination process.[13,15] The ability of the injured athlete to tolerate varying levels of resistance can indicate a great deal about the extent of the injury to the contractile units. For the athlete, the limitation in muscular strength is generally caused by pain. As pain diminishes and the healing process progresses, levels of muscular strength gradually return to normal. The development of isokinetic testing devices has enabled the athletic trainer to test levels of muscular strength objectively within the limitations of those devices.[7]

Manual muscle testing is usually performed with the athlete positioned such that individual muscles or muscle groups can be isolated and tested through a full range of motion via the application of manual resistance. The ability of the athlete to move through a full range of motion or to offer resistance to movement is subjectively graded by the athletic trainer according to various classification systems and grading criteria that have been developed. Table 13-3 indicates a commonly used grading system for manual muscle testing.

Neurologic Examination

Neurological examination:
- Cerebral function
- Cranial nerve function
- Cerebellar function
- Sensory testing
- Reflex testing

The neurologic examination usually follows manual muscle testing. It consists of five major areas: cerebral function, cranial nerve function, cerebellar function, sensory testing, reflex testing, and determining referred pain. In cases of musculoskeletal injury that does not involve head injury, it is generally not necessary to assess cerebral function, cranial nerve function, and cerebellar function. The athletic trainer should concentrate instead on sensation testing and reflex testing to determine involvement of the peripheral nervous system after injury.

TABLE 13-2 Range of Joint Motion

Joint	Action	Degrees of Motion
Shoulder	Flexion	180
	Extension	50
	Adduction	40
	Abduction	180
	Medial rotation	90
	Lateral rotation	90
Elbow	Flexion	145
Forearm	Pronation	80
	Supination	85
Wrist	Flexion	80
	Extension	70
	Abduction	20
	Adduction	45
Hip	Flexion	125
	Extension	10
	Abduction	45
	Adduction	40
	Medial rotation	45
	Lateral rotation	45
Knee	Flexion	140
Ankle	Planter flexion	45
	Dorsiflexion	20
Foot	Inversion	40
	Eversion	20

TABLE 13-3 Manual Muscle Strength Grading

Grade	Percentage (%)	Value of Concentration	Muscle Strength
5	100	Normal	Complete range of motion (ROM) against gravity, with full resistance
4	75	Good	Complete ROM against gravity, with some resistance
3	50	Fair	Complete ROM against gravity, with no resistance
2	25	Poor	Complete ROM, with gravity omitted
1	10	Trace	Evidence of slight contractility, with no joint motion
0	0	Zero	No evidence of muscle contractility

Cerebral function   Tests for general cerebral function include questions that assess general affect, level of consciousness, intellectual performance, emotional status, thought content, sensory interpretation (visual, auditory, tactile), and language skills.

Cranial nerve function   The function of the twelve cranial nerves can be quickly determined by assessing the quality of the following: sense of smell, eye tracking, imitation of facial expressions, biting down, balance, swallowing, tongue protrusion, and strength of shoulder shrugs. Table 13-4 lists the cranial nerves and their specific functions.

Cerebellar function   Because the cerebellum controls purposeful, coordinated movement, tests such as touching finger to nose, touching finger to finger of examiner, drawing alphabets in the air with the foot, heel-toe walking, and others will determine dysfunction.

TABLE 13-4 Cranial Nerves and Their Function

I.	Olfactory	Smell
II.	Optic	Vision
III.	Oculomotor	Eye movement, opening of eyelid, constriction of pupil, focusing
IV.	Trochlear	Inferior and lateral movement of eye
V.	Trigeminal	Sensation to the face, mastication
VI.	Abducens	Lateral movement of eye
VII.	Facial	Motor nerve of facial expression; taste; control of tear, nasal, sublingual salivary, and submaxillary glands
VIII.	Vestibulocochlear	Hearing and equilibrium
IX.	Glossopharyngeal	Swallowing, salivation, gag reflex, sensation from tongue and ear
X.	Vagus	Swallowing; speech; regulation of pulmonary, cardiovascular, and gastrointestinal functions
XI.	Accessory	Swallowing, innervation of sternocleidomastoid muscle
XII.	Hypoglossal	Tongue movement, speech, swallowing

Sensory testing   A major component of musculoskeletal assessment is determining the distribution of peripheral nerves and dermatomes (Figure 13-5). A dermatome is an area of skin that is innervated by the cutaneous neurons of a single spinal nerve or cranial nerve. The term *dermatome* is sometimes confused with *myotomes,* which are found in developing embryo. Segmental myotomes eventually develop into groups of muscles that are innervated by a specific spinal nerve.

Although peripheral nerve distribution varies with individuals, it is more predictable than dermatome distribution.[7] As the dermatome examination progresses, the examiner compares sensation from one side of the body to the other using the following tests:

- Superfical sensation—touch dermatomes with cotton
- Superficial pain—touch dermatomes with a pin
- Deep pressure pain—squeeze a muscle (e.g., gastrocnemius)
- Sensitivity of temperature—touch dermatomes with ice cube
- Sensitivity of vibration—touch dermatomes with a tuning fork
- Position sense—move fingers or toes passively and ask athlete to indicate direction

Reflex testing   The term *reflex* refers to an involuntary response to a stimulus. In terms of the neurological examination there are three types of reflexes: deep tendon (somatic) reflexes, superficial reflexes, and pathological reflexes.

A deep tendon reflex is caused by stimulation of the stretch reflex (see Chapter 4) and results in an involuntary contraction of a muscle because of stretch of its tendon. Deep tendon reflexes can be elicited at the tendons of the biceps (C5), brachioradialis (C6), triceps (C7), patella (L4), and Achilles (S1). Table 13-5 shows a grading system for deep reflexes.[12]

Superficial reflexes are elicited by stimulation of the skin at specific sites, which produces a reflex muscle contraction. Superficial reflexes include upper abdominal (T7, 8, 9), lower abdominal (T11, 12), cremasteric (T12, L1), plantar (S1, 2), and gluteal (L4, S3). An absence of a superficial reflex is indicative of some lesion in the cerebral cortex of the brain.[12]

Pathological reflexes are also superficial reflexes. The presence of a pathological reflex indicates a lesion in the cerebral cortex; an absence indicates integrity. Babinski's sign, in which stroking of the lateral plantar surface produces extension and splaying of the toes, is an example of a pathological reflex.[12] Chaddock's, Oppenheim's, and Gordon's are additional pathological reflexes.

13-4

Critical Thinking Exercise

A receiver in football has his feet taken out from under him by a tackler and lands flat on his low back with his legs above him. An on-the-field evaluation reveals unilateral decreased muscle strength, decreased sensation, and a decreased patellar tendon reflex in the right lower extremity.

? Based on the findings of the evaluation, how should the athletic trainer manage this injury?

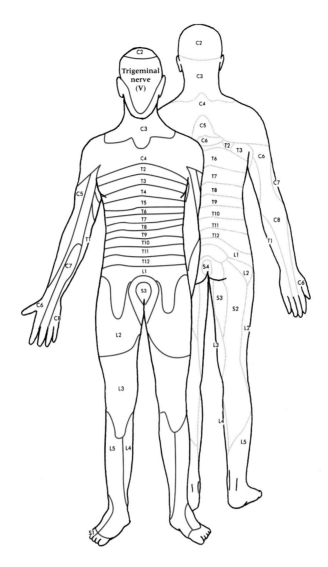

Figure 13-5

Numbness, referred pain, or other nerve involvements often follow the segmental distribution of spinal nerves on the skin's surface.

Determining projected referred pain   As discussed in Chapter 10, a complaint of deep, burning pain or of an ache that is diffused or of a painful area with no signs of disorder or malfunctioning is most likely referred pain.[5] Cyriax considers that the common sites for pain referral are, in order of importance, joint capsule, tendon, muscle, ligament, and bursa.[6] Pressures from the dura mater or nerve sheath can also produce referred pain or other sensory responses. Palpation of what is thought to be the area at fault often is misleading. Detecting the selective tension of the tissue at fault is one of the best means for gathering correct data. Some

TABLE 13-5 Reflex Grading

	Grade	Definition
Absence of a reflex	0	Areflexia
Diminished reflex	1	Hyporeflexia
Average reflex	2	
Exaggerated reflex	3	Hyperreflexia
Clonus	4	Spasmodic alteration of muscle contraction and relaxation, indicating a nerve irritation

musculoskeletal pain is caused by myofascial trigger points, which are not related to deep, referred pain. Palpation is used to determine the presence or absence of tense tissue bands and tender trigger points.

Testing Joint Stability

A number of specific tests are described in Chapters 18 through 25 for determining the integrity of the ligaments surrounding a particular joint. Joint stability tests provide information about the grade of a sprain of a particular ligament and can determine the extent of the functional instability of the joint.

Testing Accessory Motions

Accessory motions refer to the manner in which one articulating joint surface moves relative to another.[2,22] Normal accessory component motions must occur for full-range movement to take place. Accessory motions are limited by tightness of the joint capsule and/or ligaments that surround a joint. It is critical for the athletic trainer to closely evaluate the injured joint to determine whether motion is limited by tightness of the musculotendinous units or by limitation in accessory motion involving the joint capsule and ligaments. If accessory motion is limited by some restriction of the joint capsule or the ligaments, joint mobilization techniques should be incorporated into the treatment program.[14] Joint mobilization is discussed in detail in Chapter 16.

Testing Functional Performance

Functional examination determines if the athlete has full strength, joint stability, and coordination and if the part is pain free.

Functional performance testing may be done as part of an initial evaluation to determine if an injury is severe enough to keep the athlete out of practice or competition. It may also be used to evaluate progress during a rehabilitation program. Decisions for return to full sports participation following injury should be based to a large extent on performance on functional tests. Functional testing should proceed gradually from minimal stress to tests that mimic the actual stress that would normally come from full sports participation. The major concern is whether the athlete has regained full strength, range of motion, speed, endurance, and neuromuscular control and is pain free.

Postural Examination

As discussed in Chapter 25, many cases of injuries in athletes can be attributed to body malalignments. Musculoskeletal assessment might be one area of a postural examination. It is designed to test for malalignments and asymmetries by viewing the body in comparison to a grid or plumb line (see Figures 25-23 through 25-25).

Anthropometric Measurements

Anthropometry is the science of measuring the human body. Anthropometric measurements include osteometry (measurement of the dimensions of the skeletal system), craniometry (measurement of the bones of the skull), skin-fold measurements to determine body composition (see Chapter 5), and height and weight measurements (see Chapter 2). Limb girth measurements taken during a rehabilitation program would also be considered a type of anthropometric measurement.

Volumetric Measurements

Volumetric measurements can be taken to determine changes in limb volume caused by swelling, which can be attributed to hemorrhage, edema, or inflammation. Limb volume may be measured in a volumetric tank that essentially measures the amount of water displaced by immersion of the limb in the tank (Figure 13-6). *Focus Box:* "Constructing and using a volumetric tank" describes the tank and the procedure for measuring limb volume.

Figure 13-6

Tank for measuring limb volume.

PROGRESS EVALUATIONS

The athletic trainer who is overseeing a rehabilitation program must constantly monitor the progress of the athlete toward full recovery throughout the rehabilitative process. In many instances the athletic trainer will be able to treat the injured athlete on a daily basis. This close supervision affords the athletic trainer the luxury of being able to continuously adjust or adapt the treatment program based on the progress made by the athlete on a day-to-day basis.

The progress evaluation should be based on the athletic trainer's knowledge of exactly what is occurring in the healing process at any given time. The timelines of injury healing provide the framework that dictates the progress of the rehabilitation program. The athletic trainer must understand that the aggressive approach taken in rehabilitation of the injured athlete does little to speed up the healing process. Progression will be limited by the contraints of that process.

Progress evaluations will be more limited in scope than the detailed off-the-field evaulation sequence described in this chapter. The off-the-field evaluation should be thorough and comprehensive. The athletic trainer should take time to systematically rule out information that is not pertinent to the present injury. Once the extraneous information has been eliminated, the subsequent progress evaluation can focus specifically on how the injury appears today compared with yesterday. Is the athlete better or worse as a result of the treatment program rendered on the previous day?

To ensure that the progress evaluation will be complete, the athletic trainer still needs to go through certain aspects of history, observation, palpation, and special testing.

History

The athletic trainer should ask the athlete the following questions:
- How is the pain today compared to yesterday?
- Are you able to move better and with less pain?
- Do you think that the treatment done yesterday helped or made you more sore?

Observation

The athletic trainer should make the following observations:
- Is the swelling today more or less than yesterday?
- Is the athlete able to move better today?

13-5

Critical Thinking E x e r c i s e

A gymnast is four months post-ACL reconstruction. She was last seen three months ago prior to leaving for summer vacation. She has returned for the beginning of classes and comes in to see the athletic trainer to see what kind of activities she should be doing in her rehabilitation program.

? To generate a progress note, what type of information does the athletic trainer need to know?

Focus

Constructing and using a volumetric tank

A volumetric tank (see Figure 13-6) is constructed of five 0.6-centimeter sheets of acrylic plastic molded together to form a container, which is mounted on a platform. The internal dimensions of the tank are: length = 35.6 centimeters, width = 17.8 centimeters, and depth = 20.3 centimeters. All the walls form right angles with each other as well as with the floor of the tank. The bottom of the tank has three adjustable leveling screws. Two of these screws are at one end of the tank base, while the third is centrally located on the opposite end. The end with one screw is classified as the front of the tank. A piece of acrylic plastic that measures 1.3 centimeters wide by 6 centimeters long is attached to the side of the tank, 4 centimeters from the back of the tank, to ensure consistent limb positioning in the tank.

A glass tube, 7.3 millimeters in diameter by 7.6 centimeters, passes through the front of the tank. The tube extends 3.2 centimeters outside the front wall of the tank. The tube is 5.1 centimeters from the top of the front wall and is perpendicular to the wall of the tank. A 10.2-centimeter piece of rubber tubing is attached to the end of the glass tube. This tubing combination llows for displaced water to be collected. A centimeter ruler, a skin thermometer, and a 500- and 1,000-milliliter graduated cylinder is used for all measurements. A water collection container is used to catch the runoff when the tubing is unclamped.

Procedure for measuring water displacement

The volumetric tank is placed on the floor and leveled using the adjusting screws. The tank is then filled to the 17-centimeter mark on the ruler with 33.5° C water. The subject places the limb against the back wall of the tank. The tank is then shaken gently to eliminate any air bubbles in the tank or on the surface of the limb. When the water is completely motionless, the tubing is unclamped and the runoff collected in the container. Any water remaining in the tubing should be shaken out into the collection container. The amount of water collected in the runoff container is measured in the graduated cylinders and the measurements noted.

- Is the athlete still guarding and protecting the injury?
- How is the athlete's affect? Is he or she upbeat and optimistic or depressed and negative?

Palpation

The athletic trainer should palpate the injured area to determine the following:

- Does the swelling have a different consistency today, and has the swelling pattern changed?
- Is the injured structure still as tender to touch?
- Is there any deformity present today that was not obvious yesterday?

Special Tests

The athletic trainer should use special tests to make the following determinations:

- Does ligamentous stress testing cause as much pain? Has the athletic trainer's assessment of the grade of instability changed?
- How does a manual muscle test compare with yesterday?
- Has either active or passive range of motion changed?
- Does accessory movement appear to be limited?
- Can the athlete perform a specific functional test better today than yesterday?

DOCUMENTING INJURY EVALUATION INFORMATION

Complete and accurate documentation of findings from an evaluation is essential.[21] As discussed in Chapter 3, accurate documentation can be a strong ally should the athletic trainer become involved in litigation. For the athletic trainer working in a clinical setting, clear, concise, accurate record keeping is necessary for third party reimbursement. Although the process may seem at times cumbersome and time consuming, the athletic trainer must develop proficiency not only in evaluation skills, but also in the ability to generate an accurate report of the findings from that evaluation.

SOAP Notes

Documentation of acute athletic injury can be effectively accomplished through a system designed to record subjective and objective findings and to document the immediate and future treatment plan for the athlete. The SOAP note format (subjective, objective, assessment, and plan) provides a standard format for recording injury information.[22] This method combines information provided by the athlete and observations of the examiner.[16] Figure 13-7 presents a recommended injury report form that includes these components of documentation. This form also includes a provision to document findings arising from more definitive evaluation or from the examiner's subsequent evaluation.

SOAP note:
- Subjective
- Objective
- Assessment
- Plan

SUBJECTIVE: The patient is a _____-year-old athlete with the above diagnosis. The athlete notes a _____ onset on _____. Past history for this condition is remarkable for/unremarkable. Diagnostic testing of _____ . Medications include _____ . The athletes' goals are to _____ . General medical history is remarkable for/unremarkable. The athlete will follow with MD on _____ .

OBJECTIVE: Measurable, Reproducible, Observable findings—Be Objective
OBSERVATION: Be descriptive
ROM: AROM/PROM—Measure with goniometer
STRENGTH: Strength to MMT—Use grading system 1 to 5
FLEXIBILITY: Try to document with goniometer if possible
PALPATION:
SENSATION:
SPECIAL TEST:
GAIT:
FUNCTIONAL TESTS:
TREATMENT:

ASSESSMENT: Your professional opinion of the athlete's problem
The athlete presents with the following problems (1) _____ , (2) _____ , (3) _____ , (4) _____ .

PLAN: Describe how you will manage the athlete regarding frequency of treatment, what the treatment will include (i.e., modalities, therapeutic exercise, home program, and follow up with you).
Short-term goals include (1) _____ , (2) _____ , (3) _____ , (4) _____ .
Long-term goals include _____ .

Signature _____ ATC

Figure 13-7

SOAP note form.

S (Subjective)

This component includes the subjective statements provided by the injured athlete. History taking is designed to elicit the subjective impressions of the athlete relative to time, mechanism, and site of injury. The type and course of the pain and the degree of disability experienced by the athlete are also noteworthy.

O (Objective)

Objective findings result from the athletic trainer's visual inspection, palpation, and assessment of active, passive, and resistive motion. Findings of special testing should also be noted here. Thus the objective report would include assessment of posture, presence of deformity or swelling, and location of point tenderness. Also, limitations of active motion and pain arising or disappearing during passive and resistive motion should be noted. Finally, the results of special tests relative to joint stability or apprehension are also included.

A (Assessment)

Assessment of the injury is the athletic trainer's professional judgment with regard to impression and nature of injury. Although the exact nature of the injury will not always be known initially, information pertaining to suspected site and anatomical structures involved is appropriate. A judgment of severity may be included but is not essential at the time of acute injury evaluation.

P (Plan)

The plan should include the first aid treatment rendered to the athlete and the sports therapist's intentions relative to disposition. Disposition may include referral for more definitive evaluation or simply application of splint, wrap, or crutches and a request to report for reevaluation the next day. If the injury is chronic, the examiner's plan for treatment and therapeutic exercise would be appropriate. The treatment plan should establish specific short-term goals for the rehabilitation program and should provide criteria-based guidelines for accomplishing these goals.

Progress Notes

Progress notes should be routinely written after each progress evaluation done throughout the course of the rehabilitation program. Progress notes can follow the SOAP format as indicated in the previous sections. They can be generated in the form of an expanded treatment note or done as a weekly summary. Information in the progress note should concentrate on the types of treatment received and the patient's response to that treatment, progress made toward the short-term goals established in the SOAP note, changes in the previous treatment plan and goals, and the course of treatment over the next several days.[1]

ADDITIONAL DIAGNOSTIC TESTS USED BY A PHYSICIAN

The physician, like the athletic trainer, often performs a detailed musculoskeletal examination on the injured athlete. Often, the physician and the athletic trainer will discuss and compare their individual findings. Because the physician is legally charged with determining a diagnosis and deciding on a course of treatment, he or she may have to acquire and compare additional information. This information can come from imaging techniques that may include plain film radiographs (X rays), arthrography, arthroscopy, myelography, computed tomography, bone scanning, magnetic resonance imaging, ultrasonography, and echocardiography.[19] Other tests might include electrocardiography, electroencephalography, electromyography, nerve conduction velocity, synovial fluid analysis, blood testing, and urinalysis.

13-6

Critical Thinking Exercise

A field hockey player is tripped, twists her knee, and falls hard on artificial turf on that same knee. There is immediate swelling and pain. After evaluation, the athletic trainer is not sure what the injury is and sends the athlete directly to the physician for diagnosis. The physician decides that additional diagnostic tests are necessary to determine the exact pathology.

? What diagnostic tests is the physician likely to order to determine the exact nature and extent of the knee injury?

Imaging Techniques

Plain Film Radiography (X rays)

An X-ray examination assists the physician in determining fractures and dislocations or any bone abnormality that may be present. It may also be used to rule out serious disease such as an infection or neoplasm. A trained radiologist can detect some soft-tissue factors, such as joint swelling and ectopic bone development in ligaments and tendons (Figure 13-8A).[4]

Arthrography

Arthrography is the visual study of a joint via X ray after injection of an opaque dye, air, or a combination of air and opaque dye into the joint space. This procedure can show the disruption of soft tissue and loose bodies in the joint.

Arthroscopy

The fiber-optic arthroscope is widely used by orthopedists in surgery. It is considered more accurate than the arthrogram but is more invasive, requiring anesthesia and a small incision for the introduction of the arthroscope (endoscope) into the joint space. While the arthroscope is in the joint, the surgeon can perform surgical procedures such as removing loose bodies and, in some cases, suturing torn tissues.[19]

Arthroscopy uses a fiber-optic arthroscope to view the inside of a joint.

Myelography

During myelography, an opaque dye is introduced into the spinal canal (epidural space) through a lumbar puncture. While the patient is tilted, the dye is allowed to flow to different levels of the spinal cord. Using this contrast medium, physicians can detect conditions such as tumors, nerve root compression, and disk disease as well as other diseases within the spinal cord.

Computed Tomography

Computed tomography (CT) penetrates the body with a thin, fan-shaped X-ray beam, producing a cross-sectional view of tissues. Unlike X-ray images, CT images allow the injured structure to be viewed from many angles. As the machine scans, a computer compares the many views; these electrical signals are then processed by a computer into a visual image (Figure 13-8B).

Bone Scanning

A bone scan involves the intravenous introduction of a radioactive tracer such as technetium-99. By imaging the entire skeleton or part of a skeleton, bony lesions in which there is some inflammation, such as stress fractures, can be detected (Figure 13-8C).

Magnetic Resonance Imaging

Magnetic resonance imaging (MRI) surrounds the body with powerful electromagnets, creating a field as much as 600,000 times as strong as that of the earth.[2] The magnetic current focuses on hydrogen atoms in water molecules and aligns them; when the current is shut off, the atoms continue to spin, emitting an energy that is detected by the computer. The hydrogen atoms in different tissue spin at different rates, thus producing different images. In many ways, MRI provides clearer images than does CT scanning. Despite the expense of MRI, it is currently the test of choice by physicians for detecting soft-tissue lesions (Figure 13-8D).

Ultrasonography

Ultrasonography is the use of ultrasound to view location, measurement, or delineation of an organ or tissue by measuring the reflection or transmission of high-frequency ultrasound waves. A computer calculates the distance from the sound-reflecting or sound-absorbing surface and creates a two-dimensional image.

Figure 13-8

Examination of the knee.
A, X ray. **B,** CT scan. **C,** Bone
scan. *(continued)*

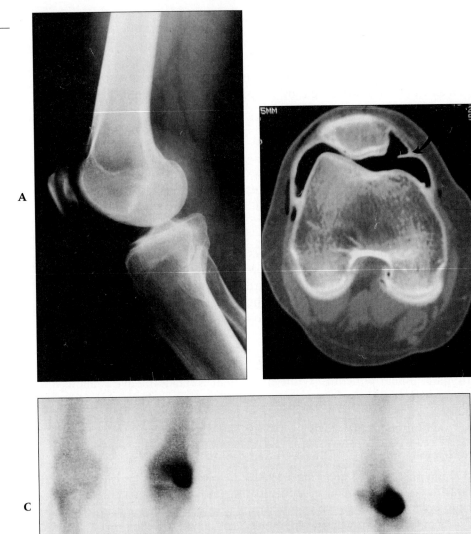

Echocardiography

Echocardiography uses ultrasound to produce a graphic record of internal cardiac structures. An echocardiogram is most often used to visualize the cardiac valves and to determine the dimensions of the left atrium and both ventricles.

Other Diagnostic Tests

Electrocardiography

An electrocardiogram (ECG) records the electrical activity of the heart to determine whether impulse formation, conduction, and depolarization and repolarization of the atria and ventricles follows a normal pattern. It is of value in diagnosing causes of abnormal cardiac rhythm and myocardial damage.

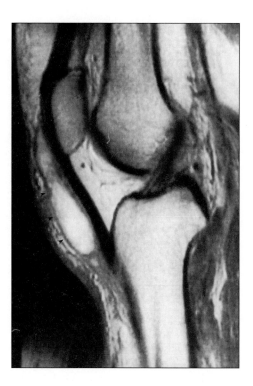

Figure 13-8—cont'd

D, MRI.

Electroencephalography

The electroencephalogram (EEG) records electrical potentials produced in the brain on an instrument called an electroencephalograph. It is used to detect changes or abnormalities in brain wave patterns.

Electromyography

Electromyography (EMG) involves the graphic recording of a muscle contraction and the amount of electrical activity generated in muscle using either surface or needle electrodes. Motor unit potentials can be observed on an oscilloscope screen or from a graphic recording called an electromyogram. Various muscular conditions can be evaluated.

Nerve Conduction Velocity

Determining the conduction velocity of a nerve may provide key information to the physician about a number of neuromuscular conditions. After a stimulus is applied to a peripheral nerve, the speed with which a muscle action occurs is measured. Delays in conduction might indicate nerve compression or other muscular or nerve disease.

Synovial Fluid Analysis

The primary purpose of synovial fluid analysis is to detect the presence of an infection in the joint. The test also confirms the diagnosis of gout and differentiates noninflammatory joint disease such as degenerative arthritis from inflammatory conditions such as rheumatoid arthritis.[4]

Analysis of synovial fluid and blood can be used to detect musculoskeletal infections.

Blood Testing

The physician may decide to run a complete blood count (CBC) on the athlete for many different reasons. The most common reasons are to screen for anemia (too few red cells) or infection (too many white cells).[25] Samples may be taken in a syringe

TABLE 13-6 Normal Laboratory Values of a Complete Blood Count

Test	Normal Values
Red blood cell count	Males 5.4 million/mm^3
	Females 4.8 million/mm^3
White blood cell count	5,000–9,000/mm^3
Platelet count	250,000–400,000/mm^3
Hematocrit	Male 40%–54%
	Female 38%–47%
Hemoglobin	Male 14–16.5 g/100 ml
	Female 12–15 g/100 ml
Cholesterol	<200 mg/dl

from a vein in the arm or from a needle stick in the finger. A routine CBC addresses the following:

- The red blood cell count looks at the number of cells per unit volume to detect anemias, prolonged infections, iron deficiencies, internal bleeding, and certain types of cancers.
- Hemoglobin levels are closely associated with red blood cell count and tend to reflect overall blood volume.
- The hematocrit measures how much of the total blood volume is made up of red blood cells. A low hematocrit indicates certain types of anemias.
- The white blood cell count is used to determine the presence of bacteria. Differentiation of white cell types microscopically can identify specific types of infection.
- A deficiency in the platelet count can lead to dangerous internal bleeding.
- Blood testing can also measure levels of serum cholesterol. The recommended desirable range is <200 mg/dL.

Normal laboratory values for the CBC are summarized in Table 13-6.

Urinalysis

Urinalysis is a common test that can yield a large quantity of information.[20] In most cases a sample of urine in a small dry container is all that is needed. If the urine will not be analyzed within one hour, the sample should be refrigerated. A routine urinalysis addresses the following:[25]

- Specific gravity indicates the ability of the kidney to concentrate and dilute fluids.
- The pH refers to how acid or alkaline the urine is. It may be acidic in cases of diabetes or dehydration. Alkaline urine is present in urinary tract infections and kidney disease. Presence of glucose may indicate diabetes.
- Presence of ketones, a by-product of fat metabolism, may also indicate diabetes.
- Hemoglobin may appear in urine after intense exercise or from kidney disease.
- Presence of protein indicates kidney disease.
- Presence of nitrate indicates infection.
- A small amount of urine is examined under a microscope to find red blood cells, white blood cells, and bacteria.
- If bacteria are present, a urine culture may be necessary to determine the specific bacteria causing an infection.
- Many additional tests may also be done on urine, including electrolytes, hormones, and drug levels.

Normal laboratory values for a standard urinalysis are listed in Table 13-7.

TABLE 13-7 Normal Laboratory Values of a Urinalysis

Test	Normal Values
Output	1,000–1,500 ml
Color	Yellow to amber and clear
Specific gravity	1.010–1.025
Osmolality	500–800 mosm/kg water
pH	4.6–4.8
Uric acid	0.6–1 g/24 hr
Urea	23–25 g/24 hr
Creatine	1–2 g/24 hr

SUMMARY

- Once the athlete has been transported from the site of initial injury, a detailed off-the-field injury evaluation may be performed on the sidelines, in the training room, in an emergency room, or in a sports medicine clinic.
- Athletic trainers evaluate sports injuries whereas physicians diagnose injuries.
- To accurately evaluate an injury, the athletic trainer must possess a thorough background in human anatomy, including surface anatomy, body planes, and anatomical directions; and an in-depth understanding of the musculoskeletal system, with special focus on adverse biomechanical forces, which become pathomechanical. After they are assessed, sports injuries must be described using appropriate terminology.
- The off-the-field evaluation scheme is divided into four broad categories: history, observation, palpation, and a number of special tests that provide additional information about the extent of injuries.
- The progress evaluation focuses specifically on how the injury appears today compared with yesterday and are more limited in scope than the detailed off-the-field evaluation sequence is.
- The SOAP note (subjective, objective, assessment, and plan) provides a standard format for documenting and recording injury information. Progress notes may also be recorded in the SOAP format.
- To make an accurate diagnosis, the physician may need to use a particular imaging technique or one of several additional tests.

Web Sites

Cramer First Aider: http://www.ccsd.k12.wy.us/cchs_web/cramerfirstaider/fstaider.htm

National Athletic Trainers' Association: http://www.nata.org

Solutions to Critical Thinking EXERCISES

13-1 The athletic trainer must realize that the physician has more training and is usually more skilled in injury diagnosis. Although the athletic trainer correctly identified the MCL sprain, the meniscus tear was completely overlooked. The athletic trainer should routinely refer an injured athlete to the physician for diagnosis. The injury evaluation done by the athletic trainer should reveal the same results as the physician diagnosis.

13-2 The athletic trainer should first take a subjective history from the injured athlete, and follow that with an objective examination that includes observation, palpation, range-of-motion testing, manual muscle testing, a neurological examination, special tests, tests for joint stability, and a functional performance evaluation.

13-3 In this case, a ligamentous injury is more likely. A lesion of inert tissue will elicit pain on active and passive movement in the same direction. If a lesion is present in contractile tissue, pain will occur on active motion in one direction and on passive motion in the opposite direction. A sprain of a ligament will result in pain whenever that ligament is stretched either through active contraction or passive stretching.

13-4 Generally, injury to the spinal cord would result in bilateral symptoms. Unilateral changes are more indicative of peripheral nerve injury. However, any change in the neurological status of the athlete is cause for great concern. The athletic trainer should remove the athlete from the playing field using a stretcher or, preferably, a spine board.

13-5 To ensure that the progress evaluation will be complete, the athletic trainer needs to go through history, observation, palpation, and special testing. The athlete should be asked pertinent questions such as "What types of exercises have you done for the past three months?" and "What type of pain, if any, are you still experiencing?" Observation of the symmetry to the other knee and palpation of the injured structures should be done. Range of motion, muscle strength, joint stability, and neuromuscular control should also be assessed.

13-6 Initially, it is likely that standard knee X rays would be used to determine the presence of a fracture. An MRI is widely used by sports medicine physicians to determine injury to ligamentous, meniscal, or other soft tissues. On occasion, a diagnostic arthoscopy might be done to allow direct observation of the injured structures.

REVIEW QUESTIONS AND CLASS ACTIVITIES

1. Differentiate between injury evaluation and diagnosis.
2. What basic knowledge must the examiner have before making an injury assessment?
3. Explain the key terminology necessary to communicate the results of an assessment.
4. Identify the various descriptive assessment terms.
5. How should an examiner take a history? What questions should be asked?
6. Describe palpation and when and how it should be performed.
7. What can be ascertained from active, passive, and resisted isometric movement?
8. Explain how muscle testing, reflex testing, and sensation testing are performed.
9. What part do special tests play in injury assessment?
10. When should a functional evaluation be given?
11. What information should be included in a SOAP note?
12. What insights can a physician gain by having special laboratory tests performed? Describe each test in detail.

REFERENCES

1. Arrigo C: Clinical documentation. In Konin J: *Clinical athletic training*, Thorofare, NJ, 1997, Slack.
2. Barak T, Rosen E, Sofer R: Mobility: passive orthopedic manual therapy. In Gould J, Davies G, editors: *Orthopedic and sports physical therapy*, St Louis, 1994, Mosby.
3. Bates B: *A guide to physical examination and history taking*, Philadelphia, 1991, Lippincott.
4. Birnbaum JS: *The musculoskeletal manual*, Orlando, 1986, Grune & Stratton.
5. Clarkson H, Gilewich G: *Musculoskeletal assessment: joint range of motion and manual muscle strength*, Baltimore, 1989, Williams & Wilkins.
6. Cyriax J: *Textbook of orthopaedic medicine*, ed 8, London, 1982, Bailliere Tindale.
7. Daniels L, Worthingham C: *Muscle testing: techniques of manual examination*, Philadelphia, 1997, Saunders.
8. Ellison AE, chairman, editorial board: *Athletic training and sports medicine*, Chicago, 1984, American Academy of Orthopaedic Surgeons.
9. Evans R: *Illustrated essentials in orthopedic physical assessment*, St Louis, 1994, Mosby.
10. Gehring P: Physical assessment begins with a history, *RN* 54(11): 27, 1991.
11. Gross J, Fetto J, Rosen E: *Musculoskeletal examination*, Cambridge, Mass, 1996, Blackwell Scientific.
12. Hartley A: *Practical joint assessment*, St Louis, 1991, Mosby.
13. Hoppenfeld S: *Physical examination of the spine and extremities*, New York, 1976, Appleton-Century-Crofts.
14. Kaltenborn FM: *Mobilization of the extremity joints: examination and basic treatments*, Oslo, 1980, Olaf Norlis Bokhandel.
15. Kendall F, Kendall E: *Muscles testing and function*, Baltimore, 1983, Williams & Wilkins.
16. Kettenbach G: *Writing SOAP notes*, Philadelphia, 1990, Davis.
17. Lynch MK, Kessler RM: Pain. In Kessler RM, Hertling D, editors: *Management of common musculoskeletal disorders*, Philadelphia, 1983, Harper & Row.
18. Magee DL: *Orthopedic physical assessment*, Philadelphia, 1997, Saunders.
19. Milbauer D: Principles of radiographic evaluation and imaging techniques. In Nicholas J, Hershman E: *The lower extremity and spine in sports medicine*, St Louis, 1995, Mosby.
20. Peterson M, Holbrook J, Von-Hales D: Contributions of the history, physical examination, and laboratory investigation in making medical diagnosis, *West J Med* 156(2):163, 1992.
21. Post M: *Physical examination of the musculoskeletal system*, Chicago, 1987, Year Book.
22. Prentice W: *Rehabilitation techniques in sports medicine*, Dubuque, 1999, WCB/McGraw-Hill.
23. Starkey C, Ryan J: *Evaluation of orthopedic and athletic injuries*, Philadelphia, 1996, FA Davis.
24. Wadsworth C: *Manual examination and treatment of the spine and extremities*, Baltimore, 1988, Williams & Wilkins.
25. Wurman R: *Medical access*, Los Angeles, 1985, Access Press.

ANNOTATED BIBLIOGRAPHY

Birnbaum JS: *The musculoskeletal manual*, Orlando, 1986, Grune & Stratton.

This text is written for medical professionals who require a direct and simple approach for recognizing and managing musculoskeletal problems. A great number of the conditions discussed relate to sports trauma.

Booher JM, Thibodeau GA: *Athletic injury assessment*, ed 3, St Louis, 1994, Mosby.

This outstanding text is addressed directly to the practitioner in sports medicine or athletic training. All aspects of musculoskeletal and internal sports injuries are considered.

Cyriax J, Cyriax P: *Illustrated manual of orthopaedic medicine*, London, 1983, Butterworth.

This beautifully color-illustrated text is designed for diagnosing and providing Cyriax management to musculoskeletal conditions.

Gross J, Fetto J, Rosen E: *Musculoskeletal examination*, Cambridge, Mass, 1996, Blackwell Scientific.

This evaluation text is written primarily for physicians.

Hoppenfeld S: *Physical examination of the spine and extremities*, New York, 1976, Appleton-Century-Crofts.

This text presents an easy-to-follow, methodical, and in-depth procedure for examining musculoskeletal conditions.

Konin J, Wiksten D, Isear J: *Special tests for orthopedic examination*, Thorofare, NJ, 1997, Slack.

This well-illustrated text details examination techniques used in evaluating musculoskeletal injuries.

Magee DJ: *Orthopedic physical assessment*, Philadelphia, 1997, Saunders.

The strength of this extremely well-illustrated book with excellent depth of coverage lies in its coverage of injuries commonly found during athletic training.

Post M: *Physical examination of the musculoskeletal system*, Chicago, 1987, Year Book.

This text contains contributions by many experts in the field of orthopedic examination. Each major joint is covered in detail.

Starkey C, Ryan J: *Evaluation of orthopedic and athletic injuries*, Philadelphia, 1996, FA Davis.

This detailed, well-illustrated text addresses all aspects of injury assessment for the athletic trainer.

Bloodborne Pathogens

When you finish this chapter you should be able to

- Explain what bloodborne pathogens are and how they can infect athletes and athletic trainers.
- Describe the transmission, symptoms, signs, and treatment of hepatitis B virus.
- Describe the transmission, symptoms, and signs of human immunodeficiency virus.
- Explain how human immunodeficiency virus is most often transmitted.
- List the pros and cons of sports participation of athletes with hepatitis B virus or human immunodeficiency virus.
- Discuss universal precautions as mandated by the Occupational Safety and Health Administration and how they apply to the athletic trainer.

Bloodborne pathogens are transmitted through contact with blood or other bodily fluids. Hepatitis, especially the hepatitis B virus (HBV), and human immunodeficiency virus (HIV) are of special concern.[3] Despite the media attention given to bloodborne pathogens in recent years, many athletic trainers have only moderate understanding of the magnitude of the problem.[10]

It has always been important for the athletic trainer as a health care provider to be concerned with maintaining an environment in the athletic training room that is as clean and sterile as possible.[1,16] In our society it has become critical for everyone in the population to take measures to prevent the spread of infectious diseases.[12] Failure to do so may predispose any individual to life-threatening situations. The athletic trainer must take every precaution to minimize the potential for exposure to blood or other infectious materials (Figure 14-1).

VIRUS REPRODUCTION

A virus is a submicroscopic parasitic organism that is dependent on the nutrients within cells. A virus consists of a strand of either deoxyribonucleic acid (DNA) or ribonuleic acid (RNA). A virus contains one or the other, but not both. A virus consists of a shell of proteins surrounding genetic material. It is a parasite dependent on a host cell for metabolic and reproductive requirements. In general, viruses make their cell hosts ill by redirecting cellular activity to create more viruses (Figure 14- 2).

Figure 14-1

The athletic trainer must take precautions to prevent exposure to and transmission of bloodborne pathogens.

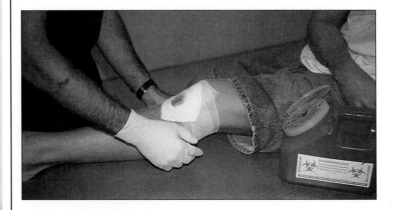

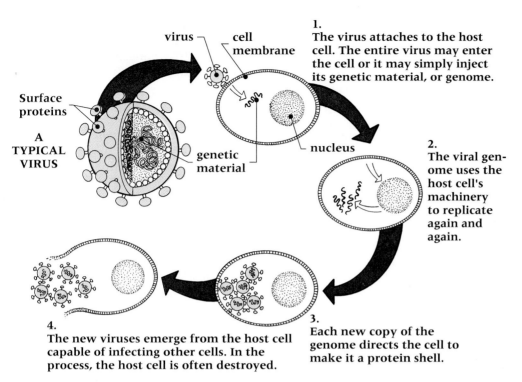

virus ─── cell membrane

1. The virus attaches to the host cell. The entire virus may enter the cell or it may simply inject its genetic material, or genome.

Surface proteins

A TYPICAL VIRUS

genetic material ── nucleus

2. The viral genome uses the host cell's machinery to replicate again and again.

4. The new viruses emerge from the host cell capable of infecting other cells. In the process, the host cell is often destroyed.

3. Each new copy of the genome directs the cell to make it a protein shell.

Figure 14-2

The reproducing virus.

BLOODBORNE PATHOGENS

Bloodborne pathogens are pathogenic microorganisms that can potentially cause disease and are present in human blood and other body fluids, including semen, vaginal secretions, cerebrospinal fluid, synovial fluid, and any other fluid contaminated with blood. The two most significant bloodborne pathogens are HBV and HIV. A number of other bloodborne diseases exist, including hepatitis C, hepatitis D, and syphilis. Hepatitis A virus (HAV) is spread by lack of personal hygiene and can be transmitted during unprotected sexual intercourse, from contact with feces of infected persons, and from shellfish taken from contaminated water.[15] Good sanitation, personal hygiene, and properly cooking shellfish at high temperatures are essential for prevention.

Although HIV has been widely addressed in the media, HBV has a higher possibility for spread than HIV, and thus athletic trainers should be more concerned about contracting HBV.[14] Hepatitis B virus is stronger and more durable than HIV and can be spread more easily via sharp objects, open wounds, and bodily fluids.[18]

Hepatitis B Virus

Hepatitis B virus is a major cause of viral infection; it results in swelling, soreness, and loss of normal function in the liver. The number of cases of HBV has risen dramatically during the last ten years. It has been estimated that 1.25 million people in the United States have chronic hepatitis and can potentially infect others. New cases are occurring at rates as high as 300,000 per year.[27]

Symptoms and Signs

The symptoms and signs in a person infected with HBV include flulike symptoms such as fatigue, weakness, nausea, abdominal pain, headache, fever, and possibly jaundice. It is possible that an individual infected with HBV will exhibit no signs or symptoms, and the virus may go undetected. In these individuals, the HBV antigen will always be present. Thus the disease may be unknowingly transmitted to others through exposure to blood or other body fluids or through intimate contact. Cases of

Mode of transmission includes:
- Human blood
- Semen
- Vaginal secretions
- Cerebrospinal fluid
- Synovial fluid

Bloodborne pathogens include:
- Hepatitis B virus
- Human immunodeficiency virus

14-1

Critical Thinking Exercise

The athletic trainer is responsible for taking every precaution in preventing infection by bloodborne pathogens.

? How are bloodborne pathogen infections prevented from spreading from one athlete to another?

chronic active hepatitis may occur because of a problem with the immune system that prevents the complete destruction of virus-infected liver cells.

An infected person's blood may test positive for the HBV antigen within two to six weeks after the symptoms develop. Approximately 85 percent of those infected recover within six to eight weeks.

Prevention

Good personal hygiene and avoiding high-risk activities is the best way to avoid HBV.[13] Hepatitis B virus can survive for at least one week in dried blood or on contaminated surfaces and may be transmitted through contact with these surfaces. Caution must be taken to avoid contact with any blood or other fluid that potentially contains a bloodborne pathogen.

Management

Vaccination against HBV must be made available by the employer at no cost to any individual who may be exposed to blood or other body fluids and may thus be at risk of contracting HBV. All athletic trainers, as well as any individual working in an allied health care profession, should receive immunization. An estimated 8,700 health care workers contract HBV each year, and as many as 200 of these cases end in death.[27] The vaccine is given in three doses over a six-month period. Approximately 87 percent will be immune after the second dose, and 96 percent develop immunity after the third dose. Postexposure vaccination is available when individuals have come into direct contact with bodily fluids of an infected person.[8]

Human Immunodeficiency Virus

Human immunodeficiency virus is a **retrovirus** that combines with a host cell. A number of cells in the immune system may be infected, such as T_4 blood cells, B cells, and monocytes (macrophages), which decreases their effectiveness in preventing disease. It has been estimated that 1 in 250 people in the United States is infected with HIV.[27] Approximately 1 of every 100 adult males between the ages of twenty and forty-nine is HIV positive. There are 40,000 to 50,000 new cases each year.[25] The World Health Organization estimates that, worldwide, 10 to 12 million adults carry the virus; 40 million carriers are estimated by the year 2000.[36]

Symptoms and Signs

As is the case with HBV, HIV is transmitted by exposure to infected blood or other body fluids or by intimate sexual contact.[38] Symptoms of HIV include fatigue, weight loss, muscle or joint pain, painful or swollen glands, night sweats, and fever. Antibodies to HIV can be detected in a blood test within one year after exposure. As with HBV, people with HIV may be unaware that they have contracted the virus and may go for eight to ten years before developing any signs or symptoms. Unfortunately most individuals who test positive for HIV will ultimately develop acquired immunodeficiency syndrome (AIDS). Table 14-1 summarizes information on HBV and HIV.

14-2

Critical Thinking E x e r c i s e

A wrestler has been diagnosed with hepatitis B virus.

? What are the symptoms and signs of HBV infection?

retrovirus
A virus that enters a host cell and changes its RNA to a proviral DNA replica.

TABLE 14-1 Transmission of Hepatitis B Virus and Human Immunodeficiency Virus

Disease	Symptoms and Signs	Mode of Transmission	Infectious Materials
Hepatitis B virus	Flulike symptoms, jaundice	Direct and indirect contact	Blood, saliva, semen, feces, food, water, and other products
Human immunodeficiency virus/ acquired immunodeficiency syndrome	Fever, night sweats, weight loss, diarrhea, severe fatigue, swollen lymph nodes, lesions	Direct and indirect contact	Blood, semen, vaginal fluid

Acquired Immunodeficiency Syndrome

A syndrome is a collection of signs and symptoms that are recognized as the effects of an infection. An individual with AIDS has no protection against even the simplest infections and thus is extremely vulnerable to developing a variety of illnesses, opportunistic infections, and cancers (such as Kaposi's sarcoma and non-Hodgkin's lymphoma) that cannot be stopped.[8,22]

Acquired immunodeficiency syndrome is the disease of the 1990s. According to the Centers for Disease Control and Prevention (CDC), 641,086 Americans have been reported with AIDS as of December 1997. At least 385,000 of those people have died. Estimates suggest that 650,000 to 900,000 Americans are now living with HIV, and at least 40,000 new infections occur each year.

A positive HIV test cannot predict when the individual will show the symptoms of AIDS.[31] About 50 percent of people develop AIDS within ten years of becoming HIV-infected. Those individuals who develop AIDS generally die within two years after the symptoms appear.

Management

Unlike HBV, there is no vaccine for HIV. Even though some drug therapy may extend their lives, there is currently no available treatment to cure patients with AIDS. Much research is being done to find a preventive vaccine and an effective treatment. Presently, the most effective treatment seems to be a therapy consisting of a combination of three drugs. One drug blocks the action of an enzyme that the virus needs to make some of the components for new virus cells. A second drug blocks the copying of viral genes that can enter the host cell's nucleus (a process called reverse transcription) and thus disables the synthesis of new viruses. A third drug helps protect the T cells and thus slows the progression of HIV.[31]

Although new treatments have extended the healthy life span of many people with AIDS, HIV prevalence has continued to increase. As the number of AIDS cases declines because of these new treatments, the number of people with HIV will increase, which means a greater need for both prevention and treatment services.

Prevention

Athletes must understand that their greatest risk for contracting HIV is through intimate sexual contact with an infected partner.[21] Practicing safe sex is of major importance. The athlete must choose nonpromiscuous sex partners and use condoms for vaginal or anal intercourse. Latex condoms provide a barrier against both HBV and HIV. Male condoms should have reservoir tips to reduce the chance of ejaculate being released from the sides of the condom. Condoms that are prelubricated are less likely to tear. Water-based, greaseless spermicides or lubricants should be avoided.[36] If the condom tears, a vaginal spermicide should be used immediately. The condom should carefully be removed and discarded.[36] Additional ways to reduce risk of HIV infection can be found in *Focus Box:* "HIV risk reductions."

BLOODBORNE PATHOGENS IN ATHLETICS

In general the chances of transmitting HIV among athletes is low.[11,19,33] There is minimal risk of on-field transmission of HIV from one player to another in sports.[15,33] One study involving professional football estimated that the risk of transmission from player to player was less than 1 per 1 million games.[7] At this writing there have been no validated reports of HIV transmission in sports.[25]

Some sports may have a potentially higher risk for transmission because of close contact and possibility of passing blood on to the other person.[15] Sports such as the martial arts, wrestling, and boxing have more theoretical potential for transmission (see *Focus Box:* "Risk categories for HIV transmission in sports").[25]

Human immunodeficiency virus is most often transmitted through intimate sexual contact.

The use of latex condoms can reduce the chances of contracting HIV.

14-3

Critical Thinking Exercise

A wrestler comes into the training room very concerned that his wrestling partner got a bloody nose and that he came in contact with a few drops of that athlete's blood.

? What should the athletic trainer tell the athlete about the transmission of HIV from this type of contact?

HIV risk reduction

- Avoid contact with others' bodily fluids, feces, and semen.
- Avoid sharing needles (e.g., when injecting anabolic steroids or human growth hormones).
- Choose nonpromiscuous sex partners.
- Limit sex partners.
- Consistently use condoms.
- Avoid drugs that impair judgment.
- Avoid sex with known HIV carriers.
- Get regular tests for sexually transmitted diseases.
- Practice good hygiene before and after sex.

Policy Regulation

Athletes participating in organized sports are subject to procedures and policies relative to transmission of bloodborne pathogens. The National Athletic Trainers' Association, U.S. Olympic Committee, National Collegiate Athletic Association, National Federation of State High School Athletic Associations, National Basketball Association, National Hockey League, National Football League, and Major League Baseball all have established policies to help prevent the transmission of bloodborne pathogens. These organizations have also initiated programs to help educate athletes under their control. The Centers for Disease Control and Prevention is another useful resource for the athletic trainer seeking information and guidelines for medical assistance on disease control, epidemic prevention, and notification.

All institutions should take responsibility for educating their student athletes about how bloodborne pathogens are transmitted. In the case of a high school athlete, efforts should also be made to educate the parents.[6] Professional, collegiate, and high school athletes should be made to understand that the greatest risk of contracting HBV or HIV is through their off-the-field activities, which may include unsafe sexual practices and sharing of needles, particularly in the use of steroids. Athletes, perhaps more than other individuals in the population, think that they are immune and that infection will always happen to someone else. The athletic trainer should also assume the responsibility of educating and informing student trainers of exposure control policies.

Risk categories for HIV transmission in sports[12]

- Highest risk: boxing, martial arts, wrestling, rugby
- Moderate risk: basketball, field hockey, football, ice hockey, judo, soccer, team handball
- Lowest risk: archery, badminton, baseball, bowling, canoeing/kayaking, cycling, diving, equestrianism, fencing, figure skating, gymnastics, modern pentathalon, racquetball, rhythmic gymnastics, roller skating, rowing, shooting, softball, speed skating, skiing, swimming, synchronized swimming, table tennis, volleyball, water polo, weight lifting, yachting

Each institution should implement policies and procedures concerning blood-borne pathogens.[33] A recent survey of NCAA institutions found that a large number of athletic trainers and other health care providers at many colleges and universities demonstrated significant deficits in following the universal guidelines mandated by OSHA. Universal precautions in a sports medicine or other health care setting protect both the athlete and the health care provider.[23]

OSHA
Occupational Safety and Health Administration.

Human Immunodeficiency Virus and Athletic Participation

There is no definitive answer as to whether asymptomatic HIV carriers should participate in sports.[37] Bodily fluid contact should be avoided, and the participant should also avoid engaging in exhaustive exercise that may lead to an increased susceptibility to infection.[37]

The Americans with Disabilities Act of 1991 says that athletes infected with HIV cannot be discriminated against and may be excluded from participation only with a medically sound basis.[25] Exclusion must be based on objective medical evidence and must take into consideration the extent of risk of infection to others and potential harm to self and what means can be taken to reduce this risk.[17]

Testing Athletes for Human Immunodeficiency Virus

Testing for HIV should not be used as a screening tool to determine if an athlete can participate in sports.[9,33] Mandatory testing for HIV may not be allowed because of legal reasons related to the Americans with Disabilities Act.[33] In terms of importance, mandatory testing should be secondary to education to prevent transmission of HIV.[24] Neither the NCAA nor the Centers for Disease Control and Prevention recommends mandatory HIV testing for athletes.[33]

Athletes who engage in high-risk activities should be encouraged to seek voluntary anonymous testing for HIV.[35] A blood test analyzes serum using enzyme-linked immunosorbent assay (ELISA). The ELISA test detects antibodies to HIV proteins. Positive ELISA tests should be repeated to rule out false-positive results. A second positive test requires the Western blot examination, which is a more sensitive test.[8] Detectable antibodies may appear from three months to one year after exposure. Testing therefore should occur at six weeks, three months, and one year.[36]

Many states have enacted laws that protect the confidentiality of the HIV-infected person. The athletic trainer should be familiar with state law and make every effort to guard the confidentiality and anonymity of HIV testing for athletes.

For additional information on HIV and AIDS care, contact the CDC National AIDS Hotline: 1 (800) 342-2437.

UNIVERSAL PRECAUTIONS IN AN ATHLETIC ENVIRONMENT

In 1991 the Occupational Safety and Health Administration **(OSHA)** established standards for an employer to follow that govern occupational exposure to bloodborne pathogens.[30]

The guidelines instituted by OSHA were developed to protect the health care provider and the patient against bloodborne pathogens.[27] It is essential that every sports program develop and carry out a bloodborne pathogen exposure control plan.[34] The NATA has established specific guidelines for athletic trainers.[20,26] (See Appendix B for the NATA's policy statement.) This plan should include counseling, education, volunteer testing, and the management of bodily fluids.[33]

These guidelines should be followed by anyone coming into contact with blood or other bodily fluids.[4,28] Following are considerations specifically in the sports arena.

14-4

Critical Thinking Exercise

A sports program must initiate and carry out a bloodborne pathogen exposure control plan.

? What are the universal precautions in an athletic environment as proposed by OSHA?

Preparing the Athlete

Before an athlete participates in practice or competition, all open skin wounds and lesions must be covered with a dressing that is fixed in place and does not allow for transmission to or from an athlete.[32] An occlusive dressing lessens the chances of cross-contamination. One example is the hydrocolloid dressing, which is considered a superior barrier. This type of dressing also reduces the chances that the wound will reopen because it keeps the wound moist and pliable.[32]

When Bleeding Occurs

As mandated by the NCAA and the USOC, open wounds or other skin lesions considered a risk for disease transmission should be given aggressive treatment. Athletes with active bleeding must be removed from participation as soon as possible and returned only when it is deemed safe by the medical staff.[7] Uniforms containing blood must be evaluated for infectivity. A uniform that is saturated with blood must be removed and changed before the athlete can return to competition. All personnel managing potential infective wound exposure must follow universal precautions.[7,27]

Personal Precautions

Latex gloves should be worn whenever the athletic trainer handles blood or bodily fluids.

The health care personnel working directly with bodily fluids on the field or in the athletic training facility must make use of the appropriate protective equipment in all situations in which there is potential contact with bloodborne pathogens. Protective equipment includes disposable latex gloves, gowns or aprons, masks and shields, eye protection, nonabsorbent gowns, and disposable mouthpieces for resuscitation devices.[5] Equipment for dealing with bloodborne pathogens should be included in sideline emergency kits.[29] Disposable latex gloves are used when handling any potentially infectious material. Double gloving is suggested when there is heavy bleeding or sharp instruments are used. Gloves are always carefully removed after use. In cases of emergency, heavy toweling may be used until gloves can be obtained.[1] (See *Focus Box:* "Glove use and removal.")

Hands and all skin surfaces that come in contact with blood or other bodily fluids should be washed immediately with soap and water or other antigermicidal agents. Hands should also be washed between each patient treatment. If there is the possibility of bodily fluids becoming splashed, spurted, or sprayed, the mouth, nose, and eyes should be protected. Aprons or nonabsorbent gowns should be worn to avoid clothing contamination.

First aid kits must contain protection for hands, face, and eyes and contain resuscitation mouthpieces. Kits should also make towelettes available for cleaning skin surfaces.[3]

14-5

Critical Thinking Exercise

An athletic trainer manages a facial laceration.

? What personal precautions must be taken by the athletic trainer when managing this facial laceration?

Availability of Supplies and Equipment

In keeping with universal precautions, the sports program must also have available chlorine bleach, antiseptics, proper receptacles for soiled equipment and uniforms, wound care bandages, and a designated container for sharps disposal such as needles, syringes, and scalpels.[7]

Universal precautions minimize the risk of exposure and transmission.

Biohazard warning labels should be affixed to containers for regulated wastes, refrigerators containing blood, and other containers used to store or ship potentially infectious materials (Figure 14-3). The labels are fluorescent orange or red. Red bags or containers should be used for disposal of potentially infected materials.

Focus

Glove use and removal
1. Avoid touching personal items when wearing contaminated gloves.
2. Remove first glove and turn inside out, beginning at wrist to peel off without touching skin.
3. Remove second glove, making sure not to touch ungloved hand to soiled surfaces.
4. Discard gloves that have been used, discolored, torn, or punctured.
5. Wash hands immediately after glove removal.

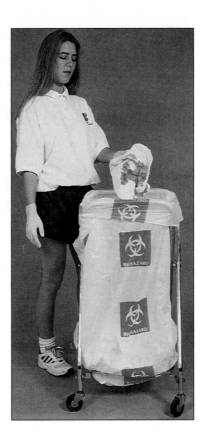

Figure 14-3

Soiled linens should be placed in a leakproof bag marked as a biohazard.

Disinfectants

All contaminated surfaces such as treatment tables, taping tables, work areas, and floors should be cleaned immediately with a solution consisting of one part bleach to ten parts water (1:10) or with a disinfectant approved by the Environmental Protection Agency.[6] Disinfectants should inactivate the HIV virus. Towels or other linens that have been contaminated should be bagged and separated from other laundry. Soiled linen is to be transported in red containers or bags that prevent soaking or leaking and are labeled with biohazard warning labels (see Figure 14-3). Contaminated laundry should be washed in hot water (71°C/159.8° F for 25 minutes) using a detergent that deactivates the virus. Laundry done outside the institution should be sent to a facility that follows OSHA standards. Gloves must be worn during bagging and cleaning of contaminated laundry.

Sharps

Sharps refers to sharp objects used in athletic training, such as needles, razor blades, and scalpels. Extreme care should be taken when handling and disposing of sharps to minimize risk of puncturing or cutting the skin. Athletic trainers rarely use needles, but it is not unusual for them to use scalpels or razor blades. Whenever needles are used, they should not be recapped, bent, or removed from a syringe. Sharps should be disposed of in a leakproof and puncture-resistant container.[6] The container should be red and labeled as a biohazard (Figure 14-4). Scissors and tweezers are not as likely to cause injury as sharps are, but they should be sterilized with a disinfecting agent and stored in a clean place after use.

Sharps include:
- Scalpels
- Razor blades
- Needles

Protecting the Coach and Athletic Trainer

OSHA guidelines for bloodborne pathogens are intended to protect the coach, athletic trainer, and other employees and not the athlete.[30] Coaches do not usually come in contact with blood or other bodily fluids from an injured athlete, so their

Figure 14-4

Sharps should be disposed of in a red puncture-resistant plastic container marked as a biohazard.

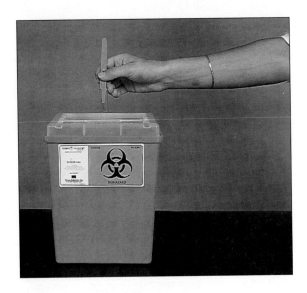

risk is considerably reduced. It is the responsibility of the high school, college, professional team, or clinic to ensure the safety of the athletic trainer as a health care provider by instituting and annually updating policies for education on the prevention of transmission of bloodborne pathogens through contact with athletes. The institution must provide the necessary supplies and equipment to carry out these recommendations.

The athletic trainer has the personal responsibility of adhering to these policies and guidelines and enforcing them in the training room. Athletic trainers may further minimize risk of exposure in the athletic training setting by not eating, drinking, applying cosmetics or lip balm, handling contact lenses, and touching the face before washing hands. Food products should never be placed in a refrigerator containing contaminated blood.[2]

Protecting the Athlete from Exposure

Several additional recommendations may further help protect the athlete. The USOC supports the required use of mouthpieces in high-risk sports. It is also recommended that all athletes shower immediately after practice or competition. Athletes who may be exposed to HIV or HBV should also be evaluated for immunization against HBV.

POSTEXPOSURE PROCEDURES

After a report of an exposure incident, the athletic trainer should have a confidential medical evaluation that includes documentation of the exposure route, identification of the source individual, a blood test, counseling, and an evaluation of reported illness. Again, the laws that pertain to reporting and notification of the test results relative to confidentiality vary from state to state.[30]

SUMMARY

- Bloodborne pathogens are microorganisms that can potentially cause disease and are present in human blood and other bodily fluids, including semen, vaginal secretions, cerebrospinal fluid, synovial fluid, and any other fluid contaminated with blood. Hepatitis B virus and HIV are bloodborne pathogens.
- A virus is a submicroscopic parasitic organism that contains either DNA or RNA, but not both. It is dependent on the host cell to function and reproduce.
- A vaccine is available to prevent HBV. Currently no effective vaccine exists for treating HIV.
- An individual infected with HIV may develop AIDS, which is fatal.

- The risks of contracting HBV or HIV may be minimized by avoiding exposure to blood and other bodily fluids and by practicing safe sex.
- The risk of an athlete being exposed to bloodborne pathogens on the field is minimal. Off-field activities involving risky sexual behaviors pose the greatest threat for transmission.
- Various national medical and sports organizations have established policies and procedures for dealing with bloodborne pathogens in the athletic population.
- The Occupational Safety and Health Administration has established rules and regulations that protect the health care employee.
- Universal precautions must be taken to avoid bloodborne pathogen exposure. All sports programs must carry out a plan for counseling, education, volunteer testing, and the management of exposure.

Web Sites

Occupational Safety and Health Administration (OSHA): http://www.osha.gov

Department of Health and Human Services: http://www.os.dhhs.gov

HIV/AIDS Prevention: http://cdc.gov/nchstp/hiv_aids/dhap.htm

Centers for Disease Control and Prevention: http://www.cdc.gov

National Institutes of Health: http://www.nih.gov

Solutions to Critical Thinking EXERCISES

14-1 During competition or practice the athlete should be most concerned about coming in contact with blood from another athlete. There should be little or no concern about exposure to sweat or saliva. The chances of contracting HIV during athletic participation are minimal. Certainly, the athlete is most likely to be exposed to HIV during unprotected intimate sexual contact.

14-2 The wrestler complained of flulike symptoms such as headache, fever, fatigue, weakness, nausea, and some abdominal pain. A blood test reveals the presence of the HBV antigen.

14-3 The greatest risk of contracting HIV is through intimate sexual contact with an infected partner. The athletic trainer should explain to the athlete that there is little chance of HIV transmission among athletes. There is a theoretical potential risk of transmission among athletes in close contact who pass blood from one to the other.

14-4 Universal precautions should be practiced by anyone coming in contact with blood or other bodily fluids. This plan must include counseling, education, volunteer testing, and management of bodily fluids.

14-5 The athletic trainer wears one-time-use latex gloves. All materials used in cleaning and managing the laceration are disposed of in a red biohazard container.

REVIEW QUESTIONS AND CLASS ACTIVITIES

1. Define and identify the bloodborne pathogens.
2. Describe HBV transmission, symptoms, signs, prevention, and treatment.
3. Explain the pros and cons of allowing the participation of an athlete who is an HBV carrier.
4. Describe HIV transmission, symptoms, signs, prevention, and treatment.
5. How is HIV transmitted, and why is it eventually fatal at this time?
6. Should an athlete who tests positive for HBV or HIV be allowed to participate in sports? Why or why not?
7. How can an athlete reduce the risk of HIV infection?
8. Define OSHA universal precautions for preventing bloodborne pathogen exposure.
9. What precautions would you, as an athletic trainer, take when caring for a bleeding wound on the field?

REFERENCES

1. American Academy of Pediatrics: Human immunodeficiency virus (acquired immunodeficiency syndrome [AIDS] virus) in athletic settings, *Pediatrics* 88:640, 1991.
2. American College Health Association: *General statement of institutional response to aids*, 1–6, Rockville, MD, 1988, Task Force on Aids, American College Health Association.
3. American Medical Association Department of HIV, Division of Health Science: *Digest of HIV/AIDS policy*, 1–15, Chicago, Ill, 1993, Department of HIV, American Medical Association.
4. American Red Cross: *Emergency response*, St Louis, 1993, Mosby Lifeline.
5. American Red Cross: *First aid: responding to emergencies*, St Louis, 1991, Mosby–Year Book.
6. Arnold BL: A review of selected blood-borne pathogen position statements and federal regulations, *J Ath Train* 30(2):171, June 1995.
7. Benson MT, editor: National Collegiate Athletic Association 1990–2000 NCAA sports medicine handbook, Overland Park, Kan, 1999, National Collegiate Athletic Association.
8. Berkow R, editor: *The Merck manual diagnosis of therapy*, ed 16, Raway, NJ, 1992, Merck Sharp and Dohne Research Laboratories.
9. Bitting LA, Trowbridge CA, Costello LE: A model for a policy on HIV/AIDS and athletics, *J Ath Train* 31(4):356, 1996.
10. Boyle M, Sitler M, Rogers K: Knowledge and attitudes of certified athletic trainers in Pennsylvania toward HIV/AIDS and treating HIV-positive athletes, *J Ath Train* 32(1):40, 1997.
11. Brown L, Dortman P: What is the risk of HIV infection in athletic competition? 19939:PO-C21-3102, International Conference on AIDS, 1993.
12. Brown LS, Phillips RY, Brown CL: HIV/AIDS policies and sports: the National Football League, *Med Sci Sports Exerc* 26(4):403, 1994.

13. Buxton BP et al: Prevention of hepatitis B virus in athletic training, *J Ath Train*, 29(2):107, 1994.

14. Coorts J, Michael T, Whitehill W: Hepatitis B immunization of athletic trainers in District IX, *J Ath Train* 32(4):315, 1997.

15. Garl T, Hrisomalos T, Rink R: *Transmission of infectious agents during athletic competition*, USOC Sports Medicine and Science Committee, 1991.

16. Hamann B: *Disease: identification, prevention, and control*, St Louis, 1994, Mosby.

17. Herbert DL: Mandatory testing for HIV and exclusion from athletic participation, *Sports Med Stand Malpract Report* 8(4):59, 1996.

18. Hunt BP, Pujol TJ: Athletic trainers as HIV/AIDS educators, *J Ath Train* 29(2):102, 1994.

19. Kleiner DM, Holcomb WR: Bloodborne pathogens: current information for the strength and conditioning professional, *Strength Cond* 17(4):42, 1995.

20. Knight K: Guidelines for preventing bloodborne pathogen diseases, *J Ath Train* 30:197, 1995.

21. Landry GL: HIV infection and athletes, *Sports Med Digest* 15(4):1, 1993.

22. LaPerriere A, Klimas N, Major P: Acquired immune deficiency syndrome. In American College of Sports Medicine: *ACSM's exercise management for persons with chronic disease and disabilities*, Champaign, Ill, 1997, Human Kinetics.

23. McGrew C: HIV and HBV in sports medicine. Part 2. *Sports Medicine in Primary Care* 1(4):29, 1995.

24. McGrew C, Dick R, Schneidewind K: Survey of NCAA institutions concerning HIV/AIDS policies and universal precautions, *Med Sci Sports Exerc* 25:917, 1993.

25. Mitten MJ: HIV-positive athletes, *Physician Sportsmed*, 22(10):63, 1994.

26. National Athletic Trainers' Association: Blood-borne pathogens guidelines for athletic trainers, *J Ath Train* 30(3):203, 1995.

27. National Safety Council: *Bloodborne pathogens*, Boston, 1993, Jones & Bartlett.

28. National Safety Council: *First aid and CPR*, Boston, 1997, Jones & Bartlett.

29. Nelson RC, Rinn TB: Sideline emergency kits and the need to include universal precautions against blood-borne pathogens, *J Sports Chiropractic & Rehabilitation* 10(1):32, 1996.

30. OSHA: The OSHA bloodborne pathogens standard, *Federal Register* 55(235):64175, 1991.

31. Payne W, Hahn D: *Understanding your health*, Dubuque, 1998, WCB/McGraw-Hill.

32. Rheinecker SB: Wound management: the occlusive dressing, *J Ath Train* 30(2):143, 1995.

33. Rogers KJ: Human immunodeficiency virus in sports. In Torg JS and Shephard RJ, editors: *Current therapy in sports medicine*, St Louis, 1995, Mosby.

34. Ross CM, Young SJ: Understanding the OSHA bloodborne pathogens standard and its impact upon recreational sports, *NIRSA J* 19(2):12, 1995.

35. Sankaran G, Volkwein KAE, Bonsall DR: HIV infection: risk, right to know, and requirement to divulge, *Athletic Therapy Today* 1(3):49, 1996.

36. Seltzer DG: Educating athletes on HIV disease and AIDS, *Physician Sportmed* 21(1):109, 1993.

37. Thomas CE: The HIV athlete: policy, obligations, and attitudes, *Sport Science Review* 5(2): 12, 1996.

38. Zeigler T: *Management of bloodborne infections in sport*, Champaign, Ill, 1997, Human Kinetics.

ANNOTATED BIBLIOGRAPHY

Benson MA, editor: *National Collegiate Athletic Association 1999–2000 sports medicine handbook*, Overland Park, Kan, 1999, National Collegiate Athletic Association.

This text offers a complete discussion of bloodborne pathogens and intercollegiate athletic policies and administration.

Berkow R, editor: *The Merck manual of diagnosis and therapy*, ed 16, Rahway, NJ, 1992, Merck Sharp and Dohne Research Laboratories.

This excellent guide discusses diagnosis, symptoms, signs, and treatment of bloodborne pathogens.

Bradley-Springer L, Fendrick RA: *AIDS/HIV instant instructor*, El Paso, Texas, 1994, Skidmore-Roth.

This excellent card system covers transmission, transmission prevention, occupational exposure prevention, testing, counseling, disease progression, and treatment of HIV and AIDS.

Hall K et al: *Bloodborne pathogens*, Boston, 1993, Jones & Bartlett.

This manual is dedicated to presenting OSHA regulations specific to bloodborne pathogens.

Hamann B: *Disease: identification, prevention, and control*, St Louis, 1994, Mosby.

This text is designed for health educators; AIDS and hepatitis are covered in detail.

Zeigler T: *Management of bloodborne infections in sport*, Champaign, Ill, 1997, Human Kinetics.

Perhaps the most comprehensive single text available on dealing with bloodborne pathogens in an athletic population, this text contains procedure and policy statements from several different sport and health organizations on managing bloodborne pathogens in the athletic environment.

Using Therapeutic Modalities

When you finish this chapter you should be able to

- Discuss the legal ramifications of treating the athlete with therapeutic modalities.
- Explain the relationship of most therapeutic modalities relative to electromagnetic energy.
- Describe the theoretical uses of the various types of modalities.
- Correctly demonstrate a variety of thermotherapy and cryotherapy techniques.
- Discuss the use of ultrasound in an athletic training setting.
- Discuss the physiological basis and therapeutic uses of electrical stimulating currents.
- Describe how massage, traction, and intermittent compression can be used as therapeutic agents.

Most athletic trainers routinely incorporate the use of therapeutic modalities into their rehabilitation programs. When used appropriately, therapeutic modalities can be an effective adjunct to various techniques of therapeutic exercise. This chapter is an introduction to the therapeutic modalities most commonly used by an athletic trainer, including cryotherapy, thermotherapy, diathermy, ultrasound, electrotherapy, lasers, massage, traction, and intermittent compression.

LEGAL CONCERNS

Therapeutic modalities must be used in sports medicine with the greatest care possible. At no time should there be an indiscriminate use of any therapeutic modality. Specific laws governing the use of therapeutic modalities vary considerably from state to state. The athletic trainer must follow laws that specifically dictate how athletic trainers can use certain therapeutic modalities. An athletic trainer who uses any type of therapeutic modality must have a thorough understanding of the functions and the indications or contraindications for its use.[38]

The athletic trainer should avoid using a shotgun approach when deciding to incorporate therapeutic modalities into a treatment program. Selection of the appropriate modality should be based on an accurate evaluation of the injury and a decision about which modality can most effectively reach the desired target tissue to achieve specific results. If used appropriately, modalities can be an integral part of a treatment and rehabilitation program.[38]

> The athletic trainer must carefully follow laws that prohibit him or her from use of certain therapeutic modalities.

HOW ARE THE MODALITIES RELATED?

Electrical stimulating currents, shortwave and microwave diathermy, the infrared modalities (e.g., hot packs, cold packs), ultraviolet therapy, and the low-powered laser are all therapeutic agents that emit or produce similar types of radiation and can be classified as electromagnetic energy. Ultrasound is a form of radiation that must be classified as acoustic energy rather than electromagnetic energy.[39]

The common characteristics of electromagnetic energy are as follows: it can be transmitted without a medium for support; all forms of electromagnetic energy travel at 300 million meters per second in a vacuum; energy waveforms travel in a straight line; and depending on the medium with which the waveform comes into contact, it may be reflected, refracted, absorbed, or transmitted. The electromagnetic radiation spectrum represents various regions classified according to specific wavelengths and frequencies. The lower the frequency, the longer the wavelength, and vice versa. Generally the longer the wavelength of the radiation, the greater the depth of penetration. In human tissue, the energy must be absorbed before any physiological changes can take place.[39]

TRANSMISSION OF THERMAL ENERGY

Thermal energy is transmitted through **conduction, convection, radiation,** and **conversion.**

Conduction

conduction
Heating through direct contact with a hot medium.

Conduction occurs when heat is transferred from a warmer object to a cooler one. The ratio of this heat exchange is dependent on the temperature and the exposure time. Skin temperatures are influenced by the type of heat or cold medium, the conductivity of the tissue, the quantity of blood flow in the area, and the speed at which heat is being dissipated.[23] To avoid tissue damage, the temperature should never exceed 116.6° F (47° C). An exposure that includes close contact with a hot medium that has a temperature of 113° F (45° C) should not exceed thirty minutes. Examples of conductive therapeutic modalities are moist hot packs, paraffin baths, electric heating pads, ice packs, and cold packs.

Convection

convection
Heating indirectly through another medium such as air or liquid.

Convection refers to the transference of heat through the movement of fluids or gases. Factors that influence convection heating are temperature, speed of movement, and the conductivity of the part.[40] The best example of a modality that uses convection is the whirlpool bath.

Radiation

radiation
Transfer of heat through space from one object to another.

Radiation is the process whereby heat energy is transferred from one object through space to another object. Shortwave and microwave diathermy, infrared heating, and ultraviolet therapy all rely on the process of radiation for energy transfer.

Conversion

conversion
Heating through other forms of energy.

Conversion refers to the generation of heat from another energy form such as sound, electricity, and chemical agents. The mechanical energy produced by high-frequency sound waves changes to heat energy at tissue interfaces (ultrasound therapy).[40] The deep heat of diathermy can be produced by applying electrical currents of specific wavelengths to the skin. Chemical agents such as liniments and balms create a heating sensation through counterirritation of sensory nerve endings.[40]

CRYOTHERAPY

Application of cold for the first aid of trauma to the musculoskeletal system is a widely used practice in sports medicine. When applied intermittently after injury, along with compression, elevation, and rest, it reduces many of the adverse conditions related to the inflammatory or reactive phase of an acute injury.[22,27] Depending on the severity of the injury, rest, ice, compression, and elevation (RICE) may be used from the first day to as long as two weeks after injury.

Physical Principles

The major therapeutic value of cold is its ability to produce anesthesia, allowing pain-free exercise.

Cold as a therapeutic agent is a type of electromagnetic energy classified specifically as infrared radiation. When a cold object is applied to a warmer object, heat is abstracted. In terms of cryotherapy, the most common method for cold transfer to tissue is through conduction. The extent to which tissue is cooled depends on the cold medium that is being applied, the length of cold exposure, and the conductivity of the area being cooled.[31] In most cases the longer the cold exposure, the deeper the cooling. At a temperature of 38.3° F (3.5° C), muscle temperatures can be reduced as deep as four centimeters. Cooling is dependent on the type of tissue. For example, tissue with a high water content, such as muscle, is an excellent cold conductor, whereas fat is a poor conductor. Because of fat's low cold conductivity, it acts as the body's insulator.[31] Tissue that has previously been cooled takes longer to return to a normal temperature than does tissue that has been heated.

The two most common means used to deliver cold as therapy to the body are ice or cold packs and immersion in cool or cold water. The most effective type of pack contains wet ice rather than ice in a plastic container or in a commercial chemical pack (e.g., Cryogen).[3] Wet ice is a more effective coolant because of the extent of internal energy needed to melt the ice.[40]

Physiological Effects of Cold

When cold is applied to skin for fifteen minutes or less at a temperature of 50° F (10° C) or less, vasoconstriction of the arterioles and venules in the area occurs. This vasoconstriction is caused in part by the reflex action of the smooth muscles, which can result from stimulation of the sympathetic nervous system and adrenal medulla, causing a secretion of norepinephrine and epinephrine.[40] Also causing vasoconstriction is cooled blood circulating to the anterior hypothalamus. If cold is continuously applied for fifteen to thirty minutes, an intermittent period of vasodilation occurs for four to six minutes. This period is known as the **hunting response,** a reaction against tissue damage from too much cold exposure.[22] When the hunting response occurs, the tissue temperature does not return to preapplication levels. This response has primarily been observed in the appendages. Cold during this period also causes an increase in blood viscosity and a decrease in vasodilator metabolites.[40]

hunting response
Causes a slight temperature increase during cooling.

Much of the damage done to cells after trauma occurs as a result of compromised circulation, which decreases the amount of oxygen being delivered to the cells in the area of injury. The immediate use of ice after injury decreases the extent of hypoxic injury to those cells on the periphery of the primary injury by slowing their metabolic rate. This slowdown results in less damage to the tissues and thus decreases rehabilitation time.[22]

Because cold lowers the metabolic rate and produces vasoconstriction, swelling will be reduced in an acute inflammatory response. Cold does not reduce swelling that is already present.[22]

Cooling tissues can directly decrease a muscle spasm by slowing metabolism in the area, thus decreasing the waste products that may have accumulated, waste products that act as muscle irritants and cause spasm. A muscle spasm can also be decreased when cold is applied to decrease the gamma motor neuron activity and also to decrease afferent muscle spindle and GTO activity as well as when cold increases the muscle's viscosity, slowing its ability to contract.[19]

Because the local application of cold can decrease an acute muscle spasm, the muscle becomes more amenable to stretch. A gentle stretch of a spastic muscle after an acute injury may be indicated; however, the stretching of long-standing contractures is contraindicated. Cold tends to cause collagen stiffness.[24]

Cold decreases free nerve ending excitability as well as the excitability of peripheral nerves. Analgesia is caused by raising the nerve's threshold.[19,49] Nerve fiber response to cold depends mainly on the presence of myelination and the diameter of the fiber. For example, most sensitive to cold are the small, light-touch, cold, and gamma efferent myelinated fibers to the muscle spindles.[19] The next most sensitive to cold are the large myelinated fibers of the proprioceptors and alpha motor nerves.[19] The least sensitive to cold are the unmyelinated pain fibers and postganglionic sympathetic nerves.[19] Table 15-1 indicates the usual outward sequential response to cold application.

Cold, in general, is more penetrating than heat. Once a muscle has been cooled through the subcutaneous fat layer, cold's effects last longer than heat effects do because fat acts as an insulator against rewarming.[24] The major problem is to penetrate the fat layer initially so that muscle cooling occurs. In individuals with less than

The extent of cooling depends on the thickness of the subcutaneous fat layer.

TABLE 15-1 Skin Response to Cold

Stage	Response	Estimated Time after Initiation
1	Cold sensation	0 to 3 minutes
2	Mild burning, aching	2 to 7 minutes
3	Relative cutaneous anesthesia	5 to 12 minutes

TABLE 15-2 Physiological Variables of Cryotherapy

Variable	Response to Therapy
Muscle spasm	Decreases
Pain perception	Decreases
Blood flow	Decreases up to 10 minutes
Metabolic rate	Decreases
Collagen elasticity	Decreases
Joint stiffness	Increases
Capillary permeability	Increases
Edema	Controversial

$^1/_2$ inch (1.25 cm) of subcutaneous fat, significant muscle cooling can occur after ten minutes of cold application. In persons with more than $^4/_5$ inch (2 cm) of subcutaneous fat, muscle temperatures barely drop after ten minutes (Table 15-2).[19]

Another unique quality of cooling is its ability to decrease muscle fatigue and increase and maintain muscular contraction. This ability is attributed to the decrease of the local metabolic rate and the tissue temperature.[24]

Special Considerations

Raynaud's phenomenon
Condition in which cold exposure causes vasospasm of digital arteries.

Although adverse reactions to therapeutic cold application are uncommon, they do happen and are described as follows:

- Cooling for an hour at 30.2° to 15.8° F (–1° to –9° C) produces redness and edema that lasts for twenty hours after exposure.[17] Frostbite has been known to occur in subfreezing temperatures of 26.6° to 24.8° F (–3° to –4° C).[22]
- Immersion at 41° F (5° C) increases limb fluid volume by 15 percent.
- Exposure for ninety minutes at 57.2° to 60.8° F (14° to 16° C) can delay resolution of swelling up to one week.[22]
- Some individuals are allergic to cold and react with hives and joint pain and swelling.[40]
- Icing through a towel or an elastic bandage limits the reduction in temperature, which could influence the effectiveness of the treatment.[52]
- **Raynaud's phenomenon** is a condition that causes vasospasm of digital arteries lasting for minutes to hours, which could lead to tissue death. The early signs of Raynaud's phenomenon are attacks of intermittent skin blanching or cyanosis of the fingers or toes, skin pallor followed by redness, and finally a return to normal color. Pain is uncommon, but numbness, tingling, or burning may occur during and shortly after an attack.
- Paroxysmal cold hemoglobinuria is a rare disease that occurs minutes after cold exposure and may lead to renal dysfunction, secondary hypertension, and coma. Early symptoms are severe pain in the back and legs, headache, vomiting, diarrhea, and dark brown urine.
- Although it is relatively uncommon, application of ice can cause nerve palsy. Nerve palsy occurs when cold is applied to a part that has motor nerves close to

the skin surface, such as the peroneal nerve at the fibular head. Usually the condition resolves spontaneously with no significant problem. As a general rule, ice should not be applied longer than twenty to thirty minutes at any one time.

Cryotherapeutic Methods

A number of methods of cold applications can be used therapeutically. The ones most commonly used in sports medicine are ice massage, cold or ice water immersion, ice packs, and vapocoolant sprays.

Ice Massage

Ice massage is a cryotherapeutic method that is performed on a small body area. It can be applied by the athletic trainer and the athlete alike.

Equipment Water is frozen in a foam cup, which forms a cylinder of ice. The foam is removed approximately an inch from the top of the cup. The remaining foam provides a handle for the athletic trainer to grasp while massaging. Another method is to fill a paper cup with water and insert a tongue depressor to act as a handle when the water is frozen. A towel should be present to absorb the water that is collected.

Indications Ice massage is commonly used over a small muscle area such as the tendons, the belly of the muscle, or the bursa or over myofascial trigger points.

Application Grasping the ice cylinder, the athletic trainer rubs the ice over the athlete's skin in overlapping circles in a ten- to fifteen-centimeter area for a period of five to ten minutes. The athlete should experience the sensations of cold, burning, aching, and numbness. When analgesia has been reached, the athlete can engage in stretching or exercise (Figure 15-1).

Special considerations In an athlete with normal circulation, tissue damage seldom occurs from cold application. The temperature of the tissue seldom goes below 59° F (15° C). The comfort of the athlete must be considered at all times.

Cold or Ice Water Immersion

Cold water immersion is a relatively simple means for treating a distal body part.

Equipment Depending on the body part to be immersed, a variety of containers or basins can be used. In some cases, a small whirlpool can be used. Water and crushed ice are mixed together to reach a temperature of 50° F (10° C) to 60° F (15° C). Towels must be available for drying.

Indications Where circumferential cooling of a body part is desired, cold or ice water immersion is preferred.

Application The athlete immerses the body part in the water and proceeds through the four stages of cold response. This process may take ten to fifteen minutes. When the pain cycle has been interrupted, the part is removed from the water, and normal movement patterns are conducted. When pain returns, the part is reimmersed. This procedure may be repeated three times.

Special considerations Because cold makes collagen tissue brittle, caution should be taken in allowing the athlete to return to full sports performance after receiving cold treatment. Overcooling can lead to frostbite. Any allergic response to cold should also be noted.

Ice Packs (Bags)

The use of ice packs is another way to apply cryotherapy.

Equipment There are a number of types of ice packs. Wet ice packs provide the best cooling properties. Flaked or crushed ice can be encased in a wet towel and placed on the part to be treated. A pack can be made by placing crushed or chipped ice in a self-sealing plastic bag; this method is not as efficient but is less messy. If isopropyl alcohol is added at a two to one ratio, the packs can be put into a freezer and

Cold therapy can begin one to three days after injury.

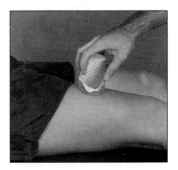

Figure 15-1

Ice massage can lead to an analgesia that can be followed by gentle muscle stretching.

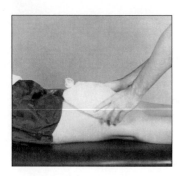

Figure 15-2

Ice packs can be another way to apply cryotherapy.

Fluori-methane spray is used in the spray and stretch technique.

not completely frozen. When they are removed from the freezer, the packs easily fit the contour of the body part. These packs are useful for approximately fifteen or twenty minutes.[40] When the plastic packs are used, a wet towel should be placed between the skin and the pack. Besides toweling, an elastic wrap should be available; it should be used to hold the pack firmly in place.

Two different types of chemical cold packs are available. One is a gel pack that may be refrozen after use and is hypoallergenic. The gel pack is commonly used in many athletic training settings. The other type is a liquid bag within a bag of crystals. When the inner bag is ruptured the chemicals mix, causing an endothermic reaction. If allowed contact with the skin, these chemicals can cause a chemical burn and a liability problem.[3]

Indications The athlete experiences the four stages of cold that were described earlier in this section and then proceeds with normal movement patterns (Figure 15-2).

Special considerations Excessive cold exposure must be avoided. With any indication of allergy to cold or of abnormal pain, the therapy should be discontinued.

Vapocoolant Sprays

Increasingly, vapocoolant sprays are being used for treatment of musculoskeletal conditions attributed to sports activity.

Equipment Currently the most popular vapocoolant is fluori-methane, a non-flammable, nontoxic substance. Under pressure in a bottle, it gives off a fine spray when it is inverted and an emitter is pressed.

Indications The major value of a vapocoolant spray is its ability to reduce muscle spasm and increase range of motion. It is also a major treatment for myofascial pain and trigger points.[35] Care must be taken, however, to avoid frostbite.

Application When vapocoolant spray is used to increase the athlete's range of motion in an area in which there is no trigger point, the following procedure is performed:

1. Hold the vapocoolant at a 30-degree angle, 12 to 18 inches (30 to 47 cm) from the skin.
2. Spray the entire length of the muscle from its proximal attachment to its distal attachment.
3. Cover the skin at a rate of approximately 4 inches (10 cm) per second; apply the spray two or three times as a gradual stretch is applied.

When dealing with a possible trigger point, the procedure is first to determine its presence, then to alleviate it. One method by which the athletic trainer can determine an active trigger point is to reproduce the injured athlete's major pain complaint by pressing firmly on the site for five to ten seconds. Another assessment technique used by the athletic trainer is to elicit a jump response by placing the athlete's muscle under moderate tension, applying firm pressure, and briskly pulling a finger across the tight band of muscle. This procedure causes the tight band of muscle to contract and the athlete to wince or cry out.[32]

The spray and stretch method for treating trigger points and myofascial pain has become a major approach (Figure 15-3) and is performed as follows:[31]

1. Position the athlete in a relaxed but well-supported position. The muscle that contains the trigger point is stretched (an exception to this is the sternocleidomastoid muscle).
2. Alert the athlete that the spray will feel cool.
3. Hold the fluori-methane bottle approximately 12 inches (30 cm) away from the skin to be sprayed.
4. Direct the spray at an acute angle in one direction toward the reference zone of pain.
5. Direct the spray to the full length of the muscle, including the reference zone of pain.

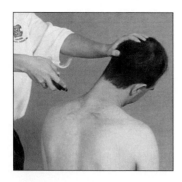

Figure 15-3

A vapocoolant spray such as fluori-methane can assist in reducing muscle spasm.

6. Begin firm stretching that is within the athlete's pain tolerance.

7. Continue spraying in parallel sweeps that are approximately ¼ inch (0.6 cm) apart at a speed of approximately 4 inches (10 cm) every second.

8. Cover the skin area one or two times.

9. Continue passive stretching while spraying (do not force the stretch; allow time for the muscle to let go).

10. After the first session of spraying and stretching, warm the muscle with a hot pack or by vigorous massage.

11. If necessary, perform a second session after step 10.

12. When a stretch has been completed, have the athlete actively but gently move the part in a full range of motion.

13. Do not overload a muscle with strenuous exercise immediately after a stretch.

14. After an initial spraying and stretching session, instruct the athlete about stretch exercises that should be performed at home on a daily basis.

Cryokinetics

Cryokinetics is a technique that combines cryotherapy, or the application of cold, with exercise.[22] The goal of cryokinetics is to numb the injured part to the point of analgesia and then work toward achieving normal range of motion through progressive active exercise.

The technique begins by numbing the body part via ice immersion, cold packs, or ice massage. Most athletes report a feeling of numbness within twelve to twenty minutes. If numbness is not perceived within twenty minutes, the athletic trainer should proceed with exercise regardless. The numbness usually lasts for three to five minutes, at which point ice should be reapplied for an additional three to five minutes until numbness returns. This sequence should be repeated five times (see *Focus Box:* "Summary of cryokinetics").

Exercises are performed during the periods of numbness. The exercises selected should be pain free and progressive in intensity; the concentration should be on both flexibility and strength. Changes in the intensity of the activity should be limited by both the nature of the healing process and by individual patient differences in perception of pain. However, progression always should be encouraged within the framework of those limiting factors; the ultimate goal is to return the athlete to full sport activities.[22]

cryokinetics
Combines cryotherapy with exercise.

Focus

Summary of cryokinetics

1. Immerse ankle in ice water until numb (12 to 20 min).
2. Exercise within limits of pain (see progression below) (3 to 5 min).
3. Renumb ankle by immersion (3 to 5 min).
4. Exercise within limits of pain (3 to 5 min).
5. Repeat steps 3 and 4 three more times.
6. Principles of exercising:
   a. All exercise should be active, that is, performed totally by the patient.
   b. All exercise must be pain free.
   c. All exercise must be performed smoothly, without limping, twitching, or any other abnormal motion.
   d. The exercise must be aggressively progressive, that is, progress to more complex and difficult levels as quickly as possible (remember—*no pain*).

THERMOTHERAPY

The application of heat to treat disease and traumatic injuries has been used for centuries. Recently, however, its use in the immediate treatment phase of musculoskeletal injury has been replaced with cold application. Heat is an energy form that increases molecular activity by conduction, convection, conversion, and radiation.[40] Thermotherapy modes are moist, dry, superficial, and deep.

Physiological Effects of Heat

The body's response to heat depends on the type of heat energy applied, the intensity of the heat energy, the duration of application, and the unique tissue response to heat. For a physiological response to occur, heat must be absorbed into the tissue, causing an increase in molecular activity. After the tissue's absorption of heat energy, heat is spread to adjacent tissue. To effect a therapeutic change that results in normal function of the absorbing tissue, the correct amount of heat must be applied. With too little, no change occurs; with too much, the tissue is damaged further.

There are still many unanswered questions about how heat produces therapeutic responses and what types of thermotherapy are most appropriate for a given condition. The desirable therapeutic effects of heat include increasing the extensibility of collagen tissues; decreasing joint stiffness; reducing pain; relieving muscle spasm; reducing inflammation, edema, and exudates in the postacute phase of healing; and increasing blood flow.[40]

Heat affects the extensibility of collagen tissue by increasing the viscous flow of collagen fibers and subsequently relaxing the tension. From a therapeutic point of view, heating contracted connective tissue permits an increase in extensibility through stretching. Muscle fibrosis, a contracted joint capsule, and scars can be effectively stretched while being heated or just after the heat is removed.[40] An increase in extensibility does not occur unless heat treatment is associated with stretching exercises.

Both heat and cold relieve pain, stimulating the free nerve endings and peripheral nerves by a gating mechanism or secretion of endorphins (see Chapter 10). Muscle spasm caused by **ischemia** can be relieved by heat, which increases blood flow to the area of injury. Heat is also believed to assist inflammation and swelling by a number of related factors such as raising temperature, increasing metabolism, reducing oxygen tension, lowering the pH level, increasing capillary permeability, and releasing histamine and bradykinin, which cause vasodilation. Histamine and bradykinin are released from some cells during acute and chronic inflammation. Heat is also produced by axon reflexes and vasomotor reflex change. Parasympathetic impulses stimulated by heat are believed to be one reason for vasodilation (Table 15-3).[25]

Superficial Heat

The superficial heating modalities, along with the cold modalities discussed previously, are all considered to be forms of electromagnetic energy whose wavelengths and frequencies are classified in the infrared region of the electromagnetic spectrum.

Heat has the capacity to increase the extensibility of collagen tissue.

ischemia
Lack of blood supply to a body part.

TABLE 15-3 Physiological Variables of Thermotherapy

Variable	Response to Therapy
Muscle spasm	Decreases
Pain perception	Decreases
Blood flow	Increases
Metabolic rate	Increases
Collagen elasticity	Increases
Joint stiffness	Decreases
Capillary permeability	Increases
Edema	Increases

Heat applied superficially to the skin directly increases the subcutaneous temperature and indirectly spreads to the deeper tissues. Muscle temperature increases through a reflexive effect on circulation and through conduction.[40] Comparatively, when heat is applied at the same temperature, moist heat causes a greater indirect increase in the deep-tissue temperature than does dry. Dry heat, in contrast to moist heat, can be tolerated at higher temperatures.

Special Considerations in the Use of Superficial Heat

In general, superficial heating of the skin is a safe therapeutic medium, assuming of course that the heat is kept at a reasonable intensity and that application does not occur for too long a period. The following are important contraindications and precautions to be taken when superficial heat is used:

- Never apply heat when there is a loss of sensation.
- Never apply heat immediately after an injury.
- Never apply heat when there is decreased arterial circulation.
- Never apply heat directly to the eyes or the genitals.
- Never heat the abdomen during pregnancy.
- Never apply heat to a body part that exhibits signs of acute inflammation.

Moist Heat Therapies

Heated water is one of the most widely used therapeutic modalities in sports medicine. It is readily available for use in any sports medicine program. The greatest disadvantage of hydrotherapy is the difficulty in controlling the therapeutic effects, primarily as a result of the rapid dissipation of heat, which makes maintaining a constant tissue temperature difficult.

For the most part, moist heat aids the healing process in some local conditions by causing higher superficial tissue temperatures; however, joint and muscle circulation increase little in temperature. Superficial tissue is a poor thermal conductor, and temperature rises quickly on the skin surface as compared with the underlying tissues.

Superficial tissue is a poor thermal conductor.

Moist Heat Packs

Commercial moist heat packs, sometimes called hydrocollator packs, heat by conduction.

Equipment   Moist heat packs contain silicate gel in a cotton pad, which is immersed in thermostatically controlled hot water at a temperature of 160° F (71.1° C) to 170° F (76.7° C). Each pad retains water and a constant heat level for twenty to thirty minutes. Six layers of toweling or commercial terry cloth are used between the packs and the skin (Figure 15-4).

Indications   The major value of the moist heat pack is that its use results in general relaxation and reduction of the pain-spasm-ischemia-hypoxia-pain cycle. There are limitations of the moist heat pack and all other superficial heating modalities: "the deeper tissues, including the musculature, are usually not significantly heated because the heat transfer from the skin surface into deeper tissues is inhibited by the subcutaneous fat, which acts as a thermal insulator, and by the increased skin flow, which cools and carries away the heat externally applied."[25]

Application
1. Remove pack from water and allow to drain for a few seconds.
2. Cover pack with six layers of dry toweling or commercial cover.
3. Treat the area for fifteen to twenty minutes.
4. As pack cools, remove layers of toweling to continue the heating.

Special considerations
- The athlete should not be lying on packs.
- Be sure the athlete is comfortable at all times.

15-1

Critical Thinking Exercise

A volleyball player has an elbow sprain that occurred five days ago. To this point he has been using cryotherapy as exclusive treatment. His elbow is still tender with some minimal swelling. He says that he really hates the ice and wants to know if he can switch over to some form of heat, which he feels will be more comfortable.

? In the course of an injury rehabilitation program, when should the athletic trainer change from using cold to using heat?

Figure 15-4

At least two protective layers of toweling must be applied between the skin and a moist heat pack.

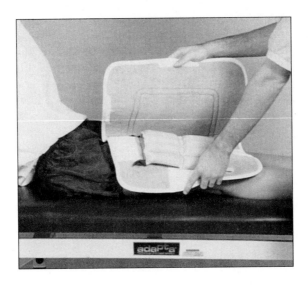

Whirlpool Baths

Whirlpool therapy is a combination of massage and water immersion. It has become one of the most popular thermotherapies used in sports medicine.

Equipment   There are generally three types of whirlpools: the extremity tank, which is used for treating legs and arms and is 15 inches wide, 28 to 32 inches long, and 18 to 25 inches deep; the lowboy tank, which is 24 inches wide, 52 to 62 inches long, and 18 inches deep and is used for full-body immersion; and the highboy tank, which is designed for the hip or the leg and is 20 to 24 inches wide, 36 to 48 inches long, and 28 inches deep.[53]

The whirlpool is essentially a tank and a turbine motor, which regulates the movement of water and air. The amount of movement (agitation) is controlled by the amount of air that is emitted. The more air there is, the more water movement.[53] The turbine motor can be moved up and down on a tubular column. It can also be rotated on the column and locked in place at a specific angle.

The whirlpool bath combines heated water and massaging action.

Indications   The whirlpool provides both conduction and convection. Conduction is achieved by the skin's contact with the higher water temperature. As the water swirls around the skin surface, convection occurs (Figure 15-5).

Figure 15-5

A whirlpool bath provides therapy through heat conduction and convection.

TABLE 15-4 Whirlpool Temperatures

Descriptive Terms	Temperature
Very cold	>55° F (12.8° C)
Cold	55°–65° F (12.8°–18.3° C)
Tepid	80°–90° F (27°–33.5° C)
Neutral	92°–96° F (33.5°–35.5° C)
Warm	96°–98° F (35.5°–36.5° C)
Hot	98°–104° F (36.5°–40° C)

This medium assists the body part by reducing swelling, muscle spasm, and pain. Because of the buoyancy of the water, active movement of the part is also assisted.

Application

1. The water temperature should be set according to Table 15-4. Some athletic trainers prefer to perform only cold water treatments, whereas others prefer to increase the temperature according to the healing phase of an acute injury. Chronic conditions normally require a higher water temperature.
2. Once the tank has been filled with water at the desired temperature, the athlete is comfortably positioned so that the part to be treated can be easily reached by the agitated water. In many cases, the water jet should not be placed directly on the part but to the side of the tank. This placement is particularly relevant in the early stages of the acute injury. In cases in which the stream is concentrated directly toward the injury site, the site should be at least eight to ten inches from the jet.
3. The duration of treatment is of major concern for the athletic trainer. The maximum length of treatment time for acute injuries should not exceed twenty minutes. In the early stages of acute injury treatment, a graduated program should be implemented. Treatment time should be increased slowly on a daily basis—to five minutes, ten minutes, fifteen minutes, and finally to twenty minutes. A duration of twenty minutes is usually recommended for treatment of chronic injuries.

Special considerations

1. Great caution should be taken when an athlete undergoes full-body immersion because of the possibility that the athlete will experience light-headedness.[4]
2. Proper whirlpool maintenance is necessary to avoid infection. The following procedures should be adhered to:
   a. Empty tank after use.
   b. Scrub inside of tank with a commercial disinfectant, rinse with clean water, and dry.
   c. Polish external surface of tank with a commercial stainless steel polish.
3. Safety is of major importance in the use of the whirlpool. All electrical outlets should have a ground fault circuit interrupter. At no time should the athlete turn the motor on or off. Ideally, the on/off switch should be a considerable distance from the machine.[53]

Paraffin Bath

Paraffin is a popular method for applying heat to the distal extremities.

Equipment The commercial paraffin bath is a thermostatically controlled unit that maintains a temperature of 126° to 130° F (52° to 54° C). The paraffin mixture consists of a ratio of twenty-five kilograms of paraffin wax to one liter of mineral oil. Slats at the bottom of the container protect the athlete from burns and collect the settling dirt. Also required for treatment are plastic bags, paper towels, and towels.

Paraffin bath therapy is particularly effective for injuries to the more angular body areas.

Figure 15-6

A paraffin bath is an excellent form of therapeutic heat for the distal extremities. After paraffin coating has been accomplished, the part is covered by a plastic material. When heat is no longer generated, the paraffin is scraped back into the container.

Indications   The mineral oil acts to lower the melting point of the paraffin and thus the specific heat. Consequently, the ability to tolerate the heat from the paraffin is greater than it would be from water at the same temperature.

This therapy is especially effective in treating chronic injuries occurring to the more angular areas of the body such as the hands, wrists, elbows, ankles, and feet.

Application   Therapy by means of the paraffin bath can be delivered in several ways. The body part can be dipped and wrapped in a plastic bag, or it can be dipped and reimmersed to form eight to ten layers. The paraffin can be painted on in several layers, or the body part can be soaked in the paraffin.

Before therapy, the part to be treated is thoroughly cleaned and dried. Then the athlete dips the affected part into the paraffin bath and quickly pulls it out, allowing the accumulated wax to dry and form a solid covering. The process of dipping and withdrawing is repeated six to twelve times until the wax coating is $^1/_4$ to $^1/_2$ inch (0.6 to 1.25 cm) thick.

If the dip and wrap technique is to be employed, the accumulated wax is allowed to solidify on the last withdrawal; then the wax is completely wrapped in a plastic material that in turn is wrapped with a towel. The packed body part is placed in a position of rest for approximately thirty minutes or until heat is no longer generated. The covering is then removed and the paraffin is scraped back into the container.

If the soak technique is selected, the athlete is instructed to soak the wax-coated part in the hot wax container for twenty to thirty minutes without moving it, after which the part is removed from the container and the paraffin on it is allowed to solidify. The part can be packed in towels following the soak, or the paraffin coating can be scraped back into the container immediately after it hardens. Once the paraffin has been removed from the part, an oily residue remains that provides an excellent surface for massage (Figure 15-6).

Special considerations   Avoid paraffin bath therapy on body areas that have hemorrhaging or a decrease in normal circulation.

It is essential that the athlete clean the body part thoroughly before therapy to avoid contaminating the mixture. In most cases, if this rule is closely adhered to, the mixture will only have to be replaced approximately every six months.[40]

contrast bath procedure
Technique that uses immersion in ice slush, followed by immersion in tepid water (93° to 98° F [33.9° to 37.7° C]).

Contrast Bath

Contrasting hot and cold water is a popular therapy in sports medicine. It is primarily used in the treatment of the extremities.

Equipment   The **contrast bath** technique requires the use of two containers, one to hold hot water at 105° to 110° F (40.6° to 43.3° C) and one to hold cold water at

50° to 65° F (10° to 18° C). A whirlpool can be used for the hot container, and a basin or bucket can be used for the cold.

Indications   Contrast baths are used when changing the treatment modality from cold to heat to facilitate a mild tissue temperature increase. The use of contrast baths allows for a transitional period during which a slight rise in temperature may be effective for increasing blood flow to an injured area without causing accumulation of additional edema. Only a slight temperature change occurs superficially using the contrast technique.[28] The theory that contrast baths induce a type of pumping action by alternating vasoconstriction with vasodilation has little or no credibility.[40] Likewise, the use of hot and cold packs to produce a contrast effect has also proven to be ineffective.[29]

Application   During the initial stages of contrast bath treatment, the ratio of heat to cold treatment begins with a relatively brief exposure to heat; this exposure is gradually increased in subsequent treatments. Recommendations as to specific ratios are extremely variable. However, it appears that a 3:1 ratio (3 minutes in heat, 1 minute in cold) or 4:1 for nineteen or twenty minutes is fairly well accepted (Figure 15-7).[40] The ratio may be modified as the transition from cold to heat progresses.

Special considerations
- Care must be taken to keep the water temperature constant.
- The athlete should be kept as comfortable as possible throughout the procedure.

Alternative method   A second method of contrast that has become popular in sports medicine uses the concept of alternatively submerging the limb in an ice slush bath for two minutes and then in tepid water at 93° to 98° F (33.9° to 37.7° C) for thirty seconds. The baths are alternated for fifteen minutes, beginning and ending with cold immersion.

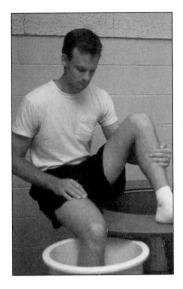

Figure 15-7

A contrast bath, which uses alternating cold water immersion and hot water immersion, is a therapy popular with many athletic trainers.

Fluidotherapy

Fluidotherapy creates a therapeutic environment with dry heat and forced convection through a suspended airstream.

Equipment   Fluidotherapy units come in a variety of sizes, ranging from ones that treat distal extremities to ones that treat large body areas. The unit contains fine cellulose particles in which warm air is circulated. As the air is circulated, the cellulose particles become suspended, giving them properties that are similar to liquid.[40] Fluidotherapy allows the athlete to tolerate much greater temperatures than would be possible using water or paraffin heat (Figure 15-8).

Indications   Fluidotherapy is successful, resulting in decreased pain, increased joint range of motion, and decreased spasm and swelling.

Application
- Treatment temperature usually ranges from 100° to 113° F (37.8° to 45° C).
- Particle agitation should be controlled for comfort.
- Exercise can be performed while the athlete is in the cabinet.
- The athlete should be positioned for comfort.
- Treatment duration is fifteen to twenty minutes.

Fluidotherapy consists of cellulose particles in which warm air is circulated.

SHORTWAVE AND MICROWAVE DIATHERMY

Shortwave and microwave diathermy are two modalities that emit electromagnetic energy that is capable of producing temperature increases in the deeper tissues. Tissues with a higher water content (e.g., muscle) selectively absorb the heat delivered by shortwave and microwave diathermies.[19] The extent of muscle heating is dependent on the thickness of the subcutaneous fat layer. Both shortwave and microwave diathermies provide less heat penetration than does ultrasound. In contrast to shortwave and microwave diathermies, ultrasonic vibration is not absorbed by fat and is therefore not influenced by its thickness.[19]

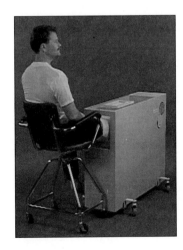

Figure 15-8

Fluidotherapy units contain fine cellulose particles in which warm air is circulated.

Shortwave Diathermy

Shortwave diathermy heats deeper tissues by introducing a high-frequency electrical current. Shortwave diathermy is in essence a radio transmitter; the Federal Communications Commission (FCC) has assigned a wavelength of 7.5 to 22 meters and a frequency of 13.56 or 27.12 megacycles per second for therapeutic purposes.[41]

Shortwave diathermy can be used two ways: through a condenser that uses electrostatic field heating or through electromagnetic or induction field heating.[41] In electrostatic field heating, the patient is a part of the circuit. Heating is uneven because of different tissue resistance to energy flow, an application of Joule's law, which states that the greater the resistance or impedance, the more heat will develop. In electromagnetic field heating, the patient is not part of the circuit but is heated by an electromagnetic field.[41]

Pulsed shortwave diathermy is a relatively new form of diathermy.[30] Pulsed diathermy is created by simply interrupting the output of continuous shortwave diathermy at consistent intervals. Pulsing reduces the likelihood of any significant tissue temperature increase and reduces the patient's perception of heat. Generators that deliver pulsed shortwave diathermy typically use a drum type of electrode. Pulsed diathermy is claimed to have therapeutic value and to produce nonthermal effects with minimal thermal physiological effects, depending on the intensity of the application. When pulsed diathermy is used in intensities that create an increase in tissue temperature, its effects are no different from those of continuous shortwave diathermy.

Equipment   In general, the shortwave diathermy unit consists of a power supply to a power amplifier and a frequency generator. It has an oscillator that produces high frequency (either 13.56 or 27.12 megacycles) and a power amplifier that converts alternating current (AC) to direct current (DC).[23] It also has a circuit that tunes in the patient automatically or manually as part of the circuitry (Figure 15-9).

The shortwave diathermy treatment applicators are either condensor or inductive types.[41] With the condensor, or field heating, the patient is a natural part of the cir-

Figure 15-9

The Magnatherm is an example of a currently used shortwave diathermy unit.

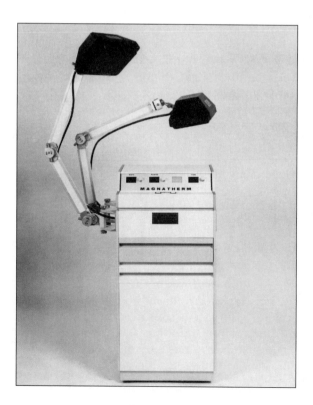

cuit. The condensor applicator consists of electrodes that are formed by sheets of flexible or rigid metal covered by heavy insulation.

There are two types of inductive electrodes: the coil and the single drum unit. The inductive coil is a cable electrode, which ranges from two to five meters (6–16 feet) long and is wound around the patient's injured part. Whereas the coil can heat generally, the single drum unit is designed to treat a more specific area.[21] Tissues with high water content such as blood and muscle are the most easily heated.

Indications   Shortwave diathermy is highly effective for bursitis, capsulitis, osteoarthritis, deep muscle spasm, and strains. The depth of the inductive technique can be as much as 2 inches (5 cm). The condensor technique penetrates from 1 to 2 inches (2.5 to 5 cm). Tissue temperature can reach 107° F (41.7° C).

Application   If more superficial heating is desired, a condensor plate is used; when deeper therapy is desired, the induction coil should be used. A double-layered towel is placed between the applicator and the skin. When the patient is as comfortable as possible, he or she is tuned in with the oscillating circuit of the unit. In most cases the treatment times range from twenty to thirty minutes.

Special considerations

- It is difficult to treat localized body areas.
- Dosage is subjective.
- There is less heating of skin and more chance for deep tissue burns.
- Towels must be placed between the applicator and the skin. Towels absorb perspiration during treatment.
- When there is loss of sensation, shortwave diathermy should not be used.
- When metal objects such as implants, pacemakers, jewelry, a metal table, intrauterine devices (IUDs), zippers on clothing, or glasses are present, shortwave diathermy should not be administered.
- Avoid use when the athlete is hemorrhaging, is pregnant, or has open wounds or contact lenses.
- Diathermy cables or coils must not touch one another or any metal.
- Avoid heating eyes, testicles, ovaries, bony prominences, and bone-growth areas.
- A deep, aching sensation during treatment may indicate overheating.

Microwave Diathermy

Clinical microwave diathermy generally has a wavelength of 12 cm to 33 cm and an FCC-assigned frequency of 915 to 2,450 megacycles. Lower microwave frequencies (e.g., 915 megacycles per second) cause less conversion of energy into the subcutaneous tissue and, as a result, produce more uniform muscle heating.[30] Microwave diathermy heats deeper tissue by conversion. It is more easily absorbed in tissue with higher water content such as muscle and blood than is shortwave diathermy.[21]

Equipment   In the microwave diathermy unit, AC is changed into DC. The unit consists of a magnetron oscillator, which is a tube that incorporates a complete oscillator circuit capable of generating a radio frequency. A *coaxial cable* transports the energy from the magnetron oscillator to the applicator head. Within the delivery head is an antenna that radiates energy to the athlete. A commonly used spaced applicator is contained within a rectangular metallic reflector. It is suggested for use on flat or concave body surfaces.[21] The further away the reflector is from the skin, the greater the body coverage will be with a proportional increase in wattage.

A coaxial cable consists of an insulated central conductor with tubular stranded conductors, which are separated by layers of insulation laid concentrically over the central conductor.

Indications   Microwave diathermy is highly effective in treating conditions such as fibrositis, myositis, osteoarthritis, bursitis, calcific tendinitis, sprains, strains, and posttraumatic joint stiffness.[23] In an athlete with a subcutaneous fat thickness of 0.5 cm or less, microwave diathermy can penetrate tissue as much as 5 cm (2 inches) thick.[41]

Application   The athlete is made comfortable, and the microwave diathermy director is positioned at right angles to the part to be treated. The athlete's subjective

TABLE 15-5 Sample Shortwave Diathermy and Microwave Diathermy Dosage

Dosage	Effect	Application
Lowest dose (I)	Just below the point of any sensation of heat (acute inflammatory process)	2 to 5 minutes daily for 2 weeks
Low dose (II)	Mild heat sensation, barely felt (subacute, resolving inflammatory process)	2 to 5 minutes daily for 2 weeks
Medium dose (III)	Moderate but pleasant heat sensation (subacute, resolving inflammatory process)	2 to 30 minutes from 2 to 3 times weekly for 1 to 4 weeks
Heavy dose (IV)	Vigorous heating that causes a sensation that is well tolerated (chronic conditions); pain threshold should not be exceeded	5 to 30 minutes for 2 to 3 times weekly for 1 to 4 weeks

heat sensation is the major guide to dosage. The therapeutic heat range for microwave diathermy, as for shortwave diathermy, is 104° to 113° F (40° to 45° C).[41] The length of treatment does not usually exceed thirty minutes. A dosage scheme has been suggested that can be used for both shortwave diathermy and microwave diathermy (Table 15-5).[21,26,48] A towel must be placed over the skin to absorb any perspiration that accumulates.

Special considerations   The same considerations given to shortwave diathermy must also be given to microwave diathermy. The applicator should never come in contact with the skin. At no time should heating exceed the athlete's pain threshold.[41]

Comparing Microwave Diathermy and Shortwave Diathermy

In general, shortwave and microwave diathermies penetrate the body to approximately the same depth; however, microwave diathermy provides deeper muscle heating and comparatively more skin heating than does shortwave diathermy.[23] Microwave diathermy heating is more localized than is shortwave diathermy heating.

ULTRASOUND THERAPY

Ultrasound is another widely used modality in athletic training. It is a valuable therapeutic tool in the rehabilitation of many different injuries because it stimulates the repair of soft tissue injuries and relieves pain.[10] Ultrasound is a deep-heating modality and is used primarily for elevating tissue temperatures. Ultrasound is a form of acoustic rather than electromagnetic energy. Ultrasound is defined as inaudible, acoustic vibrations of high frequency that may produce either thermal or nonthermal physiological effects.[7] The use of ultrasound as a therapeutic agent may be extremely effective if the athletic trainer has an adequate understanding of its effects on biological tissues and of the physical mechanisms by which these effects are produced.[11]

> Ultrasound can be applied either to the skin or through a water medium.

The number of movements, or oscillations, in one second is referred to as the frequency of a sound wave and is known as a hertz (Hz) unit. More commonly, 1 Hz equals 1 cycle per second, 1 kHz equals 1,000 cycles per second, and 1 MHz equals 1 million cycles per second.[41] The human ear cannot detect sound greater than 20,000 Hz; therefore inaudible sound is considered ultrasound. When sound scatters and absorbs as it penetrates tissue, its energy is decreased (**attenuation**). Absorption of sound increases with an increase in frequency.

> **attenuation**
> A decrease in intensity as the sound enters deeper tissues.

Tissue penetration depends on impedance or acoustical properties of the media that are proportional to tissue density.[10] Sound reflection occurs when adjacent tissues have different impedance. The greater the impedance, the greater the reflection, and more heat is produced. The greatest heat is developed between bone and the adjacent soft-tissue interface.

Equipment   The main piece of equipment for delivering therapeutic ultrasound is a high-frequency generator, which provides an electrical current through a coaxial cable to a transducer contained within an applicator. In the applicator or transducer are synthetic crystals such as barium titanate or lead zirconate titanate that possess the property of piezoelectricity. These crystals are in disks 2 to 3 mm thick and 1 to 3 cm in diameter.[51] The **piezoelectric effect** causes expansion and contraction of the crystals, which produce oscillation voltage at the same frequency as the sound wave.[7]

Therapeutic ultrasound has a frequency range between 0.75 and 3.0 MHz (megahertz). The majority of ultrasound generators are set at a frequency of 1 MHz, although there are ultrasound units that are set at a frequency of 3 MHz. A generator that can be set between 1 and 3 MHz affords the athletic trainer the greatest treatment flexibility. Ultrasound energy generated at 1 MHz is transmitted through the more superficial tissues and absorbed primarily in the deeper tissues at depths of 3 to 5 cm. A 1 MHz frequency is most useful in individuals with high percent body fat cutaneously and whenever the desired effects are in the deeper structures.[7] At 3 MHz the energy is absorbed in the more superficial tissues with a depth of penetration between 1 and 2 cm ($^1/_3$ and $^3/_4$ inch).[8]

Ultrasound beam   The portion of the surface of the ultrasound transducer that produces the sound wave is referred to as the **effective radiating area**. Energy is delivered to the tissues in a collimated cylindrical beam. The beam from ultrasound generated at 1 MHz is more divergent than at 3 MHz. Within this beam, the distribution of ultrasound energy is nonuniform. The amount of variability of intensity in the beam is indicated by the **beam nonuniformity ratio (BNR)**. The lower the BNR, the more uniform the energy output. Optimally the BNR would be 1:1.

Intensity   The intensity of the ultrasound beam is determined by the amount of energy delivered to the sound head (applicator). It is expressed in the number of watts per square centimeter (W/cm²). As a therapeutic modality used in sports medicine, the intensity ranges from 0.1 to 3 W/cm².

Pulsed versus continuous ultrasound   Virtually all therapeutic ultrasound generators can emit either continuous or pulsed ultrasound waves. If continuous ultrasound is used, the sound intensity remains constant throughout the treatment and the ultrasound energy is being produced 100 percent of the time. With pulsed ultrasound, the intensity is periodically interrupted and no ultrasound energy is produced during the off period. The percentage of time that ultrasound is being generated is referred to as the *duty cycle*. If the pulse duration is one millisecond and the total pulse period is five milliseconds, the duty cycle would be 20 percent. Therefore the total amount of energy being delivered to the tissues would be only 20 percent of the energy delivered if a continuous wave were being used.

Continuous ultrasound is most commonly used to produce thermal effects. The use of pulsed ultrasound results in a reduced average heating of the tissues. Pulsed ultrasound or continuous ultrasound at a low intensity will produce nonthermal or mechanical effects, which may be associated with soft-tissue healing.[7]

Indications   Therapeutic ultrasound produces both thermal and nonthermal effects.[11] Traditionally, ultrasound has been used primarily to produce a tissue temperature increase. The clinical effects of using ultrasound to heat the tissues are similar to other forms of superficial heat, discussed in earlier sections. For the majority of these effects to occur, the tissue temperature must be raised to a level of 104° to 113°F (40° to 45° C) for a minimum of five minutes. Temperatures below this range will be ineffective, and temperatures above 113° F (45° C) may be potentially

piezoelectric effect
Electrical current produced by applying pressure to certain crystals such as quartz.

effective radiating area
That portion of the transducer that produces sound energy.

beam nonuniformity ratio (BNR)
The amount of variability in intensity of the ultrasound beam.

Ultrasound can be pulsed or continuous.

Duty cycle indicates the percentage of time that ultrasound is being generated.

Ultrasound produces effects that are thermal or nonthermal.

damaging.[7] Ultrasound at 1 MHz with an intensity of 1 W/cm² can raise soft-tissue temperature by 0.2° C per minute, and at 3 Mhz, as much as 0.6°C per minute.[7]

Whenever ultrasound is used to produce thermal changes, nonthermal changes also occur. However, if appropriate treatment parameters are selected, nonthermal effects can occur with minimal thermal effects. The nonthermal effects of therapeutic ultrasound include cavitation and acoustic microstreaming. Cavitation is the formation of gas-filled bubbles that expand and compress because of ultrasonically induced pressure changes in tissue fluids.[11] Cavitation results in an increased flow in the fluid around these vibrating bubbles. Microstreaming is the unidirectional movement of fluids along the boundaries of cell membranes resulting from the mechanical pressure wave in an ultrasonic field.[11] Microstreaming can alter cell membrane structure and function because of changes in cell membrane permeability to sodium and calcium ions important in the healing process. As long as the cell membrane is not damaged, microstreaming can be of therapeutic value in accelerating the healing process.[11]

Nonthermal effects include cavitation and microstreaming.

The nonthermal effects of therapeutic ultrasound in the treatment of injured tissues may be as important as the thermal effects and perhaps are even more important. The nonthermal effects of cavitation and microstreaming can be maximized while the thermal effects are minimized by using an intensity of 0.1 to 0.2 W/cm² with continuous ultrasound or 1.0 W/cm² at a duty cycle of 20 percent.

Acute conditions require more frequent treatments over a shorter period of time, whereas chronic conditions require fewer treatments over a longer period of time.[35] Ultrasound treatments should begin as soon as possible after injury, ideally within hours but definitely within forty-eight hours to maximize effects on the healing process.[7] Acute conditions may be treated using low-intensity ultrasound once or twice daily for six to eight days until acute symptoms such as pain and swelling subside. In chronic conditions, when acute symptoms have subsided, treatment may be done on alternating days for a total of ten to twelve treatments.

Application   There are a number of options for using ultrasound in sports medicine.

Direct skin application   Because acoustic energy cannot travel through air and is reflected by the skin, there must be a **coupling medium** applied to the skin.[7] Coupling mediums include a variety of materials, such as mineral oil or water-soluble creams or gels. The purpose of a coupling medium is to provide an airtight contact with the skin and a slick, low-friction surface. When a water-soluble material is used, the skin should first be washed and dried to prevent air bubbles from hampering the flow of mechanical energy into the skin (Figure 15-10).

coupling medium
Used to facilitate the transmission of ultrasound into the tissues.

Underwater application   Underwater ultrasound is suggested for such irregular body parts as the wrist, hand, elbow, knee, ankle, and foot. The part is fully submerged in water; then the ultrasound head is submerged and positioned approximately 1 inch (2.5 cm) from the body part to be treated. The water medium provides an airtight coupling and allows sound waves to travel at a constant velocity. To ensure uninterrupted therapy, air bubbles that form on the skin must be continually wiped away. The sound head is moved slowly in a circular or longitudinal pattern.[7]

Underwater application should be done in a plastic or rubber nonmetal container to avoid reflection of energy off the metal walls.

Bladder technique   If, for some reason, the treatment area cannot be immersed in water, a bladder technique can be used. In this technique, a balloon is filled with water, and the ultrasound energy is transmitted from the transducer to the treatment surface through this bladder. Both sides of the balloon should be coated with gel to ensure good contact.[7]

Moving the transducer   Moving the transducer during treatment leads to a more even distribution of energy within the treatment area and can reduce the likelihood of developing hot spots. The transducer should be moved slowly at approximately 4 cm (1½ inches) per second. The transducer should be kept in maximum contact with the skin via some coupling agent throughout the treatment.

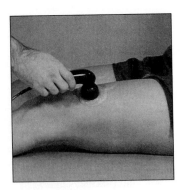

Figure 15-10

Ultrasound therapy, when applied directly to the skin, must be performed over a coupling medium because acoustical energy cannot travel through air.

Movement of the transducer can be in a circular pattern or a stroking pattern. In the circular pattern, the transducer is applied in small overlapping circles. In the stroking pattern, the transducer is moved back and forth, overlapping the preceding stroke by half. Both techniques are performed slowly and deliberately. The field covered should not exceed 3 to 4 inches (7.5 to 10 cm). The pattern is determined mainly by the skin area to be treated. For example, the circular pattern is best for highly localized areas such as the shoulder, whereas in larger, more diffuse injury areas, the stroking pattern is best used. When a highly irregular surface area is to be given therapy, the underwater method should be used.[54]

Dosage and treatment time   Dosage of ultrasound varies according to the depth of the tissue treated and the state of injury, such as subacute or chronic.[5] Basically, 0.1 to 0.3 W/cm^2 is regarded as low intensity, 0.4 to 1.5 W/cm^2 is medium intensity, and 1.5 to 3 W/cm^2 is high intensity. The duration of treatment ranges from five to ten minutes.

Special considerations   Although ultrasound is a relatively safe modality, certain precautions must be taken, and in some situations ultrasound should never be used. Great care must be taken when treating anesthetized areas because the sensation of pain is one of the best indicators of overdosage. Great precautions must be used in areas that have reduced circulation. In general, ultrasound must not be applied to highly fluid areas of the body such as the eyes, ears, testes, brain, spinal cord, and heart. Reproductive organs and women who are pregnant must not receive ultrasound. Acute injuries should not be treated with ultrasound. Epiphyseal areas in children should have only minimum ultrasound exposure.[54]

Ultrasound in Combination with Other Modalities

In an athletic training environment, it is not uncommon to combine modalities to accomplish a specific treatment goal. Ultrasound is frequently used with other modalities, including hot packs, cold packs, and electrical stimulating currents.

Hot packs and ultrasound are a useful combination because of the relaxing effects of hot packs in muscle spasm or muscle guarding. Hot packs produce more superficial heating while ultrasound produces heating in the deeper tissues. The use of a hot-pack and 1-MHz ultrasound treatments appears to have an additive effect on muscle temperature.[6]

Cold packs are frequently used before ultrasound application. However, if the treatment goal is an increase in deep tissue temperature, the use of a cold pack before ultrasound interferes with heating and is not recommended.[9,44]

Ultrasound is often used with electrical stimulating currents and is thought to be particularly effective in treating trigger points and acupuncture points. Ultrasound increases the blood flow to the deep tissues while the electrical currents produce a muscle contraction or modulate pain associated with an injury (Figure 15-11).[7]

15-2
Critical Thinking E x e r c i s e

A field hockey player has a three-week-old deep quadriceps contusion. She has returned to full practice. There is still a palpable swollen area present and some remaining purplish-yellow discoloration. The injury is no longer tender to the touch, but the athlete does not have full range of motion in flexion.

? At this point in the process of healing, what modalities would be most appropriate?

Ultrasound is commonly used in conjunction with other modalities.

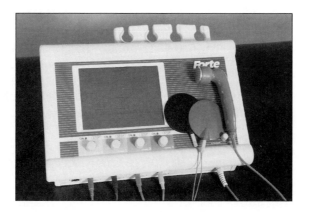

Figure 15-11

Combination ultrasound and electrical stimulator unit.

Phonophoresis

Phonophoresis is a method of driving molecules through the skin using the mechanical vibration of the ultrasound.[46] The techniques of phonophoresis and *iontophoresis* are often confused, and occasionally the two terms are erroneously interchanged. Both techniques are used to deliver chemicals to various biologic tissues. Phonophoresis involves the use of acoustic energy in the form of ultrasound to drive whole molecules across the skin into the tissues, while iontophoresis uses an electrical current to transport ions into the tissues.

Phonophoresis is designed to move medication into injured tissues. Some sports medicine personnel prefer this method to iontophoresis, indicating that it is less hazardous to the skin and that there is greater penetration.[43] As with iontophoresis, phonophoresis is predominantly used to introduce hydrocortisone and an anesthetic into the tissues. This method has been proposed for treating painful trigger points, tendinitis, and bursitis.[43] The effectiveness of phonophoresis as a treatment technique is questionable and needs further research.[34]

Many clinicians prefer to use a 10 percent hydrocortisone ointment.[43] Sometimes lidocaine is added to the cortisone to provide a local anesthetic effect. This medicine is massaged into the skin over an area of tendinitis, bursitis, or other chronic soft-tissue condition. The coupling gel is then spread over the medication, and the ultrasound is applied.

Chem-pads are commercially produced pads that are impregnated with medication; they may be used instead of the traditional medicated ointment application.

ELECTROTHERAPY

The use of electrotherapy is commonplace in the athletic training setting.[15]

Physical Principles

In general, electricity is a form of energy that displays magnetic, chemical, mechanical, and thermal effects on tissue. It implies a flow of electrons between two points. Electrons are particles of matter that have a negative electrical charge and revolve around the core, or nucleus, of an atom.

An electrical current refers to a string of electrons that pass along a conductor such as a nerve or wire. The volume or amount of the current is measured in **amperes** (A); 1 A equals the rate of flow of 1 coulomb (C) per second. A coulomb is a unit of electrical charge and is defined as the quantity of an electrical charge that can be transferred by 1 A in one second.

Resistance to the passing of an electrical current along a conductor is measured in **ohms** (Ω), and the force that moves the current along is called **voltage (V).** One volt is the amount of electrical force required to send a current of 1 A through a resistance of 1 Ω. In terms of electrotherapy, currents of 0 to 150 V are considered low-voltage currents, and currents above 150 **V** are considered high voltage. The intensity of a current varies directly with the voltage and inversely with the resistance. Electrical power is measured in **watts** (amps $\times$ volts).[50]

An electrical current applied to nerve tissue at a sufficient intensity and duration to reach that tissue's excitability threshold will result in a membrane depolarization or firing of that nerve. There are three major types of nerve fibers: sensory, motor, and pain. As current intensity or duration is increased, the threshold for depolarization will be reached first for sensory fibers, then for motor fibers, and then for pain fibers. Thus it is possible to produce different physiological responses by adjusting the treatment parameters.[16]

Electrical Stimulating Units

Electrotherapeutic devices generate three different types of current, which, when introduced into biological tissue, are capable of producing specific physiological changes. These three types of current are AC, DC, and pulsed.[36]

Figure 15-12

Many therapeutic electrical generators are transcutaneous electrical nerve stimulator (TENS) units.

A great deal of confusion has developed about the terminology used to describe electrotherapeutic currents. All therapeutic electrical generators, regardless of whether they deliver AC, DC, or pulsed currents through electrodes attatched to the skin, are *transcutaneous electrical stimulators*. The majority of these generators are used to stimulate peripheral nerves and are correctly called *transcutaneous electrical nerve stimulators (TENS)* (Figure 15-12). Occasionally the terms *neuromuscular electrical stimulator (NMES)* or *electrical muscle stimulator (EMS)* are used; however, these terms are appropriate only when the electrical current is being used to stimulate muscle directly, as would be the case with denervated muscle in which peripheral nerves are not functioning. In recent years, a new type of transcutaneous electrical stimulator has gained popularity that uses current intensities too small to excite peripheral nerves. In the past these devices have been called *microcurrent electrical nerve stimulators (MENS)*, although they are currently being referred to as *low-intensity stimulators (LIS)*.[36]

Direct Current

Direct current, or galvanic current, flows in one direction only from the positive pole to the negative pole. Direct current may be used for pain modulation or muscle contraction or to produce ion movement. Specific physiological effects are determined by how the treatment parameters are set on the stimulating unit. Most electrical stimulators currently used in athletic training settings are DC units.

Alternating Current

With AC, the direction of current flow reverses itself once during each cycle. Alternating current may be used for pain modulation or muscle contraction.

Pulsed Current

Pulsed currents usually contain three or more pulses grouped together. These groups of pulses are interrupted for short periods of time and repeat themselves at regular intervals. Pulsed currents are used in interferential and so-called Russian currents.

Current Parameters

Waveforms

Electrical stimulating units can take on various waveforms depending on the capability of the generator. A waveform is a graphic representation of the shape, direction, amplitude, and direction of a particular electrical current. Both AC and DC units can produce currents with waveforms that are either sine, square, or triangular in shape (Figure 15-13).

Modulation

Current modulation refers to the ability of the electrical stimulating unit to change or alter the magnitude or duration of a waveform. Modulation may be continuous, interrupted, or surged for both AC and DC currents (Figure 15-14).

Current parameters:
- Waveform
- Modulation
- Intensity
- Duration
- Frequency
- Polarity
- Electrode setup

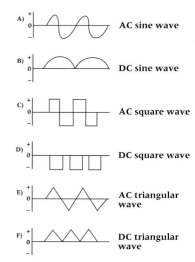

Figure 15-13

Waveforms can be either sine, square, or triangular for both AC and DC.

Intensity

Current intensity refers to the voltage output of the stimulating unit. Generators that produce voltage outputs of up to 150 V are low-voltage generators. Those that produce up to 500 V are high-voltage generators. Low-voltage generators are almost always DC; high-voltage generators may be either AC or DC. The majority of the electrical stimulators used in athletic training settings are high-voltage DC generators.

Duration

Duration refers to the length of time that current is flowing. It is also referred to as pulse width or pulse duration. Duration is preset on most of the high-voltage DC stimulators.

Frequency

Frequency refers to the number of waveforms being emitted by the electrical stimulating unit in one second. Frequency is identified in pulses per second (PPS), cycles per second (CPS), or hertz. Frequencies may range from one PPS to several thousand PPS.

Frequency
Measured in hertz (Hz), cycles per second (CPS), or pulses per second (PPS).

Polarity

Polarity refers to the direction of current flow. It may move toward either a positive or a negative pole.

Electrode Setup

In electrotherapy, moist electrode pads are fixed directly to the skin. Electrodes may be of different sizes. Using a large *(dispersive)* electrode remote from the treatment area while placing a smaller *(active)* electrode as close as possible to the nerve or muscle motor point will give the greatest effect at the small electrode. The large electrode disperses the current over a large area; the small electrode concentrates the current in the area of the motor point. The physiological effects can occur anywhere between the two pads, but they usually occur at the active electrode, because current density is greater at this point.[16] Many newer electrical stimulating units have pads that are of equal size and thus both electrodes would be considered active electrodes.

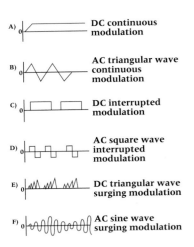

A) DC continuous modulation

B) AC triangular wave continuous modulation

C) DC interrupted modulation

D) AC square wave interrupted modulation

E) DC triangular wave surging modulation

F) AC sine wave surging modulation

Figure 15-14

Modulation may be continuous, surged, or interrupted for either AC or DC.

Indications

Alternating, direct, and pulsed currents can be used to modulate pain and to induce muscle contraction.[20] Direct current may also be used to produce ion movement (iontophoresis).[16]

Pain Modulation

Electrical stimulating currents can reduce pain associated with injury.[16] The neurophysiological mechanisms associated with pain modulation—including gate control, descending pain control (central biasing), and opiate pain control—were discussed in Chapter 10.

Gate control   Electrical stimulation of sensory nerves will evoke the gate control mechanism and diminish awareness of painful stimuli. As long as the stimulation is causing the sensory nerves to fire, the gate to pain should be closed. If the stimulus stops, the gate is then open, and pain returns to perception. The following parameters can be used for gate control: intensity should be adjusted to create a tingling sensation but should not cause a muscular contraction; both pulse duration and frequency should be set at the maximum possible on the machine.[16]

Descending pain control   Intense electrical stimulation of the smaller pain fibers at trigger and acupuncture points for short time periods causes stimulation of descending neurons, which then affect transmission of pain information by closing the gate at the spinal cord level. Current intensity should be very high, approaching a noxious level; pulse duration should be 10 msec; frequency should be 80 pulses per second.[16]

Opiate pain control theory   Electrical stimulation of sensory nerves stimulates the release of enkephalin from local sites throughout the central nervous system and the release of β-endorphins from the pituitary gland into the cerebral spinal fluid. Pain modulation is caused by applying an electrical current to areas close to the site of pain or to acupuncture or trigger points both local and distant to the pain area. A point stimulator should be used, with current intensity set as high as tolerable; pulse duration should be set at the maximum possible on the machine; frequency should be set at 1 to 5 PPS.[16]

Muscle Contraction

The quality of a muscle contraction will change according to the changes in current parameters. As the frequency of stimulation increases, the muscle will develop more tension because of progressive shortening of the muscle until a tetanic contraction is achieved. Tetany will occur for virtually all muscles at approximately 50 PPS. Increases in intensity spread the current over a larger area and increase the number of motor units activated by the current. Increases in current duration also cause more motor units to be activated. A variety of therapeutic gains can be made by electrically stimulating a muscle contraction; these gains include muscle pumping contractions, muscle strengthening, retardation of atrophy, and muscle reeducation.

A muscle contraction can be used for:
- Muscle pumping
- Muscle strengthening
- Retardation of atrophy
- Muscle reeducation

Muscle pumping   This type of contraction is used to help stimulate circulation by pumping fluid and blood through the venous and lymphatic channels back to the heart. High-voltage DC is recommended. Intensity should be increased to elicit a muscle contraction at a frequency of 20 to 40 PPS, using a surged mode with on/off times at 5 seconds each. The injured part should be elevated, and active contraction should be encouraged. Treatment time is twenty to thirty minutes.[16]

Muscle strengthening   Electrical stimulation can be used to facilitate strength gains. High-frequency AC is recommended (e.g., Electrostim 380). Intensity should be increased at a frequency of 50 to 60 PPS to elicit a tetanic muscle contraction using surging current set at 15 seconds on and 50 seconds off. Treatment should include ten repetitions three times per week. For best results, the athlete should combine this electrically induced tetanic contraction with maximal active contraction against some resistance.[16]

Retardation of atrophy   Electrically induced muscle contraction can be used to minimize atrophy and loss of muscle function that typically occurs with immobilization after injury. High-frequency AC is recommended. Intensity should be increased to 30 to 60 PPS to elicit a tetanic contraction using interrupted current mode. The athlete should incorporate voluntary isometric contraction. Treatment time should be fifteen to twenty minutes.[16]

Muscle reeducation   Muscular inhibition after surgery or injury can be reduced by electrically stimulating a muscle. Intensity should be increased to a level necessary for a comfortable contraction at 30 to 50 PPS using either interrupted or surged current. The athlete should watch and feel the contraction and attempt to initiate a voluntary contraction. Treatment time is fifteen to twenty minutes; treatment is repeated several times daily.[16]

Iontophoresis

Iontophoresis is a technique in which chemical ions are transported through the intact skin using electrical current for the purpose of treating skin infections or for a counterirritating effect.[14] The type of current used is always a low-voltage direct current set on a continuous mode because the pulse duration must be long enough to allow for migration of ions.

Iontophoresis uses electrical current to drive ions.

Figure 15-15

Pattern created by
interferential current.

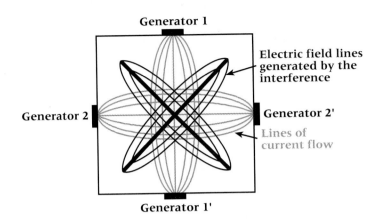

There are three techniques of application: an active pad is applied over gauze that is saturated with a solution containing the ions (this pad is positioned as close as possible to the involved tissue); the active electrode is suspended in a container of the ion solution, and then the part to be treated is immersed in the container; or a special stimulator with a specially adapted electrode containing the treatment ions is positioned as close to the involved tissue as possible. In all cases, a large dispersive pad is applied to the patient and the proper polarity of the active electrode is selected based on the polarity of the ions in the solution.

Positive ions require an active electrode that is positive; negative ions require an active electrode that is negative. Treatment time will vary. A more comprehensive source dealing with iontophoresis should be consulted before using this technique.[14]

Interferential Currents

Interferential currents make use of two separate electrical generators that emit currents at two slightly different frequencies. Two pairs of electrodes are arranged in a square pattern such that the currents cross one another, creating an interference pattern at a central point of stimulation. The interference pattern creates a broader area of stimulation (Figure 15-15).[33]

Low-Intensity Stimulators

Low-intensity stimulators (LIS) are among the newest of the electrical stimulators available to the athletic trainer. *Low-intensity stimulator* is the latest term for what used to be called microcurrent electrical nerve stimulator, or MENS. Low-intensity stimulators deliver current to the athlete at very low frequencies (1 PPS) and at extremely low intensities that are subsensory. This type of current is used to stimulate the healing process in both soft tissue and bone by altering the electrical activity of individual cells. The effectiveness of LIS therapy is currently based primarily on theory; there is little research information to support its use.[16]

Biofeedback

Biofeedback is a therapeutic procedure that uses electronic or electromechanical instruments to accurately measure, process, and feed back reinforcing information via auditory or visual signals. Perhaps the biggest advantage of biofeedback is that it provides the athlete with a chance to make correct small changes in performance that are immediately noted and rewarded so that eventually larger changes or improvements in performance can be accomplished.[37]

Several different types of biofeedback modalities are available for use in rehabilitation; EMG biofeedback is the most widely used in a clinical setting.[37] An EMG biofeedback unit measures the electrical activity produced by depolarization of a muscle fiber as an indicator of the quality of a muscle contraction. The EMG biofeed-

15-3

Critical Thinking Exercise

A female soccer player is having difficulty contracting her quadriceps muscle on the second day after a surgical reconstruction of her knee. She has some swelling in the vastus medialis, and she is still experiencing some pain.

? What modality can the athletic trainer use to help her achieve a quadriceps contraction?

back unit receives small amounts of electrical energy generated during muscle contraction through active electrodes, then separates or filters extraneous electrical energy via a differential amplifier before the signal is processed and subsequently converted to some type of information that has meaning to the user. Biofeedback information is displayed either visually using lights or meters, or auditorily using tones, beeps, buzzes, or clicks. High sensitivity levels should be used during relaxation training whereas comparatively lower sensitivity levels would be more useful in muscle reeducation.

In athletic training, biofeedback is most typically used for muscle reeducation, to decrease muscle guarding, or for pain reduction.[37]

LOW-POWER LASER

Laser is an acronym that stands for light amplification by stimulated emission of radiation.[12] The low-power laser is a relatively new device whose proposed applications in an athletic training setting include acceleration of collagen synthesis, control of microorganisms, increased vascularization, and reduction of pain and inflammation.[47]

laser
Light amplification by stimulated emission of radiation.

The helium-neon (HeNe) and the gallium-arsenide (GaAs) lasers are two low-power lasers currently being investigated by the Food and Drug Administration (FDA) for potential use in physical medicine. Currently the FDA has not approved the use of the low-power laser except in laboratory and experimental settings.[12]

MASSAGE

Massage is defined as the systematic manipulation of the soft tissues of the body. The movements of gliding, compressing, stretching, percussing, and vibrating are regulated to produce specific responses in the athlete.[13]

Massage is separated into five basic categories: effleurage, petrissage, friction, tapotement, and vibration.

Therapeutic Effects of Massage

Historically, wherever sports have been seriously undertaken, massage has been used in some form. Today sports massage seems to be regaining popularity among athletic trainers as a treatment modality. Manipulation of soft tissue by massage is a useful adjunct to other modalities. Sports massage causes mechanical, physiological, and psychological responses.

Mechanical Responses

Mechanical responses to massage occur as a direct result of the graded pressures and movements of the hand on the body. Such actions encourage venous and lymphatic drainage and mildly stretch superficial and scar tissue. Connective tissue can be effectively stretched by friction massage, which helps prevent rigidity in scar formation. When an athlete is forced to remain inactive while an injury heals or when edema surrounds a joint, the stagnation of circulation may be prevented by using certain massage techniques.

Physiological Responses

Massage can increase circulation and, as a result, increase metabolism to the musculature and aid in the removal of metabolites such as lactic acid.[13] It also helps overcome venostasis and edema by increasing circulation at and around the injury site, assisting in the normal venous blood return to the heart.

The reflex effects of massage are processes that, in response to nerve impulses initiated through rubbing the body, are transmitted to one organ by afferent nerve fibers and then back to another organ by efferent fibers. Reflex responses elicit a variety of organ reactions such as body relaxation, stimulation, and increased circulation.[42]

Possible physiological responses of massage include:
- Reflex effects
- Relaxation
- Stimulation
- Increased circulation

Relaxation can be induced by slow, superficial stroking of the skin. It is a type of massage that is beneficial for tense, anxious athletes who may require gentle treatment.

Stimulation is attained by quick, brisk action that causes a contraction of superficial tissue. The benefits derived by the athlete are predominantly psychological. He or she feels invigorated after intense manipulation of the tissue. In the early days of American sports, stimulation massage was given as a warm-up procedure, but it has gradually lost popularity because of the time involved and the recognition that it is relatively ineffectual physiologically.[42]

Increased circulation is accomplished by mechanical and reflex stimuli. Together they cause the capillaries to dilate and be drained of fluid as a result of firm outside pressure, thus stimulating cell metabolism, eliminating toxins, and increasing lymphatic and venous circulation. In this way the healing process is aided.

Psychological Responses

The tactile system is one of the most sensitive systems in the human organism. From earliest infancy, humans respond psychologically to being touched. Because massage is the act of laying on of hands, it can be an important means for creating a bond of confidence between the athletic trainer and the athlete.

Massage Strokes

Effleurage

Effleurage, or stroking (Figure 15-16), is divided into light and deep methods. Light stroking is designed primarily to be sedative. It is also used in the early stages of injury treatment. Deep stroking is a therapeutic compression of soft tissue, which encourages venous and lymphatic drainage. A different application of effleurage may be used for a specific body part.

Stroking variations   There are many variations in effleurage massage; some that are of particular value to sports injuries are pressure variations, the hand-over-hand method, and the cross-body method.[13] Pressure variations range from very light to deep and vigorous stroking. Light stroking, as discussed previously, can induce relaxation or may be used when an area is especially sensitive to touch; on the other hand, deep massage is designed to bring about definite physiological responses. Light and deep effleurage can be used alternately when both features are desired. The hand-over-hand stroking method is of special benefit to those surface areas that are particularly unyielding. It is performed by an alternate stroke in which one hand strokes, followed immediately by the other hand, somewhat like shingles on a roof (Figure 15-17). The cross-body effleurage technique is an excellent massage for the

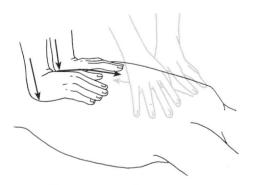

Massage procedures

Figure 15-16

Effleurage.

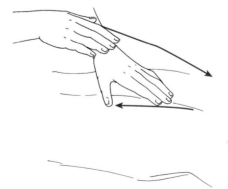

Figure 15-17

Hand-over-hand effleurage.

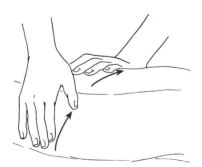

Figure 15-18

Cross-body effleurage.

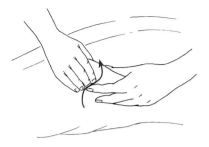

Figure 15-19

Petrissage.

Figure 15-20

Friction massage.

low back region. The operator places a hand on each side of the athlete's spine. Both hands first stroke simultaneously away from the spine, then both hands at the same time stroke toward the spine (Figure 15-18).

Petrissage

Kneading, or **petrissage** (Figure 15-19), is a technique adaptable primarily to loose and heavy tissue areas such as the trapezius, the latissimus dorsi, or the triceps muscles. The procedure consists of picking up the muscle and skin tissue between the thumb and forefinger of each hand and rolling and twisting it in opposite directions. As one hand is rolling and twisting, the other begins to pick up the adjacent tissue. The kneading action wrings out the muscle, thus loosening adhesions and squeezing congestive materials into the general circulation. Picking up skin may cause an irritating pinch. Whenever possible, deep muscle tissue should be gathered and lifted.

petrissage (**pet** tris saj)
Kneading.

Friction

The **friction** massage (Figure 15-20) is used often around joints and other areas where tissue is thin and is used on tissues that are especially unyielding such as scars, adhesions, muscle spasms, and fascia. The action is initiated by bracing with the heels of the hands, then either holding the thumbs steady and moving the fingers in a circular motion or holding the fingers steady and moving the thumbs in a circular motion. Each method is adaptable to the type of area or articulation that is being massaged. The motion is started at a central point, and then a circular movement is initiated, with the hands moving in opposite directions away from the center point. The purpose is to stretch the underlying tissue, develop friction in the area, and increase circulation around the joint.

friction
Heat producing.

Tapotement

The most popular methods of **tapotement,** or percussion, are cupping, hacking, and pincerlike or pincing movements.

Cupping   The cupping action produces an invigorating and stimulating sensation. It is a series of percussion movements rapidly duplicated at a constant tempo. The hands are cupped to such an extent that the beat emits a dull and hollow sound, unlike the sound of the slap of the open hand. The hands move alternately, from the wrist, with the elbow flexed and the upper arm stabilized (Figure 15-21A). The cupping action should be executed until the skin in the area develops a pinkish coloration.

Hacking   Hacking can be used in conjunction with cupping to bring about a varied stimulation of the sensory nerves (Figure 15-21B). Hacking is similar to cupping except that the hands are rotated externally and the ulnar, or little finger, border of the hand is the striking surface. Only the heavy muscle areas should be treated in this manner.

tapotement (ta **pote** ment)
Percussion.

Figure 15-21

Tapotement. **A**, Cupping.
B, Hacking. **C,** Pincing.

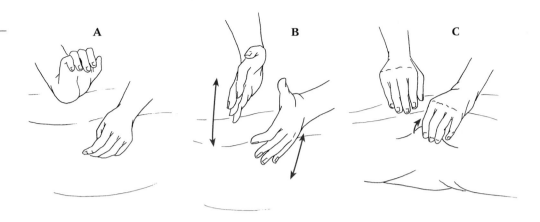

Pincing   Although pincing is not in the strictest sense percussive, it is categorized under tapotement because of the vigor with which it is applied. Alternating hands lift small amounts of tissue between the first finger and thumb in quick, gentle pinching movements (Figure 15-21C).

Vibration

vibration

Rapid shaking.

Vibration is rapid movement that produces a quivering or trembling effect. It is used in sports because of its ability to relax and soothe. Although vibration can be done manually, the machine vibrator is usually the preferred modality.

Guidelines for an Effective Massage

Besides knowing the different kinds of massage, the athletic trainer should understand how to give the most effective massage. The following rules should be used whenever possible:

1. Make the athlete comfortable.
   a. Place the body in the proper position on the table.
   b. Place a pad under the areas of the body that are to be massaged.
   c. Keep the training room at a constant 72° F (22.2° C) temperature.
   d. Respect the athlete's privacy by draping him or her with a blanket or towel, exposing only the body parts to be massaged.
2. Develop a confident, gentle approach when massaging.
   a. Assume a position that is easy both on you and on the athlete.
   b. Avoid using too harsh a stroke, or further injury may result.
3. To ensure proper lymphatic and venous drainage, stroke toward the heart whenever possible.
4. Know when not to use massage.
   a. Never give a massage if the athlete may have a local or general infection. To do so may encourage the infection's spread or may aggravate the condition.
   b. Never apply massage directly over a recent injury; limit stroking to the periphery. Massaging over recent injuries may dislodge the clot organization and start bleeding.

Sports Massage

Massage in sports is usually confined to a specific area and is seldom given to the full body. The time required for giving an adequate and complete body massage is excessive in athletics. It is not usually feasible to devote this much time to one athlete; five minutes is usually all that is required for massaging a given area.

Massage Lubricants

To enable the hands to slide easily over the body, a friction-reducing medium must be used. Rubbing the dry body can cause gross skin irritation by tearing and breaking off the hair. Many mediums (e.g., fine powders, oil liniments, or almost any substance having a petroleum base) can be used to advantage as lubricants.

Positioning of the Athlete

Proper positioning for massage is of great importance. The injured part must be made easily accessible; the athlete must be comfortable, and the part to be massaged must be relaxed.

Confidence

Lack of confidence on the part of the person doing the massage is easily transmitted through inexperienced hands. Every effort should be made to think out the procedure to be used and to present a confident appearance to the athlete.

Deep Transverse Friction Massage

The transverse, or Cyriax, method of deep friction massage is increasingly being used in sports medicine. It is a specific technique for treating muscles, tendons, ligaments, and joint capsules. The major goal of transverse massage is to move transversely across a ligament or tendon to mobilize it as much as possible. This technique often precedes active exercise. Deep transverse friction massage restores mobility to a muscle in the same way that mobilization frees a joint.[13]

The position of the athletic trainer's hands is important in gaining maximum strength and control. Four positions are suggested: index finger crossed over the middle finger, middle finger crossed over the index finger, two fingers side by side, and an opposed finger and thumb (Figure 15-22).

The massage must be directly over the site of lesion and pain. The fingers move with the skin and do not slide over it. Massage must be across the grain of the affected tissue. The thicker the structure, the more friction is given.[13] The technique is to sweep back and forth over the full width of the tissue. Massage should not be given to acute injuries or over highly swollen tissues. A few minutes of this method will produce a numbness in the area, and exercise or mobilization can be instituted.

Acupressure Massage

Acupressure is a type of massage based on the ancient Chinese art of acupuncture, which was discussed in Chapter 10. Physiological explanations of the effectiveness of acupressure massage may likely be attributed to some interaction of the various mechanisms of pain modulation.

> Transverse massage is a method of deep transverse friction massage.

Figure 15-22

Cyriax massage is a specific technique for muscle, tendons, ligaments, and joint capsules using a variety of hand positions. **A,** Index finger crossed over the middle finger. **B,** Middle finger crossed over the index finger. **C,** Two fingers side by side. **D,** Opposed finger and thumb.

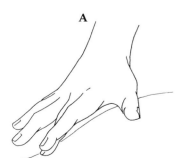
A

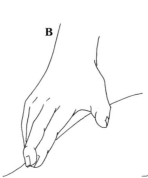
B

C

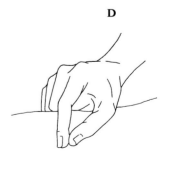
D

The athletic trainer uses acupuncture charts to select specific points that are described in the literature as having some relationship to the area of pain. The charts provide the athletic trainer with a general idea of where these points are located. Two techniques may be used to specifically locate acupressure points. Because it is known that electrical impedance is reduced at acupuncture points, an ohmmeter may be used to locate the points. Perhaps the easiest technique is for the athletic trainer simply to palpate the area until he or she feels either a small fibrous nodule or a strip of tense muscle tissue that is tender to the touch.

Once the point is located, massage is begun with the index or middle fingers, the thumb, or the elbow. Small circular motions are used on the point. The amount of pressure applied to these acupressure points should be determined by patient tolerance; however, the pressure must be intense and will likely be painful to the patient. Generally, the more pressure the patient can tolerate, the more effective the treatment is.

Effective treatment times range from one to five minutes at a single point per treatment. It may be necessary to massage several points during the treatment to obtain the greatest effects. If so, the athletic trainer should work distal points first and move proximally.

During the massage, the patient will report a dulling or numbing effect and will frequently indicate that the pain has diminished or subsided totally during the massage. The lingering effects of acupressure massage vary tremendously from patient to patient. The effects may last for only a few minutes in some but may persist in others for several hours.

TRACTION

Traction is commonly used in the cervical and lumbar spine.

Traction can be defined as a drawing tension applied to a body segment. It is most commonly used in the cervical and lumbar regions of the spine.[18]

Physiological Effects

Traction is used to produce separation of the vertebral bodies and in so doing can effect stretching of the ligaments and joint capsules of the spine, stretching of spinal and paraspinal muscles, increased separation of the articular facet joints, relief in pressure on nerves and nerve roots, decrease in the central pressure of the intervertebral disks allowing for the movement of herniated disk material back into the center of the disk, increases of and changes in joint proprioception, and relief of the compressive effects of normal posture.[18]

Indications

Traction is most commonly used for the treatment of spinal nerve root impingement, which may result from many causes, including vertebral disk herniation or prolapse and spondylolisthesis. It may also be used to decrease muscle guarding, to treat muscle strain, to treat sprain of the spinal ligaments, and to relax discomfort resulting from normal spinal compression.

Application

Traction may be applied to the spine through the use of manual techniques or traction machines, including table traction units, wall-mounted traction units, and inverted traction techniques.

Manual Traction

Manual traction is infinitely more adaptable and offers greater flexibility than mechanical traction. Changes in force, direction, duration, and patient position can be made instantaneously as the athletic trainer senses relaxation or resistance (Figure 15-23).

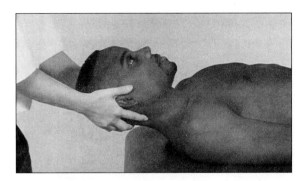

Figure 15-23

Manual cervical traction.

Mechanical Traction

For mechanical lumbar traction, a split table with a movable section to eliminate friction must be used to allow for smooth, nonrestricted traction. A nonslip traction harness applied directly to the skin is needed to transfer the traction force comfortably to the athlete and to stabilize the trunk while the lumbar spine is placed under traction (Figure 15-24). For cervical traction, the athlete may be either in the supine or sitting position. A nonslip cervical harness should be secured under the chin and back of the head.

Positional Traction

Positional traction is used on a trial-and-error basis to determine maximum position of comfort or to accomplish a specific treatment goal. For example, placing an athlete with a lumbar disc problem in a backlying position with the hips and knees flexed and supported at 90 degrees increases the opening of the foramen and takes pressure off the disk, thus minimizing pain and making the athlete more comfortable.

Wall-Mounted Traction

Cervical traction can be accomplished with a wall-mounted system. Plates, sand bags, or water bags can be used for weights. These units are relatively inexpensive and effective (Figure 15-25).

Inverted Traction

Specialized equipment or simply hanging upside down will place the person in an inverted position. The spine is lengthened because of the stretch provided by the weight of the trunk (Figure 15-26).

15-5

Critical Thinking Exercise

A gymnast has been told by a physician that she has a sprain of a ligament between two lumbar vertebrae in her low back. He tells her that it is important to stretch her low back. Because she was extremely flexible before her injury, she does not feel that the stretching she has been doing is effectively stretching the injured ligament.

? The gymnast comes to the athletic trainer and asks if any other therapeutic technique will help her stretch the injured ligament.

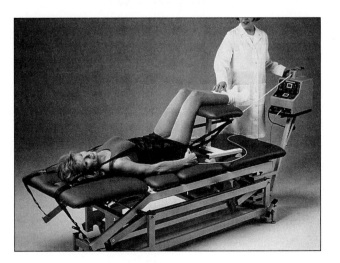

Figure 15-24

Lumbar traction using a split table and a traction machine.

Figure 15-25

Cervical traction using a wall-mounted unit.

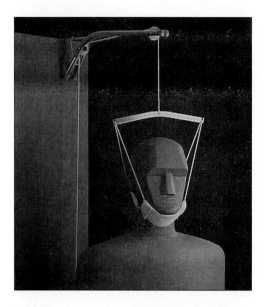

Figure 15-26

Inversion traction apparatus.

Special Considerations

- Good results have been achieved using both intermittent and sustained traction. In most cases of lumbar disk problems, sustained traction seems to be the treatment of choice. Intermittent traction is considered to be more comfortable.[18]
- Progressive traction increases the traction force gradually in a preselected number of steps, which allows the athlete to adapt slowly to the traction and helps him or her to stay relaxed.
- Recommendations on length of treatment and on/off times are extremely variable and depend on the specific problem to be treated.
- For the lumbar spine, a traction force equal to one half the athlete's body weight is a good guideline to use in selecting a force high enough to cause vertebral separation. Cervical traction forces can be adjusted from 20 to 50 pounds depending on patient comfort and response.

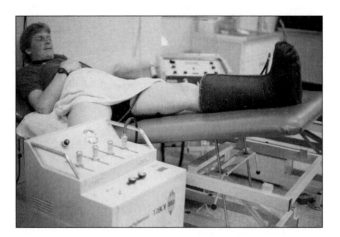

INTERMITTENT COMPRESSION UNITS

Intermittent compression units are used for controlling or reducing swelling after acute injury or for pitting edema, which tends to develop in the injured area several hours after injury.[17]

Equipment

Intermittent compression makes use of a nylon pneumatic inflatable sleeve applied around the injured extremity (Figure 15-27). The sleeve can be inflated to a specific pressure that forces excessive fluid accumulated in the interstitial spaces into vascular and lymphatic channels through which it is removed from the area of injury. Compression facilitates the movement of lymphatic fluid, which helps eliminate the by-products of the injury process.[45] The extremity should be elevated during treatment.

Treatment Parameters

Intermittent compression devices have three parameters that may be adjusted: on/off time, inflation pressures, and treatment time. Recommended treatment protocols have been established through clinical trial and error with little experimental data currently available to support any protocol.[17]

On/off times are variable, including 1 minute on, 2 minutes off; 2 minutes on, 1 minute off; and 4 minutes on, 1 minute off. Again, these recommendations are not research based. Patient comfort should be the primary guide.

Recommended inflation pressures have been loosely correlated with blood pressures. The Jobst Institute recommends that pressure be set at 30 to 50 mm Hg for the upper extremity and at 30 to 60 mm Hg for the lower extremity. Because arterial capillary pressures are approximately 30 mm Hg, any pressure that exceeds this level should encourage the absorption of edema and the flow of lymphatic fluid.[45]

Clinical studies have demonstrated a significant reduction in limb volume after thirty minutes of compression.[1,45] Thus a thirty-minute treatment time seems to be efficient in reducing edema.

Some intermittent compression units have the capability of combining cold along with compression. Compression when combined with cold is more effective in reducing edema.[1,45] It is also common to use electrical stimulating currents to produce muscle pumping, thus facilitating lymphatic flow.

MAGNET THERAPY

Recently, magnet therapy has become popular among both competitive and recreational athletes. An increasing number of athletic trainers are using magnets as a treatment modality for athletes who complain of a variety of musculoskeletal ailments. Although a wealth of anecdotical information on magnet therapy can be found in the

Figure 15-28

Therapeutic modalities treatment log.

Patient's Name _____ Sport _____

Diagnosis _____ Date of Injury _____

Athletic Trainer _____

Therapeutic Modality _____

Treatment Parameters

    Intensity/Output _____

    Frequency _____

    Duty Cycle _____

    Temperature _____

    Duration of Treatment _____

    Electrode Placement _____

Special Instructions:

Month/Year _____

Date Administered:

1 2 3 4 5 6 7 8 9 10 11 12 13 14 15 16 17 18 19 20 21 22 23 24 25 26 27 28 29 30 31

popular literature, a careful review of the medical literature indicates few data-based research articles on the efficacy or potential therapeutic benefits of using magnets.

Magnet therapy may be defined as the application of a magnetic field to the human body. A magnet is a natural ferrous material with inseparable positively and negatively charged poles that characteristically attract particles of opposite charge and repel particles of similar charge. The strength of a magnetic field is measured in Gauss units. Most therapeutic magnets range between 300 and 1,000 Gauss. The explanations of the potential beneficial physiological effects of magnets include changes in polarity within a damaged cell, increased blood flow and thus increased oxygen saturation, increased muscle strength, increased hormone secretions, increased cell division rate, increased enzyme activity, increased tissue temperature, increased lymphatic flow, and changes in blood pH.

Although magnet therapy appears to be a relatively safe treatment modality, it should be used with caution by athletic trainers until some definitive basis for use has been determined scientifically.

RECORDING THERAPEUTIC MODALITY TREATMENTS

Athletic trainers who use a therapeutic modality in treatment need to record the procedure. The specifics of the modality treatment should be recorded on the original SOAP note, on the progress note, and on a therapuetic modalities treatment log like the one shown in Figure 15-28. Changes in the treatment parameters should be noted on the treatment log so that anyone administering a modality treatment can consult the log to determine the appropriate treatment parameters.

SUMMARY

- To avoid legal problems, athletic trainers must use therapeutic modalities with extreme care. Athletic trainers must be familiar with the laws of their state regarding therapeutic modality use. Before using any modality, the athletic trainer must have a thorough understanding of its function and when it should and should not be used.
- Heat energy is transmitted through conduction, convection, radiation, and conversion. Conduction occurs when heat is transferred from a warmer object to a cooler one. Convection heating occurs by means of fluid or gas movement. Radiation is heat energy that is transmitted through empty space. Conversion is heat that is generated when one type of energy is changed to another.

- The use of cold for therapeutic purposes and as part of an emergency procedure is extremely popular in sports medicine. Cold penetrates deeper than superficial heat. Therapy is usually performed when the tissue has reached a state of relative anesthesia. Cryotherapy decreases muscle spasm, pain perception, and blood flow. It increases the inelasticity of collagen fibers, joint stiffness, and capillary permeability. Common cryotherapy procedures are cold water immersion, ice massage, ice packs, and the use of vapocoolant sprays.

- Thermotherapy increases blood flow, increases collagen viscosity, decreases joint stiffness, and reduces pain and muscle spasm. When the body's temperature is raised, tissue metabolism is increased, vascular permeability is increased, and chemicals such as histamine, bradykinin, and serotonin are released.

- Superficial therapeutic heat should not be applied under the following circumstances: when there is a loss of sensation; immediately after an acute injury; or when there is decreased arterial bleeding. Superficial therapeutic heat should not be used over the eyes or genitals or over the abdomen of a pregnant woman. Types of superficial heat are moist heat packs, whirlpool baths, paraffin baths, fluidotherapy, and contrast baths.

- Both shortwave and microwave diathermies produce heat through electromagnetic energy, whereas ultrasound produces heat through acoustical energy. The contraindications for use of shortwave diathermy and microwave diathermy are the same as for superficial heating, with the additional restrictions of no implants, jewelry, or intrauterine devices. Care must be taken not to cross the cables.

- Ultrasound is a form of acoustic energy. It creates a mechanical vibration that is converted to heat energy within the body. Heating occurs in the denser tissues such as bone and connective tissue. More heat is built up at tissue interfaces. Ultrasound has both thermal and nonthermal physiological effects. It can be combined with electrical stimulation or used to drive molecules through the skin with the method known as phonophoresis.

- The use of electrical stimulating currents is popular in sports medicine. Electrical stimulating units produce either alternating current (AC), direct current (DC), or pulsed current. Both AC and DC can be used for pain modulation and muscle contraction. Direct current can also be used for iontophoresis. The physiological effects of electrical current are determined by the treatment parameters and equipment selected. Current parameters include waveforms, modulation, intensity, duration, frequency, polarity, and electrode placement. Interferential currents and LIS are two of the newest electrical stimulating currents available to the athletic trainer.

- The low-power laser may be used to stimulate the healing process or to modulate pain. Currently it has not been approved as a treatment modality.

- Massage is a useful modality for many sport-related injuries. Techniques include effleurage, petrissage, friction, tapotement, and vibration. Deep transverse massage is used on connective tissue.

- Traction is used to produce separation of the vertebrae, most commonly for the treatment of spinal nerve root impingement and associated abnormalities. It is typically used in the cervical and lumbar spine and may involve either manual or machine-assisted traction.

- Intermittent compression devices are used to control swelling after acute injury or to reduce pitting edema.

Web Sites

Cramer First Aider: http://www.ccsd.k12.wy.us/cchs_web/
cramerfirstaider/fstaider.htm

National Athletic Trainers' Association: http://www.nata.org

Solutions to *Critical Thinking* EXERCISES

15-1 The decision is to some extent subjective. The athletic trainer must understand what is going on with the healing process. By the fifth day, the inflammatory process is ending and the fibroblastic stage is establishing itself. At this point it is still advisable to avoid any treatment that may increase swelling, which can interfere with healing. Heat would increase circulation, which might increase swelling. The athletic trainer would not likely exacerbate the injury by using heat, but the recommendation is that cold be used during this time. A rule of thumb is that when tenderness is gone, it is safe to change to some form of heat.

15-2 At this point, some form of heat to increase blood and lymphatic flow to the injured area is warranted. Increased blood flow will help facilitate the process of healing, and an increased lymphatic flow will help remove the by-products of the inflammatory process. Hot packs provide superficial heat and would not be effective in this case. Both the diathermics as well as ultrasound would be recommended because they all have a depth of penetration great enough to affect the injured area; ultrasound would be somewhat more effective. For best results, stretching and strengthening exercises should always be used along with modalities.

15-3 A biofeedback unit can help the athlete relearn how to fire the quadriceps muscle. The biofeedback unit can provide both visual and auditory feedback to indicate the strength of a contraction as well as the timing of a contraction. Biofeedback can be used almost immediately following surgery.

15-4 The athletic trainer can use cryotherapy, heat, or electrical stimulating currents to help reduce pain. Electrical stimulating currents may be the most useful if the athletic trainer wants to also elicit a muscle contraction to help decrease muscle guarding. Massage is also useful for modulating pain and for relaxing muscle. Regardless of the modality chosen, the athlete should engage in some stretching and strengthening exercises after the modality treatment.

15-5 The athletic trainer should try using manual lumbar traction techniques, which, if done properly, can be effective in isolating a specific ligament between two lumbar vertebrae. If the athletic trainer cannot manually generate enough traction force to stretch the ligament, a table traction unit or an inverted traction technique may prove to be more useful.

15-6 Proper initial management of the injury could have prevented a great deal of the swelling that has occurred. At this point, the athletic trainer should make use of ice to modulate pain; intermittent compression and electrical stimulating current to induce a muscle pumping contraction (both of which can help the lymphatic system remove the swelling); and low-intensity ultrasound (>0.2 W/cm^2), which can help facilitate the healing process. In addition, the athlete should continually wear a compressive elastic wrap. He must also progress to full weight bearing, concentrating on regaining a normal gait as soon as tolerated.

REVIEW QUESTIONS AND CLASS ACTIVITIES

1. Explain the legal factors that a coach or athletic trainer should consider before using a therapeutic modality.
2. Give examples of modalities that heat through conduction, convection, radiation, and conversion.
3. What physiological changes occur when heat is applied to the body?
4. Discuss the physiological effects of using cryotherapy.
5. Demonstrate the proper technique for a variety of cryotherapeutic approaches.
6. Compare therapy delivered through heat to that delivered through cold. When would you use each?
7. What are shortwave and microwave diathermy used for?
8. Discuss how ultrasound can be used during a rehabilitation program.
9. Compare phonophoresis with iontophoresis.
10. What is a TENS unit?
11. Identify the potential treatment goals of an electrically stimulated muscle contraction.
12. How is massage best used in a sports medicine setting?
13. List the mechanical effects of cervical and lumbar traction.
14. Explain when and how intermittent compression can best be used as a treatment modality.

REFERENCES

1. Angus J, Prentice W, Hooker D: A comparison of two external intermittent compression devices and their effect on post acute ankle edema, *J Ath Train* 29(2):178, 1994.
2. Barr J: Transcutaneous electrical nerve stimulation characteristics for altering pain perception, *Phys Ther* 66(10):1037, 1987.
3. Belitsky RB et al: Evaluation of the effectiveness of wet ice, dry ice, and Crogen packs in reducing skin temperature, *Phys Ther* 67(7):1080, 1987.
4. Bell AT, Horton PG: The use and abuse of hydrotherapy in athletics: a review, *Ath Train* 22:115, 1987.
5. Castel C, Draper D, Castel D: Rate of temperature increase during ultrasound treatments: are traditional times long enough? *J Ath Train* 29(2):156, 1994.
6. Draper DO, Harris ST, Schulthies S et al: Hot-pack and 1-MHz ultrasound treatments have an additive effect on muscle temperature, *J Ath Train* 33(1):21, 1998.
7. Draper D, Prentice W: Therapeutic ultrasound. In Prentice W, editor: *Therapeutic modalities in sports medicine*, ed 4, Dubuque, Iowa, 1999, WCB/McGraw-Hill.
8. Draper DO, Ricard M: Rate of temperature decay in human muscle following 3-Mhz ultrasound: the stretching window revealed, *J Ath Train* 30(4):304, 1995.
9. Draper D, Schulthies S, Sorvisto P: The effect of cooling the tissue prior to ultrasound treatment, *J Ath Train* 29(2):154, 1994.
10. Draper D, Sunderland S: Examination of the law of Grotthus-Draper: does ultrasound penetrate subcutaneous fat? *J Ath Train* 28(3):246, 1993.
11. Dyson M: The use of ultrasound in sports physiotherapy. In Grisogono V, editor: *Sports injuries: international perspectives in physiotherapy*, Edinburgh, 1989, Churchill Livingstone.
12. Enwemeka C: Laser biostimulation of healing wounds: specific effects and mechanisms of action, *J Orthop Sports Phys Ther* 9:333, 1988.
13. Fritz S: *Mosby's fundamentals of therapeutic massage*, St Louis, 1995, Mosby Lifeline.
14. Harris PR: Iontophoresis: clinical research in musculoskeletal inflammatory conditions, *J Orthop Sports Phys Ther* 4:109, 1982.
15. Holcomb W: A practical guide to electrical therapy, *J Sport Rehabil* 6(3):272, 1997.
16. Hooker D: Electrical stimulating currents. In Prentice W, editor: *Therapeutic modalities in sports medicine*, ed 4, Dubuque, Iowa, 1999, WCB/McGraw-Hill.
17. Hooker D: Intermittent compression devices. In Prentice W, editor: *Therapeutic modalities in sports medicine*, ed 4, Dubuque, Iowa, 1999, WCB/McGraw-Hill.
18. Hooker D: Traction as a specialized modality. In Prentice W, editor: *Therapeutic modalities in sports medicine*, ed 4, Dubuque, Iowa, 1999, WCB/McGraw-Hill.
19. Hunter LY: Physical therapy modalities. In Hunter LY, Funk FJ, editors: *Rehabilitation of the injured knee*, St Louis, 1984, Mosby.
20. Jacobs SR et al: Electrical stimulation of muscle. In Stillwell GK, editor: *Therapeutic electricity and ultraviolet radiation*, ed 3, Baltimore, 1983, Williams & Wilkins.
21. Kloth L: Shortwave and microwave diathermy. In Michlovitz SL, editor: *Thermal agents in rehabilitation*, Philadelphia, 1996, Davis.
22. Knight K: *Cryotherapy in sport injury management*, Champaign, Ill, 1995, Human Kinetics.

23. Krumholz A, Gelfand B, O'Conner P: Therapeutic modalities. In Nicholas J, Hershman EB, editors: *The lower extremity and spine in sports medicine,* vol 1, St Louis, 1995, Mosby.

24. Lehmann JF, DeLateur BJ: Cryotherapy. In Lehmann JF, editor: *Therapeutic heat and cold,* ed 3, Baltimore, 1982, Williams & Wilkins.

25. Lehmann JF, DeLateur BJ: Therapeutic heat. In Lehmann JF, editor: *Therapeutic heat and cold,* ed 3, Baltimore, 1982, Williams & Wilkins.

26. Lehmann JF et al: Comparison of relative heating patterns produced in tissues by exposure to microwave energy at frequencies of 2450 to 900 megacycles, *Arch Phys Med Rehabil* 46:307, 1965.

27. McMaster WC: Cryotherapy, *Physician Sportsmed* 10:112, 1982.

28. Myrer J, Draper D, Durrant E: Contrast therapy and intramuscular temperature in the leg, *J Ath Train* 29(4):318, 1994.

29. Myrer JW, Measom G, Durrant E, et al: Cold- and hot-pack contrast therapy: Subcutaneous and intramuscular temperature change, *J Ath Train* 32(3):238, 1997.

30. Michlovitz SL: Biophysical principles of heating and superficial heat agents. In Michlovitz SL, editor: *Thermal agents in rehabilitation,* Philadelphia, 1996, Davis.

31. Michlovitz SL: Cryotherapy: the use of cold as a therapeutic agent. In Michlovitz SL, editor: *Thermal agents in rehabilitation,* Philadelphia, 1996, Davis.

32. Nielsen AJ: Case study: myofascial pain of posterior shoulder relieved by spray and stretch, *J Orthop Sports Phys Ther* 3:21, 1981.

33. Patterson RP: Instrumentation for electrotherapy. In Stillwell GK, editor: *Therapeutic electricity and ultraviolet radiation,* ed 3, Baltimore, 1983, Williams & Wilkins.

34. Penderghest C, Kimura I, Gulick D: Double-blind clinical efficacy study of pulsed phonophoresis on perceived pain associated with symptomatic tendinitis, *J Sport Rehabil* 7(1):9, 1998.

35. Peppard A, Riegter HF: Trigger point therapy for myofascial pain, *Physician Sportsmed* 9:161, 1981.

36. Prentice W: Basic principles of electricity. In Prentice W, editor: *Therapeutic modalities in sports medicine,* ed 4, Dubuque, Iowa, 1999, WCB/McGraw-Hill.

37. Prentice W: Biofeedback. In Prentice W, editor: *Therapeutic modalities in sports medicine,* ed 4, Dubuque, Iowa, 1999, WCB/McGraw-Hill.

38. Prentice W: Preface. In Prentice W, editor: *Therapeutic modalities in sports medicine,* ed 4, Dubuque, Iowa, 1999, WCB/McGraw-Hill.

39. Prentice W: The science of therapeutic modalities. In Prentice W, editor: *Therapeutic modalities in sports medicine,* ed 4, Dubuque, Iowa, 1999, WCB/McGraw-Hill.

40. Prentice W, Bell G: Infrared modalities. In Prentice W, editor: *Therapeutic modalities in sports medicine,* ed 4, Dubuque, Iowa, 1999, WCB/McGraw-Hill.

41. Prentice W, Draper, D, Donley P: Shortwave and microwave diathermy. In Prentice W, editor: *Therapeutic modalities in sports medicine,* ed 4, Dubuque, Iowa, 1999, WCB/McGraw-Hill.

42. Prentice W, Lehn C: Therapeutic massage. In Prentice W, editor: *Therapeutic modalities in sports medicine,* ed 4, Dubuque, Iowa, 1999, WCB/McGraw-Hill.

43. Quillin WS: Ultrasonic phonophoresis, *Physician Sportsmed* 10:211, 1982.

44. Rimington S, Draper D, Durrant E: Temperature changes during therapeutic ultrasound in the precooled human gastrocnemius muscle, *J Ath Train* 29(4):325, 1994.

45. Rucinski T, Hooker D, Prentice W: The effects of intermittent compression on edema in postacute ankle sprains, *J Orthop Sports Phys Ther* 13(8):65, 1991.

46. Rusk HA: *Rehabilitation medicine,* ed 4, St Louis, 1977, Mosby.

47. Saliba E, Foreman S: Low-power laser. In Prentice W, editor: *Therapeutic modalities in sports medicine,* ed 4, Dubuque, Iowa, 1999, WCB/McGraw-Hill.

48. Schliephakle E: Carrying out treatment. In Throm H, editor: *Introduction to shortwave and microwave therapy,* ed 3, Springfield, Ill, 1966, Charles C Thomas.

49. Sherman M: Which treatment to recommend? Hot or cold? *Am Pharm* NS20:46, 1980.

50. Snyder-Mackler L, Robinson A: *Clinical electrophysiology: electrotherapy and electrophysiology,* Baltimore, 1989, Williams & Wilkins.

51. ter Harr C: Basic physics of therapeutic ultrasound, *Physiotherapy* 73(3):110, 1987.

52. Tsang K et al: The effects of cryotherapy applied through various barriers, *J Sport Rehabil* 6(4):343, 1997.

53. Walsh M: Hydrotherapy: the use of water as a therapeutic agent. In Michlovitz SL, editor: *Thermal agents in rehabilitation,* Philadelphia, 1996, Davis.

54. Ziskin MC, Michlovitz SL: Therapeutic ultrasound. In Michlovitz SL, editor: *Thermal agents in rehabilitation,* Philadelphia, 1996, Davis.

ANNOTATED BIBLIOGRAPHY

Cameron, M: *Physical agents in rehabilitation: from research to practice.* Philadelphia, 1999, W.B. Saunders.

A guide for the physical therapist using therapeutic modalities.

Knight KL: *Cryotherapy in sports injury management,* Champaign, Ill, 1995, Human Kinetics.

This text presents excellent coverage, both theoretical and practical, of one of the most widely used therapeutic approaches in sports medicine and athletic training—cryotherapy. The text is clearly written and easily applied.

Michlovitz SL, editor: *Thermal agents in rehabilitation,* Philadelphia, 1996, Davis.

This excellent text is about understanding the foundations and use of thermal agents in sports medicine and athletic training. It provides detailed discussions of inflammation, pain, superficial heat and cold, and the therapeutic use of ultrasound and shortwave and microwave diathermies.

Prentice, W: *Therapeutic modalities for allied health professionals,* New York, 1998, McGraw-Hill.

A comprehensive guide to using therapeutic modalities in treating a variety of patient populations. This text contains pertinent case studies and laboratory activities.

Prentice WE: *Therapeutic modalities in sports medicine,* ed 4, Dubuque, Iowa, 1999, WCB/McGraw-Hill.

This text is a complete and comprehensive guide about the use of therapeutic modalities in the sports medicine setting. It addresses all aspects of modality use, including massage, traction, and intermittent compression. The text is an excellent blend of theory and practical application.

Starkey C: *Therapeutic modalities for athletic trainers,* Philadelphia, 1998, Davis.

This text discusses many of the modalities used by athletic trainers in a clinical setting.

Travell JG, Simons DG: *Myofascial pain and dysfunction,* Baltimore, 1983, Williams & Wilkins.

This valuable text about myofascial trigger points provides a clear understanding of trigger-point evaluation in the upper body and the treatment of choice; it also covers muscle stretch after the application of a vapocoolant.

Using Therapeutic Exercise in Rehabilitation

When you finish this chapter you should be able to

- Explain how the athletic trainer approaches rehabilitation.
- Contrast therapeutic exercise and conditioning exercise.
- Describe the consequences of sudden inactivity and injury immobilization.
- Describe the primary components of a rehabilitation program.
- Discuss the concept of open versus closed kinetic chain exercises.
- Describe the value of aquatic exercise in rehabilitation.
- Discuss the techniques and principles of proprioceptive neuromuscular facilitation.
- Describe the use of mobilization and traction techniques for improving accessory joint motions.

O ne of the primary goals of coach and athletic trainer is to create a playing environment for the athlete that is as safe as it can possibly be. Regardless of that effort, the nature of athletic participation dictates that injuries will eventually occur. When injuries do occur, the focus of the athletic trainer shifts from injury prevention to injury treatment and rehabilitation.

THE ATHLETIC TRAINER'S APPROACH TO REHABILITATION

The process of rehabilitation begins immediately after injury. Initial first aid and management techniques can have a substantial impact on the course and ultimate outcome of the rehabilitative process. Thus, in addition to possessing sound understanding of how injuries can be prevented, the athletic trainer must also be competent in providing correct and appropriate initial care when injury occurs. In a sports medicine setting, the athletic trainer generally assumes the primary responsibility for design, implementation, and supervision of the rehabilitation program for the injured athlete.

Designing programs for rehabilitation is relatively simple and involves several basic short-term goals: controlling pain, maintaining or improving flexibility, restoring or increasing strength, reestablishing neuromuscular control, and maintaining levels of cardiorespiratory fitness. The long-term goal is to return the injured athlete to practice or competition as quickly and safely as possible. The design is the easy part of supervising a rehabilitation program. The difficult part comes in knowing exactly when and how to change or alter the rehabilitation protocols to most effectively accomplish both long- and short-term goals. Progression during the rehabilitation program should be based on specific criteria, and return to competition must be based on level of function and patient outcomes.

The approach to rehabilitation in an athletic training environment is considerably different than in most other rehabilitation settings. The competitive nature of athletics necessitates an aggressive approach to rehabilitation. Because the competitive season in most sports is relatively short, the athlete does not have the luxury of simply sitting around and doing nothing until the injury heals. The goal is for the athlete to return to activity as soon as safely possible. Thus, the athletic trainer who is supervising the rehabilitation program must perform a balancing act between not pushing the athlete hard enough and being overly aggressive. In either case, a mistake in judgment on the part of the athletic trainer may hinder the athlete's return to activity.

The athletic trainer is responsible for design, implementation, and supervision of the rehabilitation program.

The long-term goal is to return the injured athlete to practice or competition as quickly and safely as possible.

Decisions as to when and how to alter and progress a rehabilitation program should be based within the framework of the healing process. The athletic trainer must possess a sound understanding of both the sequence and time frames for the various phases of healing and must realize that certain physiological events must occur during each of the phases. Any actions taken during a rehabilitation program that interfere with this healing process will likely increase the length of time required for rehabilitation and will slow the athlete's return to full activity. The healing process must have an opportunity to accomplish what it is supposed to. At best, the athletic trainer can only try to create an environment that is conducive to the healing process. Little can be done to speed up the process physiologically, but many things can be done during rehabilitation to impede healing.

Athletic trainers have many tools at their disposal that can facilitate the rehabilitative process. How the athletic trainer chooses to use those tools is often a matter of individual preference and experience. Additionally, each individual patient is different, and the responses to various treatment protocols are variable. Thus, a cookbook approach to rehabilitation, with specific protocols that can be followed like a recipe, is impossible. In fact, use of rehabilitation recipes is strongly discouraged. Instead, the athletic trainer must develop a broad theoretical knowledge base from which specific techniques of rehabilitation may be selected and applied to each individual athlete.

THERAPEUTIC EXERCISE VERSUS CONDITIONING EXERCISE

Exercise is an essential factor in fitness conditioning, injury prevention, and injury rehabilitation. To compete successfully at a high level, the athlete must be fit. An athlete who is not fit is more likely to sustain an injury. Coaches and athletic trainers both recognize that improper conditioning is one of the major causes of sports injuries. It is essential that the athlete engage in training and conditioning exercises that minimize the possibility of injury while maximizing performance.

The basic principles of training and conditioning that were discussed in Chapter 4 also apply to therapeutic, rehabilitative, or reconditioning exercises for restoring normal body function following injury. The term *therapeutic exercise* is perhaps most widely used to indicate exercises that are used in a rehabilitation program.

SUDDEN PHYSICAL INACTIVITY AND INJURY IMMOBILIZATION

The human body is a dynamic, moving entity that requires physical activity to maintain proper physical function. When an injury occurs, two problems immediately arise that must be addressed. First is the generalized loss of physical fitness that occurs when activity is stopped, and second is the specific inactivity of the injured part, resulting from protective splinting of the soft tissue and, in some cases, immobilization by some external means.

Effects of General Inactivity

An athlete who is highly conditioned will experience a rapid, generalized loss of fitness when exercise is suddenly stopped.[13] This sudden lack of activity causes loss of muscle strength, endurance, and coordination. Whenever possible, the athlete, without aggravating the injury, must continue to exercise the entire body.

Effects of Immobilization

An injured body part that is immobilized for a period of time causes a number of disuse problems that adversely affect muscle, joints, ligaments, bone, neuromuscular efficiency, and the cardiorespiratory system.

Muscle and Immobilization

When a body part is immobilized for as short a period as twenty-four hours, definite adverse muscular changes occur.

16-1

Critical Thinking Exercise

A soccer player has been diagnosed as having a grade 2 sprain of the MCL in her knee. The team physician has referred the athlete to the athletic trainer, who is charged with the responsibility of overseeing the rehabilitation program.

? What are the short-term goals of a rehabilitation program, and how can the athletic trainer best achieve these goals?

Therapeutic exercises are concerned with restoring normal body function after injury.

A sudden loss of physical activity leads to a generalized loss of physical fitness.

Atrophy and fiber-type conversion   Disuse of a body part quickly leads to a loss of muscle mass. The greatest atrophy occurs in the type I (slow-twitch) fibers. Over time, the slow-twitch fibers develop fast-twitch characteristics. Slow-twitch fibers also diminish in number without type II (fast-twitch) fibers lessening in number.[30] A muscle that is immobilized in a lengthened or neutral position tends to atrophy less. In contrast, immobilizing a muscle in a shortened position encourages atrophy and greater loss of contractile function.[17] Atrophy can also be prevented through isometric contraction and electrical stimulation of the muscles. As the unused muscle decreases in size because of atrophy, protein is also lost. When activity is resumed, normal protein synthesis is reestablished.

Decreased neuromuscular efficiency   Immobilization causes motor nerves to become less efficient in recruiting and stimulating individual muscle fibers within a given motor unit.[2] Once immobilization ends, the original motor neuron discharge returns within about one week.

Joints and Immobilization

Immobilization of joints causes loss of normal compression, which in turn leads to a decrease in lubrication within the joint that subsequently causes degeneration. This degeneration occurs because the articular cartilage is deprived of its normal nutrition. The use of continuous passive motion, electrical muscle stimulation, or hinged casts has in some cases retarded loss of articular cartilage.[2]

Ligament and Bone and Immobilization

Both ligaments and bones adapt to normal stress by maintaining their strength or becoming stronger. However, when stress is eliminated or decreased, ligament and bone become weaker.[17] Once immobilization has been removed, high-frequency, low-duration endurance exercise positively enhances the mechanical properties of ligaments. Endurance activities tend to increase both the production and the hypertrophy of the collagen fibers. Full remodeling of ligaments after immobilization may take as long as twelve months or more.

Cardiorespiratory System and Immobilization

Like other structures, the cardiorespiratory system is adversely affected by immobilization. The resting heart rate increases approximately one-half beat per minute each day of immobilization. The stroke volume, maximum oxygen uptake, and vital capacity decrease concurrently with the increase in heart rate.

MAJOR COMPONENTS OF A REHABILITATION PROGRAM

A well-designed rehabilitation program should routinely address several key components before an injured athlete can return to preinjury competitive levels. Those components include minimizing swelling through appropriate first aid and management of initial injury, controlling pain, restoring full range of motion, restoring or increasing strength, reestablishing neuromuscular control, regaining balance, maintaining levels of cardiorespiratory fitness, and incorporating functional progressions.[23]

Minimizing Initial Swelling

The process of rehabilitation begins immediately after injury. The manner in which the injury is managed initially unquestionably has a significant impact on the course of the rehabilitative process. The one problem all injuries, regardless of type, have in common is swelling. Swelling may be caused by any number of factors, including bleeding, production of synovial fluid, an accumulation of inflammatory by-products, edema, or a combination of several factors. Once swelling has occurred, the healing process is significantly retarded. The injured area cannot return to normal until all the swelling is gone. Therefore, all first aid management of these conditions should be directed toward controlling the swelling.[1] If the swelling can be controlled initially in the acute stage of injury, the time required for rehabilitation is likely to be significantly reduced. To control and significantly limit the amount of swelling, the RICE principle—rest, ice, compression, and elevation—should be applied (see Chapter 12).

Controlling Pain

When an injury occurs, the athletic trainer must realize that the athlete will experience some degree of pain (see Chapter 10). The extent of the pain will be determined by the severity of the injury, the athlete's individual response to and perception of pain, and the circumstances under which the injury occurred. The athletic trainer can modulate acute pain by using the RICE technique immediately after injury.[23] A physician may also make use of various medications to help ease pain.

Persistent pain can make strengthening or flexibility exercises more difficult and thus interfere with the rehabilitation process. The athletic trainer should routinely address pain during each individual treatment session. Making use of appropriate therapeutic modalities, including various techniques of cryotherapy, thermotherapy, and electrical stimulating currents, will help modulate pain throughout the rehabilitation process (see Chapter 15).[26]

Restoring Range of Motion

Injury to a joint will always be associated with some loss of motion. That loss of movement may be attributed to contracture of connective tissue (i.e., ligaments, joint capsules); resistance to stretch of the musculotendinous unit (i.e., muscle, tendon, and fascia); or some combination of the two.

Physiological versus Accessory Movements

Two types of movement govern range of motion about a joint. Physiological movements result from an active muscle contraction that moves an extremity through flexion, extension, abduction, adduction, and rotation. Accessory motions refer to the manner in which one articulating joint surface moves relative to another; such motions include spin, roll, and glide.[12] Physiological movement is voluntary, and accessory movements normally accompany physiological movement. The two occur simultaneously. Normal accessory motions must occur for full-range physiological movement to take place. If any of the accessory component motions are restricted, normal physiological cardinal plane movement will not occur.[36]

Traditionally, rehabilitation programs tend to concentrate more on passive physiological movements and do not pay much attention to accessory motions. It is critical for the athletic trainer to closely evaluate the injured joint to determine whether motion is limited because of physiological movement constraints involving musculotendinous units or because of limitation in accessory motion involving the joint capsule and ligaments. If physiological movement is restricted, the athlete should engage in stretching activities designed to improve flexibility. Stretching exercises should be used whenever there is musculotendinous resistance to stretch. If accessory motion is limited because of some restriction of the joint capsule or the ligaments, the athletic trainer should incorporate mobilization techniques into the treatment program. Mobilization techniques should be used whenever there are tight articular structures.[24]

Restoring Muscular Strength, Endurance, and Power

Muscular strength is one of the most essential factors in restoring the function of a body part to preinjury status. Isometric, isotonic, isokinetic, and plyometric exercises can benefit rehabilitation. A major goal in performing strengthening exercises is for the athlete to work through a full pain-free range of motion.

Accessory motions:
- Spin
- Roll
- Glide

Restricted physiological movement = stretching.

Restricted accessory motion = joint mobilization.

Figure 16-1

Exercises using rubber tubing are used for strengthening.

Isometric Exercise

Isometric exercises are commonly performed in the early phase of rehabilitation when a joint is immobilized for a period of time. They are useful when resistance training through a full range of motion may make the injury worse. Isometrics increase static strength and assist in decreasing the amount of atrophy. Isometrics also can lessen swelling by causing a muscle pumping action to remove fluid and edema.

Strength gains are limited primarily to the angle at which the joint is exercised. No functional force or eccentric work is developed. Other major difficulties are motivation and measuring the force that is being applied.

Progressive Resistance Exercise

Progressive resistance exercise is the most commonly used strengthening technique in a reconditioning program. This exercise may be done using free weights, exercise machines, rubber tubing, or manual resistance (Figure 16-1). Progressive resistance exercise uses isotonic contractions in which force is generated while the muscle is changing in length.

Concentric and eccentric muscle contractions   Isotonic contractions may be either concentric or eccentric. Traditionally, athletes engaging in progressive resistance exercise have concentrated primarily on the concentric component without paying much attention to the importance of the eccentric component. The use of eccentric contractions, particularly in rehabilitation of various injuries related to sport, has received considerable emphasis in recent years.[20] Eccentric contractions are critical for deceleration of limb motion, especially during high-velocity dynamic activities. For example, a baseball pitcher relies on an eccentric contraction of the external rotators at the glenohumeral joint to decelerate the humerus, which may be internally rotating at speeds as high as 8,000 degrees per second. Strength deficits or an inability of a muscle to tolerate these eccentric forces can predispose an athlete to injury. Eccentric contractions are used to facilitate concentric contractions in plyometric exercises and may also be incorporated with functional proprioceptive neuromuscular facilitation strengthening exercises. Thus, the athletic trainer should incorporate both eccentric and concentric strengthening exercises in a rehabilitation program.

Both concentric and eccentric contractions are possible with free weights, with most isotonic exercise machines, and with rubber tubing or an elastic band. A disadvantage of machines and free weights is that they do not allow exercises to be performed in diagonal or functional planes. It is also difficult to exercise at functional velocities without producing additional injuries. Conversely, resistance exercise using rubber tubing allows both concentric and eccentric resistance and is not encumbered by the design of an exercise machine. It offers a wide range of usefulness at an extremely low cost.

Isokinetic Exercise

Isokinetic exercise is commonly used in the rehabilitative process.[20] It most often is incorporated during the later phases of a rehabilitation program. Isokinetics uses a fixed speed with accommodating resistance to provide maximal resistance throughout the range of motion (Figure 16-2). Isokinetic devices are generally capable of calculating measures of torque, average power, and total work and ratios of torque to body weight, each of which may be used diagnostically by the athletic trainer. Isokinetic measures are commonly used as a criterion for return of the athlete to functional activity after injury.

The speed of movement can be altered in isokinetic exercise. Gains in strength from training at slower speeds are fairly specific to the angular velocity used in training. Isokinetic machines allow the athlete to exercise at speeds that are somewhat more functional. Training at faster speeds seems to produce more general improve-

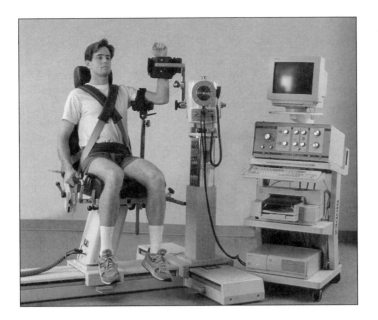

Figure 16-2

Isokinetics are primarily used as a diagnostic tool to determine levels of strength.

ment because increases in torque values can be seen at both fast and slow speeds. Isokinetic exercise performed at high speeds tends to decrease the joint's compressive forces. Comparatively, fast-speed exercises produce fewer negative effects on joints than do slow-speed exercises. Short-arc submaximal isokinetics spreads out synovial fluid that helps to nourish the articular cartilage and therefore to prevent deterioration.[20] It also develops neuromuscular patterning for functional speed and movements demanded by specific sports.

Testing Strength, Endurance, and Power

Testing for improvement in muscular strength, endurance, or power can be accomplished through manual muscle tests, isotonic resisted exercises, or isokinetic dynamometers. Isokinetic testing generally provides the most reliable objective measure of changes in strength.

Reestablishing Neuromuscular Control, Proprioception, Kinesthesia, and Joint Position Sense

After injury and subsequent rest and immobilization, the central nervous system "forgets" how to put together information coming from muscle and joint mechanoreceptors and from cutaneous, visual, and vestibular input. *Neuromuscular control* is the mind's attempt to teach the body conscious control of a specific movement.[16] Successful repetition of a patterned movement makes its performance progressively less difficult and thus requires less concentration; eventually the movement becomes automatic. Reestablishing neuromuscular control requires many repetitions of the same movement through a step-by-step progression from simple to more complex movements. Strengthening exercises, particularly those that tend to be more functional, such as closed kinetic chain exercises, are essential for reestablishing neuromuscular control.[35]

Regaining neuromuscular control means regaining the ability to follow some previously established sensory pattern. The central nervous system compares the intent and production of a specific movement with stored information, continually adjusting until any discrepancy in movement is corrected.[35] Four elements are critical for reestablishing neuromuscular control: (1) proprioceptive and kinesthetic awareness, (2) dynamic stability, (3) prepatory and reactive muscle characteristics, and (4) conscious and unconscious functional motor patterns.[34]

16-2

Critical Thinking E x e r c i s e

After an ankle sprain, a basketball player is placed in an ankle immobilizer and given crutches with instructions to begin totally non–weight bearing and progress to full weight bearing without crutches as soon as possible. After four days, the athlete is out of the immobilizer and can walk without crutches but still has a significant limp.

? What should the athletic trainer do to help the athlete regain a normal gait pattern, and why is it important to do so as soon as possible?

Relearning normal functional movement and timing after injury to a joint may require several months. Addressing neuromuscular control is critical throughout the recovery process but may be most critical during the early stages of rehabilitation to avoid reinjury.[35]

Reestablishing proprioception and kinesthesia should also be of primary concern to the athletic trainer in all rehabilitation programs.[16] **Proprioception** is the ability to determine the position of a joint in space; **kinesthesia** refers to the ability to detect movement.[9] The ability to sense the position of a joint in space is mediated by mechanoreceptors found in both muscle and joints and by cutaneous, visual, and vestibular input. Neuromuscular control relies on the central nervous system to interpret and integrate proprioceptive and kinesthetic information and then to control individual muscles and joints to produce coordinated movement.[35]

Joint Mechanoreceptors

Joint mechanoreceptors are found in ligaments, capsules, menisci, labra, and fat pads. They include Ruffini's endings, Pacinian corpuscles, and free nerve endings. These receptors are sensitive to changes in the shape of various joint structures and to the rate and direction of movement of the joint. They are most active in the end ranges of motion.[28]

Muscle Mechanoreceptors

The receptors found in muscles and tendons are the muscle spindles and the Golgi tendon organs. The muscle spindles are sensitive to changes in length of the muscle, and Golgi tendon organs are sensitive to changes in tension. The actions of these receptors are discussed in detail in Chapter 4.[28]

Regaining Balance

Balance involves the complex integration of muscular forces, neurological sensory information received from the mechanoreceptors, and biomechanical information.[11] Balance involves positioning the body's center of gravity within the base of support. When the center of gravity extends beyond the base of support, the limits of stability have been exceeded even though the base of support has not changed, and a corrective step or stumble is necessary to prevent a fall. Even when an individual appears to be motionless, the body is undergoing constant postural sway caused by reflexive muscle contractions, which correct and maintain dynamic equilibrium in an upright posture.[5] When balance is disrupted, the response to correct it is primarily reflexive and automatic. The primary mechanisms for controlling balance occur in the joints of the lower extremity.[35]

The ability to balance and maintain postural stability is essential to an athlete who is acquiring or reacquiring complex motor skills.[35] Athletes who show a decreased sense of balance or lack of postural stability after injury may lack sufficient proprioceptive and kinesthetic information or muscular strength, either of which may limit the athlete's ability to generate an effective correction response to disequilibrium. A rehabilitation program must include functional exercises that incorporate balance and proprioceptive training to prepare the athlete for return to activity. Failure to address balance problems may predispose the athlete to reinjury (Figure 16-3).

Maintaining Cardiorespiratory Fitness

Although strength and flexibility are commonly regarded as essential components in any injury rehabilitation program, relatively little consideration is given toward maintaining levels of cardiorespiratory fitness. An athlete spends a considerable amount of time preparing the cardiorespiratory system to be able to handle the increased demands made on it during a competitive season. When injury occurs and the athlete is forced to miss training time, levels of cardiorespiratory endurance may

---

proprioception
The ability to determine the position of a joint in space.

kinesthesia
The ability to detect movement.

Neuromuscular control produces coordinated movements.

Joint mechanoreceptors include Ruffini's endings, Pacinian corpuscles, and free nerve endings.

Muscle mechanoreceptors include muscle spindles and Golgi tendon organs.

Balance involves the integration of muscular, neurological, and biomechanical information.

A

B

C

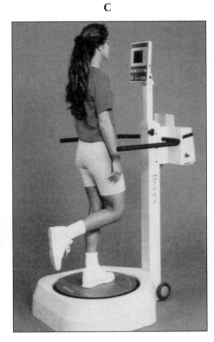

Figure 16-3

Balance training is essential in the rehabilitation program. Many balance training products are available. **A,** BAPS Board. **B,** Kinesthetic Awareness Trainer. **C,** Biodex Balance System.

decrease rapidly. Thus the athletic trainer must design or substitute alternative activities that allow the individual to maintain existing levels of cardiorespiratory fitness during the rehabilitation period.

Depending on the nature of the injury, a number of possible activities are open to the athlete. For a lower-extremity injury, non–weight bearing activities should be incorporated. Pool activities provide an excellent means for injury rehabilitation. Cycling also can positively stress the cardiorespiratory system (Figure 16-4).

Incorporating Functional Progressions

The purpose of any program of rehabilitation is to restore normal function after injury. Functional progressions involve a series of gradually progressive activities designed to prepare the individual for return to a specific sport.[35] Functional progressions should be incorporated into the treatment program as early as possible. Well-designed functional progressions will gradually assist the injured athlete in achieving normal, pain-free range of motion, restoring adequate strength levels, and regaining neuromuscular control throughout the rehabilitation program. Ultimately, the focus becomes a safe return to competition. Those skills necessary for successful participation in a given sport are broken down into component parts, and the athlete gradually reacquires those skills within the limitations of his or her individual progress.[35]

Functional activities follow a consistent progression from simple to complex skills, slow to fast speeds, short to longer distances, or light to heavy activities. Every new activity introduced must be carefully monitored by the athletic trainer to determine the athlete's ability to perform as well as his or her physical tolerance. If an activity does not produce additional pain or swelling, the level should be advanced; new activities should be introduced as quickly as possible. Thus the injured athlete would be gradually introduced to the stresses imposed by a particular demand until function is adequate for the athlete to return to *sport-specific activity.*[35]

The optimal functional progression program would be designed such that the athlete would have an opportunity to practice every possible skill that is required in a

16-3

Critical Thinking Exercise

A runner complains of anterior knee pain. She has greatly cut back on the distance of her training runs and indicates that she has been taking antiinflammatory medication to help her continue to train. However, she is frustrated because her knee seems to be getting worse instead of better.

? What can the athletic trainer recommend to most effectively help the athlete deal with her knee pain?

sport before he or she returns to competition. This program would minimize the normal anxiety and apprehension experienced by the athlete on return to a competitive environment.[19]

Supervised functional progression activities can be done during team practice sessions. This arrangement allows athletes to be around teammates and coaches, which should help them feel more accepted as team members.[19]

Functional Testing

Functional testing uses functional progression drills for the purpose of assessing the athlete's ability to perform a specific activity. Functional testing involves performance by the athlete of a single maximal effort to get some idea of how close the athlete is to full return to activity. For years athletic trainers have used a variety of functional tests to assess the athlete's progress, including sprint tests, agility runs, figure 8's, shuttle runs, carioca tests, side stepping, vertical jumps, hopping for time or distance, balance tests, and co-contraction tests (Figure 16-5).[19,35]

DEVELOPING A REHABILITATION PLAN

All exercise rehabilitation must be conducted as part of a carefully designed plan.	No rehabilitation program can be effective without a carefully designed plan. Athletic trainers overseeing a rehabilitation program must have a complete understanding of the injury, including knowledge of how the injury was sustained, the major anatomical structures affected, the grade of trauma, and the stage or phase of the injury's healing.

Exercise Phases

Phases of rehabilitation: Preoperative phase ■ Phase 1—acute phase ■ Phase 2—repair phase ■ Phase 3—remodeling	Rehabilitation progressions in sports medicine can be subdivided into three phases based primarily on the three stages of the healing process: phase 1, the acute phase; phase 2, the repair phase; and phase 3, the remodeling phase (see Chapter 10). If surgery is necessary, a fourth phase, the preoperative phase, must also be considered. Depending on the type and extent of injury and the individual response to healing, phases will usually overlap. Each phase must include carefully considered goals and criteria for advancing from one phase to another.

The Preoperative Exercise Phase

Exercise performed during the preoperative phase can often assist recovery after surgery.	The preoperative exercise phase applies only to those athletes who sustain injuries that require surgery. If surgery can be postponed, exercise may be used as a means to improve its outcome. By allowing the initial inflammatory response phase to resolve and by maintaining or increasing muscle strength and flexibility, cardiorespiratory fitness, and neuromuscular control, the athlete may be better prepared to continue the rehabilitation program after surgery.

Phase 1: The Acute Injury Phase

Phase 1 begins immediately when injury occurs and may last as long as four days. This inflammatory stage of the healing process is attempting to control and clean up the injured tissues, thus creating an environment that is conducive to the fibroblastic stage. The primary focus of rehabilitation during this phase is to control swelling and to modulate pain by using rest, ice, compression, and elevation (RICE) immediately after injury. Throughout this phase, ice, compression, and elevation should be used as much as possible.[23]

The postsurgical exercise phase should start twenty-four hours after surgery.	Rest of the injured part is critical during this phase. It is widely accepted that early mobility during rehabilitation is essential. However, if the athletic trainer becomes overly aggressive during the first forty-eight hours after injury and does not allow the injured part to rest during the inflammatory stage of healing, the inflammatory process never gets a chance to accomplish its purpose. Consequently, the length of time required for inflammation may be extended. Immobility during the first two days after injury is necessary to control inflammation.

It must be emphasized that rest does not mean that the athlete does nothing. The term *rest* applies only to the injured body part. During this period, the athlete should work on cardiorespiratory fitness and should do strengthening and flexibility exercises for the parts of the body not affected by the injury. When immobilized, muscle tensing or isometrics may be used to maintain muscle strength.

By day 3 or 4, swelling begins to subside and eventually stops altogether. The injured area may feel warm to the touch, and some discoloration is usually apparent. The injury is still painful to the touch, and some pain is elicited on movement of the injured part. At this point the athlete may begin active mobility exercises, working through a pain-free range of motion. If the injury involves the lower extremity, the athlete should be encouraged to progressively bear more weight.

The team physician may choose to have the athlete take nonsteroidal antiinflammatory drugs (NSAIDs) to help control swelling and inflammation. It is usually helpful to continue this medication throughout the rehabilitative process.

Phase 2: The Repair Phase

Once the inflammatory response has subsided, the repair phase begins. During this stage of the healing process, fibroblastic cells are laying down a matrix of collagen fibers and forming scar tissue. This stage may begin as early as four days after the injury and may last for several weeks. At this point, swelling has stopped completely. The injury is still tender to the touch but is not as painful as during the last stage. Pain is also less on active and passive motion.[23]

As soon as inflammation is controlled, the athletic trainer should immediately begin to incorporate into the rehabilitation program activities that can help the athlete maintain levels of cardiorespiratory fitness, restore full range of motion, restore or increase strength, and reestablish neuromuscular control.

Modalities in this phase, as in the acute phase, should be used to control pain and swelling. Cryotherapy should be used during the early portion of this phase to reduce the likelihood of swelling. Electrical stimulating currents can help control pain and improve strength and range of motion.[26]

Phase 3: The Remodeling Phase

The remodeling phase is the longest of the three phases and may last for several years, depending on the severity of the injury. The ultimate goal during this maturation stage of the healing process is return to activity. The injury is no longer painful to the touch, although some progressively decreasing pain may still be felt on motion. The collagen fibers must be realigned according to tensile stresses and strains placed on them during functional sport-specific exercises.[23]

The focus during this phase should be on regaining sport-specific skills. Dynamic functional activities related to individual sport performance should be incorporated into the rehabilitation program. Functional training involves the repeated performance of an athletic skill for the purpose of perfecting that skill. Strengthening exercises should progressively place on the injured structures stresses and strains that would normally be encountered during that sport. Plyometric strengthening exercises can be used to improve muscle power and explosiveness.[19] Functional testing should be done to determine specific skill weaknesses that need to be addressed before full return.

At this point, some type of heating modality is beneficial to the healing process. The deep-heating modalities, ultrasound, or the diathermies should be used to increase circulation to the deeper tissues. Massage and gentle mobilization may also be used to reduce spasm, increase circulation, and reduce pain. Increased blood flow delivers the essential nutrients to the injured area to promote healing, and increased lymphatic flow assists in breakdown and removal of waste products.[26]

Figure 16-4

Stationary cycling provides a means of maintaining cardiorespiratory fitness during rehabilitation.

Figure "8" course

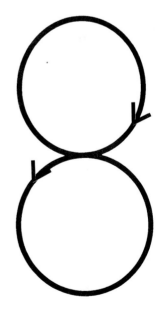

Figure 16-5

A figure-8 run is an example of a functional progression test.

Functional progressions incorporate sport-specific skills into the rehabilitation program.

Controlled Mobility during Rehabilitation

Wolff's law states that after injury both bone and soft tissue will respond to the physical demands placed on them, causing them to remodel or realign along lines of tensile force.[23] Therefore it is critical that injured structures be exposed to progressively increasing loads throughout the rehabilitation process.

Controlled mobility has been shown to be superior to immobilization for scar formation, revascularization, muscle regeneration, and reorientation of muscle fibers and tensile properties.[23] However, immobilization of the injured tissue during the acute, inflammatory response phase will likely facilitate the process of healing by controlling inflammation, thus reducing clinical symptoms. As healing progresses to the repair phase, controlled activity directed toward return to normal flexibility and strength should be combined with protective support or bracing. Generally, clinical signs and symptoms disappear at the end of this phase. As the remodeling phase begins, aggressive, active range-of-motion and strengthening exercises should be incorporated to facilitate tissue remodeling and realignment.

Early exercise rehabilitation involves submaximal exercise performed in short bouts that are repeated several times daily. Exercise intensity must be commensurate with healing. As recovery increases, the intensity of exercise also increases, with the exercise performed less often. Finally, the athlete returns to a conditioning mode of exercise, which often includes high-intensity exercise three or four times per week.

To a great extent, pain will dictate rate of progression. With initial injury, pain is intense, but it tends to decrease and eventually subside altogether as healing progresses. Engaging in exercise that is too intense or too prolonged can be detrimental to the progress of rehabilitation. Any increase in the amount of swelling, an increase in pain, a loss or a plateau in strength, a loss or a plateau in range of motion, an increase in the laxity of a healing ligament, or exacerbation of other clinical symptoms during or after a particular exercise or activity indicates that the load is too great for the level of tissue repair or remodeling.[35] The athletic trainer must be aware of the timelines required for the process of healing and realize that being overly aggressive can interfere with that process.

Adherence to a Rehabilitation Program

For a rehabilitation program to be successful, the injured athlete must comply with and adhere to the plan of rehabilitation. In the field of athletic injury, compliance is the biggest deterrent to successful rehabilitation.[7] The athletic trainer can take several steps to enhance adherence.

- The athletic trainer can provide the encouragement and positive reinforcement necessary for the athlete to make a commitment. Athletes who are committed to the rehabilitation program work harder and thus return to competition more quickly with better results than those who are nonadherents.[7]
- The athletic trainer can be creative in designing and varying the exercise routine to keep the athlete interested and motivated.[21]
- Support from peers, coaches, and rehabilitation staff is important in influencing compliance. Those athletes with support show a greater effort to fit the rehabilitation effort into their schedules.[4]
- Attitude of the athletic trainer is another important consideration when dealing with injured athletes. An athletic trainer who feels that an athlete is going to be nonadherent is less likely to motivate the athlete to comply with the treatment program.
- Treatment plan instructions that are clearly explained verbally and then written down are more likely to be followed by the athlete.[37]
- The coach must support the rehabilitation concept and must discipline the athlete for lack of participation in the rehabilitation process.
- The athletic trainer can make an effort to fit the rehabilitation program into the athlete's schedule rather than the reverse.[6]

16-4

Critical Thinking Exercise

Following a recurrent shoulder injury, a lacrosse player seems to have developed a bad attitude toward doing his injury rehabilitation.

? What can the athletic trainer do to help this athlete be more compliant and adhere to his rehabilitation program?

■ Almost all rehabilitation should be pain free. Painful exercise not only is harmful but also reduces compliance, especially in the nonadherent athlete. Rehabilitation programs should be examined to determine the aspects that may be painful.[4]

Criteria for Full Return to Activity

All exercise rehabilitation plans must determine what is meant by complete recovery from an injury. Often it means that the athlete is fully reconditioned and has achieved full range of movement, strength, neuromuscular control, cardiovascular fitness, and sport-specific functional skills. Besides physical well-being, the athlete must also have regained full confidence to return to his or her sport.

The decision to release an athlete recovering from injury to a full return to athletic activity is the final stage of the rehabilitation and recovery process. The decision should be carefully considered by each member of the sports medicine team involved in the rehabilitation process. The team physician should be ultimately responsible for deciding that the athlete is ready to return to practice or competition. The decision to return an athlete to activity should address the following concerns:

■ *Physiological healing constraints*—Has rehabilitation progressed to the later stages of the healing process?

■ *Pain status*—Has pain disappeared, or is the athlete able to play within his or her own levels of pain tolerance?

■ *Swelling*—Is there still a chance that swelling may be exacerbated by return to activity?

■ *Range of Motion*—Is the athlete's range of motion adequate to allow the athlete to perform both effectively and with minimized risk of reinjury?

■ *Strength*—Is strength, endurance, or power great enough to protect the injured structure from reinjury?

■ *Neuromuscular control/Proprioception/Kinesthesia*—Has the athlete relearned how to use the injured body part?

■ *Cardiorespiratory fitness*—Has the athlete been able to maintain cardiorespiratory fitness at or near the level necessary for competition?

■ *Sport-specific demands*—Are the demands of the sport or a specific position such that the athlete will not be at risk of reinjury?

■ *Functional testing*—Does the athlete's performance on appropriate functional tests indicate that his or her extent of recovery is sufficient to allow successful performance?

■ *Prophylactic strapping, bracing, padding*—Are any additional supports necessary for the injured athlete to return to activity?

■ *Responsibility of the athlete*—Is the athlete capable of listening to his or her body and of recognizing a potential reinjury situation?

■ *Predisposition to injury*—Is this athlete prone to reinjury or to a new injury when they are not fully recovered?

■ *Psychological factors*—Is the athlete capable of returning to activity and competing at a high level without fear of reinjury?

■ *Athlete education and preventive maintainance program*—Does the athlete understand the importance of continuing to engage in conditioning exercises that can greatly reduce the chances of reinjury?

ADDITIONAL APPROACHES TO THERAPEUTIC EXERCISE IN REHABILITATION

Open versus Closed Kinetic Chain Exercises

The concept of the kinetic chain deals with the anatomical functional relationships that exist in the upper and lower extremities. In a weight-bearing position, the lower extremity kinetic chain involves the transmission of forces among the foot,

A closed kinetic chain occurs when the foot or hand is on the ground.

An open kinetic chain occurs when the foot or hand is off the ground.

16-5

Critical Thinking Exercise

A racquetball player twists his knee during a match and sprains his ACL. Knee movement is limited because of the pain, and full weight bearing is extremely painful. He has a weekend-long racquetball tournament in two weeks and is concerned about regaining his knee motion while being able to maintain the fitness levels necessary to compete for two consecutive days.

? What type of rehabilitative technique could the athletic trainer recommend that would allow the athlete to address both his range of motion and fitness concerns even though he is unable to bear weight?

Aquatic exercise provides an excellent means for rehabilitation.

ankle, lower leg, knee, thigh, and hip. In the upper extremity, the hand as a weight-bearing surface transmits forces to the wrist, forearm, elbow, upper arm, and shoulder girdle.[22]

An open kinetic chain exists when the foot or hand is not in contact with the ground or some other surface.[22] In a closed kinetic chain, the foot or hand is weight bearing. Movements of the more proximal anatomical segments are affected by open and closed kinetic chain positions.[3] For example, the rotational components of the ankle, knee, and hip reverse direction when changing from an open to closed kinetic chain activity. In a closed kinetic chain, the forces begin at the ground and work their way up through each joint. In a closed kinetic chain, forces must be absorbed by various tissues and anatomical structures rather than simply dissipating as would occur in an open chain.[27]

The use of closed chain strengthening techniques has become the rehabilitation treatment of choice for many athletic trainers.[15] Because most sports activities involve some aspect of weight bearing with the foot in contact with the ground or with the hand in a weight-bearing position, closed kinetic chain strengthening activities are more functional than are open chain activities. Closed kinetic chain exercises are more sport or activity specific, involving exercise that more closely approximates the desired activity. Specificity of training must be emphasized to athletes for them to maximize carryover to functional activities on the playing field.[22] Therefore, the treatment program should incorporate rehabilitative exercises that emphasize strengthening the entire kinetic chain rather than an isolated body segment.

Closed kinetic chain exercises use varying combinations of isometric, concentric, and eccentric contractions, which must occur simultaneously in different muscle groups within the chain. Isolation exercises typically make use of one specific type of muscular contraction to produce or control movement.[10] Consequently, there must be some neuromuscular adaptation to this type of strengthening exercise.

In the athletic training setting, several different closed kinetic chain exercises have gained popularity and have been incorporated into rehabilitation protocols. Exercises commonly used for the lower extremity are minisquats, leg presses, forward and lateral step-ups, terminal knee extensions using tubing, and exercises that use equipment such as stair climbing or stepping machines, slide boards, and stationary bicycles.[8,38] Push-ups and weight-shifting exercises on a medicine ball are two of the more typically used upper extremity exercises (Figure 16-6).[31,32]

Aquatic Exercise

Aquatic exercise has become popular as a rehabilitative tool in sports medicine.[1] An athletic trainer who has access to a swimming pool is fortunate. Water submersion offers an excellent environment for beginning a program of exercise therapy, or it can complement all phases of rehabilitation.

Because of buoyancy and hydrostatic pressure, submersion in a pool presents a versatile exercise environment that can be easily varied according to individual needs.[29] With the proper technique, the athlete can reduce muscle spasm, relax tense muscles, increase the range of joint motion, reestablish correct movement patterns, and above all, increase strength, power, and muscular endurance.[29]

Aquatic exercise uses the water's buoyancy and pressure; it can be described as assistive, supportive, and resistive. As an assistive medium, the water's buoyancy can increase range of motion, strength, and control. The athlete starts by placing the body part below the water level and allows the part to be carried passively upward, keeping within pain-free limits. As the athlete gains strength, he or she actively engages in movement, and again the buoyancy of the water is assistive. Progression of the movement can be initiated by increasing speed and by using the water above the body part as a resistive medium (Figure 16-7).

A second use of water buoyancy is support. The limb normally will float just below the water's surface. In this position the limb is parallel to the surface of the wa-

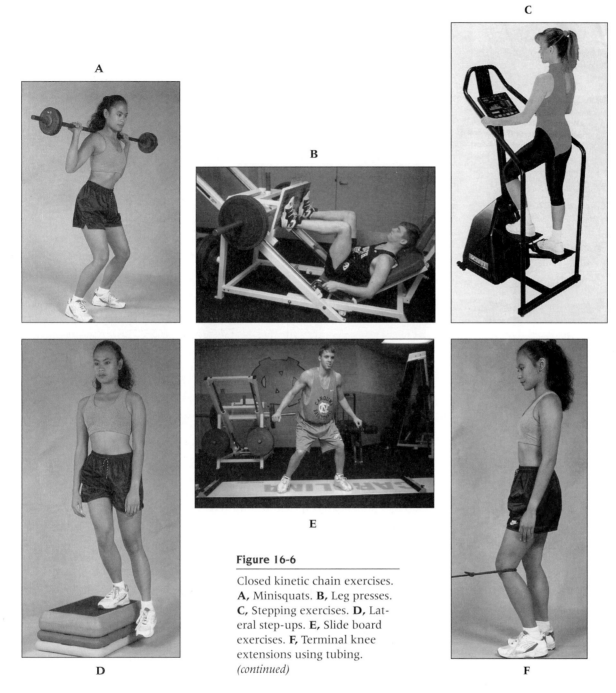

Figure 16-6

Closed kinetic chain exercises. **A,** Minisquats. **B,** Leg presses. **C,** Stepping exercises. **D,** Lateral step-ups. **E,** Slide board exercises. **F,** Terminal knee extensions using tubing. *(continued)*

ter. An increase in speed will make movement more difficult. Progression also can be accomplished if the part is less streamlined. In exercising the arm, for example, the athlete can increase the difficulty by moving across the water with the flat of the hand or by using a hand paddle or webbed glove. Flippers can increase resistance to the leg.

Resistance is the third use of water buoyancy. The injured body part is moved downward against the upward thrust of the water. Maximum resistance is attained by keeping the limb at a right angle to the water's surface. Like the supportive technique, the resistive technique can be made progressively more difficult by the use of different devices. Extra resistance is added by pushing or dragging flotation devices down into the water.

G

H

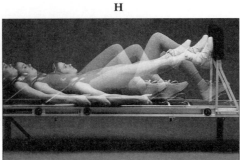

I

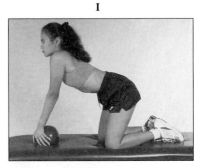

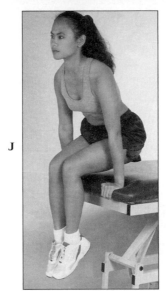

J

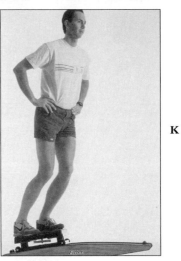

K

Figure 16-6—cont'd

G, Stationary bicycling.
H, Shuttle 2000. **I,** Weight
shifting. **J,** Push-ups. **K,** Fitter.

PNF strengthening techniques:
- Rhythmic initiation
- Repeated contraction
- Slow reversal
- Slow-reversal-hold
- Rhythmic stabilization

Besides engaging in specific exercises, the athlete can practice sports skills, using the water's buoyancy and resistance to advantage. For example, locomotor or throwing skills can be practiced to regain normal movement patterns. The swimming pool can also be an excellent medium for retaining or restoring functional capacities as well as restoring cardiovascular endurance. Wearing a flotation device around the waist, the athlete performs a variety of upper- and lower-limb movement patterns (Figure 16-8). Movements of straight-ahead running, backward running, side stepping, figure eights, and carioca can be performed by an athlete bearing full weight while in three to five feet of water.

Proprioceptive Neuromuscular Facilitation Techniques

Proprioceptive neuromuscular facilitation (PNF) is an approach to therapeutic exercise that uses proprioceptive, cutaneous, and auditory input to produce functional improvement in motor output and can be a vital element in the rehabilitation process of many sports-related injuries.[12] These techniques have been recommended and are widely used in sports medicine for increasing strength, flexibility, and coordination as well as decreasing deficits in kinesthetic sense in response to demands placed on the neuromuscular system.[33] The principles and techniques of PNF are based primarily on the neurophysiological mechanisms involving the stretch reflex (see Chapter 4).[25]

Techniques of PNF

The PNF techniques are generally used in rehabilitation for the purposes of facilitating strength and increasing range of motion. Flexibility is increased by the techniques of contract-relax, hold-relax, and slow-reversal-hold-relax. In contrast,

A

B

C

Figure 16-7

Use of the water's buoyancy and pressure for progressive exercise. **A,** Several buoyancy and resistive devices may be used in aquatic exercise. **B,** Using the water for buoyance. **C,** Using the water for resistance.

strength can be facilitated by repeated contraction and the slow-reversal, rhythmic initiation, and rhythmic stabilization techniques.[25]

Strengthening techniques   To assist the athlete in developing muscle strength, muscle endurance, and coordination, the following techniques are used.

Rhythmic initiation   Rhythmic initiation consists of a progressive series, first of passive movement, then of active assistive movement, followed by an active movement through an agonist pattern. This approach helps athletes with limited movement progressively regain strength through the range of motion.

Figure 16-8

A wet vest can facilitate exercise programs in the water by making the athlete more buoyant.

Repeated contraction   Repeated contraction of a muscle or a muscle group is used for general weakness or weakness at one specific point. The athlete moves isotonically against the maximum resistance of the athletic trainer until fatigue is experienced. At the time fatigue is felt, stretch is applied to the muscle at that point in the range to facilitate greater strength production. All resistance must be carefully accommodated to the strength of the athlete. Because the athlete is resisting as much as possible, this technique may be contraindicated for some injuries.

Slow reversal   The athlete moves through a complete range of motion against maximum resistance. Resistance is applied to facilitate antagonist and agonist muscle groups and to ensure smooth and rhythmic movement. It is important that reversals of the movement pattern be instituted before the previous pattern has been fully completed. The major benefit of this PNF technique is that it promotes normal reciprocal coordination of agonist and antagonist muscles.

Slow-reversal-hold   In this technique the athlete moves a body part isotonically using agonist muscles and immediately follows that movement with an isometric contraction. The athlete is instructed to hold at the end of each isotonic movement. The primary purpose of this technique is to develop strength at a specific point in the range of movement.

Rhythmic stabilization   Rhythmic stabilization uses an isometric contraction of the agonists, followed by an isometric contraction of the antagonist muscles. With repeated contraction of these muscles, strength is maximum at this point.

Stretching techniques   To produce muscle relaxation through an inhibitory response for purposes of increasing range of motion, the following PNF techniques may be used.

Contract-relax   The affected body part is passively moved until resistance is felt. The athlete is then told to contract the antagonistic muscle isotonically. The movement is resisted by the athletic trainer for ten seconds or until fatigue is felt. The athlete is instructed to relax for ten seconds. The athletic trainer passively moves the limb to a new stretch position. The exercise is repeated three times.

Hold-relax   The hold-relax technique is similar to contract-relax except that an isometric contraction is used. The athlete moves the body part to the point of resistance and is told to hold. The muscles are isometrically resisted by the athletic trainer for ten seconds. The athlete is then told to relax for ten seconds, and the body part is moved to a new range, either actively by the athlete or passively by the athletic trainer. This exercise is repeated three times.

Slow-reversal-hold-relax   The athlete moves the body part to the point of resistance and is told to hold. The muscles are isometrically resisted by the athletic trainer for ten seconds. The athlete is then told to relax for ten seconds, thus relaxing the antagonist while the agonist is contracted, moving the part to a new limited range (Figure 16-9).

PNF stretching techniques:
- Contract-relax
- Hold-relax
- Slow-reversal-hold-relax

Figure 16-9

The slow-reversal-hold-relax stretching technique for the hamstring muscle.

Basic Principles for Using PNF Techniques

These principles are the basis of PNF and must be used with any specific techniques. Application of the following principles may assist in promoting a desired response in the individual being treated.[14]

1. The athlete must be taught through brief, simple descriptions the PNF patterns for sequential movements from starting position to terminal positions.
2. When learning the patterns, the athlete should look at the moving limb for feedback on directional and positional control.
3. Verbal commands should be firm and simple—push, pull, or hold.
4. Manual contact with the hands can facilitate a movement response.
5. The athletic trainer must use correct body mechanics when providing resistance.
6. The amount of resistance given should facilitate a maximal response that allows smooth, coordinated motion.
7. Rotational movement is a critical component in all the PNF patterns.
8. The distal movements of the patterns should occur first and should be completed by no later than halfway through the pattern.
9. The stronger components are emphasized to facilitate the weaker components of a movement pattern.
10. Pressing the joint together causes increased stability, whereas traction pulls the joint apart and facilitates movement.
11. Giving a quick stretch causes a reflex contraction of that muscle.

PNF Patterns

The PNF exercise patterns involve three component movements: flexion-extension, abduction-adduction, and internal-external rotation. Human movement is patterned and rarely involves straight motion because all muscles are spiral in nature and lie in diagonal directions.[14]

The PNF patterns involve distinct diagonal and rotational movements of upper extremity, lower extremity, upper trunk, lower trunk, and neck. The exercise pattern is initiated with the muscle groups in the lengthened or stretched position. The muscle group is then contracted, moving the body part through the range of motion to a shortened position.

The upper and lower extremities each have two separate patterns of diagonal movement for each part of the body, which are referred to as the diagonal 1 (D1) and diagonal 2 (D2) patterns. These two diagonal patterns are subdivided into D1 moving into flexion, D1 moving into extension, D2 moving into flexion, and D2 moving into extension. The patterns are named according to the movement occurring at either the shoulder or the hip.

Figures 16-10 and 16-11 are examples of PNF patterns that may be used for rehabilitating some sports injuries. PNF techniques for specific joints will be discussed in Chapters 18 through 24.

Joint Mobilization and Traction

The techniques of joint mobilization are used to improve joint mobility or to decrease joint pain by restoring accessory movements to the joint, thus allowing for full, nonrestricted, pain-free range of motion.[24] Mobilization techniques may be used to attain a variety of treatment goals such as the following: reducing pain; decreasing muscle guarding; stretching or lengthening tissue surrounding a joint, especially capsular and ligamentous tissue; reflexogenic effects that either inhibit or facilitate muscle tone or the stretch reflex; and proprioceptive effects that improve postural and kinesthetic awareness.

Mobilization Techniques

Mobilization techniques are used to increase the accessory motions about a joint.[12] Treatment techniques designed to improve accessory motion involve small-amplitude oscillating movements called *glides* within a specific part of the range.[9]

16-6

Critical Thinking E x e r c i s e

A wrestler was immobilized in a cast for six weeks after a fracture of the olecranon process of the ulna. The cast was removed three weeks ago, and the athlete has been working hard on stretching exercises to regain elbow extension. At this point he is still lacking 16 degrees of extension and does not seem to be gaining any additional motion.

? Because the stretching seems to be ineffective at this point, what can the athletic trainer do to help the athlete regain range of motion?

Mobilization works to improve accessory motions.

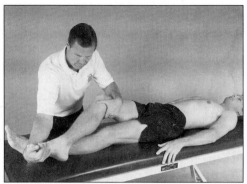

Figure 16-10

The D2 lower-extremity pattern moving into hip extension. **A,** Starting position. **B,** Terminal position.

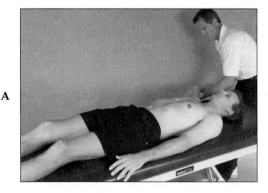
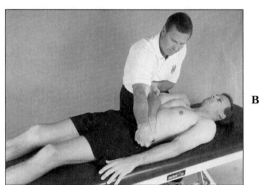

Figure 16-11

The D2 upper-extremity pattern moving into shoulder extension. **A,** Starting position. **B,** Terminal position.

Mobilization should be done with both the athlete and the athletic trainer in comfortable and relaxed positions. The athletic trainer should mobilize one joint at a time. The joint should be stabilized as near one articulating surface as possible; the other surface should be held with a firm, confident grasp.[24]

Maitland has categorized mobilization techniques into five grades as follows:[18]

- Grade I—a small-amplitude glide at the beginning of the range of movement. Used when pain and spasm limit movement early in the range of motion.
- Grade II—a large-amplitude glide within the midrange of movement. Used when spasm limits movement sooner with a quick oscillation than with a slow one, or when slowly increasing pain restricts movement halfway into the range.
- Grade III—a large-amplitude glide up to the pathological limit in the range of movement. Used when pain and resistance from spasm, inert tissue tension, or tissue compression limit movement near the end of the range.
- Grade IV—a small-amplitude glide at the end of the range of movement. Used when resistance limits movement in the absence of pain and spasm.
- Grade V—a small-amplitude, quick thrust delivered at the end of the range of movement, usually accompanied by a popping sound that is called a manipulation. Used when minimal resistance limits the end of the range. Manipulation is most effectively accomplished by the velocity of the thrust rather than by the force of the thrust. Most authorities agree that manipulation should be used only by individuals trained specifically in these techniques because a great deal of skill and judgment is necessary for safe and effective treatment.

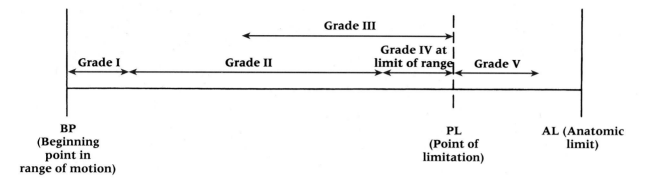

Figure 16-12

Maitland's five grades of motion.

In Maitland's system, grades I and II are used primarily for treatment of pain, and grades III and IV are used for treating stiffness. It is necessary to treat pain first and stiffness second. Figure 16-12 shows the various grades of oscillation that are used in a joint with some limitation of motion.

The shape of the articulating surfaces usually dictates the direction of the mobilization being performed.[24] Generally one articulating surface may be considered to be concave and the other to be convex. When the concave surface is stationary and the convex surface is moving, the glide should be done in the opposite direction of the bone movement. If the convex surface is stationary and the concave surface is moving, the glide should be done in the same direction as the bone movement. If mobilization in the appropriate direction exacerbates complaints of pain or stiffness, the athletic trainer should apply the technique in the opposite direction until the patient can tolerate application of the technique in the appropriate direction.

In many cases, traction can be combined with mobilization. *Traction* refers to a technique in which one articulating segment is pulled to produce some separation of the two joint surfaces. Both mobilization and traction techniques use a translational movement of one joint surface relative to the other. This translation may be in one of two directions: it may be either perpendicular or parallel to the *treatment plane.* The treatment plane falls perpendicular to, or at a right angle to, a line running from the axis of rotation in the convex surface to the center of the concave articular surface (Figure 16-13). Mobilization techniques use glides that translate one articulating

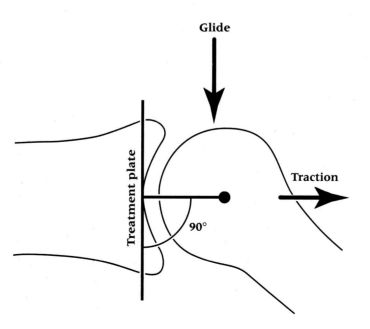

Figure 16-13

The treatment plane is perpendicular to a line drawn from the axis of rotation to the center of the articulating surface of the concave segment.

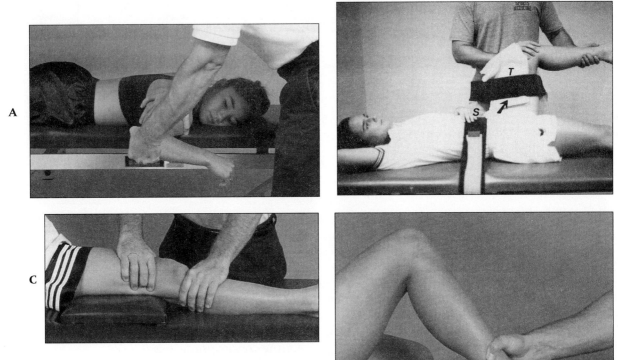

Figure 16-14

A, Anterior humeral glide (for increasing extension and lateral rotation). **B,** Inferior femoral glide (for increasing abduction and flexion). **C,** Posterior tibial glide (for increasing flexion). **D,** Posterior tibial glide (for increasing plantar flexion).

surface along a line parallel with the treatment plane. Traction techniques translate one of the articulating surfaces in a perpendicular direction to the treatment plane. Mobilization glides are done parallel to the treatment plane; traction is performed perpendicular to the treatment plane. Like mobilization techniques, traction may be used either to decrease pain or reduce to joint hypomobility.

Figure 16-14 shows examples of joint mobilization techniques for some joints and body segments. Mobilizations for specific joints are discussed further in Chapters 18 through 24.

SUMMARY

- When injuries occur in sports medicine, the focus of the athletic trainer shifts from injury prevention to injury treatment and rehabilitation. The athletic trainer usually assumes the primary responsibility for design, implementation, and supervision of the rehabilitation program for the injured athlete. Two major goals of rehabilitation are to prevent deconditioning and to restore the injured part to a preinjury state. Besides the physical aspect, the mental and emotional aspects of rehabilitation must always be considered.

- When an injured body part is immobilized for a period of time, a number of disuse problems adversely affect muscle, joints, ligaments, bone, cartilage, neuromuscular efficiency, and the cardiorespiratory system.

- Designing programs for rehabilitation is relatively simple and involves several basic components: minimizing swelling, controlling pain, maintaining or improving flexibility, restoring or increasing strength, reestablishing neuromuscular control, regaining balance, maintaining levels of cardiorespiratory fitness, and incorporating functional progressions. The long-term goal is to return the injured athlete to practice or competition as quickly and safely as possible.

- Rehabilitation programs in sports medicine can be subdivided into three phases, based primarily on the three stages of the healing process: phase 1, the acute phase; phase 2, the repair phase; and phase 3, the remodeling phase. If surgery is necessary, a fourth phase, the preoperative phase, must also be considered.

- The decision to release an athlete recovering from injury to a full return to athletic activity is the final stage of the rehabilitation and recovery process. The decision should be carefully considered by each member of the sports medicine team involved in the rehabilitation process.

- An open kinetic chain exists when the foot or hand is not in contact with the ground or some other surface. In a closed kinetic chain, the foot or hand is weight bearing. The use of closed chain strengthening techniques has become the rehabilitation treatment of choice for many athletic trainers. Closed kinetic chain strengthening activities are more functional than are open kinetic chain activities.

- Aquatic exercises can be an important rehabilitative tool for the athletic trainer, particularly with injuries involving the lower extremity. Aquatic exercises allow for resistance with motion without weight bearing.

- Proprioceptive neuromuscular facilitation is a manual therapy technique that can be used for strengthening muscle or increasing range of motion. The PNF movement patterns involve a sequential series of specific movements for the lower extremity, lower trunk, upper trunk, and upper extremity.

- Mobilization and traction are manual therapy techniques used to improve joint mobility or to decrease joint pain by restoring accessory movements to the injured joint, which allows full, pain-free range of motion.

Web Sites

Solutions to Critical Thinking EXERCISES

16-1 The short-term goals in any sports medicine rehabilitation program should include controlling pain, regaining range of motion, regaining strength, reestablishing neuromuscular control, and maintaining levels of cardiorespiratory fitness. The approach to rehabilitation should be aggressive, and decisions as to when and how to alter and progress specific components within a rehabilitation program should be based on and are limited by the healing process. The long-term goal is to return the athlete to full activity as soon as safely possible.

16-2 After injury and subsequent rest and immobilization, it is not unusual for the athlete to "forget" how to walk. The athletic trainer must help the athlete relearn neuromuscular control, which means regaining the ability to follow some previously established motor and sensory pattern by regaining conscious control of a specific movement until that movement becomes automatic. Strengthening exercises, particularly those that tend to be more functional, such as closed kinetic chain exercises, are essential for reestablishing neuromuscular control. Addressing neuromuscular control is critical throughout the recovery process but may be most critical during the early stages of rehabilitation to avoid reinjury or overuse injuries to additional structures.

16-3 Anterior knee pain can result from many different causes. Strengthening of the quadriceps can be helpful. If full range of motion strengthening exercises increase pain, the athlete should begin with positional isometric exercises done at different points in the range, progressing to full-range concentric and eccentric exercise as tolerated. Closed kinetic chain exercises such as minisquats, stepping exercises, or leg presses are excellent quadriceps-strengthening exercises and tend to be more functional in nature than are traditional open kinetic chain exercises.

16-4 The athletic trainer can provide the encouragement and positive reinforcement necessary for the athlete to make a commitment. Support from peers, coaches, and rehabilitation staff is important. Instructions should be clearly explained verbally, then written down. The rehabilitation program should fit into the athlete's schedule. The athletic trainer must be creative in designing and varying the exercise routine. The rehabilitation program should be as pain free as possible. The coach needs to support the rehabilitation process.

16-5 Perhaps the best recommendation would be to have the athlete engage in an aquatic exercise program. In the water, the athlete would not be weight bearing and could exercise the injured knee through a pain-free range of motion while simultaneously working on maintaining levels of fitness by engaging in water-resisted conditioning exercises.

16-6 To achieve a full physiological range of movement, the joint must have normal accessory motions. Stretching techniques address motion restriction caused by tightness of the musculotendinous unit. The athletic trainer should incorporate joint mobilization techniques that address restriction of motion caused by some tightness of capsular and ligamentous structures that surround the affected joint.

REVIEW QUESTIONS AND CLASS ACTIVITIES

1. What occurs physiologically when an athlete is suddenly forced to stop physical activity?
2. Discuss the physiological effects of immobilization on muscles, ligaments, joints, neuromuscular efficiency, and the cardiovascular system.
3. Discuss similarities and differences between training and conditioning exercises and therapeutic exercise.
4. Why must an athlete condition the entire body while an injury heals?
5. Why is it important to modulate pain during a rehabilitation program?
6. How is range of motion restored after an injury?
7. Critically compare the use of isometric, isotonic, and isokinetic exercises in rehabilitation.
8. Discuss the difference between proprioception and kinesthesia, and explain how they are related to neuromuscular control.
9. How and when should functional progressions be incorporated into the rehabilitation program?
10. Describe how to determine if an athlete is ready to return to activity after injury.
11. What is the importance of developing a rehabilitation plan? Include the criteria for moving to various phases.
12. What are the important considerations during each of the three phases of rehabilitation?
13. Why are closed kinetic chain exercises more useful than open kinetic chain exercises in the rehabilitation of sports injuries?
14. How may aquatic exercise be incorporated into a rehabilitation program?
15. Proprioceptive neuromuscular facilitation includes stretching, strengthening, and movement-patterning techniques. How can these techniques apply to sports injuries?
16. Explain why it is necessary to use stretching techniques to increase physiological movement and to use mobilization techniques to improve accessory motions.

REFERENCES

1. Arrigo C: Aquatic rehabilitation, *Sports Med Update* 7(2):1, 1992.
2. Barak T, Rosen E, Sofer R: Mobility: passive orthopedic manual therapy. In Gould J, Davies G, editors: *Orthopedic and sports physical therapy,* St Louis, 1990, Mosby.
3. Bunton E, Pitney W, Kane A: The role of limb torque muscle action and proprioception during closed kinetic chain rehabilitation of the lower extremity, *J Ath Train* 28(1):11, 1993.
4. Byerly P, Worrell T, Gahimer J et al: Rehabilitation compliance in an athletic training environment, *J Ath Train* 29(4):352, 1994.
5. Cox E, Lephart S, Irrgang J: Unilateral balance training of noninjured individuals and the effects on postural sway, *J Sport Rehabil* 2(2):87, 1993.
6. Fields J et al: Factors associated with adherence to sport injury rehabilitation in college age recreational athletes, *J Sport Rehabil* 4(3):172, 1995.
7. Gieck J, Hedgepath E: Psychological considerations for rehabilitating the injured athlete. In Prentice W, editor: *Rehabilitation techniques in sports medicine,* ed 3, Dubuque, Iowa, 1999, WCB/McGraw-Hill.
8. Graham V, Gehlsen G, Edwards J: Electromyographic evaluation of closed and open kinetic chain rehab exercises, *J Ath Train* 28(1):23, 1993.
9. Grigg P: Peripheral neural mechanisms in proprioception, *J Sport Rehabil* 3(1):2, 1994.
10. Hillman S: Principles and techniques of open kinetic chain rehabilitation, *J Sport Rehabil* 3(4):319, 1994.
11. Irrgang J, Whitney S, Cox E: Balance and proprioceptive training for rehabilitation of the lower extremity, *J Sport Rehabil* 3(1):68, 1994.
12. Kaltenborn F: *Mobilization of the extremity joints: examination and basic treatment techniques,* Norway, 1980, Olaf Norlis Bokhandel.
13. Knight KJ: Guidelines for rehabilitation of sports injuries. In Harvey JS, editor: *Rehabilitation of the injured athlete. Clinics in sports medicine,* vol 4, no 3, Philadelphia, 1985, Saunders.
14. Knott M, Voss EE: *Proprioceptive neuromuscular facilitation: patterns and techniques,* ed 2, Philadelphia, 1968, Harper & Row.
15. Lafree J, Mozingo A, Worrell T: Comparison of open kinetic chain knee and hip extension to closed kinetic chain leg performance, *J Sport Rehabil* 4(2):99, 1995.
16. Lephart S: Reestablishing neuromuscular control. In Prentice W, editor: *Rehabilitation techniques in sports medicine,* ed 3, Dubuque, Iowa, 1999, WCB/McGraw-Hill.
17. Magnusson P, McHugh M: Current concepts on rehabilitation in sports medicine. In Nicholas J, Hirschman E, editors: *The lower extremity and spine in sports medicine,* St Louis, 1995, Mosby.
18. Maitland G: *Extremity manipulation,* London, 1977, Butterworth.
19. McGee M: Functional progressions and functional testing in rehabilitation. In Prentice W, editor: *Rehabilitation techniques in sports medicine,* ed 3, Dubuque, Iowa, 1999, WCB/McGraw-Hill.
20. Perrin D: *Isokinetic exercise and assessment,* Champaign, Ill, 1993, Human Kinetics.
21. Pitney W, Bunton E: Improving rehabilitation effectiveness by enhancing the creative process, *J Ath Train* 30(3):261, 1995.
22. Prentice W: Closed kinetic chain exercise. In Prentice W, editor: *Rehabilitation techniques in sports medicine,* ed 3, Dubuque, Iowa, 1999, WCB/McGraw-Hill.
23. Prentice W: The healing process and pathophysiology of musculoskeletal injury. In Prentice W, editor: *Rehabilitation techniques in sports medicine,* ed 3, Dubuque, Iowa, 1999, WCB/McGraw-Hill.
24. Prentice W: Mobilization and traction techniques in rehabilitation. In Prentice W, editor: *Rehabilitation techniques in sports medicine,* ed 3, Dubuque, Iowa, 1999, WCB/McGraw-Hill.
25. Prentice W: Proprioceptive neuromuscular facilitation techniques. In Prentice W, editor: *Rehabilitation techniques in sports medicine,* ed 3, Dubuque, Iowa, 1999, WCB/McGraw-Hill.
26. Prentice W: *Therapeutic modalities in sports medicine,* ed 4, Dubuque, Iowa, 1999, WCB/McGraw-Hill.
27. Rivera J: Open vs closed kinetic chain rehabilitation of the lower extremity, *J Sport Rehabil* 3(2):154, 1994.
28. Rowinski M: Afferent neurobiology of the joint. In Gould J, Davies G: *Orthopedic and sports physical therapy,* St Louis, 1990, Mosby.

29. Selepak G: Aquatic therapy in rehabilitation. In Prentice W, editor: *Rehabilitation techniques in sports medicine,* ed 3, Dubuque, Iowa, 1999, WCB/McGraw-Hill.

30. Smith MJ: Muscle fiber types: their relationship to athletic training and rehabilitation. In Garron GW, editor: *Gymnastics. Clinics in sports medicine,* vol 4, no 1, Philadelphia, 1985, Saunders.

31. Stone J, Lueken J, Partin N: Closed kinetic chain rehabilitation of the glenohumeral joint, *J Ath Train* 28(1):34, 1993.

32. Stone J, Partin N, Lueken J: Upper extremity proprioceptive training, *J Ath Train* 2(1):15, 1994.

33. Surburg PR, Schrader JW. Proprioceptive neuromuscular facilitation technique in sports medicine: a reassessment, *J Ath Train* 32(1):34, 1997.

34. Swanik C et al: Reestablishing proprioception and neuromuscular control in the ACL-injured athlete, *J Sport Rehabil* 6(2):182, 1997.

35. Tippett S, Voight M: *Functional progressions for sport rehabilitation,* Champaign, Ill, 1995, Human Kinetics.

36. Wadsworth C: *Manual examination and treatment of the spine and extremities,* Baltimore, 1988, Williams & Wilkins.

37. Webburn A, Carbon R, Miller B: Injury rehabilitation programs: what are we talking about? *J Sport Rehabil* 6(1):54, 1997.

38. Wilk K et al: Kinetic chain exercise: implications for the anterior cruciate ligament patient, *J Sport Rehabil* 6(2):125, 1997.

ANNOTATED BIBLIOGRAPHY

Buschbacher R, Braddom R: *Sports medicine and rehabilitation: a sport specific approach,* Philadelphia, 1994, Hanley & Belfus.

This text discusses the rehabilitation of injuries that occur in specific sports.

Edmond S: *Manipulation and mobilization: extremity and spinal techniques,* St Louis, 1993, Mosby.

This text provides the entry-level student and the practicing clinician with a comprehensive text on mobilization and manipulation techniques.

Kisner C, Colby A: *Therapeutic exercise: foundations and techniques,* Philadelphia, 1996, Davis.

This clear, concise presentation of the field of therapeutic exercise is well suited to sports medicine; it covers exercise for increasing range of motion and for treating soft tissue, bone, and postsurgical problems extremely well.

Prentice W: *Mobilization and traction: principles and techniques,* video, 33 minutes, St Louis, 1993, Mosby.

This videotape presents a thorough overview of mobilization and traction and includes detailed demonstrations of various techniques.

Prentice W: *Proprioceptive neuromuscular facilitation: principles and techniques,* video, 26 minutes, St Louis, 1993, Mosby.

This videotape presents an introduction to PNF stretching and strengthening exercises complete with detailed hands-on demonstration of specific techniques.

Prentice W: *Rehabilitation techniques in sports medicine,* ed 3, Dubuque, Iowa, 1999, WCB/McGraw-Hill.

This comprehensive text deals with all aspects of rehabilitation used in a sports medicine setting.

Tippett S, Voight M: *Functional progressions for sport rehabilitation,* Champaign, Ill, 1995, Human Kinetics.

This text presents scientific principles and practical applications for using functional exercise to rehabilitate athletic injuries.

Zachazewski J, Magee D, Quillen W: *Athletic injuries and rehabilitation,* Philadelphia, 1996, Saunders.

This extremely detailed, scientifically based, advanced text deals with athletic injury rehabilitation.

Chapter

Pharmacology, Drugs, and Sports

17

When you finish this chapter you should be able to

- Define the term *drug*.
- Discuss the various methods by which drugs can be administered.
- Discuss pharmacokinetics relative to absorption, distribution, metabolism, and excretion.
- Explain the difference between administering and dispensing medications.
- Discuss legal concerns for administering medications to the athletic population.
- Describe the various protocols that the athletic trainer should follow for administering over-the-counter medications to athletes.
- Discuss the various drugs that can be used to treat infection, reduce pain and inflammation, relax muscle, treat gastrointestinal disorders, treat colds and congestion, and control bleeding.
- Discuss the problem of substance abuse in the athletic population.
- Describe the ergogenic aids used by athletes to improve performance.
- Discuss the use of alcohol, drugs, and tobacco by athletes.
- Explain the drug testing policies and procedures, and list the different types of banned drugs.

pharmacology
The study of drugs and their origin, nature, properties, and effects on living organisms.

Pharmacology is the branch of science that deals with the actions of drugs on biological systems, especially drugs that are used in medicine for diagnostic and therapeutic purposes. Pharmaceutical care is the direct provision of medication-related care for the purpose of achieving definite outcomes that improve quality of life.[16] Medications of all types, both prescription and over-the-counter, are commonly used by athletes as they are by other individuals in the population.[1]

Unfortunately, the abuse of various drugs and other substances for performance enhancement or for recreational mood alteration is also widespread among athletes. Thus the athletic trainer must be knowledgeable about drug use and substance abuse within the athletic population.

WHAT IS A DRUG?

drug
A chemical agent used in the prevention, treatment, or diagnosis of disease.

A **drug** is a chemical agent used in the prevention, treatment, or diagnosis of disease.[27] The use of substances for the express purpose of treating some infirmity or disease dates back to early history. The ancient Egyptians were highly skilled in making and using medications, treating a wide range of external and internal conditions.

Many of our common drugs, such as aspirin and penicillin, are derived from natural sources. Historically, medications were composed of roots, herbs, leaves, or other natural materials that were identified as having or believed to have medicinal properties. Today many medications that originally came from nature are produced synthetically.

PHARMACOKINETICS

pharmacokinetics
The method by which drugs are absorbed, distributed, metabolized, and eliminated.

Pharmacokinetics refers to the method by which drugs are absorbed, distributed, metabolized, and eliminated or excreted by the body. The term *pharmacodynamics* is often confused with pharmacokinetics. Pharmacodynamics refers to the actions or the effects of a drug on the body.[27,42]

Administration of Drugs

To be effective therapeutically, a drug must first enter the system and then reach a receptor in a target tissue. The administration of medications in athletes, as in any individual, can be either internal or external and is based on the type of local or general response desired.

Drugs can be administered internally or externally.

Internal Administration

Drugs and medications can be taken internally through inhalation, or they may be administered intradermally, intramuscularly, intranasally, intraspinally, intravenously, orally, rectally, or sublingually.

Inhalation is a means of bringing medication or substances to the respiratory tract. This method is most often used in sports to relieve the athlete of the symptoms of respiratory illness such as asthma. The vehicle for inhalation is normally water vapor, oxygen, or highly aromatic medications.

Intradermal (into the skin) or *subcutaneous* (under the cutaneous tissues) administration is usually accomplished through a hypodermic needle injection. Such introduction of medication is initiated when a rapid response is needed, but this method does not produce as rapid a response as intravenous injection offers.

Intramuscular injection means that the medication is given directly into the muscle tissue. The site for such an injection is usually the gluteal area or the deltoid muscle of the upper arm.

Intranasal application varies according to the condition that is to be treated. The introduction of a decongestant intranasal solution by using a dropper or an atomizer may relieve the discomfort of head colds and allergies.

Intraspinal injection may be indicated for any of the following purposes: introduction of drugs to combat specific organisms that have entered the spinal cord, injection of a substance such as procaine to anesthetize the lower limbs, or withdrawal of spinal fluid to be studied.

Intravenous injection (into a vein) is given when an immediate reaction to the medication is desired. The drug enters the venous circulation and is spread rapidly throughout the body.

Oral administration of medicines is the most common method of all. Forms such as tablets, capsules, powders, and liquids are easily administered orally.

Rectal administration of drugs is limited. In the past some medications have been introduced through the rectum to be absorbed by its mucous lining. Such methods have proved undesirable because of difficulties in regulating dosage.

Sublingual and *buccal* introductions of medicines usually consist of placing easily dissolved agents such as troches (lozenges) or tablets under the tongue. They dissolve slowly and are absorbed by the mucous lining.

External Administration

Medications administered externally include inunctions, ointments, pastes, plasters, transdermal patches, and solutions.

Inunctions are oily or medicated substances that are rubbed into the skin and result in a local or systemic reaction. Oil-based liniments and petroleum analgesic balms used as massage lubricants are examples of inunctions.

Ointments consisting of oil, petroleum jelly, or lanolin combined with drugs are applied for long-lasting topical medication.

Pastes are ointments with a nonfat base. They are spread on cloth and usually produce a cooling effect on the skin.

Plasters are thicker than ointments and are spread either on cloth or paper or directly on the skin. They usually contain an irritant, are applied as a counterirritant, and are used for relieving pain, increasing circulation, and decreasing inflammation.

TABLE 17-1 Drug Vehicles

Liquid preparations

Aqueous solution	Sterile water containing a drug substance
Elixir	Alcohol, sugar, and flavoring with a drug dissolved in solution, designed for internal consumption
Liniment	Alcohol or oil containing a dissolved drug, designed for external massage
Spirit	A drug dissolved in water and alcohol or in alcohol alone
Suspension	Undissolved powder in a fluid medium; must be mixed well by shaking before use
Syrup	A mixture of sugar and water containing a drug

Solid preparations

Ampule	A closed glass receptacle containing a drug
Capsule	A gelatin receptacle containing a drug
Ointment (emollient)	A semisolid preparation for external application of such consistency that it may be applied to the skin by inunction
Paste	An inert powder combined with water
Tablet	A solid pharmaceutical dosage compressed into a small oval, circle, square, or other form
Plaster	A substance intended for external application, made of such materials and of such consistency as to adhere to the skin and thereby attach a dressing
Powder	Finely ground drug plus vehicle or effervescent granules
Suppository	A medicated gelatin molded into a cone for placement in a body orifice (e.g., the anal canal)

Transdermal patches are patches resembling adhesive bandages that contain various types of slow-release medications. They may be left in place for several days.

Solutions can be administered externally and are extremely varied, consisting principally of bacteriostatics. Antiseptics, disinfectants, vasoconstrictors, and liquid rubefacients are examples.

Drug Vehicles

drug vehicle
The substance in which a drug is transported.

A **drug vehicle** is a therapeutically inactive substance that transports a drug. A drug is housed in a vehicle that may be either a solid or a liquid. Some of the more common drug vehicles are listed in Table 17-1.

Absorption of Drugs

Once a drug is in the system, it must be dissolved before it can be absorbed. The rate and extent of absorption is determined by the chemical characteristics of the drug, the dosage form (i.e., tablet or solution), and the gastric-emptying time. Solutions in which the drug is already dissolved have the fastest absorption rate, and time-release medications have the slowest rate.[27]

bioavailability
How completely a particular drug is absorbed by the system.

Bioavailability refers to how completely a particular drug is absorbed by the system. Bioavailability is most dependent on the characteristics of the drug and not on the dosage form, whereas absorption rate is largely determined by dosage form.

Distribution

volume of distribution
The volume of fluid through which the drug would have to be distributed to reach a therapeutic level of concentration.

Once absorbed, the drug is transported through the blood to a specific target tissue. The drug will be distributed to other parts of the body as well. **The volume of distribution** is the volume of fluid through which the drug would have to be distributed to reach a therapeutic level of concentration. The **efficacy** of a drug is its capability of producing a specific therapeutic effect once it reaches a particular receptor site in a target tissue. **Potency** is the dose of the drug that is required to produce a desired therapeutic effect.[27]

Metabolism

The **biotransformation** of drugs into water-soluble compounds that can be excreted is referred to as **metabolism.** Most of the metabolism takes place in the liver, with some occurring in the kidneys and blood. Metabolism of drugs in the liver transforms most active drugs into inactive compounds. Occasionally, when an active drug is metabolized, the metabolites may be toxic.[27]

Excretion

Excretion of a drug or its metabolites is controlled by the kidneys. Drugs are filtered through the kidneys and are usually excreted in the urine, although some may be reabsorbed. Some drugs may also be excreted in saliva, sweat, and feces.[27]

Drug Half-Life

The rate at which a drug disappears from the body, either through metabolism or excretion or a combination of the two, is called the **half-life.** This rate is the amount of time required for half the drug in the body to be eliminated. For most drugs, the half-life is measured in hours, but for some it is measured in minutes or days. Knowing the half-life of a drug is critical in determining how often and in what dosage a drug must be administered to achieve and maintain therapeutic levels of concentration. The dosage interval, or time between administration of individual doses, is equal to the half-life of that particular drug.[27]

How often a drug will be administered is determined in part by the drug's **steady-state,** which is reached when the amount that is taken is equal to the amount that is excreted. A steady-state is usually reached after five half-lives of the drug have occurred. Drugs with long half-lives may take several days to weeks to reach a steady-state.[27]

Effects of Physical Activity on Pharmacokinetics

In general, exercise decreases the absorption after oral administration of a drug, whereas exercise increases absorption after intramuscular or subcutaneous administration because of an increased blood flow in the muscle.[34] Thus, exercise has an influence on the amount of a drug that reaches a receptor site, which significantly affects the pharmacodynamic activity of that drug.[34]

LEGAL CONCERNS IN ADMINISTERING VERSUS DISPENSING DRUGS

Administering a drug is defined as providing a single dose of medication for immediate use by the patient. Dispensing refers to providing the patient with a drug in a quantity sufficient to be used for multiple doses.

Dispensing Prescription Drugs

At no time can anyone other than a person licensed by law legally prescribe or dispense prescription drugs for an athlete. An athletic trainer, unless specifically allowed by state licensure, is not permitted to dispense a prescription drug. Failure to heed this fact can be a violation of federal laws and state statutes. Table 17-2 lists information about how medication dispensing is controlled. A violation of these laws could mean legal problems for the physician, athletic trainer, school, school district, or even the league.[17]

Administering Over-the-Counter Drugs

The situation is not so clear-cut for nonprescription drugs. Basically, the athletic trainer may be allowed to administer a single dose of a nonprescription medication. For example, most secondary schools do not allow the athletic trainer to dispense nonprescription (over-the-counter [OTC]) drugs that are to be taken internally by the athlete, including aspirin and OTC cold remedies. The application of

efficacy
A drug's capability of producing a specific therapeutic effect.

potency
The dose of the drug required to produce a desired therapeutic effect.

biotransformation
Transforming a drug so it can be metabolized.

metabolism
Changing a drug into a water-soluble compound that can be excreted.

half-life
Rate at which a drug disappears from the body through metabolism, excretion, or both.

steady-state
When the amount of the drug taken is equal to the amount that is excreted.

At no time can anyone other than a person licensed by law legally prescribe or dispense drugs for an athlete.

TABLE 17-2 Agencies and Regulations That Govern the Provision of Pharmaceutical Care

Regulation	Enforced/Administered by	Purpose
Federal Food, Drug, and Cosmetic Act (FDCA) of 1938	Food and Drug Administration	Regulates the quality, strength, bioequivalence, and labeling of prescription and nonprescription drugs
Druham-Humphrey Amendment of 1951	Food and Drug Administration	Separates prescription from nonprescription drugs
Current Good Manufacturing Practice Regulations of 1962	Food and Drug Administration	Mandates standards for repackaging of medications
Federal Controlled Substances Act of 1970	Drug Enforcement Authority	Regulates controlled substances (drugs that have potential for abuse)
Poison Prevention Packaging Act (PPPA) of 1970	Food and Drug Administration	Regulates packaglng of prescription and nonprescription drugs in child-resistant safety containers
Medical Device Act of 1976	Food and Drug Administration	Regulates classffication and performance standards of medical devices.
Federal Anti-Tampering Act of 1983	Food and Drug Administration	Mandates tamper-resistant packaging on all nonprescription drugs
Fair Packaging and Labeling Act	Food and Drug Administration	Mandates labeling of the contents of nonprescription drugs to assist consumers in identifying similar products
Prescription Drug Marketing Act of 1987	Food and Drug Administration	Mandates accountability of sample drugs from receiving through administering or dispensing
Anti-Drug Abuse Act of 1988	Drug Enforcement Authority	Regulates anabolic steroids as controlled substances
Omnibus Reconciliation Act of 1990 (OBRA '90)	Food and Drug Administration	Mandates drug review, patient medication records, and verbal patient education as part of dispensing of prescription medications
State Pharmacy Practice Acts	Individual State Boards of Pharmacy	Regulates the provision of pharmaceutical care within each state. Laws and regulations may vary considerably between states
State Medical Acts	Individual State Boards of Medicine	Regulates the practice of medicine within each state

nonprescription wound medications is allowed by some secondary schools under the category of first aid. On the other hand, some high school athletic trainers in the United States are not allowed to apply even a wound medication in the name of first aid but can only clean the wound with soap and water. The athlete must then be sent to the school nurse for medication. The dispensing of vitamins and even dextrose may be specifically disallowed by some school districts. At the college or professional level, minors are not usually involved, and the administration of nonprescription medications may be less restrictive. It is assumed that athletes who are of legal age have the right to use whatever nonprescription drugs they choose. However, this right does not preclude the fact that the athletic trainer must be reasonable and prudent about the types of nonprescription drugs offered to the athlete.

Generally, the administration of single doses of nonprescription medicines by a member of the athletic staff to any athlete depends on the philosophy of the school district and must be under the direction of the team physician. In this area, as in all other areas of sports medicine and athletic training, the athletic trainer is obligated to act reasonably and prudently.

Record Keeping

Those involved in any health care profession are acutely aware of the necessity of maintaining complete, up-to-date medical records. The athletic training setting is no exception. The athletic trainer who administers medications must realize that maintaining accurate records of the types of medications administered is just as important as recording progress notes, treatments given, and rehabilitation plans. The athletic trainer may be dealing with a number of different patients simultaneously while trying to get a team ready for practice or competition. Situations may become hectic, and stopping to record each time a medication is administered is difficult. Nevertheless, the athletic trainer should include the following information on the medication administration log: name of the athlete, complaint or symptoms, current medications, any known drug allergies, name of medication given, lot number if available, expiration date, quantity of medication given, method of administration, and date and time of administration.[17,39]

Each athletic trainer should be aware of state regulations and laws that pertain to the ordering, prescribing, distributing, storing, and dispensing or administering of medications. Obtaining legal counsel, working with the state board of pharmacy or a student health clinic, working in cooperation with a team physician, and establishing strict written policies are all actions that can minimize the chances of violating state laws that regulate the use of medications.[17,39]

Labeling Requirements

OTC drugs are required to have adequate directions for use, precautions, and adequate readability. The federal eight-point label for nonprescription drugs requires the following information:

1. The name of the product
2. The name and address of the manufacturer, packer, or distributor
3. The net contents of the package
4. The established name of all active ingredients and the quantity of certain other ingredients whether active or not
5. The name of any habit-forming drug contained in the preparation
6. Cautions and warnings to protect the consumer
7. Adequate directions for safe and effective use
8. Expiration date and lot number

Nonprescription drugs may not be repackaged without meeting labeling criteria. All drugs dispensed from the athletic training room must be properly labeled. Legal violations may occur if a portion of a nonprescription drug is removed from an original, properly labeled package and dispensed to an athlete. This practice carries the same liability as does dispensing prescription drugs, because the athlete is not given the opportunity to review the label for name, contents, precautions, directions, and other information considered essential for the safe use of the product. Liability for any adverse patient outcome is therefore transferred to the dispenser of the improperly labeled OTC drug.[17]

The Safety of Pharmaceutical Drugs

No drug can be considered completely safe and harmless. If a drug is potent enough to effect some physiological action, it is also strong enough, under some conditions, to be dangerous. All persons react individually to any drug. A given amount of a specific medication may result in no adverse reaction in one athlete, whereas another athlete may experience a pronounced adverse response. Both the athlete and the athletic trainer should be fully aware of any untoward effect a drug may have. It is essential that the athlete be instructed clearly about when specifically to take medications, with meals or not, and what not to combine with the drug, such as other drugs or specific foods. Some drugs can nullify the effect of another drug or can cause a serious antagonistic reaction. For example, calcium, which is found in a variety of foods and in some medications, can nullify the effects of the antibiotic tetracycline.

Drug Responses

Individuals react differently to the same medication, and different conditions may alter the effect of a drug on the athlete. Drugs themselves can be changed through age or improper preservation, as well as through the manner in which they are administered. Response variations also result from differences in each individual's size or age.

Alcohol should not be ingested with a wide variety of drugs, both prescription and nonprescription. A fatty diet may decrease a drug's effectiveness by interfering with

17-1

Critical Thinking Exercise

A college-age softball player comes into the training room complaining of a sore throat and stuffy head and asks the athletic trainer to give her some "drugs" to get rid of her problem.

? Is the athletic trainer legally allowed to give her any type of medication, and if so, how should the athletic trainer give it to the athlete?

TABLE 17-3   General Responses Produced by Drugs and Medication

Addiction	Body response to certain types of drugs that produces both a physiological need and a psychological craving for the substance
Antagonistic action	Result observed when medications, used together, have adverse effects or counteract one another
Cumulative effect	Exaggerated drug effects, which occur when the body is unable to metabolize a drug as rapidly as it is administered; the accumulated, unmetabolized drug may cause unfavorable reactions
Depressive action	Effect from drugs that slow down cell function
Habituation	Individual's development of a psychological need for a specific medication
Hypersensitivity	Allergic response to a specific drug; such allergies may be demonstrated by a mild skin irritation, itching, a rash, or a severe anaphylactic reaction, which could be fatal
Idiosyncrasy	Unusual reaction to a drug; a distinctive response
Irritation	Process, as well as effect, caused by substances that result in a cellular change; mild irritation may stimulate cell activity, whereas moderate or severe irritation by a drug may decrease cell activity
Paradoxical reaction	A drug-induced effect that is the exact opposite of that which is therapeutically intended
Potentiating agent	A pharmaceutical that increases the effect of another; for example, codeine is potentiated by aspirin, and therefore less of it is required to relieve pain
Specific effect	Action usually produced by a drug in a select tissue or organ system
Side effect	The result of a medication that is given for a particular condition but affects other body areas or has effects other than those sought
Stimulation	Effect caused by drugs that speed up cell activity
Synergistic effect	Result that occurs when drugs given together produce a greater reaction than when given alone
Tolerance	Condition existing when a certain drug dosage is no longer able to give a therapeutic action and must therefore be increased

its absorption. Excessively acid foods such as fruits, carbonated drinks, or vegetable juice may cause adverse drug reactions.[4] Athletic trainers must thoroughly know the athletes with whom they work. The possibility of an adverse drug reaction is ever present and requires continual education and vigilance.

Table 17-3 is a list of general body responses sometimes produced by drugs and medications.

Buying Medications

One of the athletic department's best friends is the local pharmacist. The pharmacist can assist in the selection and purchase of nonprescription drugs, can save money by suggesting the lower-priced generic drugs, and can act as a general advisor on the effectiveness of drugs, the dose of a medicine, and even the inherent dangers in a specific drug.

All pharmaceuticals must be properly labeled, indicating clearly the content, expiration date, and any dangers or contraindications for use. Pharmaceutical manufacturers place the expiration date on drugs, and athletic trainers should locate this date on the package. When storing medications always keep both prescription and over-the-counter medications in a locked cabinet or secured place; keep them in the original container; store them away from heat, direct light, damp places, and extreme cold; and keep over-the-counter medications in single dose packs.[39]

SELECTED THERAPEUTIC DRUGS USED TO TREAT THE ATHLETE

The use of drugs and medicine is widespread in the athletic population, as it is in society in general. Thousands of drugs, both prescription and nonprescription, are available for physicians and consumers to choose from, and new drugs are being constantly developed. Pharmaceutical laboratories develop compounds *in vitro*, and then test, retest, and refine the drug *in vivo* before submitting it for Food and Drug Administration (FDA) approval.

in vitro = in a laboratory
in vivo = in the body

A number of texts and databases are available (i.e., *Physician's Desk Reference* and *Drug Facts and Comparisons*) and are widely used as references for comparison of **bioequivalent** drugs (drugs that produce similar biological effects) relative to their appropriateness and effectiveness in treating a specific condition or illness. Table 17-4 summarizes the various classifications of drugs available.

bioequivalence

Having a similar biological effect.

The following sections discuss the most common pharmaceutical practices in athletic training to date and the specific drugs that are in use (see also Table 17-5). The

TABLE 17-4 Pharmaceutical Classifications

Analgesics (anodynes)	Pain-relieving drugs
Anesthetics	Agents that produce local or general numbness to touch, pain, or stimulation
Antacids	Substances that neutralize acidity; commonly used in the digestive tract
Anticoagulants	Agents that prevent coagulation of blood
Antidotes	Substances that prevent or counteract the action of a poison
Antipruritics	Agents that relieve itching
Antiseptics	Agents that kill bacteria or inhibit their growth and can be applied to living tissue
Antispasmodics	Agents that relieve muscle spasm
Antitussives	Agents that inhibit or prevent coughing
Astringents	Agents that cause contraction or puckering action
Bacteriostatics and fungistatics	Agents that retard or inhibit the growth of bacteria or fungi
Carminatives	Agents that relieve flatulence (caused by gases) in the intestinal tract
Cathartics	Agents used to evacuate substances from the bowels; active purgatives
Caustics	Burning agents, capable of destroying living tissue
Counterirritants	Agents applied locally to produce an inflammatory reaction for the relief of a deeper inflammation
Depressants	Agents that diminish body functions or nerve activity
Disinfectants	Agents that kill or inhibit the growth of microorganisms; should be applied only to nonliving materials
Diuretics	Agents that increase the secretion of urine
Emetics	Agents that cause vomiting
Expectorants	Agents that suppress coughing
Hemostatics	Substances that either slow down or stop bleeding or hemorrhage
Irritants	Agents that cause irritation
Narcotics	Drugs that produce analgesic and hypnotic effects
Sedatives	Agents that relieve anxiety
Skeletal muscle relaxants	Drugs that depress neural activity within skeletal muscles
Stimulants	Agents that excite the central nervous system
Vasoconstrictors and vasodilators	Drugs that, respectively, constrict or dilate blood vessels

TABLE 17-5 Athletic Trainers' Guide to Medications Frequently Used in Sports Medicine

Generic Name	Trade Name	Primary Use of Drug/Prescription	Sports Medicine Consideration
Analagesics, antipyretics, and antinflammatories (NSAIDs)			
Aspirin	Many trade names	Analgesic, antipyretic, antinflammatory.	Gastric irritation, nausea, tinnitus, prolonged bleeding if injured in contact sports
Acetaminophen	Tylenol, Datril, others	Analgesic, antipyretic.	None
Flurbiprofen	Ansaid*	All are analgesic, antipyretic, antiinflammatory (NSAIDs).	Gastric irritation less common than with aspirin except for indomethacin. These medications should be used for reducing pain and inflammation; they should not be substituted for acetaminophen in cases of mild headache or low fever. Adequate hydration reduces the risk of adverse effects in the renal system.
Ketoprofen	Orudis*		
Indomethacin	Indocin*		
Ibuprofen	Advin, Motrin,* Nuprin	Notify doctor immediately for skin rash, itching, visual disturbances, weight gain, edema, black stools, dark urine, or persistent headache.	
Naproxen	Naprosyn,* Anaprox*		
Diflunisal	Dolobid*		
Piroxicam	Feldene*	*Drug interactions*: salicylates, other NSAIDs, probenecid, cimetidine, phenylpropanolamine, diuretics, lithium, phenytoin, beta blockers, ACE inhibitors, anticoagulants, digoxin	*NSAID hypersensitivity*: Because of cross sensitivity to aspirin and all other NSAIDs do not give these agents to athletes in whom aspirin, iodides, or other NSAIDs have caused symptoms of asthma, rhinitis, rash, nasal polyps, bronchospasm, or other symptoms of allergic reactions.
Tolmetin	Tolectin*		
Fenoprofen	Nalfon*		
Meclofenamate	Meclomen*		
Diclofenac	Voltaren*		
Ketoralac	Toradol*		
Etodolac	Lodine*		
Mefenamic acid	Ponstel*		
Nabumetone	Relafen*		
Antifungal agents			
Ketoconazole	Nizoral*	Systemic (oral) antifungal drug.	Should not be taken within two hours of antacids.
		Drug has been associated with hepatic toxicity including fatalities.	May cause dizziness or drowsiness.
		Notify doctor immediately for unusual fatigue, anorexia, nausea, jaundice, dark urine, pale stools, abdominal pain, fever, or diarrhea.	*Hypersensitivity*: Anaphylaxis has been reported.
Griseofulvin	Fulvicin P/G,* Gris-Peg*	Oral antifungal agent.	Photosensitivity may occur: Patient should avoid prolonged exposure to sunlight or sunlamps.
		Notify doctor immediately for fever, sore throat, or skin rash.	
		Reduces the effectiveness of oral contraceptives.	
Fluconazole	Diflucan*	Oral antifungal agent.	
		Warnings: hepatic injury, anaphylaxis, dermatologic changes have been reported.	
		Notify doctor immediately for skin rash.	
		Drug interactions: cimetidine, rifampin, nonsedating antihistamines. phenytoin, theophylline, zidovudine	

Generic name	Brand name(s)	Action / Drug interactions	Special considerations
Terbinafine	Lamisil*	Oral antifungal agent for treatment of toenails or fingernails, scalp, body, groin, or feet.	Weeks to months may be required to resolve infection.
Antibiotics			
Penicillins	V-Cillin-K,* Pen Vee K, Trimox*	Notify doctor immediately for skin rash, itching, aching joints, dark urine, difficulty swallowing, fever, chills, pale stool, redness, blistering, peeling or loosening of skin, unusual tiredness and yellowing of skin or eyes. *Drug interactions:* cimetidine, rifampin, terfenadine, caffeine	Alcohol consumption during treatment increases risk of liver toxicity.
Cephalosporins	Keflex,* Ceftin*	*Drug interactions:* beta blockers, oral contraceptives, erythromycin, tetracycline	If diarrhea occurs, do not give Imodium AD. Patients allergic to penicillin may have cross sensitivity to cephalosporins.
Macrolides	Ery-Tab,* Zithromax,* Biaxin,* Dynabac*	*Drug interactions:* oral contraceptives, alcohol, probenecid. *Drug interactions:* fluconazole, zidovudine, theophylline, nonsedating antihistamines, oral contraceptives, carbamazepine, ergot alkaloids, penicillins	
Fluoroquinolones	Cipro,* Noroxin,* Floxin,* Penetrex,* Maxaquin,* Zagam,* Levaquin*	Notify doctor immediately for agitation, confusion, tremors, fever, skin rash. *Drug interactions:* antacids, sucralfate, Pepto-Bismol, cimetidine, caffeine, probenecid, phenytoin, theophylline, oral contraceptives	Photosensitivity: avoid overexposure to sunlight or sunlamps. May cause dizziness. Rarely associated with pain, inflammation, or rupture of a tendon.
Tetracyclines	Sumycin,* Vibramycin*	*Drug interactions:* antacids, anticoagulants, cimetidine, insulin, lithium, oral contraceptives, penicillins, sodium bicarbonate.	Should not be taken with milk, antacids, or minerals because of reduced absorption. Photosensitivity may occur.
Drug that affect the respiratory tract			
Chlorpheniramine	Chlor-Trimeton	Antihistamine for allergies.	Used primarily for treatment of allergic rhinitis. Causes drowsiness, decreased coordination.
Cromolyn	Nasalcrom	Nasal allergy symptom controller; prevents and relieves nasal allergy symptoms.	Allergic rhinitis, seasonal allergies
Oxymetazoline	Afrin, Dristan Long Lasting, Neosynephrine 12 Hour, Allerest	Adrenergic decongestant applied topically as spray or nose drops.	Do not exceed recommended duration of treatment because of rebound congestion; may cause sneezing, dryness of nasal mucosa, and headache.
Pseudoephedrine	Sudafed, Cenafed, Oranyl, others	Adrenergic decongestant used orally.	Produces stimulation of the central nervous system; topically applied decongestants work faster, but oral decongestants are preferred for long-term use.
Diphenhydramine	Benadryl, Benylin cough syrup	Antihistamine used primarily for allergic reaction; also used for sleep.	Produces drowsiness and dry mouth; found in over-the-counter sleeping medications.

TABLE 17-5 Athletic Trainer's Guide to Medications Frequently Used in Sports Medicine—cont'd

Generic Name	Trade Name	Primary Use of Drug/Prescription	Sports Medicine Consideration
Dextromethorphan	Robitussin DM, Benylin DMO, Sucrets Lozenges	Nonnarcotic antitussive used for cough suppression.	Very effective in cases of unproductive cough; rarely produces drowsiness and other side effects.
Terfenadine	Seldane*	Antihistamine.	*Drug interaction*: newer antidepressants Nonsedating; Watch for cardiotoxic drug interactions with erythromycin, grapefruit juice, oral antifungals, and other drugs.
Cetirizine	Zyrtec*	Antihistamine; effective for some allergic reactions.	May cause some sedation but less than traditional antihistamines.
Fexofenadine Loratidine Astemizole	Allegra* Claritin* Hismanyl*	Antihistamines.	Nonsedating.
Benzonatate	Tessalon*	Peripherally acting antitussive that acts as an anesthetic.	May cause dizziness; should not be chewed.
Codeine	Robitussin AC*	Narcotic antitussive that depresses the central cough mechanism.	Used in combination with expectorant; can produce sedation, dizziness, constipation, or nausea.
Guaifenesin	Robitussin, Glyate	Expectorant used for symptomatic relief of unproductive cough.	Used for treating dry or sore throat; good hydration maximizes effects.
Drugs that affect the gastrointestinal tract			
Sodium bicarbonate	Soda Mint	Antacid used for quick relief of upset stomach.	Produces gas, belching; overuse may cause systemic alkalinity.
Aluminum hydroxide	Amphogel, Dialume	Antacid used for upset stomach.	May produce constipation: moderate acid neutralizer.
Calcium carbonate	Titralac, Mallamint	Antacid used for upset stomach and for calcium supplementation.	May produce constipation and acid rebound; high acid neutralizing capacity.
Maguesium hydroxide	Milk of Magnesia	Laxative used for constipation.	May cause diarrhea.
Cimetidine	Tagamet HB	Histamine-2 antagonist used for relief of upset stomach, heartburn, acid indigestion.	Numerous drug interactions.
Nizatidine Ranitidine Famotidine	Axid AR Zantac 75 Pepeid AC	Histamine-2 antagonist used for relief of upset stomach, heartburn, acid indigestion.	
Combination antacids	Alka-Seltzer, Digel, Gaviscon, Gelusil, Maalox, Mylanta, Wingel, others	Combination drugs for controlling gastric upset.	May produce either diarrhea or constipation.
Promethazine	Phenergan*	Antiemetic used for preventing motion sickness, nausea, and vomiting.	Produces sedation and drowsiness.
Diphenoxylate HCL Loperamide	Lomotil,* Uni-Lom* Imodium AD	Narcotic antidiarrheal. Nonnarcotic systemic antidiarrheal.	Causes dry mouth, nausea, drowsiness. Abdominal discomfort, drowsiness with large doses.
Combination antidiarrheals	Donnagel, Kaopectate	Relief of diarrhea.	All are relatively safe with few side effects; effectiveness is questionable.
	Pepto-Bismol		Effective for traveler's diarrhea.

*Requires a prescription.

discussions include both prescription and nonprescription drugs, with emphases on what should most concern the athletic trainer and what the medications or materials are designed to accomplish.

Drugs to Combat Infection

Combating infection, especially skin infection, is of major importance in sports. Serious infection can cause countless hours of lost time and has even been the indirect cause of death.

Drugs used to combat infection include local antiseptics and disinfectants, antifungal agents, and antibiotics.

Local Antiseptics and Disinfectants

Antiseptics are substances that can be placed on living tissue for the express purpose of either killing bacteria or inhibiting their growth. Disinfectants are substances that combat microorganisms but should be applied only to nonliving objects. Other general names given to antiseptics and disinfectants are germicides, which are designed to destroy bacteria; fungicides, which kill fungi; sporicides, which destroy spores; and sanitizers, which minimize contamination by microorganisms.

In sports many agents are used to combat infection. It is critical that agents have a broad spectrum of activity against infective organisms, including the human immunodeficiency virus (HIV).

Antiseptics and disinfectants include alcohol, phenol, halogens, and oxidizing agents.

Alcohol   Alcohol is one of the most widely used skin disinfectants. Ethyl alcohol (70% by weight) and isopropyl alcohol (70%) are equally effective. They are inexpensive and nonirritating; they kill bacteria immediately, with the exception of spores. However, they have no long-lasting germicidal action. Besides being directly combined with other agents to form tinctures, alcohol acts independently on the skin as an antiseptic and astringent. In a 70 percent solution, alcohol can be used for disinfecting instruments. Because of alcohol's rapid rate of evaporation, it produces a mild anesthetic action. Combined with 20 percent benzoin, it is used in athletics as a topical skin dressing to provide a protective skin coating and astringent action.

Phenol   Phenol was one of the earliest antiseptics and disinfectants used by the medical profession. From its inception to the present, phenol has been used to control disease organisms, both as an antiseptic and as a disinfectant. It is available in liquids of varying concentrations and in emollients. Substances that are derived from phenol and that cause less irritation are now used more extensively. Some of these derivatives are resorcinol, thymol, and the common household disinfectant Lysol.

Halogens   Halogens are chemical substances (chlorine, fluoride, and bromine) that are used for their antiseptic and disinfectant qualities. Iodophors, or halogenated compounds, a combination of iodine and a carrier, create a much less irritating preparation than tincture of iodine is. A popular iodophor is povidone-iodine complex (Betadine), which is an excellent germicide commonly used as a surgical scrub by surgeons. Betadine as an antiseptic and germicide in athletic training has proved extremely effective on skin lesions such as lacerations, abrasions, and floor burns.

Oxidizing agents   Oxidizing agents, as represented by hydrogen peroxide (3%), are commonly used in athletic training. Hydrogen peroxide is an antiseptic that, because of its oxidation, affects bacteria but readily decomposes in the presence of organic substances such as blood and pus. For this reason it has little effect as an antiseptic. Contact with organic material produces an effervescence, during which no great destruction of bacteria takes place. The chief value of hydrogen peroxide in the care of wounds is its ability to cleanse the infected cutaneous and mucous membranes. Application of hydrogen peroxide to wounds results in the formation of an active effervescent gas that dislodges particles of wound material and debris and, by removing degenerated tissue, eliminates the wound as a likely environment for bacterial breeding. Hydrogen peroxide also possesses compounds that are widely used as antiseptics. Because it is nontoxic, hydrogen peroxide may be used for cleansing mucous membranes. A diluted solution (50% water and 50% hydrogen peroxide) can be used for treating inflammatory conditions of the mouth and throat.

Antifungal Agents

Many medicinal agents on the market are designed to treat fungi, which are commonly found in and around athletic facilities. The three most common fungi are *Epidermophyton, Trichophyton,* and *Candida albicans.*

In recent years, there has been successful development and use of antifungal agents such as ketoconazole (Nizoral), amphotericin B (Fungizone), and griseofulvin. Both ketoconazole and amphotericin B seem to be effective against deepseated fungus infections such as those caused by *Candida albicans.* Ketoconazole, fluconazole, and griseofulvin, all of which can be administered orally, produce an effective fungistatic action against the specific fungus species of *Microsporum, Trichophyton,* and *Epidermophyton,* all of which are associated with common athlete's foot.[3] Given over a long period of time, griseofulvin becomes a functioning part of the cutaneous tissues, especially the skin, hair, and nails, producing a prolonged and continuous fungistatic action. Miconazole (Micatin), clotrimazole (Lotrimin), and tolnaftate (Tinactin, which does not treat *Candida* infections) are topical medications for a superficial fungus infection caused by *Trichophyton* and other fungi.

Mechanical antiseptics, usually soaps that provide a cleansing and detergent action, remove pathogens from the skin.

Antibiotics

Antibiotics are chemical agents that are produced by microorganisms. Their useful action is primarily a result of their interfering with the necessary metabolic processes of pathogenic microorganisms. In sports antibiotics are used by the physician as either topical dressings or systemic medications. The indiscriminate use of antibiotics can produce extreme hypersensitivity or idiosyncrasies and can prevent the development of natural immunity or resistance to subsequent infections. The use of any antibiotic must be carefully controlled by the physician, who selects the drug on the basis of the most desirable type of administration and the least amount of toxicity to the patient.

Antibiotics include penicillin, bacitracin, tetracycline, erythromycin, sulfonamides, and quinolones.

The antibiotics mentioned here are just a few of the many available. New types continue to be developed, mainly because, over a period of time, microorganisms often become resistant to a particular antibiotic, especially if it is indiscriminately used. Some of the more common antibiotics are penicillin, streptomycin, bacitracin, tetracycline, erythromycin, and the sulfonamides.[4]

Penicillin   Penicillin as a prescription medication is probably the most important of the antibiotics; it is useful in a variety of skin and systemic infections. In general, penicillin interferes with the metabolism of the bacteria.

Bacitracin   Bacitracin has a broad spectrum of effectiveness as an antibacterial agent. Bacitracin plus polymixin (Polysporin) also has a broad spectrum of effectiveness as an antibacterial agent. Adding neomycin to the product (Neosporin) does not increase effectiveness, and some individuals are allergic to neomycin.

Tetracycline   Tetracyclines consist of a wide group of antibiotics that have a broad antibacterial spectrum. Their application, which is usually oral, modifies the infection rather than eradicating it completely.

Erythromycin   Erythromycin is most often used for streptococcal infection and Mycoplasma pneumoniae. It has the same general spectrum as penicillin and is a useful alternative in the penicillin-allergic patient.

Sulfonamides   Sulfonamides are a group of synthetic antibiotics. In general, sulfonamides make pathogens vulnerable to phagocytes by inhibiting certain enzymatic actions.

Quinolones   Quinolones are a relatively new group of antibiotics. They have a broad spectrum of activity. Patients taking these antibiotics must be carefully monitored for adverse effects.

TABLE 17-6 Medications Recommended for the Management of Asthma

Long-Term Control	Quick Relief Medications
Inhaled corticosteroids	Short-acting beta 2 agonists
Beclomethasone (Beclovent, Vanceril)	Albuterol (Proventil, Ventolin)
Fluticasone propionate (Flovent)	Bitolterol mesylate (Tornalate)
Flunisolide (Aero-Bid)	Pirbuterol (Maxair)
Triamcinolone acetonide (Azmacort)	Terbutaline (Brethaire)
Cromolyn (Intal)	Anticholinergics
Nedocromil (Tilade)	Ipratropium bromide (Atrovent)
Long-acting beta 2 agonists	Oral corticosteroids
Salmeterol (Serevent)	Methylprednisolone (Medrol)
Albuterol sustained-release (Proventil Repetabs)	Prednisolone (various generics)
	Prednisone (various generics)
Theophyllin (Theodur, Theolair-SR)	
Leukotriene modifiers	
Zafirlukast (Accolate)	
Zileuton (Zyflo)	

Drugs for Asthma

Asthma is a chronic inflammatory lung disorder that is characterized by obstruction of the airways as a result of complex inflammatory processes, smooth muscle spasm, and hyperresponsiveness to a variety of stimuli.[22] Asthma triggers may include exercise, viral infection, animal exposure, dust mites, mold, air pollutants, weather, and NSAIDs as well as other drugs. The National Asthma Education and Prevention Program (NAEPP) has established international guidelines for the diagnosis and management of asthma.[23,32] The goals of asthma therapy are to prevent chronic and troublesome symptoms, maintain normal lung function and activity levels, prevent asthma exacerbations, provide optimal pharmacotherapy with minimal adverse effects, and meet athletes' expectation of and satisfaction with asthma care.

Exercise-induced bronchospasm (EIB) is a limiting and disruptive experience. Any asthma patient may be subject to EIB. A bronchospastic event caused by loss of heat, water, or both from lungs during exercise or exertion, EIB results from hyperventilation of air that is cooler and dryer than that in the respiratory tract.[2] EIB may occur during or minutes after physical activity, reaches its peak in five to ten minutes after stopping the activity, and usually resolves in twenty to thirty minutes. In some asthma patients, exercise may be the only precipitating factor.

The athlete who has asthma must be monitored carefully. The NAEPP recommends measurements of the following: asthma signs and symptoms, pulmonary function (peak flow or spirometry), quality of life/functional status, history of asthma exacerbations, and pharmacotherapy. Table 17-6 identifies medications recommended in asthma management.

Drugs that Inhibit Pain and Inflammation

Pain Relievers

Controlling pain in an athlete can involve innumerable drugs and procedures, depending on the beliefs of the athletic trainer, coach, or physician. As discussed in Chapter 9, why pain is positively affected by certain methods is not clearly understood; however, some of the possible reasons are as follows:
- The excitatory effect of an individual impulse is depressed.
- An individual impulse is inhibited.

17-2

Critical Thinking Exercise

A field hockey player has a recurrent problem in breathing, especially during high-intensity fitness training. Since the weather has gotten warmer, her symptoms have gotten worse.

? What should the athletic trainer expect is wrong with this athlete, and how should her condition be managed?

Drugs used to inhibit pain or inflammation include counterirritants and local anesthetics, narcotic analgesics, and nonnarcotic analgesics and antipyretics.

- The perceived impulse is decreased.
- Anxiety created by the pain or impending pain is decreased.

Counterirritants and Local Anesthetics

Counterirritants include spray coolants, alcohol, cold, menthol, and local anesthetics.

Analgesics give relief by causing a systemic and topical analgesia. Many chemical reactions on the skin can inhibit pain sensations by rapid evaporation, which causes a cooling action, or by counterirritating the skin. Irritating and counterirritating substances used in sports act as rubefacients (skin reddeners) and skin stimulants, although their popularity has decreased in recent years. Their application causes local increase in blood circulation, redness, and rise in skin temperature. Frequently mild pain can be reduced by a counterirritant, which produces a stimulus to the skin of such intensity that the athlete is no longer aware of the pain. Some examples of counterirritants include liniments, analgesic balms, heat, and cold.

Spray coolants Spray coolants, because of their rapid evaporation, act as topical anesthetics to the skin. Several commercial coolants are presently on the market. Chloromethane is one of the most popular spray coolants currently used in sports. Cooling results so quickly that superficial freezing takes place, inhibiting pain impulses for a short time. Athletic trainers disagree on the effectiveness of spray coolants. Some athletic trainers use them extensively for strains, sprains, and contusions. In most cases, spray coolants are useful only when other analgesics are not available.

Alcohol Alcohol evaporates rapidly when applied to the skin, causing a refreshingly cool effect that gives a temporary analgesia.

Menthol Menthol is an alcohol taken from mint oils and is principally used as a local analgesic, counterirritant, and antiseptic. In sports, menthol is used most often with a petroleum base for treating cold symptoms and in analgesic balms.

Cold Cold applications also immediately act to constrict blood vessels and to numb sensory nerve endings. Applications of ice packs or submersion of a part in ice water may completely anesthetize an area. If extreme cold is used, caution must be taken that tissue damage does not result.

Local anesthetics Local anesthetics are usually injected by the physician in and around injury sites for minor surgical procedures or to alleviate the pain of movement. Lydocaine hydrochloride is used extensively as a local anesthetic.

Narcotic Analgesics

Narcotic analgesics include codeine, propoxyphene hydrochloride, morphine, and meperidine.

Most narcotics used in medicine are derived directly from opium or are synthetic opiates. They depress pain impulses and the individual's respiratory center. The two most often used derivatives are codeine and morphine.

Codeine Codeine resembles morphine in its action but is less potent. Codeine is effective in combination with nonnarcotic analgesics. In small doses it is a cough suppressant found in many cough medicines.

Propoxyphene hydrochloride Propoxyphene hydrochloride (Darvon) is a mild analgesic narcotic that is slightly stronger than aspirin in its pain relief. It is not an antiinflammatory drug. It is addictive, and when combined with alcohol, tranquilizers, or other sedatives or depressants, it can be fatal.

Morphine Morphine depresses pain sensations to a greater extent than any other drug. It is also the most dangerous drug because of its ability to depress respiration and because of its habit-forming qualities. Morphine is never used in the following situations: before a diagnosis has been made by the physician; when the subject is unconscious; when there is a head injury; or when there is a decreased rate of breathing. It is never repeated within two hours.

Meperidine Meperidine (Demerol) is used as a substitute for morphine for the relief of mild or moderate pain and is effective only when given intravenously or intramuscularly.

Nonnarcotic Analgesics and Antipyretics

Nonnarcotic analgesics are those drugs designed to suppress all but the most severe pain, without the patient's losing consciousness. In most cases these drugs also act as antipyretics, regulating the temperature control centers.

Acetaminophen Acetaminophen (Tylenol) is an effective analgesic and antipyretic but has no antiinflammatory activity. Because it does not irritate the gastrointestinal system, it is often a replacement for aspirin in noninflammatory conditions. Overingestion could lead to liver damage. Chronic heavy alcohol users may be at risk for liver damage when taking more than the recommended dose of acetominophen.

Drugs to Reduce Inflammation

Sports physicians have a wide choice of drugs at their disposal for treatment of inflammation. A great variety of OTC drugs also claim to deal effectively with inflammation of the musculoskeletal system. The problem of proper drug selection is tenuous, even for a physician, because new drugs are continually coming to the forefront. The situation is compounded by highly advertised OTC preparations. Any drug selection, especially drugs designed to treat the inflammatory process, must be effective, must be appropriate for the highly physical athlete, and must not create any adverse reactions. These points are addressed by the following discussions of the more generally accepted antiinflammatory drugs.

Acetylsalicylic Acid (Aspirin)

Aspirin is one of the most widely used analgesics, antiinflammatories, and antipyretics. It is also one of the most abused drugs in use today. A number of medications that have salicylates act in reducing pain, fever, and inflammation. Aspirin has been associated with various adverse reactions that are primarily centered in the gastrointestinal region. Those reactions include difficulty in food digestion (dyspepsia), nausea, vomiting, and gastric bleeding.

Overingestion of aspirin can lead to serious side effects. Adverse reactions to aspirin, especially in high doses, are ear ringing or buzzing (tinnitus) and dizziness. A major problem that can arise in individuals under eighteen years of age is Reye's syndrome. The administration of aspirin to a child during chicken pox or influenza can induce Reye's syndrome. Its etiology is unknown.

Severe allergic response resulting in an anaphylactic reaction can occur in individuals who have an intolerance to aspirin. Asthmatic patients may be at greater risk for allergic reactions to aspirin. Aspirin use should be avoided by athletes in contact sports since it prolongs blood clotting time.

Nonsteroidal Antiinflammatory Drugs

Nonsteroidal drugs have antiinflammatory, antipyretic, and analgesic properties. They are strong inhibitors of prostaglandin synthesis and are effective for such chronic problems as rheumatoid arthritis and osteoarthritis.[3] Nonsteroidal antiinflammatory drugs (NSAIDs) are used primarily for reducing the pain, stiffness, swelling, redness, and fever associated with localized inflammation. Their antiinflammatory capabilities are thought to be equal to those of aspirin; their advantages are fewer side effects and relatively longer duration of action. NSAIDs are effective for patients who cannot tolerate aspirin because of gastrointestinal distress associated with aspirin use. Even though NSAIDs have analgesic and antipyretic capabilities, they should not be used in place of aspirin or acetaminophen in cases of mild headache or increased body temperature. However, they can be used to relieve many other mild to moderately painful somatic conditions, such as menstrual cramps and soft-tissue injury. Table 17-7 lists the NSAIDs commonly used in treating athletes.

Nonnarcotic analgesics include acetaminophen.

Antiinflammatories include acetylsalicylic acid (aspirin), NSAIDs, and corticosteroids.

TABLE 17-7 NSAIDs Frequently Used among Athletes

Drug/Trade Name	Dosage Range (mg) and Frequency	Maximum Daily Dose (mg)
Aspirin	325–650 mg every 4 hours	4,000
Voltaren	50–75 mg twice a day	200
Cataflam	50–75 mg twice day	200
Dolobid	500–1,000 mg followed by 250–500 mg 2 to 3 times a day	1,500
Nalfon	300–600 mg 3 to 4 times a day	3,200
Motrin, Rufin	400–800 mg 3 to 4 times a day	3,200
Indocin	5–150 mg a day in 3 to 4 divided doses	200
Orudis	75 mg 3 times a day or 50 mg 4 times a day	300
Ponstel	500 mg followed by 250 mg every 6 hours	1,000
Naprosyn	250–500 mg twice a day	1,250
Anaprox	550 mg followed by 275 mg every 6 to 8 hours	1,375
Feldene	20 mg per day	20
Clinoril	200 mg twice a day	400
Tolectin	400 mg 3 to 4 times a day	1,800
Relafen	1,000 mg once or twice a day	2,000
Ansaid	50–100 mg 2 to 3 times a day	300
Toradol	10 mg every 4 to 6 hours for pain; *Not to be used for more than 5 days*	40
Lodine	200–400 mg every 6 to 8 hours for pain	1,200

Note: Prescription required for all except aspirin.

17-3

Critical Thinking Exercise

A college-age softball player comes into the training room complaining of a headache and asks the athletic trainer to give her some ibuprofin to get rid of her headache.

? Is ibuprofin the most appropriate medication to use in this case?

The NSAIDs can produce adverse reactions and should be used cautiously. Athletes who have aspirin allergy triad of nasal polyps, associated bronchospasm or asthma, and history of anaphylaxis should not receive any NSAID. The NSAIDs can cause gastrointestinal tract reactions, headache, dizziness, depression, tinnitus, and a variety of other systemic reactions. Taking ibuprofen with heavy alcohol use may increase the risk of stomach bleeding.

Corticosteroids

Corticosteroids, of which cortisone is the most common, are used primarily for chronic inflammation of musculoskeletal and joint regions. Cortisone is a synthetic glucocorticoid that is usually given orally or by injection. More caution is taken in the use of corticosteroids than was practiced in the past. Prolonged use of corticosteroids can produce the following serious complications:

- Fluid and electrolyte disturbances (e.g., water retention caused by excess sodium levels)
- Musculoskeletal and joint impairments (e.g., bone thinning and muscle and tendon weakness)
- Dermatological problems (e.g., delayed wound healing)
- Neurological impairments (e.g., vertigo, headache, convulsions)
- Endocrine dysfunctions (e.g., menstrual irregularities)
- Ophthalmic conditions (e.g., glaucoma)
- Metabolic impairments (e.g., negative nitrogen balance, muscle wasting)

Cortisone is primarily administered by injection. Other methods of administration are iontophoresis and phonophoresis (see Chapter 15). Studies have indicated that cortisone injected directly into tendons, ligaments, and joint spaces can lead to weakness and degeneration. Strenuous activity may predispose the treated part to rupturing. Tennis elbow and plantar fasciitis have benefited from corticosteroid treatment.

Drugs that Produce Skeletal Muscle Relaxation

Drugs that produce skeletal muscle relaxation include methocarbamol (Robaxin), and carisoprodol (Soma). There is growing speculation among physicians that, because centrally acting muscle relaxants also act as sedatives or tranquilizers on the higher brain centers, these drugs are less specific to muscle relaxation than was once believed. Another major side effect is that they cause drowsiness.

Muscle spasm and guarding accompany many musculoskeletal injuries. Elimination of spasm and guarding should facilitate programs of rehabilitation. In many situations, centrally acting oral muscle relaxants are used to reduce spasm and guarding. However, to date the efficacy of using muscle relaxants has not been substantiated, and they do not appear to be superior to analgesics or sedatives in either acute or chronic conditions.

Drugs Used to Treat Gastrointestinal Disorders

Disorders of the gastrointestinal tract include upset stomach or formation of gas because of food incompatibilities and acute or chronic hyperacidity, which leads to inflammation of the mucous membrane of the intestinal tract. Poor eating habits may lead to digestive tract problems such as diarrhea or constipation. Drugs that elicit responses within the gastrointestinal tract include antacids, antiemetics, carminatives, cathartics and laxatives, antidiarrheals, and histamine-2 blockers.

> Drugs used to treat gastrointestinal disorders include antacids, antiemetics, carminatives, cathartics or laxatives, histamine-2 blockers, and antidiarrheals.

Antacids

The primary function of an antacid is to neutralize acidity in the upper gastrointestinal tract by raising the pH and inhibiting the activity of the digestive enzyme pepsin, thus reducing its action on the gastric mucosal nerve endings. Antacids are effective not only for relief of acid indigestion and heartburn but also in the treatment of peptic ulcer. Antacids available in the market possess a wide range of acid-neutralizing capabilities and side effects.

One of the most commonly used antacid preparations is sodium bicarbonate, or baking soda. Other antacids include alkaline salts, which again neutralize hyperacidity but are not easily absorbed in the blood. Ingestion of antacids containing magnesium tends to have a laxative effect. Those containing aluminum or calcium seem to cause constipation. Consequently, many antacid liquids or tablets are combinations of magnesium and either aluminum or calcium hydroxides. Overuse can cause electrolyte imbalance and other adverse effects.

Antiemetics

Antiemetics are used to treat the nausea and vomiting that may result from a variety of causes. Antiemetics act either locally or centrally. The locally acting drugs, such as most OTC medications (e.g., Pepto-Bismol), reportedly work by affecting the mucosal lining of the stomach. However, their effects of soothing an upset stomach may be more of a placebo effect. The centrally acting drugs affect the brain by making it less sensitive to irritating nerve impulses from the inner ear or stomach. A variety of prescription antiemetics can be used for controlling nausea and vomiting, including phenothiazines (Phenegran), antihistamines, anticholinergic drugs for preventing motion sickness, and sedative drugs. The primary side effect of these medications is drowsiness.

Carminatives

Carminatives are drugs that give relief from flatulence (gas). Their action on the digestive canal is to inhibit gas formation and aid in its expulsion. Simethicone is the most commonly used carminative.

Cathartics (Laxatives)

The use of laxatives in sports should always be under the direction of a physician. Constipation may be symptomatic of a serious disease condition. Indiscriminant use of laxatives may render the athlete unable to have normal bowel movements. It may also lead to electrolyte imbalance. There is little need for healthy, active individuals to rely on artificial means for stool evacuation.

Antidiarrheals

Diarrhea may result from many causes, but it is generally considered to be a symptom rather than a disease. It can occur as a result of emotional stress, allergies to food or drugs, adverse drug reactions, or many different types of intestinal problems. Diarrhea may be acute or chronic. Acute diarrhea, the most common, comes on suddenly and may be accompanied by nausea, vomiting, chills, and intense abdominal pain. It typically runs its course rapidly, and symptoms subside once the irritating agent is removed from the system. Chronic diarrhea, which may last for weeks, may result from more serious disease states.

Medications used for control of diarrhea are either locally acting or systemic. The locally acting medications most typically contain kaolin, which absorbs other chemicals, and pectin, which soothes irritated bowel. Some contain substances that add bulk to the stool. The systemic agents, which are generally antiperistaltic or antispasmodic medications, are considered to be much more effective in relieving symptoms of diarrhea, but most, except loperamide (Imodium AD), are prescription drugs. The systemic medications are either opiate derivatives or anticholinergic agents, both of which reduce peristalsis. Common side effects of the systemic antidiarrheals include drowsiness, nausea, dry mouth, and constipation. It is not advisable to treat antibiotic-induced diarrhea because diarrhea may be a protective symptom in antibiotic-induced pseudomembranous colitis.

Histamine-2 Blockers

Histamine-2 blockers (H_2 blockers) reduce stomach acid output by blocking the action of histamine on certain cells in the stomach. They are used to treat peptic and gastric ulcers and other gastrointestinal hypersecretory conditions. Cimetidine (Tagamet) and ranitidine (Zantac) are examples.

Drugs Used to Treat Colds and Allergies

Drugs on the market designed to affect colds and allergies are almost too numerous to count. In general, they fall into three categories, all of which deal with the symptoms of the condition and not the cause. Those categories are drugs that deal with nasal congestion, with histamine reactions, and with cough.

Nasal Decongestants

Topical nasal decongestants that contain mild vasoconstricting agents, such as oxymetazoline (Afrin) and xylometazoline (Otivin), are on the market. These agents are relatively safe. However, prolonged use can cause rebound congestion and dependency.

An effective oral decongestant is psuedoephedrine hydrochloride (Sudafed). Repeated dosing does not lead to rebound congestion.

Antihistamines

Antihistamines are often added to nasal decongestants. Histamine is a protein substance contained in animal tissues that, when released into the general circulation, causes the reactions of an allergy. Histamine causes dilation of arteries and capillaries, skin flushing, and a rise in temperature. An antihistamine is a substance that opposes histamine action. Antihistamines offer little benefit in treating the common

---

Drugs used to treat colds and allergies include nasal decongestants, antihistamines, cough suppressants, and sympathomimetics.

cold. They are beneficial in allergies. Examples are terfenadine (Seldane), diphenhydramine hydrochloride (Benadryl), and chlorpheniramine (Chlor-Trimeton).

Antihistamines, as well as decongestants and diuretics, can decrease the peripheral mechanisms of sweating that impair the body's ability to dissipate heat and thus predispose the athlete to heat-related illness.

Cough Medicines

Cough medicines either suppress the cough (antitussives) or increase the production of fluid in the respiratory system (expectorants). Antitussives are available in liquid, capsule, troche, or spray form. Narcotic antitussives contain codeine (Robitussin AC); nonnarcotic antitussives contain diphenhydramine (Benylin Cough Syrup), dextromethorphan (Benylin DM, Sucrets), or benzonatate (Tessalon). The advantage of nonnarcotic antitussives is that they have few side effects and are not addictive. There is little evidence that expectorants (guaifenesin) are any more effective in the control of coughing than is simply drinking water.

Sympathomimetics

Exercise-induced bronchospasm (EIB) involves spasm of smooth muscle in the bronchioles and shortness of breath. Drugs used to treat EIB are called sympathomimetics. An example is albuterol (Proventil, Ventolin). Bronchodilators generally reverse the symptoms. Sympathomimetics may cause heat-related problems if used in a hot environment.

Epinepherine In some states, the athletic trainer may receive instructions and certification for the administration of epinepherine via an injective device (Epipen) to treat anaphylaxis resulting from insect stings. Once it is clear that an athlete is having an anaphylactic reaction, the Epipen can be used to safely and easily inject medication into the thigh.

Drugs Used to Control Bleeding

Various drugs and medicines cause selective actions on the circulatory system, including vasoconstrictors and anticoagulants.

Drugs used to control bleeding include vasoconstrictors, hemostatic agents, and anticoagulants.

Vasoconstrictors

In sports, vasoconstrictors are most often administered externally to sites of profuse bleeding. The drug most commonly used for this purpose is epinephrine (adrenaline), which is applied directly to a hemorrhaging area. It acts immediately to constrict damaged blood vessels and is extremely valuable in cases of epistaxis (nosebleed) in which normal procedures are inadequate.

Hemostatic Agents

Drugs that immediately inhibit bleeding are currently being investigated. Hemostatic agents such as thrombin may prove to be useful; however, specific drug recommendations are not available at this time.

Anticoagulants

The most common anticoagulants used by physicians in sports are heparin and coumarin derivatives. Heparin prolongs the clotting time of blood but will not dissolve a clot once it has developed. Heparin is used primarily to control extension of a thrombus that is already present. Coumarin derivatives act by suppressing the formation of prothrombin in the liver. Given orally, they are used to slow clotting time in certain vascular disorders.

PROTOCOLS FOR USING OVER-THE-COUNTER MEDICATIONS

In most cases, the athletic trainer will be concerned only with nonprescription medications. A nonprescription drug is also called an over-the-counter drug; it can be bought without a prescription.

There is a major difference between prescription and nonprescription drugs. Drugs that require a prescription may pose a greater risk to the patient and therefore require the clinical skills and judgment of individuals trained to prescribe drugs.

Focus Box: "Protocols for athletic trainers for the use of over-the-counter drugs" presents guidelines for treating a number of minor illnesses or conditions seen frequently in the athletic population. The authors and publisher have exerted every effort to ensure that drug selection and dosage set forth in this text are in accord with current recommendations and practice at the time of publication. However, in view of ongoing research, changes in government regulations, and the constant flow of information relating to drug therapy and drug reactions, the reader is urged to check the package insert for each drug for any change in indications and dosage and for added warnings and precautions. Reading the package insert is especially important when the recommended agent is a new or infrequently employed drug.

SUBSTANCE ABUSE AMONG ATHLETES

Perhaps no other topic related to pharmacology has received more attention from the media during recent years than the use and abuse of drugs by athletes. Much has been written regarding the use of performance-enhancing drugs among Olympic athletes and the widespread use of street drugs by collegiate and professional athletes. Clearly, substance abuse has no place in the athletic population.[3]

Although much of the information being disseminated to the public by the media may be based on hearsay and innuendo, the use and abuse of many different types of drugs can have a profound impact on athletic performance. To say that many experts in the field of sports medicine regard drug abuse among athletes with growing concern is a gross understatement. The athletic trainer must be knowledgeable about substance abuse in the athletic population and should be able to recognize signs that may indicate when an athlete is engaging in substance abuse (see *Focus Box:* "Identifying the substance abuser").

Performance-Enhancing Substances (Ergogenic Aids)

Common ergogenic aids include stimulants, beta blockers, narcotic analgesics, diuretics, anabolic steroids, human growth hormone, and blood doping.

Ergogenic aid is a term used to describe any method, legal or illegal, used to enhance athletic performance.[38] Athletic trainers should have a primary concern about the use of various pharmacological agents by athletes for enhancing performance.

Stimulants

The intention of the athlete when he or she ingests a stimulant may be to increase alertness, reduce fatigue, or in some instances, increase competitiveness and even hostility.[14] Some athletes respond to stimulants with a loss of judgment that may lead to personal injury or injury to others.

Two major categories of stimulants are psychomotor-stimulant drugs and adrenergic (sympathomimetic) drugs. Psychomotor stimulants are of two general types: amphetamines (e.g., methamphetamine) and nonamphetamines (e.g., methylphenidate and cocaine). The major actions of psychomotor stimulants result from the rapid turnover of catecholamines, which have a strong effect on the nervous and cardiovascular systems, metabolic rates, temperature, and smooth muscle.

Sympathomimetic drugs act directly on adrenergic receptors, or those that release catecholamines (i.e., epinephrine and norepinephrine) from nerve endings, and thus act indirectly on catecholamines. Ephedrine is an example of this type of drug and can, in high doses, cause mental stimulation and increased blood flow. As a result, it may also cause elevated blood pressure and headache, increased and irregular heartbeat, anxiety, and tremor.

Amphetamines and cocaine are the psychomotor drugs most commonly used in sports. Cocaine is discussed in the section on recreational drug abuse in this chapter. Sympathomimetic drugs present an extremely difficult problem in sports medicine because they are commonly found in cold remedies.[14] The U.S. Olympic Committee

Focus

Protocols for the use of over-the-counter drugs for athletic trainers

The athletic trainer is often responsible for initial screening of athletes who have various illnesses or injuries. Frequently, the athletic trainer must make decisions regarding the appropriate use of over-the-counter medications for their athletes. Subjective findings such as onset, duration, medication taken, and known allergies must be included in the screening evaluation.

The following protocols should be viewed as guidelines to the disposition of the athelete. The protocols are aimed at clarifying the use of over-the-counter drugs in the treatment of common problems encountered by the athletic trainer while covering or traveling with a particular team. These guidelines do not cover every situation the athletic trainer encounters in assessing and managing the athlete's physical problems. Therefore, physician consultation is recommended wherever there is uncertainty in making a decision regarding the appropriate care of the athlete.

Existing Illness or Injury	Appropriate Treatment Protocol
Temperature	
Greater than or equal to 102° F orally	Consult physician ASAP.
Less than 102° F but more than 99.5° F orally	Patient may be given acetaminophen. See Acetaminophen Administration.
	Limit exercise of athlete. Do not allow participation in practice.
	If fever decreases to less than 99.5° the athlete may participate in practice.
	If athlete is to be involved in an intercollegiate event, consult with a physician concerning participation.
Less than or equal to 99.5° F orally	Follow management guidelines for fever less than 102° but allow athlete to practice and/or compete.
Throat	

History
    Sore throat
    No fever
    No chills
	Advise Saline Gargles (¹/₂ tsp. salt in a glass of warm water). Patient may also be given Cepastat®/Chloraseptic® throat lozenges. Before administering determine: Is the patient allergic to Cepastat®/Chloraseptic® (phenol containing) lozenges? If yes, do not administer.

Sore throat Fever	Determine temperature. If fever, manage as outlined in temperature protocol and consult physician ASAP.
Sore throat and/or fever and/or swollen glands	Consult physician ASAP.
Nose	
Watery discharge	Patient may be given Pseudoephedrine (Sudafed®) tablets. See Pseudoephedrine Administration Protocol.
Nasal congestion	Patient may be given Oxymetazoline HCl (Afrin®) nasal spray. See Oxymetazoline Administration Protocol.
Chest	

Cough
    Dry hacking or
    Clear mucoid
        sputum
	You may administer Robitussin DMR® (generic guaifenesin with dextromethorphan). Before administering determine: Is the patient going to be involved in practice or game within 4 hours from administration of medication? If yes, do not give Robitussin DM®.
	If indicated, you may administer one dose, 10 ml. (2 teaspoonfuls). Inform the patient that drowsiness may occur. Repeat doses may be administered every 6 hours. Push fluids, encourage patient to drink as much as possible.

Continued

Protocols for the use of over-the-counter drugs for athletic trainers—cont'd

Chest—cont'd

Green or rusty sputum | Consult physician ASAP.
Severe, persistent cough | Consult physician ASAP.

Ears

Discomfort due to ears popping | Patient may be given Pseudoephedrine (Sudafed®) tablets and/or Oxymetazoline HCl (Afrin®) nasal spray. *See Pseudoephedrine Admnistration Protocol and/or Oxymetazoline Protocol.*

Earache (or external otitis) | Patient may be given Acetaminophen. Consult physician ASAP. *See Acetaminophen Administration Protocol.*

Recurrent earache | Consult physician ASAP.

Prevention of Motion Sickness

Complaint: History of nausea, dizziness, and/or vomiting associated with travel | Patient may be given dimenhydrinate (Dramamine®) or diphenhydramine (Benadryl®). Before administering, determine:

Is the patient sensitive or allergic to Dramamine®, Benadryl® or any other antihistamine? If yes, do not administer.

Has the patient taken any other antihistamines (e.g. Actifed®, Chlor-Trimeton®, various cold medications) or other medications that cause sedation, within the last 6 hours? If yes, do not administer.

Does the patient have asthma, glaucoma, or enlargement of the prostate gland? If yes, do not administer.

Is the patient going to be involved in practice or game within 4 hours from administration of medication? If yes, do not administer.

Administer Dramamine® or Benadryl® dose based on body weight, 30 to 60 minutes before departure time: Under 125 lbs: one Dramamine® 50 mg tablet. Over 125 lbs: two Dramamine 50 mg tablets

Benadryl® dose: Under 125 lbs: one 25 mg capsule. Over 125 lbs: two 25 mg capsules.

Inform the patient that drowsiness may occur for 4–6 hours after taking this medication. Avoid alcoholic beverages. Avoid driving for 6 hours after taking. If travelling time is extended, another dose may be administered 6 hours after the first dose.

Nausea, Vomiting

Prolonged and severe | Consult physician ASAP.

Nausea, Gastric Upset, Heart-Burn, Butterflies in the Stomach, Acid Indigestion

Associated with dietary indiscretion or tension | You may administer an antacid as a single dose, as defined by label of particular antacid (e.g. Riopan®, Gelusil®, Maalox®, Pepto Bismol®, Titralac®), or a histamine (H2) antagonist (Pepcid AC®Tagamet HB®, Axid A®, Zantac 75®). *See histamine H2 antagonist protocol Pepto Bismol® Warning: Contains salicylates. Do not give to children or teenagers who have or are recovering from chicken pox or flu because of the risk of Reye syndrome. Do not use this product with aspirin.*

Continued

Focus

Protocols for the use of over-the-counter drugs for athletic trainers—cont'd

Nausea, Gastric Upset, Heart-Burn, Butterflies in the Stomach, Acid Indigestion—cont'd

Associated with abdominal or chest pain	Consult physician ASAP.
Vomiting, nausea—no severe distress	Monitor symptoms. Patient may be given dimenhydrinate (Dramamine®) or diphenhydramine (Benadryl®) orally. Same as instructions and precautions under motion sickness.
Vomiting: projectile, coffee ground, febrile	Consult physician ASAP.

Diarrhea

Associated with abdominal pain or tenderness and/or dehydration, bloody stools, febrile, recurrent diarrhea	Consult physician ASAP.
Frequent loose stools not associated with any of the above signs or symptoms	Encourage clear liquid diet. Encourage avoidance of dairy products and high fat foods for 24 hours. (BART diet—bananas, apples, rice, toast). If it persists consult physician ASAP. Patient may be given loperamide (Immodium A-D ®). Before administering, determine: How long has patient had diarrhea? If longer than 24 hours, see physician. You may administer one dose (2 caplets) of loperamide (Immodium A-D® 2 mg per caplet). One caplet may be administered after each loose stool not to exceed 8 mg (4 caplets) per 24 hours. Inform the patient that dizziness or drowsiness may occur within 12 hours after taking this medication. Avoid alcoholic beverages. Use caution while driving or performing tasks requiring alertness.

Constipation

Prolonged or severe abdominal pain or tenderness, nausea or vomiting	Consult physician ASAP.
Discomfort associated with dietary change or decreased fluid intake	You may administer milk of magnesia 30 ml as a single dose. Before administering determine: Does the patient have chronic renal disease? If yes, do not administer. Recommend increased fluid intake, increased intake of fruits, bulk vegetables or cereals.

Headache

Pain associated with elevated BP, temperature elevation, blurred vision, nausea, vomiting, or history of migraine	Consult physician ASAP.
Pain across forehead (Mild headache)	Patient may be given Acetaminophen or Patient may be given NSAID. *See Acetaminophen Adminstration or NSAID Administration Protocols.*

Continued

Focus

Protocols for the use of over-the-counter drugs for athletic trainers—cont'd

Headache—cont'd

Tension headache, occipita pain
: Patient may be given Acetaminophen. *See Acetaminophen Administration Protocol.*

Pain in antrum or forehead associated with sinus or nasal congestion
: Patient may be given Pseudoephedrine (Sudafed®) tablets and Acetaminophen. *See protocols for Pseudoephedrine and Acetaminophen Administration.*

Musculoskeletal Injuries

Deformity
: Consult physician ASAP.

Localized pain and tenderness, impaired range of motion
: First aid to part as soon as possible:
  Ice
  Compression—Ace bandage
  Elevation
  Protection—crutches or sling and/or splint

Pain with swelling discoloration, no impaired movement or localized tenderness
: If this injury interferes with the patient's normal activities, consult a physician within 24 hours.
  Patient may be given Acetaminophen or NSAID. *See Acetaminophen Administration or NSAID Administration Protocols.*

Skin

Localized or generalized rash accompanied by elevated temperature, enlarged lymph nodes, sore throat, stiff neck, infected skin lesion, dyspnea, wheezing
: Consult physician ASAP.

Mild, localized, nonvesicular skin eruptions accompanied by pruritis
: Hydrocortisone 1.0% cream may be applied.
  Before administering, determine:
    Is the patient taking any medication? If yes, do not administer. Refer to physician.
    Are eyes or any large area of the body involved? If yes, do not administer. Refer to physician.
    Is there any evidence of lice infestation?
    The cream may be repeated every 6 hours if needed. Do not use more than 3 times daily.

Abrasions
: Control bleeding. Clean with antibacterial soap and water. Apply appropriate dressing and antibiotic ointment. Monitor for signs of infection. Dressing may be changed 2–3 times a day if needed.

Localized erythema due to ultraviolet rays
: Advise application of compresses soaked in a solution of cold water.

Continued

Protocols for the use of over-the-counter drugs for athletic trainers—cont'd

Skin—cont'd

Jock itch or athlete's foot	Advise 10–15 minute application of compresses soaked in cool water to relieve intense itching. Patient may be given miconazole (Micatin®) cream topically. Before administering determine: Is the patient sensitive or allergic to miconazole? If yes, do not administer. Consult physician ASAP. Is the patient receiving other types of treatment for rash in same area? If yes, do not administer. Consult physician ASAP. Instruct patient to wash and dry area of rash, and then apply $^1/_4$–$^1/_2$ inch ribbon of cream. Give patient the cream on a clean gauze pad and rub gently on the infected area. Spread evenly and thinly over rash. The dose may be repeated in 8–12 hours (twice a day). Consult physician within 24 hours.

Skin Wounds

Lacerations	Control bleeding. Cleanse area with antibacterial soap and water. Apply steristrips. Consult physician immediately if there is any question about the necessity for suturing.
Extensive lacerations or other severe skin wounds	Control bleeding. Protect area with dressing. Refer to physician immediately.

Wound Infection

Febrile, marked cellulitis, red streaks, tender or enlarged nodes	Consult physician ASAP.
Localized inflammation, afebrile, absence of nodes and streaks	Warm soaks to affected area. Consult physician ASAP.

Burns

1st degree erythema of skin, limited area	Apply cold compresses to affected area. Dressing is not necessary on 1st degree burns. If less than 45 minutes have elapsed since burn injury, clean gently with soap and water. Patient may be given acetaminophen. *See Acetaminophen Administration Protocol.*
1st degree with extensive involvement over body	Consult physician ASAP.
2nd degree erythema with blistering	Consult physician ASAP.
3rd degree pearly white appearance of affected area, no pain	Consult physician ASAP.

Continued

Focus

Protocols for the use of over-the-counter drugs for athletic trainers—cont'd

Allergies

Athlete with known seasonal allergies who forgot to bring own medication	Patient may be given 4 mg tablet of chlorpheniramine (Chlor-Trimeton®). Before administering determine: Is the patient sensitive to chlorpheniramine? If yes, do not administer. Consult physician ASAP. Does the patient have urinary retention, or glaucoma? If yes, do not administer. Consult physician ASAP. Is patient going to be involved in training or game within four hours from administration of medication? If yes, do not administer. Consult physician ASAP. Has the patient taken any other antihistamines (e.g. Actifed®, Dramamine®, various cold medications) or other medications that cause drowsiness within the last 6 hours? If yes, do not administer. Consult physician ASAP. You may administer 1 dose of chlorpheniramine (4 mg, $^{1}/_{2}$ or 1 tablet). Repeat doses may be administered every 6 hours. Inform the patient that drowsiness may occur for 4–6 hours after taking this medication. Avoid alcoholic beverages. Avoid driving or operation of machinery for 6 hours after taking. Contact physician if symptoms do not abate.

Contact Lens Care

Note: There are 3 types of contact lenses: hard, gas permeable, soft

Solutions are labeled for use with a particular type of lens and should not be used for any other type of lens.

Do not use solutions preserved with thimersol or chlorhexidine because of possible allergy or irritation.

Lens needs rinsing/wetting before insertion	Hard lens: use all purpose wetting/soaking solution (e.g., Wet-N-Soak®). Gas permeable lens: use all purpose wetting/soaking solution (e.g., Wet-N-Soak®). Soft lens: use rinsing/soaking solution (e.g., Soft Mate ps®).
Lens needs soaking/storage	Hard lens: use all purpose wetting/soaking solution (e.g., Wet-N-Soak®). Gas permeable lens: use all purpose wetting/soaking solution (e.g., Wet-N-Soak®). Soft lens: use rinsing/soaking solution (e.g., Soft Mate ps®).
Lens needs cleaning	Hard lens: use cleaning solution (e.g., EasyClean®). Gas permeable lens: use cleaning solution (e.g., Easy Clean®). Soft lens: use cleaning solution (e.g., Lens Plus Daily Cleaner®).

Eye Care

Foreign body—minor: sand, eyelash etc.	Use eye wash irrigation solution (Dacriose®).
Irritation—minor	Use artificial tears. Do not use with contact lens in eye.
Severe irritation, foreign body not easily removed, trauma	Consult physician ASAP.

Continued

Focus

Protocols for the use of over-the-counter drugs for athletic trainers—cont'd

Administration protocols for common over-the-counter drugs used in sports medicine

Acetaminophen protocol (Tylenol®)

Before *administering,* determine:

Is the patient allergic to acetominophen? If yes, do not give acetaminophen.

You may *administer* Acetaminophen 325 mg, two tablets. Repeat doses may be *administered* every 4 hours if needed. If *dispensing* occurs, use labeled 2/pack only. Patient instructions must accompany *dispensing.*

Pseudoephedrine protocol (Sudafed®)

Before *administering,* determine:

Is the patient allergic or sensitive to pseudoephedrine? If yes, do not give pseudo-ephedrine.

Does the patient have high blood pressure, heart disease, diabetes, urinary reten-tion, glaucoma or thyroid disease? If yes, do not give pseudoephedrine.

Does the patient have problems with sweating? If yes, do not give pseudoephedrine.

Do not administer 4 hours before practice or game.

Do not administer if patient is involved in post season play.

You may *administer* pseudoephedrine (Sudafed®) 30 mg, two tablets. Repeat doses may be *administered* every 6 hours up to 4 times a day. If *dispensing* occurs use labeled 2/pack only. Patient instructions must accompany *dispensing.*

Oxymetazoline protocol (Afrin®)

Before *administering,* determine:

Is the patient allergic or sensitive to Afrin® or Otrivin®? If yes, do not administer.

Does the patient react unusually to nose sprays or drops? If yes, do not administer.

You may *administer* 2–3 sprays of Oxymetazoline (Afrin®) 0.05% nasal spray into each nostril. Repeat doses may be administered every 12 hours. (The container can be marked with the patient's name and maintained by the trainer for repeat administra-tion or *dispensed* to the patient. Patient instructions must accompany *dispensing.*

Do not use the same container for different patients.

Do not use for more than three days without MD supervision.

Use small package sizes to reduce risk of overuse/rebound congestion.

NSAID Protocol (ibuprofen: Advil®, naproxen sodium: Aleve®, ketoprofen: Orudis KT®, Actron®)

Before *administering,* determine:

Is the patient allergic to aspirin, e.g. asthma, swelling, shock or hives associated with aspirin use?* *If yes, do not give ibuprofen because even though ibuprofen con-tains no aspirin or saliculates, cross reactions may occur in patients allergic to aspirin.

Does the patient have renal disease or gastrointestinal ulcerations?* *If yes, do not administer ibuprofen.

You may *administer* ibuprofen 200 mg (Advil®) one or two tablets. Repeat doses may be *administered* every 6 hours if needed. Do not exceed 6 tablets in a 24 hour pe-riod without consulting an MD. Do not administer if patient is less than 12 years of age.

or

You may *administer* naproxen sodium 220 mg (Aleve®) one tablet every 8 to 12 hours or two tablets to start followed by 1 tablet 12 hours later. Do not exceed 3 tablets in a 24 hour period without consulting a physician. Do not administer if patient is less than 12 years of age.

or

Continued

Focus

Protocols for the use of over-the-counter drugs for athletic trainers—cont'd

NSAID Protocol (ibuprofen: Advil® , naproxen sodium: Aleve® , ketoprofen: Orudis KT® , Actron®)—cont'd

You may *administer* ketoprofen 12.5 mg (Orutis KT®, Actron®) one tablet or caplet every 4 to 6 hours if needed. If pain or fever persists after one hour, one more 12.5 mg tablet or caplet may be given. Do not exceed 6 tablets or caplets in a 24 hour period without consulting a physician. Do not administer if the patient is less than 16 years of age.

The patient should take the NSAID with a full glass of water and food if occasional and mild heartburn, upset stomach or mild stomach pain occurs. Consult MD if these symptoms are more than mild or persist. Discontinue drug if patient experiences skin rash, itching, dark, tarry stools, visual disturbances, dark urine or persistent headache. Instruct patient to avoid concurrent aspirin or alcoholic beverages.

Histamine H$_2$ Antagonist Protocol (ranitidine: Zantac 75®, nizatidine: Axid AR®, famotidine: Pepsid AC®, cimetidine: Tagamet-HB®)

Before *administering*, determine:

Is the patient less than 12 years of age? If yes, do not give H$_2$ antagonist.

Does the patient have difficulty swallowing or persistent abdominal pain? If yes, do not give H$_2$ antagonist.

You may *administer* ranitidine (Zantac 75®) one 5 mg tablet with water up to two times a day. Do not administer more than 2 tablets in a 24 hour period.

or

You may *administer* nizatidine (Axid AR®) one 75 mg tablet with water up to two times a day. Do not administer more that two tablets in a 24 hour period.

or

You may *administer* famotidine (Pepsid AC®) one 10 mg tablet with water up to two times a day. Do not administer more than 2 tablets in a 24 hour period.

or

You may *administer* cimetidine (Tagamet-HB®) one 10 mg tablet with water up to two times a day. Do not administer more than two tablets in a 24 hour period. Do not administer cimetidine if the patient is taking phenytoin (Dilantin®) or theophyllin (Theodur®).

(USOC) has approved some substances to be used by asthmatics who develop exercise-induced bronchospasms. These substances are selective B$_2$ agonists and consist of albuterol (Proventil), salbutamol (Serevent), and terbutaline (in its aerosol form). Before an athlete engages in Olympic competition, his or her team physician must notify the USOC Medical Subcommission in writing about the athlete's use of these drugs.[14]

Amphetamines   Amphetamines are synthetic alkaloids that are extremely powerful and dangerous drugs. They may be injected, inhaled, or taken as tablets. Amphetamines are among the most abused of those drugs used for the goal of enhancing sports performance. In ordinary doses, amphetamines can produce euphoria, with an increased sense of well-being and heightened mental activity, until fatigue sets in (from lack of sleep), accompanied by nervousness, insomnia, and anorexia. In high doses, amphetamines reduce mental activity and impair performance of complicated motor skills. The athlete's behavior may become irrational. The chronic user may be "hung up," that is, stuck in a repetitive behavioral sequence. This perseveration may last for hours and become increasingly more irrational. The long-term or

Identifying the substance abuser

The following are signs of drug abuse:
Sudden personality changes
Severe mood swings
Changing peer groups
Decreased interest in extracurricular and leisure activities
Worsening grades
Disregard for household chores and curfews
Feeling of depression most of the time
Breakdown in personal hygiene habits
Increased sleep and decreased eating
Smell of alcohol or marijuana on clothes and skin
Sudden weight loss
Lying, cheating, stealing
Arrests for drunk driving or for possessing illegal substances
Truancies from school
Frequent loss of change of jobs
Defensiveness at the mention of drugs or alcohol
Increased isolation (spends time in room)
Deteriorating family relationship
Drug paraphernalia (needles, empty bottles, etc.)
Observations by others about negative behavior
Signs of intoxication
Missed appointments
Falling asleep in class or at work
Financial problems
Missed assignments or deadlines
Diminished productivity

even short-term use of amphetamines can lead to amphetamine psychosis, manifested by auditory and visual hallucinations and paranoid delusions. Physiologically, high doses of amphetamines can cause mydriasis (abnormal pupillary dilation), increased blood pressure, hyperreflexia (increased reflex action), and hyperthermia.

Athletes believe that amphetamines improve sports performance by promoting quickness and endurance, delaying fatigue, and increasing confidence, thereby causing increased aggressiveness. Studies indicate that there is no improvement in performance but there is an increased risk of injury, exhaustion, and circulatory collapse.[10]

Caffeine   Caffeine is found in coffee, tea, cocoa, and cola and is readily absorbed into the body (Table 17-8).[26] Caffeine is a central nervous system stimulant and diuretic and also stimulates gastric secretion. One cup of coffee can contain from 100 to 150 milligrams of caffeine. In moderation, caffeine causes stimulation of the cerebral cortex and medullar centers, resulting in wakefulness and mental alertness. In larger amounts and in individuals who ingest caffeine daily, it raises blood pressure, decreases and then increases the heart rate, and increases plasma levels of epinephrine, norepinephrine, and renin. It affects coordination, sleep, mood, behavior, and thinking processes.[26]

In terms of exercise and sports performance, caffeine is controversial. Like amphetamines, caffeine can affect some athletes by acting as an ergogenic aid during prolonged exercise. The USOC considers caffeine a stimulant if the concentration in the athlete's urine exceeds 12 micrograms per milliliter. Some adverse effects of

TABLE 17-8 Examples of Caffeine-Containing Products

Product	Dose
Coffee (1 cup)	100.0 mg
Diet Coke (12 oz)	45.6 mg
Diet Pepsi (12 oz)	36.0 mg
No-Doz (1)	100.0 mg
Anacin (1)	32.0 mg
Excedrin (1)	65.0 mg
Midol (1)	32.4 mg
Jolt (12 oz)	200.0 mg
Mountain Dew (12 oz)	54.0 mg

caffeine ingestion are tremors, nervousness, headaches, diuresis, arrhythmias, restlessness, hyperactivity, irritability, dry mouth, tinnitus, ocular dyskinesia, scotomata, insomnia, and depression.[10] A habitual user of caffeine who suddenly stops may experience withdrawal, including headache, drowsiness, lethargy, rhinorrhea, irritability, nervousness, depression, and loss of interest in work. Caffeine also acts as a diuretic when hydration may be important.[26]

Narcotic Analgesic Drugs

Narcotic analgesic drugs are derived directly from opium or are synthetic opiates. Morphine and codeine (methylmorphine) are examples of substances made from the alkaloid of opium. Narcotic analgesics are used for the management of moderate to severe pain. Users risk physical and psychological dependency as well as many other problems stemming from the use of narcotics. It is believed that slight to moderate pain can be effectively controlled by drugs other than narcotics.

Beta Blockers

The *beta* in beta blockers refers to the type of sympathetic nerve ending receptor that is blocked.[13] Medically, beta blockers are used primarily for hypertension and heart disease. Beta blockers have been used in sports that require steadiness, such as marksmanship, sailing, archery, fencing, ski jumping, and luge.[13] Beta blockers are one class of adrenergic agents that inhibit the action of catecholamines released from sympathetic nerve endings. Beta blockers produce relaxation of blood vessels. This relaxation in turn slows heart rate and decreases contractility of heart muscle, thus decreasing cardiac output.

Diuretics

Diuretic drugs increase kidney excretion by decreasing the kidney's resorption of sodium. The excretion of potassium and bicarbonate may also be increased. Therapeutically, diuretics are used for a variety of cardiovascular and respiratory conditions (e.g., hypertension) in which elimination of fluids from tissues is necessary. Sports participants have misused diuretics mainly in two ways: to reduce body weight quickly or to decrease a drug's concentration in the urine (increasing its excretion to avoid the detection of drug misuse). In both cases, there are ethical and health grounds for banning certain classes of diuretics from use during competition.

Anabolic Steroids

Anabolic steroids are synthetically created chemical compounds whose structure closely resembles naturally occurring sex hormones—in particular, the male hormone testosterone.[9,18] Anabolic steroids have both androgenic and anabolic effects. Androgenic effects include growth development and maintenance of reproductive

Focus

Examples of deleterious effects of anabolic steroids

Teens—Premature closure of long bones, acne, hirsutism, voice deepening, enlarged mammary glands (gynecomastia) of the male

Males—Male pattern baldness, acne, voice deepening, mood swings, aggressive behavior, decreased high-density lipoprotein, increased cholesterol, reduction in size of testicle, reduced testosterone production, changes in libido

Females—Hair loss, acne, voice deepening (irreversible), increased facial hair, enlarged clitoris (irreversible), increased libido, menstrual irregularities, increased aggression, decreased body fat, increased appetite, decreased breast size

Abuse—May lead to liver tumors and cancer, heart disease, hypertension, central nervous system dysfunction, and irreversible changes to the reproductive and endocrine systems

tissues and masculinization in males. Anabolic effects promote nitrogen retention, which leads to protein synthesis in skeletal muscles and other tissues, resulting in increased muscle mass and weight, general growth, and bone maturation.[20]

Athletes who choose to take anabolic steroids are seeking to maximize the anabolic effects while minimizing the androgenic side effects. The problem is that no steroids exist that have only anabolic effects; they all also have androgenic effects.

In 1984 the American College of Sports Medicine (ACSM) reported that anabolic steroids taken with an adequate diet could contribute to an increase in body weight and, with a heavy resistance program, to a possible significant gain in strength.[33] However, when used in mass quantities, as is typically done by individual athletes, anabolic steroids can have many deleterious and irreversible side effects that constitute a major threat to the health of the athlete (see *Focus Box:* "Examples of deleterious effects of anabolic steriods").[28]

Anabolic steroids present an ethical dilemma for the sport world.[18] It is estimated that more than a million young male and female athletes are taking or have taken them, with most being purchased through the black market.[40] Approximately 6.5 percent of male athletes and 1.9 percent of female athletes are taking anabolic steroids.[6] An estimated 2.5 percent of intercollegiate athletes take anabolic steroids.[24] The more commonly used anabolic steroids include Anavar, Dianabol, Anadrol, and Finajet.[10]

Usage of anabolic steroids is a major problem in sports that involve strength.[41] Powerlifting, the throwing events in track and field, and American football are some sports in which the use of anabolic steroids is a serious problem.

Androstenedione

Androstenedione is a relatively weak androgen that is produced primarily in the testes and in lesser amounts by the adrenal cortex and ovaries. It has been used in humans to increase testosterone in men and particularly in women; however, the effect lasts only for a few hours. Currently, the FDA classifies commercially produced androstenedione as a dietary supplement. To date, there is no scientific base of research to support or rebuke the efficacy or safety of using this ergogenic aid.

Human Growth Hormone

Human growth hormone (HGH) is produced by the somatotropic cells of the anterior region of the pituitary gland from which it is released into the circulatory system. The amount released varies with age and the developmental periods of a

17-4

Critical Thinking Exercise

A football linebacker returns to school for preseason practice, and to the shock of both his teammates and the coaches, he has gained thirty pounds and greatly increased his muscle bulk since leaving in June. Even though this athlete is known to be religious about his weight training, the coaches are fairly certain that he has engaged in steroid abuse. The athlete vehemently denies taking steroids and is willing to take a drug test to prove it.

? One of the coaches approaches the athletic trainer and asks if the athlete is using steroids. Without subjecting the athlete to a definitive drug test, what physical signs are indicative of steroid abuse?

person's life. A lack of HGH can result in dwarfism. In the past, HGH was in limited supply because it was extracted from cadavers. Now, however, it can be made synthetically and is more readily available.[21,36]

Experiments indicate that HGH can increase muscle mass, skin thickness, connective tissues in muscle, and organ weight and can produce lax muscles and ligaments during rapid growth phases. It also increases body length and weight and decreases body fat percentage.[36]

The use of HGH by athletes throughout the world is on the increase because it is more difficult to detect in urine than are anabolic steroids.[19] There is currently a lack of concrete information about the effects of HGH on the athlete who does not have a growth problem. It is known that an overabundance of HGH in the body can lead to premature closure of long-bone growth sites or, conversely, can cause acromegaly, a condition that produces elongation and enlargement of bones of the extremities and thickening of bones and soft tissues of the face. Also associated with acromegaly is diabetes mellitus, cardiovascular disease, goiter, menstrual disorders, decreased sexual desire, and impotence. Acromegaly decreases the life span by up to twenty years. Like anabolic steroids, HGH presents a serious problem for the sports world. At this time there is no proof that an increase of HGH combined with weight training contributes to strength and muscle hypertrophy.[19]

Blood Reinjection (Blood Doping, Blood Packing, and Blood Boosting)

Endurance, acclimatization, and altitude make increased metabolic demands on the body, which responds by increasing blood volume and the number of red blood cells to meet the increased aerobic demands.

Recently, researchers have replicated these physiological responses by removing 900 milliliters of blood, storing it, and reinfusing it after six weeks. The reason for waiting at least six weeks before reinfusion is that it takes that long for the athlete's body to reestablish a normal hemoglobin and red blood cell concentration. Athletes using this method have significantly improved their endurance performance. From the standpoint of scientific research, such experimentation has merit and is of interest. However, not only is use of such methods in competition unethical, but use by nonmedical personnel could prove to be dangerous, especially when a matched donor is used.[14]

There are serious risks with transfusing blood and related blood products. The risks include allergic reactions, kidney damage (if the wrong type of blood is used), fever, jaundice, the possibility of transmitting infectious diseases (hepatitis B or HIV), or a blood overload, which can result in circulatory and metabolic shock.[11]

Recreational Substance Abuse among Athletes

Recreational drugs include tobacco, alcohol, cocaine, and marijuana.

Just as it is of the world in general, recreational substance abuse is a part of the world of sports.[3] Reasons that athletes use these substances may include desire to experiment, to temporarily escape from problems, or to just be part of a group (peer pressure). For some athletes, recreational drug use leads to abuse and dependence. Drug abuse may be defined as the use of drugs for nonmedical reasons, that is, with the intent of getting high, or altering mood or behavior.

Psychological versus Physical Dependence

There are two general aspects of dependence: psychological and physical. Psychological dependence is the drive to repeat the ingestion of a drug to produce pleasure or to avoid discomfort. Physical dependence is the state of drug adaptation that manifests itself as the development of tolerance and, when the drug is removed, causes a withdrawal syndrome. Tolerance of a drug is the need to increase the dosage to create the effect that was obtained previously by smaller amounts. The withdrawal syndrome consists of an unpleasant physiological reaction when the drug is abruptly stopped.

Some drugs that are abused by the athlete overlap with those thought to enhance performance. Examples include amphetamines and cocaine. Tobacco (nicotine), alcohol, cocaine, and marijuana are the most abused recreational drugs. The athletic trainer and coach might also come in contact with abuse by athletes of barbiturates, nonbarbiturate sedatives, psychotomimetic drugs, or different inhalants.

Tobacco Use

Although cigarettes, cigars, and pipes are becoming increasingly rare in the athletic population, the use of smokeless tobacco and the passive exposure to others who are smoking are ongoing problems for athletes.

Cigarette smoking   On the basis of various investigations into the relationship between smoking and performance, the following conclusions can be drawn:

1. There is individual sensitivity to tobacco that may seriously affect performance in instances of relatively high sensitivity. Because more than one third of the men studied indicated tobacco sensitivity, it may be wise to prohibit smoking by athletes.
2. Tobacco smoke has been associated with as many as 4,700 different chemicals, many of which are toxic.
3. As few as ten inhalations of cigarette smoke cause an average maximum decrease in airway conductance of 50 percent. This decrease occurs in nonsmokers who inhale smoke secondhand as well.
4. Smoking reduces the oxygen-carrying capacity of the blood. A smoker's blood carries five to ten times more carbon monoxide than normal. Carbon monoxide inhibits the capability of oxygen molecules to bind to the hemoglobin molecule. Thus, the red blood cells are prevented from picking up sufficient oxygen to meet the demands of the body's tissues. The carbon monoxide also tends to make arterial walls more permeable to fatty substances, a factor in atherosclerosis.
5. Smoking aggravates and accelerates the heart muscle cells through overstimulation of the sympathetic nervous system.
6. Total lung capacity and maximum breathing capacity are significantly decreased in heavy smokers; this fact is important to the athlete, because both changes would impair the capacity to take in oxygen and make it readily available for body use.
7. Smoking decreases pulmonary diffusing capacity.
8. After smoking, an accelerated thrombolic tendency is evidenced.
9. Smoking is a carcinogenic factor in lung cancer and is a contributing factor to heart disease.

The addictive chemical of tobacco is nicotine, which is one of the most toxic drugs. When inhaled, it causes blood pressure elevation, increased bowel activity, and an antidiuretic action. Moderate tolerance and strong physical dependence occur.

Use of smokeless tobacco   It is estimated that more than 7 million individuals use smokeless tobacco, which comes in three forms: loose-leaf, moist or dry powder (snuff), and compressed. The tobacco is placed between the cheek and the gum. Then it is sucked and chewed. Aesthetically, this habit is an unsavory one during which an athlete is continually spitting into a container. Besides the unpleasant appearance, the use of smokeless tobacco proposes an extremely serious health risk.[5] Smokeless tobacco causes bad breath, stained teeth, tooth sensitivity to heat and cold, cavities, gum recession, tooth bone loss, leukoplakia, and oral and throat cancer. Aggressive oral and throat cancer and periodontal destruction (with tooth loss) have been associated with this habit.[7]

The major substance ingested is nitrosonornicotine, which is the drug responsible for this habit's addictiveness. It is absorbed through the mucous membranes, and within a short period of time the level of nicotine in the blood is equivalent to that of a cigarette smoker. This chemical makes smokeless tobacco a more addictive habit

17-5

Critical Thinking E x e r c i s e

The baseball team has a number of players who routinely chew tobacco or use dip. The athletic trainer is extremely concerned about the possible long-term effects of using smokeless tobacco and has convinced the coach that banning chewing is in the players' best interest.

? Because many of the players know that using smokeless tobacco is a long-standing practice among players and is a part of the baseball cult, what can the athletic trainer do to help the players accept this new rule?

than smoking is. The user of chewing tobacco experiences the nicotine effects without exposure to the tar and carbon monoxide associated with a burning cigarette. Smokeless tobacco increases heart rate but does not affect reaction time, movement time, or total response time among athletes or nonathletes.[12]

Passive smoke   There are dangers associated with the passive inhalation of smoke (secondhand smoke) by nonsmokers. Both smokers and nonsmokers are exposed to smoke containing carbon monoxide, nicotine, ammonia, and cyanide. Obviously smokers inhale the greater quantity of contaminated air. However, it has been estimated that for each pack of cigarettes smoked, the nonsmoker who shares a common air supply will inhale the equivalent of three to five cigarettes. Significant numbers of individuals exposed to passive smoke develop nasal symptoms, eye irritation, headaches, cough, and in some cases, allergies to smoke. For these reasons and others, many state, local, and private sector policies have been established that restrict or ban smoking in public areas. There is little doubt that passive smoking poses a significant health threat to the nonsmoker.

Alcohol Use

Alcohol is the most widely used and abused substance among athletes.[25] Alcohol is a drug that depresses the central nervous system. Alcohol is absorbed from the digestive system into the bloodstream very rapidly. Factors that affect how rapidly absorption takes place include the number of drinks consumed, the rate of consumption, alcohol concentration of the beverage, and the amount of food in the stomach. Some alcohol is absorbed into the blood through the stomach, but the greater part is absorbed through the small intestine. Alcohol is transported through the blood to the liver, where it can be oxidized at a rate of two-thirds of an ounce per hour. An excess causes an increase in the level of alcohol circulating in the blood. As blood alcohol levels continue to increase, predictable signs of intoxication appear. At 0.1 percent, the person loses motor coordination; from 0.2 percent to 0.5 percent the symptoms become progressively more profound and perhaps even life threatening. Intoxication persists until the remainder of the alcohol can be metabolized by the liver. There is no way to accelerate the liver's metabolism of alcohol (the act of sobering up); it just takes time. Alcohol has no place in sports participation.

Approximately 20 percent of cases of alcoholism are associated with genetic reasons and 80 percent with overindulgence. The athlete who is suffering from alcohol abuse may display the following characteristics: mood changes, missed practices, isolation, attitude changes, fighting or inappropriate outbursts of violence, changes in appearance, hostility toward authority figures, complaints from family, and changes in peer group.[30]

Drug Use

Cocaine   Cocaine, also known as coke, snow, toot, happy dust, and white girl, is a powerful central nervous system stimulant with effects of very short duration. Cocaine use produces immediate feelings of euphoria and excitement, decreased sense of fatigue, and heightened sexual drive. Cocaine may be snorted, taken intravenously, or smoked (freebased). The initial effects are extremely intense, and because they are pleasurable, strong psychological dependence is developed rapidly by users who can or cannot afford to support this expensive habit.

Habitual use of cocaine will not lead to physical tolerance or dependence but will cause psychological dependence and addiction. Long-term effects include nasal congestion and damage to the membranes and cartilage of the nose if snorted, bronchitis, loss of appetite leading to nutritional deficiencies, convulsions, impotence, and cocaine psychosis with paranoia, depression, hallucinations, and disorganized mental function. An overdose can lead to overstimulation of the sympathetic nervous system and can cause tachycardia, hypertension, extra heartbeats, coronary vasoconstriction, strokes, pulmonary edema, aortic rupture, and sudden death.[29]

Crack   Crack is a rocklike crystalline form of cocaine that is heated in a small pipe and then inhaled, producing an immediate rush. The effects last for only a matter of minutes and are frequently followed by a state of depression. This sudden intense stimulation of the nervous system predisposes the user to cardiac failure or respiratory failure and makes this commonly available drug extremely dangerous.

Marijuana   Marijuana is one of the most abused drugs in Western society. It is more commonly called grass, weed, pot, dope, or hemp. The marijuana cigarette is called a joint, jay, number, reefer, or root.

Marijuana is not a harmless drug. The components of marijuana smoke are similar to those of tobacco smoke, and the same cellular changes are observed in the user. Continued use leads to respiratory diseases such as asthma and bronchitis and a decrease in vital capacity of 15 percent to 40 percent (certainly detrimental to physical performance). Among other deleterious effects are lowered sperm counts and testosterone levels. Evidence of interference with the functioning of the immune system and cellular metabolism has also been found. The most consistent sign is the increase in pulse rate, which averages close to 20 percent higher during exercise and is a definite factor in limiting performance. Some decrease in leg, hand, and finger strength has been found at higher dosages. Like tobacco, marijuana must be considered carcinogenic.

Psychological effects such as a diminution of self-awareness and judgment, a slowdown of thinking, and a shorter attention span appear early in the use of the drug. Postmortem examinations of habitual users reveal not only cerebral atrophy but alterations of anatomical structures, which suggest irreversible brain damage. Marijuana also contains unique substances (cannabinoids) that are stored, in much the same manner as are fat cells, throughout the body and in the brain tissues for weeks and even months. These stored quantities result in a cumulative deleterious effect on the habitual user.

A drug such as marijuana has no place in sports. Claims for its use are unsubstantiated, and the harmful effects, both immediate and long-term, are too significant to permit indulgence at any time.

DRUG TESTING IN ATHLETES

Drug testing of athletes for the purpose of identifying individuals who may have some problems with drug abuse is commonplace.[14] Both the NCAA and the USOC routinely conduct drug testing.[23,37] The legality and ethics of testing only those individuals involved with sports are still open to debate.[15] The pattern of drug usage among athletes may simply reflect that of our society in general. Great care must be taken that an athlete's personal rights are not violated.[35]

Both the NCAA and the USOC conduct drug testing programs.

Drug testing began with the 1968 Olympic games. In 1985 the USOC began drug testing athletes involved in both national and international competitions. In January 1986 the member institutions of the NCAA voted overwhelmingly to expand the NCAA drug education program to include mandatory random drug testing in specific sports throughout the year and during and after NCAA championship events.[23] The major goals of both organizations are to protect the health of athletes and to help ensure that competition is fair and equitable.[10]

Most professional teams and many individual colleges and universities have initiated drug testing programs for their athletes.[31] Unfortunately, drug testing is rarely done at the high school level because of cost constraints.

The Drug Test

There are some slight differences between NCAA and USOC drug testing procedures and protocols. Most of these differences have to do with how the athletes are selected for random tests. The NCAA requires all athletes to sign a consent form agreeing to participate in the drug testing program throughout the year. The USOC tests athletes on a random basis throughout the year and tests all athletes before a USOC-sanctioned competition.[10]

17-6

*Critical **Thinking*** Exercise

A university has recently implemented a drug testing program for athletes in all sports. The athletic director has decided that the athletic trainer is perhaps the best individual to supervise the program.

? Should the athletic trainer be willing to take on the additional responsibilities of overseeing the drug testing program for the athletes?

During the drug test, the athlete must first provide positive identification. Then, under direct observation, the athlete must urinate into two separate specimen bottles (labeled A and B), which are sealed and submitted to an official NCAA or USOC testing laboratory for analysis. In the laboratory, specimen A is used for both screening and confirmation tests. A confirmation test uses analysis techniques that are more sensitive and accurate should a positive test result occur during the screening test. Specimen B is used only when a reconfirmation is needed for a positive test of specimen A. The athlete is then notified of a positive test result and becomes subject to sanctions from either the NCAA or the USOC.[10]

Sanctions for Positive Tests

For a first-time positive test, the NCAA will declare the athlete ineligible for all regular and postseason competitions for a minimum of one year. During that year the athlete may be retested at any time. The athlete must be retested with a negative result and have eligibility restored before he or she may return to competition. Additional positive tests can result in a lifetime disqualification from NCAA competition.[23]

The USOC sanctions range from three to twenty-four months of disqualification, depending on the drug, for a first-time violation, and a minimum of two years to a lifetime ban for subsequent positive tests.[37]

Focus

Banned drugs

Drugs banned by both NCAA and USOC

Anabolic steroids

Diuretics

Beta blockers (used to lower blood pressure, decrease heart rate, decrease cardiac arrythmias)

Peptide hormones (human growth hormone, corticotropin, erythropoietin, human chorionic gonadotropin, etc.)

Stimulants* (amphetamines, cocaine, and anorexiants)

Caffeine (limited ingestion permits up to 12 μg/ml USOC and 15 μg/ml NCAA)

Blood doping

Drugs banned by USOC only

Narcotic analgesics (codeine is permitted)

Skeletal muscle relaxants (banned for modern pentathlon and biathlon events only)

Cough and cold decongestants (sympathomimetic drugs)

Injectable anesthetics (acceptable with prior written permission)

Corticosteroids (intramuscular, intravenous, rectal, and oral use is banned; most topical and inhaled use is permitted with written permission)

Drugs banned by NCAA only†

Substances that contain alcohol (banned for riflery)

Street drugs (heroin and marijuana)

Modified from Fuentes R, Rosenberg J, Davis A: *Allen and Hanbury's athletic drug reference*, Durham, NC, 1996, Galaxo.

*USOC permits inhaled albuterol and terbutaline with prior written permission; NCAA permits all inhalants.

†USOC reserves the right to test for alcohol and street drugs with possible sanctions for positive tests.

Banned Substances

Both the NCAA and the USOC have established lists of substances that are banned from use by athletes. The lists include performance-enhancing drugs and street, or recreational, drugs as well as many OTC and prescription drugs.

The list of drugs banned by either the NCAA or the USOC or by both is extensive and includes approximately 4,600 separate medications.[10] The list of drugs banned by the USOC is considerably more extensive than the NCAA list because the USOC is subject to internationally used drugs banned by the International Olympic Committee (IOC). *Focus Box:* "Banned drugs" summarizes the various categories of drugs that appear on the banned lists for the NCAA and the USOC.[10]

The athletic trainer working with athletes who may be tested for drugs by the NCAA or with world-class or Olympic athletes governed by the USOC should be thoroughly familiar with the list of banned drugs.[8] Having an athlete disqualified because of the indiscriminate use of some prescription or OTC medication would be most unfortunate.

Some drugs appear on the banned list for both the NCAA and the USOC.

SUMMARY

- A drug is a chemical agent used in the prevention, treatment, or diagnosis of disease that may be administered either internally or externally. It is transported in an inactive substance called a vehicle.
- Pharmacokinetics refers to the method by which drugs are absorbed, distributed, metabolized, and eliminated or excreted by the body.
- Administering a drug is defined as providing a single dose of medication for immediate use by the athlete. Dispensing refers to providing the athlete with a drug in a quantity sufficient to be used for multiple doses. At no time can anyone other than a person licensed by law legally prescribe or dispense drugs for an athlete. In certain situations, the athletic trainer may be allowed to administer a single dose of a nonprescription medication.
- Drugs used to combat infection include local antiseptics and disinfectants, antifungal agents, and antibiotics.
- Drugs used to inhibit pain or inflammation include counterirritants and local anesthetics, narcotic analgesics, nonnarcotic analgesics and antipyretics, acetylsalicylic acid (aspirin), nonsteroidal antiinflammatory drugs, and corticosteroids.
- Drugs used to treat gastrointestinal disorders include antacids, antiemetics, carminatives, cathartics or laxatives, and antidiarrheals.
- Drugs used to treat colds and allergies include nasal decongestants, antihistamines, cough suppressants, and asthma drugs.
- Drugs used to control bleeding include vasoconstrictors, hemostatic agents, and anticoagulants.
- The athletic trainer is often responsible for initial screening of athletes who have various illnesses or injuries. Frequently, the athletic trainer must make decisions regarding the appropriate use of over-the-counter medications for athletes. Specific protocols have been established that can serve as a guide for the use of these medications by the athletic trainer.
- Substance abuse involves the use of performance-enhancing drugs and the widespread use of recreational drugs, or street drugs. The athletic trainer must be knowledgeable about substance abuse in the athletic population and should be able to recognize signs that an athlete is engaging in substance abuse. Substance abuse has no place in the athletic population.
- The use of performance-enhancing drugs (ergogenic aids) by athletes must be discouraged because of potential health risks and to ensure equal competition. Among the more common ergogenic aids used by athletes are stimulants, beta blockers, narcotic analgesics, diuretics, anabolic steroids, human growth hormone, and blood doping.

- Recreational drug abuse among athletes is of major concern. It can potentially lead to serious psychological and physical health problems. The most prevalent substances that are abused are tobacco, alcohol, cocaine, and marijuana.
- Drug testing of athletes for the purpose of identifying individuals who may have some problems with drug abuse is done routinely by the NCAA and the USOC. The major goals of drug testing are to protect the health of athletes and to help ensure that competition is fair and equitable. Most professional teams and many individual colleges and universities have initiated drug testing programs for their athletes. Unfortunately, drug testing is rarely done at the high school level because of cost constraints.
- Both the NCAA and USOC have established lists of drugs that are banned for use by athletes competing in either NCAA- or USOC-sanctioned events.

Web Sites

National Athletic Trainers' Association: http://www.nata.org

Cramer First Aider: http://www.ccsd.k12.wy.us/cchs_web/cramerfirstaider/fstaider.htm

Wheeless' Textbook of Orthopaedics: http://www.medmedia.com/med.htm

Clicking on "medications" at this Web site allows the reader to search for information on dosages, indications, contraindications, and so on.

Online Pharmacology: http://www.pharmacology.com/phatyme.htm

This site allows the reader to search for various medications; it gives information about warnings, recent studies, and so on.

Solutions to Critical Thinking EXERCISES

17-1 At no time can anyone other than a person licensed by law legally prescribe or dispense drugs for an athlete. An athletic trainer is not permitted to administer or dispense a prescription drug. However, the athletic trainer may be allowed to administer a single dose of a nonprescription medication. The athletic trainer must be reasonable and prudent about the types of nonprescription drugs offered to the athlete. If medications are administered by an athletic trainer, he or she must maintain accurate records of the types of medications administered. Each athletic trainer should be aware of state regulations and laws that pertain to the use of medications.

17-2 It is possible that this athlete has exercise-induced bronchospasm (EIB). EIB may be caused by loss of heat, water, or both from lungs during exercise or exertion, resulting from hyperventilation of air that is cooler and dryer than that in the respiratory tract. The goals of asthma therapy are to prevent chronic and troublesome symptoms, maintain normal lung function and activity levels, prevent asthma exacerbations, provide optimal pharmacotherapy with minimal adverse effects, and meet athletes' expectation of and satisfaction with asthma care.

17-3 Ibuprofin is an NSAID. The NSAIDs are most effective for reducing pain, stiffness, swelling, redness, and fever associated with localized inflammation. Even though NSAIDs have anal-

gesic and antipyretic capabilities, they should not be used in cases of mild headache or increased body temperature in place of aspirin or acetaminophen. However, they can be used to relieve many other mild to moderately painful somatic conditions, such as menstrual cramps and soft-tissue injury.

17-4 The visible signs of steroid abuse include male pattern baldness, acne, voice deepening, mood swings, aggressive behavior, gynecomastia, reduction in the size of a testicle, and changes in libido. Because the athlete denies steroid abuse, the athletic trainer might suspect that human growth hormone has been used to achieve these results.

17-5 The athletic trainer should first point out the potential long-term effects of using smokeless tobacco, which include bad breath, stained teeth, tooth sensitivity to heat and cold, cavities (with tooth loss), gum recession, periodontal destruction, and oral and throat cancer. The trainer may also try to substitute for the tobacco by giving the players chewing gum or sunflower seeds so that their habitual need to chew on something and spit while playing baseball is satisfied.

17-6 In this particular case, the issue of added responsibility is irrelevant. The athletic trainer should be more concerned with how this responsibility would impact his or her ability to perform normal job functions. Athletic trainers work hard to develop a sense of trust in the athletes for whom they must provide health care. Being forced to assume roles as police officers or enforcers can only serve to undermine that trust. Thus, this athletic trainer should be adamant in recommending to the athletic director that some other individual assume the responsibility of overseeing the drug testing program.

REVIEW QUESTIONS AND CLASS ACTIVITIES

1. What is the branch of science known as pharmacology, and what is the difference between a prescription and a nonprescription drug?
2. What is a drug vehicle? Give some examples of drug vehicles.
3. By what methods can drugs be administered to an individual?
4. Describe the pharmacokinetics of how a drug is handled by the body.
5. List procedures that should be followed in the selection, purchase, storage, record keeping, and safety precautions of over-the-counter drugs.
6. What are the legal implications if an athletic trainer administers prescription and nonprescription drugs?

7. List the responses that an athlete may experience to a drug.

8. List examples of common drugs used by athletes to combat infection, to reduce pain and inflammation, to treat colds and allergies, to treat gastrointestinal disorders, to treat muscle dysfunctions, and to control bleeding.

9. Describe the specific protocols for administering over-the-counter medications to athletes.

10. Discuss the use of performance-enhancing drugs by athletes.

11. How do stimulants enhance an athlete's performance?

12. What are the purposes of narcotic analgesic drugs in sports? How do they affect performance?

13. What type of athlete would use beta blockers? Why are they used?

14. Describe why anabolic steroids, diuretics, and growth hormone are used by athletes. What are their physiological effects on the athlete?

15. Describe blood doping in sports. Why is it used? What are its dangers?

16. Contrast psychological and physical dependence, tolerance, and withdrawal syndromes.

17. List the dangers of smokeless tobacco. List the effects of nicotine on the body.

18. Why is cocaine use a danger to the athlete?

19. Select a recreational drug to research. What are the physiological responses to it, and what dangers does it pose to the athlete?

20. How can an athlete who is abusing drugs be identified? Describe behavioral identification as well as drug testing.

21. Debate the issue of drug testing in athletics.

REFERENCES

1. Almekinders L: Athletic injuries and the use of medication. In Torg J, Shephard R, editors: *Current therapy in sports medicine*, St Louis, 1995, Mosby.

2. Barnes P: Is immunotherapy for asthma worthwhile? *N Eng J Med* 334:531, 1996.

3. Blood K: Nonmedical substance use among athletes at a small liberal arts college, *Ath Train* 25(4):335, 1990.

4. Clark W: *Goth's medical pharmacology*, ed 13, St Louis, 1992, Mosby.

5. Connolly G: Use of smokeless tobacco in major league baseball, *N Engl J Med* 318:1281, 1988.

6. DuRant R: Use of multiple drugs among adolescents who use anabolic steroids, *N Engl J Med* 328:922, 1993.

7. Edwards S et al: The effects of smokeless tobacco on heart rates and neuromuscular reactivity, *Physician Sportsmed* 15(7):141, 1987.

8. Erlich N: The athletic trainer's role in drug testing, *Ath Train* 21:225, 1986.

9. Frankel M, Leffers D: Athletes on anabolic-androgenic steroids, *Physician Sportsmed* 20(6):75, 1992.

10. Fuentes R, Rosenberg J, Davis A: *Allen and Hanbury's athletic drug reference*, Durham, NC, 1995, Galaxo.

11. Gledhill N: Control of drug abuse in sports. In Torg J, Shephard R, editors: *Current therapy in sports medicine*, St Louis, 1995, Mosby.

12. Glover ED et al: Smokeless tobacco: questions and answers, *Ath Train* 25(1):10, 1990.

13. Gordon NF et al: Effect of beta-blockers on exercise physiology: implication for exercise training, *Med Sci Sports Exerc* 23(6):668, 1991.

14. *Guide to banned medications*, United States Olympic Committee, Division of Sports Medicine, Drug Education, and Doping Control Program, Nov 1, 1990.

15. Heck J: Drug testing, *J Ath Train* 28(3):197, 1993.

16. Hepler CD, Strand LM: Opportunities and responsibilities in pharmaceutical care, *Am J Hosp Pharm* 4:533, 1990.

17. Huff P: Drug distribution in the training room, *Clin Sports Med* 17(2):214, 1998.

18. Izumi H: Anabolic steroid use among athletes and the future, *Ath Train* 25(1):58, 1990.

19. Jacobson B: Effect of amino acids on growth hormone release, *Physician Sportsmed* 18(1):63, 1990.

20. Laster J, Russell J: Anabolic steroid–induced tendon pathology: a review of literature, *Med Sci Sports Exerc* 23(1):81, 1991.

21. Murray T: Human growth hormone in sports, *Physician Sportsmed* 14(5):29, 1986.

22. National Asthma Education and Prevention Coordinating Committee; National Heart, Lung, and Blood Institute; and World Health Organization: *Global initiative for asthma*, Bethesda, Md, 1995, National Institutes of Health, Publication No. NIH-95-3659.

23. National Collegiate Athletic Association: *1997–98 NCAA drug testing: education programs*, Overland Park, Kan, 1997, NCAA.

24. National Collegiate Athletic Association: Ergogenic drug use down: binge-drinking on the rise according to a national study, *NCAA Sport Sciences Education Newsletter*, Winter 4:1, 1993.

25. O'Brien C: Alcohol and sport: impact of social drinking on recreational and competitive sports performance, *Sports Med* 15:71, 1993.

26. Partin P: Effects of caffeine on athletes, *Ath Train* 23(4):12, 1988.

27. Poe TE: Pharmacology. In Malone T: *Physical and occupational therapy: drug implications for practice*, Philadelphia, 1989, JB Lippencott.

28. Potteiger J, Stilger V: Anabolic steroid use in the adolescent athlete, *J Ath Train* 29(1):60, 1994.

29. Randall T: Cocaine and alcohol mix in the body to form even longer lasting, more lethal drug, *JAMA* 267:1943, 1992.

30. Samples P: Alcoholism in athletes: new directions for treatment, *Physician Sportsmed* 17(4):192, 1989.

31. Schneider D, Morris J: College athletes and drug testing: attitudes and behaviors, by gender and sport, *J Ath Train* 28(2):146, 1993.

32. Second Expert Panel on the Management of Asthma; National Heart, Lung, and Blood Institute: *Highlights of Expert Panel Report 2: Guidelines for the Diagnosis and management of asthma*, Bethesda, Md, 1997, National Institutes of Health, Publication No. NIH 97-4051A.

33. Shroyer J: Getting tough on anabolic steroids: can we win the battle? *Physician Sportsmed* 18(2):106, 1990.

34. Somani SM, Kamimori GH: The effects of exercise on absorption, distribution, metabolism, excretion, and pharmacokinetics of drugs. In Somani SM: *Pharmacology in exercises and sports*, Boca Raton, Fla, 1996, CRC Press.

35. Starkey C, Abdenour T, Finnane D: Athletic trainers' attitudes toward drug screening of intercollegiate athletes, *J Ath Train* 29(2):120, 1994.

36. Terney R, McLain L: The use of anabolic steroids in high school students, *Am J Dis Child* 144:99, 1990.

37. US Olympic Committee: *Drug education handbook 1993–1996*, Colorado Springs, Colo, 1993, USOC.

38. Wagner J: Enhancement of sport performance with drugs: an overview, *Sports Ed* 12:250, 1991.

39. Whitehill W, Wright K, Robinson J: Guidelines for dispensing medications, *J Ath Train* 27(1):20, 1992.

40. Windsor R, Dumitru D: Prevalence of anabolic steroid use by male and female adolescents, *Med Sci Sports Exerc* 21(5):494, 1989.

41. Yesalis C: Anabolic-androgenic steroid use in the United States, *JAMA* 270:1217, 1993.

42. Young LL, Koda-Kimble MA: *Applied therapeutics: the clinical use of drugs*, Vancouver, Wash, 1995, Applied Therapeutics.

ANNOTATED BIBLIOGRAPHY

Bolling LE, editor: *1994/1995 NCAA drug testing/education programs*, Overland Park, Kan, 1994, National Collegiate Athletic Association.

This NCAA manual presents publications and educational materials, drug education programs, NCAA drug testing legislation, and suggested forms and testing protocol.

Clark WG: Goth's medical pharmacology, ed 13, St Louis, 1992, Mosby.

This text presents modern pharmacology in a readable and easily understood manner.

Fuentes R, Rosenberg J, Davis A: *Allen and Hanbury's athletic drug reference*, Durham, NC, 1996, Galaxo.

This text is perhaps the most complete resource for the use of medications, substance abuse, and drug testing in the athletic population; it has a comprehensive listing of all drugs banned by the NCAA and USOC.

Martin M, Yates W: *Therapeutic medications in sports medicine*, Baltimore, 1998, Williams & Wilkens.

This guide serves as a quick reference to therapeutic medications used in the treatment of common injuries and illnesses of the physically active population.

US Olympic Committee: *Drug education handbook 1993–1996*, Colorado Springs, Colo, 1993, USOC.

This handbook provides, in a well-written and succinct manner, the goals of the U.S. Olympic Committee's drug education program.

Specific Sports Conditions

The Foot

When you finish this chapter you should be able to

- Identify the major anatomical and functional features of the foot.
- Discuss how foot injuries may be prevented.
- Describe the process for evaluating injuries to the foot.
- Identify specific injuries that occur in the foot, and discuss plans for management.
- Discuss rehabilitation techniques for the injured foot.

Many sport activities involve some elements of running, jumping, and changing direction. The foot is in direct contact with the ground, and the forces created by these athletic movements place a great deal of stress on the structures of the foot. Consequently, the foot has a high incidence of injury.

The function of the foot is critical in running, jumping, and changing direction. In one instant, the foot must act as a shock absorber to dissipate the ground reaction forces. In the next instant, it must become a rigid lever that functions to propel the body forward, backward, or to the side.

Because of the stress that these movements place on the foot and because of the complex nature of the anatomical structures of this body part, recognition and management of injuries to the foot present a major challenge to the athletic trainer.

FOOT ANATOMY

Bones

The foot consists of 26 bones: 14 phalangeal, 5 metatarsal, and 7 tarsal (Figure 18-1).

Toes

The toes are somewhat similar to the fingers in appearance but are much shorter and serve a different function. The toes are designed to give a wider base both for balance and for propelling the body forward. The first toe, or hallux, has two phalanges, and the other toes each have three phalanges.

Two sesamoid bones are located beneath the first metatarsophalangeal joint. Their functions are to assist in reducing pressure in weight bearing, to increase the mechanical advantage of the flexor tendons of the great toe, and to act as sliding pulleys for tendons.

Metatarsals

The metatarsals are the five bones that lie between and articulate with the tarsals and the phalanges, thus forming the semimovable tarsometatarsal and metatarsophalangeal joints. Although there is little movement permitted, the ligamentous arrangement gives elasticity to the foot in weight bearing. The metatarsophalangeal joints permit hinge action of the phalanges, which is similar to the action found between the hand and fingers. The first metatarsal is the largest and strongest and functions as the main weight-bearing support during walking and running.

Tarsal Bones

The foot has seven tarsal bones, which are located between the bones of the lower leg and the metatarsals. These bones are important for support of the body and its locomotion. They consist of the calcaneus, talus, cuboid, navicular, and the first, second, and third cuneiform bones.

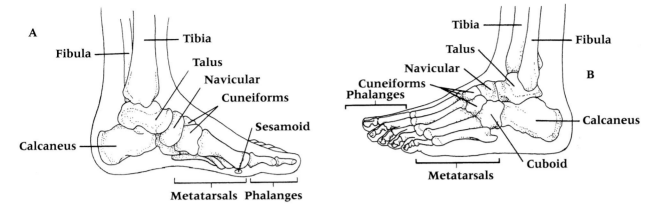

Figure 18-1

Bony structure of the foot. **A,** Medial aspect. **B,** Lateral aspect.

Calcaneus   The calcaneus is the largest tarsal bone. It supports the talus and shapes the heel; its main functions are to convey the body weight to the ground and to serve as an attachment for both the Achilles tendon and several structures on the plantar surface of the foot.

The wider portion on the posterior calcaneous is called the tuberosity of the calcaneus. The medial and lateral tubercles are located on the inferior lateral and medial aspects and are the only parts of this bone that normally touch the ground.

Talus   The irregularly shaped talus is the most superior of the tarsal bones. It is situated above the calcaneus over a bony projection called the sustentaculum tali. The talus consists of a body, neck, and head. The uppermost part of the talus is the trochlea, which articulates with the medial and lateral malleoli to form the ankle joint. The talus is broader anteriorly than posteriorly, thus preventing forward slipping of the tibia during locomotion.

Because the talus fits principally into the space formed by the malleoli, lateral movement is restricted by the stabilizing ligaments of the ankle. Because the uppermost articular surface of the talus is narrower posteriorly than anteriorly, dorsiflexion is limited. At a position of full dorsiflexion, the anterior aspect of the medial collateral ligaments is taut; whereas in plantar flexion, internal rotation occurs because of the shape of the talus. The average range of motion is 10 degrees in dorsiflexion and 23 degrees in plantar flexion.[26]

Navicular   The navicular bone is positioned anterior to the talus on the medial aspect of the foot. Anteriorly the navicular bone articulates with the three cuneiform bones.

Cuboid   The cuboid is positioned on the lateral aspect of the foot. It articulates posteriorly with the calcaneus and anteriorly with the fourth and fifth metatarsals.

Cuneiforms   The three cuneiform bones are located between the navicular and the base of the three metatarsals on the medial aspect of the foot.

Arches of the Foot

The foot is structured, by means of ligamentous and bony arrangements, to form several arches. The arches assist the foot in supporting the body weight, in absorbing the shock of weight bearing, and in providing a space on the plantar aspect of the foot for the blood vessels, nerves, and muscles.[10] There are four arches: the medial longitudinal, the lateral longitudinal, the anterior metatarsal, and the transverse (Figure 18-2).

Medial Longitudinal Arch

The medial longitudinal arch originates along the medial border of the calcaneus and extends forward to the distal head of the first metatarsal. Bony support is provided by the calcaneus, talus, navicular, first cuneiform, and first metatarsal. The main

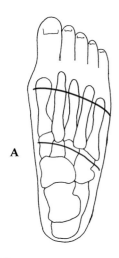
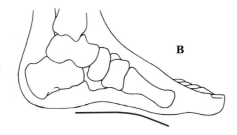
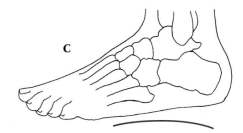

Figure 18-2

The arches of the foot. **A,** Anterior metatarsal and transverse arches. **B,** Medial longitudinal arch. **C,** Lateral longitudinal arch.

supporting ligament of the longitudinal arch is the plantar calcaneonavicular ligament, which acts as a spring by returning the arch to its normal position after it has been stretched. The tendon of the posterior tibialis muscle helps to reinforce the plantar calcaneonavicular ligament.

Lateral Longitudinal Arch

The lateral longitudinal arch is on the outer aspect of the foot and follows the same pattern as that of the medial longitudinal arch. It is formed by the calcaneus, cuboid, and fifth metatarsal bones. It is much lower and less flexible than the inner longitudinal arch.

Anterior Metatarsal Arch

The anterior metatarsal arch is shaped by the distal heads of the metatarsals. The arch has a semiovoid appearance, stretching from the first to the fifth metatarsal.

Transverse Arch

The transverse arch extends across the transverse tarsal bones, primarily the cuboid and the internal cuneiform, and forms a half dome. It gives protection to soft tissue and increases the foot's mobility.

Plantar Fascia (Plantar Aponeurosis)

The plantar fascia is a thick white band of fibrous tissue originating from the medial tuberosity of the calcaneus and ending at the proximal heads of the metatarsals. Along with ligaments, the plantar fascia supports the foot against downward forces (Figure 18-3). The plantar fascia is a distal continuation of fascia that runs posteriorly from the muscles of the thigh to the muscles of the calf and continues under the calcaneous, where it thickens to become the plantar fascia.

Figure 18-3

Plantar fascia.

Articulations

Joints of the foot are categorized into five regions: interphalangeal, metatarsophalangeal, intermetatarsal, tarsometatarsal, subtalar, and midtarsal.

Interphalangeal Joint

The interphalangeal joints are located at the distal extremities of the proximal and middle phalanges at the bases of the adjacent middle and distal phalanges. These joints are designed only for flexion and extension. All interphalangeal joints have reinforcing collateral ligaments on their medial and lateral sides. Also located between

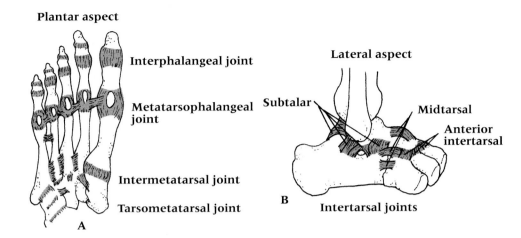

Plantar aspect

Interphalangeal joint

Metatarsophalangeal joint

Intermetatarsal joint

Tarsometatarsal joint

A

Lateral aspect

Subtalar

Midtarsal

Anterior intertarsal

B   Intertarsal joints

Figure 18-4

A, Ligaments of the interphalangeal, metatarsophalangeal, intermetatarsal, and tarsometatarsal joints. **B,** Ligaments of the intertarsal joints.

the collateral ligaments on the plantar and dorsal surface are interphalangeal ligaments (Figure 18-4).

Metatarsophalangeal Joint

The metatarsophalangeal joints are the condyloid type, which permits flexion, extension, adduction, and abduction. Each of these joints has collateral ligaments as well as plantar and dorsal metatarsophalangeal ligaments.

Intermetatarsal Joint

The intermetatarsal joints are sliding joints. They include two sets of articulations. One set consists of an articulation on each side of the base of the metatarsal bones, and the second articulations are on each side of the heads of the metatarsal bone. Each of these articulations permits only slight gliding movements. Shafts of the metatarsals are connected by interosseous ligaments. The bases are connected by plantar and dorsal ligaments, and the heads are attached by transverse metatarsal ligaments.

Tarsometatarsal Joint

The tarsometatarsal joint is formed by the junction of the bases of the metatarsal bones with the cuboid and all three cuneiforms. The slight saddle shape of this joint allows for some gliding and thus for a restricted amount of flexion, extension, adduction, and abduction. Metatarsal bones are attached to the tarsal bones by the dorsal and plantar tarsometatarsal ligaments. Interosseous ligaments connect the three cuneiforms to the metatarsals. The tarsometatarsal joint is also known as Lisfranc's joint.

Subtalar Joint

The subtalar joint is the articulation between the talus and the calcaneus. *Inversion, eversion, pronation,* and *supination* are normal movements that occur at the subtalar joint. Inversion refers to a movement of the calcaneous such that the sole of the foot turns inward or medially. Eversion refers to a movement of the calcaneous such that the sole of the foot turns outward or laterally.

In weight bearing, foot pronation refers to the combined movements of talar plantar flexion and adduction and calcaneal eversion. In contrast, foot supination is the combined movements of talar dorsiflexion and abduction and calcaneal inversion. These movements, which occur at the subtalar joint, are triplanar movements, that is, movements that occur in all three planes simultaneously.[12] The movements of the talus during pronation and supination have profound effects on the lower extremity, both proximally and distally.

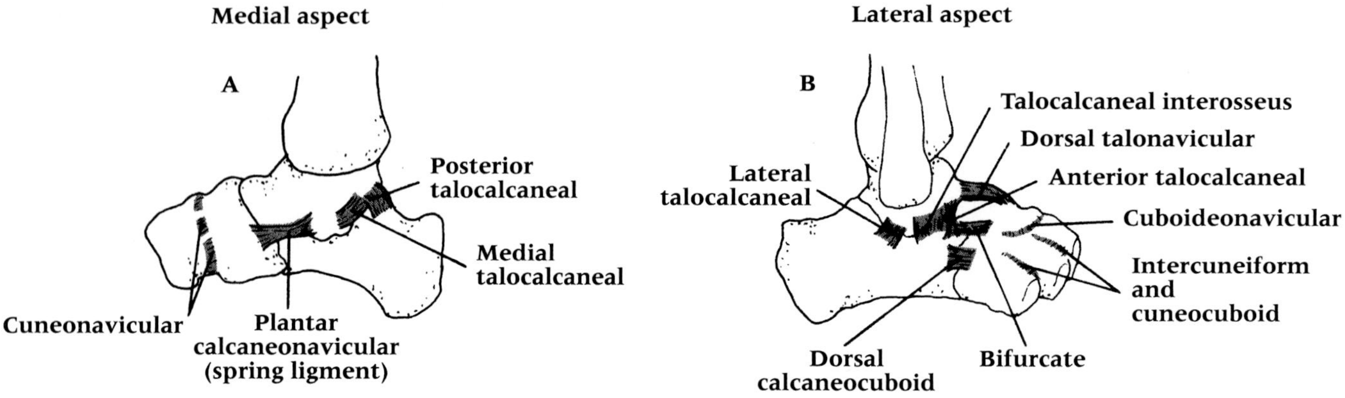

Medial aspect   **Lateral aspect**

Figure 18-5

Ligaments of the subtalar joint.
A, Medial aspect. **B,** Lateral
aspect.

Midtarsal Joint

The midtarsal joint consists of two distinct joints: the calcaneocuboid and the talonavicular joint. The midtarsal joint depends mainly on ligamentous and muscular tension to maintain position and integrity. Midtarsal joint stability is directly related to the position of the subtalar joint. If the subtalar joint is pronated, the talonavicular and calcaneocuboid joints become hypermobile. If the subtalar joint is supinated, the midtarsal joint becomes hypomobile. As the midtarsal joint becomes more or less mobile, it affects the distal portion of the foot because of the articulations at the tarsometatarsal joint.[12]

Stabilizing Ligaments

The subtalar ligaments are the talocalcaneal interosseus and the anterior, posterior, lateral, and medial talocalcaneal (Figure 18-5). A major ligament is the plantar calcaneonavicular, which passes from the medial longitudinal arch. Because of its relatively large number of elastic fibers and its primary purpose of providing shock absorption, the plantar calcaneonavicular is commonly called the spring ligament.

The primary ligaments of the midtarsal joint are the dorsal talonavicular, bifurcate, and dorsal calcaneocuboid. The midtarsal joint is given added strength in its plantar aspect by the long plantar ligaments.

Ligaments of the anterior tarsal joints are divided into those of the cuneonavicular, cuboideonavicular, intercuneiform, and cuneocuboid joints. Each of these joints has both dorsal and plantar ligaments. The intercuneiform ligaments have three transverse bands; one band connects the first cuneiform with the second and the second with the third. A ligament also connects the third cuneiform with the cuboid bone.

Muscles and Movement

The movements of the foot are produced by numerous muscles (Figures 18-6 and 18-7; Table 18-1).

Dorsiflexion and Plantar Flexion

Dorsiflexion and plantar flexion of the foot take place at the ankle joint and will be discussed in greater detail in Chapter 19. The gastrocnemius, soleus, plantaris, peroneus longus, peroneus brevis, tibialis posterior, flexor hallucis longus, and flexor digitorum longus muscles are the plantar flexors. Dorsiflexion is accomplished by the tibialis anterior, extensor digitorum longus, extensor hallucis longus, and peroneus tertius muscles (see Figure 18-6).

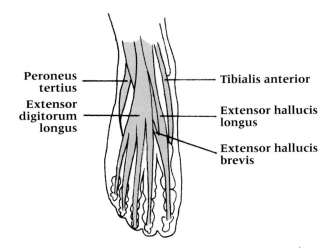

Figure 18-6

Muscles and tendons of the dorsal aspect of the ankle and foot.

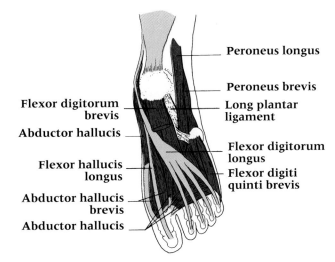

Figure 18-7

The movements of the foot are accomplished by a complex of many muscles.

TABLE 18-1 Actions of the Intrinsic Foot Muscles

Location	Muscle	Action
Dorsal surface	Extensor digitorum brevis	Extension of first through fourth toes
First layer, plantar aspect	Abductor hallucis	Abduction and flexion of big toe
	Abductor digiti minimi pedis	Abduction and flexion of little toe
	Flexor digitorum brevis	Flexion of second through fifth toes
Second layer, plantar aspect	Quadratus plantae	Flexion of second through fifth toes
	Flexor digiti minimi brevis pedis	Flexion and abduction of little toe
	Lumbricalis pedis	Flexion of proximal phalanges and extension of distal phalanges of second through fifth toes; abduction of second toe; adduction of third, fourth, and fifth toes
Third layer, plantar aspect	Adductor hallucis	Adduction and flexion of big toe
	Flexor hallucis brevis	Flexion of big toe
Fourth layer, plantar aspect	Interosseus plantaris	Adduction of third, fourth, and fifth toes; flexion of these toes when acting with dorsal interossei
	Interosseus dorsalis pedis	When acting alone, first interosseus pulls second toe toward the big toe and pulls second, third, and fourth toes away from the big toe
		When acting with plantar interossei, flexion of second, third, and fourth toes

Inversion, Adduction, and Supination

The medial movements of the foot are produced by the same muscles as inversion, adduction (medial movement of the forefoot), and supination (a combination of inversion and adduction). Muscles that produce these movements pass behind and in front of the medial malleolus. Muscles passing behind are the tibialis posterior, flexor digitorum longus, and flexor hallucis longus (see Figure 19-5D). Muscles passing in front of the medial malleolus are the tibialis anterior and the extensor hallucis longus (see Figure 19-5A).

Eversion, Abduction, and Pronation

The lateral movements of the foot are caused by the same muscles that produce eversion, abduction (lateral movement of the forefoot), and pronation (a combination of eversion and abduction). Muscles passing behind the lateral malleolus are the peroneus longus and the peroneus brevis. Muscles passing in front of the lateral malleolus are the peroneus tertius and extensor digitorum longus (see Figure 19-5B).

Movement of the Phalanges

The movements of the phalanges are flexion, extension, abduction, and adduction. Flexion of the second, third, fourth, and fifth distal digitus is executed by the flexor digitorum longus and the quadratus plantar muscles. Flexion of the middle phalanges is performed by the flexor digitorum brevis, and flexion of the proximal phalanges is by the lumbricales and the interossei. The great toe is flexed by the flexor hallucis longus. The extension of all the middle phalanges is done by the abductor hallucis and abductor digiti quanti, the lumbricales, and the interossei. Extension of all distal phalanges is effected by the extensor digitorus longus, the extensor hallucis longus, and the extensor digitorum brevis. The adduction of the foot is performed by the interossei plantares and adductor hallucis; abduction is by the interossei dorsalis, the abductor hallucis, and the abductor digiti quanti.

Nerve Supply and Blood Supply

Nerve Supply

The tibial nerve, largest division of the sciatic nerve, supplies the muscles of the back of the leg and the plantar aspect of the foot. The common peroneal nerve is a smaller division of the sciatic nerve and, with its branches, supplies the front of the leg and the foot (Figure 18-8).

Figure 18-8

The major nerves of the foot. **A,** Dorsal aspect. **B,** Plantar aspect.

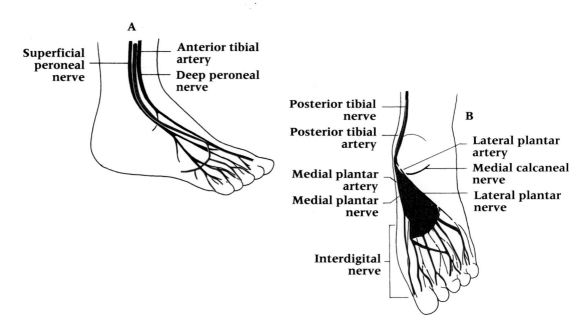

	Stance Phase		Swing Phase
25%	40%	35%	
Contact	**Midstance**	**Propulsion**	
Heel contact	Midstance	Heel off	Toe off
External rotation of leg	Internal rotation of leg		External rotation of leg
Supination	Pronation		Supination

Figure 18-9

Walking gait cycle.

Blood Supply

The major portion of the blood is supplied to the foot by the anterior and posterior tibial arteries. The dorsal venous arch and digital veins and the dorsal digital vein stem from the short and long saphenous veins.

FUNCTIONAL ANATOMY AND FOOT BIOMECHANICS

Athletic trainers must realize, when considering foot, ankle, and leg injuries, that these segments are joined together to form a kinetic chain. Each movement of a body segment has a direct effect on proximal and distal body segments.[8] A study of lower-extremity chronic and overuse injuries related to sports participation must include some understanding of the biomechanics of the foot, especially in the act of walking and running. A number of biomechanical factors may be related to injuries of the lower leg region.

Most people will at some time in their lives develop foot problems.

Normal Gait

The action of the lower extremity during a complete stride in walking and running can be divided into two phases (Figure 18-9). The first is the stance, or support, phase, which starts with initial contact at heel strike and ends at toe-off. The second is the swing, or recovery, phase. This phase represents the time immediately after toe-off in which the leg is moved from behind the body to a position in front of the body in preparation for heel strike.[2]

The foot's function during the support phase of running is twofold. At heel strike, the foot acts as a shock absorber to the impact forces and then adapts to the uneven surfaces. At push-off, the foot functions as a rigid lever to transmit the explosive force from the lower extremity to the running surface.[2] In a heel-strike running gait, initial contact of the foot is on the lateral aspect of the calcaneus with the subtalar joint in supination (Figure 18-10). It is estimated that 80 percent of distance runners use this heel-strike pattern and the remainder are either midfoot or forefoot strikers.[26] In running, both feet are off the surface at the same time (Figure 18-11). Sprinters tend to be forefoot strikers, whereas a number of joggers are midfoot strikers.

At initial contact, the subtalar joint is supinated. Associated with this supination of the subtalar joint is an obligatory external rotation of the tibia.[2] As the foot is loaded, the subtalar joint moves into a pronated position until the forefoot is in contact with the running surface. The change in subtalar motion occurs between initial

Figure 18-10

Foot bearing weight in walking as it moves from heel strike to toe-off.

Figure 18-11

Running gait cycle.

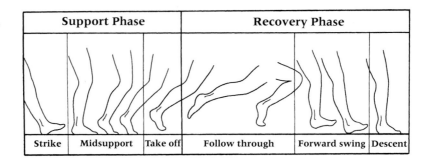

Support Phase			Recovery Phase		
Strike	Midsupport	Take off	Follow through	Forward swing	Descent

heel strike and 20 percent into the support phase of running.[2] As pronation occurs at the subtalar joint, there is obligatory internal rotation of the tibia. Transverse plane rotation occurs at the knee joint because of this tibial rotation. Pronation of the foot unlocks the midtarsal joint and allows the foot to assist in shock absorption and to adapt to uneven surfaces. It is important during initial impact to reduce the ground reaction forces and to distribute the load evenly on many different anatomical structures throughout the foot and leg. Pronation is normal and allows for this distribution of forces on as many structures as possible to avoid excessive loading on just a few structures. The subtalar joint remains in a pronated position through 55 percent to 85 percent of the support phase, with maximum pronation being concurrent with the body's center of gravity passing over the base of support.[6]

The foot begins to resupinate and will approach the neutral subtalar position at 70 percent to 90 percent of the support phase.[6] In supination, the midtarsal joints are locked and the foot becomes stable and rigid to prepare for push-off. This rigid position allows the foot to exert a great amount of force from the lower extremity to the running surface.

Subtalar Joint Pronation and Supination

Pronation and supination of the foot and subtalar joint are normal during the support phase of running. However, excessive or prolonged pronation or supination will often cause or contribute to overuse injuries. When structural or functional deformities exist in the foot or leg, compensation is likely to occur at the subtalar joint. The subtalar joint compensates in a manner that allows the foot to make stable contact with the ground and get into a weight-bearing position (Figure 18-12). This excessive motion compensates for an existing structural deformity.[12]

Structural Deformities

The most typical structural deformities of the foot that produce excessive pronation or supination include forefoot varus, forefoot valgus, and rearfoot varus (Figure 18-12).[22] Structural forefoot varus and structural rearfoot varus deformities are usually associated with excessive pronation. A structural forefoot valgus causes excessive supination. The deformities usually exist in one plane, but the subtalar joint will interfere with the normal functions of the foot and make it more difficult for the joint to act as a shock absorber, to adapt to uneven surfaces, and to act as a rigid lever for push-off. The compensation rather than the deformity itself usually causes overuse injuries.[12]

Excessive Pronation

Excessive or prolonged pronation during running is one of the major causes of stress injuries. Overload of specific structures results when excessive pronation is produced in the support phase or when pronation is prolonged into the propulsive phase of running. Excessive pronation during the support phase will cause compensatory subtalar joint motion such that the midtarsal joint remains unlocked, resulting in an

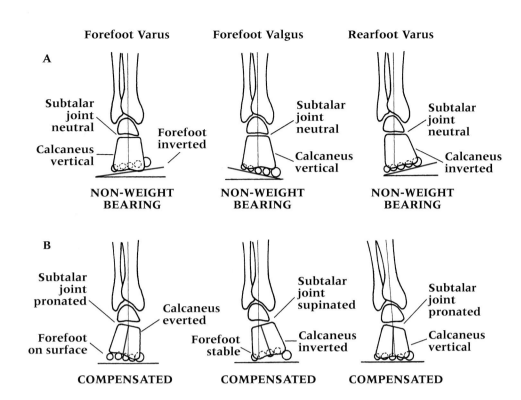

Forefoot Varus   **Forefoot Valgus**   **Rearfoot Varus**

A

Subtalar joint neutral
Forefoot inverted
Calcaneus vertical
NON-WEIGHT BEARING

Subtalar joint neutral
Calcaneus vertical
NON-WEIGHT BEARING

Subtalar joint neutral
Calcaneus inverted
NON-WEIGHT BEARING

B

Subtalar joint pronated
Calcaneus everted
Forefoot on surface
COMPENSATED

Subtalar joint supinated
Calcaneus inverted
Forefoot stable
COMPENSATED

Subtalar joint pronated
Calcaneus vertical
COMPENSATED

Figure 18-12

Structural foot deformities (posterior view). **A,** Bony alignment in a non-weight bearing position. **B,** Compensated bony alignment in a weight bearing position.

excessively loose foot. As more motion occurs at the midtarsal joint, the first metatarsal and first cuneiform become more mobile. These bones comprise a functional unit known as the first ray. With pronation of the midtarsal joint, the first ray is more mobile because of its articulations with that joint. The first ray is also stabilized by the attachment of the peroneus longus tendon, which attaches to the base of the first metatarsal.

The peroneus longus tendon passes posteriorly around the base of the lateral malleolus and then through a notch in the cuboid to cross the foot to the first metatarsal. The cuboid functions as a pulley to increase the mechanical advantage of the peroneal tendon. Stability of the cuboid is essential in this process. In the pronated position, the cuboid loses much of its mechanical advantage as a pulley; therefore the peroneus longus tendon no longer stabilizes the first ray effectively. This condition creates hypermobility of the first ray and increased pressure on the other metatarsals. There is also an increase in tibial rotation, which forces the knee joint to absorb more transverse rotation motion.[12]

Prolonged pronation of the subtalar joint will not allow the foot to resupinate in time to provide a rigid lever for push-off, resulting in a less powerful and efficient force. Thus various foot and leg problems will occur with excessive or prolonged pronation during the support phase; these problems include stress fractures of the second metatarsal, plantar fasciitis, posterior tibial tendinitis, Achilles tendinitis, tibial stress syndrome, and medial knee pain.[11]

Excessive Supination

At heel strike in prolonged or excessive supination, compensatory movement at the subtalar joint will not allow the midtarsal joint to unlock, which causes the foot to remain excessively rigid. Because less movement occurs at the calcaneocuboid joint, the cuboid becomes hypomobile. The peroneus longus tendon has a greater amount of tension because the cuboid has less mobility and thus will not allow mobility of the first ray. In this case, the majority of the weight is borne by the first and fifth metatarsals. Thus the foot cannot absorb the ground reaction forces as efficiently.[12]

Excessive supination limits tibial internal rotation. Injuries typically associated with excessive supination include inversion ankle sprains, tibial stress syndrome, peroneal tendinitis, iliotibial band friction syndrome, and trochanteric bursitis.[11]

PREVENTION OF FOOT INJURIES

Certainly the foot is highly vulnerable to a variety of injuries. The repetitive stresses and strains incurred by the foot during athletic activities are unquestionably sufficient to cause both acute traumatic and overuse injuries. Foot injuries can best be prevented by selecting appropriate footwear, by correcting biomechanical structural deformities through the use of appropriate orthotics, and by paying attention to appropriate foot hygiene and care.

Selecting Appropriate Footwear

The athletic and fitness shoe manufacturing industry has become extremely sophisticated and offers a number of options when it comes to purchasing shoes for different athletic activities. Selecting an appropriate shoe is one of the most critical considerations in preventing a foot problem. Before a shoe is selected, the athletic trainer should evaluate the athlete's foot to determine the existence of a structural deformity such as a forefoot valgus or varus or a rearfoot varus. The type of shoe selected should depend on the existing structural deformity.

As noted earlier, pronation is a problem of hypermobility. Individuals who excessively pronate need stability and firmness to reduce this excess movement. Research indicates that shoe compression, compared to a barefoot condition, may actually increase pronation.[5] The ideal shoe for a pronated foot is one that is less flexible and has good rearfoot control. Conversely, supinated feet are usually very rigid. Increased cushioning and flexibility benefit this type of foot.

Several construction factors may influence the firmness and stability of a shoe. The basic form upon which a shoe is built is called the last. The upper is fitted onto a last in several ways. Each method has its own flexibility and control characteristics. A slip-lasted shoe is sewn together like a moccasin and is very flexible. A board lasted shoe contains a piece of fiberboard to which the upper is attached, which provides a very firm, inflexible base for the shoe. A combination-lasted shoe is boarded in the back half of the shoe and slip lasted in the front, which provides rearfoot stability with forefoot mobility.

The shape of the last may also determine shoe selection. Most athletes with excessive pronation perform better in a straight-lasted shoe, that is, a shoe in which the forefoot does not curve inward in relation to the rearfoot. Midsole design also affects the stability of a shoe. The midsole separates the upper from the outsole.[11] More dense, less yielding material is often used under the medial aspect of the foot to control pronation.

In an effort to control rearfoot movement, many shoe manufacturers have reinforced the heel counter both internally and externally, often in the form of extra plastic along the outside of the heel counter. Other factors that may affect the performance of a shoe are the outsole contour and composition, lacing systems, and forefoot wedges.[12]

Using a Shoe Orthotic

Many injuries to the foot can be prevented by using an orthotic device to correct biomechanical problems that may exist in the foot and that can potentially cause an injury. The orthotic is a plastic, rubber, or leather support that is placed in the shoe as a replacement for the existing insert. Ready-made orthotics can be purchased in sporting goods or shoe stores. Some athletes will need to have orthotics that are custom fitted or made by the athletic trainer.[11]

The use of orthotics for correcting specific problems will be discussed in the section on rehabilitation at the end of this chapter.

Foot Hygiene

Athletes who perform simple tasks such as keeping the toenails trimmed correctly, shaving down excessive calluses, keeping the feet clean, wearing clean, correctly fitted socks, and keeping the feet as dry as possible to prevent the development of athlete's foot (See Chapter 28) can separately and collectively reduce a number of potential problems that can cause them to unnecessarily miss days of practice or competition.

FOOT ASSESSMENT

Athletic trainers, when assessing foot injuries, must clearly understand that the foot is part of a kinetic chain that includes both the ankle and the lower leg. Acute injuries must be differentiated from those injuries that had a relatively slow onset.[20]

History

An athletic trainer making a decision about how to manage a foot injury must perform a quick assessment to determine the type of injury and its history. The following questions should be asked:[20]

- Is this the first time this condition has occurred? If it has happened before, when, how often, and under what circumstances?
- How did the injury occur?
- Did it occur suddenly or come on slowly?
- Was the mechanism a sudden strain, twist, or blow to the foot?
- Where is the pain (ankle, heel, arches, toes)?
- What type of pain is there?
- Is there muscle weakness?
- Is there any snapping, popping, or crepitus during movement?
- Is there any alteration in sensation?
- Can the athlete point to the exact site of pain?
- When is the pain or other symptoms more or less severe?
- On what type of surface has the athlete been training?
- What type of footwear was being used during training? Is it appropriate for the type of training? Is discomfort increased when footwear is worn?

Observation

The athlete should be observed to determine the following:

- Is the athlete favoring the foot, walking with a limp, or unable to bear weight?
- Is the injured part deformed, swollen, or discolored?
- Does the foot change color when weight bearing and non–weight bearing (changing rapidly from a darker to lighter pink when not weight bearing)?
- Is there pes planus (a flatfoot) or pes cavus (a high arch)?
- Is the foot well aligned? Does it maintain its shape on weight bearing?
- Do any abnormalities exist in the toes (e.g., hammer toes, claw toes, Morton's toe, hallux valgus, corns, bunions, plantar warts)?

Looking for Structural Deformities

The first step in looking for structural deformities is to establish a position of subtalar neutral. The athlete should be prone with the distal third of the leg hanging off the end of the table (Figure 18-13). A line should be drawn bisecting the leg from the start of the musculotendinous junction of the gastrocnemius to the distal portion of the calcaneus. With the athlete still prone, the athletic trainer palpates the talus while the forefoot is inverted and everted. One finger should palpate the talus at the anterior aspect of the fibula and another finger at the anterior portion of the medial malleolus. The position at which the talus is equally prominent on both sides is

Figure 18-13

Position for assessing existing structural deformities.

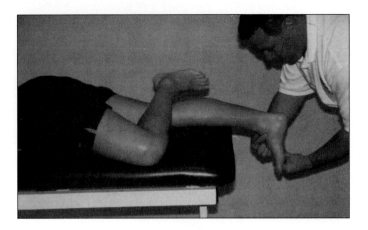

considered a neutral subtalar position in which the subtalar joint is neither pronated or supinated.

Once the subtalar joint is placed in a neutral position, the athletic trainer should apply mild dorsiflexion while observing the metatarsal heads in relation to the plantar surface of the calcaneous. Forefoot varus is an osseous deformity in which the medial metatarsal heads are inverted in relation to the plane of the calcaneus. Forefoot varus is the most common cause of excessive pronation (see Figure 18-12A). Forefoot valgus is a position in which the lateral metatarsals are everted in relation to the rearfoot (see Figure 18-12B).

These forefoot deformities are benign in a non–weight bearing position, but during weight bearing, the metatarsal heads must somehow make contact with the surface to bear weight. To accomplish this movement for a forefoot varus, the talus plantar flexes and adducts and the calcaneus everts. For the forefoot valgus, the calcaneus inverts and the talus abducts and dorsiflexes. A forefoot valgus is the most common forefoot deformity.

In a rearfoot varus deformity, when the foot is in a subtalar neutral position and non–weight bearing, the medial metatarsal heads are elevated, as in a forefoot varus, and the calcaneous is also in an inverted position (see Figure 18-12C). For the foot to bear weight, the subtalar joint must pronate.

Shoe Wear Patterns

Athletes with excessive pronation often wear out the front of the running shoe under the second metatarsal. Shoe wear patterns are commonly misinterpreted by athletes who think they must be pronators because they wear out the back outside edges of their heels. However, most people wear out the back outside edges of their shoes. Just before heel strike, the anterior tibialis fires to prevent the foot from slapping forward. The anterior tibialis not only dorsiflexes the foot but also slightly inverts it; hence the wear pattern on the back edge of the shoe. An athlete who excessively supinates tends to show a wear pattern on the lateral border of the shoe. The key to inspection of wear patterns on shoes is observation of the heel counter and the forefoot.[11]

Palpation

Besides determining pain sites, swelling, and deformities, palpation is used to determine and evaluate circulation.

Bony Palpation

The following bony landmarks should be palpated:

Medial Aspect
- Medial calcaneus
- Calcaneal dome
- Medial malleolus
- Sustentaculum tali
- Talar head
- Navicular tubercle
- First cuneiform
- First metatarsal
- First metatarsophalangeal joint
- First phalanx

Dorsal Aspect
- Second, third, fourth metatarsals
- Second, third, fourth metatarso-phalangeal joints
- Second, third, fourth phalanges
- Third and fourth cuneiform bones

Lateral Aspect
- Lateral calcaneus
- Lateral malleolus
- Sinus tarsi
- Peroneal tubercle
- Cuboid bone
- Styloid process (proximal head of the fifth metatarsal)
- Fifth metatarsal
- Fifth metatarsophalangeal joint
- Fifth phalanx

Plantar Aspect
- Metatarsal heads
- Medial calcaneal tubercle
- Sesamoid bones

Soft-Tissue Palpation

The following soft-tissue structures should be palpated:

Medial and Plantar Aspect
- Tibialis posterior tendon
- Flexor hallucis longus tendon
- Flexor digitorum longus tendon
- Deltoid ligament
- Calcaneonavicular ligament (spring ligament)
- Medial longitudinal arch
- Plantar fascia
- Transverse arch

Lateral and Dorsal Aspect
- Anterior talofibular ligament
- Calcaneofibular ligament
- Posterior talofibular ligament
- Peroneus longus tendon
- Peroneus brevis tendon
- Extensor hallucis longus tendon
- Extensor digitorum longus tendon
- Extensor digitorum brevis tendon
- Tibialis anterior tendon

Pulses

To ensure that there is proper blood circulation to the foot, the pulse is measured at the posterior tibial and dorsalis pedis arteries (Figure 18-14). Pulse in the dorsalis pedis artery is normally felt between the tendons of the extensor hallucis longus and extensor digitorum longus, on a line from the midpoint between the medial and lateral malleoli to the proximal end of the first intermetatarsal space.

Pulse in the posterior tibial artery is normally palpable behind the medial malleolus, 1 inch (2.5 cm) in front of the medial border of the Achilles tendon.[20]

Special Tests

Movement

Both the extrinsic and the intrinsic foot muscles should be assessed for pain and range of motion during active, passive, and resistive isometric movement.

Tinel's Sign

Tapping over the posterior tibial nerve produces tingling distal to that area. Numbness, tingling, and paresthesia may indicate the presence of tarsal tunnel syndrome (Figure 18-15).

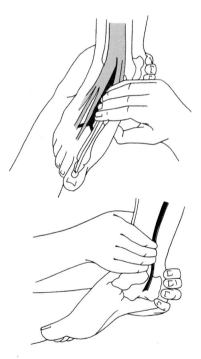

Figure 18-14

An ankle injury may impede blood flow, making routine measurement of the pulse extremely important.

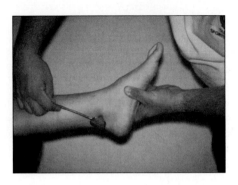

Figure 18-15

A positive Tinel's sign may indicate tarsal tunnel syndrome.

Figure 18-16

Morton's test to establish metatarsalgia or a Morton's neuroma.

neuroma
A bulging that emanates from a nerve.

metatarsalgia
A general term used to describe pain in the ball of the foot.

Morton's Test

With the foot in a supine position, transverse pressure is applied to the heads of the metatarsals, causing sharp pain in the forefoot. A positive test may indicate the presence of a **neuroma** or **metatarsalgia** (Figure 18-16).

Neurological Assessment

Reflexes and cutaneous distribution should also be tested. Skin sensation should be noted for any alteration.

Tendon reflexes such as in the Achilles tendon (S1 nerve root) should elicit a response when gently tapped. Sensation is tested by running the hands over the anterior, lateral, medial, and posterior surfaces of the foot and toes.

RECOGNITION AND MANAGEMENT OF SPECIFIC INJURIES

Most people will at some time develop foot problems that can be attributed to the use of improper footwear, poor foot hygiene, or anatomical structural deviations that result from faulty postural alignments or abnormal stresses. Many sports place exceptional demands on the feet—far beyond what is considered normal. The athletic trainer should be well aware of potential foot problems and should be capable of identifying, ameliorating, or preventing them whenever possible.

Injuries to the Tarsal Region

Fractures of the Talus

Etiology   Fractures of the dome of the talus usually occur either laterally from a severe inversion and dorsiflexion force or medially from an inversion and plantar flexion force with external rotation of the tibia on the talus.[1]

The severity of the fracture may range from a nondisplaced compression fracture to a displaced osteochondral fracture. The presence of osteochondral fragments is referred to as *osteochondritis dissecans*.

Symptoms and signs   The athlete often has a history of repeated trauma to the ankle. He or she feels pain on weight bearing and complains of catching and snapping along with intermittent swelling. The talar dome is tender on palpation over the anteromedial or anterolateral joint line.[1]

Management   For accurate diagnosis, an X ray is essential. Nonsurgical management is appropriate for nondisplaced subchondral compression fractures. Treatment should include protective immobilization with non–weight bearing progressing to full weight bearing depending on symptoms. Rehabilitation should concentrate on strengthening and regaining full range of motion in the ankle joint. If conservative treatment fails and symptoms continue or if there is a displaced osteochondral fracture, surgical removal of the loose bodies arthoscopically may be necessary. Following surgery, the athlete can expect to resume activity in six to eight months.[1]

Fracture of the Calcaneous

Etiology   A fracture of the calcaneous most often occurs from landing after a jump or fall from a height. Avulsion fractures can also occur anteriorly at the attachment of the calcaneonavicular ligament to the sustentaculum tali or posteriorly at the attachment of the talocalcaneal ligament. Anterior avulsion fractures can be misdiagnosed as tendinitis of the posterior tibialis.[9]

Symptoms and signs   There is usually immediate swelling and pain and an inability to bear weight. Deformity is not normally present unless there is a displaced comminuted fracture.

Management   RICE must be used immediately to minimize pain and swelling before referring the athlete to X ray for diagnosis. With nondisplaced fractures, immobilization and early range of motion exercises are recommended as soon as acute swelling and pain subside and motion is tolerated.[9]

Calcaneal Stress Fracture

Etiology   Calcaneal stress fractures along with stress fractures of the tibia and of the second metatarsal are among the most common stress fractures in the lower extremity. A calcaneal stress fracture occurs with repetitive impact during heel strike and is most prevalent among distance runners. It is characterized by a sudden onset of constant pain in the plantar-calcaneal area.[9]

Symptoms and signs   Weight bearing, particularly that which occurs on heel strike in running, increases pain. Complaints of pain tend to continue after exercise stops. The fracture may fail to appear during X-ray examination; a bone scan may provide a better diagnostic tool.

Management   Management is usually conservative for the first two or three weeks and includes rest and active range-of-motion exercises of the foot and ankle. Non–weight bearing cardiovascular exercise such as pool running may continue during this period. After two weeks and when pain subsides, activity within pain limits can be resumed gradually, with the athlete wearing a cushioned shoe.

Apophysitis of the Calcaneus (Sever's Disease)

Etiology   Calcaneal **apophysitis,** or *Sever's disease,* occurs in young, physically active athletes. Sever's disease is comparable to Osgood-Schlatter's disease at the tibial tubercle of the knee (see Chapter 20). Sever's disease is a traction injury at the **apophysis** of the calcaneous (bone protrusion) where the Achilles tendon attaches.[13]

Symptoms and signs   Pain occurs at the posterior heel below the attachment of the Achilles tendon insertion of the child or adolescent athlete. Pain occurs during vigorous activity and does not continue at rest.

Management   The apophysitis, like other overuse syndromes, is best treated with rest, ice, stretching (of the Achilles tendon), and antiinflammatory medications. A heel lift can take some stress off the apophysis.

Retrocalcaneal Bursitis

Etiology   Retrocalcaneal bursitis is caused by inflammation of the bursa that lies between the Achilles tendon and the calcaneous (Figure 18-17). Retrocalcaneal bursitis often occurs from the pressure and rubbing of the heel counter of a shoe. This condition is chronic, developing gradually over a long period of time, and may take many days—sometimes weeks or months—to resolve.[3]

An **exostosis** is a benign bony outgrowth or callus that protrudes from the surface of a bone and is usually capped by cartilage. An exostosis that develops on the

18-1
Critical Thinking E x e r c i s e

A twelve-year-old, physically immature baseball player complains of pain in his right heel where the Achilles tendon attaches. This condition is an apophysitis known as Sever's disease.

? Why and how does Sever's disease occur?

Figure 18-17

Retrocalcaneal bursitis.

apophysitis (a **poff** ah cytis)
Inflammation of an apophysis.

apophysis (a **poff** ah sis)
Bony outgrowth such as tubercle or tuberosity.

exostoses (ek **sos** toe ses)
Benign bony outgrowths that protrude from the surface of a bone and that are usually capped by cartilage.

Figure 18-18

Calcaneal exostoses.

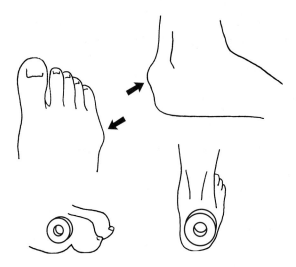

posterior aspect of the calcaneous because of ongoing inflammation of the retrocal-caneal bursa is sometimes referred to as a pump bump (Figure 18-18).[13]

Symptoms and signs   Pain may be elicited by palpating the bursa just above and anterior to the insertion of the Achilles tendon. There will likely be some swelling on both sides of the heel cord. If the source of irritation persists, a bony callus may also begin to form.

Management   Initially, RICE plus NSAIDs and analgesics are used as needed. Often, use of ultrasound can reduce the inflammation. Stretching of the Achilles tendon should be routine. A heel lift should be used to take stress off the Achilles tendon. A donut heel pad can be used to take pressure off the bursa and an existing exostosis (see Figure 18-18). If necessary, larger shoes with wider heel contours should be worn.[21]

Heel Contusion

Etiology   Sport activities that demand a sudden stop-and-go response or a sudden change from a horizontal to a vertical movement (e.g., basketball, jumping, or the land-ing in long jumping) are particularly likely to cause heel contusions. The calcaneous is protected by a thick, cornified skin layer and a heavy fat pad covering, but even this thick padding cannot always protect against the impact of jumping or running.[19]

The major function of the tissue heel pad is to sustain hydraulic pressure through fat columns. Tissue compression is monitored by pressure nerve endings from the skin and plantar aponeurosis. Often, the irritation is on the lateral aspect of the heel because of the heel strike in walking or running.

Symptoms and signs   When injury occurs, the athlete complains of severe pain in the heel and is unable to withstand the stress of weight bearing. Often there is warmth and redness over the tender area.

Management   A contusion of the heel may potentially develop into chronic in-flammation of the periosteum. The athlete should not bear weight on the heel for a period of at least twenty-four hours. RICE is applied, and NSAIDs are administered. If pain when walking has subsided by the third day, the athlete may resume moder-ate activity with the protection of a heel cup or protective doughnut (Figure 18-19). The athlete should wear shock-absorbent footwear.

Cuboid Subluxation

Etiology   Pronation and trauma have been reported to be prominent causes of cuboid subluxation.[12] This condition is often confused with plantar fasciitis. The pri-mary reason for pain is the stress placed on the long peroneal muscle when the foot is in pronation. In this position, the long peroneal muscle allows the cuboid bone to move downward medially.

Symptoms and signs   This displacement of the cuboid causes pain along the fourth and fifth metatarsals as well as over the cuboid. This problem often refers pain to the heel area as well. Many times this pain is increased when the athlete rises after a prolonged non–weight bearing period.

Management   Dramatic treatment results may be obtained by manipulating to restore the cuboid to its natural position (Figure 18-20). Once the cuboid is manipulated, an orthotic often helps to support it in its proper position. If manipulation is successful, quite often the athlete can return to play immediately with little or no pain. The athlete should wear an appropriately constructed orthotic when practicing or competing to reduce the chances of recurrence.

Tarsal Tunnel Syndrome

Etiology   The tarsal tunnel is a loosely defined area behind the medial malleolus that forms a tunnel with an osseous floor and the roof composed of the flexor retinaculum. Through this tunnel passes the tibialis posterior, flexor hallucis longus, and flexor digitorum muscles with their surrounding synovial sheaths and the tibial nerve artery and vein. Any condition that compromises the structures within this tunnel can cause tarsal tunnel syndrome, including tenosynovitis, previous fractures, excessive pronation, or any acute trauma.[13]

Symptoms and signs   Complaints of pain and paresthesia are typical, particularly along the medial and plantar aspects of the foot.[12] Complaints of increased pain at night are also common. Tinel's sign will be positive in cases of tarsal tunnel syndrome (see Figure 18-15). If the condition persists, motor weakness and atrophy may gradually appear, following the course of the tibial nerve.

Management   Initial conservative management includes the use of antiinflammatory medication and other antiinflammatory modalities. The use of an appropriate orthotic to correct excessive pronation may effectively reduce the symptoms. Surgery may be necessary if the symptoms become recurrent.[13]

Injuries to the Metatarsal Region

Pes Planus Foot (Flatfoot)

Etiology   The term *pes planus* refers to a type of foot in which the medial longitudinal arch appears to be flat and is sometimes said to be fallen (Figure 18-21). In general, pes planus is associated with excessive foot pronation and may be caused by a number of factors, including a structural forefoot varus deformity, the wearing of shoes that are tight, trauma that weakens supportive structures such as muscles and ligaments, overweight, or excessive exercise that repeatedly subjects the arch to severe pounding on an unyielding surface.[21]

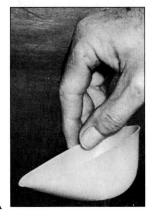
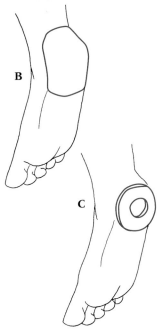

Figure 18-19

A and **B,** Heel protection achieved through the use of a heel cup. **C,** Protective heel doughnut.

Figure 18-20

A cuboid manipulation is done with the athlete prone. The plantar aspect of the forefoot is grasped by the thumbs, with the fingers supporting the dorsum of the foot. The thumbs should be over the cuboid. The manipulation should be a thrust downward to move the cuboid into its more dorsal position. Often, a pop is felt as the cuboid moves back into place.

Figure 18-21

Fallen medial longitudinal arch.

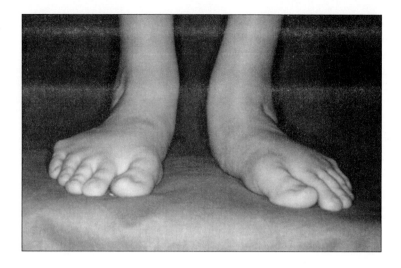

Figure 18-22

Pes cavus.

Critical Thinking Exercise

An athlete enters the training room complaining of her flat feet and that she has pain in her knees and a big callus under her second metatarsal.

? What is likely causing this problem, and how can it usually be corrected?

Symptoms and signs   The athlete may complain of pain and a feeling of weakness or fatigue in the medial longitudinal arch. There may be calcaneal eversion, a bulging of the navicular bone, a flattening of the medial longitudinal arch, and dorsiflexing with lateral splaying of the first metatarsal.

Management   The single most important point that must be emphasized is that regardless of how flattened the medial longitudinal arch appears to be, if it is not causing the athlete any pain or related symptoms, then absolutely nothing should be done to try to correct the apparent problem. Attempts to do so may in fact create an unnecessary problem. However, if the athlete is experiencing pain, an appropriately constructed orthotic designed to correct excessive pronation by using a medial wedge will most likely alleviate symptoms. In certain cases, incorporating an arch support into the orthotic or taping the arch for support may be helpful (see Figures 8-15 through 8-18).

Pes Cavus Foot (High Arch Foot)

Etiology   The term *pes cavus* refers to a type of foot that has an arch that is higher than normal (Figure 18-22). Sometimes called *clawfoot* or *hollow foot*, pes cavus is not as common as pes planus. A pes cavus is generally associated with excessive supination. The accentuated high medial longitudinal arch may be congenital or may indicate a neurological disorder.[13]

Symptoms and signs   In cases of pes cavus, shock absorption is poor, and thus problems such as general foot pain, metatarsalgia, and clawed or hammer toes are seen. Commonly associated with this condition are a structural forefoot valgus deformity and an abnormal shortening of the Achilles tendon. The Achilles tendon is directly linked with the plantar fascia (Figure 18-23). Also, because of the abnormal distribution of body weight, heavy calluses develop on the ball and heel of the foot.[21]

Management   As is the case with pes planus, pes cavus may be asymptomatic, in which case no attempt should be made to correct the problem. If there are associated problems, then an orthotic should be constructed using a lateral wedge to correct a structural forefoot valgus deformity. Stretching of the Achilles tendon and the plantar fascia may also be helpful.

Longitudinal Arch Strain

Etiology   Longitudinal arch strain is usually an early-season injury caused by subjecting the musculature of the foot to increased stress produced by repetitive contact with hard playing surfaces. In this condition, there is a flattening or depression

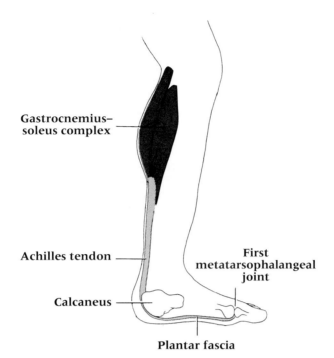

Gastrocnemius–
soleus complex

Achilles tendon

Calcaneus

First
metatarsophalangeal
joint

Plantar fascia

Figure 18-23

The Achilles tendon is directly
linked with the plantar fascia.
Achilles tendon stretching releases a tight medial longitudinal arch.

of the longitudinal arch while the foot is in the midsupport phase, resulting in a strain to the arch. Such a strain may appear suddenly, or it may develop slowly over a considerable length of time.

Symptoms and signs   As a rule, pain is experienced only during running or jumping. The pain usually appears just below the posterior tibialis tendon and is accompanied by swelling and tenderness along the medial aspects of the foot. This injury may also be associated with a sprain of the calcaneonavicular ligament as well as a strain of the flexor hallucis longus tendon.

Management   The management of a longitudinal arch strain involves immediate care, consisting of RICE, followed by appropriate therapy and reduction of weight bearing. Weight bearing must be performed pain free. Arch taping technique no. 1 or 2 might be used to allow earlier pain-free weight bearing (see Figures 8-15 through 8-18).

Plantar Fasciitis

Heel pain is a very common problem in the athletic and nonathletic population. This phenomenon has been attributed to several etiologies, including heel spurs, plantar fascia irritation, and bursitis.[8] *Plantar fasciitis* is a catch-all term that is commonly used to describe pain in the proximal arch and heel. The plantar fascia (plantar aponeurosis) runs the length of the sole of the foot (see Figure 18-3). It is a broad band of dense connective tissue that is attached proximally to the medial surface of the calcaneus. It fans out distally, with fibers and their various small branches attaching to the metatarsophalangeal articulations and merging into the capsular ligaments. The function of the plantar fascia is to assist in maintaining the stability of the foot and in securing or bracing the longitudinal arch.[14]

Etiology   Tension develops in the plantar fascia both during extension of the toes and during depression of the longitudinal arch as the result of weight bearing. When the weight is principally on the heel, as in ordinary standing, the tension exerted on the fascia is negligible. However, when the weight is shifted to the ball of the foot (on the heads of the metatarsals), fascial tension is increased. In running, because the push-off phase involves both a forceful extension of the toes and a powerful

18-3
Critical Thinking Exercise

A distance runner is experiencing pain in the left arch. There is palpable tenderness in the left foot's aponeurosis, primarily in the epicondyle region of the calcaneus.

? What condition does this scenario describe, and how should it be managed?

Plantar Fasciitis

Injury Situation A male cross-country runner injured the proximal arch and heel when he stepped into a hole during a meet. The athlete continued to run and work out for a week before reporting to the athletic trainer.

Symptoms and Signs The athlete complained of early pain in the medial arch and medial distal heel that tended to move centrally as the week progressed. He complained of severe pain when rising in the morning and after sitting for a long period. The area appeared slightly swollen with a severe sharp pain on palpation at the plantar fascia insertion and medial aspect of the calcaneus. Pain increased with passive dorsiflexion of the great toe. An X ray showed the beginning of a heel spur. The athlete was found to have a cavus foot.

Management Plan The athlete was diagnosed as having plantar fasciitis (heel spur syndrome), and a conservative plan was chosen.

Phase 1 *Acute Injury* **GOALS**: Minimize inflammation and pain.
ESTIMATED LENGTH OF TIME (ELT): 1 week.

■ **Therapy** RICE plus NSAID as needed to reduce pain and inflammation. Injection therapy consisting of a steroid and anesthetic for trigger points.

■ **Exercise rehabilitation** Toe touch crutch walking. Begin heel cord stretching and rolling pin exercise to increase fascia flexibility.

Phase 2 *Repair* **GOALS**: Gain full weight bearing and walking pattern.
ELT: 1 to 3 weeks.

■ **Therapy** Ultrasound to increase blood flow. Cross friction massage over injury site. Apply shock absorption shoe insert with cutout (3 to 5 cm) in the tender area. Apply arch taping.

■ **Exercise rehabilitation** Continue heel cord stretching and rolling pin exercise to stretch the plantar fascia. Begin a program of gradual pain-free weight bearing. Begin a program of foot flexor strengthening.

Phase 3 *Remodeling* **GOALS**: Focus on full pain-free weight bearing while engaged in running.
ELT: 2 weeks.

■ **Therapy** Ultrasound as warranted. Continue cross friction massage. Use of a heel cup and arch taping when athlete is supporting weight.

■ **Exercise rehabilitation** Heel cord and plantar fascia stretching continues. Use of shoes with a reinforced heel counter for heel control. Foot flexor strengthening against tubular resistance is initiated. General exercise is performed to the lower leg. The athlete begins a running program that is pain free.

Criteria for Return to Competitive Cross-Country Running

1. Proximal arch and heel are pain free.
2. Heel cord and plantar fascia are stretched.
3. Lower leg has maximum strength.
4. Athlete is able to run competitively without pain.
5. Athlete is psychologically ready for competition.

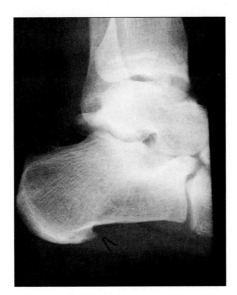

Figure 18-24

X ray of a large plantar cal-caneal exostotic spur.

thrust by the ball of the foot (on the heads of the metatarsals), fascial tension is increased to approximately twice the body weight.

Street shoes, by nature of their design, take on the characteristics of splints and tend to restrict foot action to such an extent that the arch may become somewhat rigid. This rigidity occurs because of shortening of the ligaments and other mild abnormalities. The athlete, changing from such footwear into a flexible gymnastic slipper or soft track shoe, often experiences trauma when the foot is subjected to stress. Trauma may also result from poor running technique.

A number of anatomical and biomechanical conditions have been studied as possible causes of plantar fasciitis. Those conditions include leg length discrepancy, excessive pronation of the subtalar joint, inflexibility of the longitudinal arch, and tightness of the gastrocnemius-soleus unit. Wearing shoes without sufficient arch support, running with a lengthened stride, and running on soft surfaces are also potential causes of plantar fasciitis.[24]

Symptoms and signs   The athlete complains of pain in the anterior medial heel, usually at the attachment of the plantar fascia to the calcaneus. The pain eventually moves into the central portion of the plantar fascia. This pain is increased when the athlete rises in the morning or bears weight after sitting for a long period. However, the pain lessens after a few steps. Pain also will be intensified when the toes and forefoot are forcibly dorsiflexed. If irritation persists, a painful heel spur will probably develop at the attachment of the plantar fascia to the medial aspect of the calcaneous; the heel spur will be visible on an X ray (Figure 18-24).

Management   Management of plantar fasciitis will generally require an extended period of treatment. It is not uncommon for symptoms to persist for as long as eight to twelve weeks. Orthotic therapy is very useful in the treatment of this problem. A soft orthotic works better than a hard orthotic. An extra-deep heel cup should be built into the orthotic. The orthotic should be worn at all times, especially when the athlete rises from bed in the morning.[12] Use of a heel cup compresses the fat pad under the calcaneous, providing a cushion under the area of irritation. When soft orthotics are not feasible, taping may reduce the symptoms. A simple arch taping or alternative taping often allows pain-free ambulation.[8] The use of a night splint to maintain a position of static stretch has also been recommended. In some cases, the athlete may need to use a short leg walking cast for four to six weeks.

The athlete should engage in vigorous heel cord stretching and in exercises that stretch the plantar fascia in the arch. Exercises that increase dorsiflexion of the great

18-4

Critical Thinking Exercise

A basketball player sustains a grade 2 lateral sprain of the left ankle.

? What metatarsal fracture may be associated with this type of sprain?

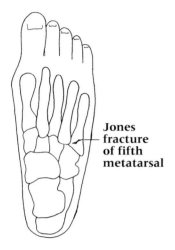

Figure 18-25

A Jones fracture occurs at the neck of the fifth metatarsal.

A cross-country runner changes her running patterns by increasing distance and performing more hill work. She complains to the athletic trainer of a gradually worsening pain in her forefoot. Inspection reveals point tenderness in the region of the fourth metatarsal bone. X ray reveals a stress fracture.

? How should this condition be managed?

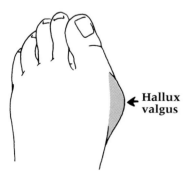

← **Hallux valgus**

Figure 18-26

Bunion, or hallux valgus deformity.

toe also may be of benefit to this problem. Stretching should be done at least three times a day. Antiinflammatory medications are recommended. Steroidal injection may be warranted at some point if symptoms fail to resolve.

Jones Fracture

Etiology Fractures may occur to any of the metatarsals and can be caused by inversion and plantar flexion of the foot; by direct force, such as being stepped on by another player; or by repetitive stress. By far the most common acute fracture is to the diaphysis at the base of the fifth metatarsal, which is referred to specifically as a Jones fracture (Figure 18-25).[23]

Symptoms and signs A Jones fracture is characterized by immediate swelling and pain over the fifth metatarsal. Healing of a Jones fracture is slow and frustrating for the athlete. This injury has a high nonunion rate, and the course of healing is unpredictable.[4]

Management Treatment for a Jones fracture is controversial but it appears that the use of crutches with no immobilization, gradually progressing to full weight bearing as pain subsides, may allow the athlete to return to activity in about six weeks. However, nonunion may cause a refracture to occur. It has been recommended that athletes be treated more aggressively using early internal fixation.[9]

Metatarsal Stress Fractures

Etiology The most common metatarsal stress fracture in the foot involves the shaft of the second metatarsal and is often referred to as a *march fracture*. It occurs in the runner who has suddenly changed patterns of training, such as increasing mileage, running hills, or running on a harder surface. An athlete who has an atypical condition such as a structural forefoot varus, hallux valgus, flatfoot, or a short first metatarsal is more predisposed to a second metatarsal stress fracture.[17]

An athlete can also experience a stress fracture of the fifth metatarsal at the insertion of the peroneus brevis tendon, but this injury should not be confused with a Jones fracture.

Management A bone scan is the best way to detect the presence of a stress fracture. Management of a metatarsal stress fracture usually consists of three or four days partial weight bearing followed by two weeks of rest. Return to running should be very gradual. An orthotic that corrects excessive pronation can help take stress off the second metatarsal.[3]

Bunion (Hallux Valgus Deformity) and Bunionettes (Tailor's Bunions)

Etiology A bunion, one of the most frequent painful deformities, occurs at the head of the first metatarsal (Figure 18-26). The term *bunion* is often used to refer to an exostosis. Commonly, a bunion is associated with a structural forefoot varus in which the first ray tends to splay outward, putting pressure on the first metatarsal head. Bunions are often caused by shoes that are pointed, too narrow, or too short. It is generally believed that women's shoes play a predominant role in the development of a hallux valgus deformity.[15]

The bursa over the first metatarsophalangeal joint becomes inflamed and eventually thickens. The joint becomes enlarged and the great toe becomes malaligned, moving laterally toward the second toe, sometimes to such an extent that it eventually overlaps the second toe. This type of bunion is also associated with a depressed or flattened transverse arch and a pronated foot.

The bunionette, or tailor's bunion, is much less common than hallux valgus and affects the fifth metatarsophalangeal joint. In this case, the little toe angulates toward the fourth toe, causing an enlarged metatarsal head.[5]

In all bunions, both the flexor and extensor tendons are malaligned, creating more angular stress on the joint. NOTE: Sesamoid fractures and sesamoiditis could be secondary to hallux valgus.

Symptoms and signs In the beginning of bunion formation, there is tenderness, swelling, and enlargement of the joint. Poorly fitting shoes increase the irritation and pain. As the inflammation continues, angulation of the toe progresses, eventually leading to painful ambulation.

Management Each bunion has unique characteristics. Early recognition and care can often prevent increased irritation and deformity. Following are some management procedures:

1. Wear correctly fitting shoes with a wide toe box.
2. Wear an appropriate orthotic to correct a structural forefoot varus deformity.
3. Place a felt or sponge rubber doughnut pad over the first and/or fifth metatarsophalangeal joint.
4. Wear a tape splint along with a resilient wedge placed between the great toe and the second toe (see Figure 8-21).
5. Engage in daily foot exercises to strengthen the extensor and flexor muscles.

Ultimately, a surgical procedure called a bunionectomy may be necessary to correct the problem.

Sesamoiditis

Etiology Two sesamoid bones lie within the flexors and adductor tendons of the great toe. These sesamoids function to transmit forces from the ground to the head of the first metatarsal. Sesamoiditis is caused by repetitive hyperextension of the great toe that eventually results in inflammation. Sesamoiditis is most common in dancing and basketball. It is estimated that 30 percent of sesamoid injuries are sesamoiditis.[18] Fractures of the sesamoids are also common.

Symptoms and signs The athlete complains of pain under the great toe, especially during a push-off. There is palpable tenderness under the first metatarsal head.

Management Sesamoiditis is treated with a variety of orthotic devices, including metatarsal pads, arch supports, and most often, a metatarsal bar (Figure 18-27). Activity should be decreased to allow inflammation to subside.

Metatarsalgia

Etiology Although *metatarsalgia* is a general term used to describe pain in the ball of the foot, it is more commonly associated with pain under the second and sometimes the third metatarsal head. A heavy callus often forms in the area of pain (Figure 18-28).[27]

One of the causes of metatarsalgia is restricted extensibility of the gastrocnemius-soleus complex. Because of this restriction, the athlete shortens the midstance phase of the gait and emphasizes the toe-off phase, causing excessive pressure under the forefoot. This excess pressure over time causes a heavy callus to form in this region. As the forefoot bears weight, normal skin becomes pinched against the inelastic callus and produces pain.[18]

Another cause of matatarsalgia is a fallen metatarsal arch.

Symptoms and signs As the transverse arch becomes flattened and the heads of the second, third, and fourth metatarsal bones become depressed, pain can result. A cavus deformity can also cause metatarsalgia.

Management Management of metatarsalgia usually consists of applying a pad to elevate the depressed metatarsal heads. See *Focus Box:* "Metatarsal pad support." NOTE: The bar is placed behind and not under the metatarsal heads (see Figure 18-27). Abnormal callus buildup should be removed by paring or filing. An athlete for whom the etiology of metatarsalgia is primarily a gastrocnemius-soleus contracture should perform a regimen of static stretching several times per day. An athlete whose metatarsal arch is depressed as a result of weakness should practice a daily regimen of exercise, concentrating on strengthening flexor and intrinsic muscles and stretching the Achilles tendon. A Thomas heel (Figure 18-29), which elevates the

18-6

Critical Thinking E x e r c i s e

A field hockey player complains to the athletic trainer of swelling, tenderness, and aching in the head of the first metatarsophalangeal joint of her left foot. On inspection, the athletic trainer observes that the great toe is deviated laterally.

? What is this condition commonly called, and why does it occur?

Figure 18-27

Metatarsal bar to treat both metatarsalgia and sesamoiditis.

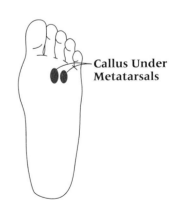

Callus Under Metatarsals

Figure 18-28

A heavy callus often forms under the metatarsal heads in metatarsalgia.

Focus

Metatarsal pad support

The purpose of the metatarsal pad is to reestablish the normal relationships of the metatarsal bones. It can be purchased commercially or constructed out of felt or sponge rubber (see Figure 18-31).

Materials needed

One roll of 1-inch (2.5 cm) tape, a 1/8-inch (0.3 cm) adhesive felt oval cut to a 2-inch (5 cm) circumference, and tape adherent.

Position of the athlete

The athlete sits on a table or chair with the plantar surface of the affected foot turned upward.

Position of the operator

The operator stands facing the plantar aspect of the athlete's foot.

Procedure

1. The circular pad is placed just behind the metatarsal heads.
2. Approximately two or three circular strips of tape are placed loosely around the pad and foot.

---

medial aspect of the heel from $^1/_8$ to $^3/_{16}$ inch (0.3 to 0.47 cm), also could prove beneficial.

Metatarsal Arch Strain

Etiology   The athlete who has a fallen metatarsal arch or who has a pes cavus is susceptible to strain.[3] Normally, the heads of the first and fifth metatarsal bones bear slightly more weight than the heads of the second, third, and fourth metatarsal bones. The first metatarsal head bears two-sixths of the body weight, the fifth bears slightly more than one-sixth, and the second, third, and fourth each bear approximately one-sixth. If the foot tends to excessively pronate or if the intermetatarsal ligaments are weak, allowing the foot to spread abnormally (splayed foot), a fallen metatarsal arch may result (Figure 18-30).

Symptoms and signs   The athlete has pain or cramping in the metatarsal region. There is **point tenderness** and weakness in the area. Morton's test may produce pain in the metatarsals (see Figure 18-16).

Management   Treatment of a metatarsal arch strain usually consists of applying a pad to elevate the depressed metatarsal heads. The pad is placed in the center and just behind the ball of the foot (metatarsal heads) (Figure 18-31).

Morton's Neuroma

Etiology   A neuroma is a mass that occurs about the nerve sheath of the common plantar nerve at the point at which it divides into the two digital branches to adjacent toes. A neuroma usually occurs between the metatarsal heads and is the most common nerve problem of the lower extremity.[25] A Morton's neuroma is located between the third and fourth metatarsal heads where the nerve is the thickest because it receives branches from both the medial and lateral plantar nerves (Figure 18-32).

Irritation increases with the collapse of the transverse arch of the foot, which puts the transverse metatarsal ligaments under stretch and thus compresses the common digital nerve and vessels. Excessive foot pronation can also be a predisposing factor, because more metatarsal shearing forces occur with the prolonged forefoot abduction.

---

point tenderness
Pain produced when an injury site is palpated.

18-7

Critical Thinking Exercise

A football player who commonly plays on artificial turf complains of pain in his right great toe.

? What type of injury frequently occurs to the great toe of an athlete who plays on artificial turf?

Symptoms and signs   The athlete complains of a burning paresthesia and severe intermittent pain in the forefoot that is often localized to the third web space and radiating to the toes. The pain is often relieved when non–weight bearing.[12] Hyperextension of the toes on weight bearing, as in squatting, stair climbing, or running, can increase the symptoms. Wearing shoes with a narrow toe box or high heels can increase the symptoms. If there is prolonged nerve irritation, the pain can become constant.

Management   A bone scan is often necessary to rule out a metatarsal stress fracture. A teardrop-shaped pad is placed between the heads of the third and fourth metatarsals in an attempt to splay the metatarsals apart during weight bearing, which decreases pressure on the neuroma. Often this teardrop pad will markedly reduce pain, and the athlete can continue to play despite this condition. Shoe selection also plays an important role in treatment of neuromas. Narrow shoes, particularly women's shoes that are pointed in the toe area and certain men's boots, may squeeze the metatarsal heads together and exacerbate the problem. A shoe that is wide in the toe box area should be selected. A straight-laced shoe often provides increased space in the toe box.[25] On rare occasions, surgical excision may be required.

Injuries to the Toes

Sprained Toes

Etiology   Sprains of the phalangeal joints of the toes are caused most often by kicking some nonyielding object. Sprains result from a considerable force applied in such a manner as to extend the joint beyond its normal range of motion (jamming it) or to impart a twisting motion to the toe, thereby twisting and tearing the ligaments and joint capsule.

Symptoms and signs   Pain is immediate and intense but is generally short lived. There is immediate swelling with discoloration appearing during the first or second day. There will be stiffness and residual pain that may last for several weeks.

Management   RICE must be applied immediately to minimize swelling. Casting or splinting of the small toes is difficult. Thus, buddy taping the injured toe to the adjacent toes is an effective technique of immobilization. The athlete may begin weight bearing as soon as tolerated and may not need to be on crutches at all.

Turf Toe

Etiology   Turf toe is a hyperextension injury resulting in a sprain of the metatarsophalangeal joint of the great toe, either from a single trauma or from repetitive overuse.[15] Typically, this injury occurs on unyielding synthetic turf although it can occur on grass also. Many of these injuries occur because sports shoes made for use on artificial turf often are more flexible and allow more dorsiflexion of the great toe.

Symptoms and signs   There is significant pain and swelling in and around the metatarsophalangeal joint of the great toe. Pain is exacerbated when the athlete tries to push off the foot in walking and certainly in running and jumping.

Management   Some shoe companies have addressed this problem by adding steel or other materials to the forefoot of their turf shoes to stiffen them. Flat insoles that have thin sheets of steel under the forefoot are also available. When commercially made products are not available, a thin, flat piece of thermoplastic (e.g. Orthoplast) may be placed under the shoe insole or may be molded to the foot. Taping the toe to prevent dorsiflexion may be done separately or with one of the shoe stiffening suggestions (see Figure 8-22). Modalities of choice include ice and ultrasound. One of the major ingredients in any treatment for turf toe is rest. The athlete should be discouraged from returning to activity until the toe is pain free.

Fractures and Dislocations of the Phalanges

Etiology   Fractures of the phalanges (Figure 18-33) usually occur either by kicking an object, stubbing a toe, or being stepped on. Dislocations of the phalanges are less common than fractures. If one occurs, it is most likely to be a dorsal dislocation

Figure 18-29

The Thomas heel elevates the medial aspect of the calcaneus $1/8$ to $3/16$ inch (0.3 to 0.47 cm), which can help relieve pronation and metatarsalgia.

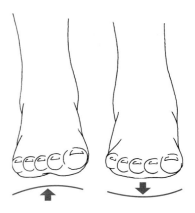

Figure 18-30

Normal and fallen metatarsal arch.

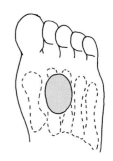

Figure 18-31

Metatarsal pad.

Fractures and dislocations of the foot phalanges can be caused by kicking an object or by stubbing a toe.

18-8

Critical Thinking Exercise

While roughhousing in the locker room, an athlete inadvertently kicks a locker and injures his right great toe.

? What should the athletic trainer be concerned with in this type of injury mechanism?

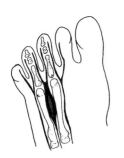

Figure 18-32

Morton's neuroma.

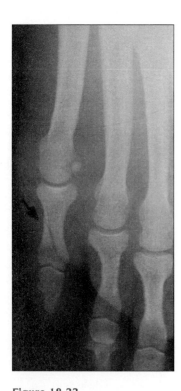

Figure 18-33

Fracture of the fifth phalanx.

of the middle phalanx proximal joint. The mechanism of injury is the same as for fractures. Frequently, fractures and dislocations accompany one another.[9]

Symptoms and signs   There is immediate intense pain, which is increased when the toes are moved. In the case of a dislocation, deformity will be obvious. Swelling of the joint occurs rapidly, and there is subsequent discoloration in the area of injury.

Management   Toe dislocations should be reduced by a physician. Casting of toe fractures and dislocations is unnecessary unless multiple toes are involved or unless the injury is a great toe fracture, in which case a cast may occasionally be applied for as long as three weeks. Otherwise buddy taping of the injured toe to adjacent toes usually provides sufficient support.

Morton's Toe

Etiology   Normally, the first metatarsal is longer than the second. Morton's toe is a condition in which there is an abnormally short first metatarsal, and thus the second toe appears to be longer than the great toe (Figure 18-34). Much of the weight bearing is ordinarily on the first metatarsal. Because the first metatarsal is short, however, more weight must be borne by the second metatarsal instead. This uneven weight distribution becomes even more of a problem in a running gait, during which weight bearing tends to shift more to the second metatarsal.

A Morton's toe can be a benign condition that causes no problems. However, if the second metatarsal is subjected to more stress, particularly during running, a stress fracture could develop.

Symptoms and signs   Symptoms are those of stress fractures in general. The athlete complains of pain both during and after activity, and there may be an area of point tenderness. A bone scan would be positive for a stress fracture. A callus is likely to form under the second metatarsal head.

Management   If a Morton's toe is not causing any symptoms, nothing should be done to try and correct the problem. If a Morton's toe is associated with a structural forefoot varus deformity, an orthotic with a medial wedge would likely be helpful.

Hallux Rigidus

Etiology   Hallux rigidus is a painful condition caused by the proliferation of bony spurs on the dorsal aspect of the first metatarsophalangeal joint that results in impingement and a loss of both active and passive dorsiflexion.[15] Hallux rigidus is a degenerative arthritic process resulting in changes to the articular cartilage of the metatarsal head and also in synovitis. In running and jumping activities, dorsiflexion of the metatarsophalangeal joint in the great toe is essential and, if restricted, causes the foot to roll onto the lateral border to compensate.

Symptoms and signs   The great toe is unable to dorsiflex, causing the athlete to toe off on the second, third, fourth, and fifth toes. Forced dorsiflexion increases pain. Walking becomes awkward because weight bearing is on the lateral aspect of the foot.

Management   Management usually includes a stiffer shoe with a larger toe box. An orthosis similar to that worn for a turf toe may also be helpful. Antiinflammatory medication may help reduce the inflammatory response. An osteotomy to surgically remove the mechanical obstruction to dorsiflexion may allow the athlete to return to a normal level of function.[15]

Hammer or Clawed Toes

Etiology   Hammer or clawed toes may be congenital, but more often the conditions are caused by wearing shoes that are too short over a long period of time, thus cramping the toes. Hammer toe usually involves the second or third toe; clawed toes involve more than one toe.

Symptoms and signs   In both conditions, the metatarsophalangeal and proximal interphalangeal joints become malaligned; flexor tendons become overly contracted, and extensor tendons become overly stretched. Such deformities eventually result in the formation of hard corns or calluses on the deformed joints.

Management   Often, surgery is the only cure. However, wearing proper shoes and using protective taping (see Figure 8-24) can help prevent irritation.

Overlapping Toes

Etiology   Overlapping of the toes (Figure 18-35) may be congenital or may be brought about by improperly fitting footwear, particularly shoes that are too narrow.

Symptoms and signs   At times, the condition indicates an outward projection of the great toe articulation or a drop in the longitudinal or metatarsal arch.

Management   As in the case of hammer toes, surgery is the only cure, but some therapeutic modalities such as a whirlpool bath can assist in alleviating inflammation. Taping may prevent some of the contractural tension within the sport shoe.

FOOT REHABILITATION

It is critical that the athletic trainer incorporates appropriate rehabilitation techniques in managing injuries of the foot. The foot is the base of support for the entire kinetic chain. Thus, injuries to the foot can affect the biomechanics of not only the foot, but also the ankle, knee, hip, and spine.

General Body Conditioning

Rehabilitation techniques for managing injuries to the lower extremity in general and to the foot in particular often require that the athlete be non–weight bearing for some period of time. Even if weight bearing is allowed, the injured athlete will not be able to maintain his or her level of fitness by engaging in running activities. Thus it becomes necessary to substitute alternative conditioning activities such as running in a pool or working on an upper extremity ergometer (Figure 18-36).[7] The athlete should certainly continue to engage in strengthening and flexibility exercises as allowed by the constraints of the injury.

Weight Bearing

If the athlete is unable to walk without a limp, non–weight bearing or limited weight-bearing crutch walking might be employed. Using incorrect gait mechanics will certainly affect other joints within the kinetic chain, causing unnecessary pain, and tends to do more harm than good. Progressing to full weight bearing as soon as it may be tolerated is generally recommended.

Joint Mobilization

Manual joint mobilization techniques are useful in maintaining or normalizing joint motions (Figure 18-37). The following joint mobilization techniques can be used in the foot:

- Anterior/posterior calcaneocuboid glides are used for increasing adduction and abduction. The calcaneus should be stabilized while the cuboid is mobilized.
- Anterior/posterior cuboidmetatarsal glides are done with one hand stabilizing the cuboid and the other gliding the base of the fifth metatarsal. These glides are used for increasing mobility of the fifth metatarsal.
- Anterior/posterior tarsometatarsal glides decrease hypomobility of the metatarsals.
- Anterior/posterior talonavicular glides also increase adduction and abduction. One hand stabilizes the talus while the other mobilizes the navicular bone.
- With anterior/posterior metatarsalphalangeal glides, the anterior glides increase extension and the posterior glides increase flexion. Mobilizations are accomplished by isolating individual segments.

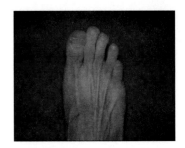

Figure 18-34

In a Morton's toe, there is a short first metatarsal.

Figure 18-35

Overlapping toes.

18-9

Critical Thinking Exercise

A tennis player complains of pain in the ball of the right foot. Inspection reveals a heavy callus formation under the second metatarsal head. This condition produces a metatarsalgia.

? What is the probable cause of this condition?

Figure 18-36

Pool exercises are useful in maintaining fitness while non–weight bearing.

Critical Thinking E x e r c i s e

A defensive lineman on a college football team complains of severe intermittent pain in the region between the third and fourth toes of the left foot. Inspection reveals that the pain radiates from the base to the tip of the toes. There is numbness of the skin between the toes.

? What is this condition, and how should it be conservatively managed?

Flexibility

Maintaining normal flexibility is critical in the foot. Of particular importance is restoring full range of motion following various injuries to the phalanges. It is also critical to engage in stretching activities in the case of plantar fasciitis (Figure 18-38). Stretching of the gastrocnemius-soleus complex is also important for a number of injuries (see Figures 19-30B and C).

Muscular Strength

Strength exercises for the foot can be done using a variety of resistance methods, including rubber tubing, towel exercises, and manual resistance.

Exercises commonly used in strengthening the muscles involved in foot motion include:

- Writing the alphabet—With the toes pointed, the athlete writes the complete alphabet in the air three times.
- Picking up objects—The athlete picks up small objects such as marbles with the toes and places them in a container.
- Ankle circumduction—The ankle is circumducted in as extreme a range of motion as possible (ten circles in one direction and ten circles in the other).
- Gripping and spreading of the toes— Gripping and spreading is repeated for up to ten repetitions (Figure 18-39).
- Towel gathering—A towel is extended in front of the feet. The heels are firmly planted on the floor with the forefoot on the end of the towel. The athlete then attempts to pull the towel with the feet without lifting the heels from the floor. As execution becomes easier, a weight can be placed at the other end of the towel for added resistance. Each exercise should be performed ten times (Figure 18-40A). This exercise can also be used for exercising the foot in abduction and adduction.
- Towel scoop—A towel is folded in half and placed sideways on the floor. The athlete places the heel firmly on the floor and the forefoot on the end of the towel. To ensure the greatest stability of the exercising foot, it is backed up with the other foot. Without lifting the heel from the floor, the athlete scoops the towel forward with the forefoot. Again, a weight resistance can be added to the end of the towel. The exercise should be repeated up to ten times (Figure 18-40B).

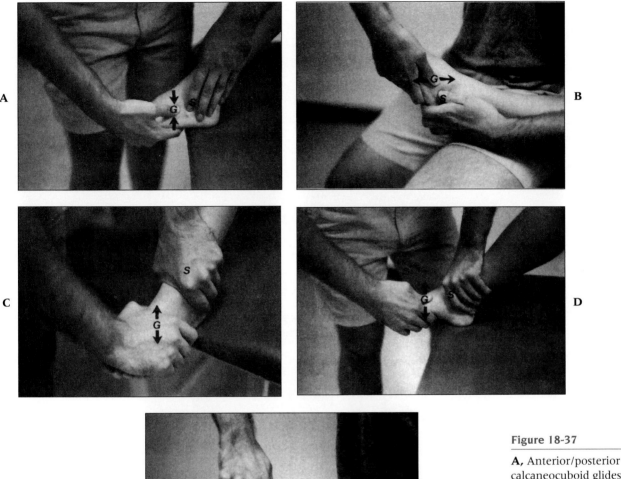

Figure 18-37

A, Anterior/posterior calcaneocuboid glides.
B, Anterior/posterior cuboidmetatarsal glides.
C, Anterior/posterior tarsometatarsal glides.
D, Anterior/posterior talonavicular glides.
E, Anterior/posterior metatarsophalangeal glides.

Neuromuscular Control

Reestablishing neuromuscular control following foot injury is a critical component in the rehabilitative process and should not be overlooked. Although maintaining neuromuscular control while weight bearing may appear to be a rather simple motor skill for uninjured athletes, neuromuscular control is compromised when injuries occur. Muscular weakness, proprioceptive deficits, and range of motion deficits may challenge an athlete's ability to maintain a center of gravity within the body's base of support, causing the athlete to lose balance. Neuromuscular control in the foot is the single most important element dictating movement strategies within the closed kinetic chain. The capability of adjusting and adapting to changing surfaces while creating a stable base of support is perhaps the single most important function of the foot in weight bearing.[12]

Neuromuscular control involves a highly integrative, dynamic process involving multiple neurological pathways. Neuromuscular control relative to joint position

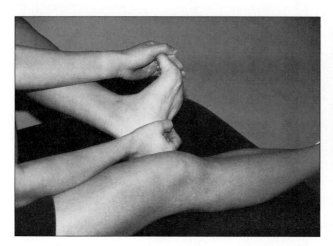

Figure 18-38

Plantar fascia stretches.

Figure 18-39

Gripping and spreading of the toes can be an excellent rehabilitation exercise for the injured foot.

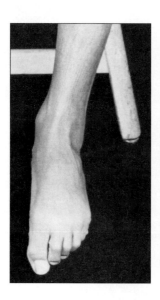
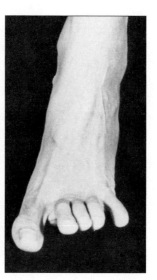

sense, proprioception, and kinesthesia is essential to all athletic performance but is particularly important to those athletic activities that require weight bearing. Current rehabilitation protocols are therefore focusing more on closed kinetic chain exercises, and neuromuscular control is receiving more attention in the sports medicine community.

Exercises for reestablishing neuromuscular control in the foot should expose the injured athlete to a variety of walking, running, and hopping exercises involving directional changes performed on varying surfaces. Balance board or wobble exercises can be useful in establishing a dynamic base of support (Figure 18-41).

Foot Orthotics and Taping

Throughout this chapter, references have been made to taping techniques and to the use of orthotics as means of providing additional support or correcting biomechanical abnormalities. Taping techniques have been thoroughly discussed in Chapter 8, and the use of orthotics was discussed briefly earlier in this chapter. This section expands on the discussion of orthotic use relative to the various injuries discussed in this chapter.

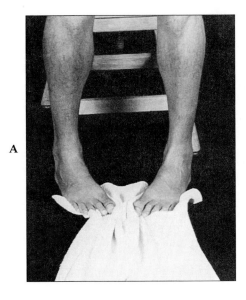

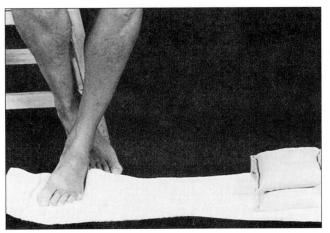

Figure 18-40

A, The towel gathering exercise. **B,** The towel scoop exercise.

The use of orthotics to correct foot deformities is a common practice in athletic training. The normal foot functions most efficiently when no deformities are present that predispose it to injury or exacerbate existing injuries. Orthotics are used to control abnormal compensatory movements of the foot by "bringing the floor up to meet the foot."[11]

The foot functions most efficiently in a neutral position. By providing support so that the foot does not have to move abnormally, an orthotic should help prevent compensatory problems. For problems that have already occurred, the orthotic provides a platform of support so that soft tissues can heal properly without undue stress.

Basically, there are three types of orthotics:[11]

1. Pads and soft flexible felt supports. These soft inserts are readily fabricated and are advocated for mild overuse syndromes. Pads are particularly useful in shoes, such as spikes and ski boots, that are too narrow to hold orthotics.

2. Semirigid orthotics made of flexible thermoplastics, rubber, or leather. These orthotics are prescribed for athletes who have increased symptoms. These orthotics are molded from a neutral cast. They are well tolerated by athletes whose sports require speed or jumping.

3. Functional or rigid orthotics are made from hard plastic and also require neutral casting. These orthotics allow control for most overuse symptoms.

Many athletic trainers make a neutral mold, put it in a box, mail it to an orthotic laboratory, and several weeks later, receive an orthotic back in the mail. Others like to construct the entire orthotic from start to finish, which requires a more skilled technician than does the mail-in method.

Figure 18-41

BAPS board exercises.

Orthotics for Correcting Excessive Pronation and Supination

To correct a structural forefoot varus deformity in which the foot excessively pronates, the orthotic should be the rigid type and should have a medial wedge under the head of the first metatarsal. It is also advisable to add a small wedge under the medial calcaneous to make the orthotic more comfortable (Figure 18-42A).

Conversely, to correct a structural forefoot valgus deformity in which the foot excessively supinates, the orthotic should be semirigid and have a lateral wedge under the head of the fifth metatarsal. Again, adding a small wedge under the lateral calcaneous will make the orthotic more comfortable (Figure 18-42B).

Figure 18-42

A, Medial wedge for forefoot varus. **B,** Lateral wedge for forefoot valgus. **C,** Medial wedge for rearfoot varus.

A. Forefoot Varus   **B. Forefoot Valgus**   **C. Rearfoot Varus**

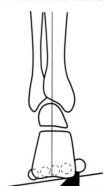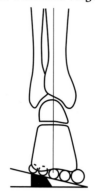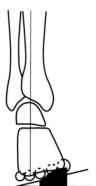

To correct a structural rearfoot varus deformity, the orthotic should be semirigid and have a wedge under the medial calcaneous and a small wedge under the head of the first metatarsal (Figure 18-42C).

Functional Progressions

Athletes engage in functional progression following injury to the foot in order to gradually regain the ability to walk, jog, run, change directions, and hop.[16] *Focus Box: "Functional progression for the foot"* details an appropriate functional progression for an injury to the foot.

Focus

Functional progression for the foot

- Non–weight bearing
- Partial weight bearing
- Full weight bearing
- Walking
    Normal
    Heel
    Toe
    Side Step/Shuffle Slides
- Jogging
    Straightaways on track
    Walk turns
    Jog complete oval of track
- Short sprints
- Acceleration/deceleration sprints
- Carioca
- Hopping
    Two feet
    One foot
    Alternate
- Cutting, jumping, hopping on command

SUMMARY

- The function of the foot is critical in running, jumping, or changing direction, and the complex nature of the anatomical structures of this body part makes recognition and management of foot injuries a major challenge to the athletic trainer.

- Many chronic and overuse injuries to the lower extremity can be related to faulty biomechanics of the foot because the foot is the part of the kinetic chain that is in direct contact with the ground.

- Essential movements that occur in the foot include pronation and supination, dorsiflexion and plantar flexion, adduction and abduction, and inversion and eversion.

- Foot injuries can best be prevented by selecting appropriate footwear, by correcting biomechanical structural deformities through the use of appropriate orthotics, and by paying attention to appropriate foot hygiene and care.

- Assessment of an injury to the foot includes a history and a palpation of soft-tissue and bony structures. In addition, observation should include a check for existing structural deformities including forefoot varus, which might cause excessive pronation, forefoot valgus, which causes excessive supination, and rear foot varus, which contributes to excessive pronation.

- Injuries to the foot can best be classified into three categories: injuries to the tarsal region, injuries to the metatarsal region including the arches, and injuries to the toes.

- An athlete engaging in rehabilitation of an injury to the foot should maintain general body conditioning and should engage in exercises designed to regain essential joint mobility, strength, flexibility, and neuromuscular control through a series of functional progressions that gradually increase stress to the injured structures.

- The use of orthotics and taping techniques can be essential in treating many of the injuries that occur in the foot.

Web Sites

Foot and Ankle Web Index: http://www.footandankle.com
The foot and ankle link library of this site is very helpful.

Premiere Medical Search Engine: http://www.medsite.com
This site allows the reader to enter any medical condition and it will search the net to find relevant articles.

Dr. Pribut's Running Injuries Page: http://www.clarknet/pub/pribut/spsport.html
This page lists common running injuries to the foot, ankle, knee, and hip.

Wheeless' Textbook of Orthopaedics: http://www.medmedia.com/med.htm
This Web page is great for injuries, anatomy, and X rays.

North Shore Podiatry Foot Care Center: http://www.bunionbusters.com
This site provides information about foot care and includes surgical care and abnormalities of the foot.

Solutions to Critical Thinking EXERCISES

18-1 Sever's disease is a traction injury to the apophysis of the calcaneal tubercle where the Achilles tendon attaches. The circulation becomes disrupted, resulting in a degeneration of the epiphyseal region.

18-2 It is likely that this athlete has a forefoot varus. To correct a structural forefoot varus deformity where the foot excessively pronates, the orthotic should be the rigid type and should have a medial wedge under the head of the first metatarsal. It is also advisable to add a small wedge under the medial calcaneous to make the orthotic more comfortable. The athletic trainer should also recommend that this athlete purchase a board-lasted shoe with a medial heel wedge and a firm heel counter.

18-3 This condition is characteristic of a plantar fascial strain. It should be managed symptomatically. A doughnut placed over the epicondyle region, a heel lift, and a shoe with a stiff shank may relieve some pain. The athlete should stretch the plantar muscles and gastrocnemius and perform arch exercises. Application of LowDye taping for pronation can also relieve pain.

18-4 A lateral sprain can produce an avulsion fracture of the proximal head of the fifth metatarsal bone.

18-5 Management of this stress fracture usually consists of three or four days partial weight bearing followed by two weeks of rest. Return to running should be very gradual. An orthotic that corrects excessive pronation can help take stress off the second metatarsal.

18-6 This condition is a bunion, or hallux valgus deformity. It is associated with wearing shoes that are too pointed, narrow, or short. It may begin with an inflamed bursa over the metatarsophalangeal joint. It can be associated with a depressed transverse arch or a pronated foot.

18-7 A sprain of the first metatarsophalangeal joint (turf toe) stems from hyperextension, usually because of the unyielding surface of artificial turf. This injury is a tear of the joint capsule from the metatarsal head.

18-8 Kicking the locker with the great toe could cause a fracture of the proximal or distal phalanx. This injury may develop swelling, discoloration, and point tenderness.

18-9 Metatarsalgia can be caused by a restricted gastrocnemius-soleus complex that produces a pes cavus. It can also be caused by a fallen metatarsal arch that abnormally depresses the second or third metatarsal heads and causes a heavy callus to be developed.

18-10 The defensive lineman has a Morton's neuroma. Conservatively, it is treated by having the athlete wear a broad-toed shoe, a transverse arch support, and a metatarsal bar or teardrop pad.

REVIEW QUESTIONS AND CLASS ACTIVITIES

1. Describe the anatomy of the foot.
2. How does the foot function during the gait cycle?
3. How can an injury on the plantar surface of the foot cause soreness and pain in the knee?
4. Demonstrate an appropriate procedure for assessing injuries of the foot.
5. How does a structural forefoot varus deformity cause an individual to excessively pronate?
6. Identify the types of acute strains that occur in the region of the foot. How can they be prevented? How can they be managed?
7. What are the common fractures that occur in the foot, and how can they be managed?
8. How does plantar fasciitis occur, and what measures should be taken to treat it?
9. Where are the two most likely places for an exostosis to occur in the foot?
10. What is the difference between a pes cavus and a pes planus foot?
11. What is the difference between a Morton's toe and a Morton's neuroma?
12. How is a hallux valgus deformity related to excessive pronation?
13. Why does a Jones fracture often take such a long time to heal?
14. How would you construct the most appropriate orthotic for an athlete who excessively supinates, and why?

REFERENCES

1. Baker C, Deese M: Diagnostic and operative ankle arthroscopy. In Baxter DE: *The foot and ankle in sport,* St Louis, 1995, Mosby.
2. Benda C: Stepping in the right sock, *Physician Sportsmed* 19 (12):125, 1991.
3. Candelora PD, Hunter SC: Overuse foot injuries. In Baker CL et al, editors: *The Hughston Clinic sports medicine book,* Baltimore, Md, 1995, Williams & Wilkins.
4. Collins KS, Streitz W: Bilateral Jones fractures in a high school football player, *J Ath Train* 31(3):253, 1996.
5. Coughlin MJ: Forefoot disorders. In Baxter DE, editor: *The foot and ankle in sports,* St Louis, 1995, Mosby.
6. Craik R, Oatis C: *Gait analysis: theory and application,* St Louis, 1995, Mosby.
7. Davis P et al: Rehabilitation strategies and protocols for the athlete. In Sammarco GJ, editor: *Rehabilitation of the foot and ankle,* St Louis, 1995, Mosby.
8. Denegar CR, Siple B: Bilateral foot pain in a collegiate distance runner, *J Ath Train* 31(1): 61, 1996.
9. Glick J, Sampson T: Ankle and foot fractures in athletics. In Nicholas J, Herschman E: *The lower extremity and spine in sports medicine,* St Louis, 1995, Mosby.
10. Hamill J et al: Biomechanics of the foot and ankle. In Sammarco GJ, editor: *Rehabilitation of the foot and ankle,* St Louis, 1995, Mosby.
11. Hunter S, Dolan M, Davis M: *Foot orthotics in therapy and sport,* Champaign, Ill, 1996, Human Kinetics.
12. Hunter S, Prentice W: Rehabilitation of foot injuries. In Prentice WE, editor: *Rehabilitation techniques in sports medicine,* ed 3, Dubuque, Iowa, 1999, WCB/McGraw-Hill.
13. Jones D, Singer K: Soft tissue conditions of the foot and ankle. In Nicholas J, Herschman E: *The lower extremity and spine in sports medicine,* St Louis, 1995, Mosby.
14. Kaya R: Plantar fasciitis in athletes, *J Sport Rehabil* 5(4):305, 1996.
15. Mann RA: Great toe disorders. In Baxter DE, editor: *The foot and ankle in sports,* St Louis, 1995, Mosby.
16. McGee M: Functional progressions and functional testing in rehabilitation. In Prentice WE, editor: *Rehabilitation techniques in sports medicine,* ed 3, Dubuque, Iowa, 1999, WCB/McGraw-Hill.
17. Moul J, Massey A: Recurrent metatarsal stress fractures in a college football lineman, *J Ath Train* 30(1):72, 1994.
18. Petrizzi MJ: Foot injuries. In Birrer RB, editor: *Sports medicine for the primary care physician,* ed 2, Boca Raton, Fla, 1994, CRC Press.
19. Pfeffer GB: Plantar heel pain. In Baxter DE, editor: *The foot and ankle in sport,* St Louis, 1995, Mosby.
20. Reynolds JC: Functional examination of the foot and ankle. In Sammarco GJ, editor: *Rehabilitation of the foot and ankle,* St Louis, 1995, Mosby.
21. Sammarco GJ: Soft tissue injuries. In Torg JS, Shephard RJ, editors: *Current therapy in sports medicine,* ed 3, St Louis, 1995, Mosby.
22. Tiberio D: Pathomechanics of structural foot deformities, *Phys Ther* 68:1840, 1988.
23. Torg JS: Jones fractures. In Torg JS, Shephard RJ, editors: *Current therapy in sports medicine,* ed 3, St Louis, 1995, Mosby.
24. Torg JS: Plantar fasciitis. In Torg JS, Shephard RJ, editors: *Current therapy in sports medicine,* ed 3, St Louis, 1995, Mosby.

25. Turco V: Injuries to the foot and ankle. In Nicholas J, Herschman
    E: *The lower extremity and spine in sports medicine*, St Louis, 1995,
    Mosby.
26. Valmassy R: Clinical biomechanics of the lower extremities, St
    Louis, 1996, Mosby.
27. Welsh RP: Metatarsalgia problems. In Torg JS, Shephard RJ,
    editors: *Current therapy in sports medicine*, ed 3, St Louis, 1995,
    Mosby.

ANNOTATED BIBLIOGRAPHY

Baxter DE: *The foot and ankle in sport*, St Louis, 1995, Mosby.

*This complete medical text addresses all aspects of the foot and ankle. It covers
common sports syndromes, anatomical disorders in sports, unique problems,
athletic shoes, orthoses, and rehabilitation.*

Donatelli R: *The biomechanics of the foot and ankle*, Philadelphia, 1990, Davis.

This practical book is for the therapist working directly with the patient.

The Ankle and Lower Leg

When you finish this chapter you should be able to

- Identify the major anatomical components of the ankle and lower leg that are commonly injured in sports.
- Accurately assess ankle and lower leg injuries.
- Discuss the etiology, symptoms and signs, and management of injuries occurring to the ankle and lower leg.
- Discuss a rehabilitation plan for various injuries to the ankle and lower leg.

L
ike the foot, the ankle and lower leg are common sites of injury in the athletic population.[2] Ankle injuries, especially to the stabilizing ligaments, are the most frequent injuries in sports. This chapter focuses on acute and chronic sports injuries in the ankle and lower leg (Figure 19-1).

ANATOMY OF THE LOWER LEG AND ANKLE

Bones

The portion of the lower extremity that lies between the knee and the ankle is defined as the lower leg and contains two bones, the tibia and the fibula. The bones that form the ankle joint are the distal portion of the tibia, the distal portion of the fibula, and the talus. The calcaneous also plays a critical role in the function of the ankle joint (Figure 19-2).

Tibia

With the exception of the femur, the tibia is the longest bone in the body. It serves as the principal weight-bearing bone of the leg. It is located on the medial side of the lower leg. The tibia is triangularly shaped in its upper two thirds but is rounded and more constricted in the lower third. The most pronounced change occurs in the lower third of the shaft and produces an anatomical weakness that establishes this area as the site of most fractures occurring to the leg. The shaft of the tibia has three surfaces: posterior, medial, and lateral. The posterior and lateral surfaces are covered by muscle; the medial surface is subcutaneous and as a result vulnerable to outside trauma.

Fibula

The fibula is long and slender and is located along the lateral aspect of the tibia, joining it in an arthrodial articulation at the upper end, just below the knee joint, and as a syndesmotic joint at the lower end. Both the upper and the lower tibiofibular joints are held in position by strong anterior and posterior ligaments. The main function of the fibula is to provide for the attachment of muscles.

Tibial and fibular malleoli   The thickened distal ends of both the tibia and the fibula are referred to, respectively, as the medial malleolus and lateral malleolus. The lateral malleolus of the fibula extends further distally so that the stability created by the bony arrangement at the ankle joint is greater on the lateral aspect of the ankle than on the medial.

Talus

The talus, the second largest tarsal and the main weight-bearing bone of the articulation, rests on the calcaneus and receives the articulating surfaces of the lateral and medial malleoli. The talus forms a link between the lower leg and the foot, or tarsus.

Figure 19-1

The ankle and lower leg are common sites of injury in sports.

Calcaneous

The calcaneous is one of the tarsal bones and was discussed in Chapter 18. The calcaneous is the bone that forms the heel to which attach many of the supporting ligaments of the ankle joint as well as the Achilles tendon.

Articulations

Superior and Inferior Tibiofibular Joints

The tibia and fibula articulate with one another superiorly and inferiorly (tibiofibular joints). The superior tibiofibular joint is diarthrotic, allowing some gliding movements. The articulation is formed by the tibia's lateral condyle and the head of the fibula. It is surrounded by a fibrous capsule reinforced with anterior and posterior ligaments. The superior tibiofibular joint is stronger in front than in back.

The inferior tibiofibular joint is a fibrous articulation. The articulation is between the lateral malleolus and the distal end of the tibia. The joint is reinforced by the ankle ligaments.

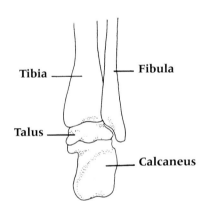

Figure 19-2

The ankle is a hinge joint formed by the tibia, fibula, and talus.

Talocrural Joint

The ankle joint, or talocrural joint, is a hinge joint (ginglymus) that is formed by the articular facet on the distal portion of the tibia, which articulates with the superior articular surface (trochlea) of the talus; the medial malleolus, which articulates with the medial surface of the trochlea of the talus; and the lateral malleolus, which articulates with the lateral surface of the trochlea (see Figure 19-2). This bony arrangement is typically referred to as the *ankle mortise.* Ankle movements that occur at the talocrural joint include plantar flexion and dorsiflexion.

Subtalar Joint

The anatomy and function of the subtalar joint was discussed in Chapter 18. The subtalar joint consists of the articulation between the talus and the calcaneus. Ankle movements that occur at the subtalar joint include inversion and eversion.

Figure 19-3

Major lateral ligaments of the
ankle.

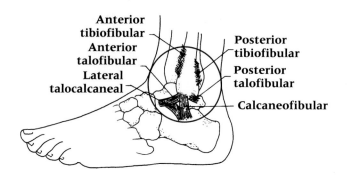

Anterior tibiofibular
Anterior talofibular
Lateral talocalcaneal
Posterior tibiofibular
Posterior talofibular
Calcaneofibular

Stabilizing Ligaments

Tibiofibular Ligaments

Joining the tibia and fibula is a strong interosseous membrane. The fibers display an oblique downward-and-outward pattern. The oblique arrangement aids in diffusing the forces placed on the leg. The membrane completely fills the tibiofibular space except for a small area at the superior aspect that is provided for the passage of the anterior tibial vessels. The anterior and posterior tibiofibular ligaments, which hold the tibia and fibula together and form the distal portion of the interroseous membrane, are sometimes referred to as the syndesmotic ligaments.

Ankle Ligaments

In addition to the tibiofibular ligaments, the ligamentous support of the ankle consists of three lateral ligaments and the medial, or deltoid, ligament (Figure 19-3).

Lateral ligaments   The three lateral ligaments include the anterior talofibular, the posterior talofibular, and the calcaneofibular (Table 19-1).

Medial ligaments   The deltoid ligament is triangular. It attaches superiorly to the borders of the medial malleolus; it attaches inferiorly to the medial surface of the talus, to the sustentaculum tali of the calcaneus, and to the posterior margin of the navicular bone. The deltoid ligament is the primary resistance to foot eversion. It, along with the plantar calcaneonavicular (spring) ligament, also helps maintain the inner longitudinal arch. Although it should be considered as one ligament, the deltoid ligament includes superficial and deep fibers (Figure 19-4). Anteriorly are the anterior tibiotalar part and the tibionavicular part. Medially is the tibiocalcaneal part, and posteriorly is the posterior tibiotalar part.

Joint Capsule

A thin articular capsule encases the ankle joint and attaches to the borders of the bone involved. It is somewhat different from most other capsules in that it is thick on the medial aspects of the joint but becomes a thin, gauzelike membrane at the back.

TABLE 19-1 Function of Key Ankle Ligaments

Ligament	Primary Function
Anterior talofibular	Restrains anterior displacement of talus
Calcaneofibular	Restrains inversion of calcaneus
Posterior talofibular	Restrains posterior displacement of talus
Deltoid	Prevents abduction and eversion of ankle and subtalar joint
	Prevents eversion, pronation, and anterior displacement of talus

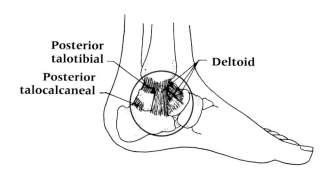

Figure 19-4

Major medial ligaments of the ankle.

Ankle Musculature

The movements of the talocrural joint are dorsiflexion (flexion) and plantar flexion (extension). Inversion and eversion occur at the subtalar joint. Tendons of muscles passing posterior to the malleoli will produce ankle plantar flexion along with toe flexion in the foot. Muscles and their tendons passing anterior to the talocrural joint function to dorsiflex the foot and to produce toe extension. The muscles that cross the ankle joint laterally cause eversion, while the muscles that cross the ankle joint medially cause inversion (Figure 19-5).

Muscle Compartments

The musculature of the lower leg is contained within four distinct compartments, which are bounded by heavy fascia (Figure 19-6). Acute or chronic trauma to any of these compartments can lead to swelling and neurological motor and sensory deficits.

The *anterior compartment* contains those muscles that dorsiflex the ankle and extend the toes—the tibialis anterior, extensor hallucis longus, and extensor digitorum longus muscles—and contains the anterior tibial nerve and the tibial artery.

The *lateral compartment* contains the peroneus longus and brevis, which evert the ankle; the peroneus tertius muscle, which assists in dorsiflexion; and the superficial branch of the peroneal nerve.

The *superficial posterior compartment* contains the gastrocnemius muscle and the soleus muscle. These muscles plantar flex the ankle.

The *deep posterior compartment* contains the tibialis posterior, flexor digitorum longus, and flexor hallucis longus muscles, which invert the ankle, and the posterior tibial artery.

Nerve and Blood Supply

The major nerves of the lower leg are the tibial and common peroneal, stemming from the large sciatic nerve. The major arteries often accompany the nerves and are the posterior and anterior tibial arteries (Figure 19-7). The primary veins consist of the popliteal peroneal and the anterior and posterior tibial veins.

FUNCTIONAL ANATOMY

The biomechanical motions occurring at the ankle and rear foot are complex. Anatomically, the ankle is a stable hinge joint in which the dome of the talus articulates with the distal ends of the tibia and fibula. Medial or lateral displacement of the talus is prevented by the malleoli. The arrangement of the ankle ligaments permits flexion and extension at the talocrural joint while limiting inversion and eversion at the subtalar joint (see Chapter 18).[29]

The square shape of the talus contributes to ankle stability. Because the talus is wider anteriorly than posteriorly, the most stable position of the ankle is with the foot in dorsiflexion. In this position, the wider anterior aspect of the talus comes in

Because the talus is wider anteriorly than posteriorly, the most stable position of the ankle is with the foot in dorsiflexion.

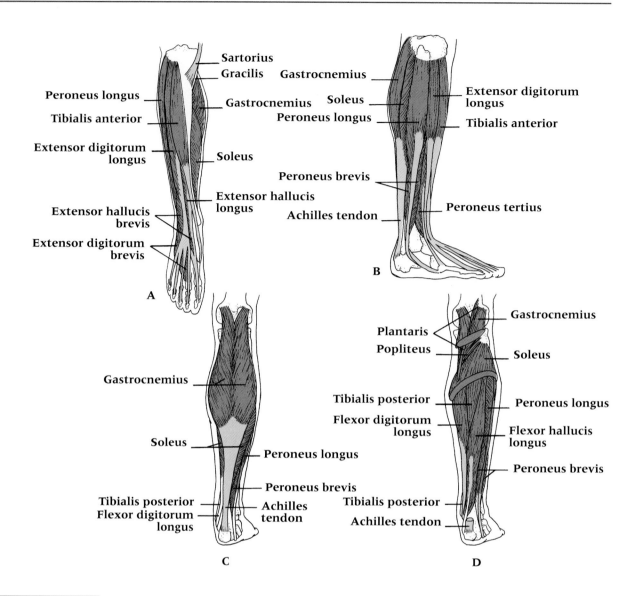

Figure 19-5

Muscles of the lower leg.
A, Anterior view. **B,** Lateral view. **C,** Posterior view (superficial structures). **D,** Posterior view (deep structures).

Preventing ankle sprains is achieved by:

- Stretching the Achilles tendon
- Strengthening key muscles
- Obtaining proprioceptive training
- Wearing proper footwear
- Taping when appropriate

contact with the narrower portion lying between the malleoli, gripping it tightly. By contrast, as the ankle moves into plantar flexion, the wider portion of the tibia is brought in contact with the narrower posterior aspect of the talus, which makes plantar flexion a much less stable position than dorsiflexion.

The degree of motion for the ankle joint ranges from 10 degrees of dorsiflexion to 50 degrees of plantar flexion. Normal gait mechanics require at least 20 degrees of plantar flexion and 10 degrees of dorsiflexion with the knee extended.[19]

Normal ankle function depends on the joints of the rearfoot, the most important of which is the subtalar joint. The movements of the talus during pronation and supination have profound effects on the lower extremity both proximally and distally.

PREVENTING INJURY IN THE LOWER LEG AND ANKLE

Many lower leg and ankle conditions, especially sprains, can be reduced if the athlete engages in the following: stretching the Achilles tendon, strengthening key muscles, learning neuromuscular and proprioceptive control, wearing proper footwear, and in some cases, being proper taped.

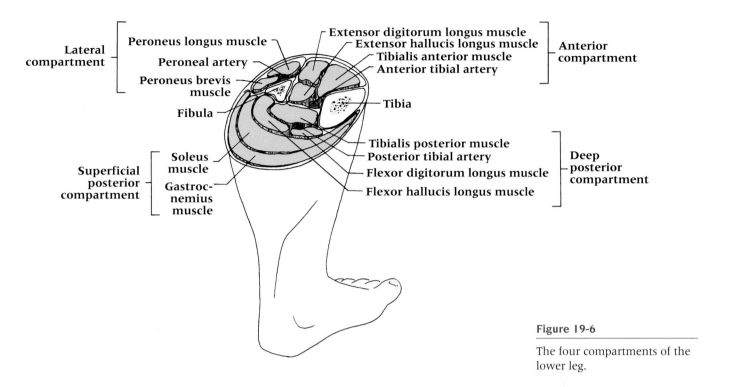

Figure 19-6

The four compartments of the lower leg.

Achilles Tendon Stretching

It is critical for normal gait that the ankle dorsiflex at least 10 degrees or more. A tight heel cord may limit dorsiflexion and may predispose the athlete to ankle injury. The athlete, especially one with tight Achilles tendons, should routinely stretch before and after practice (see Figure 19-30). To adequately stretch the Achilles tendon complex, stretching should be performed both with the knee extended and then with it flexed 15 to 30 degrees.

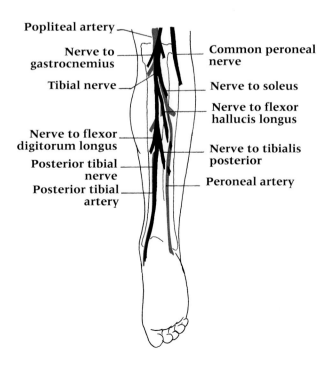

Figure 19-7

Blood and nerve supply of the lower leg.

Strength Training

Of major importance in ankle injury prevention is the achievement of both static and dynamic joint stability (see Figure 19-32). A normal range of motion must be maintained, and the muscles and tendons that surround the talocrural joint must be kept strong.

Neuromuscular Control Training

Athletes must develop neuromuscular control at the ankle joint. Neuromuscular control involves the capability of adapting to uneven surfaces by controlling motion at the ankle joint. Athletes can enhance ankle neuromuscular control by training in controlled activities on uneven surfaces or by spending time each day on a balance board (wobble board), (see Figure 19-31), a BAPS board or a Kinesthetic Awareness Trainer (KAT) system (see Figure 16-3B).

Footwear

As discussed in Chapter 7, proper footwear can be an important factor in reducing injuries to both the foot and the ankle. Shoes should not be used in activities for which they were not intended—for example, running shoes designed for straight-ahead activity should not be used to play tennis, a sport that demands a great deal of lateral movement. Cleats on a shoe should not be centered in the middle of the sole but should be placed far enough on the border to avoid ankle sprains. High-top shoes, when worn by athletes with a history of ankle sprain, can offer greater support than low-top shoes do.

Preventive Ankle Taping and Orthoses

Chapter 8 discussed the doubt surrounding the benefits of routinely taping ankles that have no history of sprain. There is some indication that tape, properly applied, can provide some prophylactic protection.[14] However, tape that constricts soft tissue or disrupts normal biomechanical function can create unnecessary injuries. Although taping is preferred, a much cheaper cloth muslin wrap may provide some protection (see Chapter 8). Lace-up supports and semirigid ankle braces are increasingly being used in place of tape. The sport-stirrup orthosis has been found superior to taping in preventing recurrent ankle sprains (see Figure 7-24).[24,25]

ASSESSING THE LOWER LEG AND ANKLE

History

The athlete's history may vary depending on whether the problem is the result of sudden trauma or is chronic. The athlete with an acute injury to the lower leg or ankle should be asked the following questions:[5]

- Have you ever hurt your ankle before?
- How did you hurt your ankle?
- What did you hear when the injury occurred—a crack, snap, or pop?
- How bad was the pain and how long did it last?
- Is there any sense of muscle weakness or difficulty in walking?
- How disabling was the injury? Could you walk right away, or were you not able to bear weight for a period of time?
- Has a similar injury occurred before?
- Was there immediate swelling, or did the swelling occur later (or at all)?
- Where did the swelling occur?

The athlete with a chronic painful condition might be asked the following:

- How much does it hurt?
- Where does it hurt?

- Under what circumstances does pain occur—when bearing weight, after activity, or when arising after a night's sleep?
- What past ankle injuries have occurred?
- What first aid and therapy, if any, were given for these previous injuries?

Observation

In looking initially at the ankle, the athletic trainer determines the following:[30]

- Are there any postural deviations? (Toeing in may indicate tibial torsion or genu valgum or varum; foot pronation should also be noted.)
- Is there any difficulty in walking?
- Is there an obvious deformity or swelling?
- Are the bony contours of the ankle normal and symmetrical, or is there a deviation such as a bony deformity?
- Are the color and texture of the skin normal?
- Is there crepitus or abnormal sound in the ankle joint?
- Is heat, swelling, or redness present?
- Is the athlete in obvious pain?
- Does the athlete have a normal ankle range of motion?
- If the athlete is able to walk, is there a normal walking pattern?

Palpation

The area of injury should be palpated to determine obvious structural deformities, areas of swelling, or points of tenderness.

Bony Palpation

The following bony landmarks should be palpated:

Anterior Aspect
- Fibular head
- Fibular shaft
- Lateral malleolus
- Tibial plateau
- Tibial shaft
- Medial malleolus
- Dome of the talus
- Posterior Aspect
- Medial malleolus
- Lateral malleolus
- Dome of the talus

Posterior Aspect
- Medial malleolus
- Lateral malleolus
- Dome of the talus
- Calcaneous

Soft-Tissue Palpation

The following soft tissue structures should be palpated:

Lateral Aspect
- Lateral compartment
  Peroneus longus muscle
  Peroneus brevis muscle
  Peroneus tertius muscle
- Peroneus longus tendon
- Peroneus brevis tendon
- Anterior talofibular ligament
- Calcaneofibular ligament
- Posterior talofibular ligament

Medial Aspect
- Deep posterior muscle
  Posterior tibialis muscle
  Flexor digitorum longus muscle
  Flexor hallicus muscle
- Posterior tibialis tendon
- Flexor digitorum longus tendon
- Flexor hallucis tendon
- Deltoid ligament

Anterior Aspect

- Anterior compartment
  Anterior tibialis muscle
  Extensor hallicus longus muscle
  Extensor digitorum longus muscle
- Anterior tibialis tendon
- Extensor hallucis longus tendon
- Extensor digitorum longus tendon
- Peroneus tertius tendon
- Anterior tibiofibular ligament

Posterior Aspect

- Superficial posterior compartment
  Gastrocnemius muscle
  Soleus muscle
- Achilles tendon
- Posterior tibiofibular ligament

Special Tests

Lower Leg

Lower leg alignment tests   Determining malalignment of the lower leg can reveal the causes of abnormal stresses applied to the foot, ankle, and lower leg as well as the knees and hip. In normal alignment of the lower extremity, anteriorly, a straight line can be drawn from the anterior superior iliac spine of the pelvis, through the patella, and to the web between the first and second toes. Laterally, a straight line can be drawn from the greater trochanter of the femur, through the center of the patella, and to just behind the lateral malleolus. Posteriorly, a straight line can be drawn from the center of the lower leg to the midline of the Achilles tendon and calcaneus.[6] A common malalignment of the lower leg is internal or external tibial torsion.

Percussion and compression tests   When fracture is suspected, a gentle percussive blow can be given to the tibia or fibula below or above the suspected site. Percussion can also be applied upward on the bottom of the heel. Such blows set up a vibratory force that resonates at the fracture, causing pain (Figure 19-8).

In a compression test, the tibia and fibula are compressed either above or below the fracture site (Figure 19-9). Increased pain over the area of point tenderness may be indicative of a fracture, and referral should be made for X rays.

Thompson test   The Thompson test (Figure 19-10) is performed by squeezing the calf muscle while the leg is extended and the foot is hanging over the edge of the table. A positive Thompson sign is one in which squeezing the calf muscle does not cause the heel to move or pull upward or causes the heel to move less when compared with the uninjured leg.

Homan's sign   The test for Homan's sign gives some indication of the presence of a deep vein thrombophlebitis. With the athlete in a supine position with the knee fully extended, the ankle is passively dorsiflexed so that the calf muscles are

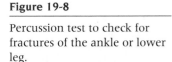

Figure 19-8

Percussion test to check for fractures of the ankle or lower leg.

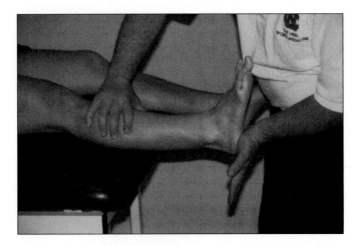

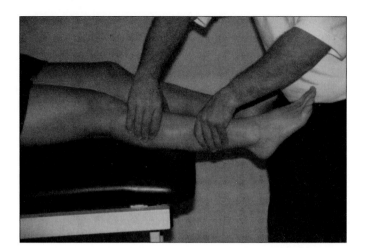

Figure 19-9

Compression test to check for fractures of the tibia or fibula.

stretched. Pain in the calf is a positive sign (Figure 19-11). The athlete should be referred immediately to the physician for further diagnosis.

Ankle Stability Tests

Anterior drawer test   The anterior drawer test is used to determine the extent of injury to the anterior talofibular ligament primarily and to the other lateral ligaments secondarily (Figure 19-12). The athlete sits on the edge of a treatment table with legs and feet relaxed. The athletic trainer grasps the lower tibia in one hand and the calcaneus in the palm of the other hand. The tibia is then pushed backward as the calcaneus is pulled forward. A positive anterior drawer sign occurs when the foot slides forward, sometimes making a clunking sound as it reaches its end point, and generally indicates a tear in the anterior talofibular ligament.

Talar tilt test   Talar tilt tests are used to determine the extent of inversion or eversion injuries. With the foot positioned at 90 degrees to the lower leg and stabilized, the calcaneous is inverted. Excessive motion of the talus indicates injury to the calcaneofibular and possibly the anterior and posterior talofibular ligaments as well (Figure 19-13).

The deltoid ligament can be tested in the same manner except that the calcaneous is everted.

Functional Tests

Muscle function is important in evaluating the ankle injury (Figure 19-14). *If the following movements aggravate a recent injury, they should be avoided.* While bearing weight on both feet, the athlete does the following:
- Walks on toes (tests plantar flexion)
- Walks on heels (tests dorsiflexion)
- Walks on lateral border of feet (tests inversion)
- Walks on medial border of feet (tests eversion)
- Hops on the injured ankle

Passive, active, and resistive movements should be manually applied to determine joint integrity and muscle function.

RECOGNITION OF SPECIFIC INJURIES

Ankle Injuries

Ankle sprains are perhaps the single most common injury in the athletic population. Ankle sprains are generally caused by sudden inversion or eversion, often in combination with plantar flexion or dorsiflexion (Table 19-2). Injuries may be classified according to either location or mechanism of injury.

A positive anterior drawer sign of ankle stability is when the foot slides forward, sometimes making a clunking sound as it reaches its end point.

A positive talar tilt occurs when the calcaneofibular ligament is sprained.

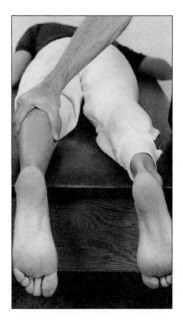

Figure 19-10

The Thompson test to determine an Achilles tendon rupture by squeezing the calf muscle. A positive result to the test is one in which the heel does not move.

Figure 19-11

Homan's sign may indicate a deep vein thrombophlebitis.

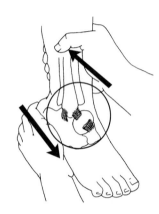

Figure 19-12

Anterior drawer test for ankle ligament instability.

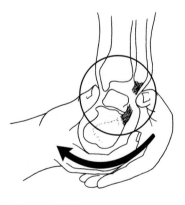

Figure 19-13

Talar tilt testing for lateral ankle instability.

Inversion Sprain

Inversion ankle sprains are the most common and result in injury to the lateral ligaments. The anterior talofibular ligament is the weakest of the three lateral ligaments. Its major function is to stop forward subluxation of the talus. It is injured in an inverted, plantar flexed, and internally rotated position (Figure 19-15). The calcaneofibular and posterior talofibular ligaments may also be injured in inversion sprains as the force of inversion is increased.

Occasionally an inversion force could be of sufficient magnitude to cause a portion of bone to be avulsed from the lateral malleolus (Figure 19-16).[30] It is also possible that inversion can cause both an avulsion of the lateral malleolus and a fracture of the medial malleolus. This injury is known as a *bimalleolar fracture*.[30]

The severity of lateral ankle sprains is classified according to grades. A grade 1 sprain usually involves the anterior talofibular ligament; a grade 2, the anterior talofibular and calcaneofibular ligaments; and a grade 3, the anterior talofibular, calcaneofibular, posterior talofibular, and frequently the anterior tibiofibular ligaments. In each instance, the foot is forcefully inverted such as when a basketball player jumps and comes down on the foot of another player. Inversion sprains can also occur when an individual is walking or running on an uneven surface or suddenly steps into a hole.

Grade I Inversion Ankle Sprain

The grade 1 ankle sprain is the most common type of sprain. Lateral sprains are probably the most frequent injury in sports in which running and jumping occur.[4]

Etiology   The inversion sprain occurs with the foot in inversion, plantar flexion, and adduction with a mild stretching of the anterior talofibular ligament.

Symptoms and signs   Mild pain and disability occur. Weight bearing is minimally impaired. Signs are point tenderness and swelling over the ligament with no joint laxity.[28]

Management   Rest, ice, compression, and elevation (RICE) are used for twenty minutes every few hours for one to two days. The application of a horseshoe pad may also help control hemorrhage (Figure 19-17).[42] It may be advisable for the athlete to limit weight-bearing activities for one to two days, after which rehabilitation may become more aggressive. An elastic wrap might provide comfortable pressure when weight bearing begins. When the athlete's ankle is pain free and not swollen, a routine of circumduction is begun several times per day. When the athlete returns to weight bearing, application of tape may provide an extra measure of protection. Usually an athlete can return to activity in seven to ten days.[33]

Grade 2 Inversion Ankle Sprain

A grade 2 ankle sprain has a high incidence among sports participants and causes a great deal of disability with many days of lost time.[36]

Etiology   Moderate force on the ankle while it is in a position of inversion, plantar flexion, and adduction can cause a grade 2 sprain.

Symptoms and signs   The athlete usually complains that a pop or snap was felt on the lateral side of the ankle. There is moderate pain and disability, and weight bearing is difficult. There is tenderness and edema with blood in the joint. Ecchymosis may occur, as well as a positive talar tilt test. There is also a positive anterior drawer sign between 4 and 14 mm (.16–.55 inch).[4] A grade 2 ankle sprain may be a complete tear of the anterior talofibular ligament and a stretch and tear of the calcaneofibular ligament. The anterior drawer test will elicit slight to moderate abnormal motion. This injury degree can produce a persistently unstable ankle that recurrently becomes sprained and later develops traumatic arthritis.[36]

Management   RICE should be used intermittently for at least seventy-two hours. X-ray examination should be routine for this grade of injury. The athlete should use

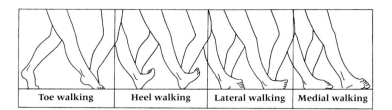

| Toe walking | Heel walking | Lateral walking | Medial walking |

Figure 19-14

Evaluating ankle function during walking.

crutches for five to ten days, gradually progressing to full weight bearing during that period. The athlete will need to wear some type of protective immobilization device for one to two weeks.[4] Plantar and dorsiflexion exercises in a pain-free range should begin forty-eight hours after the injury occurs. Early movement helps maintain range of motion and normal proprioception. Proprioceptive neuromuscular facilitation (PNF) exercise improves strength, range of motion, and proprioception. Exercise should include isometrics while the ankle is immobilized, followed by range-of-motion exercises, progressive resistance exercise (PRE), and balance activities lasting up to four weeks.[9]

Taping in a closed basket weave technique may protect the ankle during the early stages of walking (see Figure 8-26). The athlete must be instructed to avoid walking or running on uneven surfaces for two to three weeks after weight bearing has begun.

NOTE: The long-term effects of a grade 2 sprain are likely to include chronic instability with a recurrence of injury. Over a period of time, this instability can lead to joint degeneration and osteoarthritis. Once a grade 2 sprain has occurred, the athlete must continue to engage in rehabilitative activities to minimize recurrence of injury.[43]

Grade 3 Inversion Ankle Sprain

The grade 3 inversion ankle sprain is relatively uncommon in sports. When it does happen, it is extremely disabling. Often the force causes the ankle to subluxate and then spontaneously reduce.

Etiology   The grade 3 sprain is caused by a significant inversion force to the ankle, usually combined with plantar flexion, and adduction. This injury involves varying grades of damage to the anterior talofibular, calcaneofibular, and posterior talofibular ligaments as well as the joint capsule.

Symptoms and signs   The athlete complains of severe pain in the region of the lateral malleolus. Weight bearing is not possible because of the great amount of swelling, with or without pain. Hemarthrosis, discoloration, a positive talar tilt, and a positive anterior drawer test are present.[41]

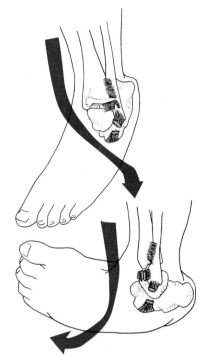

Figure 19-15

Mechanism of an inversion ankle sprain.

TABLE 19-2 Mechanisms of Ankle Sprain and Ligament Injury

Mechanisms	Area Injured
Plantar flexion or inversion	Anterior talofibular ligament
	Calcaneofibular ligament
	Posterior talofibular ligament
	Tibiofibular ligament (severe injury)
Inversion (uncommon)	Calcaneofibular ligament (along with anterior or posterior talofibular ligament)
Dorsiflexion	Tibiofibular ligament
Eversion	Deltoid ligament
	Tibiofibular ligament (severe injury)
	Interosseous membrane (as external rotation increases)
	Possible fibular fracture (proximal or distal)

Management PLAN

Grade 2 Inversion Ankle Sprain

Injury Situation A male, college senior lacrosse player stepped into a rut on the field, causing a major twist of the left ankle. At the time of injury, the athlete felt a severe pain on the lateral aspect of the ankle before he fell to the ground.

Symptoms and Signs After the injury, the athlete complained of moderate pain on the outside of his left ankle. Initially, it was painful to move the ankle. Walking on the left foot was very difficult. There was moderate tenderness over the lateral aspect of the ankle. Swelling rapidly occurred around the lateral malleoli. The ankle displayed a slight positive talor tilt and a positive anterior drawer test of 4 mm.

Phase **1** *Acute Injury* **GOALS:** To control hemorrhage, swelling, pain, and spasm.
ESTIMATED LENGTH OF TIME (ELT): 2–3 days.

■ **Therapy** Ice packs are applied (20 minutes) intermittently 6 to 8 times daily. X-ray examination rules out fracture. Athlete wears elastic wrap during waking hours and elevates leg. The leg is elevated during sleep. Nonsteroidal antiinflammatory drugs and analgesics are given. An air splint is used during this period for support and compression. No weight bearing is allowed. Crutches are used to avoid weight bearing for at least 3 or 4 days or until athlete can walk without a limp with lateral support.

■ **Exercise rehabilitation** The athlete begins exercise by toe gripping and spreading if there is no pain (10 to 15 times) every waking hour starting on the second day of injury. General body maintenance exercises are conducted 3 times a week as long as they do not aggravate the injury.

Phase **2** *Repair* **GOALS:** To decrease swelling, permit secondary healing to occur, restore full muscle contraction without pain, restore 50% pain-free movement.
ELT: 3 weeks.

■ **Therapy** All treatment is immediately followed by exercise. Use ice pack (5 to 15 minutes), ice massage (7 minutes), cold whirlpool (60° F, 10 minutes), or massage above and below injury site (5 minutes). When hemorrhage is completely controlled, use whirlpool (90° to 100° F, 10 to 15 minutes).

■ **Exercise rehabilitation** Crutch walking with a toe touch if athlete is unable to walk without a limp while wearing an air cast, tape, or both for 3 weeks. First 2 weeks, toe griping and spreading (10 to 15 times) every waking hour. Active PNF ankle patterns 3 or 4 times daily for a pain-free range of motion. Any exercise that produces pain or swelling is avoided. Ankle circumduction (10 to 15 times each direction) 2 or 3 times daily. Achilles tendon stretch from the floor (30 seconds) in each foot position (toe in, toe out, straight ahead) 3 or 4 times daily. Toe raises (10 times, 1 to 3 sets) 3 or 4 times daily. Eversion exercise using a towel or rubber tube or tire resistance 3 or 4 times daily. Shifting body weight between injured and noninjured ankle (up to 20 times 2 or 3 times daily). Wobble board exercise (1 to 3 minutes) 2 or 3 times daily. Progress to straight-ahead short-step walking if it can be done without a limp. General body maintenance exercises are conducted 3 times a week as long as they do not aggravate injury.

Phase **3** *Remodeling* **GOALS:** To restore symptom-free full range of motion, power, endurance, speed, and agility.
ELT: 3–5 weeks.

■ **Therapy** Therapeutic modalities such as whirlpool (100° to 105° F) (20 minutes) or ultrasound (0.5 W/cm²) (5 minutes) are used symptomatically.

Continued

Grade 2 Inversion Ankle Sprain—*cont'd*

■ **Exercise rehabilitation** Achilles tendon stretch using slant board (30 seconds each foot position) 2 or 3 times daily. Toe raises using slant board and resistance (10 repetitions, 1 to 3 sets) 2 or 3 times daily. Resistance ankle device to strengthen anterior, lateral, and medial muscles (starting with 2 lb and progressing to 10 lb) (1 to 3 sets) 2 or 3 times daily. Wobble board for ankle proprioception (begin at 1 minute in each direction, progress to 5 minutes) 3 times daily. Walk-jog routine as long as athlete is symptom free: begin with alternate walk-jog-run-walk 25 yards straight ahead, jog 25 yards straight ahead; progress to walk 25 yards in lazy S or to perform five figure eights, progress to figure-eight running as fast as possible; progress to run 10 figure eights or Z cuts as fast as possible and to spring up in the air on the injured leg 10 times without pain.

Criteria for Return to Competitive Lacrosse

1. The ankle is pain free during motion and no swelling is present.
2. Full ankle range of motion and strength have been regained.
3. The athlete is able to run, jump, and make cutting movements as well as before injury.

Management Normally RICE is used intermittently for at least three days. It is not uncommon for the physician to apply a dorsiflexion cast or weight-bearing brace for three to six weeks, followed by taping for three to six weeks.[20,37] Crutches are usually given to the athlete when the cast is removed. Isometric exercise is carried out while the cast is on, followed by range-of-motion, PRE, and balance exercises. In some cases surgery is warranted to stabilize the athlete's ankle. NOTE: A grade 3 ankle sprain creates significant joint laxity and instability. Because of this laxity, the ankle joint is prone to degenerative processes.

Eversion Ankle Sprain

Etiology Eversion ankle sprains represent only about 5 percent to 10 percent of all ankle sprains. The eversion ankle sprain is less common than the inversion ankle sprain largely because of the bony and ligamentous anatomy (Figure 19-18). As mentioned previously, the fibular malleolus extends further inferiorly than does the tibial malleolus. This protection, combined with the strength of the thick deltoid ligament, prevents excessive eversion. More often, eversion injuries involve an avulsion fracture of the tibia before the deltoid ligament tears.[19] The deltoid ligament may also be contused in inversion sprains due to impingement between the fibular malleolus and the calcaneous. Despite the fact that eversion sprains are less common, the severity is such that these sprains may take longer to heal than inversion sprains.

A foot that is pronated, hypermobile, or has a depressed medial longitudinal arch is more predisposed to eversion ankle injuries (Figure 19-19).[4]

Symptoms and signs Depending on the grade of injury, the athlete complains of pain, sometimes severe, that occurs over the foot and lower leg. Usually the athlete is unable to bear weight on the foot. Both abduction and adduction cause pain, but pressing directly upward against the bottom of the foot will not produce pain.

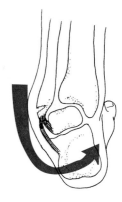

Figure 19-16

The same mechanism that produces an ankle sprain can also cause an avulsion fracture of the malleolus.

19-1

Critical Thinking Exercise

Following a grade 1 ankle sprain, a football player is rehabilitating his injury.

? What would be an appropriate progression for him to use to get from non–weight bearing to sprinting?

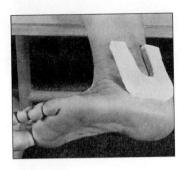

Figure 19-17

A horseshoe-shaped pad provides an excellent compress when held in place by an elastic wrap.

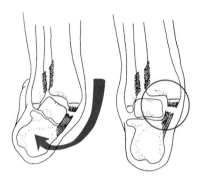

Figure 19-18

An eversion ankle sprain that creates a space between the medial malleolus and the talus.

Figure 19-19

A pronated foot can lead to an eversion ankle sprain.

Management   X rays are often necessary to rule out fracture. Initially, RICE and no weight bearing are recommended, and a posterior splint tape is applied. NSAIDs and analgesics are given as needed. Management of eversion sprain will follow the same course described for inversion sprains. The athlete engages in a PRE program for the posteromedial ankle muscles, engages in balance activities, and is fitted with an inner heel wedge shoe insert. NOTE: An eversion sprain with a severity of grade 2 or more can produce significant joint instability. Because the deltoid ligament helps support the medial longitudinal arch, a sprain can cause weakness in this area, leading to excessive pronation or a fallen arch.

Syndesmotic Sprain

Etiology   Isolated injuries to the distal tibiofemoral joint are referred to as syndesmotic sprains.[11] The anterior and posterior tibiofibular ligaments are found between the distal tibia and fibula and extend up the lower leg as the interosseous ligament, or syndesmotic ligament. Sprains of the ligaments are more common than has been realized in the past. These ligaments are torn with increased external rotational or forced dorsiflexion and are often injured in conjunction with a severe sprain of the medial and lateral ligament complexes (see Figure 19-18).[39] Initial rupture of the ligaments occurs distally at the tibiofibular ligament above the ankle mortise. As the force of disruption is increased, the interosseous ligament is torn more proximally.

Symptoms and signs   The athlete complains of severe pain and loss of function in the ankle region. When the ankle is passively externally rotated or dorsiflexed, there is a major pain in the lower leg indicating a syndesmotic sprain or possibly a lateral malleolar fracture. Pain normally occurs along the anterolateral leg.

Management   Sprains of the syndesmotic ligaments are extremely hard to treat and often take months to heal.[39] Treatments for this problem are essentially the same as for medial or lateral sprains, with the difference being an extended period of immobilization. Functional activities and return to sport may be delayed for a longer period of time than for inversion or eversion sprains.

Ankle Fracture

Etiology   There are a number of mechanisms through which an ankle can be fractured or dislocated.[13] A foot that is forcibly abducted can produce a transverse fracture of the distal tibia and fibula. In contrast, a foot that is planted in combination with a forced internal rotation of the leg can produce a fracture to the distal and posterior tibia (Figure 19-20).

Avulsion fractures, in which a chip of bone is pulled off by resistance of a ligament, are common in grade 2 and 3 degree eversion or inversion sprains.

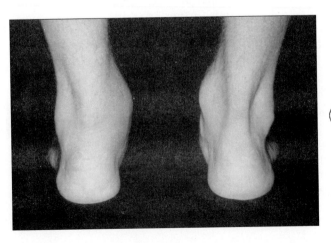

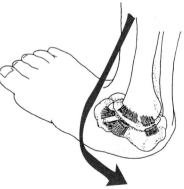

Figure 19-20

Ankle fractures or dislocations can be major sports injuries.

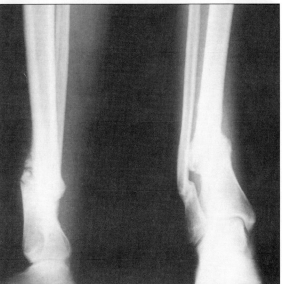

Symptoms and signs   In most cases of fracture, swelling and pain may be extreme. There may be some or no deformity; however, if a fracture is suspected, splinting is essential.

Management   RICE is used as soon as possible to control hemorrhage and swelling. Once swelling is reduced, a walking cast or brace may be applied. Immobilization will usually last for at least six to eight weeks.[30]

Lower Leg Injuries

Acute Achilles Tendon Strain

Etiology   Achilles tendon strains are common in sports and occur most often after ankle sprains or sudden excessive dorsiflexion of the ankle.

Symptoms and signs   The resulting injury may be mild to severe. The most severe injury is a partial or complete avulsion or rupturing of the Achilles tendon. While

19-2

Critical Thinking Exercise

A basketball player has a history of numerous lateral ankle sprains.

? How may this player reduce the incidence of these ankle sprains?

19-3

Critical Thinking Exercise

A tennis player sustains a grade 2 lateral sprain of the left ankle while making a sudden stop.

? Assuming good immediate care was carried out, how should this condition be managed ten days after injury?

19-4

Critical Thinking Exercise

A football player, while lying on the field, has his ankle forced into external rotation by another player.

? What type of injury is sustained by this mechanism? What is a characteristic sign of this injury?

sustaining this injury, the athlete feels acute pain and extreme weakness on plantar flexion.

Management   Initially, as with other acute conditions, pressure is first applied with an elastic wrap together with the application of cold. Unless the injury is minor, hemorrhage may be extensive, requiring RICE over an extended period of time. After hemorrhaging has subsided, an elastic wrap should be applied for continued pressure. Because of the tendency for acute Achilles tendon trauma to become a chronic condition, a conservative approach to therapy is required. The athlete should begin stretching and strengthening the heel cord complex as soon as possible. A lift should be placed in the heel of each shoe to decrease stretching of the tendon and thus relieve some stress that contributes to chronic inflammation.

Achilles Tendinitis

Etiology   Achilles tendinitis is an inflammatory condition that involves the Achilles tendon and/or its tendon sheath, the paratenon. Often, the tendon is overloaded because of excessive tensile stress placed on it during movements of a repetitive nature, such as running or jumping. Achilles tendinitis will often present with a gradual onset over a period of time. The condition worsens with repetitive weight-bearing activities such as running or early season conditioning in which the duration and intensity are increased too quickly with insufficient recovery time. Decreased gastrocnemius and soleus complex flexibility can also increase symptoms.

Symptoms and signs   The athlete often complains of generalized pain and stiffness about the Achilles tendon region that, when localized, is usually just proximal to the calcaneal insertion. Uphill running or hill workouts will usually aggravate the condition. There may be reduced gastrocnemius and soleus muscle flexibility in general that may worsen as the condition progresses. Muscle testing may show a deficit when the athlete performs toe raises. Initially, the athlete may ignore symptoms that present at the beginning of activity and resolve as the activity progresses. Symptoms may progress to morning stiffness and discomfort with walking after periods of prolonged sitting. The tendon may be warm and painful to palpation as well as thickened, which may indicate the chronicity of the condition. Crepitus may be palpated with active plantar flexion and dorsiflexion, and pain will be elicited with passive stretching. Chronic inflammation of the Achilles tendon may lead to thickening when compared with the uninvolved side (Figure 19-21).[18]

Figure 19-21

A thickened Achilles tendon caused by tendinitis.

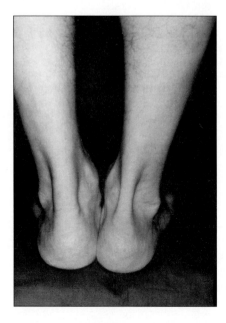

Management   Achilles tendinitis may be resistant to a quick resolution because of the slower healing response of tendinous tissue. It is important to create a proper healing environment by reducing stress on the tendon. Addressing structural faults that may be causing the irritation should be done through proper shoeware and foot orthotics as well as flexibility exercises for the heel cord complex. Modalities such as ice can help reduce pain and inflammation early on, and ultrasound can facilitate an increased blood flow to the tendon in the later stages of rehabilitation. Cross friction massage may be used to break down adhesions that may have formed during the healing response and further improve the gliding ability of the paratenon. Strengthening of the gastrocnemius-soleus musculature must be progressed carefully so as not to cause a recurrence of the symptoms.[18]

Achilles Tendon Rupture

A rupture of the Achilles tendon (Figure 19-22) is a possibility in sports that require stop-and-go action. Although most common in athletes who are thirty years of age or older, rupture of the Achilles tendon can occur in athletes of any age. It usually occurs in an athlete with a history of chronic inflammation and gradual degeneration caused by microtears.[1]

Etiology   The initial insult normally is the result of sudden pushing-off action of the forefoot with the knee being forced into complete extension.

Symptoms and signs   When the rupture occurs, the athlete complains of a sudden snap that felt like something kicked him or her in the lower leg. Pain is immediate but rapidly subsides. Point tenderness, swelling, and discoloration are usually associated with the trauma. Toe raising is impossible in an Achilles tendon rupture. The major problem in Achilles tendon rupture is accurate diagnosis, especially in a partial rupture. Any acute injury to the Achilles tendon should be suspected of a rupture. Signs indicative of a rupture are obvious indentation at the tendon site and a positive Thompson test (see Figure 19-10). An Achilles tendon rupture usually occurs 2 to 6 cm (.78–2.34 inches) proximal to its insertion onto the calcaneus.

Management   Usual management of a complete Achilles tendon rupture is surgical repair.[10] Nonoperative treatment consists of RICE, NSAIDs, and analgesics with a non–weight bearing cast for six weeks followed by a short-leg walking cast for two weeks. With this approach, there is 75 percent to 80 percent return of normal function.[4] Surgery is usually the choice for serious injuries, providing 75 percent to 90 percent return of function. Exercise rehabilitation lasts for about six months and consists of range-of-motion exercises, PRE, and the wearing of a 2 cm heel lift in both shoes.[4]

Peroneal Tendon Subluxation/Dislocation

The peroneus longus and brevis tendons pass through a common groove located behind the lateral malleolus. The tendons are held in place by the peroneal retinaculum.

Etiology   This injury most often occurs in sports that apply dynamic forces to the foot and ankle (e.g., turning and sharply cutting). Wrestling, football, ice skating, skiing, basketball, and soccer have the highest incidence. Another mechanism is a direct blow to the posterior lateral malleolus. A moderate to severe inversion sprain or forceful dorsiflexion of the ankle can tear the peroneal retinaculum, allowing the peroneal tendon to dislocate out of its groove. As discussed previously, one of the major functions of the peroneus longus muscle is to pull the first metatarsal into plantar flexion.

Symptoms and signs   The athlete complains that in running or jumping the tendons snap out of the groove and then back in when stress is released. Eversion against manual resistance will often replicate the subluxation. The athlete experiences recurrent pain, snapping, and ankle instability. The lateral aspect of the ankle may show ecchymoses, edema, tenderness, and crepitus over the peroneal tendon.

19-5

Critical Thinking Exercise

A thirty-five-year-old racquetball player, while moving backward, experiences a sudden snap and pain in the left Achilles tendon.

? What type of injury does this mechanism describe, and how should it be examined?

A ruptured Achilles tendon may occur because of chronic inflammation.

Figure 19-22

Achilles tendon rupture.

Figure 19-23

Common tendinitis of the foot and ankle region.

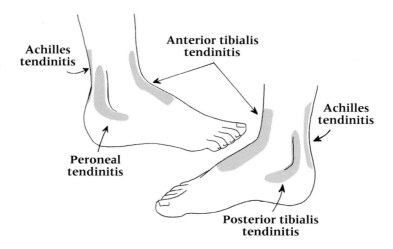

19-6

Critical Thinking Exercise

A volleyball player with a history of repeated ankle sprains complains of a snapping sensation in the right ankle.

? What procedures should be followed when managing a subluxated peroneal tendon?

19-7

Critical Thinking Exercise

A jogger, after running downhill for an extended period of time, experiences pain in the anterior medial aspect of the left foot. The condition is diagnosed as anterior tibialis tendinitis.

? How should this condition be managed?

Management A conservative approach should be used first and should include compression with a felt pad cut in a horseshoe-shaped pattern that surrounds the lateral malleolus. This compression can be reinforced with a rigid plastic or plaster splint until acute signs have subsided, and RICE, NSAIDs, and analgesics are given as needed. The time period for this conservative care is five to six weeks, followed by a gradual exercise rehabilitation program that includes range-of-motion exercises, PRE, and balance training. If a conservative approach fails, surgery is required.

Anterior Tibialis Tendinitis

Etiology Anterior tibialis tendinitis is a common condition of athletes and joggers who run downhill for an extended period of time.

Symptoms and signs There is point tenderness over the anterior tibialis tendon (Figure 19-23).

Management The athlete should be advised to rest (or at least decrease running time and distance) and to avoid hills. In more serious cases, ice packs, coupled with stretching before and after running, should help reduce the symptoms. A daily strengthening program also should be conducted. Oral antiinflammatory medications may be required.[32]

Posterior Tibial Tendinitis

Etiology Posterior tibialis tendinitis is a common overuse condition among runners with hypermobility or pronated feet. It is a repetitive microtrauma occurring during pronation in movements such as jumping, running, or cutting.

Symptoms and signs The athlete complains of pain and swelling in the area of the medial malleolus (see Figure 19-23). Inspection reveals edema and point tenderness directly behind the medial malleolus. In serious cases, the pain becomes more intense during resistive inversion and plantar flexion.

Management Initially, RICE, NSAIDs, and analgesics are given as needed. A non–weight bearing short-leg cast with the foot in inversion may be used. Management consists of correcting the problem of pronation with LowDye taping or an orthotic device.

Peroneal Tendinitis

Etiology Although not particularly common, peroneal tendinitis can be a problem in athletes with pes cavus. In pes cavus, the foot tends to excessively supinate, which causes weight bearing on the outside of the foot and thus places stress on the peroneal tendon.

Symptoms and signs The athlete complains of pain behind the lateral malleolus when rising on the ball of the foot during jogging, running, cutting, or turning activities. Tenderness is noted over the tendon located at the lateral aspect of the calcaneus distally to beneath the cuboid bone (see Figure 19-23).[32]

Management   Initially, management consists of RICE and NSAIDs as required, taping with elastic tape, and appropriate warm-up and flexibility exercises. LowDye taping (see Figure 8-19) or an orthosis to help support the foot and prevent excessive pronation may help.

Shin Contusion

Etiology   The anterior aspect of the lower leg is often referred to as the shin. The tibia, lying just under the skin, is exceedingly vulnerable and sensitive to blows or bumps. Because of the absence of muscular or adipose padding, the periosteum receives the full force of any impact delivered to the shin. The periosteum is a membrane that surrounds all bony surfaces except articulating surfaces, which are covered by hyaline cartilage. The periosteum is composed of two fibrous layers that adhere closely to the bone and act as a bed for nerves, blood vessels, and bone-forming osteoblasts.

Symptoms and signs   The athlete complains of intense pain when the shin is contused. A hematoma forms rapidly and tends to exhibit a jellylike consistency.[15] There could also be an associated compartment syndrome, particularly in the anterior compartment, as well as a potential tibial fracture.

Management   RICE, NSAIDs, and analgesics are administered as needed. Maintaining compression in the area of the hematoma is critical. In some cases, the hematoma may need to be aspirated. The athlete, within pain limitations, engages in range-of-motion and PRE exercises. The athlete is fitted with a doughnut padding under an orthoplast shell for protection.[15]

An inappropriately managed injury to the periosteum may develop into osteomyelitis, a serious condition that results in the destruction and deterioration of bone (Figure 19-24).

In sports such as football and soccer in which the shin is particularly vulnerable, adequate protective padding should be used. All injuries in this area are potentially serious; therefore even minor shin bruises should never be permitted to go untended.

Muscle Contusions

Etiology   Contusions of the leg, particularly in the area of the gastrocnemius muscle, are common in sports. Most often, contusions occur from being kicked in the back of the leg.

A forceful blow to an unprotected shin can lead to a severe contusion.

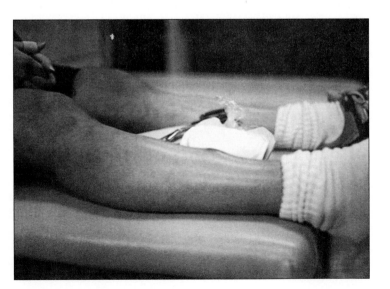

Figure 19-24

A poorly cared-for shin bruise can lead to osteomyelitis.

Symptoms and signs A bruise in this area can produce an extremely handicapping injury for the athlete. A bruising blow to the leg will cause pain, weakness, and partial loss of the use of the limb. Palpation may reveal a hard, rigid, and somewhat inflexible area because of internal hemorrhage and muscle guarding.

Management When this condition occurs, it is advisable to stretch the muscles in the region immediately to prevent spasm and then to apply a compression wrap and ice to control internal hemorrhaging.

If cold therapy or other superficial therapy such as massage and whirlpool do not return the athlete to normal activity within two to three days, the use of ultrasound may be warranted. An elastic wrap or tape support will stabilize the part and permit the athlete to participate without aggravation of the injury.

Leg Cramps and Spasms

Spasms are sudden, violent, involuntary contractions of one or several muscles and may be either clonic or tonic. A *clonic* spasm is identified by intermittent contraction and relaxation. A *tonic* spasm is identified by constant muscle contraction without an intervening period of relaxation. The clonic spasm has a neurological basis and is seen less often in sports.

Etiology The specific cause of a muscle cramp is often difficult to determine. Fatigue, excess loss of fluid through sweating, and inadequate reciprocal muscle coordination are some of the factors that may predispose an individual to tonic muscle spasm. The gastrocnemius muscle is particularly prone to this condition.

Symptoms and signs The athlete has considerable muscle cramping and pain with the tonic contraction of the calf muscle.

Management Management in such cases includes trying to help the athlete relax to relieve the muscle cramp. A firm grasp of the contracted muscle, together with mild, gradual stretching, relieves most acute spasms. An ice pack or gentle ice massage may also be helpful in reducing spasm. In cases of recurrent spasm, the athletic trainer should make certain that fatigue or abnormal water or electrolyte loss is not a factor.

Gastrocnemius Strain

Etiology The medial head of the gastrocnemius is particularly susceptible to muscle strain near its musculotendinous attachment. Sports that require quick starts and stops or occasional jumping can cause this gastrocnemius strain. Usually the athlete makes a quick stop with the foot planted flat and suddenly extends the knee, placing stress on the medial head of the gastrocnemius (Figure 19-25).

Symptoms and signs Depending on the grade of injury, there is a variable amount of pain, swelling, and muscle disability. The athlete may complain of a sensation of having been "hit in the calf with a stick." Examination reveals edema, point tenderness, and a functional strength loss.[15]

Management Initially, RICE, NSAIDs, and analgesics are given as needed. A grade 1 calf strain should be given a gentle, gradual stretch after muscle cooling. Weight bearing can take place as tolerated. A heel wedge may help reduce stretching of the calf muscle during walking. Appropriate elastic wrap may serve to support the muscle while active. A gradual program of range-of-motion exercises and PRE should be instituted.

Acute Leg Fractures

Etiology Of all leg fractures, the fibular fracture has the highest incidence. It occurs principally in the middle third, while fractures of the tibia occur predominantly in the lower third. Fractures of the shaft of both the tibia and fibula result from either direct or indirect trauma (Figure 19-26). There may be bony displacement with deformity that results in overriding of the bone ends, particularly if the athlete attempts to move or to stand on the limb after the injury. Crepitus and a temporary loss of limb function are usually present.

19-8

Critical Thinking Exercise

A football running back receives a hard low tackle. He hears a loud pop and feels a sharp pain in his right lower leg. Weight bearing is impossible.

? In this situation, what type of injury is suspected?

Figure 19-25

Calf strain.

Figure 19-26

Fracture of the tibia.

Symptoms and signs   This injury causes soft-tissue insult and hemorrhaging. The athlete complains of severe pain and disability. The leg appears hard and swollen, which may indicate the beginning of Volkmann's contracture. Volkmann's contracture is the result of internal tension caused by hemorrhage and swelling within closed fascial compartments, which inhibits the blood supply and results in necrosis of muscles and contractures.

Management   In most cases, fracture reduction and cast immobilization are applied up to six weeks, depending on the extent of the injury and any complications.

Medial Tibial Stress Syndrome

Etiology   Medial tibial stress syndrome (MTSS) has in the past been referred to as shinsplints, which is a catchall term that indicates pain in the anterior part of the shin. Conditions such as stress fractures, muscle strains, and chronic anterior compartment syndromes have all been termed shinsplints. MTSS accounts for approximately 10 percent to 15 percent of all running injuries and up to 60 percent of all conditions that cause pain in athletes' legs.[22] MTSS is caused by a repetitive microtrauma. It is seen commonly in basketball, running, and gymnastics. Factors that can contribute to MTSS include weakness of leg muscles, shoes that provide little support or cushioning, and training errors such as running on hard surfaces or overtraining. Malignment problems such as varus foot, a tight heel cord, a hypermobile pronated foot, or a forefoot supination can also lead to MTSS.[22]

MTSS may involve one of two syndromes: a tibial stress fracture or an overuse syndrome that can progress to an irreversible, exertional compartment syndrome.

Symptoms and signs   Four grades of pain can be attributed to medial tibial stress syndrome: grade 1 pain occurring after athletic activity; grade 2 pain occurring before and after activity but not affecting performance; grade 3 pain occurring before, during, and after athletic activity and affecting performance; and grade 4 pain, so severe that performance is impossible.

Management   Management of this condition should include physician referral to rule out the possibility of stress fracture via the use of bone scans and X rays. Activity modification along with measures to maintain cardiovascular fitness are set in place immediately. Correction of abnormal pronation during walking and running must also be addressed with shoes and if needed, custom foot orthotics. Ice massage

19-9

Critical Thinking Exercise

A gymnast complains of pain in the medial aspect of her right tibia. There is pain before, during, and after activity. Assessment rules out a stress fracture, and the injury is determined to be a grade 3 medial tibial stress syndrome.

? What could be the cause of this condition?

Medial Tibial Stress Syndrome

Injury Situation A female college field hockey player at the end of the competitive season began to feel severe discomfort in the medial aspect of the right shin.

Symptoms and Signs The athlete complained that her shin seemed to ache all the time but the pain became more intense after practice or a game. During palpation there was severe point tenderness approximately 2 inches (5 cm) in length, beginning $4^{1}/_{2}$ inches (11.25 cm) from the tip of the medial malleolus. The pain was most severe along the medial posterior edge of the tibia. Further evaluation showed that the athlete had pronated feet. X-ray examination showed no indication of stress fracture.

Management Plan The injury was considered to be a medial tibial stress syndrome (shinsplints) involving the long flexor muscle, the great toe, and the posterior tibial muscle.

Phase **1** *Acute Injury* **GOALS:** To reduce inflammation, pain, and point tenderness.
ESTIMATED LENGTH OF TIME (ELT): 1–2 weeks.

■ **Therapy** Initially RICE, NSAIDs, and analgesics are given as needed. The athlete is instructed to rest and avoid weight bearing as much as possible. Ice massage (7 minutes) is performed, followed by gentle static stretching to the anterior and posterior muscles 2 to 3 times daily. A LowDye taping or orthotic device is applied to the arch to correct pronation during weight bearing.

■ **Exercise rehabilitation** Static stretch of Achilles tendon and anterior part of low leg; stretch is held 30 seconds (2 or 3 times); set is repeated 3 or 4 times daily. General body maintenance exercises are conducted 3 times weekly if they do not aggravate injury.

Phase **2** *Repair* **GOALS:** To heal injury, help athlete become symptom free, return athlete to walking, jogging, and finally, running.
ELT: 2–3 weeks.

■ **Therapy** Cold application (5 to 15 minutes) to shin area before and after walking 1 time daily. Activity is stopped if there is shin pain. Ultrasound (0.5 to 0.075 W/cm²) (5 to 10 minutes) 1 to 2 times daily. Transverse friction massage is given to prevent adhesions. The athlete wears LowDye taping or orthoses when weight bearing. A counterforce bracing with tape is also worn 2 to 4 inches (5 to 10 cm) proximal to the malleoli.

■ **Exercise rehabilitation** Ankle range-of-motion exercises plus PRE with rubber tubing to the anterior and posterior leg muscles. Static stretch of lower leg followed by arch and plantar flexion exercises. Towel gathering exercise (10 repetitions, 1 to 3 sets); progress from no resistance to 10 lb of resistance, 3 times daily. Towel scoop exercise (10 repetitions, 1 to 3 sets); progress to 10 lb, 3 times daily. Marble pickup, 3 times daily. General body maintenance exercises are conducted 3 times weekly if they do not aggravate injury. Athlete engages in a program of progressive weight bearing and locomotion within pain-free limits starting with slow heel-toe walking, fast walking, jogging, and finally, running. As pain decreases, activity can increase.

Phase **3** *Remodeling* **GOALS:** Return to full-field hockey activity.
ELT: 3–6 weeks.

■ **Therapy** The athlete carries out cryokinetics before and after practice. The athlete continues to wear counterforce brace and LowDye taping or orthoses for foot pronation.

Continued

■ **Exercise rehabilitation** The athlete continues a daily program of lower leg static stretch after ice application before and after activity. The athlete carries out a program of ankle range-of-motion exercises and lower leg PRE 3 days a week.

Criteria for Return to Competitive Field Hockey

1. Leg is symptom free after prolonged activity.
2. The lower leg and ankle have full strength and range of motion.
3. Hyperpronation is controlled to prevent reoccurrence.

to the area may be helpful in the reduction of localized pain and imflammation. A flexibility program for the gastrocnemius-soleus musculature should be initiated. Arch taping and circumferential tape applied around the area of pain have also been used.

Compartment Syndromes

As discussed earlier in this chapter, the leg is composed of four compartments. Each compartment is bound by fascial sheaths or by fascial sheaths and bone (see Figure 19-6). Compartment syndromes may be classified as either acute traumatic or chronic exertional.

Etiology The rare acute traumatic syndrome occurs either after being kicked in the lower leg or after excessive exercise in an untrained individual. Excessive swelling within the confines of a fascial compartment compress muscles, blood vessels, and nerves. With the increase in fluid pressure, muscle ischemia that could lead to permanent disability occurs creating a medical emergency that requires immediate decompression to prevent permanent damage.

A chronic exertional compartment syndrome occurs most frequently among runners and athletes in sports that involve extensive running, such as soccer. Normally internal pressures within the lower leg compartments rise slowly during exercise and subside after exercise is stopped. Chronic exertional compartment syndrome occurs when the tissue fluid pressure increases too much and/or remains elevated after exercise stops producing ischemia and pain, but neurological involvement is rare. Chronic exertional compartment syndrome is often confused with shinsplints by the athletic trainer. It may also be confused with a stress fracture.

The compartments most often affected are the anterior and deep posterior, with the anterior having by far the highest incidence.[25] On occasion, the lateral compartment may be involved.

Symptoms and signs The more common chronic exertional compartment syndrome symptoms are usually bilateral. The incidence of bilaterality in chronic exertional compartment syndrome is 50 percent to 60 percent.[8] The athlete complains of pain during exercise in the anterolateral region of the leg. Gradually, over time the pain will occur in a predictable manner after running a specific distance or length of time. The athlete commonly complains of an ache or sharp pain and pressure in the

Chronic exertional compartment syndromes occur most commonly in runners, while acute compartment syndromes occur in soccer players.

Figure 19-27

Tibial stress fracture

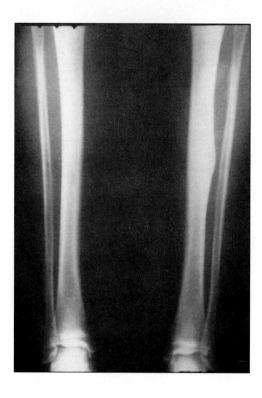

19-10

Critical Thinking Exercise

A soccer player complains of recurrent pain in the anterolateral region of the leg during practice and competition. The pain is described as an ache and a feeling of pressure.

? This condition is determined to be an exertional compartment syndrome. How should it be managed?

19-11

Critical Thinking Exercise

A novice and poorly conditioned recreational runner with a pes cavus experiences pain and discomfort in the lower third of the left lower leg after three weeks of running. The pain and discomfort become more intense immediately after running.

? An X ray shows the beginning of a stress fracture. How should it be managed?

region of the anterior compartment when performing a particular activity. The symptoms subside or go away completely when resting. When major symptoms are present, weakness in foot and toe extension and numbness in the dorsal region may occur.

Management Often initial symptoms are aided by the application of RICE, NSAIDs, and analgesia as needed. However, recurrent conditions may require surgical release of the associated fascia. Once surgery is performed, the athlete is allowed to return home and begin a light program of exerise in 10 days.

Stress Fracture of the Tibia or Fibula

Etiology Stress fractures to the tibia or fibula are a common overuse stress condition, especially among distance runners (Figure 19-27). Stress fractures of the lower leg, like many other overuse syndromes, are more likely to occur in athletes who have structural deformities of the foot. Athletes who have hypermobile pronated feet are more susceptible to fibular stress fracture, whereas those with rigid pes cavus are more prone to tibial stress fractures. The wider the tibia, the lower the incidence of stress fractures. Runners frequently develop a stress fracture in the lower third of the leg; ballet dancers more commonly acquire one in the middle third. Stress fractures often occur to nonexperienced and nonconditioned individuals.[38] Training errors are often the cause.[38] Other causes may include amenorrhea and nutritional deficiencies.

Symptoms and signs The athlete complains of pain in the leg that is more intense after than during the activity. There is usually point tenderness, but it may be difficult to discern the difference between bone pain and soft-tissue pain. One technique for distinguishing bone pain from soft-tissue pain is bone percussion. The fibula or tibia is tapped firmly above the level of tenderness. Vibration travels along the bone to the fracture, which may respond with pain. Another percussive technique is to hit the heel upward from below, which causes pain to occur at the fracture site.

Diagnosis of a stress fracture may be extremely difficult. X-ray examination may or may not detect the problem. A bone scan will more accurately assess the presence of a stress fracture but does not clearly distinguish between a stress fracture and periostitis.

Management   The following regimen may be used for a stress fracture of the tibia or fibula:

- Running and other stressful locomotor activities should be discontinued for at least fourteen days.
- When pain is severe, the athlete should use a crutch for walking or wear a cast.
- Weight bearing may be resumed as pain subsides.
- Bicycling may be done before the athlete returns to running.
- After a pain-free period of at least two weeks, running can gradually begin again.[12]
- Biomechanical foot corrections should be made.

REHABILITATION TECHNIQUES FOR THE LOWER LEG AND ANKLE

General Body Conditioning

Cardiorespiratory conditioning should be maintained during the entire rehabilitation process. Pedaling a stationary bike or using an upper extremity ergometer with the hands provides the athlete with excellent cardiovascular exercise without placing stress on the lower leg or ankle (Figure 19-28). Pool running with a float vest and swimming are also good cardiovascular exercises.

Weight Bearing

During the period of maximum protection immediately following injury, the athlete should be either non–weight bearing or perhaps partial weight bearing on crutches. Early limited stress following the initial period of inflammation may promote faster and stronger healing.[19] Partial weight bearing with crutches helps control several complications to healing, including muscle atrophy, proprioceptive loss, circulatory stasis, and tendinitis. For these reasons, early ambulation, even if only touch down weight bearing, is essential.[7] Protected motion facilitates proper collagen reorientation and thus increases the strength of the healing ligament.

Joint Mobilizations

Movement of an injured joint can be improved by manual joint mobilization techniques (Figure 19-29). Joint mobilizations that concentrate on increasing dorsiflexion and plantar flexion should be started first.[26] Posterior tibial glides and anterior

Figure 19-28

Exercises to maintain cardiorespiratory endurance can be done on an upper extremity ergometer.

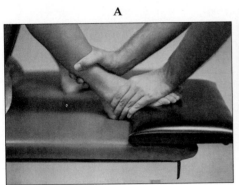
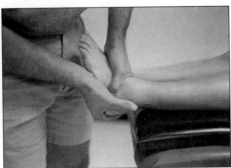
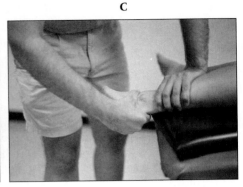

Figure 19-29

Ankle joint mobilization techniques. **A,** posterior tibial glides. **B,** posterior talar glides. **C,** Subtalar joint medial and lateral glides.

talar glides can be used to improve plantar flexion. Anterior tibial glides and posterior talar glides will increase dorsiflexion. Subtalar joint medial and lateral glides can be used to increase inversion and eversion.

Flexibility

In the early stages of rehabilitation, inversion and eversion should be minimized. Exercises such as towel stretching for the plantar flexors and standing or kneeling stretches for the dorsiflexors can improve range of motion. Athletes are encouraged to do these exercises slowly and without pain and to use high repetitions (two sets of 40). Vigorous heel cord stretching should be initiated as soon as possible (Figure 19-30).

As tenderness decreases, inversion-eversion exercises may be initiated. Such exercises include pulling a towel from one side to the other by alternately inverting and everting the foot, and drawing the alphabet while the foot is in an ice bath. The alphabet should be done in capital letters to ensure that full range is used.

Exercises performed on a BAPS board, wedge board, or KAT system may be beneficial for range of motion and for regaining neuromuscular control (Figure 19-31).[3] The athlete begins these exercises seated and progresses to standing. Initially, the

Figure 19-30

Flexibility exercises. **A,** Kneeling stretch for dorsiflexors. **B,** Gastrocnemius stretch with knee straight. **C,** Soleus stretch with knee bent.

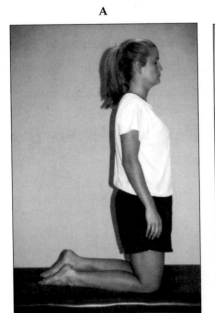
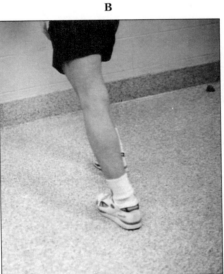
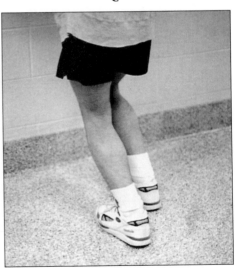

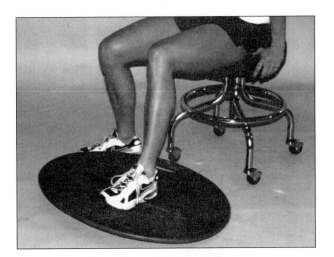

Figure 19-31

BAPS board exercises are used for reestablishing neuro-muscular control.

athlete should start in the seated position and move a wedge board in the plantar flexion–dorsiflexion direction. As pain decreases and healing progresses, the board may be turned in the inversion-eversion direction. When seated exercises are performed with ease, standing balance exercises should be initiated. They may be started with the athlete on one leg, standing, without a board. The athlete then supports weight with the hands and maintains balance on a wedge board in either plantar flexion–dorsiflexion or inversion-eversion directions. Next, hand support may be eliminated while the athlete balances on the wedge board. The same sequence is then used on the BAPS board. The BAPS board is initially used with assistance from the hands. Then balance is practiced on the BAPS board unassisted.

Strengthening

Isometric strengthening exercises may be done in the four major ankle motion planes. They may be accompanied early in the rehabilitative phase by plantar flexion and dorsiflexion isotonic exercises. As healing progresses and range of motion increases, strengthening exercises may be begun in all planes of motion (Figure 19-32).[27] Care must be taken when exercising in inversion and eversion to avoid tibial rotation as a substitute movement. Pain should be the basic guideline for deciding when to start inversion-eversion isotonic exercises. Light resistance with high repetitions has fewer detrimental effects on the ligaments (two to four sets of 10 repetitions). Resistive tubing exercises, ankle weights around the foot, or a balance board are excellent methods of strengthening inversion and eversion. Tubing has advantages in that it may be used both eccentrically and concentrically. Isokinetics have advantages in that more functional speeds may be obtained. PNF strengthening exercises that isolate the desired motions at the talocrural joint can also be used.

Proprioception and Neuromuscular Control

Early weight bearing has previously been mentioned as a method of reducing proprioceptive loss. It has been shown that deficits in ankle proprioception can predispose an athlete to ankle injury.[31] During the rehabilitation phase, an athlete can recoup proprioception by standing on both feet with closed eyes and progressing to standing on one leg.[17] This exercise may be followed by standing and balancing on a BAP board, which should be done initially with support from the hands. As a final exercise, the athlete can progress to free standing and controlling the board through all ranges.

Other closed kinetic chain exercises may be beneficial. Leg presses and minisquats (Figure 19-33) on the involved leg will encourage weight bearing and increase proprioceptive return. Single leg standing kicks using abduction, adduction, extension,

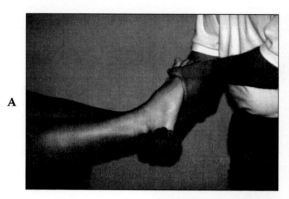

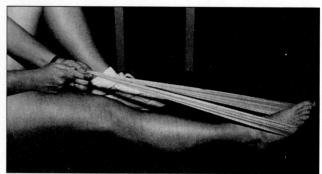

Figure 19-32

Ankle strengthening exercises. **A,** manually resisted strengthening exercises can be done in all four directions. **B,** resisted tubing exercises. **C,** Ankle weights.

and flexion of the uninvolved side while weight bearing on the affected side will increase both strength and proprioception. These kicks may be performed with the athlete either standing free or on a machine (Figure 19-34).

Taping and Bracing

It is most desirable to have the athlete return to sport without the aid of ankle support. However, it is common practice that some type of ankle support be worn initially.[21] Ankle taping does appear to have a stabilizing effect on unstable ankles with-

Figure 19-33

Minisquats are helpful both in regaining range of motion and in strengthening.

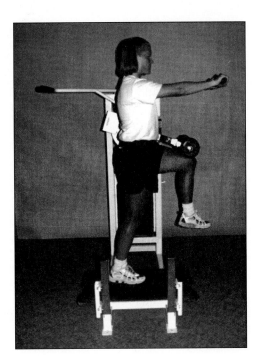

Figure 19-34

Single leg standing kicks on an exercise machine.

out interfering with motor performance.[35,40] The athletic trainer can tape the ankle and can also tape the shoe onto the foot to make the shoe and ankle function as one unit. High-topped footwear may further stabilize the ankle.[23] If cleated shoes are worn, cleats should be outset along the periphery of the shoe to provide stability. An Aircast or some other supportive ankle brace can also be worn as a substitute for taping (Figure 19-35).[14,16,24,34]

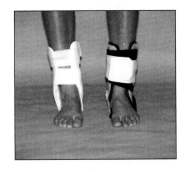

Figure 19-35

A number of ankle support devices are available.

Functional Progressions

Functional progressions may be as complex or simple as needed. More severe injuries need a more detailed functional progression. The typical progression begins early in the rehabilitation process as the athlete becomes partially weight bearing. Full weight bearing should be started when ambulation is performed without a limp.

Running may begin as soon as ambulation is pain free. Pain-free hopping on the affected side may also be a guideline to determine when running is appropriate. Exercising in a pool allows for early running. The athlete is placed in the pool in a swim vest that supports the body in water. The athlete then runs in place without touching the bottom of the pool. Proper running form should be stressed. Eventually the athlete is moved into shallow water so that more weight is placed on the ankle. Progression is then to running on a smooth, flat surface, ideally a track. Initially the athlete should jog the straights and walk the curves and then progress to jogging the entire track. Speed may be increased to a sprint in a straight line. The cutting sequence should begin with circles of diminishing diameter. Cones may be set up for the athlete to run figure eights as the next cutting progression. The crossover or sidestep is next.[1] The athlete sprints to a predesignated spot and cuts or sidesteps abruptly. When this progression is accomplished, the cut should be done without warning on the command of another person. Jumping and hopping exercises should be started on both legs simultaneously and gradually reduced to only the injured side.[19]

The athlete may perform at different levels for each of these functional sequences. One functional sequence may be done at half speed while another is done at full speed. For example, an athlete may run full speed on straights of the track but do figure eights at only half speed. Once the upper levels of all the sequences are reached, the athlete may return to limited practice, which may include early teaching and fundamental drills.

Return to Activity

The athlete should have complete range of motion and at least 80 percent to 90 percent of preinjury strength before considering a return to the sport.[19] Finally, if full practice is tolerated without insult to the injured part, the athlete may return to competition. Returning to full activity must include a gradual progression of functional activities that slowly increase the stress on the injured structure. The specific demands of each individual sport dictate the individual drills of this progression.

SUMMARY

- The portion of the lower extremity that lies between the knee and the ankle is defined as the lower leg and contains two bones, the tibia and the fibula. The bones that form the ankle joint, or talocrural joint, are the distal portion of the tibia, the distal portion of the fibula, and the talus. The calcaneous also plays a critical role in the function of the ankle joint.
- The ligamentous support of the ankle consists of the tibiofibular ligaments, three lateral ligaments, and the medial, or deltoid, ligament.
- The musculature of the lower leg is contained within four distinct compartments: muscles of the anterior compartment dorsiflex the ankle; muscles of the lateral compartment evert the ankle; muscles of the superficial posterior compartment plantar flex the ankle; and muscles of the deep posterior compartment invert the ankle.
- Athletes can prevent many lower leg and ankle conditions, especially sprains, by stretching the Achilles tendon, strengthening key muscles, engaging in neuromuscular and proprioceptive training, wearing proper footwear, and using taping and ankle support devices appropriately.
- Ankle sprains are the single most common injury in the athletic population. Ankle sprains are classified as inversion, eversion, or syndesmotic injuries. Occasionally, ankle fractures occur along with ankle sprains.
- The Achilles tendon, or heel cord complex, is subject to acute strain that may lead to a chronic tendinitis. A rupture of the Achilles tendon is common in the older athlete.
- Tendinitis of the anterior tibialis, posterior tibialis, and peroneal tendons are all common around the ankle joint.
- Shin contusions, muscle contusions, muscle cramps, gastrocnemius strains, and fractures of the tibia or fibula are all traumatic injuries that can occur in the lower leg.
- Chronic overuse conditions of the lower leg include medial tibial stress syndrome (shinsplints), exertional compartment syndrome, and stress fractures of the tibial and fibula.
- Perhaps the most important consideration in the rehabilitation of injuries to the lower leg and ankle is to use a gradual progression, beginning with non–weight bearing and subsequently incorporating the appropriate strengthening, range-of-motion, neuromuscular control, and joint mobilization techniques to facilitate the athlete's return to full activity.

Web Sites

Cramer First Aider: http://www.ccsd.k12.wy.us/cchs_web/cramerfirstaider/fstaider.htm

The University of Texas Anatomy of The Human Body: http://rpiwww.mdacc.tmc.edu/mmlearn/anatomy.html

American Orthopaedic Foot and Ankle Society: http://www.aofas.org

World Ortho: http://www.worldortho.com

Readers can use the search engine in this site to locate relevant information.

Solutions to Critical Thinking EXERCISES

19-1 The typical progression begins when the athlete becomes partially weight bearing. Full weight bearing should be started when ambulation is performed without a limp. Walking may begin as soon as ambulation is pain free. The athlete then progresses to running on a smooth, flat surface, ideally a track. Initially the athlete should jog the straights and walk the curves and then progress to jogging the entire track. The cutting sequence should begin with circles of diminishing diameter, figure eights, and crossover or side steps. Jumping and hopping exercises should be started on both legs simultaneously and gradually reduced to only the injured side.

19-2 The athletic trainer takes a multifaceted approach to reducing ankle sprains. The Achilles tendon is stretched to allow at least 10 degrees of dorsiflexion. Strength training is carried out to the peroneals, plantar flexors, and dorsiflexors. Proprioceptive training is performed on a balance board. The athlete wears high-top shoes. Ankle taping with an orthosis can also be employed.

19-3 The athlete continues to wear a stirrup brace for one to three weeks longer. Taping at 90 degrees will be conducted for two to four weeks. The athlete engages in pain-free plantar flexion and dorsiflexion exercises. The athlete also engages in proprioceptive exercises on a balance board.

19-4 The mechanism describes a syndesmotic ankle sprain. The athlete experiences severe pain in the anterolateral leg region when the ankle is externally rotated.

19-5 This injury is a possible partial or complete rupture of the Achilles tendon. The athletic trainer should look for pain that eventually subsided, an inability to perform a toe raise, point tenderness, swelling, discoloration, an obvious indentation at the tendon site, and a positive Thompson test.

19-6 The athletic trainer applies compression with a horseshoe-shaped felt pad around the lateral malleoleus. This pad is reinforced by a rigid splint. RICE, NSAIDs, and analgesics are given as needed. An exercise program is employed to strengthen, stretch, and enhance balance training.

19-7 The athlete is instructed to rest or reduce the stress of running. Application of ice packs followed by stretching is carried out before and after activity. A strengthening program is carried out along with treatment by oral antiinflammatory medications as needed.

19-8 The athlete has sustained a lower leg fracture. The most common site is in the middle third of the fibula.

19-9 In gymnastics, athletes often run on hard surfaces wearing shoes with little cushioning. This, combined with overtraining and fatigue, could lead to MTSS. Other reasons are a varus or pronated hypermobile foot.

19-10 The conservative approach is the application of RICE and NSAIDs and rest. With weakness in toe extension and numbness in the dorsal region, surgery may be warranted.

19-11 The runner should avoid stressful locomotor activities for at least fourteen days. Bicycling and swimming can be engaged in if pain free. Running can be resumed after a pain-free period of two weeks.

REVIEW QUESTIONS AND CLASS ACTIVITIES

1. Identify and describe the anatomy of the ankle and lower leg.
2. How can ankle injuries be prevented?
3. Demonstrate the steps that should be taken when assessing ankle and lower leg injuries.
4. Describe the three different types of ankle sprains.
5. Contrast the management of grade 1, 2, and 3 ankle sprains.
6. What is the usual mechanism for fractures of the ankle?
7. Describe the various injuries that can occur to the Achilles tendon. Indicate their etiology and symptoms and signs.
8. What tendons are most likely to develop tendinitis around the ankle?
9. Discuss the etiology, symptoms and signs, and management of the various acute or traumatic injuries that can occur in the lower leg.
10. What are the possible causes of medial tibial stress syndrome?
11. Contrast the acute anterior compartment syndrome with the chronic type.
12. Describe the various chronic overuse problems that can occur in the lower leg.
13. Describe the appropriate progression of treatment that should be used in the rehabilitation of ankle and lower leg injuries.

REFERENCES

1. Anderson DL: Surgical management of chronic Achilles tendinitis, *Cl J Sports Med* 2(1):38, 1992.
2. Baxter D: *The foot and ankle in sport,* St Louis, 1995, Mosby.
3. Bernier JN, Perrin DH, Rijke A: Effect of unilateral functional instability of the ankle on postural sway and inversion and eversion strength, *J Ath Train* 32(3):226, 1997.
4. Birrer RB: Ankle injuries. In Birrer RB, editor: *Sports medicine for the primary care physician,* ed 2, Boca Raton FL CRC Press, 1995, Mosby.
5. Booher JM, Thibodeau GA: *Athletic injury assessment,* ed 3, St Louis, 1994, Mosby.
6. Brosky T et al: The ankle ligaments: considerations of syndesmotic injury and implications for rehabilitation, *J Orthop Sports Phys Ther* 21(1):197, 1995.
7. Brotzman B, Brasel J: Foot and ankle rehabilitation. In Brotzman B: *Clinical orthopaedic rehabilitation,* St Louis, 1996, Mosby.
8. Brown DE: Exertional leg pain. In Brown DE, Neuman RD, editors: *Orthopedic secrets,* Philadelphia, 1995, Hanley & Belfus.
9. Case WS: Recovering from ankle sprains, *Physician Sportsmed* 21(11):43, 1993.
10. Dugan D, Hobler C: Progressive management of open surgical repair of Achilles tendon rupture, *J Ath Train* 29(4):349, 1994.

11. Fischer DA: Syndesmotic ankle sprain. In Torg JS, Shephard RJ, editors: *Current therapy in sports medicine*, ed 3, St Louis, 1995, Mosby.

12. Giladi M et al: Stress fractures, *Am J Sports Med* 19(6):647, 1991.

13. Glick J, Sampson T: Ankle and foot fractures in athletics. In Nicholas J, Hershman E: *The lower extremity and spine in sports medicine*, St Louis, 1996, Mosby.

14. Gross M, Lapp A, Davis M: Comparison of Swed-O-Universal ankle support and Aircast Sport Stirrup orthoses and ankle tape in restricting eversion-inversion before and after exercise, *J Orthop Sports Phys Ther* 13(1):11, 1991.

15. Hacut JE: General types of injuries. In Birrer RB, editor: *Sports medicine for the primary care physician*, Boca Raton, Fla, 1994, CRC Press.

16. Heit E, Lephart S, Rozzi S: The effects of ankle bracing and taping on joint position sense in the stable ankle, *J Sport Rehabil* 5(3):206, 1996.

17. Hertel J et al: Effect of lateral ankle joint anesthesia on center of balance, postural sway, and joint position sense, *J Sport Rehabil* 5(2):111, 1996.

18. Hirth C: Rehabilitation of lower leg injuries. In Prentice WE, editor: *Rehabilitation techniques in sports medicine*, ed 3, Dubuque, Iowa, 1999, WCB/McGraw-Hill.

19. Hunter S, Prentice W: Rehabilitation of ankle injuries. In Prentice WE, editor: *Rehabilitation techniques in sports medicine*, ed 3, Dubuque, Iowa, 1999, WCB/McGraw-Hill.

20. Jepson KK: The use of orthoses for athletes. In Birrer RB, editor: *Sports medicine for the primary care physician*, ed 2, Boca Raton, Fla, 1994, CRC Press.

21. Kinzey SJ, Ingersoll CD, Knight KL: The effects of selected ankle appliances on postural control, *J Ath Train* 32(4):300, 1997.

22. Levandowski R, Di Frori JP: Leg injuries. In Birrer RB, editor: *Sports medicine for the primary care physician*, ed 2, Boca Raton, Fla, 1994, CRC Press.

23. Lindley T: Taping and semirigid bracing may not affect ankle functional range of motion, *J Ath Train* 30(2):109, 1995.

24. Locke A et al: Long-term use of a softshell prophylactic ankle stabilizer on speed, agility, and vertical jump performance, *J Sport Rehabil* 6(3):235, 1997.

25. Lokiec F, Sievner I, Pritsch M: Chronic compartment syndrome of both feet, *J Bone Joint Surg*, 738:178, 1991.

26. Loudin J, Bell S: The foot and ankle: an overview of arthrokinematics and selected joint techniques, *J Ath Train* 31(2):173, 1996.

27. McKnight C, Armstrong C: The role of ankle strength in functional ankle instability. *J Sport Rehabil* 6(1):21, 1997.

28. McMullen ST: Foot and ankle trauma. In Brown DE, Neuman RD, editors: *Orthopedic secrets*, Philadelphia, 1995, Hanley & Belfus.

29. McPoil Jr TG, Brocoto RS: The foot and ankle: biomechanical evaluation and treatment. In Gould III JA, editor: *Orthopaedic and sports physical therapy*, ed 2, St Louis, 1990, Mosby.

30. Mehlman CT: Ankle fractures: common mechanisms, classifications, complications, *Ath Train* 23(2):110, 1988.

31. Payne KA, Berg K, Latin RW: Ankle injuries and ankle strength, flexibility, and proprioception in college basketball players, *J Ath Train* 32(3):221, 1997.

32. Sammarco GJ: Injuries to the tibialis anterior, peroneal tendons, and long flexors and extensions of the toes. In Baxter DE, editor: *The foot and ankle in sport*, St Louis, 1995, Mosby.

33. Scotece SG, Guthrie MR: Comparison of three treatment approaches for grade I and II ankle sprains in active-duty soldiers, *J Orthop Sports Phys Ther* 15(1):819, 1992.

34. Sharpe SR, Knapik J, Jones B: Ankle braces effectively reduce recurrence of ankle sprains in female soccer players, *J Ath Train* 32(1):21, 1997.

35. Simoneau GG, Degner RM, Kramper CA et al: Changes in ankle joint proprioception resulting from strips of athletic tape applied over the skin, *J Ath Train* 32(2):141, 1997.

36. Stanish WD: Lower leg, foot, and ankle injuries in young athletes. In Micheli LJ, editor: T*he young athlete. Clinics in sports medicine*, vol 14, no 3, Philadelphia, 1995, Saunders.

37. Surve I et al: A fivefold reduction in the incidence of recurrent ankle sprains in soccer players using the sport-stirrup orthosis, *Am J Sports Med* 22(5):601, 1994.

38. Taube RR, Wadsworth LT: Managing tibial stress fractures, *Physician Sportsmed* 21(4):123, 1993.

39. Taunton J, Smith C, Magee D: Leg, foot, and ankle injuries. In Zachazewski J, Magee D, Quillen W: *Athletic injuries and rehabilitation*, Philadelphia, 1996, WB Saunders.

40. Vaes P, DeBoeck H, Handleberg F et al: Comparative radiologic study of the influence of ankle joint bandages on ankle stability, *Am J Sports Med* 13:46, 1985.

41. Vegso JJ: Ankle sprain: nonoperative management injuries to lower extremity. In Torg JS, Shephard RJ, editors: *Current therapy in sports medicine*, ed 3, St Louis, 1995, Mosby.

42. Wilkerson GB: Treatment of the inversion ankle sprain through synchronous application of focal compression and cold, *Ath Train* 26(3):220, 1991.

43. Zecher SB, Leach RE: Lower leg and foot injuries in tennis and other racquet sports. In Lehman RC, editor: *Racquet sports. Clinic in sports medicine*, vol 14, no 1, Philadelphia, 1995, Saunders.

ANNOTATED BIBLIOGRAPHY

Baxter D: *The foot and ankle in sport*, St Louis, 1995, Mosby.

This comprehensive text is edited by an orthopedist who specializes in foot and ankle injuries.

Sammarco GJ: Rehabilitation of the foot and ankle, St Louis, 1995, Mosby.

This text specifically addresses the aspects of rehabilitation directed at both the foot and ankle.

Prentice WE, editor: *Rehabilitation techniques in sports medicine*, ed 3, Dubuque, Iowa, 1999, WCB/McGraw-Hill.

Chapters 24 and 25 of this text are dedicated to a discussion of rehabilitation techniques for injuries to the lower leg and ankle. The text first covers the pathomechanics and mechanisms of various injuries and then presents in specific detail rehabilitation concerns and progressions.

The Knee and Related Structures

When you finish this chapter you should be able to

- Describe the normal structural and functional knee anatomy and relate it to major sports injuries.
- Assess the knee and related structures after injury.
- Establish a knee injury prevention program.
- Discuss etiological factors, symptoms and signs, and management procedures for major conditions involving the knee joint and related structures.
- Discuss considerations for rehabilitation of the injured knee.

The knee is one of the most complex joints in the human body. Because so many sports place extreme stress on the knee, it is also one of the most traumatized joints. The knee is commonly considered a hinge joint because its two principal movements are flexion and extension. However, because rotation of the tibia is an essential component of knee movement, the knee is not a true hinge joint. The stability of the knee joint depends primarily on the ligaments, the joint capsule, and muscles that surround the joint (Figure 20-1). The knee is designed primarily to provide stability in weight bearing and mobility in locomotion; however, it is especially unstable laterally and medially (Figure 20-2).

Muscles and ligaments provide the main source of stability in the knee.

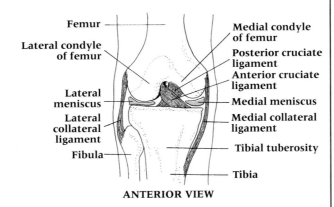

Femur — **Medial condyle of femur**
Lateral condyle of femur — **Posterior cruciate ligament**
Anterior cruciate ligament
Lateral meniscus — **Medial meniscus**
Lateral collateral ligament — **Medial collateral ligament**
Fibula — **Tibial tuberosity**
Tibia

ANTERIOR VIEW

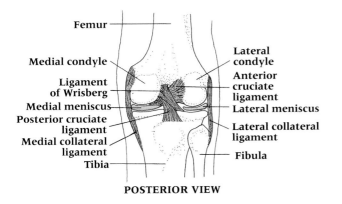

Femur
Medial condyle — **Lateral condyle**
Ligament of Wrisberg — **Anterior cruciate ligament**
Medial meniscus — **Lateral meniscus**
Posterior cruciate ligament — **Lateral collateral ligament**
Medial collateral ligament — **Fibula**
Tibia

POSTERIOR VIEW

Figure 20-1

The bony and ligamentous arrangement of the knee.

Figure 20-2

The knee is a highly complicated joint that is often traumatized during competitive sports.

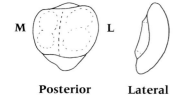

M   L

Posterior   Lateral

Figure 20-3

Patella.

ANATOMY

Bones

The knee joint complex consists of the femur, the tibia, the fibula, and the patella. The distal end of the femur expands and forms the convex lateral and medial condyles, which are designed to articulate with the tibia and the patella. The articular surface of the medial condyle is longer from front to back than is the surface of the lateral condyle. Anteriorly, the two condyles form a hollowed groove to receive the patella. The proximal end of the tibia, the tibial plateau, articulates with the condyles of the femur. On this flat tibial plateau are two shallow concavities that articulate with their respective femoral condyles and are divided by the popliteal notch. Separating these concavities, or articular facets, is a roughened area where the cruciate ligaments attach and from which a process commonly known as the tibial spine arises.

Patella

The patella is the largest sesamoid bone in the human body. It is located in the tendon of the quadriceps femoris muscle and is divided into three medial facets and a lateral facet that articulate with the femur (Figure 20-3). The lateral aspect of the patella is wider than the medial aspect. The patella articulates between the concavity provided by the femoral condyles. Tracking within this groove depends on the pull of the quadriceps muscle and patellar tendon, the depth of the femoral condyles, and the shape of the patella.

Articulations

The knee joint complex consists of several articulations between the femur and the tibia, the femur and the patella, the femur and the fibula, and the tibia and fibula.

Menisci

The menisci (Figure 20-4) are two oval (semilunar) fibrocartilages that deepen the articular facets of the tibia, cushion any stresses placed on the knee joint, and maintain spacing between the femoral condyles and tibial plateau. The consistency of the menisci is much like that of the intervertebral disks. They are located medially and laterally on the tibial tuberosity. The menisci transmit one half of the contact force in

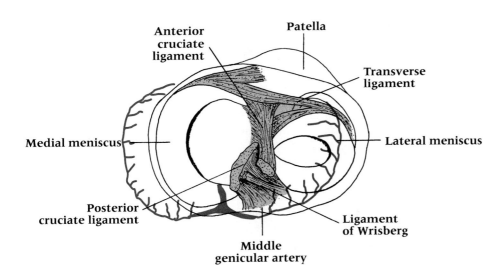

Figure 20-4

Menisci and blood supply of the knee.

the medial compartment and an even higher percentage of the contact load in the lateral compartment. The menisci help stabilize the knee, especially the medial meniscus, when the knee is flexed at 90 degrees.

Medial Meniscus

The medial meniscus is a C-shaped fibrocartilage, the circumference of which is attached firmly to the medial articular facet of the tibia and to the joint capsule by the coronary ligaments. Posteriorly, it is also attached to fibers of the semimembranous muscle.

Lateral Meniscus

The lateral meniscus is more O-shaped and is attached to the lateral articular facet on the superior aspect of the tibia. The lateral meniscus also attaches loosely to the lateral articular capsule and to the popliteal tendon. The ligament of Wrisberg is the part of the lateral meniscus that projects upward, close to the attachment of the posterior cruciate ligament. The transverse ligament joins the anterior portions of the lateral and medial menisci.

Meniscal Blood Supply

Blood is supplied to each meniscus by the medial genicular artery. Each meniscus can be divided into three circumferential zones: the red-red zone is the outer, or peripheral, one-third and has a good vascular supply; the red-white zone is the middle one-third and has minimal blood supply; and the white-white zone on the inner one-third is **avascular** (Figure 20-5).

Generally, the meniscus has a poor blood supply.

avascular
Devoid of blood circulation.

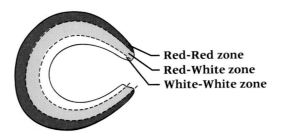

Figure 20-5

The meniscus has three vascular zones.

Stabilizing Ligaments

The major stabilizing ligaments of the knee include the cruciate ligaments, the collateral ligaments, and the capsular ligaments (see Figure 20-1).

Cruciate Ligaments

The cruciate ligaments account for a considerable amount of knee stability. They are two ligamentous bands that cross one another within the joint cavity of the knee. The anterior cruciate ligament (ACL) attaches below and in front of the tibia; then, passing backward, it attaches laterally to the inner surface of the lateral condyle. The posterior cruciate ligament (PCL), the stronger of the two, crosses from the back of the tibia in an upward, forward, and medial direction and attaches to the anterior portion of the lateral surface of the medial condyle of the femur.

Anterior cruciate ligament The anterior cruciate ligament comprises three twisted bands: the anteromedial, intermediate, and posterolateral bands. In general, the anterior cruciate ligament prevents the femur from moving posteriorly during weight bearing. It also stabilizes the tibia against excessive internal rotation and serves as a secondary restraint for valgus or varus stress with collateral ligament damage.

When the knee is fully extended, the posterolateral section of the cruciate ligament is tight. In flexion the posterolateral fibers loosen and the anteromedial fibers tighten.[46] The anterior cruciate ligament works in conjunction with the thigh muscles, especially the hamstring muscle group, to stabilize the knee joint.

Posterior cruciate ligament Some portion of the posterior cruciate ligament is taut throughout the full range of motion. It acts as a drag during the gliding phase of motion and resists internal rotation of the tibia. In general, the posterior cruciate ligament prevents hyperextension of the knee and femur, sliding forward during weight bearing.

Capsular and Collateral Ligaments

Additional stabilization of the knee is provided by the capsular and collateral ligaments. Besides providing stability, they also direct movement in a correct path. Although they move in synchrony, they are divided into the medial and lateral complexes.

Medial collateral ligament The superficial position of the medial (tibial) collateral ligament (MCL) is separate from the deeper capsular ligament at the joint line. It attaches above the joint line on the medial epicondyle of the femur and below on the tibia, just beneath the attachment of the pes anserinus. The posterior aspect of the ligament blends into the deep posterior capsular ligament and semimembranous muscle. Fibers of the semimembranous muscle go through the capsule and attach to the posterior aspect of the medial meniscus, pulling it backward during knee flexion. Some of its fibers are taut through flexion and extension. Its major purpose is to prevent the knee from valgus and external rotating forces. The medial collateral ligament was thought to be the principal stabilizer of the knee in a valgus position when combined with rotation. It is now known that other structures, such as the anterior cruciate ligament, play an equal or greater part in this function.[48]

Deep medial capsular ligaments The deep medial capsular ligament is divided into three parts: the anterior, medial, and posterior capsular ligaments. The anterior capsular ligament connects with the extensor mechanism and the medial meniscus through the coronary ligaments. It relaxes during knee extension and tightens during knee flexion. The primary purposes of the medial capsular ligaments are to attach the medial meniscus to the femur and to allow the tibia to move on the meniscus inferiorly. The posterior capsular ligament is sometimes called the posterior oblique ligament and attaches to the posterior medial aspect of the meniscus and intersperses with the semimembranous muscle.[3]

Lateral collateral ligament and related structures   The lateral (fibular) collateral ligament (LCL) is a round, fibrous cord that is shaped like a pencil. It is attached to the lateral epicondyle of the femur and to the head of the fibula. The lateral collateral ligament is taut during knee extension but relaxed during flexion.

Another stabilizing ligament of importance is the arcuate ligament. It is formed by a thickening of the posterior articular capsule. Its posterior aspect attaches to the fascia of the popliteal muscle and the posterior horn of the lateral meniscus.

Other structures that stabilize the knee laterally are the iliotibial band, popliteus muscle, and biceps femoris. The iliotibial band, a tendon of the tensor fascia latae and gluteus medius, attaches to the lateral epicondyle of the femur and lateral tibial tubercle (Gerdy's tubercle). It becomes tense during both extension and flexion. The popliteus muscle stabilizes the knee during flexion and, when contracting, protects the lateral meniscus by pulling it posteriorly.

The biceps femoris muscle also stabilizes the knee laterally by inserting into the fibular head, iliotibial band, and capsule.

Joint Capsule

The articular surfaces of the knee joint are completely enveloped by the largest joint capsule in the body. Anteriorly, the joint capsule extends upward underneath the patella to form the suprapatellar pouch. The inferior portion contains the infrapatellar fat pad and the infrapatellar bursa. Medially, a thickened section of the capsule forms the deep portion of the medial collateral ligament. Posteriorly, the capsule forms two pouches that cover the femoral condyles and the tibial plateau. The capsule thickens medially to form the posterior oblique ligament and laterally to form the arcuate ligament.

The joint capsule is divided into four regions: the posterolateral, posteromedial, anterolateral, and anteromedial. Each of these four "corners" of the capsule is reinforced by other anatomical structures. The posterolateral corner is reinforced by the iliotibial band, the popliteus, the biceps femoris, the LCL, and the arcuate ligament. The MCL, the pes anserinus tendons, the semimembranosus, and the posterior oblique ligament reinforce the posteromedial corner. The anterolateral corner is reinforced by the iliotibial band, the patellar tendon, and the lateral patellar retinaculum. The superficial MCL and the medial patellar retinaculum reinforce the anteromedial corner.

Synovial membrane lines the inner surface of the joint capsule, except posteriorly where it passes in front of the cruciates, making them extrasynovial (Figure 20-6).

Knee Musculature

For the knee to function properly, a number of muscles must work together in a highly complex fashion. The following is a list of knee actions and the muscles that initiate them (Figure 20-7):

- Knee flexion is executed by the biceps femoris, semitendinosus, semimembranosus, gracilis, sartorius, gastrocnemius, popliteus, and plantaris muscles.
- Knee extension is executed by the quadriceps muscle of the thigh, consisting of three vasti—the vastus medialis, vastus lateralis, and vastus intermedius—and by the rectus femoris.
- External rotation of the tibia is controlled by the biceps femoris. The bony anatomy also produces external tibial rotation as the knee moves into extension.
- Internal rotation is accomplished by the popliteal, semitendinosus, semimembranosus, sartorius, and gracilis muscles. Rotation of the tibia is limited and can occur only when the knee is in a flexed position.
- The iliotibial band on the lateral side primarily functions as a dynamic lateral stabilizer.

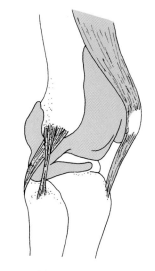

Figure 20-6

Synovial membrane of the knee.

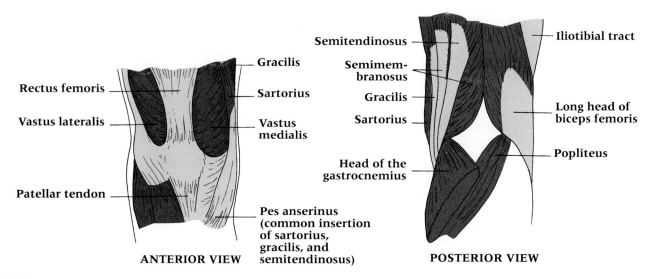

Figure 20-7

Musculature of the knee.

Bursae

A bursa is a flattened sac or enclosed cleft composed of synovial tissue that is separated by a thin film of fluid. The function of a bursa is to reduce the friction between anatomical structures. Bursae are found between muscle and bone, tendon and bone, tendon and ligament, and so forth. As many as two dozen bursa have been identified around the knee joint. The suprapatellar, prepatellar, infrapatellar, pretibial, and gastrocnemius bursae are perhaps the most commonly injured about the knee joint (Figure 20-8).

Fat Pads

There are several fat pads around the knee. The infrapatellar fat pad is the largest. It serves as a cushion to the front of the knee and separates the patellar tendon from the joint capsule. Other major fat pads in the knee include the anterior and posterior suprapatellar and the popliteal. Some fat pads occupy space within the synovial capsule.

Nerve Supply

The tibial nerve innervates most of the hamstrings and the gastrocnemius. The common peroneal nerve innervates the short head of the biceps femoris and then courses through the popliteal fossa and wraps around the proximal head of the

Figure 20-8

Common bursae of the knee.

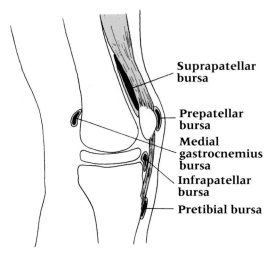

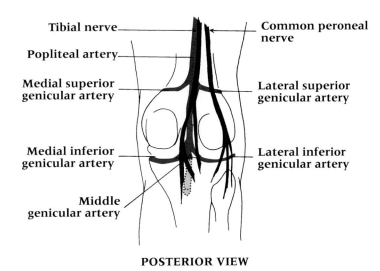

Figure 20-9

Blood and nerve supply to the knee.

POSTERIOR VIEW

fibula. Because the peroneal nerve is exposed at the head of the fibula, contusion of the nerve can cause distal sensory and motor deficits. The femoral nerve innervates the quadriceps and the sartorius muscles (Figure 20-9).

Blood Supply

The main blood supply to the knee comes from the popliteal artery, which stems from the femoral artery. From the popliteal artery, five branches supply the knee: the medial and lateral superior genicular, middle genicular, and medial and lateral inferior genicular arteries (see Figure 20-9).

FUNCTIONAL ANATOMY

Movement between the tibia and the femur involves the physiological motions of flexion, extension, and rotation as well as arthrokinematic motions, including rolling and gliding. As the tibia extends on the femur, the tibia glides and rolls anteriorly. If the femur is extending on the tibia, gliding occurs in an anterior direction, whereas rolling occurs posteriorly.

Axial rotation of the tibia relative to the femur is an important component of knee motion. In the "screw home" mechanism of the knee, as the knee extends, the tibia externally rotates. Rotation occurs because the medial femoral condyle is larger than the lateral condyle. Thus, when weight bearing, the tibia must rotate externally to achieve full extension. The rotational component gives a great deal of stability to the knee in full extension. When weight bearing, the popliteus muscle must contract and externally rotate the femur to "unlock" the knee so that flexion can occur.

The capsular ligaments are taut during full extension and to some extent relaxed during flexion. This is particularly true of the lateral collateral ligament; however, portions of the medial collateral ligament relax as flexion occurs. Relaxation of the more superficial collateral ligaments allows rotation to occur. In contrast, the deeper capsular ligament tightens to prevent excessive rotation of the tibia.

During the last 15 degrees of extension, the tibia externally rotates and the anterior cruciate ligament unwinds.[36] In full extension the anterior cruciate ligament is taut, and it loosens during flexion. As the femur glides on the tibia, the posterior cruciate ligament becomes taut and prevents further gliding. In general, the anterior cruciate ligament stops excessive internal rotation, stabilizes the knee in full extension, and prevents hyperextension. The posterior cruciate ligament prevents excessive internal rotation, guides the knee in flexion, and acts as a drag during the initial glide phase of flexion.

Major actions of the knee:
- Flexion
- Extension
- Gliding
- Rotation

In complete flexion, approximately 140 degrees, the range of the knee movement is limited by the extremely shortened position of the hamstring muscles, the extensibility of the quadriceps muscles, and the bulk of the hamstring muscles. In this position, the femoral condyles rest on their corresponding menisci at a point that permits a small degree of inward rotation.

The patella aids the knee during extension by lengthening the lever arm of the quadriceps muscle. It distributes the compressive stresses on the femur by increasing the contact area between the patellar tendon and the femur.[46] It also protects the patellar tendon against friction. During full extension, the patella lies slightly lateral and proximal to the trochlea. At 20 degrees of knee flexion, there is tibial rotation, and the patella moves into the trochlea. At 30 degrees, the patella is most prominent. At 30 degrees and more, the patella moves deeper into the trochlea. At 90 degrees, the patella again becomes positioned laterally. When knee flexion is 135 degrees, the patella has moved laterally beyond the trochlea.[46]

Kinetic Chain

The knee is part of the kinetic chain that was discussed in Chapter 16. It is directly affected by motions and forces occurring to and being transmitted from the foot, ankle, and lower leg. In turn, the knee must transmit forces to the thigh, hip, pelvis, and spine. Abnormal forces that cannot be distributed must be absorbed by the tissues. When the foot is in contact with the ground, a closed kinetic chain exists. In a closed kinetic chain, forces must either be transmitted to proximal segments or be absorbed in a more distal joint. The inability of this closed system to dissipate these forces typically leads to a breakdown in some part of the system. As part of the kinetic chain, the knee joint is susceptible to injury resulting from absorption of these forces.[59]

ASSESSING THE KNEE JOINT

It is the responsibility of the team physician to diagnose the severity and exact nature of a knee injury. Although the physician is charged with the final evaluation, the athletic trainer is usually the first person to observe the injury; therefore he or she is charged with initial evaluation and immediate care. The most important aspect of understanding what pathological process has taken place is to become familiar with the traumatic sequence and mechanisms of injury, either through having seen the injury occur or through learning its history (Figure 20-10). Often the team physician is not present when the injury occurs, and the athletic trainer must relate the pertinent information.[17]

History

To determine the history and major complaints involved in a knee injury, the following questions should be asked.

Figure 20-10

It is extremely important that the sequence and mechanism of the knee injury be known before the pathological process can be understood.

Current Injury

- What were you doing when the knee was hurt?
- What position was your body in?
- Did the knee collapse?
- Did you hear a noise or feel any sensation at the time of injury, such as a pop or crunch? (A pop could indicate an anterior cruciate tear, a crunch could be a sign of a torn meniscus, and a tearing sensation might indicate a capsular tear.)
- Could you move the knee immediately after the injury? If not, was it locked in a bent or extended position? (Locking could mean a meniscal tear.) After being locked, how did it become unlocked?
- Did swelling occur? If yes, was it immediate, or did it occur later? (Immediate swelling could indicate a cruciate or tibial fracture, whereas later swelling could indicate a capsular, synovial, or meniscal tear.)
- Where was the pain? Was it local, all over, or did it move from one side of the knee to the other?
- Have you hurt the knee before?

When first studying the injury, the athletic trainer should observe whether the athlete is able to support body weight flat-footed on the injured leg or whether the athlete needs to stand and walk on the toes. Toe walking is an indication that the athlete is holding the knee in a splinted position to avoid pain or that the knee is being held in a flexed position by a wedge of dislocated meniscus. In first-time acute knee sprains, fluid and blood effusion is not usually apparent until after a twenty-four-hour period. However, in an anterior cruciate ligament sprain, a hemarthrosis may occur during the first hour after injury. Swelling and ecchymosis will occur unless the effusion is arrested through the use of compression, elevation, and cold packs.

Recurrent or Chronic Injury

- What is your major complaint?
- When did you first notice the condition?
- Is there recurrent swelling?
- Does the knee ever lock or catch? (If yes, it may be a torn meniscus or a loose body in the knee joint.)
- Is there severe pain? Is it constant, or does it come and go?
- Do you feel any grinding or grating sensations? (If yes, it could indicate chondromalacia or traumatic arthritis.)
- Does your knee ever feel like it is going to give way, or has it actually done so? (If yes and often, it may be a capsular, cruciate, or meniscal tear, a loose body, or a subluxating patella.)
- What does it feel like to go up and down stairs? (Pain may indicate a patellar irritation or meniscal tear.)
- What past treatment, if any, have you received for this condition?

Observation

A visual examination should be performed after the major complaints have been determined. The athlete should be observed in a number of situations: walking, half squatting, and going up and down stairs. The leg also should be observed for alignment and symmetry or asymmetry.

If possible, the athlete with an injured knee should be observed in the following actions:
- Walking
- Half squatting
- Going up and down stairs

Walking

- Does the athlete walk with a limp, or is the walk free and easy? Is the athlete able to fully extend the knee during heel strike?
- Can the athlete fully bear weight on the affected leg?
- Is the athlete able to perform a half-squat to extension?
- Can the athlete go up and down stairs with ease? (If stairs are unavailable, stepping up on a box or stool will suffice.)

Leg Alignment

The athlete should be observed for leg alignment. Anteriorly, the athlete is evaluated for genu valgum, genu varum, and the position of the patella. Next, the athlete is observed from the side to ascertain conditions such as the hyperflexed or hyperextended knee.

Deviations in normal leg alignment may or may not be a factor in knee injury but should always be considered as a possible cause. Like alignment in any other body segment, leg alignment differs from person to person; however, obvious discrepancies could predispose the athlete to an acute or chronic injury.

Anteriorly, with the knees extended as much as possible, the following points should be noted:
- Are the patellas level with each other?
- Are the patellas facing forward?
- Can the athlete touch the medial femoral condyles and medial malleoli?

Looking at the athlete's knees from the side:
- Are the knees fully extended with only slight hyperextension?
- Are both knees equally extended?

Leg alignment deviations that may predispose to injury   Four major leg deviations could adversely affect the knee and patellofemoral joints: patellar malalignment, genu valgum (knock-knees), genu varum (bowlegs), and genu recurvatum (hyperextended knees).

Patellar malalignment   A patella that is rotated inward or outward from the center may be caused by a complex set of circumstances. For example, a combination of genu recurvatum, genu varum, and internal rotation, or anteversion, of the hip and internal rotation of the tibia could cause the patella to face inward. Internal rotation of the hip also may be associated with knock-knees, along with external rotation of the tibia, or tibial torsion. Athletes who toe-out when they walk may have an externally rotated hip, or retroversion. The normal angulation of the femoral neck after eight years of age is 15 degrees; an increase of this angle is considered anteversion, and a decrease is considered retroversion. If an abnormal angulation seems to be a factor with the patella, malalignment or tibial torsion angles should be measured.

MEASURING FOR TIBIAL TORSION, FEMORAL ANTEVERSION, AND FEMORAL RETROVERSION   Tibial torsion is determined by having the athlete kneel on a stool with the foot relaxed. An imaginary line is drawn along the center of the thigh and lower leg, bisecting the middle of the heel and the bottom of the foot. Another line starts at the center of the middle toe and crosses the center of the heel. The angle formed by the two lines is measured (Figure 20-11); an angle measuring more or less than 15 degrees is a sign of tibial torsion.

Femoral anteversion or retroversion can be determined by the number of degrees the thigh rotates in each direction. As a rule, external rotation and internal rotation added together equal close to 100 degrees. If internal rotation exceeds 70 degrees, there may be anteversion of the hip.[53]

Hyperextension of the knee may result in internal rotation of the femur and external rotation of the tibia. Internal rotation at the hip is caused by weak external rotator muscles or foot pronation.

Genu valgum   The causes of genu valgum, or knock-knees, can be multiple. Normally, toddlers and very young children display knock-knees. When the legs have strengthened and the feet have become positioned more in line with the pelvis, the condition is usually corrected. Commonly associated with knock-knees are pronated feet. Genu valgum places chronic tension on the ligamentous structures of the medial part of the knee, abnormal compression of the lateral aspect of the knee surface, and abnormal tightness of the iliotibial band. One or both legs may be affected, and the hip's external rotator muscles may be weak.

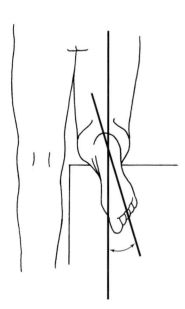

Figure 20-11

Measuring for tibial torsion.

Genu varum   The two types of genu varum, or bowlegs, are structural and functional. The structural type, which is seldom seen in athletes, reflects a deviation of the femur and tibia. The more common functional, or postural, type usually is associated with knees that are hyperextended and femurs that are internally rotated. Often when genu recurvatum is corrected, so is genu varum.

Genu recurvatum   Genu recurvatum, or hyperextended knees, commonly occurs as a compensation for lordosis, or swayback. There is notable weakness and stretching of the hamstring muscles. Chronic hyperextension can produce undue anterior pressure on the knee joint and posterior ligaments and tendons.

Knee Symmetry or Asymmetry

The athletic trainer must establish whether both of the athlete's knees look the same:
- Do the knees appear symmetrical?
- Is one knee obviously swollen?
- Is muscle atrophy apparent?

Leg-Length Discrepancy

Discrepancies in leg length can occur as a result of many causes, either anatomical or functional. True anatomical leg length can be measured from the anterior superior iliac spine (ASIS) to the lateral malleolus. Functional leg length can be measured from the umbilicus to the medial malleolus.

Anatomical differences in leg length can potentially cause problems in all weight-bearing joints. Functional differences can be caused by rotations of the pelvis or malalignments of the spine.

Palpation

Bony Palpation

The bony structures of the knee are palpated for pain and deformities that might indicate a fracture or dislocation. The athlete sits on the edge of the training table or a bench. With the athlete's knee flexed to 90 degrees, the athletic trainer palpates the following bony structures:

Medial Aspect
- Medial tibial plateau
- Medial femoral condyle
- Adductor tubercle
- Gerdy's tubercle

Lateral Aspect
- Lateral tibial plateau
- Lateral femoral condyle
- Lateral epicondyle
- Head of the fibula

Anterior Aspect
- Tibial tubercle

Patella
- Superior patellar border
- Inferior patellar border
- Around periphery with the knee relaxed
- Around periphery with the knee in full extension

Soft-Tissue Palpation

The following soft tissue structures should be palpated:

Anterior
- vastus medialis
- vastus lateralis

Figure 20-12

Typical pain sites around the knee.

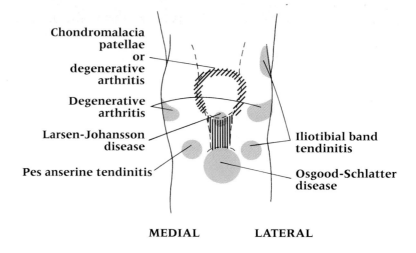

Chondromalacia patellae or degenerative arthritis

Degenerative arthritis

Larsen-Johansson disease

Pes anserine tendinitis

Iliotibial band tendinitis

Osgood-Schlatter disease

MEDIAL   LATERAL

- vastus intermedialis
- rectus femoris
- quadriceps tendon
- sartorius
- medial patellar plica
- patellar tendon
- anterior joint capsule

Medial
- medial collateral ligament superficial portion
- medial collateral ligament-capsular portion
- pes anserinus insertion (sartorius, gracilis, semimembranosus)
- medial joint capsule

Posterior
- semitendinosus
- popliteus
- medial and laterals heads of the gastrocnemius
- biceps femoris
- posterior oblique ligament

Lateral
- lateral collateral ligament
- iliotibial band
- lateral joint capsule
- arcuate complex

Palpation of Swelling Patterns

Of major importance to knee inspection and evaluation is palpating for joint effusion (Figure 20-13). Swelling may be *intracapsular* (inside the joint capsule) or *extracapsular* (outside the joint capsule). Intracapsular swelling may also be referred to as a *joint effusion*. A moderate amount of swelling that occurs immediately following injury and that is caused by synovial fluid and by blood in the joint is called a **hemarthrosis.** A hemarthrosis can only be identified by having the team physician aspirate the joint with a needle. With intracapsular joint effusion, the fluid in the joint can be moved manually from one side of the joint to the other. In a *sweep maneuver,* pressure applied from superior to the patella downward moves fluid into the center of the joint capsule; then pressure from the medial side of the joint line will cause a bulging laterally. Joint effusion can also cause what has been referred to as a *ballotable patella.* With the knee in full extension and the quadriceps relaxed, a release of downward pressure on the patella sitting on top of the joint capsule causes the patella to bounce back to its normal position.

hemarthrosis (hem **are** throsis) Blood in a joint cavity.

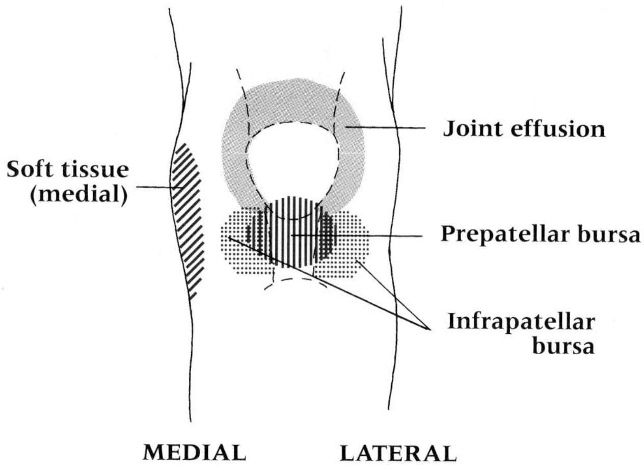

Figure 20-13

Typical swelling sites around the knee.

Joint effusion

Soft tissue (medial)

Prepatellar bursa

Infrapatellar bursa

MEDIAL   LATERAL

Extracapsular swelling from bursitis, tendinitis, or injury to one of the collateral ligaments tends to localize over the injured structure and then gradually migrate downward toward the foot and ankle because of the effects of gravity.

Special Tests for Assessment of Knee Joint Instability

Both acute and chronic injury to the knee can produce ligamentous instability.[57] It is advisable that the injured knee's stability be evaluated as soon after injury as possible. However, tests of this type should be performed only by well-trained professionals. The injured knee and uninjured knee are tested and contrasted to determine any differences in their stability.

Determination of the degree of instability is made by the endpoint felt during stability testing. As stress is applied to a joint, there will be some motion, which is limited by an intact ligament. In a normal joint, the endpoint will be abrupt with little or no give and no reported pain. With a grade 1 sprain, the endpoint will still be firm with little or no instability and some pain will be indicated. With a grade 2 sprain, the endpoint will be soft with some instability present and a moderate amount of pain. In a grade 3 complete rupture, the endpoint will be very soft with marked instability, and pain will be severe initially, then mild.[32]

The use of magnetic resonance imaging (MRI) as a diagnostic tool has aided tremendously in the classification of ligamentous sprains. Despite its expense, MRI is being widely used by physicians to detect ligament injuries.

Table 20-1 provides a summary of the various tests and what a positive test indicates in terms of the injured structures.

Classification of Knee Joint Instabilities

A good deal of controversy exists over the most appropriate terminology for classifying instabilities in the knee joint.[40] For years the American Orthopedic Society for Sports Medicine has classified knee laxity as either a straight or a rotatory instability. A straight instability implies laxity in a single direction, either medial, lateral, anterior, or posterior. Rotatory instabilities refer to excessive rotation of the tibial plateau relative to the femoral condyles and are identified as anterolateral, anteromedial, posterolateral, or rarely, posteromedial. It is not unusual to see combined instabilities, depending on the structures that have been injured. This classification system is still the most widely used and accepted by the athletic trainer (Table 20-2).

Recently, the concept of tibial translation has been proposed.[43] **Translation** refers to the amount of gliding of the medial tibial plateau as compared with the lateral tibial plateau relative to the femoral condyles. For example, in anterolateral rotatory instability, the anterior translation of the lateral tibial plateau would be much greater than the more stable medial tibial plateau. The amount of anterior translation is

20-2

Critical Thinking Exercise

A cross-country runner is complaining of nonspecific anterior knee pain. She indicates that not only do her knees hurt during her training sessions, but they also bother her when ascending or descending stairs, when she squats and then tries to stand, and when she sits for long periods of time.

? What anatomical and biomechanical factors that might be contributing to the athlete's anterior knee pain should be assessed by the athletic trainer?

translation
Refers to anterior gliding of tibial plateau.

TABLE 20-1 Knee Stability Tests

Test	If Positive
Valgus stress test at 0°	Torn MCL and possibly ACL, PCL, PMC
Valgus stress test at 20°/30°	Torn MCL (if grade 3 check ACL, PCL, PMC)
Varus stress test at 0°	Torn LCL and possibly ACL, PCL, PLC
Varus stress test at 20°/30°	Torn LCL (if grade 3 check ACL, PCL, PLC)
Anterior drawer test (neutral)	Torn ACL
Anterior drawer test (15° ER)	Torn PMC, ACL, and possibly MCL
Anterior drawer test (30° IR)	Torn PLC, ACL
Lachman drawer test (20°/30° flexion)	Torn ACL, PCL (positive more often than anterior drawer because hamstrings are relaxed and medial meniscus/collateral ligaments do not block anterior displacement at 20°)
Pivot-shift tests (Galaway and McIntosh) Extension/IR/valgus (tibia subluxated) → flexion (tibia reduces at 20°)	Torn ACL, ALC
Slocum's test Sidelying extension/IR/valgus (tibia subluxated) → flexion (tibia reduces at 20°)	Torn ACL, ALC
Jerk test (Hughston) Flexion/IR/valgus (tibia reduced) → extension (tibia subluxates at 20°)	Torn ACL, ALC
Losee test 45° flexion/ER/valgus (tibia subluxated anteriorly) → extension (tibia reduces at 20°)	Torn ACL, ALC
Flexion-rotation drawer test 15° flex (tibia subluxated anteriorly/femur ER) → flexion (tibia reduces posteriorly/femur IR)	Torn ACL
Posterior drawer test 90°	Torn PCL
External rotation recurvatum test (tibia ER)	Torn PCL, PLC
Posterior sag test 90°	Torn PCL
Reverse pivot-shift test (Jakob) Extension (tibia reduced) → flexion (tibia subluxated posteriorly with ER)	Torn PCL
McMurray's test (IR)	Torn LM
(ER)	Torn MM
Apley's grinding test	Torn MM

ACL, Anterior cruciate ligament; *ER*, external rotation; *IR*, internal rotation; *LCL*, lateral collateral ligament; *LM*, lateral meniscus; *MCL*, medial collateral ligament; *MM*, medial meniscus; *PCL*, posterior cruciate ligament; *PLC*, posterior lateral corner; *PMC*, posterior medial corner.

20-3

Critical Thinking E x e r c i s e

A football running back is hit on the lateral surface of his knee by an opponent making a tackle. He has significant pain and some immediate swelling on the medial surface of his knee. The athletic trainer suspects that the athlete has sustained a sprain of the MCL.

? What are the most appropriate tests that the athletic trainer should do to determine the exact nature and extent of the injury?

determined by the integrity of the anatomical restraints that normally restrict excessive translation. More ligamentous, tendinous, and capsular structures will be damaged as the severity of the injury increases. Classification of knee injury relative to tibial translation is likely to gain popularity among sports medicine professionals.

Valgus and Varus Stress Tests

Valgus and varus stress tests are intended to reveal laxity of the medial and lateral stabilizing complexes, especially the collateral ligaments. The athlete lies supine with the leg extended. To test the medial side, the examiner holds the ankle firmly with one hand while placing the other over the head of the fibula. The examiner then places a force inward in an attempt to open the side of the knee. This valgus stress is applied with the knee fully extended, or at 0 degrees, and at 30 degrees of flexion (Figure 20-14A). The examination in full extension tests the MCL, posteromedial capsule, and the cruciates. At 30 degrees flexion, the MCL is isolated. The examiner reverses hand positions and tests the lateral side with a varus force on the fully extended knee and then with 30 degrees of flexion (Figure 20-14B). With the knee ex-

TABLE 20-2 Classification of Instabilities

Straight Instabilities	Rotary Instabilities
Medial	Anterolateral
Lateral	Anteromedial
Anterior	Posterolateral
Posterior	

tended, the LCL and posterolateral capsule are examined. At 30 degrees of flexion, the LCL is isolated.[32] NOTE: The lower limb should be in neutral with no internal or external rotation.

Anterior Cruciate Ligament Tests

A number of tests are currently being used to establish the integrity of the cruciate ligaments.[25] They are the drawer test at 90 degrees of flexion, the Lachman drawer test, the pivot-shift test, the jerk test, and the flexion-rotation drawer test.

Drawer test at 90 degrees of flexion   The athlete lies on the training table with the injured leg flexed. The examiner stands facing the anterior aspect of the athlete's leg, with both hands encircling the upper portion of the leg, immediately below the knee joint. The fingers of the examiner are positioned in the popliteal space of the affected leg, with the thumbs on the medial and lateral joint lines (Figure 20-15A). The index fingers of the examiner are placed on the hamstring tendon to ensure that it is relaxed before the test is administered. The tibia's sliding forward from under the femur is considered a positive anterior drawer sign.[36] If a positive anterior drawer sign occurs, the test should be repeated with the athlete's leg rotated internally 30 degrees and externally 15 degrees (Figure 20-15B and C). A sliding forward of the tibia when the leg is externally rotated is an indication that the posteromedial aspect of the joint capsule, the anterior cruciate ligament, or possibly the medial collateral ligament could be torn. Movement when the leg is internally rotated indicates that the anterior cruciate ligament and posterolateral capsule may be torn. A normal anterior shear is 5 mm. Cailliet indicates that shears of $^1/_2$ inch, $^1/_2$ to $^3/_4$ inch, and $^3/_4$ inch or more (1.25 cm, 1.25 to 1.9 cm, and 1.9 cm or more) correspond to grades 1, 2, and 3, respectively.[9]

Lachman drawer test   The Lachman drawer test is considered to be a better test than the drawer test at 90 degrees of flexion (Figure 20-16).[57] This preference is especially true for examinations immediately after injury. One reason for using it immediately after an injury is that it does not force the knee into the painful 90-degree position but tests it at a more comfortable 20 to 30 degrees. Another reason for its

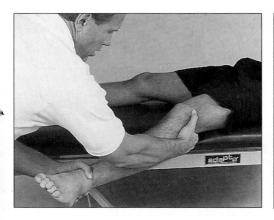

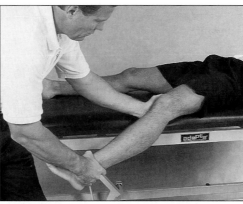

Figure 20-14

Valgus and varus knee stress tests. **A,** Valgus. **B,** Varus.

B

Figure 20-15

Drawer test for cruciate laxity.
A, Knee at 90 degrees, with the foot pointing straight.
B, Knee at 90 degrees, with the leg internally rotated.
C, Knee at 90 degrees, with the leg externally rotated.

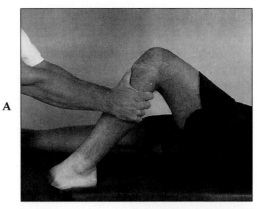

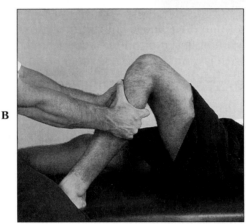

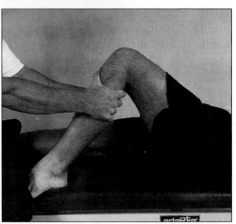

increased popularity is that it reduces the contraction of the hamstring muscles.[13] That contraction causes a secondary knee-stabilizing force that tends to mask the real extent of injury. The Lachman drawer test is administered by positioning the knee in approximately 30 degrees of flexion. One hand of the examiner stabilizes the leg by grasping the distal end of the thigh, and the other hand grasps the proximal aspect of the tibia and attempts to move it anteriorly. A positive Lachman's test indicates damage to the anterior cruciate.

Pivot-shift test   The pivot-shift test is designed to determine anterolateral rotary instability (Figure 20-17). It is most often used in chronic conditions and is a sensitive test when the anterior cruciate ligament has been torn. The athlete lies supine; one hand of the examiner is pressed against the head of the fibula, and the other hand grasps the athlete's ankle. To start, the lower leg is internally rotated and the knee is fully extended. The thigh is then flexed 30 degrees at the hip while the knee is also flexed, and a simultaneous valgus force and axial load are applied by the examiner's upper hand. If the anterior cruciate ligament is damaged, the lateral tibial plateau will be subluxated in the fully extended position. As the knee is flexed to be-

Figure 20-16

Lachman drawer test for cruciate laxity.

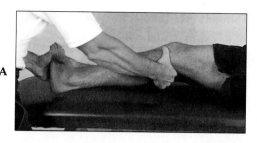

Figure 20-17

Pivot-shift test for anterolateral rotary instability. **A,** The tibia is subluxated in extension. **B,** It reduces at 20 degrees of flexion.

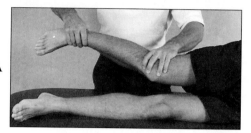
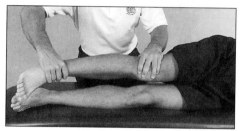

Figure 20-18

Jerk test for anterolateral rotary instability. **A,** The tibia is reduced in flexion. **B,** It subluxates at 20 degrees of extension.

tween 20 and 40 degrees, the lateral tibial plateau will reduce itself, producing a palpable shift or clunk.[56] A variation of the pivot-shift test is Slocum's test, which is done in a side-lying position.[56]

Jerk test   The jerk test reverses the direction of the pivot shift.[32] The position of the knee is identical to that for the pivot-shift test except that the knee is moved from a position of flexion into extension with the lateral tibial plateau in a reduced position. If there is anterior cruciate insufficiency, as the knee moves into extension the tibia will subluxate at about 20 degrees of flexion, once again producing a palpable shift or clunk (Figure 20-18).

Flexion-rotation drawer test   With this test, the lower leg is cradled with the knee flexed between 15 and 30 degrees. At 15 degrees, the tibia is subluxated anteriorly with the femur externally rotated. As the knee is flexed to 30 degrees, the tibia reduces posteriorly and the femur rotates internally (Figure 20-19).[56]

Posterior Cruciate Ligament Tests

Tests for posterior cruciate ligament instability include the posterior drawer test, the external rotation recurvatum test, and the posterior sag test.

Posterior drawer test   The posterior drawer test is performed with the knee flexed at 90 degrees and the foot in neutral. Force is exerted in a posterior direction at the proximal tibial plateau. A positive posterior drawer test indicates damage to the posterior cruciate ligament (Figure 20-20).

20-4

Critical Thinking E x e r c i s e

A lacrosse player carrying the ball attempts to avoid a defender by planting his right foot firmly on the ground and cutting hard to his left. His knee immediately gives way, and he hears a loud pop. He has intense pain immediately, but after a few minutes he feels as if he can get up and walk.

? What ligament has most likely been injured? What stability tests should be done by the athletic trainer to determine the extent of the injury to this ligament?

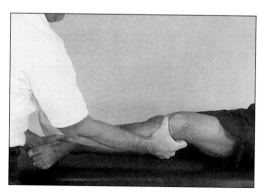

Figure 20-19

Flexion-rotation drawer test.

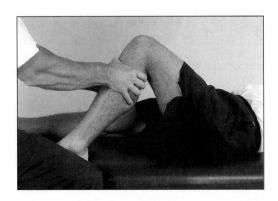

Figure 20-20

Posterior drawer test.

Figure 20-21

External rotation recurvatum test.

Figure 20-22

Posterior sag test.

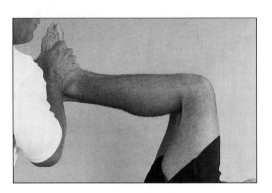

External rotation recurvatum test The athletic trainer grasps the great toe and lifts the leg off the table. If the tibia externally rotates and slides posteriorly, there may be injury to the posterior cruciate ligament and posterolateral corner of the joint capsule, creating posterolateral instability (Figure 20-21).[56]

Posterior sag test (Godfrey's test) With the athlete supine, both knees are flexed to 90 degrees. Observing laterally on the injured side, the tibia will appear to sag posteriorly when compared with the opposite extremity if the posterior cruciate ligament is damaged (Figure 20-22).[56]

Instrument Assessment of Cruciate Laxity

Several ligament-testing devices are currently available that objectively quantify the anterior or posterior displacement of the knee joint, thus reducing much of the subjectivity associated with the previously described tests.[22] The KT-2000 arthrometer, the Stryker knee laxity tester, and the Genucom are three such testing devices (Figure 20-23).

Measurements taken postoperatively and at periodic intervals throughout the rehabilitation process provide an objective indication to the athletic trainer about the effectiveness of the treatment program in maintaining or reducing anterior or posterior translation.[57]

Meniscal Tests

Determining a torn meniscus often can be difficult. The three most commonly used tests are McMurray's test, the Apley compression test, and the Apley distraction test.

McMurray's meniscal test McMurray's test (Figure 20-24) is used to determine the presence of a displaceable meniscal tear within the knee. The athlete is posi-

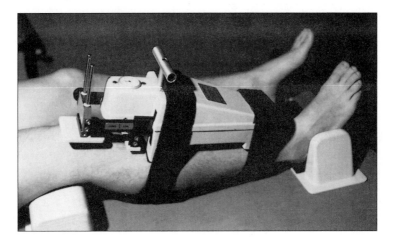

Figure 20-23

The KT-2000 knee arthrometer.

tioned face up on the table with the injured leg fully flexed. The examiner places one hand on the foot and one hand over the top of the knee, fingers touching the medial joint line. The ankle hand scribes a small circle and pulls the leg into extension. As this occurs, the hand on the knee feels for a clicking response. Medial meniscal tears can be detected when the lower leg is externally rotated, and internal rotation allows detection of lateral tears.

Apley compression test   The Apley compression test (Figure 20-25) is performed with the athlete lying face down and the affected leg flexed to 90 degrees. While stabilizing the thigh, the examiner applies a hard downward pressure to the leg. The leg is then rotated back and forth. If pain results, a meniscal injury has occurred. A medial meniscal tear is noted by external rotation, and a lateral meniscal tear is noted by internal rotation of the lower leg.

Figure 20-24

The McMurray meniscal test. **A** and **B,** Internal rotation of the lower leg into knee extension. **C** and **D,** External rotation of the lower leg into knee extension.

A
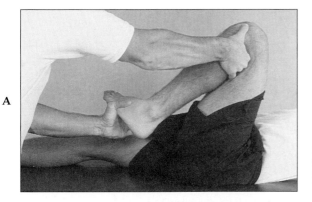

B
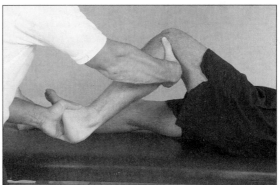

C
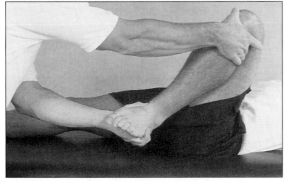

D
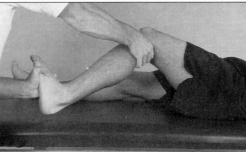

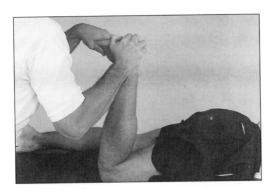

Figure 20-25

The Apley compression test.

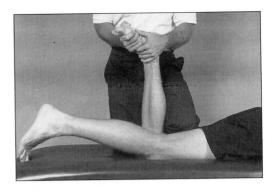

Figure 20-26

The Apley distraction test.

Apley distraction test   With the athlete in the same position as for the Apley compression test, the examiner applies traction to the leg while moving it back and forth (Figure 20-26). This maneuver distinguishes collateral ligamentous tears from capsular and meniscal tears. If the capsule or ligaments are affected, pain will occur; if the meniscus is torn, no pain will occur from the traction and rotation.[32]

Girth Measurement

A knee injury is almost always accompanied by an eventual decrease in the girth of the thigh musculature. The muscles most affected by disuse are the quadriceps group, which are antigravity muscles and assist humans in maintaining an erect, straight-leg position. They are in constant use in effecting movement. Atrophy results when a lower limb is favored and is not used to its potential. Measurement of the circumference of both thighs can often detect former leg injuries or determine the extent of exercise rehabilitation. Five sites have been suggested for girth measurement: the joint line (tibial plateau), 8 to 10 cm above the tibial plateau; the level of the tibial tubercle; the belly of the gastrocnemius muscle measured in centimeters from the tibial tubercle; and 2 cm above the superior border of the patella recorded in centimeters above the tibial tubercle (Figure 20-27).

Because the musculature of the knee atrophies so readily after an injury, girth measurements must be routinely taken.

Subjective Rating Scales

On occasion, subjective rating scales such as the Lysholm Scale and the Knee Function Rating Form have been used to determine the patients perception of how well the injured knee is doing relative to pain, stability, and functional performance. The information obtained from these rating scales can be combined with findings from stability testing to help with an initial diagnosis or evaluation of progress in rehabilitation.

Functional Examination

It is important that the athlete's knee also be tested for function. The athlete should be observed walking and, if possible, running, turning, performing figure-8s, backing up, and stopping. The co-contraction test, vertical jump, and single-leg hop test are also useful functional tests. If the athlete can do a deep knee bend or duck walk without discomfort, it is doubtful that there is a meniscal tear. The resistive strength of the hamstring and quadriceps muscles should be compared with the strength of the knee known to be uninjured (Figure 20-28).

Patellar Examinations

Any knee evaluation should include inspection of the patella. Numerous evaluation procedures are associated with the patella and its surroundings. The following evaluation procedures can provide valuable information about possible reasons for knee discomfort and problems in functioning.[56]

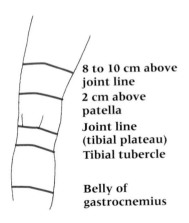

8 to 10 cm above joint line
2 cm above patella
Joint line (tibial plateau)
Tibial tubercle

Belly of gastrocnemius

Figure 20-27

The five sites for girth measurement.

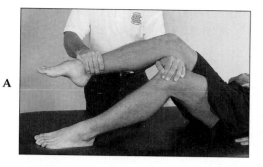 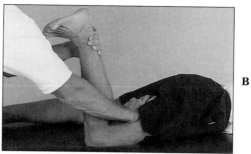

A

B

Figure 20-28

A, Testing quadriceps strength.
B, Testing hamstring strength.

Observation of the Patellar Position, Shape, and Alignment

The first aspect of examining the patella is one of observation. In terms of position, the patella may ride higher than usual (patella alta) or lower than normal (patella infera), causing a tendency toward abnormal articulation when the athlete sits with the legs hanging over the end of a table and with the knees flexed at a 45-degree angle. Observation can also tell the shape and size of the patella. Some patellas are smaller or larger than usual, and some display an abnormal shape, especially at the inferior pole. The symptomatic patella also should be observed for alignment with the nonsymptomatic patella. As discussed earlier, leg alignment problems such as hip anteversion, genu valgum, tibial torsion, and foot pronation can cause the patella to rotate inward, creating a tracking problem within the femoral groove.

The Q Angle

The Q angle is created when lines are drawn from the middle of the patella to the anterosuperior spine of the ilium and from the tubercle of the tibia through the center of the patella (Figure 20-29). It should be measured with the knee fully extended and with the knee flexed at 30 degrees. The normal Q angle is 10 degrees for males and 15 degrees for females. Q angles that exceed 20 degrees are considered excessive and could lead to a pathological condition associated with improper patellar tracking in the femoral groove.

A Q angle greater than 20 degrees could predispose the athlete to patellar femoral pathology.

The A Angle

The A angle measures the patellar orientation to the tibial tubercle. It is created by the intersection of a line that bisects the patella longitudinally and a line from the tibial tubercle to the apex of the inferior pole of the patella (Figure 20-30).[2] An A angle of 35 degrees or greater has been correlated with patellofemoral pathomechanics that seems to result in constant patellofemoral pain. The A angle serves as a quantitative measure of patellar realignment after rehabilitative intervention.

Palpation of the Patella

With the athlete's quadriceps muscle fully relaxed, the examiner palpates the patella for pain sites around its periphery and under its sides (Figure 20-31).

Patellar Compression, Patellar Grinding, and Apprehension Tests

With the knee held to create approximately 20 degrees of flexion, the patella is compressed downward into the femoral groove; it is then moved forward and backward (Figure 20-32). If the athlete feels pain or if a grinding sound is heard during the patellar grind test, a pathological condition is probably present. With the knee still flexed, the patella is forced forward and is held in this position as the athlete extends the knee (Figure 20-33). A positive Clark's sign is present when pain and grinding are experienced by the athlete. Another test that indicates whether the patella can easily be subluxated or dislocated is known as the patellar apprehension test (Figure 20-34). With the knee and patella in a relaxed position, the examiner pushes the patella laterally. The athlete will express sudden apprehension at the point at which the patella begins to dislocate.[26]

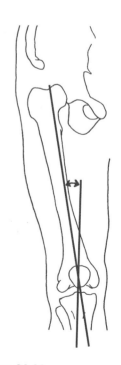

Figure 20-29

Measuring the Q angle of the knee.

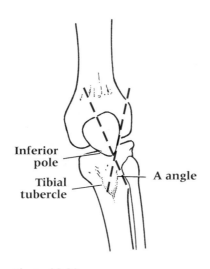

Figure 20-30

Determining the A angle.

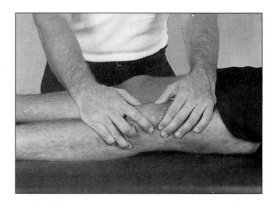

Figure 20-31

Palpating the periphery of the patella while the quadriceps muscle is fully relaxed.

PREVENTION OF KNEE INJURIES

Preventing knee injuries in sports is a complex problem. Of major importance are effective physical conditioning, rehabilitation and skill development, and shoe type. A questionable practice may be the routine use of protective bracing.

Physical Conditioning and Rehabilitation

To avoid knee injuries, the athlete must be as highly conditioned as possible, which means total body conditioning that includes strength, flexibility, cardiovascular and muscle endurance, agility, speed, and balance.[48] Specifically, the muscles surrounding the knee joint must be strong and flexible. The joints and soft tissue that make up the kinetic chain of which the knee is a part must also be considered sources of knee injury and therefore must be specifically conditioned for strength and flexibil-

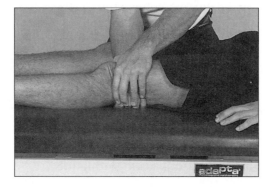

Figure 20-32

Patellar compression test. The patella is pressed downward in the femoral groove and moved forward and backward to elicit pain or crepitus.

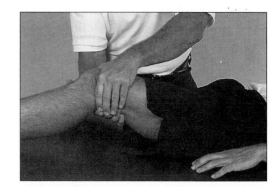

Figure 20-33

Patellar grind test. While the knee is flexed, the patella is forced forward; the athlete then actively contracts the quadriceps. The test reveals a positive Clark's sign if the athlete feels pain or grinding.

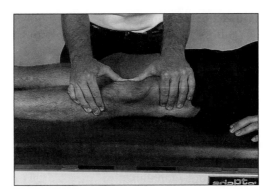

Figure 20-34

Patellar apprehension test for the easily subluxated or dislocated patella.

ity.[51] Athletes participating in a particular sport should acquire a strength ratio between the quadriceps and hamstring muscle groups. For example, the hamstring muscles of football players should have 60 percent to 70 percent of the strength of the quadriceps muscles.[48] The gastrocnemius muscle should also be strengthened to help stabilize the knee. Although maximizing muscle strength may prevent some injuries, it fails to prevent rotary-type injuries.

Avoiding abnormal contraction of the muscles through flexibility exercises is a necessary protection for the knee. Gradual stretching of the knee musculature helps the muscle fibers become more extensible and elastic.[48] Of special concern in preventing knee injuries is extensibility of the hamstrings, erector spinae, groin, quadriceps, and gastrocnemius muscles.

Knees that have been injured must be properly rehabilitated. Repeated minor injuries to a knee make it susceptible to a major injury. (See the section on knee joint rehabilitation later in this chapter.)

Shoe Type

During recent years, collision sports such as football have been using soccer-style shoes. The change from a few long conical cleats to a large number of cleats that are short (no longer than 1/2 inch [1.25 cm]) and broad has significantly reduced knee injuries in football. A shoe with more and shorter cleats is better because the foot does not become fixed to the surface and the shoe still allows controlled running and cutting.

Functional and Prophylactic Knee Braces

Functional and prophylactic knee braces are discussed in Chapter 7. These braces have been designed to prevent or reduce the severity of knee injuries.[41] Prophylactic knee braces are worn on the lateral surface of the knee to protect the medial collateral ligament.[18] Functional knee braces are used to protect grade 1 or 2 sprains of the ACL or, most commonly, a surgically reconstructed ACL. These braces are custom molded and are designed to control rotational stress or tibial translation. The effectiveness of protective knee braces is at best controversial (Figure 20-35).[49,52]

RECOGNITION AND MANAGEMENT OF SPECIFIC INJURIES

Ligament Injuries

The major ligaments of the knee can be torn in isolation or in combination. Depending on the application of forces, injury can occur from a direct straight-line or single-plane force, from a rotary force, or from a combination of the two.[4]

Medial Collateral Ligament Sprain

Etiology   Most knee sprains affect the MCL as a result either of a direct blow from the lateral side, in a medial direction, or of a severe outward twist. Greater injury results from medial sprains than from lateral sprains because of their more

20-5

Critical Thinking Exercise

A baseball player is six months post-ACL reconstruction. He has been cleared by the team physician to return to activity. However, he still has a concern about his knee being reinjured. He wants to know whether he should be wearing a functional knee brace.

? What should the athletic trainer recommend to this athlete?

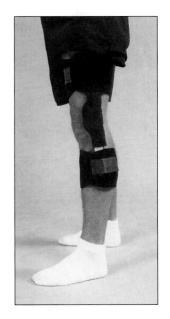

Figure 20-35

Prophylactic knee brace.

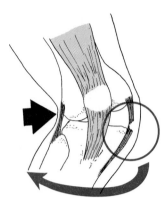

Figure 20-36

A valgus force with the tibia in external rotation injures the medial collateral and capsular ligaments, the medial meniscus, and sometimes the anterior cruciate ligaments.

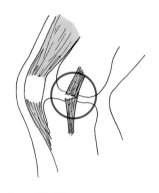

Figure 20-37

Grade 1 medial collateral ligamentous sprain.

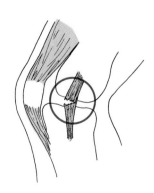

Figure 20-38

Grade 2 medial collateral ligamentous sprain.

direct relation to the articular capsule and the medial meniscus (Figure 20-36). Medial and lateral sprains occur in varying degrees, depending on knee position, previous injuries, the strength of muscles crossing the joint, the force and angle of the trauma, fixation of the foot, and conditions of the playing surface.

The position of the knee is important in establishing its vulnerability to traumatic sprains. Any position of the knee, from full extension to full flexion, can result in injury if there is sufficient force. Full extension tightens both lateral and medial ligaments. Flexion affords a loss of stability to the lateral ligament but maintains stability in various portions of the broad medial ligament.[22] Medial collateral ligamentous sprains result most often from a violently adducted and internally rotated knee. The most prevalent mechanism of a lateral collateral ligamentous or capsular sprain is one in which the foot is everted and the knee is forced laterally into a varus position.

Speculation among medical authorities is that torn menisci seldom happen as the result of an initial trauma; most occur after the collateral ligaments have been stretched by repeated injury. Many mild to moderate sprains leave the knee unstable and thus vulnerable to additional internal derangements. The strength of the muscles crossing the knee joint is important in assisting the ligaments to support the articulation. These muscles should be conditioned to the highest possible degree for sports in which knee injuries are common. With the added support and protection of muscular strength, a state of readiness may be developed through proper athletic training.

The force and angle of the trauma usually determine the extent of injury that takes place. Even after an athletic trainer witnesses the occurrence of a knee injury, it is difficult to predict the amount of tissue damage. The most revealing time for testing joint stability is immediately after injury before effusion masks the extent of derangement.

GRADE 1 MEDIAL COLLATERAL LIGAMENT SPRAIN   A grade 1 MCL injury of the knee has the following characteristics (Figure 20-37):

- A few ligamentous fibers are torn and stretched.
- The joint is stable during valgus stress tests.
- There is little or no joint effusion.
- There may be some joint stiffness and point tenderness just below the medial joint line.
- Even with minor stiffness, there is almost full passive and active range of motion.

Management   Immediate care consists of RICE for at least twenty-four hours. After immediate care, the following procedures should be undertaken:

- Crutches are prescribed if the athlete is unable to walk without a limp.
- Follow-up care may involve cryokinetics, including five minutes of ice pack treatment before exercise or a combination of cold and compression or pulsed ultrasound.
- Proper exercise is essential, starting with phase 1 of the knee joint rehabilitation procedures on page 555.

Isometrics and straight-leg exercises are important until the knee can be moved without pain. The athlete then graduates to stationary bicycle riding or a high-speed isokinetic program. Exercises for regaining neuromuscular function should also be incorporated.

The athlete is allowed to return to full participation when the knee has regained normal strength, power, flexibility, endurance, and coordination. Usually a period of one to three weeks is necessary for recovery. When returning to activity, the athlete may require tape support for a short period.

GRADE 2 MEDIAL COLLATERAL LIGAMENT SPRAIN   Grade 2 MCL knee sprain indicates both microscopic and gross disruption of ligamentous fibers (Figure 20-38). The only structures involved are the medial collateral ligament and the medial capsular ligament. A grade 2 sprain is characterized by the following:

- A complete tear of the deep capsular ligament and partial tear of the superficial layer of the medial collateral ligament or a partial tear of both areas.
- No gross instability, but minimum or slight laxity during full extension. However, at 30 degrees of flexion and when the valgus stress test is performed, laxity may be as much as 5 to 15 degrees.
- Slight or absent swelling unless the meniscus or anterior cruciate ligament has been torn. An acutely torn or pinched synovial membrane, subluxated or dislocated patella, or an osteochondral fracture can produce extensive swelling and hemarthrosis.
- Moderate to severe joint tightness with an inability to fully, actively extend the knee. The athlete is unable to place the heel flat on the ground.
- Definite loss of passive range of motion.
- Pain in the medial aspect, with general weakness and instability.

Management   Management consists of the following:

- RICE for forty-eight to seventy-two hours.
- Crutches are used with a three-point gait until the acute phase of injury is over and the athlete can walk without a limp.
- Depending on the severity and possible complications, a full-leg cast or postoperative knee-immobilizing splint (Figure 20-39) may be applied by the physician for two to five days, after which range-of-motion exercises are begun.
- Modalities should be used two to three times daily to modulate pain and to control inflammation.
- Isometric exercise emphasizing quadriceps strengthening (quad sets, straight leg lifts) should progress to active resisted full-range exercise as soon as possible.
- Closed kinetic chain exercises such as cycling on a stationary bike, stair climbing, and resisted flexion and extension should be used as early as possible.
- Functional progression activities should be incorporated early in the rehabilitation program.
- Use of tape or perhaps a hinged brace when the athlete attempts to return to running activities is encouraged.

Conservative care of the grade 2 medial collateral ligament sprain has been successful. Studies show that there can be spontaneous ligament and capsular healing because other structures, such as the anterior cruciate ligament, also protect the knee against valgus and rotary movement.[22]

GRADE 3 MEDIAL COLLATERAL LIGAMENT SPRAIN   Grade 3 MCL sprain means a complete tear of the supporting ligaments (Figure 20-40). The following are major symptoms and signs:

- Complete loss of medial stability.
- Minimum to moderate swelling.
- Immediate severe pain followed by a dull ache.
- Loss of motion because of effusion and hamstring guarding.
- A valgus stress test that reveals some joint opening in full extension and significant opening at 30 degrees of flexion.

Isolated grade 3 sprains of the MCL occur most often when the mechanism of injury involves a direct valgus force with the foot fixed and loaded. MCL tears resulting from rotation combined with valgus stress with the foot fixed but not loaded virtually always result in ACL and occasionally PCL tears. Thus, testing must include evaluation of ACL and PCL integrity.[50]

Management   Immediate and follow-up care (RICE for twenty minutes every two hours during the waking day) should be performed for at least seventy-two hours. Conservative nonoperative treatment is now recommended for isolated grade 3 MCL sprains. The question of repair or nonoperative management of MCL tears with associated ACL or PCL tears remains controversial. Recovery times and long-term results regarding knee function and stability appear to be better than with surgical repair. It is necessary to rule out ACL damage before beginning conservative

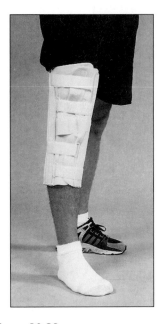

Figure 20-39

Knee immobilizer used after a ligamentous injury.

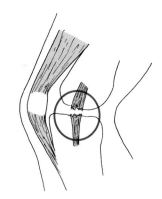

Figure 20-40

Grade 3 medial collateral ligamentous sprain.

treatment. Conservative treatment usually involves limited immobilization in a hinged rehabilitation brace set to allow 30 to 90 degrees of motion and progressive weight bearing for two to three weeks with motion increase to 0 to 90 degrees for another two to three weeks. The rehabilitation program would be similar to that for grade 1 and 2 sprains, although recovery time would be greater.

Lateral Collateral Ligament Sprain

Sprain of the lateral collateral ligament of the knee is much less prevalent than sprain of the medial collateral ligament.

Etiology   The force required to tear this ligament is varus, often with the tibia internally rotated (Figure 20-41). Because of the usually inaccessible medial aspect, a direct blow is rare. In skiing, the LCL can be injured when the skier fails to hold a snowplow and the tips cross, throwing the body weight to the outside edge of the ski. If the force or blow is severe enough, both cruciate ligaments, the attachments of the iliotibial band, and the biceps muscle may be torn. This same mechanism could also disrupt the lateral and even the medial meniscus. If the force is great enough, bony fragments can be avulsed from the femur or tibia. An avulsion can also occur through the combined pull of the lateral collateral ligament and biceps muscle on the head of the fibula.

Symptoms and signs   The major signs include the following:

- Pain and tenderness over the LCL. With the knee flexed and internally rotated, the defect may be palpated.
- Swelling and effusion over the LCL.
- Some joint laxity with a varus stress test at 30 degrees. If laxity exists in full extension, ACL and possibly PCL injury should be evaluated.
- Pain. Pain will be greatest with grade 1 and grade 2 sprains. In grade 3 sprains, pain will be intense initially, and then there will be a dull ache.

An injury can also occur to the peroneal nerve, causing temporary or permanent palsy. The common peroneal nerve originates from the sciatic nerve. It lies behind the head of the fibula and winds laterally around the neck of the fibula, where it branches into deep and superficial peroneal nerves (see Figure 20-9). Tears or entrapment of this nerve can produce varying weaknesses and paralysis of the lateral aspect of the lower leg. Injury of the peroneal nerve requires immediate medical attention.

Management   Management of the lateral collateral ligamentous injury should follow procedures similar to those for medial collateral ligamentous injuries.

Anterior Cruciate Ligament Sprain

The anterior cruciate ligament sprain is the most serious ligament injury in the knee.[37]

Etiology   The ACL is most vulnerable to injury when the tibia is externally rotated and the knee is in a valgus position. The ACL can sustain injury from a direct blow to the knee or from a single-plane force. The single-plane injury occurs when the lower leg is rotated while the foot is fixed (Figure 20-42). In this situation, the ACL becomes taut and vulnerable to sprain. An example occurs when an athlete who is running fast suddenly decelerates and makes a sharp cutting motion, causing an isolated tear of the ACL. The same mechanism could be true of the skier when his or her ski catches in the snow and the body twists medially or laterally.

Tears of the ACL combined with injury to other supporting structures in the knee can produce rotatory instabilities. Anterolateral rotatory instability may involve injury to the anterolateral joint capsule, the LCL, and possibly the PCL and structures in the posterolateral corner. Anteromedial rotatory instability usually involves injury to the anteromedial capsule, the MCL, and possibly the PCL and posteromedial corner.[1]

Hyperextension from a force to the front of the knee with the foot planted can tear the ACL (Figure 20-43) and, if severe enough, can also sprain the MCL.

A lateral knee sprain can be caused by a varus force when the tibia is internally rotated.

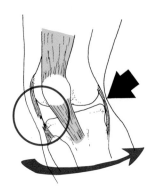

Figure 20-41

A varus force with the tibia internally rotated injures the lateral collateral ligament; in some cases both the cruciate ligaments and the attachments of the iliotibial band and biceps muscle of the thigh may be torn.

20-6

Critical Thinking E x e r c i s e

A soccer player has suffered an isolated grade 2 sprain of his anterior cruciate ligament. At this point, the physician feels that surgery is not required and decides to try to rehabilitate the athlete and have him return to practice. It is likely that when the athlete returns to full activity, he will experience some feeling of instability when stopping, starting, and cutting.

? What can the athletic trainer recommend to the athlete to help him minimize feelings of instability and to prevent the occurrence of additional injury to the ACL?

Symptoms and signs   The athlete with a torn ACL will experience a pop followed by immediate disability and will complain that the knee feels like it is "coming apart." Anterior cruciate ligament tears produce rapid swelling at the joint line. The athlete with an isolated ACL tear will exhibit a positive anterior drawer sign and a positive Lachman's sign. The pivot-shift test, jerk test, and flexion-rotation drawer test may be positive even with an isolated ACL tear.

Management   Even with application of proper first aid and immediate RICE, swelling begins within one to two hours and becomes a notable hemarthrosis within four to six hours.[7] The athlete typically cannot walk without help. If a clinical evaluation is inconclusive, an arthroscopic examination may be warranted to make a proper diagnosis.

Anterior cruciate ligamentous injury could lead to serious knee instability; an intact anterior cruciate ligament is necessary for a knee to function in high-performance situations. Controversy exists among physicians about how best to treat an acute anterior cruciate ligamentous rupture and when surgery is warranted.[43,58] It is well accepted that an unsatisfactorily treated anterior cruciate ligamentous rupture will eventually lead to major joint degeneration.[24] Therefore, a decision for or against surgery must be based on the athlete's age, the type of stress applied to the knee, and the amount of instability present, as well as the techniques available to the surgeon.[34,54] A simple surgical repair of the ligament may not establish the desired joint stability.[21]

Surgery may involve joint reconstruction, with transplantation of some external structure—such as the pes anserinus, semitendinosus muscle, tensor fasciae latae, or most commonly, the patellar tendon—to replace the lost anterior cruciate support. This type of surgery involves a brief hospital stay, three to five weeks in braces, and four to six months of rehabilitation.[54] A detailed rehabilitation program for an ACL reconstruction is provided in the accompanying management plan.

Little scientific evidence exists to support the use of functional knee braces, yet many physicians feel that the braces can provide some protection during activity.[10,42]

Posterior Cruciate Ligament Sprain

The PCL has been called the most important ligament in the knee, providing a central axis for rotation.[53] The PCL provides about 95 percent of the total restraining force to straight posterior displacement of the tibia.

Etiology   The PCL is most at risk when the knee is flexed to 90 degrees. A fall with full weight on the anterior aspect of the bent knee with the foot in plantar flexion or receipt of a hard blow to the front of the bent knee can tear the PCL (Figure 20-44). In addition, it can be injured by a rotational force, which also affects the medial or lateral side of the knee.[53]

Symptoms and signs   Major signs and symptoms include the following:
- The athlete will report feeling a pop in the back of the knee.
- Tenderness and relatively little swelling will be evident in the popliteal fossa.
- Laxity will be demonstrated in a posterior sag test. The posterior drawer test is fairly reliable; however, an abduction stress test that is positive at both 30 degrees and in full extension is considered to be a definitive test for a torn PCL.

Management   RICE should be initiated immediately. If clinical evaluation is inconclusive, arthroscopic evaluation may be warranted.

Nonoperative rehabilitation of grade 1 and 2 injuries should focus on quadriceps strengthening. As with isolated tears of the ACL, tears to the PCL elicit controversy as to whether the injury should be treated nonoperatively or with surgical intervention. Satisfactory outcomes achieved by nonoperative means have been reported.[12] Although techniques for repairing the torn PCL are technically difficult, surgery is occasionally recommended. Rehabilitation after surgery generally involves six weeks of immobilization in extension with full weight bearing on crutches. Range-of-motion exercises are begun at six weeks, progressing to the use of PRE at four months.[48]

Figure 20-42

A major mechanism causing an anterior cruciate tear occurs when a running athlete suddenly decelerates and makes a sharp cutting motion.

Simple surgical repair of the torn anterior cruciate ligament may not establish proper stability.

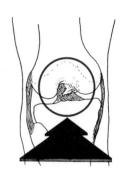

Figure 20-43

An anterior force with the foot planted can tear the anterior cruciate ligament.

Surgical Repair of Anterior Cruciate Ligament

Injury Situation A female college soccer player injured her right knee while cutting to her left with her right foot planted. There was no contact.

Symptoms and Signs She stated that she felt a pop and severe pain immediately. A few minutes later she felt that she could walk on it; however, it gave way as she put weight on it. Swelling was apparent at the joint line and over the medial aspect of the knee. Stability tests demonstrated positive anterior drawer, positive Lachman's, positive pivot-shift, positive flexion-rotation drawer, and positive valgus stress test at 0 and 30 degrees.

Management Plan She was diagnosed as having torn the ACL, MCL, and possibly the medial meniscus. Surgical repair was performed using an intraarticular ACL repair with a bone–patellar tendon–bone graft.

Preoperative Phase (3 to 6 weeks after injury) The goal during this phase is resolution of postinjury swelling and pain and restoration of full range of motion. Strengthening exercises through a full pain-free range of motion should begin as soon as can be tolerated. The athlete should be psychologically prepared for surgery during this phase.

Phase 1 *Acute Injury* **GOALS:** Minimize swelling, pain, and hemorrhage after surgery; establish and maintain full knee extension; achieve good quadriceps control; begin working on regaining knee flexion; regain neuromuscualr control. **ESTIMATED LENGTH OF TIME (ELT):** 1 week.

■ **Therapy** RICE during the entire first week 3 to 4 times per day to control swelling. Electrical muscle stimulation to control pain and elicit muscle contraction. Constant passive motion machine.

■ **Exercise rehabilitation** Achieve full extension by end of first week. Weight shifting on crutches. Early quadriceps activity is important. Perform straight leg raises and multiangle submaximal isometrics at 90, 60, and 40 degrees. Perform knee extensions in 90 to 30 degrees arc. Hip exercises, especially adduction, for VMO function. Active isotonic hamstring contractions to achieve 90 degrees of flexion by end of second week. Mobilize patella. Weight bearing as tolerated with brace locked in full extension.

Phase 2 *Repair* **GOALS:** Achieve a normal gait pattern; maintain full extension; strengthen quadriceps and hamstrings; increase knee flixion; maintain cardiorespiratory endurance; improve neuromuscular control. Begin light functional activities. **ELT:** 1 to 6 weeks.

■ **Therapy** Electrical muscle stimulation; RICE to control swelling initially and after each treatment session. The amount of swelling will determine the ability to contract the quadriceps. Electrical muscle stimulation to facilitate muscle contraction and for reeducation. Ultrasound to increase blood flow.

■ **Exercise rehabilitation** Ambulation with brace locked in full extension initially. Progressively increase range of motion in brace as tolerated by the patient. Remove brace by week 3 or 4. Full weight bearing without a limp at the end of 4 weeks. Full range of motion should be attained before athlete engages in intense strength training. Concentrate on hamstring strengthening. Use closed kinetic chain activities and cocontractions as much as possible. Strengthening exercises: minisquats, step-ups, hamstring and hip leg presses, and standing knee flexion and extension using surgical tubing. Multidirection patellar mobilization; mobilize tibia. Stationary bike as soon as range of motion permits. Proprioceptive activities on BAPS board and KAT. Instrument assessment of cruciate laxity every 2 weeks for up to 12 weeks.[21] Continue bicycling and use step climbing.

Continued

Phase 3 *Remodeling*   **GOALS:** Concentrate on functional progressions and return to high-demand activity.

ELT: Week 7 to 4 months.

■ **Therapy** Electrical muscle stimulation to facilitate contraction. Ultrasound to facilitate blood flow. Massage to decrease scar. Mobilization techniques as needed.

■ **Exercise rehabilitation** Isokinetic testing. High-speed training using rubber tubing. Begin hop training. Work on balance. Incorporate sport-specific activities. Begin a return to running program at about 4 months. Return to sport activity; injury maintenance.

Criteria for Return to Competitive Soccer

1. Knee is symptom free.
2. Appropriate isokinetic evaluation.
3. Appropriate arthrometer measurement.
4. Appropriate performance in functional tests.
5. Athlete is psychologically prepared for return.

Meniscal Lesions

The medial meniscus has a much higher incidence of injury than does the lateral meniscus because coronary ligament attaches the medial meniscus peripherally to the tibia and also to the capsular ligament. The lateral meniscus does not attach to the capsular ligament and is more mobile during knee movement. Because of the attachment to the medial structures, the medial meniscus is prone to disruption from valgus and torsional forces.

Etiology   A valgus force can adduct the knee, often tearing and stretching the medial collateral ligament; meanwhile, its fibers twist the medial meniscus outward. Repeated mild sprains reduce the strength of the knee to a state favorable for a cartilaginous tear through lessening its normal ligamentous stability. The most common mechanism is weight bearing combined with a rotary force while the knee is extended or flexed. A cutting motion made by the athlete while running can distort the medial meniscus. Stretching of the anterior and posterior horns of the meniscus can produce a vertical-longitudinal, or "bucket-handle," tear (Figure 20-45). Another way that a longitudinal tear occurs is if the knee is forcefully extended from a flexed position while the femur is internally rotated. During extension the medial meniscus is suddenly pulled back, causing the tear (see Figure 20-45). In contrast, the lateral meniscus can sustain an oblique tear by a forceful knee extension with the femur externally rotated.[7] A large number of medial meniscus lesions are the outcome of a sudden, strong internal rotation of the femur with a partially flexed knee while the foot is firmly planted. As a result of the force of this action, the meniscus is pulled out of its normal bed and pinched between the femoral condyles.

Meniscal lesions can be longitudinal, oblique, or transverse. Because of its blood supply, tears in the outer one third of a meniscus may heal over time if stress in the

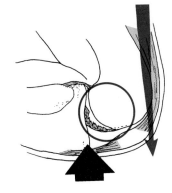

Figure 20-44

A fall on or a blow to the anterior aspect of the bent knee can tear the posterior cruciate ligament.

Figure 20-45

Common mechanisms of injury to the meniscus. Forced flexion produces a peripheral tear. Cutting with the foot fixed is likely to produce a "bucket-handle" tear.

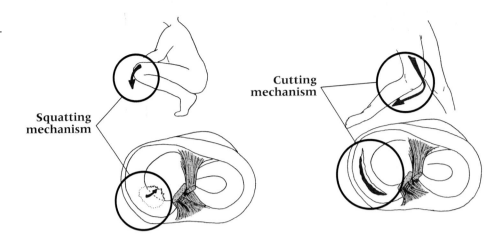

Squatting mechanism

Cutting mechanism

area is kept to a minimum.[3] Tears that occur within the midsubstance of the meniscus often fail to heal because of lack of adequate blood supply.[3]

Symptoms and signs   An absolute diagnosis of meniscal injury is difficult. To determine the possibility of such an injury, a complete history should be obtained, which consists of information about past knee injury and an understanding of how the present injury occurred. Diagnosis of meniscal injuries should be made immediately after the injury has occurred and before muscle spasm and swelling obscure the normal shape of the knee.

A meniscal tear may or may not result in the following:

- Effusion developing gradually over forty-eight to seventy-two hours.
- Joint-line pain and loss of motion.
- Intermittent locking and giving way of the knee.
- Pain when the athlete squats.

Once a meniscal tear occurs, the ruptured edges harden and may eventually atrophy. On occasion, portions of the meniscus may become detached and wedge themselves between the articulating surfaces of the tibia and femur, thus imposing a locking, catching, or giving way of the joint. Chronic meniscal lesions may also display recurrent swelling and obvious muscle atrophy around the knee. The athlete may complain of a sense of the knee collapsing, of a popping sensation, or of an inability to perform a full squat or to change direction quickly without pain when running. Such symptoms and signs usually warrant surgical intervention. NOTE: Symptomatic meniscal tears can eventually lead to serious articular degeneration with major impairment and disability.

Management   If the knee is not locked but shows indications of a tear, the physician might initially obtain an MRI. A diagnostic arthroscopic examination may also be performed.

The knee that is locked by a displaced meniscus may require unlocking with the athlete under anesthesia so that a detailed examination can be conducted. If discomfort, disability, and locking of the knee continue, arthroscopic surgery may be required to remove a portion of the meniscus.

Surgical management of meniscal tears should make every effort to minimize loss of any portion of the meniscus.[28] The menisci are critical in preventing degenerative joint disease. Healing of the torn meniscus is dependent on where the tear has occurred. Tears in the red-red or red-white zones may heal well after surgical repair because they have a good vascular supply. Tears in the inner white-white zone will have to be resected because they are unlikely to heal, even with surgical repair, due to avascularity (see Figure 20-5). Resection, or a partial meniscectomy, involves removing as little as possible of the meniscus through an arthroscope. Partial meniscectomy of a torn meniscus is much more common than meniscal repair is.

20-7

Critical Thinking Exercise

A wrestler is diagnosed by the team physician as having a torn medial meniscus. On evaluation, McMurray's test was positive, and a subsequent MRI revealed a longitudinal bucket-handle tear in the posterior horn of the medial meniscus.

? What are the typical mechanisms of injury that can result in a tear of a meniscus?

Postsurgical management for a partial meniscectomy does not require bracing and allows partial to full weight bearing on crutches as quickly as can be tolerated for about two weeks. It is not uncommon for an athlete to return to full activity in as little as six to fourteen days.

A repaired meniscus requires immobilization in a rehabilitative brace for five to six weeks. The athlete should be on crutches, progressing from partial to full weight bearing at six weeks. During immobilization, active ROM exercises between 0 and 90 degrees should be done. At six weeks, full ROM resistive exercises can begin. Rehabilitation should concentrate on endurance.[31]

Joint Injuries

Knee Plica

The fetus has three synovial knee cavities whose internal walls, at four months, are gradually absorbed to form one chamber; however, in 20 percent of all individuals, the knee fails to fully absorb these cavities.[6] In adult life, these septa form synovial folds known as plicae.

Etiology   The most common synovial fold is the infrapatellar plica, which originates from the infrapatellar fat pad and extends superiorly in a fanlike manner. The second most common synovial fold is the suprapatellar plica, located in the suprapatellar pouch. The least common, but most subject to injury, is the mediopatellar plica, which is bandlike and begins on the medial wall of the knee joint and extends downward to insert into the synovial tissue that covers the infrapatellar fat pad.[6] Because most synovial plicae are pliable, most are asymptomatic; however, the mediopatellar plica may be thick, nonyielding, and fibrotic, causing a number of symptoms. The mediopatellar plica is associated with chondromalacia of the medial femoral condyle and patella (Figure 20-46).[6]

Symptoms and signs   The athlete may or may not have a history of knee injury. If symptoms are preceded by trauma, it is usually from blunt force, such as a fall on the knee, or from a twist with the foot planted. A major complaint is recurrent episodes of painful pseudolocking of the knee when the athlete has been sitting for a period of time. As the knee passes 15 to 20 degrees of flexion, a snap may be felt or heard. Such characteristics of locking and snapping could be misinterpreted as a torn meniscus. The athlete complains of pain while ascending or descending stairs or when squatting. Unlike meniscal injuries, there is little or no swelling and no ligamentous laxity.

Management   A knee plica that becomes inflamed as a result of trauma is usually treated conservatively with rest, antiinflammatory agents, and local heat. If the condition recurs, causing a chondromalacia of the femoral condyle or patella, the plica will require surgical excision.

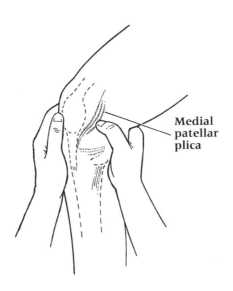

Figure 20-46

Knee plica.

Medial patellar plica

Osteochondral Knee Fractures

Etiology   Occasionally the same mechanisms that produce collateral ligamentous, cruciate ligamentous, or meniscal tears can shear off either a piece of bone attached to the anterior cartilage or cartilage alone. Twisting, sudden cutting, or being struck directly in the knee are typical causes of this condition.

Symptoms and signs   The athlete commonly hears a snap and feels the knee give way. Swelling is immediate and extensive because of hemarthrosis, and there is considerable pain.

Management   The diagnosis is usually confirmed by arthroscopic examination. Surgery is performed to replace the fragment as soon as possible to avoid joint degeneration and arthritis. The femoral condyles and the patella are affected.

Osteochondritis Dissecans

Osteochondritis dissecans is a painful condition involving partial or complete separation of a piece of articular cartilage and subchondral bone. Both teenagers and adults can have this condition. The vast majority of fragments, more than 85 percent, occur in the lateral portion of the medial femoral condyle.[11] Clinically, osteochondral detachments are seen wherever there is osteochondritis dissecans. Typically, the lesion results in normal articular cartilage with dead subchondral bone underneath separated by a layer of fibrous tissue.

Etiology   The exact cause of osteochondritis dissecans is unknown. It usually has a very slow onset. Possible etiological factors include the following:

- Direct or indirect trauma.
- Association with certain familial skeletal or endocrine abnormalities.
- A prominent tibial spine impinging on the medial femoral condyle.
- A facet of the patella impinging on the medial femoral condyle.

Symptoms and signs   The athlete with osteochondritis dissecans complains of a knee that aches, swells recurrently, and on occasion, may catch or lock. There may be atrophy of the quadriceps muscle and point tenderness.

Management   For children, rest and immobilization using a cylinder cast are usually prescribed. This management affords proper resolution of the injured cartilage and normal ossification of the underlying bone. Like many other osteochondroses, osteochondritis dissecans may take as long as one year to resolve. This condition in the teenager and adult may warrant surgery such as multiple drilling in the area to stimulate healing, pinning loose fragments, or bone grafting.

Loose Bodies within the Knee

A knee that locks and unlocks during activity may indicate a torn meniscus.

Etiology   Because of repeated trauma to the knee during sports activities, osteochondral fragments, or loose bodies ("joint mice"), can develop within the joint cavity. Loose bodies can stem from osteochondritis dissecans, fragments from the menisci, pieces of torn synovial tissue, or a torn cruciate ligament.

Symptoms and signs   The loose body may move in the joint space and become lodged, causing locking and popping. The athlete will complain of pain and a feeling of instability with giving way.

Management   When the loose body becomes wedged between articulating surfaces, irritation can occur. If not surgically removed, the loose body can create conditions that lead to joint degeneration.

Joint Contusions

Etiology   A blow struck against the muscles crossing the knee joint can result in a handicapping condition. One of the muscles frequently involved is the vastus medialis of the quadriceps group, which is primarily involved in locking the knee in a position of full extension.

Symptoms and signs   Bruises of the vastus medialis produce all the appearances of a knee sprain, including severe pain, loss of movement, and signs of acute inflammation.

Such bruising is often manifested by swelling and discoloration caused by the tearing of muscle tissue and blood vessels. If adequate first aid is given immediately, the knee will usually return to functional use twenty-four to forty-eight hours after the trauma.

Bruising of the capsular tissue that surrounds the knee joint is often associated with muscle contusions and deep bone bruises. A traumatic force delivered to capsular tissue may cause capillary bleeding, irritate the synovial membrane, and result in profuse fluid effusion into the joint cavity and surrounding spaces, thereby producing intraarticular swelling. Effusion often takes place slowly and almost imperceptibly. It is advisable to prevent the athlete from engaging in further activity for at least twenty-four hours after he or she receives a capsular bruise. Activity causes an increase in circulation and may cause extensive swelling and hematoma at the knee joint. Scar tissue develops wherever internal bleeding with clot organization is present. If this condition is repeated time after time, chronic synovitis or an arthritic sequela may develop.

Because the knee joint and patella are poorly padded, they are prone to bruising.

Management   Care of a bruised knee depends on many factors. However, management principally depends on the location and severity of the contusion. The following procedures are suggested:

- Apply compression bandages and cold until resolution has occurred.
- Prescribe inactivity and rest for twenty-four hours.
- If swelling occurs, continue cold application for seventy-two hours. If swelling and pain are intense, refer the athlete to the physician.
- Once the acute stage has ended and the swelling has diminished to little or none, conduct cold application with active ROM exercises within a pain-free range. If a gradual use of heat is elected, great caution should be taken to prevent swelling.
- Allow the athlete to return to normal activity, with protective padding, when pain and the initial irritation have subsided.
- If swelling is not resolved within a week, it is possible that a chronic condition of either synovitis or bursitis may exist, indicating the need for rest and medical attention.

Bursitis

Bursitis in the knee can be acute, chronic, or recurrent. Although any one of the numerous knee bursae can become inflamed, anteriorly the prepatellar, deep infrapatellar, and suprapatellar bursae have the highest incidence of irritation in sports (see Figure 20-8).

The knee has many bursae; the prepatellar, deep infrapatellar, and suprapatellar bursae are most often irritated.

Etiology   The prepatellar bursa often becomes inflamed from continued kneeling, and the deep infrapatellar becomes irritated from overuse of the patellar tendon.

Symptoms and signs   Prepatellar bursitis results in localized swelling above the knee that is ballotable. Swelling is not intraarticular, and there may be some redness and increased temperature. Swelling in the popliteal fossa does not necessarily indicate bursitis but could instead be a sign of Baker's cyst (Figure 20-47). A Baker's cyst is connected to the joint, which swells because of a problem in the joint and not because of bursitis. A Baker's cyst is commonly painless, causing no discomfort or disability. Some inflamed bursae may be painful and disabling because of the swelling and should be treated accordingly.

Management   Management usually follows a pattern of eliminating the cause, prescribing rest, and reducing inflammation. Perhaps the two most important techniques for controlling bursitis are the use of elastic compression wraps and antiinflammatory medication. When the bursitis is chronic or recurrent and the synovium has thickened, use of aspiration and a steroid injection may be warranted.

Patellar Conditions

The position and function of the patella expose it to a variety of traumas and diseases related to sports activities.[23]

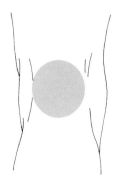

Figure 20-47

Baker's cyst in the popliteal fossa.

Knees that give way or catch have a number of possible pathological conditions:
- Subluxating patella
- Meniscal tear
- Anterior cruciate ligamentous tear
- Hemarthrosis

Figure 20-48

Fracture and dislocation of the patella.

Patellar Fracture

Etiology   Fractures of the patella can be caused by either direct or indirect trauma (Figure 20-48). Most patellar fractures are the result of indirect trauma in which a severe pull of the patellar tendon occurs against the femur when the knee is semi-flexed. This position subjects the patella to maximum stress from the quadriceps tendon and the patellar ligament. Forcible muscle contraction may then fracture the patella at its lower half. Direct injury most often produces fragmentation with little displacement. Falling, jumping, or running may result in a fracture of the patella. NOTE: Approximately 3 percent of the population has a bipartite patella, meaning there are two portions of the patella. This condition can be misdiagnosed as a patellar fracture.

Symptoms and signs   The fracture causes hemorrhage and joint effusion, resulting in generalized swelling. Indirect fracture causes capsular tearing, separation of bone fragments, and possible tearing of the quadriceps tendon. Direct fracture involves little bone separation.

Management   Diagnosis is accomplished through use of the history, palpation of separated fragments, and an X-ray confirmation. As soon as the examiner suspects a patellar fracture, a cold wrap should be applied, followed by an elastic compression wrap and splinting. The athletic trainer should then refer the athlete to the team physician. The athlete will normally be immobilized for two to three months.

Acute Patellar Subluxation or Dislocation

Etiology   When an athlete plants his or her foot, decelerates, and simultaneously cuts in an opposite direction from the weight-bearing foot, the thigh rotates internally while the lower leg rotates externally, causing a forced knee valgus. The quadriceps muscle attempts to pull in a straight line and as a result pulls the patella laterally—a force that may dislocate the patella. As a rule, displacement takes place outwardly, with the patella resting on the lateral condyle (Figure 20-48).

With this mechanism, the patella is forced to slide laterally into a partial or full dislocation. Some athletes are more predisposed to this condition than others because of the following anatomical structures:
- A wide pelvis with anteverted hips
- Genu valgum, which increases the Q angle
- Shallow femoral grooves
- Flat lateral femoral condyles
- High-riding and flat patellas
- Vastus medialis and ligamentous laxity with genu recurvatum and externally rotated tibias

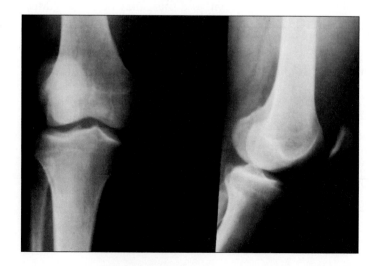

- Pronated feet
- Externally pointing patellas

A patella that subluxates repetitively places abnormal stress on the patellofemoral joint and the medial restraints. The knee may be swollen and painful. Pain is a result of swelling but also results because the medial capsular tissue has been stretched and torn. Because of the associated swelling, the knee is restricted in flexion and extension. There may also be a palpable tenderness over the adductor tubercle where the medial retinaculum (patellar femoral ligament) attaches.

An acute patellar dislocation is often associated with sudden twisting of the body while the foot or feet are planted and is associated with a painful giving way episode.

Symptoms and signs The athlete experiences pain, swelling, and a complete loss of knee function, and the patella rests in an abnormal position. The physician immediately reduces the dislocation by applying mild pressure on the patella with the knee extended as much as possible. If a period of time has elapsed before reduction, a general anesthetic may have to be used. After aspiration of the joint hematoma, ice is applied, and the joint is splinted. A first-time patellar dislocation is sometimes associated with a chondral or osteochondral fracture. X-ray evaluation is performed before and after reduction.

Management To reduce a dislocation, the hip is flexed, and the patella is gently moved medially as the knee is slowly extended. After reduction, the knee is immobilized in extension for four weeks or longer, and the athlete is instructed to use crutches when walking. During immobilization, isometric exercises are performed at the knee joint. After immobilization, the athlete should wear a horseshoe-shaped felt pad that is held in place around the patella by an elastic wrap or that is sewn into an elastic sleeve that is worn while the athlete runs or performs in sports (Figure 20-49). Commercial braces are also available.

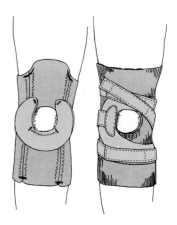

Figure 20-49

Special pads for the dislocated patella.

Muscle rehabilitation should focus on all the musculature of the knee, thigh, and hip. Knee exercise should be confined to straight-leg raises.

If surgery is performed, it is usually to release constrictive ligaments or to reconstruct the patellofemoral joint. It is important to strengthen and to balance the strength of all musculature associated with the knee joint. Postural malalignments must be corrected as much as possible. Shoe orthotic devices may be used to reduce foot pronation, tibial internal rotation, and subsequently, stress to the patellofemoral joint.

Injury to the Infrapatellar Fat Pad

The two most important fat pads of the knee are the infrapatellar fat pad and the suprapatellar fat pad. The infrapatellar fat pad lies between the synovial membrane on the anterior aspect of the joint and the patellar tendon, and the suprapatellar fat pad lies between the anterior surface of the femur and the suprapatellar bursa. Of the two pads, the infrapatellar is more often injured in sports, principally as a result of its large size and particular vulnerability during activity.

Etiology The infrapatellar fat pad may become wedged between the tibia and the patella, irritated by chronic kneeling pressures, or traumatized by direct blows.

Symptoms and signs Repeated injury to the fat pad produces capillary hemorrhaging and swelling of the fatty tissue; if the irritation continues, scarring and calcification may develop. The athlete may complain of pain below the patellar ligament, especially during knee extension, and the knee may display weakness, mild swelling, and stiffness during movement.

Management Care of acute fat pad injuries involves rest from irritating activities until inflammation has subsided, heel elevation of $1/2$ to 1 inch (1.25 to 2.5 cm), and the therapeutic use of cold. Heel elevation prevents added irritation during full extension; the application of hyperextension taping may also be necessary to prevent occurrence of full extension.

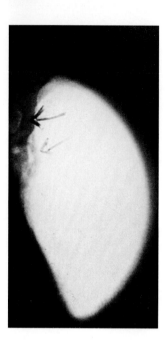

Figure 20-50

Chondromalacia with chipping away of the articular surface of the patella.

Critical Thinking Exercise

A triathlete has been complaining of knee pain for several months. She has never had an acute injury to the knee, but her training regimen is intense, involving three hours of training each day. She has been diagnosed by a physician as having chondromalacia patella.

? She has been referred to the athletic trainer for evaluation and rehabilitation. What can the athletic trainer do to help reduce the athlete's symptoms and signs?

Patellofemoral Arthralgia

The patella, in relation to the femoral groove, can be subject to direct trauma or disease that leads to chronic pain and disability.[55] Of major importance among athletes are those conditions that stem from abnormal patellar tracking within the femoral groove, of which the three most common are chondromalacia patella, degenerative arthritis, and patellofemoral stress syndrome.[27] Patellofemoral arthralgia is a catchall term that is used to refer to any type of pain that occurs in or around the patellofemoral joint.

Chondromalacia patella

Etiology   Chondromalacia patella is a softening and deterioration of the articular cartilage on the back of the patella (Figure 20-50). Cailliet describes chondromalacia as undergoing three stages:[9]

- Stage 1—swelling and softening of the articular cartilage
- Stage 2—fissuring of the softened articular cartilage
- Stage 3—deformation of the surface of the articular cartilage caused by fragmentation

The exact cause of chondromalacia is unknown. As indicated previously, abnormal patellar tracking could be a major etiological factor;[61] however, individuals with normal tracking have acquired chondromalacia, and some individuals with abnormal tracking are free of it.[9] Abnormal patellofemoral tracking can be produced by genu valgum, external tibial torsion, foot pronation, femoral anteversion, a quadriceps Q angle greater than 15 to 20 degrees, patella alta, a shallow femoral groove, a shallow articular angle of the patella, an abnormal articular contour of the patella, or laxity of the quadriceps tendon.

Symptoms and signs   The athlete may experience pain in the anterior aspect of the knee while walking, running, ascending and descending stairs, or squatting. There may be recurrent swelling around the kneecap and a grating sensation when flexing and extending the knee.

The patella displays crepitation during the patellar grind test. During palpation, there may be pain on the inferior border of the patella or when the patella is compressed within the femoral groove while the knee is passively flexed and extended. The athlete has one or more lower-limb alignment deviations.

Degenerative arthritis occurs on the medial facet of the patella, which makes contact with the femur when the athlete performs a full squat.[9] Degeneration first occurs in the deeper portions of the articular cartilage, followed by blistering and fissuring that stems from the subchondral bone and appears on the surface of the patella.[7,9]

Management   In some cases, patellofemoral arthralgia is initially treated conservatively as follows:

- Avoidance of irritating activities such as stair climbing and squatting
- Isometric exercises that are pain free to strengthen the quadriceps and hamstring muscles
- Oral antiinflammatory agents and small doses of aspirin
- A neoprene knee sleeve
- An orthotic device to correct pronation and reduce tibial torsion

If conservative measures fail to help, surgery may be the only alternative. Some of the following surgical measures may be indicated:[7]

- Moving the insertion of the vastus medialis muscle forward through realignment procedures such as lateral release of the retinaculum
- Shaving and smoothing the irregular surfaces of the patella, femoral condyle, or both
- In cases of degenerative arthritis, removing the blister through drilling
- Elevating the tibial tubercle
- As a last resort, completely removing the patella

Patellofemoral stress syndrome

Etiology   Patellofemoral stress syndrome results from some lateral deviation of the patella as it tracks in the femoral groove. This tendency toward lateral tracking may be the result of several factors:[48]

- Tightness of the hamstrings and gastrocnemius
- Tightness of the lateral retinaculum, which compresses the lateral facet of the patella against the lateral femoral condyle
- Increased Q angle
- Tightness of the iliotibial band
- Pronation of the foot
- Patella alta (the patellar tendon is longer than the patella)
- Vastus medialis oblique (VMO) insufficiency caused by imbalance with the strength of the vastus lateralis (VL) or by inhibition resulting from the presence of 20 to 30 milliliters of effusion in the knee[27]
- Weak hip adductors to which the VMO is attached

Symptoms and signs   There will be tenderness of the lateral facet of the patella and some swelling associated with irritation of the synovium as well as reports of a dull ache in the center of the knee. Patellar compression will elicit pain and crepitus. The athlete will be apprehensive when the patella is forced laterally.

Management   The causes underlying patellofemoral pain as identified during the evaluation process should provide the basis for treatment.[47] The athlete must engage in a strengthening program for the adductor muscles and for correcting the imbalance between the VMO and the VL through the use of biofeedback techniques.[29,39] Stretching exercises for the hamstrings, gastrocnemius, and iliotibial band are also necessary. Orthotics can be used to correct pronation and other malalignments.[19] The McConnell taping technique (see Chapter 8) has been demonstrated to be extremely effective in regaining proper patellar alignment and thus a more symmetrical loading on the lower extremity.[19] Taping is designed to correct the orientation of the patella.

If conservative treatment measures fail, lateral retinacular release has been advocated by some physicians.

Extensor Mechanism Injuries

Many extensor mechanism problems can occur in the physically active individual.[38] They can occur in the immature adolescent's knee or as a result of jumping and running.

Osgood-Schlatter Disease and Larsen-Johansson Disease

Etiology   Two conditions common to the immature adolescent's knee are Osgood-Schlatter disease and Larsen-Johansson disease. Osgood-Schlatter disease is an apophysitis characterized by pain at the attachment of the patellar tendon to the tibial tubercle. This condition most often represents an avulsion fracture of the tibial tubercle. This fragment is cartilaginous initially, but with growth a bony callus forms and the tuberosity enlarges. This condition usually resolves when the athlete reaches the age of eighteen or twenty. The only remnant is an enlarged tibial tubercle.

The most commonly accepted cause of Osgood-Schlatter disease is repeated avulsion of the patellar tendon at the apophysis of the tibial tubercle. Complete avulsion of the patellar tendon is a major complication of Osgood-Schlatter disease.

Larsen-Johansson disease is similar to Osgood-Schlatter disease, but it occurs at the inferior pole of the patella (Figure 20-51). Like the cause of Osgood-Schlatter disease, the cause of Larsen-Johansson disease is believed to be excessive repeated strain on the patellar tendon. Swelling, pain, and point tenderness characterize Larsen-Johansson disease. Later, degeneration can be noted during X-ray examination.

Conditions that may be mistaken for one another:
- Osgood-Schlatter disease
- Larsen-Johansson disease
- Jumper's or kicker's knee

Patellofemoral Pain

Injury Situation A 16-year-old high school female basketball player complains of pain in her left anterior knee. She has been experiencing this pain for several weeks. At first, pain was present only during and immediately after practice, but lately her knee seems to ache all the time. Her pain has increased to the point where she now has difficulty completing a practice session.

Symptoms and Signs The athlete complains of pain in the anterior aspect of the knee while walking, running, ascending and descending stairs, or squatting. Pain is increased during the patellar grind test. During palpation, there may be pain on the inferior border of the patella or when the patella is compressed within the femoral groove while the knee is passively flexed and extended. She has tightness of the hamstrings, an increased Q angle, excessive pronation in her left foot, and weakness in her vastus medialis obliques (VMO).

Management Plan The goal is to reduce pain initially and then to identify and correct faulty biomechanics that may collectively contribute to her anterior knee pain.

Phase 1 *Acute Injury* **GOALS:** Modulate pain; begin appropriate strengthening exercises.
ESTIMATED LENGTH OF TIME (ELT): Day 1 to Day 4.

■ **Therapy** Use ice and electrical stimulation to decrease pain. If there appears to be inflammation, antiinflammatory medications may be helpful. McConnell taping should be used to try and correct any patellar malalignment. She may need to sit out of practice for a couple of days to remove the source of irritation.

■ **Exercise rehabilitation** An orthotic insert should be constructed to correct the excessive pronation that occurs during gait. Quadriceps strengthening begins with isometric exercises, specifically, quad sets. Isometric contractions may be done at several positions throughout the range from 90 degrees of flexion to full extension.

Phase 2 *Repair* **GOALS:** Increase VMO strength and improve hamstring flexibility.
ELT: Day 5 to 2 Weeks.

■ **Therapy** Ice and electrical stimulation may be continued. McConnell taping technique should also be continued, with day-to-day reassessment of its effectiveness. The use of biofeedback may help the athlete to learn to contract the VMO.

■ **Exercise rehabilitation** The effectiveness of the orthotic should be reassessed with appropriate correction adjustments. Aggressive hamstring stretching exercises should be used. Quadriceps strengthening exercises should concentrate on the VMO and should progress from isometrics to full-range isotonics as soon as full range of motion resisted exercise no longer causes pain. Closed kinetic chain exercises, particularly minisquats and lateral step-ups, should be recommended. The athlete may resume practice; however, those activities that seem to increase pain should be modified or replaced with alternative activities. Fitness levels must be maintained by either stationary cycling or aquatic exercise.

Phase 3 *Remodeling* **GOALS:** Complete elimination of pain and full return to activity.
ELT: 2 Weeks to full return.

■ **Therapy** The athlete can be gradually weaned from McConnell taping. She may find it helpful to wear a neoprene sleeve during activity.

Continued

■ **Exercise rehabilitation** The athlete must continue quadriceps strengthening and hamstring stretching exercises. The athlete should now be accustomed to the orthotic insert. It may be necessary to continue to use alternative fitness activities indefinitely.

Criteria for Return to Competitive Basketball

1. Pain is eliminated in squatting and in ascending or descending stairs.
2. Athlete has good hamstring flexibility.
3. Quadriceps strength, particularly VMO strength, is good.

Symptoms and signs Repeated irritation causes swelling, hemorrhage, and gradual degeneration of the apophysis as a result of impaired circulation. The athlete complains of severe pain when kneeling, jumping, and running. There is point tenderness over the anterior proximal tibial tubercle (see Figure 20-51).

Management Management is usually conservative and includes the following:

■ Stressful activities are decreased until the epiphyseal union occurs, within six months to one year.
■ Severe cases may require a cylindrical cast.
■ Ice is applied to the knee before and after activities.
■ Isometric strengthening of quadriceps and hamstring muscles is performed.

Patellar Tendinitis (Jumper's and Kicker's Knee)

Etiology Jumping, as well as kicking or running, may place extreme tension on the knee extensor muscle complex. As a result of one or more commonly repetitive injuries, tendinitis occurs in the patellar or quadriceps tendon.[5] On rare occasions, a patellar tendon may completely fail and rupture. Sudden or repetitive forceful extension of the knee may begin an inflammatory process that will eventually lead to tendon degeneration.

Symptoms and signs The athlete will report pain and tenderness at the inferior pole of the patella on the posterior aspect. Patellar tendinitis has three stages of pain:

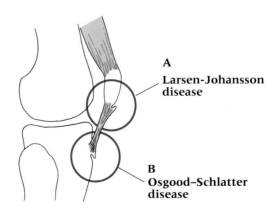

A
Larsen-Johansson disease

B
Osgood–Schlatter disease

Figure 20-51

Two conditions of the immature extensor mechanism. **A,** Larsen-Johansson disease. **B,** Osgood-Schlatter disease.

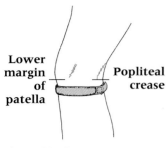

Figure 20-52

The tenodesis strap for patellofemoral pain brace.

Critical Thinking Exercise

A high jumper has been diagnosed as having patellar tendinitis, or jumper's knee. In three weeks, he has two important track meets and wants to know what he can do to get rid of the problem as soon as possible.

? What options does the athletic trainer have in treating the athlete with patellar tendinitis?

iliotibial band friction syndrome (ill ee **oh** tibial) Runner's knee.

- Stage 1—pain after sports activity
- Stage 2—pain during and after activity (the athlete is able to perform at the appropriate level)
- Stage 3—pain during activity and prolonged after activity (athletic performance is hampered); may progress to constant pain and complete rupture

Management   Any pain in the patellar tendon must preclude sudden explosive movement such as that characterized by heavy plyometric-type exercising. Many approaches to treating athletes with inflammation associated with jumper's knee have been reported, including the use of ice, phonophoresis, iontophoresis, ultrasound, and various forms of superficial heat modalities such as whirlpool together with a program of exercise. A patellar tendon tenodesis brace or strap may also be used (Figure 20-52).

Deep transverse friction massage has been used successfully for treating jumper's knee.[45] Friction is created by firm massage of the patellar tendon at the inferior patellar pole perpendicular to the direction of the fibers. Friction massage is used to increase the process of inflammation so that healing may progress to the fibroblastic phase. Thus, when transverse friction massage is used, other techniques for reducing inflammation should not be used.

Patellar Tendon Rupture

Etiology   A sudden powerful contraction of the quadriceps muscle with the weight of the body applied to the affected leg can cause a rupture.[60] The rupture may occur to the quadriceps tendon or to the patellar tendon. Usually rupture does not occur unless there has been an inflammatory condition over a period of time in the region of the knee extensor mechanism, causing tissue degeneration. Seldom does a rupture occur in the middle of the tendon, but usually it is torn from its attachment. The quadriceps tendon ruptures from the superior pole of the patella, whereas the patellar tendon ruptures from the inferior pole of the patella.

Symptoms and signs   The patella moves upward toward the thigh and the defect can be palpated. The athlete cannot extend the knee. There is considerable swelling with significant pain initially, followed by a feeling that the injury may not be all that serious.

Management   A rupture of the patellar tendon usually requires surgical repair. Proper conservative care of jumper's knee can minimize the chances of patellar tendon rupture. Athletes who use antiinflammatory drugs such as steroids must avoid intense exercise involving the knee. Steroids injected directly into these tendons weaken collagen fibers and mask pain.[41]

Runner's Knee (Cyclist's Knee)

Etiology   Runner's knee is a general expression for many repetitive and overuse conditions. Many runner's knee problems can be attributed to malalignment and structural asymmetries of the foot and lower leg, including leg-length discrepancy. Common are patellar tendinitis and patellofemoral problems that may lead to chondromalacia. Two conditions that are prevalent among joggers, distance runners, and cyclists are iliotibial band friction syndrome and pes anserinus tendinitis or bursitis.

ILIOTIBIAL BAND FRICTION SYNDROME   **Iliotibial band friction syndrome** is an overuse condition commonly occurring in runners and cyclists who have genu varum and pronated feet.[35] Irritation develops at the band's insertion and, where friction is created, over the lateral femoral condyle.[44] Ober's test (see Chapter 21) will cause pain at the point of irritation. Treatment includes stretching the iliotibial band and reducing inflammation.[30]

PES ANSERINUS TENDINITIS OR BURSITIS   The **pes anserinus** is where the sartorius, gracilis, and semitendinosus muscles join to the tibia (see Figure 20-7). Associated with pes anserinus tendinitis is pes anserinus bursitis. Inflammation results from excessive genu valgum and weakness of the vastus medialis muscle. This condition is commonly produced by running on a slope with one leg higher than the other.

Management   Management of runner's or cyclist's knee involves correction of foot and leg alignment problems. Therapy includes cold packs or ice massage before and after activity, proper warm-up and stretching, and avoidance of activities, such as running on inclines, that aggravate the problem. Other management procedures may include antiinflammatory medications and orthotic shoe devices to reduce leg conditions such as genu varum.

The Collapsing Knee

Knee collapse can stem from a variety of reasons. The most common causes of frequent knee collapse include a weak quadriceps muscle; chronic instability of the medial collateral ligament, anterior cruciate ligament, or posterior capsule; a torn meniscus; loose bodies within the knee; a subluxating patella; chondromalacia; and meniscal tears. Frequently, the knee will give way in response to pain produced by one of these conditions.

KNEE JOINT REHABILITATION

Rehabilitation of the injured knee joint in an athlete presents a challenge to the athletic trainer who is overseeing the rehabilitation process.[33] The goal of every rehabilitation program is to achieve return to normal activity. For the athlete, "normal" activity involves psychological and physiological stresses that are at a considerably higher level than those on the average person in the population. The athletic trainer must assume the responsibility for rehabilitating the whole athlete and not just the injured knee.

Every athlete who is injured must be treated individually. The athletic trainer who attempts to use a cookbook approach to rehabilitation protocols will become frustrated because a rehabilitation program needs the flexibility to be altered based on the specific needs of the individual athlete.[48]

It is difficult for anyone supervising rehabilitation programs to stay abreast of the newest techniques and philosophies, which are constantly being updated or altered. This difficulty is perhaps more true for injuries involving the knee joint than any other body part. Rapid advances in technology and surgical techniques, along with an ever-increasing understanding of the physiological, biomechanical, and neural components of knee function, have drastically and repeatedly changed the approach to knee rehabilitation in recent years.

General Body Conditioning

The athlete must work hard to maintain levels of cardiorespiratory endurance. Full return to activity will be delayed if endurance levels must be improved after the injured knee is rehabilitated. The athlete can engage in non–weight bearing activities such as using an upper-extremity ergometer, aquatic exercise, and if range of motion permits, riding a stationary bicycle. It is essential for the athlete to concentrate on maintaining existing levels of strength, flexibility, and proprioception in all other areas of the body throughout the rehabilitation process.

Weight Bearing

Generally, it is best for the athlete to go non–weight bearing on crutches for at least one to two days after acute injury to the knee. This precaution will allow the healing process to progress well into the inflammatory stage before the athlete does anything that may interfere with healing. Frequently the athlete will be allowed to progress gradually to weight bearing while continuing to wear a rehabilitative brace. The athlete should then progress to touch down weight bearing, to three-point gait, to four-point gait, and finally, to full weight bearing as soon as the healing constraints of the particular injury allow. Injured structures in the knee joint will not heal fully until they are subjected to normal tensile forces and strains.

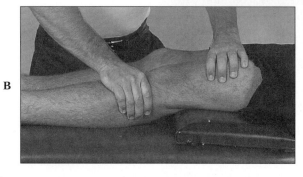
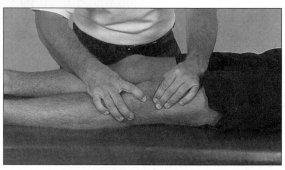

Figure 20-53

Knee mobilization techniques.
A, Posterior femoral glides.
B, Posterior tibial glides.
C, Patellar glides.

Knee Joint Mobilization

Mobilization techniques should be incorporated as early as possible to reduce the arthrofibrosis that normally occurs with immobilization.[48] After surgery, patellar mobility is generally considered to be the key to regaining normal knee motion. Patellar mobilizations that include medial, lateral, superior, and inferior glides should be used along with anterior and posterior tibial glides to ensure the return of normal joint arthrokinematics (Figure 20-53). Constant passive motion (CPM) machines are commonly used to maintain motion in a pain-free arc immediately after surgery (Figure 20-54).

Figure 20-54

Constant passive motion for the knee.

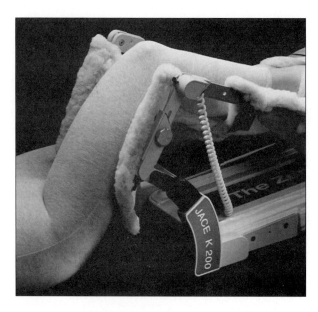

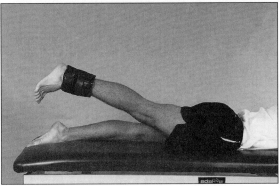

Figure 20-55

Straight-leg raising. **A,** Hip flexion. **B,** Hip abduction. **C,** Hip extension. **D,** Hip adduction.

Flexibility

Regaining full range of motion after knee injury is one of the most critical aspects of a knee rehabilitation program. Regardless of whether an injury is treated conservatively or surgically, efforts toward achieving full range of movement are begun on the first day. The athletic trainer should emphasize active ROM exercises throughout the rehabilitation program. Once normal movement of the knee joint has been achieved, efforts should be directed toward maintaining or improving flexibility of each of the muscle groups surrounding the knee joint through stretching. PNF stretching techniques are most effective.[14,15]

Muscular Strength

Strengthening generally follows a progression from isometric exercise (i.e., straight-leg raises, quad setting) (Figure 20-55), to isotonic exercise stressing both concentric and eccentric components, to isokinetic exercise, to plyometric exercise. It is essential to concentrate on strengthening all the muscle groups that have some function at the knee joint, including the quadriceps, hamstrings, abductors, adductors, and gastrocnemius.[48]

Eccentric muscle contraction should be routinely incorporated into strengthening programs through both isotonic and isokinetic exercise. Eccentric contraction of the quadriceps is necessary for deceleration of the lower leg during running. Conversely, the hamstrings must decelerate the lower leg in a kicking motion.[58] Plyometric exercises used during the later phases of rehabilitation use a quick, eccentric muscle contraction to facilitate a concentric contraction.

Traditionally, rehabilitation has tended to make use of the open kinetic chain strengthening exercises that use ankle band weights, free weights, machines, and so on. It is important to emphasize closed kinetic chain exercises, in which the foot is in

20-11
Critical Thinking Exercise

A field hockey player is three days postop after reconstruction of her knee using a patellar tendon graft. It is essential that she begin active range-of-motion and strengthening exercises as soon as possible.

? What type of strengthening exercises should the athletic trainer recommend?

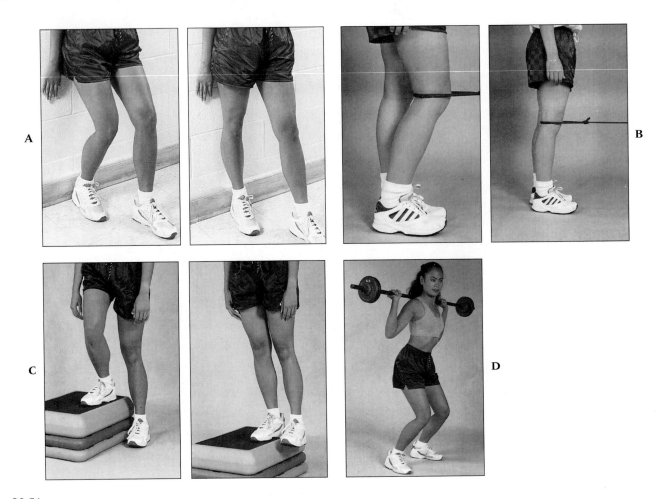

Figure 20-56

Terminal knee extension—closed kinetic chain. **A,** Wall standing— starting position; stopping position. **B,** Using rubber tubing— starting position; stopping position. **C,** Lateral step-ups— starting position; stopping position. **D,** Minisquats.

contact with the ground.[16] Closed chain activities are more functional and eliminate many of the stress and shearing forces associated with an open-lever system. Thus, they are safer than open chain exercises. Minisquats, step-ups onto a box, leg presses on a machine, and the use of stationary bicycles, stair climbing machines, and exercise tubing are examples of closed chain activities (Figure 20-56).[58] These exercises also emphasize and facilitate cocontraction of antagonistic muscle groups (e.g., quadriceps and hamstrings). This cocontraction aids in providing appropriate neuromuscular control of opposing muscle groups and thus promotes stability about the joint.[20]

PNF strengthening techniques using D1 and D2 lower-extremity patterns allow the athletic trainer to work on coordinated movement patterns and, in particular, emphasize the tibial rotation component of knee motion (Figure 20-57).[48]

Neuromuscular Control

Regaining neuromuscular control of joint motion after injury is also important. The athlete quickly "forgets" how to contract a muscle after injury. Loss of neuromuscular control usually occurs because of pain inhibition or swelling. Efforts directed toward proprioceptive control are begun immediately after injury to the knee with weight-shifting exercises on crutches, straight-leg lifts, and quad sets. Strengthening and flexibility exercises mentioned previously will help facilitate return of proprioception. The BAPS board and the KAT system (see Figures 15-4A and B), a mini tramp, and a slide board can all be used to improve proprioception and balance, as well as the NeuroCom and the Chattex (Figure 20-58).

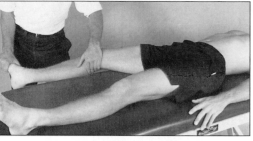

A

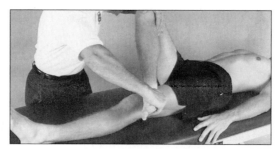

B

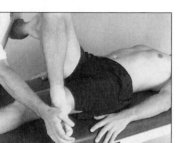

C

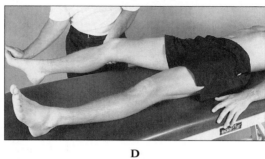

D

E

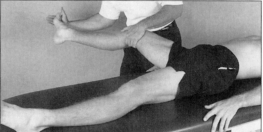

F

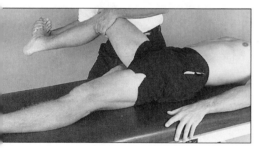

G

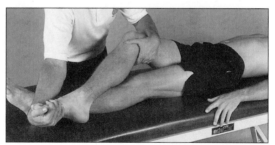

H

Figure 20-57

D1 lower-extremity pattern moving into: **A,** flexion-starting position; **B,** flexion-terminal position; **C,** extension-starting position; **D,** extension-terminal position. D2 lower-extremity pattern moving into: **E,** flexion-starting position; **F,** flexion-terminal position; **G,** extension-starting position; **H,** extension-terminal position.

Figure 20-58

Balance devices. **A,** Neuro-Com. **B,** Chattex.

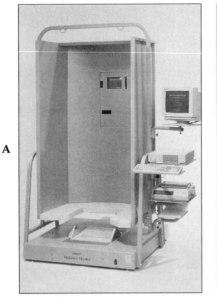

A

B

Figure 20-59

A, Rehabilitative knee brace. **B, C,** Functional knee braces.

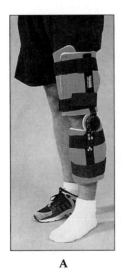

A   B   C

Bracing

Rehabilitative knee braces have been designed to allow protected motion of either operative or nonoperative knees.[26] Braces enclose the thigh and calf with fabric fasteners, are lightweight, and are hinged such that motion can be limited within a specific degree range (see Figure 20-59A). Depending on the specific injury or the surgical technique used, the knee must be protected in limited ranges for some period of time. The braces are removed during rehabilitation sessions to allow the athlete to work in the greatest range of motion possible. Rehabilitative braces are typically worn for three to six weeks after surgery.

Functional knee braces are worn to provide support to the unstable knee on return to activity.[26] All functional braces are custom fitted to some degree and use hinges and posts for support. Some braces use custom-molded thigh and calf enclosures to hold the brace in place, whereas others rely on straps for suspension (Figure 20-59B and C). Among the functional braces currently available are the Lennox Hill, CTI, Can-AM, Don Joy RKS, Feaney, Omni TS7, OTI Performer, and Townsend.

Braces are designed to improve stability of the ACL-deficient knee by preventing full extension. Some braces attempt to control rotation or varus force. Functional knee braces alone do not seem to be able to control pathological laxity associated with ACL deficiency. However, if combined with an appropriate rehabilitation program, these braces have been shown to restrict anterior-posterior translation of the tibia at low loads.

Functional Progression

Sport-specific skills should be broken down into component parts, and the athlete should be gradually reintroduced to them and progressed through their individual components. For the athlete with an injured knee, a gradual return to running is essential. The athlete should begin with walking (forward, backward, straight line, curve) and progress to jogging (straight, curve, uphill, downhill), running (forward, backward), and then sprinting (straight, curve, large figure-8, small figure-8, zigzag, carioca).

Return to Activity

The decision to permit the athlete to return to full activity should be based on a number of criteria.[8] It is perhaps most important to make sure that the healing process has been given a sufficient chance to repair the injured structure. Objective criteria for return include isokinetic evaluation (torque values at least 90 percent of the uninjured extremity), arthrometer measurement, and functional performance tests (figure-8s at speed, carioca, hop test, etc.).

SUMMARY

- The knee is one of the most complex joints in the human body. As a hinge joint that also glides and has some rotation, it is also one of the most traumatized joints in sports. Three structures are most often injured: the medial and lateral collateral capsules and ligaments, the menisci, and the cruciate ligaments.
- Knee injuries may be avoided if athletes maximize muscle strength and wear appropriate shoes. Use of protective knee bracing is questionable.
- Ligamentous and capsular sprains occur frequently to the medial aspect of the knee and less often to the lateral aspect. The most common ligamentous injury occurs to the anterior cruciate ligament.
- A meniscus can be injured in a variety of ways, including a rotary force to the knee with the foot planted, a sudden valgus or varus force, or sudden flexion or extension of the knee. There may be severe pain and loss of motion, locking of the knee, and pain in the area of the tear.
- The patella and its surrounding area can develop a variety of injuries from sports activities. Some of these injuries are fracture, dislocation, and chronic articular degeneration such as chondromalacia. Other conditions in the region include Osgood-Schlatter disease and jumper's knee.
- The goal of the knee rehabilitation program is to restore the athlete's muscular strength, power, endurance, flexibility, neuromuscular control, and functional capability. The program varies according to the sport and condition.

Web Sites

◪ *Solutions to Critical Thinking* E X E R C I S E S

20-1 When the athlete is weight bearing with the knee in full extension, the femur is internally rotated relative to the tibia and is "locked" in this position. The collateral, the cruciates, and the capsular ligaments are tightest in full extension and tend to become more relaxed when moving into flexion. It is possible to injure any of the ligaments in full extension. The posterior cruciate has the least chance of being injured when the knee is fully extended.

20-2 During the evaluation, the athletic trainer should look for tightness of the hamstrings or gastrocnemius, tightness of the lateral retinaculum, increased Q angle, tightness of the iliotibial band, pronation of the foot, patella alta, VMO insufficiency, inhibition resulting from the presence of effusion in the knee, or weak hip adductors to which the VMO is attached.

20-3 A valgus stress test should be used to test the MCL. The examination in full extension tests the MCL, posteromedial capsule, and the cruciates. At 30 degrees of flexion, the MCL is isolated. If some instability is present with the knee in full extension, the athletic trainer should closely evaluate the integrity of the cruciate ligaments.

20-4 This mechanism is typical for a sprain of the anterior cruciate ligament, although other ligamentous, capsular, and meniscal structures may be injured as well. Appropriate stability tests for the ACL include the anterior drawer test done in neutral, internal, and external rotation; Lachman's test; pivot-shift test; jerk test; and the flexion-rotation drawer test.

20-5 If the baseball player still has personal concerns about his knee not being ready to return to full activity, then he is certainly not ready regardless of whether he is wearing a knee brace. The athletic trainer should design a series of functional progression activities that will help the athlete gain confidence in his abilities while continuing to work on strengthening and on neuromuscular control exercises. If the athlete feels strongly about wearing a brace, the athletic trainer should make every effort to provide him with one despite the fact that the literature supporting the use of functional knee braces is unclear.

20-6 It is important to understand that once a ligament has been sprained, the inherent stability provided to the joint by that ligament has been lost and will never be totally regained. Thus, the athlete must rely on the other structures that surround the joint, the muscles and their tendons, to help provide stability. It is essential for the athlete to work hard on strengthening exercises for all the muscle groups that play a role in the function of the knee joint.

20-7 The most common mechanism is weight bearing combined with a rotary force while the knee is extended or flexed. A large number of medial meniscus lesions are the outcome of a sudden, strong internal rotation of the femur with a partially flexed knee while the foot is firmly planted. Another way a longitudinal tear occurs is by forceful extension of the knee from a flexed position while the femur is internally rotated. During extension, the medial meniscus is suddenly pulled back, causing the tear.

20-8 It is likely that the athlete has an inflamed or irritated mediopatellar plica. The mediopatellar plica may be thick, nonyielding, and fibrotic, which can cause a number of symptoms. The presence of an inflamed mediopatellar plica is sometimes associated with chondromalacia of the medial femoral condyle and patella.

20-9 The athletic trainer should recommend a reduction in the length of the training sessions, in particular, a limit to the running phase of training. Pain-free isometric exercises to strengthen the quadriceps and hamstring muscles can be used initially, and the athlete can progress to closed kinetic chain strengthening exercises. Oral antiinflammatory agents and small doses of aspirin may also be helpful. A neoprene knee sleeve may also help modulate pain. Use of an orthotic device to correct pronation and reduce tibial torsion can sometimes help eliminate pain.

20-10 A conservative approach would be to use the normal techniques to reduce inflammation, such as rest, ice, ultrasound, and antiinflammatory medications. An alternative and more aggressive technique would be to use a deep transverse friction massage technique to increase the inflammatory response, which will ultimately facilitate healing. If successful, the more aggressive treatment may allow a quicker return to full activity.

20-11 Closed kinetic chain strengthening exercises such as minisquats, lateral or forward step-ups onto a box, leg presses on a machine, terminal knee extensions using exercise tubing, and use of stationary bicycles, stair climbing machines, and stepping machines are all appropriate exercises that can be used safely and effectively almost immediately after surgery. Limitation in range of motion secondary to pain and swelling may restrict the athlete's ability to perform these strengthening exercises.

REVIEW QUESTIONS AND CLASS ACTIVITIES

1. Describe the major structural and functional anatomical features of the knee.
2. Explain how a knee injury can best be prevented. What injuries are most difficult to prevent?
3. Demonstrate the steps that should be taken when assessing the knee.
4. Describe the symptoms, signs, and management of knee contusions and bursitis.
5. Distinguish collateral ligament sprains from cruciate sprains.
6. What is the difference between a meniscal lesion and a knee plica?
7. Explain how different fractures (e.g., patellar and epiphyseal fractures) may occur in the knee.
8. Describe the relationship of loose bodies within the knee to osteochondritis dissecans.
9. How do the patella fracture and the patellar dislocation occur?

10. Compare the causes of patellofemoral arthralgia.
11. What types of injuries can occur to the extensor mechanism in a physically immature athlete?
12. Describe and compare the iliotibial band friction syndrome and pes anserinus tendinitis or bursitis.
13. What causes the knee to collapse?
14. Describe knee rehabilitation after conservative treatment of a second-degree medial collateral sprain and after surgical repair of a torn anterior cruciate ligament.

REFERENCES

1. Arangio G, Cohen E: Incidence of associated knee lesions with torn anterior cruciate ligament: retrospective cohort assessment, *J Sport Rehabil* 7(1):1, 1998.
2. Arno S: The A angle: a quantitive measurement of patella alignment and realignment, *J Orthop Sports Phys Ther* 12(6):237, 1990.
3. Arnoczky SP, Warren RF: Microvasculature of the human meniscus, *Am J Sports Med* 10:90, 1982.
4. Arnosky P: Physiologic principles of ligament injuries and healing. In Scott N, editor: *Ligament and extensor mechanism injuries of the knee: diagnosis and treatment,* St Louis, 1991, Mosby.
5. Bazluki J: Surgical intervention and rehabilitation of chronic patellar tendinitis, *J Ath Train* 31(1):65, 1996.
6. Blackburn TA Jr et al: An introduction to the plica, *J Orthop Sports Phys Ther* 3:171, 1982.
7. Boland AL Jr: Soft tissue injuries of the knee. In Nicholas JA, Hershman EB, editors: *The lower extremity and spine in sports medicine,* St Louis, 1995, Mosby.
8. Borsa PA, Lephart SM, Irrgang JJ: Sport-specificity of knee scoring systems to assess disability in anterior cruciate ligament-deficient athletes, *J Sport Rehabil* 7(1):44, 1998.
9. Calliet R: *Knee pain and disability,* Philadelphia, 1983, FA Davis.
10. Coughlin L et al: Knee bracing and anterolateral rotary instability, *Am J Sports Med* 15:161, 1987.
11. DeStefano V: Skeletal injuries of the knee. In Nicholas J, Hershman E, editors: *The lower extremity and spine in sports medicine,* St Louis, 1995, Mosby.
12. Doberstein ST, Schrodt J: Partial posterior cruciate ligament tear in a collegiate basketball player: a case report, *J Ath Train* 32(2):155, 1997.
13. Draper D, Schultheis S: A test for eliminating false positive anterior cruciate ligament injury diagnosis, *J Ath Train* 28(4):355, 1993.
14. Engle B, Canner C: PNF and modified procedures for ACL instability, *J Orthop Sports Phys Ther* 11(6):230, 1990.
15. Engle B, Canner C: Rehabilitation of symptomatic anterolateral knee instability, *J Orthop Sports Phys Ther* 11(6):237, 1990.
16. Escamilla RF, Fleisig GS, Zheng N: Biomechanics of the knee during closed kinetic chain and open kinetic chain exercises, *Med Sci Sports Exerc* 30(4):556, 1998.
17. Fadale PD, Hulstyn MJ: *Common athletic knee injuries. Clinics in sports medicine* 16(3):479, 1997.
18. Fujiwara L et al: Effect of three lateral knee braces on speed and agility in experienced and nonexperienced wearers, *Ath Train* 25(2):160, 1990.
19. Gilleard W, McConnell J, Parsons D: The effect of patellar taping on the onset of vastus medialis obliquus and vastus lateralis muscle activity in persons with patellofemoral pain, *Phys Ther* 78(1):25, 1998.
20. Gryzlo S, Patek R, Pink M: Electromyographic analysis of knee rehabilitation exercises, *J Orthop Sports Phys Ther* 20(1):36, 1994.
21. Harter R et al: A comparison of instrumented and manual Lachman test results in ACL-reconstructed knees, *Ath Train* 25(4):330, 1990.
22. Indelicato P: Isolated MCL tear: nonoperative management. In Torg J, Shephard R, editors: *Current therapy in sports medicine,* St Louis, 1995, Mosby.
23. Ingersoll CD: Assessment of patellofemoral pain, *Athletic Therapy Today* 3(2):45, 1998.
24. Irrgang J, Harner C: Recent advances in ACL rehabilitation: clinical factors that influence the program, *J Sport Rehabil* 6(2):111, 1997.
25. Jensen K: Manual laxity tests for anterior cruciate ligament injuries, *J Orthop Sports Phys Ther* 11(10):474, 1990.
26. Johnson C, Bach B: Use of knee braces in athletic injuries. In Scott N, editor: *Ligament and extensor mechanism injuries of the knee: diagnosis and treatment,* St Louis, 1991, Mosby.
27. Kramer PG: Patella malalignment syndrome: rationale to reduce excessive lateral pressure, *J Orthop Sports Phys Ther* 8:301, 1986.
28. Kuhlman K: Meniscal repair. In Torg J, Shephard R, editors: *Current therapy in sports medicine,* St Louis, 1995, Mosby.
29. Laprade J, Culham E, Brouwer B: Comparison of five isometric exercises in the recruitment of the vastus medialis oblique in persons with and without patellofemoral pain syndrome, *J Orthop Sports Phys Ther* 27(3):197, 1998.
30. Lebsack D et al: Iliotibial band friction syndrome, *Ath Train* 25(4):356, 1990.
31. Lutz G, Warren R: Meniscal injuries. In Griffin L, editor: *Rehabilitation of the injured knee,* St Louis, 1995, Mosby.
32. Lynch M, Henning C: Physical examination of the knee. In Nicholas J, Hershman E, editors: *The lower extremity and spine in sports medicine,* St Louis, 1995, Mosby.
33. Mangine R: The knee. In Sanders B, editor: *Sports physical therapy,* Norwalk, Conn, 1990, Appleton & Lange.
34. Mangine R, Kremchek T: Evaluation-based protocol of the anterior cruciate ligament, *J Sport Rehabil* 6(2):157, 1997.
35. Martens M: Iliotibial band friction syndrome. In Torg J, Shephard R, editors: *Current therapy in sports medicine,* St Louis, 1995, Mosby.
36. Martin D, Guskiewicz K, Perrin D: Tibial rotation affects anterior displacement of the knee, *J Sport Rehab* 3(4):275, 1994.
37. McCarthy M, Buxton B, Hiller D: Current protocols and procedures for anterior cruciate ligament reconstruction and rehabilitation, *J Sport Rehab* 3(3):204, 1994.
38. Merchant A: Extensor mechanism injuries: classification and diagnosis. In Scott N, editor: *Ligament and extensor mechanism injuries of the knee: diagnosis and treatment,* St Louis, 1991, Mosby.
39. Miller JP, Sedory D, Croce RV: Vastus medialis obliquus and vastus lateralis activity in patients with and without patellofemoral pain syndrome, *J Sport Rehabil* 6(1):1, 1997.
40. Mont M, Scott N: Classification of ligament injuries. In Scott N, editor: *Ligament and extensor mechanism injuries of the knee: diagnosis and treatment,* St Louis, 1991, Mosby.
41. Montgomery D: Prophylactic knee braces. In Torg J, Shephard R, editors: *Current therapy in sports medicine,* St Louis, 1995, Mosby.
42. Nichols C, Johnson R: Cruciate ligament injuries: nonoperative treatment. In Scott N, editor: *Ligament and extensor mechanism injuries of the knee: diagnosis and treatment,* St Louis, 1991, Mosby.
43. Noyes F, Grood E: Classification of ligament injuries: why an anterolateral or anteromedial laxity is not a diagnostic entity. In Griffin P, editor: *Instructional course lectures,* Parkridge, Ill, 1987, American Academy of Orthopaedic Surgeons.
44. Olson DW: Iliotibial band friction syndrome, *Ath Train* 21(1):32, 1986.
45. Pellecchia G, Hame H, Behnke P: Treatment of infrapatellar tendinitis: a combination of modalities and transverse friction massage, *J Sport Rehab* 3(2):125, 1994.
46. Pitman M, Frankel V: Biomechanics of the knee in athletics. In Nicholas J, Hershman E, editors: *The lower extremity and spine in sports medicine,* St Louis, 1995, Mosby.
47. Post WR: Patellofemoral pain: let the physical exam define treatment, *Physician Sportsmed* 26(1):68, 1998.
48. Prentice W, Davis M: Rehabilitation of the knee. In Prentice W, editor: *Rehabilitation techniques in sports medicine,* Dubuque, Iowa, 1999, WCB/McGraw-Hill.

49. Prentice W, Toriscelli T: The effects of lateral knee stabilizing braces on running speed and agility, *Ath Train* 21(2):112, 1986.

50. Rettig A: Medial and lateral ligament injuries. In Scott N, editor: *Ligament and extensor mechanism injuries of the knee: diagnosis and treatment*, St Louis, 1991, Mosby.

51. Ryder S, et al: Prevention of ACL injuries, *J Sport Rehabil* 6(2):80, 1997.

52. Salvaterra G, Wang M, Morehouse C: An in vitro biomechanical study of the static stabilizing effect of lateral prophylactic knee bracing on medial stability, *J Ath Train* 28(2):133, 1993.

53. Shelbourne D, Klootwyk T, De Carlo M: Ligamentous injuries. In Griffin L, editor: *Rehabilitation of the injured knee*, St Louis, 1995, Mosby.

54. Shelbourne D, Trumper R: Accelerated rehabilitation after ACL reconstruction. In Torg J, Shephard R, editors: *Current therapy in sports medicine*, St Louis, 1995, Mosby.

55. Somes S, Worrell TW, Corey B, Ingersol CD: Effects of patellar taping on patellar position in the open and closed kinetic chain: a preliminary study, *J Sport Rehabil* 6(4):299, 1997.

56. Tria A, Hosea T: Clinical diagnosis of knee ligament injuries. In Scott N, editor: *Ligament and extensor mechanism injuries of the knee: diagnosis and treatment*, St Louis, 1991, Mosby.

57. Weiss J et al: A functional assessment of anterior cruciate ligament deficiency in an acute and clinical setting, *J Orthop Sports Phys Ther* 11(8):372, 1990.

58. Wilk K, Andrews J: Current concepts in the treatment of anterior cruciate ligament disruption, *J Orthop Sports Phys Ther* 15(6):279, 1992.

59. Wilk K, et al: Kinetic chain exercise: implications for the anterior cruciate ligament patient, *J Sport Rehabil* 6(2):125, 1997.

60. Woodall W, Welsh J: A biomechanical basis for rehabilitation programs involving the patellofemoral joint, *J Orthop Sports Phys Ther* 11(11):535, 1990.

61. Zarins B, Boyle J: Knee ligament injuries. In Nicholas J, Hershman E, editors: *The lower extremity and spine in sports medicine*, St Louis, 1995, Mosby.

ANNOTATED BIBLIOGRAPHY

Grelsamer R, McConnell J: *The patella: a team approach*, Gaithersburg, Md, 1998, Aspen.

This text provides a comprehensive discussion that concentrates specifically on the patella from both a physician's and a physical therapist's perspective.

Griffin L: *Rehabilitation of the knee*, St Louis, 1995, Mosby.

This text incorporates new advances in rehabilitation techniques and equipment and gives emphasis to sport-specific functional rehabilitation programs.

Nicholas J, Hershman E: *The lower extremity and spine in sports medicine*, St Louis, 1995, Mosby.

This two-volume set looks at the entire lower extremity and spine; an excellent comprehensive reference for all joints.

Prentice W: *Rehabilitation techniques in sports medicine*, Dubuque, Iowa, 1999, WCB/McGraw-Hill.

This text is a comprehensive, well-illustrated text on rehabilitation techniques used in sports medicine. Chapter 23 deals specifically with rehabilitation of the knee and provides up-to-date recommendations for a rehabilitation program.

Scott N: *Ligament and extensor mechanism injuries of the knee*, St Louis, 1991, Mosby.

This comprehensive text looks at all aspects of the knee joint, including anatomy, biomechanics, ligamentous stability testing, injuries, surgical procedures, bracing, and rehabilitation; provides an outstanding review of the existing literature on all topics.

The Thigh, Hip, Groin, and Pelvis

When you finish this chapter you should be able to

- Describe the major anatomical features of the thigh, hip, and pelvis as they relate to sports injuries.
- Discuss the techniques used to evaluate injuries to the thigh, hip, and pelvis.
- Identify and evaluate the major sports injuries to the thigh, hip, and pelvis.
- Establish a management and rehabilitation plan for a sports injury to the thigh, hip, or pelvis.

Although the thigh, hip, and pelvis have relatively lower incidences of injury than the knee and lower limb, they do receive considerable trauma from a variety of sports activities. Of major concern are thigh strains and contusions and chronic and overuse stresses affecting the thigh and hip.

ANATOMY OF THE THIGH

The thigh is generally considered that part of the leg between the hip and the knee. Several important anatomical units must be considered in terms of their relationship to sports injuries: the shaft of the femur, musculature, nerves and blood vessels, and the fascia that envelops the thigh.

The Femur

The femur (Figure 21-1) is the longest and strongest bone in the body and is designed to permit maximum mobility and support during locomotion. The cylindrical shaft is bowed forward and outward to accommodate the stresses placed on it during bending of the hip and knee and during weight bearing.

Musculature

The muscles of the thigh may be categorized according to their location: anterior, posterior, and medial.

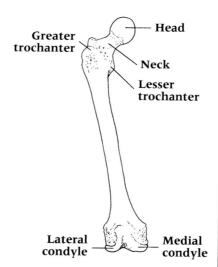

Figure 21-1

Femur (os femoris).

Anterior Thigh Muscles

The anterior thigh muscles consist of the sartorius and the quadriceps femoris group.

Sartorius   The sartorius muscle (Figure 21-2) consists of a narrow band that is superficial throughout its whole length. It stems from the anterosuperior iliac spine and crosses obliquely downward and medially across the anterior aspect of the thigh where it attaches to the anteromedial aspect of the tibial head. It helps flex the thigh at the hip joint, abducts and outwardly rotates the thigh at the hip joint, and inwardly rotates the flexed knee. When the legs are stabilized, the sartorius acts to flex the pelvis on the thigh. When the sartorius muscle contracts, the pelvis is rotated.

Quadriceps femoris   Normally the strongest of the thigh muscles, the quadriceps femoris muscle group (Figure 21-3) consists of four muscles: rectus femoris, vastus medialis, vastus lateralis, and vastus intermedius. These four muscles form a common tendon that attaches distally at the superior border of the patella and indirectly into the patellar ligament, which attaches to the tibial tuberosity. The rectus femoris muscle is attached superiorly to the anterior inferior iliac spine and the ilium above the acetabulum and inferiorly to the patella and patellar ligament. The vastus medialis and vastus lateralis muscles originate from the lateral and medial linea aspera of the femur. The vastus intermedius muscle originates mainly from the anterior and lateral portion of the femur. Inferiorly, the three vastus muscles are attached to the rectus femoris muscle and to the lateral and proximal aspects of the patella. Of particular importance is the vastus medialis muscle, which serves as a major stabilizer for patellar tracking.

Posterior Thigh Muscles

The posterior thigh muscles include the popliteus and the hamstring muscles.

Hamstring muscles   Located posteriorly, the hamstring muscle group (Figure 21-4) consists of three muscles: the biceps femoris, semimembranosus, and semitendinosus muscles.

The biceps femoris muscle, as its name implies, has two heads. Its long head originates with the semitendinosus at the medial aspect of the ischial tuberosity. Its short head is attached to the linea aspera below the gluteus maximus attachment on the femur and medial to the attachment of the vastus lateralis. Both muscle heads attach with a common tendon to the head of the fibula.

The semitendinosus muscle originates at the medial aspect of the ischial tuberosity along with the biceps femoris muscle. Together with the semimembranosus muscle, the semitendinosus muscle attaches to the medial aspect of the proximal tibia. This attachment is just behind those of the sartorius and gracilis muscles, which all together form the pes anserinus tendon. The tibial branch of the sciatic nerve supplies this muscle.

Figure 21-2

Sartorius.

Figure 21-3

Quadriceps femoris.

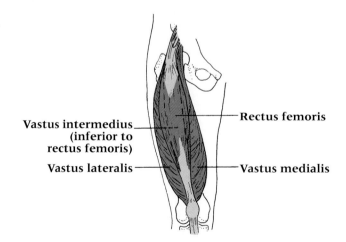

Vastus intermedius (inferior to rectus femoris)

Vastus lateralis

Rectus femoris

Vastus medialis

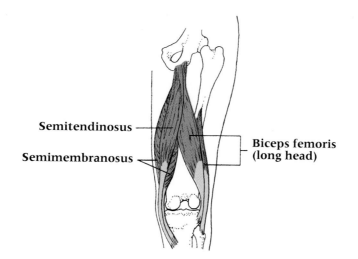

Figure 21-4

Hamstring muscles.

The semimembranosus muscle originates from the lateral aspect of the upper half of the ischeal tuberosity. Moving downward, it attaches into the medial femoral condyle. It also attaches to the medial side of the tibia, the popliteus muscle fascia, and the posterior capsule of the knee joint. The tibial branch of the sciatic nerve supplies this muscle.

Medial Thigh Muscles

The medial thigh muscles include the gracilis, sartorius, pectineus, and three adductor muscles. All act as adductors and lateral rotators of the thigh at the hip joint (Figure 21-5).

The gracilis muscle is attached superiorly to the body of the inferior ramus of the pubis and inferiorly to the medial aspect of the proximal tibia. It is a relatively narrow-appearing muscle that adducts the thigh at the hip and flexes and medially rotates the leg at the knee joint. The anterior branch of the obturator nerve serves this muscle.

The pectineus muscle arises from the pectineal crest of the pubis and attaches distally on the pectineal line of the femur. As one of the adductors, it also flexes and outwardly rotates the thigh.

The adductor longus, brevis, and magnus muscles originate at the ramus of the pubis and attach inferiorly on the linea aspera of the femur. The muscles adduct the

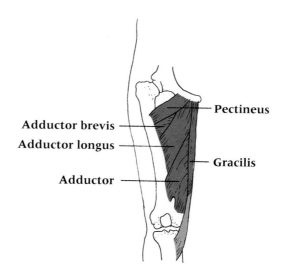

Figure 21-5

Hip adductors.

thigh at the hip and outwardly rotate the thigh. All these muscles assist in the flexion of the thigh.

Nerve Supply

Among nerves that emerge from the sacral plexus are the tibial and common peroneal nerves, which in the thigh form the largest nerve in the body, the greater sciatic nerve. The sciatic nerve supplies the muscles of the thigh and lower leg (see Figure 21-16).

Blood Supply

The main arteries that supply the thigh are the deep medial circumflex femoral, deep femoral, and femoral artery. The two main veins are the superficial great saphenous and the femoral vein (see Figure 21-18).

Fascia

The fascia lata femoris is that part of the deep fascia that invests the thigh musculature. It is relatively thick anteriorly, laterally, and posteriorly but thin on the medial side where it covers the adductors. On its most lateral part, the iliotibial track, an attachment is provided for the tensor fascia lateral and greater aspect of the gluteus maximus.

FUNCTIONAL ANATOMY OF THE THIGH

The function of the quadriceps femoris muscle group is extension of the lower leg. The rectus femoris muscle, with its pelvic attachment of the quadriceps muscles, is the only flexor of the thigh at the hip joint. The common peroneal nerve innervates the short head of the rectus femoris muscle, and the tibial portion of the sciatic nerve innervates the long head. The remainder of the quadriceps are innervated by the femoral nerve.

The hamstring muscles are biarticular; they act as extensors at the hip and flexors at the knee joint. Assisting the hamstrings in knee flexion are the sartorius, gracilis, popliteus, and gastrocnemius muscles. At the hip, hamstrings work in cooperation with the gluteus maximus to extend the hip. Lateral rotation of the leg at the knee is conducted by the biceps femoris muscle. Medial rotation is caused by both the semitendinosus and semimembranosus muscles.

ASSESSMENT OF THE THIGH

History

The athletic trainer should ask the following questions:
- Was the onset sudden or slow?
- Has this injury occurred before?
- How was the thigh injured?
- Can the athlete describe the intensity or duration of the pain?
- Is the pain constant? If not, when does it occur?
- Can the athlete specify exactly where the pain is?
- Is the pain related to risk?
- What type of pain is there? Muscle pain is dull, achy, and hard to localize. Vascular pain is sharp, bright, and sometimes burning. Bone pain feels deep, penetrating, and highly localized.

Observation

The athletic trainer should compare the thighs:
- Are they symmetrical?
- Are both the same size? Is there swelling?
- Are the skin color and texture normal?

- Is the athlete in obvious pain?
- Is the athlete willing to move the thigh?

Palpation

Both thighs should be palpated for comparison while the athlete is as relaxed as possible.

Bony Palpation

The following bony landmarks should be palpated:
- Medial femoral condyle
- Lateral femoral condyle
- Greater trochanter
- Lesser trochanter
- Anterior superior iliac spine
- Medial tibial plateau
- Fibular head

Soft Tissue Palpation

The following soft tissue structures should be palpated:

Anterior
- Sartorious
- Rectus femoris
- Vastus lateralis
- Vastus medialis
- Vastus intermedialis

Posterior
- Semimembranosis
- Semitendinosis
- Biceps femoris

Medial
- Adductor brevis
- Adductor longus
- Adductor magnus
- Gracilis
- Pectineus

Lateral
- Iliotibial band
- Gluteus medius
- Tensor fasciae latae

Special Tests

NOTE: If a fracture is suspected, the following tests are not performed.
- Beginning an extension, the knee is passively flexed. A normal muscle will elicit full range of motion that is pain free. A muscle that has swelling or spasm will have restricted passive motion.
- Active movement from flexion to extension that is strong and painful may indicate muscle strain. A movement that is weak and pain free may indicate a third-degree or partial muscle rupture.[17]
- Muscle weakness against an isometric resistance may indicate a nerve injury.[1]

PREVENTION OF THIGH INJURIES

Like all other muscles in sports, the thigh must have maximum strength, endurance, and extensibility to withstand strain. In collision sports such as football, thigh guards are mandatory.

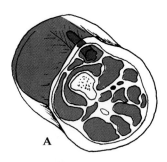

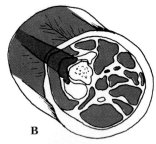

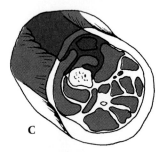

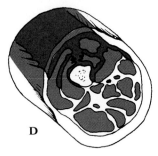

Figure 21-6

Quadriceps contusion.
A, Grade 1, mild hemorrhage.
B, Grade 2, mild pain and point tenderness. **C,** Grade 3, moderate pain and swelling.
D, Grade 4, deep intramuscular hematoma.

RECOGNITION AND MANAGEMENT OF THIGH INJURIES

Injuries to the thigh muscles are among the most common in sports. Contusions and strains occur most often, with the former having the higher incidence.

Quadriceps Contusions

Etiology The quadriceps group is continually exposed to traumatic blunt blows in a variety of vigorous sports. Contusions usually develop as the result of a severe impact to the relaxed thigh that compresses the muscle against the hard surface of the femur. The extent of the force and the degree of thigh relaxation determine the depth of the injury and the amount of structural and functional disruption that take place.[4]

Symptoms and signs Contusions of the quadriceps display all the classic symptoms of most muscle bruises. Pain, a transitory loss of function, and immediate capillary effusion usually occur at the instant of trauma. The athlete usually describes having been hit by a sharp blow to the thigh, which produced intense pain and weakness. Early detection and avoidance of profuse internal hemorrhage are vital, both in effecting a fast recovery by the athlete and in the prevention of widespread scarring. Palpation may reveal a circumscribed swollen area that is painful to the touch.

The grade 1 quadriceps contusion is a superficial intramuscular bruise that produces mild hemorrhage, little pain, no swelling, and mild point tenderness at the site of the trauma. There is no restriction of the range of motion (Figure 21-6A; Table 21-1). The grade 2 contusion is deeper than grade 1 and produces mild pain, mild swelling, and point tenderness, with the athlete able to flex the knee no more than 90 degrees (Figure 21-6B). The grade 3 quadriceps contusion is of moderate intensity, causing pain, swelling, and a range of knee flexion that is 90 to 45 degrees with an obvious limp present (Figure 21-6C). The severe, or grade 4, quadriceps contusion represents a major disability. A blow may have been so intense as to split the fasciae latae, allowing the muscle to protrude (muscle herniation) (Figure 21-6D). A characteristic deep intramuscular hematoma with an intermuscular spread is present. Pain is severe, and swelling may lead to hematoma. Movement of the knee is severely restricted with 45 degrees or less flexion, and the athlete has a decided limp.

Management The leg should be immediately placed in flexion with an ice pack to avoid muscle shortening (Figure 21-7). RICE, NSAIDs, and analgesics are given as needed. Crutches may be warranted in second- or third-degree contusions. A hematoma that develops may have to be aspirated.[12] One or two units of blood may be lost into the anterior thigh. After exercise or reinjury, RICE must be routinely applied to the thigh. Follow-up care consists of range of motion (ROM) exercises and PRE within a pain-free limitation. Heat, massage, and ultrasound should be avoided to prevent the possibility of myositis ossificans (Figure 21-8).

Generally, the rehabilitation of a thigh contusion should be handled conservatively. Cold packs combined with gentle stretching may be the preferred treatment. If heat therapy is used, it should not be initiated until the acute phase of the injury has clearly passed. An elastic bandage should be worn to provide constant pressure and mild support to the quadriceps area. Exercise should be graduated from mild

TABLE 21-1 Thigh Contusions and Restricted Knee Flexion

Degree of Flexion	Injury Severity
>90°	Grade 2
>45°, <90°	Grade 3
<45°	Grade 4

Figure 21-7

Immediate care of the thigh contusion includes RICE and a constant stretch of the quadriceps muscle.

stretching of the quadriceps area in the early stages of the injury to swimming, if possible, and then to jogging and running. Exercise should not be conducted if it produces pain.

Medical care of a thigh contusion may include surgical repair of a herniated muscle or aspiration of a hematoma. Some physicians administer enzymes either orally or through injection for the dissolution of the hematoma.

Once an athlete has sustained a grade 3 or grade 4 thigh contusion, great care must be taken to avoid sustaining another contusion. The athlete should routinely wear a protective pad held in place by an elastic wrap while engaged in sports activity.

Myositis Ossificans Traumatica

Etiology   A severe blow or repeated blows to the thigh, usually to the quadriceps muscle, can lead to ectopic bone production, or myositis ossificans. This condition commonly follows bleeding into the quadriceps muscle and a hematoma. The contusion to the muscle causes disruption of the muscle fibers, capillaries, fibrous connective tissue, and periosteum of the femur. Acute inflammation follows resolution of hemorrhage. The irritated tissue may then produce calcified formations that resemble cartilage or bone. Particles of bone may be noted during X-ray examination two to six weeks after the injury. If the injury is to a muscle belly, complete absorption or a decrease in the size of the formation may occur. This decrease is less likely, however, if calcification is at a muscle origin or insertion. In terms of bone attachment, some formations are completely free of the femur, some are stalklike, and some are broadly attached (see Figure 21-8).

Improper care of a thigh contusion can also lead to myositis ossificans. The following can initially cause the condition or, once present, can aggravate it, causing it to become more pronounced:

- Attempts to "run off" a quadriceps contusion
- Too-vigorous treatment of a contusion—for example, massage directly over the contusion, ultrasound therapy, or superficial heat to the thigh

Symptoms and signs   The athlete complains of pain, muscle weakness, soreness, swelling, and decreased muscle function. On examination there is tissue tension and point tenderness along with a decreased ROM.

Management   Once myositis ossificans is apparent, treatment should be extremely conservative. If the condition is painful and restricts motion, the formation may be surgically removed after one year with much less likelihood of its return. Too-early removal of the formation may cause it to return. Recurrent myositis ossificans may indicate a blood-clotting problem such as hemophilia, which is a rare condition.

After sustaining an initial contusion to the anterior thigh, the athlete should wear a protective pad constructed to disperse the forces of subsequent impacts away from the contused area. This padding may prevent the development of myositis ossificans.

Myositis ossificans can occur from:
- A single severe blow
- Many blows to a muscle area
- Improper care of a contusion

21-1

Critical Thinking Exercise

A basketball player performing a layup shot receives a sharp blow to the right quadriceps muscle.

? How may the grade of this contusion be determined?

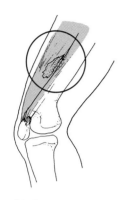

Figure 21-8

Myositis ossificans.

In order of incidence of sports injury to the thigh, quadriceps contusions rank first and hamstring strains rank second.

Quadriceps Muscle Strain

Quadriceps tendon strain is discussed in the section on jumper's knee in Chapter 20.

Etiology On occasion, the rectus femoris muscle will become strained by a sudden stretch, such as when an athlete falls on a bent knee, or a sudden contraction, such as when an athlete jumps in volleyball or kicks in soccer. Usually the strain is associated with a muscle that is weakened or one that is overly constricted.

A tear in the region of the rectus femoris muscle may cause partial or complete disruption of muscle fibers (Figure 21-9). The incomplete tear may be located centrally within the muscle or more peripheral to the muscle.

Symptoms and signs A peripheral quadriceps femoris muscle tear causes fewer symptoms than the deeper tear. In general, there is less point tenderness and a smaller hematoma. A more centrally located partial muscle tear causes the athlete more pain and discomfort than the peripheral tear does. With the deep tear there is a great deal of pain, point tenderness, spasm, and loss of function but little discoloration from internal bleeding. In contrast, complete muscle tear of the rectus femoris muscle may leave the athlete with little disability and discomfort but with some deformity of the anterior thigh.

Management Initially, RICE, NSAIDs, and analgesics are given as needed. The extent of the tear should be ascertained as soon as possible before swelling. Swelling can mask the grade of injury. Crutches may be warranted for the first, second, and third days. After the acute inflammatory phase has progressed to resolution and healing has begun, a regimen of isometric muscle contraction, within pain-free limits, can be initiated along with cryotherapy. Other therapy approaches such as cold whirlpool and ultrasound may also be used. Gentle stretching should not be started until the thigh is pain free. A neoprene or elastic sleeve may be worn for support (Figure 21-10).

Hamstring Strains

Hamstring strains are the second most prevalent sports injury to the thigh. Athletes suffer more strains to the hamstrings than to any other thigh muscle.

Etiology The exact cause of hamstring strain is not known. One theory is that the short head of the biceps femoris muscle is subject to the highest incidence of hamstring strain because, as a result of an idiosyncracy of nerve innervation, it contracts at the same time that the quadriceps muscle does. Another speculation is that a quick change of the hamstring muscle from the role of knee stabilization to that of

Figure 21-9

Rupture of the rectus femoris.

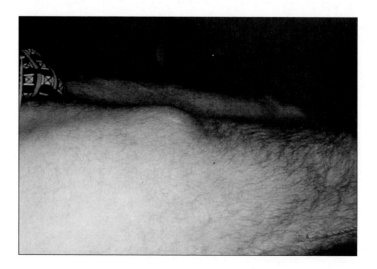

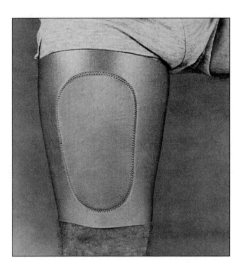

Figure 21-10

A neoprene sleeve may be worn for soft-tissue support.

extending the hip when running could be a major cause of strain (Figure 21-11). What leads to this muscle failure and deficiency in the complementary action of opposing muscles is not clearly understood. Possible reasons include muscle fatigue, faulty posture, leg-length discrepancy, tight hamstrings, improper form, adverse neural tension,[21] or an imbalance of strength between hamstring muscle groups. NOTE: Hamstring muscles function as decelerators of leg swing and commonly become injured when an athlete suddenly changes direction or starts to slow. In most athletes, the hamstring muscle group should have a strength 60 percent to 70 percent of that of the quadriceps group.[4]

Symptoms and signs   Hamstring strain can involve the muscle belly or bony attachment. The extent of injury can vary from the pulling apart of a few muscle fibers to a complete rupture or an avulsion fracture (Figure 21-12).[3]

Capillary hemorrhage, pain, and immediate loss of function vary according to the degree of trauma. Discoloration may occur a day or two after injury.

Figure 21-11

There is a high incidence of hamstring strain in hurdling and sprinting.

Figure 21-12

Hamstring tear.

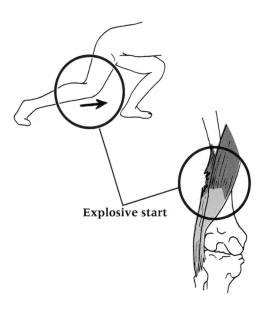

Explosive start

Grade 1 hamstring strain usually is evidenced by muscle soreness during movement, accompanied by point tenderness. These strains are often difficult to detect when they first occur. Not until the athlete has cooled down after activity do irritation and stiffness become apparent. The soreness of the mild hamstring strain in most instances can be attributed to muscle spasm rather than to the tearing of tissue. Fewer than 20 percent of fibers are torn in a grade 1 hamstring strain.

A grade 2 hamstring strain represents a partial tearing of muscle fibers, identified by a sudden snap or tear of the muscle accompanied by severe pain and a loss of function during knee flexion. Fewer than 70 percent of fibers are torn in a grade 2 hamstring tear.

A grade 3 hamstring strain constitutes the rupturing of tendinous or muscular tissue, involving major hemorrhage and disability. With more than 70 percent of fibers torn, there is severe edema, tenderness, loss of function, ecchymosis, and a palpable mass or palpable gap in the muscle.[16]

Management   Initially, RICE, NSAIDs, and analgesics are given as needed. Activity should be reduced until soreness has been completely alleviated. An athlete with a grade 1 hamstring strain, as with the other grades of strain, should not be allowed to resume full sports participation until complete function of the injured part is restored.

Grade 2 and 3 strains should be treated extremely conservatively. For grade 2 strains, RICE should be used for twenty-four to forty-eight hours, and for grade 3 strains, for forty-eight to seventy-two hours. After the early inflammatory phase of injury has stabilized, a treatment regimen of isometric exercise, cryotherapy, and ultrasound may be of benefit. In later stages of healing, gentle stretching within pain limits, jogging, stationary cycling, and isokinetic exercise at high speeds may be used. After elimination of soreness, the athlete may begin isotonic knee curls. Full recovery may take from one month to a full season.

Strains are always a problem to the athlete because they tend to recur as a result of the inelastic, fibrous scar tissue that sometimes forms during the healing process. The higher the incidence of strains at a particular muscle site, the greater the amount of scar tissue and the greater the likelihood of further injury will be. The fear of another pulled muscle becomes, to some individuals, almost a neurotic obsession, which is often more handicapping than the injury itself.

21-2

Critical Thinking Exercise

A sprinter competing in a 100-yard dash experiences a sudden snap, severe pain, and weakness in the left hamstring muscle. Examination reveals a grade 2 strain.

? In terms of exercise, how should this injury be managed?

TABLE 21-2 Management of Muscle-Tendon Injuries of the Hip, Groin, and Pelvis

	Stage of Healing		
Management	Phase I Acute, 1 to 72 hr	Phase II Healing and Repair	Phase III Maturation and Remodeling
Ice	X		
Compression	X		
Elevation	X		
Rest	X		
Nonsteroidal antiin- flammatory medica- tion	X		
Contrast baths		X	
Whirlpool hydro- therapy		X	
Active range of motion		X	X
Ultrasound		X	X
Muscle stimulation		X	X
Isometric exercise		X	X
Isokinetic/isotonic exercise			X
Stretching			X
Aerobic exercise			X
Proprioceptive activities			X
Agility training			X
Sport-specific activities			X
Jogging			X
Straight-ahead sprint			X
Return to sport			X
Strength and flexibility maintenance			X

Muscle rehabilitation after injury should emphasize eccentric exercise (Table 21-2).

Acute Femoral Fractures

Etiology In sports, fractures of the femur occur most often in the shaft rather than at the bone ends and are almost always caused by a great force such as falling from a height or being hit directly by another participant. A fracture of the shaft most often takes place in the middle third of the bone because of the anatomical curve at this point as well as because the majority of direct blows are sustained in this area.[13]

Symptoms and signs The athlete complains of pain over the fracture site. There is severe pain if weight bearing is attempted. On examination there is swelling and bone movement causing crepitus. Deformity of the thigh may be apparent.

Management Initially, the athlete is treated for shock. Neurovascular status is verified and a splint applied before the athlete is moved. The X-ray examination that verifies the fracture is followed by reduction and the application of a cast. Analgesics and NSAIDs are given as needed. Shock generally accompanies a fracture of the femur. Bone displacement is usually present as a result of the strength of the quadriceps muscle, which causes overriding of the bone fragments. Direct violence produces extensive soft-tissue injury, with lacerations of the vastus intermedius muscle, hemorrhaging, and major muscle spasms.[19]

Femoral Stress Fracture

Etiology   Femoral overuse fractures represent 10 percent to 25 percent of all stress fractures.[16] A stress fracture often stems from excessive downhill or mountain running or in jumping activities. A compression fracture occurs horizontal to the trabeculae, which are small pieces of spongy, bony substances that are usually interconnected with other, similar pieces. In a distraction fracture, the fracture line occurs perpendicular to the trabeculae of the femoral neck.[15] Stress fractures of the femur are being diagnosed more often than in the past.

Symptoms and signs   The athlete complains of a persistent pain in the thigh. An X ray or bone scan reveals the stress fracture. The most common site is in the area of the femoral neck.

Management   Analgesics, RICE, and NSAIDs are given as needed. Range-of-motion exercises and PRE are carried out within pain-free limits. For incomplete fractures, rest and limited weight bearing constitute the usual treatment of choice.[6,11] Complete stress fractures may have to be surgically pinned.

ANATOMY OF THE HIP, GROIN, AND PELVIC REGION

Normal function of the hip and pelvis is necessary for sports performance. Normal body movement is highly important for sports that predominantly use the lower extremities or the upper extremities. It must be remembered that the hip and pelvis are part of the kinetic chain that transmits a load from the foot to the spine and vice versa in all three planes of movement.[20]

Bones

The pelvis is a bony ring formed by the two innominate bones, the sacrum and the coccyx (Figure 21-13). Each innominate bone is composed of an ilium, ischium, and pubis. The functions of the pelvis are to support the spine and trunk and to transfer their weight to the lower limbs. In addition to providing skeletal support, the pelvis serves as a place of attachment for the trunk and thigh muscles and as protection for the pelvic viscera. The basin formed by the pelvis is separated into a false and a true pelvis. The false pelvis is composed of the wings of the ilium. The true pelvis is composed of the coccyx, the ischium, and the pubis.

Femoral stress fractures are becoming more prevalent because of the increased popularity of repetitive, sustained activities such as distance running.

Figure 21-13

Pelvis.

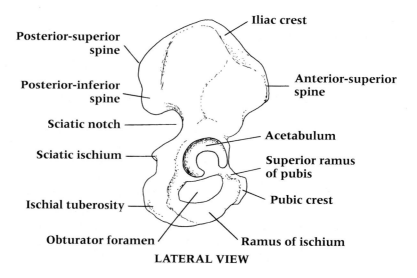

LATERAL VIEW

The innominate bones are three bones that ossify and fuse early in life. They include the ilium, which is positioned superiorly and posteriorly; the pubis, which forms the anterior part; and the ischium, which is located inferiorly. Lodged between the innominate bones is the wedge-shaped sacrum, composed of five fused vertebrae.

Articulations

Sacroiliac Joint and Coccyx

The sacrum is joined to other parts of the pelvis by strong ligaments, forming the sacroiliac joint. A small backward-forward movement is present at the sacroiliac junction. The coccyx is composed of four or five small fused vertebral bodies that articulate with the sacrum. The sacroiliac joint is discussed in detail in Chapter 25.

Hip Joint

The hip joint is formed by articulation of the femur with the innominate, or hip, bone. The articulating, spherical head of the femur fits into a deep socket in the innominate bone called the acetabulum, which is padded at its center by a mass of fatty tissue, ligaments, and capsule. The acetabulum forms an incomplete bony ring that is interrupted by a notch on the lower aspect of the socket. The ring is completed by the transverse ligament that crosses the notch. The socket faces forward, downward, and laterally. The femoral head is a sphere that fits into the acetabulum in a medial, upward, and slightly forward direction.

Ligaments, Joint Capsule, and Synovial Membrane

Surrounding its rim is a fibrocartilage known as the glenoid labrum. A loose sleeve of articular tissue is attached to the circumference of the acetabulum above and to the neck of the femur below. The capsule is lined by an extensive synovial membrane, and the iliofemoral, pubocapsular, and ischiocapsular ligaments give it strong reinforcement. Hyaline cartilage completely covers the head of the femur, with the exception of the fovea capitis, a small area in the center to which the ligamentum teres is attached. The ligamentum teres gives little support to the hip joint; its main function is the transport of nutrient vessels to the head of the femur. Because of its bony, ligamentous, and muscular arrangements, this joint is considered by many to be the strongest articulation in the body.

The synovial membrane is a vascular tissue enclosing the hip joint in a tubular sleeve, with the upper portion surrounding the acetabulum. The lower portion is fastened to the circumference of the neck of the femur. Except for the ligamentum teres, which lies outside the synovial cavity, the membrane lines the acetabular socket.

The articular capsule is a fibrous, sleevelike structure covering the synovial membrane; its upper end attaches to the cartilaginous labrum and its lower end to the neck of the femur. The circular fibers that surround the femoral neck serve as a tight collar. This area is called the zona orbicularis, and it holds the femoral head in the acetabulum. Many strong ligaments—the iliofemoral, the pubofemoral, and the ischiofemoral—reinforce the hip joint (Figure 21-14).

The iliofemoral ligament (Y ligament of Bigelow) is the strongest ligament of the body. It prevents hyperextension, controls external rotation and adduction of the thigh, and limits the pelvis during any backward rolling of the femoral head during weight bearing. It reinforces the anterior aspect of the capsule and is attached to the anterior iliac spine and the intertrochanteric line on the anterior aspect of the femur.

The pubofemoral ligament prevents excessive abduction of the thigh and is positioned anterior and inferior to the pelvis and femur.

The ischiofemoral ligament prevents excessive internal rotation and adduction of the thigh and is located posterior and superior to the articular capsule.

Figure 21-14

Ligaments of the hip.

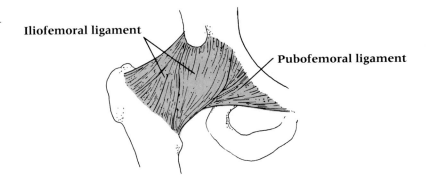

Hip Musculature

The muscles of the hip can be divided into anterior and posterior groups. The anterior group includes the iliacus and psoas muscles. The posterior group's muscles include the tensor fasciae latae, gluteus maximus, gluteus medius, gluteus minimus, and the six deep outward rotators—the piriformis, superior gemellus, inferior gemellus, obturator internus, obturator externus, and quadratus femoris.

Anterior Hip Muscles

The iliacus and psoas muscles are the anterior hip muscles. The triangular-shaped iliacus is contained within the iliac fossa within the abdomen. Its tendon merges with the psoas major muscles, forming a common tendon that is called the iliopsoas. The iliopsoas attaches on the iliac fossa and part of the inner surface of the sacrum proximally, and it attaches distally on the lesser trochanter of the femur. The psoas muscle attaches proximally on the transverse processes and bodies of the lumbar vertebrae. Its distal attachment is on the lesser trochanter. The iliopsoas muscle flexes the thigh at the hip joint and tends to rotate the thigh outwardly and to adduct the thigh when free to move. When fixed, the iliopsoas assists in flexing the trunk and hip.

Posterior Hip Muscles

The posterior muscles of the hip consist of the tensor fasciae latae, the three gluteal muscles, and the six deep outward rotators.

The tensor fasciae latae muscle is located on the upper anterior aspect of the lateral thigh (Figure 21-15). It is attached superiorly to the iliac crest just behind the anterior superior iliac spine and is inserted inferiorly into the iliotibial tract. Its primary action is flexion and medial rotation of the thigh. It is innervated by the superior gluteal nerve.

The gluteus maximus muscle forms the buttocks in the hip region. Lateral to and underneath the gluteus maximus are the gluteus medius and the gluteus minimus muscles (Figure 21-16). The gluteus maximus muscle is attached above to the posterior aspect of the iliac crest, the sacrum, and the coccyx as well as to the fascia in the area. Inferiorly, this muscle attaches to the iliotibial tract and into the gluteal tuberosity of the femur between the linea aspera and greater trochanter. The gluteus maximus muscle acts as a lateral rotator of the thigh at the hip joint and allows the body to rise from a sitting to a standing position. Through its attachment to the iliotibial tract, the muscle helps extend the flexed knee. The inferior gluteal nerve supplies this muscle. The gluteus medius muscle is located lateral to the hip. It is attached superiorly to the lateral aspect of the ilium and inferiorly to the lateral aspect of the trochanter. The gluteus maximus muscle covers this muscle posteriorly, and it is covered anteriorly by the tensor fasciae latae. The gluteus medius muscle acts primarily as a thigh abductor at the hip, with some flexion and medial rotation occurring from its anterior aspect and some extension and lateral rotation occurring from

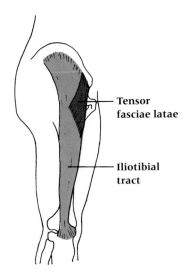

Figure 21-15

Tensor fasciae latae.

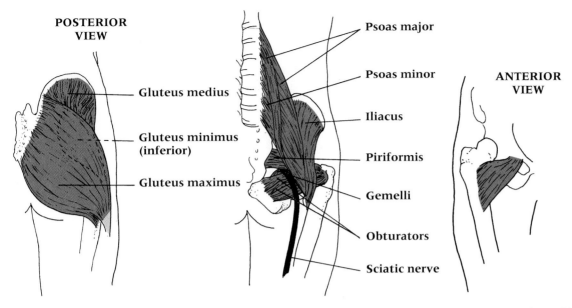

Figure 21-16

Hip muscles.

its posterior aspect. It is innervated by the superior gluteal nerve. The gluteus minimus muscle originates above the lateral aspect of the ilium and attaches inferiorly to the anterior aspect of the greater trochanter of the femur. Its main action is to cause medial rotation at the hip joint; its secondary action is abduction of the thigh at the hip joint. It is innervated by the superior gluteus nerve.

Underneath these larger muscles are much smaller muscles that, along with the gluteus maximus, laterally rotate the hip: the piriformis, the quadratus femoris, the obturator internus and externus, and the gemellus superior and inferior (Figure 21-17). Collectively, they stabilize the head of the femur in the acetabulum.

Bursae

The hip joint has many bursae. Clinically, the most important of them are the iliopsoas bursa and the deep trochanteric bursa. The iliopsoas bursa is located between the articular capsule and the iliopsoas muscle on the anterior aspect of the joint. The deep trochanteric bursa lies between the greater trochanter and the deep fibers of the gluteus maximus muscle.

Figure 21-17

The six deep, outward rotators of the hip.

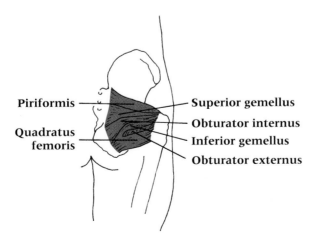

Figure 21-18

Blood and nerve supply to the hip region.

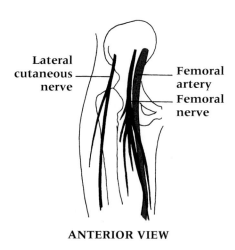

Figure 21-18

Blood and nerve supply to the hip region.

Nerve Supply

The lumbar plexus is created by the intertwining of the fibers stemming from the first four lumbar nerves. The femoral nerve, a major nerve emerging from this plexus, later divides into many branches to supply the thigh and lower leg. Nerve fibers from the fourth and fifth lumbar nerves and the first, second, and third sacral nerves form the sacral plexus within the pelvic cavity, anterior to the piriformis muscle. Along with other nerves, the tibial and common peroneal nerves emerge from the sacral plexus and form the large sciatic nerve in the thigh (see Figure 21-18).

Blood Supply

Arteries

Opposite the fourth lumbar vertebra, the aorta divides to become the two common iliac arteries (Figure 21-18). They in turn pass downward to divide, opposite the sacroiliac joint, into the internal and external iliac arteries. Most of the branches of the internal iliac artery supply blood to the pelvic viscera. The external iliac artery is the primary artery to the lower limb.

Veins

Three major veins are found in the region of hips, groin, and pelvis. The first is the common iliac vein, which stems from the inferior vena cava on both sides draining the lower body. The second is the internal iliac vein, which ascends behind its iliac artery to the brim of the true pelvis, where it joins the external vein to form the common iliac vein. Its tributaries drain the pelvis and adjoining area. Third is the external iliac vein, which passes upward from the femoral vein behind the inguinal ligament and follows the brim of the true pelvis, where it joins the internal iliac vein.

FUNCTIONAL ANATOMY OF THE HIP, GROIN, AND PELVIC REGION

The hip joint is a ball-and-socket joint that has maximum stability because of deep insertion into the acetabulum. The acetabulum faces outward, forward, and downward. The capsular pattern of the hip is flexion, abduction, and medial rotation. The forces involved in the hip are as follows: standing—one third of the body weight; standing on one foot—2.4 to 2.6 times the body weight; walking—1.3 to 5.8 times the body weight; and running—4.5 times the body weight.[17]

The sacroiliac joints and symphysis pubis do not have direct control of their own movements. They are influenced by the same muscles that influence the lumbar spine and hip. Many of these muscles attach to the sacrum and pelvis. Movement occurring in the sacroiliac and symphysis pubis joints is slight when compared with the hip and spinal joints.[16]

ASSESSMENT OF THE HIP AND PELVIS

The hip and pelvis form the body's major power source for movement. The body's center of gravity is located just in front of the upper part of the sacrum. Injuries to the hip or pelvis cause the athlete major disability in the lower limb, trunk, or both.

Because of the close proximity of the hip and pelvis to the low back region, many evaluative procedures overlap.

History

The following information is determined:
- What are the athlete's symptoms (e.g., weakness, disability, pain)?
- When did the athlete first notice a problem with the hip or pelvis?
- Describe types of pain (hip pain is felt mainly in the groin and medial or frontal side of thigh; hip pain may also be referred to the knee).
- Describe the sacroiliac pain; does it radiate in the posterior thigh, iliac fossa, or buttock on the affected side?
- When does the pain occur (e.g., during activity, while turning in bed)?
- Age and gender of the athlete (e.g., boys three to twelve years old can have Legg-Calvé-Perthes disease; distance-running amenorrheic girls may develop a hip stress fracture).

Observation

The athlete should be observed for postural asymmetry and while standing on one leg and during ambulation.

> The athlete with an external pelvic pain must be observed for postural asymmetry.

Postural Asymmetry

From the front view, do the hips look even? A laterally tilted hip could mean a leg-length discrepancy or abnormal muscle contraction on one side of the hip or low back region.
- From the side view, is the pelvis abnormally tilted anteriorly or posteriorly? This tilting may indicate lordosis or flat back, respectively.
- In lower-limb alignment, is there indication of genu valgum, genu varum, foot pronation, or genu recurvatum? The patella should also be noted for relative position and alignment.
- The posterior superior iliac spines, represented by the skin depressions above the buttocks, should be horizontal to one another. Uneven depressions could indicate that the pelvis is laterally tilted.

Standing on One Leg

Standing on one leg may produce pain in the hip, abnormal movement of the symphysis pubis, or a fall of the pelvis on the opposite side as a result of abductor weakness.

Ambulation

The athlete should be observed during walking and sitting. Pain in the hip and pelvic region will normally be reflected in movement distortions.

Palpation

The following bony landmarks should be palpated:

Bony Palpation

- Iliac crest
- Greater trochanter
- Anterior superior iliac spine
- Femoral neck
- Anterior inferior iliac spine
- Lesser trochanter

- Pubic symphysis
- Ischial tuberosity
- Posterior inferior iliac spine
- Posterior superior iliac spine

Soft-Tissue Palpation

The soft-tissue sites of major concern are in the regions of the groin, femoral triangle, sciatic nerve, and major muscles. Groin pain could result from swollen lymph glands, indicating an infection, or from an adductor muscle strain.

The following soft tissue structures should be palpated:

Anterior
- Rectus femoris
- Sartorius
- Iliopsoas
- Inguinal ligament

Medial
- Gracilis
- Adductor magnus
- Adductor longus
- Adductor brevis
- Pectineus

Posterior
- Gluteus maximus
- Piriformis
- Hamstrings

Lateral
- Gluteus medius
- Gluteus minimus
- Tensor fasciae latae
- Iliotibial band

Special Tests

Functional Evaluation

The athlete is led through all possible hip movements, both passive and active, to evaluate range of motion and active and resistive strength (Figure 21-19). These movements are as follows: hip abduction, hip adduction, hip flexion, hip extension, and internal and external hip rotation.

Tests for Hip Flexor Tightness

Contractures of the hip flexors are major causes of lordosis and susceptibility to groin pain and discomfort. Two tests can be used: the Kendall test and the Thomas test.

Kendall test   The athlete lies supine on a table with one knee flexed on the chest and the back completely flat (Figure 21-20). The other knee is flexed over the table's end. Normal extensibility of the hip flexors allows the thigh to touch the table with the knee flexed approximately 70 degrees. Tight hip flexors are revealed by the inability of the thigh to lie flat on the table. If only the rectus femoris muscle is tight, the thigh will touch the table, but the knee will extend more than 70 degrees (Figure 21-21).

Thomas test   The Thomas test indicates whether hip contractures are present (Figure 21-22). The athlete lies supine on a table, arms across the chest, legs together and fully extended. The athletic trainer places one hand under the athlete's lumbar curve; one thigh is brought to the chest, flattening the spine. In this position, the extended thigh should be flat on the table. If not, there is a hip contracture. When the athlete fully extends the leg again, the curve in the low back returns.

21-3

Critical Thinking E x e r c i s e

A gymnast has a history of moderate groin pain. She is susceptible to strains in that region. The athlete also appears to have an exaggerated lumbar lordotic curve.

? What tests should be given to evaluate the tightness of the groin region?

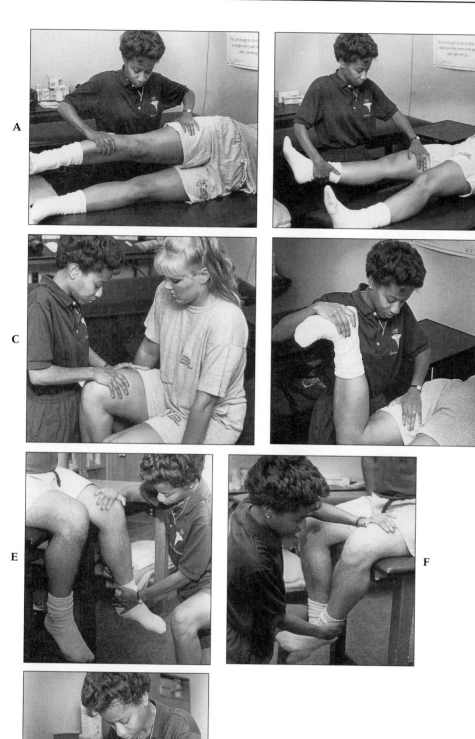

Figure 21-19

Manual muscle tests of the hip.
A, Abduction. **B,** Adduction.
C, Flexion (iliopsoas muscle).
D, Extension. **E,** Internal
rotation. **F,** External rotation.
G, Knee extension to isolate
the rectus femoris.

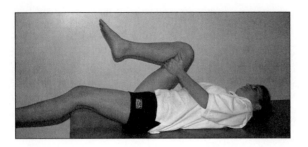

Figure 21-20

Kendall test for hip flexor tightness.

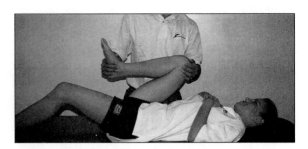

Figure 21-21

Demonstrating tight hip flexors.

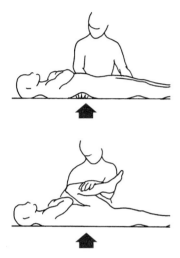

Figure 21-22

Thomas test for hip contractures.

Femoral Anteversion and Retroversion

The athlete with a painful hip problem may also have a discrepancy in the relationship between the neck of the femur and the shaft of the femur. The normal angle of the femoral neck is 15 degrees anterior to the long axis of the shaft of the femur and femoral condyles. Athletes who walk in a toe-in manner may be reflecting a hip deformity in which the femoral neck is directed anteriorly (femoral anteversion). In contrast, athletes who walk in a pronounced toe-out manner may be displaying a condition in which the femoral neck is directed posteriorly (femoral retroversion) (Figure 21-23). Internal hip rotation in excess of 35 degrees is characteristic of femoral anteversion, and an excess of the normal 45 degrees of external rotation is characteristic of femoral retroversion.

Test for the Hip and Sacroiliac Joint

Patrick test (FABER)   The Patrick test, or FABER test (flexion, abduction, external rotation of the hip), detects pathological conditions of the hip and sacroiliac joint (Figure 21-24). The athlete lies supine on the examining table. The foot on the side of the painful sacroiliac is placed on the opposite extended knee. Pressure is then applied downward on the bent knee. Pain may be felt in the hip or sacroiliac joint.

Gaenslen's test   In a supine position, with the affected side on the edge of the table, the unaffected thigh is flexed toward the abdomen. Pressure is applied to the knee on the affected side, moving the sacroiliac joint into extension. The test is positive if hyperextension on the affected side increases pain (Figure 21-25)

Figure 21-23

A, Anteversion of the femoral neck. When the knee is directed anteriorly, the femoral neck is directed anteriorly to some degree. **B,** Retroversion of the femoral neck. When the knee is directed posteriorly, the femoral neck is directed posteriorly to some degree.

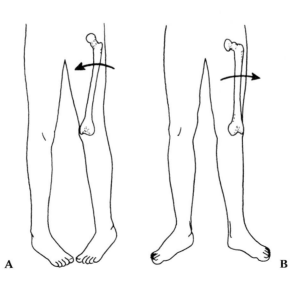

A   B

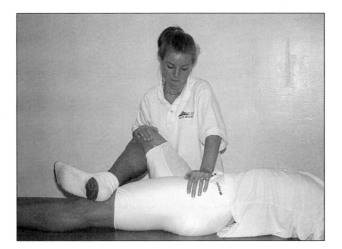

Figure 21-24

The Patrick test for a pathological condition of the hip and sacroiliac joint.

Testing the Tensor Fasciae Latae and Iliotibial Band

Three tests that can be used to discern iliotibial band tightness and inflammation of the bursa overlying the lateral femoral epicondyle or direct irritation of the iliotibial band and periosteum are Renne's test, Nobel's test, and Ober's test.[2]

Renne's test   The athlete stands and supports full weight on the affected leg with the knee bent at 30 degrees to 40 degrees. A positive response of fasciae latae tightness occurs when pain is felt at the lateral femoral condyle.

Nobel's test   Lying supine, the athlete's knee is flexed to 90 degrees, and pressure is applied to the lateral femoral epicondyle while the knee is gradually extended. A positive response occurs when severe pain is felt at the lateral femoral epicondyle with the knee at 30 degrees of flexion.

Ober's test   The athlete lies on the unaffected side. With the knee flexed at 90 degrees, the affected thigh is abducted as far as possible. With the pelvis stabilized, the abducted thigh is then relaxed and allowed to drop into adduction. A contracted tensor fasciae latae or iliotibial band will keep the thigh in an abducted position, not allowing it to fall into adduction (Figure 21-26).

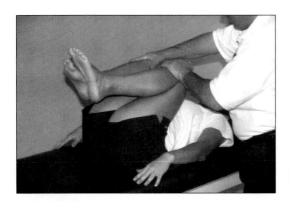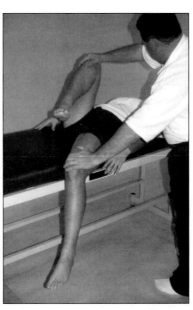

Figure 21-25

Gaenslen's test.

Figure 21-26

Ober's test for iliotibial band tightness.

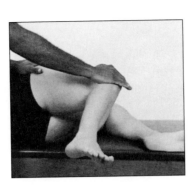

Figure 21-27

Trendelenburg's test.

Trendelenburg's Test

While the athlete stands, the foot on the unaffected side is lifted so that the hip flexes. Normally in this position, the iliac crest on the unaffected side will be higher than on the affected side. If the iliac crest on the affected side is higher than on the unaffected side, the test is positive, indicating weakness in the hip abductors, particularly the gluteus medius (Figure 21-27).

Piriformis Test

The athlete lies on the unaffected side with the affected leg in 60 degrees of hip flexion and the knee relaxed. The pelvis is stabilized and pressure is applied downward on the knee, rotating the hip internally. Tightness or pain is indicative of piriformis tightness.

Ely's Test

While the athlete lies in a prone position, the pelvis is stabilized and the knee on the affected side is flexed. If the hip on that side extends as the knee is flexed, there is tightness of the rectus femoris (Figure 21-28).

Measuring Leg-Length Discrepancy

In individuals who are not physically active, leg-length discrepancies of more than one inch may produce symptoms; however, shortening of as little as 3 mm ($1/8$ inch) may cause symptoms in highly active athletes. Such discrepancies can cause cumulative stresses to the lower limbs, hip, and pelvis, or low back.

There are two types of leg-length discrepancy: true, or anatomical, shortening and apparent, or functional, shortening. X-ray examination is the most valid means of measurement. It is difficult to be completely accurate because of mobility of the soft tissue over bony landmarks (Figure 21-29A).

Anatomical discrepancy   In an anatomical discrepancy, shortening may be equal throughout the lower limb or localized within the femur or lower leg. The athlete lies supine and fully extended on the table. Measurement is taken between the lateral malleoli and the anterior superior iliac spine of each leg (Figure 21-29B).

Figure 21-28

Ely's test.

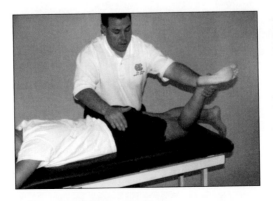

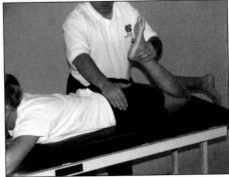

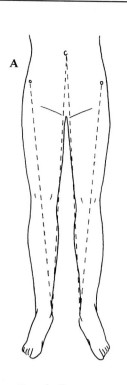

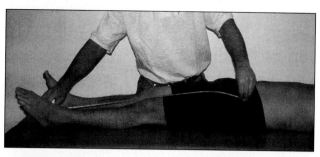

Figure 21-29

A, Measuring for leg-length discrepancy. **B,** Anatomical discrepancy. **C,** Functional discrepancy.

Functional discrepancy Functional leg shortening can occur as the result of lateral pelvic tilt (obliquely) or from a flexion or adduction deformity. Measurement is taken from the umbilicus to the medial malleoli of each ankle (Figure 21-29C).

RECOGNITION AND MANAGEMENT OF SPECIFIC HIP, GROIN, AND PELVIC INJURIES

Hip Joint

Groin Strain

Etiology The groin is the depression that lies between the thigh and the abdominal region. The musculature of this area includes the iliopsoas, the rectus femoris, and the adductor group (the gracilis, pectineus, adductor brevis, adductor longus, and adductor magnus). Groin pain is one of the more difficult problems to diagnosis, especially if chronic in nature.[1]

Any one of the muscles in the region of the groin can be torn during sports activity and elicit what is commonly considered a groin strain (Figure 21-30). The adductor longus muscle is most often strained.[8] Running, jumping, or twisting with external rotation can produce such injuries.

Symptoms and signs The groin strain is one of the most difficult injuries to care for in sports. The strain can be felt as a sudden twinge or feeling of tearing during an active movement, or the athlete may not notice it until after termination of activity.[8] Like most tears, the groin strain produces pain, weakness, and internal hemorrhage.

Management If it is detected immediately after it occurs, the strain should be treated by RICE, NSAIDs, and analgesics as needed for forty-eight to seventy-two hours. Passive, active, and resistive muscle tests should be given to ascertain the exact muscle or muscles that are involved.

The athletic trainer frequently encounters difficulty when attempting to care for a groin strain. Rest has been the best treatment. Daily whirlpool therapy or cryotherapy are palliative; ultrasound offers a more definite approach. Exercise should be delayed until the groin is pain free. Exercise rehabilitation should emphasize gradual stretching and restoration of the normal range of motion. Until normal flexibility and strength are developed, a protective spica bandage or a commercial brace should be applied (Figure 21-31).

Leg-length discrepancy in an athlete can lead to stress-related physical injuries.

Acute Groin Strain

Injury Situation A female varsity basketball player had a history of tightness in her groin. During a game she suddenly rotated her trunk while also stretching to the right side. The athlete experienced a sudden, sharp pain and a sense of "giving way" in the left side of the groin that caused her to immediately stop play and limp to the sidelines.

Symptoms and Signs As the athlete described it to the athletic trainer, there was severe pain when rotating her trunk to the right and flexing her left hip. Inspection revealed the following:
1. There was major point tenderness in the groin, especially in the region of the adductor magnus muscle.
2. There was no pain during passive movement of the hip, but severe pain did occur during both active and resistive motion.
3. When the groin and hip were tested for injury, the hip joint, illiopsoas, and rectus femoris muscles were ruled out as having been injured; however, when the athlete adducted the hip from a stretch position, it caused her extreme discomfort.

Management Plan Based on the athletic trainer's inspection, with findings confirmed by the physician, it was determined that the athlete had sustained a grade 2 strain of the groin, particularly to the adductor magnus muscle.

Phase 1 *Acute Injury* **GOALS:** To stop hemorrhage, reduce pain, and stop muscle spasms.
ESTIMATED LENGTH OF TIME (ELT): 2 to 3 days.

■ **Therapy** Careful physical examination plus MRI to rule out conditions other than a strain. IMMEDIATE CARE: RICE (20 min) intermittently, 6 to 8 times daily. When weight bearing, the athlete wears a 6-inch elastic hip spica.

■ **Exercise rehabilitation** No exercise—as complete rest as possible.

Phase 2 *Repair* **GOALS:** To reduce pain, control spasm, and restore full ability to contract and stretch the adductor longus muscle. Maintain cardiorespiratory fitness.
ELT: 2 to 3 weeks.

■ **Therapy** Ice massage (1 min) 3 to 4 times daily followed by hip ROM movements. Muscle electrical stimulation using the surge current at 7 or 8, depending on athlete's tolerance, together with ultrasound, set at 1 W/cm² (7 min), once daily. Cold therapy in the form of ice massage (7 min) or ice packs (10–15 min) followed by exercise, 2 to 3 times daily.

■ **Exercise rehabilitation** Proprioceptive neuromuscular facilitation hip patterns 2 to 3 times daily after cold application, progressing to PRE using pulley, isokinetic, or free weights (10 repetitions, 3 sets) once daily. Jogging in chest-level water (10 to 20 min) 1 or 2 times daily for first exercise rehabilitation week followed by flutter kick swimming (pain free) once daily during subsequent weeks. General body maintenance exercises are conducted 3 times a week as long as they do not aggravate the injury.

Phase 3 *Remodeling* **GOALS:** To restore full power, endurance, and muscle extensibility. The athlete gradually returns to precompetition exercise and finally competition, wearing a groin restraint.
ELT: 3 to 6 weeks.

■ **Therapy** If symptom free, precede exercise with ice massage (7 min) or ice pack (5 to 15 min).

Continued

Acute Groin Strain—*cont'd*

■ **Exercise rehabilitation** Engage in ROM exercise and PRE. Begin a program of jogging on flat course, slowly progressing to a 3-mile run once daily and then progressing to figure-eights, starting with obstacles 10 feet apart and gradually shortening distance to 5 feet, from one-half speed to full speed.

Criteria for Return to Competitive Basketball

1. As measured by an isokinetic dynamometer, the athlete's injured hip should have strength equal to that of the uninjured hip.
2. Hip has full range of motion.
3. The athlete is able to run figure-eights around obstacles set 5 feet apart at full speed.

Trochanteric Bursitis

Etiology Trochanteric bursitis is a relatively common condition of the greater trochanter of the femur (Figure 21-32). Although commonly called bursitis, the condition also could be an inflammation at the site where the gluteus medius muscle inserts or the iliotibial band passes over the trochanter.

Symptoms and signs The athlete complains of pain in the lateral hip. Pain may radiate down to the knee, causing a limp. Palpation reveals tenderness over the lateral aspect of the greater trochanter. Tests for tensor fasciae latae and iliotibial tightness should be carried out.

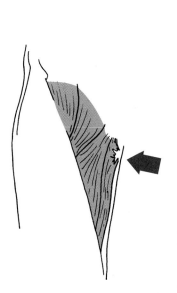

Figure 21-30

Many sports that require severe stretch of the hip region can cause a groin strain.

Figure 21-31

Commercial restraints such as the Sawa groin and thigh braces are increasingly being utilized by athletic trainers.

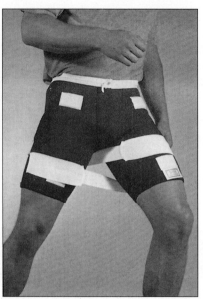

An increased Q angle or leg-length discrepancy can lead to trochanteric bursitis in women runners.

21-4

Critical Thinking Exercise

A gymnast performs a dismount from the rings. Landing off balance, he violently twisted his right hip.

? From the information provided, what type of injury could have been sustained?

Management   Therapy initially includes RICE, NSAIDs, and analgesics as needed. ROM exercises and PRE directed toward hip abductors and external rotators should follow. Phonophoresis may be added if the athlete does not respond in three to four days. The athlete's return to running should be cautious; the athlete should avoid running on inclined surfaces. Faulty running form, leg-length discrepancy, and faulty foot biomechanics must be taken into consideration. The condition is most common among women runners who have an increased Q angle or a leg-length discrepancy.

Sprains of the Hip Joint

Etiology   The hip joint, the strongest and best-protected joint in the human body, is seldom seriously injured during sports activities.[10] The hip joint is substantially supported by the ligamentous tissues and muscles that surround it, so any unusual movement that exceeds the normal range of motion may result in tearing of tissue. Such an injury may occur as the result of a violent twist, produced either via an impact force delivered by another participant, via forceful contact with another object, or via a situation in which the foot is firmly planted and the trunk is forced in an opposing direction.

Symptoms and signs   A hip sprain displays all the signs of a major acute injury but is best revealed through the athlete's inability to circumduct the thigh. Symptoms

Figure 21-32

Tenderness sites in the region of the hip and pelvis.

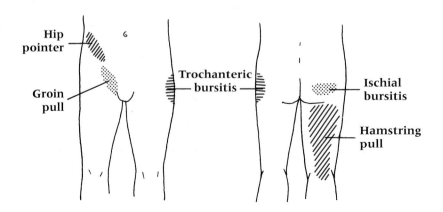

are similar to a stress fracture. There is significant pain in the hip region. Hip rotation increases pain.

Management   X rays or MRIs should be done to rule out fracture; RICE, NSAIDs, and analgesics are given as needed. Depending on the grade of sprain, weight bearing is restricted. Crutch walking is used for grade 2 and 3 sprains. ROM exercises and PRE are delayed until the hip is pain free.

Subluxation—Dislocated Hip Joint

Etiology   Dislocation of the hip joint rarely occurs in sports and then usually only as the end result of traumatic force directed along the long axis of the femur. Such dislocations are produced when the knee is bent. The most common displacement is one posterior to the acetabulum, with the femoral shaft adducted and flexed.

Symptoms and signs   The injury presents a picture of a flexed, adducted, and internally rotated thigh. Palpation will reveal that the head of the femur has moved to a position posterior to the acetabulum. A hip dislocation causes serious pathology by tearing capsular and ligamentous tissue. A fracture is often associated with this injury, accompanied by possible damage to the sciatic nerve.

Management   Medical attention must be secured immediately after displacement, or muscle contractures may complicate the reduction. Immobilization usually consists of two weeks of bed rest and the use of a crutch for walking for a month or longer.

Complications   Complication of the posterior hip dislocation is likely, with such possibilities as a palsy of the sciatic nerve and later the development of osteoarthritis. Hip dislocation also can lead to disruption of the blood supply to the head of the femur, which eventually leads to the degenerative condition known as avascular necrosis.[7]

Hip Joint Problems in the Young Athlete

The athletic trainer working with a child or adolescent should understand three major problems. They are Legg-Calvé-Perthes slipped capital femoral epiphysis, the snapping hip.

Legg-Calvé-Perthes Disease (Coxa Plana)

Etiology   Legg-Calvé-Perthes disease is avascular necrosis of the femoral head (Figure 21-33). It occurs in children ages four to ten and in boys more often than in girls. For the most part this condition is not clearly understood. Trauma accounts for 25 percent of the cases seen.[2] It is listed under the broad heading of osteochondrosis. Because of a disruption of circulation at the head of the femur, articular cartilage becomes necrotic and flattens.[9]

Symptoms and signs   The young athlete commonly complains of pain in the groin that sometimes is referred to the abdomen or knee. Limping is also typical. The condition can have a rapid onset, but more often it comes on slowly over a number of months. Examination may show limited hip movement and pain.

Management   Care of this condition could mean complete bed rest to alleviate synovitis. A special brace to avoid direct weight bearing on the hip may have to be worn. If treated in time, the head of the femur will revascularize and reossify.

Complications   If the condition is not treated early enough, the head of the femur will become ill shaped, creating problems of osteoarthritis in later life.

Slipped Capital Femoral Epiphysis

Etiology   The problem of a slipped capital femoral epiphysis (Figure 21-34) is found mostly in boys between the ages of ten and seventeen who are characteristically tall and thin or obese. Although idiopathic, it may be related to the effects of a growth hormone. One quarter of the cases seen have the condition in both hips. Trauma accounts for 25 percent of the cases seen.[2] X-ray examination may show femoral head slippage posteriorly and inferiorly.

21-5

Critical Thinking Exercise

A field hockey player has been determined to have a Q angle of 22 degrees. Her left leg is ³/₄ inch shorter than her right leg. She complains of pain at the point just over the left greater trochanter when she runs.

? Based on the information provided, what could the condition be?

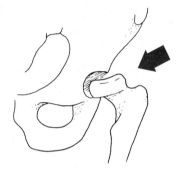

Figure 21-33

Legg-Calvé-Perthes disease (coxa plana). Arrow indicates avascular necrosis of the femoral head.

A young athlete complaining of pain in the groin, abdomen, or knee and walking with a limp may display signs of Legg-Calvé-Perthes disease or a slipped capital femoral epiphysis.

21-6

Critical Thinking Exercise

A fifteen-year-old male football player complains of pain in his hip off and on during the season. There is increasing hip and knee pain during movement. The athlete has a restriction of hip abduction, flexion, and medial rotation. He is beginning to walk with a limp.

? What should the athletic trainer be concerned about in this fifteen-year-old, and what steps should be taken?

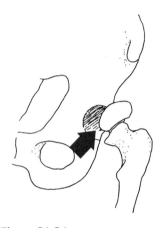

Figure 21-34

Slipped capital femoral epiphysis (arrow).

21-7

Critical Thinking Exercise

A young female gymnast complains to the athletic trainer that her hip snaps when she stands on one leg.

? What is the possible cause of this snapping hip phenomenon?

Symptoms and signs Like Legg-Calvé-Perthes disease, a slipped capital femoral epiphysis causes the athlete pain in the groin that comes on suddenly as a result of trauma or over weeks or months as a result of prolonged stress. In the early stages of this condition, signs may be minimal. In its most advanced stage, however, there is hip and knee pain during passive and active motion; limitations of abduction, flexion, and medial rotation; and a limp.[14]

Management In minor slippage, rest and non–weight bearing may prevent further slipping. Major displacement usually requires corrective surgery.

Complications If the slippage goes undetected or if surgery fails to properly restore normal hip mechanics, severe hip problems may occur in later life.

The Snapping Hip Phenomenon

Etiology The snapping hip phenomenon is common to young female dancers, gymnasts, and hurdlers, who make similar use of their hips. The problem stems from habitual movements that predispose muscles around the hip to become imbalanced.[13] This condition commonly occurs when the individual laterally rotates and flexes the hip joint as part of the exercise or dance routine. This condition is related to a structurally narrow pelvic width, greater range of motion of hip abduction, and less range of motion in lateral rotation. With hip stability becoming lessened, the hip joint capsule and ligaments and adductor muscles become less stable.

Symptoms and signs The athlete complains that snapping occurs, especially when balancing on one leg. Such a problem should not go unattended, especially if pain and inflammation are associated with the snapping.

Management Management should focus on cryotherapy and ultrasound to stretch tight musculature and strengthen weak musculature in the hip region.

Pelvic Conditions

Athletes who perform activities that involve jumping, running, and violent collisions can sustain serious acute and overuse injuries to the pelvic region. When an athlete runs, the pelvis rotates along a longitudinal axis proportionate to the amount of arm swing. It also tilts up and down as the leg engages in support and nonsupport. This combination of motion causes shearing at the sacroiliac joint and symphysis pubis. Tilting of the pelvis also produces both a decrease and an increase in lumbar lordosis, depending on the slant of the running surface. Running downhill increases lumbar lordosis, and running uphill decreases it.

Contusion (Hip Pointer)

Etiology Iliac crest contusion and contusion of the abdominal musculature, commonly known as a hip pointer, occurs most often in contact sports (Figure 21-35). The hip pointer results from a blow to an inadequately protected iliac crest. The hip pointer is considered one of the most handicapping injuries in sports and one that is difficult to manage. A direct force to the unprotected iliac crest causes severe pinching action to the soft tissue of that region.

Symptoms and signs A hip pointer produces immediate pain, spasms, and transitory paralysis of the soft structures. As a result, the athlete is unable to rotate the trunk or to flex the thigh without pain.

Management RICE should be applied immediately after injury and should be maintained intermittently for at least forty-eight hours. In severe cases, bed rest for one to two days will speed recovery. It should be noted that the mechanisms for the hip pointer are the same as those for an iliac crest fracture or epiphyseal separation.

Referral to a physician must be made, and an X-ray examination must be performed. A variety of treatment procedures can be used for this injury. Ice massage and ultrasound have been found beneficial. Initially the injury may be injected with a steroid. Later, oral antiinflammatory agents may be used. Recovery time usually ranges from one to three weeks.

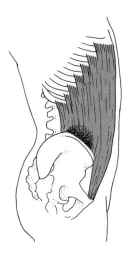

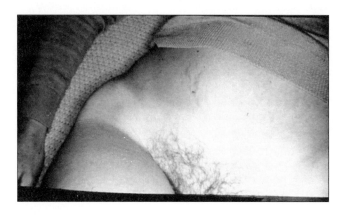

Figure 21-35

A blow to the pelvic rim can cause a bruise and hematoma known as a hip pointer.

Osteitis Pubis

Etiology   Because the popularity of distance running has increased, a condition known as osteitis pubis has become more prevalent. It is also caused by the sports of soccer, football, and wrestling. As the result of repetitive stress on the pubic symphysis and adjacent bony structures by the pull of muscles in the area, a chronic inflammatory condition is created (Figure 21-36).

Symptoms and signs   The athlete has pain in the groin region and in the area of the symphysis pubis. There is point tenderness on the pubic tubercle, and the athlete experiences pain while running, doing sit-ups, and doing squats. Acute osteitis pubis may occur as a result of pressure from a bicycle seat.

Management   Follow-up care usually consists of rest, an oral antiinflammatory agent, and a gradual return to activity.

Stress Fractures

Etiology   Stress fractures in the pelvic area are seen mostly in distance runners. Repetitive cyclical forces created by ground reaction forces can produce stress fractures in the pelvis and the proximal femur. They constitute approximately 16 percent of all stress fractures and are more common in women than in men. The most common sites are the inferior pubic ramus and the femoral neck and subtrochanteric area of the femur.

Symptoms and signs   Commonly, the athlete complains of groin pain along with an aching sensation in the thigh that increases with activity and decreases with rest. Standing on one leg may be impossible for the athlete. Deep palpation will cause severe point tenderness. Pelvic stress fracture has a tendency to occur during intensive interval training or competitive racing. For the ischium and the pubis, crutch walking is recommended.[2]

Management   Rest is usually the treatment of choice for two to five months. X-rays are usually normal for six to ten weeks. Normally a bone scan will pick up osteoclastic activity early.[2] Freestyle swimming can be performed for aerobic exercise. The breast stroke must be avoided.

Avulsion Fractures and Apophysitis

Etiology   The pelvis has a number of apophyses where major muscles make their attachments. An apophysis, or traction epiphysis, is a bony outgrowth and is contrasted to pressure epiphyses, which are the growth plates for long bones. The three most common sites for avulsion fractures and apophysitis in the pelvic region are the ischial tuberosity and the hamstring attachment, the anterior inferior iliac spine and the rectus femoris muscle attachment, and the anterior superior iliac spine where

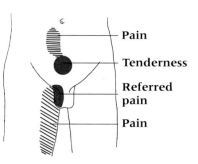

Figure 21-36

Osteitis pubis and other pain sites in the region of the pelvis and groin.

21-8
Critical Thinking Exercise

A football player who was not wearing hip pads receives a hard compressive hit to his left iliac crest region.

? What injury has this athlete sustained? What are the expected symptoms and signs?

Figure 21-37

Avulsion fractures to the pelvic apophyses.

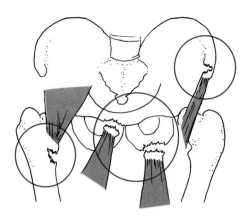

the sartorius muscle makes its attachment (Figure 21-37). Sports that have sudden acceleration or deceleration, such as football, soccer, and basketball, can cause a convulsion, a fracture, or an apophysitis.

Symptoms and signs   The athlete complains of a sudden localized pain with limited movement. There is swelling and point tenderness. Muscle testing increases pain.

Management   X-ray examination is routinely given with apophysical pain. Uncomplicated conditions can be treated with RICE and crutches with toe-touch weight bearing for one to two months.[2] After the control of pain and inflammation (two to three weeks), a gradual stretch program is begun. When 80 degrees of range of motion have been returned, a PRE program is instituted.[1] When full range of motion and strength have been regained, the athlete can return to competition.

THIGH AND HIP REHABILITATION TECHNIQUES

General Body Conditioning

After a thigh or hip injury, as after other sports injuries, the athlete must retain cardiorespiratory fitness, muscle endurance, and strength of the total body. Pool running and swimming provide a maintenance of total body conditioning. One-legged stationary bicycle and upper body ergometer (UBE) activities can maintain cardiorespiratory fitness.

Flexibility

A major concern of rehabilitation in the thigh region is the restoration of quadriceps and hamstring extensibility. Stretching exercises usually progress from proprioceptive neuromuscular facilitation relaxation stretching to gentle passive stretching to gradual static stretching, all within pain-free limits. Range-of-motion exercises must include all major movements of the hip and groin region: internal rotation, external rotation, adduction, abduction, extension, flexion, and the combined movement of internal and external circumduction. Stretching in all ranges of movement must also be performed after hip injury. Like the thigh, the hip should undergo a progressive stretching program that includes proprioceptive neuromuscular facilitation relaxation methods, passive stretching, and active static stretching within pain-free limits.[18]

Joint Mobilization

Mobilizing accessory movements of the hip after injury is essential. Figures 21-38 through 21-41 demonstrate some key hip mobilization techniques.

Strength

Normally the progression for strength is, first, muscle setting and isometric exercise until the muscle can be fully contracted; second, active isotonic contraction; and third, isotonic progressive resistance exercise or isokinetic exercise. Proprioceptive neuromuscular facilitation that uses both knee and hip patterns is also an excellent

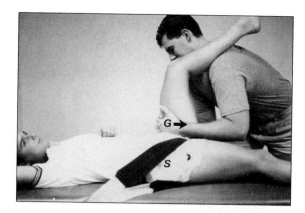

Figure 21-38

Inferior femoral glides. Inferior femoral glides at 90 degrees of hip flexion may also be used to increase abduction and flexion.

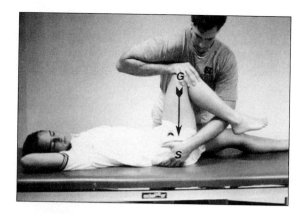

Figure 21-39

Posterior femoral glides. With the athlete supine, a posterior femoral glide can be done by stabilizing underneath the pelvis and using the body weight applied through the femur to glide posteriorly. Posterior glides are used to increase hip flexion.

means of thigh rehabilitation. Because of the wide variety of possible movements, it is essential that exercise be conducted as soon as possible after injury without aggravating the condition. When exercise is begun, it should be practiced within a pain-free range of movement. The athlete should follow a program that is organized to start with free movement and leads up to resistance exercises. A general goal is to have the athlete perform each exercise for ten to fifteen repetitions, progressing from one set to three sets two or three times daily (Figure 21-42). (Because of the relationship between the thigh and the knee region, more information on rehabilitation can be found in Chapter 20.)

Neuromuscular Control

To maintain or restore neuromuscular control to the thigh or hip region, the athlete should focus on balance and closed kinetic chain exercises. For balance, the athlete can engage in weight bearing on just the affected leg using the balance board. Closed

21-10

Critical Thinking E x e r c i s e

A soccer player sustains a stress fracture to the right subtrochanter.

? As the stress fracture heals, what should be the neuro-muscular control concerns?

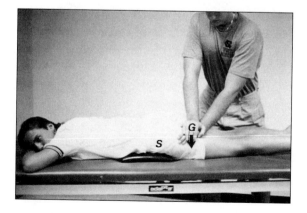

Figure 21-40

Anterior femoral glides. Anterior femoral glides increase extension and are accomplished by using some support to stabilize under the pelvis and applying an anterior glide posteriorly on the femur.

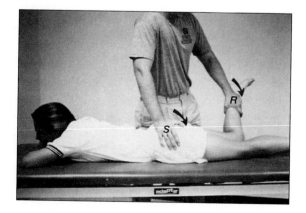

Figure 21-41

Medial femoral rotations. Medial femoral rotations may be used for increasing medial rotation and are done by stabilizing the opposite innominate while internally rotating the hip through the flexed knee.

A

B

C

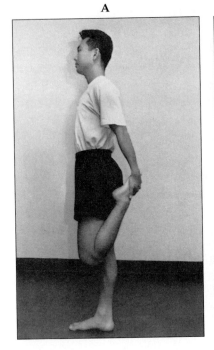

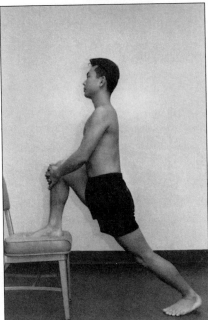

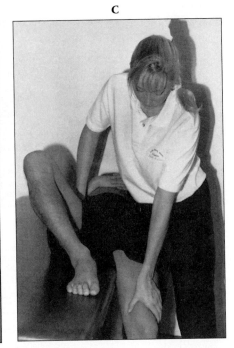

Figure 21-42

Selected basic exercises for hip rehabilitation. **A,** Active hip flexor standing stretch. **B,** Active hip flexor chair stretch. **C,** Manual hip flexor stretch **D,** Hip abduction and adduction. **E,** Hip adduction against gravity. **F,** Hip adduction against a resistance.

D

E

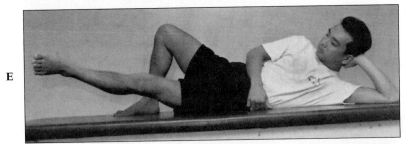

F

kinetic chain exercises might include minisquats, leg presses, and workouts on stair climbing or stepping machines.

Functional Progressions

Functional progression might begin in a pool, where non–weight bearing running can be performed. Depending on the sport, weight-bearing progression might consist of walking, jogging, slow running, zigzag running, figure-eight running, and sprinting.

Return to Activity

Before returning to activity and competition, the athlete must demonstrate full pain-free function of the thigh and hip region. The athlete must have full range of motion, strength, balance, and agility.

SUMMARY

- The thigh is composed of the femoral bone, musculature, nerves, blood vessels, and fascia that envelops the soft tissue. The thigh is considered that part of the leg between the hip and the knee. The quadriceps contusion and the hamstring strain represent the most common sports injuries to the thigh; the quadriceps contusion has the highest incidence. Of major importance in acute thigh contusion is early detection and the avoidance of internal bleeding. One major complication to repeated contusions is myositis ossificans.

- Jumping or falling on a bent knee can strain the quadriceps muscle. A more common strain is that of the hamstring muscle; however, it is not clearly known why hamstring muscles become strained. Strain occurs most often to the short head of the biceps femoris muscle.

- The femur can sustain both acute fractures and stress fractures. Acute fractures occur most often to the femoral shaft, usually from a direct blow. Femoral stress fractures are most common in the femoral neck.

- The groin is the depression that lies between the thigh and the abdominal region. Groin strain can occur to any one of a number of muscles located in this region. Running, jumping, or twisting can produce a groin strain.

- A common problem among women runners is trochanteric bursitis. An irritation occurs in the region of the greater trochanter of the femur.

- The hip joint, the strongest and best-protected joint in the human body, has a low incidence of acute sports injuries. More common are conditions stemming from an immature hip joint. They include Legg-Calvé-Perthes disease (coxa plana) and the slipped capital femoral epiphysis.

- The snapping hip phenomenon is one in which hip stability is lessened as a result of laxity of the hip joint, ligaments, and adductor muscles.

- A common problem in the pelvic region is the hip pointer. This condition results from a blow to an inadequately protected iliac crest. The contusion causes pain, spasm, and malfunction of the muscles in the area. The pelvis can also sustain overuse conditions such as osteitis pubis as well as acute fractures and stress fractures.

21-11

Critical Thinking Exercise

An athlete has successfully completed the rehabilitation process after a hip injury.

? What are the criteria for this athlete's return to activity?

Web Sites

Cramer First Aider: http://www.ccsd.k12.wy.us/cchs_web/cramerfirstaider/fstaider.htm

World Ortho: http://www.worldortho.com

Wheeless' Textbook of Orthopaedics: http://www.medmedia.com/med.htm

American Orthopaedic Society for Sports Medicine: http://www.sportsmed.org

OrthoNet: http://www.orthonet.com

This new site may offer a helpful search engine and useful information.

Solutions to *Critical Thinking* EXERCISES

21-1 One of the best ways to determine the grade of a contusion to the quadriceps muscle is through the degree of restriction of knee flexion. With a grade 1 contusion, there is no restriction to the range of motion. With a grade 2 contusion, the range of knee flexion is more than 90 degrees. With a grade 3 contusion, the range is between 45 and 90 degrees. With a grade 4 contusion, the range is less than 45 degrees.

21-2 Initially, activity is significantly reduced. Isometric exercise is carried out after the early inflammatory phase. In later stages of healing, pain-free exercise such as gentle stretching, jogging, stationary cycling, and high-speed isokinetics may be employed.

21-3 The two tests that can be used for hip flexion tightness are the Kendall and Thomas tests. The Kendall test evaluates the athlete's ability to place her thigh flat on the table while the other is flexed on her chest. The Thomas test evaluates whether the athlete can lay on the table with her legs fully extended and at the same time keep her lumbar spine flat.

21-4 The off-balanced dismount could have created a sprain of the hip joint.

21-5 This condition could be an inflammation of the gluteus medius muscle or iliotibial band, or it could be trochanteric bursitis caused by the increased Q angle and short leg.

21-6 Because of the age of the athlete, the athletic trainer should consider the possibility of a growth problem, most likely a slipped capital femoral epiphysis. The athletic trainer must refer this athlete immediately to a physician for X rays.

21-7 A likely cause of this problem is a strength imbalance of those muscles that help to stabilize the hip joint while flexing and rotating. There also could be a structurally narrow pelvis, greater than usual ROM of hip abduction, or a restricted ROM during lateral rotation.

21-8 This athlete has sustained a hip pointer, or contusion to the skin and musculature in the region of the iliac crest. The athlete most likely will experience severe pain, muscle spasm, and an inability to rotate his trunk or flex his hip without pain.

21-9 This athlete's complaints represent a number of possible conditions: osteitis pubis, stress fracture of the inferior pubic ramus, a possible avulsion apophysis fracture, or an apophysitis.

21-10 As the stress fracture heals, the athlete must maintain and restore neuromuscular control of the thigh and hip region. The focus should be on balance and closed kinetic chain exercises. Balance board exercises and affected leg weight-bearing activities can also be conducted. Minisquats, leg presses, and stair climbing and stepping are other possible closed kinetic chain exercises.

21-11 The athlete must demonstrate pain-free movement of the thigh and hip. There must be full ROM, strength, balance, and agility along with a preinjury level of cardiorespiratory fitness.

REVIEW QUESTIONS AND CLASS ACTIVITIES

1. Describe the major injuries to the thigh, including contusions and strains. How are they sustained and cared for?
2. How may hamstring strains be recognized and cared for?
3. How is a groin strain typically recognized and cared for?
4. What are the similarities and differences between coxa plana and a slipped capital femoral epiphysis?

REFERENCES

1. Amoral JF: Thoracoabdominal injuries in the athlete. In Fadale PD and Hulstyn MJ, editors: *Primary care of the injured athlete, part II. Clinics in sports medicine,* vol 16, no 4, Oct 1997.
2. Bielak JM, Henderson JM: Injuries of the pelvis and hip. In Birrer PB, editor: *Sports medicine for the primary care physician,* ed 2, Boca Raton, Fla, 1994, CRC Press.
3. Booher J, Moran B: Evaluation and management of the acute hamstring injury, *Sports Med Guide* 4:2, 1993.
4. Bradshaw C et al: Obturator nerve entrapment, *Am J Sports Med* 25(3):May/June 1997, pp. 402–408.
5. Bull RC: Soft tissue injury to the hip and thigh. In Torg JS, Shephard RJ, editors: *Current therapy in sports medicine,* St Louis, 1995, Mosby.
6. Casterline M et al: Femoral stress fracture, *J Ath Train* 31(1):53, 1996.
7. Cooper DE: Traumatic subluxation of the hip. In Torg JS, Shephard RJ, editors: *Current therapy in sports medicine,* St Louis, 1995, Mosby.
8. Estwanik JJ et al: Groin strain and other possible causes of groin pain, *Physician Sportsmed* 18(2):54, 1990.
9. Gerberg LF, Micheli LJ: Nontraumatic hip pain in active children, *Physician Sportsmed* 24 (1):69, 1996.
10. Greenwood MJ et al: Differential diagnosis of the hip vs lumbar spine: five case reports, *J Orthop Sports Phy Ther* 27(4):308, 1998.
11. Hacutt JE: General types of injuries. In Birrer RB, editor: *Sports medicine for the primary care physician,* ed 2, Boca Raton, Fla, 1994, CRC Press.
12. Hasselman CT et al: When groin pain signals an adductor strain, *Physician Sportsmed* 23(7):53, 1995.
13. Jackson DL: Stress fracture of the femur, *Physician Sportsmed* 19(7):39, 1991.
14. Johnson BC, Klabunde LA: The elusive slipped capital femoral epiphysis, *J Ath Train* 20(2):124, 1995.
15. Kaeding CC: Quadriceps strains and contusions, *Physician Sportsmed* 23(1):59, 1995.
16. Levandowski R, Difiori JP: Thigh injuries. In Birrer RB, editor: *Sports medicine for the primary care physician,* ed 2, Boca Raton, Fla, 1994, CRC Press.
17. Magee DJ: *Orthopedic physical assessment,* Philadelphia, 1993, Saunders.
18. Paletta GA et al: Injuries about the hip and pelvis in the young athlete. In Michile LJ, editor: *The young athlete. Clinics in sports medicine,* vol 14, no 3, Philadelphia, 1995, Saunders.

19. Prentice WE: Mobilization and traction techniques in rehabilitation. In Prentice WE, editor: *Rehabilitation techniques in sports medicine* ed 2, St Louis, 1999, Mosby.

20. Ruane J, Rossi TA: When groin pain is more than just a strain, *Physician Sportsmed* 26(4):78, 1996.

21. Turl SE, George KP: Adverse neural tension: a factor in repetitive hamstring strain? *J Orthop Sports Phys Ther* 27(1):16, 1998.

ANNOTATED BIBLIOGRAPHY

Torg JS, Shephard RJ, editors: *Current therapy in sports medicine,* ed 3, St Louis, 1995, Mosby.

This detailed sports medicine text contains extensive coverage of thigh, hip, and pelvic injuries.

The Shoulder Complex

When you finish this chapter you should be able to

- Identify the major anatomical and functional features of the shoulder complex.
- Discuss how shoulder injuries may be prevented.
- Describe the process for evaluating injuries to the shoulder.
- Explain how shoulder stability is maintained by the joint capsule ligaments and muscles.
- Identify specific injuries that occur around the shoulder joint, and discuss plans for management.
- Discuss rehabilitation techniques for the injured shoulder.

The shoulder complex, as the name implies, is an extremely complicated region of the body. Because of its anatomical structure, the shoulder complex has a great degree of mobility. This mobility requires some compromise in stability, and thus the shoulder is highly susceptible to injury. Many sport activities, in particular those that involve repetitive overhead movements such as throwing, swimming, or serving in tennis or volleyball, place a great deal of stress on the supporting structures (Figure 22-1). Consequently, injuries related to overuse in the shoulder are commonplace in the athlete. Some understanding of the anatomy and mechanics of this joint is essential for the athletic trainer.

ANATOMY

Bones

The bones that make up the shoulder complex and shoulder joint are the clavicle, scapula, and humerus (Figure 22-2).

Clavicle

The clavicle is a slender, S-shaped bone approximately 6 inches (15 cm) long. It supports the anterior portion of the shoulder, keeping it free from the thoracic cage. It extends from the sternum to the tip of the shoulder, where it joins the acromion process of the scapula. The shape of the medial two-thirds of the clavicle is primarily circular, and its lateral third assumes a flattened appearance. The medial two-thirds bend convexly forward, and the lateral third is concave. The point at which the clavicle changes shape and contour presents a structural weakness, and the largest number of fractures to the bone occur at this point. Lying superficially with no muscle or fat protection makes the clavicle subject to direct blows.

Scapula

The scapula is a flat, triangular-shaped bone that serves mainly as an articulating surface for the head of the humerus. It is located on the dorsal aspect of the thorax and has three prominent projections: the spine, the acromion, and the coracoid process. The spine divides the posterior aspect unequally. The superior dorsal aspect is a deep depression called the supraspinous fossa, and the area below, a more shallow depression, is called the infraspinous fossa. The acromion is a process at the lateral tip of the spine. A hooklike projection called the coracoid process arises anteriorly from the scapula. It curves upward, forward, and outward in front of the glenoid fossa, which is the articulating cavity for the reception of the humeral head. The glenoid cavity is situated laterally on the scapula below the acromion and is relatively shallow. However, the presence of the fibrocartilagenous glenoid labrum increases the depth of articulation. The scapula serves as a site of attachment for many muscles that act to move the shoulder complex.

Humerus

The head of the humerus is spherical, with a shallow, constricted neck; it faces upward, inward, and backward, articulating with the scapula's shallow glenoid fossa. Circumscribing the humeral head is a slight groove called the anatomical neck, which is the attachment for the articular capsule of the glenohumeral joint. The greater and lesser tuberosities are located adjacent and immediately inferior to the head. The lesser tuberosity is positioned anteriorly and medially, with the greater tuberosity placed somewhat higher and laterally. Lying between the two tuberosities is a deep groove called the bicipital groove, which retains the long tendon of the biceps brachii muscle.

Articulations

There are four major articulations associated with the shoulder complex: the sternoclavicular joint, the acromioclavicular joint, the glenohumeral joint, and the scapulothoracic joint (Figure 22-2).

Sternoclavicular Joint

The clavicle articulates with the manubrium of the sternum to form the sternoclavicular (SC) joint, the only direct connection between the upper extremity and the trunk. The sternal articulating surface is larger than the sternum, causing the clavicle to rise much higher than the sternum. A fibrocartilaginous disk is interposed between the two articulating surfaces. It functions as a shock absorber against the medial forces and also helps prevent any displacement upward. The articular disk is placed so that the clavicle moves on the disk and the disk in turn moves separately on the sternum. The clavicle is permitted to move up and down, forward and backward, in combination, and in rotation.

Acromioclavicular Joint

The acromioclavicular (AC) joint is a gliding articulation of the lateral end of the clavicle with the acromion process. It is a rather weak junction. A fibrocartilaginous disk separates the two articulating surfaces. A thin, fibrous capsule surrounds the joint.

Figure 22-1

Vigorous overhead activities can produce a number of shoulder problems.

Shoulder complex articulations:
- Sternoclavicular
- Acromioclavicular
- Glenohumeral
- Scapulothoracic

Figure 22-2

Skeletal anatomy of the shoulder complex.

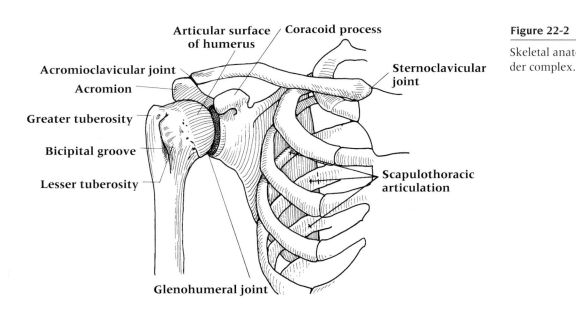

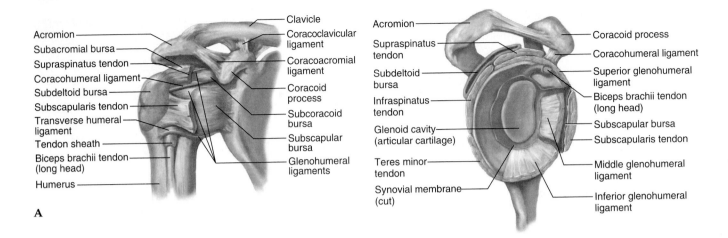

A

B

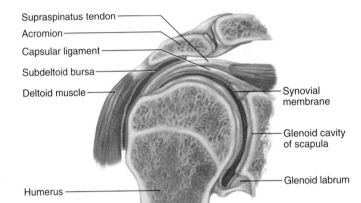

C

Figure 22-3

Shoulder complex articulations and ligaments. **A,** Anterior view. **B,** Lateral view. **C,** Frontal section.

Glenohumeral Joint

The glenohumeral joint (shoulder joint) is an enarthrodial, or ball-and-socket, joint in which the round head of the humerus articulates with the shallow glenoid cavity of the scapula. The cavity is deepened slightly by a fibrocartilaginous rim called the glenoid labrum. The glenohumeral joint is maintained by both a passive and an active mechanism; the passive mechanism relates to the glenoid labrum and capsular ligaments, and the active mechanism relates to the deltoid and rotator cuff muscles.

Scapulothoracic Joint

The scapulothoracic joint is not a true joint; however, the movement of the scapula on the wall of the thoracic cage is critical to shoulder joint motion. Contraction of the scapular muscles, which attach the scapula to the axial skeleton, is critical in stabilizing the scapula and thus in providing a base on which a highly mobile joint can function.

Ligaments

Figure 22-3 shows the ligamentous arrangement of the shoulder complex.

Sternoclavicular Joint Ligaments

The sternoclavicular joint is extremely weak because of its bony arrangement, but it is held securely by strong ligaments that tend to pull the sternal end of the clavicle downward and toward the sternum, in effect, anchoring it. The main ligaments are the anterior sternoclavicular, which prevents upward displacement of the clavicle; the posterior sternoclavicular, which also prevents upward displacement of the clavicle; the interclavicular, which prevents lateral displacement of the clavicle; and the costoclavicular, which prevents lateral and upward displacement of the clavicle.[2]

Acromioclavicular Joint Ligaments

The acromioclavicular ligament consists of anterior, posterior, superior, and inferior portions. In addition to the acromioclavicular ligament, the coracoclavicular ligament joins the coracoid process and the clavicle and helps maintain the position of the clavicle relative to the acromion. The coracoclavicular ligament is further divided into the conoid and trapezoid ligaments. The coracoclavicular ligament, because of the rotation of the clavicle on its long axis, develops some slack, which permits movement of the scapula at the acromioclavicular joint to take place. The coracoacromial ligament connects the coracoid to the acromion. This ligament along with the acromion forms the coracoacromial arch.

Glenohumeral Joint Ligaments

Surrounding the glenohumeral articulation is a loose, articular capsule. This capsule is strongly reinforced by the superior, middle, and inferior glenohumeral ligaments and by the tough coracohumeral ligament, which attaches to the coracoid process and to the greater tuberosity of the humerus.[27] The glenohumeral ligaments appear to produce a major restraint in shoulder flexion, extension, and rotation. The anterior glenohumeral ligament is tense when the shoulder is in extension, abduction, or external rotation. The posterior glenohumeral ligament's greatest tension is in extension with external rotation. The middle glenohumeral ligament is in greatest tension when in flexion and external rotation. The inferior glenohumeral ligament is most tense when the shoulder is abducted, extended, or externally rotated. The posterior capsule is tense when the shoulder is in flexion, abduction, internal rotation, or any combination of these. The superior and middle segment of the posterior capsule has the greatest tension while the shoulder is internally rotated. The inferior glenohumeral ligament is primarily a check against both anterior and posterior dislocation of the humeral head. The long tendon of the biceps brachii muscle passes across the head of the humerus and then through the bicipital groove. In the anatomical position, the long head of the biceps moves in close relationship with the humerus. The transverse ligament retains the long biceps tendon within the bicipital groove by passing over it from the lesser and the greater tuberosities, converting the bicipital groove into a canal.

Musculature

Muscles Acting on the Glenohumeral Joint

The muscles that cross the glenohumeral joint produce dynamic motion and establish stability to compensate for a bony and ligamentous arrangement that allows for a great deal of mobility (Figure 22-4). Movements at the glenohumeral joint include flexion, extension, abduction, adduction, horizontal adduction/abduction, internal/external rotation, and circumduction. The muscles acting on the glenohumeral joint may be separated into two groups. The first group consists of muscles that originate on the axial skeleton and attach to the humerus and includes the latissimus dorsi and the pectoralis major. The second group originates on the scapula and attaches to the humerus and includes the deltoid, the teres major, and the coracobrachialis. Additionally, the subscapularis, the supraspinatus, the infraspinatus, and the teres minor muscles constitute the short rotator muscles, commonly called the rotator cuff, whose tendons adhere to the articular capsule and serve as reinforcing structures (Figure 22-5). The biceps and triceps muscles attach on the glenoid and effect elbow motion.

22-1

Critical Thinking Exercise

A football quarterback has a multidirectional instability of the glenohumeral joint resulting from a series of two anterior dislocations. He is just beginning preseason practice and wants to know what he can do to strengthen his shoulder so that it does not dislocate again.

? What muscles are important in providing dynamic stability specifically to the glenohumeral joint, and will strengthening these muscles prevent a subsequent dislocation?

Glenohumeral joint movements:
- Flexion
- Extension
- Abduction
- Adduction
- External rotation
- Internal rotation
- Horizontal abduction
- Horizontal adduction
- Circumduction

Rotator cuff muscles:
- Subscapularis
- Supraspinatus
- Infraspinatus
- Teres minor

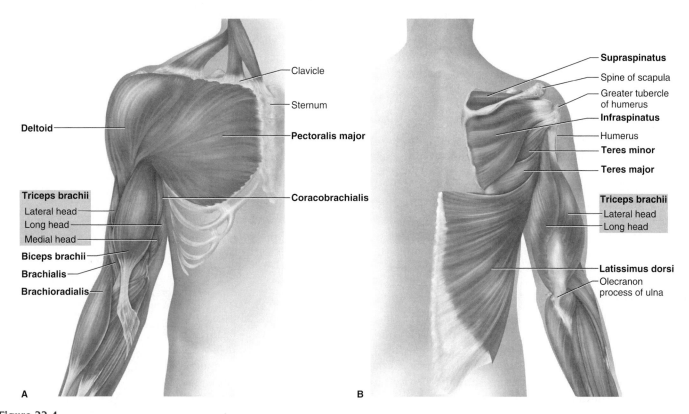

Clavicle

Sternum

Deltoid

Pectoralis major

Triceps brachii
Lateral head
Long head
Medial head

Coracobrachialis

Biceps brachii

Brachialis

Brachioradialis

A

Supraspinatus

Spine of scapula

Greater tubercle
of humerus

Infraspinatus

Humerus

Teres minor

Teres major

Triceps brachii
Lateral head
Long head

Latissimus dorsi
Olecranon
process of ulna

B

Figure 22-4

Shoulder musculator. **A**, Anterior. **B,** Posterior.

Scapular Muscles

A third group of muscles attaches the axial skeleton to the scapula and includes the levator scapula, the trapezius, the rhomboids, and the serratus anterior and posterior. The scapular muscles are important in providing dynamic stability to the shoulder complex.

Bursae

Several bursae are located around the shoulder joint, the most important of which is the subacromial (subdeltoid) bursa (Figure 22-6), located between the coracoacromial arch and the glenohumeral capsule and reinforced by the supraspinous tendon. The subacromial bursa is easily subjected to trauma when the humerus is in the overhead position because it becomes compressed under the coracoacromial arch.

Nerve Supply

The spinal nerve roots from the fifth cervical vertebra through the first thoracic vertebra to create the complex nerve network called the brachial plexus, which is discussed in Chapter 25 (Figure 22-7). Stemming from this plexus are the peripheral nerves that innervate muscles of the upper extremity, including the axillary (C5–6), the musculocutaneous (C5–7), the subscapular (C5–6), the suprascapular (C5–6), the dorsal scapular (C5), the pectoral (C5–T1), and the radial (C5–T1) nerves.

Blood Supply

The subclavian artery, which lies distal to the sternoclavicular joint, arches upward and outward, passes the anterior scalene muscle, and then moves downward laterally behind the clavicle and in front of the first ribs (see Figure 22-7). The subclavian artery continues on to become the axillary artery at the outer border of the first rib and to become the brachial artery in the region of the teres major muscle in the upper arm.

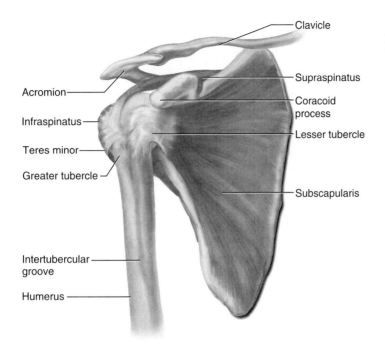

Figure 22-5

Rotator cuff muscles.

FUNCTIONAL ANATOMY

The anatomy of the shoulder complex allows for a great degree of mobility.[29] To achieve this mobility, stability of the complex is sometimes compromised. Instability of the shoulder frequently leads to injury, particularly in those sports that involve overhead activity. In the glenohumeral joint, the rounded humeral head articulates with a relatively flat glenoid on the scapula. Thus, in movement of the shoulder joint, it is critical to maintain the positioning of the humeral head relative to the glenoid. The muscles of the rotator cuff—the subscapularis, infraspinatus, supraspinatus, and teres minor—along with the long head of the biceps function to provide dynamic stability, to control the position, and to prevent excessive displacement of the humeral head relative to the position of the glenoid. The supraspinatus compresses the humeral head into the glenoid while cocontraction of the infraspinatus, teres minor, and subscapularis depresses the humeral head during overhead movements.[27]

The glenohumeral joint capsule also helps control humeral head movement. The tendons of the rotator cuff blend into the glenohumeral joint capsule. As the muscles contract, they dynamically tighten the joint capsule, which helps center the humeral head relative to the glenoid.

Dynamic movement, as well as stabilization of the shoulder complex, requires integrated function of not only the glenohumeral joint, but also of the scapulothoracic, acromioclavicular, and sternoclavicular joints.[28] The muscles that produce movement of the scapula on the thorax help maintain the position of the glenoid relative to the moving humerus and include the levator scapula and upper trapezius, which elevate the scapula; the middle trapezius and rhomboids, which adduct the scapula; the lower trapezius, which adducts and depresses the scapula; and the serratus anterior, which abducts and upwardly rotates the scapula.[30]

Scapulohumeral Rhythm

Scapulohumeral rhythm describes the movement of the scapula relative to the movement of the humerus throughout a full range of abduction (Figure 22-8). As the humerus elevates to 30 degrees, there is no movement of the scapula. This phase is referred to as the setting phase, during which a stable base is being established on

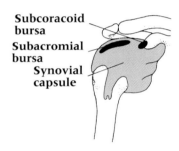

Figure 22-6

Synovial capsule and bursae of the shoulder.

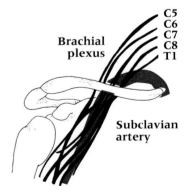

Figure 22-7

Brachial plexus and subclavian artery.

Figure 22-8

Scapulohumeral rhythm.

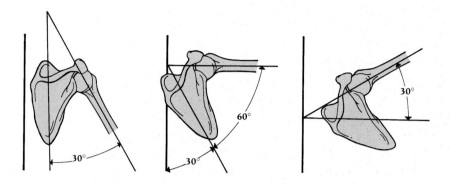

the thoracic wall. From 30 to 90 degrees, the scapula abducts and upwardly rotates 1 degree for every 2 degrees of humeral elevation. From 90 degrees to full abduction, the scapula abducts and upwardly rotates 1 degree for each 1 degree of humeral elevation.

For the scapula to abduct and upwardly rotate throughout 180 degrees of humeral abduction, clavicular movement must occur at both the sternoclavicular and acromioclavicular joints. The clavicle must elevate approximately 40 degrees and must rotate in a posterosuperior direction at least 10 degrees.[2]

PREVENTION OF SHOULDER INJURIES

Proper physical conditioning is of major importance in preventing many shoulder injuries. Like all preventive conditioning programs, the shoulder program should be directed toward general body development and development of specific body areas for a given sport. If a sport places extreme, sustained demands on the arms and shoulders or if the shoulder is at risk for sudden traumatic injury, extensive conditioning must be used. Strengthening through a full range of motion of all the muscles involved in movement of the shoulder complex is essential.

Proper warm-up must be performed gradually before explosive arm movements are attempted. This warm-up includes a general increase in body temperature, followed by sport-specific stretching of selected muscles.

All athletes in collision and contact sports should be instructed and drilled on how to fall properly. They must be taught not to try to catch themselves with an outstretched arm. Performing a shoulder roll is a safer way to absorb the shock of the fall. Specialized protective equipment such as shoulder pads must be properly fitted to help prevent shoulder injuries in tackle football.

To avoid overuse shoulder injuries, it is essential that athletes be correctly taught the appropriate techniques of throwing, spiking, overhead smashing, overhand serving, and tackling and blocking, and the proper swimming strokes.

ASSESSMENT OF THE SHOULDER COMPLEX

The shoulder complex is one of the most difficult regions of the body to evaluate. One reason for this difficulty is that the biomechanical demands placed on these structures during overhand accelerations and decelerations are not yet clearly understood.[26]

History

It is essential that the evaluator understand the athlete's major complaints and the possible mechanism of the injury. It is also necessary to know whether the condition was produced by a sudden trauma or was of slow onset. If the injury was sudden, the evaluator must determine whether the precipitating cause was from external and direct trauma or from some resistive force. The following questions can help the evaluator determine the nature of the injury:

- What happened to cause this pain?
- Have you ever had this problem before?
- What are the duration and intensity of the pain?
- Where is the pain located?
- Is there crepitus during movement, numbness, or distortion in temperature such as a cold or warm feeling?
- Is there a feeling of weakness or a sense of fatigue?
- What shoulder movements or positions seem to aggravate or relieve the pain?
- If therapy has been given before, what, if anything, offered pain relief (e.g., cold, heat, massage, or analgesic medication)?

Observation

The athlete should be generally observed while walking and standing. Observation during walking can reveal asymmetry of arm swing or a lean toward the painful shoulder. The athlete is next observed from the front, side, and back while in a standing position. The evaluator looks for any postural asymmetries, bony or joint deformities, or muscle spasm or guarding patterns.

Anterior Observation

- Are both shoulder tips even with one another, or is one depressed?
- Is one shoulder held higher because of muscle spasm or guarding?
- Is the lateral end of the clavicle prominent (indicating a step deformity caused by acromioclavicular sprain or dislocation)?
- Is one lateral acromion process more prominent than the other (indicating a possible glenohumeral dislocation)?
- Does the clavicular shaft appear deformed (indicating possible fracture)? Is there loss of the normal lateral deltoid muscle contour (indicating glenohumeral dislocation)?
- Is there an indentation in the upper biceps region (indicating rupture of biceps tendon)?
- Are the deltoid muscles symmetrical?

Lateral Observation

- Is there thoracic kyphosis, or shoulders slumped forward (indicating weakness of the erector muscles of the spine and tightness in the pectoral region)?
- Is the position of the head normal or is it forward?
- Is there forward or backward arm hang (indicating possible scoliosis)?

Posterior Observation

- Is there asymmetry such as a low shoulder, and are the scapulae even? (One scapula being unusually high may indicate Sprengel's deformity, which is a congenital deformity in which the scapula does not descend.)
- Is the scapula protracted because of constricted pectoral muscles?
- Is there a distracted or winged scapula on one or both sides? (A winged scapula on both sides could indicate a general weakness of the serratus anterior muscles; if only one side is winged, the long thoracic nerve may be injured. Winging of one scapular and not the other may indicate scoliosis.)
- Are the muscles symmetrical on both sides?
- Is there normal scapulohumeral rhythm?

Palpation

Bony Palpation

Palpation of the bony structures should be done with the athletic trainer standing in front of and then behind the athlete. Both shoulders are palpated at the same time for pain sites and deformities.

Anterior structures
- Sternoclavicular joint
- Clavicular shaft
- Acromioclavicular joint
- Coracoid process
- Acromion process
- Humeral head
- Greater tuberosity of the humerus
- Lesser tuberosity of the humerus
- Bicipital groove

Posterior structures
- Scapular spine
- Scapular vertebral border
- Scapular lateral border
- Scapular superior angle
- Scapular inferior angle

Soft-Tissue Palpation

Palpation of the soft tissue of the shoulder detects pain sites, abnormal swelling or lumps, muscle spasm or guarding, and trigger points. Trigger points are commonly found in the following muscles: levator scapulae, lesser rhomboid, supraspinous, infraspinous, scalene, deltoid, subscapular, teres major, trapezius, serratus anterior, and pectoralis major and minor. The shoulder is again palpated anteriorly and posteriorly.

Anterior palpation
- Sternoclavicular ligament
- Acromioclavicular ligament
- Coracoclavicular ligament
- Anterior and middle deltoid muscle
- Rotator cuff tendons
- Subacromial bursa
- Pectoralis major muscle
- Sternocleidomastoid muscle
- Biceps muscle and tendon
- Coracoacromial ligament
- Glenohumeral joint capsule

Posterior palpation
- Posterior deltoid
- Rhomboids
- Latissimus dorsi
- Serratus anterior
- Levator scapulae
- Trapezius
- Supraspinatus
- Infraspinatus
- Teres major and minor

Special Tests

A number of special tests can help determine the nature of an injury to the shoulder complex.

Active and Passive Range of Motion

The shoulder's active and passive range of motion should be noted and compared with the opposite side. The following are normal ranges for shoulder motion:
- Flexion = 180 degrees
- Extension = 50 degrees
- Abduction = 180 degrees
- Adduction = 40 degrees
- Internal rotation = 90 degrees
- External rotation = 90 degrees

Muscle Testing

Strength of the shoulder musculature should be assessed by manual muscle testing. Both the muscles that act on the glenohumeral joint and the muscles that act on the scapula should be tested. Muscle actions were described in the section on anatomy.

Test for Sternoclavicular Joint Instability

With the athlete sitting, pressure is applied anteriorly, then superiorly, and then inferiorly to the proximal clavicle to determine any instability or increased pain associated with a sprain (Figure 22-9A). Pressure applied to the tip of the shoulder in a medial direction may also increase pain.

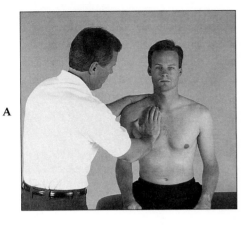

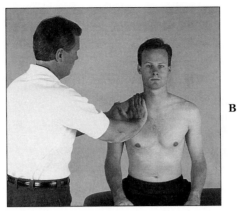

Figure 22-9

A, Assessing sternoclavicular joint stability. **B,** Assessing acromioclavicular joint stability.

Test for Acromioclavicular Joint Instability

The acromioclavicular joint is first palpated to determine if there is any displacement of the acromion process and the distal head of the clavicle. Next, pressure is applied to the distal clavicle in all four directions to determine stability and any associated increase in pain (Figure 22-9B). Pressure is applied to the tip of the shoulder, which compresses the acromioclavicular joint and may also increase pain.[27]

Tests for Glenohumeral Instability

Glenohumeral translation (load and shift test)   This test may be done with the athlete either sitting or supine. First, one hand is placed over the shoulder to stabilize the scapula (Figure 22-10). The other hand grasps the humeral head between the thumb and index finger. A stress load is applied and translation of the humerus is assessed in both an anterior and a posterior direction.

Anterior and posterior drawer tests   The anterior drawer test checks for anterior glenohumeral instability. The athlete lies supine with the arm abducted 80 degrees, horizontally adducted 10 degrees, and externally rotated 10 degrees. The scapula is stabilized, and the humeral head is glided anteriorly while slight distraction is applied to the glenohumeral joint (Figure 22-11A).

The posterior drawer test checks for posterior glenohumeral instability. The athlete lies supine with the arm abducted 90 degrees and horizontally adducted 20 degrees, and the elbow flexed at 90 degrees. The scapula is stabilized, and the humerus is internally rotated as the humeral head is glided posteriorly (Figure 22-11B).

Sulcus test   The elbow is grasped and traction is applied in an inferior direction. With excessive inferior translation, a depression occurs just below the acromion. The appearance of this sulcus is a positive sign (Figure 22-12).[22]

Tests for glenohumeral instability:
- Load and shift test
- Anterior drawer test
- Posterior drawer test
- Sulcus test
- Clunk test
- Relocation test
- Apprehension test

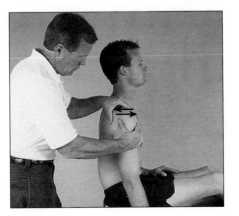

Figure 22-10

Test for anterior-posterior translation.

Figure 22-11

A, Anterior drawer test.
B, Posterior drawer test.

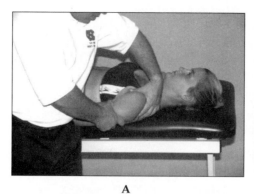

A

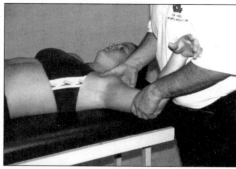

B

Clunk test   While the athlete lies supine, one hand of the evaluator grasps the elbow, and the other is placed on the posterior humerus. The arm is passively abducted and externally rotated with an anterior force applied to the humeral head. The arm is then circumducted while the evaluator feels for a clunking sensation. A positive test may indicate the presence of a tear in the glenoid labrum (Figure 22-13).[2]

Apprehension test (crank test) and relocation test   With the arm abducted 90 degrees, the shoulder is slowly and gently externally rotated as far as the athlete will allow. The athlete with a history of anterior glenohumeral instability will show great apprehension that is reflected by a facial grimace before an endpoint can be reached. At no time should the evaluator force this movement (Figure 22-14A).

Posterior instability also can be determined through an apprehension maneuver. With the athlete in a supine position, the shoulder is flexed to 90 degrees and internally rotated while a force is applied through the long axis of the humerus (Figure 22-14B).

The relocation test is done with the athlete lying supine, the shoulder at 90 degrees, and the elbow at 90 degrees. As the shoulder is externally rotated, pressure is applied anteriorly to stabilize the humeral head, which allows for a greater degree of external rotation than does the apprehension test (Figure 22-14C).[2]

Tests for Shoulder Impingement

In Neer's test, forced flexion of the humerus in the overhead position may cause impingement of soft-tissue structures between the humeral head and the coracoacromial arch (Figure 22-15A). The Hawkins-Kennedy impingement test involves horizontal adduction with forced internal rotation of the humerus, which also produces

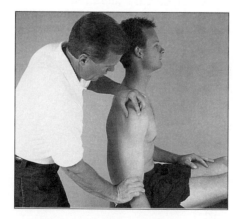

Figure 22-12

Test for sulcus sign.

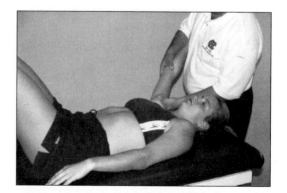

Figure 22-13

Clunk test.

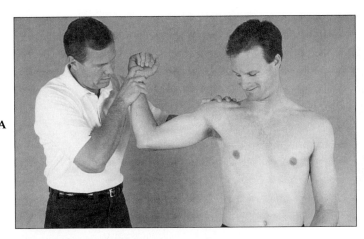

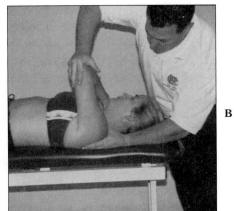

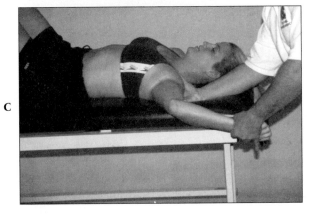

Figure 22-14

A, Shoulder apprehension test.
B, Posterior apprehension test.
C, Relocation test.

impingement (Figure 22-15B). A positive sign is indicated if the athlete feels pain and reacts with a grimace.[21]

Tests for Supraspinatus Muscle Weakness

Drop arm test   The drop arm test is designed to determine tears of the rotator cuff, primarily of the supraspinatus muscle. The athlete abducts the arm as far as possible and then slowly lowers it to 90 degrees. From this position the athlete with a torn supraspinatus muscle will be unable to lower the arm further with control (Figure 22-16A). If the athlete can hold the arm in a 90-degree position, pressure on the wrist will cause the arm to fall.

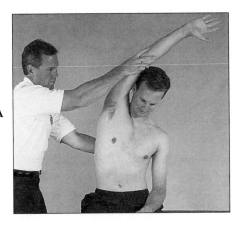

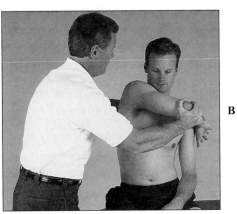

Figure 22-15

Shoulder impingement test.
A, Full elevation. **B,** Horizontal adduction with internal rotation.

Figure 22-16

Supraspinatus tests. **A,** Drop arm test. **B,** Empty can test.

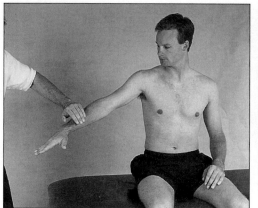

A

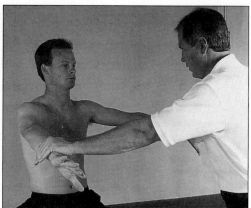

B

Tests for supraspinatus weakness:
- Drop arm test
- Empty can test

Empty can test   The empty can test for supraspinatus muscle strength has the athlete bring both arms into 90 degrees of forward flexion and 30 degrees of horizontal abduction (Figure 22-16B). In this position, the arms are internally rotated as far as possible, thumbs pointing downward. A downward pressure is then applied by the evaluator. Weakness and pain can be detected as well as comparative strength between the two arms.

Test for Serratus Anterior Muscle Weakness

The athlete performs a push-up movement against a wall. Winging of the scapula indicates weakness of the serratus anterior muscle. Winging of only one scapula could indicate an injury to the long thoracic nerve.

Tests for biceps tendon irritation
- Yergason's test
- Speed's test
- Ludington's test

Tests for Biceps Tendon Irritation

Yergason's test involves keeping the elbow at 90 degrees with the forearm pronated while the athlete attempts to actively supinate against the resistance of the evaluator as the humerus is also being pulled downward (Figure 22-17A). *Speed's test* is performed with the elbow extended, the forearm supinated, and resistance applied as the humerus elevates to 60 degrees (Figure 22-17B). Both tests are positive if pain is felt in the region of the bicipital groove. If there is instability, the tendon may subluxate out of its groove. *Ludington's test* is performed with the athlete in a seated position with hands clasped behind the head. The biceps muscles are alternately contracted and relaxed. The athletic trainer palpates the bicep muscles, and if no contraction is felt on one side, there is likely a rupture (Figure 22-17C).

Circulatory Assessment

It is essential that athletes with shoulder complaints be evaluated for impaired circulation. Pulse rates are routinely obtained over the axillary, brachial, and radial arteries. The axillary artery is found in the axilla against the shaft of the humerus. The brachial artery is a continuation of the axillary artery and follows the medial border of the biceps brachii muscle toward the elbow. The radial pulse is found at the anterior lateral aspect of the wrist over the radius. Taking the radial pulse provides an indication of the total circulation of the shoulder and arm.

Skin temperature is subjectively assessed by a comparison of the back of the athlete's hands. A cold temperature can be an indication of blood vessel constriction.[36]

Tests for Thoracic Outlet Compression Syndrome

Anterior scalene syndrome test (Adson's test)   The purpose of this test is to indicate whether the subclavian artery is being compressed as it enters into the outlet canal that lies between the heads of the anterior and middle scalene muscles. Compression can also occur between the cervical rib and the anterior scalene muscle.

22-3

Critical Thinking Exercise

A wrestler comes into the training room complaining of paresthesia and pain extending down the arm, of a sensation of cold, impaired circulation in the fingers, and of muscle weakness. During the evaluation it also becomes apparent that the wrestler has some muscle atrophy in the affected extremity. The athletic trainer suspects that the wrestler may have thoracic outlet compression syndrome.

? What specific tests should the athletic trainer do to determine whether thoracic outlet compression syndrome is present, and what do those tests indicate?

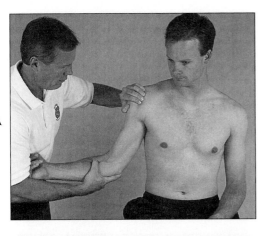

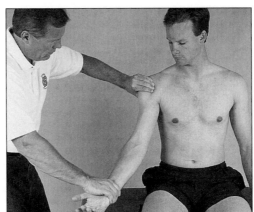

Figure 22-17

Bicipital tendinitis and subluxation tests. **A,** Yergason's test. **B,** Speed's test. **C,** Ludington's test.

This maneuver is performed with the athlete seated on a stool with one hand resting on the thigh. The athlete's radial pulse is taken, first with the arm relaxed and then extended, while at the same time the athlete elevates the chin, turns the face toward the extended hand, and holds the breath (Figure 22-18A). A positive test is one in which the pulse is depressed or stopped completely in the testing position.[16]

Costoclavicular syndrome test (Roo's test)   This test indicates whether the subclavian artery is being compressed between the first rib and the clavicle. While the athlete is in a sitting position, both arms are abducted to 90 degrees and externally rotated (Figure 22-18B). The athlete opens and closes the hand and fingers, making a fist for three minutes. Loss of strength in the hands or loss of sensation in the upper extremity are indicative of thoracic outlet syndrome.

The military brace position test also indicates costoclavicular compression of the subclavian artery. While the athlete stands, the shoulders are retracted as if coming to attention. The arm is abducted to 30 degrees and extended, and the head is turned to the opposite shoulder (Figure 22-18C). If the test is positive, the radial pulse disappears.

Hyperabduction syndrome test (Allen test)   In an athlete with hyperabduction syndrome, the subclavian and axillary vessels and the brachial plexus are compressed as they move behind the pectoralis minor muscle and beneath the coracoid process. To test for this syndrome, the athlete's radial pulse is taken while the arm is fully extended overhead (Figure 22-18D).

Sensation Testing

When there is injury to the shoulder complex, a routine test of cutaneous sensation should be performed. Dermatome levels are tested for pain and light pressure (see Figure 13-5).

Tests for thoracic outlet compression syndrome:
- Adson's test
- Roo's test
- Military brace position test
- Allen test

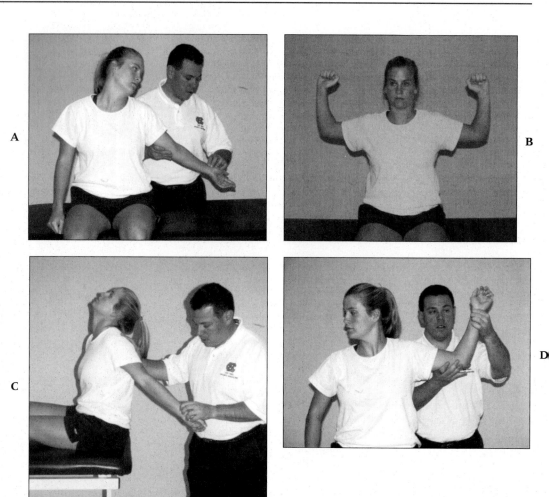

Figure 22-18

Thoracic outlet compression syndrome tests. **A,** Adson's test. **B,** Costoclavicular syndrome test (Roo's test). **C,** Military brace position test. **D,** Hyperabduction syndrome test (Allen test).

RECOGNITION AND MANAGEMENT OF SPECIFIC INJURIES

Clavicular Fractures

Etiology   Clavicular fractures are one of the most frequent fractures in sports (Figure 22-19). Fractures of the clavicle result from a fall on the outstretched arm, a fall on the tip of the shoulder, or a direct impact. The majority of clavicle fractures occur in the middle third from a direct impact. In young athletes, these fractures are usually of the greenstick type.

Symptoms and signs   The athlete with a fractured clavicle usually supports the arm on the injured side and tilts his or her head toward that side, with the chin turned to the opposite side. During inspection the injured clavicle appears slightly lower than the unaffected side. Palpation may also reveal swelling, point tenderness, and mild deformity.

Management   The clavicular fracture is cared for immediately by applying a sling and swathe bandage and by treating the athlete for shock, if necessary. If X-ray examination reveals a fracture, a closed reduction should be attempted by the physician followed by immobilization with a figure-eight wrap. Immobilization should be maintained for six to eight weeks. After this period of immobilization, gentle isometric and mobilization exercises should begin while the athlete wears a sling for an additional three to four weeks to provide protection. Occasionally, clavicle fractures may require operative management.[10]

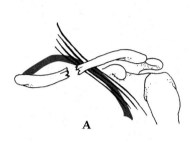

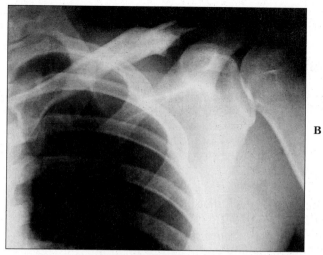

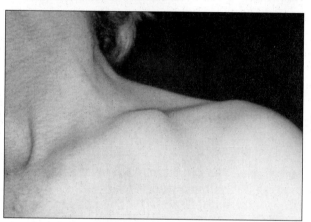

Figure 22-19

Clavicular fracture. **A,** Associated brachial blood vessels and nerves. **B,** X-ray film of a comminuted clavicular fracture. **C,** Typical appearance of clavicular fracture with obvious bone deformity.

Scapular Fractures

Etiology   Fracture of the scapula is an infrequent injury in sports (Figure 22-20). Although the scapula appears extremely vulnerable to trauma, it is well protected by a heavy outer bony border and a cushion of muscle above and below. Those fractures that do occur happen as a result of a direct impact or when the force is transmitted through the humerus to the scapula. Fractures may occur to the body, the glenoid, the acromion, and the coracoid.[6]

Symptoms and signs   Such a fracture may cause the athlete to have pain during shoulder movement as well as swelling and point tenderness.

Management   When this injury is suspected, the athlete should be given a supporting sling and sent directly to the physician for X rays. The arm should be supported in a sling for three weeks with overhead strengthening exercises beginning at week 1.

Fractures of the Humerus

Fractures can occur to the humeral shaft, proximal humerus, and head of the humerus (epiphyseal fracture).

Etiology   The etiology of a fracture of the humerus varies with the type of fracture.

HUMERAL SHAFT   Fractures of the humeral shaft (Figure 22-21A) happen occasionally in sports, usually as the result of a direct blow or a fall on the arm. The type of fracture is usually comminuted or transverse, and a deformity is often produced because the bone fragments override each other as a result of strong muscular pull.

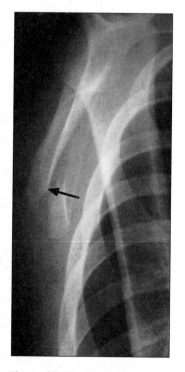

Figure 22-20

Fractures of the scapula are infrequent in sports.

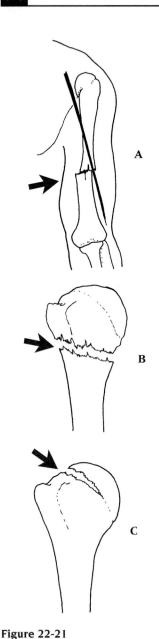

Figure 22-21

Humeral fractures. **A,** Shaft fracture. **B,** Upper humerus. **C,** Epiphyseal fracture.

The pathological process is characteristic of most uncomplicated fractures, except that there may be a tendency for the radial nerve, which encircles the humeral shaft, to be severed by jagged bone edges, resulting in radial nerve paralysis and causing wrist drop and inability to perform forearm supination.

PROXIMAL HUMERUS   Fractures of the proximal humerus (Figure 22-21B) pose considerable danger to nerves and vessels of that area. Fractures of the humerus can result from a direct blow, a dislocation, or the impact received by falling onto the outstretched arm. Various parts of the end of the humerus may be involved, such as the anatomical neck, tuberosities, or surgical neck. This fracture may be mistaken for a shoulder dislocation. The greatest number of fractures take place at the surgical neck.

EPIPHYSEAL FRACTURE   Epiphyseal fracture of the head of the humerus (Figure 22-21C) is much more common in the young athlete than is a bone fracture. An epiphyseal injury in the shoulder region occurs most frequently in individuals ten years of age and younger. It is caused by a direct blow or by an indirect force traveling along the length of the axis of the humerus. This condition causes shortening of the arm, disability, swelling, point tenderness, and pain. There also may be a false joint. This type of injury should be suspected when the aforementioned signs appear in young athletes.

Symptoms and signs   It may be difficult to recognize a fracture of the humerus by visual inspection alone; therefore, X-ray examination gives the only positive proof. Some of the more prevalent signs that may be present are pain, inability to move the arm, swelling, point tenderness, and discoloration of the superficial tissue. Because of the proximity of the axillary blood vessels and the brachial plexus, a fracture to the upper end of the humerus may result in severe hemorrhaging or paralysis.

Management   Recognition of humeral shaft fractures requires immediate application of a splint, treatment for shock, and referral to a physician. The athlete with a fracture to the humeral shaft will be out of competition for approximately three to four months.

A suspected fracture of the proximal humerus warrants immediate support with a sling and swathe bandage and referral to a physician. Incapacitation may last for two to six months.

Initial treatment for epiphyseal fractures should include splinting and immediate referral to a physician. Healing is initiated rapidly; immobilization is necessary for only approximately three weeks. The main danger of this injury lies in the possibility of damage to the epiphyseal growth centers of the humerus.

Sternoclavicular Sprain

Etiology   A sternoclavicular sprain (Figure 22-22) is a relatively uncommon occurrence in sports, but occasionally this sprain may result from one of the various traumas affecting the shoulder complex. The mechanism of the injury can be initiated by an indirect force transmitted through the humerus of the shoulder joint by direct violence such as a blow that strikes the poorly padded clavicle or by twisting or torsion of a posteriorly extended arm. Depending on the direction of force, the medial end of the clavicle can be displaced upward and forward, slightly anteriorly.

Symptoms and signs   Trauma resulting in a sprain to the sternoclavicular joint can be described in three degrees. A grade 1 sprain is characterized by little pain and disability, with some point tenderness but no joint deformity. A grade 2 sprain displays subluxation of the sternoclavicular joint with visible deformity, pain, swelling, point tenderness, and an inability to abduct the shoulder in full range or to bring the arm across the chest, indicating disruption of stabilizing ligaments.

The grade 3 sprain, which is the most severe, presents a picture of complete dislocation with gross displacement of the clavicle at its sternal junction, swelling, and disability, indicating complete rupture of the sternoclavicular and costoclavicular lig-

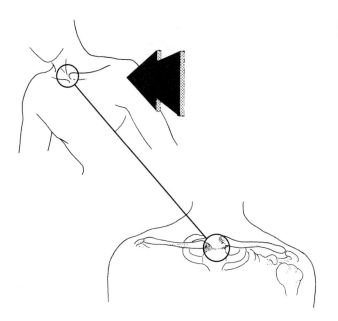

Figure 22-22

Sternoclavicular sprain and dislocation.

aments. If the clavicle is displaced posteriorly, pressure may be placed on the blood vessels, esophagus, or trachea, causing a life-or-death situation.

Management   RICE should be used immediately after injury. Care of this condition is based on reducing a displaced clavicle to its original position, which is done by a physician, and immobilizing it at that point so that healing may take place. A deformity, primarily caused by formation of scar tissue at that point, is usually apparent after healing is completed. There is no loss of function. Immobilization is usually maintained for three to five weeks, followed by graded reconditioning exercises. There is a high incidence of recurrence of sternoclavicular sprains.

Acromioclavicular Sprain

Etiology   The acromioclavicular joint is extremely vulnerable to sprains among active sports participants, especially in collision sports (Figure 22-23).[33] The mechanism of an acromioclavicular sprain is most often induced by a direct impact to the tip of the shoulder that forces the acromion process downward, backward, and inward while the clavicle is pushed down against the rib cage. Injury may also occur

22-4

Critical Thinking Exercise

A soccer player is tripped to the ground on a hard tackle and lands on the tip of her left shoulder. She complains of pain both in the tip of her shoulder and in her chest. She has difficulty lifting her arm above her shoulder because of the pain.

? What injuries might result from this mechanism of injury?

Figure 22-23

Direct impact is a primary mechanism for an acromioclavicular sprain.

Figure 22-24

Rockwood's classification of acromioclavicular joint sprains. **A,** Grade 1. **B,** Grade 2. **C,** Grade 3. **D,** Grade 4. **E,** Grade 5. **F,** Grade 6.

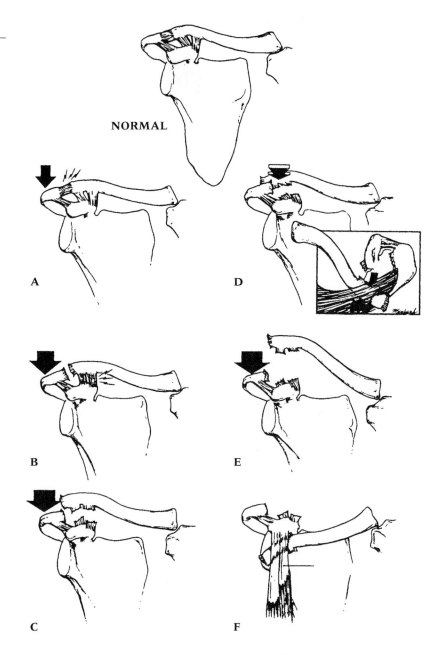

when an upward force is exerted against the long axis of the humerus by a fall on an outstretched arm. The position of the arm during indirect injury is one of adduction and partial flexion. Depending on the extent of ligamentous involvement, the acromioclavicular sprain may be classified as grades 1 through 6 (Figure 22-24).[31] Direct impact injuries usually cause more severe injury.

A program of prevention should entail proper fitting of protective equipment, conditioning to provide a balance of strength and flexibility to the entire shoulder complex, and teaching proper techniques of falling and the use of the arm in sports.

CONTUSION TO THE DISTAL END OF THE CLAVICLE Contusions of this type are often called shoulder pointers and cause a bone bruise and subsequent irritation to the periosteum. During initial inspection, this injury may be mistaken for a grade 1 acromioclavicular sprain. In most cases, these conditions are self-limiting. When the athlete is able to move the shoulder freely, he or she can return to sports activities.

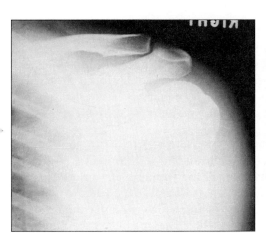 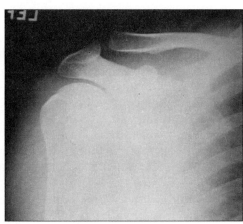

B

Figure 22-25

Comparison of **A**, a normal
shoulder with **B,** a grade 2
acromioclavicular sprain.

Symptoms and signs   The grade 1 acromioclavicular sprain reflects point tenderness and discomfort during movement at the junction between the acromion process
and the outer end of the clavicle. There is no disruption of the acromioclavicular
joint, indicating only mild stretching of the acromioclavicular and coracoclavicular
ligaments (see Figure 22-24A).

A grade 2 sprain indicates tearing or rupture of acromioclavicular ligaments with
associated stretching of the coracoclavicular ligament. There is partial displacement
and prominence of the lateral end of the clavicle when compared with the unaffected side, especially when the acromioclavicular stress test is initiated (Figure 22-25). In this moderate sprain, there is point tenderness during palpation of the
injury site, and the athlete is unable to fully abduct through a full range of motion
or to bring the arm completely across the chest (see Figure 22-24B).

Although occurring less frequently, the grade 3 sprain involves complete rupture
of the acromioclavicular and coracoclavicular ligaments (see Figure 22-24C).

A grade 4 sprain exhibits posterior dislocation of the clavicle with complete disruption of the acromioclavicular ligament (see Figure 22-24D). In some grade 4
sprains, the coracoclavicular ligaments may remain intact.

In a grade 5 sprain, there is complete loss of both the acromioclavicular and coracoclavicular ligaments in addition to tearing of the trapezius and deltoid attachment
to the clavicle and acromion. Such an injury reflects gross deformity and prominence of the distal clavicle, severe pain, loss of movement, and instability of the
shoulder complex (see Figure 22-24E).

A grade 6 injury is very rare in the athletic setting and involves the clavicle being displaced inferior to the coracoid behind the coracobrachialis tendon (see Figure 22-24F).

Management   Immediate care of the acromioclavicular sprain involves three basic
procedures: (1) application of cold and pressure to control local hemorrhage, (2) stabilization of the joint by a sling and swathe bandage, and (3) referral to a physician
for definitive diagnosis and treatment.

A grade 1 sprain requires use of a sling for three or four days. A grade 2 sprain requires ten to fourteen days of protection in a sling. The current recommended management for a grade 3 sprain is nonoperative with approximately two weeks of protection in a sling. Grades 4 through 6 require surgical intervention using open
reduction with internal fixation.[35] If there is posterior displacement of the clavicle,
surgical reduction and fixation will be necessary. With all grades, an aggressive rehabilitation program involving joint mobilization, flexibility exercises, and strengthening exercises should begin immediately after the recommended period of protection.
Progression should be as rapid as the athlete can tolerate without increased pain or
swelling. The joint should also be protected with appropriate padding until a pain-
free, full range of motion returns.[3]

Glenohumeral Joint Sprain

Etiology　The mechanism of this injury is similar to that which produces dislocations and strains. Anterior capsular sprains occur when the arm is forced into abduction (e.g., when making an arm tackle in football). Sprains can also occur from external rotation of the arm. A direct blow to the shoulder could also result in a sprain. The pathological process of a sprain to the glenohumeral joint often involves the rotator cuff muscles.

The infraspinatus–teres minor muscle group is the most effective in controlling external rotation of the humerus and in reducing ligamentous injury.[7] The posterior capsule can be sprained by a forceful movement of the humerus posteriorly when the arm is flexed.

Symptoms and signs　The athlete complains of pain during arm movement, especially when the sprain mechanism is reproduced. There may be decreased range of motion and pain during palpation.

Management　Care after acute trauma to the shoulder joint requires the use of a cold pack for twenty-four to forty-eight hours, elastic or adhesive compression, rest, and immobilization by a sling. After hemorrhage has subsided, a program of cryotherapy or ultrasound and massage may be added, and mild passive and active exercise is advocated for regaining full range of motion. Once the athlete can execute full shoulder range of movement without signs of pain, a resistance exercise program should be initiated. Any traumatic injury to the shoulder joint can lead to a subacute and chronic condition of either synovitis or bursitis, which in the absence of shoulder movement will allow muscle contractures, adhesions, and atrophy to develop, resulting in an ankylosed shoulder joint.

Acute Subluxations and Dislocations

Shoulder dislocations account for up to 50 percent of all dislocations. The extreme range of mobility in the normal shoulder creates an inherent instability in the joint, which is thus susceptible to dislocation. The most common kind of displacement is that occurring anteriorly. Posterior dislocations account for 1 percent to 4.3 percent of all shoulder dislocations. Inferior dislocations are extremely rare. Of dislocations caused by direct trauma, 85 percent to 90 percent recur.[37]

Etiology

SUBLUXATIONS　With glenohumeral subluxations, there is excessive translation of the humeral head without complete separation of the joint surfaces. Subluxation is a brief, transient occurrence in which the humeral head quickly returns to its normal position relative to the glenoid. Subluxation can occur anteriorly, posteriorly, or inferiorly.

ANTERIOR GLENOHUMERAL DISLOCATION　An anterior glenohumeral dislocation may result from direct impact to the posterior or posterolateral aspect of the shoulder. The most common mechanism is forced abduction, external rotation, and extension that forces the humeral head out of the glenoid cavity (Figure 22-26).[12] An arm tackle in football or rugby or abnormal forces created in executing a throw can produce a sequence of events resulting in dislocation.

In an anterior glenohumeral dislocation, the head of the humerus is forced out of its articular capsule in an anterior direction past the glenoid labrum and then downward to rest under the coracoid process. The scope of the pathological process is extensive, with torn capsular and ligamentous tissue, possibly tendinous avulsion of the rotator cuff muscles or long head of the biceps, possibly injury to the brachial plexus, and profuse hemorrhage.

A tear or detachment of the glenoid labrum may occur.[39] Healing is usually slow, and the detached labrum and capsule can produce a permanent anterior defect on the labrum called a *Bankart lesion*. Another defect that can occur after dislocation is found on the posterior lateral aspect of the humeral head and is referred to as a *Hill-*

22-5

Critical Thinking Exercise

A football player has suffered an anterior dislocation of the glenohumeral joint while making a tackle. He is really concerned about missing the remainder of the season and is the type of athlete who wants to know everything there is to know about the injury. He asks the athletic trainer to explain to him exactly what has happened and what potential other problems might exist along with this injury.

? What should the athletic trainer tell this player about the possible ramifications of this injury?

Anterior Glenohumeral Dislocation

Injury Situation A male rugby player was attempting to tackle a ball carrier. At the last second, the ball carrier cut to the right to avoid the tackle. The tackler did not make contact with his left shoulder, but instead with his left arm only. The shoulder was in a position of abduction and external rotation and was forced backward into extension as the ball carrier ran by.

Symptoms and Signs The athlete felt his shoulder give way and felt a pop and a tearing sensation with intense pain. There was a flattened deltoid contour. Palpation of the axilla revealed prominence of the humeral head. The dislocated arm was in slight abduction and external rotation, and the athlete was unable to touch the opposite shoulder with the hand of the affected arm.

Management Plan The athletic trainer immediately immobilized the dislocated shoulder without attempting reduction. The rugby player was then referred to a physician for reduction after X rays ruled out fracture. After the dislocation was reduced and immobilized, muscle reconditioning was initiated as soon as possible.

Phase 1 *Acute Injury* **GOALS:** Control pain and swelling and begin to regain range of motion.
ESTIMATED LENGTH OF TIME (ELT): 1 to 5 days.

■ **Therapy** RICE should be applied immediately and should continue to be used for the next several days. Initial management of an anterior shoulder dislocation requires immediate immobilization in a position of comfort using a sling with a folded towel or small pillow placed under the arm. Protective sling immobilization should continue for approximately one week after reduction. In anterior dislocations, the arm should be maintained in a relaxed position of adduction and internal rotation.

■ **Exercise rehabilitation** While the shoulder is immobilized, the athlete is instructed to perform isometric exercises for strengthening the internal and external rotator muscles. Codman's pendulum exercises and sawing exercises can help the athlete regain range of motion as pain allows.

Phase 2 *Repair* **GOALS:** Achieve full range of motion and increase strength.
ELT: 5 to 12 days.

■ **Therapy** Ice and electrical stimulation should be used to modulate pain. Low-intensity ultrasound may also be used to facilitate healing. The athlete may continue to wear the sling but should be progressively weaned from it as pain allows.

■ **Exercise rehabilitation** Range-of-motion exercises using a T-bar can be instituted as early as tolerated. Wall climbing and rope-and-pulley exercises can also be used to regain motion. Progress the strengthening program from isometrics to resistive rubber tubing and then to dumbbells and other resistance devices as quickly as can be tolerated. Exercises should concentrate on strengthening the rotator cuff. Weight shifting with the hands on the ground can help the athlete begin strengthening the scapular stabilizers and reestablishing neuromuscular control.

Phase 3 *Remodeling* **GOALS:** Regain normal strength and return to full activity.
ELT: 12 days to 3 weeks.

■ **Therapy** Electrical stimulation can be used for muscle reeducation. Ultrasound can be used for deep heating to increase blood flow to clean up the injured area. Ice should be used after exercise.

■ **Exercise rehabilitation** Strengthening exercise should progress from resisted isotonics to isokinetics at greater speeds. Functional D1 and D2 PNF strengthening patterns should be used, adjusting resistance to the athlete's capabilities. Plyometric activities using weighted balls can be used to work on more

Continued

dynamic control. Closed kinetic chain exercises using weight shifting on a ball or balance device improves neuromuscular control. Functional progressions utilize various activities that require overhead motion and throwing.

Criteria for Return to Competitive Rugby

1. The shoulder should have full range of motion and be pain free.
2. Shoulder strength should be near normal.
3. Throwing and catching activities do not produce pain.
4. Protective shoulder braces may be worn to help limit shoulder motion.

Sachs lesion. It is caused by the compression of the cancellous bone of the head of the humerus against the anterior glenoid rim that creates a divot in the humeral head. A *SLAP lesion* is another defect that may occur in the labrum. This defect is caused by an injury to the superior aspect of the labrum that begins posteriorly and extends anteriorly and affects the attachment of the long head of the biceps to the superior labrum.

Additional complications may arise if the head of the humerus comes into contact with and injures the brachial nerves and vessels. Rotator cuff tears may also occur with anterior dislocations. The bicipital tendon also may be subluxated from its canal as the result of a rupture of its transverse ligament.[37]

Figure 22-26

Anterior shoulder subluxation and dislocation.

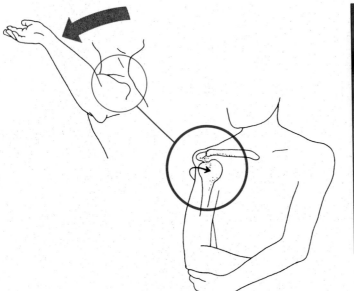
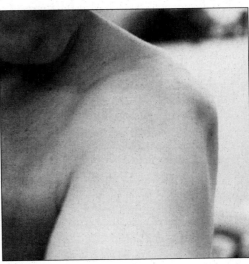

POSTERIOR GLENOHUMERAL DISLOCATION   The mechanism of injury is usually forced adduction and internal rotation of the shoulder or a fall on an extended and internally rotated arm. As with anterior dislocations, posterior dislocations will exhibit significant soft-tissue damage. Tears of the posterior glenoid labrum are common in posterior dislocation. A fracture of the lesser tuberosity may occur as the subscapularis tendon avulses its attachment.

Symptoms and signs   The athlete with an anterior dislocation displays a flattened deltoid contour. Palpation of the axilla will reveal prominence of the humeral head. The athlete carries the affected arm in slight abduction and external rotation and is unable to touch the opposite shoulder with the hand of the affected arm. There is often moderate pain and disability.

Posterior glenohumeral dislocation produces severe pain and disability. The arm is often held in adduction and internal rotation. The anterior deltoid muscle is flattened, the acromion and coracoid processes are prominent, and the head of the humerus also may be seen posteriorly. There is limited external rotation and elevation.

Management   Initial management of the shoulder dislocation requires immediate immobilization in a position of comfort using a sling with a folded towel or small pillow placed under the arm; immediate reduction by a physician; and control of the hemorrhage by cold packs. Physicians generally agree that a first-time dislocation may be associated with a fracture and therefore should not be reduced by the athletic trainer. Ideally, X rays should be taken before the physician attempts to reduce the dislocated shoulder.[32]

Often a physician will attempt an immediate reduction of anterior dislocations on the field using a method of elevation and internal "derotation" of the arm placed in minimal traction. If unsuccessful, the physician may suggest other methods that use a muscle relaxant. Recurrent dislocations do not present the same complications or attendant dangers as the acute type. However, risk is always involved. Reducing the anterior dislocation usually can be accomplished by applying traction to the abducted and flexed arm.

Reduction of posterior dislocation may have to be performed with the athlete under anesthesia. The procedure usually involves traction on the arm with the elbow bent, followed by adduction of the arm, with posterior pressure being applied to the humeral head anteriorly. While in traction, the arm is slowly externally rotated and then internally rotated.

After the dislocation has been reduced and immobilized, muscle reconditioning should be initiated as soon as possible.[34] Protective sling immobilization should continue for approximately three weeks after reduction.[35] In anterior dislocations, the arm should be maintained in a relaxed position of adduction and internal rotation. In posterior dislocations, the shoulder is immobilized in a position of external rotation and slight abduction. While immobilized, the athlete is instructed to perform isometric exercises for strengthening the internal and external rotator muscles. The strengthening program should progress from isometrics to resistive rubber tubing and then to dumbbells and other resistance devices as quickly as pain will allow. A major criterion for the athlete's return to sports competition is that internal and external rotation strength be equal to 20 percent of the athlete's body weight. Protective shoulder braces may help limit shoulder motion (see Figure 22-30).

Chronic Recurrent Instabilities of the Shoulder

Chronic or recurrent shoulder instabilities can occur after acute subluxation or dislocation. Recurrent instabilities may be either anterior, posterior, inferior, or multidirectional. Anterior instability accounts for 95 percent of all recurrent instabilities and usually results after an acute anterior dislocation. With anterior instability, repeated episodes of anterior dislocation have a high probability of occurrence. Posterior instability usually reoccurs as a subluxation rather than a dislocation. Shoulders that

Recurrent instabilities may be either anterior, posterior, inferior, or multidirectional.

have either anterior or posterior instabilities may also subluxate or dislocate inferiorly.[27] If this occurs, a multidirectional instability exists in which there is instability in more than one plane of motion. Multidirectional instabilities most often involve a combination of anteroinferior or posteroinferior laxity but can involve all three directions. It is also possible for a shoulder to dislocate in one direction and subluxate in another.[37]

Etiology   The causes of shoulder instabilities may be traumatic (macrotraumatic), atraumatic, microtraumatic (repetitive use), congenital, and neuromuscular. As discussed earlier, traumatic episodes occur from one or more traumatic situations that cause a complete or partial joint displacement. Atraumatic episodes occur in an athlete who either voluntarily or involuntarily displaces the shoulder joint because of inherent ligamentous laxity.[37]

Microtraumatic episodes are created by repetitive use of the shoulder, usually involving some faulty biomechanics, that leads to soft-tissue laxity. Sports activities such as baseball pitching, tennis serving, and freestyle swimming may produce anterior shoulder instabilities; swimming the backstroke or a backhand stroke in tennis can produce posterior instability. As the supporting tissue becomes increasingly lax, more mobility of the glenohumeral head is allowed, eventually damaging the glenoid labrum. Increased laxity of the supportive capsular and tendinous structures leads to more instability and thus increases the likelihood of recurrent subluxations and dislocations.

Symptoms and signs

RECURRENT ANTERIOR INSTABILITY   Recurrent anterior instability may cause the athlete who throws to complain of pain or clicking or to experience what is described as a dead arm syndrome in the cocking phase of the overhead throwing motion. Pain is often posterior and may last for several minutes, followed by extreme weakness of the entire arm. Anterior instability may permit excessive translation of the humeral head on the glenoid.[19] This translation can produce repetitive compression of the rotator cuff, which consequently causes impingement of soft tissues under the coracoacromial arch. Tests for apprehension may be positive. Range of motion should be assessed because of the possible decrease in external rotation.[41]

RECURRENT POSTERIOR INSTABILITY   A recurrent posterior instability may cause pain to occur posteriorly, anteriorly, or both as a result of subluxation. Joint laxity in a posterior instability, like in an anterior instability, can produce impingement, which is often more of a problem than the subluxation. Crepitation may also be noted on certain movements. There may be a loss of internal rotation when the arm is positioned at 90 degrees of abduction. Stress applied with the arm at 90 degrees of abduction and at 90 degrees of forward flexion along with abduction and internal rotation will allow the degree of posterior humeral head translation to be graded.

MULTIDIRECTIONAL INSTABILITY   Multidirectional instability will cause some inferior laxity, which will exhibit a positive sulcus sign. There is usually some pain and clicking when the arm is held by the side. Any of the symptoms and signs associated with anterior and posterior recurrent instability may be present with multidirectional instability.[43]

Management   Recurrent instabilities may be managed either conservatively or surgically. The initial choice is usually always conservative. Strengthening of all the muscles surrounding the glenohumeral joint, as well as the muscles acting on the scapula, is critical to the success of the rehabilitative program. In particular, strengthening exercises should concentrate on the rotator cuff muscles, which provide dynamic stability in the glenohumeral joint, as well as on the scapular stabilizing muscles. With anterior instability, strengthening should focus on the internal rotators and the long head of the biceps; the external rotators should be strengthened with posterior instability. Joint mobilization and flexibility exercises should be avoided regardless of the type of recurrent instability. Various types of shoulder harnesses and restraints may be used to limit shoulder motion.[40]

Shoulder instabilities may be attributed to traumatic (macrotraumatic), atraumatic, microtraumatic (repetitive use), congenital, and neuromuscular causes.

Surgical stabilization may be necessary if the strengthening program fails to improve shoulder function and comfort. Strengthening exercises should be continued for a reasonable period of time before surgery is considered. A physician may choose a variety of surgical techniques or procedures to enhance shoulder stability.

Shoulder Impingement Syndrome

Etiology   Shoulder impingement involves a mechanical compression of the supraspinatus tendon, the subacromial bursa, and the long head of the biceps tendon, all of which are located under the coracoacromial arch (Figure 22-27). This mechanical compression is due to a decrease in space under the coracoacromial arch. Repetitive compression eventually leads to irritation and inflammation of these structures. Impingement most often occurs in repetitive overhead activities such as throwing, swimming, serving a tennis ball, or spiking a volleyball.[25]

Shoulder impingement is closely related to shoulder instability.[8] Athletes involved with overhead activities often exhibit hypermobility and significant capsular laxity. Failure by the rotator cuff muscles to maintain the position of the humeral head relative to the glenoid in overhead activities allows for excessive translation of the humeral head. Eventually this repetitive stress leads to inflammation of those structures under the coracoacromial arch. Prolonged inflammation causes decreased muscular efficiency, and a progressively worsening cycle is created, which can ultimately result in rupture of the supraspinatus or biceps tendons.[21]

Postural malalignments such as a forward head, round shoulders, and an increased kyphotic curve that cause the scapular glenoid to be positioned such that the space under the coracoacromial arch is decreased can also contribute to impingement. Individuals who have a hook-shaped acromion are more likely to have problems with impingement.[13]

ROTATOR CUFF TEARS   Tears of the rotator cuff muscles are almost always near their insertion on the greater tuberosity. They can be either partial-thickness or complete-thickness tears, with partial-thickness tears occurring twice as often.[21] Most full-thickness tears appear in individuals with a long history of shoulder injury and are relatively uncommon under the age of forty years. The primary mechanism of injury usually involves either acute trauma or impingement.[44] A rotator cuff tear nearly always involves the supraspinatus muscle.[42] A tear or complete rupture of the other rotator cuff tendons—the subscapularis, infraspinatus, or teres minor—is extremely rare.

Shoulder impingement involves a mechanical compression of the supraspinatus tendon, the subacromial bursa, and the long head of the biceps tendon under the coracoacromial arch.

22-6

Critical Thinking Exercise

A javelin thrower has been forced to cease his training activity because of pain in his shoulder. He also feels that his shoulder is very loose and unstable. He has been diagnosed by the team physician as having both shoulder impingement syndrome and a multidirectional instability.

? Often, impingement and instability are thought of as being completely separate and unrelated when in fact it is common to find that athletes who engage in overhead motions exhibit signs and symptoms of both problems. How are impingement and instability related to one another?

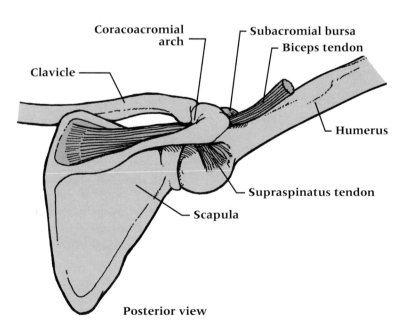

Figure 22-27

Shoulder impingement compresses soft tissue structures under the coracoacromial arch during humeral elevation.

Coracoacromial arch ⎤   ⎡ **Subacromial bursa**
                              ⎣ **Biceps tendon**

Clavicle

Humerus

Supraspinatus tendon

Scapula

Posterior view

Shoulder Impingement

Injury Situation An eighteen-year-old female middle distance swimmer is in the third week of her preseason training program. She has significantly increased the distance she has been swimming during the last three weeks. Her workouts have increased to twice a day and she has been swimming all freestyle. She is complaining of an aching pain in her left shoulder.

Symptoms and Signs The swimmer complains of diffuse pain around the acromion with point tenderness over the supraspinatus or biceps tendons. Palpation of the subacromial space increases the pain. Overhead activities also increase the pain. There is an achy feeling when she finishes her workout. The external rotators are generally weaker than the internal rotators. There is tightness in the posterior and inferior joint capsule. There is a positive impingement sign, and both the empty can test and the drop arm test increase pain.

Management Plan Management involves restoring normal biomechanics to the shoulder joint in an effort to maintain space under the coracoacromial arch during her swimming workout.

Phase **1** *Acute Injury* **GOALS**: Control pain and inflammation.
ESTIMATED LENGTH OF TIME (ELT): Day 1 to day 6.

■ **Therapy** RICE and electrical stimulating currents can be used to modulate pain initially. Ultrasound and antiinflammatory medications should be used to reduce inflammation.

■ **Exercise rehabilitation** Her aggressive swimming workout, which caused the problem in the first place, should be modified so that there is some initial control over the frequency and the duration of the workout with a gradual and progressive increase in distance. It may be necessary to keep her out of the pool during phase 1 and allow the inflammation to subside. To maintain her level of fitness, she should substitute running or exercising on a stationary bike for her swimming workout. She may continue her strengthening program, but she must discontinue any strengthening exercise using her sore shoulder.

Phase **2** *Repair* **GOALS**: Alter joint biomechanics to reduce the likelihood of impingement.
ELT: 1 to 2 weeks.

■ **Therapy** Continue using electrical stimulation and ice to modulate pain. Ultrasound is also helpful in reducing inflammation. Continue antiinflammatory medication.

■ **Exercise rehabilitation** She may now get back into the pool and begin with a short workout initially and then gradually progress the duration and intensity, using increased pain or stiffness as a guide for progression. Exercises should concentrate on strengthening the rotator cuff. Strengthening of the muscles that abduct, elevate, and upwardly rotate the scapula should also be used. The external rotators should also be strengthened. It may be necessary to limit strengthening exercises in flexion or abduction. Any exercise that places the shoulder in impingement should be avoided. Posterior and inferior glenohumeral joint mobilizations should be done to reduce tightness in the posterior and inferior joint capsule.

Phase **3** *Remodeling* **GOALS**: Full return to unrestricted activity.
ELT: 2 weeks to full return.

■ **Therapy** Use ultrasound before the workout and ice after completing the workout. Continue antiinflammatory medication.

Continued

Shoulder Impingement—*cont'd*

■ **Exercise rehabilitation** Strengthening exercises should progress to full-range overhead activities. PNF D1 and D2 strengthening patterns may be used with either manual or surgical tubing resistance. She must continue to work on strengthening the appropriate scapular muscles as she did in phase 2. Exercises designed to stretch the inferior and posterior capsule should also be continued.

Criteria for Return to Competitive Swimming

1. The gradual program that has been used to increase the duration and intensity of the workout has allowed her to complete a workout without pain.
2. She exhibits improved strength in the rotator cuff and the scapular muscles.
3. She no longer has a positive impingement sign, drop arm test, or empty can test.
4. She can discontinue use of antiinflammatory medications without a return of pain.

Symptoms and signs The athlete complains of diffuse pain around the acromion. Palpation of the subacromial space increases the pain. Overhead activities also increase the pain.[36] The external rotators are generally weaker than the internal rotators. There may be some tightness in the posterior and inferior joint capsule. There will usually be a positive impingement sign, and both the empty can test and the drop arm test may increase pain.

Neer has described a series of progressive stages of shoulder impingement.[21] Stage I occurs in athletes less than twenty-five years of age. An initial injury to the supraspinatus or long head of the biceps tendon will produce aching after activity, point tenderness over the supraspinatus or biceps tendons, pain during abduction that becomes worse at 90 degrees, pain during straight-arm full flexion or resisted supination with external rotation, no palpable muscle defect, inflammation with edema, temporary thickening of the rotator cuff and the subacromial bursa, and possible atrophy and constriction of muscles in the region of the shoulder joint.

Stage II involves a permanent thickening and fibrosis of the supraspinatus and biceps tendons and at times the subacromial bursa. Symptoms include aching during activity that becomes worse at night, some restriction of arm movement, and no obvious muscle defect.

Stage III occurs in athletes between the ages of twenty-five and forty years. In this stage, the athlete has a long history of shoulder problems, shoulder pain during activity with increased pain at night, a tendon defect of ³/₈ inch (1 cm) or less, a possible partial muscle tear, and permanent thickening of the rotator cuff and the acromial bursa with scar tissue.

Stage IV occurs in athletes over the age of forty years. In this stage, there is obvious infraspinatus and supraspinatus wasting, a great deal of pain when the arm is abducted to 90 degrees, a tendon defect greater than ³/₈ inch (1 cm), limited active and full passive range of motion, weakness during abduction and external rotation, and possible degeneration of the clavicle.

Management Management of stage I and II impingement involves restoring normal biomechanics to the shoulder joint in an effort to maintain space under the coracoacromial arch during overhead activities. Exercises should concentrate on

22-7

Critical Thinking Exercise

A volleyball player consistently experiences pain when serving the ball overhead. She also indicates that most of the time when she spikes a ball at the net she experiences pain. During an evaluation, the athletic trainer observes that when the humerus is flexed and internally rotated, the pain is worse.

? What is most likely causing this athlete's pain when her shoulder is placed in the overhead position?

22-8

Critical Thinking Exercise

A swimmer is complaining of shoulder pain, particularly when her arm is in the overhead position during her swimming stroke. She has been diagnosed as having an impingement syndrome and the team physician has referred her to the athletic trainer for rehabilitation.

? What general considerations must the athletic trainer take into account when treating shoulder impingement syndrome?

strengthening the rotator cuff muscles, which act to both compress and depress the humeral head relative to the glenoid. Strengthening of the muscles that abduct, elevate, and upwardly rotate the scapula should also be emphasized.[17] The external rotators should also be strengthened. Strengthening of the lower extremity and trunk muscles to reduce the strain placed on the shoulder and arm is also important for the throwing athlete. Posterior and inferior glenohumeral joint mobilizations should be done to reduce tightness in the posterior and inferior joint capsule. Initially, RICE and electrical stimulating currents can be used to modulate pain. Ultrasound and antiinflammatory medications should be used to reduce inflammation. The activity that caused the problem in the first place should be modified so that there is some initial control over the frequency and the level of the activity with a gradual and progressive increase in intensity.

Stages III and IV may require immobilization and complete rest. An athlete who wants to continue activity may require surgical intervention.[15]

Shoulder Bursitis

Etiology   The shoulder joint is subject to chronic inflammatory conditions resulting from trauma or from overuse. Inflammation may develop from a direct impact, a fall on the tip of the shoulder, or shoulder impingement. The bursa that is most often inflamed is the subacromial bursa. The pathological process in this condition involves fibrous buildup and fluid accumulation developing from a constant inflammatory state.

Symptoms and signs   The athlete has pain when trying to move the shoulder, especially in abduction or with flexion, adduction, and internal rotation. There will also be tenderness to palpation in the subacromial space. Impingement tests will be positive.

Management   The use of cold, ultrasound, and antiinflammatory medications to reduce inflammation is necessary. If impingement is the primary mechanism precipitating bursitis, the measures described in the previous section should be taken to correct it. The athlete must maintain a consistent program of exercise, with emphasis placed on maintaining a full range of motion, so that muscle contractures and adhesions do not immobilize the joint.

Frozen Shoulder (Adhesive Capsulitis)

Adhesive capsulitis is also called a frozen shoulder.

Etiology   Adhesive capsulitis, or frozen shoulder, is a condition more characteristic of an older person, but occasionally it occurs in the younger athlete. The exact cause of adhesive capsulitis is unclear. However, it involves a contracted and thickened joint capsule that is tight around the humeral head with little synovial fluid. There is also chronic inflammation with some fibrosis. The rotator cuff muscles are also contracted and inelastic. Constant, generalized inflammation causes pain on both active and passive motion. Thus the individual will progressively resist moving the joint because of pain. The result is a stiff or frozen shoulder.

Symptoms and signs   Pain is reported in all directions of movement about the shoulder with restriction or limitation of both active and passive movement.

Management   The objectives are to relieve discomfort and restore motion. Treatment usually involves aggressive joint mobilizations and stretching of tight muscles. Electrical stimulating currents may be used to reduce pain. Ultrasound is useful in providing penetrating heat to the area.

Thoracic Outlet Compression Syndrome

Etiology   Thoracic outlet compression syndromes involve compression of the brachial plexus, subclavian artery, and subclavian vein (neurovascular bundle) in the neck and shoulder.[20] Neurovascular compression can occur as a result of the following conditions:

- Compression of the neurovascular bundle in the narrowed space between the first rib and clavicle (costoclavicular syndrome)
- Compression between the anterior and middle scalene muscles
- Compression by the pectoralis minor muscle as the neurovascular bundle passes beneath the coracoid process or between the clavicle and first rib
- The presence of a cervical rib (an abnormal rib originating from a cervical vertebra and the thoracic rib)

Symptoms and signs   Abnormal pressure on the subclavian artery, subclavian vein, and brachial plexus produces a variety of symptoms, including paresthesia and pain, a sensation of cold, impaired circulation in the fingers, muscle weakness, muscle atrophy, and radial nerve palsy. Three tests described earlier in this chapter can be used to determine thoracic outlet compression syndrome: the anterior scalene test, the costoclavicular test, and the hyperabduction test.

Management   A conservative approach should be taken with early and mild cases of thoracic outlet compression syndromes. Conservative treatment is favorable in 50 percent to 80 percent of cases.[20] It involves correcting the anatomical condition that is responsible for this syndrome with a series of stretching and strengthening exercises. Exercises should be done to strengthen the trapezius, rhomboids, serratus anterior, and erector muscles of the spine. Stretching exercises for the pectoralis minor and the scalene muscles should also be used.

Biceps Brachii Ruptures

Etiology   Ruptures of the biceps brachii (Figure 22-28) can occur in any athlete who is performing a powerful concentric or eccentric contraction of the muscle. The rupture commonly occurs near the origin of the muscle in the bicipital groove.

Symptoms and signs   The athlete usually hears a resounding snap and feels a sudden, intense pain at the point of injury. A protruding bulge may appear near the middle of the biceps. When asked to flex the elbow joint of the injured arm and supinate the forearm, the athlete displays a definite weakness.

Management   Treatment should include immediately applying a cold pack to control hemorrhage, placing the arm in a sling, and referring the athlete to the physician. In most instances, the athlete with a ruptured bicep will require surgery to repair it. Older individuals may not require surgical repair because the brachialis muscle is the primary flexor of the elbow joint and many nonathletes will be able to function without their biceps.

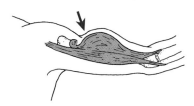

Figure 22-28

Biceps brachii rupture.

Bicipital Tenosynovitis

Etiology   Tenosynovitis of the long head of the biceps muscle is common among athletes engaged in overhead activities. Bicipital tenosynovitis is more prevalent among pitchers, tennis players, volleyball players, and javelin throwers. The repeated stretching of the biceps in these highly ballistic activities may eventually cause an irritation of both the tendon and its synovial sheath as it passes under the transverse humeral ligament in the bicipital groove. Complete rupture of the transverse ligament, which holds the biceps in its groove, may take place, or a constant inflammation may result in degenerative scarring or a subluxated tendon.

Symptoms and signs   There will be tenderness in the anterior upper arm over the bicipital groove. There may also be some swelling, increased warmth, and crepitus because of the inflammation. The athlete may complain of pain when performing dynamic overhead throwing-type activities.

Management   Bicipital tenosynovitis is best cared for by complete rest for several days, with daily applications of cryotherapy or ultrasound to reduce inflammation. Antiinflammatory medications are also beneficial in reducing inflammation. After the inflammation is controlled, a gradual program of strengthening and stretching for the biceps should be initiated.

Contusions of the Upper Arm

Etiology Contusions of the upper arm are frequent in contact sports. Although any muscle of the upper arm is subject to bruising, the area most often affected is the lateral aspect, primarily the brachial muscle and portions of the triceps and biceps muscles. Repeated contusions to the lateral aspect of the upper arm can lead to myositis ossificans, more commonly known as linebacker's arm or blocker's exostosis. Myositis ossificans is a condition in which calcifications or bone fragments occur in a muscle or in soft tissues adjacent to bone.

Symptoms and signs Bruises to the upper arm area can be particularly handicapping, especially if the radial nerve is contused through forceful contact with the humerus, which produces transitory paralysis and consequent inability to use the extensor muscles of the forearm.

Management RICE should be applied for a minimum of twenty-four hours after injury. In most cases this condition responds rapidly to treatment, usually within a few days. The key to treatment is to provide protection to the contused area to prevent repeated episodes that increase the likelihood of myositis ossificans. It is also important to maintain a full range of motion through stretching of the contused muscle.

Peripheral Nerve Injuries

Etiology Sports injuries about the shoulder can produce and cause serious nerve injuries. Injuries to shoulder nerves commonly stem from blunt trauma or a stretch type of injury. Nerve injury must be considered when there is constant pain, muscle weakness, paralysis, or muscle atrophy.[23]

Symptoms and signs Peripheral nerve injuries can result in muscle weakness as follows:

- Suprascapular—supraspinatus and infraspinatus
- Superior subscapular—subscapularis
- Inferior subscapular—subscapularis and teres minor
- Thoracodorsal—latissimus dorsi
- Medial pectoral—pectoralis major and minor
- Lateral pectoral—pectoralis major
- Axillary—deltoid and teres minor
- Dorsal scapular—rhomboids major and minor and levator scapula
- Long thoracic—serratus anterior
- Spinal accessory—trapezius
- Musculocutaneous—biceps, coracobrachialis, brachialis
- Radial—triceps and muscles of the forearm and hand
- Median—muscles of the forearm and hand
- Ulnar—muscles of the forearm and hand

Management If the injury results from blunt trauma, there may also be associated contusion. Thus RICE should be applied immediately. In many instances, muscle weakness will be transient with a relatively quick return to normal function. If muscle weakness persists or if there is any muscle wasting or atrophy, referral to a physician is essential.

THROWING MECHANICS

Throwing activities account for a considerable number of acute and chronic injuries to the shoulder joint. Throwing is a unilateral action that subjects the arm to repetitive stresses of great intensity, particularly in repetitive overhead motions in activities such as throwing a baseball or football, throwing a javelin, serving or spiking a volleyball, and serving or hitting an overhead smash in tennis. If the thrower uses faulty technique, the joints are affected by atypical stresses that result in trauma to the joint and its surrounding tissues.

Throwing is a sequential pattern of movements in which each part of the body must perform a number of carefully timed and executed acts. For example, throwing a ball or javelin uses one particular pattern of movements; hurling the discus or hammer makes use of a similar complex, but with centrifugal force substituted for linear force and the type of terminal movements used in release being different. Putting the shot—a pushing rather than a throwing movement—has in its overall pattern a number of movements similar to those used in throwing.

In the act of throwing, momentum is transferred from the thrower's body to the object that is thrown. Basic physics dictates that the greater and heavier the mass, the greater the momentum needed to move it. Hence, as the size and weight of the object increase, more parts of the body are used to effect the summation of forces needed to accomplish the throw. The same is true in respect to the speed of the object: the greater the speed, the more body parts that must come into play to increase the body's momentum. Timing and sequence of action are of the utmost importance. They improve with correct practice.

In throwing, the arm acts as a sling or catapult, transferring and imparting momentum from the body to the ball. There are various types of throwing; the overhand, sidearm, and underarm styles are the most common. The act of throwing is fairly complex and requires considerable coordination and timing if success is to be achieved.

In throwing, the most powerful muscle groups are brought into play initially, and the emphasis progresses ultimately to the least powerful but the most coordinated (i.e., the legs, trunk, shoulder girdle, arm, forearm, and finally, hand). The body's center of gravity is transported in the direction of the throw as the leg opposite the throwing arm is first elevated and then moved forward and planted on the ground, thus stopping the forward movement of the leg and permitting the body weight to be transferred from the supporting leg to the moving leg. Initially, the trunk rotates backward as the throwing arm and wrist are cocked, then rotates forward, continuing its rotation beyond the planted foot as the throwing arm moves forcibly from a position of extreme external rotation, abduction, and extension through flexion to forcible and complete extension in the terminal phase of the delivery, bringing into play the powerful internal rotators and adductors. These muscles exert a tremendous force on the distal and proximal humeral epiphysis and over a period of time create cumulative microtraumas that can result in shoulder problems.

Relative to the shoulder complex, throwing or pitching involves five distinct phases: windup, cocking, arm acceleration, arm deceleration, and follow-through (Figure 22-29).[2]

The throwing mechanism consists of five phases:
- Windup
- Cocking
- Acceleration
- Deceleration
- Follow-through

Figure 22-29

Phases of throwing from left to right: windup, cocking, acceleration, deceleration, and follow-through.

Windup Phase

The windup, or preparation, phase lasts from the first movement until the ball leaves the gloved hand. During this phase, the lead leg strides forward. Both shoulders abduct, externally rotate, and horizontally abduct.

Cocking Phase

The cocking phase begins when the hands separate and ends when maximum external rotation of the humerus has occurred. During this phase, the lead foot comes in contact with the ground.

Acceleration Phase

The acceleration phase lasts from maximum external rotation until ball release. The humerus abducts, horizontally abducts, and internally rotates at velocities approaching 8,000 degrees per second. The scapula elevates, abducts, and rotates upward.

Deceleration Phase

The deceleration phase lasts from ball release until maximum shoulder internal rotation. During this phase, the external rotators of the rotator cuff contract eccentrically to decelerate the humerus. The rhomboids contract eccentrically to decelerate the scapula.

Follow-Through Phase

The follow-through phase lasts from maximum shoulder internal rotation until the end of the motion, when the athlete is in a balanced position.

REHABILITATION OF THE SHOULDER COMPLEX

Rehabilitation of the shoulder joint after injury requires that the athletic trainer have a sound understanding of the complex anatomical and biomechanical functions of the shoulder girdle. As emphasized earlier, the shoulder is capable of a wide range of movement and consequently sacrifices some degree of stability for the sake of mobility.[18] Achieving the necessary balance between the two is essential in the high-performance athlete.

In recent years, the shoulder joint, like the knee joint, has received considerable attention within the sports medicine community. The philosophy of and approach to treatment, management, and rehabilitation continue to change rapidly.[35] Attempts by athletic trainers to use cookbook approaches to rehabilitation protocols sometimes fail to allow for essential alteration of those protocols in response to the specific needs of the individual athlete.

Immobilization after Injury

Rehabilitation programs should be tailored to the individual athlete's needs. An aggressive approach should be used for throwers and swimmers. The length of the immobilization period will vary depending on the structures injured, the severity of the injury, and whether the injury is treated conservatively or surgically by the physician. Regardless of the injury, the injured athlete usually begins to exercise isometrically while wearing an immobilization device (Figure 22-30).[11] For certain injuries, it may be unnecessary to wear a sling or brace at all. Other injuries may require that a sling be worn twenty-four hours a day and removed only for rehabilitative exercises. Certain injuries may require that a sling be worn only at night in the early stages of healing, that a motion-limiting brace be worn during competition only, or in some cases, that no sling or brace be worn after the first couple of weeks, but that motion above an angle of 90 degrees be limited for a certain number of weeks. Progression in range of motion and strengthening techniques should be dictated by an understanding of the physiological process of healing and is generally determined by a lack of pain and swelling associated with increased activity.[24]

22-9

Critical Thinking Exercise

A baseball pitcher is throwing a fastball. To effectively execute this motion, the pitcher must develop significant velocity in glenohumeral internal rotation during the acceleration phase. During the follow-through phase, this high-velocity internal rotation must quickly decelerate.

? What muscles function to actively internally rotate the glenohumeral joint during the acceleration phase, and what muscles decelerate internal rotation during follow-through?

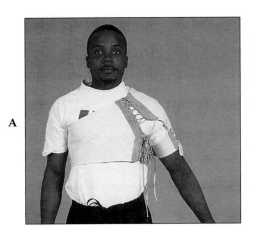

A   B

Figure 22-30

Protective braces for the shoulder.

General Body Conditioning

It is essential for the athlete to maintain a high level of cardiorespiratory endurance throughout the rehabilitation process. For shoulder joint injuries, activities such as running, speed walking, or riding an exercise bike may be used to maintain cardiorespiratory endurance. Because many athletic activities involve some running, engaging in such training for a shoulder injury is more useful than, for example, swimming for the rehabilitation of an ankle sprain. Athletes engaged in sports that require upper-extremity endurance, such as swimming and throwing, should be progressed to these activities as soon as the activities can be tolerated. Training and conditioning activities may be modified such that the athlete can continue to maintain strength, flexibility, and neuromuscular control throughout the rest of the body during the period of shoulder rehabilitation.

Shoulder Joint Mobilization

Normal joint arthrokinematics must be maintained for the athlete to regain normal full-range physiological movement. Mobilization techniques should be used whenever there is some limitation in motion that can be attributed to tightness of the joint capsule or surrounding ligaments rather than to tightness of the musculotendinous units. Mobilization techniques, including inferior, anterior, and dorsal humeral glides; anterior-posterior and inferior-superior glides of the clavicle at both the acromioclavicular and sternoclavicular joints; and generalized scapulothoracic mobilizations, can be incorporated into the early stages of rehabilitation as needed (Figure 22-31).

Flexibility

Regaining a full, nonrestricted, pain-free range of motion is one of the most important aspects of shoulder rehabilitation. Because the shoulder consists of four separate joints that must all function together, the athletic trainer must make certain that normal movement occurs at each joint individually and that the athlete eventually regains normal scapulohumeral rhythm. Gentle ROM exercises such as Codman's pendulum exercises (Figure 22-32) and a sawing motion (Figure 22-33) should be started immediately. Exercises can be progressed to a series of active assisted ROM exercises that use a T-bar and are done in a pain-free arc for all the cardinal plane movements (Figure 22-34). Cardinal plane movements at the shoulder include flexion, extension, abduction, adduction, internal and external rotation, and horizontal adduction and abduction. Rope-and-pulley exercises (Figure 22-35) or wall-climbing exercises (Figure 22-36) are particularly effective in regaining flexion and abduction.

Figure 22-31

Shoulder complex joint mobilizations. **A,** Sterno-clavicular joint. **B,** Acromio-clavicular joint. **C,** Scapular mobilizations. **D,** Anterior humeral glides. **E,** Posterior humeral glides. **F,** Inferior humeral glides.

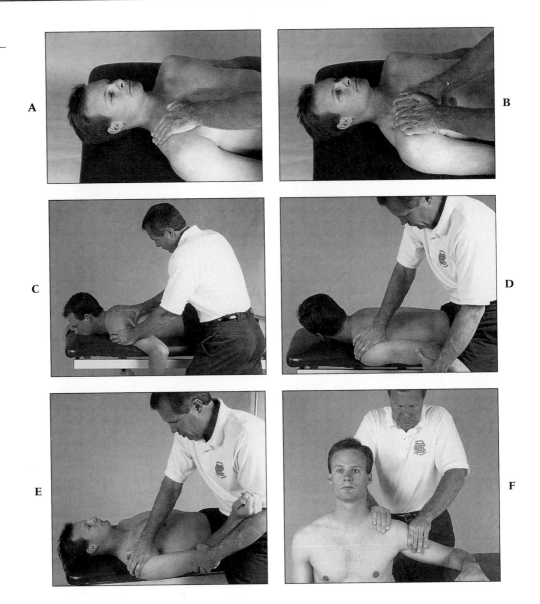

Figure 22-32

Codman's pendulum exercise may be begun immediately after injury.

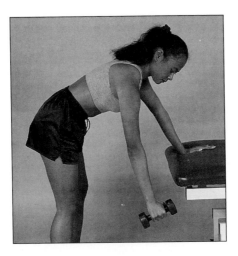

Figure 22-33

Sawing exercises are used as a gentle range-of-motion activity for the glenohumeral joint.

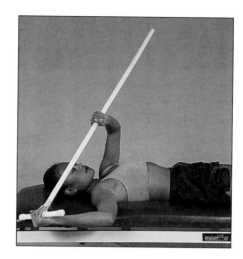

Figure 22-34

T-bar exercises are active assisted range-of-motion exercises that should be done for each of the cardinal plane movements.

Figure 22-35

Rope-and-pulley exercises for regaining flexion and abduction.

Figure 22-36

Wall-climbing exercises are useful in regaining abduction and flexion.

Figure 22-37

Isotonic exercises. **A,** Bench press (pectoralis major, triceps). **B,** Flexion to 90 degrees (anterior deltoid, coracobrachialis, deltoid, pectoralis major, biceps). **C,** Extension (latissimus dorsi, teres major, posterior deltoid). **D,** Abduction to 90 degrees (middle deltoid, supraspinatus, anterior deltoid). **E,** Horizontal abduction (posterior deltoid, infraspinatus, teres minor). **F,** Horizontal adduction (pectoralis major, anterior deltoid). **G,** External rotation (infraspinatus, teres minor, posterior deltoid). **H,** Internal rotation (subscapularis, pectoralis major, latissimus dorsi, teres minor, anterior deltoid).

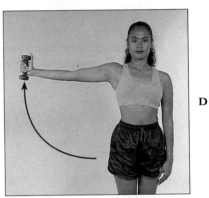

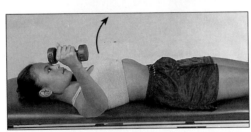

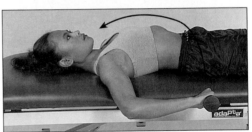

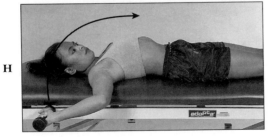

Figure 22-38

Exercises that use surgical tubing emphasize both eccentric and concentric strengthening contractions and can be done in all cardinal planes.

Muscular Strength

Strengthening exercises in the shoulder generally follow a progression from positional isometrics, to full-range isotonics that concentrate on both eccentric and concentric contractions, to isokinetics, to plyometrics. Gentle isometrics should begin immediately after injury or after surgery while the arm is still immobilized at the side.

Isotonic exercise may be incorporated with the use of different types of resistance, including dumbbells and barbells (Figure 22-37), surgical tubing or Theraband (Figure 22-38), or manual resistance techniques including PNF strengthening techniques (Figure 22-39).[14] Resistance exercises should include all cardinal plane movements. Athletic trainers should give particular attention to strengthening the scapular stabilizers by incorporating exercises to resist scapular abduction, adduction, elevation, depression, upward rotation, downward rotation, protraction, and retraction (Figure 22-40). Strengthening the muscles that control the stability of the scapula helps provide a base for the function of the highly mobile glenohumeral joint.

Isokinetic exercises are used to exercise the muscles of the shoulder girdle at varying speeds (Figure 22-41). It must be emphasized that the maximum angular velocities currently available on existing isokinetic devices (approximately 600 degrees per second) do not approach functional speeds of the throwing shoulder; the latter may be as great as 8,000 degrees per second of internal rotation.

For both isotonic and isokinetic training, concentric and eccentric components should be emphasized. Eccentric contraction of the external rotators is essential during the deceleration phase of throwing.[4] Plyometric exercises incorporated in the later stages of a rehabilitation program use a quick eccentric stretch of a muscle to facilitate a concentric contraction. Plyometric exercises for the upper extremity can be done with a weighted ball (Figure 22-42).[9]

Figure 22-39

D1 upper-extremity pattern moving into: **A,** flexion-starting position; **B,** flexion-terminal position; **C,** extension-starting position; **D,** extension-terminal position. D2 upper-extremity pattern moving into: **E,** flexion-starting position; **F,** flexion-terminal position; **G,** extension-starting position; **H,** extension-terminal position.

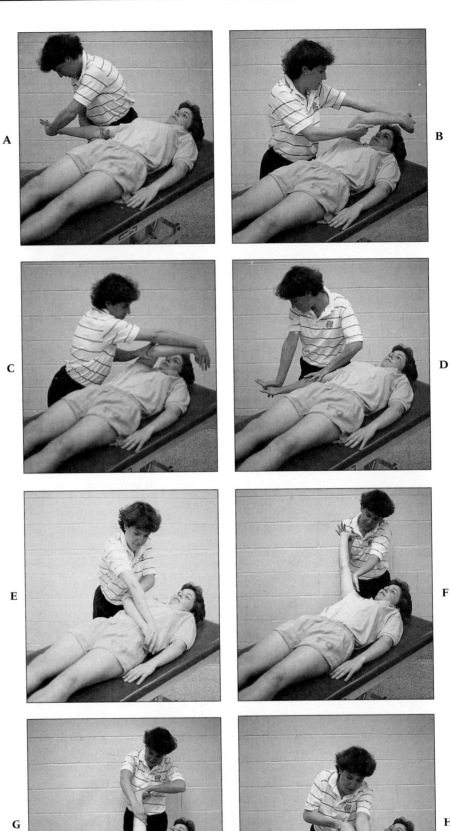

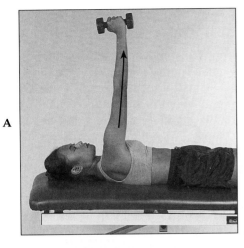

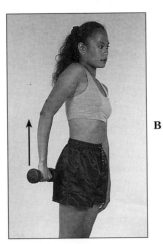

A **B**

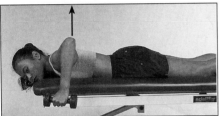

C **D**

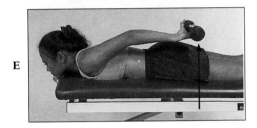

E

Figure 22-40

Strengthening exercises for the scapular stabilizers. **A,** Scapular abduction and upward rotation (serratus anterior). **B,** Scapular elevation (upper trapezius, levator scapulae). **C,** Scapular adduction (middle trapezius). **D,** Scapular depression and adduction (inferior trapezius). **E,** Scapular adduction and downward rotation (rhomboids, inferior trapezius).

Figure 22-41

Isokinetic exercises may be incorporated in the later stages of a rehabilitation program.

Figure 22-42

Plyometric exercise for shoulder strengthening using a weighted ball.

Neuromuscular Control

After injury and some period of immobilization, the athlete must relearn how to use the injured extremity. Coordinated, highly skilled movement about the shoulder joint is essential for successful return to activity. The athlete must not only regain strength and range of motion but must also develop a firing sequence for the specific muscles that are necessary to perform a highly skilled movement.[5] Biofeedback techniques can help the athlete regain control of specific muscle actions. Efforts toward regaining proprioception should begin immediately in the rehabilitation program.[1]

Closed kinetic chain activities are believed to be important for the lower extremity. However, athletes such as gymnasts, wrestlers, and weight lifters frequently work the upper extremity in a closed kinetic chain. Activities that stress closed kinetic chain function include weight shifting on the hands or on a ball (Figure 22-43) and push-ups. These exercises also emphasize cocontraction of antagonistic muscle groups and thus provide neuromuscular control of opposing muscle groups and promote stability about the shoulder joint.[38]

Figure 22-43

Closed kinetic chain activities such as weight shifting may be functionally important for certain athletes. **A,** Weight shifting on a plyoball. **B,** Weight shifting in a four-point position.

Figure 22-44

Surgical tubing attached to a tennis racket may be used as a functional progression for strengthening overhead motions.

Functional Progressions

For the athlete with an injured shoulder joint, functional progressions usually incorporate some sport-specific skill that involves overhead motions such as those required in throwing, swimming, and serving in tennis or volleyball. Strengthening activities should make use of the D2 upper-extremity PNF pattern, which closely resembles overhead throwing and serving motions (see Chapter 16). Attaching surgical tubing to a baseball or tennis racket and having the athlete move through the throwing or serving motion will help increase the athlete's strength both concentrically and eccentrically (Figure 22-44). Throwing and serving motions require high-speed angular velocities. Thus functional progressions should concentrate on a gradual and progressive increase in these angular velocities. Throwing programs, for example, should increase the throwing distance and the throwing velocity through a series of progressive stages. Progression to a more advanced stage is dictated by lack of pain and swelling at the previous stage.[2]

Return to Activity

Decisions to return an athlete to full activity should be based on preestablished criteria that can be clearly demonstrated by functional performance. Isokinetic testing can provide at least some objective measure of strength. The athletic trainer must have a clear understanding of the healing process and the general time frames required for rehabilitation. Return to full activity should be based on mutual agreement among the athlete, team physician, athletic trainer, and coach.

SUMMARY

- The shoulder complex has a great degree of mobility. This mobility, however, requires some compromise in stability, and thus the shoulder is highly susceptible to injury. Many sport activities that involve repetitive overhead movements place a great deal of stress on the shoulder joint.

- Four major articulations are associated with the shoulder complex: the sternoclavicular joint, the acromioclavicular joint, the glenohumeral joint, and the scapulothoracic joint. The muscles that act on the shoulder joint consist of those that originate on the axial skeleton and attach to the humerus, those that originate on the scapula and attach to the humerus, and those that attach the axial skeleton to the scapula.

- Dynamic movement and stabilization of the shoulder complex require integrated functions of the rotator cuff muscles, the joint capsule, and the muscles that stabilize and position the scapula. In movement of the shoulder joint, it is critical to maintain the positioning of the humeral head relative to the glenoid.

- The athletic trainer, when evaluating injuries to the shoulder complex, must take into consideration all four joints. A number of special tests can provide insight relative to the nature of a particular injury.

- Fractures may occur to the clavicle, scapula, or humerus. Sprains may occur at the sternoclavicular, acromioclavicular, or glenohumeral joints.

- Shoulder dislocations and subluxations are relatively common, with an anterior dislocation and posterior subluxation being the most likely to occur. After a dislocation has been reduced and immobilized, muscle reconditioning should be initiated as soon as possible.

- Chronic or recurrent shoulder instability can occur after acute subluxation or dislocation. Recurrent instabilities may be either anterior, posterior, inferior, or multidirectional. The causes of shoulder instabilities may be traumatic (macrotraumatic), atraumatic, microtraumatic (repetitive use), congenital, or neuromuscular.

- Shoulder impingement is closely related to shoulder instability. Athletes involved with overhead activities often exhibit hypermobility and significant capsular laxity. Shoulder impingement involves a mechanical compression of the supraspinatus

22-10

Critical Thinking Exercise

A gymnast has a recurrent anterior dislocation of the glenohumeral joint. She has excellent muscular strength in both the glenohumeral muscles and the scapular muscles. She has had no problem regaining full range of motion. She is extremely worried that her shoulder will dislocate again.

? Because strength and range of motion are not a concern in this athlete, what type of activities should the athletic trainer concentrate on during rehabilitation to help reduce the likelihood of a subsequent dislocation?

22-11

Critical Thinking Exercise

After a grade 1 sprain of the acromioclavicular joint, a lacrosse player is having a difficult time regaining full range of motion in both flexion and abduction. When doing his exercises, he can elevate his arm above 90 degrees.

? What types of activities should the athletic trainer incorporate in the rehabilitation program to help the athlete regain a full range of motion?

tendon, the subacromial bursa, and the long head of the biceps tendon under the coracoacromial arch.

- A number of injuries, including subacromial bursitis, contusions, bicipital tenosynovitis, adhesive capsulitis, peripheral nerve injuries, and thoracic outlet compression syndromes, are common injuries of the shoulder complex in athletes.
- Rehabilitation after injury to the shoulder joint may require a brief period of immobilization. Joint mobilization, flexibility, and strengthening exercises should be initiated as soon as possible after injury. Progression in range of motion and strengthening techniques should be dictated by a lack of pain and swelling associated with increased activity. Activities that stress closed kinetic chain function emphasize cocontraction of antagonistic muscle groups, and thus provide neuromuscular control of opposing muscle groups and promote stability about the shoulder joint. For the athlete with an injured shoulder joint, functional progressions usually incorporate some sport-specific skill that involves overhead motions.

Web Sites

Cramer First Aider: http://www.ccsd.k12.wy.us/cchs_web/cramerfirstaider/fstaider.htm

World Ortho: http://www.worldortho.com

Wheeless' Textbook of Orthopaedics: http://www.medmedia.com/med.htm

American Orthopaedic Society for Sports Medicine: http://www.sportsmed.org

MedFacts Sports Doc: http://www.medfacts.com

Readers can click on the medical library for information about common injuries.

OrthoNet: http://www.orthonet.com

Solutions to Critical Thinking EXERCISES

22-1 The athletic trainer should point out to the athlete that regardless of the strengthening exercises, there is still a high probability that a recurrent dislocation will occur. The dynamic stabilizers of the glenohumeral joint include the subscapularis, infraspinatus, teres minor, and supraspinatus. Remember, it is perhaps just as important to strengthen the scapular muscles.

22-2 Normal scapulohumeral rhythm exhibits no movement of the scapula as the humerus elevates to 30 degrees. As the humerus elevates from 30 degrees to 90 degrees, the scapula should abduct and upwardly rotate 1 degree for every 2 degrees of humeral elevation. From 90 degrees to full abduction of the humerus, the scapula should abduct and rotate upward 1 degree for each 1 degree of humeral elevation.

22-3 Thoracic outlet compression syndromes involve compression of the brachial plexus, subclavian artery, and subclavian vein. The anterior scalene syndrome test, or Adson's test, tests for compression by the heads of the anterior and middle scalene muscles or between the cervical rib and the anterior scalene muscle. The costoclavicular syndrome test (Roo's test or the military brace position test) tests for compression between the first rib and the clavicle. The hyperabduction syndrome test, or

Allen test, tests for compression behind the pectoral muscle and beneath the coracoid process.

22-4 Falling on the tip of the shoulder is a typical mechanism of injury for a sprain of both the acromioclavicular and sternoclavicular joints. It is also possible that a clavicular fracture has occurred.

22-5 In an anterior glenohumeral dislocation, the head of the humerus is forced out of its articular capsule in an anterior direction past the glenoid labrum and then downward to rest under the coracoid process. Torn capsular and ligamentous tissue, a possible tendinous avulsion of the rotator cuff muscles or long head of the biceps, a possible tear or detachment of the glenoid labrum, a possible injury to the brachial plexus, and profuse hemorrhage are all potential problems.

22-6 If the dynamic stabilizers (rotator cuff) and the static stabilizers (joint capsule) of the glenohumeral joint cannot maintain the position of the humeral head relative to the glenoid, there will be excessive translation of the humeral head. Excessive translation of the humerus in the overhead position can result in mechanical impingement of those structures under the coracoacromial arch. If the scapular muscles do not function to maintain the position of the glenoid relative to the humerus, impingement can result.

22-7 Her pain is probably due to mechanical impingement or compression of the supraspinatus tendon, the subacromial bursa, or the long head of the biceps under the coracoacromial arch as the arm moves into a fully abducted or flexed position. The space under the arch becomes even more compressed as the humerus is internally rotated, as would occur during the follow-through.

22-8 Restoring normal biomechanics to the shoulder joint in an effort to maintain space under the coracoacromial arch during overhead activities is critical. The athletic trainer should use techniques that strengthen the rotator cuff muscles, which act to both compress and depress the humeral head relative to the glenoid, and strengthen the scapular muscles, which abduct, elevate, and upwardly rotate the scapula. The athletic trainer should also incorporate posterior and inferior glenohumeral joint mobilizations to reduce tightness in the posterior and inferior joint capsule.

22-9 The subscapularis, pectoralis major, latissimus dorsi, teres major, and anterior deltoid must all contract concentrically to produce internal rotation during the acceleration phase. The infraspinatus, teres minor, and posterior deltoid must contract eccentrically during the follow-through to decelerate internal rotation.

22-10 Efforts toward regaining neuromuscular control should begin immediately in the rehabilitation program. Closed kinetic chain exercises emphasize cocontraction of antagonistic muscle groups, which provides neuromuscular control of opposing muscle groups and promotes stability about the shoulder joint. Activities that stress closed kinetic chain function include weight shifting on the hands or on a ball and push-ups. Biofeedback techniques can help the athlete regain control of specific muscle actions.

22-11 Because the athlete is having difficulty in regaining active range of motion, the athletic trainer might try using diagonal 1 and 2 upper-extremity PNF patterns with rhythmic initiation. This technique involves a progression from passive to active assisted to active contraction throughout a functional range. The trainer should also utilize joint mobilization techniques for not only the acromioclavicular joint but also for the sternoclavicular, glenohumeral, and scapulothoracic joints if needed.

REVIEW QUESTIONS AND CLASS ACTIVITIES

1. Explain why a full range of motion of the shoulder joint requires motion at all four joints in the shoulder complex.
2. Explain how the positioning of the humeral head is maintained relative to the glenoid in overhead throwing motions.
3. What is the relationship between shoulder instability and shoulder impingement?
4. What are the mechanisms of an anterior dislocation and a posterior dislocation?
5. How do recurrent instabilities develop?
6. What can be done to minimize the chances of a baseball pitcher developing shoulder impingement?
7. What is myositis ossificans, and how can its development be prevented?
8. How may an athlete acquire bicipital tenosynovitis? How does this condition lead to a ruptured biceps tendon?
9. Describe the various tests for thoracic outlet compression syndrome.
10. Discuss the mechanics involved in throwing a baseball.
11. Explain why closed kinetic chain exercises are useful in rehabilitation of shoulder injuries.
12. Develop an exercise rehabilitation program for a rotator cuff injury, a glenohumeral dislocation, and an acromioclavicular sprain.

REFERENCES

1. Allegrucci M, Whitney S, Lephart S: Shoulder kinesthesia in healthy unilateral athletes participating in upper extremity sports, *J Orthop Sports Phys Ther* 22(4):220, 1995.
2. Andrews J, Wilk K: *The athlete's shoulder,* New York, 1994, Churchill Livingstone.
3. Bach B, VanFleet T, Novak P: Acromioclavicular joint injuries: controversies in treatment, *Physician Sportsmed* 20(12):87, 1992.
4. Blackburn T, McLeod W: EMG analysis of posterior rotator cuff exercises, *Ath Train* 25(1):40, 1990.
5. Brosa P, Lephart S, Kocher M: Functional assessment and rehabilitation of shoulder proprioception for glenohumeral instability, *J Sport Rehabil* 3(1):84, 1994.
6. Butters K: The scapula. In Rockwood C, Masten F, editors: *The shoulder,* Philadelphia, 1990, Saunders.
7. Cain TA et al: Anterior stability of the glenohumeral joint, *Am J Sports Med* 15:144, 1987.
8. Cavallo RJ, Speer KP: Shoulder instability and impingement in throwing athletes, *Med Sci Sports Exerc* 30(4 suppl.):S18, 1998.
9. Cordasco FA, Wolfe IN, Wootten ME, Bigliani LU: An electromyographic analysis of the shoulder during a medicine ball rehabilitation program, *Am J Sports Med* 24(5):386, 1996.
10. Craig E: Fractures of the clavicle. In Rockwood C, Masten F, editors: *The shoulder,* Philadelphia, 1990, Saunders.
11. DeCarlo M, Malone K, Gerig B, Hunker M: Evaluation of shoulder instability braces, *J Sport Rehabil* 5(2):143, 1996.
12. Grana WA et al: How I manage acute anterior shoulder dislocations, *Physician Sportsmed* 15(4):88, 1987.
13. Greenfield B, Catlin P, Coats P: Posture in patients with shoulder overuse injuries and healthy individuals, *J Orthop Sports Phys Ther* 22(5):287, 1995.
14. Hillman S: Principles and techniques of open kinetic chain rehabilitation: the upper extremity, *J Sport Rehabil* 3(4):319, 1994.
15. Irrgang J, Whitney S, Harner C: Nonoperative treatment of rotator cuff injuries in throwing athletes, *J Sport Rehabil* 1(3):197, 1992.
16. Karas S: Thoracic outlet syndrome. In Hershman E, editor: *Clinics in sports medicine,* Philadelphia, 1990, Saunders.
17. Kibler WB: The role of the scapula in athletic shoulder function, *Am J Sports Med* 26(2):325, 1998.
18. Kibler WB: Shoulder rehabilitation: principles and practice, *Med Sci Sports Exerc* 30(4 suppl):S40, 1998.
19. Li et al: Shoulder function in patients with unoperated anterior shoulder instability, *Am J Sports Med* 19(5):469, 1992.
20. Lutz F, Gieck J: Thoracic outlet compression syndrome, *Ath Train* 22:302, 1986.
21. Masten F, Arntz C: Subacromial impingement. In Rockwood C, Masten F, editors: *The shoulder,* Philadelphia, 1990, Saunders.
22. Masten F, Thomas S, Rockwood C: Glenohumeral instability. In Rockwood C, Masten F, editors: *The shoulder,* Philadelphia, 1990, Saunders.
23. Mendoza F, Main K: Peripheral nerve injuries of the shoulder in the athlete. In Hershman EB, editor: *Neurovascular injuries. Clinics in sports medicine,* vol 9, no 2, Philadelphia, 1990, Saunders.
24. Mendoza F et al: Principles of shoulder rehabilitation in the athlete. In Nicholas JA, Hershman EB, editors: *The upper extremity in sports medicine,* St Louis, 1990, Mosby.
25. Mulligan E: Conservative management of shoulder impingement syndrome, *Ath Train* 23(4):348, 1988.
26. Norris T: History and physical examination of the shoulder. In Nicholas JA, Hershman EB, editors: *The upper extremity in sports medicine,* St Louis, 1990, Mosby.
27. O'Brien S et al: The anatomy and histology of the inferior glenohumeral ligament complex of the shoulder, *Am J Sports Med* 18(5):449, 1990.
28. Perry J et al: The painful shoulder during backstroke: an EMG and cinematographic analysis of 12 muscles, *Clinics J Sports Med* 2(1):13, 1992.
29. Pink M et al: The normal shoulder during freestyle swimming, *Am J Sports Med* 19(6):569, 1991.
30. Plafcan DM, Turczany PJ, Guenin BA, Kegerreis S, Worrell TW: An objective measurement technique for posterior scapular displacement, *J Orthop Sports Phys Ther* 25(5):336, 1997.
31. Rockwood CA, Williams GR, Young DC: Injuries to the acromioclavicular joint. In Rockwood CA, Green DP, Bucholz RW: *Rockwood and Green's fractures in adults,* Philadelphia, 1991, JB Lippincott.
32. Rofii M et al: Computed tomography (CT) arthrography of shoulder instabilities in athletes, *Am J Sports Med* 16(4):353, 1988.

33. Salter E et al: Anatomical observations on the acromioclavicular joint and supporting ligaments, *Am J Sports Med* 15(3):199, 1987.

34. Sawa T: An alternate conservative management of shoulder dislocations and subluxations, *J Ath Train* 27(4):366, 1992.

35. Schneider R, Prentice W: Rehabilitation of shoulder injuries. In Prentice W: *Rehabilitation techniques in sports medicine,* Dubuque, Iowa, 1999, WCB/McGraw-Hill.

36. Scovaggo ML et al: The painful shoulder during freestyle swimming, *Am J Sports Med* 19(6):577, 1991.

37. Skyhar M, Warren R, Altcheck D: Instability of the shoulder. In Nicholas JA, Hershman EB, editors: *The upper extremity in sports medicine,* St Louis, 1990, Mosby.

38. Stone J, Lueken J, Partin N: Closed kinetic chain rehabilitation for the glenohumeral joint, *J Ath Train* 28(1):34, 1993.

39. Taylor M, Fruth S, Kegerreis S: The glenoid labrum: basic science and clinical correlation, *J Sport Rehabil* 4(1):42, 1995.

40. Terry G et al: The function of passive shoulder restraints, *Am J Sports Med* 19(1):26, 1991.

41. Warner J et al: Patterns of flexibility, laxity, and strength in normal shoulders and shoulders with instability and impingement, *Am J Sports Med* 18(4):366, 1990.

42. Watson K: Impingement and rotator cuff lesions. In Nicholas JA, Hershman EB, editors: *The upper extremity in sports medicine,* St Louis, 1990, Mosby.

43. Wilk KE, Arrigo CA, Andrews JR: Current concepts: the stabilizing structures of the glenohumeral joint, *J Orthop Sports Phys Ther* 25(6):364, 1997.

44. Wolin PM, Tarbet JA: Rotator cuff injury: addressing overhead overuse, *Physician Sportsmed* 25(6):54, 1997.

ANNOTATED BIBLIOGRAPHY

Andrews J, Wilk K: *The athlete's shoulder,* New York, 1994, Churchill Livingstone.

This text concentrates on both conservative and surgical treatment of shoulder injuries that occur specifically in the athletic population.

Cailliet R: *Shoulder pain,* ed 3, Philadelphia, 1991, Davis.

This text provides excellent coverage of the fundamental principles for assessing and treating shoulder pain syndromes.

Hartley A: *Practical joint assessment: a sports medicine manual,* St Louis, 1991, Mosby.

This concise manual of joint assessment includes detailed shoulder evaluation.

Hawkins RJ, editor: *Basic science and clinical application in the athlete's shoulder. Clinics in sports medicine,* vol 10, no 4, Philadelphia, 1991, Saunders.

This detailed monograph is dedicated to all aspects of the shoulder in sports.

Nicholas JA, Hershman EB, editors: *The upper extremity in sports medicine,* St Louis, 1995, Mosby.

This text has a great deal of information on the recognition, evaluation, and management of shoulder injuries in addition to injuries of the elbow, wrist, and hand.

Rockwood C, Masten F: *The shoulder,* Philadelphia, 1990, Saunders.

This complete, two-volume set covers every subject relative to the shoulder complex.

The Elbow

When you finish this chapter you should be able to

- Describe the structural and functional anatomy of the elbow and relate it to sports injuries.
- Explain the process for assessing the injured elbow.
- Demonstrate proper immediate and follow-up management of elbow injuries.
- Discuss rehabilitation techniques that can be used following injury to the elbow.

ANATOMY OF THE ELBOW JOINT

Bones

The elbow joint is composed of three bones: the humerus, the radius, and the ulna (Figure 23-1). The distal end of the humerus forms two articulating condyles. The lateral condyle is the capitulum, and the medial condyle is the trochlea.

Articulations

The convex capitulum articulates with the concave head of the radius. The trochlea, which is spool shaped, fits into an articulating groove, the semilunar notch, which is provided by the ulna between the olecranon and coronoid processes. Above each condyle is a projection called the epicondyle. The structural design of the elbow joint permits flexion and extension through the articulation of the trochlea with the semilunar notch of the ulna. Forearm pronation and supination are made possible because the head of the radius rests against the capitulum freely without any bone limitations.

Ligaments and Capsule

The capsule of the elbow, both anteriorly and posteriorly, is relatively thin and is covered by the brachialis muscle in front and the triceps brachii behind. The capsule is reinforced by the ulnar and radial collateral ligaments. The ulnar collateral ligament is composed of a strong anterior band with weaker transverse and middle sheets. The radial collateral ligament does not attach to the radius, which is free to rotate. The radius rotates in the radial notch of the ulna and is stabilized by a strong annular ligament. The annular ligament is attached to the anterior and posterior margins of the radial notch and encircles the head and neck of the radius.

Valgus elbow stability depends mainly on the integrity of the medial collateral ligament. Lateral elbow stability has two factors: stabilization by the annular ligament maintains the relationship of the radial head to the proximal radioulnar joints. This ligament is of major importance in activities that produce forceful flexion-supination movements. Varus elbow joint forces are uncommon. The main stability of the elbow is contingent on the integrity of radiocapitular articulation, the trochlear-ulnar joint with its coronoid process, and intact medial and lateral ligaments. Additional elbow support is provided by the muscle tendons.

Synovium and Bursae

A common synovial membrane invests the elbow and the superior radioulnar articulations, lubricating the deeper structures of the two joints; a sleevelike capsule surrounds the entire elbow joint. The most important bursae in the area of the elbow are the bicipital and olecranon bursae. The bicipital bursa lies in the anterior aspect of the bicipital tuberosity and cushions the tendon when the forearm is pronated. The olecranon bursa lies between the olecranon process and the skin (Figure 23-2).

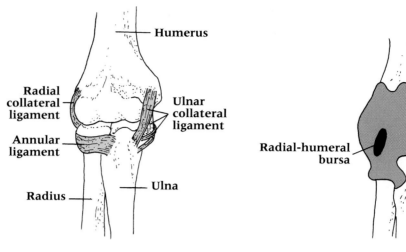

Figure 23-1

Bones and ligaments of the elbow.

Figure 23-2

Synovium and bursae of the elbow.

Musculature

The muscles of the elbow consist of the biceps brachii and the brachialis and brachioradial muscles, all of which in some way act in flexion. Extension is controlled by the triceps brachii muscle (Figure 23-3). The biceps brachii and supinator muscles allow supination of the forearm; the pronator teres and pronator quadratus act as pronators.

Nerve Supply

Nerves stemming from the fifth to eighth cervical vertebrae and the first thoracic vertebra control the elbow muscles. In the cubital fossa, these nerves become the musculocutaneous, radial, and median nerves (Table 23-1).

Figure 23-3

Muscles of the elbow joint. **A,** Anterior view. **B,** Posterior view. **C,** Forearm pronators.

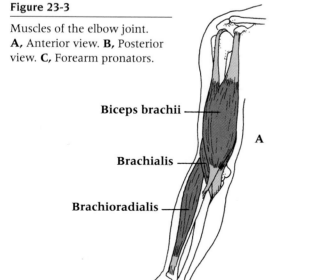

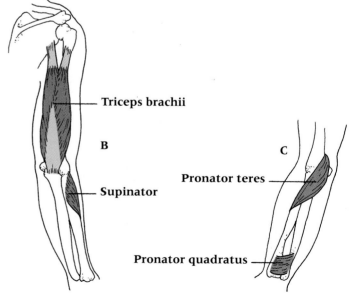

ANTERIOR VIEW   **POSTERIOR VIEW**   **ANTERIOR VIEW**

TABLE 23-1 Resistive Motion to Determine Muscle Weakness Related to Elbow Injury

Resistive Motion	Major Muscles	Involved Nerves
Elbow flexion	Biceps brachii	Musculocutaneous (cervical 5 and 6)
	Brachial	Musculocutaneous (cervical 5 and 6)
	Brachioradial	Radial (cervical 5 and 6)
Elbow extension	Triceps brachii	Radial (cervical 7 and 8)
Forearm supination	Biceps brachii	Musculocutaneous (cervical 5 and 6)
	Supinator	Radial (cervical 6)
Forearm pronation	Pronator teres	Median (cervical 6 and 7)
	Pronator quadratus	Median (cervical 8, thoracic 1)

Blood Supply

Superficial and close to the skin in front of the elbow lie the veins that return the blood of the forearm to the heart. Deep within the antecubital fossa lie the brachial and medial arteries that supply the area with oxygenated blood (Figure 23-4).

FUNCTIONAL ANATOMY

The elbow joint is considered to be a complex rather than a simple joint because the humerus articulates with the radius and ulna. Flexion and extension of the forearm are carried out in the sagittal plane, and supination and pronation occur in the transverse plane.

ASSESSMENT OF THE ELBOW

History

Like all sports injuries, an elbow injury requires the athletic trainer to first understand the possible mechanism of injury. The following questions are commonly asked in the evaluation of the elbow:

- Is the pain or discomfort caused by a direct trauma such as falling on an outstretched arm or landing on the tip of a bent elbow?
- Can the problem be attributed to sudden overextension of the elbow or to repeated overuse of a throwing motion?
- What is the location and duration of the pain? Like shoulder pain, elbow pain or discomfort could be from internal organ dysfunction or referred from a nerve root irritation or nerve impingement.
- Are there movements or positions of the arm that increase or decrease the pain?
- Has a previous elbow injury been diagnosed or treated?
- Is there a feeling of locking or crepitation during movement?

Observation

The athlete's elbow should be observed for obvious deformities and swelling. The carrying angle, flexion, and extensibility of the elbow should be observed. If the carrying angle is abnormally increased, a cubitus valgus is present; if it is abnormally decreased, a cubitus varus is present (Figure 23-5). Too great or too little of an angle may be an indication of a bony or epiphyseal fracture. The athlete is next observed for the extent of elbow flexion and extension. Both elbows are compared (Figure 23-6). A decrease in normal flexion, an inability to extend fully, or extending beyond normal extension (cubitus recurvatus) could be precipitating reasons for joint problems (Figure 23-7). Next, the elbow is bent to a 45-degree angle and observed from the rear to determine whether the two epicondyles and olecranon process form an isosceles triangle (Figure 23-8).

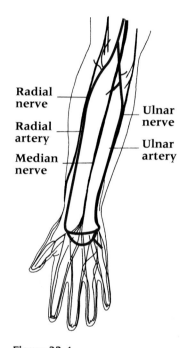

Radial nerve

Radial artery

Median nerve

Ulnar nerve

Ulnar artery

Figure 23-4

Arteries and nerves supplying the elbow joint, wrist, and hand.

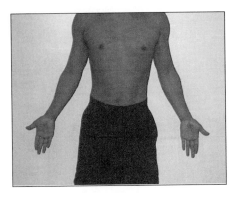

Figure 23-5

Testing for elbow carrying angle and the extent of cubitus valgus and cubitus varus.

Figure 23-6

Testing for elbow flexion and extension.

Figure 23-7

Testing for cubitus recurvatus (elbow hyperextension).

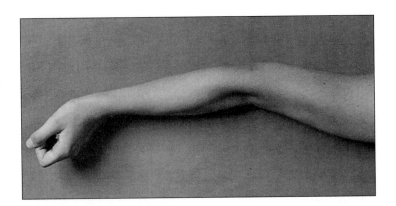

Figure 23-8

Determining whether the lateral and medial epicondyles, along with the olecranon process, form an isosceles triangle.

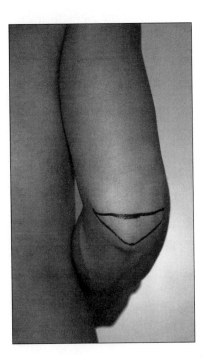

Palpation

Bony Palpation

The following bony landmarks should be palpated:

- Medial epicondyle
- Lateral epicondyle
- Olecranon process
- Radial head
- Radius

Soft Tissue Palpation

The following soft tissue structures should be palpated:

Anterior
- Biceps brachii
- Brachialis
- Brachioradialis
- Pronator teres
- Pronator quadratus

Posterior
- Triceps
- Supinator
- Biceps femoris
- Gracilis
- Pectineus

Medial
- Ulnar collateral ligament
- Wrist flexor muscles

Lateral
- Radial collateral ligament
- Annular ligament
- Wrist extensor muscles

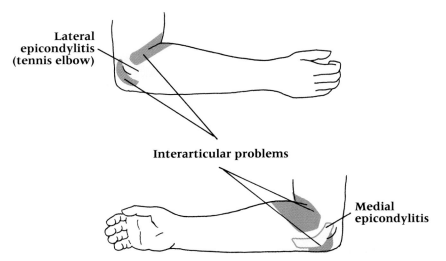

Figure 23-9

Typical pain sites in the elbow region.

Figure 23-10

Tinel's sign.

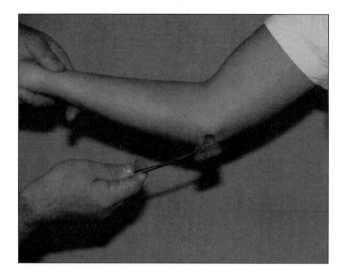

Figure 23-11

Testing for capsular pain after hyperextension of the elbow. **A,** Wrist flexion. **B,** Wrist extension.

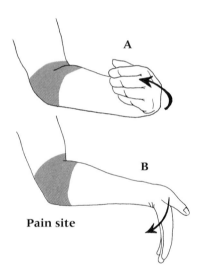

Pain site

A

B

23-1

Critical Thinking Exercise

An athlete sustains a serious sprain to the left elbow.

? What tests and basic examination procedures should be performed to determine the nature of this injury?

Special Tests

Circulatory and Neurological Evaluation

With an elbow injury, a pulse routinely should be taken at the brachial artery, which is located in the antecubital fossa, and at the radial artery at the wrist. Alteration of skin sensation also should be noted, which could indicate nerve root compression or irritation in the cervical or shoulder region or in the elbow itself. Additional nerve evaluation is made through testing active and resistive motion (see Table 23-1).

Tinel's sign   Tinel's test is designed to determine ulnar nerve compromise. The subject is seated with the elbow in slight flexion. The evaluator stands and grasps the athlete's wrist and, with the other hand, taps the ulnar notch between the olecranon process and medial epicondyle with the reflex hammer or the index finger. A positive Tinel's sign is when the athlete complains of a tingling sensation along the forearm, hand, and fingers (Figure 23-10).[13]

Tests for Capsular Injury

To test for capsular pain after hyperextension of the elbow, the elbow is flexed in a 45-degree position. The wrist is flexed as far as possible and then extended as far as possible (Figure 23-11). If joint pain is severe during this test, a moderate to severe sprain or fracture should be suspected.

Valgus/Varus Stress Test

A valgus stress test checks for sprain of the medial collateral ligament. A varus stress test checks for sprain or instability of the lateral collateral ligament. The evaluator grasps the athlete's wrist and extends the arm in an anatomical position. The other hand of the evaluator is placed over either the lateral or medial epicondyle. While the hand that is over the epicondyle acts as a fulcrum, the hand holding the athlete's wrist attempts to move the forearm. In applying the stress, the evaluator notices whether there is gapping of the lateral or medial collateral ligament (Figure 23-12).

The athlete complains of severe pain on the medial aspect of the elbow that becomes relieved by flexing the elbow. There is point tenderness on the medial epicondyle, distal aspect of the ulna, or lateral collateral ligament.

Medial and Lateral Epicondylitis Tests

The elbow is flexed to 45 degrees and wrist extension is resisted, which increases pain at the lateral epicondyle (Figure 23-13). When wrist flexion is resisted, pain is increased at the medial epicondyle.

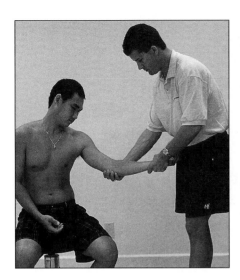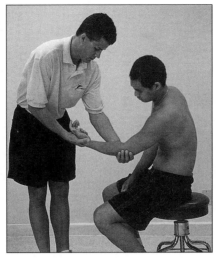

Figure 23-12

Collateral ligament test of the elbow.

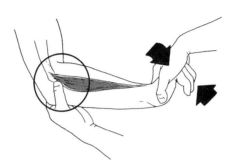

Figure 23-13

Tennis elbow test.

Pinch Grip Test

The athlete is instructed to pinch the tips of the thumb and index finger together. An inability to touch the thumb and index finger indicates entrapment of the anterior interrosseous nerve between the two heads of the pronator muscle (Figure 23-14).

Pronator Teres Syndrome Test

While the athlete is in a seated position, the athletic trainer resists forearm pronation. Increased pain proximally over the pronator teres would indicate a positive test (Figure 23-15).

Functional Evaluation

The joint and the muscles are evaluated for pain sites and weakness through passive, active, and resistive motions consisting of elbow flexion and extension (Figure 23-16) and forearm pronation and supination (see Figure 23-15). Range of motion is particularly noted in passive and active pronation and supination (Figure 23-17).

Figure 23-14

Pinch grip test.

RECOGNITION AND MANAGEMENT OF INJURIES TO THE ELBOW

The elbow is subject to injury in sports because of its broad range of motion, weak lateral bone arrangement, and relative exposure to soft-tissue damage.[27] Many sports place excessive stress on the elbow joint. Locking of the elbow in gymnastics or using implements such as racquets, golf clubs, and javelins can cause injuries. The throwing mechanism in baseball pitching can injure the elbow during both the acceleration and follow-through phases.

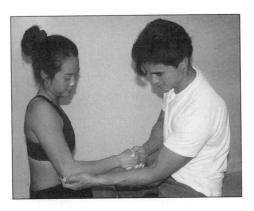

Figure 23-15

Elbow evaluation includes performing passive, active, and resistive forearm pronation and supination.

Figure 23-16

Functional evaluation includes performing passive resistance flexion and extension to determine joint restrictions and pain sites.

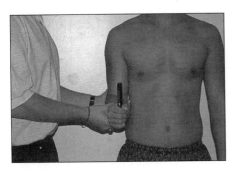
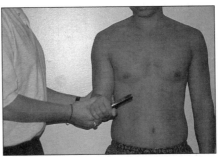
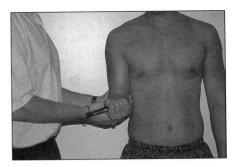

Figure 23-17

The range of motion of forearm pronation and supination is routinely tested in athletes with elbow conditions.

The two most common mechanisms of elbow injury:
- Throwing
- Falling on the outstretched hand

Contusions

Etiology   Because of its lack of padding and its general vulnerability, the elbow often becomes contused during contact sports. Bone bruises arise from a deep penetration or a succession of blows to the sharp projections of the elbow.

Symptoms and signs   A contusion of the elbow may swell rapidly after an irritation of the olecranon bursa or the synovial membrane.

Management   The contused elbow should be treated immediately with cold and pressure for at least twenty-four hours. If injury is severe, the athlete should be referred to a physician for X-ray examination to determine whether a fracture exists.

Olecranon Bursitis

Etiology   The olecranon bursa, lying between the end of the olecranon process and the skin, is the most frequently injured bursa in the elbow (Figure 23-18).[19] Its superficial location makes it prone to acute or chronic injury, particularly as the result of direct blows.[5]

Symptoms and signs   The inflamed bursa produces pain, severe swelling, and point tenderness. Occasionally, swelling will appear almost spontaneously and without the usual pain and heat.

Management   If the condition is acute, a cold compress should be applied for at least one hour. Chronic olecranon bursitis requires a program of superficial therapy primarily involving compression. If swelling fails to resolve, in some cases aspiration will hasten healing. Although seldom serious, olecranon bursitis can be annoying and should be well protected by padding while the athlete is engaged in competition.

Strains

Etiology   The acute mechanisms of muscle strain associated with the elbow joint are usually excessive resistive motions such as a fall on the outstretched hand with the elbow in extension, which forces the joint into hyperextension. Repeated microtears that cause chronic injury are discussed in the section on epicondylitis.[18]

The biceps, brachialis, and triceps muscles should be tested through active and resistive movement. The muscles of pronation and supination are also tested. Rupture of the distal biceps brachii at its radial attachment is the most common muscle rupture in the upper extremity.[23]

Symptoms and signs   During active or resistive movement, the athlete complains of pain. There is usually point tenderness in the muscle, tendon, or lower part of the muscle belly.

Management   Immediate care includes RICE as well as sling support for the most severe cases. Follow-up management may include cryotherapy, ultrasound, and rehabilitative exercises. Conditions that cause moderate to severe loss of elbow function should routinely be referred for X-ray examination. It is important to rule out the possibility of an avulsion or epiphyseal fracture.

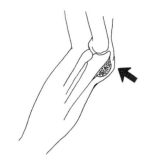

Figure 23-18

Olecranon bursitis.

Elbow Sprains

Etiology   Sprains to the elbow are usually caused by hyperextension or valgus forces.

Symptoms and signs   The athlete complains of pain and an inability to throw or grasp. Inspection displays a point tenderness over the medial collateral ligament. Flexor tendinous injury can also be present. A valgus stress test shows ligamentous disruption. Injuries frequently occur to the ulnar collateral ligament in athletes who throw, because of constant valgus stresses that eventually result in a laxity.[11]

Management   Immediate care for elbow sprains consists of cold and a pressure bandage for at least twenty-four hours with sling support fixed at 45 degrees of flexion. After hemorrhage has been controlled, superficial heat treatments in the form of whirlpool may be started and combined with massage above and below the injury. Like fractures and dislocations, strains also may result in abnormal bone proliferation if the area is massaged directly and too vigorously or is exercised too soon. The main concern should be to gently aid the elbow in regaining a full range of motion and then, when the time is right, to commence active exercises until full mobility and strength have returned. Taping can help and should restrain the elbow from further injury, or it may be used while the athlete is participating in sports (see Figure 8-8).[8]

Lateral Epicondylitis

Epicondylitis is a chronic condition that may affect athletes who execute repeated forearm flexion and extension movements such as are performed in tennis, pitching, golf, javelin throwing, and fencing. The elbow is particularly predisposed to mechanical trauma in the activities of throwing and striking.[21]

Etiology   Lateral epicondylitis is one of the most common problems of the elbow occurring in sports. It is most often seen in tennis players and is also seen in baseball, swimming, gymnastics, fencing, golfing, and hammer throwing.[14] The cause of lateral epicondylitis is repetitive microtrauma to the insertion of the extensor muscle of the lateral epicondyle. Hyperextension is the primary action.[14] Tennis elbow is another name for lateral epicondylitis that stems from a backhand stroke involving wrist overextension.[21]

Symptoms and signs   The athlete complains of an aching pain in the region of the lateral epicondyle during and after activity. The pain gradually becomes worse, and weakness develops in the hand and wrist. Inspection reveals tenderness at the lateral epicondyle and pain on resisted dorsiflexion of the wrist and full extension of the elbow. The elbow has decreased range of motion.

23-3

Critical Thinking Exercise

A tennis player complains of an aching pain around the lateral epicondyle. She indicates that the pain seems to be worse when she tries to hit a backhand shot.

? What is likely the cause of her pain, and how should the athletic trainer choose to treat this problem?

Lateral epicondylitis:
- Tennis elbow

23-4

Critical Thinking Exercise

A gymnast sustains a serious injury to his right elbow following a fall from the parallel bars.

? The athletic trainer, after ruling out fracture, should provide what immediate and follow-up care to this injury?

Management   Treatment includes immediate use of RICE, NSAIDs, and analgesics as needed. Rehabilitation includes ROM exercises, PRE, deep friction massage, hand grasping while in supination, and avoiding pronation movements. Mobilization and stretching may be used within pain-free limits. The athlete may wear a counterforce or neoprene elbow sleeve for one to three months. The athlete must be taught proper skill techniques and the proper use of equipment to avoid recurrence of the injury.[14]

Medial Epicondylitis

Etiology   Irritation and inflammation of the medial epicondyle may result from a number of different sport activities that require repeated forceful flexions of the wrist and extreme valgus torques of the elbow.[27] Pitcher's elbow, racquetball elbow, golfer's elbow, and javelin-thrower's elbow are names used to refer to medial epicondylitis.[16] Young baseball pitchers learning to throw a curveball or screwball tend to use excessive wrist flexions when imparting a spin on the baseball.[12] A forehand stroke in racquetball requires an explosive wrist flexion at impact to achieve maximum velocity. Golfers may use too much wrist flexion on the trail arm on follow-through. Throwing the javelin requires powerful wrist flexion at release (Figure 23-19).

Symptoms and signs   Regardless of the sport or exact location of the injury, the symptoms and signs of epicondylitis are similar. Pain around the epicondyles of the humerus can be produced during forceful wrist flexion or extension. The pain may be centered at the epicondyle, or it may radiate down the arm. There is usually point tenderness and, in some cases, mild swelling. Passive movement of the wrist into extension or flexion seldom elicits pain, although active movement does.

Management   Conservative management of moderate to severe epicondylitis usually includes use of sling rest, cryotherapy, or heat through the application of ultrasound. Analgesics and antiinflammatory agents may be prescribed. A curvilinear

---

Medial epicondylitis:
- Pitcher's elbow
- Racquetball elbow
- Golfer's elbow
- Javelin-thrower's elbow

23-5

Critical Thinking Exercise

A golfer is complaining of pain on the medial aspect of the trail arm during follow-through on the golf swing. When not playing golf, the athlete has a constant aching feeling.

? What is the most likely cause of this medial elbow pain?

Figure 23-19

Repeated overhand throwing actions can cause epicondylitis.

brace applied just below the bend of the elbow is highly beneficial in reducing elbow stress. This brace provides a counterforce, disseminating stress over a wide area and relieving the concentration of forces directly on the bony muscle attachments (Figure 23-20). For more severe cases, elbow splinting and complete rest for seven to ten days may be warranted.[15]

Elbow Osteochondritis Dissecans

Etiology   Although osteochondritis dissecans is more common in the knee, it also occurs in the elbow. Its cause is unknown; however, impairment of the blood supply to the anterior surfaces leads to fragmentation and separation of a portion of the articular cartilage and bone, which creates loose bodies within the joint.[4] Elbow osteochondritis dissecans is seen in the young athlete ten to fifteen years of age who throws or engages in racquet sports. A repetitive microtrauma in the movements of elbow rotation, extension, and valgus stress leads to a compression of the radial head and shearing of the radiocapitular joint.[14] Osteochondritis in children younger than ten years is usually referred to as Panner's disease.[28]

Symptoms and signs   The child or young adolescent athlete usually complains of sudden pain and locking of the elbow joint. Range of motion returns slowly over a few days. Swelling, pain, and crepitation may also occur. There is a decreased ROM, especially in full extension, and tenderness at the radiohumeral joints. There may be a grating sensation on pronation or supination. X-ray examination shows a flattening of the capitellum, a crater in the capitellum, and loose bodies.

Management   In the beginning stage of this condition, activity is restricted for six to twelve weeks, and NSAIDs are administered. With increased degeneration, activity is restricted and a splint or cast is applied along with physical therapy. If there are loose bodies with repeated locking, fragments are removed surgically.[3]

Little League Elbow

Etiology   Little League elbow occurs in 10 percent to 25 percent of young pitchers.[14] It is caused by repetitive microtrauma that occurs from throwing and not from the type of pitch thrown.[3,22] Little League elbow includes many disorders of growth in the pitching elbow.[24] These disorders may include the following:

- An accelerated apophyseal growth region plus a delay in the medial epicondylar growth plate.
- A traction apophysitis with a possible fragmentation of the medial epicondylar apophysis.
- An avulsion of the medial epicondyle of the radial head.
- Osteochondrosis of the humeral capitellum.
- A nonunion stress fracture of the olecranon epiphysis.[22,24]

Symptoms and signs   Injury onset is usually slow. In the beginning, the athlete may have a flexion contraction, which includes a tightness of the anterior joint capsule and a weakness of the triceps muscle.[26] The athlete may complain of a locking or catching sensation. There is decreased ROM of forearm pronation and supination.[7]

Management   Initially, RICE, NSAIDs, and analgesics are given as needed.[14] Throwing is stopped until pain is resolved and full ROM is returned. Gentle stretching and triceps strengthening are carried out. Surgical removal of loose bodies may be required.[7] Good throwing mechanics must be taught.

Cubital Tunnel Syndrome

Etiology   Because of the exposed position of the medial humeral condyle, the ulnar nerve is subject to a variety of problems. The athlete with a pronounced cubitus valgus may develop a friction problem. The ulnar nerve can also become recurrently dislocated because of a structural deformity. The ulnar nerve can become impinged by the arcuate ligament during flexion activities.[9] In a problem of the ulnar nerve

Osteochondritis dissecans in the elbow is similar to that in the knee but is less common.

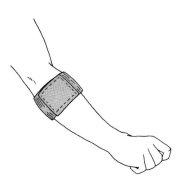

Figure 23-20

Counterforce brace for treatment of elbow epicondylitis.

23-6

Critical Thinking Exercise

A Little League pitcher complains of pain, swelling, and grating in the pitching elbow.

? What might this condition be?

23-7

Critical Thinking Exercise

A javelin thrower with a pronounced elbow cubitus valgus places abnormal pressure on the ulnar nerve.

? What nerve involvement could possibly occur from this situation?

seen in sports such as baseball, tennis, racquetball, and javelin throwing, fascial bands forming the roof of the cubital tunnel compress the ulnar nerve.[2]

Normally, four factors can lead to cubital tunnel syndrome: traction injury from a valgus force, irregularities within the tunnel, subluxation of the ulnar nerve because of a lax ligament, or a progressive compression of the ligament on the nerve.

Symptoms and signs   The athlete complains of pain on the medial aspect of the elbow that may be referred proximally or distally. Palpation indicates tenderness in the cubital tunnel, primarily on hyperflexion. There is intermittent paresthesia reflected by a burning and tingling in the fourth and fifth fingers.[1]

Management   Initially, rest and immobilization for two weeks is recommended, along with NSAIDs. Splinting or surgical decompression or transposition of a subluxating ulnar nerve may be necessary. The athlete must avoid elbow hyperflexion and valgus stresses.[14]

Dislocation of the Elbow

Etiology   Dislocation of the elbow (Figure 23-21) has a high incidence in sports activity and is caused most often either by a fall on the outstretched hand with the elbow in a position of hyperextension or by a severe twist while it is in a flexed position.[2] The bones of the ulna and radius may be displaced backward, forward, or laterally. By far the most common dislocation is one in which both the ulna and the radius are forced backward.[6] The forward-displaced ulna or radius appears deformed. The olecranon process extends posteriorly, well beyond its normal alignment with the humerus. The athletic trainer can distinguish this dislocation from the supracondylar fracture by observing that the lateral and medial epicondyles are normally aligned with the shaft of the humerus.

Symptoms and signs   Elbow dislocations involve rupturing and tearing of most of the stabilizing ligamentous tissue, accompanied by profuse hemorrhage and swelling. There is severe pain and disability. The complications of such traumas include injury to the median and radial nerves as well as to the major blood vessels and arteries and include—in almost every instance—myositis ossificans. Elbow dislocation is often associated with a radial head fracture.

Management   The primary responsibility is to apply cold and pressure immediately, then a sling, and to refer the athlete to a physician for reduction. The neurovascular status of the brachial artery and the median and ulnar nerves must be evaluated before and after reduction.[17] Reducing an elbow dislocation should never be attempted by anyone other than a physician. It must be performed as soon as possible to prevent prolonged derangement of soft tissue. In most cases, the physician will administer an anesthetic before reduction to relax muscles spasms. After reduction, the physician will often immobilize the elbow in a position of flexion and apply a sling suspension, which should be used for approximately three weeks

Figure 23-21

Elbow dislocation

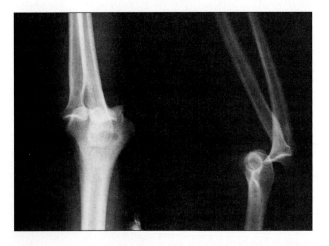

Management PLAN

Posterior Elbow Dislocation

Injury Situation A female athlete fell from the uneven bars and landed on her outstretched left hand. The elbow was forced into hyperextension, dislocating the radial head posteriorly.

Symptoms and Signs The athlete complained of extreme pain in the elbow region and numbness in the forearm and hand. From the side, the forearm appeared shortened. An obvious deformity was that the radial head stuck out beyond the posterior aspect of the elbow. The neurovascular status was assessed and found to be normal.

Management Plan The athlete was referred immediately to a physician who performed an X-ray examination of the elbow to rule out fracture. After the X-ray examination, the elbow was reduced by the physician and placed in a cast and sling at 60 degrees for 6 weeks.

Phase 1 *Acute Injury* **GOAL DURING IMMOBILIZATION PHASE**: To maintain wrist and hand strength and shoulder range of motion while elbow is immobilized.
ESTIMATED LENGTH OF TIME (ELT): 6 weeks.

■ **Exercise rehabilitation** Ball squeeze (10 to 15 repetitions), each waking hour. Shoulder circles in all directions (10 to 15 repetitions), each waking hour. General body maintenance exercises are conducted 3 times a week as long as they do not aggravate injury.

Phase 2 *Repair* **GOAL AFTER CAST IS REMOVED**: Increase range of motion 50% strength and coordination 50%.
ELT: 4 to 6 weeks.

■ **Therapy** Ice (5 to 15 minutes) before and after exercise, electrical stimulation to modulate pain, and low-intensity ultrasound to facilitate healing.

■ **Exercise rehabilitation** Continue exercises performed during immobilization phase, 3 to 4 times daily. Isometric exercise (2 to 3 times), every waking hour. Pain-free active flexion and extension and forearm pronation and supination (10 to 15 repetitions), every waking hour; avoid forcing movements. PNF also can be beneficial. Isokinetic exercise or isotonic exercise against dumbbell resistance, once daily, using daily adjustable progressive resistance exercise (DAPRE). General body maintenance exercises are conducted 3 times a week as long as they do not aggravate injury.

Phase 3 *Remodeling* **GOALS**: To restore 90% of elbow ROM and strength, including power, endurance, and neuromuscular control, and to reenter competition.
ELT: 3 to 6 weeks.

■ **Therapy** Electrical stimulation for muscle reeducation. Ultrasound or massage to increase blood flow in the area. Follow exercise with cryotherapy.

■ **Exercise rehabilitation** Continue phase 2 exercises and add isotonic machine resistance or free-weight barbell exercises; bar dips and chin-ups (10 repetitions), 3 to 4 times a week, can be added to routine. Return to daily gymnastic practice within pain-free limits. If elbow becomes symptomatic in any way, such as pain, swelling, or decreased range of motion, athlete is to return to phase 2 exercises.

Continued

Posterior Elbow Dislocation—*cont'd*

Criteria for Return to Competitive Gymnastics

The athlete must be able to do the following:

1. Extend and flex the elbow to at least 95% of the uninjured elbow.
2. Pronate and supinate the forearm to at least 95% of the uninjured arm.
3. Perform an elbow curl 10 times, for 3 sets, against a resistance equal to or greater than that which can be handled by the uninjured elbow (this resistance could be measured by an isokinetic testing device).
4. Perform an elbow extension 10 times, for 3 sets, against a resistance equal to or greater than that which can be handled by the uninjured elbow (this resistance also can be measured by an isokinetic testing device).
5. Pronate and supinate the forearm against a resistance equal to or greater than that which can be handled by the uninjured forearm.
6. Perform 10 full bar dips.
7. Perform 10 chin-ups.
8. Perform a full routine on the uneven bars without causing discomfort.

(Figure 23-22). While the arm is maintained in flexion, the athlete should execute hand gripping and shoulder exercises. Once initial healing has occurred, heat and gentle, passive exercise may be applied to help regain a full range of motion. Above all, massage and joint movements that are too strenuous should be avoided before complete healing has occurred because of the high probability of encouraging myositis ossificans. Both range of movement and a strength program should be initiated by the athlete, but forced stretching must be avoided.

Fractures of the Elbow

Etiology   An elbow fracture can occur in almost any sports event and is usually caused by a fall on the outstretched hand or the flexed elbow or by a direct blow to the elbow (Figure 23-23). Children and young athletes have a much higher rate of

Figure 23-22

Dynasplint for the reduction of elbow flexion contraction.

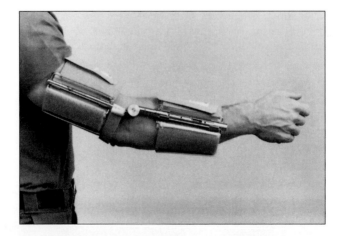

Figure 23-23

A fall on the outstretched hand can produce an elbow fracture.

this injury than do adults. A fracture can take place in any one or more of the bones that compose the elbow.[8]

A fall on the outstretched hand often fractures the humerus above the condyles, the condyles proper, or the area between the condyles. A condylar fracture at the elbow may cause a *gunstock deformity* in which the forearm, when extended, creates an angle with the upper arm relative to the log axis of the upper arm that resembles a gunstock. The ulna and radius also may be the recipients of trauma, and direct force delivered to the olecranon process of the ulna or a force transmitted to the head of the radius may cause a fracture.

Symptoms and signs   An elbow fracture may or may not result in visible deformity. There usually will be hemorrhage, swelling, and muscle spasm in the injured area.

Management   Like a dislocation, an elbow fracture can be associated with certain complications. One major complication is decreased ROM. The neurovascular status of the injury must be continually monitored. Surgery is used to stabilize an adult unstable elbow fracture and is followed by early ROM exercises. Stable fractures do not require surgery. Removable splints are used for six to eight weeks.[21]

Volkmann's Contracture

Etiology   It is essential that athletes who sustain a serious elbow injury have their brachial or radial pulse monitored periodically to rule out the possibility of a Volkmann's contracture. This condition is most often associated with a humeral supracondylar fracture, which causes muscle spasm, swelling, or bone pressure on the brachial artery and inhibits blood circulation to the forearm, wrist, and hand.

Symptoms and signs   Such a contracture can become permanent. The first indication of this problem is pain in the forearm that becomes greater when the fingers are passively extended. This pain is followed by cessation of the brachial and radial pulses.

Management   Management of the athlete with beginning signs of tissue pressure reflected by pain, coldness, and decreased motion includes the removing of elastic wraps or casts and elevation of the part. Close monitoring must occur.

> Volkmann's contracture is a major complication of a serious elbow injury.

REHABILITATION OF THE ELBOW

Rehabilitation of the elbow depends on the type of injury incurred, the specific sport played, and whether conservative or postsurgical care is involved. In general, the entire upper-arm kinetic chain, as well as the trunk and lower extremities, must be considered.

General Body Conditioning

While the elbow is being specifically rehabilitated, the athlete is directed to perform general body exercises to main preinjury fitness level.

23-8

Critical Thinking Exercise

An athlete sustains a serious elbow injury that requires immobilization by casting.

? What major concerns should the athletic trainer have if swelling occurs within the cast?

Figure 23-24

Inferior humeroulnar glides. This technique increases elbow flexion and extension. It is performed using the body weight to stabilize proximally with the hand grasping the ulna and gliding inferiorly.

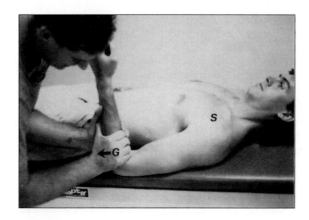

Figure 23-25

Humeroradial inferior glides. This technique increases the joint space and improves flexion and extension.

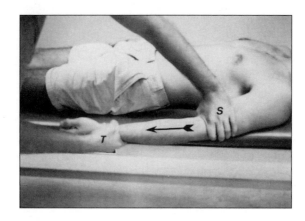

23-9

Critical Thinking Exercise

An athlete has completed physical rehabilitation following an elbow dislocation.

? What is the rehabilitative criteria for this athlete to return to full competition?

Elbow Joint Mobilization

An elbow that is immobilized and has restricted motion for a period of time develops orthrofibrosis and adhesive capsulitis as well as calcific tendinitis. It is therefore important that early ROM and mobilizations be instituted. Mobilization and traction techniques increase joint mobility and decrease pain by restoring accessory movements (Figures 23-24 and 23-25).[20]

Flexibility

As mentioned, restoring normal ROM is important early in elbow rehabilitation. A variety of approaches can be applied as long as they do not force the joint. One example is a slow passive stretch with a low force and a long duration. Active assistive or partner stretching can follow passive stretching (Figures 23-26 and 23-27). PNF exercise also aids in restoring a normal ROM (Figure 23-28).

After a severe injury, such as a dislocation, or after a surgical procedure, initial rehabilitation is directed toward regaining or maintaining normal range of motion. After surgery, a continuous passive movement could be used.

Strengthening

Beginning strengthening is achieved by low-resistance, high-repetition exercise of the biceps brachialis, triceps, pronators, supinators, wrist flexors, and wrist extensors.[25] Grip and shoulder exercises are also performed to increase strength and range of motion. All activities must be pain free.[10]

Two procedures may be used to maintain elbow mobility following surgery: the use of the continuous passive machine immediately after surgery, followed by the use of a dynamic splint. In some cases, isometric exercise is appropriate while the el-

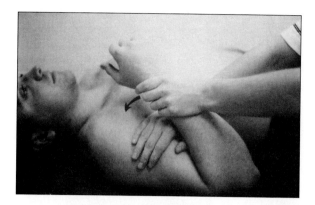

Figure 23-26

Partner stretching of triceps (medial and lateral head) and anconeus. The biceps muscle is stretched when the elbow is moved in the opposite direction.

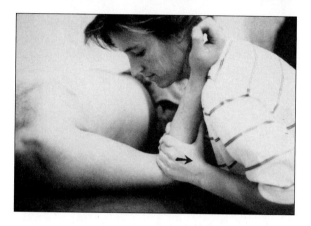

Figure 23-27

Position for humeroulnar joint traction.

bow is immobilized. Maintaining the strength of these articulations will speed the recovery of the elbow.[28] After the elbow has healed and free movement is permitted by the physician, the first consideration should be restoration of the normal range of movement. PNF and isokinetic exercises are valuable in the early and intermediate active stage of rehabilitation. Isokinetic exercise is valuable because of its speed control, its use of concentric and eccentric work, and its endurance development. Isokinetic exercise should be begun when the athlete has a full ROM; it is a good beginning to functional retraining.

Closed kinetic chain exercises are used for athletes who perform in open kinetic chain sports such as throwing. Closed kinetic chain exercises help provide both static and dynamic stability to the elbow. Proprioceptive conditioning of the elbow must be considered (Figures 23-29 and 23-30).

23-10

Critical Thinking Exercise

A wrestler is rehabilitating the elbow following a posterior dislocation.

? What exercises should this athlete do to strengthen the musculature around the elbow joint?

Functional Progressions

When the athlete has full elbow mobility, no pain or swelling, and 90 percent of preinjury strength, he or she can engage in the following functional progressions:

Figure 23-28

PNF exercises for the elbow.

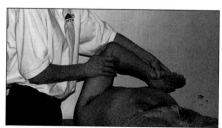
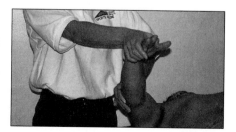

Figure 23-29

Sitting push-up.

Figure 23-30

Wall push-up.

- Open kinetic chain activities with a controlled ROM
- Open kinetic chain activities through pain-free ROM
- Closed kinetic chain exercises for stability and neuromuscular control
- Plyometrics
- Mimicry of functional activity

Return to Activity

The athlete can return to activity after achieving full ROM, joint stability, and functional strength. The athlete must maintain a high level of conditioning. Inadequate rest must be avoided to prevent a recurrence of an overuse injury. When full ROM has been regained, a graded, progressive, resistive exercise program should be initiated, including flexion, extension, pronation, and supination (Figure 23-31).

Protective Taping and Bracing

Protective taping must be continued until full strength and flexibility have been restored. Long-standing chronic conditions of the elbow usually cause gradual debilitation of the surrounding soft tissue. Elbows with conditions of this type should be re-

Figure 23-31

A gradual program of progressive resistance is important to elbow rehabilitation.

stored to the maximum state of conditioning without encouraging postinjury aggravation.

SUMMARY

- The elbow is anatomically one of the more complex joints in the human body. The elbow joint allows the movements of flexion and extension, and the radioulnar joint allows forearm pronation and supination.
- Osteochondritis dissecans affects the lateral aspect of the elbow. It is associated with a loose body in the joint and in young athletes is called Panner's disease.
- In athletes, the ulnar collateral ligament is injured as a result of a valgus force from the repetitive trauma of overhead throwing.
- Medial epicondylitis is also called golfer's elbow, racquetball elbow, and pitcher's elbow and occurs because of repetitive forced flexion of the wrist.
- Lateral epicondylitis, or tennis elbow, occurs with repetitive wrist extension.
- Elbow dislocations result from elbow hyperextension. The typical injury is a fall on an extended arm that dislocates the radius and ulna posteriorly. The degree of stability present will determine the course of rehabilitation. If the elbow is stable, a brief period of immobilization is followed by rehabilitation.
- Fractures in the elbow may occur from a direct blow or from falling on an outstretched hand. They may be treated by casting or, in some cases, by surgical reduction and fixation.

Web Sites

Cramer First Aider: http://www.ccsd.k12.wy.us/cchs_web/
    cramerfirstaider/fstaider.htm

World Ortho: http://www.worldortho.com

Wheeless' Textbook of Orthopaedics: http://www.medmedia.
    com/med.htm

American Orthopaedic Society for Sports Medicine: http://
    www.sportsmed.org

MedFacts Sports Doc: http://www.medfacts.com

OrthoNet: http://www.orthonet.com

Solutions to *Critical Thinking* EXERCISES

23-1 The athletic trainer performs tests for ligamentous and capsular stability. Pulses are taken at the wrist and antecubital fossa. Changes of skin sensation and the athlete's pain reaction to passive, active, and resistive exercise are noted.

23-2 Swelling in the region of the olecranon process following irritation may indicate olecranon bursitis. This condition is best treated with a compression wrap and antiinflammatory medications.

23-3 It is likely that this tennis player has an inflammation of the lateral epicondyle, which is typically called tennis elbow. Tennis elbow occurs from repeated and forceful hyperextension of the wrist. It is best treated using rest, ice compression, and antiinflamatory medications.

23-4 Immediate care consists of RICE and NSAIDs. More definitive management can include ROM exercises, PRE, friction massage, and hand grasping exercises while the elbow is in supination. Pronation movements are avoided. Mobilization and stretching can also be employed within pain-free limits.

23-5 This injury is most likely an inflammation of the medial epicondyle that is caused by forceful hyperflexion of the wrist. Often called golfer's elbow, this condition almost always occurs in the trail arm (for a right-handed golfer, the trail arm would be the right arm). Rest, antiinflammatory medication, and ice should be used to treat this problem.

23-6 The young pitcher's condition indicates the possibility of an elbow osteochondritis dissecans, sometimes called Panner's disease.

23-7 This javelin thrower has sustained a cubital tunnel syndrome. Because of a pronounced elbow cubitus valgus, the ulnar recurrently subluxates. Because of ligamentous laxity, there is nerve impingement and compression.

23-8 The concern of the athletic trainer is that this injury can cause a Volkmann's ischemic contracture. The brachial and radial pulses must be monitored for the possibility of a decreasing normal circulation.

23-9 This athlete must have regained full ROM in flexion, extension, pronation, and supination and must have regained full strength in these muscles.

23-10 This wrestler should do bicep curls to strengthen the biceps brachii and the brachialis and brachioradial muscles, all of which in some way act in flexion; tricep extensions to strengthen the triceps muscle; supination to strengthen the biceps brachii and supinator muscles; and pronation to strengthen the pronator teres and pronator quadratus.

REVIEW QUESTIONS AND SUGGESTED ACTIVITIES

1. Describe the procedures for assessing an elbow injury.
2. Describe the mechanism and management of elbow strains and sprains.
3. Describe how and why the elbow becomes chronically strained from throwing mechanisms.
4. Describe a dislocated elbow—its cause, appearance, and care.
5. How does the elbow sustain epicondylitis? Describe its appearance and management.
6. Compare elbow osteochondritis dissecans and knee osteochondritis dissecans. How does each occur?
7. What are the symptoms and signs of the elbow osteochondritis dissecans?
8. What causes a Volkmann's contracture? How may it be detected early?
9. Discuss the many aspects of elbow exercise rehabilitation.

REFERENCES

1. Allman FL, Carlson CA: Rehabilitation of elbow injuries. In Nicholas JA, Hershman EB, editors: *The upper extremity in sports medicine,* St Louis, 1995, Mosby.
2. Andrews JR, Whiteside JA: Common elbow problems in the athlete, *J Orthop Sports Phys Ther* 17(6):289, 1993.
3. Andrish JT: Osteochondritis dissecans in a young pitcher, *Physician Sportsmed* 25(3):85, 1997.
4. Barrett J: Reflex sympathetic dystrophy, *Physician Sportsmed* 23(4):51, 1995.
5. Bennett JB: Acute injuries to the elbow. In Nicholas JA, Hershman EB, editors: *The upper extremity in sports medicine,* St Louis, 1995, Mosby.
6. Blackard D, Sampson J: Management of an uncomplicated posterior elbow dislocation, *J Ath Train* 32(1):63, 1997.
7. Boyd Jr DW: Osteochondritis dissecans of the elbow, *Sports Med Digest* 15(7):2, 1993.
8. Brown DE et al: *Orthopedic secrets,* Philadelphia, 1995, Hanley & Belfus.
9. Bruce SL, Wasielewski N, Hawke RL: Cubital tunnel syndrome in a collegiate wrestler: a case report, *J Ath Train* 32(2):151, 1997.
10. Cordasco F, Parkes J: Overuse injuries of the elbow. In Nicholas JA, Hershman EB, editors: *The upper extremity in sports medicine,* St Louis, 1995, Mosby.
11. Ellenbecker TS et al: Medial elbow joint laxity in professional baseball pitchers, *Am J Sports Med* 26(3):420, 1998.
12. Fleisig GS et al: Kinetics of baseball: pitching with implications about injury mechanisms, *Am J Sports Med* 23(2):233, 1995.
13. Glousman RE: Ulnar nerve problems in the athlete's elbow. In Hershman EB, editor: *Neurovascular injuries. Clinics in sports medicine,* vol 9, no 2, Philadelphia, 1990, Saunders.
14. Halperin BC: Elbow and arm injuries. In Birrer RB, editor: *Sports medicine for the primary care physician,* ed 2, Boca Raton, Fla, 1994, CRC Press.
15. Hannafin JA: How I manage tennis and golfer's elbow, *Physician Sportsmed* 24(2):63, 1996.
16. Hocutt JE: General type injuries. In Birrer RB, editor: *Sports medicine for the primary care physician,* ed 2, Boca Raton, Fla, 1994, CRC Press.
17. Hoffman DF: Elbow dislocations, *Physician Sportsmed* 21(11):57, 1993.
18. Nirschl RP, Kraushaar BS: Guidelines for elbow injuries, *Physician Sportsmed* 24(5):43, 1996.
19. Nuber GW, Bower MK: Olecranon stress fracture in throwing athletes. In Torg JS, Shephard RJ, editors: *Current therapy in sports medicine,* ed 3, St Louis, 1995, Mosby.
20. Prentice WE: Mobilization and traction techniques. In Prentice WE, editor: *Rehabilitation techniques in sports medicine,* ed 3, Dubuque, Iowa, 1999, WCB/McGraw-Hill.
21. Regan WD: Lateral elbow pain in the athlete: a clinical review, *Clin Sports Med* 1(1):53, 1991.
22. Rettig AC et al: Epidemiology of elbow, forearm, and wrist injuries in the athlete. In Plancher KD, editor: *The athletic elbow and wrist. Part I. Clinics in sports medicine,* vol 14, no 2, Philadelphia, 1995, Saunders.
23. Thompson KL: Rupture of the distal biceps tendon in a collegiate football player: a case report, *J Ath Train* 33(1):62, 1998.
24. Torg JS: Injuries to the upper extremity—Little League elbow. In Torg JS, Shephard RJ, editors: *Current therapy in sports medicine,* St Louis, 1995, Mosby.
25. Tracy J, Obuchi S, Johnson B: Kinematic and electromyographic analysis of elbow flexion during inertial exercise, *J Ath Train* 30(3):254, 1995.
26. Wells M, Bell G: Concerns on Little League elbow, *J Ath Train* 30(3):249, 1995.
27. Werner SL: Biomechanics of the elbow during baseball pitching, *J Orthop Sports Phys Ther* 17(6):274, 1993.
28. Zulia P, Prentice W: Rehabilitation of elbow injuries. In Prentice W: *Rehabilitation techniques in sports medicine,* Dubuque, Iowa, 1999, WCB/McGraw-Hill.

ANNOTATED BIBLIOGRAPHY

Plancher KD, editor: *The athletic elbow and wrist. Part I. Clinics in sports medicine,* vol 14, no 2, Philadelphia, 1995, Saunders.

This in-depth monograph covers the diagnosis and conservative treatment of athletic elbow and wrist injuries.

Plancher KD, editor: *The athletic elbow and wrist. Part II. Clinics in sports medicine,* vol 15, no 2, Philadelphia, 1996, Saunders.

This monograph offers detailed discussions of the most common injuries and of overuse injuries to the elbow and wrist that occur in sports.

Winkle D et al: *Diagnosis and treatment of the upper extremity,* Amsterdam, 1997, Aspen.

This text is a detailed discussion of the orthopedic examination and treatment based on the Cyriax model.

The Forearm, Wrist, Hand, and Fingers

When you finish this chapter you should be able to

- Describe the structural and functional anatomy of the forearm, wrist, hand, and fingers.
- Describe the process of assessment for injuries to the forearm, wrist, hand, and fingers.
- Discuss management techniques for dealing with injuries to the forearm, wrist, hand, and fingers.
- Discuss the appropriate rehabilitation techniques for dealing with injuries to the forearm, wrist, hand, and fingers.

ANATOMY OF THE FOREARM

Bones

The bones of the forearm are the ulna and the radius (Figure 24-1).The ulna, which may be thought of as a direct extension of the humerus, is long, straight, and larger proximally than distally. The radius, considered an extension of the hand, is thicker distally than proximally.

Articulations

The forearm has three articulations: the superior, middle, and distal radioulnar joints. The superior radioulnar articulation is a pivot joint that moves in a ring formed by the ulna and the annular ligament.

The middle radioulnar joint, which is the junction between the shafts of the ulna and the radius, is held together by an oblique ligamentous cord and the interosseous membrane. The oblique cord is a small band of ligamentous fibers that are attached to the lateral side of the ulna and pass downward and laterally to the radius. The interosseous membrane is a thin sheet of fibrous tissue that runs downward between the radius and the ulna and transmits forces directly through the hand from the radius to the ulna. The middle radioulnar joint provides a surface for muscle attachments, and there are openings for blood vessels at the upper and lower ends.

The distal radioulnar joint is a pivot joint formed by the articulation of the head of the ulna with a small notch on the radius. It is held securely by the anterior and posterior radioulnar ligaments. The inferior ends of the radius and ulna are bound by an articular, triangular disk that allows radial movement of 180 degrees into supination and pronation.

Musculature

The forearm muscles consist of flexors and pronators that are positioned anteriorly and extensors and supinators that lie posteriorly. The flexors of the wrist and fingers are separated into superficial muscles and deep muscles (Figure 24-2). The deep flexors arise from the ulna, the radius, and the interosseous tissue anteriorly, and the superficial flexors come from the internal humeral condyle. The extensors of the wrist and fingers originate on the posterior aspect and the external condyle of the humerus.

Nerve and Blood Supply

Except for the flexor carpi ulnaris and half of the flexor digitorum profundus, most of the flexor muscles of the forearm are supplied by the median nerve. The majority of the extensor muscles are controlled by the radial nerve. The major blood supply stems from the brachial artery, which divides into the radial and ulnar arteries in the forearm.

ASSESSMENT OF THE FOREARM

History

The following questions are asked to determine forearm injuries:

- What caused the injury (e.g., blunt trauma, throwing, or chronic overuse)?
- What were the symptoms at the time of injury? Did symptoms occur later?
- Were symptoms localized or diffused?
- Was there swelling or discoloration?
- Was there immediate loss of function?
- What treatment was given?
- How does the forearm feel now?

Observation

The entire forearm, including the wrist and elbow, is first visually inspected for obvious deformities, swelling, and skin defects. If a deformity is not present, the athlete then is observed pronating and supinating the forearm.

Palpation

The injured forearm is palpated at distant sites as well as at the point of injury. Palpation can reveal tenderness, edema, fracture deformity, change in skin temperature, a false joint, bone fragments, or a lack of continuity between bones.

Bony Palpation

The following bony landmarks should be palpated:

- Proximal radial head
- Olecranon process
- Radial shaft

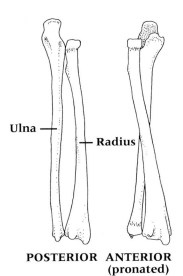

POSTERIOR ANTERIOR (pronated)

Figure 24-1

Bones of the forearm.

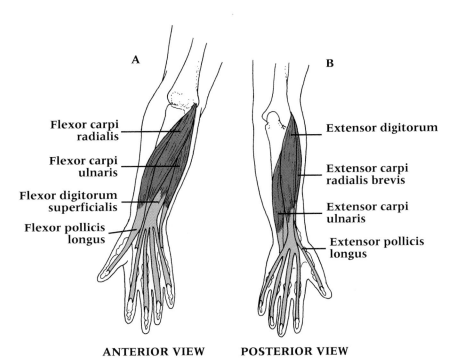

Figure 24-2

Muscles of the forearm. **A,** Anterior view. **B,** Posterior view.

A

Flexor carpi radialis
Flexor carpi ulnaris
Flexor digitorum superficialis
Flexor pollicis longus

B

Extensor digitorum
Extensor carpi radialis brevis
Extensor carpi ulnaris
Extensor pollicis longus

ANTERIOR VIEW   **POSTERIOR VIEW**

- Ulnar shaft
- Distal radius
- Radial styloid process
- Ulnar head
- Ulnar styloid

Soft-Tissue Palpation

The following soft tissue structures should be palpated:

Articulations
- Distal radioulnar joint
- Radiocarpal joint
- Extensor retinaculum
- Flexor retinaculum

Extensor muscles (posterolateral)
- Extensor carpi radialis longus
- Extensor carpi radialis brevis
- Extensor carpi ulnaris
- Brachioradialis
- Extensor pollicis longus
- Extensor pollicis brevis
- Abductor pollicis longus
- Extensor indicus supinator

Flexor muscles (anteromedial)
- Flexor carpi radialis
- Flexor carpi ulnaris
- Palmaris longus
- Flexor digitorum superficialis
- Flexor digitorum profundus
- Flexor pollicis longus
- Pronator quadratus
- Pronator teres

RECOGNITION AND MANAGEMENT OF INJURIES TO THE FOREARM

The forearm, lying between the elbow joint and the wrist, is indirectly influenced by injuries to these areas; however, direct injuries can also occur.

Contusions

Etiology   The forearm is constantly exposed to bruising in contact sports such as football. The ulnar side receives the majority of blows in arm blocks and, consequently, the greater amount of bruising. Bruises to this area may be classified as acute or chronic. The acute contusion can result in a fracture, but this happens only rarely.

Symptoms and signs   Most often a muscle or bone develops varying degrees of pain, swelling, and hematoma. The chronic contusion develops from repeated blows to the forearm with attendant multiple irritations. Heavy fibrosis may take the place of the hematoma, and a bony callus has been known to arise out of this condition.

Management   Care of the contused forearm requires proper attention in the acute stages through application of RICE for at least one hour, followed the next day by cryotherapy. Protection of the forearm is important for athletes who are prone to this condition. The best protection consists of a full-length sponge rubber pad for the forearm early in the season.

Forearm Splints

Etiology   Forearm strain can occur in a variety of sports; most such injuries come from a severe static contraction. Repeated static contraction can lead to forearm splints. Forearm splints, like the medial tibial stress syndrome (shinsplints), are diffi-

Forearm splints, like shin-splints, commonly occur either early or late in the sports season.

cult to manage. They occur most often in gymnasts, particularly those who perform on the side horse, and in wrestlers.[2]

Symptoms and signs   The main symptom is a dull ache between the extensor muscles, which cross the back of the forearm. There also may be weakness and extreme pain during muscle contraction. Palpation reveals an irritation of the interosseous membrane and surrounding tissue. The cause of this condition is uncertain; like shinsplints, forearm splints usually appear either early or late in the season, which indicates poor conditioning or fatigue, respectively. The pathological process is believed to result from the constant static muscle contractions of the forearm (e.g., those contractions required to stabilize the side horse participant). Continued isometric contraction causes minute tears in the area of the interosseous membrane.

Management   Care of forearm splints is symptomatic. If the problem occurs early in the season, the athlete should concentrate on increasing the strength of the forearm through resistance exercises, but if it arises late in the season, emphasis should be placed on rest and cryotherapy or heat and use of a supportive wrap during activity.

The forearm can also sustain an acute or chronic exertional compartment syndrome, although this condition is much less common than in the lower leg. It can occur in sports such as gymnastics and weight lifting and can result from direct injuries such as muscle avulsion, distal radius fracture, or a crushing injury. The deep forearm compartment containing the flexor digitorum profundus, flexor pollicus longus, and pronator quadratus is most susceptible to changes of muscle and nerve ischemia. Detection and management of this condition are the same as for the lower leg condition.

Forearm Fractures

Etiology   Fractures of the forearm (Figure 24-3) are particularly common among active children and youths and occur as the result of a blow or a fall on the outstretched hand.[12] Fractures to the ulna or the radius alone are much rarer than simultaneous fractures to both. A direct blow to the forearm usually results in a fracture to the ulna. The forearm break usually presents all the features of a long-bone fracture: pain, swelling, deformity, and a false joint. If the break is in the upper third, the pronator teres muscle has a tendency to pull the forearm into an abduction deformity, whereas fractures of the lower portion of the arm are often in a neutral position. The older the athlete, the greater the danger of extensive damage to soft tissue and the greater the possibility of paralysis from Volkmann's contractures.

Symptoms and signs   The athlete experiences an audible pop or crack followed by moderate to severe pain, swelling, and disability. There is localized tenderness, edema, and ecchymosis with possible crepitus.[12]

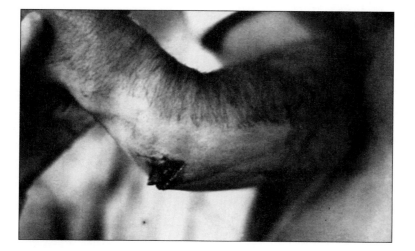

Figure 24-3

An open fracture of the ulna.

Figure 24-4

Common appearance of the forearm in Colles' fracture.

Management   Initially, RICE is applied, followed by splinting until definitive care is available. Definitive care consists of a long-arm plaster or fiberglass cast followed by a program of rehabilitation.

Colles' Fracture

Etiology   Colles' fractures are among the most common types of forearm fractures and involve the lower end of the radius or ulna (Figure 24-4). The mechanism of injury is usually a fall on the outstretched hand, forcing the radius and ulna backward and upward (hyperextension). Much less common is the reverse of Colles' fracture. The mechanism of this fracture is the result of a fall on the back of the hand.[19]

Symptoms and signs   In most cases, there is forward displacement of the radius that causes a visible deformity to the wrist, which is commonly called a *silver fork* deformity. Sometimes no deformity is present, and the injury may be passed off as a bad sprain—to the detriment of the athlete. Bleeding is profuse in this area, and the extravasated fluids can cause extensive swelling in the wrist and, if unchecked, in the fingers and forearm. Ligamentous tissue is usually unharmed, but tendons may be torn and avulsed, and there may be median nerve damage.[19]

Management   The main responsibility is to apply a cold compress, splint the wrist, put the limb in a sling, and then refer the athlete to a physician for X-ray examination and immobilization. Severe sprains should always be treated as possible fractures. Lacking complications, the Colles' fracture will keep an athlete out of sports for one to two months. It should be noted that what appears to be a Colles' fracture in children and youths is often a lower epiphyseal separation.[22]

ANATOMY OF THE WRIST, HAND, AND FINGERS

Bones

The wrist, or carpus, is the region that connects the distal forearm to the hand. It is formed by the distal aspect of the radius and the ulna with a proximal row of four and a distal row of four carpal bones that articulate with five metacarpals. Appearing in order from the radial to the ulnar side in the first, or proximal, row of carpal bones are the scaphoid (navicular), lunate, triquetral, and pisiform bones; the distal row consists of the greater multangular (trapezium), lesser multangular (trapezoid), capitate, and hamate bones (Figure 24-5).

Figure 24-5

Bones of the wrist and hand.

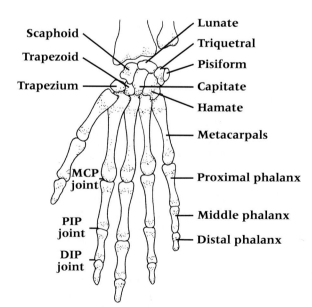

The concave surfaces of the lower ends of the radius and ulna articulate with the convex surfaces of the first row of carpal bones, with the exception of the pisiform, which articulates with the triangular fibrocartilage complex (TFCC) interposed between the head of the ulna and the triquetral bone.

Articulations

Radiocarpal Joints

The radiocarpal joint is a condyloid joint and permits flexion, extension, abduction, and circumduction. Its major strength is drawn from the great number of tendons that cross it rather than from its bone structure or ligamentous arrangement. The articular capsule is a continuous cover formed by the merging of the radial and the ulnar collateral, volar radiocarpal, and dorsal radiocarpal ligaments.

Carpal Joints

The carpal bones articulate with one another in arthrodial, or gliding, joints and combine their movements with those of the radiocarpal joint and the carpometacarpal articulations. They are stabilized by anterior, posterior, and connecting interosseous ligaments.

Metacarpal Joints

The metacarpal bones are five bones that join the carpal bones above and the phalanges below, forming metacarpophalangeal (MCP) articulations of a condyloid type and permitting flexion, extension, abduction, adduction, and circumduction. The thumb varies slightly at its carpometacarpal joint and is classified as a saddle joint that allows rotation on its long axis in addition to the other metacarpophalangeal movements.

Phalangeal Joints

Each phalangeal joint, like the carpal joints, has an articular capsule that is reinforced by collateral and accessory volar ligaments. The interphalangeal articulations are of the hinge type, permitting only flexion and extension. Their ligamentous and capsular support is basically the same as that of the MCP joints.

Ligaments

There are numerous wrist, hand, and finger ligaments; however, only those most likely to be injured in sports are discussed here.

Ligaments of the Wrist

The wrist is composed of many ligaments that bind the carpal bones to one another, to the ulna and radius, and to the proximal metacarpal bones. Of major interest in wrist injuries are the collateral ulnar ligament, which extends from the tip of the styloid process of the ulna to the pisiform bone, and the triquetral bone and radial collateral ligament that extends from the styloid process to the radius to the navicular bone (scaphoid). Crossing the volar aspect of the carpal bones is the transverse carpal ligament. This ligament serves as the roof of the carpal tunnel, in which the median nerve is often compressed (Figure 24-6).

Ligaments of the Phalanges

The proximal interphalangeal (PIP) joints have the same design as the MCP joints. They comprise the collateral ligaments, palmar fibrocartilages, and a loose posterior capsule or synovial membrane protected by an extensor expansion (Figure 24-7).

Musculature

The wrist and hand are a complex of extrinsic and intrinsic muscles. See Table 24-1 on page 676 for the major muscles in the hand and wrist (Figure 24-8).

Figure 24-6

Ligaments of the wrist.

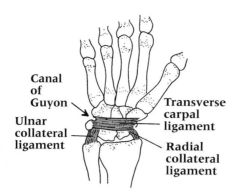

Canal
of
Guyon

Ulnar
collateral
ligament

Transverse
carpal
ligament

Radial
collateral
ligament

Circulation impairment must be noted as soon as possible in any wrist and hand injury.

Blood and Nerve Supply

The three major nerves of the hand are the ulnar, radial, and median nerves. The ulnar nerve comes to the hand by passing between the pisiform bone and the hook of the hamate bone. The radial nerve enters the wrist from the back of the forearm between the superficial and deep extensor muscles, where it terminates in the back of the carpus. The median nerve enters the palm of the hand through the carpal tunnel (see Figure 24-12). The sensory pattern of peripheral nerves can be seen in Figure 24-9. The radial nerve may or may not follow this pattern.

The arteries that supply the wrist and the hand are the radial and ulnar arteries. They create two arterial arches: the superficial palmar arch, which is the largest and most distal to the hand, and the deep palmar arch.

ASSESSMENT OF THE WRIST, HAND, AND FINGERS

History

The evaluator asks about the location and type of pain:

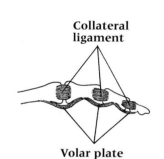

Collateral ligament

Volar plate

Figure 24-7

Ligaments of the phalanges.

- What increases or decreases the pain?
- Has there been a history of trauma or overuse?
- What therapy or medications, if any, have been given?

Observation

As the athlete is observed, arm and hand asymmetries are noted:

- Are there any postural deviations?
- Does the athlete hold the part in a stiff or protected manner?
- Is the wrist or hand swollen?

Hand usage such as writing or unbuttoning a shirt is noted. The general attitude of the hand is observed (Figure 24-10). When the athlete is asked to open and close the hand, the evaluator notes whether this movement can be performed fully and rhythmically. Another general functional activity is to have the athlete touch the tip of the thumb to each fingertip several times. The last factor to be observed is the color of the fingernails. Nails that are very pale instead of pink may indicate a problem with blood circulation.[12]

Palpation

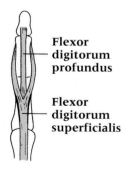

Flexor digitorum profundus

Flexor digitorum superficialis

Figure 24-8

Tendons of the phalanges.

Bony palpation

The following bony landmarks should be palpated:

- Scaphoid
- Trapezoid
- Trapezium
- Lunate
- Capitate

- Triquetral
- Pisiform
- Hamate (hook of the hamate)
- Metacarpals 1–5
- Proximal, middle, and distal phalanges of the fingers
- Proximal and distal phalanges of the thumb

Soft Tissue Palpation

The following soft tissue structures should be palpated:

General
- Triangular fibrocartilage
- Ligaments of the carpal bones
- Carpometacarpal joints and ligaments
- Metacarpophylangeal joints and collateral ligaments
- Proximal interphylangeal joints and collateral ligaments
- Distal interphylangeal joints and collateral ligaments

Anterior
- Flexor carpi radialis tendon
- Flexor carpi ulnaris tendon
- Lumbricale muscles
- Flexor digitorum superficialis tendons
- Flexor digitorum profundus tendons
- Palmer interossi muscles
- Flexor pollicus brevis
- Flexor pollicus longus tendon
- Abductor pollicus brevis
- Opponens pollicus muscle
- Opponens digiti minimi muscle

Posterior
- Extensor carpi radialis longus tendon
- Extensor carpi radialis brevis tendon
- Extensor carpi ulnaris tendon
- Extensor digitorum tendons
- Extensor indicis tendon
- Extensor digiti minimi tendon
- Dorsal interossi muscles
- Extensor pollicus brevis tendon
- Extensor pollicus longus tendon
- Abductor pollicus longus tendon

Special Tests

Finklestein's Test

Finklestein's test is a test for de Quervain's syndrome (Figure 24-11). The athlete makes a fist with the thumb tucked inside. The wrist is then deviated into ulnar flexion. Sharp pain is evidence of stenosing tenosynovitis. Pain over the carpal tunnel could mean a carpal tunnel syndrome affecting the median nerve. On occasion, the flexor tendons also become trapped, making finger flexion difficult. Any symptoms of carpal tunnel syndrome are an indication for testing, using Tinel's sign and Phalen's test.[14]

Tinel's Sign

Tinel's sign is produced by tapping over the transverse carpal ligament of the carpal tunnel, which causes tingling and parasthesia over the thumb, index finger, middle finger, and the lateral half of the ring finger. This sensory distribution of the median nerve indicates the presence of carpal tunnel syndrome (Figure 24-12).

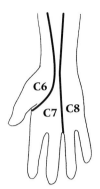

Figure 24-9

Sensory patterns of peripheral nerves in the hand.

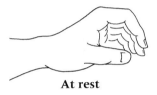

At rest

Normal fist   Clenched fist

Figure 24-10

General normal attitudes of the hand.

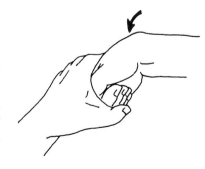

Figure 24-11

De Quervain's test.

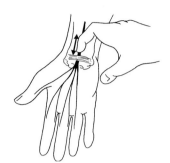

Figure 24-12

Tapping over the transverse carpal ligament to test for carpal tunnel syndrome (Tinel's sign).

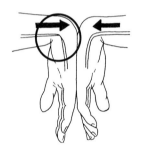

Figure 24-13

Wrist press for carpal tunnel syndrome (Phalen's test).

Phalen's Test

Another common test for carpal tunnel syndrome is Phalen's test. The athlete is instructed to flex both wrists as far as possible and press them together. This position is held for approximately one minute. If this test is positive, pain will be produced in the region of the carpal tunnel (Figure 24-13).[14]

Valgus/Varus and Glide Stress Tests for Wrist, Metacarpophalangeal, and Interphalangeal Joints

A series of tests can be done to stress the ligamentous integrity of the joints in the hand and fingers. Applying valgus and varus stress as well as anterior and posterior glides collectively determine whether a sprain has occurred to one of the many ligaments that connect the carpal bones (Figure 24-14A). Valgus/varus stress to the interphalangeal joints of the fingers stress the collateral ligaments, while anterior/posterior glides stress the joint capsule (Figure 24-14B). Increased pain or instability with any of these tests usually indicates a ligament sprain.[13]

Lunotriquetral Ballotment Test

This test requires the examiner to stabilize the lunate with thumb and index finger while sliding the triquetrum anteriorly and posteriorly to look for laxity, pain, and crepitus. A positive test indicates instability of the lunotriquetral joint that often results in dislocation of the lunate.

Circulatory and Neurological Evaluation

The hands should be inspected to determine whether circulation is being impeded. The hands should be felt for their temperature. A cold hand or portion of a hand is a sign of decreased circulation. Pinching the fingernails can also help detect circulatory problems. Pinching will blanch the nail, and on release, there should be rapid return of a pink color. Another objective test is the Allen's test.

Allen's test   The Allen's test is used to determine the function of the radial and ulnar arteries supplying the hand. The athlete is instructed to squeeze the hand tightly into a fist and then open it fully three or four times. While the athlete is holding the last fist, the evaluator places firm pressure over each artery. The athlete is then instructed to open the hand. The palm should now be blanched. One of the arteries is then released, and if normal, the hand will instantly become red. The same process is repeated with the other artery (Figure 24-15).

The hand is next evaluated for sensation alterations, especially in cases of suspected tunnel impingements. Nerve involvements will be further evaluated when active and resistive movements are initiated.

Figure 24-14

A, Valgus/varus stress to the wrist. **B,** Anterior/posterior glide to the PIP joint.

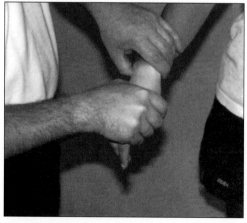

A

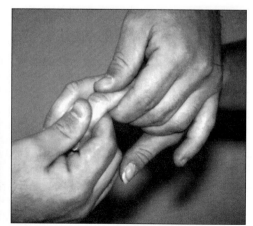

B

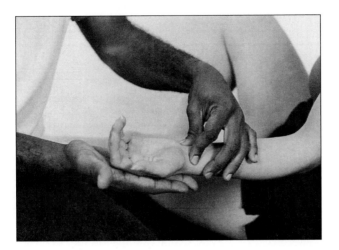

Figure 24-15

Testing the radial and ulnar arteries of the hand (Allen's test).

Functional Evaluation

Range of motion is noted in all movements of the wrist and fingers. Active and resistive movements are then compared with those of the uninjured wrist and hand.[13] The following sequence should be conducted:

- Wrist: flexion, extension, radial and ulnar deviation
- MCP joint: flexion, extension
- PIP and DIP joints: flexion, extension
- Finger: abduction, adduction
- MCP, PIP, and DIP joints of the thumb: flexion and extension
- Thumb: abduction, adduction, opposition
- Fifth finger: opposition

Passive, active, and resistive movements are performed in the wrist and hand. Table 24-1 indicates resistive motions to use to determine the extent of strength of the major wrist and hand muscles.

RECOGNITION AND MANAGEMENT OF INJURIES TO THE WRIST, HAND, AND FINGERS

Wrist Injuries

Injuries to the wrist usually occur from a fall on the outstretched hand or from repeated flexion, extension, or rotary movements (Figure 24-16).[18]

Wrist Sprains

Etiology   It is often difficult to distinguish between injury to the wrist's muscle tendons and to the supporting structure of the carpal region. This section emphasizes the condition of wrist sprain; tendon injuries will be addressed in the discussion of the hand.

A sprain is by far the most common wrist injury and, in most cases, is the most poorly managed injury in sports. It can arise from any abnormal, forced movement of the wrist.

Falling on the hyperextended wrist is the most common cause of wrist sprain, but violent flexion or torsion will also tear supporting tissue. Because the main support of the wrist is derived from posterior and anterior ligaments that transport the major nutrient vessels to the carpal bones and stabilize the joint, repeated sprains may disrupt the blood supply and, consequently, circulation to the carpal bones.

Symptoms and signs   The athlete complains of pain, swelling, and difficulty moving the wrist. On examination there is tenderness, swelling, and limited ROM. All

24-3

Critical Thinking Exercise

An athlete who sustained a major wrist sprain complains of a decrease in hand circulation.

? How should this injury be evaluated for a circulation problem?

TABLE 24-1 Resistive Motion to Determine Muscle Weakness Related to Wrist and Hand Injury

Resistive Motion	Major Muscles Involved	Nerves
Wrist flexion	Flexor carpi radialis	Median, cervical 6 and 7
	Flexor carpi ulnaris	Ulnar, cervical 8, thoracic 1
Wrist extension	Extensor carpi radialis longus	Radial, cervical 6 and 7
	Extensor carpi radialis brevis	Radial, cervical 6 and 7,
		Radial, cervical 6–8
	Extensor carpi ulnaris	
Flexion of MCP joints of fingers	Lumbricalis manus	Radial, cervical 6–8
	Interossei dorsalis manus	Median, ulnar, cervical 6–8
	Interossei palmares	Ulnar, cervical 8, thoracic 1
		Ulnar, cervical 8, thoracic 1
Flexion of PIP and DIP joints of fingers	Flexor digitorum superficialis	Median, cervical 7 and 8, thoracic 1
Extension of MCP joints of fingers	Extensor digitorum	Radial, cervical 6–8
	Extensor indicis	Radial, cervical 6–8
	Extensor digiti minimi	Radial, cervical 6–8
Finger abduction	Interossei dorsalis	Ulnar
	Abductor digiti	Cervical 8, thoracic 1
Finger adduction	Interossei palmares	Ulnar, cervical 8, thoracic 1
Thumb flexion	Flexor pollicis brevis	Median, cervical 6 and 7
	Lateral portion	Ulnar, cervical 8, thoracic 1
	Medial portion	Cervical 8, thoracic 1
	Flexor pollicis longus	
Thumb extension	Extensor pollicis brevis	Radial, cervical 6 and 7
	Extensor pollicis longus	Radial, cervical 6–8
Thumb abduction	Abductor pollicis longus	Radial, cervical 6 and 7
	Abductor pollicis brevis	Median, cervical 6 and 7
Thumb adduction	Adductor pollicis	Ulnar, cervical 8, thoracic 1
Thumb opposition	Opponens pollicis	Median, cervical 6 and 7
Fifth-finger opposition	Opponens digiti minimi	Ulnar, cervical 6 and 7

athletes having severe sprains should be referred to a physician for X-ray examination to determine possible fractures.

Management   Mild and moderate sprains should initially be given RICE, splinting, and analgesics. It is desirable to have the athlete start hand-strengthening exercises almost immediately after the injury has occurred. Taping for support can benefit healing and help prevent further injury (see Figures 8-40 and 8-41).

Triangular Fibrocartilage Complex (TFCC) Injury

Etiology   Injury to the TFCC usually occurs through forced hyperextension of the wrist, as in falling on an outstretched hand, that compresses the TFCC between the radioulnar joint and the proximal row of carpal bones. TFCC injury is often associated with sprain of the ulnar collateral ligament.

Symptoms and signs   It is common for the athlete not to immediately report this injury. There is pain along the ulnar side of the wrist. Wrist extension is difficult and painful. There will be considerable swelling around the wrist, although there may not be much swelling initially.

Management   The athlete with TFCC injury should be referred to a physician for treatment. If not properly managed, permanent loss of motion and disability can occur.

24-4

Critical Thinking E x e r c i s e

A soccer player complains of pain in the wrist caused by falling on the hand with forced hyperextension of the wrist several days earlier. There is pain along the ulnar side of the wrist. Wrist extension is difficult and painful. There is considerable swelling around the wrist.

? What should the athletic trainer suspect has happened to this athlete?

Figure 24-16

Wrist injuries commonly occur from falls on the outstretched hand or from repeated flexion, extension, lateral, or rotary movements.

Tenosynovitis

Etiology   Wrist tenosynovitis occurs to the extensor carpi radialis longus or brevis in weight lifters and rowers.[18] Other sports that cause wrist tenosynovitis are those that require the athlete to perform repetitive wrist accelerations and decelerations. The cause of tenosynovitis is the repetitive and overuse of the wrist tendons and their sheaths.

Symptoms and signs   The athlete complains of pain with use or pain in passive stretching. There is tenderness and swelling over the tendon.

Management   Acute pain and inflammation are managed by ice massage for ten minutes four times a day for the first forty-eight to seventy-two hours, NSAIDs, and rest. When swelling has subsided, range of motion is promoted with contrast baths. Ultrasound or phonophoresis can be used for their antiinflammatory effects. When pain and swelling have subsided, PRE can be instituted.[18]

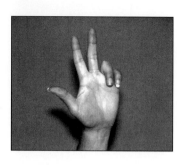

Figure 24-17

Bishop's, or benediction, hand.

Figure 24-18

Claw hand.

Figure 24-19

Drop wrist.

Figure 24-20

Ape hand.

Tendinitis

Etiology   Tendinitis of the flexor carpi radialis is common in racquet sports. Flexor ulnaris pisiform tendinitis is also common. Sports that require repetitive pulling movements and sports that place prolonged pressure on the palms, such as cycling, can cause flexor digitorum tendinitis. The primary cause of tendinitis is overuse of the wrist.

Symptoms and signs   The athlete complains of pain on active use or passive stretching of the involved tendon. Isometric resistance to the involved tendon produces pain, weakness, or both.

Management   Acute pain and inflammation are managed with ice massage for ten minutes four times daily for forty-eight to seventy-two hours, NSAIDs, and rest. A wrist splint may protect the injured tendon. After swelling has subsided, a program of contrast baths and ROM exercises can be begun. When the athlete is pain free, a high-repetition, low-resistance PRE program can be instituted.

Nerve Compression, Entrapment, Palsy

Etiology   Because of the narrow spaces that some nerves must travel through the wrist to the hand, compression neuropathy or entrapment can occur. The two most common entrapments are of the median nerve, which travels through the carpal tunnel, and the ulnar nerve, which is compressed in the tunnel of Guyon between the pisiform bone and the hook of the hamate bone. Nerve palsy occurs because of direct trauma to the nerves. The radial and median nerves are most likely to exhibit nerve palsy.

Symptoms and signs   Such compression causes a sharp or burning pain that is associated with an increase or decrease in skin sensitivity or with paresthesia. A characteristic deformity of the hand known as a *benediction* deformity or a *bishop's* deformity results from damage to the ulnar nerve that affects the hypothenar and intrinsic muscles of the ring and little fingers (Figure 24-17). Compression of both the median and ulnar nerves causes a *claw hand* deformity (Figure 24-18).

A palsy of the radial nerve produces a *drop wrist* deformity, which is caused by paralysis of the extensor muscles such that the wrist and fingers cannot be extended (Figure 24-19). Palsy of the median nerve can cause an *ape hand,* in which the thumb is pulled backward in line with the other fingers by the extensor muscles (Figure 24-20).

Management   If the possibility exists that chronic entrapment will cause irreversible nerve damage and if conservative treatment is unsuccessful, surgical decompression may be necessary.

Carpal Tunnel Syndrome

Etiology   The carpal tunnel is located on the anterior aspect of the wrist. The floor of the carpal tunnel is formed by the carpal bones and the roof by the transverse carpal ligament (Figure 24-21). A number of anatomical structures course through this limited space, including eight long finger flexor tendons, their synovial sheaths, and the median nerve.[23] Carpal tunnel syndrome results from an inflammation of the tendons and synovial sheaths within this space, which ultimately leads to compression of the median nerve.[4] Carpal tunnel syndrome most often occurs in athletes who engage in activities that require repeated wrist flexion, although it can also result from direct trauma to the anterior aspect of the wrist.

Symptoms and signs   Compression of the median nerve will usually result in both sensory and motor deficits. Sensory changes could result in tingling, numbness, and paresthesia in the arc of median nerve innervation over the thumb, index and middle fingers and palm of the hand. The median nerve innervates the lumbrical muscles of the index and middle fingers and three of the thenar muscles. Thus, weakness in thumb movement is associated with this condition.[23]

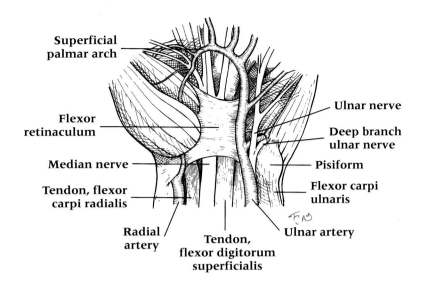

Figure 24-21

The transverse carpal ligament lies over the median nerve at the carpal tunnel.

Superficial palmar arch

Flexor retinaculum

Median nerve

Tendon, flexor carpi radialis

Radial artery

Tendon, flexor digitorum superficialis

Ulnar nerve

Deep branch ulnar nerve

Pisiform

Flexor carpi ulnaris

Ulnar artery

Management   Initially, conservative treatment involving rest, immobilization, and nonsteroidal antiinflammatory medication is recommended. If the syndrome persists, injection with a corticosteroid and possible surgical decompression of the transverse carpal ligament may be necessary.

de Quervain's Disease

Etiology   de Quervain's disease (also called Hoffman's disease) is a stenosing tenosynovitis in the thumb. The first tunnel of the wrist becomes contracted and narrowed as a result of inflammation of the synovial lining. The tendons that go through the first tunnel are the extensor pollicis brevis and abductor pollicis longus, which move through the same synovial sheath. Because the tendons move through a groove of the radiostyloid process, constant wrist movement can be a source of irritation.

Symptoms and signs   Athletes who use a great deal of wrist motion in their sport are prone to de Quervain's disease. Its primary symptom is an aching pain, which may radiate into the hand or forearm. Movements of the wrist tend to increase the pain, and there is a positive Finklestein's test. There is point tenderness and weakness during thumb extension and abduction, and there may be a painful snapping and catching of the tendons during movement. Finklestein's test will be positive (see Figure 24-11).

Management   Management of de Quervain's disease involves immobilization, rest, cryotherapy, and antiinflammatory medication. Ultrasound and ice massage are also beneficial.

Dislocation of the Lunate Bone

Etiology   Dislocations in the wrist are infrequent in sports activity. Most occur from a forceful hyperextension of the wrist. Dislocation of the lunate (Figure 24-22) is considered the most common dislocation of a carpal bone.[6] Dislocation occurs as a result of a fall on the outstretched hand, which forces open the space between the distal and proximal carpal bones. When the stretching force is released, the lunate bone is dislocated anteriorly (palmar side).

Symptoms and signs   The primary signs of this condition are pain, swelling, and difficulty in executing wrist and finger flexion. There also may be numbness or even paralysis of the flexor muscles because of lunate pressure on the median nerve.[6]

Management   This condition should be treated as acute, and the athlete should be sent to a physician for reduction of the dislocation. If the dislocation is not

24-5

Critical Thinking Exercise

A shot-putter is beginning to feel tingling, numbness, and paresthesia in the thumb, index, and middle fingers and palm of the right hand.

? The athlete is demonstrating a carpal tunnel syndrome. What factors could produce this problem?

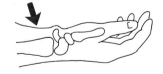

Figure 24-22

Dislocation of the lunate bone.

A soccer player falls on the outstretched left hand, causing a major compression force to the scaphoid bone between the radius and the second row of the carpal bones.

? What wrist injury is most likely?

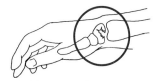

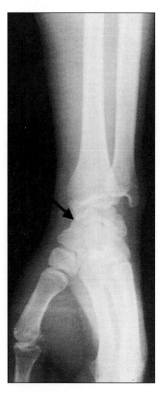

Figure 24-23

Carpal scaphoid fracture.

recognized early enough, bone deterioration may occur, requiring surgical removal. The usual time of disability and subsequent recovery is one to two months.

Scaphoid Fracture

Etiology   The scaphoid bone is the most frequently fractured of the carpal bones. The injury is usually caused by a force on the outstretched hand, which compresses the scaphoid bone between the radius and the second row of carpal bones (Figure 24-23). This condition is often mistaken for a severe sprain, and as a result, the required complete immobilization is not performed. Without proper splinting, the scaphoid fracture often fails to heal because of an inadequate supply of blood; thus degeneration and necrosis occur. This condition is called aseptic necrosis of the scaphoid bone. It is necessary to try, in every way possible, to distinguish between a wrist sprain and a fracture of the scaphoid bone because a fracture necessitates immediate referral to a physician.

Symptoms and signs   The signs of a recent scaphoid fracture include swelling in the area of the carpal bones, severe point tenderness of the scaphoid bone in the anatomical snuffbox (Figure 24-24), and scaphoid pain that is elicited by upward pressure exerted on the long axis of the thumb and by radial flexion.

Management   With these signs present, cold should be applied, the area splinted, and the athlete referred to a physician for X-ray study and casting. In most cases, cast immobilization lasts for approximately six weeks and is followed by strengthening exercises coupled with protective taping. Immobilization is discontinued for rehabilitation. The wrist needs protection against impact loading for an additional three months.[11]

Hamate Fracture

Etiology   A fracture of the hamate bone and in particular of the hook of the hamate can occur from a fall but more commonly occurs from contact while the athlete is holding a sports implement such as a tennis racket, a baseball bat, a lacrosse stick, a hockey stick, or a golf club.

Symptoms and signs   Wrist pain and weakness and point tenderness are experienced. Pull of the muscular attachments can cause nonunion.

Management   Casting of the wrist is usually the treatment of choice. The hook of the hamate can be protected by a donut-type pad that takes pressure off the area.

Wrist Ganglion

Etiology   The wrist ganglion, which is a synovial cyst, is often seen in sports (Figure 24-25). It is considered by many to be a herniation of the joint capsule or of the synovial sheath of a tendon; other authorities believe it to be a cystic structure. The wrist ganglion usually appears slowly, after a wrist strain, and contains a clear, mucinous fluid. The ganglion most often appears on the back of the wrist but can appear at any tendinous point in the wrist or hand.

Symptoms and signs   The athlete complains of occasional pain with a lump at the site. Pain increases with use. There is a cystic structure that may feel soft, rubbery, or very hard.[11]

Management   An old method of treatment was to first break down the swelling through digital pressure and then apply a felt pressure pad for a period of time to encourage healing. A newer approach is a combination of aspiration and chemical cauterization, with subsequent application of a pressure pad. Neither of these methods prevents the ganglion from recurring. Ultrasound can be used to reduce the size of the ganglion cyst. Surgical removal is the most effective of the various methods of treatment.

Hand and Finger Injuries

The hand is one of the most commonly injured sites in sports, yet it is probably the most poorly managed. Immediate evaluation must be afforded to avoid any delay in proper management. When it comes to improper care, the hand is notoriously unforgiving.[7]

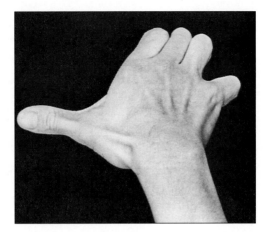

Figure 24-24

Anatomical snuffbox formed by extensor tendons of the thumb.

Contusions and Pressure Injuries of the Hand and Phalanges

Etiology   The hand and phalanges, having an irregular bony structure combined with little protective fat and muscle padding, are prone to bruising in sports.

Symptoms and signs   This condition is easily identified from the history of trauma and the pain and swelling of soft tissues.

Management   Cold and compression should be applied immediately until hemorrhage has ceased, and is followed by gradual warming of the part in whirlpool or immersion baths. Soreness may still be present, and protection should be given by a sponge rubber pad (see Figure 8-42).

A particularly common contusion of the finger is bruising of the distal phalanx, which results in a subungual hematoma (contusion of the fingernail). This extremely painful condition occurs because of the accumulation of blood underneath the fingernail. The athlete should place the finger in ice water until the hemorrhage ceases, and the pressure of blood should then be released (Figure 24-26; see also *Focus Box:* "Releasing blood from beneath the fingernail").[15]

Figure 24-25

Wrist ganglion.

Bowler's Thumb

Etiology   A perineural fibrosis of the subcutaneous ulnar digital nerve of the thumb can occur from the pressure of a bowling ball thumbhole and cause the development of fibrotic tissue around the ulnar nerve.[10]

Symptoms and signs   The athlete senses pain, tingling during pressure to the irritated area, and numbness.

Management   Early management includes padding of the thumbhole and a decrease in the amount of bowling. If the condition continues, however, surgery may be warranted.

Trigger Finger or Thumb

Etiology   Repeated movement can cause the tendons of the wrist and hand to sustain irritation that results in tenosynovitis. An inflammation of the tendon sheath leads to swelling, crepitation, and painful movement. Most commonly affected are the extensor tendons of the wrist: the extensor carpi ulnaris, extensor pollicis longus, extensor pollicis brevis, and abductor pollicis longus.[21]

The trigger finger or thumb is an example of stenosing tenosynovitis. It most commonly occurs in a flexor tendon that runs through a common sheath with other tendons. Thickening of the sheath or tendon can occur, which constricts the sliding tendon. A nodule in the synovium of the sheath adds to the difficulty of gliding.[8] The cause of trigger finger or thumb is nonspecific overuse.

Symptoms and signs   The athlete complains that when the finger or thumb is flexed, there is resistance to reextension, producing a snapping that is both palpable

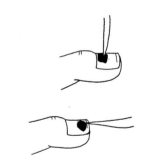

Figure 24-26

Releasing blood from beneath the fingernail, technique no. 1.

Focus

Releasing blood from beneath the fingernail

The following are two common methods for releasing the pressure of the subungual hematoma.

MATERIALS NEEDED: Scalpel, small-gauge drill or paper clip, and antiseptic.

POSITION OF ATHLETE: The athlete sits with the injured hand palm downward on the table.

TECHNIQUE 1

1. The injured finger should first be coated with an antiseptic solution.
2. A sharp scalpel point, small-gauge drill, or paper clip is used to penetrate the injured nail through a rotary action. If the hematoma extends as far as the end of the nail, it may be best to release the blood by slipping the scalpel tip under the end of the nail.

TECHNIQUE 2

1. The injured finger should first be coated with an antiseptic solution.
2. A paper clip is heated to a red-hot temperature.
3. The red-hot paper clip or small-gauge drill is laid on the surface of the nail with moderate pressure, resulting in melting a hole through the nail to the site of the bleeding.

and audible. During palpation, tenderness is produced, and a lump can be felt at the base of the flexor tendon sheath.

Management   Treatment initially is the same as for de Quervain's disease; however, if treatment is unsuccessful, steroid injections may produce relief. If steroid injections do not provide relief, splinting the tendon sheath is the last option.

Mallet Finger

Etiology   The mallet finger, common in sports, is sometimes called baseball finger or basketball finger. It is caused by a blow from a thrown ball that strikes the tip of the finger, jamming and avulsing the extensor tendon from its insertion along with a piece of bone.

Symptoms and signs   The athlete complains of pain at the distal interphalangeal joint. X-ray examination may show a bony avulsion from the dorsal proximal distal phalanx. The athlete is unable to extend the finger, carrying it at approximately a 30-degree angle. There is also point tenderness at the site of the injury, and the avulsed bone often can be palpated (Figure 24-27).

24-7

Critical Thinking Exercise

A baseball catcher receives a pitch that jams and avulses the extensor tendon of the distal interphalangeal joint of the second finger.

? How should this condition be managed?

Figure 24-27

Mallet finger.

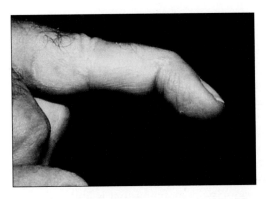

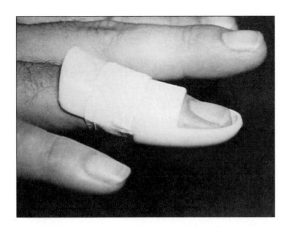

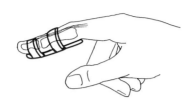

Figure 24-28

Splinting of the mallet finger.

Management   RICE is given for the pain and swelling. If there is no fracture, the distal phalanx should immediately be splinted in a position of extension for a period six to eight weeks (Figure 24-28).

Boutonniere Deformity

Etiology   The boutonniere, or buttonhole, deformity is caused by a rupture of the extensor tendon dorsal to the middle phalanx. Trauma occurs to the tip of the finger, which forces the DIP joint into extension and the PIP joint into flexion.

Symptoms and signs   The athlete complains of severe pain and inability to extend the DIP joint. There is swelling, point tenderness, and an obvious deformity (Figure 24-29).

Management   Management of the boutonniere deformity includes cold application followed by splinting of the PIP joint in extension. NOTE: If this condition is inadequately splinted, the classic boutonniere deformity will develop. Splinting is continued for five to eight weeks. While the finger is splinted, the athlete is encouraged to flex the distal phalanx (Table 24-2).

Jersey Finger

Etiology   Jersey finger is a rupture of the flexor digitorum profundus tendon from its insertion on the distal phalanx. This condition most often occurs in the ring finger when the athlete tries to grab the jersey of an opponent and either ruptures the tendon or avulses a small piece of bone.[20]

Symptoms and signs   Because the tendon is no longer attached to the distal phalanx, the DIP joint cannot be flexed and the finger is in an extended position. There is pain and point tenderness over the distal phalanx.

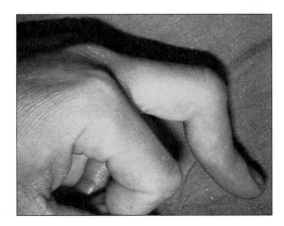

Figure 24-29

Boutonniere deformity.

TABLE 24-2 Conservative Treatment and Splinting of Finger Injuries

Injury	Constant Splinting	Begin Motion	Additional Splinting during Competition	Joint Position
Mallet finger	6–8 wk	6–8 wk	6–8 wk	Slight DIP hyperextension
Collateral ligament sprains	3 wk	2 wk	4–6 wk	30-degree flexion
PIP and DIP dislocations	3 wk	3 wk	3 wk	30-degree flexion
Phalangeal fractures	4–6 wk	4–6 wk	3 wk	N/A
PIP and DIP fractures	9–11 wk	3 wk	3 wk	30-degree flexion
Pseudoboutonniere volar plate injuries	5 wk	3 wk	3 wk	20- to 30-degree flexion
Boutonniere deformity	6–8 wk	6–8 wk	6–8 wk	PIP in extension; DIP and MCP not included
MCP fractures	3 wk	3 wk	4–6 wk	30-degree flexion
Flexor digitorum profundus repair	5 wk	3 wk	3 wk	Depends on repair

Management   If the tendon is not surgically repaired, the athlete will never be able to flex the DIP joint, causing weakness in grip strength; otherwise, function will be relatively normal. If surgery is done, the course of rehabilitation requires about twelve weeks, and there is often poor gliding of the tendon with the possibility of rerupture.[20]

Dupuytren's Contracture

Etiology   The cause of Dupuytren's contracture is unknown. Nodules develop in the palmer aponeurosis that limit finger extension and eventually cause a flexion deformity.

Symptoms and signs   A flexion deformity most often develops in which the ring or little finger moves into the palm of the hand and cannot be extended (Figure 24-30).

Management   A flexion contracture deformity of this type can significantly interfere with normal hand function. The tissue nodules causing the contracture must be removed surgically.

Sprains, Dislocations, and Fractures of the Phalanges

Etiology   The phalanges, particularly of the thumb, are prone to sprains caused by a blow delivered to the tip or by violent twisting (Figure 24-31). The mechanism of injury is similar to that of fractures and dislocations. The sprain, however, mainly affects the capsular, ligamentous, and tendinous tissues.

Symptoms and signs   Recognition is accomplished primarily through the history and the sprain symptoms: pain, severe swelling, and hematoma.

Gamekeeper's Thumb

Etiology   A sprain of the ulnar collateral ligament of the MCP joint of the thumb is common among athletes, especially skiers and tackle football players.[3]

The mechanism of injury is usually a forceful abduction of the proximal phalanx, which is occasionally combined with hyperextension (Figure 24-32).[9]

Symptoms and signs   The athlete complains of pain over the ulnar collateral ligament in addition to a weak and painful pinch. Inspection demonstrates tenderness and swelling over the medial aspect of the thumb.[11]

Management   Because the stability of pinching can be severely deterred, proper, immediate, and follow-up care must be performed. If there is instability in the joints, the athlete should be immediately referred to an orthopedist. If the joint is stable, X-ray examination should be performed to rule out fracture. A thumb splint should

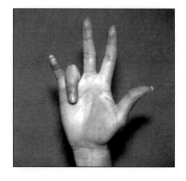

Figure 24-30

Dupuytren's contracture.

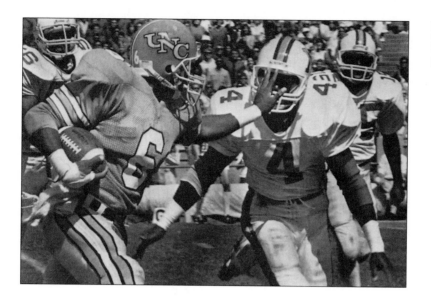

Figure 24-31

Football often places the phalanges at risk of severe injury.

be applied for protection for three weeks or until the thumb is pain free. The splint, extending from the end of the thumb to above the wrist, is applied with the thumb in a neutral position. After the splint is removed, thumb spica taping should be worn during sports participation (see Figure 8-43).

Sprains of the Interphalangeal Joints of the Fingers

Etiology   Interphalangeal finger sprains can include the PIP joint or the DIP joint. Injury can range from minor to complete tears of the collateral ligament, a volar plate tear, or a central extensor slip tear (see Table 24-2).[9] A collateral ligament sprain of the interphalangeal joint is common in sports such as basketball, volleyball, and football. A common cause is an axial force that produces a jammed finger. This mechanism places valgus or varus stress on the interphalangeal joint.

Symptoms and signs   The athlete complains of pain and swelling at the involved joint. There is severe point tenderness at the joint site, especially in the region of the collateral ligaments. There may be a lateral or medial instability when the joint is in 150 degrees of flexion. Collateral ligamentous injuries may be evaluated by the application of a valgus and varus joint stress test.

Management   Management includes RICE for the acute stage, X-ray examinations, and splinting. Splinting of the PIP joint is usually at 30 to 40 degrees of flexion for ten days. If the sprain is to the DIP joint, splinting a few days in full extension assists in the healing process. If the sprains are minor, taping the injured finger to a noninjured one will provide protective support. Later, a protective checkrein can be applied for either thumb or finger protection (see Figure 8-45).

Swan Neck Deformity and PseudoBoutonniere Deformity

Etiology   The volar plate of the PIP joint is most commonly injured in sports from a severe hyperextension force. A distal tear may cause a swan neck deformity, whereas injury to the proximal part of the plate may cause a pseudoboutonniere deformity.

Symptoms and signs   There is pain and swelling at the PIP joint, and it displays varying degrees of hyperextension. Tenderness is over the volar aspect of the PIP. A major indication of a tear is that the PIP joint can be passively hyperextended in comparison with other PIP joints.

Management   Initially, the athlete is treated with RICE and analgesics as required. Management consists of splinting at 20 to 30 degrees of flexion for three weeks, followed by buddy taping and then PRE.

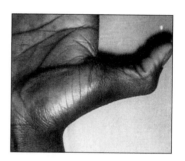

Figure 24-32

Gamekeeper's thumb.

24-8

Critical Thinking Exercise

A volleyball player, going up to block a spike, receives an axial force to the middle finger, which causes a valgus force.

? What soft tissue injuries would be expected with such a force?

Figure 24-33

Open dislocation of the interphalangeal joint of a thumb.

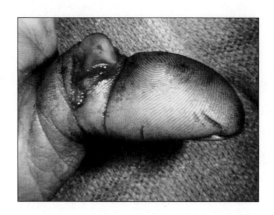

PIP Dorsal Dislocation

Etiology   Dislocations of the phalanges have a high rate of occurrence in sports (Figure 24-33). Dislocations can occur at a number of joints, for example, PIP dorsal dislocation, PIP palmar dislocation, and MCP dislocation. Most dislocations are seen in collision or contact sports. The mechanism that produces a PIP dislocation is hyperextension that produces a disruption of the volar plate at the middle phalanx.

Symptom and signs   The athlete complains of pain and swelling over the PIP. There is an obvious avulsion deformity and disability.

Management   Initially, the athlete is treated with RICE, splinting, and analgesics, followed by reduction by a physician. After reduction, the finger is splinted at 20 to 30 degrees of flexion for three weeks. After splint removal, buddy taping is used.

PIP Palmar Dislocation

Etiology   The cause is a twist of a finger while it is semiflexed.

Symptoms and signs   The athlete complains of pain and swelling over the PIP. There is point tenderness over the PIP, primarily on the dorsal side. The finger displays an angular or rotational deformity.

Management   The finger is treated with RICE, splinting, and analgesics, followed by reduction. It is then splinted in full extension for four to five weeks, after which it is protected for six to eight weeks during activity.

MCP Dislocation

Etiology   The cause of the MCP dislocation is a twisting or shear force.

Symptoms and signs   The athlete complains of pain, swelling, and stiffness at the MCP joint. The proximal phalanx is dorsally angulated at 60 to 90 degrees.[11]

Management   Initially, the injury is treated with RICE, splinting, and analgesics. It is then reduced, buddy taped, and given early ROM.[1]

Metacarpal Fracture

Etiology   Contact and collision sports produce not only dislocations but also a high number of hand and finger fractures (Table 24-3).[5] The cause of metacarpal fractures is commonly a direct axial force or a compressive force, such as being stepped on (Figure 24-34). Fractures of the fifth metacarpal are associated with boxing and the martial arts and are usually called a boxer's fracture.

Symptoms and signs   The athlete complains of pain and swelling. The injury may appear to be an angular or rotational deformity.

24-9

Critical Thinking Exercise

A football player gets into a fistfight on the field and injures his right hand through an axial force to the fifth metacarpal bone.

? What type of injury should be suspected, and how should it be managed?

TABLE 24-3 Avulsion Fractures

Avulsion Fracture	Corresponding Sprain
Corner of base of middle phalanx	Collateral ligament
Volar base of middle phalanx	Volar plate injury
Dorsal base of middle phalanx	Central extensor slip tear
Volar base of distal phalanx	Flexor profundus tear
Dorsal base of distal phalanx	Mallet finger

Management   Initially, RICE and analgesics are given, followed by X-ray examinations. Deformity is reduced, followed by splinting. A splint is worn for four weeks, after which early ROM is carried out.

Bennett's Fracture

Etiology   A Bennett's fracture occurs at the carpometacarpal (CMC) joint of the thumb as the result of an axial and abduction force to the thumb.[5]

Symptoms and signs   The athlete complains of pain and swelling over the base of the thumb. The thumb's CMC appears deformed. An X ray shows fracture.

Management   This condition is structurally unstable and must be referred to an orthopedic surgeon.

Distal Phalangeal Fracture

Etiology   The primary cause of distal phalangeal fracture is a crushing force.

Symptoms and signs   There is a complaint of pain and swelling of the distal phalanx. A subungual hematoma is often seen in this condition.

Management   Initially, RICE and analgesics are given. A protective splint is applied as a means for relief of pain. The subungual hematoma is drained.

Middle Phalangeal Fracture

Etiology   A middle phalangeal fracture occurs from a direct trauma or twist.

Symptoms and signs   There is pain and swelling with tenderness over the middle phalanx. There may be deformity. X rays show bone displacement.

Management   RICE and analgesics are given as needed. Depending on the fracture site and if there is no deformity, a buddy tape may be used with a thermoplastic splint for sport activity. If there is deformity, immobilization is applied for three to four weeks and a protective splint for an additional nine to ten weeks.[11]

Proximal Phalangeal Fracture

Etiology   Fractures of the proximal phalanges may be spiral and angular.

Symptoms and signs   The athlete complains of pain, swelling, and deformity. Inspection reveals varying degrees of deformity.

Management   RICE and analgesics are given as needed. Fracture stability is maintained by immobilization of the wrist in slight extension, MCP in 70 degrees of flexion, and buddy taping.

PIP Fracture and Dislocation

Etiology   The cause of this combination of fracture and dislocation is an axial load on a partially flexed finger.

Symptoms and signs   This condition causes pain and swelling in the region of the PIP joint. There is localized tenderness over the PIP joint.

Management   RICE and analgesics are given initially, followed by reduction of the fracture. If there is a small fragment, buddy taping is used. If there is a large fragment, a splint of 30 to 60 degrees of flexion is applied.

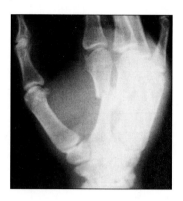

Figure 24-34

Transverse fractures of the second, third, and fourth metacarpals.

24-10

Critical Thinking Exercise

A wrestler sustains an axial force to the thumb, producing a Bennett's fracture.

? What symptoms and signs should the athletic trainer expect in such an injury?

Fingernail Deformities

Changes in the normal appearance of the fingernails can be indicative of a number of different diseases. Some of the more common changes in the fingernails and causes are listed here:

- Scaling or ridging—psoriasis
- Ridging and poor development—hyperthyroidism
- Clubbing and cyanosis—congenital heart disorders or chronic respiratory disease
- Spooning or depression—chronic alcoholism or vitamin deficiencies

REHABILITATION OF INJURIES TO THE FOREARM, WRIST, HAND, AND FINGERS

Reconditioning of the hand, wrist, and forearm must commence as early as possible. Immobilization of the forearm or wrist requires that the muscles be exercised almost immediately after an injury occurs if atrophy and contracture are to be prevented.

General Body Conditioning

Athletes who sustain forearm, wrist, or hand injuries must maintain their preinjury level of conditioning. This conditioning includes cardiorespiratory fitness, strength, flexibility, and neuromuscular control.[16] Athletes have many exercise options, such as walking, running, stair climbing, aerobics, cycling, and a variety of resistance and flexibility activities. Modified sports activities can be adapted to the individual injury.[16]

Joint Mobilization

Wrist and hand injuries respond to traction and mobilization techniques. Figure 24-35 shows one of these techniques.[17]

Flexibility

A full pain-free ROM is a major goal of rehabilitation of the lower arm. Joint function is increased when the athlete works in conjunction with traction and mobilization (Figures 24-36 and 24-37). The flexibility program should include active assisted and active pain-free stretching exercises.[20]

Strength

Strength exercises for the wrist must be cautiously carried out so as to not irritate the healing process. A variety of resistance approaches are available (Figures 24-38 through 24-43). The flexibility program should include active assisted and active

Figure 24-35

Distal anterior-posterior radial glide. The athletic trainer increases pronation by utilizing distal anterior-posterior radial glides, with one hand stabilizing the ulna and the other gliding the radius. Glides are performed in all four directions.

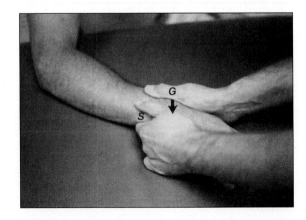

Figure 24-36

Active assisted wrist extension stretching. The athlete uses the uninvolved hand to help stretch the involved wrist.

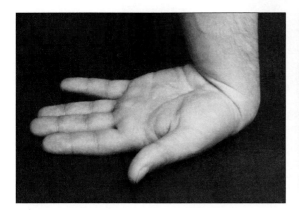
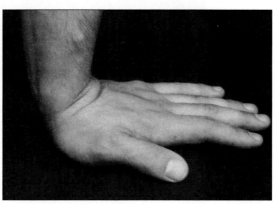

Figure 24-37

Static wrist stretching.

pain-free stretching exercises.[17] The strength principles of hand injuries are consistent with the rehabilitation for most other injuries. Restoring grip strength is essential. It can be regained by gripping a number of different devices (Figure 24-44).

Neuromuscular Control

Hand and finger rehabilitation requires a restoration of dexterity, which includes pinching and other fine motor activities such as buttoning buttons, tying shoes, and picking up small objects (Figure 24-45). A variety of customized bracing splints

Figure 24-38

Towel twist exercise. The athlete twists the towel in each direction as if wringing out water.

Figure 24-39

Wrist roll. The athlete rolls a weight both quickly and slowly.

Figure 24-40

Dumbbell wrist flexion exercise.

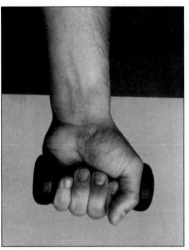

Figure 24-41

Dumbbell wrist extension exercise.

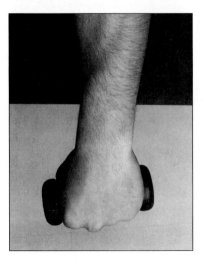

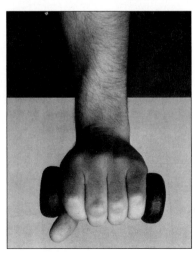

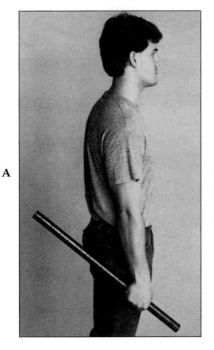
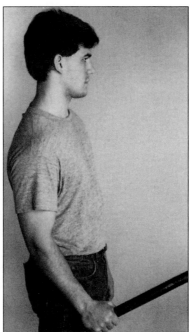

Figure 24-42

Wrist deviation strengthening. **A,** Ulnar deviation. **B,** Radial deviation.

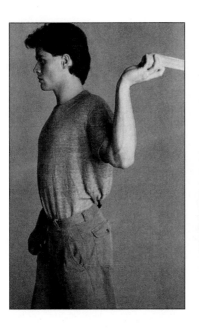

Figure 24-43

Sport-specific wrist- and hand-strengthening exercise.

and taping techniques are available to protect the injured wrist and hand (see Figure 8-9).

Return to Activity

Criteria for the return to a sport after wrist or hand injury are grip strength equal to the unaffected limb, full range of motion, and full dexterity. The thumb has unique strength requirements. A manual resistance program can be instituted to strengthen adduction, abduction, flexion, extension, opposition, and circumduction of the thumb. Rubber bands may be used to progressively strengthen the fingers' intrinsic muscles (Figure 24-46). It must be remembered that a primary goal of forearm,

Figure 24-44

A variety of resistance devices are available for restoring hand grip function.

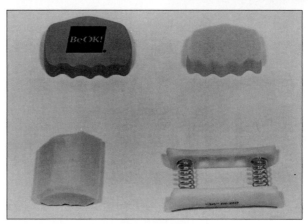

Figure 24-45

Developing finger dexterity.

Figure 24-46

Finger strengthening using rubber bands. **A,** Finger abduction exercise. **B,** Thumb abduction exercise. **C,** Thumb opposition exercise.

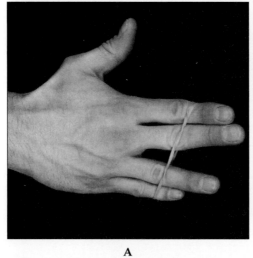
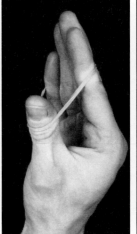
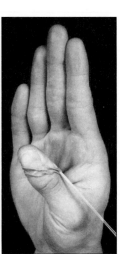

A   B   C

wrist, and hand rehabilitation is to return the athlete to preinjury grip strength (Figure 24-47).

SUMMARY

- The forearm is composed of two bones, the ulna and the radius, as well as associated soft tissue. Sports injuries to the region commonly consist of contusions, chronic forearm splints, acute strains, and fractures.
- Injuries to the wrist usually occur as the result of a fall on an outstretched hand or repeated movements of flexion, extension, and/or rotation. Common injuries are sprains, lunate dislocations, scaphoid fractures, and hamate fractures.
- Injuries to the hand occur frequently in sports activities. Common injuries include those caused by contusions and chronic pressure; by tendons receiving sustained irritation, which leads to tenosynovitis; and by tendon avulsions. Sprains, dislocations, and fractures of the fingers are also common.

Figure 24-47

Increases in grip strength can be measured using a dynamometer.

Web Sites

Cramer First Aider: http://www.ccsd.k12.wy.us/cchs_web/ cramerfirstaider/fstaider.htm

World Ortho: http://www.worldortho.com

Wheeless' Textbook of Orthopaedics: http://www.medmedia. com/med.htm

American Orthopaedic Society for Sports Medicine: http:// www.sportsmed.org

MedFacts Sports Doc: http://www.medfacts.com

OrthoNet: http://www.orthonet.com

Solutions to Critical Thinking EXERCISES

24-1 This condition is commonly called forearm splints. Its mechanism is from static contractions of the extensor forearm muscles. As a result, minute tears are produced in the interosseous membrane.

24-2 This is a silver fork deformity, which is caused by the fracture displacement of the distal radius. Another name for this injury is Colles' fracture. The athletic trainer applies an ice compress, a splint, and a sling. The athlete is then referred to a physician for an X ray and definitive treatment.

24-3 The athlete's hand is cold to the touch. Pinching a fingernail makes it blanch, and when released, it does not return to a pink color. Allen's test is carried out last, verifying a problem with hand circulation.

24-4 It is likely that the soccer player has injured the triangular fibrocartilage complex (TFCC) between the radioulnar joint and the proximal row of carpal bones. TFCC injury is often associated with sprain of the ulnar collateral ligament. The athlete with TFCC injury should be referred to a physician for treatment.

24-5 The shot-putter's repeated wrist flexions against a resistance have caused an inflammation of the tendons and synovial sheaths within the carpal tunnel. This inflammation in turn causes a compression of the median nerve and the subsequent symptoms experienced by the athlete.

24-6 The compression force is likely to cause a scaphoid fracture, which is often mistaken for a sprained wrist.

24-7 RICE is applied immediately. An X ray is done to rule out a fracture of the distal phalanx. The injury should be splinted in extension.

24-8 The suspected injuries from such a mechanism could be a complete tear of the collateral ligament, a volar plate tear, or a central extensor slip tear.

24-9 The athletic trainer should suspect a fracture of the fifth metacarpal bone. The injury may appear as an angular or rotational deformity. RICE and analgesics are given along with an X-ray examination. The injury is splinted for about four weeks, and the athlete engages in early ROM exercises.

24-10 With such a fracture, the athlete would complain of pain and swelling at the base of the thumb.

REVIEW QUESTIONS AND CLASS ACTIVITIES

1. Compare forearm splints and shinsplints. How does each occur?
2. Describe the Colles' fracture of the forearm—its cause, appearance, and care.
3. Demonstrate the major tests for hand and wrist conditions.
4. Describe the mechanism, symptoms, and signs of a wrist sprain.
5. Distinguish between the symptoms and signs of the wrist strain and sprain.

6. What healing problems occur with navicular carpal fractures? Why?

7. How can a subungual hematoma be released?

8. What causes stenosing tenosynovitis in the hand?

9. Describe the circumstances that can produce a mallet finger and a boutonniere deformity in baseball players. What care should each condition receive?

10. A sprained thumb is common in sports activities. How does it occur, and what care should it receive?

11. Should a dislocated finger be reduced by the athletic trainer? Explain your answer.

REFERENCES

1. Beam JW, Hechtman KS: Felt augmentation for thumb dislocation, *J Ath Train* 32(1):68, 1997.

2. Black KP et al: Compartment syndrome in athletes. In Hershman EB, editor: *Neurovascular injuries. Clinics in sports medicine,* vol 9, no 2, Philadelphia, 1990, Saunders.

3. Campbell JD et al: Ulnar collateral ligament injury of the thumb, *Am J Sports Med* 20(1):29, 1992.

4. Case WS: Carpal tunnel syndrome, *Physician Sportsmed* 33(1):27, 1995.

5. Caso JT, Hastings H: Metacarpal and phalangeal fractures in athletics. In Rettig AC, editor: *Hand and wrist. Clinics in sports medicine,* vol 17, no 3, Philadelphia, 1998, Saunders.

6. Guskiewicz K, Degnan G, Schildwatcher T: Scapholunate dissociation and dorsal intercalated segmental instability in an adolescent football player, *J Sport Rehabil* 4(2):116, 1995.

7. Jebson PJ, Steyers CM: Hand injuries in rock climbing, *Physician Sportsmed* 25(5):54, 1997.

8. Kielhaber TR et al: Upper extremity tendinitis and overuse syndrome in the athlete. In Culver JE, editor: *Injuries of the hand and wrist. Clinics in sports medicine,* vol 11, no 1, Philadelphia, 1992, Saunders.

9. Laimore JR, Enger WD: Serious, often subtle finger injuries, *Physician Sportsmed* 26(6):57, 1996.

10. Langford SA, Whitaker JH, Toby ER: Thumb injuries in athletics. In Rettig AC, editor: *Hand and wrist injuries. Clinics in sports medicine,* vol 17, no 3, Philadelphia, 1998, Saunders.

11. Lillegrad WA: Hand. In Birrer RB, editor: *Sports medicine for the primary care physician,* ed 2, Boca Raton, Fla, 1994, CRC Press.

12. Lord JL: Forearm injuries. In Birrer RB, editor: *Sports medicine for the primary care physician,* ed 2, Boca Raton, Fla, 1994, CRC Press.

13. Mirabello ST et al: The wrist field evaluation and treatment. In Culver JE, editor: *Injuries of the hand and wrist. Clinics in sports medicine,* vol 11, no 1, Philadelphia, 1992, Saunders.

14. Nguyen DT et al: Evaluation of the injured wrist on the field and in the office. In Rettig AC, editor: *Hand and wrist injuries. Clinics in sports medicine,* vol 17, no 3, Philadelphia, 1998, Saunders.

15. Palmer RE: Joint injuries of the hand in athletics. In Rettig AC, editor: *Hand and wrist injuries. Clinics in sports medicine,* vol 17, no 3, Philadelphia, 1998, Saunders.

16. Prentice WE: Maintenance of cardiorespiratory endurance. In Prentice WE, editor: *Rehabilitation techniques in sports medicine,* ed 3, Dubuque, Iowa, 1999, WCB/McGraw-Hill.

17. Prentice WE: Mobilization and traction techniques. In Prentice WE, editor: *Rehabilitation techniques in sports medicine,* ed 3, Dubuque, Iowa, 1999, WCB/McGraw-Hill.

18. Rettig AC: Epidemiology of hand and wrist injuries in sports. In Rettig AC, editor: *Hand and wrist injuries. Clinics in sports medicine,* vol 17, no 3, Philadelphia, 1998, Saunders.

19. Rettig AC: Dassa GL, Raskin KB, Melone CP: Wrist fractures in the athlete. In Rettig AC, editor: *Hand and wrist injuries: Clinics in sports medicine,* vol 17, no 3, Philadelphia, 1998, Saunders.

20. Schneider AM: Injuries to the hand and wrist. In Prentice WE, editor: *Rehabilitation techniques in sports medicine,* ed 3, Dubuque, Iowa, 1999, WCB/McGraw-Hill.

21. Servi JT: Wrist pain from overuse, *Physician Sportsmed* 25(12):41, 1997.

22. Weinstein SM, Herring SA: Nerve problems and compartment syndrome in the hand, wrist, and forearm. In Culver JE, editor: *Injuries of the hand and wrist. Clinics in sports medicine,* vol 11, no 1, Philadelphia, 1992, Saunders.

23. Zimmerman G: Carpal tunnel syndrome, *J Ath Train* 29(1):22, 1994.

ANNOTATED BIBLIOGRAPHY

Chan KM, editor: *Sports injuries of the hand and upper extremity,* New York, 1995, Churchill Livingstone.

This text covers basic orthopedic principles and introduces recent literature on the management of upper extremity injuries.

Clark GL, Shaw-Wilgis EF, Aiello B, Eckhaus D, Eddington LV, editors: *Hand rehabilitation: a practical guide,* ed 2, New York, 1997, Churchill Livingstone.

This major reference is devoted to treatment goals and purposes, indications, precautions for therapy, nonoperative therapy, postoperative therapy, postoperative complications, and evaluation.

Rettig AC, editor: *Hand and wrist injuries. Clinics in sports medicine,* vol 17, no 3, Philadelphia, 1998, Saunders.

This monograph covers all aspects of sports injuries to the hands and wrists.

Tubiana R, Thomine JM, Machin E: *Examination of the hand and wrist.* St Louis, 1996, Mosby Year-Book.

This excellent book combines examination of the anatomy and function of the hand and upper extremity and function with clinical evaluation.

The Spine

When you finish this chapter you should be able to

- Describe the anatomy of the cervical, thoracic, and lumbar spine.
- Understand how the nerve roots from the spinal cord combine to form specific peripheral nerves.
- Describe a process to assess injuries of the cervical, thoracic, and lumbar spine.
- Explain how to evaluate and identify various postural deformities.
- Describe measures to prevent injury to the spine.
- Discuss specific injuries that can occur to the various regions of the spine in terms of their etiology, symptoms and signs, and management.
- Discuss the techniques of rehabilitation for the injured neck.
- Explain the rehabilitation goals for managing low back injuries.

T he spine is one of the most complex regions of the body.[19] It contains a multitude of bones, joints, ligaments, and muscles, all of which are collectively involved in spinal movement. The proximity to and relationship of the spinal cord, the nerve roots, and the peripheral nerves to the vertebral column adds to the complexity of this region. Injury to the cervical spine has potentially life-threatening implications. Low back pain is one of the most common ailments known to humans. Thus, the athletic trainer requires an in-depth understanding of the anatomy of the spine, the techniques to assess the spine, the various injuries that can occur to different regions of the spine, and rehabilitative techniques.

ANATOMY

Bones of the Vertebral Column

The spine, or vertebral column, is composed of thirty-three individual bones called vertebrae. Twenty-four are classified as movable, or true, and nine are classified as immovable, or false. The false vertebrae, which are fixed by fusion, form the sacrum and the coccyx. The design of the spine allows a high degree of flexibility forward and laterally and limited mobility backward. Rotation around a central axis in the areas of the neck and the lower back is also permitted.

The movable vertebrae are separated into three different divisions, according to location and function. The first division comprises the seven cervical vertebrae; the second, the twelve thoracic vertebrae; and the third, the five lumbar vertebrae. As the spinal segments progress downward from the cervical region, they grow increasingly larger to accommodate the upright posture of the body and to contribute in weight bearing. The shape of the vertebrae is irregular, but the vertebrae possess certain characteristics that are common to all. Each vertebra consists of a neural arch, through which the spinal cord passes, and several projecting processes that serve as attachments for muscles and ligaments. Each neural arch has two laminae and two pedicles. The latter are bony processes that project backward from the body of the vertebrae and connect with the laminae. The laminae are flat bony processes occurring on either side of the neural arch; they project backward and inward from the pedicles. Spina bifida occulta is a congenital condition in which the lamina of the vertebrae, usually in the lumbar region, do not unite. In spina bifida cystica, a cyst, formed because of this lack of union, exposes part of the spinal cord. With the exception of the first and second cervical vertebrae, each vertebra has a spinous and transverse process for muscular and ligamentous attachment, and all vertebrae have an articular process.

Regions of the spinal column:
- Cervical
- Thoracic
- Lumbar
- Sacrum
- Coccyx

The Cervical Spine

The cervical spine consists of seven vertebrae, with the first two differing from the other true vertebrae (Figure 25-1A). These first two are called the atlas and the axis, respectively, and they function together to support the head on the spinal column and to permit cervical rotation. The atlas, named for its function of supporting the head, displays no body or spinous processes and is composed of lateral masses that are connected to the anterior and posterior arches. The upper surfaces articulate with the occipital condyles of the skull and allow flexion and extension along with some lateral movement. The arches of the atlas form a bony ring sufficiently large to accommodate the odontoid process and the medulla of the spinal cord. The axis, or epistropheus, is the second cervical vertebra and is designed to allow the skull and atlas to rotate on it. Its primary difference from a typical vertebra is the presence of a toothlike projection from the vertebral body that fits into the ring of the atlas. This projection is called the odontoid process. The great mobility of the cervical spine is attributed to the flattened, oblique facing of the spine's articular facets and to the horizontal positioning of the spinous processes.

The Thoracic Spine

The thoracic spine consists of twelve vertebrae. Thoracic vertebrae have long transverse processes and prominent but thin spinous processes (Figure 25-1B). Thoracic vertebrae 1 through 10 have articular facets on each transverse process to which the

Figure 25-1

A, Cervical vertebrae (atlas and axis). **B,** Thoracic vertebrae. **C,** Lumbar vertebrae.

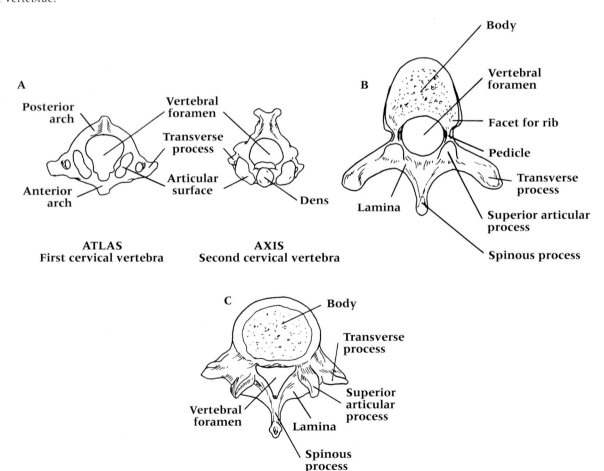

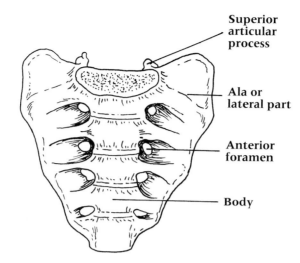

Superior articular process

Ala or lateral part

Anterior foramen

Body

Figure 25-2

The sacrum.

ribs articulate. The head of the rib articulates between two vertebrae and thus shares half of an articular facet.

The Lumbar Spine

The lumbar spine is composed of five vertebrae. These vertebrae are the major support of the low back and are the largest and thickest of the vertebrae, with large spinous and transverse processes (Figure 25-1C). The superior articular processes face medially while the inferior processes face laterally. The articular processes of the superior vertebrae articulate with the articular processes of the inferior vertebrae. Movement occurs in all the lumbar vertebrae; however, there is much less flexion than extension.

The Sacrum

The sacrum is formed in the adult by the fusion of five vertebrae (Figure 25-2) and, with the two hip bones, comprises the pelvis. The roots of the lumbar and sacral nerves, which form the lower portion of the cauda equina, pass through four foramina lateral to the five fused vertebrae.

The sacrum articulates with the ilium to form the sacroiliac (SI) joint, which has a synovium and is lubricated by synovial fluid. During both sitting and standing, the body's weight is transmitted through these joints. A complex of numerous ligaments serves to make these joints very stable.

The Coccyx

The coccyx, or tailbone, is the most inferior part of the vertebral column and consists of four or more fused vertebrae. The gluteus maximus muscle attaches to the coccyx posteriorly.

Curves of the Spine

Physiological curves are present in the spinal column for adjusting to the upright stresses. These curves are, respectively, the cervical, thoracic, lumbar, and pelvic, or sacrococcygeal, curves. The cervical and lumbar curves are convex anteriorly, whereas the thoracic and pelvic curves are convex posteriorly (Figure 25-3).

Intervertebral Disks

Between each of the cervical, thoracic, and lumbar vertebrae lie fibrocartilaginous intervertebral disks (Figure 25-4). Each disk is composed of the annulus fibrosus and the nucleus pulposus. The annulus fibrosus forms the periphery of the intervertebral

25-1

Critical Thinking Exercise

While assessing complaints of back pain in a swimmer, the athletic trainer notes that on lateral observation the low back appears to be excessively curved and the thoracic spine seems to have a curved, rounded appearance.

? When assessing posture laterally, the evaluator will normally see curves in various regions of the spine. What are the normal curves and their shape within the spine?

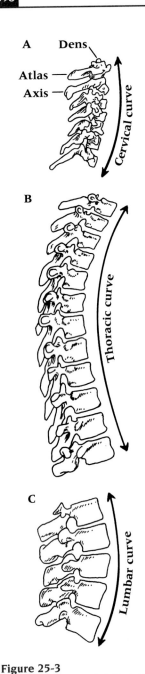

Figure 25-3

A, Cervical curve. **B,** Thoracic curve. **C,** Lumbar curve.

disk and is composed of strong, fibrous tissue, with its fibers running in several different directions for strength. In the center, the semifluid nucleus pulposus is compressed under pressure. The disks act as important shock absorbers for the spine.

Intervertebral Articulations

Intervertebral articulations are between vertebral bodies and vertebral arches. The articulation between the vertebral bodies is a cartilaginous joint. Motions between articulating vertebrae include forward gliding, lateral gliding, compression, and distraction. Besides motion at articulations between the bodies of the vertebrae, movement takes place at four articular processes that derive from the pedicles and laminae. These facet joints are synovial joints except for those between the first and second cervical vertebrae. The direction of movement of each vertebra is somewhat dependent on the direction in which the articular facets face.

Ligamentous Structures

The major ligaments that join the various vertebral parts are the anterior longitudinal, the posterior longitudinal, and the supraspinous (Figure 25-5). The anterior longitudinal ligament is a wide, strong band that extends the full length of the anterior surface of the vertebral bodies. It attaches to both the vertebral bodies and the disks and restricts extension. The posterior longitudinal ligament is contained within the vertebral canal; it extends the full length of the posterior aspect of the bodies of the vertebrae and acts to limit flexion. The supraspinous ligament attaches to each spinous process and is referred to as the ligamentum nuchae in the cervical region. The interspinous ligament between the spinous processes limits rotation and flexion of the spine.

The sacroiliac joint is maintained by the extremely strong dorsal sacral ligaments. The sacrotuberous and the sacrospinous ligaments attach the sacrum to the ischium.

Muscles of the Spine

The muscles that extend the spine and rotate the vertebral column can be classified as either superficial or deep (Figure 25-6). The superficial muscles extend from the vertebrae to ribs. The erector spinae make up the superficial muscles. The erector spinae are a group of paired muscles that consist of three columns, or bands: the longissimus group, the iliocostalis group, and the spinalis group. Each of these groups is further divided into regions: the cervicis region in the neck, the thoracis region in the middle back, and the lumborum region in the low back. The erector spinae muscles extend the spine.

The deep muscles extend from one vertebra to another. The deep muscles include the interspinales, multifidus, rotatores, and semispinalis. The semispinalis is divided into the cervicis, thorasis, and capitis regions. These muscles extend and rotate the spine.

Spinal Cord

The spinal cord is that portion of the central nervous system that is contained within the vertebral canal of the spinal column. It extends from the foramen magnum of the cranium to the filum terminale in the vicinity of the first or second lumbar vertebra. The lumbar roots and the sacral nerves form a horselike tail called the cauda equina.

Spinal Nerves and Peripheral Branches

Thirty-one pairs of spinal nerves extend from the sides of the spinal cord: eight cervical, twelve thoracic, five lumbar, five sacral, and one coccygeal (Figure 25-7). Each of these nerves has an anterior root (motor root) and a posterior root (sensory root).

POSTERIOR

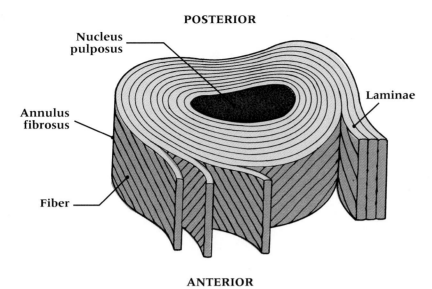

Figure 25-4

Intervertebral disk.

Nucleus pulposus

Laminae

Annulus fibrosus

Fiber

ANTERIOR

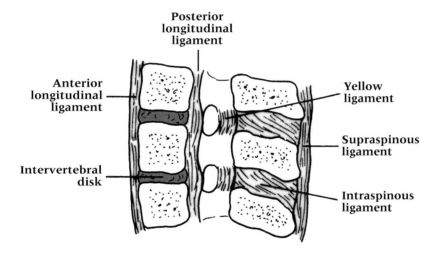

Figure 25-5

Ligaments of the spine.

Posterior longitudinal ligament

Anterior longitudinal ligament

Yellow ligament

Supraspinous ligament

Intervertebral disk

Intraspinous ligament

The two roots in each case join together and form a single spinal nerve, which passes downward and outward through the intervertebral foramen. As the spinal nerves are conducted through the intervertebral foramina, they pass near the articular facets of the vertebrae. Any abnormal movement of these facets, such as in a dislocation or a fracture, may expose the spinal nerves to injury. Injuries that occur below the third lumbar vertebra usually result in nerve root damage but do not cause spinal cord damage.

Each pair of spinal nerves, with the exception of C1, has a specific area of cutaneous sensory distribution called a *dermatome*. Figure 13-5 shows the dermatomes. Loss of sensation in a specific dermatome can provide information about the location of nerve damage.

The spinal nerve roots combine to form a network of nerves, or a plexus. There are five nerve plexuses: *cervical, brachial, lumbar, sacral,* and *coccygeal.* The cervical plexus originates from spinal nerves C1 through C4; the brachial plexus, from C5 through T1; the lumbar plexus, from L1 through L4; the sacral plexus, from L4 through S4; and the coccygeal plexus, from S4 through S5 and the coccygeal nerve. Tables 25-1 and 25-2 indicate each nerve, its nerve roots, the muscle it innervates and accompanying action, and the cutaneous innervation for the brachial plexus, the lumbo plexus and the sacral plexus, respectively.

Figure 25-6

Deep and superficial muscles of the spine.

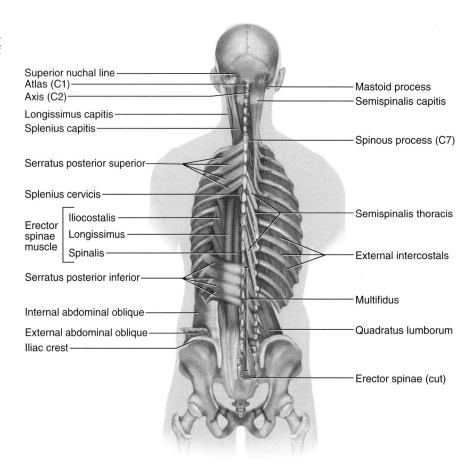

Superior nuchal line
Atlas (C1)
Axis (C2)
Longissimus capitis
Splenius capitis

Serratus posterior superior

Splenius cervicis

Erector spinae muscle
Iliocostalis
Longissimus
Spinalis

Serratus posterior inferior

Internal abdominal oblique

External abdominal oblique
Iliac crest

Mastoid process
Semispinalis capitis

Spinous process (C7)

Semispinalis thoracis

External intercostals

Multifidus

Quadratus lumborum

Erector spinae (cut)

FUNCTIONAL ANATOMY

Movements of the Vertebral Column

Movements of the vertebral column:
- Flexion
- Extension
- Lateral flexion
- Rotation

The movements of the vertebral column are flexion and extension, right and left lateral flexion, or bending, and rotation to the left and right. The degree of movement differs in the various regions of the vertebral column. The cervical and lumbar regions allow extension and flexion. Although the thoracic vertebrae have minimal movement, their combined movement between the first and twelfth thoracic vertebrae can account for 20 to 30 degrees of flexion and extension.

Flexion of the cervical region is produced primarily by the sternocleidomastoid muscles and the scalene muscle group on the anterior aspect of the throat. The scalenes flex the head and stabilize the cervical spine as the sternocleidomastoids flex the neck. The upper trapezius, semispinalis capitis, splenius capitus, and splenius cervicis muscles extend the neck. Lateral flexion of the neck is accomplished by all the muscles on one side of the vertebral column contracting unilaterally. Rotation is produced when the sternocleidomastoid, the scalenes, the semispinalis cervicis, and the upper trapezius on the side opposite the direction of rotation contract in addition to a contraction of the splenius capitus, splenius cervicis, and longissimus capitus on the same side as the direction of rotation.

Flexion of the trunk involves the lengthening of the deep and superficial back muscles and the contraction of the abdominal muscles (rectus abdominus, internal oblique, external oblique) and hip flexors (rectus femoris, iliopsoas, tensor fasciae latae, sartorius). Seventy-five percent of flexion occurs at the lumbosacral junction (L5–S1), whereas 15 percent to 20 percent occurs between L4 and L5. The rest of

25-2

***Critical* Thinking** E x e r c i s e

A wrestler has normal neck flexion and extension and lateral flexion but is having difficulty rotating his head toward his left shoulder. The athletic trainer suspects a strain of one of the muscles that rotate the head.

? Which muscles rotate the head to the left?

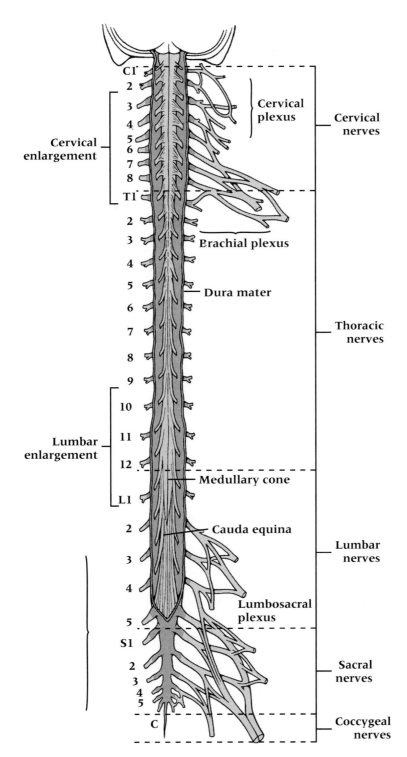

Figure 25-7

Spinal cord and spinal nerves.

the lumbar vertebrae execute 5 percent to 10 percent of flexion.[8] Extension involves the lengthening of the abdominal muscles and the contraction of the erector spinae and the gluteus maximus, which extends the hip. Trunk rotation is produced by the external obliques and the internal obliques. Lateral flexion is produced by the quadratus lumborum muscle along with the obliques, latissimus dorsi, iliopsoas, and the rectus abdominus on the side of the direction of movement.

TABLE 25-1 Brachial Plexus

Nerve	Origin	Function, Muscle Innervated	Cutaneous Innervation

Axillary	Posterior cord, C5–C6	Abduct arm
		    Deltoid
		Laterally rotate arm
		    Teres minor
			Inferior lateral shoulder

Radial	Posterior cord, C5–T1	Extend forearm
		    Triceps brachii
		    Anconeus
		Flex forearm
		    Brachialis (part)
		    Brachioradialis
		Supinate forearm
		    Supinator
		Extend wrist
		    Extensor carpi radialis longus (also abducts wrist)
		    Extensor carpi radialis brevis (also abducts wrist)
		    Extensor carpi ulnaris (also adducts wrist)
		Extend fingers
		    Extensor digitorum
		    Extensor digiti minimi
		    Extensor indicis
		Thumb muscles
		    Abductor pollicis longus
		    Extensor pollicis longus
		    Extensor pollicis brevis
			Posterior surface of arm and forearm, lateral two-thirds of dorsum of hand

Musculocu-taneous	Lateral cord, C5–C7	Flex arm
		    Coracobrachialis
		Flex forearm
		    Biceps brachii (also supinates)
		    Brachialis (also small amount of innervation from radial)
			Lateral surface of forearm

Ulnar	Medial cord, C8–T1	Flex wrist
		    Flexor carpi ulnaris (also adducts wrist)
		Flex fingers
		    Part of flexor digitorum profundus (distal phalanges of little and ring finger)
		Abduct/adduct fingers
		    Interossei
		Thumb muscle
		    Adductor pollicis
		Hypothenar muscles
		    Flexor digiti minimi brevis
		    Abductor digiti minimi
		    Opponens digiti minimi
		Midpalmar muscles
		    Two medial lumbricals
		    Interossei
			Medial one-third of hand, little finger, and medial one-half of ring finger

Median	Medial and lateral cord, C8–T1	Pronate forearm
		    Pronator teres
		    Pronator quadratus
		Flex wrist
		    Flexor carpi radialis (also abducts wrist)
		    Palmaris longus
		Flex fingers
		    Part of flexor digitorum profundus (distal phalanges of middle and index finger)
		    Flexor digitorum superficialis
			Lateral two-thirds of palm of hand, including lateral half of ring finger and tarsal tips of the same finger

Continued

TABLE 25-1 Brachial Plexus—cont'd

Nerve	Origin	Function, Muscle Innervated	Cutaneous Innervation
		Thumb muscle	
		Flexor pollicis longus	
		Thenar muscles	
		Abductor pollicis brevis	
		Opponens pollicis	
		Flexor pollicis brevis	
		Midpalmar	
		Two lateral lumbricals	

PREVENTION OF INJURIES TO THE SPINE

Cervical Spine

Acute traumatic injuries to the spine can be potentially life threatening, particularly if the cervical region of the spinal cord is involved. Thus the athlete must do everything possible to minimize the possibility of injury.

Muscle Strengthening

Strengthening of the musculature of the neck is critical. The neck muscles can function to protect the cervical spine by resisting excessive hyperflexion, hyperextension, or rotational forces. During participation, the athlete should constantly be in a state of readiness and, when making contact with an opponent, should "bull" the neck. This action is accomplished when the athlete elevates both shoulders and isometrically cocontracts the muscles surrounding the neck. Protective cervical collars can also help limit movement of the cervical spine. Athletes with long, weak necks are especially at risk. Tackle football players and wrestlers must have highly stable necks. Specific strengthening exercises are essential for the development of this stability. A variety of different exercises that incorporate isotonic, isometric, or isokinetic contractions can be used. One of the best methods is manual resistance by the athlete or by a partner who selectively uses isometric and isokinetic resistance exercises. Manual resistance should not be performed just before an individual engages in a collison sport such as football or ice hockey because of the danger of participating in these activities with fatigued neck muscles.

Range of Motion

In addition to strong muscles, the athlete's neck should have a full range of motion. Ideally, the athlete should be able to place the chin on the chest and to extend the head back until the face is parallel with the ceiling. There should be at least 40 to 45 degrees of lateral flexion and enough rotation to allow the chin to reach a level even with the tip of the shoulder. Flexibility is increased through stretching exercises and strength exercises that are in full range of motion. Where flexibility is restricted, manual static stretching can be beneficial.

Using Correct Techniques

Athletes involved in collision sports—in particular, American football and rugby, which involve tackling an opponent—must be taught and required to use techniques that reduce the likelihood of cervical injury. The head, especially one in a helmet, should not be used as a weapon. Football helmets do not protect players

TABLE 25-2 Lumbo and Sacral Plexuses

Nerve	Origin	Function, Muscle Innervated	Cutaneous Innervation

Obturator	L2–L4	Adduct thigh
		  Adductor magnus
		  Adductor longus
		  Adductor brevis
		  Gracilis (also flexes thigh)
		Rotate thigh laterally
		  Obturator externus
			Superior medial side of thigh

Femoral	L2–L4	Flex thigh
		  Iliacus
		  Psoas major
		  Pectineus
		  Sartorius (also flexes leg)
		Extend leg
		  Rectus femoris (also flexes thigh)
		  Vastus lateralis
		  Vastus medialis
		  Vastus intermedius
			Anterior and lateral branches supply the thigh; the saphenous branch supplies the medial leg and foot

Tibial	L4–S3	Extend thigh, flex leg
		  Biceps femoris (long head)
		  Semitendinosus
		  Semimembranosus
		  Adductor magnus
		Flex leg
		  Popliteus
		Plantar flex foot
		  Gastrocnemius
		  Soleus
		  Plantaris
		  Tibialis posterior
		Flex toes
		  Flexor hallucis longus
		  Flexor digitorum longus
			None

Medial and lateral plantar	Tibial	Plantar muscles of foot	Medial and lateral sole of foot
Sural	Tibial	None	Lateral and posterior one-third of leg and lateral side of foot
Common peroneal	L4–S2	Extend thigh, flex leg Bicep femoris (short head)	Lateral surface of knee

Deep peroneal	Common peroneal	Dorsiflex foot
		  Tibialis anterior
		  Peroneus tertius
		Extend toes
		  Extensor hallucis longus
		  Extensor digitorum longus
			Skin over great and second toe

Superficial peroneal	Common peroneal	Plantar flex and evert foot
		  Peroneus longus
		  Peroneus brevis
		Extend toes
		  Extensor digitorum brevis
			Distal anterior third of leg and dorsum of foot

against neck injury. In the illegal spearing maneuver, the athlete uses the helmet as a weapon by striking the opponent with its top. Most serious cervical injuries in football result from deliberate axial loading while spearing.[36]

In other sports, such as diving, wrestling, and bouncing on a trampoline, the athlete's neck can be flexed at the time of contact. Energy of the forward-moving body mass cannot be fully absorbed, and fracture or dislocation or both can occur. Diving into shallow water causes many catastrophic neck injuries.[5] Most accidents happen when the diver dives into water that is less than five feet deep and fails to keep the arms extended in front of the face. The head strikes the bottom, which produces a cervical fracture at the C5 or C6 level. Many of the same forces are applied in wrestling. In such trauma, paraplegia, quadriplegia, or death can result. Coaches cannot stress enough to the athlete the importance of using appropriate tackling techniques.

Lumbar Spine

Low back pain is one of the most common and disabling ailments known to humans. In the athlete, however, most cases of low back pain do not involve serious or long-lasting pathology.

Avoiding Stress

The athlete, like everyone else in the population, can prevent low back pain by avoiding unnecessary stresses and strains that are associated with activities of daily living. The back is subjected to these stresses and strains when one is standing, sitting, lying, working, or exercising. Care should be taken to avoid postures and positions that can cause injuries (see *Focus Box:* "Recommended postures to prevent low back pain").

Correction of Biomechanical Abnormalities

The athletic trainer should be aware of any biomechanical anomalies that the athletes possess. This knowledge helps the athletic trainer establish individual corrective programs. Basic conditioning should include an emphasis on trunk flexibility. Every effort should be made to produce maximum range of motion in rotation and both lateral and forward flexion. Both strength and flexibility should be developed in the spinal extensors (erector spinae). Abdominal strength is essential to ensure proper postural alignment.

Using Correct Lifting Techniques

Weight lifters can minimize their chance of injury to the lumbar spine by using proper lifting techniques. They can help stabilize the spine by incorporating appropriate breathing techniques that involve inhaling and exhaling deeply during lifting. Weight belts can also help stabilize the lumbar spine. Spotters can greatly enhance safety by helping lift and lower the weight.

Core Stabilization

Core stabilization, dynamic abdominal bracing, and maintaining a neutral position are all aspects of a technique that can be used by an athlete to increase the stability of the trunk. This increased stability helps the athlete maintain the spine and pelvis in a comfortable and acceptable mechanical position that will control the effects of repetitive microtrauma and protect the structures in the back from further damage. Abdominal muscle control also gives the athlete the ability to stabilize the trunk and control posture.[20,49]

ASSESSMENT OF THE SPINE

Assessment of injuries to the spine is somewhat more complex than assessment of injuries to the joints of the extremities because of the number of articulations involved in spinal movement.[27] It is also true that injury to the spine, or in particular the spinal cord, may have life-threatening or life-altering implications. Thus, the athletic trainer must be systematic and detailed in the evaluation process.

History

The most critical part of the evaluation is to rule out the possibility of spinal cord injury. Questions that address this possibility should first establish the mechanism of injury.

Recommended postures to prevent low back pain

Sitting

1. Do not sit for long periods.
2. Avoid sitting forward on a chair with back arched.
3. Sit on a firm, straight-backed chair.
4. Sit with the low back slightly rounded or positioned firmly against the back of the chair.
5. Sit with the feet flat on the floor and the knees above the level of the hips (if unable to adequately raise the knees, place the feet on a stool).
6. Avoid sitting with legs straight and raised on a stool.

Standing

1. If standing for long periods:
   a. Shift position from one foot to another.
   b. Place one foot on a stool.
2. Stand tall, flatten low back, and relax knees.
3. Avoid arching back.

Lifting and carrying

1. To pick up an object:
   a. Bend at knees and not the waist.
   b. Do not twist to pick up an object—face it squarely.
   c. Tuck in buttocks and tighten abdomen.
2. To carry an object:
   a. Hold object close to body.
   b. Hold object at waist level.
   c. Do not carry object on one side of the body—if it must be carried unbalanced, change from one side to the other.

Sleeping

1. Do not stay in one position too long.
2. Use a bed that is flat and firm yet comfortable.
3. Do not sleep on the abdomen.
4. Do not sleep on the back with legs fully extended.
5. If sleeping on the back, place a pillow under the knees.
6. Ideally, sleep on the side with the knees drawn up.
7. Never extend the arms overhead.
8. Remember that the least strain on the back is in the fully recumbent position with the hips and knees at angles of 90 degrees. In the case of a chronic or a subacute lower back condition, use a firm mattress—it will afford better rest and relaxation of the lower back. Placing $^3/_4$-inch plywood underneath the mattress gives a firm, stable surface for the injured back. Sleeping on a water bed will often relieve low back pain, because a water bed supports the body curves equally and decreases abnormal pressures to any one body area.

- What do you think happened?
- Did you hit someone with, or land directly on, the top of your head?
- Were you knocked out or unconscious? (Anytime an impact is sufficient to cause unconsciousness, the potential for injury to the spine exists.)
- Do you have any pain in your neck?
- Do you have tingling, numbness, or burning in your shoulders, arms, or hands?

- Do you have equal muscle strength in both hands? (Any sensory or motor change bilaterally may indicate a spinal cord injury.)
- Are you unable to move your ankles and toes?

A yes response to any of these questions will necessitate extreme caution when the athlete is moved. The athletic trainer who is handling a suspected cervical spine injury should err only in being overly cautious. Emergency care of the athlete with suspected cervical spine injury was discussed in detail in Chapter 12.

Once cervical spine injury has been ruled out, other general questions may provide some indication as to the nature of the problem.

- Where is the pain located?
- What kind of pain do you have?
- What were you doing when the pain began?
- Were you standing, sitting, bending, or twisting?
- Did the pain begin immediately?
- How long have you had this pain?
- Do certain movements or positions cause more pain?
- Can you assume a position that gets rid of the pain?
- Is there any tingling or numbness in the arms or legs?
- Is there any pain in the buttocks or the back of the legs?
- Have you ever had any back pain before?
- What position do you usually sleep in? How do you prefer to sit?

It is important to remember that pain in the back may be caused by many different conditions. The source may be musculoskeletal or visceral, or it may be referred.

Observation

Observing the posture and movement capabilities of the athlete during the evaluation can help clarify the nature and extent of the injury.

Posture Evaluation

It is important to observe the athlete's total static posture, with special attention paid to the low back, pelvis, and hips. The athletic trainer should also make some decision about somatotype (i.e., ectomorph, mesomorph, or endomorph). When observing the athlete's standing static posture, the athletic trainer must accept the fact that postural alignment varies considerably among individuals; therefore only obvious asymmetries should be considered. The entire body should be observed from all angles—lateral, anterior, and posterior (Figure 25-8). To ensure accuracy of observation, a plumb line or posture screen may be of use (Figure 25-9). A trained observer with a good background in postural observation may not require any special devices. Figure 25-10 shows typical vertical alignment landmarks from a lateral view. In the anterior and posterior assessment, the evaluator looks for asymmetries or differences in height between anatomical landmarks on each side (Figure 25-11).

General observations relative to posture include the following:

- Head is tilted to one side.
- Shoulder is lower on one side.
- One shoulder is carried forward.
- One scapula is lower and more prominent than the other.
- Trunk is habitually bent to one side.
- Space between the body and arm is greater on one side.
- One hip is more prominent than the other.
- Hips are tilted to one side.
- Ribs are more pronounced on one side.
- One arm hangs longer than the other.
- One arm hangs farther forward than the other.
- One patella is lower than the other.

Classic postural deviations include kyphosis, forward head posture, lordosis, flatback posture, swayback posture, and scoliosis.

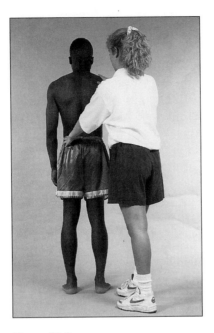

Figure 25-8

Observing spinal alignment.

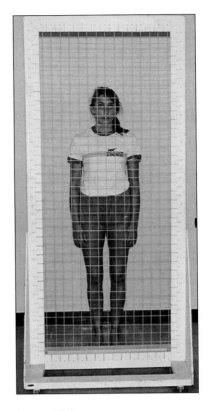

Figure 25-9

Using a grid can produce more accurate results during posture screening.

Back of ear

Middle of shoulder

Middle of greater trochanter

Back of patellae

Front of malleolus

Figure 25-10

Typical vertical alignment landmarks.

Classic postural deviations include kyphosis, forward head posture, lordosis, flatback posture, swayback posture, and scoliosis.

Kyphosis   Kyphosis is characterized by an increased thoracic curve and by scapulae that are protracted, which produces a rounded shoulder appearance (Figure 25-12A). Kyphosis is usually associated with a forward head posture.

Scheuermann's disease is a disease of unknown etiology that usually affects adolescent males. This condition is not only painful but also may cause progressive thoracic or lumbar kyphosis.

Forward head posture   If the upper back exhibits a kyphotic posture in standing or sitting, there will be a compensatory change in the position of the head and neck. To keep the eyes level in spite of a slumped or rounded shoulder posture, the athlete must extend the cervical spine, which tends to produce short but strong neck extensors and weak, long neck flexors. Thus, the head will be held in a forward position (Figure 25-12B).

Lordosis   Lordotic posture is characterized by an increased curve in the lumbar spine and an increase both in anterior tilt of the pelvis and in hip flexion (Figure 25-12E). Lordosis combined with kyphosis and a forward head posture is referred to as a kypho-lordotic posture.

Flatback posture   Flatback posture is caused by a decreased lumbar curve and an increase in posterior pelvic tilt and in hip flexion (Figure 25-12C).

Swayback posture   A swayback posture involves an anterior shifting of the entire pelvis that results in hip extension. The thoracic segment shifts posteriorly, causing flexion of the thorax on the lumbar spine. Thus, there is a decrease in lordosis in the lumbar spine and an increase in kyphosis in the thoracic spine (Figure 25-12D).

Scoliosis   Scoliosis is a lateral curvature of the spine (Figure 25-12F). The athlete with scoliosis exhibits a recognizable abnormal curve in one direction and a compen-

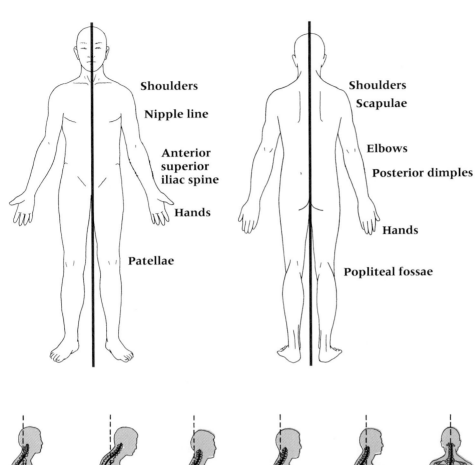

Figure 25-11

Typical horizontal alignment landmarks. (Colored line indicates vertical landmarks.)

Shoulders

Nipple line

Anterior superior iliac spine

Hands

Patellae

Shoulders

Scapulae

Elbows

Posterior dimples

Hands

Popliteal fossae

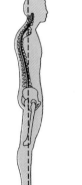 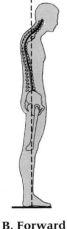 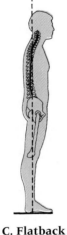  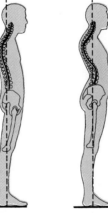 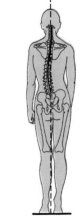

A. Kyphosis   **B. Forward Head**   **C. Flatback**   **D. Swayback**   **E. Lordosis**   **F. Scoliosis**

Figure 25-12

Postural malalignments. **A,** Kyphosis. **B,** Forward head. **C,** Flatback. **D,** Swayback. **E,** Lordosis. **F,** Scoliosis.

satory secondary curve in the opposite direction. Scoliosis can be functional or structural. A functional scoliosis can be caused by some nonspinal defect such as unequal leg length, muscle imbalance, or nutritional deficiency. Structural scoliosis is caused by some defect in the bony structure of the spine. When the athlete bends forward, the spine with a functional scoliosis may straighten, whereas the spine with a structural scoliosis remains twisted. With the athlete in this position, one side of the spine may be more prominent than the other.

Cervical Spine Observation

When evaluating a case of cervical injury, the athletic trainer should look at the position of the head and neck. Are the shoulders level and symmetrical? Is the athlete willing to move the head and neck freely? The athletic trainer should check passive,

Figure 25-13

Checking neck range of motion. **A,** Flexion. **B,** Extension. **C,** Lateral flexion. **D,** Rotation.

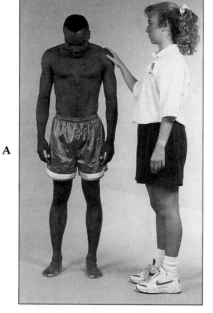
A

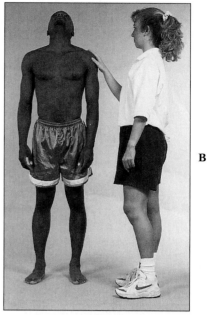
B

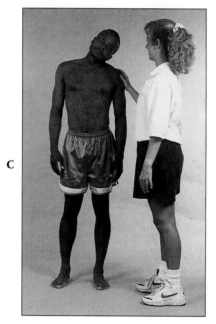
C

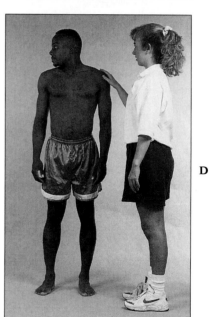
D

active, and resisted range of motion in the neck including flexion, extension, rotation, and lateral bending (Figure 25-13).

Thoracic Spine Observation

The athlete is first asked to flex, extend, laterally flex, and rotate the neck. Pain accompanying the movement in the upper back region could be referred from a lesion of the cervical disk. Additionally, pain in the scapular area could stem from an irritation of a myofascial trigger point or from irritation of the long thoracic or suprascapular nerves, which requires evaluation of the shoulder complex (see Chapter 22). The athlete should also be asked to flex forward and laterally and to extend and rotate the trunk. Pain felt during movement may indicate nerve root irritation to the lower thoracic region.

The most common cause of thoracic pain is dysfunction of one or more joint articulations and usually involves the facet joints. Increased pain upon placing the chin on the chest or upon deep inspiration is often indicative of a facet joint problem.

Lumbar Spine and Sacroiliac Joint Observation

Normal functional movement in the low back region depends on coordinated motion of the lumbar vertebrae, the sacrum, and the pelvis. The pelvis and shoulders should be level. Both the soft tissue and bony structures on both sides of the midline should be symmetrical. Any unusual curve in the lumbar area that is observed when the athlete is standing or walking could be due to muscular, capsular, or ligamentous injuries, to disk-related problems, or to some idiopathic or structural problem.

The athlete should be observed in standing, sitting, supine, side-lying, and prone positions, and special tests should be done in each of those positions to determine the nature of the problem.[33]

Palpation

Palpation should be performed with the athlete lying prone and the spine as straight as possible. The head and neck should be slightly flexed. In cases of low back pain, a pillow placed under the hips might make the athlete more comfortable. Palpation should progress from proximal to distal as the evaluator attempts to identify points of tenderness, muscle spasm or guarding, or defects in bone or soft tissue.

The musculature on each side of the spine should be palpated for tenderness or guarding. It should be remembered that referred pain can produce tender areas. At some point in the evaluation of the lumbar spine, the abdominal musculature should also be palpated; the athlete should perform a partial sit-up to determine symmetry and tone.

The spinous processes are the easiest landmark to locate. Pressure and release should be applied to the spinous process of each vertebrae in an anterior direction to determine if pain is increased either centrally or laterally. The gaps between the spinous processes should be palpated. Tenderness may indicate some ligamentous or disk-related problem. Each spinous process should be in a direct line with the one directly above and directly below (Figure 25-14). Misalignment usually occurs in the cervical or lumbar areas, indicating some rotation of an individual vertebral segment. The transverse processes on both sides of each vertebrae can also be palpated. Pressure on one side only produces rotation of that segment, which can increase pain. The facet joints and laminae are difficult to palpate because of the paraspinal muscles.

The sacroiliac joints should be palpated bilaterally for tenderness. Posterior pressure on the sacrum may increase pain if the sacroiliac joint is involved.

Special Tests for the Cervical Spine

Special tests for the cervical spine should not be done until trauma to either the vertebrae or the spinal cord has been ruled out.

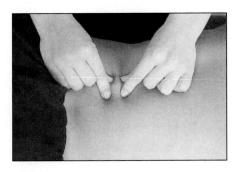

Figure 25-14

Each spinous process should be in a direct line with the one above and below.

Figure 25-15

Brachial plexus test.

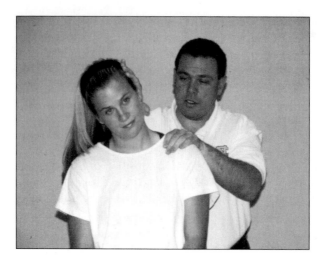

Brachial Plexus Test

Lateral flexion or bending of the cervical spine by the application of pressure on both the head and the shoulder duplicates the mechanism of injury to the brachial plexus (Figure 25-15). If the cervical spine is flexed to the right and pain radiates to the right shoulder and arm, a compression injury exists. Conversely, if the pain radiates to the left shoulder and arm, a traction or stretch injury has occurred.

Cervical Compression and Spruling's Tests

Axial compression of the cervical spine by the application of a downward force compresses cervical facet joints and the cervical spinal nerve roots (Figure 25-16). The level of the associated pain will determine specifically which nerve root has been injured. Spruling's test also uses cervical compression but with lateral bending and slight extension, which produces pain in the shoulder and arm on the side of flexion (Figure 25-17). Pain is caused by impingement of the nerve root.

Vertebral Artery Test

This test is done with the athlete supine. The athletic trainer extends, then laterally bends and rotates the cervical spine in the same direction (Figure 25-18). Dizziness or abnormal movement of the eyes (nystagmus) indicates that the cervical vertebral

Figure 25-16

Cervical compression test.

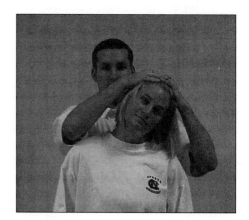

Figure 25-17

Spruling's test.

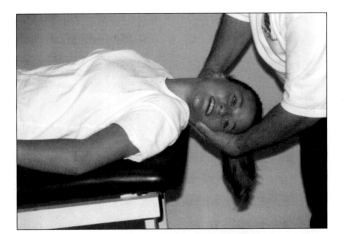

Figure 25-18

Vertebral artery test.

Figure 25-19

Shoulder abduction test.

artery is being partially occluded because of some abnormal compression. The athlete should be immediately referred to a physician for additional testing and diagnosis.

Shoulder Abduction Test

The athlete abducts the shoulder, placing the hand on top of the head (Figure 25-19). A decrease in symptoms may indicate the presence of a nerve root compression, possibly due to a herniated disk.

Special Tests for the Lumbar Spine

Special tests for the lumbar spine should be performed in standing, sitting, supine, side-lying, and prone positions.[13]

Tests Done in Standing Position

The evaluator should observe the athlete's gait. Is the patient's trunk bent, or are the hips shifted to one side? Is there a limp or any difficulty in walking? The evaluator should check the alignment and symmetry of the malleoli, popliteal crease, trochanters, anterior and posterior superior iliac spines (ASIS and PSIS), and iliac crests.

Forward bending   Forward bending involves stretching of the posterior spinal ligaments (Figure 25-20A). With forward bending or flexion, the PSISs on each side should move together. If one moves further than the other, a motion restriction is likely present on the side that moves most. If they move at different times, the side that moves first usually has a restriction.

25-3

Critical Thinking Exercise

A cross country runner stepped in a hole while running. He immediately felt pain in his left low back below his waist and had to stop running. He comes to the athletic trainer, who suspects that the mechanism of injury has caused a problem with the sacroiliac joint.

? What signs should the athletic trainer look for during the evaluation that would likely indicate some injury to the sacroiliac joint?

Figure 25-20

Checking lumbar range of motion in standing. **A,** Forward bending. **B,** Backward bending. **C,** Side bending.

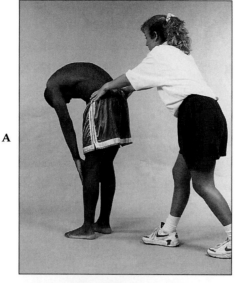

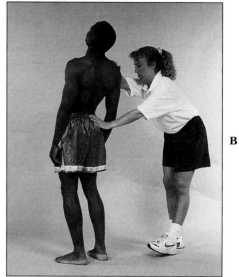

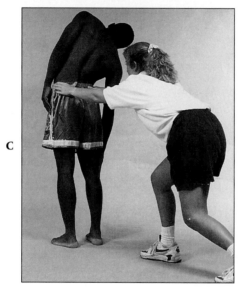

Backward bending   Backward bending places the spine in a hyperextended position and stretches the anterior ligaments of the spine (Figure 25-20B). Restrictions or pain present in backward bending are usually associated with a disk problem. However, the pain may also be related to spondylolysis or spondylolisthesis (to be discussed later in this chapter). Extension done in the one-leg standing position (stork position) is a good indicator of a spondylolysis (Figure 25-21).

Side bending   For the athlete with a lumbar lesion or with sacroiliac dysfunction, side bending toward the painful side will increase the pain (Figure 25-20C). In the case of a herniated disk, the athlete will usually side bend toward the side of the herniation to relieve the nerve from external compression by the disk.

Tests Done in Sitting Position

Forward bending   In seated forward bending or flexion, like in standing forward bending, the PSISs should move together. If one moves further than the other, a motion restriction is likely present on the side that moves most.

Rotation   The athlete sits with arms folded across the chest and rotates the trunk to the left and then to the right while the evaluator checks the movement of the lumbar spine for symmetry (Figure 25-22A).

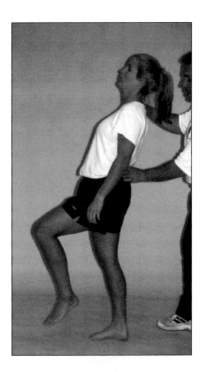

Figure 25-21

One-leg standing extension test (stork test).

Hip rotation   With the athlete in the same sitting position, the hip should be rotated internally and externally (Figures 25-22B and C). Internal rotation that produces pain will likely be a piriformis irritation (discussed later in this chapter), and pain is produced as the muscle is stretched.

Slump test   The slump test begins with the athlete sitting with both arms behind the back, knees flexed, and feet on the ground (Figure 25-23). The thoracic and lumbar spines are flexed with overpressure. Pain is assessed first in this starting position. From this starting position, the following series of positional changes occurs, with pain being assessed in each position: (1) The cervical spine is flexed, (2) one knee is extended, (3) the ankle is dorsiflexed, (4) neck flexion is released, (5) both legs are extended simultaneously, and (6) steps 1 through 4 are repeated with the other leg. This test is done to detect an increase in nerve root tension that has recently been labeled *neural tension*, which may be caused by spinal stenosis, lateral disk herniation, nerve root adhesions, or vertebral impingement.[22]

Tests Done in Supine Position

Straight leg raises   The *straight leg raising* test applies pressure to the sacroiliac joint and may indicate a problem in either the sciatic nerve, the sacroiliac joint, or the lumbar spine (Figure 25-24). Pain at 30 degrees of straight leg raising indicates either a hip problem or an inflamed nerve. Pain from 30 degrees to 60 degrees indicates some sciatic nerve involvement. If dorsiflexing the ankle at maximum straight leg raising increases the pain, the problem is likely due to some nerve root (L3–4, S1–3) or sciatic nerve irritation (Laseague's sign). Pain between 70 degrees and 90 degrees is indicative of a sacroiliac joint problem.

Kernig's test   In Kernig's test, the athlete performs a unilateral straight leg raise with the knee extended, which creates lumbar pain that possibly radiates into the buttocks. Pain indicates some impingement of the nerve root that is caused by a bulging disk or bony entrapment or by irritation of the meninges (Figure 25-25).

Brudzinski's test   Brudzinski's test is a modification of Kernig's test. Pain that increases when the neck is flexed may indicate either a lumbar disk or some nerve root irritation (Figure 25-26).[19]

25-5

C*ritical Thinking* E x e r c i s e

A volleyball player comes to the athletic trainer complaining of recurring low back pain. She has been seen by a therapist in her hometown who has told her that she has a positive straight leg raising test, but the athlete still does not understand what is causing her pain.

? How should the athletic trainer explain what having a positive straight leg raising test means?

Figure 25-22

Checking lumbar range of motion in sitting. **A,** Rotation. **B,** Internal hip rotation. **C,** External hip rotation.

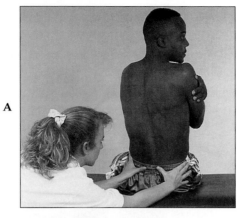

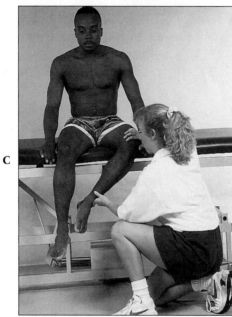

Figure 25-23

Slump test.

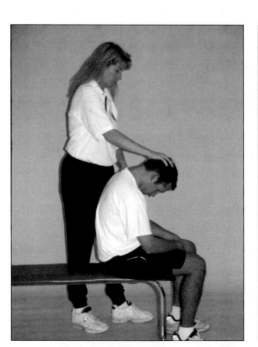

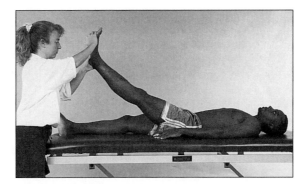

Figure 25-24

Straight leg raising test.

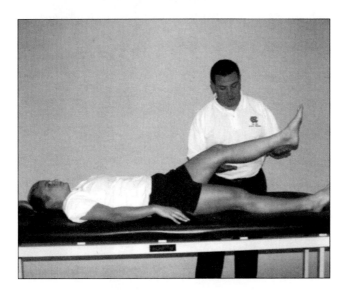

Figure 25-25

Kernig's test.

Well straight leg raising test   The well straight leg raising test, done on the unaffected side, may also produce pain in the low back on the affected side as well as radiating along the sciatic nerve. This test provides additional proof of nerve root inflammation (Figure 25-27).

Milgram and Hoover straight leg raising tests   An inability to hold both legs off the treatment table for thirty seconds on the Milgram straight leg raising test

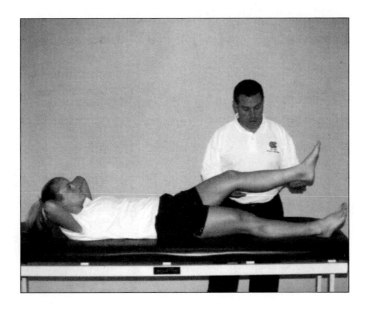

Figure 25-26

Brudzinski's test.

Figure 25-27

Well straight leg raising test.

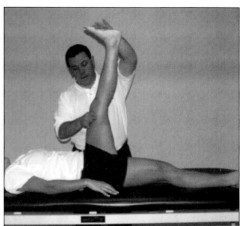

indicates some problem with the lumbar spine. This test increases intrathecal pressure that causes a disk to put pressure on a lumbar nerve root (Figure 25-28A). The Hoover test is a variation of the Milgram test; it uses a unilateral straight leg raise to check for nerve root problems (Figure 25-28B).

Bowstring test   The bowstring test is another way to determine sciatic nerve irritation. The leg on the affected side is lifted until pain is felt. The knee is then flexed until the pain is relieved, at which time pressure is applied to the popliteal fossa. The

Figure 25-28

A, Milgram straight leg raising test. **B,** Hoover test.

A
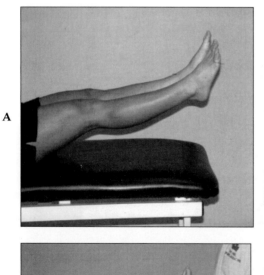
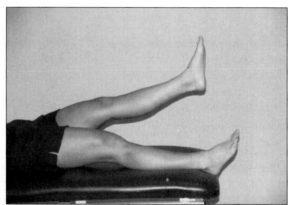

B
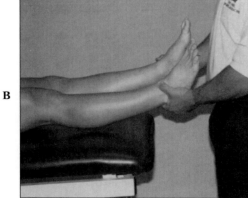
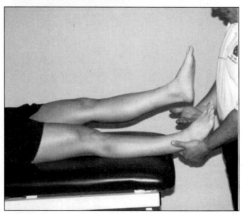

Figure 25-29

Bowstring test for sciatic nerve irritation.

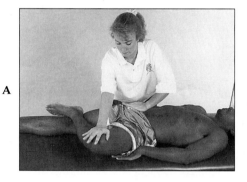

A

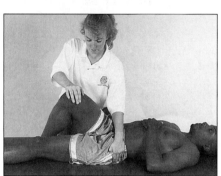

B

Figure 25-30

A, Patrick test (FABER).
B, FADIR test.

test result is positive if pain is felt during palpation along the sciatic nerve (Figure 25-29). To confirm that the pain stems from a nerve root involvement and not from hamstring tightness, the leg is lowered to a point at which pain ceases. In this position, the foot is dorsiflexed and the neck flexed. If pain returns, it is a verification of a pathological condition of the nerve root.

FABER and FADIR tests   A FABER (flexion, abduction, external rotation of the hip), or Patrick test, indicates a problem with the hip or sacroiliac joint (Figure 25-30A). A FADIR test (flexion, adduction, internal rotation of the hip) indicates a problem in the lumbar area (Figure 25-30B).

Knees to chest tests   Pulling the knees to the chest bilaterally will increase symptoms in the lumbar spine (Figure 25-31A). If pulling a single knee to the chest causes pain in the posterolateral thigh, there may be some irritation to the sacrotuberous ligament (Figure 25-31B). If pain is reported in the area of the PSIS when pulling a single knee to the opposite shoulder, there may be sacroiliac ligament irritation (Figure 25-31C).

SI compression and distraction tests   Sacroiliac compression and distraction tests are useful in determining if there is a problem in the sacroiliac joint (Figure 25-32).

Pelvic tilt tests   Anterior and posterior pelvic tilts that increase the pain on the side being stressed indicate irritation of the sacroiliac joint (Figure 25-33). Occasionally this test may be done on an athlete in a side-lying position.

Tests Done in a Prone Position

Press-ups   Press-ups, which extend the spine, are done to see if pain radiates into the buttocks or thigh, which may indicate a herniated disk. If pain localizes in this position, conservative care is recommended. If pain is more generalized, surgical care may be required (Figure 25-34).

Reverse straight leg raise test   In a reverse straight leg raise, the athlete lies prone and lifts the affected leg. If pain occurs in the low back, an L4 nerve root irritation may be present (Figure 25-35).

Figure 25-31

A, Bilateral knees to chest.
B, Single knee to chest.
C, Knee to opposite shoulder.

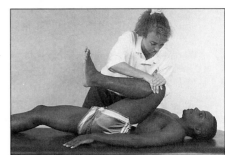

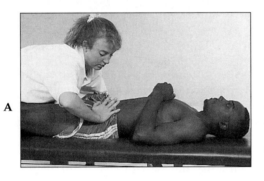

Figure 25-32

A, Sacral compression.
B, Sacral distraction.

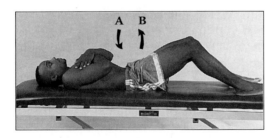

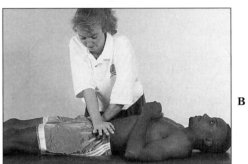

Figure 25-33

A, Anterior pelvic tilt. **B,** Posterior pelvic tilt.

Figure 25-34

Press-ups.

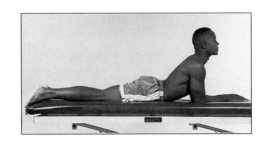

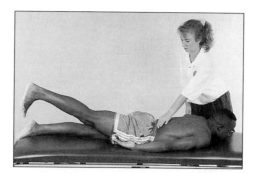

Figure 25-35

Reverse straight leg raise.

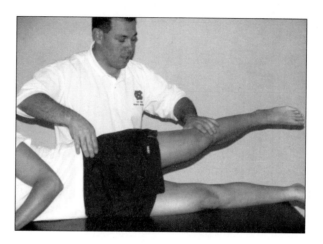

Figure 25-36

Femoral nerve traction test.

Spring test   In the spring test, a downward pressure is applied through the spinous process of each vertebra to assess anterior/posterior motion. The spring test can also be done on the transverse process to assess rotational movement. This test can determine either hypermobility or hypomobility of a specific vertebral segment.

Tests Done in a Side-Lying Position

Femoral nerve traction test   The femoral nerve traction test is done with the hip extended and the knee flexed to 90 degrees. As the hip is extended, pain occurs in the anterior thigh, which indicates nerve root impingement in the lumbar area. This test may also be done in a prone position (Figure 25-36).

Neurological Exam

The neurological exam was discussed in detail in Chapter 13. In cases in which the spinal cord and associated nerve roots are potentially injured, sensation testing and reflex testing should be a routine aspect of the assessment process.

Sensation testing   When there is a nerve root involvement, sensation can be partially or completely disrupted in dermatomal patterns. Figures 25-37A and B indicate the locations of general disruption or loss of sensation as a result of cervical and lumbosacral nerve root involvement.

Reflex testing   Deep tendon reflexes were discussed in Chapter 13. Three reflexes in the upper extremity are the biceps, brachioradialis, and triceps reflexes. In the biceps reflex, the C5 nerve root is being tested. The brachioradialis reflex assesses the C6 nerve root. C7 nerve root dysfunction is indicated by the triceps reflex.

Two reflexes in the lower extremity are the patellar and the Achilles tendon reflexes. A diminished or absent patellar reflex is an indication of an S1 nerve root

Figure 25-37

A, Upper extremity. **B,** Lower extremity.

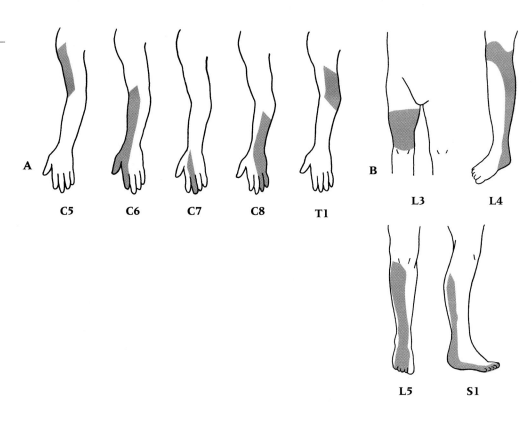

problem. The Achilles tendon reflex can determine the presence or absence of an L4 nerve root problem.

Table 25-3 summarizes the special tests for the spine.

RECOGNITION AND MANAGEMENT OF SPECIFIC INJURIES AND CONDITIONS

Cervical Spine Conditions

Because the neck is so mobile, it is extremely vulnerable to a wide range of sports injuries.[47] Severe sports injury to the neck, although relatively uncommon, can produce catastrophic impairment of the spinal cord (Figure 25-38).[48] The neck can be seriously injured by the following traumatic events (Figure 25-39): an axial load force to the top of the head, a flexion force, a hyperextension force, a flexion-rotation force, a hyperextension-rotation force, or a lateral flexion force.[41] The neck is also prone to subtle injuries stemming from stress, tension, and postural malalignments.

Cervical Fractures

Etiology   Fortunately, the incidence of neck fracture is relatively uncommon in athletics. The spinal cord is well protected by a bony vertebral canal, a connective tissue sheath, fat, and fluid cushioning. Despite this protection, vertebral dislocations and fractures have the potential to result in paralysis. The athletic trainer must constantly be prepared to handle such a situation should it arise. Sports that have the highest incidence of cervical fracture are gymnastics, ice hockey, diving, football, and rugby.[42]

Axial loading of the cervical vertebra from a force to the top of the head combined with flexion of the neck can result in an anterior compression fracture or possibly a dislocation.[40] Fractures are most common in the fourth, fifth, or sixth cervical vertebra. If the head is also rotated when contact is made, a dislocation may occur

TABLE 25-3 Special Tests for the Spine

Test	A Positive Test Indicates
Cervical Spine	
Brachial plexus test	Brachial plexus injury
Cervical compression test	Nerve root impingement
Spruling's test	Nerve root impingement
Vertebral artery test	Occluded cervical vertebral artery
Shoulder abduction test	Nerve root impingement
Lumbar Spine	
Standing Position	
Forward bending	Restriction in PSIS
Backward bending	Disk problem; spondylolysis
Side bending	Herniated disk; SI dysfunction
Stork test	Spondylolysis
Sitting Position	
Forward bending	Restriction in PSIS
Rotation	Asymmetry in lumbar spine
Internal hip rotation	Piriformis injury
Slump test	Increased neural tension
Supine Position	
Straight leg raising 30°	Hip problem; nerve root impingement
Straight leg raising 30–60°	Sciatic nerve; nerve root impingement
Straight leg raising 70–90°	SI joint dysfunction
Kernig's test	Nerve root irritation
Brudzinski's test	Lumbar disk; Nerve root irritation
Well straight leg raising	Nerve root irritation
Milgram straight leg raising	Lumbar disk
Hoover test	Nerve root irritation
	Bow string
Patrick test/FABER	SI joint dysfunction
FADIR test	Lumbar strain
Bilateral knees to chest	Lumbar sprain
Single knee to chest	Sacrotuberous ligament sprain
Single knee to opposite shoulder	Sacroiliac ligament sprain
SI joint compression	SI joint dysfunction
SI joint distraction	SI joint dysfunction
Pelvic tilt	SI joint irritation
Prone Position	
Press-ups	Herniated disk
Reverse straight leg raise	L4 nerve root irritation
Spring test	Vertebral hypermobility/hypomobility
Side-Lying Position	
Femoral nerve traction test	Nerve root irritation

along with the fracture. Fractures can also occur during a sudden forced hyperexten-sion of the neck (Figure 25-40).

Symptoms and signs   The athlete may have one or more of the following signs of cervical fracture: neck point tenderness and restricted movement, cervical muscle spasm, cervical pain and pain in the chest and extremities, numbness in trunk and/or limbs, weakness or paralysis in limbs and/or trunk, loss of bladder and/or bowel control.

Management   An unconscious athlete should be treated as if a serious neck in-jury is present until this possibility is ruled out by the physician.[46] Extreme caution must be used in moving the athlete.[1] The athletic trainer must always be aware that

Figure 25-38

The possibility of cervical neck injury is always present in sport.

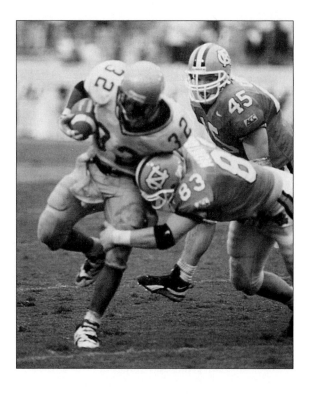

an athlete can sustain a catastrophic spinal injury from improper handling and transportation (see Chapter 12 for emergency care of spinal injuries).

Cervical Dislocations

Etiology   Cervical dislocations are not common, but they do occur much more frequently in sports than do fractures. Cervical dislocations usually result from violent flexion and rotation of the head. Most injuries of this type happen in pool diving accidents. The mechanism is analogous to the situation that occurs in football when blocks and tackles are poorly executed. The cervical vertebrae are

Figure 25-39

Mechanisms of cervical neck injury.

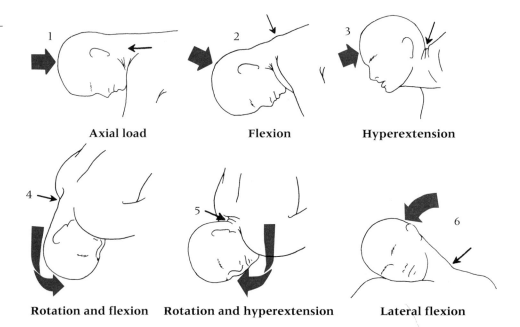

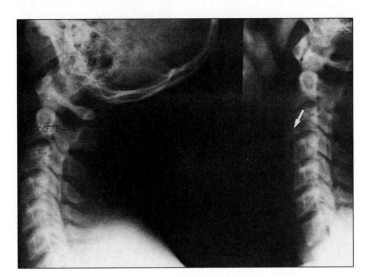

Figure 25-40

Fracture of C3 resulting from a football injury.

more easily dislocated than are the vertebrae in other spinal regions, principally because of their horizontally arranged articular facets. The superior articular facet moves beyond its normal range of motion and either completely passes the inferior facet (luxation) or catches on its edge (subluxation). The latter is far more common and, as in the case of the complete luxation, most often affects the fourth, fifth, or sixth vertebra.

Symptoms and signs   For the most part, a cervical dislocation produces many of the same signs as a fracture. Both can result in considerable pain, numbness, and muscle weakness or paralysis. The most easily discernible difference is the position of the neck in a dislocation: a unilateral dislocation causes the neck to be tilted toward the dislocated side with extreme muscle tightness on the elongated side and a relaxed muscle state on the tilted side.

Management   Because a dislocation of a cervical vertebra has a greater likelihood of causing injury to the spinal cord, even greater care must be exercised when moving the patient. Again, the procedures described in Chapter 12 should be applied to cervical dislocations.

Acute Strains of the Neck and Upper Back

Etiology   In a strain of the neck or upper back, the athlete has usually turned the head suddenly or has forced flexion, extension, or rotation. Muscles involved are typically the upper trapezius, sternocleidomastoid, the scalenes, and the splenius capitis and cervicis.[31]

Symptoms and signs   Localized pain, point tenderness, and restricted motion are present. Muscle guarding resulting from pain is common, and there is a reluctance to move the neck in any direction.

Management   Care usually includes use of RICE immediately after the strain occurs and the application of a cervical collar. Follow-up management may include ROM exercises, followed by isometric exercises, and progressing to full-range isotonic strengthening exercises; cryotherapy or superficial heat; and analgesic medications as prescribed by the physician.

Cervical Sprain (Whiplash)

Etiology   A cervical sprain can occur from the same mechanism as the strain but usually results from a more violent motion. More commonly, cervical sprain occurs from a sudden snap of the head, such as when the athlete is tackled or blocked while unprepared (Figure 25-41). Frequently, muscle strains occur with ligament sprains. A sprain of the neck produces tears in the major supporting tissue of the anterior or

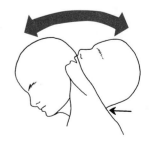

Figure 25-41

Whiplash injury.

Cervical Sprain (Whiplash)

Injury Situation While at practice, a male ice hockey player was checked hard against the boards. Because he was not properly set for the force, his head was snapped vigorously backward into extension and forward into flexion. In this process the athlete experienced a sudden sharp pain and a tearing sensation at the base of the posterior neck region.

Symptoms and Signs The athlete complained to the athletic trainer that immediately after the injury there was a dull ache, stiffness, and weakness in the neck region. He also complained of headache, dizziness, and nausea approximately 1 hour after the injury.

Palpation revealed severe muscle spasm and point tenderness of the erector spinae muscles and the lateral aspect of the neck and upper shoulder. A neurologic exam did not reveal any changes in motor or sensory abilities. X-ray examination ruled out fracture, dislocation, or spinal cord injury. Gentle passive movement produced some pain. A soft neck collar was applied for immobilization. During further evaluation, there was pain during both gentle active and resistive movement. The condition was considered to be a second-degree neck sprain with muscle involvement produced by a whiplash mechanism.

Management Plan The nature of a neck sprain dictates that management should follow a conservative course. A soft cervical collar was to be worn 24 hours a day for comfort until the athlete was symptom free. Wearing this collar could be followed by wearing the brace just during the waking hours for 1 or 2 additional weeks.

Phase **1** *Acute Injury*   **GOALS:** To control initial hemorrhage, swelling, spasm, and pain.
              ESTIMATED LENGTH OF TIME (ELT): 2 to 3 days.

■ **Therapy** Apply ice pack (20 min) intermittently 6 to 8 times daily. Transcutaneous electrical nerve stimulation (TENS) was used successfully to reduce spasm and pain in the early stages of injury.

■ **Exercise rehabilitation** Wear soft cervical collar. Athlete is taught to hold head in good alignment in relation to shoulder and spine; this alignment should be practiced every waking hour. Begin gentle grade 1 and 2 cervical mobilizations as tolerated.

Phase **2** *Repair*   **GOALS:** To restore 90% neck range of motion and 50% strength.
              ELT: 7 to 11 days.

■ **Therapy** Ice pack (5 to 15 min) or ice massage (7 min) 3 or 4 times; precedes active motion.

■ **Exercise rehabilitation** Active stretching 2 or 3 times daily, including neck flexion with depressed shoulders, lateral neck flexion, and right and left head rotation; each position held 5 to 10 seconds and repeated 5 times or within pain-free limits. Gentle passive static stretching within pain-free limits (2 to 3 times each direction) once daily; each stretch held for 20 to 30 seconds. Manual isotonic resistive exercise to the neck performed once daily by the athlete or athletic trainer (5 repetitions). Progress to grade 3 and 4 cervical mobilizations as tolerated.

Phase **3** *Remodeling*   **GOALS:** To restore full range of motion and full strength. To return to ice hockey competition and full neck muscle bulk.
              ELT: 4 to 7 days.

■ **Therapy** Ice pack (5 to 15 min) or ice massage (7 min) once daily preceding exercise.

Continued

posterior longitudinal ligaments, the interspinous ligament, and the supraspinous ligament.

Symptoms and signs The sprain displays all the signs of the strained neck but the symptoms persist longer. There may also be tenderness over the transverse and spinous processes that serve as sites of attachment for the ligaments.

Pain may not be experienced initially but always appears the day after the trauma. Pain stems from the inflammation of injured tissue and a protective muscle spasm that restricts motion.

Management As soon as possible, the athlete should have a physician evaluation to rule out the possibility of fracture, dislocation, or disk injury.[19] Neurological examination is performed by the physician to ascertain spinal cord or nerve root injury. A soft cervical collar may be applied to reduce muscle spasm. RICE is used for forty-eight to seventy-two hours while the injury is in the acute stage of healing. For an athlete with a severe injury, the physician may prescribe two to three days of bed rest along with analgesics and antiinflammation agents. Therapy might include cryotherapy or heat and massage. Mechanical traction may also be prescribed to relieve pain and muscle spasm.

Acute Torticollis (Wryneck)

Etiology Acute torticollis, a very common condition, is more frequently called wryneck or stiff neck. The athlete usually complains of pain on one side of the neck upon awakening. Wryneck usually occurs when a small piece of synovial membrane lining the joint capsule is impinged or trapped within a facet joint in the cervical vertebra. This problem can also occasionally follow exposure to a cold draft of air or the holding of the head in an unusual position over a period of time.

Symptoms and signs During inspection, there is palpable point tenderness and muscle spasm. Head movement is restricted to the side opposite the irritation with marked muscle guarding. X-ray examination will rule out a more serious injury.

Management Various therapeutic modalities may be used to modulate pain in an attempt to break a pain-spasm-pain cycle. Muscle guarding can be reduced through joint mobilizations that involve gentle traction, rotation, and lateral bending, first in the pain-free direction, then in the direction of pain. The athlete may find it helpful to wear a soft cervical collar for comfort (Figure 25-42). This muscle

Figure 25-42

A soft collar can make the neck feel more comfortable.

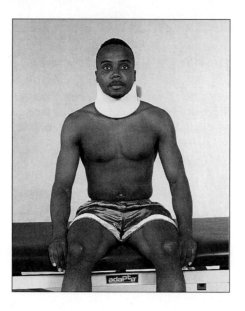

guarding will generally last for two to three days while the athlete progressively regains motion.

Cervical Cord and Nerve Root Injuries

Etiology   The spinal cord and nerve roots may be injured via four basic mechanisms: laceration by bony fragments, hemorrhage (hematomyelia), contusion, and shock. These mechanisms may be combined into a single trauma or may act as separate conditions.

LACERATION   Laceration of the cord is usually produced by the combined dislocation and fracture of a cervical vertebra. The jagged edges of the fragmented vertebral body cut and tear nerve roots or the spinal cord and cause varying degrees of paralysis below the point of injury.

HEMORRHAGE   Hemorrhage develops from all vertebral fractures and from most dislocations as well as from sprains and strains. It seldom causes harmful effects in the musculature extradurally or even within the arachnoid space, where it dissipates faster than it can accumulate. However, hemorrhage within the cord itself causes irreparable damage.

CONTUSION   Contusion in the cord or nerve roots can arise from any force that is applied to the neck violently but does not cause a cervical dislocation or fracture. Such an injury may result from sudden displacement of a vertebra that compresses the cord and then returns to its normal position. This compression causes edematous swelling within the cord, resulting in various degrees of temporary and/or permanent damage.

SPINAL CORD SHOCK   Occasionally a situation arises in which an athlete, after receiving a severe twist or snap of the neck, presents all the signs of a spinal cord injury. The athlete is unable to move certain parts of the body and complains of a numbness and a tingling sensation in the arms. After a short while, all these signs leave. The athlete is then able to move the limbs quite freely and has no symptoms other than a sore neck. This condition is considered a spinal cord shock and is caused by a mild contusion of the spinal cord or by cervical spine stenosis. In such cases, athlete should be cared for in the same manner used for any severe neck injury.

Symptoms and signs   Each of these situations can result in various types of paralysis that affect the motor and/or sensory systems. The level of the injury obviously will determine the extent of the functional deficits. Spinal cord lesions may be either complete or incomplete. A complete lesion is one in which the spinal cord has been

The spinal cord and nerve roots may be injured via four basic mechanisms: laceration by bony fragments, hemorrhage, contusion, and shock.

totally severed and there is a complete loss of all motor function and sensation below the level of the injury. Recovery of significant function below the level of the injury is unlikely, although some nerve root function may eventually recover one to two levels below the injury. Complete cord lesions at or above C3 will impair respiration and result in death. Lesions at spinal segment levels below C4 will allow for return of some nerve root function as follows:

- C4–C5—Return of deltoid function
- C5–C6—Return of elbow flexion and wrist extension
- C6–C7—Return of elbow and finger extension and wrist flexion
- C7–T1—Return of grip function

Incomplete lesions can result in central cord syndrome, Brown-Sequard syndrome, anterior cord syndrome, or posterior cord syndrome.[30] Central cord syndrome is caused by hemorrhage or ischemia in the central portion of the cord and results in complete quadriplegia with nonspecific sensory loss and in sexual as well as bowel-bladder dysfunction. Brown-Sequard syndrome is caused by an injury to one side of the spinal cord that results in loss of motor function, touch, vibration, and position sense on one side of the body, and loss of pain and temperature sensation on the other side. Anterior cord syndrome is caused by an injury to the anterior two-thirds of the cord that results in loss of motor function and pain and temperature sensation. However, sexual and bowel-bladder function is present. Posterior cord syndrome, although rare, is caused by injury to the posterior cord. Motor function is completely intact.

Management   Like suspected cervical fractures and dislocations, suspected injuries to the spinal cord must be handled with extreme caution. Care is taken to minimize potential damage to the spinal cord. In cases in which evidence of spinal cord damage accompanied by varying degrees of paralysis exists immediately with injury, management efforts must attempt to minimize additional trauma to the cord.[15] Chapter 12 presents a detailed discussion of the recommended procedures for managing athletes with suspected spinal cord injury.

Cervical Spine Stenosis

Etiology   Cervical spine stenosis is a syndrome characterized by a narrowing of the spinal canal in the cervical region that can impinge the spinal cord. This stenosis occurs either as a congenital variation or from some change in the vertebrae, including the development of bone spurs, osteophytes, or disc bulges. A sagittal canal diameter to anteroposterior width of same vertebrae at midpoint ratio less than .80 suggests cervical stenosis.[42]

Symptoms and signs   Transcient quadriplegia may occur from axial loading, hyperextension, or hyperflexion. Neck pain may be absent initially. The symptoms may be purely sensory with burning or tingling, or the athlete may have some associated motor weakness in either the arms or the legs or all four extremities. Complete recovery normally occurs within ten to fifteen minutes but may be delayed. Following neurologic recovery, full neck ROM is possible.

Management   Cervical spine stenosis may be present without any symptoms and signs. The presence of transcient quadriplegia necessitates extreme caution initially. The athlete must have diagnostic tests, including X rays or MRI to determine the extent of the problem. Athletes, particularly those in contact sports, who have been identified as having some degree of cervical stenosis should be advised of the potential risks of continued participation in that sport. There is a growing consensus among physicians that continued participation should be discouraged.[8]

Brachial Plexus Neurapraxia (Burner)

Etiology   Transcient neurapraxia, resulting from stretching or compression of the brachial plexus, is the most common of all cervical neurological injuries in the athlete.[30] Neurapraxia involves a disruption in normal function of a peripheral nerve

---

25-6

Critical Thinking Exercise

A football linebacker is making a tackle. Initial contact on the ball carrier is with the head, and the neck is forced into hyperflexion. The athlete immediately has transcient quadriplegia with burning and tingling and associated motor weakness in the arms and legs. Neck pain is absent initially. Within fifteen minutes, the athlete recovers completely and has full range of motion.

? What type of injury should the athletic trainer suspect with this athlete, and how should this condition be managed?

without any degenerative changes. Other terms commonly used to indicate this condition are *stinger, burner,* or *pinched nerve.*[43] The primary mechanism of injury is stretching of the brachial plexus when the neck is forced laterally to the opposite side while the shoulder is depressed, as would occur with a shoulder block in football. A second mechanism compresses the brachial plexus when the neck is extended, compressed, and rotated toward the affected side.

Symptoms and signs   The player complains of a burning sensation, numbness and tingling, and pain extending from the shoulder down to the hand, with some loss of function of the arm and hand that lasts for several minutes.[17] Rarely, symptoms may persist for several days. Neck range of motion is usually normal. Repeated brachial plexus nerve stretch injuries may result in neuritis, muscular atrophy, and permanent damage.[25]

Management   Once the symptoms have completely resolved and there are no associated neurological symptoms, the athlete may return to full activity. Thereafter the athlete should begin strengthening and stretching exercises for the neck musculature.[26] A football player should be fitted with shoulder pads and a cervical neck roll to limit neck range of motion during impact.[44]

Cervical Disk Injuries

Etiology   Herniation of a cervical disk is relatively common and can affect athletes in any sport. A herniation usually develops from an extruded posterolateral disk fragment or from degeneration of the disk. The primary mechanism involves sustained repetitive cervical loading during contact sports.

Symptoms and signs   The symptoms and signs include neck pain with some restriction in neck motion. There is radicular pain (nerve root) in the upper extremity with associated motor weakness or sensory changes.

Management   Initial treatment involves rest and immobilization of the neck to decrease discomfort. Neck mobilizations may help the athlete regain some range of motion. Cervical traction may also help reduce symptoms. If conservative treatment is not helpful or if the neurologic deficits increase, surgery may be necessary.

Thoracic Spine Conditions

Injuries to the thoracic region of the spine have a much lower rate of incidence than do injuries to the cervical or lumbar regions. This lower rate of injury is due to the articulation of the thoracic vertebrae with the ribs, which acts to stabilize and limit motion of the vertebrae and thus minimizes the likelihood of injury to this area. Thoracic fractures, therefore, are relatively rare and occur in high-impact sports such as skiing, tobogganing, skydiving, or automobile racing.

Scheuermann's Disease (Dorsolumbar Kyphosis)

Etiology   Scheuermann's disease is characterized by kyphosis that results from wedge fractures of 5 degrees or greater in three or more consecutive vertebral bodies with associated disk space abnormalities and irregularity of the epiphyseal endplates.[32] This degeneration allows the disk's nucleus pulposus to prolapse into a vertebral body. Characteristically, there is an accentuation of the kyphotic curve and backache in the young athlete. Adolescents engaging in sports such as gymnastics and swimming—the butterfly stroke particularly—are prone to this condition. Scheuermann's disease is idiopathic, but the occurrence of multiple minor injuries to the vertebral epiphyses seems to be an etiological factor. These injuries apparently disrupt circulation to the epiphyseal endplate, causing avascular necrosis.

Symptoms and signs   In the initial stages, the young athlete will have kyphosis of the thoracic spine and lumbar lordosis without back pain. In later stages, there is point tenderness over the spinous processes, and the young athlete may complain of backache at the end of a very physically active day. Hamstring muscles are characteristically very tight.

Management   The major goal of management is to prevent progressive kyphosis. In the early stages of the disease, extension exercises and postural education are beneficial. Bracing, rest, and antiinflammatory medication may also be helpful. The athlete may stay active but should avoid aggravating movements.

Lumbar Spine Conditions

Mechanisms of Low Back Pain

Pain in the low back is second only to foot problems in order of incidence in humans throughout their life span.[28] In sports, back problems are relatively common and are most often the result of either congenital or idiopathic (i.e., mechanical or traumatic) causes.[4] Congenital back disorders are conditions that are present at birth. Many authorities think that the human back is still undergoing structural changes as a result of its upright position and, therefore, humans are prone to slight spinal defects at birth that may cause pain later in life. The usual cause of back pain among athletes is overuse that produces strains and/or sprains of paravertebral muscles and ligaments.

Congenital anomalies   Anomalies of bony development are the underlying cause of many back problems in sports. Such conditions would have remained undiscovered had it not been for some abnormal stress or injury in the area of the anomaly. The most common causes of these anomalies are excessive length of the transverse process of the fifth lumbar vertebra, incomplete closure of the neural arch (spina bifida occulta), nonconformities of the spinous processes, atypical lumbosacral angles or articular facets, and incomplete closures of the vertebral laminae. All these anomalies may produce mechanical weaknesses that make the back prone to injury when it is subjected to excessive postural strains.

An example of a congenital defect that may develop into a more serious condition when aggravated by a blow or a sudden twist in sports is the condition of spondylolisthesis. Spondylolisthesis is a forward subluxation of the body of a vertebra, usually the fifth lumbar.

Mechanical defects of the spine   Mechanical back defects are caused mainly by faulty posture, obesity, or faulty body mechanics—all of which may affect the athlete's performance in sports. Traumatic forces produced in sports, either directly or indirectly, can result in contusions, sprains, strains and/or fractures. Sometimes even minor injuries can develop into chronic and recurrent conditions, which may have serious complications for the athlete. To fully understand a back complaint, the athletic trainer should make a logical investigation into the history and the site of any injury, the type of pain produced, and the extent of impairment of normal function.

Maintaining proper segmental alignment of the body during standing, sitting, lying, running, jumping, and throwing is of utmost importance for keeping the body in good condition. Habitual violations of the principles of good body mechanics occur in many sports and produce anatomical deficiencies that subject the body to constant abnormal muscular and ligamentous strain.[45] In all cases of postural deformity, the athletic trainer should determine the cause and attempt to rectify the condition through proper strength and mobilization exercises.[2]

Back trauma   It is of vital importance that the athletic trainer possess skill in recognizing and evaluating the extent of a sports injury to the back. Every football season seems to generate a story of an athlete who is paralyzed because of the mishandling of a fractured spine. Such episodes could be greatly reduced if field officials, coaches, and athletic trainers would use discretion, exercise good judgment, and be able to identify certain gross indications of serious spine involvement.[15]

Recurrent and chronic low back pain   Repeated strains or sprains in the low back can cause the supporting tissues to lose their ability to stabilize the spine and thus produce tissue laxity. After repeated episodes, the athlete may develop what is referred to as chronic low back pain.[6] Recurrent or chronic low back pain can have

Low back problems are most often either congenital or idiopathic.

many possible causes, including malalignment of the vertebral facets, discogenic disease, or nerve root compression, all of which can result in pain. Gradually this problem could lead to muscular weakness and impairment of sensation and reflex responses. The older the athlete, the more prone he or she is to developing chronic low back pain. The incidence of this condition at the high school level is relatively low but becomes progressively greater with increasing age. An acute back condition is the culmination of a progressive degeneration of long duration that is aggravated or accentuated by sudden flexion, extension, or rotation.

Lumbar Vertebrae Fracture and Dislocation

Etiology   Fractures of the vertebral column, in terms of bone injury, are not serious in themselves; but they pose dangers when related to spinal cord damage. Vertebral fractures of the greatest concern in sports are compression fractures and fractures of the transverse and spinous processes.

The compression fracture may occur as a result of hyperflexion of the trunk (Figure 25-43). Falling from a height and landing on the feet or buttocks may also produce a compression fracture. The vertebrae that are most often compressed are those in the dorsolumbar curves. The vertebrae usually are crushed anteriorly by the traumatic force of the body above the site of injury. The crushed vertebral body may spread out fragments and protrude into the spinal canal, compressing and possibly even cutting the cord.

Fractures of the transverse and spinous processes result most often from kicks or other direct impact to the back. Because these processes are surrounded by large muscles, fracture produces extensive soft-tissue injury. The fractures themselves present little danger and will usually permit the athlete considerable activity within the range of pain tolerance. Most care and treatment will be oriented toward therapy of the soft-tissue pathology.

Dislocations of the lumbar vertebrae in sports are rare and occur only with an associated fracture. This infrequency is due to the orientation of the facet joints in the lumbar vertebrae.

Figure 25-43

Lumbar compression fracture.

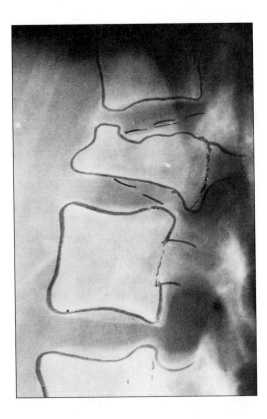

Symptoms and signs   Recognition of the compression fracture is difficult without an X-ray examination. A basic evaluation may be made through knowledge of the history and through point tenderness over the affected vertebrae. Fractures of the transverse and spinous processes may be directly palpable. There will be point tenderness with some localized swelling along with muscle guarding to protect the area.

Management   If the symptoms and signs associated with a fracture are present, the injured athlete should be x-rayed. Transporting and moving the athlete should be done on a spine board as described in Chapter 12 in an effort to minimize movement of the fractured segment.

Low Back Muscle Strains

Etiology   There are two mechanisms of the typical lower back strain in sports activities.[7] The first happens from a sudden extension contraction on an overloaded, unprepared, or underdeveloped spine, usually in combination with trunk rotation. The second is the chronic strain, commonly associated with faulty posture, that involves excessive lumbar lordosis. However, other postures such as flatback posture or scoliosis can also predispose an athlete to strain.

Symptoms and signs   Evaluation should be performed immediately after injury to rule out the possibility of fracture. Discomfort in the low back may be diffused or localized in one area. In the case of muscle strain, pain will be present on active extension and with passive flexion. There is no radiating pain farther than the buttocks or thigh and no neurological involvement that causes muscle weakness, sensation impairment, or reflex impairments.

Management   In the acute phase of this injury, it is essential that cold packs and/or ice massage be used intermittently throughout the day to decrease muscle spasm. An elastic wrap or corset-type brace will help to compress the area. A graduated program of stretching and strengthening begins slowly during the acute stage. Progressive strengthening exercises should concentrate on extension, whereas stretching should focus on both flexion and extension. Injuries of moderate-to-severe intensity may require complete bed rest to help break the pain–muscle spasm cycle. The physician may prescribe oral analgesic medication. Cryotherapy, ultrasound, and an abdominal support (Figure 25-44) are often beneficial following the acute phase. Exercise must not cause pain.

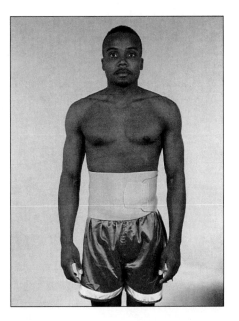

Figure 25-44

An abdominal brace helps support the lumbar area.

Lumbosacral Strain

Injury Situation A high school shot-putter came into the athletic training room complaining of a very sore back. He indicated that he woke up with the problem and was not sure how it occurred. Perhaps he had hurt it by doing dead lifts the day before or by throwing the shot incorrectly.

Symptoms and Signs The athlete complained of a constant dull ache and an inability to flex, extend, or rotate the trunk without increasing the pain. Inspection of the injury indicated the following:

1. The athlete had a pronounced lumbar lordosis.
2. There was an obvious muscle contraction of the right erector spinae.
3. There was severe point tenderness in the right lumbar region.
4. The right pelvis was elevated.
5. Passive movement did not cause pain; however, active and resistive movements produced severe pain.
6. Range of movement in all directions was restricted.
7. All tests for nerve root, hip joint, and sacroiliac joint were negative.
8. Leg length was measured, and the athlete had a functional shortening but no apparent structural shortening.
9. Both the left and right hamstring muscle groups and iliopsoas muscles were abnormally tight.
10. X-ray examination showed no pathological conditions of the lumbar vertebrae.

Based on the examination, it was concluded that the athlete had sustained a first- to second-degree strain of the lumbar muscles, primarily in the right erector spinae region.

Phase 1 *Acute Injury*   **GOALS:** To relieve muscle spasm and pain.
   ESTIMATED LENGTH OF TIME (ELT): 2 or 3 days.

■ **Therapy** Ice pack (20 min) followed by exercise and then by TENS (15 to 20 min) 3 to 4 times daily.

■ **Exercise rehabilitation** Following cold application, gentle passive stretch of low back region and hamstring and iliopsoas muscles—all within pain tolerance levels—3 to 4 times daily, along with grade 1 and 2 mobilization of affected segments.

Phase 2 *Repair*   **GOALS:** To increase low back, hamstring, and iliopsoas ROM to at least begin postural correction. 50% normal extensibility of the low back, hamstring, and iliopsoas muscles. Appropriate abdominal strength.
   ELT: 4 to 12 days.

■ **Therapy** Ice massage followed by exercise 2 to 3 times daily. If still painful, TENS therapy should be used. Ultrasound 1 to 1.5 watts/cm^2 once daily.

■ **Exercise rehabilitation** Repeat Phase 1 exercise and begin PNF to hip and low back regions 2 to 3 times daily; or static low back, hamstring, and iliopsoas stretching (2 to 3 repetitions) and lower abdominal strengthening 2 to 3 times daily. Continue grade 1 and 2 mobilizations, progressing to grades 3 and 4 as tolerated. Practice realigning pelvis. General body maintenance exercises are conducted (as long as they do not aggravate the injury) 3 times a week.

Continued

Lumbosacral Strain—*cont'd*

Phase 3 Remodeling **GOALS:** To restore 90% of ROM, strength, and proper back alignment.

■ **Exercise rehabilitation** Return to weight training and shot put program 3 times a week. Athlete is instructed about proper back alignment when throwing the shot. Athlete is to avoid dead lifting and to wear a lifting belt while weight training. Begin spinal stabilization program. Return to normal training 3 times a week. Gradual reentry into competition. Using an abdominal support belt is advisable during practice and competition.

Criteria for Return to Competitive Shot Put

1. The athlete's back must be pain free and spasm free.
2. The athlete must be near normal in hamstring, low back, and iliopsoas extensibility.
3. The athlete must be making good progress toward correcting lumbar lordosis.
4. The athlete must be able to perform the shot put with the spine and pelvis in good alignment.

Myofascial Pain Syndrome

Etiology Myofascial pain syndrome is defined as a regional pain with referred pain to a specific area that occurs with pressure or palpation of tender spots or trigger points within a specific muscle.[20] A trigger point is an area of tenderness in a tight band of muscle. Palpation of the trigger point produces pain in a predictable distribution of referred pain.[29] There may also be some restricted range of motion because of pain. Pressure on the trigger point produces a twitch or jump response from the pain. Pain can be increased by passive or active stretching of the involved muscle. In the athlete, painful or active trigger points most often develop because of some mechanical stress to the muscle. This stress could involve either an acute muscle strain or static postural positions that produce constant tension in the muscle.[12] Trigger points occur most typically in the neck, upper back, and lower back. In the lower back, there are two muscles in which trigger points commonly occur: the piriformis and the quadratus lumborum.

The piriformis muscle was discussed in Chapter 21. It is an external rotator of the thigh and is located posterior to the hip joint in the sciatic notch. The piriformis muscle is important because of its proximity to the sciatic nerve. The sciatic nerve either pierces the piriformis or courses directly above or below it.

The quadratus lumborum originates on the twelfth rib and the transverse processes of L1 through L4. It inserts on the iliac crest. The quadratus functions to elevate the pelvis.

Symptoms and signs Palpation of or pressure on a trigger point in the piriformis muscle in the sciatic notch refers pain to the posterior sacroiliac region, to the buttocks, and occasionally down to the posterior or posterolateral thigh. Pain is a deep ache that increases with exercise or with prolonged sitting while the hip is adducted, flexed, and medially rotated. Isometric abduction and passive internal rotation will increase pain. Sciatic pain may also occur with diminished sensation in the leg.

A trigger point in the quadratus lumborum produces a sharp, aching pain in the lateral lower back or flank. Pain may be referred to the upper buttocks and posterior sacroiliac region and sometimes to the abdominal wall. Pain increases when the athlete stands for long periods, moves from sitting to standing, or coughs or sneezes. There will be muscle spasm with pain that is localized to one side. Pain increases when the athlete side bends toward the side of the trigger point.

Management   Rehabilitation exercises should include both stretching and strengthening of the involved muscle. The key in treating myofascial pain is to stretch the muscle back to a normal resting length and thus relieve the irritation that created the trigger point.[14] The athlete should be placed in a comfortable position that also stretches the involved muscle. Active stretching should be mild and progressive. The use of electrical stimulation in combination with ultrasound is helpful in relieving the pain associated with a trigger point. A spray and stretch technique has also been used successfully (see Chapter 15). Progressive strengthening exercises should also be included.

Lumbar Sprains

Etiology   Sprains may occur in any of the ligaments in the lumbar spine. The most common sprain involves lumbar facet joints. Facet joint sprain typically occurs when the athlete bends forward and twists while lifting or moving some object. It can occur with a single episode or with chronic repetitive stress that causes a gradual onset that becomes progressively worse with activity.

Symptoms and signs   The pain is localized and is located just lateral to the spinous process. Pain becomes sharper with certain movements or postures, and the athlete will limit movement in painful ranges. Passive anteroposterior or rotational movement of the vertebrae will increase pain.

Management   Like sprains to other joints in the body, the lumbar sprain will require some time for healing. Initial treatment should include RICE to reduce pain. Joint mobilizations that use anteroposterior and rotational glides can be used to help decrease pain. Strengthening exercises for abdominals and back extensors as well as stretches in all directions should be limited to a pain-free range. The athlete should be instructed in trunk stabilization exercises. A brace or support should be worn to limit movement during early return to activity. It is important to guard against the development of postural changes that may occur in response to pain.

Back Contusions

Etiology   Back contusions rank second to strains and sprains in incidence. Because of its surface area, the back is quite vulnerable to bruises in sports. Football produces the greatest number of these injuries. A history that includes a significant impact to the back could indicate an extremely serious condition. Contusion of the back must be distinguished from a vertebral fracture. In some instances, this distinction is possible only through an X-ray examination.

Symptoms and signs   The bruise causes local pain, muscle spasm, and point tenderness. A swollen, discolored area may be visible also.

Management   Cold and pressure should be applied immediately for approximately seventy-two hours or longer, along with rest. Ice massage combined with gradual stretching benefits soft-tissue contusion in the region of the lower back. Recovery usually ranges from two days to two weeks. Ultrasound is effective in treating the deep muscles.

Sciatica

Etiology   Sciatica is an inflammatory condition of the sciatic nerve that can accompany recurrent or chronic low back pain. The term *sciatica* has been incorrectly used as a general term to describe all low back pain without reference to exact causes. Sciatica is commonly associated with peripheral nerve root compression from

25-7

Critical Thinking E x e r c i s e

A swimmer complains of an area of tenderness in a tight band of muscle in the middle of her upper back. Palpation of the trigger point refers pain around the chest wall. Pain is increased by both passive and active stretching of the involved muscle. Pain is usually increased following a long training workout in the pool.

? What type of muscular problem frequently develops in the middle or low back of athletes who engage in repetitive motions that fatigue a muscle? How is this problem best managed?

intervertebral disk protrusion, structural irregularities within the intervertebral foramina, or tightness of the piriformis muscle. The sciatic nerve is particularly vulnerable to torsion or direct blows that tend to impose abnormal stretching and pressure on it as it emerges from the spine, thus effecting a traumatic condition.[18]

Symptoms and signs   Sciatica may begin either abruptly or gradually. It produces a sharp shooting pain that follows the nerve pathway along the posterior and medial thigh. There may also be some tingling and numbness along its path. The nerve may be extremely sensitive to palpation. Straight leg raising usually intensifies the pain.

Management   In the acute stage, rest is essential. The cause of the inflammation must be identified and treated. If there is a disk protrusion, lumbar traction may be appropriate. Stretching of a tight piriformis muscle may also decrease symptoms. Since recovery from sciatia usually occurs within two to three weeks, surgery should be delayed to see if symptoms resolve. Oral antiinflammatory medication may help reduce inflammation.

Herniated Lumbar Disk

Etiology   The lumbar disks are subject to constant abnormal stresses that stem from faulty body mechanics, trauma, or both, which, over a period of time, can cause degeneration, tears, and cracks in the annulus fibrosus.[9] The disk most often injured lies between the L4–L5 vertebrae. The L5–S1 disk is the second most commonly affected.

In sports, the mechanism of a disk injury is the same as for the lumbosacral sprain—forward bending and twisting that places abnormal strain on the lumbar region. The movement that produces herniation or bulging of the nucleus pulposus may be minimal, and associated pain may be significant. Besides injuring soft tissues, such a stress may herniate an already degenerated disk by causing the nucleus pulposus to protrude into or through the annulus fibrosis (Figure 25-45). A disk that progressively degenerates may develop into a prolapsed disk, in which the nucleus moves completely through the annulus. If the nucleus moves into the spinal canal and comes in contact with a nerve root, the result is an extruded disk. This protrusion of the nucleus pulposus may place pressure on the cord of spinal nerves and thus cause radiating pains similar to those of sciatica. A sequestrated disk occurs when the material of the nucleus separates from the disk and begins to migrate.

Pressure within the intervertebral disks changes with various positions or postures. Studies that used intervertebral pressure in the standing position as a constant found that pressure was decreased by 75 percent when the spine was in the supine position and by 25 percent when the spine was in the side-lying position. Pressure was increased by 33 percent while the athlete was sitting, by 33 percent while the athlete was standing slightly bent forward, by 45 percent while

> A herniated lumbar disk can be prolapsed, extruded, or sequestrated.

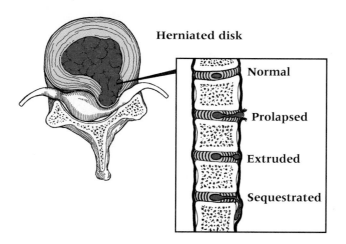

Herniated disk

Normal

Prolapsed

Extruded

Sequestrated

Figure 25-45

A herniated lumbar disk. Further degeneration can lead to a prolapsed disk, an extruded disk, or a sequestrated disk.

the athlete was sitting slightly bent forward, 52 percent while the athlete was standing bent far forward, and 63 percent while the athlete was sitting bent well forward.

Symptoms and signs   There is usually centrally located pain that radiates unilaterally in a dermatomal pattern to the buttocks and down the back of the leg, or pain that spreads across the back. Symptoms are worse in the morning when the athlete gets out of bed. Onset may be sudden or gradual, and pain may increase after the athlete sits and then tries to resume activity. Forward bending and sitting increases pain. Backward bending reduces pain. The athlete's posture will exhibit a slight forward bend with side bending away from the side of pain. Side bending toward the side of pain is limited and increases pain. There is tenderness around the painful area. Straight leg raising to 30 degrees increases pain. Tendon reflexes may be diminished. Muscle testing may reveal weakness with bilateral differences. A Valsalva maneuver increases the pain.

Management   Initial treatment should involve pain-reducing modalities such as ice or electrical stimulation. Manual traction combined with passive backward bending or extension makes the athlete more comfortable. The goal is to reduce the protrusion and restore normal posture. Thus, the athlete should be taught appropriate posture self-correction exercises. As pain and posture return to normal, back extensor and abdominal strengthening should be used.[11]

If the disk is extruded or sequestrated, all the athlete trainer can do is to modulate pain with electrical stimulation. Flexion exercises and lying supine in a flexed position may help with comfort. Sometimes the symptoms will resolve with time. But if there are signs of nerve damage, surgery may be required to eliminate pain and dysfunction.[50]

Spondylolysis and Spondylolisthesis

Etiology   Spondylolysis refers to a degeneration of the vertebrae and, more commonly, a defect in the pars interarticularis of the articular processes of the vertebrae (Figure 25-46).[21] The condition is often attributed to a congenital weakness, and the defect occurs as a stress fracture. It is more common among boys.[23] Spondylolysis may produce no symptoms unless a disk herniation occurs or there is sudden trauma such as hyperextension. Sports movements that characteristically hyperextend the spine, such as the back arch in gymnastics, the lifting of weights, the football block, the tennis serve, the volleyball spike, and the butterfly stroke in swimming, are most likely to cause this condition.

Figure 25-46

Spondylolysis of L5.

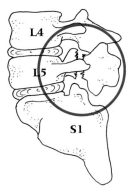

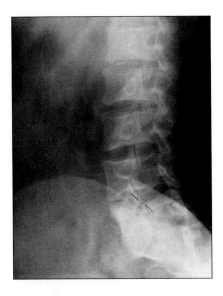

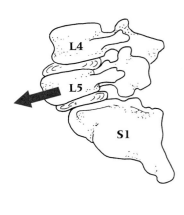

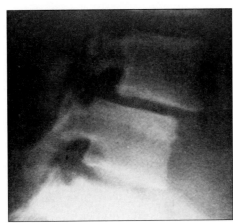

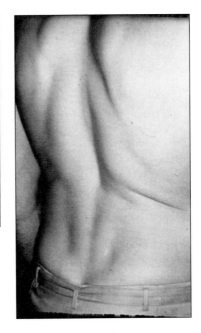

Figure 25-47

Spondylolisthesis.

Commonly, spondylolysis begins unilaterally. If it extends bilaterally, however, there may be some slipping of one vertebra on the one below it. This condition, called a spondylolisthesis, is considered to be a complication of spondylolysis that often results in hypermobility of a vertebral segment, called a step deformity.[18] Spondylolisthesis's highest incidence is with L5 slipping on S1 (Figure 25-47).[39] Although pars interarticularis defects are more common among boys, the incidence of slippage is higher in girls. It is possible that a spondylolisthesis may be asymptomatic. The athlete with this condition will usually have a lumbar hyperlordosis postural impairment. A direct blow or sudden twist or chronic low back strain may cause the defective vertebra to displace itself forward on the sacrum. A spondylolisthesis is easily detectable on X ray.

Symptoms and signs   The athlete complains of persistent aching pain across the low back or a stiffness in the low back with increased pain after, but not usually during, physical activity. The athlete feels the need to change positions frequently or to self-manipulate the low back to reduce the pain. Movements of the trunk are full range and painless with some hesitation in forward bending. At extreme ranges held for thirty seconds, an aching pain develops. The athlete feels weak when straightening from forward bending. There may be tenderness localized to one segment. When applying posteroanterior pressure to the spinous process during palpation, the athletic trainer may note some segmental hypermobility. If displacement is great enough, there may be some neurological signs.

Management   Bracing and, occasionally, bed rest for one to three days will help reduce pain. The major focus in rehabilitation should be directed toward exercises that control or stabilize the hypermobile segment. Progressive trunk strengthening exercises, especially through the midrange, should be incorporated. Dynamic core stabilization exercises that concentrate on abdominal muscles should also be used. Braces are most helpful during high-level activities. Hypermobility of a lumbar vertebra may make the athlete more susceptible to lumbar muscle strains and ligament sprains. Thus, it may be necessary for the athlete to avoid vigorous activity.

Sacroiliac Joint Dysfunction

The sacroiliac is the junction formed by the ilium and the sacrum, and it is fortified by strong ligaments that allow little motion to take place. Because the sacroiliac joint is a synovial joint, disorders can include sprain, inflammation, hypermobility, and hypomobility.

Spondylolisthesis is considered to be a complication of spondylolysis.

25-8

Critical Thinking E x e r c i s e

A gymnast constantly hyperextends her low back. She complains of stiffness and persistent aching pain across the low back with increased pain after, but not usually during, practice. The athlete feels that she needs to change positions frequently or self-manipulate her low back to reduce the pain. She is beginning to develop pain in her buttock and some muscle weakness in her leg.

? What type of injury should the athletic trainer suspect the gymnast has, and can anything be done about it?

Sacroiliac Sprain

Etiology   A sprain of the sacroiliac joint may result when the athlete twists with both feet on the ground, stumbles forward, falls backward, steps too far down and lands heavily on one leg, or bends forward with the knees locked during lifting.[34] Any of these mechanisms can produce irritation and stretching of the sacrotuberous or sacrospinous ligaments. These mechanisms may also cause either an anterior or posterior rotation of one side of the pelvis relative to the other. With rotation of the pelvis, there is hypomobility. As healing occurs, the joint on the injured side may become hypermobile, allowing that joint to sublux in either an anteriorly or posteriorly rotated position.

Symptoms and signs   With a sprain of the sacroiliac joint, there may be palpable pain and tenderness directly over the joint just medial to the PSIS with some associated muscle guarding. The athletic trainer may observe that the ASIS and/or PSIS may be asymmetrical when compared to the opposite side, which is caused by either anterior or posterior rotation of one side of the pelvis relative to the other (Figure 25-48). There may also be a measurable leg length difference. Forward bending reveals a block to normal movement, and the PSIS on the injured side moves sooner than the one on the normal side. Straight leg raising increases pain after 45 degrees. Side bending toward the painful side will increase pain.

Management   Modalities can be used to reduce pain. A supportive brace is also helpful in an acute sprain. The sacroiliac joint should be mobilized to correct the existing asymmetry. If one side of the pelvis is posteriorly rotated, it should be mobilized in an anterior direction. Strengthening exercises should be incorporated to improve stability to a hypermobile joint.

Coccyx Injuries

Etiology   Coccygeal injuries in sports are prevalent and occur primarily from direct impact, which may result from forcibly sitting down, falling, or being kicked by an opponent. Injuries to the coccyx includes sprains, subluxations, or fractures. With healing, the sacrococcygeal joint may become hypermobile and thus restrict passive motion.

Figure 25-48

The right PSIS is anteriorly rotated relative to the left.

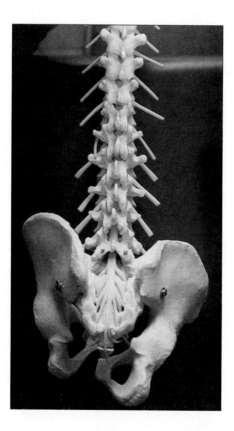

Symptoms and signs   Athletes with persistent coccyalgia should be referred to a physician for X rays and rectal examinations. Pain in the coccygeal region is often prolonged and at times chronic. Such conditions are identified by the term *coccygodynia* and occur as a result of an irritation to the coccygeal plexus.

Management   Treatment consists of analgesics and a ring seat to relieve the pressure on the coccyx while sitting. It should be noted that pain from a fractured coccyx may last for many months. Once a coccygeal injury has healed, the athlete should be protected against reinjury by appropriately applied padding.

REHABILITATION TECHNIQUES FOR THE NECK

Joint Mobilizations

Mobilization techniques for the cervical spine are extensively used in rehabilitating the injured neck. Mobilization can decrease pain, restore mobility, and increase range of motion. The most common joint mobilization techniques for the cervical spine include (Figure 25-49):

1. Cervical flexion mobilizations, which increase forward bending and flexion
2. Cervical extension mobilizations, which increase backward bending and extension
3. Cervical rotation mobilizations, which treat pain or stiffness when there is some resistance in the same direction as the rotation
4. Cervical side bending mobilizations, which treat pain and stiffness when there is some resistance to side bending of the neck
5. Cervical traction, which is used to relieve discogenic pain or increase range of motion

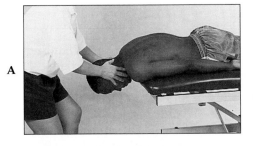
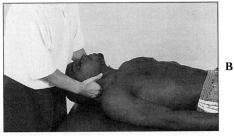

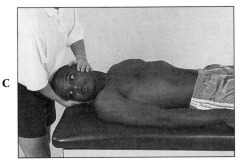
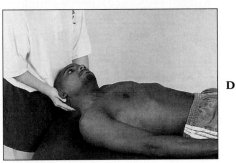
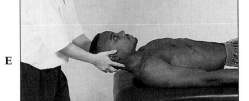

Figure 25-49

Cervical mobilizations. **A,** Cervical flexion. **B,** Cervical extension. **C,** Cervical rotation. **D,** Cervical side bending. **E,** Cervical traction.

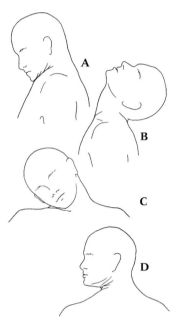

Figure 25-50

Active neck stretching is important in increasing neck mobility after injury. **A,** Forward flexion. **B,** Extension. **C,** Lateral flexion. **D,** Rotation.

Figure 25-51

Stretching the lateral neck flexors by the Billig procedure.

Flexibility Exercises

The first consideration in neck rehabilitation should be restoration of the neck's normal range of motion. The athlete who had a prior restricted range of motion should work on increasing it to a more normal range. A second goal is to strengthen the neck as much as possible. All mobility exercises should be performed pain free. Stretching exercises include passive and active movement.[38]

The athlete sits in a straight-backed chair while the athletic trainer applies a gentle passive stretch through a pain-free range. Extension, flexion, lateral flexion, and rotation in each direction is sustained for a count of six and repeated three times. Passive stretching should be conducted daily.

The athlete is also instructed to actively stretch the neck two to three times daily. Each exercise is performed for eight to ten repetitions, with each endpoint held for a count of six. All exercises are performed without force. Figure 25-50 shows forward flexion, extension, lateral flexion, and rotation.

Stretching can progress gradually to a more vigorous procedure, such as the Billig procedure. In this exercise, the athlete sits on a chair with one hand firmly grasping the seat of the chair. The other hand, over the top of the head, is placed on the ear on the side of the support hand. Keeping that hand in place, the athlete gently pulls the opposite side of the neck. The stretch should be held for six seconds (Figure 25-51). A rotary stretch in each direction can also be applied in the same manner by the athlete.

Strengthening Exercises

When the athlete has gained near-normal range of motion, a strength program should be instituted. All exercises should be conducted pain free. In the beginning, each exercise is performed with the head in an upright position facing straight forward. Exercises are performed isometrically; each resistance is held for a count of six. The athlete should start with five repetitions and progressing to ten repetitions (Figure 25-52).

1. Flexion—press forehead against palm of hand.
2. Extension—lace fingers behind head and press head back against hands.
3. Lateral flexion—place palm on side of head and press head into palm.
4. Rotation—put one palm on side of forehead and the other at back of the head. Push with each hand, attempting to rotate head. Change hands and reverse direction.

Strengthening progresses to isotonic exercises through a full range of motion using manual resistance, special equipment such as a towel, or weighted devices (Figure 25-53). Each exercise is performed for ten repetitions and two to three sets. NOTE: The athlete must be cautioned against overstressing the neck and must be encouraged to increase resistance gradually.

REHABILITATION TECHNIQUES FOR THE LOW BACK

Over the years many different techniques relative to the treatment and rehabilitation of low back pain have been recommended. Individuals such as Williams, McKenzie, Cyriax, Maitland, Paris, and Saal have proposed effective yet specific philosophical approaches for managing individuals with low back pain. In some instances, a particular approach tended to use the same exercises for all low back pain patients regardless of the existing etiology. Today the techniques for treating low back pain incorporate a more eclectic approach and utilize a combination of most applicable and useful aspects of each of the philosophic approaches.[3]

The initial treatment for low back pain should focus on modulating pain. Following acute injury, ice should be used along with electrical stimulating currents for analgesia. Rest is also helpful in allowing the injured structures to begin the healing process. It is essential that the athletic trainer avoid movements or positions that in-

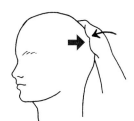

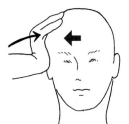

A. Flexion   **B. Extension**   **C. Lateral flexion**   **D. Rotation**

Figure 25-52

Manual neck-strengthening exercises. **A,** Flexion. **B,** Extension. **C,** Lateral flexion. **D,** Rotation.

crease pain while positioning the athlete in a posture that minimizes pain and discomfort.

Analgesics and oral antiinflammatory agents are commonly given to inhibit pain and reduce inflammation in the athlete with a low back problem. If muscle spasm or guarding is severe, muscle relaxants may be prescribed.

Progressive relaxation techniques can also be useful in treating low back pain. With constant pain comes anxiety and increased muscular tension that compounds the low back problem. By systematically contracting and completely "letting go" of the body's major muscles, the athlete learns to recognize abnormal tension and to relax the muscles consciously. Various relaxation techniques are discussed in Chapter 11.

General Body Conditioning

The low back pain that athletes most often encounter is an acute, painful experience that rarely lasts longer than three weeks. In the initial stages of acute injury, however, there can be a great deal of pain and disability. In some of the conditions described in this chapter, any movement at all can produce incapacitating low back pain. Thus, athletes with certain conditions may find it difficult to maintain general body conditioning, particularly during the acute stage of healing. It may be necessary to eliminate any type of conditioning during the first several days. The athlete should resume conditioning activities as soon as the condition has resolved to the point at which discomfort can be tolerated. The athlete may find it helpful to utilize aquatic exercise as a method for maintaining cardiorespiratory endurance, because the pain that often occurs with weight bearing may be minimized.

Figure 25-53

Neck strengthening using resistive devices. **A,** Towel. **B,** Free weight. **C,** Exercise machine.

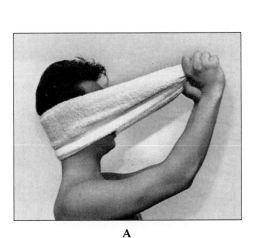

A   **B**   **C**

Joint Mobilizations

Joint mobilization of the lumbar spine may be used to improve joint mobility or to decrease joint pain by restoring to the joint accessory movements that will help the athlete achieve a full, nonrestricted, pain-free range of motion.[16] Vertebral joints in the lumbar region are capable of both anterior and posterior gliding or rotation, or some combination of the two; mobilization techniques should address all restricted joint motions. Grade 1 and 2 mobilizations may be incorporated early in the rehabilitation program for managing pain. Mobilization may progress to grades 3 and 4 once pain and muscle guarding are decreased. For best results, mobilization should be combined with manual traction techniques.

Joint mobilization techniques for the low back are indicated when

- Pain is centralized at a specific joint and increases with activity and decreases with rest.
- Active and passive range of motion is decreased.
- There is muscle tightness.
- Forward and backward bending deviates from the midline.
- Rotation and side bending produce asymmetrical movements.
- Accessory motion at individual spinal segments is decreased.

Specific mobilization techniques for the low back include (Figure 25-54):

1. Anterior/posterior lumbar vertebrae mobilizations to decrease pain and increase mobility of individual vertebrae
2. Lumbar lateral distraction to reduce pain associated with some compression of a spinal nerve

Figure 25-54

Low back mobilizations.
A, Anteroposterior lumbar vertebrae mobilization.
B, Lumbar lateral distraction.
C, Lumbar vertebral rotation.
D, Anterior sacral mobilization. **E,** Anterior rotation mobilization. **F,** Posterior rotation mobilization.

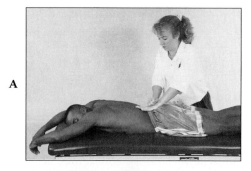
A

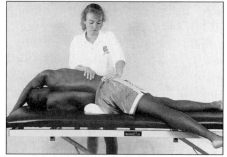
B

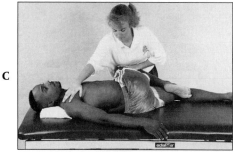
C

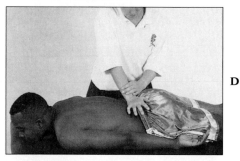
D

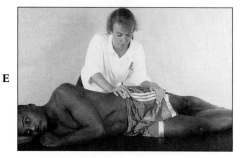
E

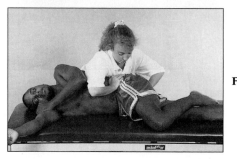
F

3. Lumbar vertebral rotation mobilizations to decrease pain and increase mobility of individual vertebrae
4. Anterior sacral mobilizations to reduce pain and muscle guarding around the sacroiliac joint
5. Anterior rotation mobilizations to correct a unilateral posterior rotation
6. Posterior rotation mobilizations to correct a unilateral anterior rotation

Traction

Traction is the treatment of choice when there is a small protrusion of the nucleus pulposus. Through traction, the lumbar vertebrae are distracted; a subatmospheric pressure is created, which tends to pull the protrusion to its original position; and there is tightening of the longitudinal ligament, which tends to push the protrusion toward its original position within the disk.[4] Traction may be done manually or with a traction machine. Sustained traction for at least thirty minutes with a force commensurate with body weight is preferred. An 80-pound (35-kilogram) force would be the minimum for a small woman, and a 180-pound (80-kilogram) force would be the minimum for a large man.[4] Traction is usually applied daily (five times per week) for two weeks.

Flexibility Exercises

Back pain may be caused by tightness or a lack of flexibility in a number of different muscle groups related to movement of the low back. An assessment of the flexibility of the muscle groups will indicate which ones are tight and need to be stretched. The following muscle groups may need to be stretched (Figure 25-55):
1. Low back extensors
2. Lumbar rotators
3. Hip abductors
4. Lumbar lateral flexors
5. Hip adductors
6. Hip rotators
7. Hip flexors
8. Hamstrings

Strengthening Exercises

Strengthening exercises should routinely be incorporated into the rehabilitation program to encourage the athlete to remain active and also to regain lumbar motion.[35] Strengthening exercises that reinforce pain-reducing movements and postures should be used, particularly in cases of low back pain. Any exercise or movement that causes pain to spread over a larger area should be avoided. Thus, selection of the correct strengthening exercises should centralize or diminish pain.

Flexion versus Extension Exercises

Generally, strengthening exercises can involve either extension or flexion exercises.[37] Extension exercises are used to strengthen the back extensors, to stretch the abdominals, and to reduce the pressure on the intervertebral disks (Figure 25-56).[24] Athletes should engage in extension exercises when:
- Back pain diminishes when the athlete is lying down and increases when the athlete is sitting.
- Backward bending is limited, yet the movement diminishes pain.
- Forward bending is extremely limited and increases pain.
- Straight leg raising is limited and painful.

Flexion exercises are used to strengthen the abdominal muscles, to stretch the back extensors, and to take pressure off a nerve root by separating the lumbar facet

25-9

Critical Thinking Exercise

During a back evaluation on a soccer player, the athletic trainer finds that backward bending is limited, yet the movement diminishes pain; straight leg raising is limited and painful; forward bending is extremely limited and increases pain; and back pain diminishes when the athlete is lying down but increases in sitting.

? What routine rehabilitative exercises should the athletic trainer recommend to the athlete?

25-10

Critical Thinking Exercise

An evaluation of a swimmer who is complaining of low back pain when swimming a freestyle stroke finds that back pain is diminished when the athlete is sitting and increased when lying down or standing; forward bending decreases the pain; the lordotic curve in the lumbar area does not reverse itself in forward bending; backward bending is painful, especially at the end range; and there is poor abdominal muscle strength.

? What type of exercises should the athletic trainer recommend?

Extension exercises are used to strengthen the back extensors, to stretch the abdominals, and to reduce the pressure on the intervertebral disks.

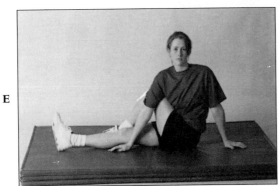

Figure 25-55

Low back stretching exercises.
A, Low back extensors.
B, Lumbar rotators and hip
abductors. **C,** Lumbar lateral
flexors. **D,** Hip adductors.
E, Hip rotators. **F,** Hip flexors.
G, Hamstrings.

joints and opening the intervertebral foramina (Figure 25-57). Athletes should engage in flexion exercises when:

- Back pain diminishes when the athlete is sitting and increases when the athlete is lying down or standing.
- Forward bending decreases the pain.
- The lordotic curve in the lumbar area does not reverse itself in forward bending.

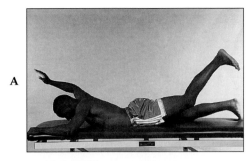

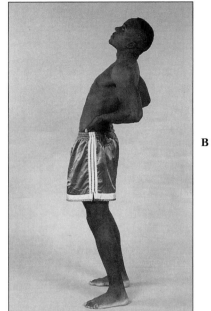

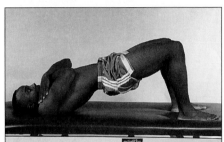

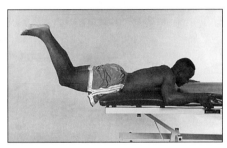

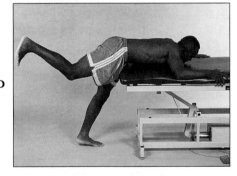

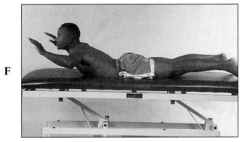

Figure 25-56

Extension strengthening exercises. **A,** Alternating leg extension. **B,** Standing extension. **C,** Supine hip extension. **D,** Prone single hip extension. **E,** Prone double-leg hip extension. **F,** Trunk extension.

- Backward bending is painful, especially at the end range.
- There is poor abdominal muscle strength.

PNF Exercises

PNF upper trunk chopping and lifting patterns may be used to strengthen the trunk musculature. Besides increasing strength, PNF exercises can help establish neuromuscular control and proprioception. Rhythmic stabilization, using isometric exercise, can facilitate cocontraction of antagonistic muscle groups (see Chapter 16).

Neuromuscular Control

Despite the fact that the athlete may have adequate strength and flexibility, he or she may have difficulty controlling the spine if the athlete does not learn to contract the appropriate muscles in a desired sequence.[10] Stabilization, especially during

Figure 25-57

Flexion strengthening exercises. **A,** Posterior pelvic tilt. **B,** Partial sit-up. **C,** Partial sit-up with rotation.

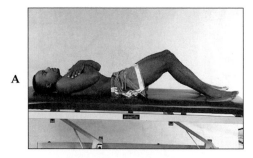
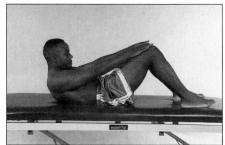

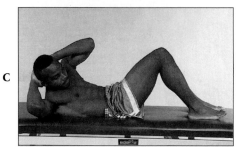

Dynamic stabilization involves the maintaining of a controlled range of motion that varies with the position and the activity being performed.

25-11

Critical Thinking Exercise

A basketball player has been told by his family physician that he has an unstable back. The physician referred him to a therapist who recommended that the athlete perform dynamic stabilization exercises. Unfortunately, the athlete had to leave home and return to college before he had a chance to learn the exercises.

? The athlete asks the athletic trainer to show him the appropriate dynamic stabilization exercises. What progression should the athletic trainer recommend?

complex functional movements, relies heavily on a learned response by the athlete to control the movement. Stabilization exercises for the trunk and spine may help minimize the cumulative effects of repetitive microtrauma to the spine. Spinal stabilization does not mean that the athlete maintains a static position. *Dynamic,* or *core, stabilization* involves the maintaining of a controlled range of motion that varies with the position and the activity being performed. Core stabilization is achieved by conscious repetitive training that, over time, becomes an unconscious natural response.[49] Core stabilization techniques are widely used in rehabilitation programs for the low back.[20]

The first step in core stabilization is for the athlete to learn to control the pelvis in a neutral position.[49] A posterior tilt of the pelvis, which flattens the lumbar curve, is caused by a simultaneous cocontraction of the abdominal and gluteal muscles. Once the athlete has learned to control pelvic tilt, progressively more advanced activities should be incorporated that involve movements of both the spine and extremities while the pelvis is maintained in a neutral position (Figure 25-58).[20]

Abdominal muscle control is another key to stabilization of the low back.[13] Abdominal bracing exercises focus attention on motor control of the external oblique muscles in different positions. There should also be cocontraction of the abdominal muscles and lumbar extensors to maintain a "corset" control of the lumbar spine.[20]

Functional Progressions

The progression of stabilization exercises should be from supine activities, to prone activities, to kneeling activities, and eventually, to weight-bearing activities, all performed while the athlete actively stabilizes the trunk. The athlete should be taught to perform a stabilization contraction before starting any movement. As the movement begins, he or she will become less aware of the stabilization contraction. The athlete may begin by incorporating stabilization into every movement performed in the strengthening exercises. Stabilization contractions can also be used in aerobic conditioning activities. The exercises should include those activities that replicate the demands of the athlete's individual sport. The various components of a sport activity should be broken down into separate activities or skills that allow the athlete to consciously practice the stabilization technique with each drill. Each individual athlete

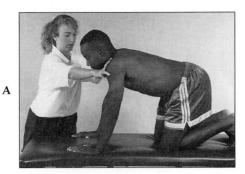

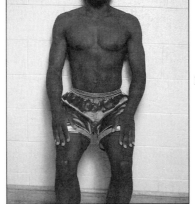
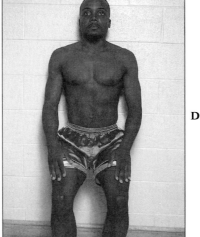
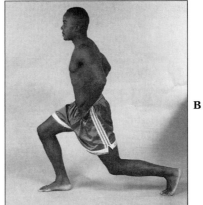

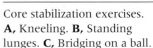

Figure 25-58

Core stabilization exercises. **A,** Kneeling. **B,** Standing lunges. **C,** Bridging on a ball. **D,** Wall slides. **E,** Alternating arm and leg extension.

will differ in degree of control and in the speed at which the skills of dynamic core stabilization are acquired.[20]

Return to Activity

Most acute muscular strains or ligament sprains in the low back take as long to heal as acute strains and sprains in the extremities do. However, if the injury becomes recurrent or the problem becomes chronic, achieving full return to activity may be frustrating to both the athlete and the athletic trainer. Injuries to the low back can be incapacitating for anyone, but the physical demands of sport activity increase the likelihood of recurrent injury. Thus, the athletic trainer must take whatever time is required to fully rehabilitate the athlete with a low back problem and must educate the athlete about the skills and techniques that can minimize additional injury.

SUMMARY

- The spine, or vertebral column, is composed of thirty-three individual vertebrae. The design of the spine allows for flexion, extension, lateral flexion, and rotation. The movable vertebrae are separated by intervertebral disks, and position is maintained by a series of muscular and ligamentous supports. The spine can be divided into three different regions: cervical, thoracic, and lumbar. The sacrum and coccyx are fused vertebrae within the vertebral column.

- The spinal cord is that portion of the central nervous system that is contained within the vertebral canal of the spinal column. Thirty-one pairs of spinal nerves extend from the sides of the spinal cord. The spinal nerve roots combine to form the peripheral nerves, which provide motor and sensory innervation. Each pair of spinal nerves has a specific area of cutaneous sensory distribution called a dermatome.

- Acute traumatic injuries to the spine can be potentially life threatening, particularly if the cervical region of the spinal cord is involved. Thus the athlete must do everything possible to minimize the possibility of injury. Strengthening of the musculature of the neck is critical. In addition to strong muscles, the athlete's neck should have a full range of motion. Athletes involved in collision sports must be taught and required to use techniques that reduce the likelihood of cervical injury.

- Low back pain is one of the most common and disabling ailments known to humans. The athlete, like everyone else in the population, can prevent low back pain by avoiding unnecessary stresses and strains that are associated with standing, sitting, lying, working, or exercising. Care should be taken to avoid postures and positions that can cause injuries.

- The most critical part of the evaluation of injuries to the spine is to rule out the possibility of spinal cord injury. Observing the posture and movement capabilities of the athlete during the evaluation can help clarify the nature and extent of the injury. Classic postural deviations include kyphosis, forward head posture, lordosis, flatback posture, swayback posture, and scoliosis. Special tests may be performed with the athlete in standing, sitting, supine, side-lying, and prone positions.

- Because the cervical and lumbar regions of the spine are so mobile, they are extremely vulnerable to a wide range of sports injuries including fractures, dislocations, strains, sprains, contusions, lesions of the intervertebral disks, and injuries to spinal nerves and to degenerative conditions. Although relatively uncommon, severe sports injury to the neck can produce catastrophic impairment of the spinal cord.

- The first consideration in neck rehabilitation should be restoration of the neck's normal range of motion. When the athlete has gained near-normal range of motion, a strength program should be instituted. Mobilization techniques for the cervical spine are extensively used in rehabilitating the injured neck.

- Rehabilitation of low back pain focuses on teaching the athlete dynamic stabilization techniques that involve exercises for the trunk and spine to minimize the cumulative effects of repetitive microtrauma to the spine. Exercises are designed to strengthen or stretch specific muscles of spinal movement and are divided into extension and flexion exercises.

Web Sites

World Ortho: http://www.worldortho.com

Wheeless' Textbook of Orthopaedics: http://www.medmedia. com/med.htm

American Orthopaedic Society for Sports Medicine: http:// www.sportsmed.org

Spinal Cord 101: http://www.goes.com/billr/html/_spinal_ cord_101.html

This site gives basic information about spinal cord structure, function, and injury.

Solutions to Critical Thinking EXERCISES

25-1 The normal curves include the cervical, thoracic, lumbar, and sacrococcygeal curves. The cervical and lumbar curves are convex anteriorly, whereas the thoracic and sacrococcygeal curves are convex posteriorly. Lordotic posture is characterized by an increased curve in the lumbar spine with an increase in both anterior tilt of the pelvis and hip flexion. When combined with kyphosis and a forward head posture, this condition is referred to as a kypho-lordotic posture.

25-2 Left rotation is produced when the sternocleidomastoid, scalenes, semispinalis cervicis, and upper trapezius on the right side contract in addition to contractions of the left splenius capitus, splenius cervicis, and longissimus capitus.

25-3 The athletic trainer should look for symmetry of the ASIS, PSIS, and iliac crests. Sacroiliac compression and distraction tests and a positive Patrick, or FABER, test are all useful in determining a problem in the sacroiliac joint. In forward bending or flexion, the PSISs on each side should move together. If one moves further than the other, a motion restriction is likely present in the sacroiliac joint on the side that moves most. If they move at different times, the side that moves first usually has a restriction.

25-4 Pain present in forward bending and restriction in backward bending with radiating pain are usually associated with a disk problem. However, such pain may also be related to spondylolysis or spondylolisthesis.

25-5 Straight leg raising applies pressure to the sacroiliac joint and may indicate a problem in the sciatic nerve, sacroiliac joint, or lumbar spine. Pain at 30 degrees of straight leg raising indicates either a hip problem or an inflamed nerve. Pain from 30 to 60 degrees indicates some sciatic nerve involvement. Pain between 70 and 90 degrees is indicative of a sacroiliac joint problem. Pain on bilateral straight leg raising indicates some problem with the lumbar spine.

25-6 The athlete may have cervical spine stenosis, which involves a narrowing of the spinal canal in the cervical region that can impinge the spinal cord. The presence of cervical stenosis is determined by an X ray that measures the canal diameter and divides that by the anteroposterior width of the same vertebral body. The athlete should be advised of the potential risks of continued participation in football.

25-7 The athlete has most likely developed a myofascial trigger point. The key in treating myofascial pain is to stretch the muscle back to a normal resting length and thus relieve the irritation that created the trigger point. Active stretching should be mild and progressive. The use of electrical stimulation in combination with ultrasound is helpful in relieving the pain associated with a trigger point. Progressive strengthening exercises should also be included.

25-8 The gymnast likely has a spondylolisthesis that has resulted in hypermobility of a vertebral segment. Initially rest will help reduce pain. The major focus in rehabilitation should be directed toward exercises that control or stabilize the hypermobile segment. Progressive trunk strengthening exercises, especially to the abdominal muscles through the midrange, should be incorporated. A brace can be helpful during practice.

25-9 Given this set of existing conditions, the athletic trainer should have the athlete engage in extension exercises to strengthen the back extensors, to stretch the abdominals, and to reduce the pressure on the intervertebral disks.

25-10 It is likely that some pressure on the nerve root is causing this pain. The athletic trainer should recommend using flexion exercises to strengthen the abdominal muscles, to stretch the back extensors, and to take pressure off a nerve root by separating the lumbar facet joints and opening the intervertebral foramina.

25-11 The first step in dynamic stabilization is for the athlete to learn to control the pelvis in a neutral position. Once the athlete has learned to control pelvic tilt, the athletic trainer should incorporate progressively more advanced activities that involve movements of both the spine and extremities while the pelvis is maintained in a neutral position. Abdominal muscle control is another key to stabilization of the low back. Stabilization exercises include weight shifting in kneeling, standing lunges, bridging on a ball, wall slides, and alternating arm and leg extensions.

REVIEW QUESTIONS AND CLASS ACTIVITIES

1. Identify the various regions of the spine.
2. Describe the mechanisms of a catastrophic neck injury.
3. What is the relationship between the spinal cord, the nerve roots, and the peripheral nerves?
4. Describe the various postural abnormalities.
5. Describe the special tests used in evaluating the lumbar and sacroiliac portions of the spine.
6. Discuss the various considerations in prevention of cervical injuries.
7. What are the mechanisms of injury to the spinal cord?
8. What can be done to minimize the incidence of low back pain?
9. Describe the various types of herniated disks.
10. How does a spondylolysis become a spondylolisthesis?
11. What is the usual mechanism for injury to the sacroiliac joint?
12. Explain when flexion exercises should be used and when extension exercises should be used in treating conditions of the low back.
13. Explain the rationale for using dynamic stabilization to rehabilitate low back pain.

REFERENCES

1. Anderson C: Neck injuries, backboard, bench, or return to play, *Physician Sportsmed* 21(8):23, 1993.
2. Ashmen KJ, Swanik CB, Lephart SM: Strength and flexibility characteristics of athletes with chronic low-back pain, *J Sport Rehabil* 5(4):275, 1996.
3. Beattie P: The use of an eclectic approach for the treatment of low back pain: a case study, *Phys Ther* 72(12):923, 1992.
4. Binkley J, Finch E, Hall J: Diagnostic classification of patients with low back pain: a survey of physical therapy experts, *Phys Ther* 73(3):138, 1993.
5. Blanksby BA, Wearne FK, Elliott BC, Blitvich JD: Etiology and occurrence of diving injuries: a review of diving safety, *Sports Med* 23(4):228, 1997.
6. Brolinson PG: Practical approach to low back pain, *Sports Medicine in Primary Care* 3(4):30, 1997.
7. Cailliet R: *Low back pain,* ed 3, Philadelphia, 1988, FA Davis.
8. Cantu R: Functional cervical spinal stenosis: a contraindication to participation in contact sports, *Med Sci Sports Exerc* 25(3):316, 1993.
9. Cibulka M: The treatment of the sacroiliac joint component to low back pain, *Phys Ther* 72(12):917, 1992.
10. Cottingham JT, Maitland J: A three-paradigm treatment model using soft-tissue mobilization and guided movement-awareness techniques for a patient with chronic low back, *J Orthop Sports Phys Ther* 26(3):155, 1997.
11. Cyriax J: Refresher course for general practitioners: the treatment of lumbar disk lesions, *J Orthop Sports Phys Ther* 12(4):163, 1990.
12. Denegar CR, Peppard A: Evaluation and treatment of persistent pain and myofascial pain syndrome, *Athletic Therapy Today* 2(4):40, 1997.
13. DeRosa C, Poterfield J: A physical therapy model for the treatment of low back pain, *Phys Ther* 72(4):261, 1992.
14. Fomby EW, Mellion MB: Identifying and treating myofascial pain syndrome, *Physician Sportsmed* 25(2):67, 1997.
15. Fourre M: On-site management of cervical spine injuries, *Physician Sportsmed* 19:4, 1991.

16. Haldeman S: Spinal manipulative therapy in sports medicine. In Spencer III CW: *Injuries to the spine: clinics in sports medicine,* vol 5, no 2, Philadelphia, 1986, Saunders.

17. Haynes S: Systematic evaluation of brachial plexus injuries, *J Ath Train* 28(3):263, 1993.

18. Herring S, Weinstein S: Assessment and neurological management of athletic low back injury. In Nicholas J, Herschman E: *The lower extremity and spine in sports medicine,* St Louis, 1995, Mosby.

19. Holland B, Sacco D: Imaging of the spine. In White A, Schofferman J: *Spine care: diagnosis and conservative treatment,* vol 1, St Louis, 1995, Mosby.

20. Hooker D, Prentice W: Back rehabilitation. In Prentice W: *Rehabilitation techniques in sports medicine,* Dubuque, Iowa, 1999, WCB/McGraw-Hill.

21. Ikata T, Miyake R, Katoh S, Morita T, Murase M: Pathogenesis of sports-related spondylolisthesis in adolescents: radiographic and magnetic resonance imaging study, *Am J Sports Med* 24(1):94,1996.

22. Johnson EK, Chiarello CM: The slump test: the effects of head and lower extremity position on knee extension, *J Orthop Sports Phys Ther* 26(6):310, 1997.

23. Johnson R: Low back pain in sports: managing spondylolysis in young athletes, *Physician Sportsmed* 21(4):53, 1993.

24. Kuritzky L, White J: Low-back pain: consider extension education, *Physician Sportsmed* 25(1):56, 1997.

25. Markey K, Benedetto M, Curl W: Upper trunk and brachial plexopathy, *Am J Sports Med* 21(5):650, 1993.

26. Nissen SJ, Laskowski ER, Rizzo TD: Burner syndrome: recognition and rehabilitation, *Physician Sportsmed* 24(6):57, 1996.

27. Nuber G, Bowen M, Schaffer M: Diagnosis and treatment of lumbar and thoracic spine injuries. In Nicholas J, Herschman E: *The lower extremity and spine in sports medicine,* St Louis, 1995, Mosby.

28. Oldridge NB, Stoll JE: Low back pain syndrome. In American College of Sports Medicine: *ACSM's exercise management for persons with chronic disease and disabilities,* Champaign, Ill, 1997, Human Kinetics.

29. Perle SM: Myofascial trigger points, *Chiropractic Sports Medicine* (Baltimore, Md) 9(3):1, 1995.

30. Rapport L, O'Leary P, Cammisa F: Diagnosis and treatment of cervical spine injuries. In Nicholas J, Herschman E: *The lower extremity and spine in sports medicine,* St Louis, 1995, Mosby.

31. Rimoldi RL: Cervical injuries. In Baker, CL et al, editors: *The Hughston Clinic sports medicine book,* Baltimore, Md, 1995, Williams & Wilkins.

32. Ritz S, Lorren T, Simpson S: Rehabilitation of degenerative diseases of the spine. In Hochschuler S, Cotler H, Guyer R: *Rehabilitation of the spine: science and practice,* St Louis, 1993, Mosby.

33. Rodriquez J: Clinical examination and documentation. In Hochschuler S, Cotler H, Guyer R: *Rehabilitation of the spine: science and practice,* St Louis, 1993, Mosby.

34. Saunders D: *Evaluation, treatment, and prevention of musculoskeletal disorders,* Bloomington, Minn, 1985, Educational Opportunities.

35. Shiple B: Relieving low-back pain with exercise, *Physician Sportsmed* 25(8):67, 1997.

36. Storey MD: Anterior neck trauma, *Physician Sportsmed* 17(9):85, 1993.

37. Szajnuk TL: Low back pain in athletes: flexion or extension? *Athletic Therapy Today* 1(3):47, 1996.

38. Teitz CC: Rehabilitation of neck and low back injuries. In Harvey JS, editor: *Symposium on rehabilitation of the injured athlete. Clinics in sports medicine,* vol 4, no 3, Philadelphia, 1985, Saunders.

39. Tonks SM: Spondylolysis and spondylolisthesis, *Sports Medicine in Primary Care* 1(3):18, 1995.

40. Torg JS et al: The axial load teardrop fracture, *Am J Sports Med* 19(4):355, 1991.

41. Torg JS et al: The epidemiologic, pathologic, biomechanical, and cinematographic analysis of football-induced cervical spine trauma, *Am J Sports Med* 18(1):50, 1990.

42. Torg J, Fay C: Cervical spinal stenosis with cord neurapraxia and transcient quadriplegia. In Torg J: *Athletic injuries to the head, neck, and face,* St Louis, 1991, Mosby.

43. Vereschagin KS et al: Burners, *Physician Sportsmed* 1(9):96, 1991.

44. Watkins RG: Acute cervical spine injuries in the adult competitive athlete: football injuries (burners), *Sports Med Arthroscopy Review* 5(3):182, 1997.

45. Weber MD, Woodall WR: Spondylogenic disorders in gymnasts, *J Orthop Sports Phys Ther* 14(1):6, 1991.

46. Wiesenfarth J, Briner W: Neck injuries: urgent decisions and actions, *Physician Sportsmed* 24(1):35, 1996.

47. Wilkerson JE, Maroon JC: Cervical spine injuries in athletes, *Physician Sportsmed* 18(3):57, 1990.

48. Winkelstein BA, Myers BS: The biomechanics of cervical spine injury and implications for injury prevention, *Med Sci Sports Exerc* 29(7 suppl):S246, 1997.

49. Wisbey-Roth T: Dysfunctional muscle recruitment patterns affecting core stability: the theory of synergistic stabilizer retraining. Abstract from Australian Conference of Science and Medicine in Sport, National Convention Centre, Canberra, October 1996.

50. Young JL, Press JM, Herring SA: The disk at risk in athletes: perspectives on operative and nonoperative care, *Med Sci Sports Exerc* 29(7 suppl):S222, 1997.

ANNOTATED BIBLIOGRAPHY

Cailliet R: *Low back pain syndrome,* ed 3, Philadelphia, 1988, FA Davis.

This text presents the subject of low back pain in a clear, concise, and interesting manner.

Hochschuler S, Cotler H, Guyer R: *Rehabilitation of the spine: science and practice,* St Louis, 1993, Mosby.

This comprehensive text focuses on all aspects of treatment and rehabilitation of the spine. Injuries specific to individual sports are discussed.

McCulloch J: *Backache,* ed 2, Baltimore, 1990, Williams & Wilkins.

This in-depth text is about the evaluation and treatment of back conditions.

Nicholas J, Herschman E: *The lower extremity and spine in sports medicine,* St Louis, 1995, Mosby.

This two-volume text discusses all aspects of injury to the extremities and the spine. The section on evaluation and treatment of spinal conditions is concise but thorough.

Saunders D: *Evaluation, treatment, and prevention of musculoskeletal disorders,* Bloomington, Minn, 1985, Educational Opportunities.

This text takes a manual therapy approach to treating and rehabilitating musculoskeletal injuries in general and injuries to the spine in specific.

Torg JS, editor: *Head and neck injuries. Clinics in sports medicine,* vol 6, no 1, Philadelphia, 1991, Saunders.

This text provides in-depth coverage of head and neck injuries stemming from sports activities.

White A, Schofferman J: *Spine care: diagnosis and conservative treatment,* St Louis, 1995, Mosby.

This two-volume set looks at both conservative and surgical management of back injuries.

The Thorax and Abdomen

When you finish this chapter you should be able to

- Understand the anatomy of the thorax and abdomen.
- Identify the location and function of the heart and lungs.
- Be aware of the location and function of the abdominal viscera related to the urinary system, the digestive system, the reproductive system, and the lymphatic system.
- Be familiar with techniques for assessing thoracic and abdominal injuries.
- Identify various injuries to the structures of the thorax.
- Discuss various injuries and conditions in structures of the abdomen.

This chapter deals with major sports injuries to the thorax and abdomen. In an athletic environment, injuries to the thorax and abdomen have a lower incidence than do injuries to the extremities. However, unlike the musculoskeletal injuries to the extremities discussed to this point, injuries to the heart, lungs, and abdominal viscera can be potentially serious and even life threatening if not recognized and managed appropriately. It is imperative for the athletic trainer to be familiar with the anatomy and more common injuries seen in the abdomen and thorax (Figure 26-1).

ANATOMY OF THE THORAX

The thoracic cavity is that portion of the body commonly known as the chest, which lies between the base of the neck and the diaphragm. It consists of the thoracic vertebrae, the twelve pairs of ribs with their associated costal cartilages, and the sternum (Figure 26-2). Its main functions are to protect the vital respiratory and circulatory organs and to assist the lungs in inspiration and expiration during the breathing process. Within the thoracic cage lie the lungs, the heart, and the thymus.

The thoracic cage protects the heart and lungs.

Ribs, Costal Cartilage, and Sternum

The ribs are flat bones that are attached to the thoracic vertebrae in the back and to the sternum in the front. The upper seven ribs are called sternal, or true, ribs, and each rib is joined to the sternum by a separate costal cartilage. The eighth, ninth, and tenth ribs (false ribs) have a common cartilage that joins the seventh rib before attaching to the sternum. The eleventh and twelfth ribs (floating ribs) remain unattached to the sternum but do have muscle attachments. The individual rib articulation produces a slight gliding action.

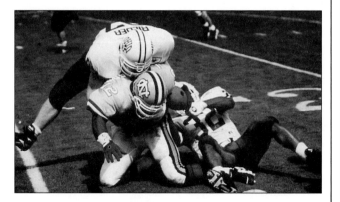

Figure 26-1

Collision sports can produce serious trunk injuries.

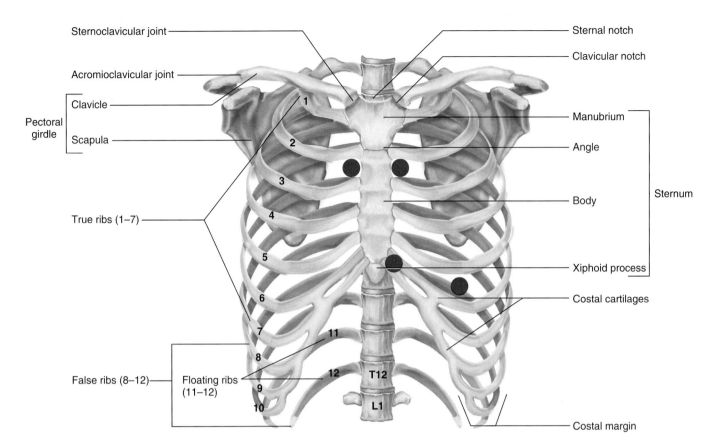

Sternoclavicular joint

Acromioclavicular joint

Pectoral
girdle
    Clavicle

    Scapula

True ribs (1–7)

False ribs (8–12)   Floating ribs
(11–12)

Sternal notch

Clavicular notch

Manubrium

Angle   Sternum

Body

Xiphoid process

Costal cartilages

Costal margin

Figure 26-2

The thoracic cage. (The colored dots indicate the points for auscultation of heart sounds through a stethoscope.)

The inside of the thoracic cage is lined with the pleura, a thin double-layer membrane filled with pleural fluid that permits the lungs to slide along the thoracic cage.

Thoracic Muscles

There are eleven pairs of both external intercostal muscles and internal intercostal muscles between the ribs (Figure 26-3). They attach on the inferior border of the rib above and the superior border of the rib below. The external intercostals function to elevate the diaphragm during inspiration, whereas the internal intercostals depress the rib cage to assist with expiration. The intercostal muscles are innervated by the intercostal nerves.

The pectoralis minor, trapezius, serratus anterior, serratus posterior, levator scapula, and rhomboids are muscles that originate on the thorax and were discussed in Chapter 22. Their primary function is controlling movement of the scapula.

Lungs

The trachea, or windpipe, branches into right and left primary bronchi, which branch into smaller divisions and ultimately terminate in clusters of air sacs called alveoli within the lungs (Figure 26-4). Alveoli facilitate the exchange of oxygen and carbon dioxide with the capillaries. The lungs are elastic and expand and constrict in response to contraction of the diaphragm muscle.

Respiratory Muscles

The diaphragm is a large, dome-shaped muscle that separates the thoracic cavity from the abdominal cavity. When the diaphragm contracts, the dome flattens, which increases the volume of the thorax and results in inspiration of air. Expiration occurs when the diaphragm relaxes and the elastic components of the lungs and thoracic cage passively decrease thoracic volume.

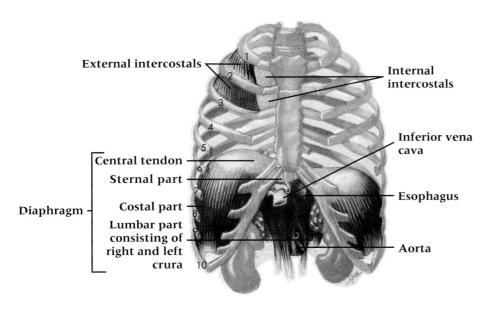

Figure 26-3

Anatomy of the thoracic muscles.

Blood Supply

Blood flows to the lungs through the pulmonary arteries to the alveoli, where it is oxygenated and returns to the heart through the pulmonary veins. The bronchi are supplied with oxygenated blood through the bronchial arteries that branch from the aorta. Deoxygenated blood returns to the heart from the bronchi via both the bronchial and pulmonary veins.

Figure 26-4

Anatomy of the trachea, lungs, and alveoli.

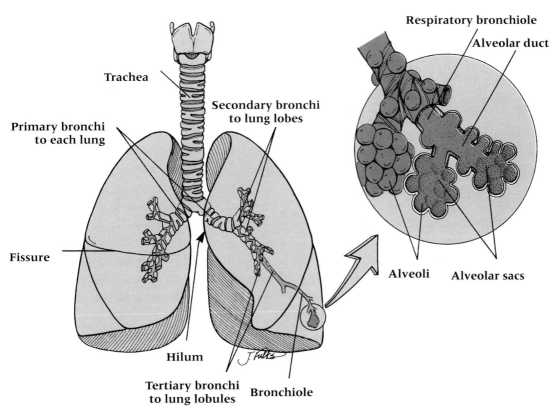

Heart

The heart is the main pumping mechanism and functions to circulate oxygenated blood throughout the body to the working tissues. The transport of oxygen involves the coordinated function of the heart, the blood vessels, the blood, and the lungs.

The adult heart lies under the sternum, slightly to the left, between the lungs, and in front of the vertebral column (Figure 26-5). It is about the size of a clenched fist. It extends from the first rib to the space between the fifth and sixth ribs.

The heart muscle consists of four chambers: the right and left atria and the right and left ventricles (Figure 26-6). Deoxygenated blood returns from all parts of the body through the venous system to the right atrium and passes through the tricuspid valve to the right ventricle. The right ventricle pumps the blood through the pul-

Figure 26-5

Location of the heart in the thorax.

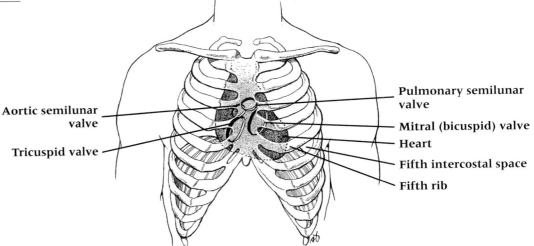

Figure 26-6

Anatomy of the heart and blood flow.

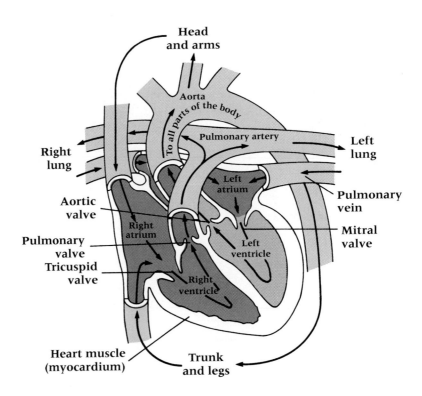

monary valve to the pulmonary artery and into the lungs, where it is oxygenated. Blood returns from the lungs via the pulmonary vein to the left atrium and passes through the mitral valve into the left ventricle. Blood is ejected past the aortic valve into the aorta, which supplies the entire body through the arterial system.

A single heartbeat consists of a contraction of both atria followed immediately by a contraction of both ventricles. Contraction of the chambers is referred to as systole, and relaxation as diastole.

Blood Supply

The heart is supplied by right and left coronary arteries branching from the aorta. Cardiac veins drain into the right atrium.

Thymus

The thymus is located in the thorax just anterior to and above the heart. The function of the thymus is to produce lymphocytes, which migrate to other lymphatic tissues to respond to foreign substances. The thymus is relatively large in the infant and after puberty gradually decreases in size.

ANATOMY OF THE ABDOMEN

The abdominal cavity lies between the diaphragm and the bones of the pelvis and is bounded by the margin of the lower ribs, the abdominal muscles, and the vertebral column. The abdominal cavity is sometimes called the abdominopelvic cavity, although there is no physical separation between the abdominal and pelvic cavities.

Abdominal Muscles

The abdominal muscles are the rectus abdominis, the external oblique, the internal oblique, and the transverse abdominis (Figure 26-7). They are invested with both superficial and deep fasciae.

The rectus abdominis muscle, a trunk flexor, is attached to the rib cage above and to the pubis below. It is divided into three segments by transverse tendinous inscriptions; longitudinally it is divided by the linea alba. It functions in trunk flexion, rotation, and lateral flexion and in compression of the abdominal cavity. A heavy fascial sheath encloses the rectus abdominis muscle, holding it in its position but in no way restricting its motion. The inguinal ring, which serves as a passageway for the spermatic cord, is formed by the abdominal fascia.

The external oblique muscle is a broad, thin muscle that arises from slips attached to the borders of the lower eight ribs. It runs obliquely forward and downward and inserts on the anterior two-thirds of the crest of the ilium, the pubic crest, and the

Figure 26-7

The abdominal musculature.

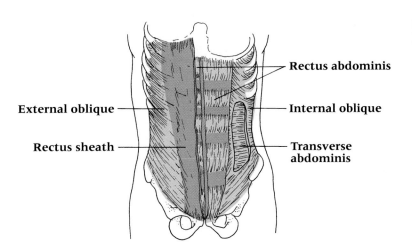

External oblique

Rectus sheath

Rectus abdominis

Internal oblique

Transverse abdominis

fascia of the rectus abdominis and the linea alba at their lower front. Its principal functions are trunk flexion, rotation, lateral flexion, and compression.

The internal oblique muscle forms the anterior and lateral aspects of the abdominal wall. Its fibers arise from the iliac crest, the upper half of the inguinal ligament, and the lumbar fascia. It runs principally in an obliquely upward direction to the cartilages of the tenth, eleventh, and twelfth ribs on each side. The main functions of the internal oblique are trunk flexion, lateral flexion, and rotation.

The transverse abdominis is the deepest of the abdominal muscles. Its fibers run transversely across the abdominal cavity, arising from the outer third of the inguinal ligament, the iliac crest, the lumbar fascia of the back, and the lower six ribs. It inserts into the linea alba and the front half of the iliac crest. The main functions of the transverse abdominis are to hold the abdominal contents in place and to aid in forced expiration. All the abdominal muscles work together in performing defecation, micturition, and forced expiration.

Abdominal Viscera

Abdominal viscera are part of the urinary, digestive, reproductive, and lymphatic systems.

The abdominal viscera are composed of both hollow and solid organs. The solid organs are the kidneys, spleen, liver, pancreas, and adrenal glands. The hollow organs include vessels, tubes, and receptacles such as the stomach, intestines, gallbladder, and urinary bladder (Figure 26-8). Organs in the abdominal cavity may be classified as being part of the urinary system, the digestive system, the reproductive system, or the lymphatic system.

Urinary System Organs

The kidneys, the ureters, and the urinary bladder are the urinary system organs.

Kidneys The kidneys are situated on each side of the spine, approximately in the center of the back. They are bean shaped, approximately $4^{1}/_{2}$ inches (11.25 cm) long, 2 inches (5 cm) wide, and 1 inch (2.5 cm) thick. The right kidney is usually slightly lower than the left because of the pressure of the liver. The uppermost surfaces of the kidneys are connected to the diaphragm by strong, ligamentous fibers. As breathing occurs, the kidneys move up and down as much as $^{1}/_{2}$ inch (1.25 cm). The inferior aspect is positioned 1 to 2 inches (2.5 to 5 cm) above the iliac crest. Resting anterior to the left kidney are the stomach, spleen, pancreas, and small and large intestines. Organs that are situated anterior to the right kidney are the liver and the intestines. The kidneys lie posterior to the abdominal cavity. Their primary function is to filter metabolic wastes, ions, or drugs from blood and expel them from the body via urination.[30]

Adrenal glands Although part of the endocrine system rather than the urinary system, the adrenal glands, also called the suprarenal glands, are located on top of each kidney. They secrete the hormones epinephrine, norepinephrine, cortisol,

26-I

Critical Thinking Exercise

A soccer player is kicked in the abdomen above the umbilicus. Initially, she had the wind knocked out of her. Now, she is complaining of pain and her abdomen is tight on palpation.

? What should the athletic trainer be most concerned about and what organs may potentially be involved?

Figure 26-8

Abdominal viscera.

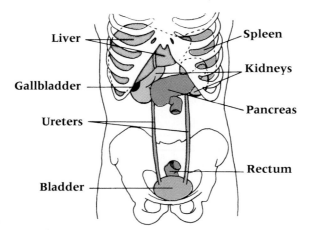

Liver
Spleen
Gallbladder
Kidneys
Pancreas
Ureters
Rectum
Bladder

estrogen, aldosterone, and androgen, which have a variety of physiologic functions throughout the body.[34]

Ureters and urinary bladder   The ureters are small tubes that extend inferiorly from the kidney to the urinary bladder, which functions to store urine. The bladder is a hollow container that lies posterior to the pubic symphysis. In the male, the bladder is anterior to the rectum, and in the female, it is anterior to the vagina and inferior to the uterus.

Digestive System Organs

The liver, gallbladder, pancreas, stomach, small intestine, and large intestine are digestive system organs.

Liver   The liver is the largest internal organ of the body. It lies in the upper right quadrant of the body against the inferior surface of the diaphragm and weighs about three pounds. It consists of two major right and left lobes. The liver performs digestive and excretory functions; absorbs and stores excessive glucose; processes nutrients; and detoxifies harmful chemicals. It secretes bile, which is essential in neutralizing and diluting stomach acid and for digesting fat in the small intestine during the digestive process.[25]

Hepatitis is an inflammation of the liver caused by viral infection or alcohol consumption. If is not corrected, the cells in the liver may die and be replaced by scar tissue, which can lead to cirrhosis or impaired liver function.[30] Cirrhosis is a progressive disease of the liver that results in diffuse scarring and fibrosis and disruption of hepatic blood flow that can eventually result in liver failure. Cirrhosis can have many causes but it is most often associated with chronic alcoholism.[34]

Gallbladder   The gallbladder is a pear-shaped, saclike structure located on the inferior surface of the liver. It serves as a storage reservoir for bile secreted from the liver. Shortly after a meal, the gallbladder secrets the stored bile into the small intestine. Cholesterol, which is secreted by the liver, may cause the gallbladder to produce a gallstone, which can potentially block the release of bile. The gallstone interferes with digestion and must usually be removed surgically.[34]

Pancreas   The pancreas is located between the small intestine and the spleen. It secretes pancreatic juice, which is critical in the digestion of fats, carbohydrates, and proteins. It also produces insulin and glucagon, which are hormones that control the amount of glucose and amino acids in the blood.

Stomach   The stomach is found primarily in the upper left quadrant between the esophagus and the small intestine. It functions mainly as a storage and mixing chamber of food that has been ingested. Some digestion and absorption occurs in the stomach. Gastric secretions assist in the partial digestion of protein and the absorption of alcohol and caffeine. Ingested food is mixed with secretions from the stomach glands to form a semifluid material called chyme, which passes from the stomach into the small intestine.[30]

Small intestine   The small intestine is connected to the stomach via a series of tubelike folds. The small intestine has three portions: the duodenum, the jejunum, and the ileum. In total, it is approximately 20 feet (6 m) in length. Secretions from the liver and pancreas mix with secretions from the small intestine, which are essential to the process of digestion. Mucus is secreted in large amounts to lubricate and protect the wall of the intestinal as a mixture of chyme and the digestive enzymes is propelled through the small intestine by a series of peristaltic contractions. Chyme moves through the small intestine over a period of three to five hours. Most of the digestion and absorption of food occurs in the small intestine.[29]

Large intestine   The large intestine is that portion of the digestive tract that extends from the small intestine to the anus and is approximately $6^{1}/_{2}$ feet (2 m) in length. It has three divisions: the cecum, the colon, and the rectum. The veriform appendix extends from the cecum. In the colon, chyme is converted to feces through absorption of water, secretion of mucus, and activity of microorganisms. Feces remain in the colon and rectum until the time of defecation.

Lymphatic System Organs

The spleen and the thymus, which is discussed in the section on the thoracic cavity, are organs of the lymphatic system.

Spleen   The spleen is the largest lymphatic organ in the body. It weighs approximately 6 ounces (170 grams) and is approximately 5 inches (12.5 cm) long. It lies under the diaphragm on the left side and behind the ninth, tenth, and eleventh ribs. It is surrounded by a fibrous capsule that is firmly invested by the peritoneum. The spleen's main functions are to serve as a reservoir of red blood cells; to regulate the number of red blood cells in the general circulation, to destroy ineffective red cells, to produce antibodies for immunological function, and to produce lymphocytes.[34]

Reproductive System Organs

Unlike the other organ systems discussed to this point, the reproductive system for males and females differs considerably. The female reproductive organs include the ovaries, uterus, uterine tubes (fallopian tubes), and vagina. The male reproductive organs include the seminal vesicles, prostate gland, testes, vas deferens, epididymis, urethra, and the penis.

Female reproductive organs   The reproductive organs in the female are between the urinary bladder and the rectum; the uterus and vagina are in the midline, and the uterine tubes and ovaries extend to either side (Figure 26-9). Their position is maintained by a group of ligaments, the primary one being the broad ligament. The vagina is a receptacle for sperm, which swim upward into the uterus to fertilize the egg.

The ovaries produce and store the female eggs (ova) which are released one at a time each month into the uterine tubes. The uterine tubes transport the ovum to the uterus, where a fertilized ovum attaches to the uterine wall and becomes a developing embryo. If the ovum is not fertilized, the process of menstruation begins.

The reproductive organs in the female are well protected by the pelvis. Thus, traumatic injury to these structures is rare in the athletic population.

Male reproductive organs   The reproductive organs in the male are found both inside and outside the abdominal cavity (Figure 26-10). The prostate is dorsal to the pubic symphysis and inferior to the bladder. The urethra and the ejaculatory ducts pass through the prostate. The prostate is made of both glandular and muscular tissue and is similar in size to a walnut. The prostate secretes a milky fluid that is discharged by twenty to thirty ducts into the prostatic portion of the urethra as a component of semen. The seminal vesicles are also glandular structures found posterior and superior to the prostate gland under the bladder. The seminal vesicles contribute the majority of the fluid to the semen through the ejaculatory ducts.

The remainder of the male reproductive organs are exposed outside the abdominal cavity and are more susceptible to injury. The testes are the primary male sex

Figure 26-9

Female reproductive organs.

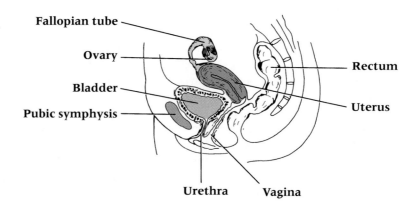

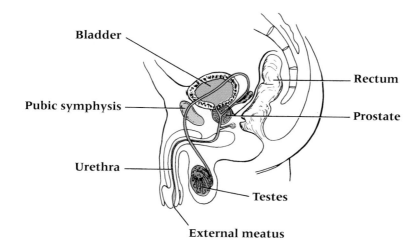

Figure 26-10

Male reproductive organs.

organs. They are located within the scrotum and produce spermatozoa and testosterone. The epididymis is a comma-shaped structure connected to the posterior surface of the testis in which the sperm are stored until mature. The vas deferens is a duct running from the epididymis to the ejaculatory duct. The urethra runs from the bladder to the tip of the penis and serves as a pathway through which both urine and semen are ejected through the penis. The penis consists of three layers of erectile tissue, which, when engorged with blood, cause an erection.

PREVENTION OF INJURIES TO THE THORAX AND ABDOMEN

Injuries to the thorax may be prevented by appropriate protective equipment, particularly in collision sport activities. In football, for example, shoulder pads are usually designed to extend to at least below the level of the sternum. Rib protectors may be worn to cover the entire thoracic cage if necessary.

The muscles of the abdomen should be strengthened to provide protection to the underlying viscera. A consistent regimen of sit-up exercises done in various positions can markedly increase the strength and size of the abdominal musculature.

Making sure that the hollow organs, in particular the stomach and bladder, are emptied prior to competition can reduce the chance of injury to those structures. Meals should be eaten at least three to four hours prior to competition to allow foods to clear the stomach. Urination immediately prior to stepping onto the field or court will protect the bladder from injury.

ASSESSMENT OF THE THORAX AND ABDOMEN

Injuries to the thorax and abdomen can produce potentially life-threatening situations. An injury that may seem to be relatively insignificant at first may rapidly develop in one that requires immediate and appropriate medical attention.[4] Thus, the athletic trainer's primary survey should focus on those signs and symptoms that indicate some life-threatening condition. The injured athlete should be continually monitored by the athletic trainer to identify any disruption of normal breathing or circulation or any indication of internal hemorrhage that could precipitate shock.

History

The questions that are asked to determine a history for thoracic and abdominal injuries are somewhat different than the questions that are pertinent to musculoskeletal injuries of the extremities.[26] The primary mechanism of injury should be determined first.
- What happened to cause this injury?
- Was there direct contact or a direct blow?

- What position were you in?
- What type of pain is there (sharp, dull, localized, etc)?
- Was the pain immediate or gradual?
- Do you feel any pain other than in the area where the injury occurred?
- Has there been any difficulty breathing?
- Are certain positions more comfortable than others?
- Do you feel faint, light-headed, or nauseous?
- Do you feel any pain in your chest?
- Did you hear or feel a pop or crack in your chest?
- Have you had any muscle spasms?
- Have you noticed any blood in your urine?
- Is there any difficulty or pain in urinating?
- Was the bladder full or empty?
- How long has it been since you have eaten?
- Is there a personal or family history of any heart problems, any abdominal problems, or any other diseases involving the thorax and abdomen?

Observation

If the athlete is observed immediately following injury, the athletic trainer should check for normal breathing and respiratory patterns.

- Most importantly, is the athlete breathing at all?
- Is the athlete having difficulty breathing deeply, or is he or she catching the breath?
- Does breathing cause pain?
- Is the athlete holding the chest wall?
- Is there symmetry in movement of the chest during breathing?
- If the athlete's wind was knocked out, is normal breathing returning rapidly or is there prolonged difficulty? Prolonged difficulty may indicate a more severe injury.

The body position of the athlete should be observed. An athlete who has sustained some type of thoracic injury will often be leaning toward the side that is injured, holding or splinting the area with the opposite hand (Figure 26-11A). In the case of an abdominal injury, the athlete will typically lie on the side with the knees pulled up toward the chest (Figure 26-11B).[34] The male who has sustained an injury

Figure 26-11

Body positions after injury. **A,** Thoracic injury. **B,** Abdominal injury. **C,** External genitalia injury.

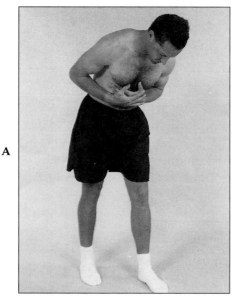

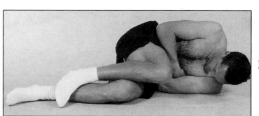

to the external genitalia will be lying on his side holding the scrotum (Figure 26-11C).

The athletic trainer checks for areas of discoloration, swelling, or deformities that may produce asymmetries. Discoloration or ecchymosis around the umbilicus is indicative of intraabdominal bleeding, whereas ecchymosis on the flanks may indicate swelling outside the abdomen.

- Is there protrusion or swelling of any portion of the abdomen? Such swelling may indicate internal bleeding.
- Does the thorax appear to be symmetrical? Rib fractures can cause one side to appear different.
- Are the abdominal muscles tight and guarding?
- Is the athlete holding or splinting a specific part of the abdomen?

Other observable signs and symptoms may indicate the nature of a thoracic or abdominal injury. Bright red blood being coughed up indicates some injury to the lungs. Bright red frothy blood being vomited may indicate injury to the esophagus or stomach, although the blood may also be swallowed from the mouth or nose and then vomited. Cyanosis generally indicates some respiratory difficulty, whereas pale, cool, clammy skin indicates lowered blood pressure.

It is important to monitor vital signs, including pulse, respirations, and blood pressure (see Chapter 12). A rapid, weak pulse and/or a significant drop in blood pressure is an indication of some potentially serious internal injury that very often involves loss of blood.

Palpation

Thorax

The hands should first be placed on either side of the chest wall to check for symmetry in chest wall movement during deep inspiration and expiration and to begin to isolate areas of tenderness (Figure 26-12). Once a tender area is identified, the athletic trainer should palpate along the rib, in the intercostal space between the ribs, and at the costochondral junction to locate a specific point of tenderness. Applying anterioposterior compression to the thoracic cage is done to identify potential rib fractures (Figure 26-13A). Transverse compression applied laterally identifies costochondral injuries (Figure 26-13B). If the athlete is having difficulty breathing, it may be helpful to use a semireclining position for these tests.

Abdomen

For abdominal palpation, the athlete should be supine with the arms at the side and with the hips and knees flexed to relax the abdominal muscles. Palpation should occur in a systematic manner using the four abdominopelvic quadrants that were discussed in Chapter 13 (see Figure 13-3). Palpation should begin in the right upper

26-2

Critical Thinking E x e r c i s e

A basketball player goes for a rebound and is accidentally hit in the abdomen by an opponent's elbow. He is lying on the court on his side with his legs drawn up. The athletic trainer decides to remove him from the court on a stretcher and evaluate him in the training room. On palpation, the abdomen feels extremely tight.

? How can the athletic trainer differentiate between muscle guarding, rigidity, and rebound tenderness in the athlete who has sustained an abdominal injury?

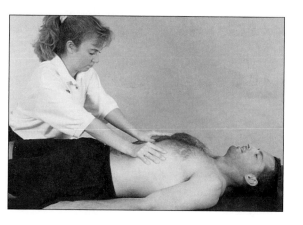

Figure 26-12

Checking asymmetry of the chest wall during breathing.

Figure 26-13

A, Checking for rib fractures. **B,** Checking for costochondral injuries.

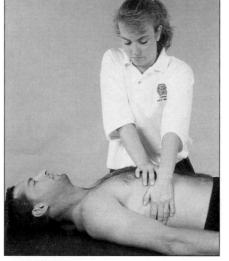
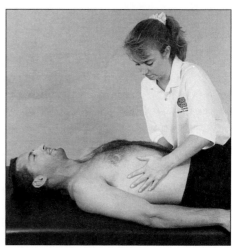

Figure 26-14

Palpating the abdomen for guarding or rigidity.

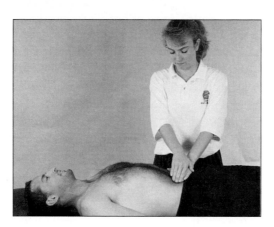

quadrant and move clockwise to the left upper quadrant, the left lower quadrant, and finally, the right lower quadrant (appendix). The evaluator should begin palpating uninjured areas first, using the tips of the fingers to feel for any tightness or rigidity (Figure 26-14). An athlete with an abdominal injury will voluntarily contract the abdominal muscles to guard or protect the tender area. If there is bleeding or irritation inside the abdominal cavity, the abdomen will exhibit boardlike rigidity and cannot be voluntarily relaxed. Rebound tenderness may also accompany intraabdominal bleeding. The evaluator can produce rebound tenderness by pressing firmly on the abdomen and then quickly releasing pressure, which causes intense pain. If the athlete is exhibiting only voluntary guarding, the evaluator can palpate over the liver, gallbladder, spleen, stomach, small intestine, large intestine, veriform appendix, and bladder while searching for tenderness, swelling, or enlargement. The kidneys should be palpated with the athlete in a prone position.

Pressure on the abdominal organs may elicit referred pain in predictable patterns away from the source. Figure 26-15 identifies patterns of referred pain.

Auscultation

Auscultation involves listening to body sounds through a stethoscope. Auscultation is often used to listen to heart sounds, breathing sounds, or bowel sounds (Figure 26-16A).

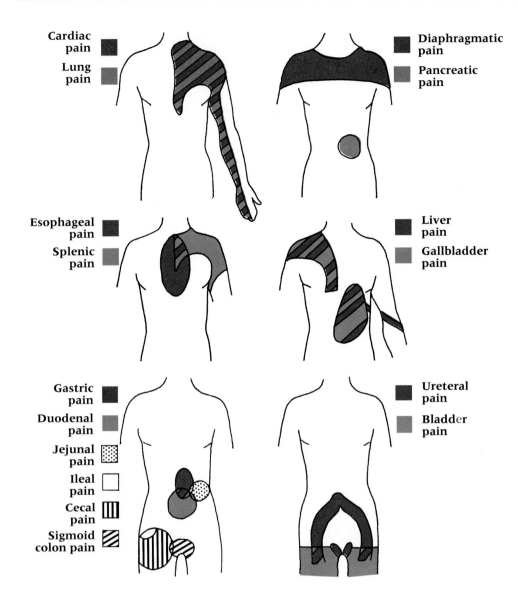

Cardiac pain

Lung pain

Diaphragmatic pain

Pancreatic pain

Esophageal pain

Splenic pain

Liver pain

Gallbladder pain

Gastric pain

Duodenal pain

Jejunal pain

Ileal pain

Cecal pain

Sigmoid colon pain

Ureteral pain

Bladder pain

Figure 26-15

Patterns of referred pain. *(continued)*

Heart sounds   A normal cardiac cycle includes two sounds, often called "lubb-dupp," which are caused by the turbulance of the blood as the valves close. In children, it is not unusual to hear a third sound.29 An abnormal periodic sound that occurs in auscultation of the heart is called a murmur. A murmur often occurs because of some defect in one of the valves within the heart. Murmurs can sound soft and blowing or loud and booming. A murmur does not necessarily mean that some pathogenic condition exists in the heart. A murmur that exists in the absence of any organic disease in the heart is called a *functional murmur.*34 Figure 26-2 shows the positions for auscultation of the heart with a stethoscope.

Breath sounds   The rate of breathing patterns should be even and consistent. Abnormal breathing patterns include *Cheyne-Stokes* breathing, in which the rate speeds up and then slows down over a one- to three-minute period; *Biot's* breathing, in which a series of breaths at the normal rate are followed by complete cessation of breathing; *apneustic* breathing, in which there are pauses in the respiratory cycle at full inspiration; and thoracic breathing, which occurs without diaphragmatic breathing. Abnormal breathing sounds are often superimposed on normal breathing sounds. Adventitious breath sounds are those that are not normally heard and may be either continuous musiclike sounds with a high pitch, called *wheezes* or *rhonchi,* or

26-3

Critical Thinking Exercise

A crew athlete complains that when she takes a deep breath she feels some funny crackling sensations in her lungs. The athletic trainer wants to listen to the athlete's chest with a stethoscope.

? What sounds should the athletic trainer listen for?

Figure 26-15—cont'd

Patterns of referred pain.

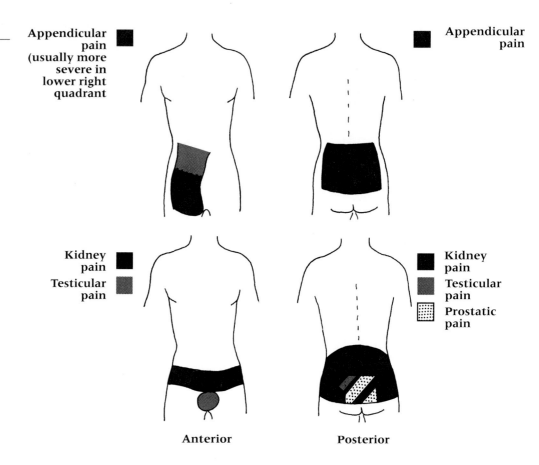

Appendicular pain (usually more severe in lower right quadrant)

Appendicular pain

Kidney pain

Testicular pain

Kidney pain

Testicular pain

Prostatic pain

Anterior   Posterior

crackling or bubbling sounds, called *rales.* Positions for auscultation should be over the apex, centrally, and at the base of each lung, both anteriorly and posteriorly.[32]

Bowel sounds   Bowel sounds are liquidlike gurgling sounds created by normal peristaltic actions that propel intestinal contents through the lower gastrointestinal tract. Following abdominal injury, bowel signs may be absent. The stethoscope can be placed in multiple positions anywhere over the lower abdomen.[32]

Percussion

The evaluator performs percussion by placing a finger of one hand over an organ and then using one or two fingers from the other hand to strike that finger (Figure 26-16B). The resulting sound may provide some indication as to the status of the or-

Figure 26-16

A, Auscultation. **B,** Percussion.

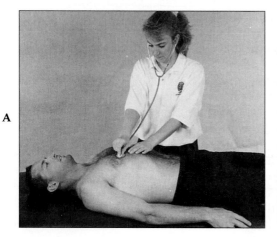

A

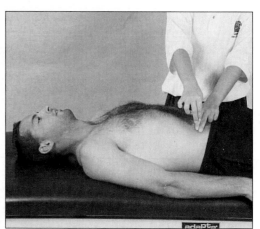

B

gan being percussed. A solid organ such as the liver will produce a dull sound, whereas a hollow organ like a lung will produce a tympanic or resonant sound.

Some special training is required to know exactly what to listen for in auscultation and percussion. The athletic trainer should know what sounds are normal and be able to determine when something sounds abnormal. The physician is certainly better qualified to make diagnostic decisions based on auscultation and percussion.

RECOGNITION AND MANAGEMENT OF SPECIFIC INJURIES

Injuries and Conditions of the Thoracic Region

The thorax is vulnerable to a variety of injuries to the ribs, the costochondral junction, and the muscles. Injuries to the lungs and heart are more serious and require special attention.[39]

Rib Contusions

Etiology   A blow to the rib cage can contuse intercostal muscles or, if severe enough, produce a fracture. Because the intercostal muscles are essential for the breathing mechanism, both expiration and inspiration become very painful when they are bruised.

Symptoms and signs   Characteristically the pain is sharp during breathing, there is point tenderness, and pain is elicited when the rib cage is compressed. X-ray examination should be routine in such an injury.

Management   RICE and antiinflammatory agents are commonly used. Like most rib injuries, contusions to the thorax are self-limiting; they respond best to rest and to cessation of sports activities.

Rib Fractures

Etiology   Rib fractures (Figure 26-17) are not uncommon in sports and have their highest incidence in collision sports, particularly wrestling and football. Fractures can be caused by either direct or indirect traumas and can, infrequently, be the result of violent muscular contractions.[11] A direct injury is caused by a kick or a well-placed block, with the fracture developing at the site of force application. An indirect fracture is produced as a result of general compression of the rib cage such as may occur in football or wrestling. Ribs have also been known to fracture from forces caused by coughing and sneezing. Ribs 5 through 9 are the most commonly fractured. Multiple rib fractures can be severe. A flail chest involves a fracture of three or more consecutive ribs on the same side.

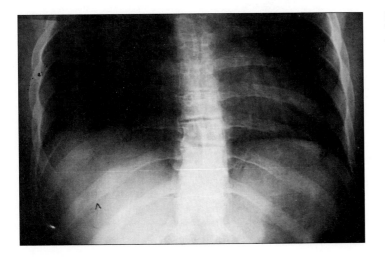

Figure 26-17

A rib fracture.

The structural and functional disruption sustained in a rib fracture varies according to the type of injury that has been received.[22] The direct fracture causes the most serious damage, because the external force fractures and displaces the ribs inwardly. Such a mechanism may completely displace the bone and cause an overriding of fragments. The jagged edges of the fragments may cut, tear, or perforate the tissue of the pleurae, causing hemothorax, or they may collapse one lung (pneumothorax). Contrary to the direct injury, the indirect fracture usually causes the rib to spring and fracture outward, producing an oblique or transverse fissure. Stress fracture of the first rib is becoming more prevalent. It can result from repeated arm movements such as those used in pitching or in rowing. Stress fractures to other ribs have resulted from repeated coughing or laughing. Injury to the pectoral muscles may mask signs of rib fracture.[27]

Symptoms and signs   The rib fracture is usually quite easily detected. The history informs the athletic trainer of the type and degree of force to which the rib cage has been subjected. After trauma, the athlete complains of severe pain during inspiration and has point tenderness. A fracture of the rib will be readily evidenced by a severe, sharp pain and possibly crepitus during palpation.

Management   The athlete should be referred to the team physician for X-ray examination if there is any indication of fracture.

An uncomplicated rib fracture is often difficult to identify on an X ray. Therefore, the physician plans the treatment according to the symptoms presented. The rib fracture is usually managed with support and rest. Simple transverse or oblique fractures heal within three to four weeks. A rib brace can offer the athlete some rib cage stabilization and comfort (Figure 26-18). However, rib supports may predispose the athlete to the development of hypostatic pneumonia, which has the potential to occur whenever an individual does not take full inspirations because of pain and some mechanical restriction.[34]

Costochondral Separation and Dislocation

Etiology   In sports activities, the costochondral separation or dislocation has a higher incidence than do fractures (Figure 26-19). This injury can occur from a direct blow to the anterolateral aspect of the thorax or indirectly from a sudden twist or a fall on a ball that compresses the rib cage. The costochondral injury displays

---

A rib fracture may be indicated by a severe, sharp pain during breathing.

26-4

Critical Thinking Exercise

An ice hockey player is checked into the boards by an opponent. He has the wind knocked out of him and, on recovery, says that he feels pain when he tries to take a deep breath. The athletic trainer suspects an injury to the thoracic cage.

? How can the athletic trainer differentiate between a rib fracture and a costochondral injury?

Figure 26-18

A commercial rib brace can provide moderate support to the thorax.

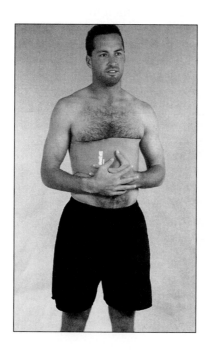

many signs that are similar to the rib fracture, with the exception that pain is localized in the junction of the rib cartilage and rib.

Symptoms and signs   The athlete complains of sharp pain during sudden movement of the trunk and has difficulty breathing deeply. There is point tenderness with swelling. In some cases, there is a rib deformity and a complaint that the rib makes a crepitus noise as it moves in and out of place.

Management   Like a rib fracture, the costochondral separation is managed by rest and immobilization by rib brace. Healing takes anywhere from one to two months and precludes any sports activities until the athlete is symptom free.

Sternum Fracture

Etiology   Fracture of the sternum results from a high impact blow to the chest. Sternum fractures are more likely to occur in automobile accidents than in athletics.[17] Injuries to the ribs or the costochondral junction are much more likely in the athlete. An impact severe enough to cause fracture of the sternum may also cause contusion to the underlying cardiac muscle.

Symptoms and signs   There may be point tenderness over the sternum at the site of the fracture that is exacerbated by deep inspiration or forceful expiration. Signs of shock or a weak, rapid pulse may indicate more severe internal injury.

Management   The athlete should be sent for X rays and should be closely monitored for signs of trauma to the heart.

Muscle Injuries

Etiology   The muscles of the thorax are all subject to contusions and strains in sports. The intercostals are especially vulnerable. Traumatic injuries occur most often from direct blows or sudden torsion of the athlete's trunk.

Symptoms and signs   Pain occurs on active motion. Injuries to muscles in this region, however, are particularly painful during inspiration and expiration, laughing, coughing, or sneezing.

Management   Care of thoracic muscle injuries requires immediate pressure and applications of cold for approximately one hour. After hemorrhaging has been controlled, immobilization should be used to make the athlete more comfortable.

Breast Injury

Etiology   Many female athletes can have breast problems in connection with their sports participation. Violent up-and-down and lateral movements of the breasts, such as are encountered in running and jumping, can bruise and strain the breast, especially in large-breasted women. Constant uncontrolled movement of the breast over a period of time can stretch the Cooper's ligament, which supports the breast at the chest wall, and lead to premature ptosis of the breasts (see Figure 7-14).

Another condition that occurs to the breasts is runner's nipples, in which the shirt rubs the nipples and causes an abrasion. Runner's nipples can be prevented by placing an adhesive bandage over each nipple before participation. Bicyclist's nipples occur as the result of a combination of cold and evaporation of sweat, which causes the nipples to become painful. Wearing a windbreaker can prevent this problem.[10]

Management   Female athletes should wear a well-designed bra that has minimum elasticity and allows little vertical or horizontal breast movement (see Figure 7-15).[14] Breast injuries usually occur during physical contact with either an opponent or equipment. In sports such as fencing or field hockey, female athletes should protect themselves by wearing plastic cup–type brassieres.

Breast Cancer

Breast cancer should be of great concern to all women. Breast cancer is the most common cancer in the female. To reduce the likelihood of breast cancer, women over twenty years of age should perform breast self-examinations every month and

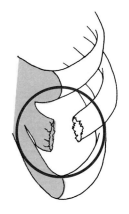

Figure 26-19

Costochondral separation.

have clinical examinations every three years. It must be stressed that a lump in the breast is not necessarily cancer. Many lumps are benign fibrous cysts. Except in women with increased risk, mammograms are not recommended until age forty.[34]

Injuries to the Lungs

Fortunately, injuries to the lungs resulting from sports trauma are rare.[38] However, because of the seriousness of this injury, the athletic trainer should be able to recognize the basic signs. The most serious of the conditions are pneumothorax, tension pneumothorax, hemothorax, or hemorrhaging into the lungs, and traumatic asphyxia.

Etiology

PNEUMOTHORAX   Pneumothorax is a condition in which the pleural cavity becomes filled with air that has entered through an opening in the chest (Figure 26-20A).[31] As the negatively pressured pleural cavity fills with air, the lung on that side collapses. The loss of one lung may produce pain, difficulty in breathing, and anoxia.[5]

TENSION PNEUMOTHORAX   A tension pneumothorax occurs when the pleural sac on one side fills with air and displaces the lung and the heart toward the opposite side, which compresses the opposite lung (Figure 26-20B).[37] There will be shortness of breath and chest pain on the side of the injury. There may be absence of breath sounds, cyanosis, and distention of neck veins. The trachea may deviate away from the side of injury. A total collapse of the opposite lung is possible; therefore, medical attention is required immediately.[16]

HEMOTHORAX   Hemothorax is the presence of blood within the pleural cavity (Figure 26-20C). It results from the tearing or puncturing of the lung or pleural tissue, which involves the blood vessels in the area. Like pneumothorax, hemothorax produces pain, difficulty in breathing, and cyanosis.

A violent blow or compression of the chest without an accompanying rib fracture may cause a lung hemorrhage. This condition results in severe pain during breathing, dyspnea (difficult breathing), coughing up of frothy blood, and signs of shock. If these signs are observed, the athlete should be treated for shock and immediately referred to a physician.

TRAUMATIC ASPHYXIA   Traumatic asphyxia occurs as the result of a violent blow to or a compression of the rib cage that causes a cessation of breathing.[18] Signs include purple discoloration of the upper trunk and head, and the conjunctivas of the eyes display a bright red color. A condition of this type demands immediate mouth-to-mouth resuscitation and medical attention.

Management

Each of these conditions is a medical emergency that requires immediate physician attention.[6] The athlete must be transported to a hospital emergency room as quickly as possible.

Heart Contusion

Etiology

A heart contusion may occur when the heart is compressed between the sternum and the spine by a strong outside force. Examples are if an athlete is hit by a pitched ball or bounces a barbell off the chest in a bench press. The right ventri-

---

Lung injuries can result in pneumothorax, tension pneumothorax, hemothorax, and traumatic asphyxia.

26-5

Critical Thinking E x e r c i s e

A lacrosse player is hit in the thorax with an opponent's stick. He has immediate localized pain over his ribs and within minutes begins to develop some respiratory difficulty. The athletic trainer suspects that the player has likely fractured a rib and is extremely concerned that the fracture has damaged the lungs.

? What lung injuries are possible, and how should this injury be managed?

Figure 26-20

A, Pneumothorax. **B,** Tension pneumothorax. **C,** Hemothorax.

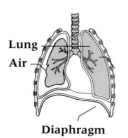
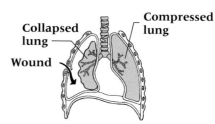
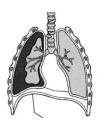

A

B

C

cle is most often injured. The most severe consequence of a violent impact to the heart would be a rupture of the aorta, which would be immediately life threatening.[40]

Symptoms and signs   This injury produces severe shock and heart pain. The heart may exhibit certain arrhythmias that cause a decrease in cardiac output, which is followed by death if medical attention is not administered immediately.[20]

Management   The athlete should be taken immediately to a hospital emergency room. The athletic trainer should be prepared to administer CPR and treat for shock.

Sudden Death Syndrome in Athletes

Etiology   It is indeed catastrophic when a young athlete dies suddenly for no apparent reason. It is estimated that 1 in 280,000 men under age thirty experience sudden death each year.[7] In athletes thirty-five years and younger, the most common cause of exercise-induced sudden death is some congenital cardiovascular abnormality.[36] The three most prevalent conditions are hypertrophic cardiomyopathy, anomalous origin of the coronary artery, and Marfan's syndrome.

Hypertrophic cardiomyopathy (HCM) is a condition in which there is thickened cardiac muscle, with no evidence of chamber enlargement, and extensive myocardial scarring. With this condition, there is an increased frequency of ventricular arrhythmia.[19] In an anomalous origin of the coronary artery, one of the two coronary vessels originates in a different site than normal, which compromises or obstructs that artery because of its unusual course. People with Marfan's syndrome have an abnormality of the connective tissue that results in a weakening of the structure of the aorta and cardiac valves, which can lead to a rupture of either a valve or the aorta itself.[36] Mitral valve prolapse has been associated with both HCM and Marfan's syndrome.[36]

Other potential cardiac causes of sudden death in athletes include coronary artery disease (CAD), which results from atherosclerosis, in which there is a narrowing of the coronary arteries that is usually due to hypercholesterolemia in the young athlete; right ventricular dysplasia, in which enlargement of the right ventricle causes a potentially lethal disturbance in heartbeat; cardiac conduction system abnormalities, which can result from abnormalities of the sinus or atrioventricular nodes; aortic stenosis, which is usually associated with a heart murmur that can cause a fall in blood pressure and cardiac collapse during exercise; Wolff-Parkinson-White syndrome, in which an abnormality in cardiac rhythm manifests itself as ventricular tachycardia; and myocarditis, an inflammation of the heart associated with a viral condition.[2,7,9,24,28,35]

Noncardiac causes of sudden death have been attributed to the use of certain drugs, including alcohol, cocaine, amphetamines, and erythropoietin (stimulates red blood cell production). A vascular event—bleeding in the brain caused by a cerebral aneurysm, for example, or head trauma that causes intracranial bleeding—may also result in sudden death. Obstructive respiratory diseases such as asthma can result in sudden death because of drug toxicity or undertreatment.[7]

Symptoms and signs   Common symptoms and signs associated with cardiac causes of sudden death include chest pain or discomfort during exertion, heart palpitations or flutters, syncope, nausea, profuse sweating, heart murmurs, shortness of breath, general malaise, and fever.[33]

Occasionally the symptoms and signs of athletic heart syndrome raise concern when there is no disease present.[3] Athletic heart syndrome is normal for any individual who is exercising. Like skeletal muscle, cardiac muscle will hypertrophy in response to exercise. It is characterized by a heart enlargement, a systolic heart murmur, slow heart rate, and electrocardiogram changes.

Prevention   It has been suggested that a major number of deaths could be avoided by counseling, screening, and early identification of preventable causes of sudden death.[15] Initial screening should include the following questions:

The most common causes of sudden death syndrome include hypertrophic cardiomyopathy, anomalous origin of the coronary artery, and Marfan's syndrome.

26-6

Critical Thinking Exercise

A basketball player collapses during a practice session when running sprints. The player is conscious and complains of chest pain, heart palpitations or flutters, syncope, nausea, profuse sweating, shortness of breath, and general malaise. The athletic trainer suspects some cardiac-related problem yet the player has no history of such a condition.

? What can cause these symptoms, and how can the athletic trainer provide the most appropriate and immediate care for this athlete?

- Has a physician ever told you that you have a heart murmur?
- Have you had chest pain during exercise?
- Have you fainted during exercise?
- Has anyone in your family under age thirty-five ever died suddenly?
- Has anyone in your family been diagnosed with a thickened heart?
- Does anyone in your family have Marfan's syndrome?

If the answer to any of these questions is yes, a more in-depth medical examination should be performed. Resting and exercise electrocardiograms and echocardiograms may be necessary to determine existing pathology.

Abdominal Injuries

Although abdominal injuries comprise only about 10 percent of sports injuries, they can require long recovery periods and can be life threatening.[8,12] The abdominal area is particularly vulnerable to injury in all contact sports. A blow can produce superficial or even deep internal injuries, depending on its location and intensity.[13] In internal injuries of the abdomen that occur in sports, the solid organs are most often affected. Strong abdominal muscles give good protection when they are tensed, but when relaxed, they are easily damaged. It is very important to protect the trunk region properly against the traumatic forces of collision sports. Good conditioning is essential, as is the use of proper protective equipment and the application of safety rules.

Injuries and Conditions Related to the Urinary System

Kidney Contusion

Etiology   The kidneys are seemingly well protected within the abdominal cavity. However, on occasion, contusions and even ruptures of these organs occur. The kidney may be susceptible to injury because of its normal distention by blood. An external force, usually one applied to the back of the athlete, will cause abnormal extension of an engorged kidney, resulting in injury. The degree of renal injury depends on the extent of the distention and the angle and force of the blow.[10]

Symptoms and signs   An athlete who has received a contusion of the kidney may display signs of shock, nausea, vomiting, rigidity of the back muscles, and hematuria (blood in the urine). Like injuries to other internal organs, kidney injuries may cause referred pain to the outside of the body. Pain may be felt high in the costovertebral angle posteriorly and may radiate forward around the trunk into the lower abdominal region. Any athlete who reports having received a severe blow to the abdomen or back region should be instructed to urinate two or three times and to look for the appearance of blood in the urine. If there is any sign of hematuria, immediate referral to a physician must be made.[34]

Management   Medical care of the contused kidney usually consists of a twenty-four-hour hospital observation and a gradual increase of fluid intake. If the hemorrhage fails to stop, surgery may be indicated. Controllable contusions usually require two weeks of bed rest and close surveillance after activity is resumed. In questionable cases, complete withdrawal from one active playing season may be required.

Kidney Stones

A kidney stone, or calculus, is usually composed of crystalline mineral salts (calcium, phosphate, uric acid) that form in the urinary tract. The cause of kidney stones is unknown. Kidney stones eventually pass through the urethra and are excreted. "Passing a kidney stone" is an extremely painful process.[34]

Contusion of the Ureters, Bladder, and Urethra

Etiology   On rare occasions, a blunt force to the lower abdominal region may avulse a ureter or contuse or rupture the urinary bladder. Injury to the urinary bladder usually occurs only if it is distended by urine. Hematuria is often associated with

Kidney and bladder contusions can cause hematuria.

26-7

Critical Thinking Exercise

A football receiver jumps to catch a high pass thrown over the middle. A defensive back hits the receiver in the low back. The athlete does not seem to have a specific injury. After the game, the player notices blood in the urine and gets really worried.

? Is blood in the urine a cause for concern? What should the athletic trainer do to manage this condition?

contusion of the bladder during running and has been referred to as a runner's bladder.[41] Abnormal concentrations of protein in urine is referred to as proteinuria. Injury to the urethra is more common in men, because the male's urethra is longer and more exposed than is the female's. Injury may produce severe perineal pain and swelling.

Symptoms and signs   After a severe blow to the pelvic region, the athlete may display the following recognizable signs: pain and discomfort in the lower abdomen; abdominal rigidity; nausea, vomiting, and signs of shock; blood coming from the urethra; and the passing of a great quantity of bloody urine, which indicates possible injury to the kidney. With a bladder contusion, the athlete will be able to urinate. With a bladder rupture, the athlete will be unable to urinate. Bladder injury commonly causes referred pain to the lower trunk, including the upper thigh anteriorly and suprapubically.

Prevention   With any impact to the abdominal region, the possibility of internal damage must be considered; after such trauma, the athlete should be instructed to check periodically for blood in the urine. To lessen the possibility of rupture, the athlete must always empty the bladder before practice or game time. The bladder can also be irritated by intraabdominal pressures during long-distance running. In this situation, repeated impacts to the bladder's base are produced by the jarring of the abdominal contents, resulting in hemorrhage and blood in the urine.

Cystitis

Cystitis is an inflammation of the bladder that most often occurs because of some urinary tract infection. The kidney, prostate, and urethra may also be involved. Acute cystitis causes frequent painful urination, chills, and fever. Antibiotics are used to treat cystitis.[32]

Urinary Tract Infections

Infection of the urinary tract (UTI) is usually caused by staphylococcus bacteria or chlamydia. It is much more likely to occur in females. UTI causes frequent, burning, painful urination and is treated with antibiotics. Athletes may prevent UTI by increasing fluid intake, practicing sanitary bowel and bladder habits, washing the genital area before intercourse, emptying the bladder after intercourse, and immediately removing contraceptive diaphragms and sponges following intercourse.[34]

Urethritis

Urethritis is an inflammation of the urethra that is most often caused by gonorrhea or occasionally by other, nongonococcal organisms. The symptoms include pain on urination along with a urethral discharge. Urethritis is treated by antibiotic therapy.[34]

Injuries and Conditions Related to the Digestive System

Like any other individual, the athlete may develop various complaints of the digestive system. The athlete may display various disorders of the gastrointestinal tract as a result of poor eating habits or the stress engendered from competition. The responsibility of the athletic trainer in such cases is to recognize the more severe conditions so that early referrals to a physician can be made.

Gastrointestinal Bleeding

Gastrointestinal bleeding that is reflected in bloody stools occurs in a variety of athletes. Distanmce runners often have blood in their stools during and following a race. The causes of gastrointestinal bleeding can vary. Possible reasons are gastritis, iron-deficiency anemia, ingestion of aspirin or other antiinflammatory agents, stress, bowel irritation, and colitis. Colitis is an inflammation of the colon, usually caused by an ulceration of the mucosal lining of the colon. Signs of colitis include abdominal pain with colic, watery stools that contain pus, dehydration, intermittent fever, and possible hemorrhage and perforation. Athletes displaying gastrointestinal bleeding must be referred immediately to a physician.[26]

Liver Contusion

Etiology   Compared to other organ injuries from blunt trauma, injuries to the liver rank second.[34] In sports activities, however, liver injury is relatively infrequent. A hard blow to the right side of the rib cage can tear or seriously contuse the liver, especially if it has been enlarged as a result of some disease, such as hepatitis. Hepatitis is an inflammation of the liver caused by either viral infection or alcohol consumption. If not corrected, hepatitis can lead to cirrhosis of the liver, in which liver function is impaired because liver cells die and are replaced by scar tissue.

Symptoms and signs   Liver injury can cause hemorrhage and shock, requiring immediate surgical intervention. Liver injury commonly produces a referred pain that is just below the right scapula, right shoulder, and substernal area and, on occasion, a referred pain located in the anterior left side of the chest.

Management   A liver contusion requires immediate referral to a physician for diagnosis and treatment.

Pancreatitis

Etiology   Inflammation of the pancreas may be acute or chronic and is often related to obstruction of the pancreatic duct. An acute inflammation leads to necrosis, suppuration, gangrene, and hemorrhage. Chronic inflammation results in formation of scar tissue that causes malfunction of the pancreas; inflammation may occur gradually from chronic alcoholism.[34]

Symptoms and signs   Acute epigastric pain causes vomiting, belching, constipation, and potentially, shock. There may also be tenderness and rigidity to palpation. Chronic pancreatitis causes jaundice, diarrhea, and mild to moderate pain that radiates to the back.

Management   Acute pancreatitis requires rehydration, pain reduction, treatment of shock, reduction of pancreatic secretions using medication, and prevention of secondary infection. Surgery would be indicated only if the pancreatic duct is blocked. Treatment of chronic pancreatitis is difficult and requires large doses of analgesics, administration of pancreatic enzymes, and a low-fat diet.

Indigestion (Dyspepsia)

Etiology   Some athletes have certain food idiosyncrasies that cause them considerable distress after eating. Others develop reactions when eating before competition. The term given to digestive upset is *indigestion* (dyspepsia). Indigestion can be caused by any number of conditions. The most common in sports are emotional stress, esophageal and stomach spasms, and/or inflammation of the mucous lining of the esophagus and stomach.

Symptoms and signs   Dyspepsia causes an increased secretion of hydrochloric acid (sour stomach), nausea, and flatulence (gas).

Management   Care of acute dyspepsia involves the elimination of irritating foods from the diet, development of regular eating habits, and avoidance of anxieties that may lead to gastric distress.

Constant irritation of the stomach may lead to chronic and more serious disorders, such as gastritis, an inflammation of the stomach wall, or ulcerations of the gastrointestinal mucosa. Athletes who appear nervous and high-strung and suffer from dyspepsia should be examined by the sports physician.

Vomiting

Etiology   Vomiting results from some type of irritation, most often in the stomach. This irritation stimulates the vomiting center in the brain to cause a series of forceful contractions of the diaphragm and abdominal muscles, thus compressing the stomach and forcefully expelling the contents.[30]

Hepatitis can cause enlargement of the liver.

Indigestion, vomiting, diarrhea, and constipation are common problems in the athlete.

Management   Antinausea medications should be administered (see Chapter 17). Fluids to prevent dehydration should be administered by mouth if possible. If vomiting persists, fluids and electrolytes must be administered intravenously.

Food Poisoning (Gastroenteritis)

Etiology   Food poisoning, which may range from mild to severe, results from infectious organisms (bacteria of the salmonella group, certain staphylococci, streptococci, or dysentery bacilli) that enter the body in either food or drink. Foods become contaminated, especially during warm weather, when improper food refrigeration permits the organisms to multiply rapidly. Contamination can also occur if the food is handled by an infected food handler.

Symptoms and signs   Infection results in nausea, vomiting, cramps, diarrhea, and anorexia. The symptoms of staphylococcal infections usually subside in three to six hours. Salmonella infection symptoms may last from twenty-four to forty-eight hours or more.

Management   Management requires rapid replacement of lost fluids and electrolytes, which, in severe cases, may need to be replaced intravenously. Bed rest is desirable in all but mild cases; as long as the nausea and vomiting continue, nothing should be given by mouth. If tolerated, light fluids or foods such as clear, strained broth, bouillon with a small amount of added salt, soft-cooked eggs, or bland cereals may be given.

Peptic Ulcer

Etiology   A peptic ulcer is a condition in which the acids secreted in the stomach destroy the mucous lining either in the stomach or the small intestine. Peptic ulcers most often occur in people who experience severe anxiety for long periods of time.[30]

Symptoms and signs   A gnawing pain, localized in the epigastric region, usually appears between one and three hours following a meal. Other symptoms include dyspepsia, heartburn, nausea, or vomiting. Pain usually lasts for minutes rather than hours.[34]

Management   Occasionally, symptoms may disappear without the aid of medication. Antacids may be helpful in neutralizing gastric secretions. Altering the diet has not proven to be effective in managing the peptic ulcer. If hemorrhaging or perforation occur, surgery may be necessary.

Diarrhea

Etiology   Diarrhea is abnormal stool looseness or passage of a fluid, unformed stool and is categorized as acute or chronic, according to the type present. Diarrhea can be caused by problems in diet, inflammation of the intestinal lining, gastrointestinal infection, ingestion of certain drugs, and psychogenic factors.[30]

Symptoms and signs   Diarrhea is characterized by abdominal cramps, nausea, and possibly vomiting, coupled with frequent elimination of stools, ranging from three to twenty a day. The infected person often has a loss of appetite and a light brown or gray, foul-smelling stool. Extreme weakness caused by fluid dehydration is usually present.

Management   The cause of diarrhea is often difficult to establish. The loose stool may be caused by any irritant, including an infestation of parasitic organisms or an emotional upset. Management of diarrhea requires a knowledge of its cause. The athletic trainer can care for less severe cases by having the athlete omit foods that cause irritation, drink boiled milk, eat bland food until symptoms have ceased, and use pectins two or three times daily for the absorption of excess fluid.

Constipation

Etiology   Some athletes are subject to constipation, which is the failure of the bowels to evacuate feces. There are numerous causes of constipation, the most common of which are lack of abdominal muscle tone; insufficient moisture in the feces, causing it to be hard and dry; lack of a sufficient proportion of roughage and bulk in the diet to stimulate peristalsis; poor bowel habits; nervousness and anxiety; and overuse of laxatives and enemas.[34]

Symptoms and signs　Constipation results in a feeling of fullness, with occasional cramping and pain in the lower abdomen. When the athlete strains hard to defecate, some vessels may be ruptured in the rectum and bleeding from the anus may occur.

Management　The best means of overcoming constipation is to regulate eating patterns to include foods that will encourage normal defecation. Cereals, fruits, vegetables, and fats stimulate bowel movement, whereas sugars and carbohydrates tend to inhibit it. Some persons become constipated as the result of psychological factors. In such cases, the athletic trainer may try to determine the causes of stress and, if need be, refer the athlete to a physician or school psychologist for counseling. Above all, laxatives or enemas should be avoided unless their use has been prescribed by a physician.

Appendicitis

Etiology　Inflammation of the vermiform appendix can be chronic or acute. It is caused by a variety of conditions, such as a fecal obstruction, lymph swelling, or even a carcinoid tumor. Its highest incidence is in males between the ages of fifteen and twenty-five. Appendicitis can be mistaken for a common gastric complaint. In early stages, the appendix becomes red and swollen; in later stages, it may become gangrenous, rupturing into the bowels or peritoneal cavity and causing peritonitis.[34] Bacterial infection is a complication of rupture of the inflamed appendix.

Symptoms and signs　The athlete may complain of a mild-to-severe pain in the lower abdomen, associated with nausea, vomiting, and a low-grade fever ranging from 99° to 100° F (37° to 38° C). Later, the cramps may localize into a pain in the right side, and palpation may reveal abdominal rigidity and tenderness at a point (McBurney's point) between the anterior superior spine of the ilium and the umbilicus, about 1 to 2 inches (2.5 to 5 cm) above the latter.[34]

A strain of the psoas muscle or an abcess in the sheath of the psoas can sometimes be mistaken for appendicitis.

Management　Surgical removal of the appendix is often necessary. If the bowel is not obstructed, there is no need to rush surgery. However, an obstructed bowel with an acute rupture is a life-threatening condition.

Hemorrhoids (Piles)

Etiology　Hemorrhoids are varicosities of the hemorrhoidal venous plexus of the anus. There are both internal and external anal veins. Chronic constipation or straining at the stool may stretch the anal veins, resulting in either a protrusion (prolapse) and bleeding of the internal or external veins or a thrombus in the external veins.

Symptoms and signs　Hemorrhoids are painful nodular swellings near the sphincter of the anus. They may cause slight bleeding and itching. The majority of hemorrhoids are self-limiting and spontaneously heal within two to three weeks.

Management　The management of hemorrhoids is mostly palliative and serves to eliminate discomfort until healing takes place. The following measures can be suggested: use of proper bowel habits, ingestion of one tablespoon of mineral oil daily to assist in lubricating dry stool, application of an astringent suppository (tannic acid), and application of a local anesthetic to control pain and itching (dibucaine). If palliative measures are unsuccessful, surgery may be required.

Injuries and Conditions Related to the Reproductive Organs

Injuries to the reproductive organs in sports are much more likely to occur in the male because the genitalia is more exposed.

Appendicitis is often mistaken for a common gastric problem.

26-8
Critical Thinking E x e r c i s e

Immediately after finishing a meal, a fencer begins to complain of a mild-to-severe pain in the lower abdomen. She has nausea, vomiting, and a low-grade fever. The athletic trainer suspects that she may have indigestion; in about an hour, however, the cramps begin to localize into a pain in the right side, and palpation reveals abdominal rigidity and tenderness at McBurney's point.

? What should the athletic trainer suspect is wrong with this athlete, and what will likely be necessary in management?

Injuries to the reproductive organs in sports are much more likely to occur in the male because the genitalia is more exposed.

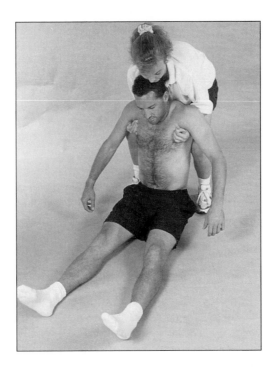

Figure 26-21

Position for reducing testicular spasm.

Scrotal Contusion

Etiology   As the result of its considerable sensitivity and particular vulnerability, the scrotum may sustain a contusion that causes a very painful, nauseating, and disabling condition.

Symptoms and signs   Like any other contusion or bruise, the scrotal contusion causes hemorrhage, fluid effusion, and muscle spasm, the degree of which depends on the intensity of the impact to the tissue.

Management   Immediately following a scrotal contusion, the athlete must be put at ease and testicular spasms must be reduced. The following technique is used to relieve testicular spasm. With the athlete in a sitting position, lift him a few inches and drop him to the ground (Figure 26-21). This maneuver will aid in reducing discomfort and relax the muscle spasm. After the pain has diminished, the athlete is helped from the playing area, and a cold pack is applied to the scrotum. Increasing or unresolved pain after fifteen to twenty minutes requires prompt referral to a physician for evaluation.

Spermatic Cord Torsion

Etiology   Torsion of the spermatic cord results from the testicle's revolving in the scrotum after a direct blow to the area or as a result of coughing or vomiting.

Symptoms and signs   Cord torsion produces acute testicular pain, nausea, vomiting, and inflammation in the area.

Management   In this case, the athlete must receive immediate medical attention to prevent irreparable complications. Twisting of the spermatic cord may present the appearance of a cluster of swollen veins and may cause a dull pain combined with a heavy, dragging feeling in the scrotum. This condition may eventually lead to atrophy of the testicle. A physician should be consulted when this condition is suspected.

Traumatic Hydrocele of the Tunica Vaginalis

Etiology   Traumatic hydrocele of the tunica vaginalis is an excess of fluid accumulation caused by a severe blow to the testicular region. The venous plexus on the posterior aspect of the testicle can become engorged, creating a varicocele. A rupture of this plexus results in a rapid accumulation of blood in the scrotum called a hematocele.

Symptoms and signs After trauma, the athlete complains of pain. Swelling in the scrotum can significantly increase the size of the sac.

Management Cold packs should be applied to the scrotum, and referral to the physician should be made. Irreversible damage can occur to the testicle if medical treatment is delayed.

Contusion of the Female Genitalia

The female reproductive organs have a low incidence of injury in sports. By far the most common gynecologic injury in the female athlete involves a contusion to the external genitalia, or vulva, which includes the labia, clitoris, and the vestibule of the vagina. A hematoma results from the contusion, which most often occurs with a direct impact to this area. A contusion of this area may also injure the pubic symphysis, producing osteitis pubis (discussed in Chapter 21).

Vaginitis

Etiology Vaginitis is an inflammation of the vagina that may be caused by a variety of microorganisms, many of which are associated with sexually transmitted diseases (STDs; discussed in Chapter 29). Other, non-STD causes may exist, however, including bacterial infection, strong chemicals from douching, irritation from a tampon, and poor hygiene habits.

Symptoms and signs There will be purulent (filled with pus) and, occasionally, bloody vaginal discharge. There may also be a strong odor with vaginal itching. Urination is frequent and painful. The vagina is red and painful to touch.

Management For vaginitis caused by an STD, appropriate antibiotic or antifungal medications should be given. The athlete should also be instructed in correct bowel and bladder hygiene and cleanliness and counseled regarding sexual behavior.

Injury to Lymphatic Organs

Injury of the Spleen

Etiology Injuries to the spleen are relatively uncommon. If injury does occur, it is most often due to a fall or a direct blow to the left upper quadrant of the abdomen (see Figure 13-3) when some existing medical condition has caused splenomegaly (enlargement of the spleen). Infectious mononeucleosis is the most likely cause of spleen enlargement. Athletes with mononeucleosis should not engage in any activity for three weeks because approximately 50 percent of sufferers exhibit splenomegaly, which is difficult to diagnose clinically (see Chapter 29).

Symptoms and signs The gross indications of a ruptured spleen must be recognized so that an immediate medical referral can be made. Indications include a history of a severe blow to the abdomen and possibly signs of shock, abdominal rigidity, nausea, and vomiting. There may be a reflex pain occurring approximately thirty minutes after injury, called Kehr's sign, which radiates to the left shoulder and one-third of the way down the left arm.

Complications The great danger with a ruptured spleen lies in its ability to splint itself and then produce a delayed hemorrhage. Splinting of the spleen is effected by a loose hematoma formation and the constitution of the supporting and surrounding structures. Any slight strain may disrupt the splinting effect and allow the spleen to hemorrhage profusely into the abdominal cavity, causing the athlete to die of internal bleeding days or weeks after the injury.[1]

Management Conservative, nonoperative treatment is recommended initially with a week of hospitalization.[23] At three weeks, the athlete can engage in light conditioning activities, and at four weeks, the athlete can return to full activity as long as no symptoms appear. If surgical repair is necessary, the athlete will require three

26-9
Critical Thinking Exercise

A baseball player is hit with a pitch in the left upper quadrant. Initially he appears to be all right, but toward the end of the game, he becomes nauseous and starts to vomit. He complains of pain in the left upper quadrant and also pain in his left shoulder extending down his arm. The athletic trainer palpates the abdomen and detects rigidity. Within a matter of minutes, the player begins to develop shock-like symptoms.

? What should the athletic trainer suspect has happened to this athlete, and how should the injury be treated?

Infectious mononeucleosis can cause spleen enlargement.

Athletes who complain of external pain in the shoulders, trunk, or pelvis after a severe blow to the abdomen or back may be describing referred pain from an injury to an internal organ.

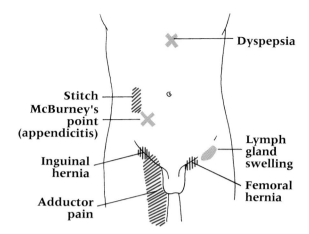

Figure 26-22

Common sites of abdominal pain.

months to recover, whereas removal of the spleen will require six months before the athlete can return to activity.

Injuries to the Abdominal Wall

A number of other abdominal pain sites can be disabling to the athlete. The athletic trainer should be able to discern the pain sites that are potentially more serious and refer the athlete accordingly. Figure 26-22 shows some of the pain sites in the abdomen.

Abdominal Muscle Strains

Sudden twisting of the trunk or reaching overhead can tear an abdominal muscle. These injuries can be very incapacitating, with severe pain and hematoma formation. The rectus abdominus is the most commonly strained abdominal muscle. Initially, ice and an elastic compression wrap should be used. Treatment should be conservative, with exercise staying within pain-free limits.

Contusions of the Abdominal Wall

Etiology   Compressive forces that injure the abdominal wall are not common in sports. When they do happen, they are more likely to occur in collision sports such as football or ice hockey; however, any sports implements or high-velocity projectiles can injure. Hockey goalies and baseball catchers would be very vulnerable to injury without their protective torso pads. Contusion may occur superficially to the abdominal skin or subcutaneous tissue or much deeper to the musculature. The extent and type of injury vary, depending on whether the force is blunt or penetrating.

Symptoms and signs   A contusion of the rectus abdominis muscle can be very disabling. A severe blow may cause a hematoma that develops under the fascial tissue surrounding this muscle. The pressure that results from hemorrhage causes pain and tightness in the region of the injury.

Management   A cold pack and a compression elastic wrap should be applied immediately after injury. Signs of possible internal injury must also be looked for.

Hernia

Etiology   The term *hernia* refers to the protrusion of abdominal viscera through a portion of the abdominal wall. Hernias may be congenital or acquired. A congenital hernial sac is developed before birth, and an acquired hernia develops after birth. Structurally, a hernia has a mouth, a neck, and a body. The mouth, or hernial ring, is the opening from the abdominal cavity into the hernial protusion; the neck is the portion of the sac that joins the hernial ring and the body. The body is the sac that protrudes outside the abdominal cavity and contains portions of the abdominal organs.[21]

Inguinal hernias usually occur in males; femoral hernias usually occur in females.

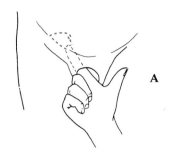

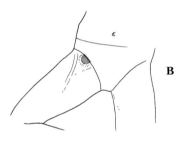

Figure 26-23

A, Inguinal hernia. **B,** Femoral hernia.

A blow to the solar plexus can lead to transitory paralysis of the diaphragm and to unconsciousness.

Hernias resulting from sports most often occur in the groin area. Inguinal hernias (Figure 26-23A), which occur in men (more than 75%), and femoral hernias (Figure 26-23B), most often occurring in women, are the most prevalent types. Externally, the inguinal and femoral hernias appear similar because of the groin protrusion, but a considerable difference is indicated internally. The inguinal hernia results from an abnormal enlargement of the opening of the inguinal canal, through which the vessels and nerves of the male reproductive system pass. In contrast, the femoral hernia arises in the canal that transports the vessels and nerves that go to the thigh and lower limb.[21]

Under normal circumstances, the inguinal and femoral canals are protected by muscle control against abnormal opening. When intraabdominal tension affects these areas, muscles produce contractions around these canal openings. If the muscles fail to react or if they prove inadequate in their shutter action, abdominal contents may be pushed through the opening. Repeated protrusions serve to stretch and increase the size of the opening. Most physicians think that any athlete who has a hernia should be prohibited from engaging in hard physical activity until surgical repair has been made.

One danger of a hernia in an athlete is the possibility that it may become irritated by falls or blows. Besides the hernial aggravations caused by trauma, another concern that athletic trainers need to be aware of is the development of a strangulated hernia, in which the inguinal ring constricts the protruding sac and occludes normal blood circulation. If the strangulated hernia is not surgically repaired immediately, gangrene and death may ensue.

Symptoms and signs   The acquired hernia occurs when a natural weakness is further aggravated by either a strain or a direct blow. Athletes may develop this condition as the result of violent activity. An acquired hernia may be recognized by the following signs: previous history of a blow or strain to the groin area that has produced pain and prolonged discomfort, superficial protrusion in the groin area that is increased by coughing, or reported feeling of weakness and pulling sensation in the groin area.

Management   The treatment preferred by most physicians is surgery. Mechanical devices, which prevent hernial protrusion, are for the most part unsuitable in sports because of the friction and irritation they produce. Exercise has been thought by many to be beneficial to a mild hernia, but such is not the case. Exercise will not affect the stretched inguinal or femoral canals positively.

Blow to the Solar Plexus

Etiology   A blow to the sympathetic celiac plexus (solar plexus) produces a transitory paralysis of the diaphragm ("wind knocked out").

Symptoms and signs   Paralysis of the diaphragm stops respiration and leads to anoxia. When the athlete is unable to inhale, hysteria because of fear may result. These symptoms are usually transitory. It is necessary to allay such fears and instill confidence in the athlete.

Management   In dealing with an athlete who has had the wind knocked out of him or her, the athletic trainer should adhere to the following procedures: help the athlete overcome apprehension by talking in a confident manner; loosen the athlete's belt and the clothing around the abdomen; have the athlete bend the knees; and encourage the athlete to relax by initiating short inspirations and long expirations.

Because of the fear of not being able to breathe, the athlete may hyperventilate. Hyperventilation is an increased rate of ventilation that results in a lowered carbon dioxide level. It causes a variety of physical reactions, such as dizziness, a lump in the throat, pounding heart, and fainting.

The athletic trainer should always be concerned that a blow hard enough to knock out the wind could also cause internal organ injury.

Stitch in the Side

Etiology   A "stitch in the side" is the name given an idiopathic condition that occurs in some athletes. The cause is obscure, although several hypotheses have been advanced. Among these possible causes are the following: constipation, intestinal gas, overeating, diaphragmatic spasm as a result of poor conditioning, lack of visceral support because of weak abdominal muscles, distended spleen, breathing techniques that lead to a lack of oxygen in the diaphragm, and ischemia of either the diaphragm or the intercostal muscles.

Signs and symptoms   A stitch in the side is a cramplike pain that develops on either the left or right costal angle during hard physical activity. Sports that involve running apparently produce this condition.

Management   Immediate care of a stitch in the side demands relaxation of the spasm, for which two methods have proved beneficial. First, the athlete is instructed to stretch the arm on the affected side as high as possible. If this method is inadequate, flexing the trunk forward on the thighs may prove of some benefit.

Athletes with recurrent abdominal spasms may need special study. The identification of poor eating habits, poor elimination habits, or an inadequate athletic training program may explain the athlete's particular problem. A stitch in the side, although not considered serious, may require further evaluation by a physician if abdominal pains persist.

SUMMARY

- Injuries to the heart, lungs, and abdominal viscera can be potentially serious and even life threatening if not recognized and managed appropriately.

- The thorax is that portion of the body commonly known as the chest, which lies between the base of the neck and the diaphragm. Its main functions are to protect the vital respiratory and circulatory organs and to assist the lungs in inspiration and expiration during the breathing process. Within the thoracic cage lie the lungs, the heart, and the thymus.

- The abdominal cavity lies between the diaphragm and the bones of the pelvis and is bounded by the margin of the lower ribs, the abdominal muscles, and the vertebral column. The abdominal viscera are composed of both hollow and solid organs. Organs in the abdominal cavity may be classified as being part of the urinary system, the digestive system, the reproductive system, or the lymphatic system.

- The primary survey by the athletic trainer who is evaluating an injury to the abdomen or thorax should focus on those signs and symptoms that indicate some life-threatening condition. Asking pertinent questions, observing body positioning, and palpation of the injured structures are critical in assessing the nature of the injury.

- Rib fractures and contusions, costochondral junction separations, sternum fractures, muscle strains, and breast injuries are all common injuries to the chest wall.

- Injuries involving the lungs include pneumothorax, tension pneumothorax, hemothorax, and traumatic asphyxia.

- The most common cause of exercise-induced sudden death is some congenital cardiovascular abnormality. The three most prevalent conditions are hypertrophic cardiomyopathy, anomalous origin of the coronary artery, and Marfan's syndrome.

- With any injury to the abdominal region, internal injury to the abdominal viscera must be considered. Injuries to the liver, spleen, and kidneys are among the more common injuries to the abdominal viscera associated with athletics.

- A number of conditions of the digestive system, such as diarrhea, constipation, and gastroenteritis, commonly affect the athletic population.

26-10

Critical Thinking Exercise

A wrestler is engaged in a strenuous off-season weight-lifting program. Recently he has begun to experience pain in his groin. It seems that whenever he strains hard to lift a weight and especially if he holds his breath, the pain appears. He is concerned that he has developed a hernia.

? What symptoms and signs should the athletic trainer look for that would indicate that the athlete does in fact have a hernia?

26-11

Critical Thinking Exercise

A cross-country runner complains of a recurring stitch in the side. She has a cramplike pain that develops on the left costal angle during a hard run. She indicates that when she stops running, the cramp disappears, but it comes back when she starts to run again.

? What can the athletic trainer recommend that might help this runner alleviate this problem?

- Injuries to the reproductive organs in sports are much more likely to occur in the male because the genitalia is more exposed.
- Injuries to the abdominal wall include muscle strains, getting the wind knocked out, and the development of an inguinal or femoral hernia.

Web Sites

Acute Appendicitis: http://www.healthanswers.com/database/ami/converted/000256.html

Anatomy of the Human Body: http://rpiwww.midacc.tmc.edu/mmlearn/anatomy.html

Chest Trauma: http://www.madsci.com/manu/trau_che.htm#30

A description of myocardial contusion, flail chest, hemothorax, and pneumothorax are included in this site.

National Heart, Lung, and Blood Institute: http://www.nhlbi.nih.gov/nhlbi/nhlbi.htm

Solutions to Critical Thinking EXERCISES

26-1 The athletic trainer should be concerned about the possibility of injury to an organ that can potentially lead to internal blood loss and eventually result in shock. It is possible that the spleen, liver, stomach, small intestine, pancreas, or gallbladder may all be injured. It is also possible that there may be a contusion to the muscles of the abdominal wall that is causing muscle guarding.

26-2 To palpate the abdominal structures, the athlete should be supine with the hips and knees flexed. An athlete with an abdominal injury will voluntarily contract the abdominal muscles to guard or protect the tender area. If there is bleeding or irritation inside the abdominal cavity, the abdomen will exhibit boardlike rigidity and cannot be voluntarily relaxed. The athletic trainer can produce rebound tenderness by pressing firmly on the abdomen and then quickly releasing pressure, which causes intense pain.

26-3 The athletic trainer should know what sounds are normal and be able to determine when something sounds abnormal. Abnormal breathing sounds are often superimposed on normal breathing sounds. Adventitious breath sounds are those that are not normally heard and may be either continuous music-like sounds with a high pitch, called wheezes or rhonchi, or crackling or bubbling sounds, called rales.

26-4 The athletic trainer should palpate along the rib, in the intercostal space between the ribs, and at the costochondral junction to locate a specific point of tenderness. The athletic trainer should also apply anterioposterior compression to the thoracic cage to identify potential rib fractures. If the athlete complains of increased pain or tenderness on transverse compression applied laterally to the rib cage, a costochondral injury is more likely.

26-5 Injuries severe enough to cause a rib fracture might also result in pneumothorax, tension pneumothorax, hemothorax, or traumatic asphyxia. Any of these conditions should be considered life threatening, and the athletic trainer should access the rescue squad immediately. The trainer should also be prepared to initiate CPR if indicated.

26-6 Potential causes could include myocardial infarction, hypertrophic cardiomyopathy, Marfan's syndrome, coronary artery disease resulting from atherosclerosis, right ventricular dysplagia, cardiac conduction system abnormalities, aortic stenosis, or myocarditis. All these causes have been attributed to sudden death syndrome in athletes. The athletic trainer is dealing with a life-threatening situation and must seek emergency medical care as soon as possible.

26-7 Anytime blood appears in the urine, there is cause for concern. In this case it is likely that the kidneys have been contused, and the blood that appears in the urine will usually disappear over the next couple of days. Nevertheless, the athlete should be referred to the team physician for diagnosis.

26-8 It is possible that the athlete has an inflamed veriform appendix. Most often, surgical removal of the appendix is necessary. Occasionally, an inflamed appendix results from an obstructed bowel. A rupture of the appendix because of bowel obstruction becomes a life-threatening emergency.

26-9 The athlete is exhibiting the symptoms and signs of a ruptured spleen. The spleen has the ability to splint itself and stop hemorrhage. However, because of the potential of shock, the athletic trainer should treat this injury as life threatening. Usually, treatment will be conservative and involve brief hospitalization, but surgical management is necessary when the spleen has ruptured and is hemorrhaging.

26-10 Most often the athlete will have some previous history of a blow or strain to the groin area that has produced pain and prolonged discomfort. There may be a superficial protrusion in the groin area that is increased when the athlete coughs, or the athlete may experience a feeling of weakness and a pulling sensation in the groin area. An inguinal hernia results from an abnormal enlargement of the opening of the inguinal canal through which the abdominal contents may be pushed.

26-11 The athletic trainer should try to modify the athlete's eating habits, which might produce constipation or gas. Cramps can be caused by improper breathing techniques, which may cause a lack of oxygen in the diaphragm and ischemia of either the diaphragm or the intercostal muscles. Cramps may also be caused by diaphragmatic spasm that results from poor conditioning or by a lack of visceral support because of weak abdominal muscles. Athletes with recurrent abdominal spasms should have further evaluation by a physician if abdominal pains persist.

REVIEW QUESTIONS AND CLASS ACTIVITIES

1. Describe the anatomy of the thorax.
2. Differentiate among rib contusions, rib fractures, and costochondral separations.
3. Compare the signs of pneumothorax, tension pneumothorax, hemothorax, and traumatic asphyxia.

4. Identify the possible causes of sudden death syndrome among athletes.

5. List the abdominal viscera and other structures associated with the urinary system, the digestive system, the lymphatic system, and the reproductive system.

6. What muscles protect the abdominal viscera?

7. What conditions of the abdominal viscera produce pain in the abdominal region?

8. Contrast the signs of a ruptured spleen with the signs of a severely contused kidney.

9. What are the most common sports injuries and conditions related to the digestive system?

10. How do you manage an athlete who has had his or her wind knocked out?

11. Distinguish an inguinal hernia or a femoral hernia from a groin strain.

12. Describe the signs of a stitch in the side.

REFERENCES

1. Affleck TP: Severe sports-related spleen injury: Not all patients require surgery, *Physician Sportsmed* 20(9):109, 1992.

2. Allison T: Counseling athletes at risk for sudden death, *Physician Sportsmed* 20(6):140, 1992.

3. Alpert J, Pape L, Ward A: Athletic heart syndrome, *Physician Sportsmed* 17(7):103, 1989.

4. Bergman RT: Assessing acute abdominal pain: a team physician's challenge, *Physician Sportsmed* 26(4):72, 1996.

5. Cvengros RD, Lazor JA: Pneumothorax—a medical emergency, *J Ath Train* 31(2):167, 1996.

6. Erickson SM, Rich BS: Pulmonary and chest wall emergencies: Onsite treatment of potentially fatal conditions, *Physician Sportsmed* 23(11):95, 1995.

7. Falsetti H: Sudden death syndrome, *Training and Conditioning* 5(3):26, 1995.

8. Fillion DT: Abdominal injuries: subtle symptoms may indicate a serious condition, *Sports Med Update* 12(3):12, 1997.

9. Franklin BA, Fletcher GF, Gordon NF: Cardiovascular evaluation of the athlete: issues regarding performance, screening, and sudden cardiac death, *Sports Med* 26(2):97, 1997.

10. Freitas JE: Renal imaging following blunt trauma, *Physician Sportsmed* 17(12):59, 1989.

11. Hammond S: Chest injuries in the trauma patient, *Nurs Clin N Amer* 25(1):35, 1990.

12. Haycock CE: Abdominal injuries. In Fu FH, Stone DA, editors: *Sports injuries: mechanisms, prevention, and treatment*, Baltimore, Md, 1994, Williams & Wilkins.

13. Haycock CE: How I manage abdominal injuries, *Physician Sportsmed* 14(6):86, 1986.

14. Haycock CE: How I manage breast problems in athletes, *Physician Sportsmed* 15(3):89, 1987.

15. Herbert DL: Preparticipation cardiovascular screening: toward a national standard, *Physician Sportsmed* 25(3):112, 1997.

16. Johnson MB, Haines M, Barry B: Recognizing pneumothorax—a case study, *Athletic Therapy Today* 1(6):42, 1996.

17. Jones H, McBride G, Murphy R: Sternal fractures associate with spinal injury, *J Trauma* 29(3):360, 1989.

18. Lee M, Wong S, Chu J: Traumatic asphyxia, *Ann Thoracic Surg* 51(1):86, 1991.

19. Maron B: Hypertrophic cardiomyopathy in athletes: catching a killer, *Physician Sportsmed* 21(9):83, 1993.

20. Maron B, Liviu C, Kaplan J, Mueller F: Blunt trauma to the chest leading to sudden death from cardiac arrest during sports activities, *N Engl J Med* 333(6):337, 1995.

21. McCarthy P: Hernias in athletes: what you need to know, *Physician Sportsmed* 18(5):115, 1990.

22. Miles J, Barrett G: Rib fractures in athletes, *Sports Med* 12(1):66, 1991.

23. Morden R, Berman B, Nagle C: Spleen injury in sports: avoiding splenectomy, *Physician Sportsmed*, 20(4):126, 1992.

24. Newsham KR: Exertional chest pain in an intercollegiate athlete, *J Ath Train* 32(1):59, 1997.

25. Ray R, Lemire JE: Liver laceration in an intercollegiate football player, *J Ath Train* 30(4):326, 1995.

26. Reid D: *Sports injury assessment*, New York, 1992, Churchill & Livingstone.

27. Reut R, Bach B, Johnson C: Pectoralis major rupture, *Physician Sportsmed* 19(3):89, 1991.

28. Rink LD: Cardiac problems and sudden death in athletes. In Baker CL et. al., editors: *The Hughston Clinic sports medicine book*, Baltimore, 1995, Williams & Wilkins.

29. Saladin K: Anatomy and physiology: the unity of form and function, Dubuque, IA, 1998, WCB/McGraw-Hill.

30. Seeley R, Stephens T, Tate P: *Anatomy and physiology*, ed 3, St Louis, 1995, Mosby.

31. Simoneauz S, Murphy B, Tehranzadeh J: Spontaneous pneumothorax in a weight lifter, *Am J Sports Med* 18(6):647, 1990.

32. *Stedman's concise medical dictionary for the health professions*, Baltimore, 1997, Williams & Wilkins.

33. Steine H: Chest pain and shortness of breath in a collegiate basketball player: case report and literature review, *Med Sci Sports Exerc* 26:504, 1992.

34. *Taber's cyclopedic medical dictionary*, Philadelphia, 1997, FA Davis.

35. Van Camp S: Sudden death. In Puffer J, editor: *Clinics in sports medicine*, Philadelphia, 1992, Saunders.

36. Van Camp S, Bloor C, Mueller F: Nontraumatic sports death in high school and college athletes, *Med Sci Sports Exerc* 27(9):641, 1995.

37. Volk CP, McFarland EG, Horsmon G: Pneumothorax: on-field recognition, *Physician Sportsmed* 23(10):43, 1995.

38. Wagner R, Sidhu G, Radcliffe W: Pulmonary contusion in contact sports, *Physician Sportsmed* 20(2): 126, 1992.

39. Widner PE: Thoracic injuries: mechanisms, characteristics, management, *Ath Train* 23(2):148, 1988.

40. Yates M, Aldrete V: Blunt trauma causing aortic rupture, *Physician Sportsmed* 19(11):96, 1991.

41. York J: Bladder trauma from jogging, *Physician Sportsmed* 18(9):116, 1990.

ANNOTATED BIBLIOGRAPHY

Taber's cyclopedic medical dictionary, Philadelphia, 1997, FA Davis.

Despite the dictionary format, this guide is excellent for the athletic trainer who is searching for clear, concise descriptions of various injuries and illnesses accompanied by brief recommendations for management and treatment.

Seeley R, Stephens T, Tate P: *Anatomy and physiology*, ed 3, St Louis, 1995, Mosby.

This anatomy text helps clarify anatomy of the various systems of the abdomen and thorax and also provides clinical correlations for specific injuries and illnesses.

The Head, Face, Eyes, Ears, Nose, and Throat

When you finish this chapter you should be able to

- Describe the anatomy of the head, face, eyes, ears, nose, and throat.
- Explain how injuries to the head, face, eyes, ears, nose, and throat can be prevented.
- Discuss the assessment process in dealing with injuries to the head and face.
- Discuss recognition and management of concussions and mild head injuries.
- Recognize common injuries to the face, eyes, ears, nose, and throat.

Injuries to the region of the head, face, eyes, ears, nose, and throat are common in sports. The severity of injuries to this region can vary from something as benign as a nosebleed to severe concussions of the cortex.

PREVENTION OF INJURIES TO THE HEAD, FACE, EYES, EARS, NOSE, AND THROAT

Although injuries to the head and face are more prevalent in collision and contact sports, the potential for head injuries exists in all sports (Table 27-1).[23] The use of helmets or protective headgear and, in some instances, face masks in sports like football, ice hockey, lacrosse, wrestling, and baseball has dramatically reduced the incidence of injuries to the head, face, eyes, ears, and nose. Some have argued that if the face mask were eliminated in a sport like football, the number of cervical spine and head injuries would be reduced, because the athlete would be less likely to use the head when making contact. It is certain, however, that the incidence of injuries to the face, eyes, ears, and nose would significantly increase. A helmet can do only so much in preventing injury to the brain.

Unquestionably, the single most important consideration in reducing injuries to this region is to teach the athletes to use correct techniques when initiating contact. All football helmets have written warnings that discourage the use of the head as a weapon. The athletic trainer has a responsibility to make certain that coaches are teaching and athletes are using correct and safe techniques.

THE HEAD

Head injuries occur from direct and blunt forces to the skull. It is estimated that at least thirty to forty major head injuries and occasionally a death occur during sport-related activities each year.[41]

TABLE 27-1 Sports with a High Risk for Head Injury[23]

Boxing	Wrestling	Motorcycle racing
Football	Soccer	Diving
Ice hockey	Auto racing	Bicycling
Martial arts	Equestrian events	Snow skiing
Rugby		

Anatomy

Bones

The skull is composed of twenty-two bones. With the single exception of the mandible, all the bones of the skull are joined together in immovable joints called sutures. The cranial vault, which houses the brain, is enclosed by the cranium, or skull, and is made up of the frontal, ethmoid, sphenoid, two parietal, two temporal, and occipital bones. The skull's thickness varies in different locations; it is thinner over the temporal regions (Figure 27-1).[41]

Scalp

The scalp is the covering of the skull. It has five layers of soft tissue. The skin, connective tissue, and aponeurosis epicranalis are the three outermost tissue layers. They are fused and move as a single layer. The aponeurosis epicranalis is a thick connective tissue sheet that acts as an attachment for the occipitalis and frontalis muscles. Between the first three tissue layers and the periosteum lies a loose connective tissue layer.[41]

Brain

The *brain,* or encephalon, is the part of the central nervous system that is contained within the bony cavity of the cranium and is divided into four sections. The *cerebrum* is the largest part of the brain and is divided into two hemispheres that are separated by a deep longitudinal fissure. The cerebrum, also referred to as the *cortex,* coordinates all voluntary muscle activities and interprets sensory impulses in addition to controlling higher mental functions, including memory, reasoning, intelligence, learning, judgment, and emotions. The *cerebellum* controls synergistic movements of skeletal muscle and plays a critical role in the coordination of voluntary muscular movements. The *pons* controls sleep, posture, respiration, swallowing, and the bladder. The *medulla oblongata* is the lowest part of the brain stem and regulates heart rate, breathing, and blood pressure as well as coughing, sneezing, and vomiting.[43]

Meninges

Investing the spinal cord and the brain are the *meninges,* which are the three membranes that protect the brain and the spinal cord. Outermost is the dura mater, consisting of a dense, fibrous, and inelastic sheath that encloses the brain and cord. In some places it is attached directly to the vertebral canal, but for the most part, a layer of fat that contains the vital arteries and veins separates this membrane from the bony wall and forms the epidural space. The arachnoid, an extremely delicate

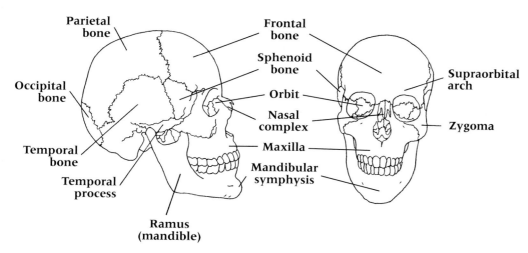

Figure 27-1

Bones of the skull and face.

Figure 27-2

The scalp and meningeal membranes covering the brain.

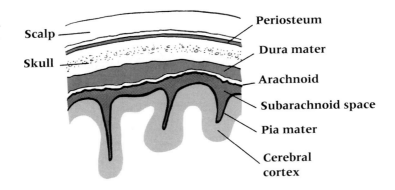

sheath, lines the dura mater and is attached directly to the spinal cord by many silk-like tissue strands. The space between the arachnoid and the pia mater, the membrane that helps contain the spinal fluid, is called the *subarachnoid space*. The subarachnoid cavity projects upward and, running the full length of the spinal cord, connects with the ventricles of the brain. The pia mater is a thin, delicate, and highly vascularized membrane that adheres closely to the spinal cord and to the brain (Figure 27-2).[43]

Cerebrospinal fluid is contained between the arachnoid and the pia mater membrane and completely surrounds and suspends the brain. Its main function is to act as a cushion, helping diminish the transmission of shocking forces.

Assessment of Head Injuries

An athlete who receives either a direct blow to the head or body contact that causes the head to snap forward, backward, or rotate to the side must be carefully evaluated for injury to the brain. Injuries to the brain may or may not result in unconsciousness; disorientation or amnesia; motor, coordination, or balance deficits; and cognitive deficits.

The Unconscious Athlete

On-the-field management of the unconscious athlete was discussed in detail in Chapter 12. The athletic trainer must be adept at recognizing and interpreting the signs that an unconscious athlete presents. Priority first aid for any head injury must always deal with any life-threatening condition, but in particular with loss of breathing. When assessing an unconscious athlete, the athletic trainer must always suspect a cervical neck injury and manage the situation accordingly, as described in Chapter 12.[9] An athlete who has been unconscious should be removed from the field on a spine board.

If no life-threatening condition exists, the athletic trainer should note the length of time that the athlete is unconscious and should not move the athlete until consciousness is regained. Once the athlete regains consciousness, or if the athlete never lost consciousness, the athletic trainer should obtain a history from the athlete.

If neck injuries are suspected in the unconscious athlete, the jaw is brought forward but the neck is not hyperextended to clear the airway.

History

An athlete who has sustained a head injury may or may not be able to respond to questions about exactly what happened to cause the loss of consciousness. Nevertheless, the following questions should be asked:
- Do you know where you are?
- Can you tell me what happened to you?
- Can you remember if you have ever been knocked out before?
- Does your head hurt?
- Do you have any pain in your neck?
- Can you move your hands and feet?

Observation

The athletic trainer who is usually around the athlete both on and off the field has the advantage of knowing what the athlete's affect is normally like and how he or she normally acts. The following observations should be made:

- Is the athlete disoriented and unable to tell where he or she is, what time it is, what date it is, who the opponent is?
- Is there a blank or vacant stare? Is there difficulty keeping the eyes open?
- Is there slurred or incoherent speech?
- Are there delayed verbal and motor responses (slow to answer questions or follow instructions)?
- Is there gross disturbance to coordination (i.e., stumbling, inability to walk a straight line, can't touch finger to nose)?
- Is there an inability to focus attention, and is the athlete easily distracted?
- Does there appear to be a memory deficit exhibited by the repeated asking of the same questions or no knowledge of what happened?
- Does the athlete have normal cognitive function (serial 7s, assignment on a particular play)?
- Is there a normal emotional response from the athlete?
- How long was the athlete's affect abnormal?
- Is there any swelling or bleeding from the scalp?
- Is there a clear or straw-colored fluid in the ear canal (cerebrospinal fluid that would occur with skull fracture)?

Palpation

Palpation of the skull should be performed in a systematic manner to identify areas of point tenderness or deformity to the skull that may indicate the presence of a skull fracture.

Special Tests

Neurologic exam   In all cases of head injury, the athletic trainer should administer an on-the-field neurological exam. The neurological exam was discussed in detail in Chapter 13. It consists of five major areas: cerebral testing, which assesses cognitive function; cranial nerve testing; cerebellar testing, which assesses coordination and motor function; sensory testing; and reflex testing.

Eye function   Abnormal function of the eyes is often related to head injury. The following conditions should be tested:

1. Pupils equal and reactive to light (PEARL).
   a. Dilated or irregular pupils. Checking pupil sizes may be particularly difficult at night and under artificial lights. To ensure accuracy, the athlete's pupil size should be compared with that of an official or another player present. It should be remembered, however, that some individuals normally have pupils that differ in size.[50]
   b. Inability of the pupils to accommodate rapidly to light variance. The evaluator can test eye accommodation by covering one eye of the athlete with a hand. The covered eye normally will dilate, whereas the uncovered pupil will remain the same. When the hand is removed, the previously covered pupil normally will accommodate readily to the light. A slow-accommodating pupil may be an indicator of cerebral injury.[50]
2. Eyes track smoothly. The athlete is asked to hold the head in a neutral position, eyes looking straight ahead. The athlete is then asked to follow the top of a pen or pencil, first up as far as possible, then down as far as possible. The eyes are observed for smooth movement and any signs of pain. Next, the tip of the pen or pencil is slowly moved from left to right to determine whether the eyes follow the tip smoothly across the midline of the face or whether they

27-1
Critical Thinking Exercise

An athlete falls and hits her head, incurring a possible cerebral injury.

? Initially, what observational signs may indicate a cerebral injury?

27-2
Critical Thinking Exercise

A football player sustains a cerebral concussion during a game.

? How should the athletic trainer determine the athlete's level of orientation and memory?

Checking eye signs can yield crucial information about possible brain injury.

Figure 27-3

A tandem Rhomberg test standing on an unstable foam surface.

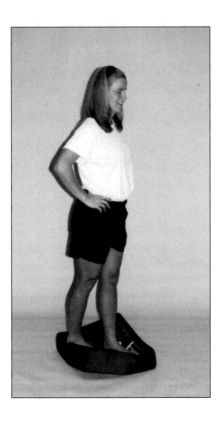

make involuntary movements. A constant involuntary back and forth, up and down, or rotary movement of the eyeball is called *nystagmus* and indicates possible cerebral involvement.[14]

3. Vision blurred. The evaluator can test for blurred vision by determining if the athlete has difficulty reading or is unable to read a game program or the scoreboard.

Balance tests If the athlete is capable of standing, a Rhomberg test can be used to assess static balance. The original test had the athlete shut the eyes and stand erect with the hands at the side. A positive sign is one in which the athlete begins to sway, cannot keep the eyes closed, or obviously loses balance.

There have been several variations and modifications to the original Rhomberg test, most involving changes in foot positions during static stance to alter the base of support. The most commonly used variations involve a single leg stance and a tandem (heel to toe) stance. Recent evidence suggests that the best on-the-field balance test uses a tandem stance performed on a foam surface (Figure 27-3).[36]

More sensitive balance testing can be done off the field with sophisticated balance systems such as those manufactured by Neurocom, Biodex, Chattex, and Breg.

Coordination tests A number of tests have been used to determine whether the head injury has affected coordination. These tests include the finger-to-nose test, heel-to-toe walking, and the standing heel to knee test. Inability to perform any of these tests may be indicative of injury to the cerebellum.

Cognitive tests The purpose of cognitive testing is to establish the effects of head trauma on various cognitive functions and to obtain an objective measure for assessment of the patient's status and improvement.[23] Cognitive tests may be performed as part of the on-the-field neurological exam. Two commonly used on-the-field cognitive tests are serial 7s, in which the athlete counts backward from 100 by 7s and the name of the months in reverse order. Recently, other cognitive tests, also referred to as neuropsychological assessments, have been developed for use in off-the-field evaluations. Neuropsychological assessments focus on memory, attention span, in-

Focus

Commonly used cognitive function tests[32]

Test	Cognitive ability assessed
1. Hopkins Verbal Learning Test	Verbal memory (word list)
2. Digit Span (WMS-R)	Attention span
3. Trail-Making Test	Visual scanning, mental flexibility
4. Stroop Test	Mental flexibility, attention
5. Controlled Oral Word Association Test	Word fluency, word retrieval
6. Symbol Digit Modalities	Visual scanning, attention
7. Grooved Pegboard Test	Fine motor coordination

Where to Get Tests

1. Hopkins Verbal Learning Test from Brandt J: Development of a new memory test with six equivalent forms, *Clinical Neuropsychologist* 5:125, 1991.
2. Digit Span subtest from Wechsler Memory Scale–Revised, The Psychological Corporation, Order Service Center, PO Box 839954, San Antonio TX (1-800-228-0752).
3. Trail-Making Test from Reitan Neuropsychology Laboratory, 2920 South 4th Ave, Tucson AZ 85713-4819 (602-882-2022).
4. Stroop Test from Stoeling Co., 620 Wheat Lane, Wood Dale, IL 60191.
5. Controlled Oral Word Association Test from Psychological Assessment Resources, Inc., PO Box 998, Odessa FL 33556-9901.
6. Symbol Digit Modalities from Western Psychological Services, 12031 Wilshire Blvd, Los Angeles CA 90025-1251.
7. Grooved Pegboard Test from Lafayette Instrument Co., Sagamore and N Ninth St, Box 5729, Lafayette IN 47903.

formation processing, concentration, and verbal learning. Neuropsychological assessment scores can be used as part of the decision for returning an athlete to play after a head injury.[32] *Focus Box:* "Commonly used cognitive function tests" lists some of the more commonly used cognitive tests.[32]

Recognition and Management of Specific Head Injuries

Skull Fracture

Etiology   Skull fractures occur most often from a blunt trauma, such as a baseball to the head, a shot put to the head, or a fall from a height.

Symptoms and signs   The athlete complains of severe headache and nausea. Palpation may infrequently reveal a defect such as a skull indentation. There may be blood in the middle ear, blood in the ear canal, bleeding through the nose, ecchymosis around the eyes that has been called raccoon eyes, or ecchymosis behind the ear that has been called a battle sign. Cerebrospinal fluid (straw-colored fluid) may appear in the ear canal and nose.[15]

Management   It is not the skull fracture itself that causes the most serious problem but complications that stem from intracranial bleeding, bone fragments embedded in the brain, and infection.[15] Such an injury requires immediate hospitalization and referral to a neurosurgeon.

Cerebral Concussions (Mild Head Injuries)

Etiology   Concussion has traditionally been defined as a clinical syndrome characterized by immediate and transient posttraumatic impairment of neural functions—such as alterations of consciousness, disturbance of vision, loss of equilibrium,

TABLE 27-2 Glasgow Coma Scale

		Points
Best motor response		
To verbal command	Obeys	6
To painful stimulus*	Localizes pain	5
	Flexion—withdraws	4
	Flexion—abnormal (decerabrate)	3
	Extension (decerabrate)	2
	No response	1
Best verbal response		
With a painful stimulus if necessary	Oriented/converses	5
	Disoriented and converses	4
	Inappropriate	3
	Incomprehensible sounds	2
	No response	1
Eye opening		
	Spontaneously	4
	To verbal command	3
	To pain	2
	No response	1
	TOTAL	3–15**

*Apply knuckles to sternum.
**Score of 7 or less indicates coma.

and so on—due to brain stem involvement.[7] It is important to realize that in the athletic population, the majority of concussions do not involve loss of consciousness.[25]

Early estimates of the incidence of concussion indicated that more than 250,000 concussions occur annually to football players alone and that as many as 20 percent of athletes suffer concussions each year.[16] More recent data suggests that the incidence of concussion is considerably lower, approximately 6 percent.[17]

Direct blows usually occur when the athlete is struck in the head by some object (e.g., a ball, a baseball bat, a lacrosse stick, or another player). A direct blow may also occur when the athlete's moving head strikes some fixed object (e.g., the floor, a goalpost), which results in impact deceleration of the brain.[31] A blow to the head can produce an injury to the brain either at the point of contact or on the opposite side of the head, which is referred to as a *contrecoup* injury. Acceleration/deceleration forces and particularly rotational forces produce shaking of the brain within the skull, which results in shearing forces that disrupt diffuse axonal connections running between the cortex and midbrain. These injuries are not visible lesions.[15]

Recently the term *mild head injury* (MHI) has gained popularity in the sports medicine community and is broadly defined as immediate, transient impairment of cerebral function.[14] MHI is characterized by the following symptoms:[1]

1. head trauma caused by acceleration/deceleration forces or contact forces
2. a brief period of either diminished consciousness or unconsciousness that last for seconds or minutes
3. a Glasgow Coma Scale score of 13 to 15 (Table 27-2)
4. posttraumatic amnesia lasting less than twenty-four hours
5. no signs of focal injury (subdural or epidural hematoma)
6. negative CT or MRI imaging studies

Symptoms and signs   Symptoms and signs of concussion or mild head injury are highly variable but generally may include headache, tinnitus, nausea, irritability, confusion, disorientation, dizziness, loss of consciousness, posttraumatic or antero-grade amnesia (can't remember anything that occurred after the injury), retrograde amnesia (can't remember things that occurred before injury), concentration diffi-culty, blurred vision, photophobia, and sleep disturbance.

In recent years, considerable debate has raged over a variety of classifica-tion systems that have been proposed for determining severity of concus-sion.[3,6,15,22,23,24,26,31,33,34,40,45,49] To date, none of these classification systems has been universally endorsed, and thus debate continues. Table 27-3 compares the various classification systems that have been proposed by different individuals or organiza-tions.

In these classification systems, grades of concussion range from as few as three to as many as six. Most grades are based primarily on the length of time that the ath-lete is unconscious and on the presence of additional specific symptoms and signs. The Glasgow Coma Scale is widely used to determine an athlete's level of conscious-ness after head injury (see Table 27-3).[28]

Management   Returning an athlete to competition following MHI often creates a difficult dilemma for both athletic trainers and physicians.[18] Certainly, there is a dif-ference between an athlete who has a mild head injury—who has simply had his or her bell rung—and an athlete who has experienced a loss of consciousness and shows signs of posttraumatic amnesia. Nevertheless, the decision to return an athlete who has experienced any type of injury to the brain to competition too early can be-come a very costly decision, one that could lead to death.[18]

When an athlete loses consciousness for any reason, the athletic trainer has but one choice and that is to remove the athlete from further activity immediately. If the athlete has sustained a head injury that causes unconsciousness, the athletic trainer must always suspect that the athlete may also have a cervical neck injury and must remove the athlete from the field using a spine board.[46]

The decision to allow an athlete with a mild head injury to return to play is more difficult and to date has been based primarily on the subjective judgment of the ath-letic trainer or physician. Table 27-4 provides recommendations for return to play following head injury.

For a number of years, tests for determining when an athlete may return to play following concussion (e.g., Rhomberg's test among others) have been criticized for their lack of sensitivity and objectivity. Recent studies have indicated that the recov-ery period following even a mild head injury may take longer than has been thought in the past.[19] When tested on more sensitive devices for measuring balance and pos-tural sway (e.g., Neurocom or Chattex systems), even those athletes with mild head injury do not return to baseline until approximately three to five days following in-jury.[19]

Athletes who have sustained a mild head injury should not be permitted to return to activity until all postconcussive symptoms, including visual, motor, or sensory changes and difficulty with thought or memory, have resolved. Permitting an ath-lete, particularly one in a contact sport, to return before symptoms resolve may place the athlete at risk for second impact syndrome.[19]

Even after postconcussive symptoms have disappeared and the athlete has re-turned to play, there is still the danger of recurrent concussions, which can produce cumulative traumatic injury to the brain. If more than one concussion occurs during a season, decisions must be made as to whether to allow the athlete to continue to compete. Table 27-5 provides some recommendations for return to play after recur-rent concussions.

Postconcussion Syndrome

Etiology   Postconcussion syndrome is a poorly understood condition that occurs following concussion. It may occur in cases of mild head injury that do not involve loss of consciousness or in cases of severe concussions.

27-3

Critical Thinking E x e r c i s e

A football player receives a grade 2 concussion. It is his second concussion this season.

? What guidelines should be followed regarding his return to play?

27-4

Critical Thinking E x e r c i s e

An athlete with a history of numerous grade 1 concussions begins to complain of memory difficulty, difficulty in concentrating, and on occasion, some irritability as well as some problems in visual focusing.

? What problem does this athlete have? How should it be managed?

After a cerebral injury, an ath-lete must be free of symptoms and signs before returning to competition.

TABLE 27-3 Grading Systems for Severity of Concussion

Grade or Level	Cantu (1986)[3]	Colorado Medical Society (1991)[6]	American Academy of Neurology (1997)[24]	Jordan (1989)[23]	Guskiewicz/University of North Carolina (1998)[17]	Saal (1991)[40]
0					Only symptom is mild confusion, but is asymptomatic within 10 min. Passes functional tests without recurrence of symptoms. Possibly develops headache after participation	
1	Normal consciousness; no LOC or PTA < 30 min. Observe on sidelines. RTP in "selected circumstances"	No LOC. Confusion. No amnesia. RTP after 20 min with normal exam	Transient confusion. No LOC. Symptoms & mental status abnormalities resolve < 15 min	Confusion. No amnesia. No LOC	No LOC. Any of 3 Cs abnormal: cranial nerves (II, III, VII, VIII) < 1 hr; cognition (memory & concentration) < 1 hr; coordination & balance < 3 days	Normal consciousness; no LOC. Mild headache. No amnesia. Unsteadiness on feet. RTP if symptoms clear
2	LOC < 5 min or PTA 30 min–24 hr. No RTP. Evaluate in medical facility	No LOC. Confusion. Amnesia. No RTP that day	Transient confusion. No LOC. Symptoms & mental status abnormalities last > 15 min	Confusion. Amnesia lasts < 24 hr. No LOC	LOC 10 sec–1 min or altered consciousness < 2 min or. Any of 3 Cs abnormal: cranial nerves (II, III, VII, VIII) > 1 hr; cognition (memory, concentration) > 1 hr; coordination & balance > 3 days	Momentary LOC. Unsteadiness of gait. Headache. No amnesia. RTP if all symptoms clear after 30 min
3	LOC > 5 min or PTA > 24 hr. Transport to emergency medical facility with full neck injury precautions. Neurosurgical evaluation	LOC. Transport to emergency medical facility with full neck injury precautions. Neurosurgical evaluation	Any LOC; brief (seconds) or prolonged (minutes)	LOC with an altered level lasting < 3 min. PTA lasts > 24 hr	LOC lasts > 1 min or altered consciousness > 2 min or 2 of 3 Cs abnormal for > 24 hr: cranial nerves (II, III, IV, VII, VIII); cognition (memory, concentration) coordination	3A: No or momentary LOC. No PTA. No play; observe closely; ? to hospital. 3B Momentary or brief LOC. Retrograde and PTA. No play; RTP when neuro status WNL
4				LOC with an altered level lasting > 3 min		LOC 5–10 min. Retrograde & possible PTA. Transport to medical facility for evaluation. RTP after neurosurgeon clearance
5						LOC; not arousable. Transport to hospital immediately. Notify hospital for neurosurgical care

TABLE 27-3 Grading Systems for Severity of Concussion—cont'd

Grade or Level	Nelson (1984)[31]	Kulund (1982)[26]	Ommaya & Gennarelli (1974)[33]	Ommaya (1994)[34]	Torg (1991)[45]	Wilberger & Maroon (1989)[49]	Hugenholtz & Richard (1982)[22]
0	Head struck or moved rapidly Not stunned or dazed initially *Later* complains of headache and difficulty in concentrating						
1	No LOC Stunned or dazed initially No amnesia "Bell rung" Sensorium clears quickly (< 1 min)	Stunned, dazed No confusion, dizziness No nausea, visual disturbances Feels well after 1–2 min	Confusion Normal consciousness No amnesia	Confusion Normal consciousness No amnesia	"Bell rung" Short-term confusion Momentary LOC Dazed appearance Unsteady gait	Short-term confusion Minimal or no LOC PTA 15–20 min	Transient or no LOC PTA < 1 hr
2	No LOC Cloudy sensorium (confused) > 1 min Headache May have tinnitus or amnesia May be irritable, hyperexcitable, dizzy	LOC Mental confusion Tinnitus, dizziness Retrograde amnesia Skill recovery may be rapid	Confusion Confusion and amnesia Normal consciousness PTA only	Confusion Confusion and amnesia Normal consciousness PTA only	Vertigo PTA	Confusion PTA > 20 min LOC < 5 min	LOC < 5 min PTA 1–24 hr
3	LOC < 1 min Not comatose (arousable with noxious stimuli) Demonstrates grade 2 symptoms in recovery	Longer LOC Headache Confusion PTA Retrograde amnesia	Normal consciousness Confusion and amnesia PTA *and* Retrograde amnesia	Coma (lasting < 6 hr) PTA *and* Retrograde amnesia	Vertigo PTA Retrograde amnesia	Loss of consciousness > 5 min Severe headache PTA > 12 hr	LOC > 5 min PTA > 24 hr
4	LOC > 1 minute Not comatose Demonstrates grade 2 symptoms in recovery		Coma (paralytic) Awakens with confusion and amnesia	Coma (lasting 6–24 hr)	PTA Immediate, transient LOC		
5			Coma (> 24 hr) Persistent vegetative state	Coma (lasting > 24 hr)	Paralytic coma Cardiorespiratory arrest		
6			Coma Death	Coma Death within 24 hr	Death		

LOC = loss of consciousness; PTA = posttraumatic amnesia; RTP = return to play.

TABLE 27-4 Recommendations for Return to Play after Head Injury

Grade	Jordon[23]	Colorado Medical Society[6]	Cantu[3]
1	May return to play if asymptomatic at rest and exertion after at least 20 min of observation	May return to play if asymptomatic at rest and exertion after at least 20 min observation	May return to play if asymptomatic for 1 wk
2	May return to play if asymptomatic for 1 wk	May return to play if asymptomatic for 1 wk	May return to play if asymptomatic for 1 wk
3	Should not be allowed to play for at least 1 mo; may then return to play if asymptomatic for 1 wk	Should not be allowed to play for at least 1 mo; may then return to play if asymptomatic for 2 wk	Should not be allowed to play for at least 1 mo; may then return to play if asymptomatic for 1 wk
4	Should not be allowed to play for at least 1 mo; may then return to play if asymptomatic for 2 wks.		

Symptoms and signs The athlete complains of a range of postconcussion problems, including persistent headache, impaired memory, lack of concentration, anxiety and irritability, giddiness, fatigue, depression, and visual disturbances.[21] These symptoms can begin immediately or within several days following the initial trauma and may last for weeks or even months before resolving.

Management The athletic trainer should make an effort to treat the symptoms to the greatest extent possible. There is no clear-cut treatment for postconcussion syndrome. The athlete should not be allowed to return to play until all the symptoms of this condition have resolved.

Second Impact Syndrome

Etiology Second impact syndrome occurs because of rapid swelling and herniation of the brain after a second head injury that occurs before the symptoms of a previous head injury have resolved.[5] This second impact may be relatively minor and, in some cases, may not even involve a blow to the head. A blow to the chest or back may create enough force to snap the athlete's head and send acceleration/deceleration forces to an already compromised brain. The resulting symptoms occur

27-5

Critical Thinking Exercise

A high school football player has experienced a concussion with a brief loss of consciousness. One week later, the athlete is symptom free except for a headache.

? Should the athletic trainer allow the athlete to resume normal contact activity at this point?

TABLE 27-5 Guidelines for Return to Activity after Concussion

Grade	First Concussion	Second Concussion	Third Concussion
1 (mild)	Return to play if asymptomatic*	Return to play in 2 wk if asymptomatic for 1 wk	Terminate season; may return to play next season if asymptomatic
2 (moderate)	Return to play if asymptomatic for 1 wk	1 mo minimum restriction; may then return to play if asymptomatic for 1 wk; consider terminating season	Terminate season; may return to play next year if asymptomatic
3 (severe)	1 mo minimum restriction; may then return to play if asymptomatic for 1 wk	Terminate season; may return to play next year if asymptomatic	

*No headache or dizziness; no impaired orientation, concentration, or memory during rest or exertion.

because a disruption of the brain's blood autoregulatory system leads to swelling of the brain, which significantly increases intracranial pressure, and to herniation. Second impact syndrome is most likely to occur in athletes less than twenty years of age.

Symptoms and signs   Often, the athlete does not even lose consciousness and may look stunned. The athlete may remain standing and be able to leave the playing field under his or her own power. However, within fifteen seconds to several minutes, the athlete's condition worsens rapidly, with dilated pupils, loss of eye movement, loss of consciousness leading to coma, and respiratory failure.[4] Second impact syndrome is a life-threatening situation that has a mortality rate of approximately 50 percent.

Management   Second impact syndrome is a life-threatening emergency that must be addressed within approximately five minutes by dramatic life-saving measures performed in an emergency care facility.[5] From the athletic trainer's perspective, the best way to manage second impact syndrome is to prevent it from occurring. Thus, the decision to allow an athlete to return to play following an initial head injury must be carefully made based on the absence of postconcussive symptoms.

Cerebral Contusion

Etiology   A contusion of the cerebrum is a focal injury to the brain that involves small hemorrhages or *intracerebral bleeding* within either the cortex, the brain stem, or the cerebellum (Figure 27-4).[15] Brain contusions usually result from an impact injury in which the head strikes a stationary, immovable object such as the floor.

Symptoms and signs   Depending on the extent of trauma and the injury site, symptoms and signs may vary significantly. In most instances, the athlete experiences a loss of consciousness but subsequently becomes very alert and talkative. A neurological exam will be normal; however, symptoms such as headaches, dizziness, and nausea will persist.

Management   Hospitalization and CT or MRI tests are standard for a cerebral contusion. Treatment varies according to the clinical status of the athlete.[15] A decision to return to play can only be made when the athlete is asymptomatic and a CT scan is normal.

Epidural Hematoma

Etiology   A blow to the head or a skull fracture can cause a tear of the meningeal arteries, which are imbedded in bony grooves in the skull (Figure 27-5). Because of arterial blood pressure, blood accumulation and the creation of a hematoma are extremely fast.[29]

Symptoms and signs   In most cases, initially, there will be a loss of consciousness. In some cases, once consciousness is regained, the athlete may be lucid and show few or none of the symptoms of serious head injury. Gradually symptoms begin to worsen, and the athlete experiences severe head pains; dizziness; nausea; dilation of one pupil, usually on the same side as the injury; or sleepiness (see *Focus Box:* "Conditions indicating the possibility of increasing intracranial pressure"). Later stages of an epidural hematoma are characterized by deteriorating consciousness, neck rigidity, depression of pulse and respiration, and convulsions. An epidural hematoma is a life-threatening situation that necessitates urgent neurosurgical care.

Management   A CT scan is necessary to diagnose an epidural hematoma. The pressure of an epidural hematoma must be surgically relieved as soon as possible to avoid the possibility of death or permanent disability.

Subdural Hematoma

Etiology   Acute subdural hematomas occur much more frequently than do epidural hematomas. Subdural hematomas result from acceleration/deceleration forces that tear vessels that bridge the dura mater and the brain (Figure 27-6).[20]

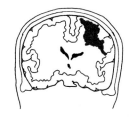

Figure 27-4

Intracerebral bleeding.

The three major types of intracranial hematomas:
- Epidural
- Subdural
- Intracerebral

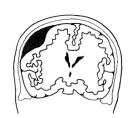

Figure 27-5

Epidural bleeding.

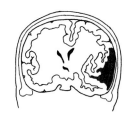

Figure 27-6

Subdural bleeding.

Focus

Conditions indicating the possibility of increasing intracranial pressure
- Headache
- Nausea and vomiting
- Unequal pupils
- Disorientation
- Progressive or sudden impairment in consciousness
- Gradual increase in blood pressure
- Decrease in pulse rate

Subdural hematomas usually involve venous bleeding, and thus symptoms and signs tend to appear more slowly. In a simple subdural hematoma, there is a collection of blood in the subdural space with no associated injury to the cerebrum. With a complicated subdural hematoma, there is both collections of blood and injury to the cortex that causes an increase in intercerebral pressure. Mortality rate for simple subdural hematomas is approximately 20 percent, whereas complicated subdural hematomas have a 50 percent mortality rate.

Symptoms and signs   With a simple subdural hematoma, the athlete is not likely to be unconscious; the athlete with a complicated subdural hematoma would almost always be unconscious and would exhibit dilation of one pupil, usually on the same side as the injury. Both types would show signs of headache, dizziness, nausea, or sleepiness.

Management   An acute subdural hematoma is a life-threatening situation that calls for immediate medical attention. A diagnostic CT scan or MRI is necessary to determine the extent and location of the hemorrhage.

Malignant Brain Edema Syndrome

Etiology   This syndrome occurs in young athletes within minutes to hours after head trauma and is caused by an intracerebral clot that results in diffuse brain swelling with little or no brain injury. Swelling is the result of hyperemia or vascular engorgement and results in increased intracranial pressure and herniation.[5]

Symptoms and signs   There is rapid neurologic deterioration from a normal alert state that progresses to coma and occasionally death.[5]

Management   This condition is a life-threatening situation that requires immediate recognition and subsequent rapid treatment in an emergency care facility.

Migraine Headaches

Etiology   Migraine is a disorder characterized by recurrent attacks of severe headache with sudden onset, with or without visual or gastrointestinal problems.[44] The athlete who has a history of repeated minor blows to the head, such as those that may occur in soccer, or who has sustained a major cerebral injury may, over a period of time, develop migraine headaches. The exact cause is unknown, but the condition is believed to be a vascular disorder.

Symptoms and signs   Flashes of light, blindness in half the field of vision (hemianopia), and paresthesia are thought to be caused by vasoconstriction of intercerebral vessels. The headache is believed to be caused by dilation of scalp arteries. The athlete complains of a severe headache that is diffused throughout the head and often accompanied by nausea and vomiting. There is evidence of a familial predisposition for those athletes who experience migraine headaches after head injury.[44]

Management   The best management of migraine is prevention. Prophylactic medications such as promethazine can help reduce the recurrence of migraines. For se-

Focus

Care of scalp lacerations

Materials needed

Antiseptic soap, water, antiseptic, 4-inch (10 cm) gauze pads, sterile cotton, and hair clippers.

Position of the athlete

The athlete lies on the table with the wound upward.

Procedure

1. The entire area of bleeding is thoroughly cleansed with antiseptic soap and water. Washing the wound to remove dirt and debris is best done in lengthwise movements.
2. After the injury site is cleansed and dried, it is exposed and, if necessary, the hair is cut away. Enough scalp should be exposed so that a bandage and tape may be applied.
3. Firm pressure or an astringent can be used to reduce bleeding if necessary.
4. Wounds that are more than $^1/_2$ inch (1.25 cm) in length and $^1/_8$ inch (0.3 cm) in depth should be referred to a physician for treatment. In less severe wounds the bleeding should be controlled and an antiseptic applied, followed by the application of a protective coating such as collodion and a sterile gauze pad. A tape adherent is then painted over the skin area to ensure that the tape sticks to the skin.

vere attacks, administration of a prescription drug, such as ergotamine tartrate or sumatriptan succinate (Imitrex), has a high success rate.

Scalp Injuries

The scalp can receive lacerations, abrasions, contusions, and hematomas.

Etiology   The cause of scalp injury is usually blunt or penetrating trauma. A scalp laceration could exist in conjunction with a serious skull or cerebral injury.

Symptoms and signs   The athlete complains of being hit in the head. Bleeding is often extensive, making it difficult to pinpoint the exact site. Matted hair and dirt can also disguise the actual point of injury.

Management   The treatment of a scalp laceration poses a special problem because of its general inaccessibility. (See *Focus Box:* "Care of scalp lacerations.")

THE FACE

Anatomy of the Face

The facial skin covers subcutaneous bone that has very little protective muscle, fascia, or fat. The supraorbital ridges house the frontal sinuses. In general, the facial skeleton is composed of dense bony buttresses combined with thin sheets of bone. The middle third of the face consists of the maxillary bone, which supports the nose and nasal passages. The lower aspect of the face consists of the lower jaw, or mandible. Besides supporting teeth, the mandible also supports the larynx, trachea, upper airway, and upper digestive tract (see Figure 27-1).

Temporomandibular Joint

The temporomandibular joint (TMJ) is the articulation between the mandibular condyle and the mandibular fossa of the temporal bone.[48] It moves in a hingelike manner when the mouth is opened and closed and glides forward, backward, and side to side when biting or chewing. The TMJ is surrounded by a joint capsule. Within the joint capsule

Figure 27-7

The temporomandibular joint (TMJ).

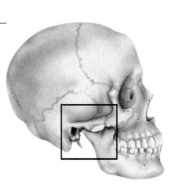

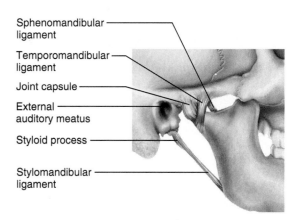

Sphenomandibular ligament

Temporomandibular ligament

Joint capsule

External auditory meatus

Styloid process

Stylomandibular ligament

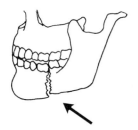

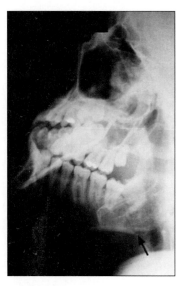

Figure 27-8

Mandibular fracture.

lies a fibrocartilaginous meniscus that separates and cushions the bones and provides for a better fit between the articulating surfaces. The joint capsule is supported by spheno-mandibular, temporomandibular, and stylomandibular ligaments (Figure 27-7).

Recognition and Management of Specific Facial Injuries

Mandible Fracture

Etiology   Fractures of the lower jaw, or mandible (Figure 27-8), occur most often in collision sports. They are second in incidence of all facial fractures. Because it has relatively little padding and sharp contours, the lower jaw is prone to injury from a direct blow. The most frequently fractured area is near the jaw's frontal angle.

Symptoms and signs   The main indications of a fractured mandible are deformity, loss of normal occlusion of the teeth, pain when biting down, bleeding around teeth, and lower lip anesthesia.[39]

Management   Fracture of the mandible requires temporary immobilization with an elastic bandage followed by reduction and fixation of the jaw by the physician. Mild repetitive activities can be carried out, such as light weight lifting, swimming, or cycling. Fixation is from four to six weeks. Full activity is resumed in two to three months with appropriate special headgear and customized mouth guard.[39]

Mandibular Dislocation

Etiology   A dislocation of the jaw, or *mandibular luxation,* involves the temporo-mandibular joint (see Figure 27-7). Because of its wide range of movement and the inequity of size between the mandibular condyle and the temporal fossa, the jaw is somewhat prone to dislocation. The mechanism of injury in dislocations is usually a side blow to the open mouth of the athlete, which forces the mandibular condyle forward out of the temporal fossa. This injury may occur as either a luxation (complete dislocation) or a subluxation (partial dislocation).

Symptoms and signs   The major signs of the dislocated jaw are a locked-open position, with jaw movement being almost impossible, and an overriding malocclusion of the teeth.

Management   Initially, cold is applied along with elastic bandage immobilization and reduction. Follow-up care includes a soft diet, NSAIDs, and analgesic when needed for one to two weeks. A gradual return to activity can begin seven to ten days after the acute period.[25] Complications of jaw dislocations are recurrent dislocation, malocclusion, and TMJ dysfunction.

Temporomandibular Joint Dysfunction

Etiology   The TMJ is important for both communication and mastication, and it has a high degree of mobility. Because of this extreme mobility, the stability of the joint is compromised. The bony configuration of the joint does not limit its mobility, so the muscles and ligaments provide the primary stability.

The most common cause of TMJ dysfunction is a disk-condyle derangement in which the disk is positioned anteriorly with respect to the condyle when the jaw is closed. As the jaw opens and the condyle translates forward, the disk relocates over the condyle, producing an audible click. A second click may occur when the jaw is closed. This chronic derangement eventually leads to deterioration of the posterior stabilizing structures and, ultimately, anterior dislocation of the disk. This chronic derangement is most typically treated through the use of a custom-designed removable mouthpiece that repositions the condyles anteriorly.[48]

A dislocation of the TMJ occurs when one or occasionally both condyles are dislocated forward and prevent the jaw from closing.

Symptoms and signs   TMJ dysfunction has been identified as a cause of various signs and symptoms within the head and neck, including headache, earache, vertigo, inflammation, and neck pain associated with trigger points and muscle guarding. Problems in and about the TMJ are similar to those of other synovial joints in that TMJ dysfunction may result from inflammation of the synovial capsule, internal disk derangement, malocclusion, hypermobility or hypomobility, muscle dysfunction, or limited mandibular joint range of motion.[48]

Management   Management of TMJ dysfunction should address the causes of the problem. Hypermobility can be corrected using strengthening exercises. Hypomobility may be corrected by using techniques of joint mobilization. Therapeutic modalities can be used to treat pain and to provide heat as needed. Often the use of a dental appliance is recommended. A custom-fitted mouth guard or even a manufactured mouth guard can be used to correct problems of occlusion. If these corrective measures fail, the athlete should be referred to a dentist for treatment.

Zygomatic Complex (Cheekbone) Fracture

Etiology   A fracture of the zygoma represents the third most common facial fracture.[13] The mechanism of injury is a direct blow to the cheekbone.

Symptoms and signs   An obvious deformity occurs in the cheek region, or a bony discrepancy can be felt during palpation. There is usually a nosebleed **(epistaxis)**, and the athlete commonly complains of seeing double **(diplopia)**. There is also numbness of the cheek.

epistaxis (epp is **tax** is)
Nosebleed.

diplopia (dip **low** peeah)
Seeing double.

Management   Care by the athletic trainer usually involves cold application for the control of edema and immediate referral to a physician. Healing takes six to eight weeks. Proper protective gear must be worn when the athlete returns to activity.

Maxillary Fracture

Etiology   A severe blow to the upper jaw, such as from a hockey puck or stick, can fracture the maxilla. This injury ranks fourth in incidence of facial fracture.

Symptoms and signs   After being struck a severe blow to the upper jaw, the athlete complains of pain while chewing, malocclusion, nosebleed, double vision, and numbness in the lip and cheek region.[39]

Management   Because bleeding is usually profuse, airway passages must be maintained. A brain injury may also be associated with this condition, as with all injuries to the face. The athlete must be immediately transported to a hospital; the conscious athlete should be transported in an upright, forward-leaning position. This position allows external drainage of saliva and blood.[39] Fracture reduction, fixation, and immobilization are carried out as specific treatment.[38]

Facial Lacerations

Etiology   Facial lacerations are common in contact and collision sports. Lacerations about the face are caused by a direct impact to the face with a sharp object or by an indirect compressive force.

Symptoms and signs   The athlete feels pain, and there is substantial bleeding and obvious tearing of the epidermis, dermis, and often the subcutaneous layer of skin (Figure 27-9).

27-6

Critical Thinking Exercise

A lacrosse player sustains a severe blow to her cheek by a stick. The blow fractures her maxilla but does not knock her unconscious.

? How should the athlete be transported to the hospital and why?

Figure 27-9

Facial laceration can be a medical emergency.

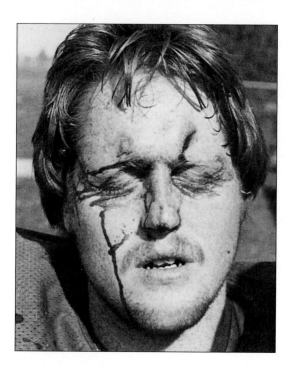

Management   The procedures for facial lacerations are presented in the section on wound care in Chapter 28. The athlete should be referred to a physician for definitive care, such as suturing. Athletic trainers should note that with *eyebrow lacerations,* they should not shave the eyebrow because it may not regrow, or if it does, it may do so in an irregular pattern.[3] Lip, oral, ear, cheek, and nasal lacerations, like all facial lacerations, are grossly contaminated and must be carefully cleaned before suturing can be successful. Infection must be avoided. Systemic antibiotics and tetanus prophylaxis may be necessary.[8]

DENTAL INJURIES

Anatomy

The tooth is a composite of mineral salts of which calcium and phosphorus are most abundant. The portion protruding from the gum, called the *crown,* is covered by the hardest substance within the body, the enamel. The portion that extends into the alveolar bone of the mouth is called the *root* and is covered by a thin, bony substance known as *cementum.* Underneath the enamel and cementum lies the bulk of the tooth, a hard material known as *dentin.* Within the dentin is a central canal and chamber containing the *pulp,* which is composed of nerves, lymphatics, and blood vessels that supply the entire tooth (Figure 27-10). With the use of face guards and properly fitting mouth guards, most dental injuries can be prevented (see Chapter 7).

Preventing Dental Injuries

There is universal agreement within the dental community that all athletes, but particularly those in contact/collision sports, should routinely wear mouth guards to prevent injuries to the teeth. Without question, the mandatory use of mouth guards in both high school and collegiate football players has significantly reduced the incidence of oral injuries in those sports. However, there is still a high incidence of dental injuries in those sports that do not require mouth guards to be worn.[12]

     Athletes should practice good dental hygiene that includes regular brushing, rinsing, and flossing. Like everyone else, athletes should have dental screenings at least

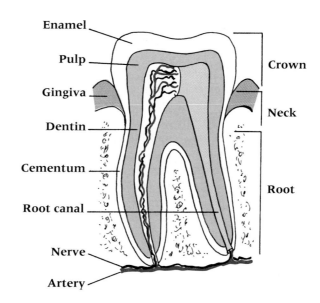

Figure 27-10

Normal tooth anatomy.

Enamel

Pulp

Gingiva

Dentin

Cementum

Root canal

Nerve

Artery

Crown

Neck

Root

once each year to prevent the development of dental caries (cavities), which is a gradual decay and degeneration of soft or bony tissue of a tooth. If this decay progresses, the tissue surrounding the tooth can become inflamed and an *abscess* forms from a bacterial infection of the tooth. Poor dental hygiene can also lead to *gingivitis,* which is an inflammation of the gums that causes swelling, redness, tenderness, and a tendency to bleed easily. Chronic gingivitis can lead to *periodontitis,* in which there is an inflammation and/or a degeneration of the dental periosteum, the surrounding bone, and the cementum; loosening of the teeth; recession of the gingiva; and infection.[43]

Recognition and Management of Specific Dental Injuries

Tooth Fractures

Etiology   Any impact to the upper or lower jaw or direct trauma can potentially fracture the teeth.[27] Three types of fractures can occur to the teeth: an uncomplicated crown fracture, a complicated crown fracture, and a root fracture (Figure 27-11).

Symptoms and signs   In an uncomplicated crown fracture, a small portion of the tooth is broken but there is no bleeding from the fracture and the pulp chamber is not exposed. In a complicated crown fracture, a portion of the tooth is broken and there is bleeding from the fracture. The pulp chamber is exposed, and there is a great deal of pain. A root fracture occurs below the gum line; therefore, diagnosis is

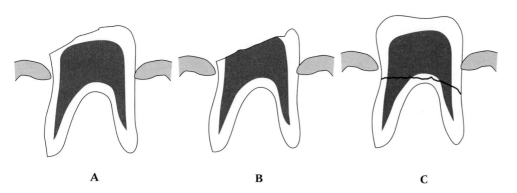

Figure 27-11

Tooth fractures. **A,** Uncomplicated crown fracture. **B,** Complicated crown fracture. **C,** Root fracture.

A   B   C

difficult and may require an X ray. Root fractures account for only 10 percent to 15 percent of all dental fractures. The tooth may appear to be in the normal position, but there is bleeding from the gum around the tooth, and the crown of the tooth may be pushed back or loose.

Any impact great enough to cause a fracture of a tooth could also produce a fracture of the mandible or even a concussion.[26]

Management   Both uncomplicated and complicated crown fractures do not require immediate treatment by a dentist. The fractured piece of tooth can simply be placed in a plastic bag, and if the fractured tooth is not extremely sensitive to air or cold, the athlete can continue to play and can see the dentist within twenty-four to forty-eight hours after the game. If there is bleeding, a piece of gauze can be placed over the fracture. For the sake of appearance, the fractured piece of tooth can be glued in place or the tooth can be capped with a synthetic composite material.

In the case of a root fracture, the athlete may continue to play but should see a dentist as soon as possible after the game. A tooth that is pushed back should not be forced forward because doing so is likely to make the fracture worse. The dentist will reposition the tooth and apply a brace to be worn for three to four months. The athlete should wear a mouth guard while competing.

Tooth Subluxation, Luxation, Avulsion

Etiology   The same mechanisms that can cause a tooth fracture may also cause loosening or dislocation of the tooth.[27] Loosening of the tooth can result in concussion or subluxation, luxation, or avulsion.

Symptoms and signs   A tooth may be slightly loosened or totally dislodged. In the case of a concussion or subluxation, the tooth is still in its normal place and is only slightly loose. The athlete feels little or no pain but indicates that the tooth just feels different. In a luxation, the tooth is not fractured but is very loose and has moved either forward to an extruded position or backward to an intruded position. In an avulsion, the tooth is knocked completely out of the mouth.

Management   For a concussion or subluxation, no immediate treatment is required, and the athlete should be referred to a dentist within forty-eight hours for evaluation only. In a luxation, the tooth should be moved back into its normal position only if it is easy to move. The athlete should be referred to a dentist as soon as possible, especially if the tooth could not be moved back to its normal position. The athletic trainer should try to reimplant an avulsed tooth. The avulsed tooth can be rinsed off but should never be scraped or scrubbed to get dirt off. If the tooth cannot be reimplanted, it should be stored in a "Save a Tooth" kit, which contains Hank's Balanced Salt Solution (HBSS), or in milk or saline.[27] The athlete should be referred to the dentist immediately. The sooner the tooth can be reimplanted, the better the prognosis.

NASAL INJURIES

Anatomy

The nose functions to clean, warm, and humidify inhaled air. The external portion of the nose is formed by a combination of bone in the superior portion and fibrocartilage inferiorly that speads laterally to form the ala. The nasal cavity extends from the nostrils posteriorly to the choanae. A nasal septum divides the nasal cavity into right and left chambers.

Recognition and Management of Specific Nose Injuries

Nasal Fractures and Chondral Separation

Etiology   A fracture of the nose is the most common fracture of the face. The force of the blow to the nose may come either from the side or from a straight frontal force. A lateral force causes greater deformity than a straight-on blow does.

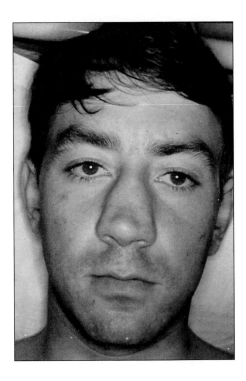

Figure 27-12

A nasal fracture may pose a serious medical problem.

Symptoms and signs   The nasal fracture appears frequently as a separation of the frontal processes of the maxilla, a separation of the lateral cartilages, or a combination of the two (Figure 27-12).

In nasal fractures, hemorrhage is profuse because of laceration of the mucous lining. Swelling is immediate. Deformity is usually present if the nose has received a lateral blow. Gentle palpation may reveal abnormal mobility and emit a grating sound (crepitus).

Management   The athletic trainer should control the bleeding and then refer the athlete to a physician for X-ray examination and reduction of the fracture. Simple and uncomplicated fractures of the nose will not hinder or be unsafe for the athlete, and he or she will be able to return to competition within a few days. Fracture deformity reduction must be performed by a trained person.[42] Adequate protection can be provided through splinting (see *Focus Box:* "Nose splinting" and Figure 27-13).

Deviated Septum

Etiology   The mechanism of injury to the septum, like that to the nasal fracture, is compression or lateral trauma.

Symptoms and signs   A careful evaluation of the nose must be made after the trauma. Injury commonly produces bleeding and, in some cases, a septal hematoma. The athlete complains of nasal pain.

Management   At the site at which a hematoma may occur, compression is applied. When a hematoma is present, it must be drained immediately via a surgical incision through the nasal septal mucosa. After surgical drainage, a small wick is inserted for continued drainage, and the nose is firmly packed to prevent the hematoma from re-forming. If a hematoma is neglected, an abscess will form, causing bone and cartilage loss and, ultimately, a difficult-to-correct deformity.

Nosebleed (Epistaxis)

Etiology   Nosebleeds in sports are usually the result of direct blows that cause varying degrees of contusion to the septum. Epistaxis can be classified as either anterior or posterior. Anterior epistaxis originates from the nasal septum, and posterior

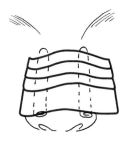

Figure 27-13

Splinting the nose fracture.

27-7

Critical Thinking E x e r c i s e

A wrestler is hit in the nose, which injures the lateral nasal wall and causes epistaxis.

? How should this nosebleed be managed?

Nose splinting

The following procedure is used for nose splinting.

Materials needed

Two pieces of gauze, each 2 inches (5 cm) long and rolled to the size of a pencil; three strips of 1½-inch (3.8 cm) tape, cut approximately 4 inches (10 cm) long; and clear tape adherent.

Position of the athlete

The athlete lies supine on the training table.

Procedure

1. The rolled pieces of gauze are placed on either side of the athlete's nose.
2. Gently but firmly, 4-inch (10 cm) lengths of tape are laid over the gauze rolls.

---

epistaxis from the lateral wall. Anterior epistaxis is more common by far and may result from a direct blow, a sinus infection, high humidity, allergies, a foreign body lodged in the nose, or some other serious facial or head injury.[47]

Symptoms and signs   Hemorrhages arise most often from the highly vascular anterior aspect of the nasal septum. In most situations, the nosebleed presents only a minor problem and stops spontaneously after a short period of time. However, there are persistent types that require medical attention and possibly cauterization. As always when blood is present, universal precautions must be used.

Management   An athlete with an acute nosebleed should sit upright with a cold compress placed over both the nose and the ipsilateral carotid artery while finger pressure is applied to the affected nostril for five minutes. It has also been suggested that a piece of rolled-up gauze be placed between the upper lip and gum, which places direct pressure on the arteries that supply the nasal mucosa.[47]

If this procedure fails to stop the bleeding within five minutes, more extensive measures should be taken. The athletic trainer uses an applicator to paint the hemorrhage point with an astringent or a styptic such as tannic acid or epinephrine hydrochloride solution. The application of a gauze or cotton pledget will provide corking action and encourage blood clotting. If a pledget is used, the ends should protrude from the nostrils at least ½ inch (1.25 cm) to facilitate removal. After bleeding has ceased, the athlete may resume activity but should be reminded not to blow the nose under any circumstances for at least two hours after the initial insult.

EAR INJURIES

Anatomy

The ear (Figure 27-14) is responsible for the sense of hearing and for equilibrium. It is composed of three parts: the external ear; the middle ear (tympanic membrane), lying just inside the skull; and the internal ear (labyrinth), which is formed in part by the temporal bone of the skull. The middle ear and internal ear are structured to transport auditory impulses to the brain. Aiding the organs of hearing and equalizing pressure between the middle and the internal ear is the eustachian tube, a canal that joins the nose and the middle ear.[37]

Sports injuries to the ear occur most often to the external portion. The external ear is separated into the auricle (pinna) and the external auditory canal (meatus). The auricle, which is shaped like a shell, collects and directs waves of sound into the

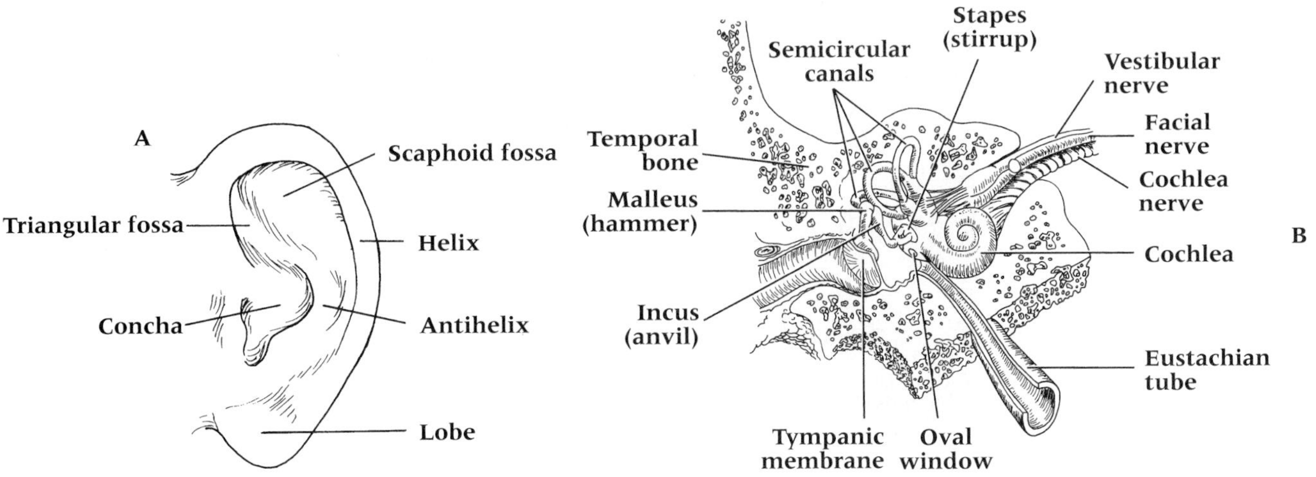

A

Triangular fossa

Scaphoid fossa

Helix

Antihelix

Concha

Lobe

Temporal bone

Malleus (hammer)

Incus (anvil)

Tympanic membrane

Oval window

Semicircular canals

Stapes (stirrup)

Vestibular nerve

Facial nerve

Cochlea nerve

Cochlea

Eustachian tube

B

Figure 27-14

Ear anatomy. **A,** External ear. **B,** Middle ear and internal ear.

auditory canal. It is composed of flexible yellow cartilage, muscles, and fat padding and is covered by a closely adhering, thin layer of skin. Most of the blood vessels and nerves of the auricle turn around its borders, with just a few penetrating the cartilage proper.

Recognition and Management of Specific Ear Injuries

Auricular Hematoma (Cauliflower Ear)

Etiology   Hematomas of the ear are common in boxing, rugby, and wrestling. They are most common in athletes who do not wear protective headgear. This condition usually occurs either from compression or from a shearing injury (single or repeated) to the auricle that causes subcutaneous bleeding into the auricular cartilage.[10]

Symptoms and signs   Trauma may tear the overlying tissue away from the cartilaginous plate, resulting in hemorrhage and fluid accumulation. A hematoma usually forms before the limited circulation can absorb the fluid. If the hematoma goes unattended, a sequence of coagulation, organization, and fibrosis results in a keloid that appears elevated, rounded, white, nodular, and firm, resembling a cauliflower (Figure 27-15). Often the keloid forms in the region of the helix fossa or concha; once developed, the keloid can be removed only through surgery.[10]

Management   To prevent this disfiguring condition from arising, some friction-reducing agent such as petroleum jelly should be applied to the ears of athletes susceptible to this condition. These athletes should also routinely wear ear guards in practice and in competition.

If an ear becomes "hot" because of excessive rubbing or twisting, the immediate application of a cold pack to the affected spot will alleviate hemorrhage. Once swelling is present in the ear, special care should be taken to prevent the fluid from solidifying; a cold pack should be placed immediately over the ear and held tightly by an elastic bandage for at least twenty minutes. If the swelling is still present at the end of this time, aspiration by a physician is required.[10] After drainage, pressure is applied to the area to prevent return of the hematoma. The physician may suture dental rolls into position to ensure uniform pressure.[10] Instead of this procedure, a collodion pack may be opted for as follows:

1. Cotton is packed into the ear canal.
2. The auricle is coated with collodion.
3. Small pieces of gauze also coated with collodion are inserted and packed into the auricle of the ear until it is completely filled.
4. A ¼-inch-thick (0.6 cm) felt piece is cut to fit and placed behind the ear.

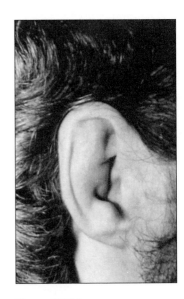

Figure 27-15

Hematoma of the auricle; also called cauliflower ear.

Figure 27-16

Positioning for an examiner using an otoscope.

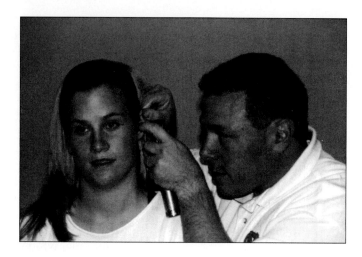

5. A pressure wrap is placed completely around the head, kept in place for two days, and then removed.
6. The collodion pack is left in place until it can be easily removed.

Rupture of the Tympanic Membrane

Etiology   Rupture of the tympanic membrane is commonly seen in contact and collision sports as well as in water polo and diving.[37] A fall or slap to the unprotected ear or sudden underwater variation can rupture the tympanic membrane.

Symptoms and signs   The athlete complains of a loud pop followed by pain in the ear, nausea, vomiting, and dizziness.[37] The athlete demonstrates hearing loss and visible rupture of the tympanic membrane. An otoscope is an instrument used to visually examine the ear canal and the tympanic membrane (Figure 27-16). Tympanic membrane ruptures can be seen through the otoscope.

Management   Small to moderate perforations of the tympanic membrane usually heal spontaneously in one to two weeks. Infection can occur and must be continually monitored.

Swimmer's Ear (Otitis Externa)

Etiology   A common condition in athletes engaged in water sports is *swimmer's ear,* or external otitis. Swimmer's ear is a general term for infection of the ear canal caused by *Pseudomonas aeruginosa,* a type of gram-negative bacillus. Contrary to current thought among swimming coaches, swimmer's ear is not usually associated with a fungal infection. Water can become trapped in the ear canal as a result of obstructions created by cysts, bone growths, plugs of earwax, or swelling caused by allergies.[30]

Symptoms and signs   The athlete complains of pain and dizziness and may also complain of itching, discharge, or even a partial hearing loss.

Management   Athletes can best prevent ear infection by drying the ears thoroughly with a soft towel, using ear drops containing a mild acid (3% boric acid) and alcohol solution before and after each swim, and avoiding situations that can cause ear infections, such as overexposure to cold wind or sticking foreign objects into the ear.

When the swimmer displays symptoms of external otitis, immediate referral to a physician must be made. Tympanic membrane rupture should be ruled out. Treatment may include acidification through drops into the ear to make an inhospitable environment for the gram-negative bacteria. Antibiotics may be used in athletes with a mild ear infection.[11] In the event of a ruptured tympanic membrane, custom-made earplugs must be used.

Middle Ear Infection (Otitis Media)

Etiology   Otitis media is an accumulation of fluid in the middle ear caused by local and systemic inflammation and infection.

Symptoms and signs   There will usually be intense pain in the ear, fluid draining from the ear canal, and a transient loss of hearing. In addition, the systemic infection may also cause fever, headache, irritability, loss of appetite, and nausea.[43]

Management   A physician may choose to draw a small amount of fluid from the middle ear to determine the most appropriate antibiotic therapy. Analgesics can be used to help reduce pain. The problem will generally begin to resolve within twenty-four hours although pain may last for seventy-two hours.

Impacted Cerumen

Etiology   Cerumen, or earwax, is secreted by glands in the outer portion of the ear canal. Occasionally, an excessive amount of earwax may accumulate, clogging the ear canal.

Symptoms and signs   Impacted cerumen causes some degree of muffled hearing or hearing loss. However, there will generally be little or no pain because no infection is involved.[43]

Management   Initially, an attempt can be made to remove excess cerumen by irrigation of the ear canal with warm water. The athlete should not attempt to remove the cerumen with a cotton tip applicator because that may increase the degree of impaction. If irrigation fails, the impacted cerumen must be physically removed by a physician using a curette.

EYE INJURIES

Eye injuries account for approximately 2 percent of all sports injuries.[35] In the United States, basketball, baseball, boxing, soccer, swimming, and racket sports have a high incidence of eye injuries (Table 27-6).[39]

Anatomy

The eye has many anatomical protective features. It is firmly retained within an oval socket formed by the bones of the head. A cushion of soft fatty tissue surrounds it, and a thin skin flap (the eyelid), which functions by reflex action, covers the eye for protection. Foreign particles are prevented from entering the eye by the lashes and eyebrows, which act as a filtering system. A soft mucous lining that covers the inner conjunctiva transports and spreads tears, which are secreted by many accessory lacrimal glands. A larger lubricating organ is located above the eye and secretes heavy quantities of fluid through the lacrimal duct to help wash away foreign particles. The eye proper is well protected by the sclera, a tough, white, outer layer possessing a transparent center portion called the *cornea*.

The cornea covers the pupil, which is the central opening of the eye. Light passes through the cornea, then through the anterior chamber past the iris and the lens,

TABLE 27-6 Percentage of Sports Eye Injuries in the United States

Sport	Percent (%)
Baseball	27
Racket sports	20
Basketball	20
Football and soccer	7
Ice hockey	4
Ball hockey	1

Figure 27-17

Eye anatomy.

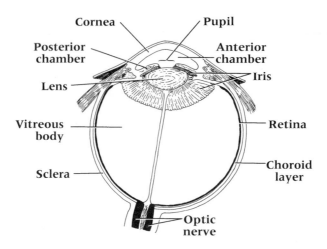

and finally through the vitreous body, all of which function collectively to focus an image on the retina, where it is detected by the optic nerve (Figure 27-17).

Preventing Eye Injuries

The eye can be injured in a number of different ways. Shattered eyeglass or goggle lenses can lacerate; ski pole tips can penetrate; and fingers, racquetball balls, and larger projectiles can seriously compress and injure the eye. High-energy sports such as ice hockey, football, and lacrosse require full-face and helmet protection, whereas low-energy sports such as racquetball and tennis require eye guards that rest on the face.[39] Protective devices must provide protection from front and lateral blows.

Sport goggles can be made with highly impact-resistant polycarbonate lenses for refraction. The major problems with sports goggles are that they distort peripheral vision and tend to become fogged under certain weather conditions (see Chapter 7).

Assessment of the Eye

It has been said that "evaluating and managing eye injuries is no place for amateurs."[2] Thus, the athletic trainer must use extreme caution in evaluating eye injuries (Figure 27-18). If any of the following conditions are evident, the athlete should be immediately referred to an ophthalmologist:[13] retinal detachment, perfo-

Figure 27-18

A serious eye injury should be treated as a major medical emergency.

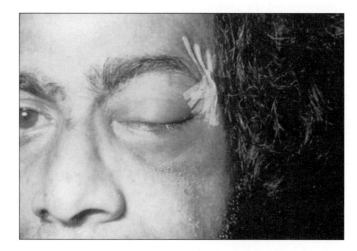

Focus

Supplies for managing eye injuries

To make an appropriate eye injury assessment, the athletic trainer must have a properly equipped first aid kit.[17] The following items should be available for use in the immediate care of eye injuries in sports:[17]

- Vision card for testing visual acuity
- Penlight
- Cotton-tipped applicators
- Sterile ocular irrigating solution
- Sterile eye patches
- Plastic eye shields
- Fluorescein strips
- Plunger for removing contact lenses

---

ration of the globe, a foreign object embedded in the cornea, blood in the anterior chamber, decreased vision, loss of the visual field, poor pupillary adaptation, double vision, laceration, or impaired lid function.

Ideally, the athlete with a serious eye injury should be transported to the hospital by ambulance in a recumbent position. Both eyes must be covered during transport. At no time should pressure be applied to the eye. In case of surrounding soft-tissue injury, a cold compress can be applied for thirty to sixty minutes to control hemorrhage. See also *Focus Box:* "Supplies for managing eye injuries."

The evaluator's first concerns are to understand the mechanism of injury and to determine if there is a related condition to the head, face, or neck. The evaluation process should include the following steps.[17]

> Extreme care must be taken with any eye injury: Transport the athlete in a recumbent position; cover both eyes, but put no pressure on the eye.

History

- What was the mechanism of injury (sharp and penetrating or blunt)?
- Was loss of vision gradual or immediate?
- What was the visual status before injury?
- Was there loss of consciousness?

Observation

- Inspect the external ocular structures for swelling and discoloration, penetrating objects, deformities, and movement of the lid.
- Inspect the globe of the eye for lacerations, foreign bodies, hyphema, or deformities.
- Inspect the conjunctiva and sclera for foreign bodies, hemorrhage, or deformities.

Palpation

Palpate the orbital rim for point tenderness or bony deformity.

Special Tests

Pupillary response   Tests to determine pupillary response were described in the section on assessment of head injuries; they include pupil dilation and accommodation by covering the eye and then exposing it to light.

Visual acuity   The evaluator determines visual acuity by asking the athlete to report what is seen when he or she looks at some object with the unaffected eye covered. A Snellen eye chart can be used to determine the extent of impairment

27-8

Critical Thinking Exercise

A wrestler gets a thumb pushed hard into the left eye.

? What symptoms indicate that this injury may be a serious eye injury?

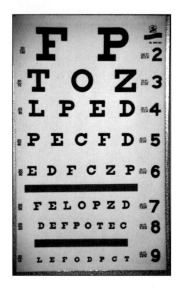

Figure 27-19

A Snellen eye chart can be used to assess visual acuity.

(Figure 27-19). There may be blurring of vision, diplopia, floating black specks, or flashes of light, all of which indicate serious eye involvement.

Ophthalmoscope An ophthalmoscope is an instrument for observing the interior of the eye, especially the retina (Figure 27-20). An athletic trainer may occasionally use an ophthalmoscope to look into the eye. Obviously, special training is necessary to recognize the presence of specific conditions or injuries.

Recognition and Management of Specific Eye Injuries

Orbital Hematoma (Black Eye)

Etiology Although well protected, the eye may be bruised during sports activity. The severity of eye injuries varies from a mild bruise to an extremely serious condition affecting vision to the fracturing of the orbital cavity. Fortunately, most eye injuries sustained in sports are mild. A blow to the eye may initially injure the surrounding tissue and produce capillary bleeding into the tissue spaces. If the hemorrhage goes unchecked, the result may be a classic "black eye."

Symptoms and signs The signs of a more serious contusion may be displayed as a subconjunctival hemorrhage or as faulty vision.

Management Care of an eye contusion requires cold application for at least half an hour, plus a twenty-four-hour rest period if the athlete has distorted vision. Under no circumstances should an athlete blow the nose after an acute eye injury. To do so might increase hemorrhaging.

Orbital Fractures

Etiology A fracture of the bony framework of the orbit surrounding the eye can occur when a blow to the eyeball forces it posteriorly, compressing the orbital fat until a blowout or rupture occurs to the floor of the orbit. Both fat and the inferior extraocular muscles can herniate through this fracture.[35]

Symptoms and signs The athlete with a fracture of the orbit will often exhibit diplopia, restricted movement of the eye, a downward displacement of the eye, and pain accompanied by soft-tissue swelling and hemorrhage. There may be numbness associated with injury to the infraorbital nerve on the floor of the orbit. An X ray must be taken to confirm the fracture.

Management A physician should administer antibiotics prophylactically to decrease the likelihood of infection. A fracture in the orbital floor allows communication with the maxillary sinus, which may contain potentially infectious bacteria. Most orbital fractures are treated surgically, although some physicians prefer to wait and see if the symptoms resolve on their own.

Figure 27-20

Positioning for an examiner using an ophthalmoscope.

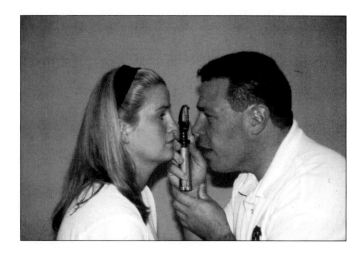

Focus

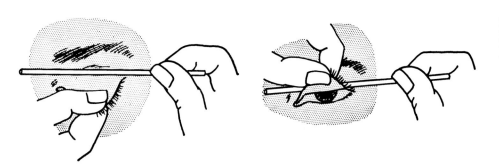

Removing a foreign body from the eye

Materials needed

Applicator stick, sterile cotton-tipped swab, eyecup, and eyewash (solution of boric acid).

Position of the athlete

The athlete lies supine on a table.

Procedure

1. Gently pull the eyelid down and place an applicator stick crosswise at its base.
2. Have the athlete look down; then grasp the lashes and turn the lid back over the stick.
3. Holding the lid and the stick in place with one hand, use the sterile cotton swab to lift out the foreign body.
4. Rinse with eyewash in an eye cup.

Foreign Body in the Eye

Etiology   Foreign bodies in the eye are a frequent occurrence in sports and are potentially dangerous.

Symptoms and signs   A foreign object produces considerable pain and disability. No attempt should be made to remove the body by rubbing or to remove it with the fingers.

Management   The athletic trainer instructs the athlete to close the eye until the initial pain has subsided and then attempts to determine if the object is in the vicinity of the upper or lower lid. Foreign bodies in the lower lid are relatively easy to remove by depressing the tissue and then wiping it with a sterile cotton applicator. Foreign bodies in the area of the upper lid are usually much more difficult to localize. Two methods may be used. The first technique is performed as follows: Gently pull the upper eyelid over the lower lid while the subject looks downward. This causes tears to be produced, which may flush the object down onto the lower lid. If this method is unsuccessful, the second technique should be used (see *Focus Box:* "Removing a foreign body from the eye" and Figure 27-21). After the foreign particle is removed, the affected eye should be washed with a saline solution. Often after removal of the foreign body there is a residual soreness, which may be alleviated by the application of petroleum jelly or some other mild ointment. If the athletic trainer encounters extreme difficulty in removing the foreign body or if the foreign body has become embedded in the eye itself, the eye should be closed and patched with a

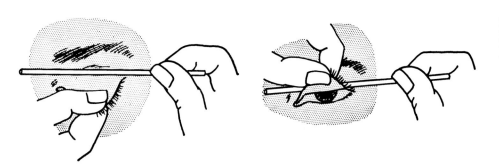

Figure 27-21

Removing a foreign body from the eye.

gauze pad held in place by strips of tape. The athlete is referred to a physician as soon as possible.[35]

Corneal Abrasions

Etiology   An athlete who gets a foreign object in his or her eye will usually try to rub it away. In doing so, the cornea can become abraded.

Symptoms and signs   The athlete will complain of severe pain and watering of the eye, photophobia, and spasm of the orbicular muscle of the eyelid.

Management   The eye should be patched, and the athlete should be sent to a physician. Corneal abrasion is diagnosed through application of a fluorescein strip to the abraded area, which stains the abrasion a bright green. Once diagnosed, the eye is dilated for further assessment. Antibiotic ointment is applied with a semipressure patch placed over the closed eyelid.

Hyphema

27-9

Critical Thinking E x e r c i s e

After receiving a blunt blow to her right eye, an athlete develops a collection of blood in the anterior chamber.

? What type of eye injury is this, and what complications may follow?

Etiology   A blunt blow to the anterior aspect of the eye can produce a hyphema, which is a collection of blood within the anterior chamber. This injury is often caused when an athlete is struck in the eye with a racquetball ball or squash ball when not wearing the appropriate protective eyeware.

Symptoms and signs   Initially there is a visible reddish tinge in the anterior chamber, and within the first two hours, the blood settles inferiorly or may fill the entire chamber. The blood may turn to a pea green color. Vision is partially or completely blocked. The athletic trainer must be aware that a hyphema is a major eye injury that can lead to serious problems of the lens, choroid, or retina.

Management   An athlete with a hyphema should be immediately referred to a physician. Conventional treatment involves hospitalization and bed rest with the head elevated 30 degrees to 40 degrees, patching of both eyes, sedation, and medication to reduce pressure in the anterior chamber. The initial hemorrhage resorbs in a few days, although occasionally there is rebleeding. If not managed properly, irreversible visual damage can occur.

Rupture of the Globe

Etiology   A blow to the eye by an object smaller than the eye orbit produces extreme pressure that can rupture the globe. A golf ball or racquetball ball fits this category. Larger objects such as a tennis ball or a fist will often fracture the bony orbit before the eye is overly compressed. Even if it does not cause rupture of the globe, such a force can cause internal injury that may ultimately lead to blindness.[35]

Symptoms and signs   The athlete complains of severe pain, decreased visual acuity, and diplopia. Inspection reveals irregular pupils, increased intraocular pressure, and orbital leakage.

Management   Treatment requires immediate rest, eye protection with a shield, and antiemetic medication to avoid increasing intraocular pressure. Immediate referral to an ophthalmologist must be made.

Retinal Detachment

Etiology   A blow to the athlete's eye can partially or completely separate the retina from its underlying retinal pigment epithelium. Retinal detachment is more common among athletes who have myopia (nearsightedness).[43]

Symptoms and signs   Detachment is painless; however, early signs include specks floating before the eye, flashes of light, or blurred vision. As the detachment progresses, the athlete complains of a "curtain" falling over the field of vision. Any athlete with symptoms of detachment must be immediately referred to an ophthalmologist.

Management   Initially, there is bed rest with patches on both eyes. The athlete should immediately be referred to an ophthalmologist to determine if surgery is required.

Acute Conjunctivitis

Etiology   The conjunctiva is the tissue that lines the back of the eyelid, moves into the space between the eyelid and eye globe, and spreads up over the sclera to the cornea.[43] Acute conjunctivitis is usually caused by various bacteria or allergens. It may begin with conjunctival irritation from wind, dust, smoke, or air pollution. It may also be associated with the common cold or other upper respiratory conditions.

Symptoms and signs   The athlete complains of eyelid swelling, sometimes with a purulent discharge. Itching is associated with allergy. Eyes may burn or itch.

Management   Acute conjunctivitis can be highly infectious. A 10 percent solution of sodium sulfacetamide is often the treatment of choice.

Hordeolum (Sty)

Etiology   A sty is an infection of the eyelash follicle or the sebaceous gland at the edge of the eyelid. The infection is usually caused by a staphylococcal organism that has been spread by rubbing or by dust particles.

Symptoms and signs   The condition starts as erythema of the eye. It localizes into a painful pustule within a few days.

Management   Treatment consists of the application of hot, moist compresses and an ointment of 1 percent yellow oxide or mercury. Recurrent sties require the attention of an ophthalmologist.

THROAT INJURIES

Contusions

Etiology   Blows to the throat do not occur frequently in sports, but occasionally an athlete may receive a kick or blow to the throat. One type of trauma is known as clotheslining, in which the athlete is struck in the throat region by another player's outstretched arm. Such a force could conceivably injure the carotid artery, causing a clot to form that occludes the blood flow to the brain. This same clot could become dislodged and migrate to the brain. In either case, serious brain injury may result.

Symptoms and signs   Immediately after throat trauma, the athlete may experience severe pain and spasmodic coughing, speak with a hoarse voice, and complain of difficulty in swallowing.

Fracture of throat cartilages of the larynx is rare, but it is possible and may be indicated by an inability to breathe and expectoration of frothy blood.[17] Cyanosis may be present. Throat contusions are extremely uncomfortable and are often frightening to the athlete.

Management   The most immediate concern is the integrity of the airway. The athlete who is experiencing difficulty in breathing should be sent to an emergency care facility immediately. In most situations, cold may be applied intermittently to control superficial hemorrhage and swelling, and after a twenty-four-hour rest period, moist hot packs may be applied. For the most severe neck contusions, stabilization with a well-padded collar is beneficial.

SUMMARY

- The skull is lined with the meninges, which collectively serve to protect the underlying cortex and midbrain from trauma.

- An athlete who receives either a direct blow to the head or body contact that causes the head to snap forward, backward, or rotate to the side must be carefully evaluated for injury to the brain. Injuries to the brain may or may not result in unconsciousness; disorientation or amnesia; motor coordination, or balance deficits; and cognitive deficits.

- It is important to realize that in the athletic population, the majority of concussions do not involve loss of consciousness.

27-10

Critical Thinking E x e r c i s e

An athlete develops an eyelash follicle infection.

? What is the cause of this condition, and how should it be treated?

27-11

Critical Thinking E x e r c i s e

While carrying the ball, a football back is clotheslined and seriously injures his throat.

? What should be the concerns of the athletic trainer in such an injury?

- Concussions usually occur as a result of a direct impact or through a combination of rotational and acceleration/deceleration forces.
- A variety of classification systems have been proposed for determining severity of concussion. To date, none of these classification systems has been universally endorsed, and thus debate continues.
- Returning an athlete to competition following concussion often creates a difficult dilemma for the athletic trainer. There must be ongoing concern for postconcussion syndrome, second impact syndrome, and epidural and subdural hematomas.
- Injuries to the face could involve fractures of the mandible, maxilla, or zygoma; dislocations of the mandible; temporomandibular dysfunction; and facial lacerations.
- Impact to the upper or lower jaw or direct trauma to the teeth can result in one or more of three types of fractures to the teeth: an uncomplicated crown fracture, a complicated crown fracture, and a root fracture. A tooth may also be subluxated, luxated, or avulsed. The athletic trainer should know when to refer an athlete for dental care.
- Most injuries to the ear involve the auricle, with cauliflower ear being the most common injury. Rupture of the tympanic membrane, swimmer's ear, and middle ear infections are common in the athletic population.
- Injuries to the eye should be treated by physicians who are specifically trained. Even injuries as simple as a black eye, a sty, or a corneal abrasion have the potential to cause some irreversible damage to vision if not properly managed. An orbital fracture, a foreign body in the eye, a hyphema, a rupture of the globe, and a retinal detachment are all considered serious injuries to the eye.
- The most serious consequence of a throat contusion is airway interference.

Web Sites

Cramer First Aider: http://www.ccsd.k12.wy.us/cchs_web/cramerfirstaider/fstaider.htm

World Ortho: http://www.worldortho.com

Wheeless' Textbook of Orthopaedics: http://www.medmedia.com/med.htm

American Orthopaedic Society for Sports Medicine: http://www.sportsmed.org

OrthoNet: http://www.orthonet.com

Solutions to Critical Thinking EXERCISES

27-1 The athlete's face color is pale and her skin moist, her pulse is rapid with shallow breathing, and her pupils may become dilated.

27-2 The athletic trainer asks the athlete questions that are related to recently acquired information. Examples are the current date, name of last week's opponent, who won that game, and who scored this game's last goal.

27-3 The athlete should be out of play for at least one month. After this period, he may return to play for one week if asymptomatic. The physician may consider terminating the athlete for the rest of the season.

27-4 This athlete is experiencing a postconcussion syndrome. The athlete cannot return completely to play until cleared by a thorough neurological examination.

27-5 In an athlete of this age, there should always be some concern about the possibility of second impact syndrome. From the athletic trainer's perspective, the decision to allow an athlete to return to play after an initial head injury must be carefully made based on the absence of postconcussive symptoms.

27-6 The conscious athlete with a fractured maxilla is transported to the hospital in a forward-leaning position. This position allows external drainage of saliva and blood.

27-7 The athlete sits up with a cold compress placed over the nose and ipsilateral carotid artery. Digital pressure can also be applied to the affected nostril for five minutes.

27-8 The symptoms that the athletic trainer looks for are blurred vision, a loss in the visual field, major pain, and double vision.

27-9 Blood in the anterior eye chamber is known as a hyphema, which could lead to major lens, choroid, or retina problems.

27-10 This sty is caused by a staphylococcal organism that is commonly spread by rubbing or by dust particle contamination. The condition should be managed with hot, moist compresses and a 1 percent yellow oxide or mercury ointment.

27-11 The compressive force of clotheslining could produce a blood clot in the carotid artery. A large enough force could fracture the larynx and cause a breathing crisis.

REVIEW QUESTIONS AND CLASS ACTIVITIES

1. What is the difference between the terms *concussion* and *mild head injury*?
2. What are the different classification systems for determining grades of concussion?

3. How are postconcussion syndrome and second impact syndrome related to concussion?

4. Demonstrate the following procedures in evaluating a concussion: testing eye signs, testing balance, testing coordination, testing cognition.

5. What immediate care procedures should be performed for athletes with facial lacerations?

6. Describe the immediate care procedures that should be performed when a tooth is fractured and when it is dislocated.

7. Describe the procedures that should be performed for an athlete with a nosebleed.

8. How can cauliflower ear be prevented?

9. How can eye injuries be prevented?

REFERENCES

1. Alexander M: Mild traumatic brain injury: pathophysiology, natural history, and clinical management, *Neurology* 45:1253, 1995.

2. Biggers P: Personal communication, 1998.

3. Cantu RC: Guidelines for return to contact sports after a cerebral concussion, *Physician Sportsmed* 14(10):75, 1986.

4. Cantu RC: Head and spine injuries in youth sports. In Michelle LJ, editor: *The young athlete. Clinics in sports medicine*, vol 14, no 3, Philadelphia, 1995, Saunders.

5. Cantu RC: Second impact syndrome. In Cantu RC: *Clinics in sports medicine*, 17(1):37, 1998.

6. Colorado Medical Society: The School Health and Sports Medicine Committee guidelines for the management of concussions in sport. In National Athletic Trainer's Association: *Proceedings of mild brain injury in sports summit*, 106–109, Dallas, 1994, NATA.

7. Committee on Head Injury Nomenclature of the Congress of Neurological Surgeons: Glossary of head injury including some definitions of injury to the cervical spine, *Clinical Neurosurgery* 12:386, 1966.

8. Crow RW: Sports-related lacerations, *Physician Sportsmed* 21(2):134, 1993.

9. Curtis SM: Disorders of brain function. In Porth CM, editor: *Pathophysiology*, ed 4, Philadelphia, 1994, Lippincott.

10. Davidson TM, Neuman TR: Managing ear trauma, *Physician Sportsmed* 22(7):27, 1994.

11. Davidson TM, Neuman TR: Managing inflammatory ear conditions, *Physician Sportsmed* 22(8):56, 1994.

12. DeYoung A, Robinson E, Godwin W: Comparing comfort and wearability: custom-made vs. self-adapted mouth guards, *J Am Dental Assoc* 125:1112, 1994.

13. Eagling EM, Roper-Hall MJ: *Eye injuries: an illustrated guide*, London, 1986, Butterworths.

14. Fick D: Management of concussion in collision sports, *Post Graduate Medicine* 97(2):53, 1995.

15. Gennarelli TA, Torg JS: Closed head injuries. In Torg JS, Shephard RJ, editors: *Current therapy in sports medicine*, St Louis, 1995, Mosby.

16. Gerberich S, Preist J, Boen C: Concussion incidences and severity in secondary school varsity football players, *Am J Public Health* 73:1370, 1983.

17. Guskiewicz K, Padua D, Weaver N: Incidence of mild head injury in high school and college football players, *Review Am J Sports Med*, 1999.

18. Guskiewicz K, Perrin D, Gansneader B: Effect of mild head injury on postural stability in athletes, *J Ath Train* 31(4):300, 1996.

19. Guskiewicz K, Riemann B, Perrin D, Nashner L: Alternative approaches to the assessment of mild head injury in athletes, *Med Sci Sports Exerc* 29(7):S213, 1997.

20. Hargarten KM: Rapid injury assessment, *Physician Sportsmed* 21(2):33, 1993.

21. Henderson JM: Head injuries in sports, *Sports Med Digest* 15(9):1, 1993.

22. Hugenholtz H, Richard M: Return to athletic competition following concussion, *Canadian Medical Assoc J* 127:827, 1982.

23. Jordan B: Head injuries in sports. In Jordan B, Tsairis P, Warren R: *Sports neurology*, Rockville, Md, 1989, Aspen.

24. Kelly JP, Rosenberg JH: Diagnosis and management of concussion in sports, *Neurology* 48:575, 1997.

25. Kinderknecht J: Head injuries. In Zachazewski J, Magee D, Quillen W: *Athletic injuries and rehabilitation*, Philadelphia, 1996, Saunders.

26. Kuland D: *The injured athlete*, Philadelphia, 1982, Lippencott.

27. Kumamoto DP et al: Oral trauma, *Physician Sportsmed* 23(5):53, 1995.

28. Maddocks DL: The assessment of orientation following concussion in athletes, *Cl J Sports Med* 5(1):32, 1995.

29. McWhorter JM: Concussions and intracranial injuries in athletics, *Ath Train* 25(2):129, 1990.

30. Mellion MB et al: Medical problems in athletes. In Birrer RB, editor: *Sports medicine for the primary care physician*, ed 2, Boca Raton, Fla, 1995, CRC Press.

31. Nelson W, Jane J, Geick J: Minor head injury in sports: A new system of classification and management, *Physician Sportsmed* 12:103, 1984.

32. Oliaro S, Guskiewicz K, Prentice W: Establishment of normative data on cognitive tests for comparison with athletes sustaining mild head injury, *J Ath Training* 33(1):36, 1998.

33. Ommaya A, Gennarelli T: Cerebral concussion and traumatic unconsciousness: correlation of experimental and clinical observations on blunt head injuries, *Brain* 97:638, 1974.

34. Ommaya A, Salazar A: A spectrum of mild head injuries in sport. In National Athletic Trainers' Association: *Proceedings of mild brain injury in sports summit*, 72–80, Dallas, 1994, NATA.

35. Pashby RC, Pashby TJ: Ocular injuries. In Torg JS, Shephard RJ, editors: *Current therapy in sports medicine*, St Louis, 1995, Mosby.

36. Reimann B, Guskiewicz K, Shields E: Relationship between clinical and forceplate measures of postural stability, *Review J Orthop Sports Phys Ther*, 1999.

37. Robinson T, Birrer RB: Ear injuries. In Birrer RB, editor: *Sports medicine for the primary care physician*, ed 2, Boca Raton, Fla, 1995, CRC Press.

38. Robinson T, Greenberg MD: Nasal injuries. In Birrer RB, editor: *Sports medicine for the primary care physician*, ed 2, Boca Raton, Fla, 1995, CRC Press.

39. Robinson T et al: Head injuries. In Birrer RB, editor: *Sports medicine for the primary care physician*, ed 2, Boca Raton, Fla, 1995, CRC Press.

40. Saal JA: Common American football injuries, *Sports Med* 12(2):132, 1991.

41. Schuller DE, Mountain RE: Auricular injury. In Torg JS, Shephard RJ, editors: *Current therapy in sports medicine*, St Louis, 1995, Mosby.

42. Swenson EJ Jr: Sports medicine emergencies. In Birrer RB, editor: *Sports medicine for the primary care physician*, ed 2, Boca Raton, Fla, 1995, CRC Press.

43. *Taber's cyclopedic medical dictionary*, Philadelphia, 1997, FA Davis.

44. Taylor LP: Neurologic disorders. In Agostini R, editor: *Medical and orthopedic issues of active and athletic women*, Philadelphia, 1994, Hanley & Belfus.

45. Torg JS: *Athletic injuries to the head, neck, and face*, St Louis, 1991, Mosby.

46. Torg JS: Emergency management of head and cervical spine injuries. In Torg JS, Shephard RJ, editors: *Current therapy in sports medicine*, St Louis, 1995, Mosby.

47. Weir J: Effective management of epistaxis in athletes, *J Ath Train* 32(3):254, 1997.

48. Weisberg J, Friedman M: The temporomandibular joint. In Gould J, Davies G, editors: *Orthopaedic and sports physical therapy*, St Louis, 1990, Mosby.

49. Wilberger JE, Maroon JC: Head injuries in athletes, *Clin Sports Med* 8:1, 1989.

50. Zagelbraum BM: Sports-related eye trauma, *Physician Sportsmed* 21(9):25, 1993.

ANNOTATED BIBLIOGRAPHY

Cantu RC: *Neurologic athletic head and neck injuries. Clinics in sports medicine*, vol 17, no 1, Philadelphia, 1998, Saunders.

This recent text looks at head and neck trauma that occurs specifically in the athletic population.

Eagling EM, Roper-Hall MJ: *Eye injuries: an illustrated guide*, London, 1986, Butterworths.

This text is a guide to the recognition and management of eye injuries.

Lehman LB, Ravich SJ: Closed head injuries in athletes. In Hershman EB, editor: *Neurovascular injuries. Clinics in sports medicine*, vol 9, no 2, Philadelphia, 1990, Saunders.

This text provides a concise description of cerebral injuries common in sports.

National Athletic Trainers' Association Research and Education Foundation: *Proceedings: Mild brain injury in sports*, Dallas, TX, 1994, NATA.

This collection of papers, presented at a conference about mild brain injuries, provides a concise summary of information on this topic.

Skin Disorders

When you finish this chapter you should be able to

- Explain the structure and function of the skin and identify the major lesions that result from skin abnormalities.
- Describe in detail how skin trauma occurs, how it may be prevented, and how it may be managed.
- Identify bacterial skin infections that are potentially contagious.
- Describe the correct hygiene practices to use to avoid fungal infections.
- Identify potentially threatening viral infections.
- Contrast allergic, thermal, and chemical reactions of the skin.
- Identify infestations and insect bites and contrast them with other skin infections.

It is essential that athletic trainers understand conditions that adversely affect the skin and mucous membranes, especially highly contagious conditions.

SKIN ANATOMY AND FUNCTION

The skin is the largest organ of the human body. The average adult skin varies in total weight from 6 to $7^1/_2$ pounds (2.7 to 3.4 kg) and is $^1/_{32}$- to $^1/_8$-inch (0.15 to 0.3 cm) thick. It is composed of three layers: the epidermis, dermis, and subcutis (Figure 28-1; Table 28-1).[19]

Epidermis

The epidermis has multiple layers. It forms the outer sheath of the body and is composed of the stratum corneum, the pigment melanin, and appendages (hair, nails, and sebaceous and sweat glands). It consists of two types of cells: keratinocytes and melanocytes. As these cells migrate outward toward the surface of the skin, the keratinocytes form the stratum corneum, which offers the greatest skin protection. The epidermis acts as a barrier against invading microorganisms, foreign particles from dirt and debris, chemicals, and ultraviolet rays and also helps contain the body's water and electrolytes. Melanin, produced by melanocytes, protects the body against ultraviolet radiation.

Dermis

The dermis is a skin layer of irregular form, situated underneath the epidermis and composed of connective tissue that contains blood vessels, nerve endings, sweat glands, hair follicles, and sebaceous glands. The dermis forms a series of projections that reach into the epidermis, resulting in an interlocking arrangement and thereby preventing the epidermis from slipping off the dermis.

Hair and Sebaceous Glands

Hair grows from hair follicles contained in the skin. Hair extends into the dermis, where it is nourished by the blood capillaries. Small muscles called arrectores pilorum connect to the hair at its root and, when contracted, serve to constrict the hair follicles and cause a "standing-on-end" effect, or goose pimples. Such contractions increase the emission of oil and thereby help protect the body from cold.

The sebaceous glands, which surround the hair, secrete an oily substance into the hair follicles. Persons who have overactive sebaceous glands may develop

Figure 28-1

The skin is the largest organ of the human body.

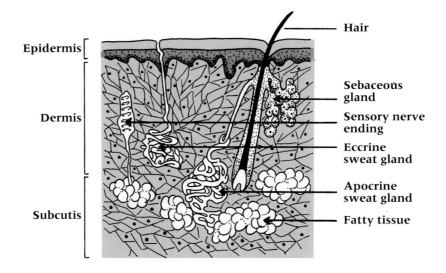

sebaceous cyst
A cyst filled with sebum; usually found in the scalp.

blackheads because of plugging of the hair follicle. A **sebaceous cyst** can develop, usually on the scalp, as a result of impairment of localized circulation and closure of the sebaceous glands, or ducts. The cyst is filled with sebum and must be surgically removed.

Sweat Glands

Sweat glands are necessary for cooling the surface of the body and the internal organs. There are two main types of sweat glands: the eccrine glands, which are present at birth and are generally present throughout the skin; and the apocrine glands, which are much larger than the eccrine and mature during adolescence in conjunction with the axillary and pubic hair. Certain individuals with undersecreting sweat glands (dry skin) may be especially susceptible to various diseases. The fluid of the sweat gland contains antibacterial agents that are essential in controlling skin infections.

Nails

The nails are special horny cell structures that come from the phalanges. They are embedded in skin at their base and along their sides and grow approximately $1/2$ inch (1.25 cm) in four months.

TABLE 28-1 Outline of the Skin's Structure and Function

Layer	Subregion	Function
Epidermis	Stratum corneum	Prevents intrusion of microorganisms, debris, chemicals, ultraviolet radiation
		Prevents loss of water and electrolytes
		Performs heat regulation for conduction, radiation, convection
	Melanin (pigmentation)	Prevents intrusion of ultraviolet radiation
Dermis		Protects against physical trauma
		Contains sensory nerve endings
		Holds water and electrolytes
	Appendages	Contains eccrine and apocrine sweat glands, hair, nails, sebaceous glands
Subcutis		Stores fat, regulates heat

Sensory Nerve Endings

Besides its many other functions, the dermis contains sensory nerve endings. These peripheral nerves provide the body with important protective information such as temperature changes and pain.

Subcutis

The subcutis region contains subcutaneous fat. This area is the primary area for fat storage; it produces internal temperature regulation and mobility of the skin over the internal body core.

SKIN LESIONS DEFINED

Skin that is healthy has a smooth, soft appearance. It is colored by a pigment known as melanin. An increased amount of blood in the skin capillaries may give the skin a ruddy appearance, and an insufficient amount may give it a pale effect.[1]

The normal appearance of the skin can be altered by external and internal factors. Some changes may be signs of other involvements. The different intensities of paleness or redness of the skin, which is related to the extent of superficial circulation, may be hereditary. Pigment variation may result from an increase of sun exposure or from organic disease; a yellowish discoloration, for example, may be indicative of jaundice. **Cellulitis,** which is an inflammation of cellular or connective tissue that spreads through the tissues, causes reddening and increased warmth.

Skin abnormalities may be divided into primary and secondary lesions. Primary lesions include macules, papules, plaques, nodules, tumors, cysts, wheals, vesicles, bullae, and pustules (Figure 28-2; Table 28-2). Secondary lesions usually develop from primary lesions (Figure 28-3; Table 28-3).

cellulitis
An inflammation of cells and connective tissue that extends deep into the tissues.

SKIN TRAUMA

Sports participation can place a great deal of mechanical force on the skin. Mechanical forces that can be applied to the skin include friction, compression, shearing, stretching, scraping, tearing, avulsing, and puncturing, all of which can lead to painful and serious injuries.[2,14]

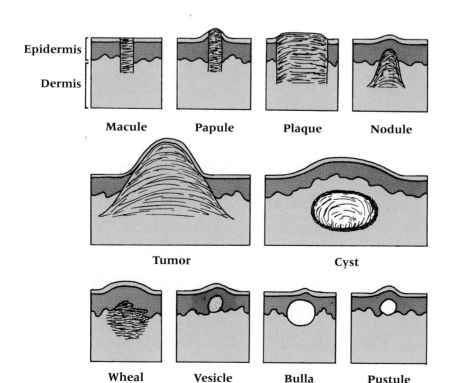

Figure 28-2

Typical primary skin lesions.

TABLE 28-2 Primary Skin Lesions

Type	Description	Example
Macule	A small, flat, circular discoloration smaller than 1 cm in diameter	Freckle or flat nevus
Papule	A solid elevation less than 1 cm in diameter	Wart
Plaque or patch	May be a macule or papule larger than 1 cm in diameter	Vitiligo patch (patches of depigmentation)
Nodule	A solid mass less than 1 cm, deeper into the dermis than a papule	Dermatofibroma (fibrosis tumor–like)
Tumor	Solid mass larger than 1 cm	Cavernous hemangioma (tumor filled with blood vessels)
Cyst	Encapsulated, fluid filled, in dermis or subcutis	Epidermoid cyst
Wheal	A papule or plaque caused by serum collection into the dermis, allergic reactions	Urticaria (hives)
Vesicle	Fluid-filled elevation less than 1 cm, just below epidermis	Smallpox, chicken pox
Bulla	Like a vesicle but larger	Second-degree burn, friction blister
Pustule	Like vesicle or bulla but contains pus	Acne

Friction and Pressure Problems

Excessive rubbing back and forth over the skin, along with abnormal pressure, can cause hypertrophy of the stratum corneum, or horny layer, of the epidermis, especially on the soles of the feet and the palms of the hands. This condition is called *keratoderma*. Another expression for this process is callosity, or **keratosis.** This same mechanism can produce corns and blisters.

Keratosis of the Feet and Hands

Skin, typically the epidermal skin layer, increases in thickness when constant friction and pressure are externally applied. Excessive callus accumulation may occur over bony protuberances.

Etiology Foot calluses may become excessive on an athlete who wears shoes that are too narrow or short. Like foot calluses, hand calluses can become painful when the subcutaneous fatty layer loses its elasticity, which is an important cushioning effect. The cal-

keratosis

Excessive growth of the horny tissue layer.

Figure 28-3

Typical secondary skin lesions.

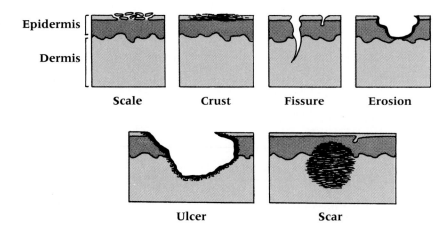

Scale   Crust   Fissure   Erosion

Ulcer   Scar

TABLE 28-3 Secondary Skin Lesions

Type	Description	Example
Scales	Flakes of skin	Psoriasis
Crust	Dried fluid or exudates on skin	Impetigo
Fissure	Skin crack	Chapping
Excoriation	Superficial scrape	Abrasion
Erosion	Loss of superficial epidermis	Scratches (superficial)
Ulcer	Destruction of entire epidermis	Pressure sore
Scar	Healing of dermis	Vaccination, laceration

lus moves as a mass when pressure and a shearing force are applied. This movement, coupled with a lack of blood supply, produces rips, tears, cracks, and ultimately, infection.

Prevention   Athletes whose shoes are properly fitted but who still develop heavy calluses commonly have foot mechanics problems that may require special orthotics. Special cushioning devices such as wedges, doughnuts, and arch supports may help distribute the weight on the feet more evenly and thus reduce skin stress. Athletes can prevent excessive callus accumulation by wearing two pairs of socks—a thin cotton or nylon pair next to the skin and a heavy athletic pair over the cotton pair—or a single doubleknit sock; wearing shoes that are the correct size and are in good condition; routinely applying materials such as a lubricant to reduce friction; and shaving the callus with a scalpel, using extreme caution.

Hand calluses can also be controlled by proper toughening procedures and by direct protection through the use of a special glove, such as is used in batting, or by the application of elastic tape or moleskin. The skin of the hands can be made more resistant to callosity by the routine application of astringents such as tannic acid or by saltwater soaks. In sports such as gymnastics, athletic trainers and athletes go to great lengths to protect the athlete's hands against tearing calluses. One protective device is a grip, which is a special type of hand covering that may include a wood dowel placed across the grip portion of the hand.

Symptoms and signs   The callus appears as a circumscribed thickening and hypertrophy of the horny layer of the skin. It may be ovular, elongated, brownish, and slightly elevated. Callus may not be painful when pressure is applied.

Management   Athletes who are prone to excess calluses should be encouraged to use an emery callus file after each shower. Massaging small amounts of lanolin into devitalized calluses once or twice a week after practice may help maintain some tissue elasticity. Once excessive formation has occurred, a keratolytic ointment, such as Whitefield's ointment, may be applied. A 5 percent to 10 percent solution of salicylic acid in a flexible collodion that is applied at night and peeled off in the morning has also been beneficial. Before application of a keratolytic ointment, the athletic trainer might manually decrease the callus's thickness by carefully paring it with a sharp scalpel, sanding it, or using pumice on its surface. Great care should be taken not to totally remove the callus and the protection it affords a pressure point. A donut pad may be cut to size and placed on a pressure point to prevent pain.

Blisters

Like calluses, blisters are often a major problem of sports participation, especially early in the season. Shearing forces produce a raised area that contains a fluid collection below or within the epidermis.

Etiology   Blisters are particularly associated with rowing, pole vaulting, basketball, football, and weight events in track and field, such as the shot put and discus. Such activities commonly cause the skin to be subjected to horizontal shearing, which produces a friction blister.

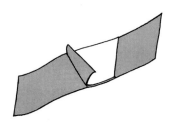

Figure 28-4

A blanked-out tape to prevent a blister.

Prevention   Soft feet and hands coupled with shearing skin stress can produce severe blisters. A dusting of talcum powder or the application of petroleum jelly can protect the skin against abnormal friction. Wearing tubular socks or two pairs of socks, as was suggested for preventing calluses, is also desirable, particularly for athletes who have sensitive feet or feet that perspire excessively. Wearing the correct-size shoe is essential. The shoes must be broken in before they are worn for long periods of time. If, however, a friction area (hot spot) does arise, the athlete has several options. The athlete can cover the irritated skin with a friction-reducing material such as petroleum jelly, place a blanked-out piece of tape tightly over the irritated area (Figure 28-4), or cover it with a piece of moleskin. Another method that has proved effective against blisters is the application of ice over skin areas that have developed abnormal friction.

Symptoms and signs   The athlete normally will feel a hot spot, that is, a sharp, burning sensation, as the blister is formed. The area of sensation should be examined immediately. The blister may be superficial, containing clear liquid. On the other hand, a blood blister may form, in which deeper tissue is disrupted, which causes blood vessels to rupture. Pain is caused by the pressure of the fluid.

Management   As stated previously, blister prevention is of paramount importance. Once developed, blisters can be a serious problem for the athlete as well as for the athletic trainer. Following are general rules for managing a blister (OSHA standards must be followed; see Chapter 14).

- The intact blister:
  1. Leave the blister intact for the first twenty-four hours. Often during that time, many of the symptoms will lessen.
  2. If the blister is large and in a place on the skin that will be continually irritated, clean it thoroughly with antiseptic soap.
  3. With a sterile scalpel, cut a small incision $^1/_8$- to $^1/_4$-inch (0.3 to 0.6 cm) long in the blister along the periphery of the raised tissue. The hole should be large enough that it will not become sealed.
  4. Disperse the fluid by applying a pressure pad, keeping the pad in place to prevent refilling.
  5. Once the fluid has been removed, clean the area again with an antiseptic such as povidone-iodine (Betadine) and cover it with an antibiotic ointment such as Polysporin.
  6. Place a doughnut pad around the dressed blister to avoid further irritation.
  7. Monitor the blistered area daily for the possibility of infection. If infection occurs, refer the athlete to a physician immediately.
  8. Replace the dressing if it becomes wet from fluid seepage. A wet environment encourages growth of bacteria and therefore infection.
  9. If there is necrotic skin, debridement can be done when the tenderness is completely gone. Debridement should not be attempted if any tenderness persists.
- The open (torn) blister:
  1. Keep the open blister clean to avoid infection. In the beginning of management, carefully and thoroughly wash with soap and water. Once cleaned, apply hydrogen peroxide or benzalkonium chloride. If the blister site is torn along less than one half of its diameter, apply a liquid antiseptic and allow to dry, then apply an antibiotic ointment.
  2. Lay the flap of skin back over the treated tissue; then apply a sterile, nonadhering dressing and a doughnut pad.
  3. Like the intact blister, the open blister should be monitored daily for the possibility of infection.
- The completely denuded blister:
  1. If the blister is torn $^1/_2$ inch (1.25 cm) or more, completely remove the flap of skin using sterile scissors.
  2. Completely clean the exposed tissue with soap and water. Apply an antiseptic liquid such as benzalkonium with occlusive dressing.[7]

28-1

C*ritical Thinking* E x e r c i s e

A basketball player wearing new shoes during a game sustains a completely denuded blister on the back of the heel.

? How should this condition be managed during and after the game?

3. If the athlete has completed his or her activity, apply a second-skin dressing such as the one manufactured by Spenco to the raw area. When applied, this gel ensures healing through the night.

Soft Corns and Hard Corns

Soft corns and hard corns are other examples of keratoses caused by abnormal skin pressure and friction.

Etiology   A hard corn (clavus durus) is the most serious type of corn. It is caused by the pressure of improperly fitting shoes and other anatomical abnormalities, the same mechanisms that cause calluses. Hammertoes are usually associated with the hard corns that form on the tops of deformed toes (Figure 28-5A). Symptoms are local pain and disability with inflammation and thickening of soft tissue. Because of the chronic nature of this condition, it requires a physician's care.

A soft corn (clavus mollis) is the result of the combination of narrow shoes and excessive foot perspiration. It is also associated with an exostosis. Because of the pressure of the shoe coupled with the exudation of moisture, the corn usually forms between the fourth and fifth toes (Figure 28-5B). A circular area of thickened, white, macerated skin appears between the toes at the base of the proximal head of the phalanges. Both pain and inflammation are likely to be present.[4]

Prevention   The primary way to prevent a soft or hard corn is to wear properly fitted shoes. Soft corns can be avoided by wearing shoes that are wide enough. Conversely, hard corns can be avoided by wearing shoes that are long enough.

Symptoms and signs   With a soft corn, the athlete complains of pain laterally on the fifth toe. During inspection, the soft corn appears as a circular piece of thickened, white, **macerated skin** on the lateral side of the fifth toe at the base of the proximal head of the phalanges. In contrast, a hard corn is on the tops of hammertoes. The bony prominence of the toe is forced up, and it presses on the inner tops of the shoe, causing the corn to form. It appears hard and dry, with a callus that is sharply demarcated.

Management   The corn is difficult to manage. If pain and inflammation are major, referral to a podiatrist for surgical removal may be advisable. The athletic trainer may ameliorate the condition by having the athlete wear properly fitting shoes and socks and may alleviate further irritation of the corn by protecting it with a small felt pad or sponge pad, which can act as a buffer between the shoe and the toe.

In caring for a soft corn, the best procedure is to have the athlete wear properly fitting shoes, keep the skin between the toes clean and dry, decrease pressure by keeping the toes separated with cotton or lamb's wool, and apply a keratolytic agent such as a 40 percent solution of salicylic acid in liquid or plasters.

Excessive Perspiration (Hyperhidrosis)

Etiology   Excessive perspiration (hyperhidrosis) occurs in a small segment of the population. This problem can make the handling of sports objects difficult, causing both performance and safety problems. Emotional excitement often makes the situation worse. The chemical composition of hyperhidrotic perspiration from palms is syruplike in appearance and extremely high in sodium chloride. This problem also increases the possibility of skin irritations and often makes adherence of bandages difficult, especially where adhesive tape is necessary. The condition makes callus development, blisters, and intertrigo (chafing) much more likely to occur.

Management   Treatment of excessive perspiration should include the use of an astringent such as alcohol or an absorbent powder (see *Focus Box:* "Foot hygiene for excessive perspiration and odor").

Chafing of the Skin

Chafing (intertrigo) of the skin is another condition that stems from friction or from rubbing the skin unduly.

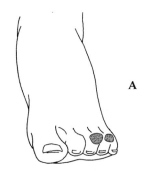

Figure 28-5

A, Hard corn (clavus durus).
B, Soft corn (clavus mollis).

macerated skin
Skin softened by exposure to water.

Excessive perspiration can be a cause of serious skin irritation.

Focus

Foot hygiene for excessive perspiration and odor

Before practice

1. Apply an astringent such as 20 percent aluminum chloride in anhydrous ethyl alcohol (Drysol) to the skin and allow it to air-dry.
2. Liberally apply a powder such as talcum, alum, or boric acid to the skin, socks, and sports footwear.

After practice

1. Thoroughly wash and dry the feet, then follow the before-practice procedure. An astringent is applied to the skin and an absorbent powder is applied to street socks and shoes.
2. Footwear should be changed frequently.
3. Sports footwear should be liberally powdered after practice to absorb moisture during storage. Ideally, a different pair of shoes should be worn daily.

28-2

Critical Thinking Exercise

A heavy-limbed shot-putter complains of a skin irritation in his groin region. The area appears red and macerated. Some of the tissue is cracked, and there are oozing sores.

? How could this chafing have been prevented?

Etiology   Chafing occurs particularly in athletes who are obese or heavy limbed. It results from friction and maceration (softening) of the skin in a climate of heat and moisture.

Prevention   To prevent intertrigo, the skin should be kept dry, clean, and friction free. For groin conditions, the athlete should wear loose, soft, cotton underwear. A male athlete should wear his supporter over a pair of loose cotton boxer shorts.

Symptoms and signs   Repeated skin rubbing, as in the groin and axilla, can separate the keratin from the granular layer of the epidermis. This separation causes oozing wounds that develop into crusting and cracking lesions.

Management   The chafed area should be cleansed once daily with mild soap and lukewarm water. Treatment of a chafed area includes the use of wet packs, moistened with a medicated solution such as Burrows, for fifteen to twenty minutes, three times daily. Each treatment is followed by the application of a 1 percent hydrocortisone cream.

Xerotic (Dry) Skin

Dry skin is a condition that athletes commonly experience during the winter months.[11]

Etiology   Athletes who are exposed to weather and bathe often commonly develop dry or chapped skin. The drying cold of winter tends to dehydrate the stratum corneum. Some athletes naturally have fewer skin lipids, which increases the tendency toward water loss.[11] A decrease in humidity along with cold winds causes the skin to lose water.

Symptoms and signs   The skin appears dry with variable redness and scaling. It occurs first on the shins, forearm, back of the hands, and face and may include itching. The skin may crack and develop fissures.

Management   The major goals in treatment are to prevent water loss and to replace lost water.[11] The following treatment procedures should be followed:

- Bath in tepid water and shower one time per day.
- Use moisturizing soaps such as Dove or Aveeno. Avoid soaping dry areas. Restrict washing to genitalia, underarms, hands, feet, and face.
- Use emollient lotions, which hydrate the skin. They should be applied after each washing.
- When the condition is more severe, the athlete should be referred to a physician for antipruritics, alpha-hydroxy acids, and perhaps topical corticosteroids.[11]

Ingrown Toenails

An ingrown toenail is a common condition among athletes. The large toe is the most often affected. The nail grows into the lateral nailfold and enters the skin.[6]

Etiology   In general, the ingrown nail results from the lateral pressure caused by poorly fitting shoes, from improper toenail trimming, or from trauma, such as repeated pressure due to the foot's sliding to the front of the shoe (Color Plate, Figure A).

Prevention   Because of the handicapping nature of this condition, prevention of ingrown toenails is much preferred over management. Properly fitted shoes and socks are essential. The toenails should be trimmed weekly by cutting straight across, avoiding rounding so that the margins do not penetrate the tissue on the side (Figure 28-6). The nail should be left sufficiently long so that it is clear of the underlying skin, but it should be cut short enough so as not to irritate the skin by pushing against shoes or socks.

Symptoms and signs   The first indications of an ingrown toenail are pain and swelling. If not treated early, the penetrated skin becomes severely inflamed and purulent. The lateral nailfold is swollen and irritated.

Management   There are a number of ways to manage the ingrown toenail. If it is in the first stages of inflammation, a more conservative approach can be taken.

- Soak the inflamed toe in warm water (105° to 110° F/40.5° to 43.3° C) for approximately twenty minutes.
- After soaking, the nail will be soft and pliable and may be pried out of the skin. Using sterile forceps or scissors, lift the nail from the soft tissue and insert a piece of cotton to keep the nail out of the skin (Figure 28-7). This cotton also relieves the pain. Perform this procedure daily until the corner of the nail has grown past the irritated tissue.

If the condition becomes chronically irritated, a more aggressive approach is likely to be taken by a physician.

- After applying an anesthetic (e.g., 1% or 2% lidocaine), slip the nail-splitting scissor under the ingrown nail.[9]
- With the scissor inserted to the point of resistance, cut away and remove the wedge-shaped nail. Keep a moist antiseptic compress in place until the inflammation has subsided.

Athletes with recurrent ingrown nails may require the use of phenol for permanent destruction of the lateral portion of the nail.

Wounds

Traumatic skin lesions, commonly termed *wounds,* are extremely prevalent in sports; abrasions, lacerations, incisions, and punctures are daily occurrences (Figure 28-8). To avoid infection, any wound, no matter how slight, must be cared for immediately (Table 28-4). In general, all wounds must be cleansed with soap and water to rid them of microorganism contamination. After cleansing, a dressing containing an antiseptic is applied. However, if the wound is to be examined by a physician, no medication should be added to the dressing. Most lacerations and puncture wounds should be treated by a physician. Uninfected abrasions are not usually referred to a physician. They are managed by debridement and thorough cleansing with soap and water, followed by the application of an occlusive dressing.[8] Using an antibiotic ointment prevents accumulation of a crust and secondary infection. It is advisable that abrasions be allowed to heal from the inside out to avoid the formation of scabs, which serve only to cover infected areas and are easily torn off by activity. Generally, lacerations, incisions, and puncture wounds require an innoculation with tetanus toxoid if a booster has not been given within ten years.

Abrasions

Abrasions are common and occur when the skin is scraped against a rough surface. The top layer of skin is worn away, thus exposing numerous blood capillaries. This general exposure, with dirt and foreign materials scraping and penetrating the skin,

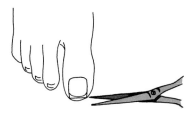

Figure 28-6

Preventing an ingrown toenail requires proper trimming.

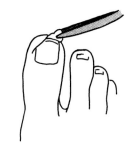

Figure 28-7

Application of a wisp of cotton under the ingrown side.

Signs of wound infection, which appear two to seven days after injury:

- Red, swollen, hot, and tender wound
- Swollen and painful lymph glands near the area of infection (groin, axilla, or neck)
- Mild fever and headache

28-3

Critical Thinking Exercise

A baseball player slides into second base and sustains a serious slide burn on the left side.

? What are the major concerns with this type of injury, and how should it be managed?

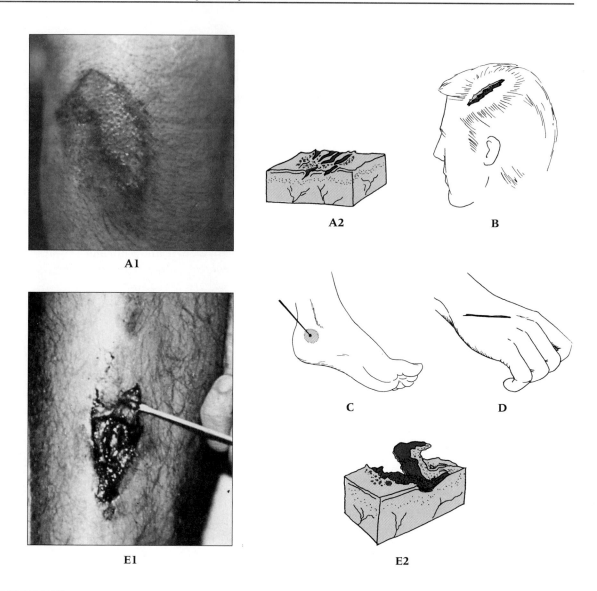

Figure 28-8

Wounds occurring in sports can present a serious problem of infection. **A1** and **A2,** Abrasion. **B,** Laceration. **C,** Puncture. **D,** Incision. **E1** and **E2,** Avulsion.

increases the probability of infection unless the wound is properly debrided and cleansed.

Punctures

Puncture wounds can easily occur during physical activities and have a high potential for infection. Direct penetration of tissues by a pointed object such as a track shoe spike can introduce the tetanus bacillus into the bloodstream. All puncture wounds and severe lacerations should be referred immediately to a physician.[15]

Lacerations

Lacerations are also common in sports and occur when a sharp or pointed object tears the tissues, giving the wound the appearance of a jagged-edged cavity. Blunt trauma over a sharp bone can also cause a wound that is similar in appearance to a laceration. Like abrasions, lacerations present an environment conducive to severe infection. The same mechanism that causes a laceration can also cause a skin avulsion, in which a piece of skin is completely ripped from its source.

TABLE 28-4 Care of Open Wounds

Type of Wound	Action of Coach or Athletic Trainer	Initial Care	Follow-up Care
Abrasion	Provide initial care. Wound seldom requires medical attention unless infected.	Cleanse abraded area with mild soap and water; debride with brush. Apply solution of hydrogen peroxide over abraded area; continue until foaming has subsided. Follow with povidone-iodine. Apply medicated ointment to keep abraded surface moist—in sports, it is not desirable for abrasions to acquire a scab. Place a nonadhering sterile pad over the ointment.	Change dressing daily; look for signs of infection.
Laceration	Cleanse around wound; avoid wiping more contaminating agents into the area. Apply dry, sterile compress pad; refer to physician.	Complete cleansing and suturing are performed by physician; injections of tetanus toxoid are given if needed.	Change dressing daily; look for signs of infection.
Puncture	Cleanse around wound; avoid wiping more contaminating agents into the area. Apply dry, sterile compress pad; refer to physician.	Complete cleansing and injections of tetanus toxoid, if needed, are performed by physician.	Change dressing daily; look for signs of infection.
Incision	Clean around wound. Apply dry, sterile compress pad to control bleeding; refer to physician.	Cleanse wound. Suturing and injection of tetanus toxoid, if needed, are performed by physician.	Change dressing daily; look for signs of infection.
Avulsion	Clean around wound; save avulsed tissue. Apply dry, sterile compress pad to control bleeding; refer to physician.	Wound is cleansed thoroughly; avulsed skin is replaced and sutured by a physician; tetanus toxoid injection is administered if needed.	Change dressing daily; look for signs of infection.

Skin Incisions

Incisions are similar to lacerations; instead of a jagged cut, however, the wound is smooth, as though it were created with a knife or piece of glass. Incision wounds in sports often occur when a blow is delivered over a sharp bone or over a bone that is poorly padded.

Skin Avulsions

Avulsion wounds occur when skin is torn from the body; they are frequently associated with major bleeding. The avulsed tissue should be placed on moist gauze that is saturated with saline solution. The tissue and gauze are put into a plastic bag that is then immersed in cold water and taken, along with the athlete, to the hospital for possible reattachment.

Skin Bruises

The consequence of a sudden compressive, blunt force to the skin is a bruise. The skin is not broken, but the soft tissue is traumatized. A first-degree bruise (ecchymosis) causes, in most cases, broken blood vessels and discoloration (black and blue). A great force affects the underlying structures, producing a bone or muscle contusion. RICE is the treatment of choice to control the hemorrhage that may occur.

bandage
A strip of cloth or other material used to cover a wound.

dressing
Covering, protective or supportive, that is applied to an injury or wound.

Wound Dressings

A **bandage,** when properly applied, can contribute decidedly to an athlete's recovery from sports injuries. Bandages carelessly or improperly applied can cause discomfort, allow wound contamination, or even hamper repair and healing. In all cases, bandages must be firmly applied—neither so tight that circulation is impaired nor so loose that the **dressing** is allowed to slip (see Chapter 8). Skin lesions are extremely prevalent in sports; abrasions, lacerations, and puncture wounds are almost daily occurrences. It is of the utmost importance to the well-being of the athlete that open wounds be cared for immediately. All wounds, even those that are relatively superficial, must be considered contaminated by microorganisms and therefore must be cleansed, medicated (when called for), and dressed. Wound dressing requires a sterile environment to prevent infections. Individuals who perform wound management in sports often do not follow good principles of cleanliness. To alleviate this problem, athletic trainers must adhere to standard procedures in the prevention of wound contamination.

Training room practices in wound care   The following are suggested procedures to use in the athletic training room to cut down the possibility of wound infections. See Table 28-4 for more specific suggestions regarding the care of external wounds.

1. Make sure all instruments such as scissors, tweezers, and swabs are sterilized.
2. Clean hands thoroughly.
3. Clean in and around a skin lesion thoroughly.
4. Place a nonmedicated dressing over a lesion if the athlete is to be sent for medical attention.
5. Avoid touching any part of a sterile dressing that may come in contact with a wound.
6. Place medication on a pad rather than directly on a lesion.
7. Secure the dressing with tape or a wrap; always avoid placing pressure directly over a lesion.

In caring for wounds that involve bleeding and other body fluids, the athletic trainer must be concerned with the chance of becoming infected by the human immunodeficiency virus (HIV) or by hepatitis B (see Chapter 14).

BACTERIAL INFECTIONS

Bacteria are single-celled microorganisms that can be seen only with a microscope after they are stained with specific dyes. They are of three major shapes: spherical (cocci), which occur in clumps; doublets, or chains, and rods (bacilli); and spirochetes, which are corkscrew shaped.

Athletes with bacterial infections associated with pus may pass the infection onto other athletes through direct contact.

staphylococcus
Genus of gram-positive bacteria normally present on the skin and in the upper respiratory tract and prevalent in localized infections.

streptococcus
Genus of gram-positive bacteria found in the throat, respiratory tract, and intestinal tract.

Staphylococcus is a genus of gram-positive bacteria that commonly appear in clumps on the skin and in the upper respiratory tract. It is the most prevalent cause of infections in which pus is present.

Streptococcus is also a genus of gram-positive bacteria, but unlike staphylococci, it appears in long chains. Most species are harmless, but some are among the most dangerous bacteria affecting humans. Streptococci can be associated with serious systemic diseases such as scarlet fever and can be associated with staphylococci in skin diseases.

Bacillus is a genus of bacteria belonging to the family *Bacillaceae*. Bacilli are spore forming, aerobic, gram-positive, and nonpathogenic, and some are mobile. Most bacilli are not pathological; those that are can cause major systemic damage.

Impetigo Contagiosa

Impetigo contagiosa is an extremely common skin disease, primarily observed in children, with the greatest number of cases occurring in late summer and early fall.

Etiology   Impetigo contagiosa is caused by group A beta-hemolytic streptococci, by *S. aureus,* or by a combination of these two bacteria. It is spread rapidly when athletes are in close contact with one another. Wrestling is a sport that is particularly at risk for spreading this disease.[18]

Focus

Symptoms and signs Impetigo contagiosa is first characterized by mild itching and soreness, which are followed by the eruption of small vesicles that form into pustules and later into yellow crustations (Color Plate, Figure B). Up to 20 percent of people carry staphylococcus in and about their nostrils. In general, impetigo develops in body folds that are subject to friction.[16]

Management Impetigo usually responds rapidly to proper treatment. This treatment consists of thorough cleansing of the crusted area followed by the application of a topical antibacterial agent such as Bactroban (see *Focus Box: "Management of impetigo"*). Systemic antibiotics also are used.

Furuncles and Carbuncles

Two major skin problems affecting athletes are furuncles and carbuncles. Both, if traumatized, could lead to a serious systemic infection.

Furunculosis

Furuncles (boils) are common among athletes.

Etiology Furuncles and carbuncles are complications of folliculitis that result from friction or blunt trauma. The predominant infectious organisms are staphylococci, which produce a pustule.

Symptoms and signs The areas of the body most affected are the back of the neck, the face, and the buttocks. The pustule becomes enlarged, reddened, and hard from internal pressure. As pressure increases, extreme pain and tenderness develop (Color Plate, Figure C). Most furuncles will mature and rupture spontaneously, emitting the contained pus. NOTE: Furuncles should not be squeezed, because squeezing forces the infection into adjacent tissue or extends it to other skin areas.[10] Furuncles on the face can be dangerous, particularly if they drain into veins that lead to venous sinuses of the brain. Such conditions should immediately be referred to a physician.

Management Care of the furuncle involves protecting it from additional irritation, referring the athlete to a physician for antibiotic treatment, and keeping the athlete from contact with other team members while the boil is draining. The common practice of hot dressings or special drawing salves is not beneficial to the maturation of the boil.

Carbuncles

Etiology Carbuncles are similar to furuncles in their early stages because they also develop from staphylococci.

Symptoms and signs The principal difference between a carbuncle and a furuncle is that the carbuncle is larger and deeper and usually has several openings in the skin. It may produce fever and elevation of the white cell count. A carbuncle starts as a painful node that is covered by tight, reddish skin that later becomes very thin.

28-4

Critical Thinking Exercise

A wrestler first experiences a mild itching and soreness in his left axillary region. Later, small pustules form that develop into yellow crusts.

? How should the athletic trainer handle this problem?

The site of greatest occurrence is the back of the neck, where it appears early as a dark red, hard area and then in a few days emerges into a lesion that discharges yellowish-red pus from a number of places.

The dangers inherent in carbuncles are that the athlete may develop an internal infection or the carbuncle may spread to adjacent tissue or to other athletes.

Management   The most common treatment of carbuncles is surgical drainage combined with the administration of antibiotics. A warm compress is applied to promote circulation to the area.

Folliculitis

Folliculitis is an infection of the hair follicle. It is most prevalent in the hair follicles of the beard and the scalp (Figure 28-9). However, it can occur anywhere that hair exists on the body.

Etiology   Folliculitis can be caused by a comedo (blackhead) or, more commonly, by the "ingrown" hair, which grows inward and curls up to form an infected nodule. The infection occurs most often in areas in which hair is shaved or rubs against clothing, such as the neck, face, buttocks, or thigh.[16]

Many hair follicles may become involved through the extension of infection to contiguous sebaceous glands. Such spreading causes a general condition called *pseudofolliculitis barbae,* or barber's itch. Barber's itch frequently occurs on the neck and forms a red, swollen area that exhibits tenderness during palpation. Pus collects around the exposed hair, making the hair easy to remove. This condition should always be referred to a physician for treatment.

Figure 28-9

Folliculitis.

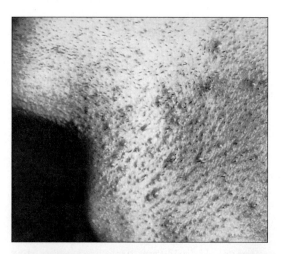

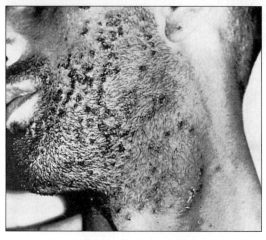

COMMON BACTERIAL INFECTIONS

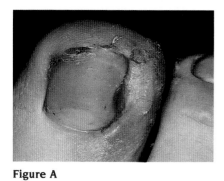

Figure A

Ingrown toenail.

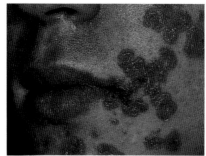

Figure B

Impetigo contagiosa.

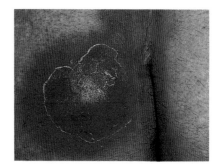

Figure C

Furuncle.

COMMON FUNGAL INFECTIONS

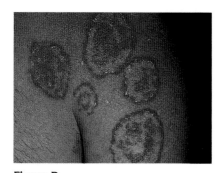

Figure D

Tinea of the body (tinea corporis).

Figure E

Tinea of the groin (tinea cruris).

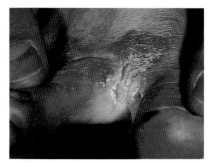

Figure F

Athlete's foot (tinea pedis).

COMMON VIRAL INFECTIONS

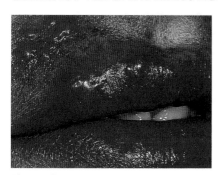

Figure G

Herpes simplex labialis.

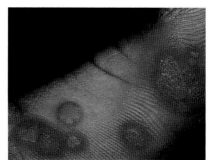

Figure H

Common warts.

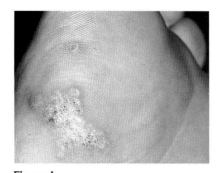

Figure I

Plantar warts on ball of foot.

COMMON SKIN REACTIONS

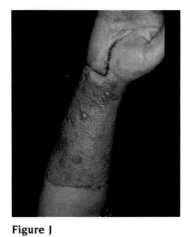

Figure J

Contact dermatitis.

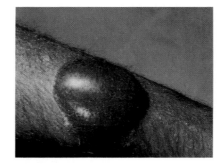

Figure K

Cold reaction.

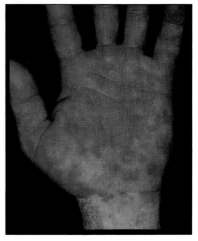

Figure L

Hives.

COMMON SEXUALLY TRANSMITTED INFECTIONS

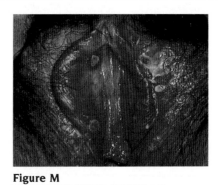

Figure M

Genital herpes simplex.

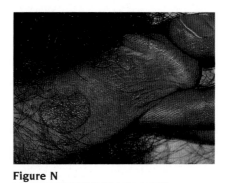

Figure N

Genital warts.

Symptoms and signs   The condition starts with inflammation that leads to development of a papule or pustule at the mouth of the hair follicle and is followed by development of a crust that may later slough off along with the hair. A deeper infection may cause scarring and permanent baldness (alopecia) in that area. The most common microorganism associated with this condition is staphylococcus.

Management   The management of acute folliculitis is similar to that of impetigo. Moist heat is applied intermittently to increase local circulation. Antibiotic medication may be applied locally, as well as systemically, depending on the scope of the condition.

Hidradenitis Suppurativa

Hidradenitis suppurativa is a chronic inflammatory condition of the apocrine glands, or large sweat glands commonly found in the axilla, scrotum, labia majora, and nipples.

Etiology   The exact cause of this condition is unclear. Most authorities believe it is caused by blockage of the apocrine gland ducts as a result of an inflammation. Some authorities believe it is a keratinous plug of a hair follicle. The role of bacteria is not exactly known.

Symptoms and signs   The condition begins as a small papule and grows to the size of a small tumor that is filled with purulent material. Deep dermal inflammation can occur, resulting in large abscesses that create bands of scar tissue.[6] The contents of this lesion are highly infectious to the athlete and, when discharged, can infect other members of the team.

Management   To treat this problem, athletes should avoid the use of antiperspirants, deodorants, and shaving creams; use medicated soaps such as those containing chlorhexidine or povidone-iodine (Betadine); and apply a prescribed antibiotic lotion. In some severe cases, surgical excision of the apocrine glands may be considered.

Acne Vulgaris

Acne vulgaris is an inflammatory disease that involves the hair follicles and the sebaceous glands. It occurs near puberty and usually is less active after adolescence. Acne is characterized by blackheads, cysts, and pustules.

Etiology   Although most adolescents experience some form of acne, only a few develop an extremely disfiguring case (Figure 28-10). Its cause is not definitely known, but it has been suggested that sex hormone imbalance may be the major causal factor.

Symptoms and signs   Acne begins as an improper functioning of the sebaceous glands with the formation of blackheads and inflammation, which in turn produces pustules on the face, neck, and back in varying depths. The superficial lesions usually dry spontaneously, whereas the deeper ones may become chronic and form disfiguring scars.[6]

The athlete with a serious case of acne vulgaris has a scarring disease and because of it may have serious emotional problems. The individual may become nervous, shy, and even antisocial and may develop feelings of inferiority in interpersonal relations with peer groups. The athletic trainer's major responsibility in aiding athletes with acne is to help the athlete perform the wishes of the physician and to give constructive guidance and counsel.[6]

Management   The care of acne is usually symptomatic. The majority of cases follow a similar pattern of hormone therapy given by a physician and a routine of washing three times daily with a mild soap followed by the application of a drying agent. Other methods may be required, such as the nightly application of keratolytic lotions (sulfur zinc or sulfur resorcinol), individual drainage of crusts or blackheads by the physician, and ultraviolet treatment. In severe cases, antibiotics can also be useful.

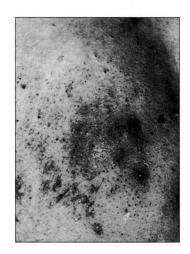

Figure 28-10

Acne vulgaris.

A

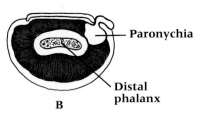

Paronychia

Distal
phalanx
B

Figure 28-11

A, Paronychia is a common infection of the skin surrounding the nail. **B,** Cross section of finger.

tetanus (lockjaw)
An acute, sometimes fatal condition characterized by tonic muscular spasm, hyperreflexia, and lockjaw.

tinea (ringworm)
Common name given to many superficial fungal infections of the skin.

Paronychia and Onychia

Fingernails and toenails are continually subject to injury and infection in sports. A common infection is paronychia, which is a purulent infection of the skin surrounding the nail (Figure 28-11).

Etiology   Paronychia and onychia develop from staphylococci, streptococci, and fungal organisms that accompany the contamination of open wounds or hangnails.[12] These infections are common in football linemen, who regularly stick their fingers in dirt.

Symptoms and signs   Acute paronychia has a rapid onset with painful, bright red swelling of the proximal and lateral nail. An accumulation of purulent material occurs behind the cuticle.[6] The infection may spread and cause onychia, an inflammation of the nail bed.

Management   The athletic trainer should recognize paronychia early and have the athlete soak the affected finger or toe in a hot solution of Epsom salts or boric acid three times daily. Topical antibiotics are often used between soakings. Every protection must be given the infected nail while the athlete is competing. Uncontrollable paronychia may require medical intervention, which consists of pus removal through a skin incision or the removal of a portion of the infected nail.

Tetanus Infection

Etiology   **Tetanus (lockjaw)** is an acute infection of the central nervous system caused by the tetanus bacillus. The bacteria can enter the blood through an open wound.

Symptoms and signs   The first sign of a tetanus infection is stiffness of the jaw and muscles of the neck. The muscles of facial expression produce contortion and become painful. The muscles of the back and extremities become tetanic. Fever becomes markedly elevated. It is possible that tetanus can be fatal.

Management   The patient with an acute tetanus infection should be treated in an intensive care unit. Initial childhood immunization by tetanus toxoid is usually completed by the time a child reaches six years of age. Boosters should be given every five to ten years. An athlete not immunized should receive an injection of tetanus immune globulin (Hyper-Tet) immediately after injury.

FUNGAL INFECTIONS

Fungi are a group of organisms that include yeast and molds and that are usually not pathogenic. However, some fungi will attack skin, hair, and nails. *Candida,* for example, a yeastlike fungus that is normally part of the flora of the skin, mouth, intestinal tract, and vaginal area, can lead to a variety of infections.

Fungi grow best in unsanitary conditions combined with warmth, moisture, and darkness. Three categories of superficial fungal infections are discussed: dermatophytes, candidiasis (moniliasis), and tinea. The fungus attacks mainly the keratin of the epidermis but may go as deep as the dermis through hair follicles. These organisms are given the common name of **ringworm (tinea)** and are classified according to the area of the body infected. Infection takes place within superficial keratinized tissue such as hair, skin, and nails. The extremely contagious spores of these fungi may be spread by direct contact, contaminated clothing, or dirty locker rooms and showers.

Dermatophytes (Ringworm Fungi)

Etiology   Dermatophytes, also known as *ringworm fungi* are the cause of most skin, nail, and hair fungal infections. They belong to three genera: *Microsporum, Trichophyton,* and *Epidermophyton.*

Tinea of the Scalp (Tinea Capitis)

Symptoms and signs   Tinea of the scalp, which begins as a small papule of the scalp and spreads peripherally, is most common among children. The lesions appear as small grayish scales that result in scattered bald patches. The primary sources of tinea capitis infection are contaminated animals, barber clippers, hairbrushes, and combs.

Management   Griseofulvin is usually the treatment of choice. It is given in small doses over a period of time or in one large dose. A topical cream such as 1 percent clotrimazole (Micatin, Tinactin) may be used to help prevent the spread of the disease.

Tinea of the Body (Tinea Corporis)

Symptoms and signs   Tinea of the body mainly involves the upper extremities and the trunk. The lesions are characterized by ring-shaped, reddish, vesicular areas that may be scaly or crusted (Color Plate, Figure D). Excessive perspiration and friction increase susceptibility to the condition.

Management   Treatment usually consists of antifungal medication such as 2 percent miconaxole cream or 1 percent clotrimazole cream or lotion.

Tinea of the Nail (Tinea Unguium)

Symptoms and signs   Tinea of the nail is a fungus infection of the toenails and fingernails. It is often seen among athletes who are involved in water sports or who have chronic athlete's foot. Trauma predisposes the athlete to infection. It is often difficult for a physician to determine accurately what is the real cause of the disease. Many different organisms can adversely affect the nail plate. When infected, the nail becomes thickened, brittle, and separated from its bed (Figure 28-12).

Management   The treatment of tinea unguium can be difficult. Newer drugs such as Sporonox are showing promise, but unfortunately, treatment lasts for months. Topical creams or lotions do not penetrate the nail. Surgical removal of the nail may have to be performed on the athlete who has extremely infected nails.[13]

Tinea of the Groin (Tinea Cruris)

Etiology   Tinea of the groin, more commonly called jock itch, appears as a bilateral and often symmetrical brownish or reddish lesion resembling the outline of a butterfly in the groin area (Color Plate, Figure E).

Symptoms and signs   The athlete complains of mild to moderate itching, resulting in scratching and the possibility of a secondary bacterial infection.

Management   The athletic trainer must be able to identify lesions of tinea cruris and handle them accordingly. Conditions of this type must be treated until cured (Figure 28-13). Infection not responding to normal management must be referred to the team physician. Most ringworm infections will respond to the many nonprescription medications that are available as aerosol sprays, liquids, powders, or ointments. Ointments are perhaps the most commonly used medication. Medications that are irritating or tend to mask the symptoms of a groin infection must be avoided.

Atypical or complicated groin infection must receive medical attention. Presently on the market are many prescription medications that may be applied topically or orally and that have dramatic effects on skin fungus.

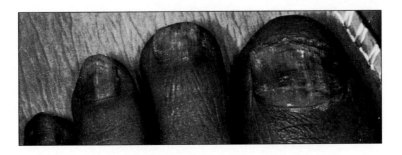

Figure 28-12

Tinea of the nail (tinea unguium).

Figure 28-13

When managing a fungal infection, the athletic trainer must break the chain of infection.

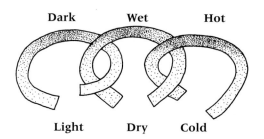

Dark   Wet   Hot

Light   Dry   Cold

Athlete's Foot (Tinea Pedis)

Etiology   The foot is the most common area of the body that is infected by dermatophytes, usually by tinea pedis, or athlete's foot (Figure 28-14). *Tricophyton mentagrophytes* infect the space between the digits and enter the plantar surface of the arch (Color Plate, Figure F). The same organism attacks toenails. *Trichophyton rubrum* causes scaling and thickening of the sole. The web space between the toes becomes macerated and infected with *Candida* yeast or gram-negative rods that are in addition to or that replace the original dermatophyte.[17] The athlete wearing shoes that are enclosed will sweat, which encourages fungal growth. However, contagion is based mainly on the athlete's individual susceptibility. Other conditions may be mistaken for athlete's foot, such as a dermatitis caused by allergy or an eczema-type skin infection.

Symptoms and signs   Athlete's foot can reveal itself in many ways but appears most often as an extreme itching on the soles of the feet and between and on top of the toes. It appears as a rash, with small pimples or minute blisters that break and exude a yellowish serum (see Figure 28-14). Scratching because of itchiness can cause the tissue to become inflamed and infected, manifesting a red, white, or gray scaling of the affected area.

Management   Griseofulvin is an effective management for tinea pedis. Of major importance is good foot hygiene. Topical medications that are also used for tinea corporis can be beneficial (see *Focus Box:* "Basic care of athlete's foot").[11]

Candidiasis (Moniliasis)

Candidiasis is a yeastlike fungus that can produce skin, mucous membrane, and internal infections.

28-5

Critical Thinking Exercise

Fungal infections are commonly found among athletes. Fungi grow best in unsanitary conditions combined with an environment of warmth, moisture, and darkness.

? What are the symptoms and signs of the fungal infection tinea pedis?

Figure 28-14

Athlete's foot (tinea pedis).

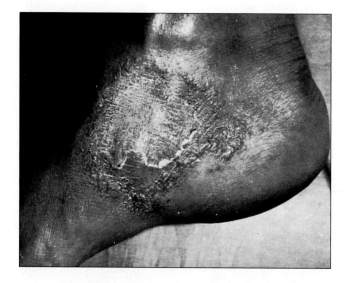

Focus

Basic care of athlete's foot

- Keep the feet as dry as possible through frequent use of talcum powder.
- Wear clean white socks to avoid reinfection, and change them daily.
- Use a standard fungicide for specific medication. Over-the-counter medications such as Desenex and Tinactin are useful in the early stages of the infection. For stubborn cases see the team physician; a dermatologist may need to make a culture from foot scrapings to determine the best combatant to be used.

The best cure for the problem of athlete's foot is *prevention*. To keep the condition from spreading to other athletes, the following steps should be faithfully followed by individuals in the sports program:

- All athletes should powder their feet daily.
- All athletes should dry their feet thoroughly, especially between and under the toes, after every shower.
- All athletes should keep sports shoes and street shoes dry by dusting them with powder daily.
- All athletes should wear clean sports socks and street socks daily.
- The shower and dressing rooms should be cleaned and disinfected daily.

Etiology   Candidiasis is caused by the yeastlike fungus *Candida albicans* and some other species. It will attack the skin, as well as other structures, if the environment is right. Weather that is hot and humid, tight clothing that rubs, and poor hygiene provide the ideal environment for fungal growth.

Symptoms and signs   Among athletes, candidiasis can occur anywhere there is intertrigo, especially under the arm and in the groin area. In other words, candidiasis can occur anywhere that skin touches skin accompanied by heat and moisture. The coach or athletic trainer may mistake this condition for simple intertrigo. It appears with a bright red, moist, glistening base.[9] The border of this lesion, in contrast to that of intertrigo, is commonly rimmed with small red pustules. If the skin is folded where the candidiasis occurs, a white, macerated border may surround the red area. Later, deep painful fissures may develop where the skin creases.

Management   The first concern in treatment is to maintain a dry area. A cool, wet, medicated compress may be applied for twenty to thirty minutes several times per day to promote dryness. Depending on the site of the disease, an antibiotic salve or lotion containing miconazole may be applied. (NOTE: Genital candidiasis is discussed in Chapter 29 in the section on sexually transmitted diseases.)

Tinea Versicolor

Tinea versicolor is a unique fungal infection and therefore is dealt with separately. It is a common fungal infection among young adults.

Etiology   Tinea versicolor is caused by a yeast called *Pityrosporum furfur*. It is a normal part of the skin's flora, appearing commonly in areas in which sebaceous glands actively secrete body oils.

Symptoms and signs   The fungus characteristically produces multiple, small, circular macules that are pink, brown, or white. They commonly occur on the abdomen, neck, and chest. The lesions do not tan when exposed to the sun and are usually asymptomatic.

Management   Treatment of tinea versicolor is difficult and recurrences are common. Numerous treatment options are available including selenium sulfide, found, for example, in Selsun shampoo. Pigment changes occur slowly even after the microorganism has been erradicated.

28-6

Critical Thinking Exercise

An athlete comes into the training room concerned about multiple, small, white, circular macules on the abdomen, neck, and chest.

? What possible infection could cause these symptoms?

VIRAL INFECTIONS

Common viruses that attack the skin of athletes:

- Herpes virus
- Verruca
- Poxvirus (molluscum contagiosum)

Viruses are ultramicroscopic organisms that do not have enzyme systems but parasitize living cells. Viruses lack independent metabolism but still have the capacity to reproduce. Entering a tissue cell, the virus exists as nucleic acid. Inside, the virus may stimulate the cell chemically to produce more virus until the host cell dies or the virus is ejected to infect additional cells. Instead of killing the cell, a budlike growth may occur, with harm to the cell, or the virus may remain within a cell without ever causing an infection. A number of skin infections are caused by viruses.

Herpes Simplex: Labialis, Gladiatorum, and Zoster

Herpes simplex is a strain of virus that is associated with skin and mucous membrane infection. Types 1 and 2 cause cutaneous lesions and are indistinguishable from one another (Color Plate, Figure G). Type 1 is found, for the most part, extragenitally and type 2 genitally.[1] Both can, however, be found anywhere on the skin or mucous membrane.

Etiology   Herpes simplex is highly contagious and is usually transmitted directly through a lesion in the skin or mucous membrane. After the initial outbreak, the virus is thought to move down a sensory nerve's neurilemmal sheath to reside in a resting state in a local ganglion. Recurrent attacks can be triggered by sunlight, emotional disturbances, illness, fatigue, infection, or other situations that may stress the organism.[5] However, sunlight does not adversely affect the reactivation rate if a sunscreen with a sun protection factor of 15 is used.

Symptoms and signs   Not all individuals infected with the virus develop overt symptoms.[5] An early indication that a herpes infection is about to erupt is a tingling or hypersensitivity in the infected area twenty-four hours before the appearance of lesions. Local swelling occurs, followed by the appearance of vesicles. The athlete may feel generally ill with a headache and sore throat, lymph gland swelling, and pain in the area of lesions. The vesicles generally rupture in one to three days, spilling out a serous material that will form into a yellowish crust. The lesions will normally heal in ten to fourteen days.

Genital herpes is discussed in Chapter 29. Of the two areas of the body most often affected, *herpes labialis* (cold sore) is usually the least symptomatic. Herpes simplex *gladiatorum* is the more serious. It commonly causes lesions to appear on the side of the face, neck, or shoulders and occurs quite often in wrestlers. Herpes simplex infection is so highly contagious that it may run rampant through an entire team in a short time. Wrestlers having any signs of a herpes infection should be disqualified from body contact until these lesions have crusted and dried. *Herpes zoster* appears in a particular pattern on the body in an area that is innervated by a specific nerve root. It may appear on the face or anywhere on the trunk. Herpes zoster is the chicken pox virus that has remained dormant for many years.

Management   Herpes simplex lesions are self-limiting. Therapy usually is directed toward reducing pain and promoting early healing. Antiviral drugs such as acyclovir are used to shorten the course and reduce the recurrence of herpes outbreaks. Quite often acyclovir is administered prophylactically.

Complications   Herpes simplex, if not carefully managed, can lead to secondary infection. A major problem is keratoconjunctivitis, an inflammation of the cornea and conjunctiva that could lead to loss of vision and that must be considered a medical emergency.

Verruca Virus and Warts

Numerous forms of verruca exist, including the verruca plana (flat wart), verruca plantaris (plantar wart), and the condyloma acuminatum (venereal wart).

28-7

Critical Thinking Exercise

An athlete experiences a tingling and sometimes painful sensation in the upper lip region. Twenty-four hours later, swelling occurs followed by the formation of vesicles. The athlete also experiences a mild headache, sore throat, and lymph gland swelling.

? What condition does this scenario describe, and how could the later symptoms have been prevented?

The papilloma virus uses the skin's epidermal layer for reproduction and growth. The verruca wart enters the skin through a lesion that has been exposed to contaminated fields, floors, or clothing. Contamination can also occur from exposure to other warts.

Common Wart

Etiology   Verruca vulgaris and plana are associated with the common wart and are prevalent on the hands of children (Color Plate, Figure H).

Symptoms and signs   This wart appears as a small, round, elevated lesion with rough, dry surfaces. It may be painful if pressure is applied. These warts are subject to secondary bacterial infection, particularly if they are located on the hands or feet, where they may be constantly irritated.

Management   Vulnerable warts must be protected until they can be treated by a physician. Application of a topical salicylic acid preparation or liquid nitrogen and electrocautering are the most common ways of managing this condition.

Plantar Warts

Etiology   Plantar warts are associated with the virus verruca plantaris and are usually found on the sole of the foot, on or adjacent to areas of abnormal weight bearing; however, they can spread to the hands and other body parts. They most commonly result from a fallen metatarsal arch or bruises to the ball of the foot, such as may be sustained during excessive jumping or running on the ball of the foot. Other names for this condition are *papilloma* and *seed warts*.

Symptoms and signs   Plantar warts are seen as areas with excessive epidermal thickening and cornification (Color Plate, Figure I). They produce general discomfort and point tenderness in the areas of excessive callus formation. Commonly the athlete complains that the condition feels as though he or she has stepped on broken glass. A major characteristic of the plantar wart is its punctuation of hemorrhages, which looks like a cluster of small black seeds.

Management   There are many different approaches to the treatment of warts. In general, while the athlete is competing, a conservative approach is taken. Concern is to protect the wart against infection and to keep the growth of the warts under control. A common approach to controlling plantar warts is the careful paring away of accumulated callous tissue and application of a keratolytic such as 40 percent salicylic acid plaster. When the competitive season is over, the physician may decide to remove the wart by freezing it with liquid nitrogen or by electrodesiccation. Until its removal, a wart should be protected by a doughnut pad.

Molluscum Contagiosum

Etiology   Molluscum contagiosum is a poxvirus infection. It is more contagious than warts, particularly during direct body contact activities such as wrestling.

Symptoms and signs   Molluscum contagiosum appears as a small, pinkish, slightly raised, smooth-domed papule with a central umbilication. When this condition is identified, it must be referred immediately to a physician.

Management   Treatment often consists of a thorough cleansing and use of a destructive procedure. Destructive procedures include powerful counterirritants such as cantharidin (Cantharone), surgical removal of the lesion, or cryosurgery utilizing nitrogen.

ALLERGIC, THERMAL, AND CHEMICAL SKIN REACTIONS

The skin can react adversely to a variety of nonpathogenic influences. Among the most common affecting athletes are allergies, temperature extremes, and chemical irritants.

28-8

Critical Thinking Exercise

A tennis player complains to the athletic trainer that she has a sharp pain in the ball of her right foot. She says that it feels as though she stepped on a piece of glass. On inspection, the athletic trainer observes excessive callus formation on the ball of the foot that is dotted with a cluster of black specks.

? What is this condition, and how should it be managed?

Skin reactions to allergy:
- Reddening
- Elevated patches
- Eczema

Allergic Reactions

An allergy is caused by an allergen, a protein toward which the body is hypersensitive. Causative factors may be food, drugs, clothing, dusts, pollens, plants, animals, heat, cold, or light, or the cause may be psychosomatic. The skin displays allergic reactions in various ways (Color Plate, Figures K and L), such as reddening and swelling of the tissue that may occur either locally or generally from an increased dilation of blood capillaries. *Urticaria,* or *hives,* occurs as a red or white elevation (wheal or papule) of the skin and is characterized by a burning or an itching sensation. *Eczema* is a skin reaction in which small papules may be produced, accompanied by itching and a reddish, dry, crusty formation.

The athletic trainer should be able to recognize gross signs of allergic reactions and should then refer the athlete to the physician. Treatment usually includes avoidance of the sensitizing agents and use of an antipruritic agent (such as calamine location) and antihistamine drugs.

Urticaria = Hives

Allergic Contact Dermatitis

There are many substances in the sports environment to which the athlete may be allergic, causing a skin reaction.

Etiology   The most common plants that cause allergic contact dermatitis are poison ivy, poison oak, sumac, ragweed, and primrose. Over time the athlete may become allergic to topical medications such as antibiotics, antihistamines, anesthetics, or antiseptics. Chemicals commonly found in soaps, detergents, and deodorants can create a reaction. Some athletes are allergic to materials in the adhesive used in athletic tape. Also, the countless chemicals used in the manufacture of shoes and clothing and other materials have been known to produce allergic contact dermatitis.

Symptoms and signs   The period of onset from the time of initial exposure may range from one day to one week. Skin that is continually warm will develop signs earlier. The skin reacts with redness, swelling, and the formation of vesicles that ooze fluid and form a crust. A constant itch develops that is increased with heat and made worse by rubbing. Secondary infection is a common result of scratching (Color Plate, Figure J).

Management   The most obvious treatment approach is to determine the irritant and avoid it. This determination may not always be simple and may require extensive testing. In the acute phase, tap water compresses or soaks can soothe and dry the vesicles. Topical corticosteroids may be beneficial.

Burns

Burns can result from excessive exposure to thermal, chemical, electrical, or radiation sources. In a sports environment, the athlete is certainly most susceptible to radiation burns from exposure to sunlight.

Actinic Dermatitis (Sunburn)

Serious skin damage can occur from overexposure to the sun's rays. Actinic dermatitis (sunburn) is a precursor to this damage.

Etiology   Sunburn is a dermatitis caused by the ultraviolet radiation from the sun, and it varies in intensity from a mild erythema (pink color) to a severe, second-degree burn represented by itching, swelling, and blistering. Every protection should be given to athletes who have thin, white skin. Their skin tends to absorb a greater amount of ultraviolet radiation than does the skin of more pigmented individuals. Individuals taking photosensitizing drugs, such as thiazide diuretics, some tetracyclines, and phenothiazine, may also be sensitive. The chemical psoralen in oil of limes, parsnips, celery, and other foods can produce a severe adverse reaction in some individuals who expose themselves to sunlight.

Symptoms and signs   If a large area of the skin is sunburned, the athlete may display all the symptoms of severe inflammation accompanied by shock. A sunburn can cause malfunctioning of the organs within the skin, which in turn may result in infection of structures such as hair follicles and sweat glands.

Sunburn appears two to eight hours after exposure. Symptoms become most extreme in approximately twelve hours and dissipate in seventy-two to ninety-six hours. After once receiving a severe sunburn, the skin is more susceptible to burning. The skin remains injured for months after a severe sunburn has been sustained. Prevention of sunburn should be accomplished by a gradual exposure to the rays of the sun combined with use of a sunscreen that will filter out most of the ultraviolet light. Individuals prone to burning should routinely wear a sunscreen such as para-aminobenzoic acid (PABA). The amount of protection provided by sunscreens is determined by the sun protection factor (SPF), which refers to the length of time a person can stay in the sun without getting sunburned. An SPF of 15 means a person wearing the sunscreen can remain exposed to the sun without suffering sunburn fifteen times longer than if that person were not wearing the sunscreen. Constant overexposure to the sun can lead to chronic skin thickening and damage.[3]

Management   A sunburn is treated according to the degree of inflammation present. Mild burns are best treated wi h cool water in a shower or bath. Aloe-based compounds have also proved beneficial. Moderate and severe burns can be relieved by a tub bath in which a pound of cornstarch is used; a vinegar solution will also help. Severe sunburn may be treated by the physician with corticosteroids and other antiinflammatory drugs.

Ultraviolet radiation is damaging—it can prematurely age the skin and can increase the chances of skin cancers. Basal cell and squamous cell carcinomas are the most common cancers.[17]

Miliaria (Prickly Heat)

Prickly heat is common in sports and occurs most often during the hot season of the year in those athletes who perspire profusely and who wear heavy clothing.

Etiology   Continued exposure to heat and moisture causes retention of perspiration by the sweat glands and subsequent miliaria.

Symptoms and signs   Miliaria results in itching and burning vesicles and pustules.[3] It occurs most often on the arms, trunk, and bending areas of the body.

Management   Care of prickly heat requires avoidance of overheating, frequent bathing with a nonirritating soap, the wearing of loose-fitting clothing, and the use of antipruritic lotions.

Chilblains

Etiology   Chilblains is a common type of dermatitis caused by excessive exposure to cold.

Symptoms and signs   The tissue does not freeze but reacts with edema, reddening, possibly blistering, and a sensation of burning and itching. The parts of the body most often affected are the ears, face, hands, and feet.

Management   Treatment consists of exercise and a gradual warming of the part. Massage and application of heat are contraindicated in cases of chilblains. (See Chapter 6 for more information about reactions to cold.)

INFESTATION AND BITES

Certain parasites cause dermatoses, or skin irritations, when they suck blood, inject venom, and even lay their eggs under the skin. Athletes who come in contact with these organisms may develop various symptoms such as itching, allergic skin reactions, and secondary infections from insult or scratching. The more common parasitic infestations in sports are caused by mites, crab lice, fleas, ticks, mosquitoes, and stinging insects such as bees, wasps, hornets, and yellow jackets.

28-9

Critical Thinking E x e r c i s e

Actinic dermatitis, or sunburn, occurs from overexposure to the sun's rays.

? What should an athlete be told about the sun's rays?

Depending on the part of the country in which the athlete resides, parasites such as mites, crab lice, fleas, ticks, mosquitoes, and stinging insects can cause serious discomfort and infection.

Focus

Treatment of scabies

- The entire body should be thoroughly cleansed, with attention to skin lesions.
- Bedding and clothing should be disinfected.
- The coating of gamma benzene hexachloride (Lindane) should be applied on the lesions for three nights.
- All individuals who have come in contact with the infected athlete should be examined by the physician.
- Locker and game equipment must be disinfected.

Seven-Year Itch (Scabies)

Etiology   Seven-year itch (scabies) is a skin disease caused by the mite *Sarcoptes scabiei,* which produces extreme nocturnal itching. The parasitic itch mite is small, and the female causes the greatest irritation. The mite burrows a tunnel approximately $1/4$- to $1/2$-inch (0.6 to 1.25 cm) long into the skin to deposit its eggs.

Symptoms and signs   The mite's burrows appear as dark lines between the fingers, toes, body flexures, nipples, and genitalia. Excoriations, pustules, and papules caused by the resulting scratching frequently hide the true nature of the disease. The young mite matures in a few days and returns to the skin surface to repeat the cycle. The skin often develops a hypersensitivity to the mite, which produces extreme itching.

Management   Gamma benzene hexachloride (Lindane) is the most effective scabicide. It is available as a cream or a shampoo. Because of the athlete's itching and scratching, secondary infections are common and must also be treated (see *Focus Box:* "Treatment of scabies").

Lice (Pediculosis)

Etiology   Pediculosis is an infestation by the louse, of which three types are parasitic to humans. The *Pediculus humanus capitis* (head louse) infests the head, where its eggs (nits) attach to the base of the hair shaft. The *Phthirus pubis* (crab louse) lives in the hair of the pubic region and lays its eggs at the hair base. The *Pediculus humanus corporis* (body louse) lives and lays its eggs in the seams of clothing.

Symptoms and signs   The louse is a carrier of many diseases; its bite causes an itching dermatitis, which, through subsequent scratching, provokes pustules and excoriations.

Management   Cure is rapid with the use of any of a number of parasiticides or lotions rubbed into the infected areas at night before retiring and again the following morning when arising. The area should be retreated after seven to ten days. The lice cannot survive dryness. Good hygiene is of paramount importance in all infestations. All clothing, bedding, and toilet seats must be kept clean and sterile.

Fleas

Etiology   Fleas are small, wingless insects that suck blood. Singly, their bites cause only minor discomfort to the recipient, unless the flea is a carrier of some contagious disease.

Symptom and signs   A large number of biting fleas can cause great discomfort. After attaching themselves to some moving object such as a dog or a human, most fleas bite in patterns of three. Fleas seem to concentrate their bites on the ankle and lower leg.

28-10

Critical Thinking Exercise

A cross-country runner complains to the athletic trainer of extreme nocturnal itching. Observation of the athlete's skin reveals dark lines in the area of the finger and toes.

? What insect infestation does this scenario describe?

Management   Once the flea bite has been incurred, an antipruritic lotion such as calamine is used to prevent the athlete from scratching the bite, because scratching could cause a secondary infection. Areas in which fleas abound can be sprayed with selected insecticides containing malathion or other effective ingredient.

Ticks

Etiology   Ticks are parasitic insects that have an affinity for the blood of many animals, including humans. They are carriers of a variety of microorganisms that can cause Rocky Mountain spotted fever or Lyme disease. Because ticks are commonly found on grass and bushes, they can easily become attached to the athlete who brushes against them.

Symptoms and signs   Rocky Mountain spotted fever and Lyme disease are characterized by headache, fever, malaise, myalgia, and a rash about the wrist and forearms.

Management   To remove a tick, mineral oil or fingernail polish is applied to its body, at which time it will withdraw its head. Grasping or pulling the tick by its head is an acceptable method for removal.

Mosquitoes

Etiology   Unless it is the carrier of a disease, the mosquito, as a bloodsucker, produces a bite that causes only mild discomfort. Mosquitoes are attracted to lights, dark clothing, and warm, moist skin.

Symptoms and signs   The mosquito bite produces a small, reddish papule. Multiple bites may lead to a great deal of itching.

Management   Itching is most often relieved by the application of a topical medication such as calamine lotion. In climates in which mosquitoes are prevalent, repellents should be used directly on the skin.

Stinging Insects

Etiology   Bees, wasps, hornets, and yellow jackets inflict a venomous sting that is temporarily painful for most individuals; however, some hypersensitive individuals respond with an allergic reaction that may be fatal. Stings to the head, face, and neck are particularly dangerous to the athlete. Athletes having a history of allergic reactions from stings must be carefully scrutinized after a sting to prevent an anaphylactic reaction. To avoid stings, the athlete should not use scented lotions or shampoos; should not wear brightly colored clothes; should not wear jewelry, suede, or leather; and should not go barefoot.[3]

Symptoms and signs   The allergic athlete may respond with an increase in heart rate, fast breathing, chest tightness, dizziness, sweating, and even loss of consciousness.

Management   In uncomplicated sting cases, the stinging apparatus must be carefully removed with tweezers, followed by the application of a soothing medication. Detergent soap applied directly on the sting often produces an immediate lessening of symptoms. In severe reactions to a sting, the athlete must be treated for severe shock and referred immediately to a physician. Sensitive athletes who perform outdoors should avoid scented cosmetics, scented soap, colognes, or aftershave lotions and colorful, floral, or dark-colored clothing.

28-11

Critical Thinking Exercise

An athlete who is allergic to bee stings is stung.

? What physical reactions should the athlete be expected to have?

SUMMARY

- The skin is the largest organ of the human body. It is composed of three layers: the epidermis, the dermis, and the subcutis. The outermost layer, the epidermis, acts as protection against infections from a variety of sources. The dermis contains sweat glands, sebaceous glands, and hair follicles. The subcutis layer is the major area for fat storage and temperature regulation.

- Primary skin lesions include the macule, papule, plaque, nodule, tumor, cyst, wheal, vesicle, bulla, and pustule. Secondary skin lesions include the scale, crust, fissure, erosion, ulcer, and scar. Skin lesions can be caused by microorganisms, trauma, allergies, temperature variations, chemicals, infestations, and insect bites.

- Sports participation can place a great deal of mechanical force on the skin, which can lead to many different problems. Abnormal friction causes keratosis, blisters, and intertrigo. Hyperhidrosis adds to the problems of skin friction and infections. A tearing force can lacerate or avulse skin. Compression can bruise, scraping abrades, and a pointed object can puncture.

- Providing immediate proper care is essential to avoid skin infections. Streptococcal and staphylococcal bacteria are associated with wound contamination, and the tetanus bacillus can cause lockjaw.

- Impetigo contagiosa is a highly infectious disease among athletes and is associated with both the staphylococcal and streptococcal bacteria. Furuncles, carbuncles, and folliculitis are staphylococcal-caused afflictions and can be spread by direct contact. Other bacterial skin conditions are hidradenitis suppurativa, acne vulgaris, and paronychia and onychia.

- The sports environment, which is often one of excessive moisture, warmth, and darkness, is conducive to fungal growth. An extremely common fungus, ringworm, is under the general heading of dermatophytes. Under the right conditions, these fungi can attack a wide variety of body tissues.

- Herpes simplex is a virus associated with herpes labialis and herpes gladiatorum. The verruca virus commonly is related to a variety of warts such as the plantar wart or the papilloma. The poxvirus causes molluscum contagiosum, a highly contagious wart spread by direct contact.

- Athletes are also subject to many other causes of skin conditions, including allergies, extremes of heat or cold, and chemical irritations. One major problem that produces an insidious destruction of the skin is prolonged overexposure to sunlight.

- Different parts of the country have problems with insect infestations and bites. Two of these problems are scabies (caused by mites) and pediculosis (from lice), and there are others that may be produced by fleas, ticks, mosquitoes, and stinging insects.

Web Sites

Dermatology Online Atlas: http://www.derms.med.uni-erlangen.de/bilddb/index_c.htm

This site allows the reader to search for skin conditions and provides excellent illustrations.

Cramer First Aider: http://www.ccsd.k12.wy.us/cchs_web/cramerfirstaider/fstaider.htm

UWEC Student Health Service Dermatology Information: http://www.uwec.edu/Admin/HlthSvs/derm.htm

Solutions to Critical Thinking EXERCISES

28-1 Initially, the skin flap is completely removed. The area is cleaned with soap and water and the antiseptic liquid benzalkonium is applied along with an occlusive dressing. After the game, a second-skin dressing is applied to the raw area.

28-2 To prevent intertrigo, the skin is kept dry, clean, and friction free. The athlete who is prone to this problem should wear

loose cotton underwear. Males should wear a supporter over underwear.

28-3 A major concern for this abrasion is infection. The abraded area is cleaned with mild soap and debrided with a brush. Hydrogen peroxide is applied to the injury, followed by povidone-iodine. The injury is covered with a medicated salve to prevent scabbing, and a nonocclusive dressing is applied.

28-4 This skin condition is the highly contagious disease impetigo contagiosa. The athlete must not have physical contact with other athletes until the disease is resolved. It is managed with daily thorough cleansing of crusted material followed by an application of an antibiotic salve or oral medication.

28-5 With tinea pedis, there is severe itching on the top of and between the toes and on the soles of the feet. A rash occurs with blisters that secrete a yellow serum. Scratching can cause an infection. A red, white, or grayish scaling may also be present.

28-6 It is likely that the athlete has tinea versicolor. Treatment of this condition is difficult and recurrences are common. Perhaps the most effective treatment is to use selenium sulfide. Pigment changes occur slowly even after the microorganism has been erradicated.

28-7 This condition is a herpes simplex viral infection. Once the herpes virus is contracted it is impossible to get rid of it. When symptoms begin to appear the athlete should be referred immediately to a physician for a prescription drug called acyclovir, which can minimize symptoms.

28-8 The black specks are plantar warts. The accumulated callus is pared down and a 40 percent salicylic acid plaster is applied. A doughnut pad is used to protect the area.

28-9 The athlete should be cautioned to use sunscreen routinely to prevent the damaging effects of overexposure to sunlight.

28-10 This scenario describes infestation by the mite *Sarcoptes scabiei.* Another name for this condition is the seven-year itch, or scabies. The mite burrows a tunnel under the skin to deposit her eggs. The eggs hatch, and the young mites return to the skin surface to repeat the cycle. A hypersensitivity develops that causes extreme itching at night.

28-11 The athlete may be expected to experience an anaphylactic reaction. There is an increase in heart rate, fast breathing, chest tightness, dizziness, sweating, and possibly a loss of consciousness. This condition is a medical emergency.

REVIEW QUESTIONS AND CLASS ACTIVITIES

1. Describe the skin's anatomy and functions. Describe lesions that are indicative of infection.
2. Contrast the microorganisms that are related to skin infections.
3. Relate the mechanical forces of friction, compression, shearing, stretching, scraping, tearing, avulsing, and puncturing to specific skin injuries.
4. List the steps to take in managing major skin traumas.
5. How should wounds be managed to avoid serious infections?
6. Characterize the different viruses that are associated with common skin infections that occur in sports.
7. What bacterial skin infections are commonly seen in athletes?
8. Tinea (ringworm) is a fungus that can be present on different parts of the body. Name the body parts.
9. How may skin infections related to microorganisms be avoided?
10. Why is candidiasis considered one of the most serious fungal infections in sports?
11. What allergic, thermal, and chemical skin reactions could an athlete sustain in the typical sports environment?
12. Different parts of the United States have their own problems with insects that infect the skin of humans. Identify the insects in your area that can cause problems to athletes. How may they be avoided?

REFERENCES

1. Allen AC: Skin. In Kissane JM, editor: *Anderson's pathology,* ed 9, vol 2, St Louis, 1990, Mosby.
2. American Academy of Orthopaedic Surgeons: *Athletic training and sports medicine,* ed 2, Park Ridge, Ill, 1991, American Academy of Orthopaedic Surgeons.
3. Arntizen KR: Dermatologic issues. In Agostini R, editor: *Medical and Orthopaedic Issues of Active and Athletic Women,* Philadelphia, 1994, Hanley & Belfus.
4. Baxter DE: *The foot and ankle in sport,* St Louis, 1995, Mosby.
5. Bergfeld WF, Munnings F: How to manage herpes in active patients, *Physician Sportsmed* 22(9):71, 1994.
6. Conklin RJ: Acne vulgaris in the athlete, *Physician Sportsmed* 16(10):65, 1988.
7. Fletcher SB et al: Medicated compress for blister treatment, *J Ath Train* 28(1):81, 1993.
8. Foster DT et al: Management of wounds, *J Ath Train* 30(2):135, 1995.
9. Habif TP: *Clinical dermatology,* St Louis, 1990, Mosby.
10. Hamann BP: *Disease: identification, prevention, and control,* St Louis, 1994, Mosby.
11. Mackey S: Relieving winter skin discomfort, *Physician Sportsmed* 23(1):53, 1995.
12. Ramsey ML: Clearing up fungal infections of the nail plate, *Physician Sportsmed* 21(2):70, 1993.
13. Rheinecker SB: Wound management: the occlusive dressing, *J Ath Train* 30(2):143, 1995.
14. Sammarco GJ: Soft tissue injuries. In Torg JS, editor: *Current therapy in sports medicine,* ed 3, St Louis, 1995, Mosby.
15. Scheinberg RS: Exercise-related skin infection, *Physician Sportsmed* 22(6):47, 1994.
16. Scheinberg RS: Stopping skin assailants: fungi, yeasts, and viruses, *Physician Sportsmed* 22(7):33, 1994.
17. Simandl G: Alterations in skin function and integrity. In Porth CM, editor: *Pathophysiology,* Philadelphia, 1994, Lippincott.
18. Thibodeau GA, Patton KT: *Anatomy and physiology,* ed 2, St Louis, 1993, Mosby.
19. Williams JGP: *Color atlas of injuries in sports,* Chicago, 1990, Year Book.

ANNOTATED BIBLIOGRAPHY

Douglas LG: Facial injuries. In Torg JS, Welsh RP, Shephard RJ, editors: *Current therapy in sports medicine,* vol 2, Philadelphia, 1990, Decker.

This text contains an excellent overview of the major open skin wounds that occur among athletes.

Habif TP: *Clinical dermatology,* St Louis, 1990, Mosby.

This excellent, in-depth text about skin disease, diagnosis, and therapy contains extensive color photos and illustrations.

Williams JGP: *Color atlas of injury in sports,* Chicago, 1990, Year Book.

This text presents extensive color illustrations for all aspects of sports injuries, including the area of dermatology.

Additional Health Conditions

When you finish this chapter you should be able to

- Describe the role of the immune system in preventing disease.
- Identify different viral infections that may affect the athlete.
- Describe symptoms and signs of respiratory infections.
- Describe disorders of the muscular system.
- Describe disorders associated with the nervous system.
- Describe disorders of the vascular and lymphatic system.
- Explain diabetes mellitus, and contrast diabetic coma and insulin shock.
- Identify the causes of epilepsy and explain how to perform the appropriate action when a seizure occurs.
- Explain what causes hypertension and how it may be controlled.
- Describe the classic signs and symptoms of cancer.
- Describe the symptoms and signs of the most common venereal diseases.
- Describe menstrual irregularities and their effect on the athlete.
- Explain female reproduction and pregnancy as they relate to the athlete.

I n addition to the many injuries that have been discussed in previous chapters, a variety of additional health-related conditions can potentially affect the athlete. Like everyone else, athletes inevitably become ill. When illnesses occur, it becomes incumbent on the athletic trainer to recognize these conditions and to follow up with appropriate care. Appropriate care for the illnesses and conditions discussed in this chapter often means referring the athlete to a physician to provide medical care that is well beyond the scope of the athletic trainer. The information provided in this chapter serves as a reference for the athletic trainer in making appropriate decisions regarding care of the sick athlete.

THE ROLE OF THE IMMUNE SYSTEM

The immune system is not an organ system but is instead a collection of disease-fighting cells that recognize the presence of foreign substances in the body and act to neutralize or destroy them.[27] Illness results when the immune system fails to neutralize or destroy the invading offender. Immunity means being protected from a disease by having been previously exposed to an invading agent, called an *antigen*. Immunity may be acquired *actively* as a result of a natural infection or invasion of antigens, or *passively* from innoculation.[29]

An immune response disposes of the antigen and thus prevents damage. The immune response may be *cell-mediated,* in which lymphocytes (T cells) are produced by the thymus in response to the antigen exposure. There may also be a *humoral immune response* in which plasma lymphocytes (B cells) are produced with subsequent formation of *antibodies.* A *nonspecific immune response,* or inflammation, is the reaction of the tissues to injury from trauma, chemicals, or ischemia. These immune responses are all positive responses that collectively act to destroy or neutralize an antigen.[28]

An autoimmune response directed against an individual's own tissues causes damage. Autoimmune diseases include, among others, diabetes mellitus, rheumatoid arthritis, multiple sclerosis, hemolytic anemia, myasthenia gravis, and HIV.

VIRAL INFECTIONS

Athletes, like everyone else, are highly susceptible to viral infection. Among the more common viral infections are rhinovirus (common cold), influenza (flu), infectious mononucleosis, rubella (German measles), rubeola (measles), mumps, and varicella-zoster (chicken pox).

Rhinovirus (Common Cold)

The common cold (coryza) is the most prevalent of all communicable diseases. It is referred to as an upper respiratory infection.

Etiology More than 100 different rhinoviruses cause colds. Colds are transmitted by either direct or indirect contact. They are spread by droplets expelled by a person with a cold who sneezes, coughs, or speaks. One method of infection is by touching a contaminated article and then rubbing the eyes.[8]

Symptoms and signs Frequently the cold begins with a scratchy or sore throat, watery discharge or stopped-up nose, and sneezing. Not all colds follow the same pattern. In some instances, a secondary bacterial infection occurs, which produces a thickened yellowish nasal discharge, watering eyes, mild fever, sore throat, headache, **malaise,** myalgia, and dry cough. Additional to the secondary infection can be laryngitis (hoarseness), tracheitis (irritation of the trachea), acute bronchitis, sinusitis, and even an inflammation of the middle ear (otitis media).

Management Treatment of the common cold is symptomatic. Most colds last for five to ten days regardless of treatment. Nonprescription cold medications may help ease some symptoms. To avoid colds, athletes should stay out of crowds, wash hands frequently, avoid sharing personal items, eat a balanced diet, and drink at least eight 8-ounce glasses of water per day. Emotional stress and extreme fatigue should be avoided as much as possible.

Recently the use of Breathe Right nasal strips has been recommended as a drug-free alternative for managing nasal congestion due to colds and allergies. When adhered to the nose, the nasal strips have two "springlike" pieces that pull upwards, mechanically "lifting" open the nasal passages. Many athletes routinely use these nasal strips to facilitate breathing (Figure 29-1).

Influenza (Flu)

Influenza, commonly known as the flu, is one of the most persistent and debilitating diseases. It usually occurs in various forms as an annual epidemic that causes severe illness among the populace.

Etiology Influenza is caused by myoviruses classified as types A, B, and C. Type A influenza is the most common and causes serious and widespread epidemics. The virus enters the cell through its genetic material. The virus multiplies and is released from the cell by a budding process, to be spread throughout the body. Not all athletes need influenza vaccines; however, athletes engaging in winter sports, basketball, wrestling, and swimming may require them.[21]

Symptoms and signs The athlete with the flu will have the following symptoms: fever, cough, headache, malaise, and inflamed respiratory mucous membranes with **coryza.** Certain viruses can increase the body's core temperature. Flu generally has an incubation period of forty-eight hours and comes on suddenly, accompanied by chills and a fever of 102° to 103° F (39° to 39.5° C), which develops over a twenty-four-hour period. The athlete complains of a headache and general aches and pains—mainly in the back and legs. The headache increases in intensity, and the athlete develops **photophobia** and an aching at the back of the skull. There is often sore throat, burning in the chest, and in the beginning, a nonproductive cough, which later may develop into bronchitis. The skin is flushed, and the eyes are inflamed and watery. The acute stage of the disease usually lasts up to five days. Weakness, sweating, and fatigue may persist for many days. Flu prevention includes avoiding infected persons and maintaining

malaise
Discomfort and uneasiness caused by an illness.

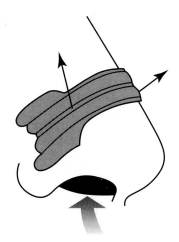

Figure 29-1

Nasal strips mechanically lift open the nasal passages.

coryza (core **eez** ah)
Profuse nasal discharge.

photophobia
Unusual intolerance to light.

29-1
Critical Thinking Exercise

A high school swimmer complains of a fever, cough, headache, malaise, aching in the back of the head, and a sore throat along with light sensitivity.

? What condition is this scenario describing, and how could it be managed?

29-2
Critical Thinking Exercise

A lacrosse player comes to the training room complaining that for the past three days he has had a headache, fatigue, loss of appetite, muscle aches, swollen lymph glands, and a sore throat. He also complains of mild tenderness in the left upper quadrant of the abdomen.

? What illness is likely to cause these symptoms?

good resistance through healthy living. Vaccines, including prevalent strains, may be recommended to individuals to decrease the incidence or severity of illness.

Management   If the flu is uncomplicated, its management consists of bed rest and supportive care. During the acute stage, the temperature often returns to normal. Symptomatic care such as aspirin should be avoided for all individuals under eighteen years of age because of Reye's syndrome. Amantadine is a medication that may be used for influenza A for individuals at risk. It also is beneficial for fever and respiratory symptoms.[4] Steam inhalation, cough medicines, and gargles may be given.

Infectious Mononucleosis

Infectious mononucleosis is an acute viral disease that affects mainly young adults and children.

Etiology   Infectious mononucleosis, commonly called mono, is caused by the Epstein-Barr virus (EBV), a member of the herpes group. It has major significance to athletes because it can produce severe fatigue and raise the risk of spleen rupture.[21] Incubation is four to six weeks. The EBV is carried in the throat and transmitted to another person through saliva. It has been called the kissing disease.[8]

Symptoms and signs   The EBV syndrome usually starts with a three- to five-day prodrome of headache, fatigue, loss of appetite, and myalgia. From days 5 to 15, there is fever, swollen lymph glands, and a sore throat.[8] By the second week 50 percent to 70 percent of those infected with EBV will have an enlarged spleen, 10 percent to 15 percent will have jaundice, and 5 percent to 15 percent will have a skin rash, a pinkish flush to the cheeks, and puffy eyelids.[21] Complications include ruptured spleen, meningitis, encephalitis, hepatitis, and anemia.[8]

Management   Treatment is supportive and symptomatic. Acetaminophen is often given for headache, fever, and malaise. Mellion indicates that "athletes may resume easy training in 3 weeks after the onset of illness if: (1) the spleen is not markedly enlarged or painful, (2) he or she is afebrile, (3) liver function tests are normal, and (4) pharyngitis and any complication have resolved."[21]

Rubella (German Measles)

Etiology   Rubella is a highly contagious viral disease that usually occurs during childhood. Infection occurs between thirteen and twenty-four days following exposure. If the disease occurs in the pregnant female, defects may occur in the developing fetus.[29]

Symptoms and signs   Slight temperature elevation, sore throat, drowsiness, swollen lymph glands, and the appearance of red spots on the palate all occur for about one to five days prior to the appearance of a rash that occurs about 50 percent of the time. The rash begins on the face and forehead, spreads down the trunk and extremities, and last for about three days.[29]

Management   Rubella may be prevented by early childhood immunization with a combination vaccine that prevents measles and mumps in addition to rubella (MMR).[28]

Rubeola (Measles)

Etiology   Like rubella, rubeola, or measles, is a highly contagious disease that often occurs during childhood. An individual who once has this disease becomes immune to further exposure. The incubation period is approximately ten days following exposure.[29]

Symptoms and signs   The onset of measles causes sneezing, nasal congestion, coughing, malaise, photophobia, spots in the mouth, conjunctivitis, and fever that may elevate to 104° at about four days. When the fever reaches that level, a rash appears, usually first on the face, as small red spots that rapidly increase in size and spread to the trunk and extremities. The rash causes an uncomfortable itching. The rash lasts for about five days, after which the temperature returns to normal.[29]

Management   Any child who has not had measles should be innoculated with the MMR vaccine at nine months and again at fifteen months. If measles do occur, bed rest, isolation in a darkened room, and the use of antipyretic and anti-itching medication can provide some relief while the disease runs its course.[28]

Mumps (Parotitis)

Etiology   Mumps is a contagious viral disease that results in inflammation of the parotid and other salivary glands. Mumps usually appears within twelve to twenty-five days following exposure.[29]

Symptoms and signs   Symptoms begin with malaise, headache, chills, and a moderate fever. There is pain in the neck below and in front of the ear that progresses to marked swelling on one or both sides. Swelling may last for as long as seven days. It is painful to move the jaw, and swallowing may be difficult. Saliva production may be either increased or decreased.[29]

Management   Immunization with MMR should be done in children older than one year to prevent the disease. If mumps does occur, the patient should be isolated while contagious, confined to bed rest, and given a soft diet. Analgesics may be used along with cold applications to control swelling; later, heat applications should be used.[29]

Varicella (Chicken Pox)

Etiology   This highly contagious viral disease is caused by the varicella-zoster virus, which also causes herpes zoster (discussed in Chapter 28). Chicken pox may occur at any age but is much more likely to occur in children under the age of fifteen years. The average incubation time is thirteen to seventeen days following exposure. An individual who has chicken pox is contagious for approximately eleven days, beginning five days before the first signs of a rash appear.[28]

Symptoms and signs   Chicken pox begins with a slight elevation in temperature for twenty-four hours, followed by an eruption of a rash. The rash first appears as individual red crops or spots, each of which progressively evolves through stages of macules, papules, vesicles, and crusts over a period of two to three days. The rash begins on the back and chest; relatively few lesions appear on the extremities. Occasionally infection occurs from scratching and rupturing the vesicles. A few scars nearly always remain. The disease may last for two to three weeks.[29]

Management   The administration of varicella-zoster immune globulin (VZIg) within seventy-two hours of exposure will prevent clinical symptoms in normal, healthy children. Acyclovir medication should be administered to adolescents and adults within twenty-four hours following the appearance of symptoms. Anti-itch medication should be used to prevent scratching.[28]

RESPIRATORY CONDITIONS

Athletes like everyone else are highly susceptible to viral infection.[14] The athlete may be prone to conditions that affect the respiratory tract, which includes the nose, sinuses, throat, larynx, trachea, and bronchi. Specific conditions discussed here are sinusitis, pharyngitis, tonsillitis, seasonal rhinitis, acute bronchitis, pneumonia, bronchial asthma, exercise-induced bronchial obstruction, and cystic fibrosis.

Respiratory tract infections can be highly communicable among sports team members.

Sinusitis

Sinusitis is an inflammation of the paranasal sinuses.

Etiology   Sinusitis can stem from an upper respiratory infection caused by a variety of bacteria. As a result, nasal mucous membranes swell and block the ostium of the paranasal sinus. A painful pressure, occurring from an accumulation of mucus, produces pain.[4]

Symptoms and signs   The skin area over the sinus may be swollen and painful to the touch. A headache and malaise may be present. A purulent nasal discharge may also occur.

Management If the infection is purulent, antibiotics may be warranted. Steam inhalation and other nasal topical sprays containing oxymetazalone (e.g., Afrin) can produce vasoconstriction and drainage.

Pharyngitis (Sore Throat)

Acute inflammation of the throat, or pharyngitis, can be related to the common cold, influenza, or a more serious condition such as mononucleosis.

Etiology Pharyngitis can be caused by a virus such as the Epstein-Barr virus of mononucleosis or by the streptococcus bacteria, as in scarlet fever or tonsillitis.[4] Approximately 95 percent of all bacterial pharyngitis is caused by a streptococcal infection.[8] Transmission is often by direct contact with an actively infected person or one who is a carrier. Ingestion of contaminated food can lead to a streptococcal sore throat.[8]

Symptoms and signs Pharyngitis is characterized by pain on swallowing, fever, inflamed and swollen lymph glands, called *lymphandentitis,* swollen tonsils, malaise, weakness, and anorexia. The mucous membranes of the throat may be severely inflamed with a covering of purulent matter.[4] A throat culture for determining the presence of a streptococcal bacterial infection may be necessary.

Management Topical gargles and rest may be warranted. Antibiotic therapy is given for a streptococcal infection to prevent scarlet fever and rheumatic fever.[4]

Tonsillitis

Etiology The tonsils are pieces of lymphatic tissue covered by epithelium that are found at the entrance of the pharynx. Within each tonsil are deep clefts, or pits, lined by lymphatic nodules. Ingested or inhaled pathogens collect in the pits and penetrate the epithelium, where they come in contact with lymphocytes and cause an acute inflammation and bacterial infection.[27] Complications include sinusitis, middle ear infections (otitis media), or tonsillar abcesses.

Symptoms and signs The tonsils appear inflamed, red, and swollen with yellowish exudate in the pits. The athlete has difficulty swallowing and may have a relatively high fever with chills. Headache and pain in the neck and back may also be present.[29]

Management The throat should be cultured to look for streptoccocal bacteria, and if positive, antibiotics should be used for ten days. Gargling with warm saline solution, a liquid diet, and antipyretic medication should all be recommended. Frequent bouts of tonsillitis may eventually necessitate surgical removal of the tonsils.[29]

Seasonal Atopic (Allergic) Rhinitis

Hay fever, or pollinosis, is an acute seasonal allergic condition that results from airborne pollens.

Etiology Hay fever can occur during the spring as a reaction to pollens from trees such as oak, elm, maple, alder, birch, and cottonwood. During the summer, grass and weed pollens can be the culprits. In the fall, ragweed pollen is the prevalent cause. Airborne fungal spores also have been known to cause hay fever. These substances act as allergens and cause an allergic reaction in susceptible people. The body's immune system produces allergic antibodies that release the chemical histamine, which produces the symptoms of hay fever.

Symptoms and signs In the early stages, the athlete's eyes, throat, mouth, and nose begin to itch; these symptoms are followed by watering of the eyes, sneezing, and a clear, watery, nasal discharge. The athlete may complain of a sinus-type headache, emotional irritability, difficulty in sleeping, red and swollen eyes and nasal mucous membranes, and a wheezing cough.[4] Other common adverse allergic conditions are asthma, anaphylaxis, urticaria, angioedema, and rhinitis.[5]

Management Most athletes obtain relief from hay fever through oral antihistamines. However, antihistamines may cause a sedating effect that the athlete must be made aware of. The use of decongestants can cause a stimulating effect.

Acute Bronchitis

An inflammation of the mucous membranes of the bronchial tubes is called bronchitis. It occurs in both acute and chronic forms. If occurring in an athlete, bronchitis is more likely to be in the acute form.

Etiology   Acute bronchitis usually occurs as an infectious winter disease that follows a common cold or other viral infection of the nasopharynx, throat, or tracheobronchial tree. Secondary to this inflammation is a bacterial infection that may follow overexposure to air pollution. Fatigue, malnutrition, or becoming chilled could be predisposing factors.

Symptoms and signs   The symptoms of an athlete with acute bronchitis usually start with an upper respiratory infection, nasal inflammation and profuse discharge, slight fever, sore throat, and back and muscle pains. A cough signals the beginning of bronchitis. In the beginning, the cough is dry, but in a few hours or days, a clear mucus secretion begins, which becomes yellowish, indicating an infection. In most cases, the fever lasts three to five days, and the cough lasts two to three weeks or longer. The athlete may wheeze, and rales may be present when auscultation of the chest is performed. Pneumonia could complicate bronchitis. To avoid bronchitis, an athlete should not sleep in an area that is extremely cold or exercise in extremely cold air without wearing a face mask to warm inhaled air.

Management   Management of acute bronchitis requires that the athlete rest until fever subsides, drink 3 to 4 quarts (3 to 4 liters) of water per day, and ingest an antipyretic analgesic, a cough suppressant, and an antibiotic (when severe lung infection is present) on a daily basis.

Pneumonia

Etiology   Pneumonia is an infection of the alveoli and bronchioles that may be caused by viral, bacterial, or fungal microorganisms. It may also be caused by irritation from chemicals, aspiration of vomitus, or other agents.[29] The alveolar spaces become filled with exudate, inflammatory cells, and fibrin.

Symptoms and signs   If the cause of pneumonia is bacterial, there will be a rapid onset. High fever with chills, pain on inspiration, decreased breath sounds and rhonchi on auscultation, and the coughing up of purulent, yellowish-colored sputum are all associated with bacterial pneumonia.

Management   Bacterial pneumonia must be treated with antibiotics. Deep breathing exercises and removal of sputum through a productive cough are helpful. Analgesic and antipyretics may also be useful for controlling pain and fever.[28]

Bronchial Asthma

Etiology   One of the most common respiratory diseases, bronchial asthma can be produced from a number of stressors, such as a viral respiratory tract infection, emotional upset, changes in barometric pressure or temperature, exercise, inhalation of a noxious odor, or exposure to a specific allergen.

Symptoms and signs   Bronchial asthma is characterized by a spasm of the bronchial smooth muscles, edema, and inflammation of the mucous membrane. In addition to asthma's narrowing of the airway, copious amounts of mucus are produced. Difficulty in breathing may cause the athlete to hyperventilate, resulting in dizziness. The attack may begin with coughing, wheezing, shortness of breath, and fatigue (see *Focus Box:* "Management of the acute asthmatic attack").

Exercise-Induced Bronchial Obstruction (Asthma)

Exercise-induced bronchial obstruction is also known as exercise-induced asthma (EIA). EIA is a form of asthma, and it may present itself exclusive of other asthma precipitators (i.e., it may be the only asthma condition the patient has).

Etiology   An exercise-induced asthmatic attack can be stimulated by exercise in some individuals; in other individuals, the attack may be provoked, only on rare

Focus

Management of the acute asthmatic attack

Athletes who have a history of asthma usually know how to care for themselves when attack occurs. However, the athletic trainer must be aware of what to look for and what to do if called on.

Early symptoms and signs

- Anxious appearance
- Sweating and paleness
- Flared nostrils
- Breathing with pursed lips
- Fast breathing
- Vomiting
- Hunched-over body posture
- Physical fatigue unrelated to activity
- Indentation in the notch below the Adam's apple
- Sinking in of rib spaces as the athlete inhales
- Coughing for no apparent reason
- Excess throat clearing
- Irregular, labored breathing or wheezing

Actions to take

- Attempt to relax and reassure the athlete.
- If medication has been cleared by the team physician, have the athlete use it.
- Encourage the athlete to drink water.
- Have the athlete perform controlled breathing along with relaxation exercises.
- If an environmental factor triggering the attack is known, remove it or the athlete from the area.
- If these procedures do not help, immediate medical attention may be necessary.

occasions, during moderate exercise. The exact cause of EIA is not clear. Metabolic acidosis, postexertional hypocapnia, stimulation of tracheal irritant receptors, adrenergic abnormalities such as a defective catecholamine metabolism, and psychological factors have been suggested as possible causes. Loss of heat and water causes the greatest loss of airway reactivity. Sinusitis can also trigger an attack in an individual with chronic asthma.

Symptoms and signs   The athlete with EIA often displays an airway narrowing caused by bronchial-wall thickening and excess production of mucus. Athletes who have a chronic inflammatory asthmatic condition (bronchiectasis) characteristically have a constant dilation of the bronchi or bronchioles. There is chest tightness, breathlessness, coughing, and wheezing.[19] The athlete with EIA may show signs of nausea, hypertension, diarrhea, fatigue, respiratory stridor (high-pitched noise on respiration), headaches, and redness of the skin. Symptoms may occur within three to eight minutes of strenuous activity.[2]

Management   Swimming produces the fewest bronchospasms, which may be a result of the moist, warm air environment. A regular exercise program can benefit asthmatics. Conditioning and running longer distances reduce EIA bouts.[13] The athlete should engage in gradual warm-ups and cooldowns. The duration of exercise should build slowly to thirty to forty minutes, four or five times a week. Exercise intensity and loading also should be graduated slowly, for example, ten to thirty seconds of work followed by thirty to ninety seconds of rest. Many athletes with chronic or exercise-induced asthma use the inhaled bronchodilator. Exercise is best performed in warm, humid conditions. A mask or scarf may be beneficial in avoiding cold, dry air. Slow nasal breathing is suggested, and athletes should avoid exercising in areas with high levels of air pollution or high pollen counts.[13] The most commonly prescribed B_2 agonist for EIA is albuterol, which acts for about two hours. Salmeterol provides a prophylaxis for up to twelve hours. Albuterol should be administered fifteen minutes before exercise, and salmeterol, thirty to sixty minutes before exercise. Cromolyn sodium should be inhaled thirty minutes before exercise. Metered-dose inhalers are preferred for administration.[19] It has also been found that prophylactic use of the bronchodilator fifteen minutes before exercise delays the symptoms by two to four hours.[4] Asthmatic athletes who receive medication for their condition should make sure that what they take is legal for competition.

Cystic Fibrosis

Etiology   Cystic fibrosis is a genetic disorder that can affect many different body systems; it can manifest itself as a type of chronic obstructive pulmonary disease, as pancreatic deficiency, as urogenital dysfunction, and as increased electrolytes in sweat.[29] It usually begins in infancy and is a major cause of severe chronic lung disease in children. Maximum life expectancy is about thirty years.

Symptoms and signs   A number of physical symptoms may exist, including bronchitis, pneumonia, respiratory failure, gallbladder diseases, pancreatitis diabetes, and nutritional deficiencies. There is an abnormally high production of mucus secretions in the lungs.

Management   Drug therapy, including ibuprofen, can help slow the progress of the disease. Antibiotics are used to control pulmonary disease. The patient must undergo consistent postural drainage, using a cupping or hacking massage technique followed by deep breathing and coughing to help mobilize secretions. High fluid intake to thin secretions and the breathing of humidified air is also recommended.[29]

MUSCULAR SYSTEM DISORDERS

The muscular system suffers from fewer disorders than other systems do. Two serious muscular disorders are muscular dystrophy and myasthenia gravis.

Duchenne Muscular Dystrophy

Etiology   Duchenne muscular dystrophy is a hereditary disease in which there is degeneration of skeletal muscle with an associated loss in strength. Muscle tissue is gradually replaced by adipose and fibrous connective tissue. This connective tissue impedes circulation, which accelerates the degenerative process. Onset is usually in early childhood, between the ages of two and ten years.[27]

Symptoms and signs   The problem begins to appear as the child learns to walk; he or she takes frequent falls and has difficulty standing up. The progressive degeneration first affects the hips, then the legs, and finally, the abdominal and spinal musculature. Muscles tend to shorten as they atrophy, which causes scoliosis and other postural abnormalities.[27]

Management   Muscular dystrophy cannot be cured; however, consistent exercise can be used to retard atrophy. Individuals may ambulate with braces for a while before they are confined to a wheelchair. Death usually occurs before the age of twenty.

Myasthenia Gravis

Myasthenia gravis is an autoimmune disease in which antibodies attack the synaptic junctions between nerves and muscles. A deficiency in aceytlcholine (a neurotransmitter) creates an abnormality that produces early fatigue of skeletal muscle.[29] Myasthenia gravis occurs most often in females between the ages of twenty and forty years.

29-3

Critical Thinking Exercise

A soccer player has a history of exercise-induced asthma (EIA).

? How should the athlete avoid incidences of EIA?

Symptoms and signs One of the first signs is a drooping of the upper eyelid and double vision due to weakness in the extraocular muscles. Following the initial symptoms, there may be difficulty in chewing and swallowing, weakness of the extremities, and a general decrease in muscular endurance.[27]

Management The disease may be treated with drugs that inhibit the breakdown of aceytlcholine, enabling it to stimulate the muscle for longer periods. Corticosteroids may also be used to suppress the immune system and thus reduce production of antibodies that destroy acetylcholine receptors.[27]

NERVOUS SYSTEM DISORDERS

Disorders that can affect the nervous system include meningitis, multiple sclerosis, and amyotrophic lateral sclerosis.

Meningitis

Etiology Meningitis is an inflammation of the meninges, or membranes, that surround the spinal cord and brain that is caused by infection, usually from the meningococcus bacteria. Bacteria may enter the central nervous system through the nose or throat following infections of the ear, throat, or respiratory tract. The bacteria gets into the arachnoid or pia mater, and inflammation spreads to the adjacent nervous tissue, causing swelling of the brain, enlargement of the ventricles, and hemorrhage of the brain stem.[27] Meningitis is a serious disease in children; it usually occurs between the ages of three months and two years.

Symptoms and signs Symptoms include a high fever, stiff neck, intense headache, and sensitivity to light and sound, and they progress to vomiting, convulsions, and coma.

Management The cerebrospinal fluid (CSF) must be analyzed for bacteria and the presence of white blood cells. CSF is taken through a puncture in the lumbar area, or spinal tap. If meningococcus bacteria is identified, isolation is necessary for at least twenty-four hours due to its highly contagious nature. Intravenous antibiotics must begin immediately. Because of the severity of this condition, the patient should be monitored and treated in an intensive care unit.

Multiple Sclerosis

Etiology Multiple sclerosis (MS) is an autoimmune inflammatory disease of the central nervous system that causes deterioration and permanent damage to the myelin sheath that surrounds a nerve cell axon. Nerve conduction is disrupted, causing diverse symptoms. MS most often affects individuals between the ages of twenty and forty years. The exact cause of MS is uncertain, but there is currently no cure.[28]

Symptoms and signs Specific signs depend on the part of the nervous system that is affected, and damage may occur in several different locations. Blurred vision with blind spots, speech defects, tremors, and muscle weakness and numbness in the extremities are common. Some people experience tremor, spasticity, and neurotic behavior that involves mood swings. The disease may progress steadily, or there may be acute attacks followed by partial or complete temporary remission of symptoms.[29]

Management Management involves dealing with the symptoms as they appear and disappear. The individual should avoid overexertion and fatigue, exposure to extreme temperatures, and stressful situations. A regular plan for daily activity and exercise should be established. Several new drugs, including interferon, appear to slow progression of the disease.[29]

Amyotropic Lateral Sclerosis

Etiology Amyotropic lateral sclerosis (ALS), also known as Lou Gehrig's disease, involves a sclerosis of the lateral regions of the spinal cord along with degeneration of motor neurons and significant atrophy of muscles.

Symptoms and signs   Symptoms include difficulty in speaking, swallowing, and use of the hands. However, sensory and intellectual function remain intact. There is rapid progression of muscle atrophy, usually resulting in paralysis and confinement to a wheelchair.[27]

Management   Although there is no cure for this devastating disease, it should be remembered that the individual who is totally incapacitated still has normal intellectual function but simply is unable to communicate feelings and ideas.[27]

Reflex Sympathetic Dystrophy

Etiology   Reflex sympathetic dystrophy (RSD) is an abnormal and excessive response of the sympathetic portion of the autonomic nervous system that occurs following injury. Most commonly it is seen in the hand or the foot resulting from immobilization of an injured part due to pain. It has been associated with injuries to bone, soft tissue, nerve, or blood vessels.

Symptoms and signs   There is a series of changes mediated by the sympathetic nervous system that progressively result in extreme hypersensitivity to touch, redness, sweating, burning/aching type pain, swelling with palpable tightness and shining of the skin, and atrophy. Symptoms may persist for months and even as long as a year. With ongoing chronic pain there is certainly the potential for psychologic depression to occur.

Management   Early recognition and intervention is essential for a good prognosis. Treatment should be directed at disrupting the abnormal sympathetic response. A sympathetic ganglion nerve block administered by a physician is critical to treatment. Active range of motion exercise through a pain free range along with the use of various therapeutic modalities for managing pain and reducing swelling have also been recommended. In cases where symptoms persist for months, anti-depressant medication may be necessary.

BLOOD AND LYMPH DISORDERS

Diseases that can affect the vascular and lymphatic systems include anemias, hemophilia, and lymphangitis.

Anemia

Anemia has been identified as the most common medical condition among athletes. It is more common in females than in males and most common among female athletes. Iron-deficiency anemia and sickle-cell anemia are two of the more common types.

Iron-Deficiency Anemia

Iron deficiency is the most common form of true anemia among athletes. Stores of iron are depleted before clinical signs occur. Iron is mainly stored in hemoglobin (64%) and bone marrow (27%).[10] Iron-deficiency anemia is most prevalent among menstruating women and males eleven to fourteen years old.[9]

Etiology   Three conditions occur during anemia: erythrocytes (red blood cells) are too small, hemoglobin is decreased, and ferritin concentration is low. Ferritin is an iron-phosphorous-protein complex that normally contains 23 percent iron. There are many ways that athletes can be iron deficient. Gastrointestinal (GI) losses are common in runners because of bowel ischemia. Aspirin or NSAIDs may cause GI blood loss. Runners absorb 16 percent of iron from the GI tract compared with 30 percent in nonathletes who are iron deficient. Menstrual losses account for most iron loss in female athletes. Average menstrual iron loss is 0.6 to 1.5 mg per day. Inadequate dietary intake of iron is the primary cause of iron deficiency. The recommended daily allowance (RDA) is 15 mg per day for females and 10 mg per day for males. The average diet contains 5 to 7 mg of iron per 100 kcal. Because female athletes often eat less than they need, they also fail to consume enough iron. Athletes who are vegetarians might lack iron.

A female athlete complains of burning thighs and nausea when she exercises. The athlete also craves ice.

? What should the athletic trainer expect from this scenario, and how should it be handled?

hemolysis
Destruction of red blood cells.

Symptoms and signs   In the first stages of iron deficiency, the athlete's performance begins to decline. The athlete may complain of burning thighs and nausea from becoming anaerobic. Ice craving is also common. Athletes with mild iron-deficiency anemia may display some mild impairment in their maximum performance. Determining serum ferritin is the most accurate test of iron status. Two factors must be checked by the physician: the athlete's mean corpuscular volume (MCV), which is the average volume of individual cells in a cubic micron, and the relative sizes of the erythrocytes.

Management   Athletes can manage iron deficiency in the following ways: eat a proper diet, including more red meat or dark poultry; avoid coffee and tea, which hamper iron absorption from grains; ingest vitamin C sources, which enhance iron absorption; and take an iron supplement (dosage depends on the degree of anemia).

Runners' Anemia

Runners' anemia, or **hemolysis,** is the second most prevalent cause of iron deficiency in athletes.

Etiology   The cause of runners' anemia, as its name implies, is the impact of the foot as it strikes the surface. Impact forces serve to destroy normal erythrocytes within the vascular system.

Symptoms and signs   Hemolysis is characterized by mildly enlarged red cells, an increase in circulatory reticulocytes, and a decrease in the concentration of haptoglobin, which is a glycoprotein bound to hemoglobin and released into the plasma. Even if the athlete wears a well-designed and well-constructed running shoe, this condition can occur. Runners anemia varies according to the amount of running performed.

Management   Athletes can manage runners' anemia by running on soft surfaces, wearing well-cushioned shoes and insoles, and running "light on the feet."

Sickle-Cell Anemia

Sickle-cell anemia is a chronic hereditary hemolytic anemia. The frequency of the genetic defect responsible for this chronic anemia disorder is highest in the African American, Native American, and Mediterranean populations.[29] In these populations, 8 percent to 13 percent are not anemic but carry this trait in their genes. If both parents carry the defective gene, the child will have sickle-cell anemia; if only one parent carries the gene, the child will have sickle-cell trait.[8] The person with sickle-cell anemia or trait can have sicklemia. The person with the sickle-cell trait may participate in sports and never encounter problems until symptoms are brought on by some unusual circumstance.

Etiology   Individuals with sickle-cell anemia have red cells that are sickle, or crescent, shaped. Within the red cells, an abnormal type of hemoglobin exists. It has been speculated that the sickling of the red blood cells results from an adaptation to malaria, which is prevalent in Africa.

The sickle cell has less potential for transporting oxygen and is fragile when compared with normal cells. A sickle cell's life span is 15 to 25 days, compared with the 120 days of a normal red cell; the short life of the sickle cell can produce severe anemia in individuals with acute sickle-cell anemia. The cell's distorted shape inhibits its passage through the small blood vessels and can cause clustering of the cells and, consequently, clogging of the blood vessels. This clogging produces **thrombi,** which block circulation. For individuals having this condition, death can occur (in the severest cases of sickle-cell anemia) from a stroke, heart disease, or an **embolus** in the lungs. Conversely, persons with sickle-cell anemia may never experience any problems. Four factors of exercise can cause sickling: acidosis; hyperthermia; dehydration of red blood cells, which increases hemoglobin concentration; and severe hypoxemia.

thrombi
Plural of thrombus; blood clots that block small blood vessels or a cavity of the heart.

embolus
A mass of undissolved matter.

Symptoms and signs   An athlete may never experience any complications from having the sickle-cell trait. However, a sickle-cell crisis can be brought on by exposure to high altitudes or by overheating of the skin, as is the case with a high fever. Crisis symptoms include fever, severe fatigue, skin pallor, muscle weakness, and severe pain in the limbs and abdomen. Abdominal pain in the right upper quadrant may indicate a splenic syndrome in which there is an infarction.[7] This syndrome is especially characteristic of a crisis triggered by a decrease in ambient oxygen while the athlete is flying at high altitudes. The athlete may also experience headache and convulsions.

Management   Treatment of a sickle-cell crisis is usually symptomatic. The physician may elect to give anticoagulants and analgesics for pain.

Hemophilia

Etiology   Hemophilia is a hereditary disease characterized by a deficiency in any one of a number of clotting factors in the blood. Consequently, there is prolonged coagulation time, failure of the blood to clot, and abnormal bleeding.[29] Hemophilia occurs predominantly in males.

Symptoms and signs   In hemophiliacs, physical exertion can cause bleeding into muscles and joints, which can be extremely painful. Eventually joints may become immobilized.[27]

Management   A hemophiliac who begins bleeding should be taken to an emergency medical care facility immediately. Unfortunately, there is no cure for hemophilia, but concentrated clotting factors have been developed that can control the bleeding for several days. Patients may be taught to self-administer these clotting factors should bleeding occur. The hemophiliac should avoid trauma and should wear a medical alert bracelet to alert care providers to his or her condition.

Lymphangitis

Etiology   Lymphangitis is an inflammation of the lymphatic channels that is most often caused by streptococcal bacteria.[27] Bacterial infection may also occur in the blood, which is referred to as **bacteremia.**

Symptoms and signs   Lymphangitis usually occurs in the extremities. There is a deep reddening of the skin, warmth, lymphandentitis, and a raised border over the affected area, particularly in cases of infection. The condition is accompanied by an onset of chills and high fever with moderate pain and swelling. In lay terms, lymphangitis is sometimes called blood poisoning.[27]

Management   The patient should be hospitalized and vital signs closely monitored.The affected extremity should be elevated and warm moist compresses applied. Antibiotics should be administered, and fluid intake is encouraged to restore fluid balance.

bacteremia (back ter ee-me ah)
Bacterial infection in the blood.

DIABETES MELLITUS

Diabetic athletes engaging in vigorous physical activity should eat before exercising and, if the exercise is protracted, should have hourly glucose supplementation. As a rule, the insulin dosage is not changed, but food intake is increased. The response of diabetics varies among individuals and depends on many variables. Although there are some hazards, with proper medical evaluation and planning by a professional, diabetics can feel free to engage in most physical activities. The most common types of diabetes are type I, insulin-dependent diabetes mellitus (IDDM), and type II, non-insulin-dependent diabetes mellitus (NIDDM). Insulin-dependent diabetes is found primarily in individuals under thirty-five years of age and represents between 5 percent and 10 percent of all cases. Non-insulin-dependent diabetes is most commonly detected after age thirty or forty, represents 80 percent of all cases, and is associated with obesity.[30]

Etiology   Diabetes is a syndrome that results from an interaction of physical and environmental factors. Its etiology is not distinct. There is a complete or partial decrease in the secretion of insulin by the pancreas.

Symptoms and signs IDDM is most commonly seen in childhood. It may occur suddenly; symptoms include frequent urination, constant thirst, weight loss, constant hunger, tiredness and weakness, itchy dry skin, and blurred vision. NIDDM occurs later in life, when the patient is forty years old or older. It is usually associated with being overweight. The pancreas does not produce enough insulin, or the body resists the insulin that is produced. Like IDDM, NIDDM can be a threat to the heart, kidneys, blood vessels, and eyes.

Management It is essential that blood glucose levels be controlled to acceptable levels. This control includes a balanced diet and, when needed, daily doses of insulin. Regular vigorous exercise can be effective in increasing peripheral insulin action to enhance glucose tolerance. Exercise, in general, improves the diabetic person's quality of life. It helps increase type I insulin sensitivity and utilization and may reduce long-term complications. In persons with type II diabetes, exercise decreases insulin resistance, improves glycemia control, and reduces or eliminates the need for insulin.[13] The athletic trainer should be aware that the diabetic athlete can adversely respond to extreme temperature variations or to an unpredictable level of activity duration or intensity and may require rapid-acting carbohydrates.

Diabetic Coma and Insulin Shock

It is important that coaches and athletic trainers who work with athletes who have diabetes mellitus be aware of the major symptoms of diabetic coma and insulin shock and the proper actions to take when either one occurs.[30]

Diabetic Coma

If diabetes is not treated adequately through proper diet or intake of insulin, the diabetic athlete can develop acidosis.

Etiology A loss of sodium, potassium, and ketone bodies through excessive urination produces a problem of ketoacidosis that can lead to coma.

Symptoms and signs Symptoms and signs include labored breathing or gasping for air, fruity-smelling breath caused by acetone, nausea and vomiting, thirst, dry mucous membrane of the mouth, flushed skin, and mental confusion or unconsciousness followed by coma.

Management Because of the life-threatening nature of diabetic coma, early detection of ketoacidosis is essential. The injection of insulin into the athlete may in part help to prevent coma.

Insulin Shock

Etiology Unlike diabetic coma, insulin shock occurs when too much insulin is taken into the body, and hypoglycemia results.

Symptoms and signs The athlete complains of tingling in the mouth, hands, or other body parts; physical weakness; headaches; and abdominal pain. It may be observed that the athlete has normal or shallow respirations, rapid heartbeat, and tremors along with irritability and drowsiness.

Management The diabetic athlete who engages in intense exercise and metabolizes large amounts of glycogen could inadvertently take too much insulin and thus have a severe reaction. To avoid this problem, the athlete must adhere to a carefully planned diet that includes a snack before exercise. The snack should contain a combination of a complex carbohydrate and protein, such as cheese and crackers. Activities that last for more than thirty to forty minutes should be accompanied by snacks of simple carbohydrates. Some diabetics carry with them a lump of sugar or have candy or orange juice readily available in the event that an insulin reaction seems imminent.[26]

SEIZURE DISORDERS (EPILEPSY)

Berkow defines seizure disorders as "a recurrent paroxysmal disorder of cerebral function characterized by sudden, brief attacks of altered consciousness, motor activity, sensory phenomena, or inappropriate behavior caused by an abnormal excessive

Focus

> **Management during a seizure**
>
> - Be emotionally composed.
> - If possible, cushion the athlete's fall.
> - Keep the athlete away from injury-producing objects.
> - Loosen restrictive clothing.
> - Prevent the athlete from biting the mouth by placing a soft cloth between the teeth.
> - Allow the athlete to awaken normally after the seizure.
> - Do not restrain the athlete during the seizure.

discharge of cerebral neurons."[4] Any recurrent seizure pattern is termed **epilepsy.** Epilepsy is not a disease but is a symptom that can be caused by a large number of underlying disorders.

epilepsy
Recurrent paroxysmal disorder characterized by sudden attacks of altered consciousness, motor activity, sensory phenomena, or inappropriate behavior.

Etiology   For some types of epilepsy, there is a genetic predisposition and a low threshold to having seizures. In others, altered brain metabolism or a history of injury may be the cause. A seizure can range from extremely brief episodes that last five to fifteen seconds (petit mal seizures) to major episodes (grand mal seizures) that last a few minutes and include unconsciousness and uncontrolled tonic-clonic muscle contractions. There are approximately 1 million epileptics in the United States, most of whom can participate in some form of physical activity.[13] Sports-related injuries are not increased in the epileptic, nor is the sudden death syndrome linked to strenuous activity by the epileptic.[13]

Symptoms and signs   Each person with epilepsy must be considered individually as to whether he or she should engage in competitive sports. If an individual has daily or even weekly major seizures, collision sports should be prohibited. This prohibition is not because a hit on the head will necessarily trigger a seizure, but because a blow during participation that causes unconsciousness could result in a serious injury. If the seizures are properly controlled by medication or occur only during sleep, little if any sports restriction should be imposed except for scuba diving, swimming alone, or participation at a great height.[13]

For individuals who have major daily or weekly seizures, collision sports may be prohibited.

Management   The athlete commonly takes an anticonvulsant medication that is specific for the type and degree of seizures that occur. On occasion, the athlete may experience some undesirable side effects from drug therapy, such as drowsiness, restlessness, nystagmus, nausea, vomiting, problems with balance, skin rash, or other adverse reactions.

When an athlete with epilepsy becomes aware of an impending seizure, he or she should take measures to avoid injury, such as immediately sitting or lying down. When a seizure occurs without warning, the athletic trainer should follow the steps in *Focus Box:* "Management during a seizure".

HIGH BLOOD PRESSURE (HYPERTENSION)

Excessive pressure applied against arterial walls while blood circulates is known as hypertension, or high blood pressure (HBP). A normal resting blood pressure is 120/80 mm Hg (systolic/diastolic), whereas the upper limit for the older adolescent and adult at rest is 140/90 mm Hg (Table 29-1).

Etiology   Hypertension is classified as primary, or essential, and secondary. Primary hypertension accounts for 90 percent of all cases and has no disease associated with it. Secondary hypertension is related to a specific underlying cause, such as kidney disorder, overactive adrenal glands (increased blood volume), hormone-producing tumor, narrowing of the aorta, pregnancy, and medications (oral contraceptives, cold

Hypertension may be a factor that excludes players from sports participation.

TABLE 29-1 Age and Blood Pressure Limits

Age	Upper Blood Pressure Limits at Rest*
<10	120/75 mm Hg
10–12	125/80 mm Hg
13–15	135/85 mm Hg
16–18	140/90 mm Hg
>18	140/90 mm Hg

*If the upper limits of blood pressure are exceeded during three measurements, the athlete may have hypertension.

remedies, etc.). The presence of prolonged high blood pressure increases the chances of premature mortality and morbidity due to such causes as coronary artery disease, congestive heart failure, and stroke.[1]

Symptoms and signs   Primary hypertension is usually asymptomatic until complications occur.[4] High blood pressure may cause dizziness, flushed appearance, headache, fatigue, epistaxis, and nervousness.

Management   High blood pressure is not determined until many pressure readings are recorded at various times. A thorough examination must be conducted to ascertain the type of hypertension. Primary hypertension may be controlled with lifestyle changes such as weight loss, salt restriction, and aerobic exercise. When the underlying condition causing secondary hypertension is cured, the blood pressure commonly returns to normal.

Endurance exercise training can lower systolic and diastolic blood pressure by 10 mm Hg in mild hypertensives (140/90 to 180/105 mm Hg). Individuals with blood pressures over 180/105 mm Hg carry out endurance exercises after pharmacological therapy. Resistive strength training, especially isometrics, is not recommended as the only form of exercise.[1]

CANCER

Etiology   Cancer is the second leading cause of death in adults, behind coronary artery disease. It is estimated that about 30 percent of all Americans will get cancer during their lifetime, and one of five will eventually die from it.[27] Cancer is a condition in which cellular behavior becomes abnormal. The cells no longer perform their normal functions. In general, cancer cells do not multiply at an increased rate. Instead, whatever causes cancer alters the cell's genetic makeup and changes the way it functions. This abnormal cell then divides, forming additional cancer cells, and over a period of time, this tumor or collection of abnormal cells tends to invade and ultimately take over normal tissue.

TUMORS   Tumors may be either benign or malignant. Benign tumors typically pose only a small threat to a tissue and tend to remain confined in a limited space. Malignant tumors, though, are cancerous; they grow out of control and spread within a specific tissue. Unfortunately, malignancies can invade surrounding tissues and can spread via the blood and lymphatic systems (metastasize) to the entire body, making it difficult to control the cancer.[27]

Malignancies are classified according to the type of tissues in which they occur and according to the rate at which they affect the tissue. Although different types of cancer cells share similar characteristics, each is separate and distinct. Some types are relatively easy to cure, whereas others are difficult to cure and are even life threatening. Skin cancer is the most common type and, fortunately, one of the easiest to detect and cure. Males and females have a different incidence of other types of cancers. In males, the highest incidence of cancer is in the prostate, followed closely by lung, colon/rectal, urinary, and leukemias/lymphomas. In females, the highest incidence is found in the breast, followed by colon/rectal, lung, uterus, and leukemias/lymphomas.

CAUSES OF CANCER   The precise causes of cancer are not easily identified. Researchers have identified more than 100 types of cancer with genetic origins. Certain cancers appear to run along family lines. The onset of most cancer has also been attributed to certain environmental factors, including viruses; exposure to ultraviolet light, radiation, and certain chemicals such as tobacco; and alcohol use. A fatty diet has been linked to cancer. It is likely that a combination of hereditary and environmental factors is responsible for the development of cancer.[27]

Symptoms and signs   Specific signs of cancer can vary tremendously, depending on the type of cancer. The American Cancer Society has identified the classic warning signs of cancer: a change in bowel and bladder habits, a sore throat that does not heal, unusual bleeding or discharge, thickening or a lump in the breast or elsewhere, indigestion or difficulty swallowing, obvious change in a wart or mole, and a nagging cough or hoarseness. The presence of any of these signs warrants immediate attention by a physician.

Management   Unquestionably, early detection and treatment of cancer markedly improves the patient's chances of beating the disease. The most effective forms of treatment involve three traditional techniques: surgery, radiation, and chemotherapy.

> Warning signs of cancer:
> - A change in bowel and bladder habits
> - A sore throat that does not heal
> - Unusual bleeding or discharge
> - Thickening or a lump in the breast or elsewhere
> - Indigestion or difficulty swallowing
> - Obvious change in a wart or mole
> - A nagging cough or hoarseness

SEXUALLY TRANSMITTED DISEASES

Sexually transmitted diseases are of major concern in sports because many athletes are at an age during which they are more sexually active than they will be at any other time in their lives. The venereal diseases with the highest incidence among the relatively young are chlamydia, genital herpes, trichomoniasis, genital candidiasis, condyloma acuminata, gonorrhea, and syphilis. HIV and hepatitis B were discussed in Chapter 14.

Chlamydia

Chlamydia is considered by many to be the most common venereal disease in the United States. It is more common than gonorrhea.[4]

Etiology   In females, chlamydia may result in pelvic inflammatory disease and is an important cause of infertility and ectopic pregnancy.

Symptoms and signs   In the male, inflammation occurs, along with a purulent discharge, seven to twenty-eight days after intercourse.[2] On occasion, painful urination and traces of blood in the urine occur. Most females with this infection are asymptomatic, but some may experience a vaginal discharge, painful urination, pelvic pain, and pain and inflammation in other sites.

Management   A bacteriological examination is given to determine the exact organisms present. Once identified, the infection must be treated promptly to prevent complications. Organism identification and treatment must take place immediately in women who are pregnant. Chlamydial ophthalmia neonatorum can cause conjunctivitis and pneumonia in the newborn from an infected mother.[2] Uncomplicated cases are usually treated with antibiotics. Approximately 20 percent of the sufferers have one or more relapses.

Chlamydia trachomatis
A genus microorganism that can cause a wide variety of diseases in humans, one of which is venereal and causes nonspecific urethritis.

Genital Herpes

Genital herpes is a venereal infection that is currently widespread.

Etiology   Type 2 herpes simplex virus is associated with genital herpes infection, which is now the most prevalent cause of genital ulcerations. Signs of the disease appear approximately four to seven days after sexual contact. Primary genital herpes crusts in fourteen to seventeen days, and secondary cases crust in ten days.

Symptoms and signs   The first signs in the male are itching and soreness, but women may be asymptomatic in the vagina and cervix. It is estimated that 50 percent to 60 percent of individuals who have had one attack of herpes genitalis will have no further episodes, or if they do, the lesions are few and insignificant. Like the lesions in herpes labialis and gladiatorum, the lesions that develop in herpes genitalis eventually become ulcerated with a red areola. Ulcerations crust and heal in approximately ten days, leaving a scar (Color Plate, Figure M). Of major importance to a pregnant woman with a history of genital herpes is whether there is an active infection when she is nearing delivery. Herpes simplex can be fatal to a newborn child. There may be some relationship between a higher incidence of cervical cancer and the incidence of genital herpes.[4]

Management   At this time, there is no cure for genital herpes. Systemic medications, specifically antiviral medications such as acycloguanosine or acyclovir (Zovirax) and vidarabine (Vira-A), are being used to lessen the early symptoms of the disease.[4]

Trichomoniasis

Trichomoniasis is an infection that affects 20 percent of all females during their reproductive years and 5 percent to 10 percent of males.

Etiology   Trichomoniasis is caused by the flagellate protozoan *Trichomonas vaginalis.*

Symptoms and signs   The female with trichomoniasis typically has a vaginal discharge that is greenish yellow and frothy. The disease causes irritation of the vulva, perineum, and thighs. The female may also experience painful urination. Males are usually asymptomatic, although some may experience a frothy, purulent urethral discharge.

Management   Two grams of metronidazole in one dose, usually the drug of choice in the treatment of trichomoniasis, cures up to 95 percent of women. Men, in contrast, should be treated with 500 milligrams twice a day for seven days. The sexual partner is treated concurrently. Complete cure is required before the individual can again engage in sexual intercourse.

Genital Candidiasis

As discussed in Chapter 28, *Candida* (a genus of yeastlike fungi) is commonly part of the normal flora of the mouth, skin, intestinal tract, and vagina.

Etiology   The *Candida* organism is one of the most common causes of vaginitis in women of reproductive age. The infection maybe transmitted sexually, but there can be numerous other causes.

Symptoms and signs   The symptoms and signs are similar to other, related conditions. The female complains of vulval irritation that begins with redness, severe pain, and a vaginal discharge (scanty). The male is usually asymptomatic but could develop some irritation and soreness of the glans penis, especially after intercourse. Rarely, a slight urethral discharge may occur.

Management   Because of the highly infectious nature of this disease, all sexual contact should cease until completion of treatment. An antifungal cream should be applied to the vagina, labia, perineum, and perianal region for three days.

Condyloma Acuminata (Venereal Warts)

Another sexually transmitted disease that should be recognized and referred to a physician is condyloma acuminata, or venereal warts.

Etiology   These warts are transmitted through sexual activity. They appear on the glans penis, vulva, or anus.

Symptoms and signs   This form of wart virus produces nodules that can have a cauliflower-like lesion or can be singular. In their early stage, the nodules are soft, moist, pink or red swellings that rapidly develop a stem with a flowerlike head. They may be mistaken for secondary syphilis or carcinoma (Color Plate, Figure N).

Management   Moist condylomas are often carefully treated by the physician with a solution containing 20 percent to 25 percent podophyllin. Dry warts may be treated with a freezing process such as liquid nitrogen.

Trichomoniasis affects 20 percent of all females and 5 percent to 10 percent of all males.

Gonorrhea

Gonorrhea, commonly called clap, is an acute venereal disease that can infect the urethra, cervix, and rectum.

Etiology The organism of infection is the gonococcal bacteria *Neisseria gonorrhoea,* which is usually spread through sexual intercourse.

Symptoms and signs In men, the incubation period is two to ten days. The onset of the disease is marked by a tingling sensation in the urethra, followed in two or three hours by a greenish-yellow discharge of pus and by painful urination. Sixty percent of infected women are asymptomatic. For those who have symptoms, onset is between seven and twenty-one days. In these cases, symptoms are mild, with some vaginal discharge. Gonorrheal infection of the throat and rectum are also possible.

Management Because of embarrassment, some individuals fail to secure proper medical help for treatment of gonorrhea, and although the initial symptoms will disappear, such an individual is not cured and can still spread the infection. Untreated gonorrhea becomes latent and will manifest itself in later years, usually causing sterility or arthritis. Treatment consists of large amounts of penicillin or other antibiotics. Recent experimental evidence suggests an increasing resistance of the gonococci to penicillin. The athletic trainer who sees evidence of any of the symptoms should immediately remand the individual to a physician for testing and treatment. *All sexual contact must be avoided* until it has been medically established that the disease is no longer active. Because of the latent residual effects, including sterility and arthritis, that are the end result of several diseases in this group, immediate medical treatment is mandatory. Although outward signs may disappear, the disease is still insidiously present in the body. Additionally, such treatment will alleviate the discomfort that accompanies the initial stages of the disease.

Syphilis

A sexually transmitted disease that is on an increase is syphilis. Reasons for this increase are high-risk sexual behavior, drug usage, and lack of knowledge about preventing infection.[8]

Etiology *Treponema pallidum,* a spirochete bacteria, is the organism related to syphilis. It enters the body through mucous membranes or skin lesions.[4]

Symptoms and signs Untreated syphilis may have a course of four stages within the body: primary; secondary; latent; and late, or tertiary. The incubation period of syphilis is normally three to four weeks but can range anywhere from one to thirteen weeks. A painless chancre, or ulceration, develops and heals within four to eight weeks. This stage is highly contagious. Ulcerations can occur on the penis, urethra, vagina, cervix, mouth, hand, or foot or around the eye.

The secondary stage of syphilis occurs within six to twelve weeks after the initial infection. It is characterized by a skin rash, lymph swelling, body aches, and mild flulike symptoms. Hair may fall out in patches.

Latent syphilis follows the secondary stage and is characterized by no or few symptoms. If untreated, approximately one-third of persons with latent syphilis will develop late, or tertiary, syphilis.

The late stage of syphilis is characterized by a deep penetration of spirochetes that damage skin, bone, and the cardiovascular and nervous systems. Tertiary syphilis can develop within three to ten years of infection. Neurosyphilis can progress into severe muscle weakness, paralysis, and various types of psychoses.

Management Penicillin is currently the appropriate antibiotic for all stages of syphilis. Those patients allergic to penicillin may be treated with erythromycin. Because *T. pallidum* can exist only in body fluids, air drying and cleaning with soap and water will destroy it. Because of the rise of penicillin resistance, ceftriaxone may be the drug of choice.

29-5

Critical Thinking Exercise

A male college basketball player confides in the athletic trainer about a greenish-yellow urethral discharge and painful urination.

? How should this situation be managed by the athletic trainer?

MENSTRUAL IRREGULARITIES AND THE FEMALE REPRODUCTIVE SYSTEM

There are special menstrual and reproductive concerns related to the female who engages in intense physical activity. This section addresses some of the more prevalent issues.

Physiology of the Menstrual Cycle

Menstruation refers to the periodic discharge of bloody fluid from the uterus, usually at regular intervals, during the life of a woman from the age of puberty to menopause.

Menarche

During the prepubertal period, girls are equal to, and often superior to, boys of the same age in activities that require speed, strength, and endurance.

Menarche—the onset of the menses—and puberty normally occur between ages nine and seventeen, with the majority of girls usually entering puberty between ages thirteen and fifteen. Puberty is that period of life in which either gender becomes able to reproduce. There is indication that strenuous sports training and competition will delay the onset of menarche. The greatest delay is related to the higher-caliber competition. In itself, a delay in the first menses does not appear to pose any significant danger to the young female athlete. Delayed menarche, or primary amenorrhea, is defined as menstruation not occurring by age sixteen or a failure to develop secondary sexual characteristics by age fourteen. The late-maturing girl commonly has longer legs, narrower hips, and less adiposity and body weight for her height, all of which are more conducive to sports.

The onset of menarche may be delayed by strenuous training and competition.

Menstruation

The effects of sustained and strenuous training and competition on the menstrual cycle and the effects of menstruation on performance still cannot be fully explained with any degree of certainty.

The classic twenty-eight-day cycle consists of the follicular and luteal phases, each of which is approximately fourteen days long. The menses vary from three to seven days, with an average of four to seven days. The majority of women tend to show some variation in the length of their cycles; these differences occur principally because of differences in duration of the preovulatory phase rather than the premenstrual phase.

With the onset of menarche, a cyclic hormone pattern commences, which establishes the menstrual cycle. These hormonal changes result from complex feedback mechanisms and specifically controlled interactions that occur between the hypothalamus, ovaries, and pituitary gland. Two gonadotropins induce the release of the egg from the mature follicle at midcycle (ovulation): follicle-stimulating hormone (FSH), which stimulates the maturation of an ovarian follicle, and luteinizing hormone (LH), which stimulates the development of the corpus luteum and the endocrine structure that secretes progesterone and estrogens. The control and eventual inhibition of the production of FSH when the follicle reaches maturity is brought about by the estrogenic steroids produced by the ovaries. Progesterone, a steroid hormone produced within the corpus luteum—a small body that develops within a ruptured ovarian follicle after ovulation—eventually inhibits production of LH. Estrogen is secreted principally by the luteal cells. Before onset of a new menstrual period, FSH levels are already rising, probably to initiate maturation of new follicles to reinstitute the next cycle.

Menstrual Cycle Irregularities

Highly active female athletes, such as those participating in ballet, gymnastics, and long-distance running, can experience irregularities in the normal menstrual cycle of twenty-five to thirty-eight days. *Oligomenorrhea* (diminished flow) refers to fewer than three to

Focus

Suggested factors in exercise-induced amenorrhea

- Competition such as long-distance running, gymnastics, professional ballet dancing, cycling, or swimming
- Low body weight with weight loss after beginning of training
- Total calorie intake inadequate for energy needs
- An eating disorder
- High incidence of menstrual abnormalities before vigorous training
- Higher levels of stress when compared with those experiencing normal menses
- Likely to have begun training at an early age
- A rapid increase in high-intensity exercise

six cycles per year.[3] **Amenorrhea** is the complete cessation of the cycle, with ovulation occurring seldom or not at all because of the low level of circulating estrogen.[3] Approximately 10 percent to 20 percent of vigorously exercising women have amenorrhea.

Etiology   The cause of exercise-related amenorrhea, or athlete's amenorrhea, is often a hypothalamic dysfunction. The gonadotropin-releasing hormone (GnRH) produced by the hypothalamus is often deficient.[20] Many factors must be ruled out by a physical examination before athlete's amenorrhea is determined. Pregnancy and abnormalities of the reproductive or genital tract must be ruled out as well as ovarian failure and pituitary tumors.[11,20]

Symptoms and signs   *Focus Box:* "Suggested factors in exercise-induced amenorrhea" includes some factors of exercise-related amenorrhea.

Management   The ideal treatment of exercise-induced amenorrhea is the reestablishment of normal hormone levels and the return of the normal menstrual cycle.[3] It is important that a medical evaluation be performed before other intervention procedures are started. Cleared of any physical abnormalities, the athlete is given nutritional counseling to balance calorie output and intake and to regulate the proper amount of nutrients. Reduction of exercise intensity and counseling to reduce emotional stress can be helpful. Estrogen replacement may be considered.[3]

amenorrhea
Absence or suppression of menstruation.

Dysmenorrhea

Dysmenorrhea (painful menstruation) apparently is prevalent among more active women; however, it is inconclusive whether specific sports participation can alleviate or produce dysmenorrhea. For girls with moderate to severe dysmenorrhea, gynecological consultation is warranted to rule out a pathological condition.[3]

Dysmenorrhea may be caused by ischemia (a lack of normal blood flow to the pelvic organs), by a possible hormonal imbalance, and by endometriosis. This syndrome, which is identified by cramps, nausea, lower abdominal pain, headache, and on occasion, emotional lability, is the most common menstrual disorder. Mild to vigorous exercises that help ameliorate dysmenorrhea are usually prescribed by physicians. Physicians generally advise a continuance of the usual sports participation during the menstrual period, provided the performance level of the individual does not drop below her customary level of ability. Among athletes, swimmers have the highest incidence of dysmenorrhea; it, along with menorrhagia, occurs most often, probably as the result of strenuous sports participation during the menses. Generally, oligomenorrhea, amenorrhea, and irregular or scanty flow are more common in sports that require strenuous exertion over a long period of time (e.g., long-distance running, rowing, cross-country skiing, basketball, tennis, field hockey, and soccer). Because great variation exists among female athletes with respect to menstrual

Girls who have moderate to severe dysmenorrhea require examination by a physician.

pattern, to its effect on physical performance, and to the effect of physical activity on the menstrual pattern, each individual must learn to make adjustments to her cycle that will permit her to function effectively and efficiently with a minimum of discomfort or restriction. Evidence to date indicates that top performances are possible in all phases of the cycle.

Bone Health

The athlete who has a prolonged decrease of FSH, LH, estrogen, and progesterone shows a profile similar to that of a postmenopausal woman.[12] Osteoporosis is most common in women older than age fifty whose bone mass (bone mineral density) has fallen below a critical threshold. Athletic women who have irregular menses because of endocrine changes are strong candidates for bone loss. Low bone mass leads to bone fragility and increased susceptibility to stress fractures in female athletes with premature osteoporosis, especially athletes with late menarche.[15] There is evidence that estrogen receptors on bone cells cause a direct relation on growth and bone function.[12] Calcium nutrition is also needed; a recommended daily allowance for adolescents through age twenty-four is 1,200 milligrams daily.[18]

An athlete experiencing loss of periods with low bone mass should decrease training intensity and volume, increase total calories, and ingest 1,200 to 1,500 milligrams of calcium daily. A program of resistance training designed for both muscle mass and strength may enhance the skeletal profile and protect against muscle injury. Estrogen replacement therapy may be warranted if other means fail.[15]

The Female Athlete Triad

The relationship of three medical disorders has been termed the *female athlete triad.* Those medical disorders are disordered eating, amenorrhea, and osteoporosis.[22,23]

Etiology   As stated by Nattiv and coworkers, "The young woman athlete, driven to excel in her chosen sport and pressured to fit a specific athletic image in order to reach her goals, is at risk for the development of disordered patterns of eating," which "may lead to menstrual dysfunction and subsequent premature osteoporosis."[22,23] This triad has the potential for serious illness and risk of death.[23]

Symptoms and signs   The components of the triad are disordered eating, amenorrhea, and osteoporosis. Disordered eating follows the same patterns of eating characteristics that anorexia nervosa and bulimia do (see Chapter 5). Amenorrhea is discussed earlier in this chapter. Osteoporosis in young women athletes refers to premature bone loss and inadequate bone development that results in low bone mass, microarchitectural destruction, increased skeletal fragility, and increased risk of fracture.[23] Physicians, athletic trainers, and coaches must be aware of the athlete's potential for risk. Special concern must be directed toward those athletes who participate in sports that focus on an ideal body type and weight, who exhibit signs of disordered eating, and who experience disruption in menarche or the menstrual cycle.

Management   Management of this triad lies in prevention. Those concerned with the athlete's total health must be educated. A concerted effort must be made to identify and screen athletes who are at risk.

Contraceptives and Reproduction

Female athletes have been known to take extra oral contraceptive pills to delay menstruation during competition. This practice is not recommended. Such practices can cause nausea, vomiting, fluid retention, amenorrhea, hypertension, double vision, and thrombophlebitis. Some oral contraceptives make women hypersensitive to the sun. Any use of oral contraceptives related to physical performance should be under the express direction and control of a physician. However, oral contraceptive use is acceptable for females with no medical problems. The new low-dose preparations, containing less than fifty milligrams of estrogen, add negligible risks to the healthy woman.

In general, athletes who wear intrauterine devices are free of such problems. However, intrauterine devices are not recommended for adolescents who are nul-

29-6

Critical Thinking E x e r c i s e

A female athlete has been diagnosed as having a serious eating disorder and amenorrhea.

? Why may these two medical disorders lead eventually to osteoporosis?

liparous (have never borne a viable child) because of the associated risk of pelvic inflammatory disease. On occasion the athlete may complain of a lower-abdominal cramp while being active. In such cases, referral to a physician should be made.

Pregnancy

Generally, participation in physical activity and even competition may be engaged in well into the third month of pregnancy, unless bleeding or cramps are present, and can frequently be continued until the seventh month if no handicapping or physiological complications arise.[17] Such activity may make pregnancy, childbirth, and postparturition less stressful. Many women athletes do not continue beyond the third month because of a drop in their performance. This decline may result from a number of causes, some related to the pregnancy, others perhaps psychological. It is during the first three months of pregnancy that the dangers of disturbing the pregnancy are greatest. After that period, there is less danger to the mother and fetus because the pregnancy is stabilized. There is no indication that mild to moderate exercise during pregnancy is harmful to fetal growth and development or causes reduced fetal mass, increased perinatal or neonatal mortality, or physical or mental retardation.[6,25] It has been found, however, that extreme exercise may lower birth weight (see *Focus Box:* "American College of Obstetricians and Gynecologists guidelines for

Focus

American College of Obstetricians and Gynecologists guidelines for exercise during pregnancy and postpartum[24]

1. During pregnancy, women can continue to exercise and derive health benefits even from a mild to moderate exercise routine. Regular exercise (at least three times per week) is preferable to intermittent activity.

2. Women should avoid exercise in the supine position after the first trimester. Such a position is associated with decreased cardiac output in most pregnant women; because the remaining cardiac output will be preferentially distributed away from splanchnic beds (including the uterus) during vigorous exercise, such regimens are best avoided during pregnancy. Prolonged periods of motionless standing should also be avoided.

3. Women should be aware of the decreased amount of oxygen available for aerobic exercise during pregnancy. They should be encouraged to modify the intensity of their exercise according to maternal symptoms. Pregnant women should stop exercising when fatigued and not exercise to exhaustion. Weight-bearing exercises may under same circumstances be continued throughout pregnancy at intensities similar to those before pregnancy. Non–weight bearing exercise such as cycling or swimming will minimize the risk of injury and facilitate the continuation of exercise during pregnancy.

4. Morphological changes in pregnancy should serve as relative contraindications to types of exercise in which loss of balance could be detrimental to maternal or fetal well-being, especially in the third trimester. Any type of exercise involving the potential for even mild abdominal trauma should be avoided.

5. Pregnancy requires an additional 300 kcal per day to maintain metabolic homeostasis. Thus women who exercise during pregnancy should be particularly careful to ensure an adequate diet.

6. Pregnant women who exercise in the first trimester should augment heat dissipation by ensuring adequate hydration, appropriate clothing, and optimal environmental surroundings during exercise.

7. Many of the physiological and morphological changes of pregnancy persist four to six weeks postpartum. Thus the woman's prepregnancy exercise routine should be resumed gradually based on her physical capability.

In general, childbirth is not adversely affected by a history of hard physical exercise.

exercise during pregnancy and postpartum"). Many athletes compete during pregnancy with no ill effects. Most physicians, although advocating moderate activity during this period, believe that especially vigorous performance, particularly in activities with severe body contact or heavy jarring or falls, should be avoided.[16] Contraindications to exercise include the following:

- Pregnancy-induced hypertension
- Preterm rupture of membranes
- Preterm labor during the prior or current pregnancy or both
- Incompetent cervix or cerclage
- Persistent second- or third-trimester bleeding
- Intrauterine growth retardation

Ectopic Pregnancy

In ectopic pregnancy, the fertilized egg is implanted outside the uterine cavity because of some inflammation of the fallopian tubes or some mechanical blockage to the normal downward movement of the ovum. The symptoms include amenorrhea, tenderness, soreness and pain on the affected side, referred pain in the shoulders, pallor, and potentially, signs of shock and hemorrhage. Operative treatment is necessary to terminate the nonviable pregnancy and to control the hemorrhage if a rupture of the tube has occurred.

SUMMARY

- The immune system is not an organ system but is instead a collection of disease-fighting cells that recognize the presence of foreign substances in the body and act to neutralize or destroy them.
- Among the more common viral infections are rhinovirus (common cold), influenza (flu), infectious mononucleosis, rubella (German measles), rubeola (measles), mumps, and varicella-zoster (chicken pox).
- Conditions that affect the respiratory system include sinusitis, pharyngitis, tonsillitis, seasonal rhinitis, acute bronchitis, pneumonia, bronchial asthma, exercise-induced bronchial obstruction, and cystic fibrosis.
- The muscular system suffers from fewer disorders than do other systems. Two serious muscular disorders are muscular dystrophy and myasthenia gravis.
- Disorders that can affect the nervous system include meningitis, multiple sclerosis, and amyotrophic lateral sclerosis.
- Diseases that can affect the vascular and lymphatic systems include anemias, hemophilia, and lymphangitis.
- Diabetes mellitus is a complex hereditary or developmental disease. Diabetics must be extremely cautious about the possibility of going into diabetic coma or insulin shock.
- Some athletes have a history of epilepsy that could lead to an alteration of consciousness. Epilepsy is not a disease, and each person with epilepsy must be considered individually.
- The athlete with high blood pressure may have to be carefully monitored by the physician. Hypertension may require the avoidance of heavy resistive activities.
- Cancer is a condition in which cellular behavior becomes abnormal. Malignant tumors are cancerous; they grow out of control and spread within a specific tissue. Skin cancer is the most common type. In males, the highest incidence of cancer is in the prostate, followed closely by lung, colon/rectal, urinary, and leukemias/lymphomas. In females the highest incidence is found in the breast, followed by colon/rectal, lung, uterus, and leukemias/lymphomas.
- The sexually transmitted diseases with the highest incidence among the young athletic population are chlamydia, genital herpes, trichomoniasis, genital candidiasis, condyloma acuminata, gonorrhea, and syphilis.

- The highly active female may have menstrual irregularities, including dysmenorrhea, amenorrhea, or oligomenorrhea. Menstrual irregularities could lead to a thinning of bone and subsequent fractures.
- Many female athletes compete during pregnancy with no ill effects. There is no indication that mild to moderate exercise during pregnancy is harmful to fetal development.

Web Sites

Cramer First Aider: http://www.ccsd.k12.wy.us/cchs_web/cramerfirstaider/fstaider.htm

Yahoo Search Engine for Diseases and Conditions: http://www.yahoo.com/Health/Diseases_and_Conditions

Karolinska Institute Library: http://www.mic.ki.se/Disease/index.html

This site allows the reader to search for related medical topics.

Health Line: http://www.mbnet.mb.ca/scip/hl/index.htm

At this site, the reader can search for answers to questions about common health conditions.

Solutions to Critical Thinking EXERCISES

29-1 This scenario describes flu symptoms. There should be symptomatic care and the avoidance of aspirin.

29-2 It is possible that this athlete has infectious mononucleosis. Treatment is supportive and symptomatic. Acetaminophen is often given for headache, fever, and malaise. The athlete may resume easy training in about three weeks after the onset of illness if: (1) the spleen is not markedly enlarged or painful, (2) he or she is afebrile, (3) liver function tests are normal, and (4) pharyngitis and any complication have resolved.

29-3 The athlete maintains a high level of conditioning, including the running of longer distances, and should always warm up and cool down gradually. All exercise intensity and loading should be graduated slowly. A bronchodilator may be employed. A mask or scarf is used in cold, dry air. The athlete should avoid exercising in areas with high levels of air pollution or when there is a high pollen count.

29-4 The athlete appears to have iron-deficiency anemia. After verification by a physician, the athlete should eat a diet rich in iron, avoid coffee and tea, eat foods high in vitamin C, and take a daily iron supplement.

29-5 This situation must be handled with the strictest confidentiality. Because this condition could be gonorrhea, immediate medical referral must be made. All sexual contact must be avoided until this condition has been resolved.

29-6 These medical disorders make up the female athlete triad. Osteoporosis is the softening and increased porosity of bones with subsequent fracturing. Athletes who have anorexia nervosa or bulimia to establish a perceived body image are at risk. Athletes who train so hard that they stop menstruating also stop their estrogen production, which results in a loss of calcium in the bones.

REVIEW QUESTIONS AND CLASS ACTIVITIES

1. Contrast the symptoms and signs of the following respiratory tract conditions: the common cold, influenza, and allergic rhinitis.
2. Discuss mononucleosis in detail, including prevention and etiology.
3. Discuss and contrast bronchial obstructive diseases such as bronchitis and asthma. How do you care for an athlete with an acute asthmatic attack?
4. Describe the most common gastrointestinal complaints. How are the conditions that produce them acquired and managed?
5. What is diabetes mellitus? What value might exercise have for the person with diabetes mellitus? How are diabetic coma and insulin shock managed?
6. In a sports setting, what are some major indications that an athlete has a contagious disease?
7. What is epilepsy? How should a grand mal seizure be managed?
8. Define hypertension. What dangers does it present to the athlete?
9. Describe the anemias that most often affect the athlete. How should each be managed?
10. What are the classic warning signs for cancer according to the American Cancer Society?
11. Discuss the etiology, symptoms and signs, and management of the most common sexually transmitted diseases. How can they be prevented?
12. Discuss menstrual irregularities that occur in highly active athletes. Why do they occur? How should they be managed? How do they relate to reproduction?
13. What are the implications of pregnancy for extensive physical activity?

REFERENCES

1. American College of Sports Medicine: Position stand: physical activity, physical fitness, and hypertension, *Med Sci Sports Exerc* 25(10):1, 1993.
2. Bartimole J: Exercise-induced asthma: pre-treating for prevention, *NATA News* 4, 1995.
3. Benson MT, editor: *1994–95 NCAA sports medicine handbook: menstrual-cycle dysfunction,* Overland Park, Kans, 1994, National Collegiate Athletic Association.
4. Berkow R, editor: *The Merck manual,* ed 16, Rahway, NJ, 1992, Merck.
5. Blumenthal MN: Sports-aggravated allergies, *Physician Sportsmed* 18(12):70, 1990.
6. Clapp JF III: A clinical approach to exercise during pregnancy. In Agostini R, editor: *The athletic woman. Clinics in sports medicine,* vol 13, no 2, Philadelphia, 1994, Saunders.

7. Eichner ER: Sickle-cell trait, heroic exercise, and fatal collapse, *Physician Sportsmed* 21(7):51, 1993.

8. Hamann B: *Disease: identification, prevention, and control,* St Louis, 1994, Mosby.

9. Harris SS: Exercise-related anemias. In Agostini R, editor: *Medical and orthopedic issues of active and athletic women,* St Louis, 1994, Mosby.

10. Harris SS: Helping active women avoid anemia, *Physician Sportsmed* 23(5):34, 1995.

11. Harter-Snow C: Athletic amenorrhea and bone health. In Agostini R, editor: *Medical and orthopedic issues of active and athletic women,* St Louis, 1994, Mosby.

12. Harter-Snow CM: Bone health and prevention of osteoporosis in active and athletic women. In Agostini R, editor: *The athletic woman. Clinics in sports medicine,* vol 13, no 2, Philadelphia, 1994, Saunders.

13. Howe WB: The athlete with chronic illness. In Birrer RB, editor: *Sports medicine for the primary care physician,* ed 2, Boca Raton, Fla, 1994, CRC Press.

14. Jong EC: Infections. In Agostini R, editor: *Medical and orthopedic issues of active and athletic women,* St Louis, 1994, Mosby.

15. Karpalcka J et al: Recurrent stress fracture in a female athlete with primary amenorrhea, *Cl J Sports Med* 4(2):136, 1994.

16. Kulpa P: Exercise during pregnancy and post partum. In Agostini R, editor: *Medical and orthopedic issues of active and athletic women,* St Louis, 1994, Mosby.

17. LeBrun CM: Effects of the menstrual cycle and birth control pills on athletic performance. In Agostini R, editor: *Medical and orthopedic issues of active athletic women,* St Louis, 1994, Mosby.

18. Lemcke DP: Osteoporosis and menopause. In Agostini R, editor: *Medical and orthopedic issues of active and athletic women,* St Louis, 1994, Mosby.

19. Mahler DA: Exercise-induced asthma, *Med Sci Sports Exerc* 25(5):554, 1993.

20. Marshall LA: Clinical evaluation of amenorrhea. In Agostini R, editor: *Medical and orthopedic issues of active and athletic women,* St Louis, 1994, Mosby.

21. Mellion MB et al: Medical problems in athletes. In Birrer RB, editor: *Sports medicine for the primary care physician,* Boca Raton, Fla, 1994, CRC Press.

22. Nattiv A, Lynch L: The female athlete triad, *Physician Sportsmed* 22(1):60, 1994.

23. Nattiv A et al: The female athletic triad. In Agostini R, editor: *Medical and orthopedic issues of active and athletic women,* St Louis, 1994, Mosby.

24. *PACOG Technical Bulletin 189. Exercise during pregnancy and postpartum period,* Washington, DC, 1994, The American College of Obstetricians and Gynecologists.

25. Partin N: The diabetic athlete, *Ath Train* 24(4):381, 1989.

26. Robbins DC, Carleton S: Managing the diabetic athlete, *Physician Sportsmed* 17(12):45, 1989.

27. Saladin K: Anatomy and physiology: the unity of form and function, Dubuque, Iowa, 1998, WCB/McGraw-Hill.

28. *Stedman's concise medical dictionary for the health professions,* Baltimore, 1997, Williams & Wilkins.

29. *Taber's cyclopedic medical dictionary,* Philadelphia, 1997, FA Davis.

30. Taunton JE, McCargarl EL: Staying active with diabetes, *Physician Sportsmed* 23(3):55, 1995.

ANNOTATED BIBLIOGRAPHY

Agostini R, editor: *Medical and orthopedic issues of active and athletic women,* St Louis, 1994, Mosby.

This text is an excellent overview of health issues facing the physically active female.

Berkow R, editor: *The Merck manual of diagnosis and therapy,* Rahway, NJ, 1992, Merck.

This text is a major reference book on etiology, symptoms and signs, and treatment of disease.

Birrer RB, editor: *Sports medicine for the primary care physician,* ed 2, Boca Raton, Fla, 1994, CRC Press.

This comprehensive review covers the important medical, orthopedic, and scientific aspects of caring for athletes.

NATA Code of Ethics

PREAMBLE

The Code of Ethics of the National Athletic Trainers' Association has been written to make the membership aware of the principles of ethical behavior that should be followed in the practice of athletic training. The primary goal of the Code is the assurance of high quality health care. The Code presents aspirational standards of behavior that all members should strive to achieve.

The principles cannot be expected to cover all specific situations that may be encountered by the practicing athletic trainer, but should be considered representative of the spirit with which athletic trainers should make decisions. The principles are written generally and the circumstances of a situation will determine the interpretation and application of a given principle and of the Code as a whole. Whenever there is a conflict between the Code and legality, the laws prevail. The guidelines set forth in this Code are subject to continual review and revision as the athletic training profession develops and changes.

PRINCIPLE 1:

Members shall respect the rights, welfare, and dignity of all individuals.

1.1 Members shall not discriminate against any legally protected class.

1.2 Members shall be committed to providing competent care consistent with both the requirements and the limitations of their profession.

1.3 Members shall preserve the confidentiality of privileged information and shall not release such information to a third party not involved in the patient's care unless the person consents to such release or release is permitted or required by law.

PRINCIPLE 2:

Members shall comply with the laws and regulations governing the practice of athletic training.

2.1 Members shall comply with applicable local, state, and federal laws and institutional guidelines.

2.2 Members shall be familiar with and adhere to all National Athletic Trainers' Association guidelines and ethical standards.

2.3 Members are encouraged to report illegal or unethical practice pertaining to athletic training to the appropriate person or authority.

2.4 Members shall avoid substance abuse and, when necessary, seek rehabilitation for chemical dependency.

PRINCIPLE 3:

Members shall accept responsibility for the exercise of sound judgment.

3.1 Members shall not misrepresent in any manner, either directly or indirectly, their skills, training, professional credentials, identity, or services.

3.2 Members shall provide only those services for which they are qualified via education and/or experience and by pertinent legal regulatory process.

3.3 Members shall provide services, make referrals, and seek compensation only for those services that are necessary.

PRINCIPLE 4:

Members shall maintain and promote high standards in the provision of services.

4.1 Members shall recognize the need for continuing education and participate in various types of educational activities that enhance their skills and knowledge.

4.2 Members who have the responsibility for employing and evaluating the performance of other staff members shall fulfill such responsibility in a fair, considerate, and equitable manner, on the basis of clearly enunciated criteria.

4.3 Members who have the responsibility for evaluating the performance of employees, supervisees, or students, are encouraged to share evaluations with them and allow them the opportunity to respond to those evaluations.

4.4 Members shall educate those whom they supervise in the practice of athletic training with regard to the Code of Ethics and encourage their adherence to it.

4.5 Whenever possible, members are encouraged to participate and support others in the conduct and communication of research and educational activities that may contribute knowledge for improved patient care, patient or student education, and the growth of athletic training as a profession.

4.6 When members are researchers or educators, they are responsible for maintaining and promoting ethical conduct in research and educational activities.

PRINCIPLE 5:

Members shall not engage in any form of conduct that constitutes a conflict of interest or that adversely reflects on the profession.

5.1 The private conduct of the member is a personal matter to the same degree as is any other person's except when such conduct compromises the fulfillment of professional responsibilities.

5.2 Members of the National Athletic Trainers' Association and others serving on the Association's committees or acting as consultants shall not use, directly or by implication, the Association's name or logo or their affiliation with the Association in the endorsement of products or services.

5.3 Members shall not place financial gain above the welfare of the patient being treated and shall not participate in any arrangement that exploits the patient.

5.4 Members may seek remuneration for their services that is commensurate with their services and in compliance with applicable law.

NATA Blood Borne Pathogens Guidelines for Athletic Trainers

The NATA recognizes that blood borne pathogens such as HIV, HBV, and HCV present many complex issues for athletic trainers, athletic administrators, and others involved with the care and training of athletes. As the primary health care professional involved with the physically active, it is important for athletic trainers to be aware of these issues. The NATA therefore offers the following guidelines and information concerning the management of blood borne pathogen–related issues in the context of athletics and settings in which the physically active are involved.

It is essential to remember, however, that the medical, legal and professional knowledge, standards and requirements concerning blood borne pathogens are changing and evolving constantly, and vary, in addition, from place to place and from setting to setting. The guidance provided in these guidelines must not, therefore, be taken to represent national standards applicable to members of the NATA. Rather, the guidance here is intended to highlight issues, problems, and potential approaches to (or management of) those problems that NATA members can consider when developing their own policies with respect to management of these issues.

ATHLETIC PARTICIPATION

Decisions regarding the participation of athletes infected with blood borne pathogens in athletic competitions should be made on an individual basis. Such decisions should be made following the standard or appropriate procedures generally followed with respect to health-related participation questions, and taking into account only those factors that are directly relevant to the health and rights of the athlete, the other participants in the competition, and the other constituencies with interests in the competition; the athletic program, the athletes, and the sponsoring schools and organizations.

The following are examples of factors that are appropriate in many settings to the decision-making process:
- The current health of the athlete
- The nature and intensity of the athlete's training
- The physiological effects of the athletic competition
- The potential risks of the infection being transmitted
- The desires of the athlete
- The administrative and legal needs of the competitive program

EDUCATION OF THE PHYSICALLY ACTIVE

In a rapidly changing medical, social, and legal environment, educational information concerning blood borne pathogens is of particular importance. The athletic trainer should play a role with respect to the creation and dissemination of educational information that is appropriate to and particularized with respect to that athletic trainer's position and responsibilities.

Athletic trainers who are responsible for developing educational programs with respect to blood borne pathogens should provide appropriate information concerning:

- The risk of transmission or infection during competition
- The risk of transmission or infection generally
- The availability of HIV testing
- The availability of HBV testing and vaccinations

Athletic trainers who have educational program responsibility should extend educational efforts to include those, such as the athletes' families and communities, who are directly or indirectly affected by the presence of blood borne pathogens in athletic competitions.

All educational activities should, of course, be limited to those within athletic trainers' scope of practice and competence, be within their job descriptions or other relevant roles, and be undertaken with the cooperation and/or consent of appropriate personnel, such as team physicians, coaches, athletic directors, school or institutional counsel, and school and community leaders.

THE ATHLETIC TRAINER AND BLOOD BORNE PATHOGENS AT ATHLETIC EVENTS

The risk of blood borne pathogen transmission at athletic events is directly associated with contact with blood or other body fluids. Athletic trainers who have responsibility for overseeing events at which such contact is possible should use appropriate preventative measures and be prepared to administer appropriate treatment, consistent with the requirements and restrictions of their job, and local, state, and federal law.

In most cases, these measures will include:

- Pre-event care and covering of existing wounds, cuts, and abrasions
- Provision of the necessary or usual equipment and supplies for compliance with universal precautions, including, for example, latex gloves, biohazard containers, disinfectants, bleach solutions, antiseptics, and sharps containers
- Early recognition and control of a bleeding athlete, including measures such as appropriate cleaning and covering procedures, or changing of blood-saturated clothes
- Requiring all athletes to report all wounds immediately
- Insistence that universal precaution guidelines be followed at all times in the management of acute blood exposure
- Appropriate cleaning and disposal policies and procedures for contaminated areas or equipment
- Appropriate policies with respect to the delivery of life-saving techniques in the absence of protective equipment
- Post-event management including, as appropriate, re-evaluation, coverage of wounds, cuts, and abrasions
- Appropriate policy development, including incorporation, with necessary legal and administrative assistance, of existing OSHA and other legal guidelines and conference or school rules and regulations

STUDENT ATHLETIC TRAINER EDUCATION

NATA encourages appropriate education of and involvement of the student athletic trainer in educational efforts involving blood borne pathogens. These efforts and programs will vary significantly based on local needs, requirements, resources, and policies.

At the secondary school level, educational efforts should include items such as the following:

- Education and training in the use of universal precautions and first aid for wounds
- Education regarding the risks of transmission/infection from the participants that they care for
- Education on the availability of HIV testing

- Education on the availability of HBV vaccinations and testing
- Education of parents or guardians regarding the students' risk of infection

At the college or university level, education efforts should include items such as those listed above, and, additionally, as appropriate, the following:

- Education in basic and clinical science of blood borne pathogens
- Discussions regarding the ethical and social issues related to blood borne pathogens
- The importance of prevention programs
- Education concerning the signs and symptoms of HBV and HIV, as consistent with the scope of practice of the athletic profession and state and local law

UNIVERSAL PRECAUTIONS AND OSHA REGULATIONS

Athletic trainers should, consistent with their job descriptions and the time and legal requirements and limitations of their jobs and professions, inform themselves and other affected and interested parties of the relevant legal guidance and requirements affecting the handling and treatment of blood borne pathogens.

Athletic trainers cannot be expected to practice law or medicine, and efforts with respect to compliance with these guidelines and requirements must be commensurate with the athletic trainer's profession and professional requirements. It may be appropriate for athletic trainers to keep copies of the Center for Disease Control regulations and OSHA regulations and guidelines available for their own and others' use.

MEDICAL RECORDS AND CONFIDENTIALITY

The security, record-keeping, and confidentiality requirements and concerns that relate to athletes' medical records generally apply equally to those portions of athletes' medical records that concern blood borne pathogens.

Since social stigma is sometimes attached to individuals infected with blood borne pathogens, athletic trainers should pay particular care to the security, record-keeping, and confidentiality requirements that govern the medical records for which they have a professional obligation to see, use, keep, interpret, record, update, or otherwise handle.

Security, record-keeping, and confidentiality procedures should be maintained with respect to the records of other athletic trainers, employees, student athletic trainers, and athletes, to the extent that the athletic trainer has responsibility for these records.

THE INFECTED ATHLETIC TRAINER

An athletic trainer infected with a blood borne pathogen should practice the profession of athletic training taking into account all professionally, medically, and legally relevant issues raised by the infection. Depending on individual circumstances, the infected athletic trainer will or may wish to:

- Seek medical care and ongoing evaluation
- Take reasonable steps to avoid potential and identifiable risks to his or her own health and the health of his or her patients
- Inform, as or when appropriate, relevant patients, administrators, or medical personnel

HIV AND HBV TESTING

Athletic trainers should follow federal, state, local, and institutional laws, regulations, and guidelines concerning HIV and HBV testing. Athletic trainers should, in appropriate practice settings and situations, find it advisable to educate or assist athletes with respect to the availability of testing.

HBV VACCINATIONS

Consistent with professional requirements and restrictions, athletic trainers should encourage HBV vaccinations for all employees at risk, in accordance with OSHA guidelines.

WITHHOLDING OF CARE AND DISCRIMINATION

NATA's policies and its Code of Ethics make it unethical to discriminate on the basis of medical conditions.

REFERENCES

American Academy of Pediatrics. Human immunodeficiency virus [acquired immunodeficiency syndrome (AIDS) virus] in the athletic setting. *Pediatrics.* 1991;88:640–641.

American Medical Association, Department of HIV, Division of Health Science. Digest of HIV/AIDS Policy. Chicago, IL: Department of HIV, American Medical Association; 1993:1–15.

American Medical Society for Sports Medicine and American Academy of Sports Medicine. Human immunodeficiency virus (HIV) and other blood-borne pathogens in sports. *American Journal of Sports Medicine.* In Press.

Benson MT, ed. Guideline 2H: blood-borne pathogens and intercollegiate athletics. NCAA Sports Medicine Handbook. 1993;24–28.

Michigan Department of Public Health. Michigan recommendations on HBV and/or HIV infected health care workers. *Triad.* 1992;4:32–34.

NATA Helmet Removal Guidelines (1998)

The National Athletic Trainers' Association has adopted the following guidelines with regard to the on-site removal of the athletic helmet.

Removing helmets from athletes with potential cervical spine injuries may worsen existing injuries or cause new ones. Removal of athletic helmets should, therefore, be avoided unless individual circumstances dictate otherwise.

Before removing the helmet from an injured athlete, appropriate alternatives such as the following should be considered:

- Most injuries can be visualized with the helmet in place.
- Neurological tests can be performed with the helmet in place. The eyes may be examined for reactivity, the nose and ears checked for fluid and the level of consciousness determined.
- The athlete can be immobilized on a spine board with the helmet in place.
- The helmet and shoulder pads elevate the supine athlete. Removal of helmet and shoulder pads, if required, should be coordinated to avoid cervical hyperextension.
- Removal of the face mask allows full airway access to be achieved. Plastic clips securing the face mask can be cut using special tools, permitting rapid removal.

In all cases, individual circumstances must dictate appropriate actions.

Health and Welfare Canada

Santé et Bien-être social Canada

CANADA'S Food Guide TO HEALTHY EATING

Enjoy a variety of foods from each group every day.

Choose lower-fat foods more often.

Grain Products
Choose whole grain and enriched products more often.

Vegetables & Fruit
Choose dark green and orange vegetables and orange fruit more often.

Milk Products
Choose lower-fat milk products more often.

Meat & Alternatives
Choose leaner meats, poultry and fish, as well as dried peas, beans and lentils more often.

Continued

CANADA'S

Food Guide

TO HEALTHY EATING

FOR PEOPLE FOUR YEARS AND OVER

Different People Need Different Amounts of Food

The amount of food you need every day from the 4 food groups and other foods depends on your age, body size, activity level, whether you are male or female and if you are pregnant or breast-feeding. That's why the Food Guide gives a lower and higher number of servings for each food group. For example, young children can choose the lower number of servings, while male teenagers can go to the higher number. Most other people can choose servings somewhere in between.

Grain Products

5-12

SERVINGS PER DAY

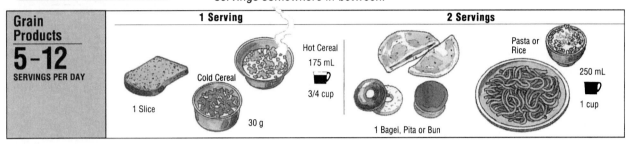

1 Serving — 1 Slice — Cold Cereal 30 g — Hot Cereal 175 mL 3/4 cup

2 Servings — 1 Bagel, Pita or Bun — Pasta or Rice 250 mL 1 cup

Vegetables & Fruit

5-10

SERVINGS PER DAY

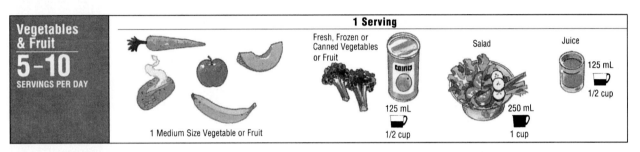

1 Serving — 1 Medium Size Vegetable or Fruit — Fresh, Frozen or Canned Vegetables or Fruit 125 mL 1/2 cup — Salad 250 mL 1 cup — Juice 125 mL 1/2 cup

Milk Products

SERVINGS PER DAY
Children 4–9 years: 2–3
Youth 10–16 years: 3–4
Adults: 2–4
Pregnant & Breast-feeding
Women: 3–4

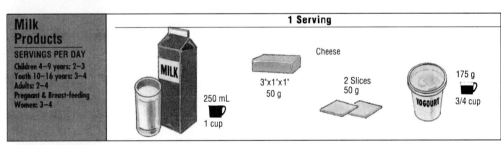

1 Serving — MILK 250 mL 1 cup — Cheese 3"x1"x1" 50 g — 2 Slices 50 g — YOGOURT 175 g 3/4 cup

Other Foods

Taste and enjoyment can also come from other foods and beverages that are not part of the 4 food groups. Some of these foods are higher in fat or Calories, so use these foods in moderation.

Meat & Alternatives

2-3

SERVINGS PER DAY

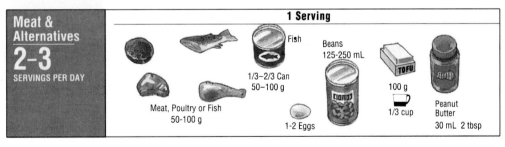

1 Serving — Meat, Poultry or Fish 50-100 g — Fish 1/3–2/3 Can 50–100 g — 1-2 Eggs — Beans 125-250 mL — TOFU 100 g 1/3 cup — Peanut Butter 30 mL 2 tbsp

Enjoy eating well, being active and feeling good about yourself. That's VITALIT

© Minister of Supply and Services Canada 1992   Cat. No. H39-252/1992E   No changes permitted. Reprint permission not required.
ISBN 0-662-19648-1

Nutrient Recommendations for Canadians

Recommended Nutrient Intake

Age	Sex	Weight (kg)	Protein (g)	Vit. A (RE[a])	Vit. D (µg)	Vit. E (mg)	Vit. C (mg)	Folate (µg)	Vit. B_{12} (µg)	Calcium (mg)	Phosphorus (mg)	Magnesium (mg)	Iron (mg)	Iodine (µg)	Zinc (mg)
Months															
0–4	Both	6.0	12[b]	400	10	3	20	25	0.3	250[c]	150	20	0.3[d]	30	2[d]
5–10	Both	9.0	12	400	10	3	20	40	0.4	400	200	32	7	40	3
Years															
1	Both	11	13	400	10	3	20	40	0.5	500	300	40	6	55	4
2–3	Both	14	16	400	5	4	20	50	0.6	550	350	50	6	65	4
4–6	Both	18	19	500	5	5	25	70	0.8	600	400	65	8	85	5
7–9	M	25	26	700	2.5	7	25	90	1.0	700	500	100	8	110	7
	F	25	26	700	2.5	6	25	90	1.0	700	500	100	8	95	7
10–12	M	34	34	800	2.5	8	25	120	1.0	900	700	130	8	125	9
	F	36	36	800	2.5	7	25	130	1.0	1100	800	135	8	110	9
13–15	M	50	49	900	2.5	9	30	175	1.0	1100	900	185	10	160	12
	F	48	46	800	2.5	7	30	170	1.0	1000	850	180	13	160	9
16–18	M	62	58	1000	2.5	10	40[e]	220	1.0	900	1000	230	10	160	12
	F	53	47	800	2.5	7	30[e]	190	1.0	700	850	200	12	160	9
19-24	M	71	61	1000	2.5	10	40[e]	220	1.0	800	1000	240	9	160	12
	F	58	50	800	2.5	7	30[e]	180	1.0	700	850	200	13	160	9
25–49	M	74	64	1000	2.5	9	40[e]	230	1.0	800	1000	250	9	160	12
	F	59	51	800	2.5	6	30[e]	185	1.0	700	850	200	13	160	9
50–74	M	73	63	1000	5	7	40[e]	230	1.0	800	1000	250	9	160	12
	F	63	54	800	5	6	30[e]	195	1.0	800	850	210	8	160	9
75+	M	69	59	1000	5	6	40[e]	215	1.0	800	1000	230	9	160	12
	F	64	55	800	5	5	30[e]	200	1.0	800	850	210	8	160	9
Pregnancy (additional)															
1st Trimester			5	0	2.5	2	0	200	0.2	500	200	15	0	25	6
2nd Trimester			20	0	2.5	2	10	200	0.2	500	200	45	5	25	6
3rd Trimester			24	0	2.5	2	10	200	0.2	500	200	45	10	25	6
Lactation (additional)			20	400	2.5	3	25	100	0.2	500	200	65	0	50	6

SOURCE: Scientific Review Committee. *Nutrition Recommendations*, Ottawa, Canada: Health and Welfare, 1990. Reproduced with permission of the Minister of Supply and Services Canada, 1996.

[a]Retinol equivalents.
[b]Protein is assumed to be from breast milk and must be adjusted for infant formula.
[c]Infant formula with high phosphorus should contain 375 mg calcium.
[d]Breast milk is assumed to be the source of the mineral.
[e]Smokers should increase vitamin C by 50%.

Continued

Nutrient Recommendations for Canadians

Energy Expressed as Daily Rates

Age	Sex	Energy (Cal)	Thiamin (mg)	Riboflavin (mg)	Niacin (NE[b])	n-3 PUFA[a] (g)	n-6 PUFA (g)
Months							
0–4	Both	600	0.3	0.3	4	0.5	3
5–12	Both	900	0.4	0.5	7	0.5	3
Years							
1	Both	1100	0.5	0.6	8	0.6	4
2–3	Both	1300	0.6	0.7	9	0.7	4
4–6	Both	1800	0.7	0.9	13	1.0	6
7–9	M	2200	0.9	1.1	16	1.2	7
	F	1900	0.8	1.0	14	1.0	6
10–12	M	2500	1.0	1.3	18	1.4	8
	F	2200	0.9	1.1	16	1.2	7
13–15	M	2800	1.1	1.4	20	1.5	9
	F	2200	0.9	1.1	16	1.2	7
16–18	M	3200	1.3	1.6	23	1.8	11
	F	2100	0.8	1.1	15	1.2	7
19–24	M	3000	1.2	1.5	22	1.6	10
	F	2100	0.8	1.1	15	1.2	7
25–49	M	2700	1.1	1.4	19	1.5	9
	F	1900	0.8	1.0	14	1.1	7
50–74	M	2300	0.9	1.2	16	1.3	8
	F	1800	0.8[c]	1.0[c]	14[c]	1.1[c]	7[c]
75+	M	2000	0.8	1.0	14	1.1	7
	F[d]	1700	0.8[c]	1.0[c]	14[c]	1.1[c]	7[c]
Pregnancy (additional)							
1st Trimester		100	0.1	0.1	1	0.05	0.3
2nd Trimester		300	0.1	0.3	2	0.16	0.9
3rd Trimester		300	0.1	0.3	2	0.16	0.9
Lactation (additional)		450	0.2	0.4	3	0.25	1.5

SOURCE: Scientific Review Committee. *Nutrition Recommendations,* Ottawa, Canada: Health and Welfare, 1990.
Reproduced with permission of the Minister of Supply and Services Canada, 1996.
[a]PUFA, polyunsaturated fatty acids.
[b]Niacin equivalents.
[c]Level below which intake should not fall.
[d]Assumes moderate physical activity.

A

abduction Movement of a body part away from the midline of the body.

accident Occurring by chance or without intention.

active range of motion Joint motion that occurs because of muscle contraction.

acute injury An injury with sudden onset and short duration.

ad libitum Amount desired.

adduction Movement of a body part toward the midline of the body.

adipose cell Stores triglyceride.

afferent nerves Nerves that transport messages toward the brain.

agonist muscles Muscles directly engaged in contraction as related to muscles that relax at the same time.

ambient Environmental (e.g., temperature or air that invests one's immediate environment).

ambulation Move or walk from place to place.

ameboid action Cellular action like that of an amoeba, using protoplasmic pseudopod.

amenorrhea Absence or suppression of menstruation.

ampere Volume or amount of electrical energy.

analgesia Pain inhibition.

analgesic Agent that relieves pain without causing a complete loss of sensation.

anaphylaxis Increased susceptibility or sensitivity to a foreign protein or toxin as the result of previous exposure to it.

androgen Any substance that aids the development and controls the appearance of male characteristics.

anemia Lack of iron.

anesthesia Partial or complete loss of sensation.

anomaly Deviation from the normal.

anorexia Lack or loss of appetite; aversion to food.

anorexia nervosa Eating disorder characterized by a distorted body image.

anoxia Lack of oxygen.

antagonist muscles Muscles that counteract the action of the agonist muscles.

anterior Before or in front of.

anteroposterior Refers to the position of front to back.

anteversion Tipping forward of a part as a whole, without bending.

antipyretic Agent that relieves or reduces fever.

anxiety A feeling of uncertainty or apprehension

apophysis Bony outgrowth to which muscles attach.

apophysitis Inflammation of an apophysis.

arrhythmical movement Irregular movement.

arthrogram Radiopaque material injected into a joint to facilitate the taking of an X ray.

arthrokinematics Physiological and accessory movements of the joint.

arthroscopic examination Viewing the inside of a joint through an arthroscope, which uses a small camera lens.

assumption of risk An individual, through express or implied agreement, assumes that some risk or danger will be involved in a particular undertaking; a person takes his or her own chances.

asymmetry (body) Lack of symmetry of sides of the body.

atrophy Wasting away of tissue or of an organ; diminution of the size of a body part.

attenuation Decrease in intensity as ultrasound enters deeper into tissues.

aura Preepileptic phenomenon, involving visual sensation of fire or glow, along with other possible sensory hallucinations and dreamlike states.

autogenic inhibition The relaxation of the antagonist muscle during contractions.

automatism Automatic behavior before consciousness or full awareness has been achieved after a brain concussion.

avascular Devoid of blood circulation.

avascular necrosis Death of tissue caused by the lack of blood supply.

avulsion Forcible tearing away of a part or a structure.

axilla Armpit.

B

bacteremia Bacterial infection in the blood.

bacteria Morphologically, the simplest group of nongreen vegetable organisms, various species of which are involved in fermentation and putrefaction, the production of disease, and the fixing of atmospheric nitrogen; a schizomycete.

bacteriostatic Halting the growth of bacteria.

ballistic stretching Older stretching technique that uses repetitive bouncing motions.

bandage Strip of cloth or other material used to cover a wound.

beam nonuniformity ratio (BNR) Amount of variability of the ultrasound beam.

beta-endorphin Chemical substance produced in the brain.

bioavailability How completely a particular drug is absorbed by the system.

bioequivalence Having a similar biological effect.

biomechanics Branch of study that applies the laws of mechanics to living organisms and biological tissues.

biotransformation Transforming a drug so it can be metabolized.

bipedal Having two feet or moving on two feet.

BMR Basal metabolic rate.

body composition Percent body fat plus lean body weight.

bradykinin Peptide chemical that causes pain in an injured area.

buccal Pertaining to the cheek or mouth.

bulimia Binge-purge eating disorder.

bursitis Inflammation of a bursa, especially those bursae located between bony prominences and a muscle or tendon such as those of the shoulder and knee.

C

calcific tendinitis Deposition of calcium in a chronically inflamed tendon, especially the tendons of the shoulder.

calisthenic Exercise involving free movement without the aid of equipment.

calorie (large) Amount of heat required to raise 1 kg of water 1° C; used to express the fuel or energy value of food or the heat output of the organism; the amount of heat required to heat 1 lb of water to 4° F.

cardiorespiratory endurance Ability to perform activities for extended periods of time.

catastrophic injury Relates to a permanent injury of the spinal cord that leaves the athlete quadriplegic or paraplegic.

catecholamine Active amines, epinephrine and norepinephrine, that affect the nervous and cardiovascular systems.

cerebrovascular accident Stroke.

chafing Superficial inflammation that develops when skin is subjected to friction.

chemotaxis Response to influence of chemical stimulation.

chiropractor One who practices a method for restoring normal condition by adjusting the segments of the spinal column.

Chlamydia trachomatis A genus microorganism that can cause a wide variety of diseases in humans, one of which is venereal and causes nonspecific urethritis.

chondromalacia Abnormal softening of cartilage.

chronic injury Injury with long onset and long duration.

cicatrix Scar or mark formed by fibrous connective tissue; left by a wound or sore.

circadian rhythm Biological time clock by which the body functions.

circuit training Exercise stations that consist of various combinations of weight training, flexibility, calisthenics, and aerobic exercises.

circumduct Act of moving a limb such as the arm or hip in a circular manner.

clonic muscle contraction Alternating involuntary muscle contraction and relaxation in quick suspension.

coenzymes Enzyme activators.

collagen Main organic constituent of connective tissue.

collision sport Sport in which athletes use their bodies to deter or punish opponents.

colloid Liquid or gelatinous substance that retains particles of another substance in a state of suspension.

commission (legal liability) Person commits an act that is not legally his or hers to perform.

communicable disease Disease that may be transmitted directly or indirectly from one individual to another.

concentric (positive) contraction The muscle shortens while contracting against resistance.

conduction Heating through direct contact with a hot medium.

conjunctiva Mucous membrane that lines the eyes.

contact sport Sport in which athletes do make physical contact but not with the intent to produce bodily injury.

contrast bath procedure Two minutes of immersion in ice slush, followed by 30 seconds in tepid water.

contrecoup brain injury After head is struck, brain continues to move within the skull, resulting in injury to the side opposite the force.

convection Heating indirectly through another medium such as air or liquid.

conversion Heating by other forms of energy (e.g., electricity).

convulsions Paroxysms of involuntary muscular contractions and relaxations.

core temperature Internal, or deep, body temperature monitored by cells in the hypothalamus, as opposed to shell, or peripheral, temperature, which is registered by that layer of insulation provided by the skin, subcutaneous tissues, and superficial portions of the muscle masses.

corticosteroid Steroid produced by the adrenal cortex.

coryza Profuse nasal discharge.

counterirritant Agent that produces mild inflammation and acts, in turn, as an analgesic when applied locally to the skin (e.g., liniment).

coupling medium Used to facilitate the transmission of ultrasound into the tissues.

crepitation Crackling sound heard during the movement of ends of a broken bone.

cryokinetics Cold application combined with exercise.

cryotherapy Cold therapy.

cubital fossa Triangular area on the anterior aspect of the forearm directly opposite the elbow joint (the bend of the elbow).

cyanosis Slightly bluish, grayish, slatelike, or dark purple discoloration of the skin caused by a reduced amount of blood hemoglobin.

D

DAPRE Daily adjustable progressive resistance exercise.

debride Removal of dirt and dead tissue from a wound.

deconditioning State in which the athlete's body loses its competitive fitness.

degeneration Deterioration of tissue.

dermatome Segmental skin area innervated by various spinal cord segments.

diagnosis Identification of a specific condition.

diapedesis Passage of blood cells, via ameboid action, through the intact capillary wall.

diarthrodial joint Ball-and-socket joint.

diastolic blood pressure The residual pressure when the heart is between beats.

DIP Distal interphalangeal joint.

diplopia Seeing double.

distal Farthest from a center, from the midline, or from the trunk.

DNA Deoxyribonucleic acid.

doping The administration of a drug that is designed to improve the competitor's performance.

dorsiflexion Bending toward the dorsum or rear; opposite of plantar flexion.

dorsum The back of a body part.

dressing Covering, protective or supportive, that is applied to an injury or wound.

drug Any substance that, when taken into the living organism, may modify one or more of its functions.

drug vehicle The substance in which a drug is transported.

dysrhythmia Irregular heartbeats.

E

eccentric (negative) contraction The muscle lengthens while contracting against resistance.

ecchymosis Black-and-blue skin discoloration caused by hemorrhage.

ectopic calcification Calcification occurring in an abnormal place.

edema Swelling as a result of the collection of fluid in connective tissue.

effective radiating area Portion of the transducer that produces sound energy.

efficacy A drug's capability of producing a specific therapeutic effect.

effleurage Stroking.

electrolyte Solution that is a conductor of electricity.

embolus A mass of undisolved matter.

emetic Agent that induces vomiting.

endurance Body's ability to engage in prolonged physical activity.

enthesitis Group of conditions characterized by inflammation, fibrosis, and calcification around tendons, ligaments, and muscle insertions.

enzyme An organic catalyst that can cause chemical changes in other substances without being changed itself.

epidemiological approach Study of sports injuries that involves the relationship of as many factors as possible.

epilepsy Recurrent paroxymal disorder characterized by sudden attacks of altered consciousness, motor activity, sensory phenomena, or inappropriate behavior.

epiphysis Cartilaginous growth region of a bone.

epistaxis Nosebleed.

ethics Principles of morality.

etiology Science dealing with causes of disease.

eversion of the foot To turn the foot outward.

excoriation Removal of a piece or strip of skin.

exostoses Benign bony outgrowths, usually capped by cartilage, that protrude from the surface of a bone.

extraoral mouth guard Protective device that fits outside the mouth.

extravasation Escape of a fluid from its vessels into the surrounding tissues.

exudate Accumulation of fluid in an area.

F

facilitation To assist the progress of.

fascia Fibrous membrane that covers, supports, and separates muscles.

fasciitis Inflammation of fascia.

fibrinogen Blood plasma protein that is converted into a fibrin clot.

fibroblast Any cell component from which fibers are developed.

fibrocartilage Type of cartilage (e.g., intervertebral disks) in which the matrix contains thick bundles of collaginous fibers.

fibrosis Development of excessive fibrous connective tissue; fibroid degeneration.

flash-to-bang Number of seconds from lightning flash until the sound of thunder divided by five.

foot pronation Combined foot movements of plantarflexion, adduction, and eversion.

foot supination Combined foot movements of dorsiflexion and inversion.

force couple Depressor action by the subscapularis, infraspinatus, and teres minor muscles to stabilize the head of the humerus and to counteract the upward force exerted by the deltoid muscle during abduction of the arm.

frequency Measured in hertz (Hz), cycles per second (CPS), or pulses per second (PPS).

friction Heat producing.

FSH Follicle-stimulating hormone.

G

GAS theory General adaptation syndrome.

genitourinary Pertaining to the reproductive and urinary organs.

genu recurvatum Hyperextension at the knee joint.

genu valgum Knock-knee.

genu varum Bowleg.

GH Growth hormone.

glycogen supercompensation High-carbohydrate diet.

glycosuria Abnormally high proportion of sugar in the urine.

H

half-life Rate at which a drug disappears from the body through metabolism, excretion, or both.

hemarthrosis Blood in a joint.

hematolytic Pertaining to the degeneration and disintegration of the blood.

hematoma Blood tumor.

hematuria Blood in the urine.

hemoglobin Coloring substance of the red blood cells.

hemoglobinuria Hemoglobin in the urine.

hemolysis Destruction of red blood cells.

hemophilia Hereditary blood disease in which coagulation is greatly prolonged.

hemopoietic Forming blood cells.

hemorrhage Discharge of blood.

hemothorax Bloody fluid in the pleural cavity.

hertz (Hz) Number of sound waves per second.

hirsutism Excessive hair growth or the presence of hair in unusual places.

homeostasis Maintenance of a steady state in the body's internal environment.

HOPS Evaluation scheme that includes history, observation, palpation, and special tests.

hunting response Causes a slight temperature increase during cooling.

hyperemia Unusual amount of blood in a body part.

hyperextension Extreme stretching of a body part.

hyperflexibility Flexibility beyond a joint's normal range.

hyperhidrosis Excessive sweating; excessive foot perspiration.

hyperkeratosis Increased callus development.

hypermobility Extreme mobility of a joint.

hyperpnea Hyperventilation; increased minute volume of breathing; exaggerated deep breathing.

hypertension High blood pressure; abnormally high tension.

hyperthermia Elevated body temperature.

hypertonic Having a higher osmotic pressure than a compared solution.

hypertrophy Enlargement of a part caused by an increase in the size of its cells.

hyperventilation Abnormally deep breathing that is prolonged, causing a depletion of carbon dioxide, a fall in blood pressure, and fainting.

hypoallergenic Low allergy producing.

hypoxia Lack of an adequate amount of oxygen.

I

idiopathic Cause of a condition is unknown.

iliotibial band friction syndrome Runner's knee.

injury Act that damages or hurts.

innervation Nerve stimulation of a muscle.

interosseous membrane Connective tissue membrane between bones.

intertrigo Chafing of the skin.

interval training Alternating periods of work with active recovery.

inunctions Oily or medicated substances (e.g., liniments) that are rubbed into the skin to produce a local or systemic effect.

inversion of the foot To turn the foot inward; inner border of the foot lifts.

ions Electrically charged atoms.

ipsilateral Situated on the same side.

ischemia Lack of blood supply to a body part.

isokinetic muscle resistance Accommodating and variable resistance.

isometric exercise Contracts the muscle statically without changing its length.

isotonic exercise Shortens and lengthens the muscle through a complete range of motion.

J

joint capsule Saclike structure that encloses the ends of bones in a diarthrodial joint.

joint play Movement that is not voluntary but accessory.

K

keratolytic Loosening of the horny skin layer.

keratosis Excessive growth of the horny tissue layer.

kilocalorie Amount of heat required to raise 1 kg of water 1° C.

kinesthesia; kinesthesis Sensation or feeling of movement; the awareness one has of the spatial relationships of one's body and its parts.

kyphosis Exaggeration of the normal curve of the thoracic spine.

L

labile Unsteady; not fixed and easily changed.

lactase deficiency Difficulty digesting dairy products.

laser Light amplification by stimulated emission of radiation.

leukocytes Consist of two types—granulocytes (e.g., basophils and neutrophils) and agranulocytes (e.g., monocytes and lymphocytes).

LH Luteinizing hormone.

liability Legal responsibility to perform an act in a reasonable and prudent manner.

load An outside force or forces acting on tissue.

lordosis Abnormal lumbar vertebral convexity.

luxation Complete joint dislocation.

lysis To break down.

M

macerated skin Skin that has been softened through wetting.

malaise Discomfort and uneasiness caused by an illness.

margination Accumulation of leukocytes on blood vessel walls at the site of injury during early stages of inflammation.

mast cells Connective tissue cells that contain heparin and histamine.

MCP Metacarpophalangeal joint.

mechanical failure Elastic limits of tissue are exceeded, causing tissue to break.

menarche Onset of menstrual function.

metabolism Changing a drug into a water-soluble compound that can be excreted.

metatarsalgia A general term to describe pain in the ball of the foot.

microtrauma Microscopic lesion or injury.

muscle contracture Permanent contraction of a muscle as a result of spasm or paralysis.

muscular endurance The ability to perform repetitive muscular contractions against some resistance.

muscular strength The maximal force that can be applied by a muscle during a single maximal contraction.

myocarditis Inflammation of the heart muscle.

myoglobin Respiratory protein in muscle tissue that is an oxygen carrier.

myositis Inflammation of muscle.

myositis ossificans Myositis marked by ossification of muscles.

N

necrosin Chemical substance that stems from inflamed tissue, causing changes in normal tissue.

negative resistance Slow eccentric muscle contraction against a resistance.

negligence The failure to use ordinary or reasonable care.

nerve entrapment Nerve compressed between bone or soft tissue.

neuritis Inflammation of a nerve.

neuroma Tumor consisting mostly of nerve cells and nerve fibers.

nociceptor Receptor of pain.

noncontact sport Sport in which athletes are not involved in any physical contact.

nystagmus Constant involuntary back and forth, up and down, or rotary movement of the eyeball.

O

obesity Excessive amount of body fat.

ohm Resistance.

omission (legal) Person fails to perform a legal duty.

orthopedic surgeon One who corrects deformities of the musculoskeletal system.

orthosis Used in sports as an appliance or apparatus to support, align, prevent, or correct deformities or to improve function of a movable body part.

orthotics Field of knowledge relating to orthoses and their use.

OSHA Occupational Safety and Health Administration.

osteoarthritis Chronic disease involving joints in which there is destruction of articular cartilage and bony overgrowth.

osteochondral Refers to relationship of bone and cartilage.

osteochondritis Inflammation of bone and cartilage.

osteochondritis dissecans Fragment of cartilage and underlying bone is detached from the articular surface.

osteochondrosis Disease state of a bone and its articular cartilage.

osteoporosis A decrease in bone density.

P

palpation Feeling an injury with the fingers.

paraplegia Paralysis of lower portion of the body and of both legs.

paresis Slight or incomplete paralysis.

paresthesia Abnormal or morbid sensation such as itching or prickling.

passive range of motion Movement that is performed completely by the examiner.

pathogenic Disease producing.

pathology Science of the structural and functional manifestations of disease.

pathomechanics Mechanical forces that are applied to a living organism and adversely change the body's structure and function.

pediatrician Specialist in the treatment of children's diseases.

pes anserinus tendinitis Cyclist's knee.

permeable Permitting the passage of a substance through a vessel wall.

petrissage Kneading.

phagocytosis Destruction of injurious cells or particles by phagocytes (white blood cells).

phalanges Bones of the fingers and toes.

phalanx Any one of the bones of the fingers and toes.

pharmacokinetics The method by which drugs are absorbed, distributed, metabolized, and eliminated.

pharmacology Science of drugs and their preparation, uses, and effects.

phonophoresis Introduction of ions of soluble salt into the body through ultrasound.

photophobia Unusual intolerance to light.

piezoelectric effect Production of an electric current as a result of pressure on certain crystals.

PIP Proximal interphalangeal joint.

plyometric exercise Type of exercise that maximizes the myotatic, or stretch, reflex.

pneumothorax Collapse of a lung as a result of air in the pleural cavity.

podiatrist Practitioner who specializes in the study and care of the foot.

point tenderness Pain is produced when an injury site is palpated.

polymers Natural or synthetic substances formed by the combination of two or more molecules of the same substance.

posterior Toward the rear or back.

potency The dose of a drug that is required to produce a desired therapeutic effect.

primary assessment Initial first aid evaluation.

prognosis Prediction as to probable result of a disease or injury.

prophylactic Refers to prevention, preservation, or protection.

prophylaxis Guarding against injury or disease.

proprioception The ability to determine the position of a joint in space.

proprioceptive neuromuscular facilitation (PNF) Stretching techniques that involve combinations of alternating contractions and stretches.

proprioceptor One of several receptors, each of which responds to stimuli elicited from within the body itself (e.g., the muscle spindles that invoke the myotatic, or stretch, reflex).

prostaglandin Acidic lipid widely distributed in the body; in musculoskeletal conditions it is concerned with vasodilation, a histamine-like effect; it is inhibited by aspirin.

prosthesis Replacement of an absent body part with an artificial part; the artificial part.

prothrombin Interacts with calcium to produce thrombin.

proximal Nearest to the point of reference.

psychogenic Of psychic origin; that which originates in the mind.

purulent Consisting of or containing pus.

Q

quadriplegia Paralysis affecting all four limbs.

R

radiation Emission and diffusion of rays of heat.

Raynaud's phenomenon Condition in which cold exposure causes vasospasm of digital arteries.

regeneration Repair, regrowth, or restoration of a part such as tissue.

residual That which remains; often used to describe a permanent condition resulting from injury or disease (e.g., a limp or a paralysis).

resorption Act of removal by absorption.

retroversion Tilting or turning backward of a part.

retrovirus A virus that enters a host cell and changes its RNA to a proviral DNA replica.

revascularize Restoration of blood circulation to an injured area.

RICE Rest, ice, compression, and elevation.

ringworm (tinea) Common name given to many superficial fungal infections of the skin.

RNA Ribonucleic acid.

rotation Turning around an axis in an angular motion.

rubefacients Agents that redden the skin by increasing local circulation through dilation of blood vessels.

S

SAID principle Specific adaptation to imposed demands.

scoliosis Lateral rotary curve of the spine.

sebaceous cyst A cyst filled with sebum; usually found in the scalp.

secondary assessment Follow-up; a more detailed examination.

seizure Sudden attack.

septic shock Shock caused by bacteria, especially gram-negative bacteria commonly seen in systemic infections.

sequela Pathological condition that occurs as a consequence of another condition or event.

serotonin Hormone and neurotransmitter.

sign Objective evidence of an abnormal situation within the body.

SPF Sun protection factor.

spica A figure-eight bandage with one of the two loops larger than the other.

Staphylococcus Genus of gram-positive bacteria normally present on the skin and in the upper respiratory tract and prevalent in localized infections.

stasis Blockage or stoppage of circulation.

static stretching Passively stretching an antagonist muscle by placing it in a maximal stretch and holding it there.

steady-state When the amount of the drug is equal to the amount that is excreted.

strain Extent of deformation of tissue under loading.

Streptococcus Genus of gram-positive bacteria found in the throat, respiratory tract, and intestinal tract.

stress Positive and negative forces that can disrupt the body's equilibrium.

stressor Anything that affects the body's physiological or psychological condition, upsetting the homeostatic balance.

subluxation Partial or incomplete dislocation of an articulation.

symptom Subjective evidence of an abnormal situation within the body.

syndrome Group of typical symptoms or conditions that characterize a deficiency or disease.

synergy To work in cooperation with.

synovitis Inflammation of the synovium.

synthesis To build up.

systolic blood pressure The pressure caused by the heart's pumping.

T

tapotement Percussion.

tendinitis Inflammation of a tendon.

tenosynovitis Inflammation of a tendon synovial sheath.

tetanus (lockjaw) An acute, often fatal condition characterized by tonic muscular spasm, hyperreflexia, and lockjaw.

tetanus toxoid Tetanus toxin modified to produce active immunity against *Clostridium tetani.*

thermotherapy Heat therapy.

thrombi Plural of thrombus; blood clots that block small blood vessels or a cavity of the heart.

tinea (ringworm) Superficial fungal infections of the skin.

tonic muscle spasm Rigid muscle contraction that lasts over a period of time.

torsion Act or state of being twisted.

torts Legal wrongs committed against a person.

training effect Stroke volume increases while heart rate is reduced at a given exercise load.

transitory paralysis Temporary paralysis.

translation Refers to anterior gliding of tibial plateau.

trauma (*pl* traumas or traumata) Wound or injury.

traumatic Pertaining to an injury or wound.

trigger points Small hyperirritable areas within a muscle.

V

valgus Position of a body part that is bent outward.

varus Position of a body part that is bent inward.

vasoconstriction Decrease in the diameter of a blood vessel.

vasodilation Increase in the diameter of a blood vessel.

vasospasm Blood vessel spasm.

vehicle The substance in which a drug is transported.

verruca Wart caused by a virus.

vibration Rapid shaking.

viscoelastic Any substance having both viscous and elastic properties.

viscosity Resistance to flow.

volar Referring to the palm or the sole.

voltage Force.

volume of distribution The volume of fluid through which the drug would have to be distributed to reach a therapeutic level of concentration.

W

Watt Power.

Y

yield point Elastic limits of tissue.

Chapter 1 *Focus boxes, pp. 4, 9, 19, 28, 30,* Courtesy, The National Athletic Trainers' Association.

Chapter 2 *Table 2-1, p. 47,* Adapted from Myers, GC, and Garrick, JG: The preseason examination of school and college athletes. In Strauss, RH (ed.): *Sports medicine,* Philadelphia: WB Saunders, 1984; *Figures 2-3, 2-4, 2-7, pp. 48, 49, 51,* Courtesy, The University of North Carolina at Chapel Hill; *Figure 2-5, p. 50,* Adapted from Tanner, M: *Growth of adolescence,* Oxford, England: Blackwell Scientific Publications, 1962; *Figure 2-8, p. 52,* Modified from *Health Style: A Self Test,* US Dep't of Health and Human Services, Public Health Service, National Clearing House, Washington, D.C.; *Tables 2-2, 2-3, pp. 53, 57,* From Committee on Sports Medicine: *Pediatrics* 81: 738, 1988, used with permission; *Figure 2-9, p. 54,* Courtesy, D. Bailey, California State University at Long Beach.

Chapter 3 *Focus box, p. 67,* Source: DeCarlo, M: Reimbursement for health care services. In Kronin, J: *Clinical athletic training,* Thorofare, NJ: Slack, 1997.

Chapter 4 *Figures 4-12G, H, I, J, pp. 94, 95,* From Prentice, WE: *Get fit stay fit,* St. Louis: Mosby, 1996; *Focus box, p. 106,* From White, T: *The wellness guide to lifelong fitness, The University of California at Berkeley Wellness Letter,* New York: Random House, 1993.

Chapter 5 *Tables 5-1, 5-2, Figures 5-1, 5-4, pp. 115, 117, 121, 132,* From Prentice, WE: *Get fit stay fit,* St. Louis: Mosby, 1996; *Table 5-3, pp. 119, 120,* Modified from *Recommended dietary allowances,* copyright 1989 by the National Academy of Sciences, National Academy Press, Washington, DC; *Figure 5-2, p. 122,* US Dept of Agriculture/US Dept of Health & Human Services, August, 1992; *Figure 5-3, p. 127,* From Prentice, WE: *Fitness for college and life,* ed. 6, Dubuque, IA: WCB/ McGraw-Hill Higher Education, 1999; *Table 5-4, p. 130,* Source: Wardlaw, GM: *Perspectives in Nutrition,* ed. 4, Dubuque, IA: WCB/ McGraw-Hill Higher Education, 1999.

Chapter 6 *Table 6-2, p. 143,* Modified from Berkow, R: *The Merck manual of diagnosis and therapy,* ed. 14, Rahway, NJ: Merck & Co, 1982; *Focus box, p. 147,* Courtesy, ER Buskirk and WC Grasley, Human Performance Laboratory, The Athletic Institute, The Pennsylvania State University.

Chapter 7 *Figure 7-1 (top), p. 161,* Courtesy, Robert Freligh, California State University at Long Beach; *Figures 7-12 and 7-13, pp. 168, 169,* From Nicholas, JA, and Hershman, EB: *The upper extremity in sports medicine,* ed. 2, St.

Louis: Mosby, 1995; *Figure 7-15, p. 169,* Photos courtesy, Denise Fandel, The University of Nebraska at Omaha; *Figures 7-19, 7-26, 7-28, 7-30, pp. 171, 175, 176, 177,* Courtesy, Mueller Sports Medicine; *Figure 7-20, p. 171,* From Prentice, WE: *Fitness for college and life,* ed. 6, Dubuque, IA: WCB/McGraw-Hill, 1999; *Figures 7-23, 7-32, 7-33, 7-34, 7-35, 7-36, 7-37, pp. 174, 178, 179, 180,* From Nicholas, JA and Hershman, EB: *The lower extremity and spine in sports medicine,* ed. 2, St. Louis: Mosby, 1995; *Figure 7-24 (left), p. 174,* Courtesy, Swedo, Inc.; *Figure 7-24 (right), p. 174,* Courtesy, Active ankle brace; *Figure 7-38, p. 182,* From Prentice, WE: *Rehabilitation techniques in sports medicine,* ed. 3, Dubuque, IA: WCB/ McGraw-Hill, 1999.

Chapter 8 *Figures 8-2, 8-6, 8-10, 8-18, 8-21, 8-25, 8-28, 8-38, 8-39, pp. 188, 190, 191, 197, 199, 200, 203, 208, 209,* From Arnheim, DD: *Essentials of athletic training,* ed. 4, Dubuque, IA: WCB/ McGraw-Hill, 1999; *Figures 8-22, 8-35, 8-36, 8-37, pp. 199, 208,* art by Donald O'Connor.

Chapter 9 *Figures 9-2, 9-3, 9-4, pp. 214, 215,* art by Don O'Connor.

Chapter 10 *Figure 10-1, p. 239,* Focus on Sports; *Figure 10-2, p. 239,* Steve Powell/ Allsport; *Figure 10-6, p. 251,* From Prentice, WE: *Therapeutic modalities in sports medicine,* ed. 4, Dubuque, IA: WCB/McGraw-Hill, 1999.

Chapter 11 *Figures 11-1, 11-2, 11-4, pp. 257, 258, 263,* Courtesy Ken Bartlett, California State University at Long Beach; *Figure 11-3, p. 259,* From Prentice, WE: *Rehabilitation techniques in sports medicine,* ed. 3, Dubuque, IA:WCB/McGraw-Hill, 1999.

Chapter 12 *Table 12-1, p. 277,* Modified from *International medical guide for ships,* Geneva: World Health Organization; *Figure 12-15, p. 292,* From Arnheim, DD: *Essentials of athletic training,* ed. 4, Dubuque, IA: WCB/McGraw-Hill, 1999; *Figure 12-17, p. 294,* Courtesy, Hartwell Medical Corp., Carlsbad, CA.

Chapter 13 *Table 13-1, p. 310,* Adapted from Post, M: *Physical examination of the musculoskeletal system,* Chicago: Yearbook Medical Publishers, 1987; *Table 13-2, p. 317,* Modified from Veterans Administration Standard Form A. Washington, DC: US Government Printing Office; *Figure 13-8, pp. 326–327,* From Nicholas, JA and Hershman, EB: *The lower extremity and spine in sports medicine,* ed. 2, St. Louis: Mosby, 1995.

Chapter 14 *Figure 14-2, p. 333,* art by Don O'Connor; *Focus box, p. 336,* From Hahn, DB and Payne, WA: *Focus on health,* ed. 4, Dubuque, IA: WCB/McGraw-Hill, 1999.

Chapter 15 *Figure 15-6, p. 343,* Courtesy, Hygenic Corp, Akron, OH; *Figure 15-8, p. 355,* Courtesy, Maxxim Medical, Sugarland, TX; *Figure 15-9, p. 356,* Courtesy, International Medical Electronics, Kansas City, MO; *Figures 15-13, 15-14, 15-15, pp. 363, 364, 365,* From Prentice, WE: *Therapeutic modalities in sports medicine,* ed. 4, Dubuque, IA: WCB/McGraw-Hill, 1999; *Figure 15-24, p. 373,* Chattanooga Corp, Hickson, TN; *Figure 15-25, p. 374,* Courtesy, Winchesters Inc., Daytona Beach, FL; *Figure 15-26, p. 374,* Courtesy, Country Technologies, Inc., Gay Mills, WI.

Chapter 16 *Figure 16-3B, p. 387,* Courtesy, BREG, Inc., Vista, CA; *Figure 16-3C, p. 387,* Courtesy, Biodex Medical Systems, Inc., Shirley, NY; *Figure 16-5, 16-13, 16-14B, pp. 389, 399, 400,* From Prentice, WE: *Rehabilitation techniques in sports medicine,* ed. 3, Dubuque, IA: WCB/McGraw-Hill, 1999; *Figures 16-6G, 16-9, pp. 394, 396,* From Prentice, WE: *Get fit stay fit,* St. Louis: Mosby, 1996; *Figure 16-6H, p. 394,* Courtesy, Contemporary Design, Glacier, WA; *Figure 16-6I, p. 394,* Courtesy, Fitter International, Calgary, Alberta; *Figure 16-7, p. 395,* Aqua Jogger courtesy Excel Sport Science, Inc., Eugene, OR; *Figure 16-12, p. 399,* Source: Maitland, G: *Extremity manipulation,* London: Butterworth, 1977, and Maitland, G: *Vertebral manipulation,* London: Butterworth, 1978.

Chapter 17 *Table 17-2, p. 408,* From Huff, P: Drug distribution in the training room, *Clinics in Sports Medicine* 17 (2): 214, 1998; *Focus box, pp. 425–432,* Adapted from Lombardo, JA: *Drugs in sports.* In Krakurer, LJ: *The yearbook of sports medicine,* Chicago: Yearbook Medical Publishers, 1986.

Chapter 18 *Figures 18-3, 18-25, 18-30, pp. 448, 468, 471,* From Arnheim, DD: *Essentials of athletic training,* ed. 4, Dubuque, IA: WCB/ McGraw-Hill, 1999; *Figures 18-21, 18-32, pp. 414, 472,* From Williams, JPG: *Color atlas of injury in sport,* ed. 2, Chicago: Yearbook Medical Publishers, 1990; *Figures 18-37, 18-38, 18-41, pp. 475–477,* From Prentice, WE: *Rehabilitation techniques in sports medicine,* ed. 3, Dubuque, IA: WCB/ McGraw-Hill, 1999.

Chapter 19 *Figures 19-3 (left), 19-24 (bottom), pp. 484, 501,* From Arnheim, DD: *Essentials of athletic training,* ed. 4, Dubuque, IA: WCB/ McGraw-Hill, 1999; *Table 19-2, p. 493,* Adapted from Singer, KM and Jones, DC: Ligament injuries of the ankle and foot. In Nicholas, JA and Hershman, EB (eds): *The lower extremity and spine in sports medicine,* vol. 1, ed. 2, St. Louis: Mosby, 1995; *Figures 19-19 (left), 19-21, 19-27, pp. 496, 498, 506,* From Williams, JPG: *Color atlas of injury in sport,* ed. 2, Chicago: Yearbook Medical Publishers,

1990; *Figure 19-20 (top), p. 497,* Courtesy, Cramer Products, Gardner, KS; Figure 19-26, p. 503, From Nicholas, JA and Hershman, EB: *The lower extremity and spine in sports medicine,* vol. 2, ed. 2, St. Louis: Mosby, 1995; *Figures 19-32C, 19-33, p. 510,* From Prentice, WE: *Rehabilitation techniques in sports medicine,* ed. 3, Dubuque, IA: WCB/McGraw-Hill, 1999.

Chapter **20**   *Figures 20-5, 20-30, 20-46, pp. 517, 536, 545,* art by Donald O'Connor; *Figure 20-23, p. 533,* Courtesy, Medmetric Corp., San Diego, CA; *Figure 20-54, p. 556,* Courtesy, Thera-Kinetics and JACE Systems, Mount Laurel, NJ.

Chapter **21**   *Figures 21-7, 21-20, 21-21, 21-24, 21-26, 21-29B and C, pp. 571, 584–587,* Courtesy Ken Bartlett, California State University at Long Beach; *Figures 21-9, 21-35 (right), pp. 572, 593,* From Williams, JPG: *Color atlas of injury in sport,* ed. 2, Chicago: Yearbook Medical Publishers; *Figure 21-10, p. 573,* Courtesy, Mueller Sports Medicine; *Table 21-2, p. 575,* From Boland, AL and Hosea, JM: *Hip and back pain in runners, Postgraduate Advances in Sports Medicine I-XII,* Pennington, NJ: Forum Medicus, 1986; *Figure 21-19, p. 583,* Courtesy, Robert Barclay and Renee Reavis Shingles, Central Michigan University; *Figure 21-30 (right), p. 589,* From Nicholas, JA and Hershman, EB: *The lower extremity and spine in sports medicine,* vol. 2, ed. 2, St. Louis: Mosby, 1995; *Figure 21-31, p. 590,* Courtesy, BRACE International, Phoenix, AZ; *Figures 21-38, 21-39, 21-40, 21-41, pp. 595,* From Prentice, WE: *Rehabilitation techniques in sports medicine,* ed. 3, Dubuque, IA: WCB/McGraw-Hill, 1999.

Chapter **22**   *Figures 22-2, 22-29, pp. 601, 631,* From Nicholas, JA and Hershman, EB: *The upper extremity in sports medicine,* ed. 2, St. Louis: Mosby, 1995; *Figures 22-3, 22-4, 22-5, pp. 602, 604, 605,* From Saladin, KS: *Anatomy & Physiology,* Dubuque, IA: WCB/McGraw-Hill, 1998; *Figures 22-8, 22-27, pp. 606, 625,* art by Donald O'Connor; *Figure 22-24, p. 618,* From Rockwood, C, and Masten, F: *The shoulder,* Philadelphia: WB Saunders, 1990; *Figure 22-34, p. 635,* Courtesy, PrePak Products, Carlsbad, CA; *Figure 22-41, p. 639,* Courtesy, Healthsouth Rehabilitation Program, Birmingham, AL.

Chapter **23**   *Figures 23-5, 23-6, 23-8, 23-12, 23-15, 23-16, 23-17, 23-19, 23-28, 23-31, pp. 648, 651, 652, 654, 661, 663,* Courtesy Ken Bartlett, California State University at Long Beach; *Figures 23-7, 23-22, pp. 648, 658,* From Nicholas, JA and Hershman, EB: *The upper extremity in sports medicine,* ed. 2, St. Louis: Mosby, 1995; *Figures 23-24, 23-25, 23-26, 23-27, 23-29, 23-30, pp. 660–662,* From Prentice, WE: Rehabilitation techniques in sports medicine, ed. 3, Dubuque, IA: WCB/ McGraw-Hill, 1999.

Chapter **24**   *Figure 24-39, 24-44, pp. 690, 692,* Courtesy Ken Bartlett, California State University at Long Beach; *Figure 24-21, 24-27 (left), 24-28 (left), 24-29, 24-31, 24-32, 24-33, 24-44, 24-47, pp. 679, 682, 683, 685, 686, 692, 693,* From Nicholas, JA and Hershman, EB: *The upper extremity in sports medicine,* ed. 2, St. Louis: Mosby, 1995; *Figure 24-35, 24-36, 24-37, 24-40, 24-41, 24-42, 24-43, 24-45, 24-46, pp. 688–692,* From Prentice, WE: *Rehabilitation techniques in sports medicine,* ed. 3, Dubuque, IA: WCB/McGraw-Hill, 1999.

Chapter **25**   *Figures 25-4, 25-12, 25-45, pp. 699, 709, 737,* art by Donald O'Connor; *Figure 25-6, p. 700,* From Saladin, KS: *Anatomy & Physiology,* Dubuque, IA: WCB/McGraw-Hill, 1998; *Figure 25-7, p. 701,* From Seeley, RR, Stephens, TD, Tate, P: *Anatomy & physiology,* ed. 3, St. Louis: Mosby, 1995; *Tables 25-1, 25-2, pp. 702–704,* From Seeley, RR, Stephens, TD, Tate, P: *Anatomy & physiology,* St. Louis: Mosby, 1989; *Figure 25-43, p. 732,* From Nicholas, JA and Hershman, EB: *The lower extremity and spine in sports medicine,* vol. 2, ed. 2, St. Louis: Mosby, 1995; *Figure 25-47 (middle & right), p. 739,* From Williams, JPG: *Color atlas of injury in sport,* ed. 2, Chicago: Yearbook Medical Publishers, 1990; *Figure 25-55, p. 746,* From Prentice, WE: *Get fit stay fit,* St. Louis: Mosby, 1996.

Chapter **26**   *Figure 26-2, p. 754,* From Saladin, KS: *Anatomy & Physiology,* Dubuque, IA: WCB/McGraw-Hill, 1998; *Figures 26-3, 26-4, 26-5, pp. 755, 756,* From Seeley, RR, Stephens, TD, Tate, P: *Anatomy & physiology,* ed. 3, St. Louis: Mosby, 1995. Art by John V. Hagen (Figure 26-3), Jody L. Fulks (Figure 26-4), Rusty Jones (Figure 26-5); *Figure 26-6, p. 756,* From Prentice, WE: *Fitness for college and life,* ed. 6, Dubuque, IA: WCB/McGraw-Hill, 1999; *Figure 26-15, pp. 764–765,* From Boyd, CE: Referred visceral pain in athletics, *Ath Train* 15:20, 1980.

Chapter **27**   *Focus box, pp. 796,* Adapted from Vegso, JJ and Lehman, RC: *Field evaluation and managment of head and neck injuries.* In Torg, JS (ed.): *Head and neck injuries, Clinics in Sports Medicine,* vol. 6, no. 1, Philadelphia: WB Saunders, 1987; *Table 27-5, p. 794,* Adapted from Cantu, RC: Guidelines for return to contact sports after a cerebral concussion. *Phys Sportsmed* 1986, 14(10): 79; *Figure 27-7, p. 798,* From Saladin, KS: *Anatomy & Physiology,* Dubuque, IA: WCB/McGraw-Hill, 1998; *Figures 27-12, 27-15, pp. 803, 805,* From Williams, JPG: *Color atlas of injury in sport,* ed. 2, Chicago: Yearbook Medical Publishers, 1990; *Table 27-6, p. 807,* Adapted from Pashby, RC and Pashby, TJ: *Ocular injuries in sport.* In Welsh, PR and Shephard, RJ (eds.): *Current therapy in sports medicine, 1985–1986,* Philadelphia: BC Decker, 1985; *Figure 27-19, p. 810,* Courtesy, Prevent Blindness America, Schaumburg, IL.

Chapter **28**   *Figure 28-8 (top left), p. 826,* From Booher, JM and Thibodeau, GA: *Athletic training assessment,* Dubuque, IA: McGraw-Hill, 2000; *Figure 28-8 (bottom left), p. 826,* Courtesy, Dr. James Garrick; *Figures 28-9, 28-10, 28-12, 28-14, pp. 830, 831, 833, 834,* From Stewart, WD, Danto, JL, Madden, S: *Dermatology: diagnosis and treatment of cutaneous disorders,* ed. 4, St. Louis: The CV Mosby Co., 1978; **Color plates,** From Habif, TP: *Clinical dermatology,* ed. 3, St. Louis: Mosby, 1996.

Field Kit Supplies

Adhesive bandages:
  regular (med., large, x-large)
  knuckle
  patch
  sterile strips
Tape cutters
Scissors
Eye cover
Save-a-tooth
Pseudoephrine (bottle and dose)
Acetominophen (bottle and dose)
Pepto-Bismol tablets
Immodium AD caplets
Ibuprophen tablets
Diphenhydramine
Dramamine
Hydrocortizone cream
A and D ointment
Petroleum jelly
Scalpels
Razor blades
Dacriose sterile eye irrigating
  solution
Latex gloves
Oral screw
QDA spray
Skin lube
Gauze pads: 2 × 2, 3 × 3, or 4 × 4
Heel cup
Sling
Hex-a-lite
Betasept
Titralac antacid
Hydrogen peroxide
Finger splints
Cotton-tipped applicators
Tongue depressors
Flex All
Lotion
EPI-PEN
Contact lens solution
CPR mask
Antiseptic hand cleaner
Sunscreen
Tape supplies: zonas, stretch, heel
  and lace pads, prewrap, 3 inch,
  2 inch, 1 inch brown, 1 inch
  white, blood tape
Ace wraps: 2 inch, 3 inch, 4 inch,
  6 inch, double 4 inch, double
  6 inch
Alcohol
Cramergesic
Flex-wrap
Adhesive foam

Adhesive felt
Moleskin
Penlight
Stethoscope
Ear thermometer
Pens
Self-stick notes
Polysporin ointment
Tongue forceps
Tweezers
Eye patch
Dental sponges
Ventolin inhaler
Contact lens cases
Contact lens wetting solution
Scalpel blades

Bruise Bag

Adhesive foam: 1 sheet, 18 inch ×
  11 inch
Adhesive felt: 1 sheet, 18 inch ×
  11 inch
Knee sleeves: large, x-large, xx-large
  (2 each)
Elbow sleeves: large, x-large,
  xx-large (2 each)
Knee brace: 2 lateral hinge
Mouth guards: 25 moldable
Ice bags: 10
Air casts: right large, right x-large,
  left large, left x-large (1 each)
Ace wraps: 2 inch, 4 inch, 6 inch,
  double 4 inch, double 6 inch
  (1 each)
Back wraps: large, x-large (1 each)
Lace-up ankle braces: right large,
  right x-large, left large, left x-large
  (1 each)
Turf toe steel plates: right and left
  sizes: 14 and 10 (2 each)
Foam padding: 24 inch x 24 inch
  roll
Philadelphia Collar
Neck roll
AC pads: 1 right, 1 left, 2 Lax pads
Soft neck collar: 1
Tape cutter: 2
Thigh sleeves: large, x-large, xx-large
  (2 each)
Spenco arch supports: size 5, size 3
  (2 each)
Spenco insoles: size 14, 11 (2 each)
Wrist splints: right and left, large,
  x-large (2 each)
Thigh pads: 2
Knee pads: 2

Sideline Emergency Supplies for the Physician

Automatic electric defibrillator
  (AED)
Battery charger
Bag mask rescusitator with oxygen
  tube
Pocket mask
Alcohol prep pads
Adhesive tape
IV starter kit
IV bag solution
Solution set (IV line)
Latex gloves
18 gauge IV catheter
14 gauge IV catheter
20cc syringe
Epinephrine

Items for the Field

6 ten-gallon coolers for water and
  electrolyte drink
4 pitchers
Ice bags and ice chest with ice for ice
  bags
Field kit
Bruise bag
Spine board
Crutches
Flatbed cart
Personal kits (fanny packs)
Emergency kit with oxygen
Physiodyne
Vacuum splints
Water bottles
Towels
Water hose
Extension cords

Seasonal Supplies

Ice towels
7-gallon coolers
Port-a-cools with needed supplies
Ice cans
Electrolyte drink
2 ten-gallon coolers for electrolyte
  drink
Cups
7-gallon cooler with ice towels
2 extra pitchers
Bee and wasp spray
Extra trash bags